COVID-19, Law & Regulation

COVID-19, Law & Regulation

Rights, Freedoms, and Obligations in a Pandemic

BELINDA BENNETT, IAN FRECKELTON AO KC,
AND GABRIELLE WOLF

Great Clarendon Street, Oxford, OX2 6DP,
United Kingdom

Oxford University Press is a department of the University of Oxford.
It furthers the University's objective of excellence in research, scholarship,
and education by publishing worldwide. Oxford is a registered trade mark of
Oxford University Press in the UK and in certain other countries

© Belinda Bennett, Ian Freckelton, Gabrielle Wolf 2023

The moral rights of the authors have been asserted

First Edition published in 2023

Impression: 1

All rights reserved. No part of this publication may be reproduced, stored in
a retrieval system, or transmitted, in any form or by any means, without the
prior permission in writing of Oxford University Press, or as expressly permitted
by law, by licence or under terms agreed with the appropriate reprographics
rights organization. Enquiries concerning reproduction outside the scope of the
above should be sent to the Rights Department, Oxford University Press, at the
address above

You must not circulate this work in any other form
and you must impose this same condition on any acquirer

Public sector information reproduced under Open Government Licence v3.0
(http://www.nationalarchives.gov.uk/doc/open-government-licence/open-government-licence.htm)

Published in the United States of America by Oxford University Press
198 Madison Avenue, New York, NY 10016, United States of America

British Library Cataloguing in Publication Data

Data available

Library of Congress Control Number: 2022932699

ISBN 978–0–19–289674–2

DOI: 10.1093/oso/9780192896742.001.0001

Printed and bound by
CPI Group (UK) Ltd, Croydon, CR0 4YY

Links to third party websites are provided by Oxford in good faith and
for information only. Oxford disclaims any responsibility for the materials
contained in any third party website referenced in this work.

*For my mother and my daughter,
both inspiring women*
BB
*For Trish and Julia, doctors in the surgery and on the wards during
the hardest of pandemic times*
IF
For Nick, Leo, and Saskia, who bring me joy each day, in and out of lockdowns
GW

Foreword

The COVID-19 pandemic has upended every corner of the world. The World Health Organization estimates the pandemic has caused nearly 15 million deaths as of May 2022, and deaths will mount further as the pandemic sweeps the globe. The virus has continually evolved, now with considerable immune escape capabilities, so we expect a future with ongoing reinfections. The pandemic has devastated national economies and disrupted global supply chains. And the pandemic has had knock-on health impacts, ranging from throwing millions back into poverty and food insecurity to setbacks on childhood vaccinations and delayed diagnosis and treatment of chronic conditions such as cancer, diabetes, and cardiovascular disease

All that is well known. Less discussed are the major threats to human rights and freedoms, not to mention a multitude of laws and litigation that have rolled back public health powers. At the end of the day, one of the major causalities of the COVID-19 pandemic may be the rule of law itself. In their important new book, *COVID-19, Law, & Regulation*, Belinda Bennett, Ian Freckelton, and Gabrielle Wolf shine a bright spotlight on this erosion of rights. These highly regarded authors systematically describe and analyse the major legal and regulatory responses around the world, while also placing them in historical context.

After the 9/11 attacks on the World Trade Center and the subsequent intentional release of anthrax packages through the United States Postal Service, the US Centers for Disease Control and Prevention (CDC) asked me to lead a team to draft a Model Health Emergency Powers Act. That model law was adopted not only in most US states, but also in countries throughout the world.

I had anticipated most responses that we have seen with COVID-19, such as testing, contact tracing, isolation, and quarantine. Vaccine and mask mandates also had been a major part of disease control historically. Masks were required even in the US during the Great Influenza Pandemic of 1918, and masks became a staple tool for other novel infectious disease outbreaks such as SARS, MERS, and Influenza A (H1N1). Vaccine mandates have been in place literally for a century or more, including requiring childhood vaccinations as a condition of school attendance. The Model Health Emergency Powers Act even anticipated large-scale orders for quarantine or *cordon sanitaire*. During the SARS epidemic, for example, Asian countries such as China and Singapore quarantined large apartment towers. Canada issued 'work quarantine' orders which restricted health workers to either be at home or in hospital. It also wasn't difficult to foresee school and business closures, which have been part and parcel of controlling widescale epidemics for many decades.

What I could not have even imagined was the full lockdown of mega-cities. But that is exactly what happened beginning in Wuhan and wider Hubei province in China, through to Rome, Paris, Berlin, London, and New York. Eventually we would see full lockdowns of Delhi, Sao Paulo, Sydney, and most of the world's metropolises. At one point or another during the pandemic, virtually the entire global population experienced lockdowns.

At the same time, autocratic rulers used the pandemic as a subterfuge for grabbing power, eroding democratic structures, imprisoning their political adversaries, and clamping down on the freedoms of press and assembly. The rule of law in many countries began to crumble. The public often lost trust in science, public health agencies, and the government itself. A key question facing societies everywhere is whether all these actions that are deeply damaging to good governance will continue beyond the pandemic, or whether we can recentre to restore core values of transparency, honest stewardship, and accountability.

And then there were the draconian measures curtailing privacy and liberty. Digital apps were used widely, especially in Asia, to facilitate contact tracing, testing, and isolation or quarantine. Those technologies worked in democratic nations with high trust in their governments, such as Japan, South Korea, and Taiwan. But in many countries, especially China, digital location technologies were used to control the population. In China, digital location devices literally controlled the lives and movements of every citizen. Digital apps were a tool that also included monitoring social media and sanctioning those who broke COVID rules, or who criticized the government. And the privacy and liberty deprivations are continuing to this day with China's 'Dynamic Zero COVID' policy.

And let's not forget the early moments of the COVID-19 pandemic which caused deep political divisions. China did not report an outbreak of SARS-like illness in Wuhan until weeks after this became apparent. The WHO discovered the Wuhan outbreak through informal sources, which China later confirmed. And China misinformed WHO, and the world, saying that there was little, or no, community spread, even though the infection was spreading widely in Wuhan, including among health workers. China sanctioned a health worker whistle blower who was concerned about the gravity of the outbreak, and the global implications.

As the pandemic dragged onto through its first year, China again was a centre of attention, as it rejected requests from WHO for an independent inquiry into the origins of SARS-CoV-2. The pandemic devolved into a nightmare for global governance, as WHO was caught between the world's two superpowers. And perhaps the low point was when President Trump announced he would be withdrawing the US from WHO membership—the unthinkable had happened. On President Biden's first day in office, he overturned the Trump Administration's threat to leave WHO. Still, Biden was so concerned with China that he instructed all US intelligence agencies to determine whether the virus originated from a natural zoonotic spill-over or from a laboratory leak at the Wuhan Institute of Virology. The intelligence community couldn't answer that question, which still remains today—even though most (but not all) public health scientists believe it was a natural zoonotic event.

Law, regulation, and governance takes place primarily at the level of sovereign nations. But there is also a framework for international law and governance, along with the role of global institutions and global public/private partnerships. This stellar book by Bennett, Freckelton, and Wolf also has deep international legal dimensions, and of course it should, and must. The principal governing instrument for global infectious disease threats is the *International Health Regulations (IHR)*. The *IHR* underwent fundamental reform in 2005 in the aftermath of the SARS epidemic. Again, China's failures of global cooperation during the SARS outbreaks precipitated the major revisions of the *IHR* in 2005.

China's failure to rapidly and accurately report early cases in Wuhan was a clear violation of the *IHR*. But the wholesale lack of compliance with the Regulations would become painfully obvious. The most conspicuous violations of the *IHR* were the travel bans and restrictions that took place. At one time or another, the vast majority of nations had large-scale travel restrictions in place. Sometimes the travel bans came early and hard, such as for Australia, which performed well during the pandemic. But most restrictions picked and chose among countries, often targeting low- and middle-income countries. What emerged was a failure of global governance. Governments, from SARS, MERS, and Zika through to Ebola, were often slack with travel or trade restrictions when they reported novel outbreaks. The *IHR* required early reporting but the incentives were perverse. COVID-19 brought this to the fore. When South African scientists identified omicron, a new variant, the country was punished with travel bans—rather than rewarding South Africa for its scientific prowess and transparency.

If I were to highlight the single most important governance failure in the pandemic—both at the national and international levels—it would be the unconscionable inequities. At the level of nations, we saw huge disparities in infection, hospitalization, and death rates—disproportionately burdening racial minorities, the poor, prisoners, nursing home residents, immigrants, and other marginalized populations. At the global level, we saw a grotesque mal-distribution of lifesaving medical resources, such as personal protective equipment, oxygen, ventilators, vaccines, and now therapeutics. Perhaps the most obvious inequality was in access to vaccines. During the first year of the pandemic, and beyond, high-income countries executed pre-purchase agreements with vaccine manufacturers, hoarding scarce vaccine supplies. By the end of 2021, most high-income countries had vaccination rates of 70% or more, while lower-income countries, for example in sub-Saharan Africa, remained largely unvaccinated. We are now seeing this play out with therapeutics, most notably the Pfizer antiviral medication Paxlovid.

WHO and partners developed new institutions and mechanisms early on to ensure a more equitable response—most notably the Act Accelerator and its vaccine arm, COVAX. While the intent was noble, the result was deeply unsatisfactory as COVAX failed to meet its targets by a long way.

All in all, we have witnessed a collapse in global solidarity during the COVID-19 pandemic. Yet, this once-in-a-lifetime crisis of health and of governance could yield an unparalleled opportunity for transformative change. Three major workstreams at WHO hold enormous promise, but will require political will, skilled diplomacy, and international cooperation. The first is WHO sustainably financing itself. The WHO has been starved of funding. Its operating budget is less than the size of a single US teaching hospital. The Organization also has control over only about one-quarter of its budget. But the World Health Assembly could change all that. WHA isn't likely to give the agency the funds it truly needs, but could respond favourably to making mandatory dues one-half of WHO's operating budget.

The WHA is also considering a US proposal for amendments of the *IHR*. As this book makes clear, those Regulations failed to ensure good governance of the pandemic. Learning from COVID-19, the international community could significantly strengthen the *IHR* to make it fit for purpose in governing future global health crises.

Finally, and most importantly, WHA charged an International Negotiating Body (INB) with the task of drafting and agreeing on a new Framework Convention for Pandemic Preparedness and Response, or another international instrument. Early proposals, especially by the European Union, are bold—covering transformational issues such as land management, climate change, and antimicrobial resistance.

Tedros Adhanom Ghebreyesus, the WHO Director-General, was re-elected at the May 2022 Assembly. He presented a blueprint for a global health architecture grounded in human rights and in equity. It is entirely possible that the post-COVID-19 world (even though the virus will almost certainly become endemic) will see a return to the old familiar pattern of governments lurching from complacency to panic—and back. But there is just a chance that the global community will come to grips with the threats we face, and transform global health law and governance. It we come together, the world will be much better prepared for the next health crisis. If we don't, let's expect a tsunami of deaths and economic destruction when the next crisis hits—and it will.

Lawrence O Gostin
Founding O'Neill Chair in Global Health Law and Director, WHO Collaborating Center on National and Global Health Law, Georgetown University, Washington, DC

Preface and Acknowledgements

In this book we analyse major legal and regulatory responses internationally to COVID-19: the most severe pandemic the world has experienced in a century. We place these responses in historical context, and evaluate their significance and impact. Drawing on key examples from most continents, we consider the implications for human rights and freedoms, governance and state obligations, of diverse laws and regulations that were implemented in an attempt to limit the spread of COVID-19 between and within countries. We also examine the roles played by the World Health Organization and the *International Health Regulations (2005)*. We have scrutinized notable legal challenges to public health measures enforced during the pandemic, such as lockdown orders, curfews, and vaccine mandates. In addition, we identify how the law has responded to particular forms of risk and vulnerability to COVID-19. We examine, in the context of the pandemic, the operation of the criminal justice system, civil litigation concerning avoidable deaths and business losses, consumer protection litigation and disciplinary regulation of health practitioners, coronial inquests and other investigations of unexpected deaths, and occupational health and safety issues posed by COVID-19. We also reflect on the role of the law in facilitating and putting into operation the remarkable scientific and epidemiological achievements during the pandemic and combatting the detrimental effects of COVID-19, and the challenges of ensuring the swift production and equitable distribution of treatments and vaccines. In our conclusion we consider the possibilities that the legal and regulatory responses to this pandemic have illuminated for effectively tackling future global health crises, and specific changes to the law that the pandemic may yield, including a pandemic treaty.

This book was conceptualized during the early months of the COVID-19 pandemic. At that stage there were many unknowns about COVID-19. Now, more than two years since the start of the pandemic, much more is known about COVID-19 and its many effects on individuals, communities, and economies. The pandemic has also raised a range of complex legal and regulatory issues. Some, such as laws relating to quarantine, were evident from an early stage. Others have emerged as important areas and have formed part of a growing body of legal scholarship across a diverse range of areas. However, the pandemic has had an impact upon every aspect of social and economic life, highlighting the importance of these issues for understanding the role of law in responding to public health emergencies. As a result, in our analysis, we have sought to engage not only with the complexities of the role of law during a public health emergency, but also with impact of the pandemic and pandemic-related laws on human rights, individual freedoms, and obligations. We have also drawn on international examples to illustrate the complexity of the ethical and legal issues presented by the pandemic, and the international responses to it.

Although the book deals with legal issues relating to COVID-19 and interprets relevant international case law, at times expressing opinions about such matters, it does not contain legal advice and should not be applied for the purposes of litigation or the provision of legal services.

We would like to express our appreciation to Oxford University Press for their enthusiasm to publish this book, and in particular Jamie Berezin, Brianne Bellio, and Matthew Williams for their support and flexibility throughout the process. We are grateful also for the co-ordination role of K. Vijayalakshmi from Newgen KnowledgeWorks and of the hard work on our manuscript by our editors, in particular Caroline Quinnell.

We would also like to thank our universities for the support they have provided during the writing of this book. Belinda would like to thank her colleagues in the School of Law at Queensland University of Technology (QUT) in Brisbane, and especially her colleagues within the Australian Centre for Health Law Research (ACHLR) at QUT, for providing a supportive, stimulating, and engaging research environment. She would also like to thank ACHLR for its support for this book, Hannah Plater for her research assistance, and Kristina Chelberg for her assistance with formatting and editing.

Ian expresses his appreciation to Melbourne Law School for its stimulating and collaborative environment, led by Dean Pip Nicholson, and latterly by Acting Dean Matthew Harding. He also is grateful to his colleagues in the Health and Medical Law postgraduate programme, in particular, his co-directors, Associate Professors Paula O'Brien and Michelle Taylor-Sands, and the students to whom he taught the 'Pandemic Law' course in 2020, 2021, and 2022, who enriched and challenged his understanding of public health law and pandemic phenomenology. He also records gratitude for the assistance given to him by Dr Pascale Chifflet of La Trobe University in relation to French law, Professor Vera Raposo of Coimbra University in relation to Portuguese and Brazilian law, Professor Pompeu Casanovas of La Trobe University in relation to Spanish law, Professor Patrick Keyzer of the Australian Catholic University in relation to constitutional law issues, especially those relating to Australia, and Daniel Beratis for assistance in locating United States citations. He expresses his appreciation also to Dr Patricia Molloy for her patient assistance in integrating corrections during the final stages of the book.

Gabrielle would like to thank her colleagues in the Deakin Law School at Deakin University for their support and Morgan Stonebridge for assisting with formatting footnotes.

All three authors would like to express their appreciation to Daniel Beratis, Danielle Feng, and Melbourne Law School Research Service, for their painstaking and high-quality work on the Bibliography, Table of Cases, and Table of Legislation and Kristina Chelberg for her assistance with formatting.

Ian expresses appreciation to Thomson Reuters for permission to draw broadly upon a series of articles he published between 2020 and 2022 in the *Journal of Law and Medicine*, including: Ian Freckelton and Gabrielle Wolf, 'Responses to Monkeypox: Learning from Previous Public Health Emergencies' (2022) 29(4) *Journal of Law and Medicine* (in press); Ian Freckelton, 'Vaccinating Children: COVID-19's Contribution to Family Law Jurisprudence' (2022) 29(3) *Journal of Law and Medicine* 645; Ian Freckelton, 'Pandemics, Polycentricity and Public Perceptions: Lessons from the Djokovic Saga' (2022) 29(1) *Journal of Law and Medicine* 9; Ian Freckelton, 'Mandatory Vaccination Litigation' (2021) 28 *Journal of Law and Medicine* 913; Ian Freckelton, 'COVID-19 as a Disruptor and a Catalyst for Change' (2021) 28(3) *Journal of Law and Medicine* 59; Ian Freckelton, 'Human Challenge Trials and COVID-19' (2021) 28 *Journal of Law and Medicine* 311; Ian Freckelton, 'COVID-19 Curfews: Kenyan and Australian Litigation and Pandemic Protection' (2020) 28(1) *Journal of Law and Medicine* 117; Ian Freckelton and Vera Raposo, 'International Access to Public Health Data: An Important Brazilian Precedent' (2020) 27(4) *Journal of Law and Medicine* 895; Ian Freckelton, 'Perils of Precipitate Publication: Fraudulent and Substandard COVID-19 Research' (2020) 27(4) *Journal of Law and Medicine* 77; Ian Freckelton, 'COVID-19, Criminal Law, Public Assemblies and and Human Rights Litigation' (2020) 27(4) *Journal of Law and Medicine* 790; Ian Freckelton, 'COVID-19 and Family Law Decision-making' (2020) 27(4) *Journal of Law and Medicine* 846; and Ian Freckelton, 'COVID-19: Negligence and Occupational Health and Safety: Ethical and Legal Issues for Hospitals and Health Centres' (2020) 27(3) *Journal of Law and Medicine* 590.

We would also like to thank the World Health Organization for permission to reproduce in Chapter 3 the decision instrument for the assessment and notification of events that may constitute a public health emergency of international concern, *International Health Regulations (2005)*, Annex 2.

Finally, we would like to thank our friends and family members for indulging our absorption with pandemic issues during COVID-19.

Belinda Bennett
Ian Freckelton
Gabrielle Wolf
February 2022

Contents

List of Abbreviations	xix
About the Authors	xxiii
Table of Cases	xxv
Table of Legislation	xxxi

1. COVID-19, Law, and Regulation	1
I. Introduction	1
II. The COVID-19 Pandemic	2
III. Key Themes	13
IV. Overview of the Book	33
2. Past Legal and Regulatory Responses to Infectious Diseases	39
I. Introduction	39
II. The Black Death, Quarantine Laws, and Changes to Labour Law	42
III. Smallpox, Inoculation, and Vaccination	47
IV. Cholera, Tuberculosis, Health Boards, and Sanitary Reform	49
V. 'Russian Flu', Disease Monitoring, and Contract Law in England	54
VI. Spanish Flu and the Use of Voluntary and Coercive Public Health Measures	55
VII. Poliomyelitis and Vaccination	60
VIII. Acquired Immune Deficiency Syndrome	61
IX. Severe Acute Respiratory Syndrome (SARS)	66
X. Bird Flu, Swine Flu, and Access to Vaccines	68
XI. Ebola Virus Disease in West Africa	71
XII. Conclusion	72
3. A Global Emergency	75
I. Introduction	75
II. The *International Health Regulations*	76
III. The *International Health Regulations (2005)*	79
IV. 2009 H1N1 Influenza Pandemic: The First Test of the *IHR (2005)*	92
V. Ebola: Another Test for the *IHR (2005)*	95
VI. COVID-19 and the *IHR (2005)*	97
VII. Proposals for a Pandemic Treaty	100
VIII. Measuring the Pandemic	103
IX. Conclusion	112
4. Restrictions on Movement	113
I. Introduction	113
II. Restrictions on Citizens' and Permanent Residents' Freedom of Movement	114

III. Closure and Patrolling of Borders to Indigenous Communities	121
IV. The Impact of Movement Restrictions on Families with Separated Parents	126
V. Extradition	132
VI. Restrictions on Non-Citizens' Freedom of Movement	136
VII. Closure of Ports to and Quarantine of Cruise Ships	143
VIII. Conclusion	144
5. Domestic Laws and Emergency Measures	**146**
I. Introduction	146
II. Emergency Laws	147
III. Travel Restrictions	153
IV. Quarantine and Isolation	154
V. Lockdowns and Stay-at-Home Orders	158
VI. Curfews	161
VII. Physical Distancing Requirements	163
VIII. Wearing of Face Masks	164
IX. Mandatory Vaccination	167
X. Vaccination Passports	176
XI. COVID-19 Testing and Contact Tracing	181
XII. Conclusion	187
6. Litigation and Legal Challenges to Emergency Orders	**188**
I. Introduction	188
II. Challenges to Border Closures	191
III. Challenges to Lockdowns	199
IV. A Challenge to Government Responses under Public Law	209
V. Challenges to Quarantine	215
VI. Challenges to Curfews	218
VII. Challenges to Physical Distancing Orders	225
VIII. Challenges to Face Mask Orders	227
IX. Challenges Arising from the Rights to Protest and Assemble	229
X. Challenges to Mandatory Vaccination Requirements	247
XI. Disputes about Vaccination of Children	263
XII. Challenges to Denial of Entry of Unvaccinated Persons	273
XIII. Conclusion	278
7. Risk, Impact, and Disadvantage	**280**
I. Introduction	280
II. The Uneven Impact of COVID-19	281
III. Prevention and Treatment	307
IV. Social Isolation	311
V. Effects of COVID-19 on Mental Health	312
VI. The Impact of COVID-19 on Economies and Employment	315
VII. Conclusion	321

8. Criminal Justice Issues and the COVID-19 Pandemic	323
I. Introduction	323
II. Changes to Substantive Aspects of Criminal Justice Systems	324
III. Issues for Criminal Justice Systems	340
IV. The Impact of COVID-19 on the Use of Detention and Incarceration	349
V. Conclusion	356
9. Civil Liability, Regulation, and Accountability	357
I. Introduction	357
II. Tort Law	359
III. Contract Law	364
IV. Construction of Insurance Contracts	370
V. Immunity for Healthcare Workers	378
VI. Vaccination Compensation	380
VII. Pathology and Medico-legal Investigations into COVID-19 Deaths	387
VIII. Consumer Protection Litigation	398
IX. Regulation of Healthcare Practitioners	407
X. Conclusion	416
10. COVID-19 and Workplace and Occupational Health and Safety	418
I. Introduction	418
II. Changing Workplace Culture	420
III. Legislative Occupational Health and Safety Obligations	422
IV. Changes to Workplace Legislation	427
V. Healthcare Workers During COVID-19	429
VI. Mandatory Vaccination in Workplaces	447
VII. Conclusion	453
11. Development of COVID-19 Treatments and Vaccines	455
I. Introduction	455
II. Research into COVID-19 Treatments and Vaccines	456
III. Participation in COVID-19 Treatments and Vaccines Research	475
IV. Publication of Results of COVID-19 Research	491
V. Conclusion	500
12. Production, Regulation, and Distribution of COVID-19 Treatments and Vaccines	502
I. Introduction	502
II. Access to COVID-19 Treatments and Vaccines	503
III. Rationing and Allocation of COVID-19 Treatments and Vaccines	516
IV. Regulation of COVID-19 Treatments and Vaccines	525
V. Intellectual Property Law and COVID-19 Treatments and Vaccines	539
VI. Conclusion	547

13. Law, Regulation, and Rights: Reflections on the COVID-19
    Pandemic   549
    I. Introduction   549
    II. Layers of Law and Polycentricity   551
    III. The Role and Scope of Law   556
    IV. Understandings of and Legal Responses to Risk   560
    V. Human Rights   567
    VI. Civil Litigation and Regulatory Obligations   573
    VII. Conclusion   578

Bibliography   581
Index   663

List of Abbreviations

ACCC	Australian Competition and Consumer Commission
ACT Accelerator	Access to COVID-19 Tools (ACT) Accelerator
AHPPC	Australia Health Protection Principal Committee
AHPRA Agency	Australian Health Practitioner Regulation
AIDS	acquired immune deficiency syndrome
AMC	Advance Market Commitment
ARDS	acute respiratory distress syndrome
ATAGI	Australian Technical Advisory Group on Immunisation
BBSI	British Board of Scholars and Imams
BORA	*New Zealand Bill of Rights Act 1990*
CARES Act 2000	*Coronavirus Aid, Relief and Economic Security Act*
CDC	United States Centers for Disease Control and Prevention
CDIT	COVID-19 Death Investigation Team
CEPI	Coalition for Epidemic Preparedness Innovations
CFR	case fatality ratio
CFS	Critical Frailty Scale
COVAX	Covid-19 Vaccines Global Access
COVID-19	coronavirus disease (2019)
CRVS	civil registration and vital statistics
C-TAP	COVID-19 Technology Access Pool
Doha Declaration	Doha Declaration on the TRIPS Agreement and Public Health
EAW	European Arrest Warrant
Ebola	Ebola virus disease
ECHR	European Court of Human Rights
EU	European Union
FAO	Food and Agriculture Organization of the United Nations
FDA	Food and Drug Administration (US)
GAVI	The Vaccine Alliance
GMOs	genetically modified organisms
GOARN	Global Outbreak Alert and Response Network
Hague Convention	Hague Convention on the Civil Aspects of International Child Abduction
HIV	human immunodeficiency virus
ICCPR	*International Covenant on Civil and Political Rights*
ICESCR	*International Covenant on Economic, Social and Cultural Rights*
ICL	independent child lawyer
ICU	intensive care unit
IEDCR	Institute of Epidemiology Disease Control and Research, Bangladesh
IFN	interferon

IFR	infection fatality ratio
IHR (2005)	*International Health Regulations (2005)*
IHR	*International Health Regulations*
ILO	International Labour Organization
IPC	infection prevention and control
IPV	intimate partner violence
IRBs	Institutional Review Boards
ISR	*International Sanitary Regulations*
MERS	Middle East Respiratory Syndrome
MHRA	Medicines and Healthcare products Regulatory Agency (UK)
MIQF	Managed Isolation and Quarantine Facility (NZ)
MIS-C	multi-inflammatory syndrome in children
MPD	Metropolitan Police Department
MSF	Médecins Sans Frontières
NASEM	National Academies of Sciences Engineering Medicine
NFP	National Focal Point
NGO	non-government organization
NICE	National Institute for Health and Care Excellence (UK)
OCI	Office of Criminal Investigations (US)
OECD	Organisation for Economic Co-operation and Development
OHCHR	United Nations Office of the High Commissioner for Human Rights
OIE	World Organisation for Animal Health
OSHA	Occupational Safety and Health Administration
PCR	polymerase chain reaction
PHE	Public Health England
PHEIC	public health emergency of international concern
PHPPA	*Public Health Protection and Promotion Act* (Can)
Polio	poliomyelitis
PPE	personal protective equipment
PREP Act	*Public Readiness and Emergency Preparation Act of 2005* (US)
RAC	Refugee Action Coalition (Aus)
REACT	real-time assessment of community transmission
RT-PCR	reverse transcription polymerase chain reaction
SAGE	Strategic Advisory Group of Experts on Immunization
SANDF	South African National Defence Force
SARS	severe acute respiratory syndrome
SARS-CoV-2	severe respiratory syndrome coronavirus 2
SAS	South African Police Service
SC	Spanish Constitution
SDGs	Sustainable Development Goals
TB	tuberculosis
TFAWs	temporary foreign agricultural workers
TRIPS	Agreement on Trade-Related Aspects of Intellectual Property Rights
UNAIDS	Joint United Nations Programme on HIV and AIDS
UNEP	United Nations Environment Programme

UNESCO	United Nations Educational, Scientific and Cultural Organization
UNHRC	United Nations Human Rights Committee
UNICEF	United Nations International Children's Emergency Fund
Values Framework	Values Framework for the Allocation and Prioritization of COVID-19 Vaccination
Venice Commission	European Commission of Democracy through Law
VICP	National Vaccine Injury Compensation Program
VoC	variants of concern
VSV	Verbraucherschutzverein
WASH	drinking water, sanitation and hygiene
WHA	World Health Assembly
WHO	World Health Organization
WPRO	Western Pacific Regional Office of the World Health Organization
WTO	World Trade Organization

About the Authors

Belinda Bennett is a Professor in the School of Law, Queensland University of Technology (QUT) in Brisbane, Australia. She is a member of the Australian Centre for Health Law Research at QUT. Her publications have analysed legal aspects of assisted reproduction, law and genetics, law and global health, and regulation of health practitioners. Her research on global health has included legal issues relevant to pandemics, and the importance of gender analysis in responding to global public health emergencies. Her publications include Belinda Bennett and Ian Freckelton (eds), *Pandemics, Public Health Emergencies and Government Powers: Perspectives on Australian Law* (Federation Press 2021); Michael Freeman, Sarah Hawkes, and Belinda Bennett (eds), *Law and Global Health: Current Legal Issues Vol 16* (OUP 2014); Belinda Bennett, Terry Carney, and Isabel Karpin (eds), *Brave New World of Health* (Federation Press 2008); Belinda Bennett, *Health Law's Kaleidoscope: Health Law Rights in a Global Age* (Ashgate Publishing 2008); and Belinda Bennett and George F Tomossy (eds), *Globalization and Health: Challenges for Health Law and Bioethics* (Springer 2006). Belinda has previously been a member and Chair of the NHMRC Embryo Research Licensing Committee. She has also previously been a Community Member of the Medical Board of Australia, and a past member of the NSW Medical Board and the Medical Council of NSW. Belinda is a member of the International Editorial Board of the *International Journal of Law in Context*; and a member of the Editorial Board for the *Journal of Law and the Biosciences*.

Ian Freckelton is a King's Counsel in full-time practice as a barrister throughout Australia and a judge of the Supreme Court of the Republic of Nauru. He has been a member of nine statutory tribunals, including the Medical Board of Victoria and the Mental Health Tribunal of Victoria. He is also a Professor of Law and a Professorial Fellow of Psychiatry at the University of Melbourne, where he is a co-director of the Health and Medical Law postgraduate programme; an Honorary Professor of Forensic Medicine at Monash University; and an Adjunct Professor at Johns Hopkins University in Baltimore, Maryland in the United States. He is an elected Fellow of the Australian Academy of Law, the Australian Academy of Health and Medical Sciences, the Academy of Social Sciences in Australia, and the Australasian College of Legal Medicine. Ian is the Editor of the *Journal of Law and Medicine* and the Founding Editor of *Psychiatry, Psychology and Law*, and the author and editor of many books, and more than 700 articles and chapters of books. Recent books include Belinda Bennett and Ian Freckelton (eds), *Pandemics, Public Health Emergencies and Government Powers: Perspectives on Australian Law* (Federation Press 2021); Ian Freckelton (ed), *Forensic Analysis* (Intech 2021); Ian Freckelton, *Expert Evidence: Law, Practice and Procedure* (6th edn, Thomson Reuters 2019; 7th edn, forthcoming 2023); Ian Freckelton and Kerry Petersen (eds), *Tensions and Traumas in Health Law* (Federation Press 2017); Ian Freckelton, *Scholarly Misconduct* (OUP 2016); Ian Freckelton and others (eds), *Expert Evidence and Criminal Jury Trials* (OUP 2016). He has given over 700 talks, orations, and presentations in over 30 countries. In 2021, Ian was appointed an Officer (AO) of the Order of Australia for distinguished service to the law and the legal profession across fields including health, medicine, and technology.

Gabrielle Wolf is an Associate Professor in Deakin University's Law School. She has published a monograph, *Make It Australian: The APG, The Pram Factory and New Wave Theatre* (Currency Press 2008), 37 articles in peer-reviewed academic journals, and four chapters in scholarly books on a range of subjects, including aspects of the current and past regulation of health practitioners in Australia, health records and confidentiality, Australian and American sentencing law, and Australian theatre history. Gabrielle previously worked as a judge's research associate and as a lawyer in private practice and in-house (at the Medical Practitioners Board of Victoria and the Australian Health Practitioner Regulation Agency). In 2019, she won the Vice-Chancellor's Mid-Career Researcher Award for Career Excellence at Deakin University.

Table of Cases

AUSTRALIA

Australian Competition and Consumer Commission v Lorna Jane Pty Ltd
  [2021] FCA 852 404
BNL20 v Minister for Home Affairs [2020] FCA 1180 301–2
Brassell-Dellow v Queensland (Queensland Police Service) [2021] QIRC 356 248–49
Clay and Dallas [2022] FCWA 18 268–69
Coco v The Queen (1994) 179 CLR 427 251
Codelfa Construction Pty Ltd v State Rail Authority of New South Wales (1982)
  149 CLR 337 366–67
Commissioner of Police (NSW) v Gibson [2020] NSWSC 953 236–37
Commissioner of Police (NSW) v Supple [2020] NSWSC 727 233–35
Commissioner of Police v Bassi [2020] NSWSC 710 231–33
Commissioner of Police v Gabriel (2004) 141 A Crim R 566 234
Commissioner of Police v Gray [2020] NSWSC 867 235–36
Construction, Forestry, Maritime, Mining and Energy Union v Mt Arthur Coal Ltd
  [2021] FWCFB 6059 .... 251–53, 424, 453
Djokovic v Minister for Immigration, Citizenship, Migrant Services and
  Multicultural Affairs [2022] FCAFC 3 .... 273–77, 371
Djokovic v Minister for Immigration, Citizenship, Migrant Services and
  Multicultural Affairs [2022] FedCFamC2G 7 273
Ellis v Medical Board of Australia (Review and Regulation) [2020] VCAT 862 413–14
Gerner v Victoria [2020] HCA 48 205–6
Gibson (on Behalf of the Dungay Family) v Commissioner of Police (NSW Police Force)
  [2020] NSWCA 160 237
HDI Global Specialty SE v Wonkana No 3 Pty Ltd [2020] NSWCA 296 373–74
Higgins v Commonwealth (1998) 79 FCR 528 205
Kardos v Harman [2020] FamCA 328 128
Karpik v Carnival PLC (The Ruby Princess) (Stay Application) [2021] FCA 1082 363
Kassam v Hazzard [2021] NSWCA 299 250–51
Kassam v Hazzard [2021] NSWCA 1320 248–49
Kimber v Sapphire Coast Community Aged Care Ltd [2021] FWCFB 6015 ..... 249–50, 448
Kontis v Coroners Court of Victoria [2022] VSC 422 397–98
LCA Marrickville Pty Ltd v Swiss Re International SE [2022] FCAFC 17 376–77
LNCP002 Pty Ltd v Feridun Akcan [2021] NSWSC 848 368
Loielo v Giles (2020) 63 VR 1 .... 221–23, 331
Majindi v Northern Territory [2012] NTSC 25 360
North Queensland Pipeline No 1 Pty Ltd v QNI Resources Pty Ltd [2021] QSC 190 368
NSW Commissioner of Police v Keep Sydney Open Ltd [2017] NSWSC 5 234
Palange & Kalhoun [2022] FedCFamC2F 149 266–68
Palmer v Western Australia [2021] HCA 5 195
Palmer v Western Australia [No 3] [2020] FCA 1220 119
Potter v Minahan (1908) 7 CLR 277 251
R v Ali (No 3) [2020] ACTSC 103 345–46
R v Macdonald [2020] NSWSC 382 .... 342, 347–48

R v UD (No 2) [2020] ACTSC 90 346
Rakielbakhour v DPP [2020] NSWSC 323 352–53
Re Broes [2020] VSC 128 352
Re Diab [2020] VSC 196 352
Re McCann [2020] VSC 138 352
Re Tong [2020] VSC 141 352
Reyes v United States of America [2020] FCAFC 149 134
Rowson v Department of Justice and Community Safety [2020] VSC 236 .... 302–4, 349
Secretary, Department of Health v Oxymed Australia Pty Ltd [2021] FCA 1518 401–5
Shehabi v Attorney General (NSW) [2016] NSWCATAP 137 481–82
South32 Aluminium (RAA) Pty Ltd v Alinta Sales Pty 368
STC3141 - An Open Label, Multi-Centre Study to Determine the Safety and Efficacy of STC3141 Administered as an Infusion for up to 5 Days in Subjects with COVID-19 Respiratory Distress Syndrome Requiring Intensive Care [2020] NSWCATGD 16 481–83
Swiss Re International Se v LCA Marrickville Pty Ltd (Second COVID-19 insurance test cases) [2021] FCA 1206 374–77
Tien v Minister for Immigration and Multicultural Affairs (1998) 89 FCR 80 274

BRAZIL

Sustainability Network v The President of the Republic of Brazil (ADPF 690 MC/DF, unreported, High Court of Brazil, 8 June 2020 per De Moraes J) 107–8

CANADA

AG of Ontario v Trinity Bible Chapel, 2021 ONSC 740 331–32
AG of Ontario v Trinity Bible Chapel, 2021 ONSC 1169 331–32
AM v CD 2022 ONSC 1516 271–72
Beaudoin v British Columbia, 2021 BCSC 512 241–42
Conseil des Juifs Hassidiques du Québec c Procureur Général du Quebec, 2021 QCCS 281 240–41
JN v CG 2022 ONSC 1198 270–71
R v Baidwan, 2020 ONSC 2349 353
R v OK, 2020 ONCJ 189 354
R v Persad, 2020 ONSC 188 354
Ribeiro v Wright, 2020 ONSC 1829 127–28
Sanctuary Ministries of Toronto v Toronto (City) (2020) 152 OR (3d) 411 ... 226–27, 296
Taylor v Newfoundland and Labrador 2020 NLSC 125 118–19
Trest v British Columbia (Minister of Health) 2020 BCSC 1524 .... 228, 562

EUROPE

Budayeva v Russia (2014) 59 EHHR 2 .... 211, 214–15
Campeanu v Romania (Application no 47848-08, European Court of Human Rights, 17 July 2014) 211
Enhorn v Sweden, Application no 56529/00, 25 January 2005 215
IB v Greece, Application no 552/10, 3 October 2013 63
Kiyutin v Russia, App no 2700/10, 15 September 2011 62
Kolyadenko v Russia (2013) 56 ECHR 2 211

Nencheva v Bulgaria (Application no 48609-06, European Court of Human
  Rights, 18 June 2013) 211
Öneryildiz v Turkey (2000) 29 ECHR 245 211
Osman v United Kingdom (2000) 29 ECHR 245 211
Terheş v Romania, Application no 49933/20, 13 April 2021 204–5
Vavřička and Others v The Czech Republic, App no 47621/13, 8 April 2021 174
Watts v United Kingdom (2010) 51 EHRR SE5 211
X v Latvia, App no 27853/09, 26 November 2013 130

FRANCE

Conseil d'État, 28 October 2020, 445441 223–24
Conseil d'État, 9 June 2021, 453247 223–24
Tribunal Administratif de Nice, Affaire N 2100056, 11 January 2021 223–24

GERMANY

F Bundesverfassungsgericht [German Constitutional Court], 1 BvQ 44/20,
  29 April 2020 240

IRELAND

C v G (Child Abduction (Poland) Grave Risk Defence) [2020] IEHC 217 .... 130, 131
Friedrich v Friedrich, 78 F 3d 1060 (6th Cir, 1996) 130
Heyns v Tifco Ltd [2021] IEHC 329 217
JV v QI [2020] IECA 302 131–32
RK v KJ (Child Abduction: Acquiescence) [2000] 2 IR 416 130
Medical Council v Waters [2021] IEHC 252 410–12
Minister for Justice and Equality v Sciuka [2021] IECA 79 134–36
O'Doherty v Minister for Health [2020] IEHC 209 199–200

KENYA

Law Society of Kenya v Mutyambai [2020] eKLR, High Court of Kenya,
  Constitutional and Human Rights Division, 16 April 2020 220–21

NEW ZEALAND

A v Ardern [2020] NZHC 796 206–7
Allen v Police [2021] NZHC 981 328–29
B v Ardern [2020] NZHC 814 206–7
Bolton v Chief Executive of Business, Innovation and Employment [2021]
  NZHC 2897; [2021] 3 NZLR 425 196
Borrowdale v Director-General of Health [2020] NZHC 2090 .... 136, 206
Four Aviation Security Service Employees v Minister of Covid-19 Response [2021]
  NZHC 3012 .... 250, 251, 253
Four Midwives v Minister for Covid-19 Response [2021] NZHC 3064 .... 251, 253
Grounded Kiwis Group Incorporated v Minister of Health [2022]
  NZHC 832 .... 118–19, 196–98
Long v Steine [2022] NZFC 251 269–70

Police v Harris [2020] NZDC 27024 325–26
Police v Woods [2020] NZDC 6614 325–26

SOUTH AFRICA

De Beer v Minister of Cooperative Governance and Traditional Affairs [2020]
ZAGPPHC 184; 2020 (11) BCLR 1349 (GP) (High Court) 156–57, 164
Khosa v Minister of Defence and Military Veterans [2020] 3 All SA 190 (GP);
[2020] ZAGPPHC 147 (High Court) 201–2, 316
Mohamed v President of the Republic of South Africa [2020] 2 All SA 844 (GP);
[2020] ZAGPPHC 120 (High Court) 156
Soobramoney v Minister of Health, KwaZulu-Natal [1997] ZACC 17; 1998 (1)
SA 765 520

SPAIN

STC 148/2021, de 14 de julio de 2021 203

TONGA

Nishi v Nishi [2021] TOSC 149 128–29

UNITED KINGDOM

BK v NK [2016] EWHC 2496 (Fam) 130
Bank of New York Mellon (International) Ltd v Cine-UK Ltd [2021] EWHC
1013 (QB) 366, 368
C (Looked After Child) (Covid-19 Vaccination) [2021] EWHC 2993 (Fam) 263–65
Carlill v Carbolic Smoke Ball Co [1892] 2 QB 484 .... 399–400, 523
Carlill v Carbolic Smoke Ball Co [1893] 1 QB 256 .... 55, 526
Channel Island Ferries Ltd v Sealink UK Ltd [1988] 1 Lloyd's Rep 323 368
Collins v Wilcock [1984] 1 WLR 1172 359–60
Commission v United Kingdom [2007] All ER 126; [2007] IRLR 720 424
Cosar v Governor of HMP Wandsworth [2020] EWHC 1142 (Admin) 132
Davis Contractors Ltd v Fareham Urban District Council [1956] AC 696 366–67
Dwyer (UK Franchising) Ltd v Fredbar Ltd [2021 EWHC 1218 (Ch) 368
E (Vaccine) [2021] EWCOP 7 263–64
Edwards v National Coal Board [1949] 1 KB 704 424
F v F [2013] EWHC 2683 (Fam) 268–69
Financial Conduct Authority v Arch Insurance (UK) Ltd [2021] UKSC 1 ...... 370–71, 374
Gardner & Harris v Secretary of State for Health and Social Care [2022]
EWHC 967 (Admin) 209–15
Gillick v West Northwick & Wisbech Health Authority [1986] AC 112 .... 264, 265
H (A Child Parental Responsibility: Vaccination) [2020] EWCA 664 263
Hirst v Chief Constable of West Yorkshire (1987) 85 Cr App R 143 234
Kaye v Robertson [1991] FSR 62 359–60
M v H (Private Law Vaccination) [2020] EWFC 93 263–64
North Yorkshire Clinical Commissioning Group v E (Covid Vaccination)
[2022] EWCOP 15 263–64
Nugent v Smith (1876) 1 CPD 423 368
Pursell v Horn (1838) 8 Ad & E 602, 112 ER 966 360

TABLE OF CASES xxix

R (AB) v Secretary of State for Justice [2021] UKSC 28; 2021] 3 WLR 494 211–12
*R (Dawson) v HM Coroner for East Riding and Kingston upon Hull Coroners
  District* [2001] EWHC Admin 352 391
R (Detention Action) v Secretary of State for the Home Department [2020]
  EWHC 732 (Admin) 298–301
R (Dolan) v Secretary of State for Health and Social Care [2020] EWHC 1786
  (Admin) 150, 202, 214–15
R (Hussain) v Secretary of State for Health and Social Care [2020] EWHC 1392
  (Admin) 238–40
R (Munjaz) v Ashworth Hospital [2006] 2 AC 148 210
R (Smith) v Oxfordshire Assistant Deputy Coroner [2011] 1 AC 1 392
R (Khalid) v Secretary of State for Health and Social Care [2021] EWHC 2156
  (Admin) 216
R v Cambridge Health Authority, Ex parte B [1995] 2 All ER 129 520
R v Cotesworth (1704) 6 Mod 180, 87 ER 928 360
Re N (a Child) [2020] EWFC 35 129–30
Re NY (A Child) [2019] UKSC 49 129
Re PT [2020] EWHC 834 (Fam) 130–31
Re S (Abduction: Hague Convention or BIIa) [2018] EWCA Civ 1226 129
Re T (a child) [2020] EWHC 220 (Fam) 263
Representation of Pearmain re St Clement Parish Elections [2021] JRC 213 368
Richards v Environment Agency [2022] EWCA Civ 26 214–15
Salam Air SAOC v Latam Airlines Groups SA [2020] EWHC 2414 (Comm) 368
Scholes v SSHD [2006] HRLR 44 392
SD v Royal Borough of Kensington and Chelsea [2021] EWCOP 14 263–64
TKC London Ltd v Allianz Insurance PLC [2020] EWHC 2710 (Comm) 366
White v General Medical Council [2021] EWHC 3286 (Admin) 409–11, 415–16

UNITED STATES OF AMERICA

Associated Acquisitions, LLC v Carbone Properties of Audobon, LLC, 962 So 2d 1102,
  (La App, 4th Cir 2007) 368
Bauer v Summey 568 F Supp 3d 573 (DSC 2021) 562
Bayley's Campground Inc v Mills 463 F Supp 3d 22 (D Me, 2020) 217–18
Bayley's Campground Inc v Mills 985 F 3d 153 (1st Cir, 2021) 217–18
Beckerich v St. Elizabeth Medical Centre, 64 NDLR P 23 (ED Ky 2021) 254
Biden v Missouri, 142 S Ct 647 (2022); 211 L Ed 433 (2022) 257, 451–52, 453, 578–79
Billo v Allegheny Steel Co, 195 A 110 (Pa, 1937) 360–61
Bissell v Davison 32 A 348 (Conn 1894) 48
Calvary Chapel Dayton Valley v Sisolak, 140 S Ct 2603 (2020); 207 L Ed
  1129 (2020) 244–45
Carmichael v Ige, 470 F Supp 3d 1133 (D Haw 2020) 218
Compagnie Francaise De Navigation A Vapeur v Louisiana State Board of Health 186
  US 380 (1902) 57–58
Cutter Incident Vaccine - Gottsdanker v Cutter Laboratories, 182 Cal App 2d 602,
  6 Cal Rptr 320, 79 ALR 2d 290 (Cal App 1 Dist 1960) 60
Florida v Department of Health and Human Services, 19 F 4th 1271 (11th Cir, 2021) ... 258
Givens v Newsom, 459 F Supp 3d 1302 (ED Cal, 2020) 207–8
Globe School District No 1 v Board of Health of City of Globe 179 P 55 (Ariz, 1919) 58
Gulf Oil Corp v FERC, 706 F 2d 444 (3rd Cir, 1983) 368
Hague v Committee for Industrial Organization 307 US 496 (1939) 230

Harsman v Cincinnati Children's Hospital Medical Center (SD Ohio, No 1:21-CV-597,
  20 September 2021) 255
Hirabayashi v United States, 320 US 81 (1943) 218–19
International Minerals & Chemical Corp v Llano, Inc, 770 F 2d 879 (10th Cir, 1989) ... 369
Jackson v Cutter Laboratories, Inc, 338 F Supp 882 (1970) 60
Jacobson v Massachusetts 197 US 11 (1905) 48, 248, 261–62
Jew Ho v Williamson 103 F 10 (ND Cal 1900) 48
John Does 1–3 v Mills, 142 S Ct 17 (2021); 211 L Ed 2d 243 (2021) 256–57
Kyocera Corp v Hemlock Semiconductor, LLC, 886 NW 2d 445
  (Mich Ct App, 2015) 368–69
Marshall v United States, 414 US 417 (1974) 243
Montana v United States 450 US 544 (1981) 125–26
Morgan's Steamship Co v Louisiana Board of Health 118 US 455 (1886) 57–58
*National Federation of Independent Business v Occupational Safety and Health
  Administration*, 142 S Ct 661 (2022); 211 L Ed 2d 448 (2022) ... 259, 261–62, 450, 453
New York State Association for Retarded Children Inc v Rockefeller,
  357 F Supp 752 (1973) 467–68
New York State Association for Retarded Children v Carey, 706 F 2d 956 (1983) 467–68
Roman Catholic Diocese of Brooklyn New York v Cuomo, 141 S Ct 63 (2020);
  208 L Ed 206 (2020) 245–46, 257
Salgo v Leland Stanford Jr University Board of Trustees 154 Cal App 2d 560,
  317 P 2d 170 (1957) 477–78
South Bay United Pentecostal Church v Newsom, 140 S Ct 1613 (2020);
  207 L Ed 154 (2020) 242–43
State v Haines 545 NE 2d 834 (Ind Ct App 1989) 63–64
Tandon v Newsom, 141 S Ct 1294 (2021); 209 L Ed 355 (2021) 246–47
United States v Grace 461 US 171 (1983) 230
Wartsila Diesel, Inc v Sierra Rutile, Ltd (ED Pa, Civ A 95-2958, 16 December 1996) 368
Wisconsin Legislature v Palm, 391 Wis 2d 497 (Sup Ct, 2020) 208
Wong Wai v Williamson 103 F 1 (ND Cal 1900) 48

Table of Legislation

INTERNATIONAL

Constitution of the World Health Organization (opened for signature 22 July 1946, entered into force 7 April 1948) 14 UNTS 185 .... 15, 66, 77, 102–3
Convention on the Rights of Persons with Disabilities (opened for signature 13 December 2006, entered into force 3 May 2008) 2515 UNTS 3
    Article 11 304
    Article 15 477
    Article 25 304
Convention Relating to the Status of Refugees (opened for signature 28 July 1951, entered into force 22 April 1954) 189 UNTS 137 ... 142–43
Council Framework Decision of 13 June 2002 on the European arrest warrant and the surrender procedures between Member States [2002] OJ L190/1 134
General Conference of the International Labour Organisation, *Indigenous and Tribal Peoples Convention 1989* (No. 169) (adopted 27 June 1989, entered into force 5 September 1991) 124
Hague Convention on the Civil Aspects of International Child Abduction (opened for signature 25 October 1980, entered into force 1 December 1983) 1343 UNTS 89 .... 129, 130
International Covenant on Civil and Political Rights (opened for signature 16 December 1966, entered into force 23 March 1976) 999 UNTS 171 ...... 90, 116–17, 118, 148, 149, 153–54, 172, 174, 475
    Article 4 .... 118, 148, 149, 150, 330–31, 568–69
    Article 6 .... 117, 121, 142–43, 148, 172, 329–30, 475, 504–5, 567–68
    Article 7 ..... 117, 148, 476, 569–70, 572
    Article 8 148
    Article 9 .... 343–44, 570
    Article 12 .... 116–17, 120, 121, 330–31, 567–68
    Article 14 .... 345–46, 348, 570
    Article 17 .... 172–73, 573
    Article 18 .... 172–73, 174, 567–68
    Article 19 .... 229, 330–31, 567–68
    Article 21 .... 229, 230–31, 330–31, 567–68
    Article 22 229
    Article 26 330–31
International Covenant on Economic, Social and Cultural Rights (opened for signature 16 December 1966, entered into force 3 January 1976) 993 UNTS 3
    Article 12 .... 30–31, 117, 121, 142–43, 172, 329–30, 475, 504–5, 567–68
    Article 15 .... 504–5, 572
International Health Regulations (2005) (adopted 23 May 2005, entered into force 15 June 2007) 2509 UNTS 79 .... 4–5, 14, 16–17, 18, 22, 23–24, 28, 29, 34–35, 41–42, 69–70, 72, 73–74, 76, 78–80, 81–93, 94, 95, 96–99, 101–2, 112, 118–19, 153–54, 178–79, 553–54, 574
    Article 1 .... 80, 82, 144
    Article 2 79
    Article 3 .... 30–31, 88–89
    Article 4 .... 87, 93
    Article 5 .... 87–88, 307–8
    Article 6 .... 81–82, 85
    Article 7 85
    Article 8 85
    Article 9 85–86
    Article 10 86
    Article 11 86–87
    Article 12 81–82
    Article 13 88
    Article 15 .... 81–82, 90

Article 17 90–91
Article 18 90
Article 23 89
Article 27 144
Article 28 144
Article 32 89
Article 42 . . . . 89, 137–38
Article 43 . . . . 91–92, 93, 118–20
Article 44 88
Article 45 89
Article 49 90
Article 59 79
Annex 1 . . . . 87, 88, 307–8
Annex 2 . . . . 81–84, 85
International Health Regulations
  (1969) (adopted 25 July 1969,
  entered into force 1 January 1971)
  764 UNTS 3 . . . . 41–42, 69, 76, 78
International Labour Organization,
  Occupational Safety and Health
  Convention (No 155) Concerning
  Occupational Safety and Health
  and the Working Environment
  (opened for signature 22 June
  1981, entered into force 11
  August 1983) 1331 UNTS 279 . . . 423
International Labour Organization,
  Promotional Framework for
  Occupational Safety and Health
  Convention (No 187) Concerning
  the Promotional Framework for
  Occupational Safety and Health
  (opened for signature 15 June
  2006, entered into force 20
  February 2009)
  2564 UNTS 291 423
International Sanitary Regulations
  (adopted 25 May 1951, entered
  into force 1 October 1952) 175
  UNTS 215 . . . . 69, 77
Marrakesh Agreement Establishing
  the World Trade Organization
  (opened for signature 15 April
  1994, entered into force 1 January
  1995) 1867 UNTS 3, Annex 1C
  ('Agreement on Trade-Related
  Aspects of Intellectual Property
  Rights') 69–70, 542–43
Regulation (EU) 2016/399 of the
  European Parliament and of
  the Council of 9 March 2016
  on a Union Code on the Rules
  Governing the Movement
  of Persons Across Borders
  (Schengen Borders Code) [2016]
  OJ L77/1 137
United Nations Convention on
  Contracts for the International
  Sale of Goods (opened for
  signature 11 April 1980, entered
  into force January 1988) 1489
  UNTS 3 365–66
United Nations Declaration on the
  Rights of Indigenous Peoples
  (Resolution A/RES/61/295, 13
  September 2007) 122–23, 125
Universal Declaration of Human
  Rights (United Nations General
  Assembly, Resolution A/RES/3/
  217A, 10 December 1948) 142
  Article 5 476
  Article 14 . . . . 117, 569–70
Universal Declaration on Bioethics
  and Human Rights (adopted 19
  October 2005)
  Article 6 476
  Article 7 477
  Article 8 477
  Article 15 505
  Article 24 505
World Medical Association,
  Declaration of Helsinki—Ethical
  Principles for Medical
  Research Involving Human
  Subjects (adopted
  June 1964) 478–79, 483
World Trade Organization,
  'Declaration on the TRIPS
  Agreement and Public Health'
  (Resolution WT/Min(01)/Dec/2,
  14 November 2001) 542–43

AUSTRALIA

Biosecurity Act 2015 (Cth) 142, 373–74
  Section 475 142
  Section 477 142
Biosecurity (Human Biosecurity
  Emergency) (Human Coronavirus
  with Pandemic Potential)
  (Emergency Requirements
  for Remote Communities)
  Determination 2020 (Cth) 287
Charter of Human Rights and
  Responsibilities Act 2006
  (Vic) 157–58, 303–4

Civil Liability Act 2002 (NSW)
  s 5B 363–64
Constitution of Australia 205, 206
  Section 92 195
  Section 117 195
Coroners Act 2008 (Vic)
  Section 1 395
Corrections Act 1986 (Vic) s 58E(1) ... 355
COVID-19 Emergency Response Act
  2020 (ACT) sch 1, cl 68BA(3) 346
Criminal Procedure Act 2009 (Vic) s
  420D(1) 346
Emergency Management Act 2005
  (WA) 123–24, 195
Extradition Act 1988 (Cth)
  Section 26 134
Guardianship Act 1987 (NSW) 481
Human Rights Act 2004 (ACT) 157–58
Human Rights Act 2019 (Qld) 157–58
Migration Act 1958 (Cth)
  Section 116 273
  Section 133C 273
Public Health (COVID-19 Restrictions
  on Gathering and Movement)
  Order (No 3) of 2020 (NSW) 232
Public Health (COVID-19 Spitting
  and Coughing) Order (No 2) 2021
  (NSW) 328–29
Public Health Act 2010 (NSW) 249
  Section 7 250–51
Public Health Amendment (COVID-19
  Spitting and Coughing) Regulation
  2020 (NSW) 328
Public Health and Wellbeing Act 2008
  (Vic) 205
Public Health and Wellbeing
  Amendment (Pandemic
  Management) Act 2021 (Vic) ....
  188, 571–72
  Section 165BN 325–26
Quarantine (Closing the Border)
  Directions (WA) 195
Quarantine Act 1908 (Cth) 373–74
Racial Discrimination Act 1975 (Cth)
  Section 18C 339–40
Remote Aboriginal Communities
  Directions (No 3) (WA) 123–24
Therapeutic Goods Act 1989
  (Cth) 404–5
Work Health and Safety Act 2011 (NSW)
  Section 47 252–53

BRAZIL

Constitution of Brazil 207

CANADA

Access to Services (COVID-19) Bill
  2021 (BC) 230
Aeronautics Act 1985 (Canada) 120
An Act Respecting the Determination of
  the Causes and Circumstances of
  Death, RSQ 1983, c R-0.2
  Section 3 395
  Section 92 395
Canadian Charter of Rights and
  Freedoms 120, 157–58, 194,
                              195, 241–42
  Section 6 .... 120, 125, 192–93
  Section 7 192–94
  Section 25 125
Constitution Act 1982 (Canada) 120
COVID-19 Emergency Response Act
  2020 (Can) s 15 543
Indian Act 1985 (Canada) 125
Occupational Health and Safety
  Regulation (British
  Columbia) 446
Patent Act 1985 (Can) s 19.4 543
Public Health Act, SBC 2008,
  c 28...................... 241–42
Public Health Protection and
  Promotion Act, SN 2018,
  c P-37.3 192–93
Quebec Charter of Human Rights and
  Freedoms, SQ 1975, c C-12 241

EUROPE

Convention for the Protection of
  Human Rights and Fundamental
  Freedoms (European Convention
  on Human Rights) (opened for
  signature 4 November 1950,
  entered into force 3 September
  1953) 213 UNTS 221 209
  Article 2 .... 202, 210–12, 214–15
  Article 5 .... 204–5, 215, 216, 343–44
  Article 6 .... 345, 348
  Article 8 174
  Article 9 238
  Article 10 410

FRANCE

French Civil Code Article 1218 365

GERMANY

German Constitution
   Article 4 240
Infectious Diseases Protection Act 428
Third Act to Protect the Public in the
   Event of an Epidemic Situation of
   National Significance 428

INDIA

Constitution of India
   Article 21 200

IRELAND

Constitution of Ireland 202–3, 217
Health (Preservation and Protection
   and other Emergency Measures in
   the Public Interest) Act 2020
   (Ireland) 202–3

NEW ZEALAND

Habeas Corpus Act 2001 (NZ) 206–7
Health Act 1956 (NZ) 206–7
   Section 70 206
New Zealand Bill of Rights
   Act 1990 . . . . 206, 269–70
   Section 5 206
   Section 18 . . . . 197, 206
Public Health Response Amendment
   Act (No 2) 2021 (NZ) 325–26

PHILIPPINES

Local Government Code of 1991 450

SOUTH AFRICA

Constitution of South Africa
   Section 10 201
   Section 11 201
   Section 12 201
   Section 199 201–2
Disaster Management Act 57 of 2002
   (South Africa) 201, 324, 328
Public Health Act 1919
   (South Africa) 59–60

Regulations Issued in Terms of Section
   27(2) of the Disaster Management
   Act 2002 (18 March 2020) 324

SPAIN

Constitution of Spain
   Article 10 203
   Article 16 203
   Article 17 203
   Article 19 203
   Article 21 203–4
   Article 23 203–4
   Article 25 203
   Article 27 203
   Article 35 203
   Article 38 203
   Article 55 203
Royal Decree 463/2020 of
   14 March 2020 203–4

UNITED KINGDOM

Coronavirus Act 2020 (UK) 391, 392
   Section 14 215
   Section 15 215
Coroners (Investigations) Regulations
   2013, SI 2013/1629 393
Coroners and Justice Act 2009 (UK)
   Section 7 392
   Regulation 28 393
   Regulation 29 393
   Schedule 5 393
Extradition Act 2003 (UK) 133
General Medical Council (Fitness to
   Practise) Rules Order of Council
   2004, SI 2004/2608 409
Health and Safety at Work Act 1974
   (UK) 422
   Section 2 423–24
   Section 3 423
   Section 7 425
Health Protection (Coronavirus,
   International Travel) (England)
   Regulations 2020, SI 2020/568 . . . 216
Health Protection (Coronavirus,
   Restrictions) (England)
   Regulations, SI 2020/350 238
Human Medicines Regulations
   2012 (UK) 531–32
Human Rights Act 1998 (UK)
   Section 12 410–11

Immigration Act 2016 (UK)
  Section 56 300
Inquiries Act 2005 (UK) ....
  213
Judicial Review and Courts Bill
  2021 (UK) 392
National Health Service (Performers Lists, Coronavirus) (England) Amendment Regulations 2021
  (Eng) 435–36
Ordinance of Labourers 1349
  (23 Edw 3 c 1) 46–47, 365–66
Statute of Labourers 1351
  (25 Edw 3 c 1) 46–47, 365–66
Vaccine Damage Payments (Specified Diseases) Order 2020,
  SI 2020/1411 (UK) 385
Vaccine Damage Payments Act 1979 (UK) 385

UNITED STATES

Americans with Disabilities Act of 1990, 42 USC §12101 254
Californian Civil Code s 1511 365
Constitution of California 207–8
Constitution of the United States 207–8,
  217–18, 244
  First Amendment 229, 243, 245,
  246, 247
Coronavirus Aid, Relief, and Economic Security Act of 2020, 15 USC
  §9001 319
  Section 3215 378–79
COVID-19 Consumer Protection Act of the 2021 Consolidated Appropriations Act, Pub L No
  116-260, 134 Stat 1182 (2021) ... 401

COVID-19 Hate Crimes Act 34 USC
  10101 (2021) 339–40
COVID-19 Religious Exemption Act,
  HB 4239, 102nd Illinois General
  Assembly (2021) 572–73
COVID-19 Vaccination and Testing; Emergency Temporary Standard,
  86 Fed Reg 61402 (5 November
  2021) 259–60
Declaration of Emergency Directive
  021: Phase Two Reopening Plan
  (Emergency Order, 28 May 2020)   244
Families First Coronavirus Response Act 319
Federal Policy for the Protection of Human Subjects, 82 Fed Reg 7149
  (19 January 2017) 478–79
Food, Drug, and Cosmetic Act 70, 532
Medicare and Medicaid Programs; Omnibus COVID-19 Health Care Staff Vaccination, 86 Fed Reg
  61555 (5 November 2021) 257
National Childhood Vaccine Injury Act of 1986, 42 USC §300aa-10 ... 384–85
National Research Act 1974 478–79
Occupational Safety and Health Act of 1970, Pub L No 91-596, 84 Stat
  1590 (1970) 259
Public Health Service Act of 1944, 42
  USC 138–39, 401
Public Readiness and Emergency Preparedness Act, 42 USC §247d-
  6d 379–80, 384–85
Sixth Amendment to Declaration
  Under the Public Readiness and
  Emergency Preparedness Act
  for Medical Countermeasures
  Against COVID-19, 86 Fed Reg
  9516 (16 February 2021) 380

1
COVID-19, Law, and Regulation

I. Introduction

The declaration on 30 January 2020 by the World Health Organization's (WHO) Director-General of a public health emergency of international concern (PHEIC) in relation to the spread of a novel coronavirus, now known as SARS-CoV-2,[1] marked the formal beginning of a global health crisis unlike any experienced since the Spanish flu in 1918. In the weeks and months following this declaration, COVID-19, the disease caused by SARS-CoV-2, would sweep the globe. In an effort to slow the rising numbers of infections and deaths, during 2020 and 2021, governments placed cities and countries into lockdown, borders were closed, and quarantine, isolation, social distancing, curfews, and the wearing of face masks all became familiar. In some countries, the scale of the pandemic overwhelmed hospitals, supplies of personal protective equipment (PPE) such as face masks became scarce, and there was unprecedented demand for intensive care beds and ventilators. As economies shut down and unemployment soared, the magnitude of the pandemic's economic and social consequences also became apparent. In its April 2020 'COVID-19 Strategy Update', WHO noted three defining characteristics of the COVID-19 pandemic: the speed and scale of the pandemic; its severity in terms of severe disease and mortality; and the societal and economic disruption caused by the pandemic.[2]

Although law often operates in the background of pandemics, COVID-19 has brought public health law into the spotlight. This book engages with the role of law, regulation, and public policy in providing a framework for responses to the pandemic at the local, national, and global levels. Throughout the pandemic, public health laws have played a key role in supporting governments' responses, for instance, by enabling the closure of borders, isolation of individuals who have tested positive for the virus, quarantine of individuals who may have been exposed to the

---

[1] World Health Organization, 'Statement on the second meeting of the International Health Regulations (2005) Emergency Committee regarding the outbreak of novel coronavirus (2019-nCoV)' (30 January 2020) <https://www.who.int/news/item/30-01-2020-statement-on-the-second-meeting-of-the-international-health-regulations-(2005)-emergency-committee-regarding-the-outbreak-of-novel-coronavirus-(2019-ncov)> accessed 20 February 2022 (hereafter World Health Organization, 'Statement on the second meeting of the IHR (2005) Emergency Committee').

[2] World Health Organization, 'COVID-19 strategy update—14 April 2020' (World Health Organization 2020) 2 <https://www.who.int/publications/m/item/covid-19-strategy-update> accessed 7 March 2022.

virus, and enforcement of curfews and physical distancing measures. They have also been the subject of litigation and challenge in the courts on many occasions. More broadly, in areas not traditionally thought of as related to health, including social security, taxation, and housing, a range of emergency provisions was enacted to support the health and well-being of citizens and economies. This book analyses the legal and regulatory responses to COVID-19 from the measures introduced in reaction to the earliest cases of persons with symptoms, to the roll-out of vaccines on the road to resumption of normality. Drawing upon examples from many countries, including the United Kingdom, Australia, New Zealand, South Africa, various European countries, the United States of America, Canada, and Brazil, it explains how law has played a critical role in supporting efforts to tackle the adverse impact of COVID-19 and its social and economic ramifications. It maintains that this experience will provide important lessons for the role of law in building more resilient public health systems for the future when, inevitably, once more we shall confront comparable public health challenges.

II. The COVID-19 Pandemic

Since early 2020, COVID-19 had a substantial adverse impact on the global community. By early December 2021, the total number of confirmed cases of COVID-19 globally exceeded 264 million with over 5 million deaths.[3] However, as we discuss in Chapter 3, it is difficult to know the actual death toll from COVID-19: the number of officially reported deaths is likely to be an under-estimate because many countries lack the capacity to collect accurate and timely data, and there is a discrepancy in many countries between the numbers of deaths formally ascribed to COVID-19 as against excess mortality, the number of deaths that would have been expected without a pandemic.[4] Healthcare workers have been particularly vulnerable to contracting and suffering from COVID-19.[5] It is estimated that globally between 80,000 and 180,000 healthcare workers died after contracting COVID-19 in the period from January 2020 to May 2021, with a population-based estimate of 115,500 deaths.[6] At the time of writing, rising rates of vaccination are slowing

[3] World Health Organization, 'Weekly operational update on COVID-19: Issue No 83' (7 December 2021) <https://www.who.int/publications/m/item/weekly-operational-update-on-covid-19---7-december-2021> accessed 11 December 2021.
[4] World Health Organization, 'The true death toll of COVID-19: Estimating global excess mortality' <https://www.who.int/data/stories/the-true-death-toll-of-covid-19-estimating-global-excess-mortality> accessed 20 February 2022.
[5] For further discussion see Chapter 10.
[6] World Health Organization, 'The impact of COVID-19 on health and care workers: a closer look at deaths' (September 2021) <https://apps.who.int/iris/handle/10665/345300> accessed 20 February 2022. See also World Health Organization, 'WHO and partners call for action to better protect health and care workers from COVID-19' News Release (21 October 2021) <https://www.who.int/news/item/21-10-2021-who-and-partners-call-for-action-to-better-protect-health-and-care-workers-from-covid-19> accessed 25 October 2021.

the pandemic in many countries. However, as discussed in Chapter 12, access to vaccines remains uneven and, at the time of writing, the world's poorest countries still lack sufficient supplies of vaccines. In May 2022, WHO announced excess mortality of approximately 14.9 million deaths between 1 January 2020 and 31 December 2021 that were directly or indirectly associated with the COVID-19 pandemic.[7]

Contagious and more severe than influenza,[8] older persons and those with underlying health conditions are at particular risk of severe disease and death from COVID-19.[9] WHO noted in January 2021 that 'Despite some improvements in treatment COVID-19 remains a severe disease, with most estimates putting the case fatality ratio greater than 10% in people over 65 years of age.'[10] For patients with COVID-19, approximately 15% will develop severe COVID-19 and will require oxygen support and 5% will 'have critical disease with complications such as respiratory failure, acute respiratory distress syndrome, sepsis and septic shock, thromboembolism, and/or multi-organ failure'.[11]

As WHO has observed, public health tools of disease surveillance, contact tracing, isolation and treatment of cases, and quarantine 'are the backbones of the COVID-19 response and the keys to controlling transmission in the absence of a widely available vaccine'.[12] Although some existing programmes, such as those directed to polio and tuberculosis (TB), have helped to support the public health response to COVID-19,[13] the pandemic has also led to disruption of these programmes. Childhood immunization programmes have also been disrupted during the pandemic,[14] and WHO's 'Global Tuberculosis Report 2021' reported that 'The COVID-19 pandemic has reversed years of progress in providing essential TB services and reducing TB disease burden.'[15]

---

[7] World Health Organization, '14.9 Million Excess Deaths Associated with the COVID-19 Pandemic in 2020 and 2021' News Release (5 May 2022) <https://www.who.int/news/item/05-05-2022-14.9-million-excess-deaths-were-associated-with-the-covid-19-pandemic-in-2020-and-2021> accessed 19 May 2022.

[8] Jovana Stojanovic and others, 'COVID-19 is Not the Flu: Four Graphs from Four Countries' (2021) 9 *Frontiers in Public Health* art 628479; Gareth Iacobucci, 'Covid and Flu: What Do the Numbers Tell Us About Morbidity and Deaths?' (2021) 375 *British Medical Journal* n2514; Lionel Piroth and others, 'Comparison of the Characteristics, Morbidity, and Mortality of COVID-19 and Seasonal Influenza: A Nation-wide, Population-based Retrospective Cohort Study' (2021) 9(3) *Lancet Respiratory Medicine* 251.

[9] World Health Organization, 'Coronavirus disease (COVID-19)' (13 May 2021) <https://www.who.int/emergencies/diseases/novel-coronavirus-2019/question-and-answers-hub/q-a-detail/coronavirus-disease-covid-19> accessed 7 March 2022.

[10] World Health Organization, 'Looking back at a year that changed the world: WHO's response to COVID-19' (22 January 2021) 4 <https://www.who.int/publications/m/item/looking-back-at-a-year-that-changed-the-world-who-s-response-to-covid-19> accessed 7 March 2022 (hereafter World Health Organization, 'Looking back at a year that changed the world').

[11] ibid 32.

[12] ibid 22.

[13] ibid 23–24.

[14] ibid 36. For further discussion see Chapter 7.

[15] World Health Organization, 'Global Tuberculosis Report 2021' (World Health Organization 2021) 1.

At a broad level, the course of the pandemic to date can be divided into three main phases with distinctive legal and regulatory responses: an initial phase with the emergence of a previously unknown virus and rising numbers of cases around the world; a second phase characterized by subsequent waves of the pandemic, a further escalation of case numbers, and a rising death toll, and the introduction of lockdowns, stay-at-home orders, and other social distancing measures; and a third phase that began with the introduction of vaccines and gradual re-opening of economies and travel, albeit with sporadic re-emergence of significant levels of the virus in some countries. As the pandemic is not yet over, there will undoubtedly be further phases, which will include the effects of COVID-19 variants such as Omicron, and issues in respect of persons who choose not to be vaccinated or not to keep their vaccination status up to date. In addition, there will be sequelae of the pandemic. A summary of the key events that occurred during the phases that have taken place at the time of writing, and some of the significant international and domestic legal and regulatory measures that were implemented in response to them, is set out below.

A. Emergence of a Previously Unknown Virus

In late December 2019, cases of a pneumonia of unknown origin emerged in Wuhan, China.[16] While the origins of the pandemic are unclear, they appear to have been zoonotic.[17] On 31 December 2019, the Wuhan Municipal Health Commission released a public bulletin confirming 27 cases of pneumonia of unknown origin.[18] On the same date, WHO China notified the WHO Western Pacific Regional Office (WPRO) International Health Regulations Focal Point.[19] On 3 January 2020, the WHO China Country Office and the Chinese National Health

---

[16] Details included in this Section are based on information provided in The Independent Panel for Pandemic Preparedness and Response, 'COVID-19: The Authoritative Chronology, December 2019–March 2020' Background paper 2a (May 2021) (hereafter Independent Panel, 'COVID-19: The Authoritative Chronology') and The Independent Panel for Pandemic Preparedness and Response, 'How an Outbreak Became a Pandemic: The Defining Moments of the COVID-19 Pandemic' (hereafter Independent Panel, 'How an Outbreak Became a Pandemic'). Both reports are available from <https://theindependentpanel.org> accessed 1 October 2022. See also Sudhvir Singh and others, 'How an Outbreak Became a Pandemic: A Chronological Analysis of Crucial Junctures and International Obligations in the Early Months of the COVID-19 Pandemic' (2021) 398(10316) *Lancet* 2109.

[17] World Health Organization, 'WHO-Convened Global Study of Origins of SARS-CoV-2: China Part, Joint WHO-China Study, 14 January–10 February 2021, Joint Report' <https://www.who.int/publications/i/item/who-convened-global-study-of-origins-of-sars-cov-2-china-part> accessed 1 October 2022; WHO Scientific Advisory Group for the Origins of Novel Pathogens (SAGO), *Preliminary Report* (9 June 2022) (World Health Organization, 2022) <https://cdn.who.int/media/docs/default-source/scientific-advisory-group-on-the-origins-of-novel-pathogens/sago-report-09062022.pdf?sfvrsn=42b55bbc_1&download=true> accessed 3 October 2022. See also Smriti Mallapaty, 'Where Did COVID Come From? Five Mysteries that Remain' (2021) 591(7849) *Nature* 188.

[18] Independent Panel, 'COVID-19: The Authoritative Chronology' (n 16) 8.

[19] ibid 8.

Commission met for a technical briefing.[20] The following day, WHO WPRO and WHO headquarters tweeted about a cluster of pneumonia cases in Wuhan, China.[21] On 5 January, WHO reported in its *Disease Outbreak News* that 44 cases had been identified by 3 January, and there was 'no evidence of significant human-to-human transmission'.[22] On the same date, WHO alerted *International Health Regulations* (*IHR*) Member States through the *IHR* Event Information System.[23] On 9 January, WHO announced that Chinese authorities had identified a novel coronavirus in a hospitalized patient in Wuhan.[24]

In response to the cases in Wuhan, measures began to be introduced at borders, with Hong Kong, Macao, Taiwan, Singapore, Turkmenistan, Vietnam, Malaysia, and the Philippines all introducing some measures by 10 January 2020.[25] WHO advised against the imposition of trade or travel restrictions on China.[26] A draft genome of the novel coronavirus was published on 11 January[27] and, on 13 January, WHO published the first protocol for a reverse transcription polymerase chain reaction (RT-PCR) assay to test for the novel coronavirus.[28]

Thailand reported its first case of the novel coronavirus on 13 January 2020 in a traveller from Wuhan.[29] Japan reported its first case two days later on 15 January.[30] On the same day, a man presented for care in Seattle in the United States of America who was later identified as the first case of coronavirus in the United States.[31] In a tweet on 19 January, WHO WPRO reported that there was evidence of limited human-to-human transmission[32] and, on 21 January, tweeted that there was evidence of human-to-human transmission.[33] The Republic of Korea reported its first cases on 20 January.[34] By 21 January, 309 cases, across 14 provinces and municipalities, had been reported in China.[35] On the same day, the Wuhan Municipal Health

---

[20] Independent Panel, 'COVID-19: The Authoritative Chronology' (n 16), 10; Independent Panel, 'How an Outbreak Became a Pandemic' (n 16) 12–13.
[21] Independent Panel, 'COVID-19: The Authoritative Chronology' (n 16) 11; Independent Panel, 'How an Outbreak Became a Pandemic' (n 16) 13.
[22] Independent Panel, 'COVID-19: The Authoritative Chronology' (n 16) 11.
[23] Independent Panel, 'COVID-19: The Authoritative Chronology' (n 16) 12; Independent Panel, 'How an Outbreak Became a Pandemic' (n 16) 13.
[24] Independent Panel, 'COVID-19: The Authoritative Chronology' (n 16) 13.
[25] ibid 14.
[26] ibid.
[27] Independent Panel, 'COVID-19: The Authoritative Chronology' (n 16) 15; Independent Panel, 'How an Outbreak Became a Pandemic' (n 16) 13.
[28] Independent Panel, 'COVID-19: The Authoritative Chronology' (n 16) 15; Independent Panel, 'How an Outbreak Became a Pandemic' (n 16) 13.
[29] Independent Panel, 'COVID-19: The Authoritative Chronology' (n 16) 15; Independent Panel, 'How an Outbreak Became a Pandemic' (n 16) 14.
[30] Independent Panel, 'COVID-19: The Authoritative Chronology' (n 16) 16; Independent Panel, 'How an Outbreak Became a Pandemic' (n 16) 14.
[31] Independent Panel, 'COVID-19: The Authoritative Chronology' (n 16) 17.
[32] ibid 18.
[33] ibid 19.
[34] ibid 18.
[35] ibid 19.

Commission reported that 15 medical staff had pneumonia caused by the novel coronavirus.[36]

WHO's International Health Regulations Emergency Committee held its first meeting about the novel coronavirus on 22–23 January.[37] At this time, there were 314 cases, 310 of which were in China. The remaining four cases all had links to Wuhan.[38] The Committee did not recommend a declaration of a PHEIC.[39]

A lockdown was introduced for the city of Wuhan on 23 January 2020.[40] Singapore reported its first case the same day.[41] Wearing of face masks in public places was made mandatory in Guangdong province on 26 January.[42] France and Vietnam reported their first cases of coronavirus on 24 January, Australia on 25 January, the United Arab Emirates on 29 January, India on 30 January, and Italy on 31 January.[43] On 1 February, Vietnam declared a national epidemic in response to the coronavirus.[44]

By the end of January 2020, there had been fewer than 8,000 confirmed cases, and most of them were in China.[45] The first death outside China due to the novel coronavirus was reported in the Philippines on 2 February.[46] On the same day, the United States introduced border measures that suspended entry of 'aliens' who had been in China during the preceding 14 days.[47] New Zealand also introduced border restrictions that prevented entry into New Zealand of foreign nationals from, or who had transited through, mainland China.[48]

By 8 February 2020, the number of reported cases in China had increased to 34,598 cases. Outside of China 288 cases had been reported in 24 countries.[49] On 11 February 2020, WHO announced that this new disease was named 'coronavirus disease 2019' or 'COVID-19'.[50] By late February, the first suspected case of

---

[36] ibid.
[37] ibid 20; Independent Panel, 'How an Outbreak Became a Pandemic' (n 16) 14.
[38] Independent Panel, 'COVID-19: The Authoritative Chronology' (n 16) 20.
[39] ibid.
[40] ibid.
[41] ibid.
[42] ibid 22.
[43] ibid 22–25.
[44] ibid 26.
[45] World Health Organization, 'Novel Coronavirus (2019-nCoV)—situation report 10' (30 January 2020) <https://www.who.int/docs/default-source/coronaviruse/situation-reports/20200130-sitrep-10-ncov.pdf> accessed 11 March 2022; Independent Panel, 'COVID-19: The Authoritative Chronology' (n 16) 25.
[46] Independent Panel, 'COVID-19: The Authoritative Chronology' (n 16) 26.
[47] ibid 27.
[48] ibid.
[49] ibid 29; World Health Organization, 'Novel Coronavirus (2019-nCoV)—situation report 19' (8 February 2020) <https://www.who.int/docs/default-source/coronaviruse/situation-reports/20200208-sitrep-19-ncov.pdf> accessed 1 October 2022.
[50] Independent Panel, 'COVID-19: The Authoritative Chronology' (n 16) 30; World Health Organization, 'Novel Coronavirus (2019-nCoV)—situation report 22' (11 February 2020) <https://www.who.int/docs/default-source/coronaviruse/situation-reports/20200211-sitrep-22-ncov.pdf> accessed 1 October 2022.

asymptomatic transmission had been reported,[51] and on 25 February the first case of coronavirus in Latin America was reported in Brazil.[52] Lockdowns and stay-at-home measures were introduced in some northern Italian municipalities.[53] In addition, there were rising case numbers on a cruise ship that had been quarantined at a port in Japan.[54]

The first case of coronavirus in sub-Saharan Africa was reported in Nigeria on 27 February 2020.[55] Japan closed schools on 2 March,[56] with school closures of various types introduced in Pakistan, Peru, Sri Lanka, and the United States during the week of 11 March.[57] On 2 March, Brazil recommended the wearing of face masks,[58] with India issuing guidance for wearing face masks a week later on 9 March.[59]

By 10 March 2020, Italy had the highest number of COVID-19 cases outside China.[60] On that day, Italy implemented a national lockdown.[61] By this date, a total of more than 80,000 confirmed cases and over 3,000 deaths had been reported in China, and a total of more than 9,000 confirmed cases and 463 deaths in Italy.[62]

On 11 March, the WHO Director-General declared that COVID-19 was a pandemic.[63] In the following week, countries began to introduce stay-at-home measures or lockdowns, school closures,[64] and border controls.[65] By 19 March 2020, the first trial of a vaccine for COVID-19 had commenced,[66] and WHO announced that with its partners it would be organizing a Solidarity Trial to compare treatments for COVID-19.[67]

---

[51] Independent Panel, 'COVID-19: The Authoritative Chronology' (n 16) 32.
[52] ibid 33.
[53] ibid.
[54] ibid; Smriti Mallapaty, 'What the Cruise Ship Outbreaks Reveal About COVID-19' (2020) 580(7801) *Nature* 18.
[55] Independent Panel, 'COVID-19: The Authoritative Chronology' (n 16) 34.
[56] ibid 35.
[57] ibid 37.
[58] ibid 36.
[59] ibid 37.
[60] ibid.
[61] ibid.
[62] World Health Organization, 'Coronavirus Disease 2019 (COVID-19)—situation report—50' (10 March 2020) <https://www.who.int/docs/default-source/coronaviruse/situation-reports/20200310-sitrep-50-covid-19.pdf> accessed 11 March 2022.
[63] WHO Director-General, 'Opening Remarks at the Media Briefing on COVID-19' (11 March 2020) <https://www.who.int/director-general/speeches/detail/who-director-general-s-opening-remarks-at-the-media-briefing-on-covid-19---11-march-2020> accessed 29 March 2022; Independent Panel, 'COVID-19: The Authoritative Chronology' (n 16) 37.
[64] Independent Panel, 'COVID-19: The Authoritative Chronology' (n 16) 39–40. For further discussion see Chapter 5.
[65] Independent Panel, 'COVID-19: The Authoritative Chronology' (n 16) 40. For restrictions on movement that were introduced in response to COVID-19, including border controls, see Chapter 4.
[66] World Health Organization, 'Coronavirus Disease 2019 (COVID-19)—situation report—60' (19 March 2020) <https://www.who.int/publications/m/item/situation-report---60> accessed 1 October 2022.
[67] ibid; Independent Panel, 'COVID-19: The Authoritative Chronology' (n 16) 41. For further discussion of the development of COVID-19 treatments and vaccines see Chapters 11 and 12.

B. Waves and Lockdowns

By 20 March 2020, Europe had become the epicentre of the pandemic,[58] with Spain having the second highest number of cases outside China after Italy.[69] By 28 March 2020, there had been a total of 86,498 confirmed cases in Italy with 9,136 deaths.[70] In Spain, there had been a total of 64,059 confirmed cases and 4,858 deaths.[71] Globally, the total number of confirmed cases had increased to 571,659, with 26,493 deaths.[72] Media reports emerged from Italy and Spain of overwhelmed hospitals,[73] high numbers of cases amongst older people,[74] and rationing of healthcare.[75] In many countries, residential aged care emerged as a particularly vulnerable sector.[76]

By the end of March, both Italy and the United States had more cases of COVID-19 than had been reported in China, with WHO recording on 30 March 2020 that there had been a total of 82,447 confirmed cases in China, a total of 97,689 confirmed cases in Italy, and a total of 122,653 confirmed cases in the United States.[77] In the United States, New York City experienced a surge in COVID-19 cases, placing hospitals and health professionals under pressure.[78] Concerns grew over supplies of ventilators and the need to ensure that health professionals had adequate

---

[68] Independent Panel, 'COVID-19: The Authoritative Chronology' (n 16) 43.

[69] ibid; World Health Organization, 'Coronavirus Disease 2019 (COVID-19)—situation report—61' (20 March 2020) <https://www.who.int/docs/default-source/coronaviruse/situation-reports/20200321-sitrep-61-covid-19.pdf> accessed 1 October 2022.

[70] World Health Organization, 'Coronavirus Disease 2019 (COVID-19)—situation report—68' (28 March 2020) <https://www.who.int/docs/default-source/coronaviruse/situation-reports/20200328-sitrep-68-covid-19.pdf> accessed 1 October 2022.

[71] ibid.

[72] ibid.

[73] Graham Keeley, 'Doctors in Spain "Totally Overwhelmed" as Hospitals Reach Coronavirus Breaking Point Amid Soaring Death Toll' *The Independent* (27 March 2020) <https://www.independent.co.uk/news/world/europe/coronavirus-spain-death-cases-hospitals-doctors-a9430026.html> accessed 1 October 2022.

[74] Marta Mas Romero and others, 'COVID-19 Outbreak in Long-Term Care Facilities from Spain. Many Lessons to Learn' (2020) 15(10) *PLoS One* art e0241030; Clara Suñer and others, 'A Retrospective Cohort Study of Risk Factors for Mortality Among Nursing Homes Exposed to COVID-19 in Spain' (2021) 1 *Nature Aging* 579.

[75] Benjamin Herreros, Pablo Gella, and Diego Real de Asua, 'Triage During the COVID-19 Epidemic in Spain: Better and Worse Ethical Arguments' (2020) 46 *Journal of Medical Ethics* 455. See Chapters 7 and 12 for further discussion of rationing.

[76] See for example, Romero and others (n 74); Suñer and others (n 74); Martha Jackman, 'Fault Lines: COVID-19, the *Charter*, and Long-Term Care' in Colleen M Flood and others (eds), *Vulnerable: The Law, Policy and Ethics of COVID-19* (University of Ottawa Press 2020).

[77] World Health Organization, 'Coronavirus Disease 2019 (COVID-19)—situation report—70' (30 March 2020) <https://www.who.int/docs/default-source/coronaviruse/situation-reports/20200330-sitrep-70-covid-19.pdf> accessed 1 October 2022.

[78] Garrett Burnett and others, 'Managing COVID-19 From the Epicenter: Adaptations and Suggestions Based on Experience' (2021) 35(3) *Journal of Anesthesia* 366; Stefan Flores and others, 'COVID-19: New York City Pandemic Notes from the First 30 Days' (2020) 38 *American Journal of Emergency Medicine* 1534.

supplies of PPE.[79] During 2020, the regions of Europe and the Americas combined accounted for approximately 70% of the reported cases and deaths from COVID-19.[80]

As with many other countries around the world, India had implemented measures in response to the first wave of the pandemic. In 2020 India implemented a national lockdown—'the largest national lockdown in the world'—in response to the first wave of COVID-19.[81] With no employment in the cities, the lockdown prompted millions of migrant workers to return to their home villages.[82]

By late June 2020, more than 9.1 million cases of COVID-19 and more than 470,000 deaths had been reported to WHO.[83] WHO's Director-General noted at his media briefing that 'In the first month of this outbreak, less than 10,000 cases were reported to WHO. In the last month, almost 4 million cases have been reported.'[84]

It appears that the pandemic contributed to a reduction in life expectancy in many countries. One study reported that, from 2018 to 2020, life expectancy in the United States decreased by 1.87 years from 78.74 years to 76.87 years.[85] This was a larger reduction in life expectancy than in 16 other peer countries. The study reported increases in life expectancies during 2018–2020 for Denmark, Finland, New Zealand, Norway, South Korea, and Taiwan. Although ten other countries (Austria, Belgium, France, Israel, Netherlands, Portugal, Spain, Sweden, Switzerland, and the United Kingdom) had reductions in life expectancies ranging from 0.12 years (Sweden) to 1.09 years (Spain), the 1.87 year reduction in the United States was the largest.[86]

The pandemic also had a disproportionate impact on some communities. In the United States, there was a disproportionate reduction in life expectancy at birth in Black and Hispanic populations, with one study[87] reporting a reduction of 3.25 years in the Black population, 2.4 times the decrease in the White population. For Black men, the reduction in life expectancy (3.56 years) was greater than the reduction for Black women (2.65 years). For the Hispanic population in the United

---

[79] See eg Megan L Ranney, Valerie Griffeth, and Ashish K Jha, 'Critical Supply Shortages—The Need for Ventilators and Personal Protective Equipment During the Covid-19 Pandemic' (2020) 328 *New England Journal of Medicine* e41.
[80] World Health Organization, 'Looking back at a year that changed the world' (n 10) 3.
[81] Editorial, 'India Under COVID-19 Lockdown' (2020) 395(10233) *Lancet* 1315.
[82] S Irudaya Rajan, P Sivakumar, and Aditya Srinivasan, 'The COVID-19 Pandemic and Internal Labour Migration in India: A "Crisis of Mobility"' (2020) 63 *Indian Journal of Labour Economics* 1021.
[83] World Health Organization, 'WHO Director-General's opening remarks at the media briefing on COVID-19–24 June 2020' (24 June 2020) <https://www.who.int/dg/speeches/detail/who-director-general-s-opening-remarks-at-the-media-briefing-on-covid-19---24-june-2020> accessed 20 February 2022.
[84] ibid.
[85] Steven H Woolf, Ryan K Masters, and Laudan Y Aron, 'Effect of the Covid-19 Pandemic in 2020 on Life Expectancy Across Populations in the USA and Other High Income Countries: Simulations of Provisional Mortality Data' (2021) 373 *British Medical Journal* n1343.
[86] ibid.
[87] ibid.

States, life expectancy decreased by 3.88 years, 2.9 times that of the White population. For Hispanic men, life expectancy decreased by 4.58 years compared to 2.94 years for Hispanic women.[88] Disparities in the impact of COVID-19 were also reported in Brazil. A study by Baqui and others found that there was a higher mortality rate for Black and *Pardo* (mixed ethnicity) Brazilians who were admitted to hospitals due to COVID-19. They also found regional disparities in mortality from COVID-19.[89] In Chapter 7 we explore the potential for the pandemic to heighten existing disparities.

In response to the crisis, lockdowns, stay-at-home orders, curfews, school closures, and physical distancing measures were introduced in many countries.[90] These measures also had a high economic and social impact. The devastating impact of the pandemic became apparent as businesses closed and workers lost their jobs or were furloughed. Affected homeowners and tenants faced financial stress, with a risk of housing insecurity. There were reports of increased rates of domestic violence and, over the course of the pandemic, increasing concerns about the impact of pandemic-related stress on people's mental health.[91] Importantly, these aspects of the pandemic were exacerbated as countries imposed, lifted, and re-imposed lockdowns and restrictions during various waves of the pandemic in 2020 and 2021. Sporting events and the performing arts were particularly affected by the lockdowns and restrictions on large gatherings of people. In March 2020, it was announced that the 2020 Summer Olympic Games and Paralympic Games, which were scheduled to be held in Japan, would be postponed.[92]

C. Variants and Vaccines

Although the roll-out of vaccines in 2021 offered some hope for an end to the pandemic, the emergence of new variants of the SARS-CoV-2 virus brought a devastating new toll during 2021.

In late 2020, concerns emerged over changes to the SARS-CoV-2 virus. WHO, in collaboration with international experts, national authorities, and others categorized these changes into 'Variants of Interest' and 'Variants of Concern' to assist

---

[88] ibid.
[89] Pedro Baqui and others, 'Ethnic and Regional Variations in Hospital Mortality from COVID-19 in Brazil: A Cross-Sectional Observational Study' (2020) 8 *Lancet Global Health* e1018. For discussion see Helena Ribeiro, Viviana Mendes Lima, and Eliseu Alves Waldman, 'In the COVID-19 Pandemic in Brazil, Do Brown Lives Matter?' (2020) 8 *Lancet Global Health* e976.
[90] For further discussion see Chapter 5.
[91] See Chapter 7.
[92] Justin McCurry and Sean Ingle, 'Tokyo Olympics Postponed to 2021 Due to Coronavirus Pandemic' *The Guardian* (25 March 2020) <www.theguardian.com/sport/2020/mar/24/tokyo-olympics-to-be-postponed-to-2021-due-to-coronavirus-pandemic> accessed 1 October 2022.

global monitoring and research.[93] WHO also convened an expert group, which recommended using the letters of the Greek alphabet as labels for the variants, as they would be easy to pronounce and would not be stigmatizing.[94]

A 'Variant of Concern' was defined as one that:

> has been demonstrated to be associated with one or more of the following changes at a degree of global public health significance:
> - increase in transmissibility or detrimental change in COVID-19 epidemiology; OR
> - increase in virulence or change in clinical disease presentation; OR
> - decrease in effectiveness of public health and social measures or available diagnostics, vaccines, therapeutics.[95]

The Alpha variant was first documented in the United Kingdom in September 2020; Beta was first documented in South Africa in May 2020; Gamma in Brazil in November 2020; Delta in India in October 2020; and Omicron reported in South Africa in November 2021.[96]

A 'Variant of Interest' was defined as one:

> - with genetic changes that are predicted or known to affect virus characteristics such as transmissibility, disease severity, immune escape, diagnostic or therapeutic escape; AND
> - Identified to cause significant community transmission or multiple COVID-19 clusters, in multiple countries with increasing relative prevalence alongside increasing number of cases over time, or other apparent epidemiological impacts to suggest an emerging risk to global public health.[97]

During the course of 2021, new coronavirus variants spread internationally, bringing new challenges for countries in their responses to the pandemic. In early 2021, the spread of the Alpha variant in the United Kingdom sent the United Kingdom into its third national lockdown.[98] In May 2021, the Delta variant

---

[93] World Health Organization, 'Tracking SARS-CoV-2 Variants' <https://www.who.int/en/activities/tracking-SARS-CoV-2-variants/> accessed 1 October 2022.
[94] ibid.
[95] ibid.
[96] ibid; World Health Organization, 'Classification of Omicron (B.1.1.529): SARS-CoV-2 Variant of Concern' Statement (26 November 2021) <https://www.who.int/news/item/26-11-2021-classification-of-omicron-(b.1.1.529)-sars-cov-2-variant-of-concern> accessed 5 December 2021; see too Promit Mukherjee and Siyanbonga Sishi, 'Botswana's Health Director Says Majority of Omicron Variant Cases Were Asymptomatic' *Reuters* (2 December 2021) <https://www.reuters.com/business/healthcare-pharmaceuticals/botswanas-health-director-says-majority-omicron-variant-cases-were-asymptomatic-2021-12-01/> accessed 6 December 2021.
[97] World Health Organization, 'Tracking SARS-CoV-2 Variants' (n 93).
[98] Tony Kirby, 'When Should the UK Lift its Lockdown?' (2021) 9 *Lancet Respiratory Medicine* e44.

sparked a deadly second wave in India. In its update as of 2 May 2021, WHO noted that 'India accounts for over 90% of both cases and deaths in the region, as well as 46% of global cases and 25% of global deaths reported in the past week.'[99] WHO figures on the number of cases showed the scale of the challenge faced by India. For example, WHO reported that as of 9 May 2021 the cumulative number of cases in India was 22,296,414, with 2,738,957 new cases in the previous seven days.[100] There were reports of oxygen shortages and of hospitals being overwhelmed;[101] calls were made for international assistance for India.[102] After this, the Delta variant spread throughout the world. It was then followed in November and December 2021 by the Omicron variant.

While the international spread of the variants brought new challenges, the roll-out of vaccines during 2021 also reduced the number of deaths due to COVID-19 and helped to lower the number of people who were hospitalized due to COVID-19.[103] However, a consequence of the introduction of vaccines was the creation of a minority in some countries of unvaccinated individuals who were increasingly deprived of the privileges in civil life enjoyed by those who had been vaccinated.[104] In many countries, the roll-out of vaccines was organized initially with some groups, such as older persons, healthcare workers, and those with immunosuppression, identified as priority groups.[105] As discussed in Chapter 12, ensuring equitable global distribution of vaccines has been an enduring challenge.

In addition, the roll-out of vaccines also became part of a dialogue with the public in some countries about the lifting of lockdowns and other restrictions.[106] Businesses were able to re-open, domestic and international travel resumed, and large sporting events once again became possible. In July 2021, the postponed 2020 Summer Olympic Games and Paralympic Games were held in Japan. Despite some opposition within Japan and calls for the Games to be postponed or cancelled,

---

[99] World Health Organization, 'COVID-19 Weekly Epidemiological Update' (4 May 2021) <https://www.who.int/publications/m/item/weekly-epidemiological-update-on-covid-19---4-may-2021> accessed 9 March 2022.
[100] World Health Organization, 'COVID-19 Weekly Epidemiological Update' (11 May 2021) <https://www.who.int/publications/m/item/weekly-epidemiological-update-on-covid-19---11-may-2021> accessed 9 March 2022.
[101] Editorial, 'India's COVID-19 Emergency' (2021) 397(10286) *Lancet* 1683.
[102] Krutika Kuppalli and others, 'India's COVID-19 Crisis: A Call for International Action' (2021) 397(10290) *Lancet* 2132.
[103] 'Covid Vaccines Have Saved 11,700 Lives and 33,000 Hospital Admissions', *BBC News* (13 May 2021) <https://www.bbc.com/news/health-57102422> accessed 16 November 2021.
[104] See Günter Kampf, 'COVID-19: Stigmatising the Unvaccinated is not Justified' (2021) 398(10314) *Lancet* 1871.
[105] For discussion of the issues relating to prioritization of COVID-19 vaccines see, Govind Persad, Monica E Peek, and Ezekiel J Emanuel, 'Fairly Prioritizing Groups for Access to COVID-19 Vaccines' (2020) 324(16) *Journal of the American Medical Association* 1601; Alberto Giubilini, Julian Savulescu, and Dominic Wilkinson, 'Queue Questions: Ethics of COVID-19 Vaccine Prioritization' (2021) 35(4) *Bioethics* 348.
[106] Kirby (n 98).

plans were made for the Games to proceed without international spectators and with a reduced number of attendees.[107]

By 5 December 2021, there had been 264,663,035 cases of coronavirus confirmed globally, with 5,247,742 deaths.[108] However, in a sign of the race against the pandemic, as of 6 December 2021, over 7.9 billion COVID-19 vaccine doses had been administered globally.[109]

The availability of vaccines and the possibility of travel and large sporting and other events have also brought new legal and ethical issues. These include whether vaccination should be mandatory for some groups such as health professionals, an issue we discuss in Chapters 5 and 10. New legal and ethical issues have also arisen around the use of immunity or vaccination passports, both for travel and for entry into cafes, restaurants, and other venues. These issues are discussed in Chapter 5.

III. Key Themes

COVID-19 has transformed significant aspects of contemporary economic and social life in many places across the globe. While the pandemic has been experienced in varied ways in different countries and communities, there are a number of common themes that cut across the broad geographic and social reach of COVID-19. Importantly, these key themes intersect and overlap to provide a rich tapestry of legal and regulatory debates surrounding COVID-19 that are analysed in this book.

The first theme relates to the layers of law and the polycentricity of the legal and regulatory pandemic response. Responding to COVID-19 has engaged all levels of government, within countries, at the national level, and at the global level. However, the response to COVID-19 has not only been a responsibility of governments and international organizations. Businesses, non-government organizations, schools and universities, and a range of others have also been part of the response to COVID-19 and have often played a key role in the practical implementation of public health measures to limit the spread of disease.

A second key theme relates to the role and scope of law. Engagement with public health law is an unsurprising aspect of the legal dimensions of a pandemic. However, as mentioned above, the pandemic response has involved laws, regulation, and policy across a broad range of areas, highlighting the important role for law in supporting community health generally. In the context of a pandemic, important questions arise about the role and scope of law within an emergency. Of

---

[107] Editorial, 'We Need a Global Conversation on the 2020 Olympic Games' (2021) 397(10291) *Lancet* 2225.
[108] World Health Organization (n 3).
[109] ibid.

particular note in this regard are questions about the role and scope of emergency laws that may limit individual freedoms, the duration of such laws, and the balancing of interests so as to avoid laws imposing disproportionate burdens.

Third, the concept of risk is central to the debates about the pandemic and legal responses to it. This includes global risks related to the threat of infectious diseases, governmental responses to risk at the national and sub-national levels, and risk to individuals. The pandemic has also shone new light on the pandemic's uneven impact, showing that some are at greater risk from COVID-19 itself or from hardship associated with measures implemented to contain its spread.[110]

Fourth, COVID-19 has provided new dimensions to the articulation of human rights in the context of a public health emergency, particularly in relation to quarantine and isolation, but also around issues such as freedom of movement, the right to assemble and protest, and broader rights relating to economic well-being, the right to life, the right to the highest attainable standard of health, and rights to the benefits of scientific progress.

Finally, COVID-19 has highlighted debates about the obligations of individuals. The debates over obligations in relation to the wearing of masks, complying with physical distancing requirements, and staying home when unwell, for example, reveal a new focus on individual obligations for public health and the challenges that arise when individuals refuse to fulfil their obligations.

Each of these themes is now discussed in more detail.

A. Layers of Law and Polycentricity

The contemporary legal regulation of public health does not simply rest with national governments. As we argue in this book, responding to the COVID-19 global public health emergency has engaged governments at all levels.

1. Global laws

WHO has played a key role in providing global leadership and global perspectives during the pandemic. As we analyse in Chapter 3, within the context of a global public health emergency, the role of WHO is central. The *International Health Regulations (2005) (IHR (2005))* provide a framework for determining whether WHO Member States are required to notify WHO of events within their territory that may amount to a PHEIC, and provide for communication and cooperation between WHO and Member States over such events, as well as the building of national core capacities in public health.

---

[110] For discussion see Chapter 7.

Drafted in the wake of World War II,[111] WHO's *Constitution* states that WHO's objective 'shall be the attainment by all peoples of the highest possible level of health'.[112] The *Constitution*'s preamble declares health to be 'a state of complete physical, mental and social well-being and not merely the absence of disease or infirmity'.[113] Gostin notes that WHO's *Constitution* 'created a normative institution with extraordinary powers'.[114] Amongst the functions of WHO, articulated in Article 2, are: 'to act as the directing and co-ordinating authority on international health work'; 'to assist Governments, upon request, in strengthening health services'; 'to furnish appropriate technical assistance and in emergencies, necessary aid upon the request or acceptance of Governments'; 'to stimulate and advance work to eradicate epidemic, endemic and other diseases'; 'to propose conventions, agreements and regulations, and make recommendations with respect to international health matters'; 'to assist in developing an informed public opinion among all peoples on matters of health'; and 'to establish and revise as necessary international nomenclatures of diseases, of causes of death and of public health practices'.[115] WHO membership is open to all States,[116] with the work of WHO carried out by the World Health Assembly, WHO's Executive Board, and WHO's Secretariat.[117] The World Health Assembly meets annually,[118] with each Member State able to send up to three delegates,[119] and with each Member having one vote.[120] Importantly, the World Health Assembly has the power to adopt, by a two-thirds vote, 'conventions or agreements with respect to any matter within the competence of the Organization'.[121] Of particular relevance in the context of global public health emergencies is the express provision in Article 21 of the WHO *Constitution* giving the World Health Assembly 'authority to adopt regulations concerning: (a) sanitary and quarantine requirements and other procedures designed to prevent the international spread of disease'.[122]

Gostin notes that in the first decades after its establishment, 'the WHO functioned as the singular global health authority that its constitution envisioned, with countries relying on its technical advice and normative leadership'.[123] However, in

---

[111] For discussion of the creation of WHO, see Lawrence O Gostin, *Global Health Law* (Harvard University Press 2014) Chapter 4 (hereafter Gostin, *Global Health Law*); Jeremy Youde, *Global Health Governance* (Polity 2012) Chapter 2.
[112] World Health Organization *Constitution of the World Health Organization* (opened for signature 22 July 1946, entered into force 7 April 1948) 14 UNTS 185, Article 1 (hereafter *Constitution of the World Health Organization*).
[113] ibid Preamble. See also Gostin, *Global Health Law* (n 111) 103.
[114] Gostin, *Global Health Law* (n 111) 103.
[115] *Constitution of the World Health Organization* (n 112) Article 2.
[116] ibid Article 3.
[117] ibid Article 9.
[118] ibid Article 13.
[119] ibid Article 11.
[120] ibid Article 59.
[121] ibid Article 19.
[122] ibid Article 21.
[123] Gostin, *Global Health Law* (n 111) 131.

recent decades, WHO's leadership has waned,[124] and, particularly in the wake of the Ebola Virus Disease (Ebola) epidemic in West Africa in 2014–16, there have been calls to revitalize WHO and ensure that it has the resources necessary to provide global health leadership.[125] Furthermore, WHO is not the only key actor in global health. Indeed, as has been pointed out by others, the landscape of contemporary global health is increasingly populated by other key international institutions, including the United Nations and the World Bank, as well as others such as Gavi—The Vaccine Alliance; and the Global Fund to Fight AIDS, Tuberculosis and Malaria.[126] With the COVID-19 pandemic, WHO has once again been the subject of debate.[127] President Trump temporarily suspended United States' funding of WHO in April 2020.[128] There have been renewed calls for increased funding and resources for WHO.[129] There is also renewed debate around the declarations of a PHEIC.[130] In the period following the pandemic, it is likely that there will once again be renewed attention on the global institutions and frameworks governing pandemics and the spread of infectious diseases. An aspect of this is a gathering momentum for a pandemic treaty—an international agreement on pandemic prevention and preparedness[131]—discussed further in Chapter 3.

2. National and sub-national laws

Although WHO's role in respect of PHEICs is one of global leadership, national governments have an essential role to play in global health. It is at the national and

---

[124] ibid 132–33. See also Lawrence O Gostin, *Global Health Security: A Blueprint for the Future* (Harvard University Press 2021) 10, 133–57.

[125] Lawrence O Gostin, 'Reforming the World Health Organization After Ebola' (2015) 313(14) *Journal of the American Medical Association* 1407; Lawrence O Gostin and Eric A Friedman, 'A Retrospective and Prospective Analysis of the West African Ebola Virus Disease Epidemic: Robust National Health Systems at the Foundation and an Empowered WHO at the Apex' (2015) 385(9980) *Lancet* 1902; Tim K Mackey, 'The Ebola Outbreak: Catalyzing a "Shift" in Global Health Governance?' (2016) 16 *BMC Infectious Diseases* art 699; Lawrence O Gostin and others, 'Toward a Common Secure Future: Four Global Commissions in the Wake of Ebola' (2016) 13(5) *PLoS Medicine* art e1002042.

[126] Lawrence O Gostin and others, 'The Legal Determinants of Health: Harnessing the Power of Law for Global Health and Sustainable Development' (2019) 393(10183) *Lancet* 1857, 1869-70. See also Gostin, *Global Health Law* (n 111); Youde (n 111); Chelsea Clinton and Devi Sridhar, *Governing Global Health: Who Runs the World and Why?* (Oxford University Press 2017).

[127] See for example, Jose E Alvarez, 'The WHO in the Age of Coronavirus' (2020) 114(4) *American Journal of International Law* 578; Eyal Benvenisti, 'The WHO—Destined to Fail? Political Cooperation and the COVID-19 Pandemic' (2020) 114(4) *American Journal of International Law* 588.

[128] Lawrence O Gostin and Sarah A Wetter, 'Using COVID-19 to Strengthen the WHO: Promoting Health and Science Above Politics' *Milbank Quarterly Opinion* (6 May 2020) <https://www.milbank.org/quarterly/opinions/using-covid-19-to-strengthen-the-who-promoting-health-and-science-above-politics/> accessed 1 October 2022.

[129] ibid.

[130] Lucia Mullen and others, 'An Analysis of International Health Regulations Emergency Committees and Public Health Emergency of International Concern Designations' (2020) 5(6) *BMJ Global Health* art e002502.

[131] See eg Ronald Labonté and others, 'A Pandemic Treaty, Revised International Health Regulations, or Both?' (2021) 17 *Globalization and Health* art 128; Lawrence O Gostin, Sam F Halabi, and Kevin A Klock, 'An International Agreement on Pandemic Prevention and Preparedness' (2021) 326(13) *Journal of the American Medical Association* 1257.

sub-national levels that public health laws and policies find their practical application. In countries, such as the United States, Canada, and Australia, that have federal legal systems, public health laws may operate at the state or provincial level, as well as sometimes at the national level.[132] Local or municipal governments may also play a role in responding to a public health emergency such as COVID-19 where physical distancing is required, as local governments may have authority in relation to areas such as public parks and playgrounds, as well as a range of civic functions within their municipalities.[133] These different layers of government may at times raise complexities, including in navigating the requirements of the *IHR (2005)*, or co-ordinating a national response to a global public health emergency such as COVID-19.[134] Furthermore, although national and international laws are clearly distinct, they are also 'interrelated and bidirectional in their impact on health and justice' with domestic laws providing models for other countries, and international laws helping to shape domestic laws and policies.[135]

The layering of different levels of law and regulation not only occurs in the field of public health law. Responding to COVID-19 has required governments to engage with public health laws broadly, across all domains of the provision of government services. In this context then, the layering of laws and regulations becomes increasingly complex as different areas of government authority at the national and sub-national levels intersect, making the response to COVID-19 one characterized by polycentricity.

3. Polycentricity and global health

Polycentric regulation focuses on 'the multiple sites in which regulation occurs at the sub-national, national and transnational levels' and the risk of consequential conflict and overlap.[136] This multiplicity of regulatory sites is evident in the layers

---

[132] For discussion of government powers at the federal, state, and local levels in the United States, see Lindsay K Cloud and others, 'A Chronological Overview of the Federal, State and Local Response to COVID-19' in Scott Burris and others (eds), *Assessing Legal Responses to COVID-19* (Public Health Law Watch 2020).

[133] ibid.

[134] For discussion of federalism and public health, see Kumanan Wilson and others, 'Strategies for Implementing the New International Health Regulations in in Federal Countries' (2008) 86(3) *Bulletin of the World Health Organization* 215; Belinda Bennett, 'Legal Rights During Pandemics: Federalism, Rights and Public Health Laws—A View from Australia' (2009) 123(3) *Public Health* 232. For discussion of federalism and COVID-19, see Carissima Mathen, 'Resisting the Siren's Call: Emergency Powers, Federalism, and Public Policy' in Colleen M Flood and others (eds), *Vulnerable: The Law, Policy and Ethics of COVID-19* (University of Ottawa Press 2020); Donald F Kettl, 'States Divided: The Implications of American Federalism for COVID-19' (2020) 80(4) *Public Administration Review* 595; Lindsay F Wiley, 'Federalism in Pandemic Prevention and Response' in Scott Burris and others (eds), *Assessing Legal Responses to COVID-19* (Public Health Law Watch 2020).

[135] Gostin and others (n 126) 1861. It has been noted that 'Rights and responsibilities are multilayered. They arise at local, national and global levels and at the intersections between these levels': Bennett (n 134) 235.

[136] Julia Black, 'Constructing and Contesting Legitimacy and Accountability in Polycentric Regulatory Regimes' (2008) 2(2) *Regulation & Governance* 137, 140; see also Keith Carlisle and Rebecca L Gruby, 'Polycentric Systems of Governance: A Theoretical Model for the Commons' (2017) 47(4) *Policy Studies Journal* 927, 930–31; Nico Steytler (ed), *Comparative Federalism and*

of law and regulation discussed above. It is also evident in the increasing number of non-government organizations at the sub-national, national, and global levels that are relevant to responding to a public health emergency.

At a global level, a range of United Nations bodies, including the Food and Agriculture Organization, United Nations International Children's Emergency Fund (UNICEF), and Joint United Nations Programme on HIV and AIDS (UNAIDS), have participated in global health initiatives, along with non-State actors such as philanthropies, public-private partnerships, and non-government organizations,[137] making the global health area an increasingly complex space. In terms of global health governance of infectious diseases, the traditional approaches were firmly state-centric in nature, focused on WHO and its Member States. This approach is best exemplified by the *IHR* as they existed prior to the 2005 reforms.[138] In these earlier *IHR*, the focus was on the obligations of Member States to report to WHO cases of a limited number of diseases and on WHO liaising with Member States.[139] The 2005 revisions to the *IHR* softened the State-centric approach by recognizing the importance of receiving information about potential public health emergencies from others.[140] Not only are the structures for global health polycentric in terms of being comprised of multiple actors but, as discussed further in Chapter 3, the decision-making processes related to global health emergencies are also polycentric in terms of the issues that may arise in relation to the international spread of disease.[141]

At the national and sub-national levels, polycentricity is evident in the complexity of the measures that may need to be taken by governments in an effort to limit the spread of disease within the community.[142] In addition, multiple actors—both State and non-State at the national and sub-national levels—have been part of the response to COVID-19, as different levels of government, businesses, charities, and others have sought to address the health and economic impact of the pandemic.

The polycentricity of decision-making in the context of COVID-19 has presented 'puzzles' in relation to the allocation of healthcare decision-making

Covid-19: Combating the Pandemic (Routledge 2021); Terry Carney and Belinda Bennett, 'Framing Pandemic Management: New Governance, Science or Culture?' (2014) 23(2) *Health Sociology Review* 136, 138. For further discussion see Chapter 13.

[137] Gostin and others (n 126) 1869–70. For further discussion of global health organizations see, Youde (n 111); Clinton and Sridhar (n 126).

[138] For discussion see David P. Fidler, *SARS, Governance and the Globalization of Disease* (Palgrave Macmillan 2004). For further discussion, see Chapter 3.

[139] See Chapter 3.

[140] See Chapter 3.

[141] Andraž Zidar, 'WHO International Health Regulations and Human Rights: From Allusions to Inclusion' (2015) 19(4) *International Journal of Human Rights* 505, 509.

[142] Colleen M Flood, Bryan Thomas, and Kumanan Wilson, 'Civil Liberties vs Public Health' in Colleen M Flood and others (eds), *Vulnerable: The Law, Policy and Ethics of COVID-19* (University of Ottawa Press 2020) 259.

authority.[143] These puzzles have included the allocation of decision-making between national and state governments within federal legal systems,[144] as well as increasing claims for local decision-making authority at the sub-national level.[145] These claims for decision-making authority have arisen in relation to a range of issues during the pandemic, including allocation of resources, border closures, curfews, authority to close parks or schools, banning of large public gatherings, and imposition of physical distancing requirements.[146] For da Silva, these claims for decision-making authority lead to two puzzles. The first is how to identify the entities with decision-making authority and what to do if multiple claims exist. The second is whether the principles for allocation of decision-making authority should be adjusted to take account of the exceptional nature of a pandemic.[147]

In relation to the first puzzle, different principles may lead to different decisions about the allocation of decision-making authority: 'interests in coordination can support federal control and interests in flexibility can support more local control'.[148] Da Silva argues, however, that allocation of decision-making authority should extend to other groups, such as cities or Indigenous communities, unless there is a reason for not applying the principles to these groups.[149] While the issue of pandemic exceptionalism addresses the role and scope of law discussed below, it also engages with the issue of whether a pandemic changes the allocation of decision-making authority.[150] Da Silva points out that, in many instances, the debates over decision-making authority during a pandemic simply reflect existing debates about such authority, which 'suggests that pandemics do not pose unique concerns in this area but merely raise existing issues'.[151] The COVID-19 pandemic has clearly generated important debates about the roles of different entities and their decision-making authority, with the multiplicity of potential actors further confirming the polycentricity of the decision-making environment.

B. The Role and Scope of Law

While management of pandemics undoubtedly presents challenges for public health and for healthcare generally, it also presents challenges for law and policy. Described as 'a key determinant of health',[152] law plays an important role in

---

[143] Michael da Silva, 'COVID-19 and Health-Related Authority Allocation Puzzles' (2021) 30(1) *Cambridge Quarterly of Health Care Ethics* 25.
[144] ibid 25–26.
[145] ibid 27.
[146] ibid 28.
[147] ibid 29.
[148] ibid 30.
[149] ibid.
[150] ibid.
[151] ibid 31.
[152] Gostin and others (n 126) 1859. For discussion see Belinda Bennett, 'Editorial: Law, Global Health and Sustainable Development: The Lancet Commission of the Legal Determinants of Health' (2020)

providing the frameworks required to achieve positive outcomes for human health.[153] Domestic/national and international laws establish rights and obligations, set norms and standards, provide tools for resolution of disputes, and provide legal frameworks for governing public and private institutions.[154] However, laws can also present barriers and obstacles to the achievement of improvements in global health, for instance, if they are 'misguided, outdated, arbitrary, or discriminatory'.[155] Looking at the 'upstream' causal factors that affect health outcomes, it has been argued that:

> National and international laws—and broader concepts of governance—have a unique and vital place in the machinery that, for better or worse, controls the floodgates that determine what happens to the people living 'down the river'.[156]

At first glance, it seems self-evident that, at least at the national and sub-national levels, the legal issues that arise in relation to pandemics are matters of public health law. Public health law is concerned with the health of populations and the public. Gostin and Wiley define public health law as:

> the study of the legal powers and duties of the state to assure the conditions for people to be healthy (e.g., to identify, prevent, and ameliorate risks to health in the population) and the limitations on the power of the state to constrain the autonomy, privacy, liberty, proprietary, or other legally protected interests of individuals for the common good.[157]

Gostin and Wiley outline 'five essential characteristics of public health law'.[158] These are: the powers and responsibilities of government; the focus on population health, including disease prevention; the relationships between the public and the State; population-based services based on public health methodologies, such as epidemiology; and the ability of the State to exercise coercive power on individuals in order to protect the community.[159] As will be clear from the discussion in this

---

27(3) *Journal of Law and Medicine* 505; Jenny C Kaldor and others, 'The *Lancet*-O'Neill Institute/Georgetown University Commission on Global Health and Law: The Power of Law to Advance the Right to Health' (2020) 13(1) *Public Health Ethics* 9.
[153] Gostin and others (n 126).
[154] ibid 1861–68.
[155] ibid 1859.
[156] John Coggon and Lawrence O Gostin, 'Global Health with Justice: Controlling the Floodgates of the Upstream Determinants of Health Through Evidence-Based Law' (2020) 13(1) *Public Health Ethics* 4, 5.
[157] Lawrence O Gostin and Lindsay F Wiley, *Public Health Law: Power, Duty, Restraint* (3rd edn, University of California Press 2016) 4.
[158] ibid.
[159] ibid 4–5.

book, responding to COVID-19 has touched on each of these characteristics. It has also required serious and sustained engagement with the tools of public health law. Matters such as quarantine, isolation, restrictions on movement of people, contact tracing, and enforcement of public health orders, have all been aspects of public health law. While many countries have used these measures, as our discussion in this book will show, there have been substantial differences between countries in the manner in which they have been used. Furthermore, some measures, such as quarantine and isolation, which had seen little use in many countries in modern times, re-emerged as important aspects of controlling the pandemic, sparking contemporary debates over the nature of individual rights in the context of a public health emergency.

Although public health law has played a central role in the domestic legal responses of countries at the national and state/provincial levels, there are two additional aspects to be considered. First is the importance of looking beyond public health and public health law. The COVID-19 pandemic has provided a dramatic illustration of the relevance of a whole-of-government approach to responding to the pandemic. Education authorities have needed to address the practical aspects of school closures and home schooling; business shut-downs and job losses have had significant impacts on income, necessitating reassessments of economic forecasts; social security payments have been needed for the rising number of unemployed individuals; changes have been made to housing laws in some countries to protect tenants who have lost their jobs from evictions; financial institutions have deferred mortgage repayments; and governments have managed border closures and restrictions. As discussed in Chapter 8, criminal laws have provided mechanisms for enforcement of public health measures and constituted both means of facilitating compliance but also deterrence of those minded not to cooperate with governments' public health initiatives. In this context, the legal responses to the pandemic are not only about managing the health aspects of the spread of disease, but also about the need for laws that support government, business, and individual responses across all aspects of contemporary social and economic life. In this sense then, law not only has a role to play in providing the necessary tools for responding to a major public health emergency, but the scope of that role must be understood broadly as encompassing all aspects of life that affect the health of individuals and populations, including housing, employment, social security, and the provision of healthcare. In the chapters that follow in this book, we seek to engage with these broader legal dimensions of the pandemic and to assess their implications for the future development of the law.

The second aspect to be contemplated is the importance of considering law within a global context. Although borders have been a key part of countries' responses to COVID-19 with travel restrictions imposed at the national and subnational levels in many countries,[160] global health is a shared concern, with global

---
[160] For discussion see Chapter 4.

cooperation required to manage the international spread of infectious diseases effectively. These global dimensions highlight the importance of considering public health law in a global context. Gostin has defined global health law as:

> the study and practice of international law—both hard law (e.g., treaties that bind states) and soft instruments (e.g., codes of practice negotiated by states) that shapes norms, processes, and institutions to attain the highest attainable standard of physical and mental health for the world's population.[161]

As Gostin's definition indicates, global health law engages with international law,[162] as well as international organizations and institutions that affect health.[163] In the chapters in this book, we seek to engage not only with formal international health law, such as the *IHR (2005)*,[164] but also with the multiple national and international organizations and policies that have shaped the responses to COVID-19.

1. Regulatory tools in a pandemic

While the role and scope of law are important aspects of the legal dimensions of COVID-19, the traditional tools of public health (including quarantine, isolation, and contact tracing) have been key aspects of the response to COVID-19 for countries around the world. However, legal responses to COVID-19 have not only engaged with public health law; they have reached law and regulation in all aspects of social and economic life.

2. The scope of law—pandemic 'exceptionalism'

In using legal and regulatory tools during the pandemic, a central issue is the scope of laws that permit extraordinary measures to be implemented in responding to an emergency. As the pandemic has constituted a major public health emergency and economic crisis, it has the potential for expansion of government powers. In Chapter 3, we discuss the designation of an emergency at an international level through the provisions in the *IHR (2005)* relating to a PHEIC.

In Chapter 5, we discuss declarations of emergency under domestic laws, and the implications of such declarations for government decision-making. We explore the use of laws to support and protect members of the community, for example, through the provision of social security payments to support those who lost employment due to economic lockdowns. We also explore the tensions that can arise through the use of law, particularly laws to enforce physical distancing, stay-at-home orders, business closures, or other measures that may be perceived by some

---

[161] Gostin, *Global Health Law* (n 111) 59.
[162] ibid 61–64.
[163] ibid 60–70.
[164] ibid 61–68. See Chapter 3 for further discussion of the *IHR (2005)*.

as infringing on their rights, analysing challenges to these restrictions in Chapter 6. In this context, the scope and limits of the law during a public health emergency become key legal questions.

While an emergency may justify an expansion of government powers to address the crisis, arguably such exceptionalism should be temporary in nature. Furthermore, as noted by Webber, 'there are situations that are neither quite normal nor exceptional'.[165] However, Webber notes that the law may not contemplate these situations, and argues that if extraordinary powers are maintained during these situations, governments 'should seek to re-establish the normal legal order where and to the extent possible'.[166]

Exceptionalism has also emerged as an important aspect of the debates over development of vaccines and treatments in the context of an emergency. As discussed in Chapter 11, the race to find a vaccine for COVID-19 has prompted debate about the extent to which requirements for clinical trials and research involving human subjects should be relaxed to permit rapid testing and implementation of promising new treatments.[167] The issue of the degree to which 'regulatory flexibility' can accommodate both the imperative for new treatments during an emergency and protection of research participants is important.[168] These debates occur in a context where a 'covidization of research' is evident as research is increasingly focused on COVID-related issues.[169] In Chapters 11 and 12, we analyse these debates and the regulation of research in the context of a public health emergency.

C. Understandings of Risk

The risks associated with infectious disease are not new. As we outline in Chapter 2, infectious disease has featured regularly throughout human history—at times with a devastating toll on human life. Developing understandings of risk in relation to infectious diseases is of importance as 'management of risk is nevertheless central to pandemic preparedness'.[170] The revisions to the *IHR* in 2005 had a major new focus on developing public health capacities at the national level[171] and, through the early 2000s, led by WHO, countries developed national plans to prepare for an

---

[165] Grégorie Webber, 'The Duty to Govern and the Rule of Law in an Emergency' in Colleen M Flood and others (eds), *Vulnerable: The Law, Policy and Ethics of COVID-19* (University of Ottawa Press 2020) 182.
[166] ibid.
[167] Alex John London and Jonathan Kimmelman, 'Against Pandemic Research Exceptionalism' (2020) 368 *Science* 476.
[168] Holly Fernandez Lynch and others, 'Regulatory Flexibility for COVID-19 Research' (2020) 7(1) *Journal of Law and the Biosciences* lsaa057.
[169] Madhukar Pai, 'Covidization of Research: What Are the Risks?' (2020) 26(8) *Nature Medicine* 1159.
[170] Belinda Bennett and Terry Carney, 'Public Health Emergencies of International Concern: Global, Regional, and Local Responses to Risk' (2017) 25(2) *Medical Law Review* 223, 225.
[171] See Chapter 3.

influenza pandemic.[172] As discussed in Chapter 3, the 2005 revisions to the *IHR* moved away from the approach of the previous *IHR*, which focused on specific, known diseases, instead adopting an approach based on assessment of the risks posed by the event and whether it could constitute a PHEIC. Such an approach is important for, as COVID-19 has demonstrated, it is not necessarily possible to foresee risk and a new, previously unknown disease may emerge and pose a major threat to human health.

1. Zoonotic diseases

Zoonotic diseases are diseases that can infect humans but have an origin in animals. These diseases can have a significant impact on human health. Indeed, it has been estimated that the majority (60.3%) of emerging infectious disease events are caused by zoonoses, and that most (71.8%) of these zoonotic diseases originate in wildlife.[173] Severe Acute Respiratory Syndrome (SARS), avian influenza, Middle East Respiratory Syndrome (MERS), and Ebola are amongst the zoonotic diseases that have emerged in recent years.[174] The intensification of livestock farming, growing urbanization of areas that were previously wilderness, climate change that affects the geographic spread of vectors, tourism into remote areas, spread of disease from companion animals, and consumption of bush meat, have all led to greater contact between people and animals, which has in turn facilitated the development of zoonotic diseases.[175]

Coker and others argue that there are three lessons from our past experiences with zoonotic diseases:

> First, that progress in public health and communicable diseases is not irreversible. Second, that more of the same tactics that have emerged in the modern era to control the emergence of new diseases in animals and human beings, and their vectors, will probably be insufficient to control future threats. Third, that a changing and increasingly interconnected world means changes in ecosystems that offer unpredictable opportunities to microbes that are more varied, numerous, and adaptable than we had once hoped, with spread occurring more rapidly.[176]

---

[172] See Chapter 3.
[173] Kate E Jones and others, 'Global Trends in Emerging Infectious Diseases' (2008) 451(7181) *Nature* 990.
[174] World Health Organization, 'How WHO is Working to Track Down the Animal Reservoir of the SARS-CoV-2 Virus' (6 November 2020) < https://www.who.int/news-room/feature-stories/detail/how-who-is-working-to-track-down-the-animal-reservoir-of-the-sars-cov-2-virus> (hereafter World Health Organization, 'How WHO is Working') accessed 1 October 2022.
[175] Richard Coker and others, 'Towards a Conceptual Framework to Support One-health Research for Policy on Emerging Zoonoses' (2011) 11(4) *Lancet Infectious Diseases* 326; Sally J Cutler, Anthony R Fooks and Wim H M Van der Poel, 'Public Health Threat of New, Reemerging, and Neglected Zoonoses in the Industrialized World' (2010) 16(1) *Emerging Infectious Diseases* 1.
[176] Coker and others (n 175) 327.

In response to COVID-19, there has been increased interest in a 'One Health' approach.[177] One Health is an interdisciplinary approach that brings together human, animal, and environmental health,[178] calling for a more holistic approach to disease surveillance and prevention. Even before COVID-19, it had been suggested that there was a need for 'enhanced longitudinal veterinary surveillance in food-producing animals and wildlife' in association with surveillance of human disease.[179] It has been argued that adoption of a One Health approach could help to build integrated disease surveillance systems, facilitate coordination and cooperation between different agencies, develop better understandings of the regulatory environment for management of zoonotic diseases, and help to provide insights into health equity and the response to COVID-19.[180]

In May 2020, the World Health Assembly requested the Director-General:

> to continue to work closely with the World Organisation for Animal Health (OIE), the Food and Agriculture Organization of the United Nations (FAO) and countries, as part of the One-Health Approach to identify the zoonotic source of the virus and the route of introduction to the human population, including the possible role of intermediate hosts, including through efforts such as scientific and collaborative field missions, which will enable targeted interventions and a research agenda to reduce the risk of similar events occurring, as well as to provide guidance on how to prevent infection with severe acute respiratory syndrome coronavirus 2 (SARS-COV2) in animals and humans and prevent the establishment of new zoonotic reservoirs, as well as to reduce further risks of emergence and transmission of zoonotic diseases.[181]

WHO has noted that 'This Resolution signifies the recognition of all 194 Member States of the importance of this work and provides WHO with a clear mandate to lead in this area.'[182] COVID-19 has dramatically illustrated the risks of zoonotic diseases for human health. In this context, the building of post-pandemic national and global public health capacities will require greater attention to surveillance and prevention of zoonotic diseases.

---

[177] Mohamed E El Zowalaty and Josef D Järhult, 'From SARS to COVID-19: A Previously Unknown SARS-related Coronavirus (SARS CoV-2) of Pandemic Potential Infecting Humans—Call for a One Health Approach' (2020) 9 *One Health* art 100124; Arne Ruckert and others, 'What Role for One Health in the COVID-19 Pandemic?' (2020) 111 *Canadian Journal of Public Health* 641.
[178] Coker and others (n 175); Chris Degeling and others, 'Implementing a One-Health Approach to Emerging Infectious Disease: Reflections on the Socio-Political, Ethical and Legal Dimensions' (2015) 15 *BMC Public Health* 1307.
[179] Cutler, Fooks, and Van der Poel (n 175) 6.
[180] Ruckert and others (n 177).
[181] World Health Assembly, 'COVID-19 Response' Resolution WHA73.1 (19 May 2020) <https://apps.who.int/gb/ebwha/pdf_files/WHA73/A73_R1-en.pdf> accessed 1 October 2022.
[182] World Health Organization, 'How WHO is Working' (n 174).

2. The social and economic context of risk

The emergence of a new, previously unknown virus to which the global population had no immunity posed a risk to all of humanity. Yet, quite early in the pandemic, it became clear that although the risk of contracting COVID-19 was shared, its burdens were uneven. Older people,[183] and those with co-morbidities and underlying health conditions such as obesity, diabetes, or heart disease[184] were quickly identified as being at heightened risk of severe outcomes and death from COVID-19. In the United States and the United Kingdom, racial minorities were also identified as having higher mortality rates from COVID-19.[185] Furthermore, physical distancing and hand hygiene necessary for protection from infection were unavailable to people who were homeless,[186] or for those living in developing countries without access to clean water.[187] Indeed, such is the combined impact of COVID-19 and existing economic and health disparities that it has been argued that 'COVID-19 is not a pandemic. It is a syndemic.'[188] It has been argued that successfully addressing COVID-19 will require successfully addressing non-communicable diseases.[189]

Even before the pandemic, it was well-recognized that there were disparities in global health. The Sustainable Development Goals (SDGs), adopted by the United Nations in 2015,[190] articulated 17 goals, a number of which are particularly relevant in the context of a global pandemic.[191] Amongst these are:

- SDG1—'to end poverty in all its forms everywhere'. Given estimates of the number of people living in extreme poverty in 2020 due to COVID-19,[192] the pandemic is likely to affect progress towards achieving this goal.

---

[183] World Health Organization, 'Coronavirus disease (COVID-19)' (n 9).
[184] ibid.
[185] Neeraj Bhala and others, 'Sharpening the Global Focus on Ethnicity and Race in the Time of COVID-19' (2020) 395(10238) *Lancet* 1673; Monica W Hooper, Anna M Nápoles, and Eliseo J Pérez-Stable, 'COVID-19 and Racial/Ethnic Disparities' (2020) 323(24) *Journal of the American Medical Association* 2466.
[186] Jack Tsai and Michael Wilson, 'COVID-19: A Potential Public Health Problem for Homeless Populations' (2020) 5(4) *Lancet Public Health* e186.
[187] Isha Ray, 'Viewpoint—Handwashing and COVID-19: Simple, Right There . . . ?' (2020) 135 *World Development* art 105086.
[188] Richard Horton, 'Offline: COVID-19 is Not a Pandemic' (2020) 396(10255) *Lancet* 874.
[189] ibid.
[190] United Nations General Assembly, *Transforming Our World: The 2030 Agenda for Sustainable Development* (A/RES/70/1) (25 September 2015). See also United Nations, 'Sustainable Development Goals' <https://sdgs.un.org/goals> accessed 29 March 2022.
[191] Kristin Heggen, Tony J Sandset, and Eivind Engebretsen, 'COVID-19 and Sustainable Development Goals' (2020) 98(10) *Bulletin of the World Health Organization* 646. On the impact of COVID-19 on the SDGs discussed below see United Nations, *Sustainable Development Goals Report 2020* (United Nations, 2020).
[192] World Bank Group, 'Poverty and Shared Prosperity 2020: Reversals of Fortune' (Report 2020).

- SDG2—'end hunger, achieve food security and improved nutrition and promote sustainable agriculture'. COVID-19 has the potential to impact food security due to disruptions to trade and agricultural labour, as well as through the impact of loss of income on the ability to buy food.[193]
- SDG3—'ensure healthy lives and promote well-being for all at all ages'. As the SDG that is primarily focused on health it is unsurprising that many of the targets of SDG3 are relevant to the COVID-19 pandemic. For example:
  - SDG3.4—'By 2030, reduce by one third premature mortality from non-communicable diseases through prevention and treatment and promote mental health and well-being' will be relevant given the relationship between COVID-19 illness and underlying health conditions such as diabetes and heart disease. In addition, the social and economic impact of COVID-19 has had significant impacts on the mental health and well-being of individuals and communities around the world.[194]
  - SDG3.7—'By 2030, ensure universal access to sexual and reproductive health-care services, including for family planning, information and education, and the integration of reproductive health into national strategies and programs.' As discussed in Chapter 7, women's access to sexual and reproductive healthcare services has been interrupted during the COVID-19 pandemic.
  - SDG3.8—'Achieve universal health coverage, including financial risk protection, access to quality essential health-care services, and access to safe, effective, quality and affordable essential medicines and vaccines for all.' The pandemic has highlighted the importance of access to affordable healthcare in wealthy and poorer countries, and the issue of equitable vaccine distribution.[195]
  - SDG3.d—'strengthen the capacity of all countries, in particular developing countries, for early warning, risk reduction and management of national and global health risks'.
- SDG5—'achieve gender equality and empower all women and girls'. As discussed in Chapter 7, the pandemic has had a gendered impact, including in relation to increased domestic violence which is relevant to SDG5.2 'eliminate all forms of violence against all women and girls'; and increases in women's unpaid caring work which is relevant to SDG5.4, 'Recognize and value unpaid care and domestic work.'

---

[193] David Laborde and others, 'COVID-19 Risks to Global Food Security' (2020) 369 *Science* 500; Channing Arndt and others, 'COVID-19 Lockdowns, Income Distribution, and Food Security: An Analysis for South Africa' (2020) 26 *Global Food Security* art 100410.
[194] For discussion see Chapter 7.
[195] For discussion see Chapter 12.

- SDG6—'Ensure availability and sustainable management of water and sanitation for all.' SDG6.2 sets the goal of 'by 2030, achiev[ing] access to adequate and equitable sanitation and hygiene for all and end open defecation, paying special attention to the needs of women and girls and those in vulnerable situations'. With hand washing and hygiene important measures in preventing COVID-19 infection, access to clean water is of particular importance.[196]
- SDG8—'promote sustained, inclusive and sustainable economic growth, full and productive employment, and decent work for all'. COVID-19 has clearly had a severe impact on national economies.
- SDG15—'protect, restore and promote sustainable use of terrestrial ecosystems, sustainably manage forests, combat desertification, and halt and reverse land degradation and halt biodiversity loss'. The protection of environment envisaged by SDG15 may help to limit the interaction of humans and wildlife and thus may be relevant to efforts to limit zoonotic diseases.
- SDG16—'promote peaceful and inclusive societies for sustainable development, provide access to justice for all and build effective, accountable and inclusive institutions at all levels'. As we argue in this book, law has played a central role in shaping the responses to COVID-19, making SDG16 directly relevant to the responses to the COVID-19 pandemic.
- SDG17—'strengthen the means of implementation and revitalize the Global Partnership for Sustainable Development'.
  o SDG17.9—'enhance international support for implementing effective and targeted capacity-building in developing countries to support national plans to implement all the Sustainable Development Goals, including through North-South, South-South, and triangular cooperation'. As discussed in Chapter 3, building of national public health capacities has been a key element of the *IHR (2005)*.

Importantly, the COVID-19 pandemic has highlighted the importance and relevance of the social determinants of health. Furthermore, the health-related consequences of lockdowns and associated social isolation, along with the stresses caused by the economic impact of the pandemic and business closures and unemployment, have highlighted the need for holistic, whole-of-government approaches to supporting population health during and after the pandemic. In Chapter 7 we analyse these supports further and review the supports that have been introduced by governments around the world in attempts to ease the impact of COVID-19-related lockdowns.

---

[196] Ray (n 187). See also the discussion in Chapter 7.

3. Mapping risk

Data have been a defining characteristic of the COVID-19 pandemic. From the earliest days of the pandemic, epidemiological data were used to track the spread of COVID-19 both globally and within countries. Numbers of infections and deaths from COVID-19 were regular features of news broadcasts from representatives of government and references to waves of infection and terms such as 'flattening the curve' and 'variants of concern' have become commonplace in the community.[197] Epidemiological data have been used by governments to inform their decision-making about the imposition or easing of restrictions.[198]

As discussed in Chapter 3, although data have been central to the mapping of risk related to COVID-19, three points are of importance. The first is that the ability to map the path of a pandemic is dependent on timely and accurate data. This presupposes that countries have the ability to test all who may have been exposed to the virus, and that their domestic health systems have the capacity to process the tests in a timely manner. In many countries neither of these is possible. Much too depends upon the integrity of data, namely, measuring phenomena in the same way and reporting on them accurately and consistently. The challenges of measuring COVID-related deaths have also raised the question of whether it is preferable to evaluate the mortality caused by COVID-19 by reference principally to excess mortality statistics, namely the extent to which deaths in a pandemic period are more numerous than in the preceding non-pandemic period. The *IHR (2005)* set out requirements for the development of national public health capacities. However, achieving these capacities has proven challenging, particularly for low-income countries.[199]

Second, the pandemic has once again highlighted the importance of disaggregated data. Disaggregation of data is essential to be able to identify the burdens of the pandemic accurately in terms of age, race, ethnicity, sex, and other factors. Without such data, it is difficult to map the burdens of the pandemic. Disaggregated data can help in the development of preventive and therapeutic strategies.[200]

---

[197] For use of language during COVID-19, see Ian Freckelton, 'COVID-19 as a Disruptor and a Catalyst for Change' (2021) 28(3) *Journal of Law and Medicine* 597, 598–601; Chun-Mei Chen, 'Public Health Messages about COVID-19 Prevention in Multilingual Taiwan' (2020) 39(5) *Multilingua* 597; Ingrid Piller, Jie Zhang, and Jia Li, 'Linguistic Diversity in a Time of Crisis: Language Challenges of the COVID-19 Pandemic' (2020) 39(5) *Multilingua* 503.

[198] Emeline Han and others, 'Lessons Learnt from Easing COVID-19 Restrictions: An Analysis of Countries and Regions in Asia Pacific and Europe' (2020) 396(10261) *Lancet* 1525; Jeconiah L Dreisbach and Sharon Mendoza-Dreisbach, 'The Integration of Emergency Language Services in COVID-19 Response: A Call for the Linguistic Turn in Public Health' (2021) 43(2) *Journal of Public Health* e248; Jeconiah L Dreisbach and Sharon Mendoza-Dreisbach, 'Unity in Adversity: Multilingual Crisis Translation and Emergency Linguistics in the COVID-19 Pandemic' (2021) 14(1) *Open Public Health Journal* 94.

[199] For discussion see Chapter 3.

[200] The Sex, Gender and COVID-19 Project, 'Gender and Sex-Disaggregated Data: Vital to Inform an Effective Response to COVID-19' (Issue Brief, September 2020) <https://globalhealth5050.org/wp-content/themes/global-health/covid/media/ISSUE%20BRIEF%20-%20Sex-Disaggregated%20Data%20&%20COVID-19%20-%20Sept%202020.pdf> accessed 1 October 2022.

Importantly, data disaggregated on the basis of sex can help to highlight disparities in access to healthcare, such as situations where women have less access to healthcare.[201] Such disparities risk under-testing of women, with the potential for a corresponding risk to others.[202] The COVID-19 Sex Disaggregated Data Tracker collects data from official national sources and also tracks the availability of disaggregated data.[203]

Third, the pandemic has once again highlighted the importance of timely data sharing to enable advances in testing, diagnosis, treatment, and vaccines during a public health emergency. Journal editors have played a key role in making data accessible during the emergency.[204] However, as discussed in Chapter 12, intellectual property laws may present barriers to data sharing.[205]

D. Human Rights

The use of public health powers by governments in response to the COVID-19 pandemic has provided a stark illustration of the potential for community interests to intrude on individual rights. One clear illustration of this has been the enforcement of stay-at-home orders and physical distancing requirements, particularly in the context of large gatherings for public protests and gatherings for religious observance. In several countries, the rights of individuals and groups to participate in congregate gatherings have raised questions that have been litigated on many occasions during the pandemic about the nature of individual and group rights during a public health emergency.[206] We discuss these issues further in Chapter 6. While the human rights dimensions of COVID-19 will be explored in more detail in later chapters of this book, there are three important points to make at this stage.

The first is the importance of acknowledging the relevance of human rights for health. This is recognized in international human rights law. The right to the highest attainable standard of health is set out in the *International Covenant on Economic, Social and Cultural Rights (ICESCR)*,[207] amongst a number of other international human rights instruments. In addition, a human rights-based approach is expressly

---

[201] ibid.
[202] ibid.
[203] See The Sex, Gender and COVID-19 Project, 'The COVID-19 Sex-Disaggregated Data Tracker' <https://globalhealth5050.org/the-sex-gender-and-covid-19-project/the-data-tracker/> accessed 1 October 2022.
[204] Vasee Moorthy and others, 'Data-sharing for Novel Coronavirus (COVID-19)' (2020) 98(3) *Bulletin of the World Health Organization* 150.
[205] Dianne Nicol and others, 'Australian Perspectives on the Ethical and Regulatory Considerations for Responsible Data Sharing in Response to the COVID-19 Pandemic' (2020) 27(4) *Journal of Law and Medicine* 829.
[206] Freckelton (n 197).
[207] *International Covenant on Economic, Social and Cultural Rights* (opened for signature 16 December 1966, entered into force 3 January 1976) 993 UNTS 3, Articles 12(1), (2)(c).

adopted in the *IHR (2005)*.[208] The United Nations Committee on Economic, Social and Cultural Rights has recognized that 'The right to health is not to be understood as a right to be *healthy*.'[209] Instead, it has interpreted the right to health as:

> an inclusive right extending not only to timely and appropriate health care but also to the underlying determinants of health, such as access to safe and potable water and adequate sanitation, an adequate supply of safe food, nutrition and housing, healthy occupational and environmental conditions, and access to health-related education and information, including on sexual and reproductive health. A further important aspect is the participation of the population in all health-related decision-making at the community, national and international levels.[210]

The responses to the COVID-19 pandemic have also raised important areas of debate relating to the relationship between health and human rights, as well as the human rights implications of restrictions on individual freedoms.[211] The United Nations has identified three rights as being 'at the frontline in the fight against COVID-19'. These are: (i) the 'right to life and the duty to protect life'; (ii) 'The right to health and access to health care'; and (iii) 'The central challenge to freedom of movement.'[212] In its 'Statement on the Coronavirus Disease (COVID-19) Pandemic and Economic, Social and Cultural Rights',[213] the Committee on Economic, Social and Cultural Rights stated:

> The COVID-19 pandemic vividly illustrates the importance of the indivisibility and interdependence of all human rights. This pandemic is essentially a global health threat. Nevertheless, it has multiple implications for the enjoyment of civil and political rights because some of the measures taken by States to combat it impose severe restrictions on the freedom of movement and on other rights. Thus, it

---

[208] World Health Organization, *International Health Regulations (2005)* (3rd edn, WHO: Geneva, 2016) Article 3(1). For further discussion see Chapter 3.
[209] Committee on Economic, Social and Cultural Rights, 'General Comment No 14: The Right to the Highest Attainable Standard of Health (Article 12 of the International Covenant on Economic, Social and Cultural Rights)' United Nations E/C.12/2000/4 (11 August 2000), para 8.
[210] ibid para 11.
[211] See eg Morten Kjaerum, Martha F Davis, and Amanda Lyons (eds), *COVID-19 and Human Rights* (Routledge 2021); Lisa Forman and Jillian C Kohler, 'Global Health and Human Rights in the Time of COVID-19: Response, Restrictions and Legitimacy' (2020) 19(5) *Journal of Human Rights* 547; Alessandra Spadaro, 'COVID-19: Testing the Limits of Human Rights' (2020) 11(2) *European Journal of Risk Regulation* 317; Karima Bennoune, '"Lest We Should Sleep": COVID-19 and Human Rights' (2020) 114(4) *American Journal of International Law* 666; Eric Mykhalovskiy and others, 'Human Rights, Public Health and COVID-19 in Canada' (2020) 111(6) *Canadian Journal of Public Health* 975.
[212] United Nations, *COVID-19 and Human Rights: We Are All in This Together* (April 2020) 4 <https://unsdg.un.org/resources/covid-19-and-human-rights-we-are-all-together> accessed 2 June 2022 (hereafter United Nations, *COVID-19 and Human Rights*).
[213] Committee on Economic, Social and Cultural Rights, 'Statement on the Coronavirus Disease (COVID-19) Pandemic and Economic, Social and Cultural Rights' United Nations, E/C.12/2020/1 (17 April 2020).

is essential that the measures adopted by States to combat this pandemic are reasonable and proportionate to ensure protection of all human rights.[214]

In the chapters of this book, we explore debates regarding the human rights implications of pandemic responses.

Second, although human rights are common to humanity, the utilization of a human rights lens does not imply the adoption of a homogenizing approach, but rather the contrary. Recognition of human rights requires consideration of the diversity of human experience and the specific needs of particular individuals and groups. Analysis of the pandemic has revealed disparities and uneven impact in terms of gender, race, age, and social and economic disadvantage. While recognizing that 'we're all in this together', the United Nations has emphasized that 'the virus does not discriminate; but its impacts do'.[215] The Committee on Economic, Social and Cultural Rights has stated that 'No one should be left behind as a result of the measures it is necessary to take to combat this pandemic'.[216] Throughout this book, we have endeavoured to include analysis of disparate impacts and their relevance to the development of law and policy.

Third, rather than characterizing individual and community rights as being in conflict with one another, a human rights-based approach provides space for recognition of the need to protect individual rights to the greatest extent possible, while recognizing that temporary limits may need to be placed on individual freedoms within the context of a pandemic. The United Nations has stated that 'Human rights are critical—for the response and the recovery'.[217]

E. Individual Obligations

One striking feature of the COVID-19 pandemic has been the reconfiguring of individual obligations in relation to public health. Although measures such as physical distancing requirements and the wearing of face masks can be mandated by law, the success of such measures depends in a large part on community compliance. Public messaging by governments and others has highlighted the importance of behaviours that individuals can adopt to protect their own health and the health of those around them: for instance, maintaining a safe physical distance from other people; wearing a face mask when in public or catching public transport; regular hand washing; adopting coughing etiquette; and getting tested for COVID-19 promptly if there is a risk of infection. Community participation and engagement

---

[214] ibid para 3.
[215] United Nations, *COVID-19 and Human Rights* (n 212) 10.
[216] Committee on Economic, Social and Cultural Rights (n 213) para 2.
[217] United Nations, *COVID-19 and Human Rights* (n 212) 2.

are essential to pandemic response and recovery.[218] Ensuring that public health information is widely available in languages spoken by different communities[219] is important for accessibility of public health messaging.

The nature of individual responsibility in the context of public health is not a new concept. Alongside the debate over individual responsibility has been debate over the role of the State in supporting people to make healthy and socially responsible choices. For some, this is viewed as a form of paternalism and reflective of 'the nanny state'.[220] Governments may choose to encourage certain behaviours by 'nudging' us in the right direction,[221] for example, by presenting information in such a way as to simplify the decision-making task.[222] Nudging has also been suggested in the context of COVID-19, for example, to increase hand hygiene.[223]

IV. Overview of the Book

In the remaining chapters of the book, we analyse the legal and regulatory dimensions of the response to the COVID-19 pandemic in detail, examining both developments in law and the role of law in providing a framework for responding to the broader social and economic aspects of the pandemic. The five themes outlined in Section III—layers of law and polycentricity; the role and scope of law; understandings of risk; human rights; and individual obligations—will provide the lenses through which we analyse the legal and regulatory responses to the pandemic.

Two further points are also important. First, we have adopted an inclusive approach to our analysis of the legal dimensions of COVID-19. In adopting this approach, we have not focused our discussion on one jurisdiction. Instead, we draw on international examples and literature, although with a primary focus on common law countries, including the United Kingdom, the United States, Canada, Australia, and New Zealand. In a work of this scope, it is not possible to provide an in-depth analysis of the full range of legal and policy developments introduced during the COVID-19 pandemic in each of the countries we consider. Instead, our

---

[218] Cicely Marston, Alicia Renedo, and Sam Miles, 'Community Participation is Crucial in a Pandemic' (2020) 395(10238) *Lancet* 1676.

[219] Leena Paakkari and Orkan Okan, 'COVID-19: Health Literacy is an Underestimated Problem' (2020) 5(5) *Lancet Public Health* e249; Hans Henri P Kluge and others, 'Refugee and Migrant Health in the COVID-19 Response' (2020) 395(10232) *Lancet* 1237.

[220] For discussion of public health and the nanny state, see Lindsay F Wiley, Micah L Berman, and Doug Blanke, 'Who's Your Nanny? Choice, Paternalism and Public Health in the Age of Personal Responsibility' (2013) 41(S1) *Journal of Law, Medicine & Ethics* 88.

[221] Richard H Thaler and Cass R Sunstein, *Nudge: Improving Decisions About Health, Wealth and Happiness* (Penguin Books 2009).

[222] Russell Korobkin, 'Three Choice Architecture Paradigms for Healthcare Policy' in I Glenn Cohen, Holly Fernandez Lynch, and Christopher T Robertson (eds), *Nudging Health: Health Law and Behavioral Economics* (Johns Hopkins University Press 2016).

[223] Robert J Weijers and Björn B de Koning, 'Nudging to Increase Hand Hygiene During the COVID-19 Pandemic: A Field Experiment' (2021) 53(3) *Canadian Journal of Behavioural Science* 353.

approach has been to provide selected examples that illustrate the social, economic, and legal developments and their implications for future legal developments.

Second, although much of the discussion in this book is necessarily about social, economic, and legal developments during the COVID-19 pandemic, this book also looks to the future and the lessons that may be learned from the experience of COVID-19. Our aim in analysing the scope and impact of the pandemic is to develop new insights and understandings of the important role that law can play in responding to emergencies.

Chapter 2 provides historical context to the legal and regulatory responses to COVID-19 at the international, national, and sub-national levels. It demonstrates how the key themes that the subsequent chapters of the book tease out in relation to the management of the current pandemic have their origins in previous experiences with pandemics. This chapter examines how different levels of government assumed responsibility for various aspects of public health during past pandemics, and traces the background to the creation of international frameworks and institutions that attempt to limit the spread of infectious diseases. It considers how laws intended to reduce the detrimental effects of pandemics affected many aspects of human life and some encouraged, while others compelled, compliance with public health measures. This chapter exposes the disproportionate impact that these laws and past pandemics had on certain populations, and considers the extent to which the law also protected some people. The chapter focuses, too, on the implications of various public health measures for civil liberties generally, including in periods before human rights were recognized in legal instruments, and the introduction of laws that reflected a burgeoning understanding of individuals' responsibility for community health.

Chapter 3 analyses the global emergency posed by COVID-19, situating it within existing international law for regulating global public health emergencies, as well as lessons from experiences with past emergencies. The chapter begins with discussion of the *IHR* and their revision in 2005. The 2005 revisions introduced a new concept of a PHEIC, new reporting requirements, and fresh requirements where Member States introduce measures that exceed WHO recommendations. Importantly, the 2005 revisions to the *IHR* included a focus on the building of national public health capacities, and expressly adopted a human rights approach. Chapter 3 also reviews the lessons learned from past public health emergencies, including the 2009 H1N1 influenza pandemic, which was the first test of the revised *IHR (2005)*, the 2014–16 Ebola crisis in West Africa, the debates over the *IHR* that have emerged during COVID-19, as well as proposals for a new pandemic treaty. The availability of accurate data has been a key part of measuring the scale and impact of the pandemic. Chapter 3 also analyses the importance of data and the challenges in accurately measuring the number of COVID-related deaths. It also considers the importance of civil registration and vital statistics for recording deaths, as well as the need for data to be disaggregated to enable identification of the pandemic's impact on different demographic groups.

Moving from Chapter 3's analysis of international law and public health emergencies, Chapter 4 analyses some of the major legal and regulatory measures that have been adopted to restrict people's movement in order to impede the transmission of COVID-19. It examines border closures that have prevented people from travelling locally, interstate or between provinces, and internationally (though some countries did repatriate citizens and permanent residents). The chapter discusses restrictions that have been imposed on entering Indigenous communities; the impact of movement restrictions on families with separated or divorced parents; and ramifications of the pandemic for extradition proceedings. Also explored in this chapter are restrictions that have been imposed on non-citizens' freedom of movement, including closure of borders to non-citizens and the impact of movement restrictions on asylum seekers, and the closure of ports to and quarantine of cruise ships. This chapter thus discusses the layers of laws that have encroached upon the legally recognized human right to freedom of movement. It touches, too, on public debates that the restrictions of movement have prompted about individuals' and communities' rights and responsibilities during public health emergencies, and the exceptional circumstances of a pandemic that have led to the imposition of highly intrusive constraints on people's lives.

Chapter 5 focuses on national responses to the pandemic within domestic law. It begins with an analysis of emergency laws and law-making during an emergency. The remaining sections of the chapter analyse the various measures that have been introduced in response to the pandemic. The measures reviewed are: travel restrictions; quarantine and isolation; lockdowns and stay-at-home orders; curfews; physical distancing requirements; wearing of face masks; and COVID testing, contact tracing, and wastewater surveillance. In addition, the chapter identifies debates about mandatory vaccination and the introduction of vaccination passports.

Chapter 6 explores the parameters that permit and set limits on the powers of governments to make emergency orders and directions during a pandemic. It does so by reference to challenges that have been mounted in diverse countries' courts during 2020 and 2021, as well as early 2022. The challenges have had in common that they have tested the power of the State to make orders in the name of public health that have significantly encroached on individuals' rights and liberties, which in some countries are constitutionally entrenched or otherwise protected. Jurisprudential considerations such as necessity, proportionality, and parsimony of interference have figured prominently in courts' decisions and what complies with such strictures has varied at different phases of the COVID-19 pandemic.

The right to life has emerged as a particularly potent consideration and has been invoked to justify many public health orders, including those that have resulted in closure of borders, imposition of quarantines, and also the requirement that populations or parts of them be locked down for periods of time. The use of curfews has been particularly contentious, but the point of greatest disputation in the courts has been orders curtailing the right to assemble—whether that be asserted for expression of views by way of civic protest or for the purposes of religious observance. Generally, orders constraining such rights have been upheld, in spite of the significant sensitivities for civil liberties attaching to such decisions. This chapter concludes with a review of decisions about the imposition of requirements that people be vaccinated in order to enjoy various ways in which they can participate in the community—from working, to attending school and childcare, to being able to go to shops, cafes, and restaurants, and to take public transport. It discusses the emergence of a preparedness of governments during 2021 to impose restrictive measures to inhibit spread of the virus and a tendency for courts to acquiesce in such measures, provided they can be shown to be required in the interests of public health.

While the pandemic has clearly been a health emergency, it has also had profound effects on people's social and economic well-being. Chapter 7 analyses these aspects of the pandemic. It begins by exploring the nature of risk and disadvantage in the pandemic, including its impact on older persons, health disparities related to race and ethnicity, the impact of COVID-19 on Indigenous Peoples, the pandemic's impact on women and children, as well as on people who are homeless, migrants, refugees, persons with disabilities, and people in detention, both prison and immigration detention. The chapter also examines access to prevention and treatment for COVID-19, social isolation, and mental health sequelae during the pandemic, and the pandemic's impact on work and employment.

The COVID-19 pandemic and efforts to reduce its detrimental impact have led to significant changes in many countries' criminal justice systems. Chapter 8 examines some important examples of these shifts and explores their ramifications for human rights and the rule of law. The chapter reviews changes to substantive aspects of criminal justice systems during the pandemic, including criminalization of conduct that has threatened to exacerbate the health crisis and shifts in the incidence and type of crimes committed. Chapter 8 also considers alterations to procedural aspects of criminal justice systems in response to the pandemic. In particular, it examines some disruptions to means of obtaining legal assistance, investigations of allegations of criminal offending, and hearing of criminal law matters. It discusses, too, issues of bail and sentencing relevant to COVID-19 and some changes to decision-making about incarcerating those charged with or convicted of criminal offending in response to the substantial risk of transmission of COVID-19 within prisons.

Chapter 9 engages with a number of the litigation and regulatory issues that have arisen during the COVID-19 period, including the bringing of actions by persons who have been detrimentally affected by lockdowns and by other public health measures. Some of these actions have been brought in tort and contract. Others have required how insurance policies are construed in the context of business and other losses. Case law in the United Kingdom and Australia is examined in this context. A number of further issues of civil liability have also arisen in the context of debates arising out of COVID-19. These have included whether immunity should be provided to health practitioners for vaccination and other provision of care during the health crisis and whether a no-fault state compensation scheme should operate.

Regulatory authorities have also been called upon to take active measures during the COVID-19 crisis. Chapter 9 describes the steps taken by consumer protection and therapeutic goods entities to inhibit the making of false representations about the efficacy of devices and medications when contemporary medical knowledge has not supported claims that have been made. In addition, regulators of health practitioners have needed to take steps to restrain the making of unscientific claims and assertions that have called into question the measures adopted by public health authorities lest they be undermined by stances expressed by some health practitioners in the media, including social media.

Chapter 10 engages with issues of workplace safety, including occupational health and safety. The COVID-19 pandemic has seen many changes to the operation of workplaces, including the adoption of working from home arrangements for many workers and hybrid arrangements for others. It has caused questioning of what constitute the occupational health and safety obligations of employers and employees alike in the context of a pandemic, as well as during the period when risks remain in spite of high levels of vaccination in some countries. This chapter reflects upon the measures that have been taken to protect particular categories of workers, including healthcare workers, but also the obligations imposed on some categories of workers who have significant contact with the public for the protection of both the public and the workers. Finally, requirements that workers be vaccinated have raised a number of issues in many countries about the extent to which such preconditions to participation in the workplace can be required by employers.

Chapter 11 examines domestic and international laws, regulations, and policies that have been relevant to research undertaken to develop treatments to cure or reduce the severity of symptoms of COVID-19, and vaccines to prevent people contracting and suffering or dying from it. The chapter considers the role played by WHO in coordinating, accelerating, and overseeing international collaboration between researchers working on treatments and vaccines to address the risks to global health posed by COVID-19. Chapter 11 also explores the risks for individual health and public health of strategies that scientists have adopted to hasten their COVID-19 research and of proposed human challenge trials. The chapter addresses challenges involved in ensuring the safety and efficacy of COVID-19 treatments and vaccines for all. This includes enrolling diverse participants in clinical trials, obtaining their informed consent to participation, and protecting those who cannot consent, but whose involvement in such trials is important. Chapter 11 also discusses the balance that has been struck between the imperative to maintain the rigour and integrity of research and the need to publish results of studies concerning treatments and vaccines as quickly as possible.

Chapter 12 examines the layers of law and regulation that have constituted obstacles to or mechanisms for facilitating the rapid production and broad distribution of COVID-19 treatments and vaccines. The chapter considers global governance structures that have been used to improve access to these medical products, but also impediments posed by some countries to their equitable and worldwide distribution. This chapter looks at the implications of these measures and also of decisions regarding allocation of scarce COVID-19 treatments and vaccines for human rights. Also explored in Chapter 12 is how regulatory authorities have managed the tension between needing to respond promptly to the risks posed by COVID-19 and ensure that treatments and vaccines released to the public are safe and efficacious. This chapter examines laws and policies that have sought to circumvent intellectual property laws which have hindered the manufacture and distribution of COVID-19 treatments and vaccines. It highlights differentials in availability of vaccines to persons in high-income countries and to those in lower- and middle-income countries.

Finally, in Chapter 13 we conclude by reflecting on the experience of the COVID-19 pandemic and the role of law and regulation in enabling responses to it. We consider the evolving nature of the pandemic and the potential responses of law and regulation to us living with the ongoing presence of COVID-19.

We hope by this book to have shone a fresh and lively light on the role of law, litigation, and legal analysis as part of the global efforts to contain the spread of the COVID-19 pandemic. The legal issues arising from the pandemic have been integral to government responses to the pandemic and to how the community has been able to respond to public health measures deployed by governments. At times, these responses have prompted high levels of contention and debate within the community, requiring us to embark on a steep learning curve.[224] They have placed legal processes and decision-making about public health measures on very public view. These matters have raised fundamental questions about the operation of law and the courts as a check and balance on government action during a pandemic but also more generally. Our aspiration is that the legal perspective will be acknowledged as an integral component of how COVID-19 has been managed and that this book will assist constructively in reflecting on the lessons that the global community can learn from responses to the COVID-19 pandemic.

---

[224] See Peter Doherty, *An Insider's Plague Year* (Melbourne University Press 2021) 78.

2
Past Legal and Regulatory Responses to Infectious Diseases

I. Introduction

Epidemiologists and medical historians find themselves strange bedfellows today. They are among the few for whom COVID-19 was not a surprise.[1] Since ancient times, people have documented the ravages of 'epidemics': diseases that spread rapidly through a population.[2] It is speculated that some of the 'plagues' narrated in the Old Testament were epidemics.[3] The first recorded pandemic—diseases that diffuse through multiple continents—commenced in 430 BCE: the 'Plague of Athens', which traversed the Mediterranean and North Africa.[4] Humans' domestication of and increased proximity to animals facilitated the transfer of pathogens from animals to humans, causing 'zoonotic diseases', which have been the bases of many epidemics.[5] Technological advances that augmented the ease and speed with which goods and people could move across land and through the seas and air exponentially increased opportunities for epidemics to develop into pandemics.[6]

---

[1] For instance, a group of scientists warned in 2007: 'Coronaviruses are well known to undergo genetic recombination which may lead to new genotypes and outbreaks. The presence of a large reservoir of SARS-CoV-like viruses in horseshoe bats ... is a time bomb. The possibility of the re-emergence of SARS and other novel viruses ... should not be ignored': Vincent CC Cheng and others, 'Severe Acute Respiratory Syndrome Coronavirus as an Agent of Emerging and Reemerging Infection' (2007) 20 *Clinical Microbiology Reviews* 660, 674. See also Joseph P Byrne and Jo N Hays, *Epidemics and Pandemics: From Ancient Plagues to Modern-Day Threats* (Greenwood 2021).

[2] Mark Honigsbaum, *The Pandemic Century: One Hundred Years of Panic, Hysteria and Hubris* (C Hurst and Company (Publishers) Limited 2019) xi (hereafter Honigsbaum, *Pandemic Century*); Sonia Shah, *Pandemic: Tracking Contagions, from Cholera to Ebola and Beyond* (Picador 2016); S Harris Ali and Roger Keil (eds), *Networked Disease: Emerging Infections in the Global City* (Wiley-Blackwell 2008); Mary Lowth, 'Plagues, Pestilence and Pandemics: Deadly Diseases and Humanity' (2012) 42(16) *Practice Nurse* 42; Jo N Hays, *Burdens of Disease: Epidemics and Human Response in Western History* (rev edn, Rutgers University Press 2009).

[3] Lowth (n 2).

[4] Honigsbaum, *Pandemic Century* (n 2) xi; David M Morens and others, 'Pandemic COVID-19 Joins History's Pandemic Legion' (2020) 11(3) *American Society for Microbiology* art e00812-20, 2–3; Robert J Littman, 'The Plague of Athens: Epidemiology and Paleopathology' (2009) 76(5) *Mount Sinai Journal of Medicine* 456; Jilene Malbeuf and others, 'The Plague of Athens Shedding Light on Modern Struggles with COVID-19' (2021) 22(43) *Journal of Classics Teaching* 47, 47–49.

[5] Honigsbaum, *Pandemic Century* (n 2) xi; Morens and others (n 4) 2–3.

[6] Honigsbaum, *Pandemic Century* (n 2) 262; S Harris Ali, 'Globalized Complexity and the Microbial Traffic of New and Emerging Infectious Disease Threats' in Tamara Giles-Vernick and Susan Craddock with Jennifer Gunn (eds), *Influenza and Public Health: Learning from Past Pandemics* (Routledge 2010) 22–23.

In the twenty-first century, infectious diseases that affected past populations have re-emerged and new diseases continue to emerge.[7] Given the unprecedented scale of globalization, a pandemic that could affect the global community has been looming.[8]

Infectious diseases are enmeshed in the story of the development of human society and the law.[9] In this chapter, we explore some examples of the interplay between law and epidemics and pandemics in different geographical regions and centuries. Those examples illustrate themes that resound in contemporary legal and regulatory responses to COVID-19 and their implications for human rights. While linear evolution of the law in this context is sometimes apparent, societies have not always learnt from the successes and failures of past legal experiments. Existing laws have been applied and adapted and new laws have been developed to contain the spread and minimize the impact of diseases.[10] In addition, laws have been amended and created in response to social, economic, and political changes, as well as developments in science, medicine, and public health prompted by epidemics.[11] On some occasions, laws have halted the advance of an epidemic,[12] while at other times, failure to use laws for this purpose has had devastating consequences.

All humans are potentially vulnerable to infectious diseases, which can wreak greater havoc than natural and man-made disasters.[13] Yet often those who are already impoverished or marginalized suffer most from epidemics and are disproportionately affected by laws designed to contain their spread.[14] Moreover, the fear that epidemics and pandemics has generated has led to scapegoating and persecution of individuals and groups, and the law has not always come to their aid.[15] Laws

---

[7] Alexandra M Stern and Howard Markel, 'International Efforts to Control Infectious Diseases, 1851 to the Present' (2004) 292(12) *Journal of the American Medical Association* 1474.

[8] Nita Madhav and others, 'Pandemics, Risks, Impacts and Mitigation' in Dean T Jamison and others (eds), *Disease Control Priorities: Improving Health and Reducing Poverty* (3rd edn, International Bank for Reconstruction and Development/World Bank 2017); Nathan Wolfe, *The Viral Storm: The Dawn of a New Pandemic Age* (Allen Lane 2011) 3.

[9] Frank M Snowden, *Epidemics and Society: From the Black Death to the Present* (Yale University Press 2019) 2.

[10] Marlene C McGuirl and Robert N Gee, 'AIDS: An Overview of the British, Australian, and American Responses' (1985) 14(1) *Hofstra Law Review* 107, 109.

[11] Susan Craddock and Tamara Giles-Vernick, 'Introduction' in Tamara Giles-Vernick and Susan Craddock with Jennifer Gunn (eds), *Influenza and Public Health: Learning from Past Pandemics* (Routledge 2010) 15.

[12] ibid.

[13] Snowden (n 9) 2–3.

[14] Craddock and Giles-Vernick (n 11) 12.

[15] Snowden (n 9) 2; Yuval Levin, 'A Mirror of the Plague: Pandemics Ancient and Modern and the Lessons They Teach' *Commentary* (May 2020) 18, 21 <www.commentarymagazine.com/articles/yuval-levin/coronavirus-mirrors-plague/> accessed 22 September 2021; Ian Freckelton, 'COVID-19: Fear, Quackery, False Representations and the Law' (2020) 72 *International Journal of Law and Psychiatry* art 101611; Steven LB Jensen, '"Human Rights against Human Arbitrariness": Pandemics in a Human Rights Historical Perspective' in Morten Kjaerum, Martha F Davis, and Amanda Lyons (eds), *COVID-19 and Human Rights* (Routledge 2021).

intended to curb dissemination of disease by separating people from one another can undermine social cohesion and responsibility.[16] People have often challenged public health laws that curtailed civic freedoms. Epidemics have also at times provoked disregard for the law generally. Indeed, Thucydides recounted 'the beginnings of a state of unprecedented lawlessness' during the Plague of Athens when 'men, not knowing what would happen next' and sensing that 'money and life alike seemed equally ephemeral', 'became indifferent to every ... law'.[17]

In this chapter, we discuss the history of legal and regulatory responses to infectious diseases, epidemics, and pandemics. In Section II, we discuss the impact of the Black Death on medieval Europe and the introduction of the term 'quarantine' and laws to enforce it. The social upheaval caused by the Black Death also led to major changes to feudal labour laws, providing an early example of the potentially far-reaching legal impacts of pandemics. In Section III, we discuss the introduction of vaccination following the work of Edward Jenner in the late eighteenth century. In Section IV, we review the nineteenth-century sanitary reforms in England, Europe, and the United States of America, led by concerns over cholera. These reforms resulted in improved urban sanitation, sewerage systems, and clean water supplies. It was also during this period that the first International Sanitary Conferences were held, which provided early foundations for the later development of the *International Health Regulations* (IHR). In Section V, we discuss the emergence of 'Russian flu' in the late nineteenth century.[18] During this period, disease monitoring was introduced and the English Court of Appeal made a landmark decision establishing fundamental rules of contract law in response to a product that was claimed to be able to prevent users from contracting influenza.

The emergence of 'Spanish flu' in 1918 also had a dramatic impact across the globe. In Section VI, we discuss the use of legal and regulatory public health measures to limit the spread of this disease, including use of face masks, quarantine, and closure of public venues. This pandemic highlighted the importance of protecting populations, including Indigenous Peoples, who were particularly vulnerable to suffering and dying from contagious diseases. Section VII discusses the emergence of polio in the late nineteenth and early twentieth centuries and international collaboration to develop the polio vaccine in the 1950s. Section VIII sets out the impact of acquired immune deficiency syndrome (AIDS), caused by the human immunodeficiency virus (HIV), on the development of discrimination laws, and

[16] Levin (n 15) 20.
[17] Thucydides, *History of the Peloponnesian War* (first published 4th century BC, Penguin Books 1972) 155.
[18] Since 2015, the World Health Organization has recommended that disease names not include geographic locations 'to minimize unnecessary negative impact of disease names on trade, travel, tourism ... and avoid causing offence to any cultural, social, national, regional, professional or ethnic groups': World Health Organization, 'World Health Organization Best Practices for the Naming of New Human Infectious Diseases' (May 2015) <www.who.int/publications/i/item/WHO-HSE-FOS-15.1> accessed 29 September 2021.

other areas of law reform. As discussed in Section IX, the emergence of Severe Acute Respiratory Syndrome (SARS) in the early 2000s provided a test for global disease surveillance systems and the *IHR*. However, the experience with SARS, and growing concerns over the spread of avian influenza (bird flu), reviewed in Section X, led to reforms of the *IHR* with revised *IHR* adopted in 2005. The experience with bird flu also demonstrated the importance of global equity in access to vaccines, an issue that was to emerge again during the 2009 'swine flu' pandemic. More recently, an outbreak of Ebola Virus Disease (Ebola) in West Africa in 2014 highlighted the importance of responding quickly to emergencies and working with communities in doing so.

II. The Black Death, Quarantine Laws, and Changes to Labour Law

During a pandemic, fear can lead to many discriminatory and violent reactions.[19] In the era of COVID-19, the term 'coronaphobia'—fear of contracting COVID-19—has been coined.[20] During the Antonine Plague of 165–180 CE (also known as the Plague of Galen),[21] there was an eruption of persecution of Christians who were blamed for the plague by reason of their rejection of local gods, their blasphemies, and their indulgence in black magic.[22] It caused devastating consequences that destabilized the fabric of the Roman Empire.[23]

More than three and half centuries later, the 'Plague of Justinian', which occurred during the reign of the last emperor of the Roman Empire in three waves from 541 CE, killed half the global population: an estimated 30 to 50 million people.[24] Another strain of the same bacterium that caused it—*Yersinia pestis*[25]—was

[19] Steven Taylor, *The Psychology of Pandemics: Preparing for the Next Global Outbreak of Infectious Diseases* (Cambridge Scholars Publishing 2019); Nidal Moukaddam, 'Fears, Outbreaks, and Pandemics: Lessons Learned' (2019) 36(11) *Psychiatric Times* 28; Freckelton (n 15); Giovanni Boccaccio, *The Decameron of Giovanni Boccaccio* (Frances Winwar tr, Modern Library 1955) xxv–xxvi.

[20] See Gordon J Asmundson and Steven Taylor, 'Coronaphobia: Fear and the 2019-nCoV Outbreak' (2020) 70 *Journal of Anxiety Disorders* art 102196; Alisha Arora and others, 'Understanding Coronaphobia' (2020) 54 *Asian Journal of Psychiatry* art 102384; Leodoro J Labrague and Janet AA De Los Santos, 'Prevalence and Predictors of Coronaphobia Among Frontline Hospital and Public Health Nurses' (2021) 38(3) *Public Health Nursing* 382.

[21] Robert J Littman and Michael L Littman, 'Galen and the Antonine Plague' (1973) 94(3) *American Journal of Philology* 243.

[22] Brenda Thacker, 'The Antonine Plague: Unknown Death within the Roman Empire, 165–180 CE' in Rebecca M Seaman (ed), *Epidemics and War: The Impact of Disease on Major Conflicts in History* (ABC-CLIO 2018) 30.

[23] Christer Bruun, 'The Antonine Plague and the "Third Century Crisis"' in Olivier Hekster, Gerda de Kleijn, and Danielle Slootjes (eds), *Crises and the Roman Empire: Proceedings of the Seventh Workshop of the International Network Impact of Empire* (Brill 2007).

[24] William Rosen, *Justinian's Flea: Plague, Empire and the Birth of Europe* (Jonathan Cape 2007) 220; Morens and others (n 4) 2.

[25] See Robert D Perry and Jacqueline D Fetherston, 'Yersinia Pestis—Etiologic Agent of Plague' (1997) 10(1) *Clinical Microbiological Reviews* 35; Marcel Keller and others, 'Ancient Yersinia Pestis Genomes from Across Western Europe Reveal Early Diversification during the First Pandemic (541–750)' (2019)

responsible for the similarly lethal 'Black Death' in the fourteenth century (possibly so called due to the necrosis of its victims' extremities).[26] This bubonic plague emerged in Central Asia in the 1330s, spread to Sicily in 1347, and then throughout Europe and Africa where it killed 40% to 60% of the population by 1353, and recurred in outbreaks for centuries thereafter.[27] The symptoms caused by this infection of the lymphatic system (including 'buboes', which are a painful swelling of lymph nodes in the armpits, neck, and groin),[28] the rapid dissemination of this disease, and its high death toll prompted significant developments in European and English public health law, some of which endure today, and labour law.[29]

It was not until 1898 that scientists discovered the pathogen that caused the Black Death and the vectors responsible for its transmission to humans: rodents and the fleas that live on them; these vectors travelled on ships, infested grain and clothing, and bit people.[30] The plague dispersed swiftly among people who lived or worked in close proximity to those who were infected, including monks, doctors, priests, and gravediggers.[31] Following Galen's theory, which was influenced by Hippocrates' hypotheses, fourteenth-century physicians believed the plague was attributable to an imbalance in the four bodily 'humours'.[32] Their purgatory treatments, designed to restore the balance, did not cure the sick.[33] Nonetheless, physicians did recognize the contagiousness of those infected (though they mistakenly attributed it to their bodies' emission of 'miasmas', noxious vapours).[34] Consequently, public health measures were introduced and legally enforced to contain its spread.[35]

116(25) *Proceedings of the National Academy of the Sciences of the United States* 12363; World Health Organization, 'Plague' (31 October 2017) <www.who.int/news-room/fact-sheets/detail/plague> accessed 17 October 2021.

[26] Morens and others (n 4) 2; Snowden (n 9) 47, 51, 83.

[27] Monica H Green, 'Editor's Introduction to Pandemic Disease in the Medieval World: Rethinking the Black Death' in Monica H Green (ed), *Pandemic Disease in the Medieval World* (Arc Medieval Press 2015) 9; David D Haddock and Lynne Kiesling, 'The Black Death and Property Rights' (2002) 31(2) *Journal of Legal Studies* S545, S554; Mark A Senn, 'English Life and Law in the Time of the Black Death' (2003) 38(3) *Real Property, Probate and Trust Journal* 507, 572.

[28] Snowden (n 9) 45, 48.

[29] See Robert C Palmer, *English Law in the Age of the Black Death, 1348–1381: A Transformation of Governance and Law* (University of North Carolina Press 1993); Senn (n 27); Katy Barnett and Matthew Harding, 'Contract in the Time of COVID-19' in Belinda Bennett and Ian Freckelton (eds), *Pandemics, Public Health Emergencies and Government Powers: Perspectives on Australian Law* (Federation Press 2021).

[30] Robert S Gottfried, *The Black Death: Natural and Human Disaster in Medieval* Europe (The Free Press 1983) xiii, 33–76; Snowden (n 9) 40, 42–43, 48; Senn (n 27) 570.

[31] Snowden (n 9) 42–43.

[32] Senn (n 27) 568; John M Barry, *The Great Influenza: The Story of the Deadliest Pandemic in History* (Penguin Books 2005) 16–17.

[33] Senn (n 27) 568.

[34] Snowden (n 9) 74, 77; Lewis C Vollmar, 'The Effect of Epidemics on the Development of English Law from the Black Death Through the Industrial Revolution' (1994) 15(3) *Journal of Legal Medicine* 385, 395 (footnote 36).

[35] Vollmar (n 34) 395 (footnote 36); Snowden (n 9) 8.

Many countries, following northern Italy's example, created boards of health whose 'health magistrates' were empowered to issue 'plague regulations'.[36] They appointed officials to confine plague victims and their contacts to their homes or transport them to 'pesthouses', hospitals on the outskirts of towns, and guards prevented anyone from leaving or entering them.[37] By the seventeenth century, an English statute created a felony for breaching such restrictions.[38] Separating people who are infected from the general population, described today as 'isolation',[39] has long been a response to epidemics. In the Old Testament, for instance, lepers were compelled to live alone to preclude them from infecting the healthy.[40]

However, the use of 'quarantine' to separate and detain people who may have been exposed to an infectious disease before permitting their entry to a new location was novel in the fourteenth century.[41] This practice was first called 'trentina', derived from the Italian word for thirty.[42] In 1377, the Rector of Ragusa (present day Dubrovnik) ordered the prevention of ships and land travellers who arrived from sites that were or were suspected to have been plague-infested from entering the port or city, respectively, for thirty days.[43] Contravention of the rules attracted fines.[44] When that time period was extended to forty days, inspired by references to the number forty in biblical purifying contexts, the term quarantine was adopted (derived from the Italian word 'quarantenaria' and the Latin 'quadraginta').[45] In 1423, Venice created 'lazaretti', quarantine stations on outlying islands where ships and their crew were detained by guards, cargo was fumigated, and passengers were separated from one another.[46] Other cities imitated Venice and further laws were developed surrounding quarantine, such as exemptions for ships that had most recently visited disease-free ports.[47]

Florence created a board of public health in 1347, initially on a provisional basis, but by the fifteenth century, due to the repeated appearance of the plague, the board had become a recurrent phenomenon with functions 'to give full authority ... for a period of three months to make provisions and issue ordinances, preserve public

---

[36] Snowden (n 9) 8, 69–70; Paul Slack, 'Responses to Plague in Early Modern Europe: The Implications of Public Health' (1988) 55(3) *Social Research* 33.
[37] Snowden (n 9) 74, 77; Vollmar (n 34) 395–96; Wendy E Parmet, 'AIDS and Quarantine: The Revival of an Archaic Doctrine' (1985) 14(1) *Hofstra Law Review* 53, 55 (hereafter Parmet, 'AIDS').
[38] 1 Jac. 1, c. 31 (1603); see Parmet, 'AIDS' (n 37) 56.
[39] Lawrence O Gostin and Lindsay F Wiley, *Public Health Law: Power, Duty, Restraint* (3rd edn, University of California Press 2016) 416.
[40] Gian Franco Gensini, Magdi H Yacoub, and Andrea A Conti, 'The Concept of Quarantine in History: From Plague to SARS' (2004) 49(4) *Journal of Infection* 257, 258.
[41] ibid 260; Gottfried (n 30) 48; Gostin and Wiley (n 39) 416.
[42] Gensini, Yacoub, and Conti (n 40) 258; Lesley E Ogden, 'A Brief Biological History of Quarantine' (2021) 71(9) *BioScience* 899.
[43] Gensini, Yacoub, and Conti (n 40) 258.
[44] ibid.
[45] ibid; Snowden (n 9) 70.
[46] Gensini, Yacoub, and Conti (n 40) 259; Snowden (n 9) 70–71.
[47] Gensini, Yacoub, and Conti (n 40) 259.

health, keep off the plague, and avoid an epidemic'.[48] Similar boards were constituted in a number of Tuscan towns, but the most effective board was that of Milan, which was staffed by physicians, surgeons, and apothecaries, horsemen used as messengers and police, an officer in charge of bills of mortality, a carter with assistants to remove dead bodies, and gravediggers.[49] The principal roles of the Italian boards were to report an outbreak and then to isolate it.[50]

The practice at the onset of the Black Death of citizens patrolling the borders of towns and preventing outsiders from entering them was later formalized into 'sanitary cordons'.[51] Military barriers were erected, troops defended territories, and military judges sentenced those who breached the cordons.[52] From 1710 to 1871, a thousand-mile-long Austrian cordon patrolled by peasants, which included lookout, sentry, and quarantine stations, defended Europe against the potential entry of travellers with plague from the Ottoman Empire.[53]

Other public health measures that were introduced to prevent the spread of plague similarly encroached on individuals' civil liberties.[54] Local governments closed schools, church services, fairs, and public assemblies.[55] The practice of trades that produced noxious odours, such as tanning and butchery, was prohibited, and the dead were buried in pits without funerals.[56] Defiance of plague regulations was common, notwithstanding the associated penalties.[57] To evade isolation and detention, people hid the sick, while merchants, resentful of interruptions to their commerce, breached quarantine.[58] The Great Plague of Marseille in 1720 may have begun after merchants convinced health authorities to release a ship's goods and crew from quarantine before the stipulated period of 40 days elapsed.[59]

When plague arrived in a community, the wealthy often fled, while some who stayed engaged in unruly behaviour, looting, and victimizing individuals and groups.[60] Authorities sometimes failed to thwart, condoned, and even sanctioned this harassment. Blamed for provoking God to punish humanity with the plague through their alleged immorality, prostitutes, lepers, beggars, and foreigners were on occasions attacked and banished.[61] Accused of poisoning wells, streams, and

---

[48] Gottfried (n 30) 123.
[49] ibid 123.
[50] ibid 124.
[51] Snowden (n 9) 72.
[52] ibid 72–73.
[53] ibid 73.
[54] ibid 78–79.
[55] Vollmar (n 34) 395.
[56] Snowden (n 9) 74, 77–78.
[57] ibid 78–79.
[58] ibid 71, 78–9; Gensini, Yacoub, and Conti (n 40) 259; Vollmar (n 34) 395 (footnote 36).
[59] Snowden (n 9) 72.
[60] ibid 59; Vollmar (n 34) 395.
[61] Anna Colet and others, 'The Black Death and its Consequences for the Jewish Community in Tàrrega: Lessons from History and Archeology' in Monica H Green (ed), *Pandemic Disease in the Medieval World* (Arc Medieval Press 2015) 64; Snowden (n 9) 62–63.

food, Jews were rounded up, tortured to confess, brutalized, and burnt, and their homes and documentation of loans they had made destroyed.[62] Initial attempts to protect Jews, for instance by a Spanish king and Duke Albrecht of Austria, were ineffective,[63] while a powerful elite encouraged their maltreatment. Emperor Charles IV of Bohemia arranged for the disposal of Jewish property, cancellation of debts owed to Jews, and immunity for those who executed them.[64] City leaders and nobles investigated and procured evidence regarding allegations of Jewish poisonings, and incited and perpetrated violence against them.[65] Believing that Jews killed Jesus Christ and sought to eradicate Christendom, 'Flagellants', who trekked across Europe, whipping their backs and reciting penitential verses, also assaulted Jews.[66]

Deaths from bubonic plague of many people of working age led to changes to the feudal economy and, consequently, labour law, which prevailed until the eighteenth century.[67] Labour shortages disrupted the feudal system, the perpetuation of which depended on a high volume of workers, low wages, and limited availability of fertile land.[68] Following the Black Death, agricultural tenants abandoned their plots of land to relocate or find alternative employment, land rentals dropped, and employees could demand higher wages for their labour and vendors higher prices for their goods.[69] Seeking to revert to pre-Black Death conditions, suppress competition, and empower employers to regulate labourers, King Edward III of England issued the *Ordinance of Labourers* in 1349, which Parliament passed as the *Statute of Labourers* in 1351.[70] It compelled servants, artisans, apprentices, and agricultural workers under 60 years of age to accept work and labour for pre-plague wages, forbade workers from leaving employers without permission or reasonable cause, and prohibited employers from paying higher wages and vendors from selling goods above 'reasonable' prices.[71] Other European governments similarly regulated wages and fixed prices.[72] The crime of vagrancy was created to punish itinerants who lacked employment, land, and/or financial support.[73] Assumpsit

---

[62] Samuel K Cohn, 'The Black Death and the Burning of Jews' (2007) 196(1) *Past and Present* 3, 3–4; Colet and others (n 61) 64, 69, 82–83; Remi Jedwab, Noel D Johnson, and Mark Koyama, 'Negative Shocks and Mass Persecutions: Evidence from the Black Death' (2019) 24(4) *Journal of Economic Growth* 345.
[63] Colet and others (n 61) 66; Cohn (n 62) 14–15.
[64] Cohn (n 62) 15.
[65] ibid 18–20, 36.
[66] Snowden (n 9) 65.
[67] Vollmar (n 34) 386, 394; Haddock and Kiesling (n 27) S555; Barnet and Harding (n 29) 220–22.
[68] Vollmar (n 34) 388, 390–91.
[69] ibid 391; Haddock and Kiesling (n 27) S586; Senn (n 27) 573–4; Palmer (n 29) 17.
[70] Senn (n 27) 573–4; Palmer (n 29) 5, 17–18, 139; Barnett and Harding (n 29) 221.
[71] Palmer (n 29) 18; Senn (n 27) 574; Vollmar (n 34) 392–93.
[72] Samuel Cohn 'After the Black Death: Labour Legislation and Attitudes Towards Labour in Late-Medieval Western Europe' (2007) 60(3) *Economic History Review* 457, 479.
[73] Robin Yeamans, 'Constitutional Attacks on Vagrancy Laws' (1968) 20(4) *Stanford Law Review* 782, 782.

writs (actions to enforce obligations) made labourers and artisans who failed to meet quality and service standards civilly liable.[74]

III. Smallpox, Inoculation, and Vaccination

By the eighteenth century, smallpox overtook bubonic plague as the dominant infectious disease, killing around 500,000 Europeans annually.[75] This highly contagious virus had long affected humanity.[76] Smallpox lesions are visible on Egyptian Pharoah Rameses V's mummy,[77] and the 15-year-long 'Antonine Plague', which from 165 CE killed five million people, was probably smallpox.[78] Traders on the silk route transported smallpox from Asia to Europe, where it became a recurrent epidemic from the eleventh century,[79] and it has been speculated that colonizing Europeans carried it across oceans where it devastated Indigenous populations, including in the United States of America and Australia.[80] Smallpox victims who did not die from internal haemorrhaging experienced a burning rash and growing red lesions that restricted swallowing.[81]

To contain the spread of smallpox, governments and their delegates enforced stringent public health measures, some of which had been deployed to address previous epidemics, while others were new. In England and the United States, smallpox victims were isolated and detained in hospitals.[82] States in the United States have 'police powers' under the Constitution, which they can rely upon to regulate public health and safety within their jurisdictions.[83] Courts referred to this authority in dismissing challenges to state officials' enforcement of quarantines on ships.[84] Following experiments with inoculation against smallpox (by injecting a small amount of smallpox matter), General George Washington ordered the inoculation of his army, while in London, the inoculated were isolated in the Smallpox and Inoculation Hospital until they were no longer infectious.[85]

---

[74] Palmer (n 29) 295; Senn (n 27) 581; Barnett and Harding (n 29) 220–23.
[75] Snowden (n 9) 97–98; Donald R Hopkins, *The Greatest Killer: Smallpox in History* (University of Chicago Press 2002); Gareth Williams, *Angel of Death: The Story of Smallpox* (Palgrave Macmillan 2010); SL Kotar and JE Gessler, *Smallpox: A History* (McFarland & Co 2013).
[76] Snowden (n 9) 89, 97.
[77] Morens and others (n 4) 3.
[78] Lowth (n 2); Rosen (n 24) 191.
[79] Harris Ali (n 6) 23; Snowden (n 9) 97–98.
[80] Alison Bashford, *Imperial Hygiene: A Critical History of Colonialism, Nationalism and Public Health* (Palgrave Macmillan 2004) 15; Harris Ali (n 6) 23; Stern and Markel (n 7) 1475. See too Peter Dowling, *Fatal Contact: How Epidemics Nearly Wiped Out Australia's First Peoples* (Monash University Publishing 2021) 16–66; Judy Campbell, 'Smallpox in Aboriginal Australia, 1829–31' (1983) 20(81) *Historical Studies* 536.
[81] Snowden (n 9) 91–92.
[82] Parmet, 'AIDS' (n 37) 71; Vollmar (n 34) 409–10.
[83] Parmet, 'AIDS' (n 37) 60.
[84] ibid 56–57, 60–61.
[85] Snowden (n 9) 104–46; Bashford (n 80) 15–16.

Inoculation was costly and carried a risk of the inoculated suffering a severe case of smallpox or spreading it.[86] In 1796, however, Dr Edward Jenner performed the first vaccination by injecting a child with cowpox, a disease of cattle that generally caused only mild illness in humans and gave them immunity against smallpox.[87] Jenner subsequently convinced authorities in England, Europe, and the United States to vaccinate their populations.[88] Some enacted legislation that mandated vaccination and stipulated penalties for breaching it.[89]

Adherents of a growing anti-vaccination movement defied use of state power to enforce smallpox vaccination.[90] Reverend Henning Jacobson, for instance, refused to be vaccinated, as required by a regulation of the Cambridge Board of Health, which was made under a Massachusetts law that authorized municipal health boards to compel vaccination and revaccination for public health and safety.[91] In response, in the 1905 case of *Jacobson v Massachusetts*,[92] the United States Supreme Court upheld the authority of state legislatures (and health boards to which they delegated it) to use their police power to protect inhabitants of their jurisdictions against epidemics, including by compelling vaccination to prevent disease transmission, provided the power was not exercised arbitrarily or unreasonably.[93] Other United States courts in the years prior to that case had similarly found that the legislature had constitutional power to require vaccination against smallpox of school students during a public health emergency.[94] United States courts nonetheless confirmed that the police power could not be used to implement discriminatory health measures. In 1900, a circuit court upheld a challenge to an ordinance issued by the San Francisco city that mandated inoculation of all Chinese residents against bubonic plague before they left the city; it found no evidence to support the city's claims that Asians were especially susceptible to contracting plague and that this measure would halt its dissemination.[95] A court also invalidated as unconstitutional the city's subsequent quarantine of an area inhabited mostly by Asian residents, in part because its exemption for houses inhabited by non-Asians indicated its discriminatory intentions.[96]

---

[86] Snowden (n 9) 106.
[87] ibid 87, 107.
[88] ibid 108.
[89] Rajaie Batniji, 'Historical Evidence to Inform COVID-19 Vaccine Mandates' (2021) 397(10276) *Lancet* 791; Alexander Grab, 'Smallpox Vaccination in Napoleonic Italy (1800–1814)' (2017) 30(3) *Napoleonica La Revue* 38; Vollmar (n 34) 409.
[90] Snowden (n 9) 108.
[91] Gostin and Wiley (n 39) 122.
[92] 197 US 11 (1905).
[93] Gostin and Wiley (n 39) 124–26; Janet L Dolgin, 'AIDS: Social Meanings and Legal Ramifications' (1985) 14(1) *Hofstra Law Review* 193, 206–67.
[94] Gostin and Wiley (n 39) 121–22. See eg *Bissell v Davison* 32 A 348 (Conn 1894).
[95] *Wong Wai v Williamson* 103 F 1 (ND Cal 1900); Parmet, 'AIDS' (n 37) 70.
[96] Parmet, 'AIDS' (n 37) 70–71; *Jew Ho v Williamson* 103 F 10 (ND Cal 1900); Dolgin (n 93) 207.

IV. Cholera, Tuberculosis, Health Boards, and Sanitary Reform

In 1959, a global mass smallpox vaccination campaign began and the last case of smallpox was reported in Somalia in 1977.[97] In 1980, the World Health Organization (WHO)—the chief health agency of the United Nations—declared that smallpox had been eliminated.[98] It remains the only infectious human disease to have been intentionally eradicated.[99] By contrast, other recurrent infectious diseases of the past, such as typhus, tuberculosis, cholera, and polio, continue to devastate some communities today.[100] Of those, tuberculosis and cholera are particularly significant. Responsible for multiple epidemics in the nineteenth century,[101] they coincided with and prompted major advances in medical knowledge, and the introduction of new national and international legal and regulatory public health measures.

Previously confined for centuries to India, in the early nineteenth century, cholera was transmitted to Europe, America, and Africa by colonial troops, Indian Muslims on pilgrimage, armies fighting wars and suppressing revolutions, and traders travelling on trains and ships.[102] During the first cholera pandemic, the English government established the Central Board of Health to recommend actions to prevent the entry to and spread within England of cholera.[103] The Board's suggestions to improve quarantine and forcefully detain cholera victims in pesthouses were unpopular with merchants and the Privy Council.[104] Nevertheless, changing understandings about cholera and its dissemination soon generated different public health law and regulation.

Humoral medicine was found to be ineffective in treating cholera's symptoms of violent expulsion of blood plasma from a victim's rectum and mouth.[105] It also could not explain cholera's sudden onset and massive death toll, and the muscular

---

[97] Snowden (n 9) 109.
[98] World Health Organization, 'Smallpox' <www.who.int/health-topics/smallpox#tab=tab_1> accessed 25 October 2021.
[99] Walter R Dowdle, 'The Principles of Disease Elimination and Eradication' *Centers for Disease Control and Prevention* (31 December 1999) <www.cdc.gov/mmwr/preview/mmwrhtml/su48a7.htm> accessed 26 September 2021; John Rhodes, *The End of Plagues: The Battle Against Infectious Diseases* (St Martin's Press 2013) 12.
[100] Anna Gorman and Kaiser Health News, 'Medieval Diseases Are Infecting California's Homeless' *The Atlantic* (8 March 2019) <www.theatlantic.com/health/archive/2019/03/typhus-tuberculosis-medieval-diseases-spreading-homeless/584380/> accessed 22 September 2020; World Health Organization, 'Cholera' (30 March 2022) <www.who.int/news-room/fact-sheets/detail/cholera> accessed 5 May 2022.
[101] Snowden (n 9) 233, 269.
[102] ibid 233–34. See also Paul A Blake, 'Historical Perspectives on Pandemic Cholera' in Kaye Wachsmuth, Paul A Blake, and Ørjan Olsvik (eds), *Vibrio Cholerae and Cholera: Molecular to Global Perspectives* (Wiley 1994); Valeska Huber, 'Pandemics and the Politics of Difference: Rewriting the History of Internationalism Through Nineteenth-Century Cholera' (2020) 15(3) *Journal of Global History* 394, 396.
[103] Vollmar (n 34) 413.
[104] ibid 414.
[105] Snowden (n 9) 236, 240–41.

contractions in the limbs of those who died from it.[106] At this time, influenced by Enlightenment thinking, Western physicians began challenging the theory of humoral imbalance and recognizing that diseases were separate entities.[107] Between 1794 and 1848, the so-called 'Paris School of Medicine', which focused on empirical observation of hospital patients, transformed Western medicine.[108] Data it collected exposed that cholera was especially prevalent in dirty, congested urban environments that were the product of industrialization and that lacked sewers, clean water, and hygienic housing.[109] Paris's foul odour and the hypothesis that waste produced miasma, which caused disease, led to the establishment of the Paris Board of Health that, from 1820, cleaned public spaces.[110] This was one of the inspirations for Edwin Chadwick, a barrister, and Dr Thomas Southwood Smith to co-found the sanitary reform movement in England in the 1830s and 1840s, which other industrial nations subsequently embraced.[111] Chadwick was influenced, too, by research he conducted during his appointment to reform England's 'poor laws' (concerning welfare for the indigent). Chadwick maintained that the high incidence of disease, especially cholera, typhoid, and smallpox, in unsanitary conditions in cities and towns caused poverty.[112] Chadwick and Southwood Smith advocated a government-sponsored, systematic urban clean-up, and Chadwick's 1842 *Report on the Sanitary Condition of the Labouring Population of Great Britain* outlined his proposals for sanitary reform.[113]

These ideas, and fears of revolution and a recurrence of cholera, drove the passage of statutes in England from 1848 that expanded state authority to improve sanitation.[114] This legislation established a General Board of Health, which could appoint inspectors to help town boards organize construction of systems for supplying clean water and removing sewage.[115] Other governments and local health boards, including in Paris, Naples, and New York, sponsored rebuilding of cities to insulate them from cholera too.[116] Some countries, such as Italy and the United States of America, also continued to use sanitary cordons, quarantine, and

---

[106] ibid 238, 240.
[107] ibid 179.
[108] ibid 168, 178, 182; Danny Dorling, *Public Health: Cholera to the Coalition* (Policy Press 2013).
[109] Snowden (n 9) 186–87, 234, 243–44.
[110] ibid 186–87.
[111] Ibid 187–90; see also EP Hennock, 'The Urban Sanitary Movement in England and Germany, 1838-1914: A Comparison' (2000) 15(2) *Continuity and Change* 269; Ian Morley, 'City Chaos, Contagion, Chadwick and Social Justice' (2007) 80(2) *Yale Journal of Biological Medicine* 61.
[112] Snowden (n 9) 187–91, 194.
[113] ibid 191–2, 194; Vollmar (n 34) 415, 419.
[114] Vollmar (n 34) 416; Snowden (n 9) 194, 203, 235; Christopher Hamlin, *Cholera: The Biography* (Oxford University Press 2009); Diane Yancey, *Cholera* (Lucent Books 2013); Amanda J Thomas, *Cholera: The Victorian Plague* (Pen & Sword History 2015).
[115] Vollmar (n 34) 416.
[116] Snowden (n 9) 256; Nancy Bristow, *American Pandemic: The Lost Worlds of the 1918 Influenza Epidemic* (Oxford University Press 2012) 18–19.

isolation, but they were often ineffective in preventing the spread of cholera and unpopular.[117]

Cholera, other epidemics such as yellow fever and plague, and the sanitary movement inspired attempts to develop international public health regulations, in part because they highlighted that individual governments' efforts were insufficient to contain infectious diseases.[118] In 1851, physicians and politicians from 12 European countries attended the first International Sanitary Conference in Paris.[119] The delegates sought to create an international surveillance system for infectious diseases by imposing obligations on member states to notify each other of any outbreaks.[120] They also discussed the potential for harmonizing countries' quarantine regulations, as variations between them were impeding trade and commerce, but the participants were unable to reach an agreement.[121] The conference generated an international network of scientists and policy-makers working to control infectious diseases, and regular further international sanitary conferences (the next three also focused on cholera).[122]

From the 1890s, acceptance of an emergent 'germ theory' of infectious disease led to greater consensus on appropriate international health regulations, including regarding quarantine, mechanisms of disease surveillance, and medical inspection and care of goods and people who travelled between nations.[123] Between 1860 and 1900, scientists led by Louis Pasteur and Robert Koch, with the aid of the recently invented microscope, proved that organisms invisible to the naked eye caused infectious diseases, and explained their contagiousness and means of constraining their transmission.[124] Koch and other bacteriologists identified the microbes responsible for causing various infectious diseases, including cholera (the bacterium *Vibrio cholera*) and tuberculosis.[125] Building on Jenner's work, Pasteur and others then developed vaccines that produced immunity against several diseases.[126] A vaccine for cholera was introduced in 1893.[127] These advances were promoted to justify the implementation of legal and regulatory measures to control the spread of infectious diseases.[128] For instance, the New York City Health Department began

---

[117] Gensini, Yacoub, and Conti (n 40) 259; Huber (n 102) 398; Snowden (n 9) 250–51.
[118] Stern and Markel (n 7) 1475; Arthur Chaslot, 'The Plague in Modern Times and the Role of Law' (2012) 2(1) *Journal of Biosecurity, Biosafety and Biodefense Law* art 10, 1, 4; David P Fidler, 'From International Sanitary Conventions to Global Health Security: The New International Health Regulations' (2005) 4(2) *Chinese Journal of International Law* 325, 329 (hereafter Fidler, 'From International Sanitary Conventions').
[119] Chaslot (n 118) 4; Stern and Markel (n 7) 1475.
[120] Fidler, 'From International Sanitary Conventions' (n 118) 329; Chaslot (n 118) 5.
[121] Chaslot (n 118) 5; Stern and Markel (n 7) 1475; Gensini, Yacoub, and Conti (n 40) 259.
[122] Stern and Markel (n 7) 1475–76.
[123] ibid; Snowden (n 9) 204.
[124] Snowden (n 9) 207–78, 215, 220–21, 225.
[125] Jim Murphy and Alison Blank, *Invincible Microbe: Tuberculosis and the Never-ending Search for a Cure* (Houghton Mifflin Harcourt 2012); Snowden (n 9) 225, 235.
[126] Snowden (n 9) 216–17.
[127] Vollmar (n 34) 418.
[128] Dolgin (n 93) 205.

requiring medical institutions and doctors to report the names of tuberculosis patients.[129] Some of the scientific developments were nonetheless achieved through unregulated experimentation on human colonial subjects in Africa, Asia, and the Caribbean.[130] These investigations were not guided by any code of ethics stipulating measures that should be taken to prevent the investigations from causing unnecessary suffering.[131]

The first International Sanitary Convention was adopted in 1892.[132] Its preamble stated that state parties had 'decided to establish common measures for protecting public health during cholera epidemics without uselessly obstructing commercial transactions and passenger traffic'.[133] From 1893, regulations were developed that prescribed principles for standardizing quarantine measures.[134] By 1897, Member States at the tenth International Sanitary Conference had established a system for notifying one another of outbreaks of plague.[135] Local and international bodies were formed to enforce the conventions, including by gathering and sharing information about infectious diseases, such as the Pan American Health Organization in the United States and the Office of the International d'Hygiène Publique in Europe.[136] Countries adopted and legalized methods of disease control that received international approval.[137] For example, the United States Public Health Service, founded in 1889, developed regulations on medical inspection of immigrants, quarantine, vaccination, and laboratory standardization.[138]

Although tuberculosis was present in the ancient world, it became especially virulent in the eighteenth and nineteenth centuries in industrialized, unsanitary, urban centres in the West.[139] Then dubbed the 'white plague' and 'consumption', it generally causes pulmonary infection, but can also harm any organ or tissue, and may rapidly kill its victim or lead to chronic, fluctuating illness.[140] As tuberculosis was initially assumed to be hereditary rather than contagious, no public health measures were implemented to contain its spread and patients were advised, amongst other things, to travel to the mountains to inhale the air.[141] Even after

---

[129] ibid 206.
[130] Stern and Markel (n 7) 1475. Chapter 11 examines how this past exploitation of people of colour in unethical medical experiments may have led to some people's reluctance to participate in COVID-19 clinical trials.
[131] Snowden (n 9) 231–32.
[132] Lawrence O Gostin, *Global Health Law* (Harvard University Press 2014) 90 (hereafter Gostin, *Global Health Law*).
[133] Fidler, 'From International Sanitary Conventions' (n 118) 329.
[134] Gensini, Yacoub, and Conti (n 40) 259.
[135] Chaslot (n 118) 5.
[136] Gostin, *Global Health Law* (n 132) 90; Chaslot (n 118) 5; Stern and Markel (n 7) 1476.
[137] Stern and Markel (n 7) 1476.
[138] ibid.
[139] Helen Bynum, *Spitting Blood: The History of Tuberculosis* (Oxford University Press 2012) 1–22; Murphy and Blank (n 125) 3–4; Snowden (n 9) 269–70.
[140] Snowden (n 9) 271–74.
[141] ibid 288–89.

Koch discovered the bacterium that causes tuberculosis, its infectiousness was not widely accepted, perhaps due to the often extended latent period of the disease.[142] In the late nineteenth and early twentieth centuries, however, when this view was overturned, in North America and Western Europe public health officials worked together with charities, educators, and various associations to tackle the disease.[143]

From 1905, International Congresses on Tuberculosis were held.[144] In many countries, public and privately run sanitoria—where tuberculosis patients were isolated in a ' "preventive-therapeutic" quarantine', rested, were well fed, and inhaled clean air—were established and dispensaries were located in urban centres to test for tuberculosis and provide therapeutic treatment for those considered too ill to attend sanitoria.[145] Tuberculosis associations and local health departments strove to educate the public to adopt hygiene practices that would prevent them from spreading the disease.[146] These campaigns were sometimes reinforced by legal measures. For instance, a municipal ordinance in New York City prohibited and imposed a fine or term of imprisonment for spitting in public.[147] Controversially, the bacillus Calmette-Guerin vaccine was tested on people in Native American reservations in the 1930s and then promulgated in a major public health campaign—the International Tuberculosis Campaign—despite limited evidence of its efficacy.[148] Allocation of resources to tackle tuberculosis diminished in the late twentieth century due to assumptions that the emergence of antibiotics would eradicate tuberculosis, but when those assumptions proved false (partly because tuberculosis was resistant to the antibiotics), it had a resurgence, particularly in developing countries where HIV/AIDS was also rife.[149] Congregate living conditions, where there are inadequate reviews of their impact on the inhabitants' health, such as in prisons, are particularly problematic for the spread of tuberculosis.[150] In 2020, it ranked as the 13th leading cause of death in the world: a total of 1.5 million people died of it, it was the second leading infectious killer after

---

[142] ibid 296.
[143] ibid 301.
[144] ibid.
[145] Gensini, Yacoub, and Conti (n 40) 260; Murphy and Blank (n 125) 56; Snowden (n 9) 301–302, 304, 306, 311, 316–17, 323.
[146] Snowden (n 9) 321.
[147] ibid 321; see too Catherine Stanton and Hannah Quirk, *Criminalising Contagion: Legal and Ethical Challenges of Disease Transmission and the Criminal Law* (Cambridge University Press 2016) 129.
[148] Snowden (n 9) 327.
[149] ibid 328–30. See also Ronald Bayer and Laurence Dupuis, 'Tuberculosis, Public Health, and Civil Liberties' (1995) 16 *Annual Review of Public Health* 307; Pranveer Singh (ed), *Tuberculosis and Co-infection with HIV-AIDS: Its History, Cause and Spread* (Cambridge Scholars Publishing 2019); James M Trauer and Allen C Cheng, 'Multidrug-resistant Tuberculosis in Australia and Our Region' (2016) 204(7) *Medical Journal of Australia* 251.
[150] See Anya Sarang and others, 'Prisons as a Source of Tuberculosis in Russia' (2016) 12(1) *International Journal of Prisoner Health* 45; Maxwell Deroznin and Asal Mohamadi Johnson, 'Multidrug Resistant Tuberculosis in Prisons Located in Former Soviet Countries: A Systematic Review' (2017) 12(3) *PLoS One* art e0174373.

COVID-19, and it was more lethal than HIV/AIDS.[151] It has been argued that drug-resistant tuberculosis poses a major risk to global health security,[152] and, in 2020, WHO classified it as a major challenge for patients and healthcare workers, and recommended a new treatment regime for its control.[153]

V. 'Russian Flu', Disease Monitoring, and Contract Law in England

Despite the advances in medicine and sanitation, influenza continued to recur regularly, its cause remained a mystery, and no cure for it was developed.[154] Nevertheless, the emergence of an influenza pandemic at the end of the nineteenth century provided an opportunity to test new methods of disease surveillance. Known as 'Russian flu', as it spread from St Petersburg and the Eurasian steppes in 1889 to Europe, Britain, and America, it killed at least one million people,[155] and for many left long-term consequences.[156] British public health authorities were initially slow to implement legal and regulatory measures that had previously succeeded in containing infectious diseases. Notwithstanding evidence of its contagiousness, they were reluctant to make influenza a notifiable disease (like cholera and smallpox), possibly to avoid burdening physicians.[157] After the 28-year-old grandson of Queen Victoria died of Russian flu, however, there was increased recognition of the importance of isolating influenza victims.[158] In addition, this was the first disease whose transmission was monitored contemporaneously.[159] The London Government Board employed epidemiologists and bacteriologists to track its progress and distributed surveys for completion by sanitary districts' health officers.[160] They identified the infectiousness of victims, including those with mild

---

[151] World Health Organization, 'Tuberculosis' (14 October 2021) <www.who.int/news-room/factsheets/detail/tuberculosis> accessed 17 October 2021. See also World Health Organization, *Global Tuberculosis Report* (WHO 2021).

[152] Eliud Wandwalo, 'Why Drug-resistant Tuberculosis Poses a Major Risk to Global Health Security' (The Global Fund, 19 November 2020) <www.theglobalfund.org/en/blog/2020-11-19-why-drug-resistant-tuberculosis-poses-a-major-risk-to-global-health-security/> accessed 14 November 2021.

[153] See Fuad Mirzayev and others, 'World Health Organization Recommendations on the Treatment of Drug-resistant Tuberculosis, 2020 Update' (2021) 57(6) *European Respiratory Journal* art e2003300.

[154] Bristow (n 116) 16; Sylvie van der Werf, 'Past Influenza Epidemics and Implications for Contemporary Influenza Research' in Tamara Giles-Vernick and Susan Craddock with Jennifer Gunn (eds), *Influenza and Public Health: Learning from Past Pandemics* (Routledge 2010) 145.

[155] Honigsbaum, *Pandemic Century* (n 2) 31; Mark Honigsbaum, 'The "Russian" Influenza in the UK: Lessons Learned, Opportunities Missed' (2011) 29S *Vaccine* B11, B11 (hereafter Honigsbaum, 'The "Russian" Influenza'); Alain-Jacques Valleron, Sofia Meurisse, and Pierre-Yves Boelle, 'Historical Analysis of the 1889-1890 Pandemic in Europe' (2008) 12(1) *International Journal of Infectious Diseases* e95.

[156] Mark Honigsbaum and Lakshmi Krishnan, 'Taking Pandemic Sequelae Seriously: From the Russian Influenza to COVID-19 Long-haulers' (2020) 396(10260) *Lancet* 1389.

[157] Honigsbaum, 'The "Russian" Influenza' (n 155) B12-13.
[158] ibid B13.
[159] ibid B13-14.
[160] ibid B11, B14.

symptoms, this virus's short incubation period, increased mortalities from its second and third waves, especially for victims with pre-existing lung problems, and its prevalence in congested environments.[161]

Russian flu also led indirectly to the articulation of some key principles of English contract law. The Carbolic Smoke Ball Company manufactured a ball from which users could inhale powdered carbolic acid, which the company claimed would prevent them from contracting Russian flu, and advertised a monetary reward for anyone who contracted it after using the ball.[162] Louisa Carlill sued the company for breach of contract after she used the ball, contracted the flu, and unsuccessfully attempted to claim the reward.[163] In 1893, the English Court of Appeal found in Carlill's favour and confirmed fundamental rules such as: an offer can be made to the whole world, but a contract only comes into existence with those who do what it requires; and inconvenience sustained by the offeree at the offeror's request can constitute consideration for the offer.[164]

VI. Spanish Flu and the Use of Voluntary and Coercive Public Health Measures

In 1918, another influenza virus rapidly swept across the globe with an estimated death toll of between 50 and 100 million people, approximately half of whom were aged in their 20s and 30s.[165] The origins of this virus have not been confirmed, though one of its first appearances was in army training camps in the American Midwest, and troops fighting in World War I carried it to Europe from where it dispersed further, including to Asia, Africa, Australia, and New Zealand.[166] It was nonetheless called 'Spanish flu' because media in Spain, which was neutral during

---

[161] ibid B11–14.
[162] *Carlill v Carbolic Smoke Ball Co* [1893] 1 QB 256 [257]; Mark Honigsbaum, *A History of the Great Influenza Pandemics: Death, Panic and Hysteria, 1830–1920* (IB Tauris 2014) 142–43 (hereafter Honigsbaum, *A History of the Great Influenza Pandemics*); Freckelton (n 15).
[163] *Carlill* (n 162) [257]; Honigsbaum, *A History of the Great Influenza Pandemics* (n 162) 142–43.
[164] *Carlill* (n 162) [268], [271] (Bowen LJ). See too Chapter 9 for an analysis of the significance of the decision for the evolution of contract law.
[165] Anthea Hyslop, 'Forewarned, Forearmed: Australia and the Spanish Influenza Pandemic, 1918–1919' in John Lack (ed), *1919: The Year Things Fell Apart?* (Australian Scholarly Publishing 2019) 2; Catharine Arnold, *Pandemic 1918: Eyewitness Accounts from the Greatest Medical Holocaust in Modern History* (St Martin's Press 2020) 298; Laura Spinney, *Pale Rider: The Spanish Flu of 1918 and How it Changed the World* (Public Affairs 2018) 167; World Health Organization, 'Past Pandemics' <www.euro.who.int/en/health-topics/communicable-diseases/influenza/pandemic-influenza/past-pandemics> accessed 29 September 2021; Patrick G Hodgson, 'Flu, Society and the State: The Political, Social and Economic Implications of the 1918–1920 Influenza Pandemic in Queensland' (PhD Thesis, James Cook University 2017) 47, 287.
[166] Mark Honigsbaum, 'Spanish Influenza Redux: Revisiting the Mother of all Pandemics' (2018) 391(10139) *Lancet* 2492, 2494; David A Relman, Eileen R Choffnes, and Alison Mack (eds), *The Domestic and International Impacts of the 2009-H1N1 Influenza A Pandemic* (The National Academies Press 2010) 4–5.

the war, were the first to report it, and Spain's King was one of its first victims.[167] Warring countries, including Germany and Britain, initially censored information about Spanish flu to avert civilian panic and lowering of morale, and maintain people's stoicism, a stoicism that some believed would reduce susceptibility to disease.[168]

Confidence that recent medical advances could prevent the spread of Spanish flu quickly evaporated, as treatments and vaccines created for it seemed ineffective and its aetiology remained unclear.[169] Physicians mistakenly believed that a bacillus caused Spanish flu.[170] It was only in 1933 that a human influenza virus was isolated and in 1997 that H1N1 avian influenza virus was identified as the cause of Spanish flu.[171] Its manifestations varied, but the most severe involved blockage of the lungs with fluid, which deprived the victims of oxygen and caused a heliotrope cyanosis, whereby their faces and/or extremities turned blue or purple.[172] Spread through droplets released into the air by victims, including when they were asymptomatic, Spanish flu dispersed quickly through crowded military training and holding camps, hospitals, and trenches.[173] A relatively mild first wave resembling seasonal influenza was succeeded by a virulent second wave and a harsh third wave.[174]

Although Spanish flu was known to be airborne and highly infectious, use of legal and regulatory mechanisms to contain its spread was inconsistent.[175] Some countries relied largely on voluntary compliance with recommended public health measures.[176] British health authorities' initial responses to Spanish flu mirrored their tardy reaction to 'Russian flu', and ignored its lessons that patients with mild or no flu symptoms could be infectious.[177] The London Government Board

---

[167] Barry (n 32) 171; Humphrey McQueen, 'The Spanish Influenza Pandemic in Australia, 1918-19' in Jill Roe (ed), *Social Policy in Australia: Some Perspectives 1901-1975* (Cassell Australia 1976) 131.

[168] Barry (n 32) 171; Mark Honigsbaum, 'Regulating the 1918-19 Pandemic: Flu, Stoicism and the Northcliffe Press' (2013) 57(2) *Medical History* 165, 174, 184 (hereafter Honigsbaum, 'Regulating the 1918-19 Pandemic').

[169] Honigsbaum, *Pandemic Century* (n 2) 8, 16-17; Jason Marisam, 'Local Governance and Pandemics: Lessons From the 1918 Flu' (2008) 85(3) *University of Detroit Mercy Law Review* 347, 359; Ilana Löwy, 'Comment: Influenza and Historians: A Difficult Past' in Tamara Giles-Vernick and Susan Craddock with Jennifer Gunn (eds), *Influenza and Public Health: Learning from Past Pandemics* (Routledge 2010) 92.

[170] Honigsbaum, *Pandemic Century* (n 2) 8.

[171] Susan K Kent, *The Influenza Pandemic of 1918-1919: A Brief History With Documents* (Bedford/St Martin's 2013) 13, 23; van der Werf (n 154) 145-46.

[172] Hyslop (n 165) 2; Bristow (n 116) 45; Honigsbaum *Pandemic Century* (n 2) 5-6; Honigsbaum, 'Regulating the 1918-19 Pandemic' (n 168) 172.

[173] Kent (n 171) 1-2, 5.

[174] ibid 8, 11.

[175] Löwy (n 169) 93.

[176] ibid 93.

[177] Honigsbaum, 'The "Russian" Influenza' (n 155) B14; Simon Heffer, 'What the Spanish Flu Pandemic Teaches us Today' *The New Statesman* (London, 8-14 May 2020) 36, 39 <www.newstatesman.com/politics/health/2020/05/what-spanish-flu-pandemic-teaches-us-today> accessed 22 September 2020.

suggested that victims sneeze and cough into handkerchiefs, and clean and disinfect their clothing and bedding, and public spaces were generally not closed.[178]

Conversely, other countries used coercive public health measures to prevent the spread of Spanish flu. The Board of Public Health in the Australian state of Victoria, for example, required citizens to report details of anyone with influenza in their homes or with whom they had contact, and prohibited people with influenza symptoms or contact with others who had them from entering public buildings or gatherings.[179] Breach of these laws attracted a fine.[180] The Premier of the state of New South Wales ordered masks to be worn in public, banned church services and outdoor meetings, and closed libraries and entertainment venues.[181]

France and Spain also used some compulsory public health measures, but enforced them haphazardly. French military authorities managed the public health response to Spanish flu initially by imposing sanitary cordons, isolating the sick, and disinfecting public spaces.[182] Nevertheless, distracted by the war effort, they abandoned these practices.[183] Spanish authorities closed universities and public schools, and prohibited public activities, including visits to hospitals, dances, and motor races.[184] Yet they succumbed to public pressure to rescind bans on football games and religious ceremonies and celebrations, and private educational institutions remained open.[185]

A number of South Pacific countries successfully used maritime quarantine to exclude Spanish flu,[186] as did Australia (at least for almost three months).[187] Rapid spread of Spanish flu in some other places, such as Western Samoa (by contrast with American Samoa) and Buenos Aires, was attributed to the neglect to impose quarantine restrictions.[188] In 1902, the United States Supreme Court had affirmed American states' authority to issue and enforce quarantine orders for public health and safety.[189] In 1918, the Surgeon General of the United States Public Health

[178] Heffer (n 177) 39; Löwy (n 169) 93.
[179] Kent (n 171) 70.
[180] ibid.
[181] ibid 81–82.
[182] Anne Rasmussen, 'Prevent or Heal, Laissez-Faire or Coerce? The Public Health Politics of Influenza in France, 1918–1919' in Tamara Giles-Vernick and Susan Craddock with Jennifer Gunn (eds), *Influenza and Public Health: Learning From Past Pandemics* (Routledge 2010) 73, 77.
[183] ibid 79.
[184] Esteban Rodriguez-Ocana, 'Barcelona's Influenza: A Comparison of the 1889–1890 and 1918 Autumn Outbreaks' in Tamara Giles-Vernick and Susan Craddock, with Jennifer Gunn (eds), *Influenza and Public Health: Learning from Past Pandemics* (Routledge 2010) 53.
[185] ibid 59, 61; Löwy (n 169) 93.
[186] Melissa A McLeod and others, 'Protective Effect of Maritime Quarantine in South Pacific Jurisdictions, 1918–19 Influenza Pandemic' (2008) 14(3) *Emerging Infectious Diseases* 468.
[187] Hyslop (n 165) 3; Marisam (n 169) 360. See also Geoffrey W Rice, 'How Reminders of the 1918–19 Pandemic Helped Australia and New Zealand Respond to COVID-19' (2020) 15(3) *Journal of Global History* 421.
[188] Geoffrey W Rice, 'Remembering 1918: Why Did Māori Suffer More Than Seven Times the Death Rate of Non-Maori New Zealanders in the 1918 Influenza Pandemic?' (2019) 53(1) *New Zealand Journal of History* 90 (hereafter Rice, 'Remembering 1918'); Kent (n 171) 71.
[189] Marisam (n 169) 356; *Compagnie Francaise De Navigation A Vapeur v Louisiana State Board of Health* 186 US 380 (1902), affirming the prior determination that quarantine did not constitute an

Service ordered medical officers operating quarantine stations in United States ports to inspect ships arriving from Europe and prevent their entry if passengers had Spanish flu until local health authorities were notified.[190] Nevertheless, a 'strict maritime quarantine on [these] ports' proved difficult to enforce, as it would also have slowed the transportation of troops and supplies out of the ports to the war front.[191]

Different United States state and local authorities adopted varied responses to Spanish flu. Some followed the advice of the United States Public Health Service to prohibit public gatherings and events, close public places such as schools, churches, and theatres, and impose quarantines and sanitary measures.[192] The New York Commissioner of Health ordered flu patients to remain isolated in hospitals or their homes, while the San Francisco Board of Health mandated mask wearing, and some towns and cities criminalized spitting in streets.[193] Citizens committees, formed at the government's request, assisted in enforcing these measures.[194] In addition, New York City's Board of Health added influenza to the list of reportable diseases.[195] Other local public health authorities, however, disregarded the recommendations made by the United States Public Health Service. Rather than closing schools, the Health Commissioner of Chicago instituted nurses' inspections of schools and homes.[196] The Illinois State Department of Public Health distributed vaccines, though the United States National Public Health Service advised that their efficacy was unproven.[197] Some defied coercive public health measures, such as closures of entertainment venues.[198] In response to the challenge to a local health board's order to close schools, Arizona's Supreme Court upheld the board's power to determine whether there is a public health emergency and make reasonable rules and regulations to enforce health laws,[199] observing that:

---

impermissible inhibition on interstate trade and commerce: *Morgan's Steamship Co v Louisiana Board of Health*, 118 US 455 (1886).

[190] Alfred W Crosby, *America's Forgotten Pandemic: The Influenza of 1918* (2nd edn, Cambridge University Press 2003) 31; Bristow (n 116) 88.

[191] Crosby (n 190) 31.

[192] Marisam (n 169) 359–61; Bristow (n 116) 84.

[193] Bristow (n 116) 94; Honigsbaum, *Pandemic Century* (n 2) 24; Marisam (n 169) 360. For a time in the state of New South Wales in Australia, too, mask wearing was compulsory: Jane Kelso, 'When Masks Were Compulsory' *Sydney Living Museums* (25 August 2020) <https://sydneylivingmuseums.com.au/stories/when-masks-were-compulsory> accessed 17 October 2020.

[194] Marisam (n 169) 362.

[195] Centers for Disease Control and Prevention, '1918 Pandemic Influenza Historic Timeline' (20 March 2018) <www.cdc.gov/flu/pandemic-resources/1918-commemoration/pandemic-timeline-1918.htm> accessed 22 September 2020.

[196] Bristow (n 116) 112.

[197] ibid 97.

[198] ibid 86, 112–13.

[199] Marisam (n 169) 364–65; *Globe School District No 1 v Board of Health of City of Globe* 179 P 55 (Ariz 1919).

The adoption by the city local board of health of ... the order closing the public schools during the rage of the said epidemic of Spanish influenza, for the purpose of preventing the spread of such epidemic, was a valid measure, adopted within the power of the local city ... Necessity is the law of time and place, and the emergency calls into life the necessity for the operation of the law. The emergency calls forth the occasion to exercise the power to protect the public health.[200]

As many doctors and nurses were serving in the war, there were shortages of medical and nursing care and also hospital beds in the United States.[201] The American Red Cross assisted state and local authorities to create makeshift emergency hospitals in public and private buildings to treat Spanish flu victims.[202] Though a voluntary organisation, at the beginning of the war, it was placed under governmental control through the creation of a War Council that conducted its operations.[203]

Few or no measures were adopted to assist populations that were especially vulnerable to contracting and dying from Spanish flu. The British Government of India made minimal efforts to help Indians, though its health officials observed that they were suffering from a famine that increased malnutrition and, consequently, susceptibility to death from Spanish flu.[204] The mortality rate from this disease among Indigenous populations in North America, South Pacific islands, South Africa, Australia, and New Zealand was disproportionately high.[205] In New Zealand, the Māori died at seven times the rate of Pākehā (white people), probably due to their high rate of co-morbidities that made them prone to developing pneumonia, communal living and sleeping in crowded accommodation that lacked adequate sanitation, and poor nutrition.[206] In some areas, separate hospitals were created for Māori and Pākehā patients.[207] Similar segregation of white and black South Africans meant that the former principally benefited from public health measures that were introduced to address Spanish flu. The *Public Health Act 1919* (SA) provided for the transfer of poor white people out of urban slums, creating racial residential segregation, which was the groundwork for apartheid.[208] Likewise, in the United States during Spanish flu, African Americans were often denied access to healthcare that was available to white Americans.[209] For instance, the

---

[200] *Globe School District No 1 v Board of Health of City of Globe* 179 P 55 (Ariz 1919) [45].
[201] Bristow (n 116) 47.
[202] ibid 47, 54.
[203] ibid 54.
[204] Maura Chhun, '"A Good Winter Rain Will Put Everything Right": The British Government in India's Response to the 1918 Influenza Pandemic and Famine' (2019–20) 19 *The Middle Ground Journal* 1, 6.
[205] Kent (n 171) 11; Rice, 'Remembering 1918' (n 188) 90; Honigsbaum, *Pandemic Century* (n 2) 27–28.
[206] Rice, 'Remembering 1918' (n 188) 90, 92, 94, 96, 101, 103.
[207] ibid 104.
[208] Kent (n 171) 15, 108–109.
[209] Bristow (n 116) 71–72.

Philadelphia Board of Health opened emergency clinics that were exclusively accessible by white Americans.[210] Impoverished, crowded reservations and boarding schools to which Native Americans were sent were conducive environments for the dissemination of Spanish flu.[211]

VII. Poliomyelitis and Vaccination

Poliomyelitis ('polio'), an infectious viral disease that can paralyse and kill its victims, emerged as an epidemic in Sweden in 1881, spread to North America and Europe and, from 1916, recurred annually, dispersed to poorer countries, and peaked in the United States between 1949 and 1954.[212] The risks associated with inadequate governmental regulatory oversight of vaccine production were exposed after Jonas Salk created the first vaccine against polio in the United States in 1955.[213] After a mass vaccination of American children commenced, two pools of the vaccine manufactured by Cutter Laboratories, one of six pharmaceutical companies contracted to produce it, were contaminated by live poliovirus.[214] Some of the vaccinated children developed abortive polio, were paralysed or died, and the contamination of vaccines triggered a polio epidemic.[215] When the problem was discovered, Cutter notified physicians, the United States Public Health Service placed an embargo on its vaccines, and the vaccination programme was halted, with litigation, including class actions, and a recalibration of legal regulation of vaccines ensuing in the United States.[216] An investigation by the United States Centers for Disease Control and Prevention reported that the Public Health Service had failed to produce comprehensive regulations and specify appropriate safeguards for vaccine production.[217] It found that Cutter's safety standards were deficient in circumstances where it attempted to produce a large quantity of vaccine in a short time period.[218]

The development of another vaccine for polio and a significant new public health strategy were the outcomes of international efforts. From 1958, Albert Sabin

---

[210] ibid 72.
[211] ibid 42–43, 70.
[212] Matthew Smallman-Raynor and others, *A World Geography: Poliomyelitis Emergence to Eradication* (Oxford University Press 2006); Bernard Seytre and Mary Shaffer, *The Death of a Disease: A History of the Eradication of Poliomyelitis* (Rutgers University Press 2005); Snowden (n 9) 386–88.
[213] Snowden (n 9) 388, 393, 396–97.
[214] ibid 393, 396–97.
[215] ibid 396–97.
[216] See Paul Offit, *The Cutter Incident* (Yale University Press 2005) 132–53; Efthimios Parasidis, 'Recalibrating Vaccination Laws' (2017) 97(6) *Boston University Law Review* 2153, 2167–72; *Cutter Incident Vaccine – Gottsdanker v Cutter Laboratories*, 182 Cal App 2d 602, 6 Cal Rptr 320, 79 ALR 2d 290 (Cal App 1 Dist 1960); *Jackson v Cutter Laboratories, Inc*, 338 F Supp 882 (1970).
[217] Snowden (n 9) 397.
[218] ibid.

and Dorothy Horstmann in the United States collaborated with Russian scientists Mikhail Chumakov and AA Smorodintsev in undertaking mass trials of Sabin's oral vaccine, which proved safe and effective.[219] The introduction of community vaccination days, first in Cuba in 1962 and then in the United States, on which people were vaccinated in their homes or at vaccination centres, resulted in the eradication of polio in Cuba and the arrest of its transmission in the United States.[220] In 1988, the World Health Assembly adopted a resolution declaring WHO's commitment to the eradication of polio.[221] In the period since this resolution, the Global Polio Eradication Initiative was formed, and cases of wild poliovirus reduced by more than 99%.[222] Despite this success, polio has not been completely eradicated and, in 2014, a public health emergency of international concern (PHEIC) was declared in relation to the spread of wild poliovirus.[223] As recently as August 2021, the IHR Emergency Committee determined that the risk of the spread of poliovirus remains a PHEIC.[224]

VIII. Acquired Immune Deficiency Syndrome

In the twentieth century, AIDS emerged as a major challenge for global health.[225] While it was never formally declared a pandemic, it is routinely, and for good reason, described in this way,[226] and has even been referred to as such by WHO.[227] Though antiretroviral therapy has been available to treat HIV since 1987, by 2015

---

[219] ibid 390, 398.
[220] ibid 398–99.
[221] World Health Assembly, *Global Eradication of Poliomyelitis by the Year 2000* (Resolution, WHA41.28, 13 May 1988).
[222] World Health Organization, *Poliomyelitis* (Fact Sheet, 22 July 2019) <https://www.who.int/news-room/fact-sheets/detail/poliomyelitis > accessed 5 May 2022.
[223] Lucia Mullen and others, 'An Analysis of International Health Regulations Emergency Committees and Public Health Emergency of International Concern Designations' (2020) 5(6) *BMJ Global Health* art e002502, 3.
[224] World Health Organization, 'Statement of the 29th Polio IHR Emergency Committee' (20 August 2021) <https://www.who.int/news/item/20-08-2021-statement-of-the-twenty-ninth-polio-ihr-emergency-committee> accessed 4 May 2022.
[225] Michael Merson and Stephen Inrig, *The AIDS Pandemic: Searching for a Global Response* (Springer 2018); Bradly J Condon and Tapen Sinha, *Global Lessons from the AIDS Pandemic: Economic, Financial, Legal and Political Implications* (Springer 2008); James Chin, *The AIDS Pandemic: The Collision of Epidemiology with Political Correctness* (Radcliffe Publishing 2007).
[226] See eg Chris Beyrer, 'A Pandemic Anniversary: 40 Years of HIV/AIDS' 397(10290) *Lancet* 2142; Robert Walter Eisinger and Anthony S Fauci, 'Ending the HIV/AIDS Pandemic' (2018) 24(3) *Emerging Infectious Diseases* 413; Anthony S Fauci and Hilary D Marston, 'Ending the HIV-AIDS Pandemic—Follow the Science' (2015) 373 *New England Journal of Medicine* 2197; Kevin M De Cock and others, 'Reflections on 40 Years of AIDS' (2021) 27(6) *Emerging Infectious Diseases* 1553; Lars Ollof Kallings, 'The First Postmodern Pandemic: 25 Years of HIV/AIDS' (2008) 263(3) *Journal of Internal Medicine* 218.
[227] See World Health Organization, 'Special Programme on AIDS: Strategies and Structure, Projected Needs' (WHO/SPA/GEN/87.1, March 1987) <http://apps.who.int/iris/bitstream/handle/10665/62299/WHO_SPA_GEN_87.1.pdf;jsessionid=F87E34E7B3CABB7A5F4C37D0DD854AA9?sequence=1> accessed 17 October 2021 (hereafter World Health Organization, 'Special Programme on AIDS').

40 million people had died of AIDS.[228] HIV emerged in Africa in the 1950s when a mutation in a disease of monkeys and apes facilitated its transmission to humans.[229] From 1981, an unusual cluster of *Pneumocystis carinii* pneumonia was reported amongst young, previously healthy men in Los Angeles.[230] After then, it spread widely,[231] eventually to most countries, although it particularly affected populations of developing countries and especially Africa;[232] at the end of 2021, over two-thirds of the estimated 38.4 million people still living with HIV resided in this continent.[233] HIV erodes its victims' immune systems, increasing their susceptibility to illness and death from infections.[234]

Those confirmed to have HIV, mainly homosexual men and intravenous drug users, were stigmatized, ostracized, and scapegoated for their illness, especially before scientists identified HIV's modes of transmission (heterosexual and homosexual intercourse, transfusion of blood, use of needles and syringes infected with HIV, and prenatally from mother to baby).[235] Their experiences prompted significant developments in anti-discrimination law. For instance, in *Kiyutin v Russia*,[236] the European Court of Human Rights found that the Russian government had unlawfully discriminated against an HIV-positive man who sought to emigrate to Russia, observing that:

> travel restrictions are instrumental for the protection of public health against highly contagious diseases with a short incubation period, such as cholera or yellow fever or, to take more recent examples, severe acute respiratory syndrome (SARS) and "avian influenza" (H5N1). Entry restrictions relating to such conditions can help to prevent their spread by excluding travellers who may transmit these diseases by their presence in a country through casual contact or airborne particles. However, the mere presence of an HIV-positive individual in a country is not in itself a threat to public health: HIV is not transmitted casually but rather through specific behaviours that include sexual relations and the sharing

---

[228] Snowden (n 9) 414; Honigsbaum, *Pandemic Century* (n 2) 139.

[229] See Jonathan Engel, *A Global History of AIDS* (HarperCollins 2006); David Quammen, *The Chimp and the River: How AIDS Emerged from an African Forest* (The Bodley Head 2015).

[230] Centers for Disease Control and Prevention, 'Pneumocystis Pneumonia—Los Angeles' (1981) 30(21) *Morbidity and Mortality Weekly Report* 250; Centers for Disease Control and Prevention, 'Pneumocystis Pneumonia—Los Angeles' (1996) 45(34) *Morbidity and Mortality Weekly Report* 729.

[231] Snowden (n 9) 408; Roger N Braden, 'AIDS: Dealing with the Plague' (1992) 19(2) *Northern Kentucky Law Review* 277, 278; McGuirl and Gee (n 10) 108.

[232] See John Iliffe, *The African AIDS Epidemic: A History* (Ohio University Press 2005).

[233] John M Dowling and Chin F Yap, *Communicable Diseases in Developing Countries: Stopping the Global Epidemics of HIV/AIDS, Tuberculosis, Malaria and Diarrhea* (Palgrave MacMillan 2014) 16; World Health Organization, 'HIV/AIDS' (30 November 2021) <https://www.who.int/news-room/fact-sheets/detail/hiv-aids> accessed 5 September 2022.

[234] Andreas Schloenhardt, 'From Black Death to Bird Flu: Infectious Diseases and Immigration Restrictions in Asia' (2006) 12(2) *New England Journal of International and Comparative Law* 263, 275.

[235] Braden (n 231) 280; Honigsbaum, *Pandemic Century* (n 2) 148.

[236] Application No 2700/10 (15 September 2011) ECHR <https://hudoc.echr.coe.int/Eng#{%22itemid%22:[%22001-103904%22]}> accessed 22 February 2022.

of syringes as the main routes of transmission. This does not put prevention exclusively within the control of the HIV-positive non-national but rather enables HIV-negative persons to take steps to protect themselves against the infection (safer sexual relations and safer injections).

Similarly, in *IB v Greece*,[237] the European Court of Human Rights held that the dismissal from employment of a man from a company on the basis of his having become known as HIV-positive in order to preserve a harmonious working environment constituted unlawful discrimination and a breach of his right to respect for his private life.

In the United States, federal, state, and local laws that prohibited discrimination against prospective and current employees based on their physical condition were applied to those with AIDS.[238] In addition, some governments passed legislation specifically protecting HIV-positive people from discrimination in employment.[239] Following the development in 1985 of a blood test that could detect antibodies to HIV, legislation was enacted banning employers from testing employees for HIV.[240] United States courts had generally permitted schools, pursuant to the police power, to exclude children who had or had been exposed to infectious diseases.[241] Yet from 1985, courts upheld challenges by HIV-positive students to prohibitions on them attending school.[242] Further, several states passed legislation forbidding people from refusing to sell or lease property to those who had or were suspected of having HIV.[243]

States in the United States, and also in Australia for a time, criminalized behaviour that could lead to HIV transmission.[244] Some United States courts held that the fact that sex offenders knew they had HIV was an aggravating factor of their offences of having sexual intercourse with non-consensual parties.[245] Ohio criminalized selling or donating blood by a person who knew they might have HIV.[246] All Australian states passed legislation providing for prison terms for individuals who did not inform their sexual partners of their HIV-positive status.[247] Some states

---

[237] Application No 552/10 (3 October 2013) ECHR <https://hudoc.echr.coe.int/fre#{%22itemid%22:[%22002-9195%22]}> accessed 22 February 2022.
[238] See Lawrence O Gostin and Zita Lazzarini, *Human Rights and Public Health in the AIDS Pandemic* (Oxford University Press 1997); Arthur S Leonard, 'AIDS and Employment Law Revisited' (1985) 14(1) *Hofstra Law Review* 11, 21, 24.
[239] Braden (n 231) 305, 332; McGuirl and Gee (n 10) 126–27.
[240] Braden (n 231) 308–9; Leonard (n 238) 11, 23.
[241] Braden (n 231) 313.
[242] ibid 314–15.
[243] ibid 316.
[244] ibid 281, 322; David J Carter, 'Transmission of HIV and the Criminal Law: Examining the Impact of Pre-Exposure Prophylaxis and Treatment-as-Prevention' (2020) 43(3) *Melbourne University Law Review* 937; *State v Haines* 545 NE 2d 834 (Ind App 1989).
[245] Braden (n 231) 330–31.
[246] ibid 285.
[247] Paul Sendziuk, *Learning to Trust: Australian Responses to AIDS* (UNSW Press 2003) 83.

also required blood donors to sign declarations that they did not belong to a social group that was at high risk of contracting HIV and penalized provision of false declarations.[248]

In the United States of America, some people who contracted HIV through blood transfusions took civil action against blood supply facilities based on negligence and product liability.[249] One court held that a surgeon could be liable for the intentional tort of battery when the patient consented to an operation on the basis that only blood donated by the patient's relatives would be used, but the surgeon transfused blood from a donor who was unrelated to the patient and that was later found to be contaminated with HIV.[250] By contrast, much civil litigation regarding transmission of HIV was averted in Australia by the early implementation of relevant regulatory and legal measures.[251] An AIDS Task Force created within the federal Department of Health and public service unions issued policy guidelines for handling HIV-positive employees in the public service.[252] From 1985, Australia instituted blood screening tests nationally, distributing testing kits to blood bank facilities, doctors, and hospitals.[253] Several states limited liability for supplying blood to an individual who contracted HIV from it to circumstances where blood testing procedures were not used or there was negligent or wilful misconduct.[254] Further, legislation in some states required doctors to inform health officials of details about HIV-positive patients.[255]

Today, South Africa has the highest population of any country of HIV-positive people, largely due to the failure of successive governments to implement legal or regulatory measures to control its spread.[256] For several reasons, HIV particularly affected developing countries. These included: challenges for the existing public health systems to respond to the rapid pace at which populations of those countries were contracting HIV and implement treatment programmes; restrictions in those countries on availability and obstacles to distribution of antiretroviral medication; insufficient foreign funding of such programmes; failure to screen donated blood for HIV antibodies prior to use of it for transfusions; and lack of protections from contracting the virus for healthcare workers who treated HIV-positive patients.[257]

Although the particular risks posed by HIV to developing countries were identified from early in the epidemic, initially some countries did not acknowledge the

---

[248] ibid 77; McGuirl and Gee (n 10) 118–19.
[249] Braden (n 231) 286, 290, footnote 81; McGuirl and Gee (n 10) 133, footnote 226.
[250] Braden (n 231) 298.
[251] McGuirl and Gee (n 10) 114.
[252] ibid 114.
[253] ibid 108, 114.
[254] ibid 116–17.
[255] ibid 114–15, 120–21.
[256] Suzuka Satoh and Elisa Boyer, 'HIV in South Africa' (2019) 394(10197) *Lancet* 467; Snowden (n 9) 416.
[257] Dowling and Yap (n 233) 16–18, 27, 29, 35; World Health Organization, 'Special Programme on AIDS' (n 227).

extent of the problem (in the case of some African countries, they feared it would harm their international reputations, tourism industries, and investment from foreign industries) and they obtained little international assistance.[258] Yet, at the First Regional Conference on AIDS in Africa in Brazzaville, Congo, in 1986, the crisis Africa was facing was publicly recognized, international help was requested, and the participants agreed to recommendations for action.[259] WHO was subsequently instrumental in co-ordinating international co-operation to address the emergency.[260] For example, in March 1987, WHO developed the Special Programme on AIDS, which sought 'to prevent HIV transmission and to reduce morbidity and mortality from HIV infections'.[261]

Other initiatives have included: the founding of UNAIDS in 1996 to '[provide] the strategic direction, advocacy, co-ordination and technical support needed to catalyse and connect leadership from governments, the private sector and communities to deliver life-saving HIV services';[262] the creation of 'Treatment 2.0' by WHO and UNAIDS in 2010 'to achieve and sustain universal access and maximize the preventive benefits of antiretroviral therapy';[263] and the launch in 2011 of UNAIDS's 'Global Plan Towards the Elimination of New HIV Infections Among Children by 2015 and Keeping Their Mothers Alive'.[264] In addition, in 2002, the Global Fund was established by an innovative partnership of governments, civil society, technical agencies, the private sector, and persons affected by AIDS, tuberculosis, and malaria to pool resources and invest in programmes to end these diseases. In its first two decades, the Global Fund disbursed more than US$20 million to strengthen health systems in 155 countries. In 2021, it reported that 'in countries where the Global Fund invests, AIDS-related deaths have been reduced by 65% and new infections have been reduced by 54% since 2002'.[265] In addition, in countries where the Global Fund invests, tuberculosis deaths (excluding HIV-positive deaths) were reduced by 28% between 2002 and 2021.[266]

---

[258] Young Soo Kim, 'World Health Organization and Early Global Response to HIV/AIDS: Emergence and Development of International Norms' (2015) 22(1) *Journal of International and Area Studies* 19, 26–28.
[259] ibid 28.
[260] ibid 29–30.
[261] World Health Organization, 'Special Programme on AIDS' (n 227).
[262] UNAIDS, 'About: Saving Lives, Leaving No One Behind' <www.unaids.org/en/whoweare/about> accessed 5 May 2022.
[263] World Health Organization and UNAIDS, 'The Treatment 2.0 Framework for Action: Catalysing the Next Phase of Treatment, Care and Support' (2011) 3 <www.unaids.org/sites/default/files/media_asset/20110824_JC2208_outlook_treatment2.0_en_3.pdf> accessed 9 September 2022.
[264] UNAIDS, *Countdown to Zero* (Report, 9 June 2011) <www.unaids.org/en/media/unaids/contentassets/documents/unaidspublication/2011/20110609_JC2137_Global-Plan-Elimination-HIV-Children_en.pdf> accessed 9 September 2022.
[265] The Global Fund, *Results Report 2021* <www.theglobalfund.org/en/results/> accessed 9 September 2022.
[266] ibid.

IX. Severe Acute Respiratory Syndrome (SARS)

Outbreaks of infectious diseases in the twenty-first century preceding COVID-19 have highlighted the importance of international co-operation for containing their spread. In conjunction with individual governments' efforts, WHO has assumed an increasingly pivotal role in tackling epidemics and pandemics. In establishing the United Nations, the Member States agreed also to create a global health organization, amongst other things, to co-ordinate international health work, support governments in managing public health and eradicating disease, and encourage collaborative health research.[267] WHO's *Constitution* (which came into force on 7 April 1948) recognized that enjoying a high standard of health is a human right and crucial for achieving world peace.[268] WHO's decision-making body, the World Health Assembly, adopts regulations, including those to prevent global transmission of disease, which are binding on WHO members, namely, the 194 United Nations Member States who have joined it.[269]

SARS demonstrated that WHO can greatly assist in combating infectious disease. SARS also provided an impetus for the updating of the *IHR*.[270] A zoonotic coronavirus, SARS was first identified in an outbreak in the Chinese province of Guangdong in November 2002, with the first reports received by WHO in February 2003.[271] In February 2003, reports of a fatal pneumonia-like illness in Guangdong were also detected by the Global Public Health Intelligence Network.[272] That month, guests in a Hong Kong hotel contracted SARS from a physician from Guangdong who was also staying there, and thereafter the disease spread internationally, including to Canada, Vietnam, and Singapore.[273] Healthcare workers appeared to be at particular risk.[274] On 12 March 2003, WHO issued a global alert

---

[267] Stern and Markel (n 7) 1477; World Health Organization, *Constitution of the World Health Organization* (opened for signature 22 July 1946, entered into force 7 April 1948) 14 UNTS 185 (hereafter World Health Organization, *Constitution of the World Health Organization*).

[268] World Health Organization, *Constitution of the World Health Organization* (n 267), Preamble.

[269] ibid; Chaslot (n 118) 9–10.

[270] See also Arthur Kleinman and James L Watson (eds), *SARS in China: Prelude to Pandemic?* (Stanford University Press 2005) 31–52, 196–204; David P Fidler, *SARS, Governance and the Globalization of Disease* (Palgrave Macmillan 2004); Sara E Davies, Adam Kamradt-Scott, and Simon Rushton, *Disease Diplomacy: International Norms and Global Health Security* (Johns Hopkins University Press 2015) 43–73.

[271] Harris Ali (n 6) 27; World Health Organization, 'Severe Acute Respiratory Syndrome (SARS)' <https://www.who.int/health-topics/severe-acute-respiratory-syndrome#tab=tab_1> accessed 27 May 2022; Fidler (n 270) 73-74.

[272] Floyd Whaley and Osman D Mansoor, 'SARS Chronology' in World Health Organization, Western Pacific Region, *SARS: How a Global Epidemic Was Stopped* (Report, 2006) 5 <https://apps.who.int/iris/bitstream/handle/10665/207501/9290612134_eng.pdf?sequence=1&isAllowed=y> accessed 13 December 2021.

[273] Honigsbaum, *Pandemic Century* (n 2) 176.

[274] World Health Organization, 'One Month Into the Global SARS Outbreak: Status of the Outbreak and Lessons for the Immediate Future' (11 April 2003) <https://www.who.int/emergencies/disease-outbreak-news/item/2003_04_11-en> accessed 2 June 2022.

about a severe atypical pneumonia and, on 15 March 2003, WHO issued a travel advisory.[275]

SARS presented the first opportunity to test the operation of the Global Outbreak Alert and Response Network (GOARN), which WHO created in 2000.[276] GOARN enables institutions and networks, including medical organizations, laboratories, and non-government humanitarian organizations (NGOs), to co-operate and share health resources to assist Member States to respond to health emergencies.[277] GOARN organized an international, online collaboration between scientists, epidemiologists, microbiologists, and laboratories, which within a month identified the cause and origin of SARS and sequenced its DNA.[278] With other organizations, GOARN monitored SARS's progress and supervised the implementation of legal and regulatory measures to contain its transmission, including isolating infected people, tracing their contacts, providing personal protective equipment to healthcare workers, screening travellers at airports, and closing schools, work sites, and public events.[279]

Affected countries, including China and also Singapore, and Toronto in Canada, implemented public health measures to contain the transmission of SARS.[280] China cordoned off some neighbourhoods, imposed quarantines, prohibited sale of civets at wet markets, and introduced infection controls in civet farms.[281] Quarantine measures were also introduced in Toronto, Hong Kong,[282] and Singapore.[283] In Hong Kong, residents in one large housing complex were quarantined, amid concerns that SARS was spreading in the building.[284] The quarantine measures used in affected areas reflected different approaches to the balancing of individual rights and community interests.[285]

SARS demonstrated the potential for an infectious disease to pose challenges for even well-resourced health systems, the potential economic impact of disease outbreaks, the importance of effective domestic public health laws, and the

---

[275] ibid; Fidler (n 270) 77–79; Whaley and Mansoor (n 272) 13, 16.
[276] Honigsbaum, *Pandemic Century* (n 2) 195; Snowden (n 9) 470.
[277] Global Outbreak Alert and Response Network, 'About Us' <https://extranet.who.int/goarn/> accessed 23 September 2020.
[278] Honigsbaum, *Pandemic Century* (n 2) 178, 191, 195.
[279] Snowden (n 9) 471–72.
[280] See Whaley and Mansoor (n 272) for a chronology of SARS. See also, Lawrence O Gostin, Ronald Bayer and Amy L Fairchild, 'Ethical and Legal Challenges Posed by Severe Acute Respiratory Syndrome: Implications for the Control of Severe Infectious Disease Threats' (2003) 290(24) *Journal of the American Medical Association* 3229.
[281] Lawrence O Gostin, *Public Health Law: Power, Duty, Restraint* (2nd edn, University of California Press 2008) 431 (hereafter Gostin, *Public Health Law*); Honigsbaum, *Pandemic Century* (n 2) 193, 195; Snowden (n 9) 473.
[282] Whaley and Mansoor (n 272) 25; Lesley A Jacobs, 'Rights and Quarantine During the SARS Global Health Crisis: Differentiated Legal Consciousness in Hong Kong, Shanghai and Toronto' (2007) 41(3) *Law & Society Review* 511.
[283] Whaley and Mansoor (n 272) 22.
[284] ibid 25; Jacobs (n 282) 531.
[285] Jacobs (n 282).

importance of international collaboration in responding to new global health challenges.[286] Davies and others have argued that the SARS crisis also represented an important point in the development of new global norms relating to management of infectious diseases:

> There was no legal obligation for states to report SARS cases under the IHR 1969, and indeed the constitutional basis for the WHO director-general issuing travel advisories was the subject of intense debate [...] Nonetheless, during the event it became clear that there was a widespread expectation that states would openly disclose SARS cases and that the WHO secretariat should be empowered to recommend appropriate travel and trade measures.[287]

Although an effective vaccine for SARS was never developed, its transmission was controlled and, on 5 July 2003, WHO announced the end of this emergency.[288] Across five continents, around 8,000 people had contracted SARS, at least 774 of whom died.[289]

X. Bird Flu, Swine Flu, and Access to Vaccines

Three years after the end of the SARS emergency, another zoonotic disease also arose in Southeast Asia, but laws facilitating culling of birds and governing humans' management of them halted its dispersion. In Hong Kong in 1997, the H5N1 strain of avian influenza A ('bird flu'), an infectious disease of birds that had affected poultry on factory farms and in live markets, was reported to have infected and killed humans.[290] Hong Kong culled chickens, but the respiratory disease reemerged in 2002 and, by early 2006, it had infected birds in 16 countries and 176 people, with a 55% mortality rate.[291] Governments ordered mass culling of poultry, prohibited selling and eating it for certain periods, and regulated its processing.[292]

---

[286] Belinda Bennett, 'Travel in a Small World: SARS, Globalization and Public Health Laws' in Belinda Bennett and George F Tomossy (eds), *Globalization and Health: Challenges for Health Law and Bioethics* (Springer 2006).
[287] Davies, Kamradt-Scott, and Rushton (n 270) 52 (citations omitted).
[288] Schloenhardt (n 234) 280; Snowden (n 9) 472.
[289] Centers for Disease Control and Prevention, 'Severe Acute Respiratory Syndrome (SARS) (Basics Fact Sheet, 13 January 2004) <www.cdc.gov/sars/about/fs-sars.html> accessed 9 September 2022; Snowden (n 9) 472.
[290] Relman, Choffnes, and Mack (n 166) 13.
[291] ibid; Schloenhardt (n 234) 280; Wendy E Parmet, 'Pandemics, Populism and the Role of Law in the H1N1 Vaccine Campaign' (2010) 4(1) *Saint Louis University Journal of Health Law and Policy* 113, 117–18 (hereafter Parmet, 'Pandemics').
[292] Annick Guenel and Sylvia Klineberg, 'Biosecurity in the Time of Avian Influenza, Vietnam' in Tamara Giles-Vernick and Susan Craddock with Jennifer Gunn (eds), *Influenza and Public Health: Learning from Past Pandemics* (Routledge 2010) 241.

The experiences of SARS and bird flu impelled the World Health Assembly to finalize a process of revising the *IHR*, which had commenced in 1995.[293] In 1951, to prevent the spread of infectious diseases, the World Health Assembly adopted the *International Sanitary Regulations*, which were an amended version of the International Sanitary Convention.[294] The World Health Assembly amended and renamed the regulations as the *International Health Regulations (IHR)* in 1969.[295] As discussed further in Chapter 3, revisions to the *IHR* in the version that the World Health Assembly adopted in 2005 (which came into effect in 2007) were intended to improve international co-operation to monitor and respond to outbreaks and constrain the transmission of infectious diseases, without unnecessarily inhibiting 'traffic and trade'.[296] These *IHR* do not pertain only to specific, named diseases, unlike previous versions.[297] They require state parties to notify WHO within 24 hours of events that 'may constitute a public health emergency of international concern' (determined according to an algorithm) and to continue to provide timely, accurate information about them and health measures they have implemented.[298] Further, the *IHR (2005)* empower WHO to undertake surveillance and gather information from unofficial sources.[299]

However, the revised *IHR* had not resolved the problem of inequitable access to vaccines for infectious diseases. Indonesia refused to provide bird flu specimens collected within its territory to WHO unless it was guaranteed that vaccines developed using them would be affordable to its citizens.[300] In 2007, the World Health Assembly recognized states' sovereign rights over their biological resources and attempted to create an intergovernmental agreement regarding sharing viruses and benefits derived from them, but negotiations ended without resolution in 2009.[301] Meanwhile, intellectual property law threatened to impede developing countries' access to 'Tamiflu', a medication that was used to treat bird flu.[302] Hoffmann-LaRoche, which held the patent to Tamiflu, confirmed that it could not manufacture enough to satisfy global demand, but refused to allow its compulsory licensing and production without its authorisation under the Agreement on Trade-Related Aspects of Intellectual Property Rights (TRIPS).[303] Nevertheless, in 2006, the

[293] Fidler, 'From International Sanitary Conventions' (n 118) 325, 343, 354; Craddock and Giles-Vernick (n 11) 8.
[294] Chaslot (n 118) 9; Schloenhardt (n 234) 282–83.
[295] Chaslot (n 118) 11.
[296] ibid 11–12.
[297] Gostin, *Global Health Law* (n 132) 181–85.
[298] World Health Organization, *International Health Regulations (2005)* (3rd edn, World Health Organization 2016).
[299] Gostin, *Global Health Law* (n 132) 192–93.
[300] Relman, Choffnes, and Mack (n 166) 77.
[301] ibid; David P Fidler, 'International Law and Equitable Access to Vaccines and Antivirals in the Context of 2009-H1N1 Influenza' in David A Relman, Eileen R Choffnes, and Alison Mack (eds), *The Domestic and International Impacts of the 2009-H1N1 Influenza A Pandemic* (The National Academies Press 2010) 146 (hereafter Fidler, 'International Law').
[302] Gostin, *Public Health Law* (n 281) 454.
[303] ibid.

Indian Drug Controller General permitted 'Cipla', an Indian laboratory, to produce a generic version of Tamiflu because Hoffmann-LaRoche's international patent was deemed insufficient under Indian law and it had not yet obtained an Indian patent.[304]

Some laws concerning licensing and distribution of vaccines were nonetheless circumvented in order to enhance access to them during another pandemic. After emerging in March 2009 near a Mexican pig farm, an H1N1 strain of influenza A ('swine flu') spread swiftly to more than 30 countries.[305] Speedy detection of reports of its outbreak by internet scanning software precipitated an early international response.[306] GOARN notified WHO headquarters and, on 11 June, its Director-General, Margaret Chan, declared a pandemic alert.[307] Scientists quickly identified that it was a different strain of the influenza virus that caused Spanish flu and incorporated segments of Eurasian and North American swine, avian, and human influenza.[308] Within six months, international collaborators had produced a vaccine, though there was insufficient supply of it during the second wave in late 2009.[309] The United States Department of Health and Human Services declared a public health emergency, which enabled its Secretary to issue 'emergency use authorizations' under the *Federal Food, Drug, and Cosmetic Act*, permitting manufacture of antiviral medications and diagnostic tests for swine flu that had not yet met licensing requirements.[310] Further, the United States Food and Drug Administration licensed the swine flu vaccine without waiting for results of full clinical trials.[311] Although they maintained control over vaccines produced within their territory, several countries promised to provide 10% of their swine flu vaccine supplies to low-income countries.[312]

During this pandemic, New York's Health Commissioner reignited debate regarding mandatory vaccination by issuing an emergency regulation requiring hospital workers with patient contact to be vaccinated for seasonal influenza and swine flu.[313] The state rescinded the regulation after healthcare workers mounted a legal challenge to it, a trial judge issued a temporary restraining order in half the cases, and the vaccine was in short supply.[314]

---

[304] Maurice Cassier, 'Flu Epidemics, Knowledge Sharing and Intellectual Property' in Tamara Giles-Vernick and Susan Craddock, with Jennifer Gunn (eds), *Influenza and Public Health: Learning from Past Pandemics* (Routledge 2010) 221–22.
[305] Relman, Choffnes, and Mack (n 166) 1; Harris Ali (n 6) 29.
[306] Honigsbaum, *A History of the Great Influenza Pandemics* (n 162) 227.
[307] ibid 227–28.
[308] ibid 229.
[309] Relman, Choffnes, and Mack (n 166) 2; Parmet, 'Pandemics' (n 291) 114; Dominic E Dwyer, 'Surveillance of Illness Associated With Pandemic (H1N1) 2009 Virus Infection Among Adults Using a Global Clinical Site Network Approach: The INSIGHT FLU 002 and FLU 003 Studies' (2011) 29S *Vaccine* B56, B56.
[310] Parmet, 'Pandemics' (n 291) 120–21, 130–31, 145.
[311] ibid, 121–22, 131.
[312] Fidler, 'International Law' (n 301) 146, 149.
[313] Parmet, 'Pandemics' (n 291) 122.
[314] ibid 122, 142.

XI. Ebola Virus Disease in West Africa

The subsequent outbreak of yet another zoonotic disease became another PHEIC, partly due to delays in implementing legal and regulatory measures to tackle it. Ebola is a highly infectious viral disease whose symptoms can include relentless vomiting, hiccoughing, and bleeding from the mouth and rectum. Ebola surfaced in the late 1970s in the Democratic Republic of the Congo and in western Sudan, re-emerged in 1996 in northeastern Congo, near the border of the Republic of the Congo, and then was the subject of serial small outbreaks.[315] Extensive deforestation led to increased contact between fruit bats infected with the virus and humans.[316] Soon after a child living in a village near the borders of Guinea, Liberia, and Sierra Leone died of Ebola in December 2013, it spread rapidly to those and other West African countries.[317] By the time the emergency ended in 2016, there were more than 28,000 suspected, probable, and confirmed cases of Ebola, and over 11,000 deaths, primarily in Guinea, Liberia, and Sierra Leone.[318]

Medical non-government organization, Médecins Sans Frontières (MSF), addressed the unfolding crisis in 2014 well before WHO and local governments.[319] From March 2014, MSF provided healthcare workers and medical supplies, opened treatment centres, and treated Ebola victims.[320] MSF's calls for help were initially unheeded despite Guinea's Ministry of Health announcing the outbreak and WHO acknowledging its notification.[321]

Despite the rising case numbers, a PHEIC, the highest alarm level, was not declared until 8 August 2014.[322] West African presidents declared states of emergency and sought international aid.[323] The United Nations Mission for Ebola Emergency Response was established on 19 September, Britain, France, and the United States sent healthcare workers and contact tracers to West Africa, and the United States Centers for Disease Control and Prevention created treatment, diagnostic, and surveillance facilities.[324]

---

[315] David Quammen, *Ebola: The Natural and Human History of a Deadly Virus* (WW Norton & Co 2014) 1, 22–29 (hereafter Quammen, *Ebola*); Adnan I Qureshi, *Ebola Virus Disease: From Origin to Outbreak* (Academic Press 2016) ch 3; Paul Farmer, *Fevers, Feuds and Diamonds: Ebola and the Ravages of History* (Farrar, Straus, and Giroux 2020) ch 1; Schloenhardt (n 234) 273; Snowden (n 9) 474–76; Honigsbaum, *Pandemic Century* (n 2) 200.
[316] Snowden (n 9) 480; Quammen, *Ebola* (n 315).
[317] Farmer (n 315), 4–6, 493–94; Snowden (n 9) 474.
[318] WHO Ebola Response Team, 'After Ebola in West Africa—Unpredictable Risks, Preventable Epidemics' (2016) 375 *New England Journal of Medicine* 587.
[319] Honigsbaum, *Pandemic Century* (n 2) 199; Qureshi (n 315) ch 3.
[320] Qureshi (n 315) ch 5; Snowden (n 9) 486–87.
[321] Snowden (n 9) 487–88; Honigsbaum, *Pandemic Century* (n 2) 202.
[322] Snowden (n 9) 491; Honigsbaum, *Pandemic Century* (n 2) 217; Lawrence O Gostin and Eric A Friedman, 'A Retrospective and Prospective Analysis of the West African Ebola Virus Disease Epidemic: Robust National Health Systems at the Foundation and an Empowered WHO at the Apex' (2015) 385(9980) *Lancet* 1902, 1902.
[323] Snowden (n 9) 491.
[324] ibid 491–92; Honigsbaum, *Pandemic Century* (n 2) 222.

In addition to closing schools and prohibiting large public gatherings in Liberia, police and soldiers patrolled streets, enforced sanitary cordons of urban communities and curfews, arrested those who breached lockdowns, guarded treatment facilities in which people with Ebola were detained, and shot people who tried to cross the border unlawfully from Sierra Leone.[325] Distrusting the authorities, some Ebola victims hid from health officials, community workers, and police who searched for them.[326] Some also avoided medical treatment and there were attacks on some teams who were implementing state decrees to disinfect the deceased and bury them quickly, contrary to customary funerary practices that involved washing and dressing corpses.[327]

The response to the Ebola outbreak demonstrated the importance of community engagement and trust in responding to public health emergencies.[328] It also highlighted the potential for disease outbreaks to compound existing disadvantage and the importance of a human rights-based approach in responding to health emergencies.[329] As discussed further in Chapter 3, the Ebola emergency also provided another test for the *IHR (2005)*, and constituted a stark reminder of the importance of building the capacity of countries to respond to public health emergencies.

XII. Conclusion

The human body and its response to infectious disease have not altered over time. Nevertheless, environmental, behavioural, and technological changes have increased the incidence, nature, and virulence of epidemics and pandemics. Today, diseases thrive in unsanitary, crowded urban slums to which large numbers of people, often originally from rural areas, have moved, particularly in the developing world.[330] Heightened production and consumption of meat and poultry, including exotic species, have led to greater contact between animals, and between animals and humans, enabling zoonotic transmission of different diseases.[331] Owing to the enhanced volume and efficiency of international travel and commerce, and the increasing porousness of national borders with globalization, diseases can move with unprecedented speed across the world.[332] Simultaneously, however, advances

---

[325] Snowden (n 9) 496–97; Odeya Cohen and others, 'Promoting Public Health Legal Preparedness for Emergencies: Review of Current Trends and Their Relevance in Light of the Ebola Crisis' (2015) 8 *Global Health Action* art 28871, 6.
[326] Snowden (n 9) 498; Cohen and others (n 325) 6.
[327] Snowden (n 9) 497–98; Honigsbaum, *Pandemic Century* (n 2) 205, 225.
[328] Ranu S Dhillon and J Daniel Kelly, 'Community Trust and the Ebola Endgame' (2015) 373 *New England Journal of Medicine* 787.
[329] Sara E Davies and Belinda Bennett, 'A Gendered Human Rights Analysis of Ebola and Zika: Locating Gender in Global Health Emergencies' (2016) 92(5) *International Affairs* 1041.
[330] Harris Ali (n 6) 26.
[331] ibid 24, 26.
[332] ibid 22–5; Honigsbaum, *Pandemic Century* (n 2) 262; Stern and Markel (n 7) 1474.

in medical science and technology have resulted in improvements in detecting, treating, and controlling the transmission of infectious diseases.[333] While these developments give rise to new legal and geopolitical challenges,[334] there is much to be learnt from national and international legal and regulatory measures that were deployed to combat past epidemics and pandemics.[335] Just as we can learn from the past about the most effective (and less effective) means of protecting public health while minimizing incursions on human rights and our way of life, so too, our current management of COVID-19 will provide lessons for the future.

This chapter has highlighted some of the significant responses to previous public health crises that laid the groundwork for the domestic and international laws and regulations that have been drawn upon to tackle the COVID-19 pandemic. As discussed in Chapter 5, many governments have relied on emergency laws to implement public health measures that have been intended to curb the transmission of COVID-19. These mirrored previous laws that similarly enforced compliance with measures, such as quarantine, isolation, mask-wearing, and closure of public venues, in order to tackle diseases including the Black Death and Spanish flu. Chapter 8 examines how some governments have criminalized behaviour that could spread disease, which occurred in the past, too, for instance, during the HIV/AIDS crisis. As Chapter 6 explores, governments today, like their predecessors, have needed to respond to public dissent and legal challenges due to their laws' encroachment on civil liberties. Laws mandating vaccination during the COVID-19 pandemic have also prompted legal action, as they did in the past (for example, smallpox vaccination requirements).

Like previous epidemics and pandemics, as discussed in Chapter 7, COVID-19 has illuminated the imperative for the law to protect those who are especially vulnerable to suffering during public health emergencies. In the COVID-19 pandemic, as was the case in the past such as at the time of Spanish flu, those who are already impoverished or marginalized have been susceptible to contracting, experiencing severe illness from, and dying of disease. In addition, at this time, as occurred during the Black Death and HIV/AIDS crises, certain social groups have been scapegoated for spreading disease. It has therefore been crucial that criminal and anti-discrimination law comes to their aid.

The COVID-19 pandemic has highlighted the importance of building countries' capacity to respond effectively through their domestic laws to infectious diseases. However, it has also demonstrated that international co-operation and collaboration is crucial for addressing global public health emergencies. Chapter 3 considers the vital role played by WHO and the *IHR (2005)* in this respect, in the past

---

[333] Stern and Markel (n 7) 1474.

[334] See David P Fidler, 'The COVID-19 Pandemic, Geopolitics and International Law' (2020) 11 *Journal of International Humanitarian Legal Studies* 237.

[335] Jonathan D Quick with Bronwyn Fryer, *The End of Epidemics: How to Stop Viruses and Save Humanity Now* (Scribe 2020).

and still today. As noted in Chapter 3, data collection and monitoring of disease transmission internationally have also been as imperative to the public health response during the COVID-19 pandemic as they were during previous epidemics, such as cholera and SARS. In addition, as Chapters 11 and 12 discuss, the COVID-19 pandemic has illuminated, as have previous epidemics from polio to HIV/AIDS, the necessity for laws and regulations to facilitate international scientific collaboration to develop treatments and vaccines, monitor their safety and efficacy, and ensure their equitable global distribution.

3
A Global Emergency

I. Introduction

On 30 January 2020, the World Health Organization (WHO) declared the international spread of COVID-19 to be a public health emergency of international concern (PHEIC),[1] with WHO stating that the Emergency Committee of the International Health Regulations 'believes that it is still possible to interrupt virus spread, provided that countries put in place strong measures to detect disease early, isolate and treat cases, trace contacts, and promote social distancing measures commensurate with the risk'.[2] According to WHO's Situation Report for 30 January 2020, there were 7,818 confirmed cases globally, with 82 confirmed cases outside China, and with cases of the disease in 18 countries.[3] WHO did 'not recommend any specific health measures for travellers'.[4] On 11 March 2020, WHO's Director-General, Dr Tedros Adhanom Ghebreyesus, declared COVID-19 to be a pandemic, noting 'we are deeply concerned both by the alarming levels of spread and severity, and by the alarming levels of inaction'.[5] By the time of this declaration, WHO's Situation Report indicated that there were 118,319 confirmed cases of COVID-19 globally, 80,995 of which were in China, and 37,364 outside of China, with cases of the disease in 113 countries, territories, and areas.[6] These declarations highlight both the seriousness of the health risks posed by COVID-19

---

[1] World Health Organization, 'Statement on the second meeting of the International Health Regulations (2005) Emergency Committee regarding the outbreak of novel coronavirus (2019-nCoV)' (30 January 2020) <https://www.who.int/news/item/30-01-2020-statement-on-the-second-meeting-of-the-international-health-regulations-(2005)-emergency-committee-regarding-the-outbreak-of-novel-coronavirus-(2019-ncov)> accessed 22 February 2022 (hereafter World Health Organization, 'Statement on the second meeting of the IHR (2005) Emergency Committee').

[2] World Health Organization, 'Novel Coronavirus (2019-nCoV)—situation report 11' (31 January 2020) <https://www.who.int/docs/default-source/coronaviruse/situation-reports/20200131-sitrep-11-ncov.pdf?sfvrsn=de7c0f7_4> accessed 28 September 2022.

[3] World Health Organization, 'Novel Coronavirus (2019-nCoV)—situation report 10' (30 January 2020) <https://www.who.int/docs/default-source/coronaviruse/situation-reports/20200130-sitrep-10-ncov.pdf?sfvrsn=d0b2e480_2> accessed 21 April 2022.

[4] ibid.

[5] World Health Organization, 'WHO Director-General's Opening Remarks at the Media Briefing on COVID-19 – 11 March 2020' <https://www.who.int/director-general/speeches/detail/who-director-general-s-opening-remarks-at-the-media-briefing-on-covid-19---11-march-2020> accessed 22 September 2022 (hereafter World Health Organization, 'WHO Director-General's Opening Remarks at the Media Briefing on COVID-19').

[6] World Health Organization, 'Coronavirus Disease 2019 (COVID-19): Situation Report 51' (11 March 2020) <https://www.who.int/docs/default-source/coronaviruse/situation-reports/20200311-sitrep-51-covid-19.pdf?sfvrsn=1ba62e57_10> accessed 21 April 2022.

even in the early phase of the pandemic, and its rapid international spread. Both of these factors have meant that COVID-19 has provided a dramatic testing of the international frameworks for managing the international spread of disease. As discussed in Chapter 2, attempts to manage the international spread of disease are not new. The use of quarantine of ships arriving at ports, and the early sanitary conventions of the 1800s are examples of the measures that have been implemented in the past to control the spread of disease.

Section II provides an overview of the background to the *International Health Regulations (IHR)*, from the international sanitary conventions in the mid-nineteenth century, through to the adoption of the *IHR* in 1969 and until the adoption of the revised *IHR* in 2005. The 2005 revisions are discussed in Section III, including the key features of the *IHR (2005)*: the declaration of a PHEIC; the reporting requirements under the *IHR (2005)*; requirements for national capacity building; the human rights approach in the *IHR (2005)*; and the provisions relating to the implementation of health measures. In Sections IV and V, we consider the role of the *IHR (2005)* in the response to two previous public health emergencies, with Section IV discussing the 2009 H1N1 influenza pandemic, and Section V discussing the 2014–16 Ebola crisis in West Africa. Section VI analyses the role of the *IHR (2005)* in the COVID-19 pandemic, and in Section VII we review proposals for a new pandemic treaty. Finally, in Section VIII we identify the important role of data in the pandemic, including use of dashboards and indicators, the role of civil registration and vital statistics, and the importance of disaggregated data in identifying the pandemic's impact on different groups within the community.

II. The *International Health Regulations*

Successive outbreaks of cholera in the early nineteenth century created an impetus for international cooperation in managing infectious diseases.[7] Although states did use measures to limit the importation of disease, such as requiring ships heading to their ports to have a clean bill of health, prior to the mid-nineteenth century there was little international co-ordination, with states needing to rely on their own resources to prevent diseases from entering via their ports.[8] Thus as Fidler has noted, during this period 'states attempted to handle the systemic effects of infectious disease transmission through the uncoordinated and unregulated exercise of national sovereignty'.[9]

---

[7] David P Fidler, *SARS, Governance and the Globalization of Disease* (Palgrave Macmillan 2004) 27. See also Amanda J Thomas, *Cholera: The Victorian Plague* (Pen & Sword History 2015).
[8] Fidler (n 7) 27.
[9] ibid.

Over the century beginning in 1851, states negotiated a number of international sanitary conventions. While a number of these conventions never entered into force, they culminated in 1951 with the adoption of the *International Sanitary Regulations* (*ISR*).[10] An important feature of this period is that concern over trade appeared to be a driver for these conventions. With increasing international trade during the nineteenth century, there were growing commercial costs associated with 'uncoordinated, unregulated national quarantine practices'.[11] Non-intervention in the sovereignty of states was also a feature of the developing system of international governance of infectious diseases.[12] This meant that there were no formal requirements for states to improve their domestic public health systems in relation to infectious diseases.[13] Although international health organizations established during the first half of the twentieth century did provide assistance with national capacity building, the decision to accept such assistance was a matter for national governments and there were no formal requirements for states in relation to their domestic infectious disease control.[14] Finally, Fidler notes that during this period, the focus was on diseases that could be spread by trade and travel, and that were external to Europe (e.g. plague, cholera, and yellow fever). Infectious diseases that were endemic to Europe (e.g. smallpox and tuberculosis) did not generally come within this system of governance.[15]

When the WHO was established in 1948, its *Constitution* gave the World Health Assembly the power to adopt regulations 'designed to prevent the international spread of disease'.[16] The adoption of the *ISR* in 1951 by the World Health Assembly has been described as one of WHO's 'earliest significant successes'.[17] As Youde has noted, five requirements were established by the *ISR*: (i) identification of six diseases to be notified to WHO: smallpox, cholera, yellow fever, typhus, relapsing fever, and plague; (ii) a requirement that governments notify any cases of these diseases in humans within their state to WHO; (iii) implementation of measures at borders, ports and airports to screen travellers and cargo for these diseases; (iv) allowing states to impose requirements for travellers to provide certificates for health and vaccination prior to entry into the state's territory; and (v) 'that the ISR were the maximum measures permissible under international law'.[18]

---

[10] ibid 28.
[11] ibid 29.
[12] ibid.
[13] ibid.
[14] ibid 30–31.
[15] ibid 31–32.
[16] World Health Organization, *International Health Regulations (2005)* (3rd edn, World Health Organization 2016) (hereafter World Health Organization, *IHR (2005)*) 1.
[17] Sara E Davies, Adam Kamradt-Scott, and Simon Rushton, *Disease Diplomacy: International Norms and Global Health Security* (Johns Hopkins University Press 2015) 5.
[18] Jeremy Youde, *Global Health Governance* (Polity 2012) 118.

In 1969, the *IHR* were adopted by the World Health Assembly.[19] Originally covering six quarantinable diseases, amendments in 1973 and 1981 reduced the number to three diseases: plague, cholera, and yellow fever.[20] However, the *IHR* came to be seen as increasingly irrelevant to global health. The small number of diseases covered by the *IHR*—only three diseases after 1981—meant that the *IHR* had little direct relevance for new and emerging diseases, including HIV/AIDS.[21] In addition, global health programmes came to be viewed more holistically, with a greater focus on primary healthcare[22] and on disease eradication programmes within states.[23] Industrialized countries viewed the battle against infectious diseases as one that had largely been won, and began shifting their attention to the rise of non-communicable diseases, while the countries that continued to have a burden of infectious diseases did not have the resources needed to address them.[24] There was also widespread non-compliance with the requirements of the *IHR*, with countries failing to report cases of disease as required by the *IHR*, or imposing measures in excess of those permitted under the *IHR*.[25] Finally, there was a growing recognition of the relevance of human rights to global health, an approach that ran against the traditional approach to infectious disease control 'because it makes the individual rather than the state the central governance focus'.[26]

It was against this backdrop that in 1995 the World Health Assembly called for revision of the *IHR*.[27] Given the challenges outlined above in the continued use of the *IHR* as a mechanism for managing the international spread of disease, the planned revision of the *IHR* was timely. However, it was to be another decade before the World Health Assembly adopted the revised *International Health Regulations (2005)*. As discussed in Chapter 2, the emergence of Severe Acute Respiratory Syndrome (SARS) in the early 2000s,[28] 'the first severe infectious disease to emerge in the twenty-first century',[29] provided an impetus for the reform efforts.[30]

---

[19] World Health Assembly, 'International Health Regulations' (Resolution WHA 22.46, 25 July 1969) cited in World Health Organization, *IHR (2005)* (n 16) 1.
[20] World Health Organization, *IHR (2005)* (n 16) 1.
[21] Fidler (n 7) 36; Youde (n 18) 121; Lawrence O Gostin, *Global Health Law* (Harvard University Press 2014) 180–81 (hereafter Gostin, *Global Health Law*).
[22] Youde (n 18) 119.
[23] Fidler (n 7) 37–38.
[24] Youde (n 18) 119.
[25] Fidler (n 7) 35–37; Youde (n 18) 119–20.
[26] Fidler (n 7) 38.
[27] World Health Assembly, 'Revision and Updating of the International Health Regulations' (Resolution WHA 48.7, 12 May 1995), cited in World Health Organization, *IHR (2005)* (n 16) 1.
[28] For discussion of SARS see Chapter 2.
[29] World Health Assembly, 'Severe Acute Respiratory Syndrome (SARS)' (Resolution WHA56.29, 28 May 2003).
[30] World Health Organization, *IHR (2005)* (n 16) 1; Gostin, *Global Health Law* (n 21) 181; Fidler (n 7).

III. The *International Health Regulations (2005)*

On 23 May 2005 the World Health Assembly adopted the *International Health Regulations (2005)*,[31] and they were to enter into force on 15 June 2007.[32] In adopting the *IHR (2005)*, the World Health Assembly urged Member States:

(1) to build, strengthen and maintain the capacities required under the International Health Regulations (2005), and to mobilize the resources necessary for that purpose;
(2) to collaborate actively with each other and WHO in accordance with the relevant provisions of the International Health Regulations (2005), so as to ensure their effective implementation;
(3) to provide support to developing countries and countries with economies in transition if they so request in the building, strengthening and maintenance of the public health capacities required under the International Health Regulations (2005);
(4) to take all appropriate measures for furthering the purpose and eventual implementation of the International Health Regulations (2005) pending their entry into force, including development of the necessary public health capacities and legal and administrative provisions, and, in particular, to initiate the process for introducing use of the decision instrument contained in Annex 2.[33]

The purpose and scope of the *IHR (2005)* 'are to prevent, protect against, control and provide a public health response to the international spread of disease in ways that are commensurate with and restricted to public health risks, and which avoid unnecessary interference with international traffic and trade'.[34] The *IHR (2005)* have been described as 'a landmark in global governance'[35] and 'a major change in the global disease outbreak surveillance and control regime'.[36] The key features of the *IHR (2005)* are outlined below.

---

[31] World Health Assembly, 'Revision of the International Health Regulations' (WHA58.3, 23 May 2005); World Health Organization, *IHR (2005)* (n 16) 1.
[32] World Health Organization, *IHR (2005)* (n 16) 1, Article 59.
[33] World Health Assembly, 'Revision of the International Health Regulations' (n 31), para 5. See also World Health Organization, *IHR (2005)* (n 16) 4.
[34] World Health Organization, *IHR (2005)* (n 16) Article 2.
[35] Gostin, *Global Health Law* (n 21) 202.
[36] Davies, Kamradt-Scott, and Rushton (n 17) 72.

A. A Public Health Emergency of International Concern

The *IHR (2005)* introduced the new concept of a 'public health emergency of international concern' (PHEIC). This is defined in the *IHR (2005)* as:

> an extraordinary event which is determined, as provided in these Regulations:
> (i) to constitute a public health risk to other States through the international spread of disease and
> (ii) to potentially require a coordinated international response.[37]

As Zidar notes, there are three elements to this definition: '(i) the concept of public health risk; (ii) implications for public health beyond the affected state's borders; and (iii) a coordinated international response led by the WHO'.[38]

WHO declared COVID-19 to be a PHEIC on 30 January 2020,[39] and declared it to be a pandemic on 11 March 2020.[40] While a PHEIC is a technical term defined under the *IHR (2005)*, with the requirements for the declaration of a PHEIC specified in the *IHR (2005)*, in recent years there has been debate over the definition of a pandemic.[41] In declaring COVID-19 to be a pandemic, the Director-General of WHO commented:

> Pandemic is not a word to use lightly or carelessly. It is a word that, if misused, can cause unreasonable fear, or unjustified acceptance that the fight is over, leading to unnecessary suffering and death.[42]

WHO's declaration of a PHEIC in relation to COVID-19 was not the first time that a PHEIC had been declared in relation to the international spread of disease.[43] Earlier PHEIC had been declared in 2009 in relation to H1N1 influenza (swine

---

[37] World Health Organization, *IHR (2005)* (n 16) Article 1.
[38] Andraž Zidar, 'WHO International Health Regulations and Human Rights: From Allusions to Inclusion' (2015) 19(4) *International Journal of Human Rights* 505, 509.
[39] See World Health Organization, 'Statement on the second meeting of the IHR (2005) Emergency Committee' (n 1).
[40] World Health Organization, 'WHO Director-General's Opening Remarks at the Media Briefing on COVID-19' (n 5).
[41] See for example Peter Doshi, 'The Elusive Definition of Pandemic Influenza' (2011) 89(7) *Bulletin of the World Health Organization* 532; Daniel J Barnett, 'Pandemic Influenza and its Definitional Implications' (2011) 89(7) *Bulletin of the World Health Organization* 539; Heath Kelly, 'The Classical Definition of a Pandemic is not Elusive' (2011) 89(7) *Bulletin of the World Health Organization* 540; Manfred S Green, 'Did the Hesitancy in Declaring COVID-19 a Pandemic Reflect a Need to Redefine the Term?' (2020) 395(10229) *Lancet* 1034.
[42] World Health Organization, 'WHO Director-General's Opening Remarks at the Media Briefing on COVID-19' (n 5).
[43] Lucia Mullen and others, 'An Analysis of International Health Regulations Emergency Committees and Public Health Emergency of International Concern Designations' (2020) 5(6) *BMJ Global Health* art e002502.

flu);[44] in 2014 in relation to the spread of polio;[45] in 2014 in relation to Ebola in West Africa;[46] in 2016 in relation to cases of microcephaly associated with Zika virus;[47] and in 2019 in relation to Ebola in the Democratic Republic of the Congo.[48] While a PHEIC was declared in the case of each of these diseases, it was not declared in relation to the spread of Middle East Respiratory Syndrome (MERS) in 2012–15, nor in relation to the spread of yellow fever in 2016.[49] Mullen and others have argued that 'Striving for more consistency and transparency in the EC [Emergency Committee] justifications around PHEIC declarations would benefit future deliberations and help to build more understanding and support for the process.'[50]

Under the *IHR (2005)*, States are required to assess events that occur within their territory and to notify WHO within 24 hours 'of all events which may constitute a public health emergency of international concern within its territory'.[51] States are also required to continue to communicate with WHO on a range of matters including case numbers, numbers of deaths, conditions that affect disease spread, health measures employed by the country, and any support needed to respond to the potential PHEIC.[52] The power to determine that a PHEIC exists rests with the Director-General of WHO.[53] In reaching a decision about whether an event constitutes a PHEIC, the Director-General is required to consider: information provided by the State; the decision instrument that is provided in Annex 2 of the *IHR (2005)*;

---

[44] ibid 3; Margaret Chan, 'World now at the start of 2009 influenza pandemic' (11 June 2009) <https://apps.who.int/mediacentre/news/statements/2009/h1n1_pandemic_phase6_20090611/en/index.html> accessed 23 February 2022.

[45] Mullen and others (n 43) 3; World Health Organization, 'WHO Statement on the second meeting of the International Health Regulations Emergency Committee concerning the international spread of wild poliovirus' (3 August 2014) <www.who.int/news/item/03-08-2014-who-statement-on-the-second-meeting-of-the-international-health-regulations-emergency-committee-concerning-the-international-spread-of-wild-poliovirus> accessed 23 February 2022.

[46] Mullen and others (n 43) 3; World Health Organization, 'Statement on the 1st meeting of the IHR Emergency Committee on the 2014 Ebola outbreak in West Africa' (8 August 2014) <www.who.int/news/item/08-08-2014-statement-on-the-1st-meeting-of-the-ihr-emergency-committee-on-the-2014-ebola-outbreak-in-west-africa > accessed 23 February 2022 (hereafter World Health Organization, 'IHR Emergency Committee on Ebola').

[47] Mullen and others (n 43) 3, 6; World Health Organization, 'WHO statement on the first meeting of the International Health Regulations (2005) (IHR 2005) Emergency Committee on Zika virus and observed increase in neurological disorders and neonatal malformations' (1 February 2016) <https://www.who.int/news/item/01-02-2016-who-statement-on-the-first-meeting-of-the-international-health-regulations-(2005)-(ihr-2005)-emergency-committee-on-zika-virus-and-observed-increase-in-neurological-disorders-and-neonatal-malformations> accessed 27 April 2022. For discussion see David L Heymann and others, 'Zika Virus and Microcephaly: Why is This Situation a PHEIC?' (2016) 387(10020) *Lancet* 719.

[48] Mullen and others (n 43) 6; World Health Organization, 'Ebola Outbreak in the Democratic Republic of the Congo Declared a Public Health Emergency of International Concern' (News Release, 17 July 2019) <www.who.int/news/item/17-07-2019-ebola-outbreak-in-the-democratic-republic-of-the-congo-declared-a-public-health-emergency-of-international-concern> accessed 13 December 2021.

[49] Mullen and others (n 43) 3, 6.
[50] ibid 9.
[51] World Health Organization, *IHR (2005)* (n 16) Article 6(1).
[52] ibid Article 6(2).
[53] ibid Article 12.

advice provided by the Emergency Committee; 'scientific principles as well as the available scientific evidence and other relevant information'; and 'an assessment of the risk to human health, of the risk of international spread of disease and of the risk of interference with international traffic'.[54] If the Director-General determines that a PHEIC exists, the Director-General shall issue temporary recommendations,[55] which may include health measures to be implemented by the State with the PHEIC, or other States to 'reduce the international spread of disease and avoid unnecessary interference with international traffic'.[56]

In contrast to the specific diseases approach in the previous *IHR*, the approach in the *IHR (2005)* is an 'all-hazards' approach.[57] Gostin argues that there was a 'conceptual shift' from a focus on trade in the previous *IHR* to a focus on health risks in the *IHR (2005)*.[58] The *IHR (2005)* define 'public health risk' as 'a likelihood of an event that may affect adversely the health of human populations, with an emphasis on one which may spread internationally or may present a serious and direct danger'.[59] While the *IHR (2005)* do adopt a broader approach than the previous *IHR*, it has been argued that provisions relating to sharing of samples and zoonotic diseases are 'major omissions'.[60]

Annex 2 of the *IHR (2005)* contains a decision instrument to assist States in determining whether an event that may constitute a PHEIC should be notified to WHO (see Fig. 3.1). The decision instrument groups events within one of three categories. The first category involves a small number of specified diseases where a case of the disease must be notified to WHO. There are four diseases listed here: smallpox; poliomyelitis due to wild-type polio virus; human influenza caused by a new sub-type; and SARS. The decision instrument indicates that a case of any of these diseases 'is unusual or unexpected and may have serious public health impact, and thus shall be notified' to WHO.[61] The second category provides an additional list of diseases and indicates that a case of any of these diseases requires that the algorithm in the decision instrument be used.[62] The diseases in this category are: 'cholera; pneumonic plague; yellow fever; viral haemorrhagic fevers (Ebola, Lassa, and Marburg); West Nile fever;' and 'other diseases of special national or regional concern, e.g. dengue fever, Rift Valley fever, and meningococcal disease'.[63] The final category of cases requires utilization of the decision instrument for 'any event of potential international public health concern,

---

[54] ibid Article 12(4). The Emergency Committee is established by the Director-General (Article 48) from a roster of experts (Article 47).
[55] ibid Article 15(1).
[56] ibid Article 15(2).
[57] Gostin, *Global Health Law* (n 21) 185.
[58] ibid.
[59] World Health Organization, *IHR (2005)* (n 16) Article 1(1).
[60] Lawrence O Gostin and Rebecca Katz, 'The International Health Regulations: The Governing Framework for Global Health Security' (2016) 94(2) *The Milbank Quarterly* 264, 281.
[61] World Health Organization, *IHR (2005)* (n 16), Annex 2.
[62] ibid.
[63] ibid.

A GLOBAL EMERGENCY 83

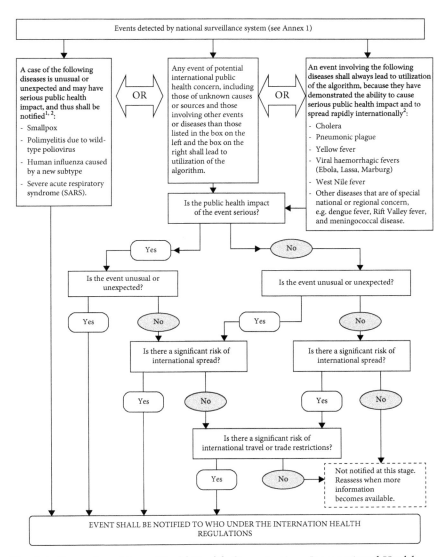

Fig. 3.1 Reproduced from World Health Organization, *International Health Regulations (2005)* (3rd edn, World Health Organization 2016) Annex 2, Decision instrument for the assessment and notification of events that may constitute a public health emergency of international concern (footnotes omitted).

including those of unknown causes or sources and those involving other events or diseases' not included in the first two categories.[64]

If the decision instrument requires utilization of the algorithm in relation to a case of a disease, there are four questions to be addressed to assist in determining whether the event must be notified to WHO. As shown in Fig. 3.1, these questions address the seriousness of the event, the unusual or unexpected nature of the event, the risk of international spread, and the risk of international travel or trade restrictions.[65] Where the answer to any two of these questions is in the affirmative, then the event must be notified to WHO. Annex 2 also provides examples to assist with interpretation of the decision instrument, although these examples are described as 'not binding' and 'for indicative guidance purposes'.[66]

Zidar has argued that each of the elements of a PHEIC is 'indeterminate'.[67] First, that the all-hazards approach to public health risk reflects the 'mutable character' of the risk.[68] In addition, the international nature of emergency is one where 'various countries or regions may be affected at different times or at different intensities' and the international response co-ordinated by WHO 'may also vary with regard to the intensity of health risks, their temporal dynamic and geographical implications' and also reflects this indeterminacy.[69] Zidar argues that together these elements make decision-making about a PHEIC an exercise in 'polycentric decision-making' which 'is a process that implies many variables that are constantly shifting and are, as such, indeterminate and elusive'.[70]

The declaration of a PHEIC is an important aspect of the *IHR (2005)*, with a report by a 2016 Review Committee describing it as 'one of the IHR's most powerful tools for warning the world about a major health threat'.[71] However, the Review Committee noted that the declaration is 'binary', that an event is either a PHEIC or it is not, and this 'can mean that the world is required to quickly switch from relative inaction to a state of emergency with little warning'.[72] To overcome this situation, an 'intermediate level of alert' was recommended.[73] There has also been

[64] ibid.
[65] ibid.
[66] ibid.
[67] Zidar (n 38) 509.
[68] ibid.
[69] ibid.
[70] ibid. See Belinda Bennett and Terry Carney, 'Public Health Emergencies of International Concern: Global, Regional and Local Responses to Risk' (2017) 25(2) *Medical Law Review* 223, 239 (hereafter, Bennett and Carney, 'Public Health Emergencies of International Concern'). For further discussion of polycentricity generally see Julia Black, 'Constructing and Contesting Legitimacy and Accountability in Polycentric Regulatory Regimes' (2008) 2(2) *Regulation & Governance* 137. See also Chapters 1 and 13.
[71] World Health Organization, 'Implementation of the International Health Regulations (2005): Report of the Review Committee on the Role of the International Health Regulations (2005) in the Ebola Outbreak and Response' Report (WHA A69/21, 13 May 2016) <https://apps.who.int/gb/ebwha/pdf_files/WHA69/A69_21-en.pdf> accessed 23 February 2022 (hereafter World Health Organization, 'Review Committee on IHR in Ebola') 63.
[72] ibid.
[73] ibid.

more recent support for the idea of a tiered approach to PHEIC declarations.[74] Wenham and others have argued, however, that:

> The problems with PHEIC declarations are not about insufficient gradients of a health emergency. Instead, the tension within this global health security mechanism results from states' refusal to engage in collective action in response to expert advice from an international organisation, particularly when seeing action as against short-term interests.[75]

B. Reporting Requirements

Using the decision instrument contained in Annex 2 of the *IHR (2005)*, States are required to assess events that occur within their territory and to notify WHO of all events that may constitute a PHEIC and any measures that have been implemented to address them.[76] States must also continue to communicate with WHO in relation to the notified event, providing information including the number of cases and deaths, 'conditions affecting the spread of the disease and the health measures employed', and any support needed to respond to the PHEIC.[77] States are also required to 'provide to WHO all relevant public health information' in relation to 'an unexpected or unusual event within its territory, irrespective of origin or source, which may constitute a public health emergency of international concern'.[78] If a State is not required to notify WHO of an event, such as if there is insufficient information to complete the decision instrument, it may nonetheless keep WHO informed and consult with WHO on the use of health measures.[79]

Adding to the polycentricity of the revised *IHR (2005)* is the expansion of the sources of information upon which WHO may rely in assessing public health events. While under the previous *IHR* WHO was reliant upon reports of disease from governments, the *IHR (2005)* expressly provides under Article 9 that 'WHO may take into account reports from sources other than notifications or consultations'.[80] This was a significant development.[81] Under the previous *IHR* countries had consistently failed to meet their *IHR* reporting obligations, and the limited number of diseases listed in the *IHR* was an additional problem.[82] As Fidler has

---

[74] For discussion see Clare Wenham and others, 'Problems with Traffic Light Approaches to Public Health Emergencies of International Concern' (2021) 397(10287) *Lancet* 1856.
[75] ibid 1858.
[76] World Health Organization, *IHR (2005)* (n 16) Article 6(1).
[77] ibid Article 6(2).
[78] ibid Article 7.
[79] ibid Article 8.
[80] ibid Article 9(1).
[81] Davies, Kamradt-Scott and Rushton (n 17) 64.
[82] Fidler (n 7) 62.

commented, 'The state-centric nature of the IHR's surveillance system was the key problem.'[83] In addition, the development of the internet and other information technologies created new possibilities to improve global surveillance of infectious diseases.[84] The new provisions that allow WHO to take reports from non-government sources into account 'introduce a host of new eyes and ears to keep watch and hold governments accountable for their response to public health emergencies'.[85]

Although the *IHR (2005)* permit WHO to receive information from other sources, WHO is obliged to consult with the relevant State and attempt to verify the information before taking any action on it.[86] States are also required, as far as practicable, to 'inform WHO within 24 hours of receipt of evidence of a public health risk identified outside their territory that may cause international disease spread'.[87] Where WHO seeks verification of reports of an event that may constitute a PHEIC, the State is required to provide WHO within 24 hours with an initial reply or acknowledgement, and 'available public health information on the status of events.' In addition, the State must provide WHO with 'information … in the context of an assessment under Article 6, including relevant information as described in that Article'.[88] Once it receives information about an event that may be a PHEIC, WHO is required to offer to collaborate with the affected State on assessment of the potential for international spread of the disease and interference with international traffic, and the adequacy of any control measures.[89] If the State does not accept WHO's offer of collaboration, 'when justified by the magnitude of the public health risk', WHO may share information about the public health event with other States while still encouraging the State to accept WHO's offer of collaboration, and taking into account the views of the State.[90]

Where WHO receives information about a possible PHEIC, it is required not to share that information with other States, unless agreed with the relevant State and until: (a) the event is determined to be a PHEIC; or (b) WHO has confirmed the international spread of infection or contamination using 'established epidemiological principles'; or (c) there is evidence either that the 'control measures against the international spread are unlikely to succeed because of the nature of the contamination, disease agent, vector, or reservoir', or the State does not have sufficient capacity to implement the measures needed to prevent further disease spread; or

---

[83] ibid.
[84] ibid 62–63.
[85] Sara E Davies and Jeremy Youde, 'The IHR (2005), Disease Surveillance, and the Individual in Global Health Politics' (2013) 17(1) *International Journal of Human Rights* 133, 139. For discussion see Bennett and Carney, 'Public Health Emergencies of International Concern' (n 70) 227.
[86] World Health Organization, *IHR (2005)* (n 16) Article 9(1).
[87] ibid Article 9(2).
[88] ibid Article 10(2).
[89] ibid Articles 10(3).
[90] ibid Article 10(4).

(d) immediate international control measures are needed because the nature and scope of the international movement of people and cargo that may be affected by infection or contamination.[91] Although these provisions require that WHO refrain from sharing information about a public health event, unless the relevant State has agreed otherwise, until one of these conditions has been satisfied, WHO may make this information available to the public if information about the event is already publicly available 'and there is a need for the dissemination of authoritative and independent information'.[92] Subject to the requirements in Article 11(2) discussed earlier, WHO must share in confidence with other States, 'and, as appropriate, to relevant intergovernmental organizations' 'public health information which it has received under Articles 5 to 10' of the *IHR (2005)*, to enable States to respond to a public health risk and prevent a similar event.[93] Where WHO proposes to share information about an event occurring within a State's territory, WHO is required to consult with the State.[94]

C. National Capacity Building

One of the key features of the *IHR (2005)* is their requirement for States to build their national capacities to detect, assess, and respond to events occurring within their territory that may constitute a PHEIC. Article 5 of the *IHR (2005)* requires that States 'develop, strengthen and maintain' their core capacity requirements, as specified in Annex 1 of the *IHR (2005)*.[95] This focus on national capacity building represented 'an "upstream" public health strategy to prevent and contain outbreaks at their source'.[96]

Upon request, WHO is to assist States in developing, strengthening, and maintaining these core capacities.[97] Each State is also required to designate or establish a National IHR Focal Point and responsible authorities within their jurisdiction for implementing the health measures under the *IHR (2005)*.[98] The National IHR Focal Points are responsible for liaising with WHO IHR Contact Points, including sending to WHO urgent communications about disease notifications required under the *IHR (2005)* as well as 'disseminating information to, and consolidating input from' the relevant parts of the State.[99]

---

[91] ibid Article 11(2).
[92] ibid Article 11(4).
[93] ibid Article 11(1).
[94] ibid Article 11(3).
[95] ibid Article 5(1).
[96] Gostin and Katz (n 60) 270.
[97] World Health Organization, *IHR (2005)* (n 16) Article 5(3).
[98] ibid Article 4(1).
[99] ibid Article 4(2).

The *IHR (2005)* require that each State assess its ability to meet the minimum core capacity requirements specified in the *IHR (2005)*, and that this assessment was to occur within two years of the *IHR (2005)* coming into force.[100] As the *IHR (2005)* entered into force on 15 June 2007,[101] this meant that countries were required to assess their core capacities by mid-2009. Within five years of the *IHR* coming into force, States were also required to develop their 'capacity to detect, assess, notify and report events' although the *IHR* did permit States to apply for an extension of two years, and 'in exceptional circumstances' to 'request a further extension not exceeding two years'.[102] Within five years of the *IHR (2005)* coming into force, States were required to develop their 'capacity to respond promptly and effectively to public health risks and public health emergencies of international concern' as specified in the core capacity requirements set out in Annex 1 of the *IHR (2005)* with the *IHR (2005)* permitting a State to apply for an initial two-year extension and, in exceptional circumstances, a further two-year extension.[103] Under the *IHR (2005)*, States 'undertake to collaborate with each other, to the extent possible',[104] including in relation to the provision of support for the 'development, strengthening and maintenance of the public health capacities required under' the *IHR (2005)*.[105] Although the *IHR (2005)* require countries to develop their public health capacities, they do not provide clear guidance for countries on how to meet the *IHR* requirements.[106]

D. A Human Rights Approach

In contrast to the previous version of the *IHR*, the *IHR (2005)* expressly adopt a human rights-based approach. Article 3(1) states that 'The implementation of these Regulations shall be with full respect for the dignity, human rights and fundamental freedoms of persons'.[107] These rights have universal application,[108] with the *IHR (2005)* requiring that their implementation is 'guided by the goal of their universal application for the protection of all people of the world from the international spread of disease'.[109] Although Article 3(1) of the *IHR (2005)* imposes an obligation on States to implement the Regulations so as to protect the human rights of persons, Zidar has observed that the scope of this obligation is 'not precisely

---

[100] ibid Annex 1, para 2.
[101] ibid 1.
[102] ibid Article 5(1), (2).
[103] ibid Article 13(1), (2).
[104] ibid Article 44(1).
[105] ibid Article 44(1)(b).
[106] For discussion of capacity building see Bennett and Carney, 'Public Health Emergencies of International Concern' (n 70) 230–34.
[107] World Health Organization, *IHR (2005)* (n 16) Article 3(1).
[108] ibid Article 3(2), (3).
[109] World Health Organization, *IHR (2005)* (n 16) Article 3(3).

delineate[d]' and therefore 'serve[s] as a guideline, a policy statement or an interpretive principle rather than a prescription'.[110] Davies and Youde have argued that 'the force of the human rights protections remains relatively underdeveloped. The rhetorical commitment does not become a vigorous international legal commitment.'[111]

While States are permitted to introduce health measures for travellers on their arrival and departure, any non-intrusive medical examination must be 'the least intrusive examination that would achieve the public health objective'.[112] If a State decides to implement additional health measures in accordance with the *IHR (2005)*, any medical examination must be 'the least intrusive and invasive' needed 'to achieve the public health objective of preventing the international spread of disease'.[113] The prior express informed consent of the traveller (or their parent or guardian) is needed before any 'medical examination, vaccination, prophylaxis, or health measure' is carried out on a traveller.[114] Travellers who are offered vaccination or prophylaxis must be informed of any risks associated with vaccination or non-vaccination,[115] and 'Any medical examination, medical procedure, vaccination or other prophylaxis which involves a risk of disease transmission' must be carried out 'in accordance with established national or international safety guidelines and standards' in order to minimize the risk.[116]

Where States implement health measures under the *IHR (2005)*, they are required to 'treat travellers with respect for their dignity, human rights and fundamental freedoms and minimize any discomfort or distress associated with such measures'.[117] Furthermore, Article 42 provides that 'Health measures taken pursuant to these Regulations shall be initiated and completed without delay, and applied in a transparent and non-discriminatory manner.'[118] Travellers must be treated 'with courtesy and respect'[119] and travellers' 'gender, sociocultural, ethnic or religious concerns' must also be taken into consideration.[120] Travellers must also be provided with a range of other supports, including food and water, accommodation, medical treatment, and a 'means of necessary communication if possible in a language that they can understand'.[121] The *IHR (2005)* also provide for protection of identifiable health information that may be collected or received from another State or from WHO.[122]

[110] Zidar (n 38) 510.
[111] Davies and Youde (n 85) 144.
[112] World Health Organization, *IHR (2005)* (n 16) Article 23(1)(a)(iii).
[113] ibid Article 23(2).
[114] ibid Article 23(3).
[115] ibid Article 23(4).
[116] ibid Article 23(5). For discussion see, Zidar (n 38) 512–13.
[117] World Health Organization, *IHR (2005)* (n 16) Article 32.
[118] ibid Article 42.
[119] ibid Article 32(a).
[120] ibid Article 32(b).
[121] ibid Article 32(c).
[122] ibid Article 45. For discussion see Zidar (n 38) 512.

The *IHR (2005)* also contain provisions that permit the use of measures that may affect the liberty or freedom of movement of persons. For example, Article 18(1) provides that WHO may make recommendations to States, including: placing 'suspect persons under public health observation', isolation and treatment of affected persons, refusal of entry of affected or suspect persons, and refusing to allow unaffected persons to enter affected areas.[123]

The new emphasis on human rights in the revised *IHR (2005)* is a significant development. Gostin has noted that the *IHR*'s 'emphasis on human dignity may suggest that international human rights law, such as the Siracusa Principles, is relevant to interpreting and implementing the IHR'.[124] The *Siracusa Principles* require that any limitation to human rights that are protected in the *International Covenant on Civil and Political Rights* (ICCPR): is prescribed by law; not arbitrary or discriminatory; necessary in the sense that it 'responds to a pressing public or social need', 'pursues a legitimate aim', and 'is proportionate to that aim'; and that the means used 'are no more restrictive ... than are required for the achievement of the purpose of the limitation'.[125]

E. Implementation of Health Measures

If the Director-General of WHO has determined that there is a PHEIC, the Director-General is required to issue temporary recommendations.[126] Before making, modifying, or terminating temporary recommendations, the Director-General must take into account:[127]

(a) the views of the affected States;
(b) advice from the Emergency Committee or Review Committee;[128]
(c) scientific principles, evidence and information;
(d) 'health measures that, on the basis of a risk assessment appropriate to the circumstances, are not more restrictive of international traffic and trade and

---

[123] World Health Organization, *IHR (2005)* (n 16) Article 18(1). For discussion see Zidar (n 38) 513–15.
[124] Gostin, *Global Health Law* (n 21) 183.
[125] United Nations Economic and Social Commission on Human Rights, *The Siracusa Principles on the Limitation and Derogation Provisions in the International Covenant on Civil and Political Rights* (Resolution E/CN.4/1985/4, 28 September 1984) (hereafter *Siracusa Principles*). For discussion see Gostin, *Global Health Law* (n 21) 256. These principles can also be relevant to the interpretation of provisions said to enable detention of persons under national public health laws: K W Todrys, E Howe, and J J Amon, 'Failing Siracusa: Governments' Obligations to Find the Least Restrictive Options for Tuberculosis Control' (2013) 3(1) *Public Health Action* 7.
[126] World Health Organization, *IHR (2005)* (n 16) Article 15(1).
[127] ibid Article 17.
[128] ibid Articles 17, 49.

are not more intrusive to persons than reasonably available alternatives that would achieve the appropriate level of health protection';
(e) 'relevant international standards and instruments';
(f) 'activities undertaken by other relevant intergovernmental organizations and international bodies'; and
(g) 'other appropriate and specific information relevant to the event'.

The Director-General's consideration of the matters outlined in paragraphs (e) and (f) above 'may be subject to limitations imposed by urgent circumstances'.[129]

Although States are permitted to implement measures that 'achieve the same or greater level of health protection than WHO recommendations', or that are 'otherwise prohibited' by the *IHR (2005)*, the measures must not be more restrictive, invasive, or intrusive than 'reasonably available alternatives'.[130] Furthermore, in deciding whether to introduce additional health measures, States are required to base their decisions on:

(a) scientific principles;
(b) available scientific evidence of a risk to human health, or where such evidence is insufficient, the available information including from WHO and other relevant intergovernmental organizations and international bodies; and
(c) any available specific guidance or advice from WHO.[131]

Where a State implements additional measures that 'significantly interfere with international traffic', it is required to notify WHO within 48 hours of the measures, and their health rationale, unless they are covered by WHO temporary or standing recommendations.[132] A 'significant interference generally means refusal of entry or departure of international travellers, baggage, cargo, containers, conveyances, goods and the like, or their delay, for more than 24 hours'.[133] After considering the information from the State, WHO may ask it to reconsider the additional measures.[134] In addition, a State that is affected by the implementation of additional health measures may ask the State implementing the measure to consult with it in order to 'clarify the scientific information and public health rationale underlying the measure and to find a mutually acceptable solution'.[135] Where a State

---

[129] ibid Article 17.
[130] ibid Article 43(1).
[131] ibid Article 43(2).
[132] ibid Article 43(5).
[133] ibid Article 43(3).
[134] ibid Article 43(4).
[135] ibid Article 43(7).

implements additional health measures, it must review the measures within three months, and consider advice from WHO and the criteria set out in Article 43(2).[136]

IV. 2009 H1N1 Influenza Pandemic: The First Test of the IHR (2005)

The 2009 H1N1 ('swine flu') influenza pandemic caused 'the first influenza pandemic of the 21st century'.[137] It also provided the first test of the revised *IHR* as it was the first PHEIC to be declared after the *IHR (2005)* came into force in 2007.[138] First identified in Mexico in early 2009, the WHO Director-General declared H1N1 to be a PHEIC on 25 April 2009[139] and on 11 June 2009 declared H1N1 to be a pandemic.[140] It is difficult to provide an accurate indication of the number of cases of H1N1, but by the end of the pandemic in August 2010, there had been approximately 18,500 laboratory-confirmed deaths caused by 2009 H1N1.[141] While the pandemic was ultimately milder than first feared, unlike seasonal influenza which typically strikes older members of the community, the disease burden of H1N1 was on younger members of the community.[142] In addition, pregnant women, individuals with compromised immune systems, and Indigenous peoples were also at risk of severe disease caused by H1N1.[143]

In assessing the role of the *IHR (2005)* in the response to the H1N1 2009 pandemic, a Review Committee convened by WHO's Director-General found that the *IHR (2005)* had led to capacity building, but 'there is wide variation in the degree of fulfilment'.[144] Amongst the Review Committee's summary conclusions was that:

> The IHR helped make the world better prepared to cope with public-health emergencies. The core national and local capacities called for in the IHR are not yet fully operational and are not now on a path to timely implementation worldwide.[145]

---

[136] ibid Article 43(6).
[137] World Health Organization, 'Strengthening Response to Pandemics and Other Public-Health Emergencies: Report of the Review Committee on the Functioning of the International Health Regulations (2005) and on Pandemic Influenza (H1N1) 2009' (2011) <https://apps.who.int/iris/handle/10665/75235> accessed 29 September 2022 (hereafter World Health Organization, 'Report of the Review Committee on H1N1') 27.
[138] ibid xiii.
[139] ibid 29–32.
[140] ibid 37.
[141] ibid 27.
[142] ibid.
[143] ibid 28.
[144] ibid 48.
[145] ibid 111.

Although the Review Committee identified a number of 'positive features of the IHR' it also acknowledged that many States Parties had not developed their *IHR* core capacities and were unlikely to meet them by the *IHR*'s 2012 deadline.[146] Amongst the Review Committee's recommendations was a recommendation for acceleration of the implementation of the *IHR* core capacities, with a focus first of all on those countries that would likely have difficulties in meeting the 2012 deadline.[147] The *IHR (2005)* required countries to establish National Focal Points (NFP) to liaise with WHO.[148] The Review Committee noted that many events are brought to WHO's awareness via unofficial sources, but that NFPs 'are important for verification and follow-up information'.[149]

The implementation of additional measures was also a concern during the 2009 H1N1 influenza pandemic, with some countries implementing trade or travel restrictions, despite such restrictions not being recommended by WHO.[150] For example, some countries implemented bans on pork imports from Mexico, the United States, and Canada.[151] However, some countries failed to comply with their *IHR (2005)* obligations to provide WHO with the scientific rationale for their additional measures, with the Review Committee noting:

> Although several countries, but not all, provided a rationale upon request by WHO, it appears that no country that implemented additional measures (i.e. measures that significantly disrupted international travel or trade by more than 24 hours) complied with their obligations under Article 43 to proactively inform WHO and provide the rationale for such measures.[152]

On the issue of human rights, the Review Committee noted that WHO did not have a mandate to investigate possible violations of the provisions of the *IHR (2005)* requiring respect for human rights.[153] However, the Committee noted that 'it is in the spirit of the IHR for WHO to consult with States Parties when the media report practices that may be seen as violations of human rights and, in turn, the IHR'.[154]

An important aspect of the global response to the H1N1 pandemic was that, following WHO guidance, most countries had already developed pandemic response plans in the years prior to the 2009 pandemic. Although the pandemic

---

[146] ibid 112.
[147] ibid.
[148] World Health Organization, *IHR (2005)* (n 16) Article 4.
[149] World Health Organization, 'Report of the Review Committee on H1N1' (n 137) 50.
[150] ibid 62.
[151] Rebecca Katz and Julie Fischer, 'The Revised International Health Regulations: A Framework for Global Pandemic Response' (2010) 3(2) *Global Health Governance* 1, 6.
[152] World Health Organization, 'Report of the Review Committee on H1N1' (n 137) 62. For discussion see Belinda Bennett and Terry Carney, 'Planning for Pandemics: Lessons from the Past Decade' (2015) 12(3) *Journal of Bioethical Inquiry* 419, 421.
[153] World Health Organization, 'Report of the Review Committee on H1N1' (n 137) 63.
[154] ibid 64.

was declared in relation to H1N1, much of the preparedness for pandemic influenza had been in preparation for a pandemic caused by H5N1 influenza.[155] H5N1 avian influenza (sometimes referred to as 'bird flu') had different characteristics from H1N1. While H5N1 was not readily transmissible to or between humans, the mortality rate for those who contracted the disease was approximately 60%.[156] As discussed in Chapter 2, it was first identified in humans in Hong Kong in 1997, and resulted in the culling of poultry in an effort to limit the spread of the disease.[157] However, from late 2003, H5N1 spread among wild and domestic birds, including migratory birds, and by February 2011 there had been approximately 500 laboratory-confirmed human cases of H5N1 across 15 countries.[158] The severity of H5N1 in humans, and the sense of a pandemic being imminent, were amongst the factors that fostered a sense of urgency in preparedness for pandemic influenza.[159] WHO provided global leadership for much of this work, publishing global pandemic preparedness plans starting in 1999 to assist countries in developing their national plans,[160] with the plans adopting a phased approach to correspond with key phases in an influenza pandemic.[161] Although the pandemic preparedness that had been undertaken for H5N1 meant that countries did have pandemic plans, it also meant that 'countries were not as prepared for a disease that was less serious but that spread more rapidly'.[162]

Despite the work that had been undertaken at a national and global level for preparedness for pandemic influenza and the *IHR (2005)* requirements for development of national public health capacities, the Review Committee concluded that the world still lacked adequate preparedness for a global public health emergency:

> The world is ill-prepared to respond to a severe influenza pandemic or to any similarly global, sustained and threatening public-health emergency. Beyond implementation of core public-health capacities called for in the IHR, global preparedness can be advanced through research, reliance on a multisectoral approach, strengthened health-care delivery systems, economic development in low- and middle-income countries and improved health status.[163]

The Review Committee made four recommendations to address this conclusion: (i) the establishment of 'a more extensive global, public health reserve workforce' that

---

[155] ibid 68. For discussion see also Bennett and Carney, 'Planning for Pandemics' (n 152).
[156] World Health Organization, 'Report of the Review Committee on H1N1' (n 137) xv.
[157] ibid 4.
[158] ibid 4–5.
[159] ibid 5.
[160] ibid 13.
[161] ibid 13–18.
[162] ibid 68. See also Bennett and Carney, 'Planning for Pandemics' (n 152) 423.
[163] World Health Organization, 'Report of the Review Committee on H1N1' (n 137) 119. See also Bennett and Carney, 'Planning for Pandemics' (n 152) 426.

could be utilized in responding to a global public health emergency;[164] (ii) the establishment of a contingency fund to support surge capacity during a PHEIC;[165] (iii) conclusion of negotiations on sharing of influenza viruses and access to vaccines;[166] and (iv) 'pursue a comprehensive influenza research and evaluation programme'.[167]

V. Ebola: Another Test for the *IHR (2005)*

The 2014 outbreak of Ebola in the West African countries of Guinea, Liberia, and Sierra Leone provided a further test of the *IHR (2005)*. In August 2014, the WHO Director-General declared the Ebola outbreak to be a PHEIC.[168] This declaration was to last until 29 March 2016.[169] The 2014–16 Ebola epidemic resulted in more than 28,000 cases and more than 11,000 deaths, with the overwhelming majority of cases being in the three most affected countries of Guinea, Liberia, and Sierra Leone.[170]

In the wake of Ebola, review committees[171] and commentators[172] reflected on the role of global health governance in responding to the crisis. As with the 2009 H1N1 pandemic, the building of national public health capacities was a common feature of much of this commentary.[173] While the Review Committee that evaluated the *IHR (2005)* and the 2009 H1N1 pandemic had called on countries to develop their capacities to meet their *IHR (2005)* core capacity requirements, many had failed to meet the 2012 deadline, and some had still failed to meet the requirements at the end of a two-year extension period.[174] Writing in the wake of the Ebola crisis, Dzau and Sands likened capacity building to preventative measures for fires:

---

[164] World Health Organization, 'Report of the Review Committee on H1N1' (n 137) 119.
[165] ibid 120.
[166] ibid.
[167] ibid 122.
[168] World Health Organization, 'IHR Emergency Committee on Ebola' (n 46).
[169] World Health Organization, 'Statement on the 9th Meeting of the IHR Emergency Committee Regarding the Ebola Outbreak in West Africa' (29 March 2016) <https://apps.who.int/mediacentre/news/statements/2016/end-of-ebola-pheic/en/index.html> accessed 21 April 2022.
[170] World Health Organization, 'Situation Report—Ebola Virus Disease' (30 March 2016) <https://apps.who.int/iris/bitstream/handle/10665/204714/ebolasitrep_30mar2016_eng.pdf> accessed 27 April 2022.
[171] For discussion see Lawrence O Gostin and others, 'Toward a Common Secure Future: Four Global Commissions in the Wake of Ebola' (2016) 13(5) *PLoS Medicine* art e1002042. See also World Health Organization, 'Review Committee on IHR in Ebola' (n 71).
[172] See for example Trygve Ottersen, Steven J Hoffman, and Gaëlle Groux, 'Ebola Again Shows the International Health Regulations are Broken: What Can Be Done Differently to Prepare for the Next Epidemic?' (2016) 42(2–3) *American Journal of Law & Medicine* 356; Lawrence O Gostin and Eric A Friedman, 'A Retrospective and Prospective Analysis of the West African Ebola Virus Disease Epidemic: Robust National Health Systems at the Foundation and an Empowered WHO at the Apex' (2015) 385(9980) *Lancet* 1902.
[173] See Ottersen, Hoffman, and Groux (n 172) 370.
[174] ibid 368.

we need to invest in the equivalent of fire-retardant furnishings, strict building codes, and the installation of smoke sensors and commercial sprinkler systems. It is the painstaking building of perhaps unglamorous capabilities related to disease surveillance, diagnostics, emergency preparedness, and infection-control protocols that will save the most lives and minimize economic disruption.[175]

Gostin too was critical of WHO's initial Ebola response, arguing that it revealed 'deep flaws' in its ability 'to lead and co-ordinate a coherent international response', resulting in the outbreak going out of control.[176] However, he argued that by the time of the 2018–20 outbreak in the Democratic Republic of the Congo, WHO 'performed far better, even though its staff were impeded by political violence and community distrust'.[177] The lesson to be learned, he urged, was that WHO's budget was 'wholly incommensurate with its global mandate, and its governance antiquated. A clear governing framework and leadership are needed to ensure coherent efforts and a functional global system.'[178]

Following a request from the 68th World Health Assembly, the WHO Director-General established a review committee to assess the role of the *IHR (2005)* in the response to Ebola.[179] The Review Committee noted that the Ebola epidemic in West Africa was the second major test of the *IHR (2005)* and that the epidemic's 'severity and duration challenged the IHR in unprecedented ways. It has shone a bright light on just how ill-prepared and vulnerable the global community remains.'[180] The Committee concluded that the *IHR (2005)* 'remain an indispensable legal framework for preventing and containing the international spread of public health risks. The overarching challenge with the IHR is poor implementation.'[181] The Review Committee did not recommend amendments to the *IHR*, but did recommend development of a 'Global Strategic Plan to improve public health preparedness and response' and 'to ensure implementation of the IHR'.[182] The Review Committee also recognized the need to increase awareness and recognition of the *IHR*.[183] Furthermore, recognizing that implementation of the *IHR* core capacities can be challenging for low-resource countries, and that some countries will need external support, the Review Committee recommended that 'WHO, States Parties and international development partners should urgently commit to providing financial support at the national, regional and international levels for the

---

[175] Victor J Dzau and Peter Sands, 'Beyond the Ebola Battle—Winning the War Against Future Epidemics' (2016) 375 *New England Journal of Medicine* 203, 204.
[176] Lawrence O Gostin, *Global Health Security: A Blueprint for the Future* (Harvard University Press 2021) (hereafter Gostin, *Global Health Security*) 12.
[177] ibid.
[178] ibid.
[179] World Health Organization, 'Review Committee on IHR in Ebola' (n 71) 8.
[180] ibid 14.
[181] ibid 56.
[182] ibid 56–57.
[183] ibid 60.

successful implementation of the Global Strategic Plan'.[184] Support for the most vulnerable countries should be prioritized.[185] In addition, external assessment of *IHR* core capacities was recommended to complement countries' self-assessment of their capacities.[186] This recommendation echoed earlier recommendations to include external evaluations in the assessment of *IHR* capacities, and the development and implementation of the Joint External Evaluation Tool.[187] However, while the Review Committee recommended the development of *IHR* core capacities, the Review Committee also recognized that 'IHR core capacities do not exist separately from national health systems' and that there was a need to strengthen health systems generally.[188]

Finally, the Review Committee made recommendations to improve compliance with the requirements of the *IHR* in relation to additional measures and temporary recommendations,[189] and to strengthen National *IHR* Focal Points,[190] as well as recommendations in relation to data sharing during public health emergencies,[191] and the need to strengthen and resource WHO's capacity in relation to implementing the *IHR* and responding to global public health emergencies.[192]

WHO established a Contingency Fund for Emergencies to enable rapid mobilization of resources when a crisis presented.[193] It also developed a Global Health Emergency Workforce with fast medical response capacity[194] and the Global Outbreak Alert and Response Network (GOARN) that had been established in 2000.[195]

VI. COVID-19 and the *IHR (2005)*

It has been asserted that 'COVID-19 exposed the extent to which pandemic preparedness was limited and disjointed, leaving health systems overwhelmed when actually confronted by a fast-moving and exponentially spreading virus'.[196] The

---

[184] ibid 59.
[185] ibid 68.
[186] ibid 61.
[187] World Health Organization, 'Joint External Evaluation Tool: International Health Regulations (2005)' (2nd edition, World Health Organization 2018) 7–9.
[188] World Health Organization, 'Review Committee on IHR in Ebola' (n 71) 69.
[189] ibid 65–67.
[190] ibid 67.
[191] ibid 70–71.
[192] ibid 71–73.
[193] World Health Organization, 'Contingency Fund for Emergencies (CFE)' <https://www.who.int/emergencies/funding/contingency-fund-for-emergencies> accessed 8 November 2021.
[194] Frederick M Burkle, 'The World Health Organization Global Health Emergency Workforce: What Role Will the United States Play?' (2016) 10(4) *Disaster Medicine and Public Health Preparedness* 531.
[195] Global Outbreak Alert and Response Network, 'About Us' <https://extranet.who.int/goarn/about-us> accessed 8 November 2021; John S Mackenzie and others, 'The Global Outbreak Alert and Response Network' (2014) 9(9) *Global Public Health* 1023.
[196] Ellen J Sirleaf and Helen Clark, 'Report of the Independent Panel for Pandemic Preparedness and Response: Making COVID-19 the Last Pandemic' (2021) 398(10295) *Lancet* 101, 102.

international alert system did not operate with sufficient speed, but the major difficulty was that 'many countries only applied the IHR in part, were not sufficiently aware of these regulations, or deliberately ignored them'.[197]

From the early days of the COVID-19 pandemic, countries introduced restrictions on travel.[198] While some of these were restrictions on domestic travel within countries, as discussed in Chapter 4, restrictions on international travel were also a feature of international responses to COVID-19.

Commentators have noted that there are challenges associated with the approach to trade and travel restrictions in the *IHR (2005)*. On the one hand, waiting until a PHEIC has been declared before issuing Temporary Recommendations, as required by the *IHR (2005)*, may risk missing the opportunity to limit the spread of disease.[199] On the other hand, recommending trade or travel restrictions in the absence of evidence that they will be effective risks negative economic impacts on affected countries.[200] States can implement health measures in addition to those recommended by WHO, but in implementing these measures they are required to follow the *IHR (2005)* requirements, basing their decisions on scientific principles, evidence and information, and ensuring that the measures are no more restrictive than reasonably available alternatives.[201] Many countries did implement travel restrictions in response to COVID-19, and it has been argued that 'It may be too early to draw definitive conclusions about the scientific justification and proportionality' of the measures States implemented.[202] This highlights the challenges for countries in assessing whether the measures they have introduced comply with the *IHR (2005)* requirements in terms of their scientific basis and being the least restrictive option. However, the failure by many countries to report promptly to WHO their implementation of measures also represents a failure by countries to comply with their obligations under the *IHR (2005)*.[203] It has been argued that in the period following the pandemic it will be necessary to evaluate the full range of trade and travel restrictions that were implemented, including those implemented by commercial companies such as airlines, which do not currently come within the *IHR (2005)*.[204]

---

[197] Preben Aavitsland and others 'Functioning of the International Health Regulations During the COVID-19 Pandemic' (2021) 398(10308) *Lancet* 1283, 1283-84; see too Gostin, *Global Health Security* (n 176) 223.

[198] Roojin Habibi and others, 'Do Not Violate the International Health Regulations During COVID-19 Outbreak' (2020) 395(10225) *Lancet* 664; see too Walter L Filho and others, 'Coronavirus: COVID-19 Transmission in Pacific Small Island Developing States' (2020) 17(15) *International Journal of Environmental Research and Public Health* art 5409.

[199] Barbara von Tigerstrom and Kumanan Wilson, 'COVID-19 Travel Restrictions and the International Health Regulations (2005)' (2020) 5 *BMJ Global Health* art e002629, 2.

[200] ibid.

[201] ibid. See also earlier discussion in Section III.

[202] von Tigerstrom and Wilson (n 199) 2.

[203] ibid; Habibi and others (n 198) 664.

[204] Habibi and others (n 198); Kelley Lee and others, 'Global Coordination on Cross-Border Travel and Trade Measures Crucial to COVID-19 Response' (2020) 395(10237) *Lancet* 1593.

In September 2020 the WHO Director-General convened the Review Committee on the Functioning of the International Health Regulations (2005) during the COVID-19 Response. The Review Committee was convened following a request from Member States in resolution WHA73.1.[205] The Committee made 40 recommendations in ten key areas,[206] and addressed key issues relating to the *IHR (2005)*. In its conclusions the Review Committee noted that:

[The *IHR (2005)*] are a pillar of global health security: the foundations of the global architecture for monitoring and responding to public health risks and emergencies, involving countries, institutions and networks coordinated by WHO. The purpose of this architecture is to enable the prevention, detection and containment of health risks and threats, the strengthening of national capacities for that purpose, and the coordination of a global alert and response system.

Despite being almost 20 years in the making, none of these elements have proved sufficient against SARS-CoV-2: since the beginning of 2020 we have been experiencing a prolonged crisis, unprecedented in our recent history.[207]

Amongst the key messages in the Review Committee's report was that 'Lack of compliance of States Parties with certain obligations under the IHR, particularly on preparedness, contributed to the COVID-19 pandemic becoming a protracted global health emergency.'[208] Looking to the future, the Review Committee concluded:

In the Committee's view, its 40 recommendations should be implemented without delay. However, it is for States Parties to decide which recommendations they will take forward and how. It is clear that sustainable national health systems, accessible to all, are an essential basis for global health emergency preparedness and response, and that the foundation of productive international collaboration is trust and transparency. Neither can be achieved without the other: they are two sides of the same coin.

The world must be prepared to respond better to the next public health emergency of international concern, especially if it has the potential to become a pandemic. The essential changes to enable effective implementation of the IHR require urgent action, not years of political negotiations.[209]

---

[205] World Health Organization, 'Report of the Review Committee on the Functioning of the International Health Regulations (2005) During the COVID-19 Response' (Report, Final Draft, 30 April 2021, WHA A74/9 Add 1) 19 <https://www.who.int/publications/m/item/a74-9-who-s-work-in-health-emergencies> accessed 21 April 2022.
[206] ibid 11.
[207] ibid 59 paras 135–36.
[208] ibid 60.
[209] ibid 63 paras 150–51.

VII. Proposals for a Pandemic Treaty

The dramatic impact of the COVID-19 pandemic has led to calls for a new pandemic treaty to ensure the world is prepared for any future pandemic. The 73rd World Health Assembly requested the WHO Director-General to initiate an independent review of the international response to COVID-19.[210] The Independent Panel for Pandemic Preparedness and Response provided its report in 2021. Describing the COVID-19 pandemic as 'the worst combined health and socio-economic crisis in living memory, and a catastrophe at every level',[211] the title of the Panel's report calls for COVID-19 to be 'the last pandemic'.[212] The Panel noted that in the period since the H1N1 influenza pandemic in 2009, 'at least 11 high-level panels and commissions have made specific recommendations in 16 reports to improve global pandemic preparedness ... Yet, despite the consistent messages that significant change was needed to ensure global protection against pandemic threats, the majority of recommendations were never implemented.'[213] The Panel's recommendations addressed a number of key areas:

- the need for improved national, regional and international leadership and co-ordination, including a new pandemic treaty;[214]
- strengthening WHO's financing, independence, and authority;[215]
- greater investment in pandemic preparedness, with new targets and benchmarks and periodic peer reviews of capacities;[216]
- a new international system for surveillance, based on state-of-the-art digital tools, and greater powers for WHO to investigate possible outbreaks and to publish information about them.[217] The Panel also recommended that 'Future declarations of a PHEIC by the WHO Director-General should be based on the precautionary principle where warranted, as in the case of respiratory infections.'[218]
- the establishment of a 'pre-negotiated platform for tools and supplies';[219]
- a new system for international financing of global preparedness and response;[220] and

---

[210] World Health Assembly, 'COVID-19 Response' (Resolution WHA73.1, 19 May 2020), para 9(10).
[211] The Independent Panel for Pandemic Preparedness and Response, 'COVID-19: Make it the Last Pandemic' (May 2021) 4 <https://theindependentpanel.org>.
[212] ibid.
[213] ibid 16.
[214] ibid 46–47.
[215] ibid 48–49.
[216] ibid 50–51.
[217] ibid 52–53.
[218] ibid 53.
[219] ibid 54.
[220] ibid 56–57.

- the development by countries of their national coordination for pandemic preparedness and response.[221]

In relation to a new treaty, the Panel recommended the adoption of a Pandemic Framework Convention, which would be 'complementary to the IHR, to be facilitated by WHO and with the clear involvement of the highest levels of government, scientific experts and civil society'.[222]

The 74th World Health Assembly requested the WHO Director-General to convene a special session of the WHA in November 2021 'dedicated to considering the benefits of developing a WHO convention, agreement or other international instrument on pandemic preparedness and response'.[223] Despite the calls for a new treaty,[224] in the absence of measures to encourage compliance or provide sanctions for non-compliance, it has been argued that it is difficult to see how a new treaty would have greater success than the *IHR (2005)* given the non-compliance with existing obligations under the *IHR (2005)*.[225] It has also been noted that treaty-making is a slow process and that 'The focus on developing a treaty could derail momentum for action on the ground to improve preparedness now'.[226] Others have argued that there is a need to learn from the COVID-19 pandemic before developing a new treaty.[227] Wenham, Eccleston-Turner, and Voss have contended, though, that a pandemic treaty is not the most effective way to achieve global equity and expressed doubts about whether the treaty will achieve what is being extolled by its proponents—'it will not solve the multiple problems of global cooperation in global health that supporters believe it will.'[228] Commentators have suggested content and key features for the proposed treaty. For example, Duff and others have proposed ten recommendations to improve global public health security, which could inform the development of a new pandemic treaty:[229] (1) ensuring that one

---

[221] ibid 58–59.
[222] ibid 47.
[223] World Health Assembly, 'Special Session of the World Health Assembly to Consider Developing a WHO Convention, Agreement or Other International Instrument on Pandemic Preparedness and Response' (Decision WHA74(16)) (31 May 2021) para 2. For discussion see Ronald Labonté and others, 'A Pandemic Treaty, Revised International Health Regulations, or Both?' (2021) 17 *Globalization and Health* art 128.
[224] For discussion see, Haik Nikogosian and Ilona Kickbusch, 'The Case for an International Pandemic Treaty' (2021) 372 *British Medical Journal* n527; Sakiko Fukuda-Parr, Paulo Buss, and Alicia Ely Yamin, 'Pandemic Treaty Needs to Start With Rethinking the Paradigm of Global Health Security' (2021) 6 *BMJ Global Health* art e006392.
[225] Clare Wenham and others, 'Preparing for the Next Pandemic' (2021) 373 *British Medical Journal* n1295.
[226] Thomas R Frieden and Marine Buissonière, 'Will a Global Preparedness Treaty Help or Hinder Pandemic Preparedness?' (2021) 6 *BMJ Global Health* art e006297, 1. See also Labonté and others (n 223).
[227] Editorial, 'Learn from COVID before Diving into a Pandemic Treaty' (2021) 592(7853) *Nature* 165.
[228] Clare Wenham, Mark Eccleston-Turner, and Maike Voss, 'The Futility of the Pandemic Treaty: Caught Between Globalism and Statism' (2022) 98(3) *International Affairs* 837, 837.
[229] Johnathan H Duff and others, 'A Global Public Health Convention for the 21st Century' (2021) 6(6) *Lancet Public Health* e428.

or more agencies have the necessary *authority* to co-ordinate global pandemic prevention, preparedness and response; (2) ensuring that the global health agency and the global health system more broadly has the flexibility needed for pandemic *responsiveness*; (3) ensuring that the global health agency has the necessary authoritative *expertise* for pandemic-related information and technical expertise; (4) the convention should provide for objective external assessments and monitoring of countries' compliance to enable *evaluations* of progress; (5) the convention should provide *enforcement* mechanisms, including incentives for compliance and penalties for non-compliance; (6) the convention should provide for the *autonomy* of the governing body; (7) the convention should provide for sustainable and independent *financing* of the global health agency; (8) the convention should provide for *representation* of all countries, as well as including other relevant stakeholders; (9) *multisectoral* engagement with different levels and parts of government, as well as engagement with other key stakeholders; and (10) *commitment* by all parties to the convention to pandemic prevention, preparedness and response.[230]

Similarly, Gostin and others have contended that the first step towards a pandemic treaty lies in acknowledgment of the 'stark failures in global governance during the COVID-19 pandemic' and that it must have as its hallmarks 'innovative norms, governance, and compliance mechanisms needed to prepare for novel outbreaks with pandemic potential'.[231]

Under the Biden administration, the United States has not been supportive of such an initiative, instead voicing concerns about a treaty on the basis of it having the potential to 'divert attention away from substantive issues regarding the response, preparedness for future pandemic threats'.[232] It remains to be seen whether the COVID-19 pandemic will lead to a sufficient impetus for global reforms supporting the need for improved pandemic preparedness.

In December 2021 the World Health Assembly met for a Special Session, only the second special session since WHO was founded in 1948, and decided to establish an intergovernmental negotiating body to draft and negotiate a new convention, agreement, or instrument on pandemic prevention, preparedness, and response for adoption under WHO's *Constitution*.[233] A progress report will be

---

[230] ibid e429–e431.
[231] Lawrence O Gostin, Benjamin M Meier, and Barbara Stocking, 'Developing an Innovative Pandemic Treaty to Advance Global Health Security' (2021) 49(3) *Journal of Law, Medicine & Ethics* 503, 503; see too Lawrence O Gostin, Sam F Halabi, and Kevin A Klock, 'An International Agreement on Pandemic Prevention and Preparedness' (2021) 326(13) *Journal of the American Medical Association* 1257.
[232] See Steven Erlanger, 'World Leaders Call for an International Treaty to Combat Future Pandemics' *New York Times* (30 March 2021, updated 4 September 2021) <https://www.nytimes.com/2021/03/30/world/europe/world-health-treaty-pandemics.html> accessed 26 September 2021.
[233] World Health Organization, 'News Release: World Health Assembly Agrees to Launch Process to Develop Historic Global Accord on Pandemic Prevention, Preparedness and Response' (News Release, 1 December 2021) <www.who.int/news/item/01-12-2021-world-health-assembly-agrees-to-launch-process-to-develop-historic-global-accord-on-pandemic-prevention-preparedness-and-response> accessed 29 September 2022.

delivered to the 76th World Health Assembly in 2023, and the outcome submitted for consideration by the 77th World Health Assembly the following year.[234]

VIII. Measuring the Pandemic

Understanding the scale and impact of the pandemic is essential for informing the development of public health, policy, and economic responses to the pandemic. However, as discussed below, the issue of pandemic-related data has, at times, been complex. While data have helped with understanding the pandemic, the vast quantities of pandemic-related information have been referred to as an 'infodemic'.[235] 'An infodemic spreads between humans in a similar manner to an epidemic, via digital and physical information systems. It makes it hard for people to find trustworthy sources and reliable guidance when they need it.'[236] Social media in particular have been noted as having played a significant role in the spread of both accurate and inaccurate information during the pandemic.[237]

Although population-level data have been important during the pandemic, civil registration and vital statistics have been disrupted during the pandemic, complicating the provision of mortality data that are essential during such a crisis. Finally, the pandemic has highlighted the need for data to be disaggregated so as to identify as accurately as possible the impact of the pandemic, particularly on disadvantaged populations.

A. The Importance of Data

During the COVID-19 pandemic, reports, indicators, and dashboards provided data at the global and country level. As Nelken has observed:

> Most commonly, they are presented as 'snapshots', illustrating diachronic developments over time or synchronic differences between countries. Alternatively, they may be displayed on so-called dashboards that focus on daily bulletins, or even minute-by-minute changes, some of which allow interaction with the user and offer the possibility of interrogating the data with respect to given localities and times.[238]

---

[234] ibid.
[235] World Health Organization, 'WHO Public Health Research Agenda for Managing Infodemics' (2021).
[236] ibid 1.
[237] Elia Gabarron, Sunday O Oyeyemi, and Rolf Wynn, 'COVID-19-related Misinformation on Social Media: A Systematic Review' (2021) 99(6) *Bulletin of the World Health Organization* 455.
[238] David Nelken, 'Between Comparison and Commensuration: A Case Study of COVID-19 Rankings' (2021) 17(2) *International Journal of Law in Context* 215, 216.

Nelken has argued that these indicators have been used to compare the successes of countries over time, and can be used by governments to help justify the need for preventive measures,[239] although there are challenges in making comparisons between countries and assessing the relevance of local and contextual factors.[240] Nelken notes that global indicators regarding the COVID-19 pandemic can be categorized as those 'aiming either to report on the progress of the epidemic or assess the success of policies in dealing with it'.[241]

Consistent and reliable reporting of data by countries[242] is also vital to being able to monitor the spread and impact of the pandemic and make appropriate, suitably tailored emergency directions:

> Having accurate data on both confirmed and provisional death statistics will enable public health researchers, policy analysts, and development partners to correctly estimate the COVID-19–related mortality rate and subsequently design data-driven pandemic preparedness efforts, early response strategies for forthcoming waves of the pandemic, and emergency actions with necessary assistance from both national and international public health organizations.[243]

Given that borders between countries are porous in many parts of the world and that variants have come into being in one country and then spread internationally, it became clear in 2020 and 2021 that what takes place in one country is relevant throughout the world. For example, the Delta variant emerged in India[244] and went on to become one of the greatest challenges posed by COVID-19. Subsequently, a new form of the Delta variant, known as 'Delta Plus', emerged and also spread internationally.[245]

In a global pandemic, accurate and timely reporting of the virus and deaths caused by the virus has important implications for the international community. As of October 2021, Turkmenistan and North Korea had not reported any cases of COVID-19.[246] On 20 February 2021 WHO Director-General, Tedros Ghebreyesus

---

[239] ibid 217. See also Nathan Genicot, 'Epidemiological Surveillance and Performance Assessment: The Two Roles of Health Indicators During the COVID-19 Pandemic' (2021) 17(2) *International Journal of Law in Context* 186.
[240] Nelken (n 238) 220–23.
[241] ibid 218.
[242] See also Chapter 1(III)(C).
[243] Mazbahul G Ahamad and others, 'Officially Confirmed COVID-19 and Unreported COVID-19–Like Illness Death Counts: An Assessment of Reporting Discrepancy in Bangladesh' (2021) 104(2) *American Journal of Tropical Medicine and Hygiene* 546, 547.
[244] See World Health Organization, 'Tracking SARS-CoV-2 Variants' <https://www.who.int/en/activities/tracking-SARS-CoV-2-variants/> accessed 29 September 2022.
[245] See Amy Barrett, 'Delta Plus: Everything You Need to Know About the New Coronavirus Variant' *Science Focus* (29 September 2021) <www.sciencefocus.com/news/delta-plus-variant/> accessed 29 September 2022.
[246] See Max Walden, 'Coronavirus Has Touched Every Corner of the Globe, But These Countries Have Reported No Cases' *ABC News* (12 November 2020) <www.abc.net.au/news/2020-11-12/what-are-the-countries-that-remain-free-of-coronavirus/12874248> accessed 29 September 2022; Timothy

noted that there had been cases of Tanzanians travelling abroad and then testing positive for the virus, and called on Tanzania 'to start reporting COVID-19 cases and share data'.[247]

Two measures are used to assess the proportion of persons who are infected with COVID-19 and have fatal outcomes: the 'infection fatality ratio' (IFR), which estimates the proportion of deaths among those who are infected; and the case fatality ratio (CFR), which estimates the proportion of deaths in identified confirmed cases.

> To measure IFR accurately, a complete picture of the number of infections of, and deaths caused by, the disease must be known ... most estimates of fatality ratios have been based on cases detected through surveillance and calculated using crude methods, giving rise to widely variable estimates of CFR by country—from less than 0.1% to over 25%.[248]

For COVID-19, the true level of transmission is frequently underestimated because a substantial proportion of people with the infection are undetected because they are asymptomatic, because they have only mild symptoms and thus are not tested, or because they choose not to report a positive test. There can also be segments of the population which are less likely to access healthcare or testing. Under-detection of cases may be exacerbated when testing capacity is limited[249] or restricted to people with severe illness and to priority risk groups (such as frontline healthcare workers, older people, and people with co-morbidities). Another factor can be false negative outcomes.[250] Cases may also be misdiagnosed and attributed to other diseases with similar clinical presentation, such as influenza. For instance, it has been reported that the Institute of Epidemiology Disease Control and Research (IEDCR), a reporting authority in Bangladesh, only reported

---

Hujar, 'No COVID-19 in Turkmenistan?' *Medical News Today* (14 October 2021) <www.medicalnewstoday.com/articles/no-covid-19-in-turkmenistan> accessed 29 September 2022; Abdujalil Abdurasulov, 'Turkmenistan: Getting Covid in a Land Where No Cases Officially Exist' *BBC News* (19 September 2021) <www.bbc.com/news/world-asia-58583212> accessed 20 September 2022; see too Aynabat Yaylymova, 'COVID-19 in Turkmenistan: No Data, No Health Rights' (2020) 22(2) *Health and Human Rights* 325.
[247] World Health Organization, 'WHO Director-General's Statement on Tanzania and COVID-19' (20 February 2021) <www.who.int/news/item/20-02-2021-who-director-general-s-statement-on-tanzania-and-covid-19> accessed 29 September 2022.
[248] World Health Organization, 'Estimating Mortality from COVID-19: Scientific Brief' (4 August 2020) <www.who.int/news-room/commentaries/detail/estimating-mortality-from-covid-19> accessed 29 September 2022 (hereafter, World Health Organization, 'Estimating Mortality from COVID-19').
[249] H Lau and others, 'Evaluating the Massive Underreporting and Undertesting of COVID-19 Cases in Multiple Global Epicenters' (2021) 27(2) *Pulmonology* 110.
[250] Jeremy S Faust and Carlos del Rio, 'Assessment of Deaths from COVID-19 and From Seasonal Influenza' (2020) 180(8) *Journal of the American Medical Association Internal Medicine* 1045.

COVID-19 deaths and not any COVID-19-like illness deaths despite the suggested guidelines.[251]

It became apparent too that during the pandemic countries were utilizing varying approaches to COVID-19 case definitions. The numerator and the denominator of any formula used to calculate fatality rate will vary according to how they are defined. A COVID-19 death was defined broadly by WHO

> for surveillance purposes as a death resulting from a clinically compatible illness in a probable or confirmed COVID-19 case, unless there is a clear alternative cause of death that cannot be related to COVID-19 disease (e.g. trauma). There should be no period of complete recovery between the illness and death.[252]

Thus, when COVID-19 is not part of the causal chain leading directly to a death, it should not be recorded as the underlying cause of death. However, COVID-19 should be recorded as the cause of death 'if accompanied by pre-existing chronic conditions or conditions capable of aggravating the clinical picture and increasing the risk of death'.[253] The issue is complicated further as

> a death caused by COVID-19 could be correctly recorded even in cases where the infection is only suspected or probable. Not only does the definition of death caused by COVID-19 admit of 'a probable case' of infection, but also the explicit instructions provided by WHO recommend that even in the case of mere suspicion of COVID-19, that is to say in the absence of swab or serological testing or other diagnostic imaging procedure that reliably confirms the infection, the disease must in any case be indicated as the underlying cause of death.[254]

These many difficulties in calculating the real numbers of deaths caused or contributed to by COVID-19 have led many, including WHO, to focus upon 'excess mortality' which is defined as 'the difference in the total number of deaths in a crisis compared to those expected under normal conditions'.[255] Such a calculation has the advantage of being more realistic as it accounts 'for both the total number of deaths directly attributed to the virus as well as the indirect impact, such as disruption to essential health services or travel disruptions'.[256] A disadvantage is that

---

[251] Ahamad and others (n 243).
[252] World Health Organization, 'Estimating Mortality from COVID-19' (n 248); European Centre for Disease Prevention and Control, 'Surveillance Definitions for COVID-19' (15 March 2021) <www.ecdc.europa.eu/en/covid-19/surveillance/surveillance-definitions> accessed 29 September 2022.
[253] See Maria C Amoretti and Elisabetta Lalumera, 'COVID-19 as the Underlying Cause of Death: Disentangling Facts and Values' (2021) 43(1) *History and Philosophy of the Life Sciences* art 4, 2.
[254] ibid.
[255] World Health Organization, 'The True Death Toll of COVID-19: Estimating Global Excess Mortality' <www.who.int/data/stories/the-true-death-toll-of-covid-19-estimating-global-excess-mortality> accessed 29 September 2022.
[256] ibid.

the methodology is to some degree undiscerning and may fail to account for the rise in other forms of death, although often these may be correlated with indirect consequences of COVID-19 and reduced availability of health resources.

Employment of the excess mortality methodology has shown that in several countries that have been particularly adversely affected by COVID-19, such as Peru, Ecuador, Bolivia, and Mexico, the excess mortality was 50% above the expected annual mortality, or above 400 excess deaths per 100,000 population in countries such as in Peru, Bulgaria, North Macedonia, and Serbia.[257] It also suggested that in countries such as Nicaragua, Russia, and Uzbekistan, there was substantial under-reporting of deaths, including by up to two orders of magnitude in Tajikistan.[258] Even in the United States, use of the methodology during 2020 showed 375,235 excess deaths. 83% were attributable to direct effects of COVID-19, and 17% were attributable to indirect effects of COVID-19, resulting in a 'decrease of life expectancy of 1.67 years, translating to a reversion of 14 years in historical life expectancy gains.'[259] The analysis of Cronin and Evans suggests that in the United States excess mortality and life years lost are disproportionately represented in minorities, particularly Black, non-Hispanic men.[260]

A significant legal development occurred when the High Court of Brazil[261] determined an application from a number of parties for a ruling that diverse forms of conduct on the part of the national Ministry of Health were unlawful. The Ministry had changed its practices in relation to daily disclosure of national COVID-19 data. Justice De Moraes granted the application on the basis that, in response to the COVID-19 pandemic, all Brazilian governments needed to introduce processes to protect public health and adopt means of sustaining the operation of the healthcare system. Dr Moraes J noted the high mortality rate in Brazil from COVID-19 and commented that:

---

[257] Ariel Karlinsky and Dmitry Kobak, 'Tracking Excess Mortality Across Countries During the COVID-19 Pandemic with the World Mortality Dataset' (2021) 10 *eLife* art e60336; see too Nazrul Islam and others, 'Excess Deaths Associated with Covid-19 Pandemic in 2020: Age and Sex Disaggregated Time Series Analysis in 29 High Income Countries' (2021) 373 *British Medical Journal* n1137. See also COVID-19 Excess Mortality Collaborators, 'Estimating Excess Mortality Due to the COVID-19 Pandemic: A Systematic Analysis of COVID-19-related Mortality, 2020–21' (2022) 399(10334) *Lancet* 1513.

[258] Karlinsky and Kobak (n 257); see too Francesco Sanmarchi and others, 'Exploring the Gap Between Excess Mortality and COVID-19 Deaths in 67 Countries' (2021) 4(7) *Journal of the American Medical Association Network Open* art e2117359.

[259] Eunice YS Chan, Davy Cheung, and Janet Martin, 'Impact of COVID-19 on Excess Mortality, Life Expectancy, and Years of Life Lost in the United States' (2021) 16(9) *PLoS One* art e0256835, 1.

[260] Christopher J Cronin and William N Evans, 'Excess Mortality from COVID and non-COVID Causes in Minority Populations' (2021) 118(39) *Proceedings of the National Academy of Sciences of the United States of America (PNAS)* art e2101386118.

[261] *Sustainability Network v The President of the Republic of Brazil* (ADPF 690 MC/DF, unreported, High Court of Brazil, 8 June 2020 per De Moraes J). See Ian Freckelton and Vera L Raposo, 'International Access to Public Health Data: An Important Brazilian Legal Precedent' (2020) 27(4) *Journal of Law and Medicine* 895. Quotations from the judgment are as translated by Professor Raposo.

It will carry disastrous consequences for the population if measures with internationally recognized effectiveness are not implemented ... Those data are necessary for the planning of public policies and decisions by public authorities, and to guarantee the full access of the population to effective knowledge about the situation experienced nationally.

De Moraes J disagreed with the submission that the circumstances of the pandemic demanded the application of any recognized exception to the usual requirement for government openness with the public and observed that:

> The disclosure of such data is important to the analysis of the situation and the planning of the necessary measures to assist public authorities in their decision-making process. Those data are also necessary to allow the general population to be fully aware of the pandemic situation existing nationally.

De Moraes J made orders to ensure publication of all epidemiological data obtained by the Ministry of Health from the time that it had changed its reporting practices. In addition, De Moraes J ordered the Ministry of Health to resume its previously candid disclosure each day, including on its public website, of epidemiological data concerning the pandemic (such as the volume of new cases) .

Although data have been vital to our understandings of the pandemic, the Independent Panel for Pandemic Preparedness and Response commented that the pandemic showed 'two worlds operating at very different speeds':[262]

> One is the world of fast-paced information and data-sharing. Open digital platforms for epidemic surveillance, in which WHO plays a leading role, constantly update and share outbreak information ... The other world is that of the slow and deliberate pace with which information is treated under the IHR (2005), with their step-by-step confidentiality and verification requirements and threshold criteria for the declaration of a PHEIC, with greater emphasis on action that should **not** be taken, rather than on action that should.[263]

To address these issues, the Panel recommended the redesign of national, regional, and global surveillance and alert systems.[264] The Panel recommended that the new system use 'state-of-the-art digital tools to connect information centres around the world and including animal and environmental health surveillance, with appropriate protections of people's rights'.[265]

---

[262] Independent Panel (n 211) 26.
[263] ibid 26–27.
[264] ibid 27.
[265] ibid 53.

B. Civil Registration and Vital Statistics

Accurate data are essential to being able to measure the scale and impact of the pandemic. Civil registration and vital statistics (CRVS) play an important role in documenting the population of a country, through registration and certification of births, deaths, marriages, and divorces, and aggregation and dissemination of statistics.[266] Although census information, household surveys, and other measures may provide some data in the absence of effective CRVS, effective CRVS can provide continuous data on causes of mortality at national and sub-national levels to inform policy development.[267] Accurate CRVS will also be key to measuring the progress of countries against SDG targets and indicators.[268] CRVS also play a vital role in providing individuals with legal recognition to enable their participation in society.[269] For example, registration of an individual's birth provides that individual with 'an identity which activates their human rights and legal status as a person, *as a human being*, before the law'.[270]

Registration of deaths is also important, not only for providing dignity to and acknowledgment of the deceased, but also giving recognition to the rights of their descendants.[271] As Brolan and Gouda note, 'In post-emergency settings, where access to resources is crucial for the survivors, benefits flowing from death certification and notification can have enormous ramification on rebuilding the lives of individuals, families, and communities who can benefit from the legal rights and entitlements they are owed on the deceased's passing.'[272] In the context of a pandemic such as COVID-19, accurate reporting of deaths will not only help to provide accurate measures of the scale of the pandemic, but will help to support the lives of the living.

A study by AbouZahr and others found that the pandemic had disrupted CRVS in a number of countries.[273] In their study of 66 countries, they found that in 11 (17%), civil registration was not seen as an essential service. In another five countries (8%), a more limited range of events was registered.[274] Of the 34 (51%) countries that regarded registration services as essential, the services were disrupted

---

[266] Claire E Brolan and Hebe Gouda, 'Civil Registration and Vital Statistics, Emergencies, and International Law: Understanding the Intersection' (2017) 25(2) *Medical Law Review* 314, 315–16.

[267] Carla AbouZahr and others, 'Towards Universal Civil Registration and Vital Statistics Systems: The Time is Now' (2015) 386(10001) *Lancet* 1407, 1409 (hereafter AbouZahr and others, 'Towards Universal Civil Registration').

[268] Brolan and Gouda (n 266) 332; AbouZahr and others, 'Towards Universal Civil Registration' (n 267) 1408–409.

[269] AbouZahr and others, 'Towards Universal Civil Registration' (n 267) 1409.

[270] Brolan and Gouda (n 266) 316.

[271] ibid 331.

[272] ibid.

[273] Carla AbouZahr and others, 'The COVID-19 Pandemic: Effects on Civil Registration of Births and Deaths and on Availability and Utility of Vital Events Data' (2021) 111(6) *American Journal of Public Health* 1123.

[274] ibid 1124.

due to pandemic-related restrictions such as travel restrictions, stay-at-home orders, or limits on in-person services.[275] In 16 countries (24%), registration services continued without interruption.[276] AbouZahr and others argue that the increased demand for accurate mortality data has been 'accompanied by a realization of the need to strengthen CRVS systems'.[277] They note that the requirement that deaths be registered within a specified period of time allows for rapid calculation of all-cause mortality, allowing for calculations of 'excess mortality' from all causes compared to previous periods.[278] Where a cause of death is provided with the registration of a death, mortality data can also help to identify increases in deaths related to COVID-19 and any increases in deaths from other causes.[279] They argue for improving CRVS systems so they have enhanced resilience and less vulnerability to service disruptions in future emergencies.[280]

C. Disaggregated Data

Just as it is important to count and record the population through CRVS, disaggregation of data is also important. Disaggregation of data by sex, race and ethnicity, age, and other measures helps to identify the impact of the pandemic and can help to inform and shape responses to it. During the COVID-19 pandemic there has been increased recognition of the importance of data that are disaggregated by sex,[281] age,[282] race and ethnicity,[283] and for Indigenous Peoples,[284] and

---

[275] ibid 1124–26.
[276] ibid 1126.
[277] ibid 1127.
[278] ibid.
[279] ibid 1128.
[280] ibid 1129-30. See also Glenn Copeland, 'Timely and Accurate Data From Vital Records Registration, Merged with Disease-Reporting System Data, Can Truly Empower Public Health Officials' (2021) 111(6) *American Journal of Public Health* 990.
[281] Nabamallika Dehingia and Anita Raj, 'Sex Differences in COVID-19 Case Fatality: Do We Know Enough?' (2021) 9(1) *Lancet Global Health* e14; Mireille Evagora-Campbell and others, 'From Routine Data Collection to Policy Design: Sex and Gender Both Matter in COVID-19' (2021) 397(10293) *Lancet* 2447–49; Clare Wenham and others, 'COVID-19: The Gendered Impacts of the Outbreak' (2020) 395(10227) *Lancet* 846 (hereafter Wenham and others, 'COVID-19: The Gendered Impacts').
[282] United Nations, *Policy Brief: The Impact of COVID-19 on Older Persons* (May 2020) <https://unsdg.un.org/resources/policy-brief-impact-covid-19-older-persons> 15; Theresa Diaz and others, 'A Call for Standardised Age-Disaggregated Health Data' (2021) 2(7) *Lancet Healthy Longevity* 436.
[283] Neeraj Bhala and others, 'Sharpening the Global Focus on Ethnicity and Race in the Time of COVID-19' (2020) 395(10238) *Lancet* 1673; Clyde W Yancy, 'COVID-19 and African Americans' (2020) 323(19) *Journal of the American Medical Association* 1891; Shaun Treweek and others, 'COVID-19 and Ethnicity: Who Will Research Results Apply To?' (2020) 395(10242) *Lancet* 1955; Grace A Noppert and Lauren C Zalla, 'Who Counts and Who Gets Counted? Health Equity in Infectious Disease Surveillance' (2021) 111(6) *American Journal of Public Health* 1004.
[284] Alistair Mallard and others, 'An Urgent Call to Collect Data Related to COVID-19 and Indigenous Populations Globally' (2021) 6(3) *BMJ Global Health* art 004655; Aggie J Yellow Horse and Kimberely R Huyser, 'Indigenous Data Sovereignty and COVID-19 Data Issues for American Indian and Alaska Native Tribes and Populations' (2021) *Journal of Population Research* <https://doi.org/10.1007/s12546-021-09261-5>.

the importance of intersectional analyses that recognize the potential for different forms of disadvantage to have a cumulative effect.[285] There has also been recognition of the importance of disaggregated data for vaccination rates.[286] There has been increased focus on disaggregation of data by sex in the context of the COVID-19 pandemic,[287] and calls for inclusion of women in clinical trials of COVID-19 treatments and vaccines.[288] A report by UN Women and others noted that 'COVID-19 may be gender blind, but it is not gender neutral.'[289] Amongst the report's recommendations were the disaggregation of all COVID-19 data 'at a minimum by sex, and ideally, by other key sociodemographic characteristics'[290] and the collection of 'standardized, comparable gender data in areas where women's and girls' lives are disproportionately affected by COVID-19'.[291]

Accurate age-related data are also important to understanding a pandemic's impact on different age groups. This has particularly been the case for older groups since persons over the age of 60 years have been at increased risk of severe disease and death as a result of COVID-19. The United Nations has noted gaps in age-related data:

> Data on older persons disaggregated by age groups, and covering all living arrangements, such as older persons in residential care facilities, are crucial to identifying the full picture of pandemic impacts and to targeting responses. Data on older persons, where they are collected, often portrays a homogenous group. For example, COVID-19 fatalities are often reported in broad age groups, such as among persons 60+ years, masking the notable differentials in COVID-19 outcomes between persons age 60–69, age 70–79, and 80+ years. Disaggregation of COVID-19 data is essential by age, sex, disability, and underlying health conditions, in order to differentiate accurately the risks to older persons.[292]

Data that are disaggregated on the basis of race, ethnicity, and for Indigenous Peoples have also been essential to identifying the disproportionate impact of

---

[285] Dehingia and Raj (n 281); Nessa E Ryan and Alison M El Ayadi, 'A Call for a Gender-Responsive Intersectional Approach to Address COVID-19' (2020) 15(9) *Global Public Health* 1404; Editorial, 'Ageing Unequally' (2021) 2(5) *Lancet Healthy Longevity* e231; Editorial, 'Compounding Inequalities: Racism, Ageism, and Health' (2021) 2(3) *Lancet Healthy Longevity* e112.
[286] Nancy Krieger and others, 'Missing Again: US Racial and Ethnic Data for COVID-19 Vaccination' (2021) 397(10281) *Lancet* 1259.
[287] Dehingia and Raj (n 281); Evagora-Campbell and others (n 281); Wenham and others, 'COVID-19: The Gendered Impacts (n 281).
[288] Melanie M Taylor and others, 'Inclusion of Pregnant Women in COVID-19 Treatment Trials: A Review and Global Call to Action' (2021) 9(3) *Lancet Global Health* e366.
[289] Lotus McDougal and others, *Strengthening Gender Measures and Data in the COVID-19 Era: An Urgent Need for Change* 4 <https://www.unwomen.org/en/digital-library/publications/2021/03/strengthening-gender-measures-and-data-in-the-covid-19-era> accessed 24 February 2022.
[290] ibid.
[291] ibid.
[292] United Nations, *Policy Brief: The Impact of COVID-19 on Older Persons* (n 282) 15.

COVID-19 on those of African-American or Asian heritage and on Indigenous communities. It has been noted that combining smaller groups into a category of 'other' makes it difficult to identify the impact on smaller groups.[293] With reports indicating that these groups have been disproportionately affected by COVID-19-related cases and deaths, data that are disaggregated on the basis of race, ethnicity, and for Indigenous Peoples are needed to be able to measure nuances in the impact of the pandemic and to be able to develop appropriate responses to it.

IX. Conclusion

As discussed in this chapter, the *IHR (2005)* have provided a global framework for responding to and tracking the international spread of disease. In 2005 the *IHR* were replaced with a new revised version that introduced the concept of a PHEIC, and an enhanced focus on human rights. However, national capacity building as required by the *IHR (2005)* has remained challenging, particularly for low resource countries. Compliance with the requirements of the *IHR (2005)* in terms of the imposition of additional measures, such as travel restrictions, has also been challenging.

The COVID-19 pandemic has once again tested the *IHR (2005)* and there have been calls for a new pandemic treaty. Finally, the quality and accuracy of data have been of central importance in being able to measure the scale and impact of the pandemic and in the development and implementation of responses to the pandemic.

---

[293] Noppert and Zalla (n 283) 1005.

4
Restrictions on Movement

I. Introduction

Soon after its emergence, it was apparent that COVID-19 was highly infectious.[1] Ostensibly to contain its spread, from the beginning of this pandemic, a variety of restrictions was imposed on people's movement around the world.[2] Borders to many areas were closed and patrolled, ensuring that people could neither leave nor enter them, in some countries interstate and international travel were banned, people were required to stay at home, those infected with COVID-19 were isolated, and those who had been or might have been exposed to the disease were quarantined.[3]

This chapter examines the nature, impact, and legality of some of the key measures that were taken in response to the COVID-19 pandemic to constrain people's movement. In so doing, it highlights the capacity of international, national, state, and local law to constitute borders and regulate people's movement across them.[4] Naturally occurring geographical boundaries—for instance, the water that surrounds an island-continent such as Australia and countries in the Pacific—can demarcate an area as separate. Communities also construct physical borders, exemplified by walls built around cities. Yet all borders are artifices that acquire significance through human imagination and capacity to include and exclude people through the law. Borders assume particular importance when a community is on guard against a threat such as a contagious disease. In these instances, laws can bring borders into service and make them and the law visible, by designating particular areas as contaminated or uncontaminated, segregating the healthy from the unhealthy, and inhibiting people's liberty to enter, exit, and move through space.[5]

---

[1] David L Heymann and Nahoko Shindo, 'COVID-19: What is Next for Public Health?' (2020) 395(10224) *Lancet* 542, 543–44.
[2] See eg Lance Gable, 'Mass Movement, Business and Property Control Measures' in Scott Burris and others (eds), *Assessing Legal Responses to COVID-19* (Public Health Law Watch 2020) 35.
[3] ibid 34–35.
[4] Robyn Bartel and others, 'Legal Geography: An Australian Perspective' (2013) 51(4) *Geographical Research* 339, 340, 343–45; Luke Bennett and Antonia Layard, 'Legal Geography: Becoming Spatial Detectives' (2015) 9(7) *Geography Compass* 406, 410; Miriam Tedeschi, 'The Body and the Law Across Boundaries During the COVID-19 Pandemic' (2020) 10(2) *Dialogues in Human Geography* 178, 178.
[5] Tedeschi (n 4) 179; Bartel and others (n 4) 341–42; Bennett and Layard (n 4) 408; Alison Bashford, 'At the Border: Contagion, Immigration, Nation' (2002) 33(120) *Australian Historical Studies* 344, 352 (hereafter Bashford, 'At the Border').

In Section II of this chapter, we analyse the border closures that governments in many countries implemented to restrict the movement of their citizens and permanent residents (though citizens and permanent residents of some countries were repatriated). Chapter 5 examines in greater detail some other movement restrictions that were imposed on citizens and permanent residents during the COVID-19 pandemic, namely, isolation and quarantine of individuals who were exposed to or who tested positive to COVID-19, lockdowns and stay-at-home orders, and curfews. Section III of this chapter explores specific measures that have been adopted to inhibit movement into areas where significant numbers of First Nations people live, highlighting the tensions involved in deployment of harsh lockdown measures in relation to these communities. In Section IV, we engage with issues that have arisen at domestic and international levels during the pandemic from inhibiting the movement of members of families where the parents are divorced or separated. In Section V of this chapter, we review the ramifications of the pandemic for applications for extradition of persons charged with criminal offences in other countries and the human rights issues that arise in their being surrendered during a pandemic. In Section VI, we scrutinize the restrictions on non-citizens' freedom of movement during the pandemic, including closure of borders to non-citizens and the impact of such measures on asylum-seekers. Section VII considers the closure of ports to and quarantine of cruise ships during the pandemic.

II. Restrictions on Citizens' and Permanent Residents' Freedom of Movement

In response to COVID-19, many governments and communities restricted the movement of their citizens and permanent residents. They applied existing laws and enacted new legislation and regulations that authorized use of these measures during a public health emergency. From the start of the pandemic, it was clear that the extensive dispersion of COVID-19 was highly probable due to its contagiousness and frequently asymptomatic presentation,[6] and that an effective vaccine would not be available for at least many months. There remains no cure for COVID-19, although, as discussed in Chapter 11, a number of improvements in treatment have been identified and used. Countries introduced various constraints on citizens' and permanent residents' movement to impede or slow the transmission of COVID-19, though their efficacy was not immediately apparent. For instance, in the first few months of the pandemic, Taiwan and Portugal imposed similarly stringent movement restrictions, yet only the former maintained a low

---

[6] Jens Ohlin, 'Pandemics, Quarantines, Utility, and Dignity' (2021) *Michigan State Law Review* 539, 549.

COVID-19 mortality rate.[7] By contrast, Sweden's Public Health Agency merely recommended that citizens and permanent residents limit their movement.[8] Several months after the pandemic began, Sweden had a relatively high death rate per population compared to some other European countries that imposed movement restrictions.[9] Nevertheless, it appears that many of Sweden's inhabitants adhered voluntarily to the recommendations.[10]

As discussed further in Chapter 6, the movement restrictions are among several matters—including the measures that at times have been used to enforce them, and their possible contravention of laws protecting people's freedom of movement—that have generated resistance and legal challenges. Concerns have been raised that certain authorities have used COVID-19 to justify suspensions of citizens' rights, suspensions that they intend to maintain once the pandemic has passed.[11] Especially troubling has been the fact that some movement restrictions have prevented citizens from contesting them. This was the case in Italy, for example, where courts suspended judicial review proceedings during a strict lockdown in the initial phase of the pandemic.[12]

A. Border Closures Restricting Local, Interstate, and International Travel

Many domestic and international laws uphold the freedom of citizens and permanent residents to move within and to leave their countries. In response to

---

[7] Irving Yi-Feng Huang, 'Fighting COVID-19 through Government Initiatives and Collaborative Governance: The Taiwan Experience' (2020) 80(4) *Public Administration Review* 665, 665, 667–69; Vera Lúcia Raposo, 'Portugal: Fighting COVID-19 in the Edge of Europe' (2020)(1S) *BioLaw Journal: Rivista di BioDiritto* 723, 723–26, 729: Raposo speculates that the high COVID-19 mortality rate in Portugal may have been attributable partly to many people's failure to distance physically from one another properly.

[8] Ana Nordberg and Titti Mattsson, 'COVID-19 Pandemic in Sweden: Measures, Policy Approach and Legal and Ethical Debates' (2020) 1 *BioLaw Journal: Rivista di BioDiritto* 731, 733–34, 738.

[9] ibid 738; Guy Davies and Bruno Roeber, 'Sweden Has Avoided a COVID-19 Lockdown so Far: Has its Strategy Worked?' *ABC News* (1 March 2021) <https://abcnews.go.com/International/sweden-avoided-covid-19-lockdown-strategy-worked/story?id=76047258> accessed 21 May 2022.

[10] Nordberg and Mattsson (n 8) 736.

[11] Klaus Dodds and others, 'The COVID-19 Pandemic: Territorial, Political and Governance Dimensions of the Crisis' (2020) 8(3) *Territory, Politics, Governance* 289, 292–93.

[12] Christos Kypraios, 'Italy' in Bonavero Institute of Human Rights, *A Preliminary Human Rights Assessment of Legislative and Regulatory Responses to the COVID-19 Pandemic Across 11 Jurisdictions* (Bonavero Report No 3/2020, 6 May 2020) 60. This was not the case in some other countries, such as New Zealand, where remote online court hearings were conducted: Lisa Hsin, 'New Zealand' in Bonavero Institute of Human Rights, *A Preliminary Human Rights Assessment of Legislative and Regulatory Responses to the COVID-19 Pandemic Across 11 Jurisdictions* (Bonavero Report No 3/2020, 6 May 2020) 66; and Brazil: Renato M Sátiro, Jessica V Martins, and Marcos de Moraes Sousa, 'The Courts in the Face of the COVID-19 Crisis: An Analysis of the Measures Adopted by the Brazilian Judicial System' (2021) 12(2) *International Journal for Court Administration* 10; João Biehl, Lucas EA Prates, and Joseph J Amon, 'Supreme Court v Necropolitics: The Chaotic Judicialization of COVID-19 in Brazil' (2021) 23(1) *Health and Human Rights Journal* 151. See also Chapter 8, Section III.

COVID-19, however, border closures have prevented citizens and permanent residents from departing from and entering local areas (such as a Spanish community), larger regions (such as China's Hubei province), and states (such as Victoria and New South Wales in Australia), that had high numbers of COVID-19 infections, and from travelling overseas.[13] Other jurisdictions, such as island nations in the Pacific, imposed border restrictions over a lengthy period in an attempt to insulate themselves from the virus, albeit at a major cost to their economies.[14] In imposing these constraints, governments sought to rely on their authority to protect the health of their inhabitants. However, as discussed in Chapter 6, some protests against and challenges to these constraints have questioned whether this authority constituted a legitimate justification for governments' infringements of protections of citizens' and permanent residents' liberty.

Though pertaining to their own citizens and permanent residents, countries' prohibitions on domestic and international travel potentially contravened their international legal obligations.[15] In imposing these bans, countries engaged Article 12 of the *International Covenant on Civil and Political Rights* (*ICCPR*),[16] which provides that 'everyone lawfully within the territory of a State shall, within that territory, have the right to liberty of movement and freedom to choose his residence', and 'everyone shall be free to leave any country, including his own'. The *ICCPR* permits a qualification on the breadth of this protection: these 'rights' may 'be subject to ... restrictions ... which are provided by law, are necessary to protect ... public health', and are 'are consistent with the other rights recognized' in the *ICCPR*.[17] The

---

[13] Ohlin (n 6) 547, 551; Kate Ogg, 'COVID-19 Travel Bans: The Right to Seek Asylum When You Cannot Leave Your Homeland' (Kaldor Centre for International Refugee Law, 16 April 2020) <www.kaldorcentre.unsw.edu.au/publication/covid-19-travel-bans-right-seek-asylum-when-you-cannot-leave-your-homeland> accessed 3 December 2021; 'Australia's State by State Coronavirus Lockdown Rules and Restrictions Explained' *The Guardian* (20 October 2020) <www.theguardian.com/australia-news/2020/oct/20/australia-covid-19-lockdown-rules-coronavirus-restrictions-by-state-how-far-can-travel-interstate-border-social-distancing-nsw-victoria-vic-queensland-qld-wa-sa-act-how-many-people-over-house> accessed 26 October 2020 (hereafter Australia's State).

[14] See Amy Remeikis, 'Pacific Nations Face "Lost Decade" Due to Economic Cost of COVID' *The Guardian* (29 September 2021) <www.theguardian.com/world/2021/sep/29/pacific-nations-face-lost-decade-due-to-economic-cost-of-covid> accessed 1 December 2021; Walter L Filho and others, 'Coronavirus: COVID-19 Transmission in Pacific Small Island Developing States' (2020) 17(15) *International Journal of Environmental Research and Public Health* art 5409; Cendra Clark and others, 'US-Affiliated Pacific Island Responses to COVID-19: Keys to Success and Important Lessons' (2022) 28(1) *Journal of Public Health Management & Practice* 10; Bernadette Carreon, 'Fear and Dread: Covid-free for Two Years: Pacific Islands Experience Explosion in Case Numbers' *The Guardian* (29 January 2022) <https://www.theguardian.com/world/2022/jan/29/fear-and-dread-covid-free-for-two-years-pacific-islands-experience-explosion-in-case-numbers> accessed 21 May 2022.

[15] Ogg (n 13).

[16] Lionel Nichols, 'Australia' in Bonavero Institute of Human Rights, *A Preliminary Human Rights Assessment of Legislative and Regulatory Responses to the COVID-19 Pandemic Across 11 Jurisdictions* (Bonavero Report No 3/2020, 6 May 2020) 26; International Covenant on Civil and Political Rights (opened for signature 16 December 1966, entered into force 23 March 1976) 999 UNTS 171, Articles 12(1)–(2) (hereafter *ICCPR*).

[17] *ICCPR* (n 16) Article 12(3); Office of the High Commissioner for Human Rights, 'CCPR General Comment No. 27: Article 12 (Freedom of Movement)' (adopted 2 November 1999, 67th Session CCPR/C/21/Rev.1/Add.9) (hereafter OHCHR, 'CCPR General Comment No. 27').

United Nations Human Rights Committee (UNHRC), which monitors State parties' implementation of the *ICCPR*,[18] clarified that this limitation will only apply if movement restrictions are 'proportionate to the interest to be protected' and constitute 'the least intrusive instrument amongst those which might achieve the desired result'.[19]

It has been argued that prohibiting citizens' and permanent residents' local, interstate, and international travel was probably not the least intrusive available measure to prevent or delay the spread of COVID-19.[20] For instance, authorities could have tested people (such as with rapid antigen testing) to ascertain whether they tested positive for COVID-19 before or after they moved across borders, isolated those who tested positive, and quarantined those who had or may have been exposed to the disease.[21] In light of these options, and especially if border closures and travel bans were maintained after COVID-19 had already spread to areas that were imposing them, it has also been questioned whether they were necessary to protect public health and proportionate to that interest.[22]

Border closures and travel bans might nonetheless be regarded as consistent with the 'inherent right to life', which is also recognized in the *ICCPR*, if they prevent people from contracting and dying from a pandemic such as COVID-19.[23] Yet the travel bans may also have violated this right, and also the *ICCPR*'s provision that 'no one shall be subjected to torture or to cruel, inhuman or degrading treatment or punishment', if they prevented people from leaving their own country in which they suffered from persecution.[24] These restrictions might have breached the *Universal Declaration of Human Rights*, too, which provides that '[e]veryone has the right to seek and to enjoy in other countries asylum from persecution';[25] people can only claim international protection once they are outside their country of origin or place of habitual residence.[26] These issues reveal the complexities of intersecting (and sometimes conflicting) rights in the context of a global public health emergency.

---

[18] United Nations Human Rights Office of the High Commissioner, 'Monitoring Civil and Political Rights' <www.ohchr.org/en/hrbodies/ccpr/pages/ccprindex.aspx#:~:text=The%20Human%20Rights%20Committee%20is,the%20rights%20are%20being%20implemented> accessed 26 October 2020.
[19] OHCHR, 'CCPR General Comment No. 27' (n 17).
[20] Ogg (n 13).
[21] ibid.
[22] ibid; Barbara von Tigerstrom and Kumanan Wilson, 'COVID-19 Travel Restrictions and the International Health Regulations (2005)' (2020) 5(5) *BMJ Global Health* art e002629, 2–3.
[23] Ogg (n 13); *ICCPR* (n 16) Article 6(1). Indeed, for the same reason, such measures may also have been justified as 'necessary for ... the prevention, treatment and control of [an] epidemic' disease and thus as 'steps ... taken' to 'achieve the full realization' of people's 'right ... to the enjoyment of the highest attainable standard of physical and mental health', which is recognized by the *International Covenant on Economic, Social and Cultural Rights* (opened for signature 16 December 1966, entered into force 3 January 1976) 993 UNTS 3, Articles 12(1), (2)(c) (hereafter *ICESCR*).
[24] Ogg (n 13); *ICCPR* (n 16) Article 7.
[25] United Nations General Assembly, *Universal Declaration of Human Rights* (Resolution A/RES/3/217A, 10 December 1948) Article 14.
[26] Ogg (n 13).

To justify their restrictions on citizens' and permanent residents' movement that would otherwise have contravened their obligations under the *ICCPR*, several countries relied on their permitted derogation from them (rather than the permitted limitation of the *ICCPR*'s protection).[27] The *ICCPR* allows such a derogation 'in time of public emergency which threatens the life of the nation ... to the extent strictly required by the exigencies of the situation, provided that such measures are not inconsistent with their other obligations under international law' and are non-discriminatory.[28] The UNHRC implied that, 'in confronting this pandemic' and 'the threat of widespread contagion', countries' restrictions on their citizens' and permanent residents' movement could constitute a legitimate derogation from their obligations under the *ICCPR* where they were used 'to protect the right to life and health of all individuals within their territory'.[29] Yet the UNHRC also emphasized that the constraints should be 'proportional in nature', 'limited in duration', and, 'where possible', 'replaced' with 'less restrictive measures that allow' the conduct of 'activities relative to the enjoyment of rights under' the *ICCPR*.[30] Further, movement restrictions that prevented people from leaving a country in which they experienced persecution were not permitted (the *ICCPR*'s protection of the right to life and prohibition of torture or cruel, inhuman or degrading treatment or punishment are non-derogable even during a public emergency).[31] Only some countries that closed borders to and imposed travel bans on their citizens and permanent residents complied with the requirement of the *ICCPR* to notify the United Nations Secretary-General of their derogation from this Covenant and their reasons for the derogation.[32]

Countries' prohibitions of their citizens' and permanent residents' travel also contradicted Temporary Recommendations issued by the World Health Organization (WHO) under the *International Health Regulations (2005)* (*IHR (2005)*) on 30 January 2020, the same day that it declared COVID-19 a public health emergency of international concern (PHEIC).[33] Those recommendations are non-binding, and countries are permitted to implement measures in response to a PHEIC that 'achieve the same or greater level of health protection than' them.[34]

---

[27] ibid; United Nations Human Rights Committee, 'Statement on Derogations From the Covenant in Connection With the COVID-19 Pandemic' (30 April 2020, CCPR/C/128/2) <www.ohchr.org/Docume nts/HRBodies/CCPR/COVIDstatementEN.pdf> (hereafter UNHRC, 'Statement on Derogations').
[28] *ICCPR* (n 16) Article 4(1).
[29] UNHRC, 'Statement on Derogations' (n 27).
[30] ibid.
[31] ibid.
[32] ibid; *ICCPR* (n 16) Article 4(3).
[33] World Health Organization, 'Statement on the second meeting of the International Health Regulations (2005) Emergency Committee regarding the outbreak of novel coronavirus (2019-nCoV)' (30 January 2020) <www.who.int/news/item/30-01-2020-statement-on-the-second-meeting-of-the-international-health-regulations-(2005)-emergency-committee-regarding-the-outbreak-of-novel-coronavirus-(2019-ncov)> accessed 26 October 2020.
[34] World Health Organization, *International Health Regulations (2005)* (3rd edn, World Health Organization 2016) (hereafter *IHR (2005)*) Articles 1 (definition of 'temporary recommendation'), 43(1).

However, countries must base their determinations whether to do so on 'scientific principles', 'available scientific evidence of a risk to human health, or where such evidence is insufficient, the available information including from WHO'.[35] That said, as Burrage J in *Taylor v Newfoundland and Labrador*[36] observed:

> In the context of such a public health emergency, with emergent and rapidly evolving developments, the time for seeking out and analyzing evidence shrinks. Where the goal is to avert serious injury or death, the margin for error may be narrow. In such a circumstance, the response does not admit of surgical precision. Rather, in public health decision making the "precautionary principle" supports the case for action before confirmatory evidence is available.

As Rangiah J in the Federal Court of Australia found, too, in an early hearing in the matter of *Palmer v State of Western Australia*, a case discussed further in Chapter 6, at least some health professionals with expertise in epidemiology and microbiology consider that border closures and travel bans can help reduce the potential for COVID-19 to be imported into an area that still has no community transmission of it.[37] Closing borders to an area that is already experiencing community transmission of COVID-19 might be less justifiable scientifically,[38] especially after the advent of vaccines and high levels of double vaccination. In any event, WHO changed its advice in April 2020 and supported movement restrictions; it listed as a 'global strategic objective' '[suppressing] community transmission through ... appropriate and proportionate restrictions on non-essential domestic and international travel'.[39]

Even if measures implemented in response to a PHEIC achieve the same or a greater level of health protection than WHO recommendations, they must still be 'consistent with' the *IHR (2005)*.[40] Therefore, they must not be 'more invasive or intrusive to persons than reasonably available alternatives that would achieve the appropriate level of health protection'.[41] It has been argued that, when authorities were striving to impede community transmission of COVID-19 (rather than prevent its introduction to communities), other less invasive measures than border closures and travel bans, such as testing, social distancing, contact tracing, isolation, and quarantine, might have helped to protect public health sufficiently.[42] In

---

[35] ibid Article 43(2).
[36] 2020 NLSC 125 [411]. See too *Grounded Kiwis Group Incorporated v Minister of Health* [2022] NZHC 832 [345]–[364].
[37] *Palmer v State of Western Australia (No 3)* [2020] FCA 1220 [48], [56], [58], [61], [151], [156], [366].
[38] von Tigerstrom and Wilson (n 22) 2–3.
[39] World Health Organization, 'COVID-19 Strategy Update' (14 April 2020) <www.who.int/docs/default-source/coronaviruse/covid-strategy-update-14april2020.pdf?sfvrsn=29da3ba0_19> accessed 3 December 2021.
[40] *IHR (2005)* (n 34) Article 43(1).
[41] ibid.
[42] Benjamin Mason Meier, Roojin Habibi, and Y Tony Yang, 'Travel Restrictions Violate International Law' (2020) 367(6485) *Science* 1436.

addition, by 7 February 2020, at least 49 countries appeared to have contravened the requirements in the *IHR (2005)* to notify WHO of their implementation of movement restrictions that 'significantly interfere[d] with international traffic', and of 'the public health rationale and relevant scientific information for' them.[43]

B. Repatriation of Citizens and Permanent Residents

Despite closing their borders to international travellers, in the early phase of the pandemic, many countries permitted and facilitated the return of their citizens and permanent residents who were living elsewhere.[44] In so doing, they complied with domestic and international human rights instruments that recognize people's 'right to return' to their country of origin or residence as a component of the right to freedom of movement.[45] Article 12(4) of the *ICCPR*, for instance, provides that 'no one shall be arbitrarily deprived of the right to enter his own country'.

The Canadian government was atypical in requiring its citizens and permanent residents to undergo health checks before permitting their repatriation.[46] Concerns were raised that this measure did not constitute a permitted limitation of Canadian citizens' right to 'enter Canada', which is protected in the *Canadian Charter of Rights and Freedoms*, on the basis that, while 'prescribed by law', it was not 'reasonable' and could not 'be demonstrably justified in a free and democratic society', as required by this Charter.[47] An interim order made under the *Aeronautics Act 1985* (Canada) required air carriers to conduct the health assessments and ban people from boarding aeroplanes travelling to Canada if they exhibited COVID-19 symptoms.[48] Particularly given that airline representatives were not necessarily medically trained, this measure could have prevented the repatriation of Canadians whose symptoms reflected conditions other than COVID-19, while permitting the re-entry to Canada of people who had COVID-19, but were asymptomatic.[49] Further, other measures could have been undertaken to prevent any repatriated citizens and permanent residents from transmitting COVID-19 to Canada, such as testing, isolation, and quarantine.[50]

---

[43] *IHR (2005)* (n 34) Articles 43(3), (5); World Health Organization, 'Novel Coronavirus (2019-nCoV) Situation Report—18' (7 February 2020) <https://www.who.int/docs/default-source/coronaviruse/situation-reports/20200207-sitrep-18-ncov.pdf> accessed 7 May 2022.

[44] Yves Le Bouthillier and Delphine Nakache, 'The Right of Citizens Abroad to Return During a Pandemic' in Colleen M Flood and others (eds), *Vulnerable: The Law, Policy and Ethics of COVID-19* (University of Ottawa Press 2020) 300, 305.

[45] ibid 300–301.
[46] ibid 306.
[47] ibid 506–507; *Constitution Act 1982* (Canada) ss 1, 6(1).
[48] Le Bouthillier and Nakache (n 44) 304–306.
[49] ibid 307.
[50] ibid 307–308.

Some countries, such as Morocco, Pakistan, and India, had ratified the *ICCPR*, but neglected, at least initially, to repatriate their citizens and permanent residents who were stranded in other countries.[51] Although the permissible limitation on protection of rights under Article 12 of the *ICCPR* does not apply to the right of return, derogation from this obligation is allowed in the circumstances outlined above, including where the derogation is necessary, proportionate, and consistent with other international legal obligations.[52] Yet, in light of alternative health measures that they could have implemented, countries' prevention of their citizens and permanent residents from returning might not have been necessary to prevent, or proportionate to the risk of, the transmission of COVID-19. Indeed, the UNHRC has confirmed that 'there are few, if any, circumstances in which deprivation of the right to enter one's own country could be reasonable'.[53] Further, if their citizens and permanent residents were at greater risk of contracting and dying from COVID-19 in the places in which they were living, denying them the opportunity to return may have been inconsistent with those countries' international legal obligations to protect the right to life under the *ICCPR*, and the right 'to the enjoyment of the highest attainable standard of . . . health' under the *International Covenant on Economic, Social and Cultural Rights*.[54]

III. Closure and Patrolling of Borders to Indigenous Communities

From the beginning of the pandemic, it was widely recognized that Indigenous communities could be particularly susceptible to contracting and experiencing poor health outcomes from COVID-19, as occurred during previous epidemics.[55] This was exacerbated by reliance on short-term or fly-in, fly-out/drive-in, drive-out staff, particularly remote area nurses.[56]

---

[51] Samir Bennis, 'Morocco Should Move to Repatriate Moroccans Stranded Overseas' *Morocco World News* (19 April 2020) <www.moroccoworldnews.com/2020/04/300036/morocco-should-moveto-repatriate-moroccans-stranded-overseas>; Dodds and others (n 11) 290.

[52] Le Bouthillier and Nakache (n 44) 301–303.

[53] UNHRC, 'Statement on Derogations' (n 27).

[54] *ICCPR* (n 16) Article 6(1); *ICESCR* (n 23) Article 12(1).

[55] United Nations Department of Economic and Social Affairs: Indigenous Peoples, 'COVID-19 and Indigenous Peoples' <www.un.org/development/desa/indigenouspeoples/covid-19.html> accessed 9 September 2022; Aimee Craft, Deborah McGregor, and Jeffery Hewitt, 'COVID-19 and First Nations' Responses' in Colleen M Flood and others (eds), *Vulnerable: The Law, Policy and Ethics of COVID-19* (University of Ottawa Press 2020) 58; Nichols (n 16) 28, 32; Kristy Crooks, Dawn Casey, and James S Ward, 'First Nations People Leading the Way in COVID-19 Pandemic Planning, Response and Management' (2020) 213(4) *Medical Journal of Australia* 151, 152; Aryati Yashadhana and others, 'Indigenous Australians at Increased Risk of COVID-19 Due to Existing Health and Socioeconomic Inequities' (2000) 1 *Lancet Regional Health Western Pacific* art 100007.

[56] See Michelle S Fitts and others, 'Health Service Vulnerabilities and Responses to the COVID-19 Pandemic' (2020) 28(6) *Australian Journal of Rural Health* 613, 614.

An especial risk was posed to Indigenous elders, whose health was vulnerable by reason of their age. Their premature passing had cultural implications for their communities given the elders' role in preserving and transmitting long-held knowledge and practices—they are often the last remaining bastions of traditional knowledge and have an important role teaching and transmitting information about conservation of biodiversity, customary law, and Indigenous languages to the next generations.[57] Disease outbreaks affect men and women differently, too, and pandemics have a tendency to deepen existing inequalities and discrimination:

> Indigenous women are over-represented in vulnerable and underpaid sectors, as daily wage earners, farmers, small business owners, domestic workers, cashiers, catering or hospitality service providers, largely within the informal economy. Indigenous women are also likely to be the caretakers of children, elderly parents and extended family members.[58]

The legacy of colonialism and removal of Indigenous people's land and resources from them has been their disproportionate economic and social disadvantage, increased risk of ill health, and inadequate access to healthcare.[59] During the COVID-19 pandemic, where they inhabited overcrowded and unhygienic accommodation, Indigenous peoples had difficulty physically distancing and isolating and quarantining individuals, as well as undertaking sanitary measures such as frequent handwashing.[60] Accurately recording data about rates of infection and of death among First Nations peoples has emerged as an important responsibility of government.[61]

The Food and Agriculture Organization of the United Nations (FAO) urged governments to take specific measures to ensure respect for Indigenous peoples' rights during the pandemic, including adopting an intercultural response when dealing with the emergency, safety, and health aspects of the response.[62] Based on the *United Nations Declaration on the Rights of Indigenous Peoples*,[63] the FAO

---

[57] United Nations Department of Economic and Social Affairs, 'The Impact of COVID-19 on Indigenous Peoples' Policy Brief No 70 (May 2020) 2 <www.un.org/development/desa/dpad/wp-content/uploads/sites/45/publication/PB_70.pdf> accessed 22 October 2021.

[58] ibid.

[59] Nichols (n 16) 28; Craft, McGregor, and Hewitt (n 55) 50–51, 53–54, 58; Tony Kirby, 'Evidence Mounts on the Disproportionate Effect of COVID-19 on Ethnic Minorities' (2020) 8(6) *Lancet Respiratory Medicine* 547, 548.

[60] Nichols (n 16) 28; Craft, McGregor, and Hewitt (n 55) 54, 56; Kirby (n 59) 548.

[61] See Stephanie R Carroll and others, 'Indigenous Peoples' Data During COVID-19 – External to Internal' (2021) 6 *Frontiers in Sociology* art 617895. For further discussion see Chapter 7.

[62] Food and Agriculture Organization of the United Nations, 'Indigenous Peoples' Health and Safety at Risk Due to Coronavirus (COVID-19)' <www.fao.org/indigenous-peoples/covid-19/en/> accessed 10 September 2022.

[63] United Nations General Assembly, *United Nations Declaration on the Rights of Indigenous Peoples* (Resolution A/RES/61/295, 13 September 2007) <www.un.org/development/desa/indigenouspeoples/wp-content/uploads/sites/19/2018/11/UNDRIP_E_web.pdf> accessed 10 September 2022.

Indigenous Persons Unit advanced a series of recommendations, including the following that pertain to movement restrictions:

8. FAO calls to not implement any policy, programme or intervention that affects indigenous peoples without obtaining previously their Free, Prior and Informed Consent.
9. The right of Indigenous Peoples to be or remain in Voluntary Isolation must be respected.
10. Several Indigenous Peoples communities have self-imposed quarantine and have established controls to limit access to their communities. These mechanisms should be respected and reinforced whenever requested.
11. FAO urges Governments to intensify protection measures to stop external farmers, settlers, private firms, industries and miners from entering indigenous peoples' territories taking advantage of the present crisis.
12. FAO has always been urging governments to stop any planned or ongoing evictions of indigenous peoples. Its call is renewed and heightened given the context of the health emergency for COVID-19.[64]

In the initial phase of the pandemic, several authorities closed the borders to Indigenous communities to prevent the transmission of COVID-19 to these communities. For instance, in Australia, the Western Australian Commissioner of Police and State Emergency Coordinator issued directions under the *Emergency Management Act 2005* (WA) to 'limit the spread of COVID-19 to protect vulnerable Aboriginal people in Remote Aboriginal Communities' (as requested by their leaders).[65] The directions restricted the people who could enter the communities' land or water (largely to those who normally resided or worked there or sought to provide medical care, goods, and services) and excluded from the communities people with COVID-19 symptoms.[66] Protocols were created for the government-funded transfer of any people who had COVID-19 and their contacts from the communities to regional centres.[67] Breach of the directions was an offence punishable by a fine.[68] The close involvement of Indigenous leaders throughout Australia in developing public health measures proved very successful at first in protecting Indigenous communities.[69] However, by the latter part of 2021, COVID-19 had penetrated some Indigenous communities in both the Northern Territory and

---

[64] Food and Agriculture Organization of the United Nations (n 62).
[65] *Remote Aboriginal Communities Directions (No 3)* (WA) cl 1 (hereafter 'Directions'); Kirby (n 59) 548.
[66] Directions (n 65) cls 5, 15.
[67] Kirby (n 59) 548.
[68] Directions (n 65).
[69] See Fiona Stanley and others, 'First Nations Health During the COVID-19 Pandemic—Reversing the Gap' in Belinda Bennett and Ian Freckelton (eds), *Pandemics, Public Health Emergencies and Government Powers: Perspectives on Australian Law* (Federation Press 2021).

New South Wales.[70] Rigorous measures were adopted in remote communities with townspeople precluded even from shopping for essentials or going for a walk, and persons who tested positive for COVID-19 being taken with assistance from the Australian Army to a quarantine facility outside Darwin in an attempt to arrest the spread of the virus.[71] Involvement of armed forces and allegations of the use of force were particularly culturally sensitive in light of the 'Stolen Generation' abuses whereby the government had removed Indigenous persons from their families.[72]

In Brazil, the Coalition of Indigenous Peoples of Brazil and others successfully applied for an injunction (initially granted by Justice Luis Roberto Barroso and ratified by a plenary decision of the Supremo Tribunal Federal) to compel the federal government to adopt measures to protect Indigenous peoples who had limited or no interaction with external society from COVID-19, including by erecting sanitary barriers isolating their lands.[73] The Supremo Tribunal Federal took into account the protection of rights to life and health by the Constitution of the Federative Republic of Brazil, and guidelines of the United Nations High Commissariat and the Inter-American Commission on Human Rights, which recognized that 'territorial isolation' was 'the most effective mechanism to protect' these communities' 'life and health' during a pandemic.[74] The Supremo Tribunal Federal also held that the option for these Indigenous people to remain isolated is a right, based on their right to self-determination, that the State is required to enforce, pursuant to the *Indigenous and Tribal Peoples Convention 1989* (No. 169) of the International Labour Organization.[75]

To prevent the spread of COVID-19 to their communities, Canadian and United States Indigenous groups closed and patrolled their borders themselves, but these actions were frequently challenged.[76] Several Canadian First Nations declared a state of emergency, enacted 'disease emergency' bylaws that confined access to

---

[70] See Sam McPhee, 'Inside the Town with the World's Strictest Lockdown' *Daily Mail Australia* (25 November 2021) <www.dailymail.co.uk/news/article-10237761/Covid-Australia-Outbreak-Indigenous-Northern-Territory-communities-spark-toughest-lockdown.html> accessed 9 September 2022; Nakari Thorpe, 'COVID-19 Cases Are Falling Across NSW But New Infections Emerging in Indigenous Communities' *ABC News* (27 October 2021) <www.abc.net.au/news/2021-10-27/covid-19-cases-still-impacting-indigenous-population/100570000> accessed 9 September 2022.

[71] See McPhee (n 70); Kassia Byrnes, '"Very Scared": What is Happening in NT's Remote Communities' *News.com.au* (24 November 2021) <www.news.com.au/national/northern-territory/very-scared-what-is-happening-in-nts-remote-communities/news-story/da0e1668c5b41c20b7bc3ead581d19e4> accessed 10 September 2022.

[72] See McPhee (n 70); Byrnes (n 71).

[73] 'STF Endorses Measures to Fight Covid-19 on Indigenous Lands: Summary of the Decision' *Federal Supreme Court* (8 May 2020) <www.stf.jus.br/repositorio/cms/portalStfInternacional/portalStfDestaque_en_us/anexo/STFdecisionindigenouspeoplesCovid.pdf> accessed 25 November 2021.

[74] ibid.

[75] ibid.

[76] In relation to the Inuit, see Andrey N Petrov and others, 'Lessons on COVID-19 from Indigenous and Remote Communities of the Arctic' (2021) 27(9) *Nature Medicine* 1491; Arctic Council, 'The Impact of COVID-19 on Inuit Communities' (16 July 2020) <https://arctic-council.org/news/the-impact-of-covid-19-on-inuit-communities/> accessed 30 November 2021.

their territories to residents, and established checkpoints to their communities.[77] People who rented cottages within First Nations' territories under leases that indicated they were 'seasonal residents' objected to the restrictions, and they and other non-residents seeking to purchase tobacco visited the communities.[78] In addition, Manitoba Hydro filed an injunction against First Nations that had constructed blockades to prevent Manitoba Hydro implementing a shift change of over 1,000 workers from other jurisdictions, which the First Nations feared would lead to the transmission of COVID-19 to their communities.[79] (The First Nations eventually agreed to remove the blockades in exchange for Manitoba Hydro minimizing its work and suspending travel to and from the construction site).[80]

The legality of the First Nations' restrictions on the movement of people who were not residents of their communities was unclear.[81] In taking these actions, they relied on the *Indian Act 1985* (Canada), which empowers them to enact bylaws, their inherent jurisdiction based on their 'unceded title to their traditional territories', and their sovereign right of self-determination, enshrined in the United Nations *Declaration on the Rights of Indigenous Peoples*.[82] Nevertheless, British Columbia is the only Canadian province to have passed legislation implementing this declaration.[83] Further, the First Nations' restrictions could be interpreted as contravening clause 6 of the *Canadian Charter of Rights and Freedoms* that recognizes the 'right' of Canadian citizens 'to move to and take up residence in any province'.[84] Clause 25 of this Charter nonetheless also states that its guarantee of rights cannot 'be construed so as to abrogate or derogate from any aboriginal, treaty or other rights or freedoms that pertain to the aboriginal peoples of Canada'.[85]

In the initial phase of the pandemic, the authority of Native American tribes in the United States to close their reservations to non-residents for non-essential travel was also challenged, as was the construction of roadblocks and checkpoints at entrances to their communities to enforce the restrictions.[86] The United States

---

[77] Craft, McGregor, and Hewitt (n 55) 59–63.
[78] ibid 60–62.
[79] ibid 64–65.
[80] Amber McGuckin, 'Deal Struck Between 4 First Nations and Manitoba Hydro to End Blockades' *Global News* (24 May 2020) <https://globalnews.ca/news/6980881/coronavirus-manitoba-hydro-4-first-nations-blockades/#:~:text=Deal%20struck%20between%204%20First%20Nations%20and%20Manitoba%20Hydro%20to%20end%20blockades,-By%20Amber%20McGuckin&text=An%20agreement%20has%20been%20reached,Manitoba%20Keewatinowi%20Okimakanak%20(MKO)> accessed 25 November 2021.
[81] Craft, McGregor, and Hewitt (n 55) 61.
[82] ibid 59.
[83] ibid 65.
[84] ibid 61.
[85] ibid.
[86] Katherine Florey, 'Toward Tribal Regulatory Sovereignty in the Wake of the COVID-19 Pandemic' (2021) 63(2) *Arizona Law Review* 399, 400–408, 419–20; Lindsey Schneider, Joshua Sbicca, and Stephanie Malin, 'Native American Tribes' Pandemic Response is Hamstrung by Many Inequities' *The Conversation* (1 June 2020) <https://theconversation.com/native-american-tribes-pandemic-response-is-hamstrung-by-many-inequities-136225> accessed 26 September 2021.

Supreme Court in the 1981 case of *Montana v United States* held that tribes have regulatory jurisdiction only over their formally enrolled members (and not over non-members even if they are residents of their reservation), except in certain circumstances, including where non-members' conduct 'threatens ... the health or welfare of the tribe'.[87] Courts have interpreted this exception narrowly to apply to regulations that are 'necessary to avert catastrophic consequences', such as circumstances that threaten the community's existence.[88] Although this exception would seem to apply to COVID-19, no case law has confirmed the actions that tribes are permitted to take during pandemics.[89]

Even if Native American tribes are authorized to establish border controls and checkpoints to protect their communities from COVID-19, they depend on governments to restrict travel in areas over which they do not have control.[90] This cooperation was not always forthcoming in the initial phase of the pandemic. For instance, the South Dakota Governor is reported as having threatened that the State would sue the Oglala Lakota Nation if it did not remove checkpoints it had established on state and federal highways that passed through its territory.[91]

IV. The Impact of Movement Restrictions on Families with Separated Parents

The closure of borders to states, lockdowns, and travel bans in the initial phase of the pandemic prevented the fulfilment of some families' pre-existing and desired shared parenting arrangements.[92] Some children were unable to move between their parents' residences, as required by parenting arrangements (often prescribed by court orders), if they were located in different jurisdictions whose borders to one another were closed, travel between those areas was prohibited, or one or both of their residences were located in areas that were subject to lockdowns.[93] The movement restrictions also disrupted some parents' plans to relocate to other jurisdictions, if the new arrangements would prevent children from visiting their other

---

[87] 450 US 544, 566 (1981); Florey (n 86) 404–405.
[88] Florey (n 86) 405.
[89] ibid 8–9.
[90] ibid 23.
[91] ibid; Nina Lakhani, 'South Dakota Governor Threatens to Sue Over Sioux's Coronavirus Roadblocks' *The Guardian* (14 May 2020) <www.theguardian.com/us-news/2020/may/14/sioux-coronavirus-roadblocks-south-dakota-governor> accessed 9 September 2022.
[92] Family Court of Australia, 'Statement from the Hon Will Alstergren—Parenting Orders and COVID-19' (*Media Release*, 26 March 2020) <www.familycourt.gov.au/wps/wcm/connect/fcoaweb/about/news/mr260320> accessed 27 October 2020; Ian Freckelton, 'COVID-19 and Family Law Decision-Making' (2020) 27(4) *Journal of Law and Medicine* 846, 846; Donna Cooper, 'Post-Separation Parenting During COVID-19' in Belinda Bennett and Ian Freckelton (eds), *Pandemics, Public Health Emergencies and Government Powers: Perspectives on Australian Law* (Federation Press 2021).
[93] Freckelton (n 92) 850.

parent who resided elsewhere.[94] Due to lockdowns, some families also faced difficulties accessing court services to seek to vary their parenting arrangements formally to accommodate the impact of the movement restrictions. Some courts, such as the Family Court of Australia, managed this problem by creating a fast-tracked COVID-19 list for hearing matters that were affected by these circumstances.[95] In the United Kingdom, the government issued guidance as early as March 2020, prompting the President of the Family Division of the High Court to state that the guidance did not mean that children must move between homes, the decision being one for parents to take after assessing their circumstances:

> Government guidance issued alongside the Stay at Home Rules on 23rd March deals specifically with child contact arrangements. It says: 'Where parents do not live in the same household, children under 18 can be moved between their parents' homes.' This establishes an exception to the mandatory 'stay at home' requirement; it does not, however, mean that children must be moved between homes. The decision whether a child is to move between parental homes is for the child's parents to make after a sensible assessment of the circumstances, including the child's present health, the risk of infection and the presence of any recognised vulnerable individuals in one household or the other.[96]

In the case of *Ribeiro v Wright*, which was heard in the Superior Court of Justice of the Canadian province of Ontario, Pazaratz J outlined principles to govern resolution of disputes regarding parenting arrangements during the pandemic, which courts in other countries, including Australia, have applied.[97] Pazaratz J emphasized that '[t]he health, safety and well-being of children and families remains the court's foremost consideration during COVID-19' and 'children's lives—and vitally important family relationships—cannot be placed "on hold" indefinitely without risking serious emotional harm and upset'.[98] Indeed, Pazaratz J noted that 'in troubling and disorienting times, children need the love, guidance and emotional support of *both* parents', so 'a blanket policy that children should never leave their primary residence—even to visit their other parent—is inconsistent with a comprehensive analysis of the best interests of the child'.[99] In light of these observations, Pazaratz J recommended that there should generally be a presumption that people must continue to comply with parental arrangements that were made

---

[94] ibid 854–55.
[95] ibid 849–50.
[96] Andrew McFarlane (President of the Family Division and Head of Family Justice, England and Wales), 'Coronavirus Crisis: Guidance on Compliance with Family Court Child Arrangement Orders' (24 March 2020) <www.judiciary.uk/announcements/coronavirus-crisis-guidance-on-compliance-with-family-court-child-arrangement-orders/> accessed 25 October 2021.
[97] 2020 ONSC 1829 (hereafter *Ribeiro*); Freckelton (n 92) 846.
[98] *Ribeiro* (n 97) [6], [10].
[99] ibid [10].

before the pandemic, subject to modifications, for instance, altering the locations for handing children over to the other parent and/or the terms for supervising parental access to children.[100] In some cases, however, such as if parents are in isolation, children may be unable to spend time with them.[101]

Kardos v Harman is an example of a case in which the Family Court of Australia applied these principles.[102] Court orders issued before the pandemic provided for a child to reside mostly with the mother, who lived in South Australia, and spend four days a month with the father in the Northern Territory.[103] To facilitate these arrangements, the orders required the mother to deliver the child to the father at airports in the Northern Territory or Queensland, and the father to return the child to the mother at an airport in South Australia.[104] The mother became concerned that the child might be exposed to COVID-19 on an interstate aeroplane flight and that border restrictions requiring her and the child to quarantine for 14 days after returning to South Australia would cause her financial problems.[105] McLelland DCJ varied the court orders so that the father could spend time with the child in South Australia.[106] Applying the approach in *Ribeiro v Wright*, McLelland DCJ sought to ensure that all reasonable efforts were made for the child to spend time with both parents, while mitigating the risk of the child contracting COVID-19 from travelling on an aeroplane, which McLelland DCJ regarded as the primary consideration (the border restrictions were a secondary consideration).[107]

Where there can be a major difference in the incidence of COVID-19 cases between one country and another, a court's decision about permitting a child to move from a country with a low incidence of COVID-19 cases to a country with a high incidence of them may be straightforward. In *Nishi v Nishi*,[108] for instance, the Supreme Court of Tonga was required to rule on whether a mother to whom custody of a child had been granted in Tonga should be permitted to take the child with her to England for a year. The application was made in September 2021 at a time when Tonga had experienced no cases of COVID-19 'to go to another where there are very severe problems with the pandemic'.[109] Whitten CJ declined the application, reasoning that in spite of:

> the mother's willingness to expose herself to what she regards as a calculated risk, her confidence or faith in the UK health care system and that Government's

---

[100] ibid [11].
[101] ibid [12].
[102] [2020] FamCA 328 [113]–[117].
[103] ibid [1].
[104] ibid.
[105] ibid [2], [76], [90].
[106] ibid [3].
[107] ibid [113], [118], [121]–[122], [126].
[108] [2021] TOSC 149.
[109] ibid [21].

responses so far, the reality is that, for the child, the choice is between a current zero risk environment in Tonga and a very real risk of exposure to infection in England. The quantification of that risk is impossible other than that ..., for now, it remains very real.[110]

Routinely, courts are asked to order the return of a child to another country under the 1980 *Hague Convention on the Civil Aspects of International Child Abduction (Hague Convention)*.[111] The *Hague Convention* is the main multilateral agreement that deals with the abduction of children from one country to another and provides means for parents to obtain contact with or access to children who are in different countries from them.[112] There are two forms of order—outward return orders, where a court orders a child to be returned to another country,[113] and inward return orders where a court orders a child to be returned from another country. During the COVID-19 pandemic, arguments were advanced by some parents that courts should not order international movement of children to or from any country, even though they may have been abducted.[114]

For instance, in *Re N (a Child)*,[115] Mostyn J was required to make a ruling in relation to a child, N, whose parents' relationship in Greece broke down in 2017. The father travelled to reside in London in 2017 and the mother and N followed in 2018. N became fully integrated into London life, but on 20 March 2020, three days before the British Prime Minister announced a national lockdown, the mother unilaterally relocated N to her mother's home on Paros in the belief that N would be much safer from the virus there.[116] Mostyn J observed that the mother's view may well have been valid, as it was 'common knowledge that by virtue of pre-emptive action Greece has a much lower rate of infection and mortality than this country';[117] yet Mostyn J also considered that this 'does not justify, in the slightest, what was a wrongful removal of N from the place of his habitual residence and, more importantly, from his father'.[118]

---

[110] ibid [22].
[111] *Hague Convention on the Civil Aspects of International Child Abduction* (opened for signature 25 October 1980, entered into force 1 December 1983) 1343 UNTS 89, see Article 1.
[112] See generally Paul R Beaumont and Peter E McEleavy, *The Hague Convention on International Child Abduction* (Oxford University Press 1999); Jeremy D Morley, *The Hague Abduction Convention: Practical Issues and Procedures for Family Lawyers* (2nd edn, American Bar Association 2017); Abubakri Yekini, *The Hague Judgments Convention and Commonwealth Model Law: A Pragmatic Perspective* (Hart 2021).
[113] See eg *Re NY (A Child)* [2019] UKSC 49 [51]–[58].
[114] See eg *Re S (Abduction: Hague Convention or BIIa)* [2018] EWCA Civ 1226 [47]–[49].
[115] [2020] EWFC 35.
[116] ibid [16].
[117] ibid.
[118] ibid.

The father then made an application under the 1980 *Hague Convention* in Greece. He also made an application to the Family Court of England and Wales for an immediate inward return order.[119] Mostyn J observed that:

> The mother attended with complete clarity from Paros. She was assisted by a Greek interpreter in London who also attended the Zoom meeting. There is no doubt that the mother was able to participate far more fully, effectively and fairly by means of the hearing proceeding by Zoom than if it had been a traditional attended hearing in court in London. She would not have been able to attend such a hearing other than, perhaps, by telephone or by (often malfunctioning) video in court (assuming that a Skype bridge to the court equipment could be established).[120]

Mostyn J observed that, even in this time of crisis, the Greek court was 'functioning relatively efficiently' and noted that it should hear any defences advanced by the mother, and '[S]hould they be rejected, and an order made for return to this country, once it is safe to do so, that court is the only court with the actual power to enforce it'.[121] To facilitate the process, Mostyn J made a declaration that N was habitually resident in England and Wales.[122]

Under Article 13(b) of the *Hague Convention*, the judicial or administrative authority of a state is not bound to order the return of an abducted child if the person opposing return establishes that 'there is a grave risk that his or her return would expose the child to physical or psychological harm or otherwise place the child in an intolerable situation'.[123] To enhance the potential for consistent international approaches, in 2020, the Hague Conference on Private International Law published a 'COVID-19 Toolkit',[124] noting that, during the pandemic, the 'grave risk exception' was more than ever likely to be raised to oppose the return of children.[125] However, the overriding considerations of the best interests of the child and a rigorous examination of what is said to constitute the grave risk to the child must be undertaken.[126]

In a number of cases, courts have been hesitant to identify the requisite risk of harm. For instance, in *Re PT*,[127] the High Court of England and Wales dealt with

---

[119] ibid [2].
[120] ibid [20].
[121] ibid [28].
[122] ibid [30].
[123] See generally *BK v NK* [2016] EWHC 2496 (Fam) [45]; *RK v KJ (Child Abduction: Acquiescence)* [2000] 2 IR 416; *Friedrich v Friedrich*, 78 F 3d 1060 (6th Cir 1996).
[124] Hague Conference in Private International Law, 'COVID-19 Toolkit' (2020) <https://assets.hcch.net/docs/538fa32a-3fc8-4aba-8871-7a1175c0868d.pdf> accessed 25 November 2021.
[125] ibid 3.
[126] See eg *C v G (Child Abduction (Poland) Grave Risk Defence)* [2020] IEHC 217 [48] applying the principles set out in *X v Latvia* (2013) 59 EHHR 100 [106]–[107].
[127] [2020] EWHC 834 (Fam).

an abduction of a 12-year-old child from Spain to England. It was argued by the mother that, at that time, the pandemic was further advanced in Spain than in the United Kingdom, PT would be at greater risk of contracting COVID-19 in Spain than in England, and PT would be at particular risk in the course of international air travel.[128] However, while Deputy Judge Rees QC accepted that the travel associated with the return of PT to Spain was likely to increase the risk that she could contract the virus, it was not sufficient to amount to a grave risk of physical harm, so he ordered her return.[129]

By contrast, in *C v G (Child Abduction (Poland): Grave Risk Defence)*,[130] Simons J of the Irish High Court concluded that the return of a child to Poland in May 2020 would have constituted a grave risk that he would have been exposed to physical and psychological harm. He noted that:

> To require a child to engage in international travel during the coronavirus pandemic would expose him to a grave risk of contracting the disease. The Irish government has advised against all unnecessary travel at this time. Indeed, there is no evidence before the court that it would even be possible to travel to Poland at this time. There is no evidence, for example, as to whether there are any commercial flights operating between Ireland and Poland. There is no evidence as to the immigration or quarantine controls, if any being imposed on passengers travelling from Ireland to Poland.[131]

Simons J noted that an order of return would also have had the effect of placing the child's mother in the invidious position of having to choose between accompanying him to Poland, thereby creating a risk to her own health, and having him travel alone to Poland, thereby depriving him of his primary carer at a time of significant change in his life.[132]

By contrast, in *JV v QI*,[133] the Irish Court of Appeal dealt with an appeal against an order that two children aged eight and eleven be returned from Ireland to Belgium over an objection by their mother, who had removed the children from Belgium to Ireland, based on the risks to them if that occurred. The Court found that the children fell into a category of 'reduced risk'.[134] It observed that primary schools were open in both Belgium and Ireland, and that the father was prepared to fly to collect the children and 'remain airside thereby obviating the legal obligation of quarantine'.[135] The Court concluded[136] that, in evaluating the claim

[128] ibid [46].
[129] ibid [47].
[130] [2020] IEHC 217.
[131] ibid [29].
[132] ibid [30].
[133] [2020] IECA 302.
[134] ibid [89].
[135] ibid [89].
[136] ibid [93].

of 'grave risk', it was obligatory for it to have regard to the Preamble to the *Hague Convention*, which states its objective as, amongst other things, 'desiring to protect children internationally from the harmful effect of their wrongful removal or retention and to establish procedures to ensure their prompt return to the State of their habitual residence'.[137] This meant that the bar to retention of the children in the country to which they had been abducted was high. Ultimately, it was held to be necessary to balance 'against hypothetical risks':

> the fact that children are in general acknowledged by experts to be at low risk of contracting Covid-19 and where contracted they normally suffer minor symptoms. Official advice in regard to Covid-19 suggests that most children with Covid-19 have mild symptoms or have no symptoms at all. However, some children can get severely ill from Covid-19. The approach of the trial judge with regard to the issues of grave risk advanced by the mother at the hearing was entirely correct and in accordance with the jurisprudence. In particular, she correctly concluded that there was no factual basis for a fear that either child would come to harm if returned to Belgium.[138]

The Court took into account that 'Travel, including international travel, must necessarily carry or import some element of risk. The necessity for travel has been brought about by the wrongful removal of the children by their mother which took place at a time when the pandemic had not abated'.[139] The Court was satisfied that in the circumstances, insofar as there were concerns surrounding the children's travel arrangements to Belgium, they could be addressed by the father's undertakings.[140] Thus, the decision was consistent with a line of authority that sought to minimize the impact of the pandemic on arrangements involving children, save where orders affecting their place of residence were absolutely necessary for their health and well-being.

V. Extradition

Attempts to curb the spread of COVID-19 have also affected legal requirements for people's movement through their impact on extradition applications and orders. At the heart of applications for extradition of a person from one country to another to face criminal charges is the need for prompt resolution of the issue.[141]

---

[137] ibid.
[138] ibid [95].
[139] ibid [97].
[140] ibid.
[141] See Miguel João Costa, *Extradition Law: Reviewing Grounds for Refusal from the Classic Paradigm to Mutual Recognition and Beyond* (Brill Nijhoff 2019); M Cherif Bassiouni, *International Extradition: United States Law and Practice* (6th edn, Oxford University Press 2016).

During the pandemic, in *Cosar v Governor of HMP Wandsworth*,[142] Irwin LJ and Lewis J of the High Court of England and Wales were required to deal with two applications for extradition. The first applicant was subject to a European arrest warrant (EAW).[143] A district judge had ordered that he be extradited to Romania and remanded him in custody pending extradition.[144] It was necessary for him to be extradited within a period of ten days from the date on which permission was refused or, if the district judge and the judicial authority issuing the EAW agreed on a later date, ten days from that later date.[145] Due to restrictions imposed as a result of COVID-19, it had not been possible to extradite him. The extradition of the second applicant had been ordered and he had been remanded in custody. Two extensions of the extradition period had been agreed to by the district judge. By the time of the appeal, the EAW had been withdrawn and he was no longer in custody but the second applicant submitted that the agreement to extend was unlawful and so his detention during the extension period was unlawful.[146]

Both applicants issued proceedings for habeas corpus, contending that their detention was unlawful. In the alternative, they sought a direction that the application be treated as an application for permission to apply for judicial review of the decisions to agree to extensions of time under Part 87.5(d) of the *Civil Procedure Rules*. Irwin LJ and Lewis J dismissed the applications for habeas corpus, holding that the applicants had been lawfully detained according to the order of the district judge made under section 21(4) of the *Extradition Act 2003* (UK).[147] The first applicant's claim was dismissed on the basis that the district judge had lawfully exercised his power to agree to a later starting date for the extradition period because of the difficulties in extraditing the first applicant due to the restrictions imposed to deal with the COVID-19 pandemic.[148] Lewis J acknowledged that the situation had given rise to serious humanitarian justifications for postponing extradition, noting that surrender may be postponed temporarily. He observed:

> This is a situation where extradition is prevented by circumstances outside the control of the United Kingdom or any member state of the European Union. The need to suspend flights between countries arises because cessation of movement is seen by some countries as one of the few ways capable of contributing to stopping the spread of coronavirus. Romania has suspended flights to prevent people entering the country who may be infected (symptomatically or asymptomatically) with coronavirus and may, therefore, pass the infection to others. The need to take

---

[142] [2020] EWHC 1142 (Admin).
[143] ibid [2].
[144] ibid.
[145] ibid [3].
[146] ibid.
[147] ibid [85].
[148] ibid [56].

such steps to address the situation created by the coronavirus pandemic is entirely beyond the control of any state.

In general terms, therefore, agreeing to extend the period for extradition as a result of the steps taken to stem the coronavirus pandemic is within the purposes permitted both by section 35 of the 2003 Act and Article 23 of the Framework Decision.[149]

A number of diverse challenges to extradition have been mounted during the COVID-19 pandemic. For instance, in *Reyes v United States of America*,[150] Andrea Reyes was taken into custody after a provisional arrest request was made by the United States of America.[151] She was found eligible for surrender and then the Attorney-General of Australia made a determination that Reyes was obliged to surrender in relation to the extradition offences and issued a warrant for that purpose.[152] Section 26(5) of the *Extradition Act 1988* (Cth) requires an order for release once a person is in custody for more than two months after the warrant is liable to be executed, but section 26(6) of that Act allows such an order not to be made if to do so would be 'dangerous to the life or prejudicial to the health of the person' or 'for any other reasonable cause'.

After two months, Ms Reyes had not been conveyed to the United States of America. Australia's Attorney-General asserted that the reason for this failure was circumstances arising from the COVID-19 pandemic, including the restrictions on movement between Australia and the United States and associated health risks for the extradition escort. The judge at first instance accepted this position.[153] The Full Court of the Federal Court of Australia found no error on the part of the first instance judge in concluding that travel by the escorts could not be undertaken without virus-related risk and that this was a plausible reason in the unprecedented times of a pandemic not to release Ms Reyes 'for any other reasonable cause'.[154] In short, the public health risks posed by COVID-19 constituted a reasonable cause to retain Ms Reyes in custody pending her removal to the extraditing country when this became feasible.

A comparable issue was confronted by the Irish Court of Appeal in *Minister for Justice and Equality v Sciuka*,[155] a decision that highlights the importance of the particular phase of a pandemic for decisions in relation to extradition. There had been a delay in surrender of Andrius Sciuka to be extradited to Lithuania to serve the remainder of his sentence for what were held at first instance to be

---

[149] ibid [56]–[57], applying Council Framework Decision, 2002/584/JHA of 13 June 2002 on the European Arrest Warrant and the Surrender Procedures Between Member States [2002] OJ L190/1.
[150] [2020] FCAFC 149.
[151] ibid [1].
[152] ibid [2].
[153] ibid [7].
[154] ibid [20].
[155] [2021] IECA 79.

'humanitarian reasons', including that a danger to Mr Sciuka's life or health would be likely to be occasioned by his surrender.[156] It was contended for Mr Sciuka that the circumstances of the pandemic did not constitute humanitarian reasons and that he should be released. However, the Minister argued that danger to health sufficed to postpone the surrender.[157]

Ultimately, the Court of Appeal affirmed that the public interest in extradition is systematically served by the extradition being carried into effect and, before there is a postponement, it must 'be demonstrated that the humanitarian grounds relied upon were so grave and of such a serious nature, and that the desirability of avoiding the apprehended prejudice is so compelling, as to render postponement [of surrender] the only effective option'.[158] It was argued for Mr Sciuka that the COVID-19 pandemic in certain circumstances could constitute an appropriate evidential basis for postponement of surrender, but that this would only be the case if the person to be extradited had the virus; in the country to which the person was to be extradited there was such an incidence of the virus that it was unsafe to transfer them to prison there; or there was a ban on all travel there due to the spread of the pandemic.[159] The Court of Appeal accepted that the reach of humanitarian grounds covered the COVID-19 pandemic in a general sense and was not restricted to the risk to life or health of the requested individual.[160] It scrutinized whether there were exceptional considerations justifying a delay in surrender and accepted that the diverse circumstances of a pandemic could be taken into account, including uncertainties in its duration and the surging nature of COVID-19: 'It is not a static event, rates of disease can decrease and rates can also increase. Variants of the virus impact on those rates. Therefore what is exceptional today may not have been exceptional at the height of last summer when rates of disease in Ireland (and much of Europe) were very low'.[161] The Court of Appeal took into account that the spread of the virus at the relevant time was such as to cause a shutdown of all flights between Ireland and the United Kingdom and Germany: 'That was exceptional and was without doubt taken in the interest of public health ie because of the risk to life and health'.[162]

The Attorney-General argued that the potential for a private or military flight should be taken into account. However, the Court did not identify any obligation for such a flight to be used to ensure that surrenders take place within a time limit: 'Given that the member states bear these costs, this would be disproportionate to smaller states who would have to hire private planes or use stretched

---

[156] ibid [1].
[157] ibid [16].
[158] ibid [23], quoting Edwards J in *Minister for Justice and Equality v DL* [2011] IEHC 248.
[159] ibid [30].
[160] ibid [32].
[161] ibid [42].
[162] ibid [44].

and expensive military options for each, generally uncontested and safe, surrender via commercial airplane'.[163] The Court affirmed the decision at first instance and concluded that, taking into account the proportionality principle, the evidence established that the serious risk to life and health arising out of the pandemic had led to an exceptional situation where the postponement of the surrender of Mr Sciuka was required in accordance with humanitarian considerations.

VI. Restrictions on Non-Citizens' Freedom of Movement

In the initial phase of the COVID-19 pandemic, many countries closed their borders to one another and denied entry to their territory of people who were not their citizens or permanent residents.[164] While domestic legislation often permitted these movement restrictions, they may have contravened some countries' international legal obligations, especially concerning human rights and treatment of asylum-seekers.[165] At first, some countries, such as South Africa and New Zealand, prohibited from crossing their borders only foreign nationals from countries with a high number of COVID-19 infections or outbreaks.[166] Nevertheless, countries, including the United States of America, continued to impose these restrictions once they, too, had a large number of COVID-19 cases and it was evident that border closures had failed to contain the spread of the virus.[167]

It has been argued that some countries relied on the pandemic to justify imposing movement restrictions that were intended to discriminate against and exclude certain people, rather than to achieve public health objectives.[168] Using borders to delineate who belongs to a nation, and associating those constructed as outsiders to the nation with disease that could compromise its health, are not new phenomena.[169] Countries' claims that they restricted non-citizens' movement to prevent the dispersion of COVID-19 sounded especially hollow when, as discussed, they simultaneously repatriated their citizens and permanent residents, who could also have imported COVID-19.[170] As noted earlier, countries could

---

[163] ibid [50].
[164] von Tigerstrom and Wilson (n 22) 1–2.
[165] Geoff Gilbert, 'Forced Displacement in a Time of a Global Pandemic' in Carla Ferstman and Andrew Fagan (eds), *Covid-19, Law and Human Rights: Essex Dialogues* (School of Law and Human Rights Centre, University of Essex 2020) 167.
[166] Melodie Labuschaigne, 'Ethicolegal Issues Relating to the South African Government's Response to COVID-19' (2020) 13(1) *South African Journal of Bioethics and Law* 23, 23; *Borrowdale v Director-General of Health, Attorney-General, and New Zealand Law Society* [2020] NZHC 2090 [11], [13].
[167] Wendy Parmet, 'Immigration Law's Adverse Impact on COVID-19' in Scott Burris and others (eds), *Assessing Legal Responses to COVID-19* (Public Health Law Watch 2020) 243.
[168] ibid 240.
[169] Alison Bashford, *Imperial Hygiene: A Critical History of Colonialism, Nationalism and Public Health* (Palgrave Macmillan 2004) 115–19; Bashford, 'At the Border' (n 5) 344–45.
[170] Dodds (n 11) 292.

have adopted other measures to minimize the risk of non-citizens transmitting COVID-19 to local populations, such as testing, isolating, and quarantining them.

A. Closure of Borders to Non-Citizens

Countries' closure of their borders to one another in response to COVID-19, even when legally permissible, sometimes created tensions. This was evident in the Schengen Area. The Schengen Agreement provides for the free movement of people between, and removal of border controls by, the 26 European countries that signed it.[171] Contrary to the spirit of this Agreement, in the initial phase of the pandemic, Schengen Member States, including Finland, Hungary, and Norway, temporarily closed their mutual borders.[172] In so doing, they relied on a provision of the Schengen Borders Code that allows Member States to reintroduce internal border control 'for a strictly limited scope and period of time' in 'exceptional circumstances' that involve a 'serious threat to public policy or internal security'.[173] Nevertheless, some Schengen Member States and their citizens objected to the border closures and queried whether they satisfied preconditions for imposing them, namely, that they constituted a 'measure of last resort', and were necessary and proportionate to the perceived threat.[174]

In addition to jeopardizing good relations with their neighbours, some countries' restrictions of non-citizens' movement appeared to reflect a nationalist agenda that was at odds with the collaborative role they were expected to play in the international community during a public health crisis.[175] Several countries seemed to base decisions about whether people could enter their territory on their nationality, and citizenship and immigration status, rather than their exposure to COVID-19 and risk of spreading it.[176] They repatriated their own citizens and

---

[171] 'Difference Between the European Union vs Schengen Area' (*ETIAS*) <www.etiasvisa.com/etias-questions/is-there-difference-between-the-european-union-and-schengen-area> accessed 25 February 2022.

[172] 'Temporary Reintroduction of Border Control' European Commission <https://ec.europa.eu/home-affairs/what-we-do/policies/borders-and-visas/schengen/reintroduction-border-control_en> accessed 10 September 2022.

[173] Regulation (EU) 2016/399 of the European Parliament and of the Council of 9 March 2016 on a Union Code on the Rules Governing the Movement of Persons Across Borders (Schengen Borders Code) cls 22–23.

[174] ibid cls 22–24; Sandor Zsiros, 'Hungary Border Closure Draws Criticism From Brussels' *Euronews* (31 August 2020) <www.euronews.com/2020/08/31/hungary-border-closure-draws-criticism-from-brussels> accessed 10 September 2022; Darren McCaffrey, 'Saving Schengen: Germany Grapples With COVID Crisis Border Closures' *Euronews* (3 September 2020) <www.euronews.com/2020/09/03/saving-schengen-germany-grapples-with-covid-crisis-border-closures> accessed 10 September 2020; 'Border Controls in Schengen due to Coronavirus: What can the EU do?' *News European Parliament* (22 June 2020) <www.europarl.europa.eu/news/en/headlines/security/20200506STO78514/reopening-schengen-borders-after-covid-19-what-can-eu-do> accessed 10 September 2022.

[175] von Tigerstrom and Wilson (n 22) 2.

[176] ibid; Parmet (n 167) 243–44.

permanent residents, as noted previously, while denying non-nationals entry to their territory.[177] In taking these measures, countries deviated from WHO's initial advice (discussed earlier) that it did 'not recommend any travel' restriction, perhaps without scientific grounds for doing so.[178] They also appear to have breached Article 42 of the *IHR (2005)*, which requires countries to apply 'health measures' in a 'non-discriminatory manner'.[179] The complexities of these issues highlight the need for an evaluation in the period following the pandemic of the trade and travel restrictions that were imposed during the pandemic.[180]

The United States federal government in particular has been accused of using COVID-19 as a justification for vigorously pursuing anti-immigration policies that it had initiated before the pandemic.[181] At the beginning of the pandemic, President Donald Trump banned entry to the United States by air, water, or land most non-nationals who had been, in the preceding 14 days, in China, Iran, the Schengen Area, the United Kingdom, Ireland, and/or Brazil.[182] United States citizens and permanent residents were nonetheless permitted to return from those countries, despite their high infection rates.[183] The Department of Homeland Security then ordered immigration officers to prevent from crossing into the United States at ports of entry on its borders with Canada and Mexico anyone who intended to undertake 'non-essential travel'.[184] Returning United States citizens and permanent residents were included amongst those deemed to be undertaking 'essential travel'.[185]

In addition, the United States Centers for Disease Control and Prevention exercised power granted under the *Public Health Service Act* (US) (delegated to it by the Surgeon General) to prohibit 'introduction' to the United States of people from countries with a communicable disease.[186] The Centers for Disease Control and Prevention claimed that, in accordance with this statute, its order was 'required in the interest of the public health' because there was 'a serious danger' of COVID-19 being introduced to the United States, which people entering from those countries would heighten.[187] The Centers for Disease Control and Prevention is empowered

---

[177] Parmet (n 167) 240–41; Ohlin (n 6) 555.
[178] World Health Organization (n 33); von Tigerstrom and Wilson (n 22) 2.
[179] von Tigerstrom and Wilson (n 22) 2.
[180] Kelley Lee and others, 'Global Coordination on Cross-Border Travel and Trade Measures Crucial to COVID-19 Response' (2020) 395(10237) *Lancet* 1593.
[181] Parmet (n 167) 241.
[182] ibid 240; Audrey Singer, 'COVID-19: Restrictions on Travelers at US Land Borders' *Congressional Research Service* (6 July 2020) 2 <https://fas.org/sgp/crs/homesec/IN11308.pdf> accessed 25 November 2021.
[183] Parmet (n 167) 240.
[184] Singer (n 182) 1.
[185] ibid.
[186] Wendy E Parmet and Michael S Sinha, 'Covid-19: The Law and Limits of Quarantine' (2020) 382(15) *New England Journal of Medicine* e28(1), e28(2); Parmet (n 167) 241; Singer (n 182) 1; *Public Health Service Act* ss 361–62, 365 (42 USC §§ 265, 268).
[187] Singer (n 182) 1; *Public Health Service Act* ss 362, 365 (42 USC §§265, 268).

to apprehend and examine those whom it 'reasonably believes' are infected with a communicable disease.[188] Yet the Centers for Disease Control and Prevention's order, which was effective from 20 March 2020, did not require assessment of foreign nationals' specific risk of having contracted and transmitting COVID-19.[189]

In later phases of the pandemic, countries' closure of their borders to non-citizens in response to risks to public health raised by the pandemic appeared generally to attract international acceptance. For example, in November 2021, governments of at least 69 countries and territories, including the United States of America, European Union, the United Kingdom, Japan, and Israel, rapidly closed their borders to non-citizens from several African countries following the reporting of a new variant of COVID-19 in South Africa: Omicron.[190] On 26 November 2021, WHO designated Omicron as a 'Variant of Concern'.[191] While WHO did not explicitly recommend border closures,[192] it seemed to condone them. It was reported that 'WHO reiterated that, pending further advice, countries should use a "risk-based approach to adjust international travel measures", while acknowledging that a rise in coronavirus cases might lead to higher morbidity and mortality rates', and WHO stated that 'the impact on vulnerable populations would be substantial, particularly in countries with low vaccination coverage'.[193] Notwithstanding this, United Nations Secretary-General, Antonio Guterres, indicated his concern about the impact of these border closures on southern African countries.[194]

---

[188] Maryam Jamshidi, 'The Federal Government Probably Can't Order Statewide Quarantines' *The University of Chicago Law Review Online* (20 April 2020) <https://lawreviewblog.uchicago.edu/2020/04/20/statewide-quarantines-jamshidi/> accessed 28 October 2020; *Public Health Service Act* s 264(d) (42 USC §§264(d)).
[189] Parmet (n 167) 241.
[190] Tim Lister, Hira Humayun, and AnneClaire Stapleton, 'At Least 69 Countries and Territories Have Imposed Travel Restrictions in Response to Omicron' *CNN* (29 November 2021) <https://edition.cnn.com/world/live-news/covid-variant-omicron-11-29-21/index.html> accessed 3 December 2021; Stephanie Nebehay, 'Omicron Poses Very High Global Risk, World Must Prepare—WHO' *Reuters* (29 November 2021) <www.reuters.com/business/healthcare-pharmaceuticals/omicron-poses-very-high-global-risk-countries-must-prepare-who-2021-11-29/> accessed 3 December 2021; Stephanie Nebehay and Alexander Winning, 'WHO Flags Omicron Risk, Travel Curbs Tighten, Biden Urges Vaccination' *Reuters* (30 November 2021) <www.reuters.com/world/spread-omicron-variant-forces-nations-rethink-plans-global-travel-2021-11-29/> accessed 3 December 2021; World Health Organization, 'Classification of Omicron (B.1.1.529: SARS-CoV-2 Variant of Concern)' (26 November 2021) <www.who.int/news/item/26-11-2021-classification-of-omicron-(b.1.1.529)-sars-cov-2-variant-of-concern> accessed 3 December 2021 (hereafter WHO, 'Classification of Omicron').
[191] World Health Organization, 'Update on Omicron' (28 November 2021) <www.who.int/news/item/28-11-2021-update-on-omicron> accessed 3 December 2021.
[192] ibid.
[193] Nebehay and Winning (n 190).
[194] ibid.

B. The Impact of Movement Restrictions on Asylum-seekers

Throughout the COVID-19 pandemic, border closures have had especially harsh effects on many people who have sought to relocate from one country to another.[195] By 22 May 2020, for in stance, 161 countries had partly or fully closed their borders and at least 99 of them made no exception for people who were seeking asylum.[196] Asylum-seekers were stranded at borders or compelled to relocate when countries prevented foreign nationals from entering their territory.[197] Some countries pushed asylum-seekers back from their frontiers.[198] For instance, purportedly to prevent the spread of COVID-19, Malaysia is reported to have turned away a boat carrying hundreds of Rohingya asylum-seekers.[199] Various countries, including Italy and Cyprus, refused to allow asylum-seekers who had been rescued at sea to disembark at their ports during the pandemic.[200] The United States forcibly deported asylum-seekers back to their countries of origin or removed them to transit locations.[201] Malta used private vessels to detain asylum-seekers at sea or transport them to Libya,[202] while other countries placed in detention facilities asylum-seekers who were unable to leave border areas.[203]

Under international law, countries have sovereign power to control their borders and take measures to protect their inhabitants' health, including by restricting non-nationals' entry to their territory.[204] Nevertheless, this power is constrained by countries' international legal obligations.[205] The measures they take to manage risks to public health must be necessary to achieve that objective and proportionate, comply with the law, and be applied in a non-discriminatory manner.[206]

---

[195] United Nations, *Policy Brief: COVID-19 and People on the Move* (June 2020) 2 <https://unsdg.un.org/resources/policy-brief-covid-19-and-people-move> accessed 23 November 2021 (hereafter United Nations, *People on the Move*).

[196] ibid 19.

[197] Bríd Ní Ghráinne, 'COVID-19, Border Closures and International Law' (Institute of International Relations Prague, 4 May 2020) 2 <www.iir.cz/covid-19-border-closures-and-international-law-2> accessed 23 November 2021.

[198] ibid 1–2; United Nations, *People on the Move* (n 195) 19.

[199] 'Rohingya Crisis: Hundreds of Refugees Stranded in Boats at Sea' *BBC News* (26 April 2020) <www.bbc.com/news/av/world-asia-52431222> accessed 28 October 2020.

[200] United Nations, *People on the Move* (n 195) 19; Daniel Ghezelbash and Nikolas F Tan, 'The End of the Right to Seek Asylum? COVID-19 and the Future of Refugee Protection' (2020) 32(4) *International Journal of Refugee Law* 668, 676.

[201] Singer (n 182) 2; Parmet (n 167) 241.

[202] Ghezelbash and Tan (n 200) 676.

[203] United Nations, *People on the Move* (n 195) 20; United Nations Human Rights Office of the High Commissioner, 'COVID-19 and the Human Rights of Migrants: Guidance' (7 April 2020) <www.ohchr.org/Documents/Issues/Migration/OHCHRGuidance_COVID19_Migrants.pdf> accessed 10 September 2022.

[204] United Nations High Commissioner for Refugees, 'Key Legal Considerations on Access to Territory for Persons in Need of International Protection in the Context of the Covid-19 Response' (16 March 2020) 1–2 <www.refworld.org/docid/5e7132834.html> accessed 10 September 2022 (hereafter UNHCR); Gilbert (n 165) 167–68.

[205] Gilbert (n 165) 168; UNHCR (n 204) 1.

[206] Ghráinne (n 197) 3–4; UNHCR (n 204) 2.

At least some countries' closure of their borders to asylum-seekers during the pandemic may not have met those requirements.[207]

It is unclear whether the shutting of their borders to asylum-seekers by some countries was necessary to control the spread of COVID-19, especially once the disease had already spread to and become established in their territory. Indeed, some countries seemingly considered such measures were unnecessary. For instance, certain Member States of the European Union, such as Sweden, complied with the European Commission's advice to exempt asylum-seekers from their border closures during the pandemic.[208] In addition, several countries created remote asylum processing systems or extended the validity of asylum-seekers' documentation and rights to remain in their territory until it was possible to process their applications safely according to usual procedures.[209]

As noted above, countries' closure of their borders to asylum-seekers may also not have been proportionate, at least in some instances, given that they could have deployed other public health measures that were as or more effective in reducing the risk of the transmission of COVID-19.[210] For instance, also as noted above, they could have tested those who arrived at their borders seeking protection, isolated any people who tested positive for COVID-19, and quarantined others who had or may have been exposed to the virus.[211] Moreover, the movement restrictions may have increased the risk of asylum-seekers contracting and spreading COVID-19, including to countries that had minimal resources to manage the pandemic.[212] Countries' border closures led some asylum-seekers to travel further, searching for a country that would grant them refuge.[213] Further, facilities in which asylum-seekers were detained were often overcrowded and lacked adequate healthcare and sanitation, increasing the risk of detainees and staff contracting COVID-19.[214] Some countries' border closures may also have been discriminatory. They prohibited entry to their territory of people of particular nationalities or asylum-seekers generally, without assessing individuals' risk of spreading COVID-19,[215] and while simultaneously repatriating their own citizens and permanent residents.

---

[207] UNHCR (n 204) 2.
[208] Ghezelbash and Tan (n 200) 675.
[209] United Nations, *People on the Move* (n 195) 22; Michelle Foster, Helene Lambert, and Jane McAdam, 'Refugee Protection in the COVID-19 Crisis and Beyond: The Capacity and Limits of International Law' (2021) 44(1) *University of New South Wales Law Journal* 104, 111–12.
[210] UNHCR (n 204) 2; European Union Agency for Fundamental Rights, 'Fundamental Rights of Refugees, Asylum Applicants and Migrants at the European Borders' (27 March 2020) 8 <https://fra.europa.eu/en/publication/2020/fundamental-rights-refugees-asylum-applicants-and-migrants-european-borders> accessed 23 November 2021.
[211] ibid.
[212] Parmet (n 167) 241; United Nations, *People on the Move* (n 195) 20.
[213] Ghráinne (n 197) 4; United Nations, *People on the Move* (n 195) 20.
[214] Parmet (n 167) 243; United Nations, *People on the Move* (n 195) 20.
[215] UNHCR (n 204) 2.

Significantly, many countries may have breached the internationally recognized human right to seek and enjoy asylum from persecution by preventing people from applying for it.[216] This right, enshrined in the *Universal Declaration on Human Rights* and regional legal instruments, involves an entitlement to make a claim for international protection and receive a fair assessment of the claim.[217] The border closures denied many people who were attempting to escape war, persecution, and other human rights violations, the opportunity to make such a claim.[218] Several countries, including Italy and France, actually suspended their processing of asylum applications in the initial phase of the pandemic.[219] These measures extended some countries' efforts preceding COVID-19 to terminate the right to seek asylum in those countries.[220] For instance, before the pandemic, Australia's federal government prevented asylum-seekers from seeking protection if they sought to access its territory by sea, but they could still arrive in Australia by aeroplane if they had valid visas and then applied for protection.[221] Nevertheless, this pathway was largely closed to asylum-seekers following the Governor-General's declaration in response to COVID-19 and pursuant to the *Biosecurity Act 2015* (Cth) that 'a human biosecurity emergency' existed.[222] Australia's borders were shut to all except citizens and permanent residents, and the government mostly suspended the granting of offshore humanitarian visas and resettlement of refugees who had already been given visas.[223]

Countries whose border closures suspended the right to seek asylum could have argued that, by preventing or delaying the spread of COVID-19, they protected other human rights such as to life and to enjoying 'the highest attainable standard of ... health'.[224] Nevertheless, especially where they compelled asylum-seekers to return to countries from which they had fled, it would have been more difficult for them to defend their possible violation of the international legal principle of *non-refoulement*, from which no derogation, exception, or limitation is permitted.[225] This principle is fundamental to the right to seek asylum and binds all states.[226] It is

---

[216] ibid 1; Gilbert (n 165) 168.
[217] Ghezelbash and Tan (n 200) 2; UNHCR (n 204) 1, endnote 1.
[218] Ghezelbash and Tan (n 200) 6.
[219] ibid 7; Ghráinne (n 197) 2.
[220] Ghezelbash and Tan (n 200) 1.
[221] ibid 5; Harriet Spinks, 'Boat Turnbacks in Australia: A Quick Guide to the Statistics since 2001' *Parliament of Australia* (20 July 2018) <www.aph.gov.au/About_Parliament/Parliamentary_Departments/Parliamentary_Library/pubs/rp/rp1819/Quick_Guides/BoatTurnbacksSince2001> accessed 10 September 2022 (hereafter Spinks, 'Boat Turnbacks').
[222] Ghezelbash and Tan (n 200) 5–6; Harriet Spinks, 'Seeking Asylum in the Time of Coronavirus: COVID-19 Pandemic Effects on Refugees and People Seeking Asylum' *Parliament of Australia* (19 May 2020) <www.aph.gov.au/About_Parliament/Parliamentary_Departments/Parliamentary_Library/FlagPost/2020/May/COVID-19_-_impacts_on_refugees_and_asylum_seekers> accessed 10 September 2022; *Biosecurity Act 2015* (Cth) ss 475, 477.
[223] Ghezelbash and Tan (n 200) 5; Spinks, 'Boat Turnbacks' (n 221).
[224] Ogg (n 13); *ICCPR* (n 16) Article 6(1); *ICESCR* (n 23) Article 12(1).
[225] European Union Agency for Fundamental Rights (n 210) 5; United Nations, *People on the Move* (n 195) 20; Ghráinne (n 197) 3; Foster, Lambert, and McAdam (n 209) 115–16.
[226] UNHCR (n 204) 1; Ghráinne (n 197) 3.

expressed in the 1951 United Nations *Convention Relating to the Status of Refugees*, which provides that 'no Contracting State shall expel or return ('refouler') a refugee in any manner whatsoever to the frontiers of territories where his life or freedom would be threatened on account of his race, religion, nationality, membership of a particular social group or political opinion'.[227]

Countries' obligations to comply with the prohibition on *refoulement* are engaged when asylum-seekers are within or arrive at the border of their territory.[228] The countries must conduct independent inquiries about the asylum-seekers' need for international protection and, if they are at risk of *refoulement*, permit them to enter their territory and not remove them from it against their will.[229] Concerned by reports that, in response to COVID-19, countries were forcibly returning asylum-seekers to their countries of origin, the United Nations Network on Migration issued a statement encouraging them to uphold the principle of *non-refoulement*.[230]

VII. Closure of Ports to and Quarantine of Cruise Ships

Transporting a high volume of passengers and crew from different countries across the world's oceans, cruise ships were potentially at great risk of disseminating COVID-19 around the globe.[231] In the initial phase of the pandemic, several countries, including Australia, New Zealand, and countries in the Pacific, Caribbean, and South America, prohibited entry of cruise ships to their ports.[232] Further, following an outbreak of COVID-19 on board several cruise ships, quarantine was also imposed in relation to the ships,[233] resulting in many people being stranded aboard them. The quarantine of the Diamond Princess cruise ship in February 2020 in a Japanese port after a passenger tested positive for COVID-19 illustrates the ethical dilemma that this restriction of non-citizens' movement posed.[234] While it prevented the transmission of COVID-19 to the mainland, confining the

---

[227] *Convention Relating to the Status of Refugees* (signed 28 July 1951, entered into force 22 April 1954) 189 UNTS 137, Article 33(1).
[228] UNHCR (n 204) 1; European Union Agency for Fundamental Rights (n 210) 5.
[229] UNHCR (n 204) 1; Ghráinne (n 197) 3.
[230] United Nations Network on Migration, 'Forced Returns of Migrants Must be Suspended in Times of COVID-19' (14 May 2020) <www.iom.int/news/forced-returns-migrants-must-be-suspended-times-covid-19#:~:text=The%20Network%20calls%20on%20States,all%20migrants%2C%20regardless%20of%20status.&text=Such%20closures%20should%20incorporate%20health,fundamental%20rights%20at%20all%20times> accessed 3 December 2021.
[231] Natalie Klein, 'International Law Perspectives on Cruise Ships and COVID-19' (2020) 11(2) *Journal of International Humanitarian Legal Studies* 282; Leah F Moriarty and others, 'Public Health Responses to COVID-19 Outbreaks on Cruise Ships—Worldwide, February-March 2020' (2020) 69(12) *Morbidity and Mortality Weekly Report* 347.
[232] Klein (n 231) 2.
[233] Ohlin (n 6) 550. See Chapter 9 in relation to litigation relating to cruise lines' liability.
[234] ibid.

passengers and crew to the close quarters of the ship, which lacked sufficient space to isolate people with COVID-19, enabled the disease to spread aboard the ship.[235] There were 700 people aboard the Diamond Princess who contracted COVID-19 and eight of them died.[236]

The legality of closures of ports to and quarantining of cruise ships in response to COVID-19 was not entirely clear. Pursuant to the law of the sea and various treaties, countries have sovereignty over their ports and can control access to and close them if their 'vital interests . . . so require', such as if they need to protect public health because ships carry infectious diseases.[237] A vessel is nonetheless allowed to enter a port it if it is in 'distress' and could refuse to leave it to avoid creating a situation of distress.[238] Yet, unless so many members of the crew were unwell with COVID-19 that they were unable to operate the ship and thereby jeopardized the safety of everyone on board, it would be difficult for a vessel to establish that it met this threshold.[239] Nevertheless, closure of ports to ships that have cases of COVID-19 among passengers and/or crew, even if they are not deemed to be in distress, appears to contravene the *IHR (2005)*. The *IHR (2005)* provide that a country cannot prevent a vessel from entering its port if there is evidence of a 'public health risk' on board (defined as 'a likelihood of an event that may affect adversely the health of human populations, with an emphasis on one which may spread internationally or may present a serious and direct danger').[240] That country can, nonetheless, determine the measures that are required to control the risk and can isolate the ship.[241]

VIII. Conclusion

Throughout the COVID-19 pandemic, many countries have restricted the movement of their citizens, permanent residents, and non-nationals. They have closed borders, prohibited travel, locked down areas, isolated infected people, and quarantined those who have been or might have been exposed to this disease. In imposing these constraints, authorities have relied upon, but, in some instances, may have contravened local, state, national, and international laws. As discussed in Chapter 6, the measures have generated much debate, resistance, and formal legal challenge, as they raise important questions about the balance that the law should strike between individuals' rights and public interests when the health of the global community is at stake.

---

[235] Klein (n 231) 2.
[236] Ohlin (n 6) 550. For further discussion see Chapter 9 in relation to the liability of cruise lines.
[237] Klein (n 231) 3.
[238] ibid 3–5.
[239] ibid 3–4.
[240] ibid 6; *IHR (2005)* (n 34) Articles 1 (definition of 'public health risk'), 28(1).
[241] Klein (n 231) 6; *IHR (2005)* (n 34) Article 27(1).

Freedom of movement is internationally recognized as a fundamental human right. Yet it can be necessary to qualify it in order to contain a highly contagious and lethal disease. COVID-19 does not recognize borders. Nevertheless, it has been assumed that, in controlling the use of spaces, keeping people in and out of them, establishing thresholds and determining who can and cannot cross them, laws can prevent its dispersion. It appears, however, that, while some movement constraints imposed during the pandemic have been effective in halting or delaying the spread of COVID-19, enabling health authorities to manage the pandemic more effectively, certain restrictions have not been as efficacious in this regard. Indeed, some authorities may even have imposed restrictions to pursue collateral objectives not related to protecting public health. Further, the impact of these constraints, including the suffering they have caused for some populations that are already vulnerable and the possible fracturing of international relations, should be factored into an assessment of their value.

In these respects, the restrictions on people's movement in the fight against COVID-19 hold crucial lessons for tackling future pandemics. For instance, once a pandemic is established, is it preferable for authorities to focus on supporting people, rather than restricting their liberty?[242] Would measures that do not constrain people's freedom promote international collaboration to manage a pandemic more effectively? How can we ensure that restrictions imposed during a pandemic do not result in 'a "new normal" of eroded rights and liberties' that prevails after the pandemic has passed?[243]

---

[242] Parmet and Sinha (n 186) e28(3).
[243] European Group on Ethics in Science and Technologies, 'Statement on European Solidarity and the Protection of Fundamental Rights in the COVID-19 Pandemic' (2 April 2020) 3 <https://ec.europa.eu/info/sites/info/files/research_and_innovation/ege/ec_rtd_ege-statement-covid-19.pdf> accessed 28 October 2020.

5
Domestic Laws and Emergency Measures

I. Introduction

Around the world the COVID-19 pandemic has required national and state or provincial governments to respond to the unfolding crisis. Governments have responded by implementing a range of measures designed to curb the spread of disease and limit rising case numbers. In countries such as Australia, Canada, New Zealand, the United Kingdom, and the United States, governments have relied in part on existing public health laws or emergency management laws. However, the extraordinary nature of the pandemic, and of the measures required to contain its spread, has meant that in some instances additional legal provisions have been needed. With many of the measures impacting upon the freedom of movement of individuals, the nature of law-making during times of emergency has been thrown into the spotlight.

This chapter reviews the measures that have been implemented domestically in response to the COVID-19 pandemic, and their legal and ethical implications. Given that these public health measures have been introduced in many countries around the world, our aim is not to provide a comprehensive analysis of the measures introduced in each country, but rather to provide examples and to consider the legal and regulatory issues they raise. The chapter begins in Section II with an analysis of law-making in an emergency, and the challenges that an emergency may pose for the regular and customary oversight of law-making processes. The remaining sections of the chapter focus on reviewing particular measures that have been introduced by domestic governments to limit the spread of COVID-19. Section III reviews the imposition of restrictions on travelling internationally and within countries. Section IV analyses the legal and ethical aspects of requirements for quarantine and isolation during the pandemic. Many countries have experienced periods of lockdown, either nationally or for designated geographical areas within the country. These measures are scrutinized in Section V, while Section VI analyses the use of curfews. In Section VII we consider the requirements for physical distancing that have been introduced in many countries, and in Section VIII we review requirements to wear face masks. In Section IX we analyse the complex legal and ethical issues that arise in relation to requirements for mandatory vaccination. Many of these issues have arisen in an occupational context and we return to this issue again in Chapter 10. Section X considers the debates that have arisen about requirements to provide proof of vaccination—known as 'vaccination passports.'

Finally, Section XI reviews measures introduced for COVID-19 testing of individuals, contact tracing of positive cases, and the public health use of wastewater surveillance. In many instances, the introduction of restrictions has been challenged in the courts. We deal with these legal challenges in Chapter 6.

II. Emergency Laws

Legislation is the orthodox regulatory tool for law. In the context of public health, existing public health powers are found in public health legislation. In addition, laws designed to support responses in other emergencies, including natural disasters, may also be relevant, by providing a legal framework for disaster declarations, which in turn may provide additional resources to support emergency responses.[1] In some countries, these existing powers have been supplemented by legislation enacting time-limited COVID-19 specific measures. Legislation has also been used to support the delivery of a wide range of other regulatory and economic measures, including the provision of social security support for individuals and economic stimulus packages for businesses.[2] Responding to a public health emergency has required engaging not only with the traditional domains of public health laws. It has also required engagement with law and regulation generally. Law and regulation have become key tools in whole-of-government responses to the crisis.

During the pandemic, law has been used to change the behaviour of individuals and organizations.[3] Anderson and Burris have suggested that four issues are relevant to research on the impact of the legal response to COVID-19: (i) whether those who are the subjects of laws understand the requirements of the law; (ii)

---

[1] For discussion of emergency laws in Australia see Belinda Bennett, Terry Carney, and Richard Bailey, 'Emergency Powers and Pandemics: Federalism and the Management of Public Health Emergencies in Australia' (2012) 31(1) *University of Tasmania Law Review* 37; Paula O'Brien and Eliza Waters, 'COVID-19: Public Health Emergency Powers and Accountability Mechanisms in Australia' (2021) 28(2) *Journal of Law and Medicine* 346; Peta Stephenson, Ian Freckelton, and Belinda Bennett, 'Public Health Emergencies in Australia' in Belinda Bennett and Ian Freckelton (eds), *Pandemics, Public Health Emergencies and Government Powers: Perspectives on Australian Law* (Federation Press 2021). In Canada see Colleen M Flood and others, 'Reconciling Civil Liberties and Public Health in the Response to COVID-19' (2020) 5(1) *FACETS* 887; Allan S Detsky and Isaac I Bogoch, 'COVID-19 in Canada: Experience and Response' (2020) 324(8) *Journal of the American Medical Association* 743. For discussion of US laws see Lawrence O Gostin and James G Hodge, 'US Emergency Legal Responses to Novel Coronavirus: Balancing Public Health and Civil Liberties' (2020) 323(12) *Journal of the American Medical Association* 1131; Lindsay F Wiley, 'Public Health Law and Science in the Community Mitigation for Covid-19' (2020) 7(1) *Journal of Law and the Biosciences* art lsaa019. For discussion of laws in the United Kingdom see Jonathan Pugh, 'The United Kingdom's Coronavirus Act, Deprivations of Liberty, and the Right to Liberty and Security of the Person' (2020) 7(1) *Journal of Law and the Biosciences* art lsaa011.

[2] For discussion see Chapter 7.

[3] Evan Anderson and Scott Burris, 'Is Law Working? A Brief Look at the Legal Epidemiology of COVID-19' in Scott Burris and others (eds), *Assessing Legal Responses to COVID-19* (Public Health Law Watch 2020) 20.

whether they are able to comply with the laws; (iii) whether they are willing to comply with the laws; and (iv) how non-compliance will be detected and corrected and how compliance will be supported.[4] While recognizing the importance of voluntary compliance, Anderson and Burris also note that 'the visible presence of enforcement authority (like police at the borders of a locked-down community) has been a feature of the COVID-19 response and may be important to compliance locally.'[5]

A. Emergency Declarations and International Law

The emergency declarations made under domestic national laws have generally imposed a range of restrictions on the rights and liberties of individuals living in affected areas. While these declarations have been made under national or subnational laws, international law is also relevant in establishing limits to restrictions on rights in emergency situations.

The *International Covenant on Civil and Political Rights (ICCPR)*[6] articulates civil and political rights. However, the *ICCPR* also recognizes that States Parties may need to derogate from some of their obligations to protect those rights during emergencies. Article 4(1) of the *ICCPR* states:

> In time of public emergency which threatens the life of the nation and the existence of which is officially proclaimed, the States Parties to the present Covenant may take measures derogating from their obligations under the present Covenant to the extent strictly required by the exigencies of the situation, provided that such measures are not inconsistent with their other obligations under international law and do not involve discrimination solely on the ground of race, colour, sex, language, religion or social origin.

While Article 4(1) permits derogations from rights recognized in the *ICCPR* in emergencies, Article 4(2) expressly provides that some rights are non-derogable. These include the right to life (protected in Article 6), protection from torture (in Article 7), and protection from slavery (Article 8).[7]

The *Siracusa Principles*[8] provide further interpretation of the permissible limitations of rights protected in the *ICCPR*. The *Siracusa Principles* provide:

---

[4] ibid 21.
[5] ibid. See Chapter 8 for further discussion of compliance with public health laws during the pandemic.
[6] *International Covenant on Civil and Political Rights* (opened for signature 16 December 1966, entered into force 23 March 1976), 999 UNTS 171.
[7] For a discussion of derogations within European human rights law see Audrey Lebret, 'COVID-19 Pandemic and Derogation to Human Rights' (2020) 7(1) *Journal of Law and the Biosciences* art lsaa015.
[8] United Nations Economic and Social Commission on Human Rights, *The Siracusa Principles on the Limitation and Derogation Provisions in the International Covenant on Civil and Political Rights*

Public health may be invoked as a ground for limiting certain rights in order to allow a State to take measures dealing with a serious threat to the health of the population or individual members of the population. These measures must be specifically aimed at preventing disease or injury or providing care for the sick and injured.

Due regard shall be had to the International Health Regulations of the World Health Organization.[9]

The *Siracusa Principles* also permit derogations to be made from obligations in the *ICCPR* when a State Party is 'faced with a situation of exceptional and actual or imminent danger which threatens the life of the nation'.[10] The *Siracusa Principles* state in cl 39 that 'A threat to the life of the nation':

(a) Affects the whole of the population and either the whole or part of the territory of the State, and
(b) Threatens the physical integrity of the population, the political independence or the territorial integrity of the State or the existence or basic functioning of institutions indispensable to ensure and protect the rights recognised in the Covenant.

A State Party that decides to derogate from its obligations under the *ICCPR* is required to make an official proclamation that a public emergency exists that threatens the life of the nation,[11] with the procedures for proclaiming a state of emergency under national laws prescribed prior to the emergency.[12] The *Siracusa Principles* also require that States which derogate from their obligations under the *ICCPR* advise other States, via the Secretary-General of the United Nations, of their decision and reasons.[13] A State is required to terminate a derogation 'in the shortest time required to bring to an end the public emergency which threatens the life of the nation'.[14]

(Resolution E/CN.4/1985/4, 28 September 1984) (hereafter *Siracusa Principles*). For discussion see Lawrence O Gostin, *Global Health Law* (Harvard University Press 2014) 256.
 [9] *Siracusa Principles* cls 25, 26.
 [10] ibid cl 39.
 [11] ibid cl 42. This is consistent with the requirement in *ICCPR* (n 6) Article 4(1) that the emergency be 'officially proclaimed'.
 [12] *Siracusa Principles* (n 8) cl 43.
 [13] ibid cls 44, 45. *ICCPR* (n 6) Article 4(3) provides: 'Any State Party to the present Covenant availing itself of the right of derogation shall immediately inform the other States Parties to the present Covenant, through the intermediary of the Secretary-General of the United Nations, of the provisions from which it has derogated and of the reasons by which it was actuated. A further communication shall be made, through the same intermediary, on the date on which it terminates such derogation.'
 [14] *Siracusa Principles* (n 8) cl 48.

Permissible derogation measures are limited to those 'strictly required by the exigencies of the situation' and must be 'proportionate to [the] nature and extent' of the emergency.[15] 'Strict necessity' is determined objectively, and each measure must be made to address 'an actual, clear, present or imminent danger and may not be imposed merely because of an apprehension of potential danger.'[16]

As noted earlier, even in an emergency, certain rights are non-derogable.[17] Importantly, a proclamation of an emergency must be made in good faith,[18] and the rule of law still prevails during an emergency.[19] However, the context of emergency laws is fundamental to their interpretation and application. As was submitted by the defendants to Lewis J in *Dolan v Secretary of State for Health and Social Care*:

> The spread of coronavirus presented a serious risk to life. The number of cases of persons infected with coronavirus, and dying, were increasing at the time that the Regulations were made. There were real fears that the National Health Service would be overwhelmed and unable to cope with the increasing number of cases. The coronavirus was a novel pathogen and scientific understanding of coronavirus was limited. Transmission from human to human was seen to be a major cause of the increase in cases of persons suffering, or dying, from coronavirus. Steps were taken to reduce transmission given the severity of the risk. As the risks have diminished, there has been a progressive easing or relaxation in the restrictions imposed.[20]

From the beginning of the pandemic, human rights organizations have highlighted the importance of respecting and protecting human rights in responding to the pandemic. While recognizing that limits can be imposed on some human rights in emergency situations, and that 'The scale and severity of COVID-19 reaches a level where restrictions are justified on public health grounds', the United Nations also noted that 'Human rights are critical—for the response and the recovery'[21] and that 'attention to human rights can shape better responses' to the pandemic.[22] In an April 2020 statement on COVID-19, the United Nations Committee on Economic, Social and Cultural Rights stated:

> The COVID-19 pandemic vividly illustrates the importance of the indivisibility and interdependence of all human rights. This pandemic is essentially a global

---

[15] ibid cl 51.
[16] ibid cl 54.
[17] *ICCPR* (n 6) Article 4(2); *Siracusa Principles* (n 8) cl 58.
[18] *Siracusa Principles* (n 8) cl 62.
[19] ibid cl 64.
[20] [2020] EWHC 1786 (Admin) [48].
[21] United Nations, *COVID-19 and Human Rights: We Are All in This Together* (April 2020) 2, 3 <https://unsdg.un.org/resources/covid-19-and-human-rights-we-are-all-together> accessed 2 June 2022.
[22] ibid 3.

health threat. Nevertheless, it has multiple implications for the enjoyment of civil and political rights because some of the measures taken by States to combat it impose severe restrictions on the freedom of movement and on other rights. Thus, it is essential that the measures adopted by States to combat this pandemic are reasonable and proportionate to ensure protection of all human rights.[23]

Given the potential significance of domestic law-making for the human rights of individuals, groups, and communities, the *Siracusa Principles* provide an important framework for law-making during emergencies by requiring that measures introduced are proportionate, necessary, and are of the shortest duration needed to bring an end to the emergency. However, it has been argued that many measures introduced in response to the pandemic 'are not of limited duration, proportionate, necessary, or non-discriminatory ... [and that] some governments have used the pandemic as a pretext to grab power, use excessive force, and harass vulnerable populations'.[24]

B. Law-making in an Emergency

Governments may need to take additional measures to respond to an emergency. There can be a need to bring such measures into operation urgently, with the result that they may be introduced and implemented without being subject to the usual processes of scrutiny by the legislature. In a number of countries, including Australia, Canada, New Zealand, and the United Kingdom, parliamentary sittings were adjourned for periods of time during the early stages of the pandemic.[25] In Europe, the European Parliament closed for a period.[26] As parliaments sought to find ways of continuing to work during the pandemic, committees were established, parliamentary sittings were moved to a virtual format, hybrid models were

---

[23] United Nations, Committee on Economic, Social and Cultural Rights, 'Statement on the Coronavirus Disease (COVID-19) Pandemic and Economic, Cultural and Social Rights' (United Nations, E/C.12/2020/1, 17 April 2020) para 3.

[24] Lisa Forman and Jillian Clare Kohler, 'Global Health and Human Rights in the Time of COVID-19: Response, Restrictions, and Legitimacy' (2020) 19(5) *Journal of Human Rights* 547, 549.

[25] Nicolas Horne, 'COVID-19 and Parliamentary Sittings (Current as at 2 April 2020)' Parliamentary Library, Parliament of Australia <https://www.aph.gov.au/About_Parliament/Parliamentary_Departments/Parliamentary_Library/FlagPost/2020/April/COVID-19_and_parliamentary_sittings> accessed 28 June 2021. For discussion of Canadian parliaments see, Jonathan Malloy, 'The Adaptation of Parliament's Multiple Roles to COVID-19' (2020) 53(2) *Canadian Journal of Political Science* 305; Erica Rayment and Jason VandenBeukel, 'Pandemic Parliaments: Canadian Legislatures in a Time of Crisis' (2020) 53(2) *Canadian Journal of Political Science* 379.

[26] See Aitor Hernández-Morales and Maia de la Baume, 'Corona-Chaos at the European Parliament' *Politico* (3 March 2020) <https://www.politico.eu/article/coronavirus-chaos-at-the-european-parliament/> accessed 2 October 2022.

used with both in person and virtual attendance by parliamentarians, or modified forms of parliament involving attendance by a smaller group of parliamentarians.[27]

Within Westminster systems of government, parliaments play a key role in approving government expenditure, law-making, and providing a framework for government accountability.[28] While measures introduced in response to the pandemic enabled national and sub-national parliaments to maintain some continuity in the context of an emergency, they also presented challenges for government accountability.[29] For example, in Australia, the National Cabinet was established to bring together the Prime Minister, state Premiers, and First Ministers of the territories to work on a co-ordinated national approach to the pandemic. However, the intergovernmental nature of the National Cabinet complicated the issue of accountability, with Boughey noting that, 'As an intergovernmental body, it is not responsible to a single parliament, but to nine separate parliaments'.[30]

The absence of parliamentary sittings represents a clear disruption to the ordinary processes of law-making within parliamentary legal systems. Importantly, these disruptions occurred at a time when the executive branch of government was exercising powers to introduce a wide range of measures that infringed civil liberties, including those that restricted freedom of movement. Webber has commented, 'Across the world, the legislative and judicial branches of government have retreated in part during the COVID-19 pandemic whereas members of the executive branch—understood to include public health officials—have assumed greater responsibilities.'[31] Declarations of emergency in many jurisdictions enabled executive decision-making and the making of declarations and orders without parliamentary oversight or at least with limited oversight.[32] It has been suggested that

---

[27] Steven Chaplin, 'Protecting Parliamentary Democracy in "Plague" Times: Accountability and Democratic Institutions During the Pandemic' (2020) 46(1) *Commonwealth Law Bulletin* 110, 119–120; Elena Griglio, 'Parliamentary Oversight Under the Covid-19 Emergency: Striving Against Executive Dominance' (2020) 8(1–2) *The Theory and Practice of Legislation* 49; Andrius Sytas, 'Lithuanian Parliament Moves Online as Coronavirus Bites' *Reuters* (12 January 2021) <https://www.reuters.com/article/health-coronavirus-lithuania-parliament-idUSL8N2JN3TO> accessed 2 October 2022; Procedure and Privileges Committee, *The Legislative Assembly's Response to the COVID-19 Pandemic* (Parliament of Western Australia, 17 November 2020) <https://www.parliament.wa.gov.au/Parliament/commit.nsf/(Report+Lookup+by+Com+ID)/D5B49310A5E6E8844825862400176FB0/$file/PPC%20-%20Report%208.pdf> (accessed 2 October 2022).

[28] Chaplin (n 27) 111–12.

[29] Janina Boughey, 'Executive Power in Emergencies: Where is the Accountability?' (2020) 45(3) *Alternative Law Journal* 168; Vanessa MacDonnell, 'Ensuring Executive and Legislative Accountability in a Pandemic' in Colleen M Flood and others (eds), *Vulnerable: The Law, Policy and Ethics of COVID-19* (University of Ottawa Press 2020).

[30] Boughey (n 29) 169. For further discussion of measures that were introduced in Australia see Anne Twomey, 'Federal and State Powers to Deal with Pandemics—Cooperation, Conflict and Confusion' in Belinda Bennett and Ian Freckelton (eds), *Pandemics, Public Health Emergencies and Government Powers: Perspectives on Australian Law* (Federation Press 2021).

[31] Grégoire Webber, 'The Duty to Govern and the Rule of Law in an Emergency' in Colleen M Flood and others (eds), *Vulnerable: The Law, Policy and Ethics of COVID-19* (University of Ottawa Press 2020) 179–80.

[32] For discussion in Australia see Boughey (n 29); Stephenson, Freckelton, and Bennett (n 1).

the extraordinary nature of law-making during a pandemic, and the need to ensure that emergency laws are proportionate and of limited duration, means that emergency laws should be drafted so as to ensure that they are 'separate and distinct from everyday laws'.[33] Proposing 'the new concept of social distancing of emergency legislation', Cormacain argues:

> that emergency laws ought to have sunset clauses, that they ought to be contained in a single legislative vehicle, that they ought to use non-textual amendments, that they don't fit the standard mosaic representation of the statute book, that they ought to use express words indicating their temporary nature, that powers are limited by definition to application solely in the emergency, and that their title indicate this limited remit.[34]

III. Travel Restrictions

As discussed in Chapter 4, travel restrictions were introduced in many countries in response to the pandemic. They included restrictions on international travel, interstate travel, and local travel. In addition, quarantine periods, usually of 14 days, were implemented in a number of countries for international travellers arriving in the country.[35] As discussed in Chapter 3, the *International Health Regulations (2005)* (*IHR (2005)*) require that World Health Organization (WHO) Member States do not unnecessarily restrict international travel. The COVID-19 pandemic has therefore raised important questions about the imposition of travel restrictions and whether they can be justified in the context of a new, previously unknown disease. Furthermore, as discussed in Chapter 4, the imposition of travel restrictions can have implications for human rights in relation to limiting freedom of movement. While some of these restrictions may be permitted derogations from obligations under the *ICCPR* in an emergency, as already discussed, such derogations must be proportionate, necessary, and of limited duration. Restrictions on international travel also presented challenges during the pandemic in terms of the rights of citizens to return to their home country. As discussed in Chapter 4, while some countries facilitated the repatriation of their citizens, for the citizens of some other countries, the repatriation process was more complex. Finally, also as discussed in Chapter 4, border closures adversely affected asylum-seekers, presenting

---

[33] Ronan Cormacain, 'Keeping Covid-19 Emergency Legislation Socially Distant from Ordinary Legislation: Principles for the Structure of Emergency Legislation' (2020) 8(3) *The Theory and Practice of Legislation* 245, 245.
[34] ibid 246.
[35] Emeline Han and others, 'Lessons Learnt from Easing COVID-19 Restrictions: An Analysis of Countries and Regions in Asia Pacific and Europe' (2020) 396(10261) *Lancet* 1525, 1527–28.

challenging issues regarding the rights of nations to control their borders, and the rights of asylum-seekers under international law.

Travel restrictions were also imposed *within* some countries. As the first country outside of China to be affected by COVID-19, Italy imposed domestic travel restrictions, limiting travel to and from areas with a high number of cases of COVID-19.[36] Australia,[37] Canada,[38] and the United States[39] were amongst a number of countries that imposed domestic travel restrictions.[40]

IV. Quarantine and Isolation

Quarantine and isolation have long been tools of public health for responding to infectious diseases for which there is no treatment, as discussed in Chapter 2. The term 'quarantine' is used for those who may have been exposed to an infectious disease, but where it is not known whether they have the disease. In contrast, 'isolation' is used to describe the separation from others of someone who is known to have an infectious disease.[41] In the Middle Ages, quarantine was a period of 40 days and implemented for incoming ships on their arrival in port.[42] Even more recently, quarantine powers have been used by governments to limit the importation of infectious disease.[43] Although quarantine and isolation might be thought of as public health tools belonging to an earlier time, in fact they have remained relevant and in use in response to the 1918 'Spanish flu', SARS in 2003, and Ebola in 2014.[44] Even if not used, the legal powers for quarantine and isolation have often remained in public health laws.[45]

---

[36] C Vicentini and others, 'Early Assessment of the Impact of Mitigation Measures on the COVID-19 Outbreak in Italy' (2020) 185 *Public Health* 99.

[37] Holly Mclean and Ben Huf, 'Emergency Powers, Public Health and COVID-19' (Research Paper No 2, Parliament of Victoria, August 2020) 36-37, 50–52.

[38] See Public Safety Canada, 'Guidance on Essential Services and Functions in Canada During the COVID-19 Pandemic' (14 October 2021) <https://www.publicsafety.gc.ca/cnt/ntnl-scrt/crtcl-nfrstrctr/esf-sfe-en.aspx> accessed 2 October 2022; Erika Ibrahim, 'Most Canadians Support Strong Travel Restrictions Amid Omicron COVID-19 Variant: Poll' *Global News* (7 December 2021) <https://globalnews.ca/news/8430507/most-canadians-support-strong-travel-restrictions-amid-omicron-covid-19-variant-poll/> accessed 2 October 2022.

[39] Ross D Silverman, 'Contact Tracing, Intrastate and Interstate Quarantine, and Isolation' in Scott Burris and others (eds), *Assessing Legal Responses to COVID-19* (Public Health Law Watch 2020); David M Studdert, Mark A Hall, and Michelle M Mello, 'Partitioning the Curve—Interstate Travel Restrictions During the COVID-19 Pandemic' (2020) 383 *New England Journal of Medicine* e83.

[40] For discussion see Chapter 4.

[41] Mark A Rothstein, 'From SARS to Ebola: Legal and Ethical Considerations for Modern Quarantine' (2015) 12(1) *Indiana Health Law Review* 227, 227.

[42] ibid 229. For further discussion see Chapter 2.

[43] For discussion see Rothstein (n 41) 230–31; Krista Maglen, 'A World Apart: Geography, Australian Quarantine, and the Mother Country' (2005) 60(2) *Journal of the History of Medicine and Allied Sciences* 196.

[44] See Rothstein (n 41) 231–32.

[45] See Chapter 2 for further historical analysis of quarantine laws.

Into the early twentieth century, individuals with tuberculosis (TB) were separated from the general community in sanitoria,[46] although even in contemporary times, non-compliance with treatment regimes,[47] or the presence of drug-resistant tuberculosis[48] led to confinement of individuals in some instances. With the emergence of SARS in 2003, quarantine again became an important public health tool for limiting the spread of a potentially fatal disease for which there was no treatment.[49] The use of quarantine within countries most affected by SARS[50] was a reminder of the continued relevance and importance of traditional public health tools in the face of a new disease. It also led to debate about the relationship between public health and human rights, and the importance of protecting the rights of those whose freedoms were curtailed for the benefit of the broader community.[51] More recently, as discussed in Chapter 2, quarantine has been used in response to the Ebola crisis in West Africa in 2014.[52]

Quarantine and isolation have once again been important public health tools in responding to COVID-19. There were two aspects of this. First was the use of powers, such as those available under public health laws or emergency laws, to require the isolation of individuals who have tested positive to COVID-19 and quarantine of those who may have been exposed to the disease.[53] Second was the use of quarantine and isolation in relation to travellers on their arrival at domestic or international borders. Some countries, such as Australia and New Zealand, required their citizens and permanent residents who returned from overseas either to remain in their homes or enter quarantine facilities for 14 days (the estimated maximum incubation period for COVID-19).[54] Many states within federal countries, including in Australia and the United States, also required those who entered

---

[46] Sheila A Rothman, *Living in the Shadow of Death: Tuberculosis and the Social Experience of Illness in American History* (Johns Hopkins University Press 1995).

[47] Sanjaya N Senanayake and Mark J Ferson, 'Detention for Tuberculosis: Public Health and the Law' (2004) 180(11) *Medical Journal of Australia* 573.

[48] Wendy E Parmet, *Populations, Public Health, and the Law* (Georgetown University Press 2009) 110; David P Fidler, Lawrence O Gostin, and Howard Markel, 'Through the Quarantine Looking Glass: Drug-Resistant Tuberculosis and Public Health Governance, Law and Ethics' (2007) 35(4) *Journal of Law, Medicine & Ethics* 616.

[49] Rothstein (n 41) 232–33.

[50] Lesley A Jacobs, 'Rights and Quarantine During the SARS Global Health Crisis: Differentiated Legal Consciousness in Hong Kong, Shanghai and Toronto' (2007) 41(3) *Law & Society Review* 511.

[51] ibid; Rothstein (n 41).

[52] Rothstein (n 41) 232. For discussion of the use of quarantine in response to Ebola, see Umberto Pellechia and others, 'Social Consequences of Ebola Containment Measures in Liberia' (2015) 10(12) *PLoS One* art e0143036; Philippe Calain and Marc Poncin, 'Reaching out to Ebola Victims: Coercion, Persuasion or an Appeal for Self-Sacrifice?' (2015) 147 *Social Science & Medicine* 126.

[53] Wendy Parmet and Michael Sinha, 'Covid-19: The Law and Limits of Quarantine' (2020) 382(15) *New England Journal of Medicine* e28(1); Silverman (n 39).

[54] Han and others (n 35) 1527–28; Yves Le Bouthillier and Delphine Nakache, 'The Right of Citizens Abroad to Return During a Pandemic' in Colleen M Flood and others (eds), *Vulnerable: The Law, Policy and Ethics of COVID-19* (University of Ottawa Press 2020) 305–306; Laurel Wamsley and Selena Simmons-Duffin, 'The Science Behind a 14-Day Quarantine After Possible COVID-19 Exposure' *npr* (1 April 2020) <www.npr.org/sections/health-shots/2020/04/01/824903684/the-science-behind-a-14-day-quarantine-after-possible-covid-19-exposure> accessed 2 October 2022.

their territory from other states with high COVID-19 infection rates to undergo quarantine.[55]

Citizens and permanent residents of some other countries who were required to quarantine or isolate were prohibited from doing so in their homes in certain circumstances. For example, Canadians returning from overseas who could only travel by public transport to their homes, as well as those who, in their homes, would have contact with vulnerable people or difficulty accessing necessities, were required to enter quarantine facilities.[56] In South Africa, Neukircher J of the North Gauteng Division of the High Court[57] placed decision-making in its larger context:

> This pandemic poses a serious threat to every person throughout South Africa and their right to life, dignity, freedom of movement, right to access healthcare and their right to a clean, safe and healthy environment. In a country where we are dominated by so much poverty, where people don't have access to basic amenities such as clean running water, housing, food and healthcare, the potential risk to those households poses a further threat which places an additional burden on the Government to combat—the risk then, in light of those circumstances rises exponentially ... In my view, in South Africa right now, every citizen is called upon to make sacrifices to their fundamental rights entrenched in the Constitution. They are called upon to do so in the name of "the greater good", the spirit of "*unubtu*" and they are called upon to do so in ways that impact on their livelihoods, their way of life and their economic security and freedom. Every citizen of this country needs to play his/her part in stemming the tide of what can only be regarded as an insidious and relentless pandemic.[58]

In a subsequent decision, Davis J of the same court scrutinized the rationality of South Africa's emergency regulations and 'their "connectivity" to the stated objectives of preventing the spread of infection'.[59] In respect of of the regulations, he observed that:

> The limitations on exercise are ... perplexing: If the laudable objective is not to have large groups of people exercising in close proximity to each other, the

---

[55] Lionel Nichols, 'Australia' in Bonavero Institute of Human Rights, *A Preliminary Human Rights Assessment of Legislative and Regulatory Responses to the COVID-19 Pandemic Across 11 Jurisdictions* (Bonavero Report No 3/2020, 6 May 2020) 26; Lawrence O Gostin and Lindsay F Wiley, 'Governmental Public Health Powers in the COVID-19 Pandemic: Stay-at Home Orders, Business Closures, and Travel Restrictions' (2020) 323(21) *Journal of the American Medical Association* 2137, 2138.
[56] Le Bouthillier and Nakache (n 54) 305.
[57] *Mohamed v President of the Republic of South Africa* [2020] 2 All SA 844 (GP); [2020] ZAGPPHC 120.
[58] ibid [62], [75].
[59] *De Beer v Minister of Cooperative Governance and Traditional Affairs* [2020] ZAGPPHC 184; 2020 (11) BCLR 1349 (GP), (High Court) [7] (hereafter *De Beer* case).

regulations should say so rather than prohibit the organizing of exercise in an arbitrary fashion ...

Restricting the right to freedom of movement in order to limit contact with others in order to curtail the risks of spreading the virus is rational, but to restrict the hours of exercise to arbitrarily determined time periods is completely irrational ...

Similarly, to put it bluntly, it can hardly be argued that it is rational to allow scores of people to run on the promenade but were one to step a foot on the beach, it will lead to rampant infection.[60]

The requirement for people to quarantine regardless of their specific risk of having contracted COVID-19 was potentially contentious, too.[61] Nevertheless, the relatively low COVID-19 infection rates in the initial phase of the pandemic in certain jurisdictions, such as Taiwan, were attributed at least partly to their effective use of these movement restrictions.[62] By 5 January 2020, Taiwan's Centers for Disease Control monitored the health of its inhabitants who had visited the Chinese city of Wuhan, from which COVID-19 emerged, in the preceding 14 days and exhibited symptoms of respiratory infection, and isolated those who tested positive for known pathogens.[63] From 14 March, people returning to Taiwan from countries with high infection rates and, subsequently, all travellers arriving in Taiwan were required to enter a 14-day quarantine.[64] To ensure that people remained in quarantine, local governments tracked their mobile telephones and arranged for officers to visit them.[65] By 18 May 2020, Taiwan had recorded just 440 cases of and seven deaths from COVID-19 in its population of over 23 million people.[66]

The use of public health powers raises important questions about human rights and the balance between individual and community interests.[67] In the United States, these issues also have constitutional law ramifications given the requirements in the *Constitution* that individual rights and freedoms not be limited without due process.[68] In Canada, the *Charter of Rights and Freedoms* is relevant,[69]

---

[60] ibid [2020] ZAGPPHC 184 [7.7]–[7.9].
[61] Gostin and Wiley (n 55) 2138.
[62] Irving Yi-Feng Huang, 'Fighting COVID-19 through Government Initiatives and Collaborative Governance: The Taiwan Experience' (2020) 80(4) *Public Administration Review* 665, 669.
[63] ibid 667.
[64] ibid.
[65] ibid.
[66] ibid 665.
[67] See eg David M Studdert and Mark A Hall, 'Disease Control, Civil Liberties, and Mass Testing—Calibrating Restrictions During the COVID-19 Pandemic' (2020) 383 *New England Journal of Medicine* 102; Ian Freckelton, 'COVID-19: Criminal Law, Public Assemblies and Human Rights Litigation' (2020) 27(4) *Journal of Law and Medicine* 790.
[68] Parmet (n 48) 118–36.
[69] Colleen M Flood, Bryan Thomas, and Kumanan Wilson, 'Civil Liberties vs Public Health' in Colleen M Flood and others (eds), *Vulnerable: The Law, Policy and Ethics of COVID-19* (University of Ottawa Press 2020).

while in Europe,[70] the United Kingdom,[71] and two states and a territory in Australia,[72] human rights legislation may also be relevant to the state's powers in relation to restrictions on individual freedoms.

V. Lockdowns and Stay-at-Home Orders

The most intrusive and restrictive non-pharmaceutical intervention to contain the spread of COVID-19 was the use of government-imposed lockdowns and stay-at-home orders, with businesses required to close and individuals required to stay at home. Other restrictions imposed included night-time curfews,[73] recommendations or restrictions on non-essential travel, and restrictions on the distance from home able to be travelled.[74] In some federal countries lockdowns were state-based rather than national, reflecting either the geographic spread of the disease and/or the distribution of decision-making powers within federal systems. In a number of countries, lockdowns and other restrictions on freedom of movement were subject to legal challenges in the courts. In Chapter 6 we analyse these challenges to lockdowns and other restrictions. The economic consequences of lockdowns and the pandemic's disruption to business were enormous with the World Bank Group stating that 'The COVID-19 pandemic jeopardizes global development gains and goals on an unprecedented scale.'[75] Around the world, millions of people lost their employment, either temporarily during lockdowns, or permanently as businesses were unable to survive prolonged closures. In response, governments in some countries introduced income support payments for businesses or those unemployed during to the pandemic.[76]

For many businesses, workers moved to working from home, creating new challenges in terms of employers' workplace health and safety obligations. However, it should also be recognized that even in wealthy countries, work from home arrangements are likely to reflect social privilege.[77] For those in essential services or in employment where the work could not be done remotely (for instance, cleaners, shop assistants, bus drivers, and others), working in person continued through the

---

[70] Rebekah McWhirter, 'The Right to Liberty in a Pandemic' (2021) 40(2) *University of Queensland Law Journal* 159.
[71] Pugh (n 1).
[72] *Charter of Human Rights and Responsibilities Act 2006* (Vic); *Human Rights Act 2019* (Qld); *Human Rights Act 2004* (ACT). For discussion see Kylie Evans and Nicolas Petrie, 'COVID-19 and the Australian Human Rights Acts' (2020) 45(3) *Alternative Law Journal* 175; McWhirter (n 70).
[73] See Section VI in this chapter.
[74] For further discussion see Chapter 4. See also Gostin and Wiley (n 55); Vicentini and others (n 36).
[75] World Bank Group, 'Saving Lives, Scaling-Up Impact and Getting Back on Track: World Bank Group COVID-19 Crisis Response Approach Paper, (June 2020) 1.
[76] See Chapter 7 for discussion of these economic measures.
[77] Clyde W Yancy, 'COVID-19 and African Americans' (2020) 323(19) *Journal of the American Medical Association* 1891.

pandemic. In the United States, for example, it has been suggested that higher numbers of COVID-19 cases amongst African Americans may, at least in part, reflect the fact that they were in employment with less opportunity to work from home, as well as having existing comorbidities, experiencing social disadvantage, and living in high-density housing.[78] In low-income countries, working from home is also not available for many.

Complicating the lockdowns in response to COVID-19 were concerns over the gendered impact of the lockdowns. In many countries hospitality and retail suffered particularly from economic lockdowns. As these industries tend to be female-dominated, there was a gendered impact to the COVID-19-related economic downturn that affected many countries.[79] Around the world concern has been expressed over the potential for women and children to be at increased risk of domestic violence during lockdowns and periods of stay-at-home orders.[80] Furthermore, women have tended to bear the brunt of school closures, with an increase in their caring-related work.[81] It has been noted that 'One of the consequences of the quarantine implemented in many countries [in] the wake of COVID-19 has been the increment in the unpaid work for women and girls within their homes.'[82]

---

[78] ibid. See also Leo Lopez III, Louis H Hart III, and Mitchell H Katz, 'Racial and Ethnic Disparities Related to COVID-19' (2021) 325 *Journal of the American Medical Association* 719; William F Owen Jr, Richard Carmona, and Claire Pomeroy, 'Failing Another National Stress Test on Health Disparities' (2020) 323 *Journal of the American Medical Association* 1905.

[79] Workplace Gender Equality Agency (Australia), 'Gendered Impact of COVID-19' (May 2020) <https://www.wgea.gov.au/publications/gendered-impact-of-covid-19> accessed 2 October 2022; OECD, 'Women at the Core of the Fight Against COVID-19 Crisis' (2020) 7 <https://www.oecd.org/coronavirus/policy-responses/women-at-the-core-of-the-fight-against-covid-19-crisis-553a8269/> accessed 2 October 2022.

[80] United Nations Development Program, 'Briefing Note: The Economic Impacts of COVID-19 and Gender Inequality: Recommendations for Policymakers' (April 2020) (hereafter UNDP, 'Briefing Note') 8 <https://www.undp.org/publications/economic-impacts-covid-19-and-gender-equality#modal-publication-download> accessed 2 October 2022; Elizabeth Roesch, Avni Amin, and Jhumka Gupta, 'Violence Against Women During COVID-19 Pandemic Restrictions' (2020) 369 *British Medical Journal* m1712; Caroline Bradbury-Jones and Louise Isham, 'The Pandemic Paradox: The Consequences of COVID-19 on Domestic Violence' (2020) 29(13–14) *Journal of Clinical Nursing* 2047; Brad Boserup, Mark McKenney, and Adel Elkbuli, 'Alarming Trends in US Domestic Violence during the COVID-19 Pandemic' (2020) 38(12) *American Journal of Emergency Medicine* 2753; Emily Leslie and Riley Wilson, 'Sheltering in Place and Domestic Violence: Evidence from Calls for Service during COVID-19' (2020) 189 *Journal of Public Economics* art 104241; Hayley Boxall, Anthony Morgan, and Rick Brown, 'The Prevalence of Domestic Violence Among Women During the COVID-19 Pandemic' (Statistical Bulletin 28, Australian Institute of Criminology, July 2020) <https://www.aic.gov.au/sites/default/files/2020-07/sb28_prevalence_of_domestic_violence_among_women_during_covid-19_pandemic.pdf> accessed 2 October 2022; Kerry Carrington and others, 'The Impact of COVID-19 Pandemic on Australian Domestic and Family Violence Services and their Clients' (2021) 56(4) *Australian Journal of Social Issues* 539; Megan L Evans, Margo Lindauer, and Maureen E Farrell, 'A Pandemic Within a Pandemic—Intimate Partner Violence during Covid-19' (2020) 383 *New England Journal of Medicine* 2302.

[81] UNDP, 'Briefing Note' (n 80) 5–6; Helen J McLaren and others, 'Covid-19 and Women's Triple Burden: Vignettes from Sri Lanka, Malaysia, Vietnam and Australia' (2020) 9(5) *Social Sciences* 87.

[82] UNDP, 'Briefing Note' (n 80) 6.

As discussed in Chapter 7, a further consequence of COVID-related lockdowns was the impact on access to healthcare generally. In an effort to preserve scarce health resources for pandemic response and to prevent hospitals and healthcare workers being overwhelmed, elective surgery and other non-essential healthcare was curtailed in many countries with a risk of increased complications and mortality.[83] In some countries, the pandemic added new complexities to accessing abortion services,[84] affecting women's access to sexual and reproductive health services. In addition, in some countries, in efforts to limit the spread of COVID-19 within hospitals, limits were placed on the number of people who could support a woman during hospital-based childbirth.[85] Even without the limits on health services there was also a noticeable decline in access to some health services. This decline was particularly evident in cancer screening, and concerns have been expressed about a post-pandemic increase in cancer diagnoses.[86]

Importantly, not all countries decided to impose national lockdowns. The efficacy of such measures has particularly been debated in the context of analysing the merits and deficits of the Swedish approach of leaving responses to the pandemic substantially to individuals.[87] During the first wave of the pandemic, Sweden notably decided against a national lockdown, deciding instead to adopt a strategy of individual responsibility, recommendations, and protection of vulnerable groups.[88]

---

[83] Mikko Uimonen and others, 'The Impact of the COVID-19 Pandemic on Waiting Times for Elective Surgery Practices: A Multicenter Study' (2021) 16(7) *PLoS One* art e0253875; Adrian Diaz and others, 'Elective Surgery in the Time of COVID-19' (2020) 219 *American Journal of Surgery* 900; K Søreide and others, 'Immediate and Long-Term Impact of the COVID-19 Pandemic on Delivery of Surgical Services' (2020) 107(10) *British Journal of Surgery* 1250.

[84] Elizabeth C Romanis, Jordan A Parsons, and Nathan Hodson, 'COVID-19 and Reproductive Justice in Great Britain and the United States: Ensuring Access to Abortion Care During a Global Pandemic' (2020) 7(1) *Journal of Law and the Biosciences* art lsaa027; Greer Donley, Beatrice A Chen, and Sonya Borrero, 'The Legal and Medical Necessity of Abortion Care Amid the COVID-19 Pandemic' (2020) 7(1) *Journal of Law and the Biosciences* art lsaa013; Bethany Bruno, David I Shalowitz, and Kavita S Arora, 'Ethical Challenges for Women's Healthcare Highlighted by the COVID-19 Pandemic' (2021) 47(2) *Journal of Medical Ethics* 69; Deborah J Bateson and others, 'The Impact of COVID-19 on Contraception and Abortion Care Policy and Practice: Experiences from Selected Countries' (2020) 46 *British Medical Journal Sexual and Reproductive Health* 241.

[85] Jeffrey L Ecker and Howard L Minkoff, 'Laboring Alone? Brief Thoughts on Ethics and Practical Answers During the Coronavirus Disease 2019 Pandemic' (2020) 2(3) *American Journal of Obstetrics and Gynecology Maternal and Fetal Medicine* art 100141.

[86] Camille Maringe and others, 'The Impact of the COVID-19 Pandemic on Cancer Deaths Due to Delays in Diagnosis in England, UK: A National, Population-Based, Modelling Study' (2020) 21(8) *Lancet Oncology* 1023; William Hamilton, 'Cancer Diagnostic Delay in the COVID-19 Era: What Happens Next?' (2020) 21(8) *Lancet Oncology* 1000. See also John M Carethers and others, 'Disparities in Cancer Prevention in the COVID-19 Era' (2020) 13(11) *Cancer Prevention Research* 893.

[87] See eg Seth Flaxman and others, 'Estimating the Effects of Non-pharmaceutical Interventions on COVID-19 in Europe' (2020) 584(7820) *Nature* 257; Kristian Soltesz and others, 'The Effect of Interventions on COVID-19' (2020) 588(7839) *Nature* art E26.

[88] Jon Pierre, 'Nudges Against Pandemics: Sweden's COVID-19 Containment Strategy in Perspective' (2020) 39(3) *Policy and Society* 478; Mariam Claeson and Stefan Hanson, 'COVID-19 and the Swedish Enigma' (2020) 397(10271) *Lancet* 259; Mariam Claeson and Stefan Hanson, 'The Swedish COVID-19 Strategy Revisited' (2021) 397(10285) *Lancet* 1619; Nicolas Banholzer and others, 'Estimating the Effects of Non-pharmaceutical Interventions on the Number of New Infections with COVID-19 During the First Epidemic Wave' (2021) 16(6) *PLoS One* e0252827.

However, with a high death toll relative to comparable countries, and a high proportion of the deaths in older Swedes, the Swedish approach has been the subject of debate.[89] While it is too early to assess definitively the relative success or failure of such a strategy, the Swedish approach highlights the importance of post-pandemic analysis of policy and regulatory options.

The issues of when and how best to ease restrictions have also been complex matters for governments in responding to the pandemic. While restrictions were eased in many countries as they gained control of the first wave of infections, during the second half of 2020, the emergence of a second wave forced some countries back into lockdown, and again in 2021 as new, more contagious variants emerged. Decisions to impose or ease restrictions have varied between countries and have generally been shaped by a mixture of matters such as the number of infections, and the social and economic impact of imposing restrictions.[90] Finally, with the increasing availability of vaccines in 2021, countries have moved to lift lockdowns and reopen, although generally with some public health restrictions in place. The notable exception to this was the United Kingdom, which lifted most of its public health restrictions in July 2021,[91] with some restrictions re-imposed in England in December 2021 in response to the spread of the Omicron variant.[92]

VI. Curfews

Curfews were used in many countries as an adjunct to COVID-19 lockdowns and stay-at-home orders.[93] They functioned to discourage social mixing and non-essential interactions, as well as to reduce mobility at night time.[94] A 2020 analysis of worldwide measures to inhibit transmission suggested that the most

---

[89] See, Michael Grothe-Hammer and Steffen Roth, 'Dying is Normal, Dying with Coronavirus is Not: A Sociological Analysis of the Implicit Norms Behind the Criticism of Swedish "Exceptionalism"' (2021) 23(Sup1) *European Societies* S332; Shina C L Kamerlin and Peter M Kasson, 'Managing Coronavirus Disease 2019 Spread with Voluntary Public Health Measures: Sweden as a Case Study for Pandemic Control' (2020) 71(12) *Clinical Infectious Diseases* 3174; Andrius Kavaliunas and others, 'Swedish Policy Analysis for COVID-19' (2020) 9(4) *Health Policy and Technology* 598; Heba Habib, 'Has Sweden's Controversial Covid-19 Strategy Been Successful?' (2020) 369 *British Medical Journal* m2376.
[90] Han and others (n 35) 1526.
[91] Samantha Hawley, 'Freedom Day Celebrated by Revellers in England, With End of Most COVID-19 Restrictions' (20 July 2021) <https://www.abc.net.au/news/2021-07-20/how-uk-freedom-day-marks-end-of-covid-19-restrictions/100294668> accessed 2 October 2022.
[92] Kate Holton and Andy Bruce, 'Johnson Imposes COVID-19 "Plan B" in England to Contain Omicron' *Reuters* (9 December 2021) <https://www.reuters.com/world/uk/britain-could-implement-covid-19-plan-b-early-thursday-times-radio-2021-12-08/> accessed 2 October 2022.
[93] Sam Jones and others, 'Curfews and Quarantines: Europe Faces Another Easter of Covid Restrictions' *The Guardian* (3 April 2021) <https://www.theguardian.com/world/2021/apr/02/europe-easter-covid-restrictions-curfews-quarantines-coronavirus> accessed 2 October 2022.
[94] See Ian Freckelton, 'COVID-19 Curfews: Kenyan and Australian Litigation and Pandemic Protection' (2020) 28(1) *Journal of Law and Medicine* 117.

effective non-pharmaceutical interventions to mitigate the spread of COVID-19 'include curfews, lockdowns and closing and restricting places where people gather in smaller or large numbers for an extended period of time'.[95] However, disaggregating the effects of curfews in slowing viral transmission, as against the impact of other public health orders, proved difficult,[96] including because exemptions were required for essential workers travelling to and from their place of employment. Curfews also tend to be paired with orders restricting movement, such as precluding leaving home save for medical care, essential work, buying food, limited exercise, or obtaining vaccinations. A consequence was that it was not easy to determine what curfews added, save that they made policing of movement restrictions at night more straightforward. Like lockdowns, curfews have also been subject to legal challenges in a number of countries. We discuss these challenges in Chapter 6.

Maria Polyakova, an economist at Stanford University questioned the logic of curfews: 'Assuming that nightclubs and such are already closed down anyway, for instance, prohibiting people from going for a walk around the block with their family at night is unlikely to reduce interactions.'[97] Statistical analyses were also undertaken in an attempt to evaluate the extent to which curfews made a difference to the spread of the virus, with a German and a German/Swiss analysis suggesting no significant effect on hospitalizations flowing from curfews.[98] An English study[99] utilized a natural experiment in Greece where curfews shifted from 9pm to 6pm in one region but not in another. It found that the 6pm curfew in Athens had no effect on time spent in grocery stores and pharmacies. As this was a result of an 18.75% reduction in hours when people were allowed to leave home, the study concluded that paradoxically the early evening curfew led to more crowding in indoor spaces and thereby had the potential to facilitate the spread of COVID-19. It argued that imposition of curfews needed to take into account the likelihood of persons engaging in substitute activities. Another study contended that a variety of adverse psychological impacts were experienced after a five-month curfew in Kuwait,[100]

---

[95] Nina Haug and others, 'Ranking the Effectiveness of Worldwide COVID-19 Government Interventions' (2020) 4(12) *Nature Human Behaviour* 1303, 1308.

[96] See Moawiah Khatatbeh, 'Efficacy of Nationwide Curfew to Encounter Spread of COVID-19: A Case from Jordan' (2020) 8 *Frontiers in Public Health* art 394; Gina Kolata, 'Do Curfews Slow the Coronavirus?' *New York Times* (23 January 2021) <https://www.nytimes.com/2021/01/23/health/coronavirus-curfews.html> accessed 2 October 2022.

[97] See Kolata (n 96).

[98] See eg Samuel de Haas, Georg Goez, and Sven Heim, 'Measuring the Effects of COVID-19-related Night Curfews: Empirical Evidence from Germany' (MGKS Discussion Paper Series in Economics, Universität Marburg, No 18-2021); Martin Huber and Henrika Langen, 'Timing Matters: The Impact of Response Measures on COVID-19-Related Hospitalization and Death Rates in Germany and Switzerland' (2020) 156(1) *Swiss Journal of Economic Statistics* art 10.

[99] Alina Velias, Sotiris Georganas, and Sotiris Vandoros, 'COVID-19: Early Evening Curfews and Mobility' (2021) 292 *Social Science & Medicine* art 114538.

[100] Ahmad Salman and others, 'The Psychological and Social Impacts of Curfew During the COVID-19 Outbreak in Kuwait: A Cross-Sectional Study' (2021) 13 *Sustainability* art 8464.

although the curfew was only one of a number of restrictions imposed during this period by the Kuwaiti government.

VII. Physical Distancing Requirements

Physical distancing requirements are often imprecisely used as a synonym for 'social distancing'. Physical distancing is the practice of staying a designated distance away from others, while social distancing is staying at home away from others with whom one does not reside.[101] Physical distancing requirements were introduced in most countries to encourage people to maintain a safe distance between themselves and others so as to limit the spread of infection. Signs advising people to maintain physical distancing became commonplace during 2020. However, the recommended distance varied between countries, with Han and others noting that Hong Kong, Singapore, and Norway recommended one metre, in Germany and Spain it was one and a half metres, and in Japan and South Korea the recommended distance was two metres. Until June 2020 the recommended distance in England was two metres and it was then reduced to at least one metre.[102] Some distancing was voluntary as people limited going out to public places such as shopping centres. In some instances, the distancing was enforced, for example, during periods of lockdown discussed at Section V. Importantly, distancing requirements often included a suite of measures designed to limit the spread of disease. At times these measures have also included mandates for the wearing of face masks, discussed later. Physical distancing requirements have also been part of the post-COVID-19 return to normality. In Australia, for example, state-based requirements for COVID-19-safe business operations have included limits on the number of people permitted to be in venues, with the calculation based on the number of people per square metre, and the requirements changing with the easing of restrictions.[103]

Distancing requirements, including lockdowns, stay-at-home orders, reductions in the number of customers permitted in venues, and other measures, have at times led to protests. As discussed in Chapter 6, these protests have raised claims

---

[101] See Reza Aminnejad and Rosa Alikhani, 'Physical Distancing or Social Distancing: That is the Question' (2020) 67(8) *Canadian Journal of Anaesthesia* 1457; Kristine Sørensen and others, 'Rebranding Social Distancing to Physical Distancing: Calling for a Change in the Health Promotion Vocabulary to Enhance Clear Communication During a Pandemic' (2021) 28(1) *Global Health Promotion* 5; Lisa L Maragakis, 'Coronavirus, Social and Physical Distancing and Self-Quarantine' (15 July 2020) *Johns Hopkins Medicine* <www.hopkinsmedicine.org/health/conditions-and-diseases/coronavirus/coronavirus-social-distancing-and-self-quarantine> accessed 24 October 2021.
[102] Han and others (n 35) 1527. In January 2022 there were further changes: see 'Covid: What are the Social Distancing Rules Across the UK?' *BBC News* (25 January 2022) <https://www.bbc.com/news/uk-51506729> accessed 18 May 2022.
[103] See eg Business Victoria, 'Density Limits to Lift on Small to Medium-Sized Venues Across Victoria' (7 May 2021) <https://business.vic.gov.au/news-and-updates/2021/density-limits-to-lift-on-small-to-medium-sized-venues-across-victoria> accessed 18 May 2022.

of a right to freedom from restrictive public health measures[104] and, at times, debate over the right to protest during a pandemic.[105] However, for others, including those who are homeless or living in congregate settings, physical distancing itself may be seen as a right to be protected from disease.[106]

Physical distancing measures are challenging in overcrowded, informal urban environments. For example, in the context of East Africa it has been noted that:

> Most East Africans depend on public transport to go to work or attend markets. Similarly, markets are focal points of trade where opportunities to keep recommended distances are limited. Living spaces and household facilities in informal settlements are often crowded and shared by multiple family members, making social distancing within a family nearly impossible. Families also share key social and hygiene-related amenities, such as water sources and toilet facilities, that lack good ventilation and are not disinfected regularly.[107]

These challenges highlight the importance of developing and implementing programmes that address local contexts and the needs of local communities.[108] As Wamoyi, Ranganathan, and Stöckl argue, 'Structural and practical limitations of physical distancing in poor urban settings in East Africa exist, as prevailing social norms encourage family togetherness and sharing of important services. Adopting the concept of physical distancing implies the acceptance of new social norms by many families.'[109]

VIII. Wearing of Face Masks

COVID-19 is not the first occasion when wearing of face masks has been considered as a strategy to respond to a public health concern. Even before this pandemic, in parts of Asia, wearing of face masks was common as a protection from seasonal influenza or high air pollution.[110] Furthermore, the wearing of face masks may also be relevant to poor air quality due to pollution, bushfires, or volcanic

---

[104] For discussion see Amy Fairchild, Lawrence Gostin, and Ronald Bayer, 'Vexing, Veiled and Inequitable: Social Distancing and the "Rights" Divide in the Age of COVID-19' (2020) 20(7) *American Journal of Bioethics* 55; Maria O'Sulllivan, 'Protest in a Pandemic—The Special Status of Public Spaces' (27 July 2020) *Australian Public Law* <https://auspublaw.org/2020/07/protest-in-a-pandemic-the-special-status-of-public-spaces/> accessed 2 October 2022.
[105] For discussion see Chapter 6.
[106] Fairchild, Gostin, and Bayer (n 104).
[107] Joyce Wamoyi, Meghna Ranganathan, and Heidi Stöckl, 'COVID-19 Social Distancing Measures and Informal Urban Settlements' (2021) 99(6) *Bulletin of the World Health Organization* 475, 475..
[108] ibid 476.
[109] ibid.
[110] Han and others (n 35) 1528.

eruptions.[111] As discussed in Chapters 6 and 8, during the COVID-19 pandemic, many governments have required people by emergency laws to wear masks and enforced these orders through criminal penalties.

During the early stages of the COVID-19 pandemic, WHO did not recommend the use of face masks in the community. At that stage, there was insufficient evidence to show that they would be effective as protection against COVID-19 infection.[112] This advice changed when research indicated that COVID-19 was largely an airborne disease, that there was a risk of transmission from asymptomatic individuals, and that use of face masks could reduce the transmission of the disease in the community.[113] In relation to the use of face masks by the community, WHO's June 2020 guidance indicated that persons with symptoms of COVID-19 should wear a mask, self-isolate, and seek medical advice, and that all members of the public, whether or not they are wearing face masks, should avoid groups and crowds; maintain physical distance from others; practise good hand and respiratory hygiene; and avoid touching their mouth, nose, and eyes.[114] WHO's advice was that the public should be encouraged to wear face masks in 'areas with known or suspected widespread transmission and limited or no capacity to implement other containment measures' in situations where it was difficult to achieve physical distancing, such as in grocery stores; in working conditions where the employees are in close contact with others; in situations of high-density living, such as refugee camps; and where there is an increased risk of negative outcomes, such as in vulnerable populations.[115] In its advice to decision-makers on the use of face masks by the general public, WHO stated:

> taking into account the available studies evaluating pre- and asymptomatic transmission, a growing compendium of observational evidence on the use of masks by the general public in several countries, individual values and preferences, as well as the difficulty of physical distancing in many contexts, WHO has updated its guidance to advise that to prevent COVID-19 transmission effectively in areas of community transmission, governments should encourage the general public

---

[111] Fiona McDonald and others, 'Facemask Use for Community Protection from Air Pollution Disasters: An Ethical Overview and Framework to Guide Agency Decision Making' (2020) 42 *International Journal of Disaster Risk Reduction* art 101376.

[112] Kar K Cheng, Tai H Lam, and Chi C Leung, 'Wearing Face Masks in the Community During COVID-19: Altruism and Solidarity' (2022) 399(10336) *Lancet* e39.

[113] Nick Scott and others, 'The Introduction of a Mandatory Mask Policy was Associated with Significantly Reduced COVID-19 Cases in a Major Metropolitan City' (2021) 16(7) *PLoS One* art e0253510; Benjamin Rader and others, 'Mask-wearing and Control of SARS-CoV-2 Transmission in the USA: A Cross-sectional Study' (2021) 3(3) *Lancet Digital Health* e148.

[114] World Health Organization, 'Advice on the Use of Masks in the Context of COVID-19: Interim Guidance' 6 (5 June 2020) <https://apps.who.int/iris/bitstream/handle/10665/331693/WHO-2019-nCov-IPC_Masks-2020.3-eng.pdf?sequence=1&isAllowed=y> accessed 2 October 2022.

[115] ibid 7.

to wear masks in specific situations and settings as part of a comprehensive approach to suppress SARS-CoV-2 transmission.[116]

WHO's guidance was that children aged up to five years should not wear face masks; for children aged between 6 and 11, a risk-based approach should be adopted in deciding whether the child should wear a mask; while children aged 12 and over should follow WHO advice and national guidance on the use of face masks by adults.[117] In its December 2020 guidance, WHO recommended that masks be worn in indoor areas with poor ventilation, even if physical distancing of at least one metre could be maintained; in indoor settings with adequate ventilation if it was not possible to maintain physical distancing of at least one metre; in outdoor settings where physical distancing was not possible; and in settings where physical distancing was not possible and the individual had an increased risk of infection or severe complications.[118]

Throughout 2020 and 2021, the wearing of face masks became commonplace, and even became mandatory in some countries when people were outside their homes.[119] They became mandatory again in England in response to the Omicron variant in December 2021 with their being required in shops, public transport and most indoor venues, including theatres and cinemas.[120] It has been argued that there should be an 'increasing focus on a previously overlooked aspect of mask usage: mask wearing by infectious people ("source control") with benefits at the population level, rather than only mask wearing by susceptible people, such as health care workers, with focus on individual outcomes'.[121] Analysis in the course of the COVID-19 pandemic has highlighted not just the advantages of wearing of masks but a need for masks to be of a particular quality to achieve their objectives.

---

[116] ibid 6.
[117] World Health Organization and UNICEF, 'Advice on the Use of Masks for Children in the Community in the Context of COVID-19: Annex to the Advice on the Use of Masks in the Context of COVID-19' (21 August 2020) 3 <https://apps.who.int/iris/bitstream/handle/10665/333919/WHO-2019-nCoV-IPC_Masks-Children-2020.1-eng.pdf?sequence=1&isAllowed=y> accessed 2 October 20212.
[118] World Health Organization, 'Mask Use in the Context of COVID-19: Interim Guidance' (1 December 2020) 9 <https://www.who.int/publications/i/item/advice-on-the-use-of-masks-in-the-community-during-home-care-and-in-healthcare-settings-in-the-context-of-the-novel-coronavirus-(2019-ncov)-outbreak> accessed 2 October 2022.
[119] Han and others (n 35) 1527–28; Wei Lyu and George L Wehby, 'Community Use of Face Masks and COVID-19: Evidence from a Natural Experiment of State Mandates in the US' (2020) 39(8) *Health Affairs* 1419. For discussion of the requirements for wearing of face masks in Australia and England see Fiona McDonald and Claire J Howell, 'Face Masks for Public Use During the COVID-19 Pandemic An Examination of Responses in Australia and England' in Belinda Bennett and Ian Freckelton (eds), *Pandemics, Public Health Emergencies and Government Powers: Perspectives on Australian Law* (Federation Press 2021).
[120] See Matthew Weaver, 'What are the Covid Rules and Guidelines in the Four Nations of the UK?' *The Guardian* (9 December 2021) <https://www.theguardian.com/world/2021/dec/09/what-are-the-covid-rules-and-guidelines-in-the-four-nations-of-the-uk> accessed 10 December 2021.
[121] See Jeremy Howard and others, 'An Evidence Review of Face Masks against COVID-19' (2021) 118(4) *Proceedings of the National Academy of Sciences of the United States of America* art e2014564118.

'The effectiveness of cloth masks to protect the wearer is lower than their effectiveness' for protecting others,[122] 'and the filtration capacity of cloth masks can be highly dependent on design, fit, and materials used.' It has been argued that formulation of standards for cloth masks is needed to help consumers choose products that are marketed during a pandemic.[123]

IX. Mandatory Vaccination

In many countries, during the second half of 2021, opening up after the previous 18 months of COVID-19 entailed limitations being placed upon freedoms, conditional upon people being able to establish that they were at reduced risk of contracting and transmitting the virus. Generally, people were permitted various freedoms if they could show proof of having been double vaccinated or at least that for a time they had been virus-free. In countries requiring double vaccination status this involved deprivation of work opportunities for some people and denial of access to venues and events unless proof could be shown of vaccination status. Litigation in respect of challenges to such requirements is discussed in Chapter 6.

A. Immunity and Vaccinations

The immune response of persons infected with COVID viruses is being researched energetically, given its importance for clinical practice, policy development, and the formulation of legally enforced restrictions. A 2020 paper published in *Nature* found that 23 patients who had recovered from severe acute respiratory syndrome (SARS) still possessed T cells 17 years after infection with SARS in the 2003 pandemic.[124] A review of 5,882 people who had recovered from COVID-19 infection found that antibodies were still present in their blood five to seven months after illness. This was true for mild and severe cases, but people with severe disease had more antibodies overall.[125]

Research has indicated that those who have been infected with COVID-19, even those with mild infections, are likely to have some protection against the virus.[126]

---

[122] See John T Brooks and Jay C Butler, 'Effectiveness of Mask Wearing to Control Community Spread of SARS-CoV-2' (2021) 325(10) *Journal of the American Medical Association* 998, 998 citing Hiroshi Ueki and others, 'Effectiveness of Face Masks in Preventing Airborne Transmission of SARS-CoV-2' (2020) 5(5) *mSphere* art e00637–20.

[123] Brooks and Butler (n 122) 998.

[124] Nina Le Bert and others, 'SARS-CoV-2-specific T Cell Immunity in Cases of COVID-19 and SARS, and Uninfected Controls' (2020) 584(7821) *Nature* 457.

[125] Tyler J Ripperger and others, 'Orthogonal SARS-CoV-2 Serological Assays Enable Surveillance of Low-prevalence Communities and Reveal Durable Humoral Immunity' (2020) 53(5) *Immunity* 925.

[126] Zijun Wang and others, 'Naturally Enhanced Neutralizing Breadth Against SARS-CoV-2 One Year After Infection' (2021) 595(7867) *Nature* 426.

It has been suggested that 'Undue public confidence in the long-term durability of immunity following natural infection by SARS-CoV-2' has contributed to vaccine hesitancy in some countries.[127] This has major ramifications for the development of public policy and for the use of legal sanctions to inhibit the participation in the community of persons who are not vaccinated, even if they have been infected with COVID: 'Maintaining public health measures that curb transmission—including among individuals who were previously infected with SARS-CoV-2—coupled with persistent efforts to accelerate vaccination worldwide is critical to the prevention of COVID-19 morbidity and mortality.'[128] It also highlights the difference between being immune and being vaccinated.

The effectiveness of vaccines against COVID-19 can be measured by reference to the potential for persons to be infected with the virus and also by reference to the incidence of symptomatic disease, hospitalization, and death. While vaccines have proved effective in providing protection against serious disease, they are less effective in protecting against asymptomatic disease and against transmission of the virus while infected.[129] However, in a retrospective cohort study of 3,436,957 individuals,[130] for fully vaccinated persons, effectiveness against SARS-CoV-2 infections was measured at 73% and against COVID-19-related hospital admissions it was 90%. After five months the effectiveness of vaccines against infection declined to 47%, compared to 88% during the first month after vaccination. The effectiveness of the vaccines against hospital admissions for infections with the Delta variant for all ages was 93% up to six months.[131] The potential for the efficacy of vaccines to decline over time has prompted implementation of vaccine booster programmes whereby those who have received double vaccination would be encouraged to receive a third (booster) vaccination.[132] However, concerns have been expressed about booster programmes when many people in some countries have not received a first dose of a COVID-19 vaccine.[133] In late October 2021, for instance, 9.4% of the population of the United Kingdom had received a booster

---

[127] Jeffrey P Townsend and others, 'The Durability of Immunity Against Reinfection by SARS-CoV-2: A Comparative Evolutionary Study' (2021) 2(12) *Lancet Microbe* e666, e673. See also Valentina Gerussi and others, 'Vaccine Hesitancy among Italian Patients Recovered from COVID-19 Infection Towards Influenza and SARS-CoV-2 Vaccination' (2021) 9(2) *Vaccines* 172.

[128] Townsend and others (n 127) e666.

[129] See Philip R Krause and others, 'Considerations in Boosting COVID-19 Vaccine Immune Responses' (2021) 398(10308) *Lancet* 1377, 1378.

[130] Sara Y Tartof and others, 'Effectiveness of mRNA BNT162b2 COVID-19 Vaccine Up to 6 Months in a Large Integrated Health System in the USA: A Retrospective Cohort Study' (2021) 398(10309) *Lancet* 1407.

[131] ibid.

[132] Claire Parker and Bryan Pietsch, 'Countries Around the World Are Debating Coronavirus Booster Shots. Here's Where They've Been Approved' *Washington Post* (12 November 2021) <https://www.washingtonpost.com/world/2021/11/12/coronavirus-vaccine-boosters-global/> accessed 9 December 2021.

[133] World Health Organization, 'Interim Statement on Booster Doses for COVID-19 Vaccination' (22 December 2021) <https://www.who.int/news/item/22-12-2021-interim-statement-on-booster-doses-for-covid-19-vaccination---update-22-december-2021> accessed 2 October 2022.

vaccination for COVID-19 whereas only 8.5% of Africa's population had received its first dose.[134]

B. Mandatory Vaccination

As discussed further in Chapters 11 and 12, during the pandemic, several COVID-19 vaccines were developed that reduced the potential for people who were vaccinated to contract the virus and, if they did become infected, to transmit it to others and develop severe illness or die from it.[135] In response to a rising incidence of COVID-19 infections, several governments decided to mandate COVID-19 vaccination.[136] Other governments significantly inhibited rights of citizens to avail themselves of freedoms if they elected not to be vaccinated. In Austria in November 2021, the government ordered a lockdown of those who had not been vaccinated, affecting up to two million people in a country of 8.9 million people[137] and then mooted the imposition of fines of up to €7,200 for those who did not submit to vaccinations.[138] In the Philippines, too, after already making vaccination or frequent testing for COVID-19 compulsory for those working in offices,[139] President Duterte signalled his preparedness to mandate universal vaccination after meeting with the country's National Task Force Against COVID-19 to discuss the emergence of the Omicron variant.[140] Reflecting global debate on the issue, Philippines

[134] See Emmanuel Akinwotu, Tobi Thomas, and Pamela Duncan, 'UK Boosters Outstripping First Jabs in Africa per Capita' *The Guardian* (30 October 2021) <https://www.theguardian.com/world/2021/oct/29/uk-covid-boosters-outstripping-first-jabs-in-africa-per-capita> accessed 2 October 2022.

[135] See eg Jamie Lopez Bernal et al, 'Effectiveness of Covid-19 Vaccines Against the B.1.617.2 (Delta) Variant' (2021) 385(7) *New England Journal of Medicine* 585, 593; Anoop SV Shah and others, 'Effect of Vaccination on Transmission of SARS-Cov-2' (2021) 385(18) *New England Journal of Medicine* 1718.

[136] Reuters, 'Factbox: Countries Making COVID-19 Vaccines Mandatory' (17 August 2021) <https://www.reuters.com/world/countries-make-covid-19-vaccines-mandatory-2021-07-13/> accessed 18 May 2022; I Glenn Cohen, 'Can Your Employer Require That You Get Vaccinated? It Depends Where You Live' *Time* (2 August 2021) <https://time.com/6086537/covid-19-vaccine-employer-required/> accessed 5 October 2021; Nathaniel Weixel, 'As COVID-19 Infections Climb, Vaccine Mandates Follow' *The Hill* (8 August 2021) <https://thehill.com/policy/healthcare/566810-as-covid-19-infections-climb-vaccine-mandates-follow?rl=1> accessed 2 October 2022.

[137] See Alan Greene, 'Austria's Lockdown for the Unvaccinated: What Does Human Rights Law Say?' *The Conversation* (18 November 2021) <theconversation.com/austrias-lockdown-for-the-unvaccinated-what-does-human-rights-law-say-171911> accessed 2 October 2022; Kirsten Greishaber, 'Austria Orders Nationwide Lockdown for Unvaccinated People' *Sydney Morning Herald* (15 November 2021) <www.smh.com.au/world/europe/austria-orders-nationwide-lockdown-for-unvaccinated-people-20211115-p598ux.html> accessed 2 October 2022.

[138] See Oliver Noyan, 'Austria Considers €7,200 Fine for Unvaccinated' *Euractiv* (30 November 2021) <www.euractiv.com/section/politics/short_news/austria-considers-e7200-fine-for-unvaccinated/> accessed 30 November 2021.

[139] See 'Philippines to Require Vaccination for Employees Working On-site' *Reuters* (12 November 2021) <www.reuters.com/world/asia-pacific/philippines-require-vaccination-employees-working-on-site-2021-11-12/> accessed 2 October 2022.

[140] See Zacarian Sarao, 'Duterte Open to Making Jabs Mandatory; Cabinet Mulls "Pressuring" the Unvaccinated' *Inquirer* (29 November 2021) <https://newsinfo.inquirer.net/1521567/duterte-says-he-agrees-with-making-vaccines-mandatory-cabinet-mulls-pressuring-the-unvaccinated> accessed 2 October 2022.

Interior Secretary Eduardo Año stated that he preferred to avoid making vaccination mandatory, but noted that several local governments had compelled vaccinations already using section 16 of the *Local Government Code* (Phil) which allowed the executive to make orders or ordinances that will protect constituents and that 'is considered legal unless stopped by the court'.[141]

Governments of some countries, including Indonesia, Turkmenistan, and Micronesia, mandated COVID-19 vaccination for the entire adult population.[142] Other governments, such as those in Fiji, Canada, and the United States, imposed vaccine mandates for all public servants (the latter also required vaccination of employees of contractors who worked with the government).[143] By contrast, some governments made vaccination mandatory principally for people who worked in industries where they had a particularly high risk of transmitting and contracting COVID-19.[144] For instance, on 1 April 2021, Italy became the first European country to mandate vaccination against COVID-19 for all healthcare workers.[145] Other countries, including France, Hungary, Greece, and Australia soon followed this example.[146] Similarly, governments of some countries, such as Australia, France, Greece, and England also required vaccination of nursing home workers.[147] The government of the Australian state of Victoria took an especially broad approach, requiring vaccination of workers in myriad industries.[148] In some countries there have been legal challenges to these mandates. These challenges are discussed in Chapter 6.

Anticipating the extensive use of COVID-19 vaccine mandates, WHO issued a policy brief on the subject on 13 April 2021.[149] It observed that 'such policies can

---

[141] ibid. The Federated States of Micronesia has also made vaccination compulsory in all contexts as a 'necessary step to achieve herd immunity': Mala Darmadi, 'Federated States of Micronesia Makes COVID-19 Vaccine Mandatory' *ABC* (30 July 2021) <www.abc.net.au/radio-australia/programs/pacificbeat/fsm-president-iv/13477078> accessed 2 October 2022.

[142] Reuters, (n 136).

[143] ibid; David Smith, 'Biden Announces New US Vaccine Mandates to "Turn the Tide of COVID-19"' *The Guardian* (10 September 2021) <www.theguardian.com/us-news/2021/sep/09/joe-biden-coronavirus-covid-pandemic-white-house> accessed 2 October 2022.

[144] Reuters (n 136).

[145] See Marta Paterlini, 'Covid-19: Italy Makes Vaccination Mandatory for Healthcare Workers' (2021) 373 *British Medical Journal* n905; Michele Massa, 'The Italian "No Jab, No Job" Law', *Verfassungblog on Matters Constitutional* (7 April 2021) <https://verfassungsblog.de/the-italian-no-jab-no-job-law/> accessed 2 October 2022; Stefano C Matteucci, 'Italy: Between Mandatory and Conditional Covid-19 Vaccination Policies' *Lex-Atlas: COVID-19* (4 May 2021) <https://lexatlas-c19.org/covid-19-vaccination-in-italy-between-compulsory-and-conditional-policies-2/> accessed 2 October 2022.

[146] Reuters (n 136); Peter Beaumont, 'Which Countries are Enforcing Mandatory Covid Jabs—and How?' *The Guardian* (16 September 2021) <www.theguardian.com/world/2021/sep/16/which-countries-enforcing-mandatory-covid-vaccination> accessed 2 October 2022; Jacqui Wise, 'France and Greece Make Vaccination Mandatory for Healthcare Workers' (2021) 374 *British Medical Journal* n1797.

[147] Reuters (n 136); Beaumont (n 146).

[148] Premier of Victoria, 'Vaccination Required to Protect Workers and Victoria' Media Release (1 October 2021) <www.premier.vic.gov.au/vaccination-required-protect-workers-and-victoria> accessed 2October 2022.

[149] World Health Organization, 'COVID-19 and Mandatory Vaccination: Ethical Considerations and Caveats Policy Brief' (13 April 2021) <https://www.who.int/publications/i/item/WHO-2019-nCoV-Policy-brief-Mandatory-vaccination-2021.1> accessed 2 October 2022.

be ethically justified, as they may be crucial to protect the health and wellbeing of the public', but they 'interfere with individual liberty and autonomy' and thus 'raise a number of ethical considerations and concerns'.[150] WHO noted that, while mandatory vaccination is 'not truly compulsory', such 'policies limit individual choice in non-trivial ways'.[151] It stated that it did 'not presently support the direction of mandates for COVID-19 vaccination, having argued that it is better to work on information campaigns and making vaccines accessible', but its policy brief did 'not provide a position that endorses or opposes mandatory COVID-19 vaccination'.[152] Instead, WHO highlighted 'important ethical considerations and caveats that should be explicitly evaluated and discussed through ethical analysis by governments and/or institutional policy-makers who may be considering mandates for COVID-19 vaccination',[153] including that:

- 'Mandatory vaccination should be considered only if it is necessary for, and proportionate to, the achievement of an important public health goal (including socioeconomic goals) identified by a legitimate public health authority. If such a public health goal (e.g., herd immunity, protecting the most vulnerable, protecting the capacity of the acute health care system) can be achieved with less coercive or intrusive policy interventions (e.g., public education), a mandate would not be ethically justified, as achieving public health goals with less restriction of individual liberty and autonomy yields a more favourable risk-benefit ratio';
- 'Data should be available that demonstrate the vaccine being mandated has been found to be safe in the populations for whom the vaccine is to be made mandatory. When safety data are lacking or when they suggest the risks associated with vaccination outweigh the risks of harm without the vaccine, the mandate would not be ethically justified, particularly without allowing for reasonable exceptions (e.g., medical contraindications)';
- 'Data on efficacy and effectiveness should be available that show the vaccine is efficacious in the population for whom vaccination is to be mandated and that the vaccine is an effective means of achieving an important public health goal';
- 'In order for a mandate to be considered, supply of the authorized vaccine should be sufficient and reliable, with reasonable, free access for those for whom it is to be made mandatory (i.e., there should be few barriers that make it difficult for populations affected by the mandate to access the vaccine)';
- 'Policy-makers have a duty to carefully consider the effect that mandating vaccination could have on public confidence and public trust, and particularly on

---

[150] ibid 1.
[151] ibid.
[152] ibid.
[153] ibid 1.

confidence in the scientific community and public trust in vaccination generally'; and
- 'Transparency and stepwise decision-making by legitimate public health authorities should be fundamental elements of ethical analysis and decision-making about mandatory vaccination'.[154]

As discussed further below, these considerations reflect some of the matters that can usefully inform determinations of whether an infringement of human rights by virtue of a COVID-19 vaccine mandate could be justifiable.

Mandatory vaccination can also be regarded as protective of some human rights.[155] For instance, by requiring people to have a COVID-19 vaccine, State Parties to the *ICCPR* might fulfil their obligation to protect 'the right to life', which Article 6 recognizes.[156] By compelling people who would have chosen not to have a vaccine to do so, it could protect from the 'reasonably foreseeable threat' of a 'life-threatening disease' imperilling their lives,[157] but also the lives of other people who are unable to have a vaccine due to their health conditions. Increasing the number of vaccinated people could have helped to control the pandemic if it assisted in reaching the threshold for 'herd immunity': the point at which enough people were vaccinated against COVID-19 to minimize the risk for those who had not been vaccinated to contract it.[158] Also for these reasons, mandatory vaccination has the potential to help protect the 'right to health'.[159] Article 12 of the *International Covenant on Economic, Social and Cultural Rights* provides that State Parties 'recognize the right of everyone to the enjoyment of the highest attainable standard of physical and mental health', and 'steps' they must take 'to achieve the full realization of this right shall include those necessary for ... control of epidemic ... diseases'.[160]

Yet COVID-19 vaccine mandates could be regarded as encroaching upon the rights to life and health if people suffer side-effects or adverse events after vaccination.[161] For instance, the AstraZeneca, Pfizer, and Moderna COVID-19

---

[154] ibid 1–3.
[155] See Gabrielle Wolf, Jason Taliadoros, and Penny Gleeson, 'A Panacea for Australia's COVID-19 Crisis? Weighing Some Legal Implications of Mandatory Vaccination' (2021) 28(4) *Journal of Law and Medicine* 993.
[156] Ashlee Beazley, 'Contagion, Containment, Consent: Infectious Disease Pandemics and the Ethics, Rights and Legality of State-enforced Vaccination' (2020) 7(1) *Journal of Law and the Biosciences* art lsaa021, 9.
[157] United Nations Human Rights Committee, 'Article 6, Right to Life' (General Comment No 36 CCPR/C/GC/36, 3 September 2019) paras 3, 18, 21, 26.
[158] Beazley (n 156) 4; Michelle M Mello, Ross D Silverman, and Saad B Omer 'Ensuring Uptake of Vaccines against SARS-CoV-2' (2020) 383(14) *New England Journal of Medicine* 1296, 1296.
[159] Beazley (n 156) 9.
[160] *International Covenant on Economic, Social and Cultural Rights* (opened for signature 16 December 1966, entered into force 3 January 1976) 993 UNTS 3.
[161] Anja Krasser, 'Compulsory Vaccination in a Fundamental Rights Perspective: Lessons from the ECtHr' (2021) 15(2) *Vienna Journal on International Constitutional Law* 207, 209–15.

vaccines have been associated with some rare health complications.[162] Mandatory vaccination might also limit the right to health if it is considered to be 'coercive medical treatment'; the United Nations Committee on Economic, Social and Cultural Rights has observed that the right to health includes the right 'to be free from ... non-consensual medical treatment' and the obligation to respect the right to health involves the 'obligation to refrain ... from applying coercive medical treatments'.[163] A COVID-19 vaccine mandate could curtail people's exercise of other human rights, too. For example, it might impinge on the right recognized in Article 17 of the *ICCPR* not to be 'subjected to arbitrary or unlawful interference with [one's] privacy', if an individual needs to disclose their vaccination status or the reasons they are seeking an exemption from a requirement to be vaccinated. If an individual's religion prohibits vaccination and/or they hold a belief that involves opposition to vaccination, mandatory COVID-19 vaccination could also engage the right recognized in Article 18 of the *ICCPR* to 'freedom of thought, conscience and religion'. This right includes freedom 'to have or to adopt a religion or belief of [one's] choice' and freedom to 'manifest' one's 'religion or belief', including through 'observance' and 'practice'.

Nevertheless, provision of exemptions from COVID-19 vaccine mandates could ensure that some human rights remain protected. For example, if a mandate provides medical exemptions for people with a predisposition to experiencing adverse side-effects from vaccination, the rights to health and life might still be protected.[164] Likewise, vaccine mandates could provide exemptions on religious grounds to ensure that they do not infringe the right to 'freedom of thought, conscience and religion' (though people may rely on such exemptions disingenuously and they might be difficult to 'police').[165]

In some countries, though, concerns have been raised that some medical practitioners may have been subverting mandatory vaccination regimes by issuing spurious exemptions. A general practitioner was referred to the medical regulator

---

[162] See generally Ian Freckelton, 'Mandatory Vaccination Tensions and Litigation' (2021) 28(4) *Journal of Law and Medicine* 913; Julia Hippisley-Cox and others, 'Risk of Thrombocytopenia and Thromboembolism After COVID-19 Vaccination and SARS-CoV2 Positive Testing: Self-Controlled Case Series Study' (2021) 374 *British Medical Journal* n1931; Australian Government, 'Is it True? Does the Vaxzevria (AstraZeneca) COVID-19 Vaccine Cause Blood Clots?' (Department of Health, 4 September 2021) <https://www.health.gov.au/initiatives-and-programs/covid-19-vaccines/is-it-true/is-it-true-does-the-vaxzevria-astrazeneca-covid-19-vaccine-cause-blood-clots> accessed 2 October 2022; Australian Government, 'Guidance on Myocarditis and Pericarditis after mRNA COVID-19 Vaccines' (30 July 2021, updated 29 April 2022) <https://www.health.gov.au/sites/default/files/documents/2021/08/covid-19-vaccination-guidance-on-myocarditis-and-pericarditis-after-mrna-covid-19-vaccines.pdf?> accessed 16 May 2022.
[163] Committee on Economic, Social and Cultural Rights, 'General Comment No 14: The Right to the Highest Attainable Standard of Health (Article 12) of the International Covenant on Economic, Social and Cultural Rights' (E/C/12/2000/4, United Nations, 11 August 2000) paras 8, 34.
[164] Krasser (n 161) 212.
[165] Dorit Rubenstein Reiss, 'Religious Exemptions to Vaccines and the Anti-vax Movement' *(Harvard Law Petrie-Flom Center*, 16 July 2021) <https://blog.petrieflom.law.harvard.edu/2021/07/16/religious-exemptions-to-vaccines-and-the-anti-vax-movement/> accessed 2 October 2022.

and his practice in Melbourne, Australia, was raided after concerns were raised about his allegedly granting fraudulent vaccination exemptions.[166] In Connecticut in the United States, the state Medical Examining Board withdrew charges against a Durham physician accused of providing fraudulent exemptions for COVID-19 vaccines after she voluntarily relinquished her medical licence.[167]

Further, restrictions on human rights through COVID-19 vaccine mandates might be justifiable. Protection of public health, which these vaccine mandates are intended to achieve, is considered a reasonable purpose of such restrictions. For instance, as already noted, the *Siracusa Principles* provide that, in certain circumstances, protecting public health can be a legitimate reason for limiting human rights and State Parties can derogate from their obligations in respect of human rights if they are seeking to achieve this objective.[168] To be justifiable, a vaccine mandate must also be necessary to achieve that objective and proportionate to it.[169] Article 18(3) of the *ICCPR*, for example, provides that 'freedom to manifest one's religion or beliefs may be subject only to such limitations as are prescribed by law and are necessary to protect public ... health'. Similarly, an interference with the right to privacy through a vaccine mandate might be justifiable if it is prescribed by law and not arbitrary because it is reasonable and proportionate.[170] The *European Convention on Human Rights* provides, similarly to the *ICCPR*, that 'everyone has the right to respect for his private ... life' and 'there shall be no interference by a public authority with the exercise of this right except such as is in accordance with the law and is necessary in a democratic society ... for the protection of health'.[171] In *Vavřička and Others v The Czech Republic*, the European Court of Human Rights held that a requirement to vaccinate children engaged this right, but was justified because it was 'in accordance with the [domestic] law' and, by addressing a 'pressing social need to protect individual and public health', pursued 'legitimate aims ... "necessary in a democratic society"'.[172]

---

[166] See Melissa Coade, 'Health Department Orders Raid on Doctor Suspected of Falsifying COVID Vaccine Exemptions' *The Mandarin* (11 November 2021) <https://www.themandarin.com.au/174784-health-department-orders-raid-on-doctor-suspected-of-falsifying-covid-vaccine-exemptions/> accessed 10 December 2021.

[167] See Lisa Backus, 'State Drops Charges Against Doctor for Issuing Fake Vaccine Exemptions' *CT Mirror* (21 October 2021) <https://ctmirror.org/2021/10/21/state-drops-charges-against-doctor-for-issuing-fake-vaccine-exemptions/> accessed 2 October 2022.

[168] *Siracusa Principles* (n 8) cls 25, 39.

[169] ibid (n 8) cls 10–11.

[170] Jacqui Wise, 'Covid-19: Is the UK Heading Towards Mandatory Vaccination of Healthcare Workers?' (2021) 373 *British Medical Journal* n1056; Sarah Joseph, 'Civil and Political Rights' in Mashood A Baderin and Manisuli Ssenyonjo (eds), *International Human Rights Law: Six Decades after the UDHR and Beyond* (Ashgate 2010).

[171] *Convention for the Protection of Human Rights and Fundamental Freedoms* (opened for signature 4 November 1950, entered into force 3 September 1953) 213 UNTS 221, Article 8.

[172] Application No 47621/13 (8 April 2021) ECHR <https://hudoc.echr.coe.int/fre#%7B%22:temid%22:[%22001-209039%22]%7D> [263]–[312]; Anna Nilsson, 'Is Compulsory Childhood Vaccination Compatible with the Right to Respect for Private Life? A Comment on *Vavřička and Others v the Czech Republic*' (2021) 28(3) *European Journal of Health Law* 323.

A COVID-19 vaccine mandate might be considered necessary to protect public health if vaccine hesitancy—which has been defined as a 'delay in acceptance or refusal of vaccination despite availability of vaccination services'—is causing low vaccine uptake and mandatory vaccination addresses the reasons for it.[173] The Working Group on Vaccine Hesitancy of the Strategic Advisory Group of Experts on Immunization, which advises WHO on policies and strategies, identified that 'complacency, convenience and confidence' can influence vaccine hesitancy.[174] If mandatory vaccination counteracts these factors, it could increase the volume of vaccinated people. Several surveys that were conducted early in the pandemic to ascertain how many people would voluntarily receive a COVID-19 vaccine yielded inconsistent results.[175] It was nonetheless apparent that anti-vaccination movements experienced a resurgence globally during this pandemic.[176] The speed at which COVID-19 vaccines were developed and circulation of misinformation about them seemed to fuel resistance to them by triggering concerns about their safety.[177]

It is futile to make vaccination mandatory until sufficient doses are available and, when that is the case, mandatory vaccination may in fact be unnecessary to achieve herd immunity.[178] In many places, and even in high-income countries such as Australia, there was initially a low supply of preferred COVID-19 vaccines and people experienced barriers to accessing them.[179] Compelling people to have COVID-19 vaccines could further lower public trust in them and intensify resistance to vaccination.[180] COVID-19 vaccine mandates might nonetheless still be considered necessary if they could increase the number of vaccinated people in settings where there is a heightened risk of contracting and suffering serious

---

[173] Noni E MacDonald and The SAGE Working Group on Vaccine Hesitancy, 'Vaccine Hesitancy: Definition, Scope and Determinants' (2015) 33(34) *Vaccine* 4161, 4163–64.

[174] 'Report of the SAGE Working Group on Vaccine Hesitancy' (12 October 2014) 7 <https://www.asset-scienceinsociety.eu/sites/default/files/sage_working_group_revised_report_vaccine_hesitancy.pdf> accessed 2 October 2022.

[175] See eg Jeffrey V Lazarus and others, 'A Global Survey of Potential Acceptance of a COVID-19 Vaccine' (2021) 27(2) *Nature Medicine* 225; Emily A Largent and others, 'US Public Attitudes Toward COVID-19 Vaccine Mandates' (2020) 3(12) *Journal of American Medical Association Network Open* art e2033324; Freckelton (n 162).

[176] Lawrence O Gostin, Safura Abdool Karim, and Benjamin Mason Meier, 'Facilitating Access to a COVID-19 Vaccine Through Global Health Law' (2020) 48(3) *Journal of Law, Medicine & Ethics* 622, 623; Lazarus and others (n 175); Philip Ball, 'Anti-Vaccine Movement Might Undermine Pandemic Efforts' (2020) 581(7808) *Nature* 251.

[177] Lazarus and others (n 175); Dorit Rubinstein Reiss and Tony Yang, 'Why a COVID-19 Vaccine Shouldn't be Mandatory' (*Harvard Law Petrie-Flom Center*, 15 September 2020) <https://blog.petrieflom.law.harvard.edu/2020/09/15/covid19-vaccine-mandate-compulsory/> accessed 15 February 2021.

[178] Reiss and Yang (n 177); Mello, Silverman, and Omer (n 158) 1297.

[179] 'Covid: Vaccines Running Out in Poorer Nations, WHO Says' *BBC News* (21 June 2021) <www.bbc.com/news/world-57558401> accessed 5 October 2021; Julie Leask and others, 'Policy Considerations for Mandatory Covid-19 Vaccination from the Collaboration on Social Science in Immunisation' (2021) 215(11) *Medical Journal of Australia* 499, 500.

[180] Lawrence O Gostin, Daniel A Salmon, and Heidi J Larson, 'Mandating COVID-19 Vaccines' (2021) 325(6) *Journal of the American Medical Association* 532, 533.

harm and/or dying from COVID-19, such as residential aged care, hospitals, and prisons. In those environments, mandatory vaccination might also be deemed to be a proportionate measure because the threat to people's health if they are exposed to COVID-19 and those who are not vaccinated is serious and it would be very difficult to reduce that risk adequately through other measures.[181] Nevertheless, in other settings, mandatory vaccination might not be deemed proportionate to the objective of protecting public health because it is more restrictive than is necessary to achieve it and other measures that are less restrictive of human rights could realize that purpose.[182] For instance, non-coercive measures, such as provision of financial incentives to have a COVID-19 vaccine and government-sponsored public education campaigns that convey the vaccines' efficacy and safety, might have increased vaccination rates to the point where public health was substantially protected.[183]

Addressing some of these concerns, Michelle Mello, Ross Silverman, and Saad Omer suggested that United States governments in particular might legitimately mandate vaccination if the following preconditions are met: as other 'less burdensome' public health measures have failed and there has been insufficient 'voluntary uptake' of vaccines to contain the transmission of COVID-19, it remains a threat to public health, so it is reasonable and necessary to encroach on individuals' autonomy; the Advisory Committee on Immunization Practices has reviewed evidence of the vaccines' safety and efficacy and recommended vaccination; the government has transparently communicated available evidence about vaccines' safety and effectiveness; vaccine supplies are sufficient to immunize the population groups for whom mandatory vaccination is proposed; and governments have arranged for those groups to access vaccination and monitor any side effects of the vaccines.[184]

X. Vaccination Passports

As countries implemented their vaccination programmes, increasing the numbers of people who became fully vaccinated and the ability to provide proof of vaccination (a vaccination passport)—the implications of being fully vaccinated became increasingly important.[185] Foremost among these issues was whether fully

---

[181] Stephen Duckett and others, *Race to 80: Our Best Shot at Living With COVID* (Grattan Institute, Report No 2021-09) (29 July 2021) 41 <https://grattan.edu.au/report/race-to-80/> accessed 2 October 2022.
[182] *Siracusa Principles* (n 8) cl 11.
[183] Anna Odone and others, 'Current Understandings of the Impact of Mandatory Vaccination Laws in Europe' (2021) 20(5) *Expert Review of Vaccines* 559, 570–71.
[184] Mello, Silverman, and Omer (n 158) 1297–98.
[185] See Mark A Hall and David M Studdert, '"Vaccine Passport" Certification—Policy and Ethical Considerations' (2021) 385 *New England Journal of Medicine* e32.

vaccinated individuals should be subject to fewer restrictions on their freedom of movement and travel than persons who were not vaccinated, or whether they would be exempt from or subject to less onerous quarantine requirements in countries that required travellers to quarantine on entry. While vaccination passports are often discussed in the context of travel, they are already being used to regulate access to services domestically, such as access to theatres, music venues, or sporting events.[186] They can take the form of paper-based documents or, more commonly, downloadable modes appropriate for mobile telephones.

It has been suggested that such passports could be granted either on the basis of vaccination or infection-related immunity.[187] However, there are challenges with these approaches given the current lack of knowledge about the length and nature of an immune response to the virus in the context of infection-related immunity and ensuring timely and equitable access to vaccines.[188] Furthermore, there remain uncertainties about whether an individual with immunity still poses a risk of transmission to others, with 'This fact [providing] the greatest challenge to the assurance that individuals who carry immunity passports would have a reduced risk to others.'[189] Concerns have also been expressed over the potential for immunity passports based on infection-related immunity to increase discrimination and disproportionately affect marginalized groups in society.[190]

A number of arguments have been advanced both for and against vaccination passports. The arguments in favour of vaccination passports include:

- That we should not impose restrictions on the freedom of movement of individuals who, because of their immunity, have a reduced risk of catching and transmitting the disease;
- Individuals who know they are immune may become less compliant with lockdown measures. As a result, they may be subject to fines or other penalties that do not accord with the harm that their behaviour may cause;
- There will be broader social benefits from allowing immune individuals to return to work and allowing them to care for others who may be vulnerable.[191]

Other concerns relating to vaccination passports include that conferring privileges on those who have been vaccinated would be unfair while vaccines supplies

---

[186] ibid.
[187] Rebecca CH Brown and others, 'The Scientific and Ethical Feasibility of Immunity Passports' (2021) 21(3) *Lancet Infectious Diseases* e58, e58–e59. In response see Françoise Baylis and Natalie Kofler, 'A Public Health Ethic Should Inform Policies on COVID-19 Immunity Passports' (2021) 21(4) *Lancet Infectious Diseases* 456.
[188] Brown and others (n 187) e59.
[189] ibid.
[190] Natalie Kofler and Françoise Baylis, 'Ten Reasons Why Immunity Passports Are a Bad Idea' (2020) 581(7809) *Nature* 379.
[191] Brown and others (n 187) e59–e60.

are low and would disproportionately impact on members of minority and low-income groups who may have lower rates of vaccination.[192] It has been pointed out that existing laws may not provide protection from discrimination on the basis of immunity status.[193]

Further issues arise regarding vaccination passports, including whether they should be issued by governments or private entities and, if issued by government, which level of government (federal, state, or local) should issue them.[194] There is also a need to consider the privacy implications of vaccine passports.[195] In the United States, Greely has observed that 'The power of the federal government to "issue" such certificates is probably not questionable but its powers to limit someone's activities based on them could be.'[196] The duration for which an immunity certificate or passport would be valid would also need to be determined,[197] along with clarity over which series of vaccines will be required.[198]

Requirements for proof of vaccination are not new.[199] For example, the *IHR (2005)* already contain provisions that allow states to require vaccination certificates from travellers for specified diseases, although this is currently limited to yellow fever.[200] However, with the introduction of vaccines for COVID-19, the debate over vaccination passports has gained momentum. Canada,[201] Australia,[202] and a number of European countries[203] committed to vaccination passports.

---

[192] Hall and Studdert (n 185) e32(1). See also Ryan Tanner and Collen M Flood, 'Vaccine Passports Done Equitably' (2021) 2(4) *Journal of the American Medical Association Health Forum* art e210972.

[193] Alexandra Phelan, 'COVID-19 Immunity Passports and Vaccination Certificates: Scientific, Equitable, and Legal Challenges' (2020) 395(10237) *Lancet* 1595, 1596–97.

[194] Henry T Greely, 'COVID-19 Immunity Certificates: Science, Ethics, Policy and Law' (2020) 7(1) *Journal of Law and the Biosciences* art lsaa035, 14.

[195] See Daniel Sleat, Kirsty Innes, and Imogen Parker, 'Are Vaccine Passports and Covid Passes a Valid Alternative to Lockdowns?' (2021) 375 *British Medical Journal* n2571; Australia Institute, 'Privacy Concerns Cast Shadow over Vaccination Passports' Media Release (10 September 2021) <https://aus traliainstitute.org.au/post/privacy-concerns-cast-shadow-over-vaccination-passports/> accessed 10 December 2021.

[196] Greely (n 194) 14.

[197] ibid 16.

[198] Kumanan Wilson and Colleen Flood, 'Implementing Digital Passports for SARS-CoV-2 Immunization in Canada' (2021) 193(14) *Canadian Medical Association Journal* E486, E487.

[199] Ahmed Sharif and others, 'A Pragmatic Approach to COVID-19 Vaccine Passport' (2021) 6 *BMJ Global Health* art e006956.

[200] ibid; Phelan (n 193) 1597.

[201] Nathan Griffiths, 'Here's What You Need to Know about Canada's New Vaccine Passports' *Times Colonist* (24 October 2021) <www.timescolonist.com/news/b-c/here-s-what-you-need-to-know-about-canada-s-new-vaccine-passports-4692984> accessed 16 May 2022.

[202] Ellen Ransley, 'Vaccine Passports to Roll Out This Week Ahead of International Travel Return' (13 October 2021) *The Australian* <https://www.theaustralian.com.au/breaking-news/vaccine-passports-to-roll-out-this-week-ahead-of-international-travel-return/news-story/d1a15faf6f5249206066b6a95 1db150f> (accessed 2 October 2022).

[203] Sylvie Corbet, 'In a Big Step, France Starts Enforcement of Coronavirus Pass for Public' (10 August 2021) *Sydney Morning Herald* <https://www.smh.com.au/world/europe/france-begins-enforcing-coro navirus-pass-for-diners-travellers-20210810-p58hdk.html> (accessed 2 October 2022).

While Britain decided against vaccination passports,[204] in December 2021, in response to the spread of the Omicron variant, it introduced requirements making the NHS COVID-19 pass mandatory for access to large venues.[205] In October 2021 Italy too extended its proof of vaccination requirements making it mandatory for all workers to have a 'green pass'.[206] From September 2021, residents in British Columbia, Ontario, and Quebec were required to show proof of vaccination before entering various non-essential locations such as restaurants, gyms, cinemas, and entertainment events.[207] By contrast, Alberta implemented an opt-in programme, whereby businesses and event venues have the choice of requiring proof of vaccination or a negative COVID-19 test result before entry, or else follow business capacity restrictions.[208] While provincial vaccine passport regimes share features such as the general definition of 'non-essential' businesses and events, each has approached the challenge of mandating the disclosure of private health information in different ways. Consequently, the personal information being disclosed, and the corresponding privacy risks, are unique to each province.

The Canadian Privacy Commissioners have issued a joint statement about their concerns about vaccination passports:

> At its essence, a vaccine passport presumes that individuals will be required or requested to disclose personal health information—their vaccine/immunity status—in exchange for goods, services and/or access to certain premises or locations. While this may offer substantial public benefit, it is an encroachment on civil liberties that should be taken only after careful consideration. This statement focuses on the privacy considerations.
>
> Vaccine passports must be developed and implemented in compliance with applicable privacy laws. They should also incorporate privacy best practices in order to achieve the highest level of privacy protection commensurate with the sensitivity of the personal health information that will be collected, used or disclosed.[209]

They have contended that:

---

[204] 'Boris Johnson Ditches UK's COVID-19 Vaccine Passports Plan Under Pressure From His Own Party' *ABC News* (13 September 2021) <https://www.abc.net.au/news/2021-09-13/britain-johnson-ditches-covid-19-vaccine-passports/100456088> (accessed 2 October 2022).
[205] Holton and Bruce (n 92); Reuters Staff, 'Fans Must Show Vaccine Pass to Attend Top-Level Games in England' *Reuters* (9 December 2021) <https://www.reuters.com/lifestyle/sports/fans-must-show-vaccine-pass-attend-top-level-games-england-2021-12-08/> accessed 2 October 2022.
[206] 'Covid: Italy to Require All Workers to Show "Green Pass" Certificate' *BBC* (16 September 2021) <https://www.bbc.com/news/world-europe-58590187> accessed 2 October 202.
[207] Griffiths (n 201).
[208] ibid.
[209] Canadian Federal, Provincial and Territorial Privacy Commissioners, 'Privacy and COVID-19 Vaccine Passports' (Joint Statement, 19 May 2021) <www.priv.gc.ca/en/opc-news/speeches/2021/s-d_20210519/> accessed 27 October 2021.

in light of the significant privacy risks involved, the necessity, effectiveness, and proportionality of vaccine passports must be established for each specific context in which they will be used:

- **Necessity:** vaccine passports must be necessary to achieve each intended public health purpose. Their necessity must be evidence-based and there must be no other less privacy-intrusive measures available and equally effective in achieving the specified purposes.
- **Effectiveness:** vaccine passports must be likely to be effective at achieving each of their defined purposes at the outset and must continue to be effective throughout their lifecycle.
- **Proportionality:** the privacy risks associated with vaccine passports must be proportionate to each of the public health purposes they are intended to address. Data minimization should be applied so that the least amount of personal health information is collected, used or disclosed.'

The necessity, effectiveness, and proportionality of vaccine passports must be continually monitored to ensure that they continue to be justified. Vaccine passports must be decommissioned if, at any time, it is determined that they are not a necessary, effective or proportionate response to address their public health purposes.[210]

However, there are other issues. For instance, with the proliferation of vaccines, each country has faced a policy question about which vaccinations should be regarded as meeting the criteria for vaccination passports. Internationally, there are differences in respect of which vaccinations are accepted as preconditions to entering various countries. This is particularly important for travel purposes but also more generally. It is an issue that may become more complex as more variants emerge which require adjustments to vaccines and the development of new vaccines, when only certain developed countries will have access to the latest vaccination options.

In addition, the potential for fraudulent creation of false immunity certificates has highlighted the importance of introducing systems to prevent this[211] because of the potential risks to public health.[212] In turn, this generated enforcement action. For instance, in Germany in November 2021 arrests were made in relation to the manufacture and sale of falsified COVID-19 vaccine documentation.[213]

---

[210] ibid.
[211] Greely (n 194) 16.
[212] ibid; Rebecca CH Brown and others, 'Passport to Freedom? Immunity Passports for COVID-19' (2020) 46 *Journal of Medical Ethics* 652, 656-57.
[213] See Alex Berry, 'Germany: Police Arrest 12 in Fake COVID Vaccine Passports Raid' *DW* (17 November 2021) <https://www.dw.com/en/germany-police-arrest-12-in-fake-covid-vaccine-passports-raids/a-59847837> accessed 2 October 2022.

Finally, the currency of vaccination passports is fundamental to their ongoing utility. The European Union has proposed setting expiry dates for the green COVID-19 pass.[214] France has announced that booster vaccinations for persons aged over 65 years will be required to extend the validity of its COVID-19 health pass.[215] It will be essential for vaccination passports to be able to be updated so as ensure review of their currency and therefore whether they are communicating the holder's present vaccination status.

XI. COVID-19 Testing and Contact Tracing

Digital technologies played an important role in the fight against COVID-19, with disease detection dashboards providing case numbers by geographic region and information about policy responses. In addition, use of digital contact tracing, mobility data, and online and social media information for communication with the public provided important information to the global community and supported decision-making.[216] The ability to test individuals who have been exposed to the virus, to identify those with a positive test result, and to be able to trace their close contacts are all central to the ability to limit the spread of the disease. The availability of testing and timely test results emerged during the COVID-19 period as an important issue. In some parts of the world, lack of capacity in diagnostic testing hampered the ability to combat the virus,[217] highlighting the importance of strong and effective public health capacities at the national and sub-national levels. Even in high-income countries, testing rates varied substantially between countries,[218] making the availability of comparative data essential to being able to compare the responses of different countries to the pandemic.[219] Also important was the increasing availability of sequencing technology with its capacity, in conjunction with epidemiological data, to identify variants of COVID-19.[220] In its 2020 report

---

[214] Silvia Amaro, 'The EU is Planning a 9-month Expiration Date on its Covid Vaccine Passports' *CBNC* (25 November 2021) <https://www.cnbc.com/2021/11/25/covid-travel-eu-proposes-a-9-month-expiration-date-on-vaccine-pass.html> accessed 2 October 2022; Bruno Waterfield, 'EU Covid Passes Set to Expire Without Booster Vaccinations' *The Times* (23 November 2021) <https://www.thetimes.co.uk/article/eu-covid-passes-set-to-expire-without-booster-vaccinations-m0pnh8gsv> accessed 2 October 2022.
[215] 'Covid: France Brings in Booster Requirements for Over 65s' *BBC News* (9 November 2021) <https://www.bbc.com/news/world-europe-59229041> accessed 2 October 2021.
[216] Jobie Budd and others, 'Digital Technologies in the Public-Health Response to COVID-19' (2020) 26(8) *Nature Medicine* 1183.
[217] OI Oyeniran, T Chia, and MI Oraebosi, 'Combating Covid-19 Pandemic in Africa: An Urgent Call to Scale Up Laboratory Testing Capacities' (2020) 15 *Ethics, Medicine and Public Health* art 100552.
[218] Tamara Kovacevic and Ben Butcher, 'Covid in Europe: How Much Testing Do Other Countries Do?' *BBC News* (9 October 2020) <https://www.bbc.com/news/54181291> accessed 2 October 2022.
[219] Joe Hassell and others, 'A Cross-Country Database of COVID-19 Testing' (2020) 7 *Scientific Data* art 345.
[220] Editorial, 'Genomic Sequencing in Pandemics' (2021) 397(10273) *Lancet* 445.

on the Sustainable Development Goals (SDGs), the United Nations noted that 'The importance of timely, quality, open and disaggregated data and statistics has never been as clear as during the COVID-19 crisis'.[221] However, the United Nations also noted that the COVID-19 'pandemic is jeopardizing the production of data central to the achievement of the SDGs'.[222]

A. Contact Tracing

Contact tracing is a well-established procedure within epidemiology and public health although it has been controversial at times.[223] Contact tracing aims to identify individuals who have been exposed to an infectious disease, whether or not they are symptomatic, and to quarantine them from those who have not been exposed to the disease, so as to break the chain of person-to-person transmission.[224] In some countries, collection of information by businesses as part of contact tracing has been mandatory. For instance, in New South Wales, Australia, as of July 2021, businesses needed to take reasonable steps to ensure that individuals entering the venue checked in so as to assist with contact tracing.[225]

However, manual contact tracing can be time-consuming, and the challenges for individuals in accurately recalling their past movements and interactions with others may result in gaps in contact tracing.[226] The effectiveness of contact tracing during the COVID-19 pandemic was variable and controversial.[227] At times when there were high numbers of infections in the community, even in countries with significant numbers of people as contact tracers with public health departments, the feasibility of contact tracing dropped substantially because of logistics.[228]

Many countries sought technological solutions to the data-intensive aspects of contact tracing and to overcome the fallibility of human memory, particularly given the potential time period between infection and onset of symptoms. For COVID-19, contact tracing may be required for up to 14 days before a person

---

[221] United Nations, *Sustainable Development Goals Report 2020* (United Nations 2020) 4.
[222] ibid. See Chapter 3 for further discussion of the impact of the pandemic on civil registration and vital statistics.
[223] See Graham Mooney, '"A Menace to the Public Health"—Contact Tracing and the Limits of Persuasion' (2020) 383 *New England Journal of Medicine* 1806.
[224] World Health Organization, 'Contact Tracing in the Context of COVID-19: Interim Guidance' (1 February 2021) <https://www.who.int/publications/i/item/contact-tracing-in-the-context-of-covid-19> accessed 12 December 2021.
[225] NSW Government, 'COVID-19 Check-in Mandate Expanded' (30 June 2021) <https://www.nsw.gov.au/media-releases/covid-check-mandate-expanded> accessed 18 May 2022.
[226] Isobel Braithwaite and others, 'Automated and Partly Automated Contact Tracing: A Systematic Review to Inform the Control of COVID-19' (2020) 2(11) *Lancet Digital Health* e607; Tyler Shelby and others, 'Lessons Learned from COVID-19 Contact Tracing During a Public Health Emergency: A Prospective Implementation Study' (2021) 9 *Frontiers in Public Health* art 721952.
[227] See eg Dyani Lewis, 'Where COVID Contact Tracing Went Wrong' (2021) 588(7838) *Nature* 384.
[228] ibid 386.

becomes symptomatic,[229] making contact tracing over such a lengthy period challenging. Mobile phone apps or the use of QR codes were identified as a potential solution to these challenges.[230] However, WHO noted that 'Digital tools should be considered a way to augment and optimize contact tracing rather than a replacement of contact tracing teams.'[231] WHO explained proximity tracking as follows:

> One form of digital technology for surveillance that has been receiving attention in many countries facing COVID-19 epidemics in recent months is proximity tracking. Proximity tracking measures signal strength to determine whether two devices [e.g. smartphones] were close enough together for their users to spread the virus from an infected individual to an uninfected person. If one user is infected, others who have been identified as within proximity of the other person can be notified, and thereby take appropriate steps to reduce health risks to themselves and others. Proximity tracking is often conflated with 'contact tracing', although contact tracing is a broad public health discipline, and proximity tracking is a new technique for aiding contact tracing.[232]

However, the use of digital contact tracing apps and QR codes may present challenges in relation to some community groups, such as older persons or socially-disadvantaged community members, amongst whom the use of smart phones may be lower, with these challenges likely to be greater in low-income countries.[233] Furthermore, these apps have not been without their own challenges, with widespread debate over the potential privacy implications of their use,[234] and issues

---

[229] See World Health Organization (n 224).
[230] Han and others (n 35) 1530.
[231] World Health Organization, 'Digital Tools for COVID-19 Contact Tracing: Annex: Contact Tracing in the Context of COVID-19' (2 June 2020) 4 <https://apps.who.int/iris/bitstream/handle/10665/339128/WHO-2019-nCoV-Contact_Tracing-2021.1-eng.pdf?sequence=24&isAllowed=y> accessed 2 October 2022.
[232] World Health Organization, 'Ethical Considerations to Guide the Use of Digital Proximity Tracking Technologies for COVID-19 Contact Tracing' (Interim Guidance, 28 May 2020) (hereafter World Health Organization, 'Ethical Considerations to Guide the Use of Digital Proximity Tracking Technologies') 1 (citation omitted) <https://www.who.int/publications/i/item/WHO-2019-nCoV-Ethics_Contact_tracing_apps-2020.1> accessed 2 October 2022.
[233] Braithwaite and others (n 226) e619.
[234] Laura Bradford, Mateo Aboy, and Kathleen Liddell, 'COVID-19 Contact Tracing Apps: A Stress Test for Privacy, the GDPR and Data Protection Regimes' (2020) 7(1) *Journal of Law and the Biosciences* art lsaa034; Alex Dubov and Steven Shoptawb, 'The Value and Ethics of Using Technology to Contain the COVID-19 Epidemic' (2020) 20(7) *American Journal of Bioethics* W7; Natalie Ram and David Gray, 'Mass Surveillance in the Age of COVID-19' (2020) 7(1) *Journal of Law and the Biosciences* art lsaa023; Gerard Goggin, 'COVID-19 Apps in Singapore and Australia: Reimagining Healthy Nations with Digital Technology' (2020) 177(1) *Media International Australia* 61; OECD, 'Tracking and Tracing COVID: Protecting Privacy and Data While Using Apps and Biometrics' (23 April 2020) <https://read.oecd-ilibrary.org/view/?ref=129_129655-7db0lu7dto&title=Tracking-and-Tracing-COVID-Protecting-privacy-and-data-while-using> accessed 2 October 2022; Normann Witzleb and Moira Paterson, 'The Australian COVIDSafe App and Privacy: Lessons for the Future of Privacy Regulation' in Belinda Bennett and Ian Freckelton (eds), *Pandemics, Public Health Emergencies and Government Powers: Perspectives on Australian Law* (Federation Press 2021).

such as whether the apps should use a centralized approach where data are collected in a central database, or a decentralized approach where contacts are notified but there is no retention of data.[235] In order to be effective, contact tracing apps are likely to require a high level of community uptake,[236] making community trust in them particularly important.[237] Public confidence that the data collected by contact tracing apps will be kept private is key to public acceptance and uptake of the apps. Concerns have been expressed, however, about the potential for digital contact tracing technologies to increase surveillance.[238] It has been argued that 'Even if COVID-19 apps are temporary, rapidly rolling out tracing technologies runs the risk of creating permanent, vulnerable records of people's health, movements and social interactions, over which they have little control.'[239] An outcome has been that in a number of countries mistrust of such matters played a role in problematic uptake of the technologies.[240]

WHO has developed ethical principles to provide guidance on the use of digital proximity tracking technologies in the context of COVID-19,[241] with the principles addressing the needs for: use of the technologies to be time limited; testing and evaluation of the technologies; collection of personal and health data to be proportionate, with a preference for use of the least intrusive measures; restrictions on the data collected and the use of such data; voluntariness about whether to use the technology; transparency and clarity about data collection and processing; privacy-preserving data storage; data security; limited retention of the data; infection reporting; notification of affected individuals; not tracking individuals after they have tested positive; accuracy; accountability; independent oversight; and engagement by civil society and the public.

---

[235] Federica Lucivero and others, 'COVID-19 and Contact Tracing Apps: Ethical Challenges for a Social Experiment on a Global Scale' (2020) 17(4) *Journal of Bioethical Inquiry* 835, 837. WHO notes that 'Proximity tracing tools can be categorized as either centralized or decentralized, meaning that contact history can either be processed centrally, typically by a health authority, or by individual devices.' World Health Organization, 'Digital Tools for COVID-19 Contact Tracing: Annex: Contact Tracing in the Context of COVID-19' (n 231) 1.

[236] Braithwaite and others (n 226).

[237] Mark Burdon and Brydon Wang, 'Implementing COVIDSafe: The Role of Trustworthiness and Information Privacy Law' (2021) 3(1) *Law, Technology and Humans* 35.

[238] For discussion see Ram and Gray (n 234); Alex Akinbi, Mark Forshaw, and Victoria Blinkhorn, 'Contact Tracing Apps for the COVID-19 Pandemic: A Systematic Literature Review of Challenges and Future Directions for Neo-liberal Societies' (2021) 9(1) *Health Information Science and Systems* 18.

[239] Jessica Morley and others, 'Ethical Guidelines for COVID-19 Tracing Apps' (2020) 582(7810) *Nature* 29, 29.

[240] See eg Anastasia Kozyreva and others, 'Psychological Factors Shaping Public Responses to COVID-19 Digital Contact Tracing Technologies in Germany' (2021) 11 *Scientific Reports* art 18716; Witzleb and Paterson (n 234); Julia Amann, Joanna Sleigh, and Effy Vayena, 'Digital Contact-tracing During the COVID-19 Pandemic: An Analysis of Newspaper Coverage in Germany, Austria, and Switzerland' (2021) 16(2) *PLoS One* art e0246524.

[241] World Health Organization, 'Ethical Considerations to Guide the Use of Digital Proximity Tracking Technologies' (n 232).

B. Wastewater Surveillance

An emerging area of data collection during the COVID-19 pandemic has been in relation to wastewater. While wastewater surveillance has long been used in public health,[242] it has acquired a new global significance in the context of COVID-19.[243] Since COVID-19 fragments can be detected in wastewater systems,[244] surveillance of wastewater may provide data in addition to testing of individuals about geographic areas with COVID-19-positive individuals.[245] Importantly, as testing of individuals is often focused on those with symptoms, close contacts of those who have tested positive, or those with a relevant travel history, wastewater surveillance may provide information on the broader community, which may include asymptomatic or mildly symptomatic individuals.[246] Wastewater surveillance also has the potential to assist in determining whether clinical testing in the community is adequate. If the results of wastewater surveillance are consistent with the number of confirmed cases in the community, the clinical testing can be used as a basis for decision-making in relation to tightening or loosening restrictions.[247] However, if wastewater surveillance suggests a higher level of infection than is evident from clinical testing, this may provide an early warning and may indicate the need for additional public health measures.[248] Early warning provided by wastewater surveillance may also be of use in countries that have contained the spread of disease and are considering easing restrictions.[249]

Wastewater surveillance also has the potential to help to detect COVID-19 in areas where there is limited clinical testing of individuals such as in low-resourced, overcrowded settings.[250] In these settings, there may be limited access to healthcare,

---

[242] World Health Organization, 'Status of Environmental Surveillance for SARS-CoV-2 Virus: Scientific Brief' (5 August 2020) <https://www.who.int/publications/i/item/WHO-2019-nCoV-sci-brief-environmentalSampling-2020-1> accessed 10 December 2021 (hereafter World Health Organization, 'Status of Environmental Surveillance for SARS-CoV-2 Virus').

[243] David A Larsen and Krista R Wigginton, 'Tracking COVID-19 with Wastewater' (2020) 38(10) *Nature Biotechnology* 1151.

[244] Warish Ahmed and others, 'First Confirmed Detection of SARS-CoV-2 in Untreated Wastewater in Australia: A Proof of Concept for the Wastewater Surveillance of COVID-19 in the Community' (2021) 728 *Science of the Total Environment* art 138764; Sandra Westhaus and others, 'Detection of SARS-CoV-2 in Raw and Treated Wastewater in Germany—Suitability for COVID-19 Surveillance and Potential Transmission Risks' (2021) 751 *Science of the Total Environment* art 141750; Jordan Peccia and others, 'Letters: Measurement of SARS-CoV-2 RNA in Wastewater Tracks Community Infection Dynamics' (2020) 38(10) *Nature Biotechnology* 1164.

[245] Janelle R Thompson and others, 'Making Waves: Wastewater Surveillance of SARS-CoV-2 for Population-Based Health Management' (2020) 184 *Water Research* art 116181; Anne Bogler and others, 'Rethinking Wastewater Risks and Monitoring in Light of the COVID-19 Pandemic' (2020) 3(12) *Nature Sustainability* 981, 985.

[246] Thompson and others (n 245) 2–3; Amy E Kirby and others, 'Using Wastewater Surveillance Data to Support the COVID-19 Response—United States, 2020–2021' (2021) 70(36) *Morbidity and Mortality Weekly Reports* 1242.

[247] Thompson and others (n 245) 3.

[248] ibid.

[249] World Health Organization, 'Status of Environmental Surveillance for SARS-CoV-2 Virus' (n 242) 1.

[250] ibid 2.

low levels of healthcare-seeking behaviour, limited testing and clinical surveillance capacities, and a higher proportion of younger people who may be only mildly symptomatic, making clinical surveillance more complex.[251] As noted by WHO, 'such settings are also unlikely to have adequate sewerage, posing challenges for sampling and analysis from open drains'.[252]

WHO has noted that 'Environmental surveillance may serve to identify circulation of SARS-CoV-2 in a community without any consent having been given for testing; and may result in stigmatization of the community',[253] although the potential for stigmatization is likely to be less than for clinical testing as wastewater samples are aggregated.[254] It has been suggested too that wastewater surveillance may have implications for the privacy of individuals living in the area under surveillance.[255] In the United States, it has been suggested that Fourth Amendment protections against unreasonable searches and seizures may be relevant, although it is acknowledged that 'Even if the Fourth Amendment applies directly to wastewater collection, however, courts are likely to uphold such efforts for COVID-19 public health surveillance under the special needs doctrine, so long as they are reasonable.'[256] Uses of wastewater surveillance may enable resources and support to be provided to affected communities, as an impetus for increased testing in particular areas, as a reason for justifying restrictive measures such as stay-at-home orders, or as a basis for the imposition of physical distancing measures,[257] although the legal bases for these measures will clearly vary according to the jurisdiction.

Wastewater surveillance is only possible if there is a sewerage system in place, yet in many low-income countries there may be inadequate sanitation systems.[258] With waterborne diseases taking a heavy toll on human health, particularly in low- and middle-income countries,[259] improving access to WASH (drinking water, sanitation and hygiene) has been a key goal within the Millennium Development Goals and, more recently, the SDGs.[260] COVID-19 has demonstrated the importance of access to clean water for handwashing in disease prevention, making access

---

[251] ibid.
[252] ibid.
[253] ibid 3.
[254] ibid.
[255] Thompson and others (n 245) 4; Lance Gable, Natalie Ram, and Jeffrey L Ram, 'Legal and Ethical Implications of Wastewater Monitoring of SARS-CoV-2 for COVID-19 Surveillance' (2020) 7(1) *Journal of Law and the Biosciences* art lsaa039.
[256] Gable, Ram, and Ram (n 255) 7.
[257] ibid 8–10.
[258] Bogler and others (n 245) 985.
[259] World Health Organization, *Health in 2015: From MDGs Millennium Development Goals to SDGs Sustainable Development Goals* (World Health Organization 2015) 122–23.
[260] ibid 102–11. SDG 6 is to 'ensure availability and sustainable management of water and sanitation for all'. SDG target 6.1 is 'By 2030, achieve universal and equitable access to safe and affordable drinking water for all.' SDG target 6.2 is 'By 2030, achieve access to universal and equitable sanitation and hygiene for all, and end open defecation, paying special attention to the needs of women and girls and those in vulnerable situations.' United Nations General Assembly, 'Transforming our World: the 2030 Agenda for Sustainable Development' (A/RES/70/1, United Nations, 25 September 2015).

to clean water a priority for those living without WASH. Further research is needed on options for wastewater surveillance in low resource settings without sewerage systems. WHO has noted:

> Most studies published to date on the use of environmental surveillance for SARS-CoV-2 have been from high-resource settings. However, approaches are needed that can be applied in lower-resource settings, where a greater proportion of the population is not connected to sewers and instead uses pit toilets or septic tanks. Possibilities include testing surface water contaminated by sewage.[261]

XII. Conclusion

As discussed in this chapter, governments around the world utilized a variety of measures to respond to the COVID-19 pandemic and to limit its spread. These measures included testing and contact tracing, quarantine and isolation, and broad-ranging initiatives such as lockdowns and curfews. Many of these measures affected the freedoms and rights of individuals and communities, raising important considerations around law-making during emergencies and highlighting the potential for public health measures to affect human rights. In Chapter 4 we discussed measures that were introduced in response to the pandemic by analysing restrictions on freedom of movement, both within and between countries and in Chapter 6 we scrutinize challenges in the courts to such measures. The social and economic impact of lockdowns, business closures, job losses, and social isolation have exacerbated existing social and economic disadvantage. We review these issues in Chapter 7.

---

[261] World Health Organization, 'Status of Environmental Surveillance for SARS-CoV-2 Virus' (n 242) 1.

6
Litigation and Legal Challenges to Emergency Orders

I. Introduction

Public support for emergency laws, orders, and directions by governments during the COVID-19 pandemic, though strong at the beginning of the pandemic,[1] waned over time and the emergency measures became increasingly contested by the second half of 2021. Demonstrators, at times needing to be dispersed by vigorous measures by police, in countries such as the Netherlands, Belgium, Germany, Austria, France, and Australia, to name but some, expressed grievances about excessive use of state power and intrusion into citizens' lives in the name of the protection of public health.[2] In Melbourne, Australia, hangman's nooses were brandished by some protesters[3] who were complaining about the bestowal of powers by controversial new legislation that recalibrated the capacity of the state government to manage pandemics and allowed imposition of new penalties on persons who were non-compliant with orders.[4]

Thus public health law and regulation became a site for community and political contestation during 2020 and 2021,[5] as well as for public unrest in some countries. Challenges to the conceptualization of the elected government as empowered to take authoritarian measures for the good of all were mounted in diverse ways. Some took the form of planned and spontaneous challenges on the streets against the anti-pandemic strategies formulated by governments. However, the principal forum of challenge was in the courts, with the opportunity being taken by citizens and a variety of entities, including civil liberties groups, to review the public

---

[1] Klaus Dodds and others, 'The COVID-19 Pandemic: Territorial, Political and Governance Dimensions of the Crisis' (2020) 8(3) *Territory, Politics, Governance* 289, 292; Jens D Ohlin, 'Pandemics, Quarantines, Utility, and Dignity' [2021] *Michigan State Law Review* 541.
[2] See Jon Henley, 'Violence in Belgium and Netherlands as COVID Protests Erupt Across Europe' *The Guardian* (22 November 2021) <www.theguardian.com/world/2021/nov/21/netherlands-arrests-second-night-covid-protests> accessed 2 December 2021.
[3] See Mostafa Rachwani, 'Melbourne Protests: Prop Gallows Seen as Thousands March Against Victoria's Covid Powers' *The Guardian* (13 November 2021) <www.theguardian.com/australia-news/2021/nov/13/melbourne-protests-prop-gallows-seen-as-thousands-march-against-victorias-covid-powers> accessed 14 September December 2022.
[4] *Public Health and Wellbeing Amendment (Pandemic Management) Act 2021* (Vic).
[5] See Sylvia Walby, 'The COVID Pandemic and Social Theory: Social Democracy and Public Health in the Crisis' (2021) 24(1) *European Journal of Social Theory* 22.

health measures adopted by government to claim that they were, variously, unconstitutional, inconsistent with human rights instruments, excessive, unnecessary, inadequate, misconceived, or not subject to required checks and balances, such as community consultation or comparison of their benefits with their detriments.

The jurisprudence that was generated by legal challenges in many countries has features in common. It constitutes a body of law that has wrestled with our fundamental values, including the extent to which extraordinary measures can or should be taken by governments in extraordinary circumstances. The language of emergencies, exceptionalism, and battlegrounds against an unseen virus was deployed to defend assertive public health measures, whereas traditional rhetoric of fundamental rights and freedoms, as well as of civil liberties, was pitted in opposition to some of the measures.[6] In the United States, in the context of limitations imposed upon religious gatherings, an influential consideration proved to be whether religious assemblies are treated more harshly than assemblies in other civic contexts.

The outcome of this substantial body of litigation was a set of rulings and decisions at superior court level which has probed the limits of the community's delegation of power to government, paralleling wartime powers jurisprudence. It has constituted a body of court-made law that has placed public health in a new spotlight, determining the protections that should be deployed when it is asserted that the health and well-being of the community should take precedence over other legal values and principles that have been developed to ensure that government power is not wielded disproportionately or for collateral reasons.[7] A further aspect of the litigation has been an analysis of when and how government is obliged to act in order to discharge its responsibilities in relation to its citizens' right to life (which is a recognized human right) and in ways which are consonant with the safety of members of the community.

At the heart of the contested hearings were questions about the appropriate role and reach of the law during a public health emergency. For instance, did the risk to public health posed by COVID-19 justify curtailing the legally recognized, fundamental human right to freedom of movement? To what extent does the right to life overtake all other rights during a pandemic? If it does, what processes of evaluation and consultation need to be utilized? When and how is government obliged to act by way of orders and directions in order to safeguard members of the community during a public health emergency? Does an individual's membership of a community carry with it a legally enforceable responsibility to relinquish their liberty if

---

[6] See generally Alan Greene, *Emergency Powers in a Time of Pandemic* (Bristol University Press 2020); Morten Kjaerum, Martha F Davis, and Amanda Lyons (eds), *COVID-19 and Human Rights* (Routledge 2021); Belinda Bennett and Ian Freckelton (eds), *Pandemics, Public Health Emergencies and Government Powers: Perspectives on Australian Law* (Federation Press 2021); Colleen M Flood and others, *Vulnerable: The Law, Policy and Ethics of COVID-19* (University of Ottawa Press 2020).

[7] See Belinda Bennett, Ian Freckelton, and Gabrielle Wolf, 'COVID-19 and the Future of Australian Public Health Law' (2022) 43(1) *Adelaide Law Review* (forthcoming).

this has the potential to reduce the transmission of a pandemic? Are movement restrictions sufficiently effective in, and necessary for, minimizing COVID-19 infection and mortality rates to warrant restricting human rights? Could such restrictions disproportionately disadvantage, but also protect, vulnerable populations? What lies at the heart of requirements that such measures be both 'necessary' and 'proportionate'? How are government powers to be balanced with obligations to comply with international legal and other obligations?

The balance between the right to life and a variety of other rights and ethical principles was particularly exemplified by the imposition of a lockdown solely for unvaccinated people in November 2021 in Austria and the preparedness in a number of countries as diverse as Greece, the Federated States of Micronesia, Turkmenistan, and the Philippines to mandate citizens' vaccination under pain of a variety of penalties.[8] This use of leverage by the State, as against the use of encouragement, guidance, and educational measures, raises the issue of when such an exercise of government power ceases to be acceptable within liberal democracies,[9] but also when it is lawful.

However, not all COVID-19-related litigation challenged the legitimacy of public health measures. Other action sought to ensure that the spirit as well as the letter of measures ordered by authorities were being implemented effectively to provide protection to the population. Examples of this are canvassed in what follows in respect of physical distancing and face masks.

Section II of this chapter reviews challenges in Canada, Australia, and New Zealand to the closure of borders, internally and externally, while Section III scrutinizes litigation calling into question the legitimacy of lockdowns ordered by governments. Section IV reviews an important decision of the English High Court on human rights and public health grounds. The judgment found the government to have failed to take certain necessary steps for safeguarding the health and safety of persons in care homes who were at identified risk early in the pandemic. Section V deals with challenges to quarantine measures imposed by national governments, as well as the phenomenon of 'hotel quarantine', which in some countries has been contentious.

Imposition of curfews has constituted a particularly resented form of governmental directive, in part because of the unfortunate history of the use of such powers in other contexts. Section VI reviews litigation challenging such public health orders in a number of countries, while Sections VII and VIII deal with challenges to requirements for physical distancing and the wearing of face masks, in

---

[8] See Chapters 5 and 10.
[9] See Klaus H Goetz and Dorte S Martinsen, 'COVID-19: A Dual Challenge to European Liberal Democracy' (2021) 44(5–6) *West European Politics* 1003; Luca Alteri and others, 'Covid-19 and the Structural Crisis of Liberal Democracies. Determinants and Consequences of the Governance of Pandemic' (2021) 14(1) *Partecipazione e Conflitto* 1; Sheena C Greitens, 'Surveillance, Security, and Liberal Democracy in the Post-COVID World' (2020) 74(S1) *International Organization* art 169.

one particular case, the failure to require wearing of face masks. Two of the most contentious issues that have resulted in significant jurisprudence during the COVID-19 era have been challenges to public health directives which have curtailed the right to assemble—whether the assembly be for reasons of civic protest or religious observance. Section IX of this chapter reviews some of the most prominent decisions by appellate courts in this context, while Section X identifies litigation that has been determined by the time of writing in relation to compulsion of vaccination for participation in the workforce.

Section XI analyses jurisprudence relating to vaccination of children in the context of family law disputes about parenting of children and Section XII utilizes the expulsion from Australia of the tennis player, Novak Djokovic, to discuss the role of law in denying entry to persons to a country where they may disrupt public health stances in relation to vaccination, as well as its ramifications through the lens of polycentricity theory. Section XIII draws together strands within the chapter in respect of litigation concerning governments' responses to the COVID-19 pandemic.

II. Challenges to Border Closures

Closures of internal borders within countries and regions have taken place in many countries in order to sequester sources of risk from other parts of those countries. However, border closures have been controversial throughout the pandemic and have prompted malcontent and criticism from some.

In Victoria, Australia, for instance, the Ombudsman reviewed 33,252 applications for exemptions to be permitted to cross a state border to enter Victoria, in a context when only 2,736 had been granted.[10] She concluded that Victoria's Border Directions were lawful but had been administered in a way that led to unjust outcomes.[11] She recommended that the Victorian government acknowledge that its narrow exercise of discretion resulted in injustice and consider measures to alleviate it,[12] finding that the exemption scheme:

> failed to comprehend the very real need for many people to come and go across the border for a wide range of reasons, even in the face of official warnings. Our state borders have been porous for over 100 years. Even in a global health emergency some people need to cross them, and too many found themselves bereft.[13]

---

[10] Victorian Ombudsman, *Investigation into Decision-making under the Victorian Border Crossing Permit Directions* (Parliamentary Paper No 309 Session 2018–21, December 2021) <https://assets.ombudsman.vic.gov.au/assets/Investigation-into-decision-making-under-the-Victorian-Border-Crossing-Permit-Directions_Dec-2021.pdf> accessed 12 December 2021.
[11] ibid 8.
[12] ibid 17.
[13] ibid 8.

In the Northern Territory of Australia, a different issue was experienced. Multiple localized lockouts from outback towns (excluding outside persons from any access to such locations) were imposed in November and December 2021 to protect residents.[14] Although they did not prompt formal legal challenges, they generated expressions of aggrievement on a range of bases from some members of First Nations communities.[15] In Brazil, though, objections to measures adopted went further—municipal authorities' restrictions of citizens' movement early in the pandemic were the subject of judicial challenges.[16] In one such case, a state court held that an order issued by the Mayor of Belo Horizonte prohibiting entrance to the city of buses from other municipalities in which stringent social distancing measures had not been imposed was an unacceptable violation of citizens' freedom of movement.[17] Later in the pandemic, states' authority to close their borders to other states in countries with federal legal systems was similarly questioned.[18] In other cases, the toll that such closures took upon grieving relatives was the subject of litigation.

A. Canadian Jurisprudence

The decision by Burridge J in the Supreme Court of Newfoundland and Labrador in *Taylor v Newfoundland and Labrador*[19] provided an extensive analysis of the issue. It took place in the tragic context of Kimberley Taylor's mother having passed away in Newfoundland on 5 May 2020. However, Ms Taylor lived in Halifax, Nova Scotia. In Newfoundland and Labrador in 2018 the Minister for Health and Community Services introduced the *Public Health Protection and Promotion Act* (the *PHPPA*), stating to the legislature, 'We are living in a world with SARS and Ebola. You are one plane flight away from a significant public health problem, and we need legislation that can adapt and deal with that.'[20] Under the *PHPPA*, the Chief Medical Officer of Health was authorized to restrict travel to the province. On 4 May 2020 he did so,

---

[14] See Serena Seyfort, 'Northern Territory Town Enters Lockdown as Three New Local COVID-19 Cases are Recorded' *9 News* (28 November 2021) <www.9news.com.au/national/northern-territory-coronavirus-outbreak-another-nt-town-enters-lockdown-as-three-new-local-covid19-cases-are-recorded/8f5d1245-bc14-4c20-af06-48e670e20a9d> accessed 1 December 2021.

[15] See Peter Hoysted, 'Freedom Movement Spreads Misinformation in the Top End' *The Australian* (2 December 2021) <www.theaustralian.com.au/commentary/freedom-movement-spreads-misinformation-in-the-top-end/news-story/1ec86f6e3a1bf8d6b3c2d667457ac2e9> accessed 2 December 2021.

[16] Victor Pinheiro, Marcelo Ilarraz, and Melissa Terni Mestriner, 'The Impacts of the COVID-19 Crisis on the Brazilian Legal System: A Report on the Functioning of the Branches of the Government and on the Legal Scrutiny of Their Activities' (2020) 8(1–2) *The Theory and Practice of Legislation* 193, 202.

[17] ibid.

[18] See eg Jeff Thaler, 'Can Governors Close Their Borders to Pandemic Risks?' *Just Security* (20 April 2020) <www.justsecurity.org/69770/can-governors-close-their-borders-to-pandemic-risks/> accessed 2 December 2021.

[19] 2020 NLSC 125 (hereafter *Taylor's case*).

[20] Newfoundland and Labrador, House of Assembly, *Hansard* 48th Leg, 3rd Sess, Vol XLVIII, 20 November 2018, quoted in *Taylor's case* (n 19) [2].

limiting entry to Newfoundland and Labrador save in extenuating circumstances. Ms Taylor's application for an exemption was initially denied on 8 May 2020. She challenged the decision as being beyond the legislative authority of the province and asserted that the travel restriction violated her right to mobility and her right to liberty as guaranteed by sections 6 and 7 of the *Canadian Charter of Rights and Freedoms* (*Charter*) respectively. The Canadian Civil Liberties Association was granted standing as a public interest litigant in support of Ms Taylor.

Extensive expert evidence in relation to the threats posed at that time by COVID-19 was adduced on behalf of the provincial government. Burridge J accepted that the COVID-19 pandemic was a public health emergency[21] and that the purpose of the legislation was the protection and promotion of the health of those in Newfoundland and Labrador.[22] He found 'plenty of room' for both the federal and provincial governments to legislate on matters of public health, given the division of powers in Canada and found a major role for the provincial government:

> Local variations in geography, population vulnerability, health care capacity, resources (human and monetary) and COVID-19 prevalence in the jurisdiction, as compared to other jurisdictions, have necessitated localized responses to the control of the virus. The decision of this province to do so by restricting the domestic travel of persons across its border is quintessentially a local response to a local situation. Put another way, the challenge posed by COVID-19 has both a national and local dimension, and the localized dimension does not admit of a national response. In responding to the pandemic the federal government cannot be all things to all people.[23]

Burridge J accepted that Ms Taylor's section 6(1) *Charter* right to mobility was infringed when she was denied entry to Newfoundland but did note that the denial was fleeting as she was permitted to enter eight days later when she was granted an exemption.[24] He found it to be an incident of citizenship of Canada that Ms Taylor had a right to travel within Canada but noted that it was not suggested (by reference to section 6(2) of the *Charter*) that she was wanting to move to or take up in residence in a part of Canada other than where she resided.

Section 7(1) of the *Charter* provides that, subject to the principles of fundamental justice, 'Everyone has the right to life, liberty and security of the person and the right not to be deprived thereof except in accordance with the principles of fundamental justice.' However, Burridge J did not find Ms Taylor's liberty interests to

---

[21] *Taylor's case* (n 19) [224].
[22] ibid [241].
[23] ibid [292].
[24] ibid [302].

be engaged so did not consider whether there had been a violation of fundamental justice in relation to her.

He concluded that the infringement of Ms Taylor's mobility right was justified as a reasonable measure to prevent the spread of COVID-19 and thus there was no breach of the *Charter*. In evaluating risk factors, he took into account that Newfoundland ranked the highest, or nearly the highest, in Canada for many of the risk factors for severe illness or death from COVID-19: asthma; chronic kidney, lung, and liver diseases; diabetes; serious heart conditions; obesity; and cancer, and had an ageing population with almost one quarter of its residents being aged 65 or older.[25] He accepted that it was incumbent upon the government to establish that a limit upon Ms Taylor's *Charter* rights was reasonable and demonstrably justified in a free and democratic society, with the result that any limitation should balance the needs of society and the individuals; that they should impair as little as possible the right in question; and that there must be proportionality between the effects of the limiting measures and their objective.[26] He accepted that the objective of the movement restriction was to protect citizens of Newfoundland from illness and death and that this was pressing and substantial,[27] as well as rationally connected, and an effective means of reducing the spread of COVID-19.[28] Importantly, in terms of his approach, he noted that the Chief Medical Officer of Health was able to draw upon specialized medical resources for decision-making[29] and that 'the courts do not have the specialized expertise to second guess the decisions of public health officials'.[30] Ms Taylor acknowledged that this legitimized 'some measure of deference' to the decisions made by the Chief Medical Officer of Health, but not abrogation of responsibility as guardian of the *Constitution* and the rule of law.[31] Burridge J concluded that the margin for error in the context of the COVID-19 pandemic with its prospect of serious injury and death was small.[32] He did not accept that voluntary self-isolation was an acceptable less intrusive option, finding it not to be a 'viable substitute for the travel restriction'.[33] He also dismissed testing incoming travellers (with then a false negative rate as high as 30%) or contact tracing as sufficient options:[34] 'Contact tracing does not prevent the importation of COVID-19. However, it can be a very effective tool when used in conjunction with the travel restriction.'[35] This led him to be satisfied that:

---

[25] ibid [412]–[413].
[26] ibid [418]–[424].
[27] ibid [436]–[437].
[28] ibid [451].
[29] ibid [457].
[30] ibid [458].
[31] ibid [460].
[32] ibid [467].
[33] ibid [477].
[34] ibid [478], [480].
[35] ibid [481].

an enemy as resilient as COVID-19 will not be kept in check through the approach advocated by the Applicants. The task of wrestling this disease into submission is no easy feat and is one that requires a dynamic and multipronged approach. The travel restriction is integral to that approach.[36]

Thus, he found there had been no violation of the *Charter*.[37]

B. Australian Jurisprudence

In the case of *Palmer v Western Australia*, the High Court of Australia needed to determine whether the state of Western Australia's border closures were invalid.[38] Through the *Quarantine (Closing the Border) Directions* (WA) and *Emergency Management Act 2005* (WA), Western Australia had prohibited any person from entering that state if they did not fall within one of the specified categories of exemption.[39] Clive Palmer, a businessman and politician, argued that these movement restrictions impermissibly infringed section 92 of the *Australian Constitution*, which states that 'trade, commerce, and intercourse among the States, whether by means of internal carriage or ocean navigation, shall be absolutely free'.[40] However, the High Court held that, although the legislation imposed a burden on interstate intercourse, it was justified, as it was intended to achieve the legitimate and reasonably necessary objective of protecting health and life, and therefore did not breach section 92.[41]

Australia's *Constitution* also provides (by section 117) that 'a subject of the Queen, resident in any State, shall not be subject in any other State to any disability or discrimination which would not be equally applicable to him if he were a subject of the Queen resident in such other State'. Western Australia avoided contravening this provision by closing its borders to all Australians equally, including people who usually resided in Western Australia.[42] In some phases of the pandemic, however, other Australian states closed their borders only to inhabitants of states that had high COVID-19 infection rates.[43] Such a distinction is likely to be regarded as justified by the facts of the pandemic.

---

[36] ibid [486].
[37] ibid [487].
[38] [2021] HCA 5 (hereafter *Palmer*).
[39] ibid [1]–[7] (Kiefel CJ and Keane J); *Quarantine (Closing the Border) Directions* (WA) cls 4, 27; *Emergency Management Act 2005* (WA) ss 56, 67.
[40] *Palmer* (n 38) [9]–[13] (Kiefel CJ and Keane J).
[41] ibid [81] (Kiefel CJ and Keane J), [166] (Gageler J), [205], [208]–[210] (Gordon J).
[42] Lionel Nichols, 'Australia' in Bonavero Institute of Human Rights, *A Preliminary Human Rights Assessment of Legislative and Regulatory Responses to the COVID-19 Pandemic Across 11 Jurisdictions* (Bonavero Report No 3/2020, 6 May 2020) 22, 26.
[43] See eg Western Australia Government, 'COVID-19 Coronavirus: Controlled Border' (20 January 2022) <www.wa.gov.au/organisation/covid-communications/covid-19-coronavirus-controlled-border> accessed 20 January 2022.

C. New Zealand Jurisprudence

Between 22 April 2020 and 28 February 2022, restrictions were placed upon overseas New Zealanders' right to re-enter their country. Amongst other things, New Zealand citizens were required to enter government-managed isolation facilities (MIQF) and to submit to medical testing. This was a key component of the government's strategy involving a zero tolerance of cases of COVID-19 in the community. It was known as the government's elimination strategy.[44] For much of the period during which the restrictions were in place, demand for MIQF outstripped capacity with the result that New Zealanders experienced difficulties and delays in the exercise of their right to return to their country. In an important decision of the High Court determined by Mallon J, a challenge was heard in relation to whether the restrictions were lawful as a justified limitation of New Zealanders' rights to enter their country during the pandemic. The case afforded an opportunity to consider the relevance of the Canadian decision of *Taylor v Newfoundland and Labrador* for New Zealand law, as well as how the proportionality test should be applied.

The challenge brought by Grounded Kiwis (a group formed to advocate for the right of New Zealanders to return home during the pandemic) focused on the restrictions placed in the three-month period from the start of September 2021 until the start of December 2021, when the restrictions in place required that a person entering New Zealand have a voucher for a place in MIQF at which they were required to isolate. Such a voucher could be obtained prior to travel to New Zealand by an online process or by application to the Ministry of Business, Innovation and Employment.[45] For the first part of the period, the isolation period was 14 days and, for the second, it changed to seven days, followed by isolation at home until receiving the result of a negative COVID-19 test.

The applicant for relief, Grounded Kiwis, challenged aspects of the system which it asserted operated as unjustified limits on the right to enter and the way decisions were made for groups entering MIQF and the approach that was taken to applications for places in MIQF under one of the emergency categories.

Mallon J observed that the MIQF system was set up under circumstances of urgency at a time of national emergency.[46] Although there were 33 facilities with 6,368 contracted rooms with an operating in the budget for 2021–2022 of just under NZ$1 billion, with 5,563 full-time equivalent workers, difficulties were encountered with implementation of the system.[47] For instance, only 50% of contracted rooms at a Wellington facility were able to be used because of poor ventilation. In

---

[44] See *Grounded Kiwis Group Incorporated v Minister of Health* [2022] NZHC 832 (*Grounded Kiwis*).
[45] See too *Bolton v Chief Executive of Business, Innovation and Employment* [2021] NZHC 2897; [2021] 3 NZLR 425.
[46] *Grounded Kiwis* (n 44) [51].
[47] ibid [52].

addition, large numbers of people complained that their particular circumstances were not properly or humanely taken into account when they were refused the right to return to New Zealand, sometimes serially.[48]

Key parts of the applicant's challenge arose from provisions under the *New Zealand Bill of Rights Act 1990* (NZ) (BORA) which includes (under section 18) the right to freedom of movement, including the right (under section 18(2)) of every New Zealand citizen to enter New Zealand. Mallon J described this right as supplementing 'the basic civil liberties of every person and its denial can affect other rights. It is therefore one of the most basic rights.'[49] She noted that to the extent that the MIQF arrangements imposed limits on the right to freedom of movement, they needed to meet the 'such reasonable limits prescribed by law as can be demonstrably justified in a free and democratic society' requirement under the BORA.[50] She concluded that in answering this question it may be appropriate to give some weight to the relevant Minister's judgment on how the balance is appropriately struck between the rights of individuals and the needs of society, and that there was also room for the operation of the precautionary principle.[51]

Mallon J accepted that during the relevant period the purpose of the MIQF regime was sufficiently important to justify the curtailment of citizens' right to return to New Zealand[52] and concluded that:

> The booking requirement was justified because in the context of an extraordinary global pandemic of a virus that has been shown to have extreme impacts on public health, public health measures can be sufficiently important to justify the right to freedom of movement. Without some form of MIQ, border cases would likely spark a resumption of community transmission. MIQFs were of paramount importance to the continuing effectiveness of New Zealand's response to the pandemic. The ability to require users to register in advance regulated demand and thereby promoted the quality and sustainability of New Zealand's MIQ system. While it 'could lead to delay for some people', it was an effective way to ensure MIQFs have sufficient capacity to meet demand at any given time. This was essential to the effective operation and integrity of the MIQ system.[53]

Ultimately, she found that the Minister failed to demonstrate that there was no reasonable alternative that was less rights-impairing than the virtual lobby system which most New Zealanders seeking to exercise their right to return were expected to use.[54] It gave no weight to users who had experienced unreasonable delay as

---

[48] ibid [52].
[49] ibid [168].
[50] ibid [170].
[51] ibid [173]–[174].
[52] ibid [254].
[53] ibid [158].
[54] ibid [342].

against those who had not. She found it to be a flawed system and to be effectively a lottery.[55]

Mallon J regarded the risk of transmission of COVID-19 to be an issue in which the Court should defer to the expert evidence adduced by epidemiologists. This led her to accept that MIQF continued to be justified on public health grounds, as least for arrivals who would not be self-isolating in Auckland. However, she found the more complex issue to be whether the compelling interests of the community generally were proportionate to the interests of individual New Zealand citizens to return to New Zealand. She accepted the submission by the applicant that a denial of the right to enter New Zealand for more than three months was not justified, concluding that the system failed to cater for individuals who were experiencing undue delay.[56] She found that government officials needed to monitor changes to MIQF settings to ensure that they remained justified but that their monitoring was insufficient, although the critical consideration under which the system operated was 'to develop and implement systems by which ... travel could be facilitated safely given the exigencies of the pandemic and Government policy at the time.'[57] She found that a wider interpretation of the exceptions permitted to the rules would have been appropriate and might have enabled at least some New Zealanders to apply for self-isolation. She commented pointedly:

> I am mindful that I am considering all of this with the benefit of hindsight and therefore must 'tread carefully'. I am also mindful that considerable work was carried out and significant funds were invested in running the MIQ system. I am also mindful that the Minister was aware of the acute MIQF supply problem and the BORA right to return and sought a good deal of advice about this that was provided on an urgent basis. I am also mindful that the public health risks of making the wrong decisions were very significant and that the Minister at all times considered the limit on citizens' right to return was justified. However, I have reached the conclusion that because, and to the extent that, the system did not sufficiently allow individual circumstances to be considered and prioritised where necessary, it operated as an unjustified limit on the right of New Zealand citizens to enter their country.

The result was that the application for declaratory relief by Grounded Kiwis was successful.

---

[55] ibid [343].
[56] ibid [362]–[365].
[57] ibid [421].

D. Overview

The approaches by the Canadian, Australian, and New Zealand courts have been similar. They have concluded that public health orders that have inhibited movement of citizens are legitimate, given the centrality of such measures for gaining and maintaining control over the pandemic. However, the important contribution made by the New Zealand *Grounded Kiwis* decision was the Court's detailed and rigorous analysis of the requirement of proportionality, when applied to the freedom of movement entitlement created by New Zealand's human rights legislation—it found that, while the system for detention of persons returning to New Zealand was justified on public health grounds, its inflexibility resulted in suffering and, as a matter of law, that it failed the proportionality requirement. Such an approach is likely to be followed in other countries.

III. Challenges to Lockdowns

Of the movement restrictions that authorities around the globe imposed on their citizens and permanent residents in the initial phase of the COVID-19 pandemic, lockdowns attracted especially strong opposition.[58] It has been suggested too that lockdowns have been a source of significantly adverse consequences for the wellbeing of some.[59]

The question of whether this infringement of the right to freedom of movement was effective in reducing transmission of COVID-19 and, if so, if it was as or more effective than other public health measures (such as physical distancing, personal hygiene, testing, contact tracing, and isolation), elicited polarized responses from members of the scientific community and the public alike.[60] In October 2020, for instance, David Nabarro, WHO's Special Envoy on COVID-19, opined that authorities should not rely on strict lockdowns as the principal method of controlling the spread of this disease, as they '[freeze] the disease in place', but do not 'eliminate'

---

[58] See eg Ben Knight, 'Germany Debates Curbing Freedom of Assembly After Coronavirus Rallies' *DW* (3 August 2020) <www.dw.com/en/germany-debates-curbing-freedom-of-assembly-after-coronavirus-rallies/a-54424215> accessed 13 September 2022.

[59] Talita Greyling, Stephanie Rossouw, and Tamanna Adhikari, 'The Good, the Bad and the Ugly of Lockdowns During COVID-19' (2021) 16(1) *PLoS One* art e0245546; Gideon Meyerowitz-Katz and others, 'Is the Cure Really Worse than the Disease? The Health Impacts of Lockdowns During COVID-19' (2021) 6(8) *BMJ Global Health* art e006653.

[60] See eg Marco Vinceti and others, 'Lockdown Timing and Efficacy in Controlling Covid-19 Using Mobile Phone Tracking' (2020) 25 *EClinical Medicine* art 100457 <www.thelancet.com/journals/eclinm/article/PIIS2589-5370(20)30201-7/fulltext> accessed 13 November 2022; cf Devi Sridhar, 'Continual Lockdowns are not the Answer to Bring Covid Under Control' *The Guardian* (10 October 2020) <www.theguardian.com/commentisfree/2020/oct/10/continual-local-lockdowns-answer-covid-control> accessed 13 September 2022.

it.[61] In Nabarro's view, these movement restrictions harmed communities that depended on tourism in particular, and increased poverty.[62]

Indeed, as discussed further in Chapter 7, from the beginning of the pandemic, it became apparent that those who were already experiencing social and/or economic disadvantage were often more likely to suffer from 'stay-at-home' orders. People who were employed in lower paid jobs before the pandemic were most at risk of being unable to work from home during lockdowns.[63] Due to its disproportionately severe impact on the poor, some queried whether India's lockdown, in particular, contravened Article 21 of its *Constitution* that guarantees the right to life, which the Supreme Court of India has interpreted as including the right to food, livelihood, and shelter.[64] Similarly controversial was the placement of nine government-funded housing commission towers in Victoria, Australia, under a 'hard lockdown', which did not apply to other citizens, after some of their residents contracted COVID-19.[65] This measure prompted significant criticism from Victoria's Ombudsman:

> The Government need not apologise for taking necessary and difficult action to keep us all safe—in the face of this pandemic, there is no alternative but to accept the advice of our State's leading infectious disease experts. But the decision to bring forward the operation to detain 3,000 people immediately did not appear to have been based on such advice, and like the virus it sought to contain, risked the health and wellbeing of many people. In a just society, human rights are not

---

[61] David Nabarro, 'COVID19: Do What Is Needed to Hold the Virus at Bay' (Skills, Systems and Synergies for Sustainable Development, 14 October 2020)<www.4sd.info/covid-19-narratives/refl ections-about-the-middle-path/> accessed 13 September 2022; Michael Doyle, 'WHO Doctor Says Lockdowns Should Not be Main Coronavirus Defence' *ABC News* (12 October 2020) <www.abc.net.au/news/2020-10-12/world-health-organization-coronavirus-lockdown-advice/12753688> accessed 13 September 2022.

[62] Doyle (n 61).

[63] Warn Lekfuangfu and others, 'On Covid-19: New Implications of Job Task Requirements and Spouse's Occupational Setting' (2020) 12 *Covid Economics* 87, 87–90, 101; Victorian Ombudsman, 'Investigation into the Detention and Treatment of the Public Housing Residents Arising from a COVID-19 "Hard Lockdown" in July 2020' (Parliamentary Paper No 192 Session 2018–20, December 2020) <www.ombudsman.vic.gov.au/our-impact/investigation-reports/investigation-into-the-detent ion-and-treatment-of-public-housing-residents-arising-from-a-covid-19-hard-lockdown-in-july-2020/#full-report> accessed 27 February 2022 (hereafter Victorian Ombudsman, *Public Housing Hard Lockdown*).

[64] Shreya Atrey, 'India' in Bonavero Institute of Human Rights, 'A Preliminary Human Rights Assessment of Legislative and Regulatory Responses to the COVID-19 Pandemic Across 11 Jurisdictions' (Bonavero Report No 3/2020, 6 May 2020) 46, 50, 53; Dodds and others (n 1) 290.

[65] Sandra Carrasco, Majdi Faleh, and Neeraj Dangol, 'Our Lives Matter: Melbourne's Public Housing Residents Talk About Why COVID-19 Hits Them Hard' *The Conversation* (24 July 2020) <https://theconversation.com/our-lives-matter-melbourne-public-housing-residents-talk-about-why-covid-19-hits-them-hard-142901> accessed 13 September 2022; David Kelly, Kate Shaw, and Libby Porter, 'Melbourne Tower Lockdowns Unfairly Target Already Vulnerable Public Housing Residents' *The Conversation* (6 July 2020) <https://theconversation.com/melbourne-tower-lockdowns-unfairly-tar get-already-vulnerable-public-housing-residents-142041> accessed 13 September 2022.

a convention to be ignored during a crisis, but a framework for how we will treat and be treated as the crisis unfolds.[66]

Some of the methods used to enforce compliance with lockdowns also generated alarm and potentially infringed human rights. Threats of fines for breaching government orders in several countries, such as Italy,[67] were mild compared with alleged abuse of citizens by police in India,[68] and by the Police Service and National Defence Force in South Africa.[69] It was reported that by 1 June 2020, more than 230,000 people had been arrested in South Africa for contravening lockdown regulations and 11 individuals had been killed by police in enforcing them.[70] Collins Khosa is an example of a person who was affected by the enforcement measures in South Africa. Suspected of violating lockdown regulations, Khosa died after he was allegedly brutalized and tortured by members of the National Defence Force during an enforcement action.[71] Khosa's death and the responses to it prompted Fabricius J to issue declarations, which included that during and notwithstanding the declaration of the State of Disaster and the Lockdown under the *Disaster Management Act 57 of 2002*:

> all persons present within the territory of the Republic of South Africa are entitled to (among others) the following rights, which are non-derogable even during states of emergency:
>
> - the right to human dignity (section 10 of the Constitution);
> - the right to life (section 11 of the Constitution);
> - the right not to be tortured in any way (section 12(1)(d) of the Constitution);
> - the right not to be treated or punished in a cruel, inhuman or degrading way (section 12(1)(e) of the Constitution);
> - under section 199(5) of the Constitution, the South African security services, which include the South African National Defence Force (SANDF), the South African Police Service (SAS), and any Metropolitan Police Department (MPD) must act and must instruct their members to act, in accordance with

---

[66] Victorian Ombudsman, *Public Housing Hard Lockdown* (n 63) 5.
[67] Christos Kypraios, 'Italy' in Bonavero Institute of Human Rights, 'A Preliminary Human Rights Assessment of Legislative and Regulatory Responses to the COVID-19 Pandemic Across 11 Jurisdictions' (Bonavero Institute of Human Rights, Bonavero Report No 3/2020, 6 May 2020) <www.law.ox.ac.uk/sites/files/oxlaw/v3_bonavero_reports_series_human_rights_and_covid_19_20203.pdf> accessed 13 September 2022, 55–57.
[68] Atrey (n 64) 50, 53.
[69] Melodie Labuschaigne, 'Ethicolegal Issues Relating to the South African Government's Response to COVID-19' (2020) 13(1) *South African Journal of Bioethics and Law* 23, 24.
[70] ibid 26.
[71] *Khosa v Ministry of Defence and Military Veterans* [2020] 3 All SA 190; [2020] ZAGPPHC 147 (H Ct), [24].

the Constitution and the law, including customary international law and international agreements binding on the Republic.[72]

Governments of several countries faced lawsuits from citizens contesting the legality of their lockdowns. The following paragraphs of this section review significant challenges determined by courts in the United Kingdom, New Zealand, Australia, Brazil, the United States and various countries in Europe.

A. United Kingdom Jurisprudence

Schools were required to close for extended periods in 2020 and 2021, with education moving to home schooling in some countries. In *Dolan v Secretary of State for Health and Social Care*,[73] one of the challenges to English public health regulations early in 2020 related to the role of government in closing and reopening schools, Article 2 of Protocol 1 to the *Convention for the Protection of Human Rights and Fundamental Freedoms*, which provides that no person shall be denied the right to education, was invoked by the applicant for relief. However, in circumstances where government policy was to encourage the return of children to school on a phased basis, the claim did not gain any traction in the High Court and was not accepted.

B. Irish Jurisprudence

In Ireland, two journalists sought leave to bring judicial review proceedings, claiming that the *Health (Preservation and Protection and other Emergency Measures in the Public Interest) Act 2020* (Ireland) and regulations made under it breached Ireland's *Constitution* of 1937.[74] This statute permitted the Minister for Health to make regulations to prevent or slow the spread of COVID-19, and the regulations prohibited people from leaving their residences without reasonable excuse, namely, to provide an essential service, or attend an essential retail outlet or medical appointment.[75] In refusing the application, Meenan J found that, although these instruments restricted citizens' constitutional rights, including to liberty, constitutional rights are not absolute, and the applicants produced no evidence

---

[72] ibid [146]. See too Melissa Parker, Hayley MacGregor, and Grace Akello, 'COVID-19, Public Authority and Enforcement' (2020) 39(8) *Medical Anthropology* 666; Cathleen Powell, 'Rule of Law Has Moved Centre Stage in Lockdown: What it Is and Why it Matters' *The Conversation* (22 May 2020) <https://theconversation.com/rule-of-law-has-moved-centre-stage-in-lockdown-what-it-is-and-why-it-matters-139045> accessed 23 October 2021.
[73] [2020] EWHC 1786 (Admin), [106]–[112].
[74] *O'Doherty v Minister for Health* [2020] IEHC 209 [1], [9]–[10], [40].
[75] ibid [15]–[16], [19].

that the restrictions were disproportionate to the incidence and effects of COVID-19.[76] Further, Meenan J held that the Minister acted constitutionally in making the regulations because the *Constitution* permits delegated legislation.[77]

C. Spanish Jurisprudence

In July 2021, the Spanish Constitutional Court delivered a long-awaited ruling (by a majority of 6:5) on the constitutionality of Articles 7, 9, 10, and 11 of *Royal Decree 463/2020* of 14 March 2020, which declared the first nationwide 'state of alarm' for the management of the COVID-19 public health crisis.[78] The decree was followed by later amendments and various extensions. The challenge was brought by the far-right parliamentary party, Vox, which asserted that the Royal Decree, which related to the period between March and June 2020, breached multiple rights in the *Spanish Constitution* (SC)—the right to freedom of movement (Article 19 SC); the right to personal freedom (Article 17 SC); the rights of assembly and demonstration (Article 21 SC); the principle of sanctioning legality (Article 25 SC), in conjunction with the principle of human dignity (Article 10(1) SC); the right to education (Article 27 SC); the right to work (Article 35 SC); the freedom to conduct a business (Article 38 SC); and the right to religious freedom (Article 16 SC).

Integral to the decision was the distinction under Spanish law amongst categories of a state of emergency: a 'state of exception' (for extraordinary and severe disruptions to public order); a 'state of siege' (for attacks against Spanish sovereignty); and a 'state of alarm' (for catastrophes and epidemics etc). The reason why the distinction was significant was that under Article 55(1) of the *Spanish Constitution*, 'suspensions' of fundamental rights are possible under a state of exception and a state of siege, but not under a state of alarm, which only permits 'limitations' of fundamental rights. In addition, more latitude is given to governmental action pursuant to a state of alarm, which can only last for a maximum of 15 days, because of its lesser degree of intrusiveness into citizens' lives.

This meant that the Spanish Constitutional Court was required to rule upon the distinction between 'suspensions' and 'limitations'; the majority concluded that a suspension is an intense limitation of a fundamental right. It concluded that Article 7 of *Royal Decree* 463/2020, which imposed a ban on freedom of movement in certain cases (through imposing a lockdown) did not infringe the right to personal freedom or the rights and guarantees with regard to penalties. It also dismissed the allegations of breach of the rights to freedom of assembly and demonstration

---

[76] ibid [60], [77].
[77] ibid [58], [77].
[78] Sentencia 148/2021, de 14 de julio de 2021 (BOE núm. 182, de 31 de julio de 2021). <www.tribunalconstitucional.es/NotasDePrensaDocumentos/NP_2021_074/2020-2054STC.pdf> accessed 13 September 2022.

(Article 21 SC) and to freedoms which guarantee the functioning of political parties and trade unions or the fundamental right of political participation (Article 23 SC). However, the Court ruled that an order prohibiting the movement of all people, anywhere and at any time, except in designated circumstances, constitutes a suspension of the right to freedom of movement and therefore under the *Spanish Constitution* was not lawful. Therefore, the right to freedom of movement and the right to freedom of residence had been breached. It found the containment measures in respect of education and training to have a sufficient basis to be in accordance with the *Constitution*. It concluded that there was no violation of the freedom of religion by making it a condition to adopt physical distancing measures to attend places of worship and religious ceremonies. However, while it rejected the argument that the right to work had been unlawfully infringed by the limitations, it found that, insofar as the law had permitted the head of a ministerial department to restrict the right to conduct a business, this was in breach of the *Constitution*. It concluded that it would have been possible to justify a 'state of exception', thus legitimizing the adoption of extreme limitations.

There were five dissenting opinions from members of the Constitutional Court on the basis that the measures in *Royal Decree* 463/2020 constituted impermissible limitations of fundamental rights. Spain's Justice Minister stated that the government respected the ruling by the majority of the Constitutional Court, but observed that '[T]he confinement measures had saved several hundred thousands of lives'.[79] In October 2021, a decision by the same court (by six votes to four) held that the part of the state of alarm that existed from November 2020 to May 2021 was unconstitutional, undermining the functions of parliament, and handing undue powers to autonomous regional governments.[80] A consequence is that the Spanish government was obliged to repay extensive numbers of fines it collected from persons who breached lockdown orders.[81]

D. European Court of Human Rights Jurisprudence

The European Court of Human Rights has not ruled extensively on the legitimacy of lockdowns. However, in *Terheş v Romania*[82] Cristian-Vasile Terheş, a Romanian national who had been elected a member of the European Parliament, challenged

---

[79] 'Spanish Court Rules COVID-19 Home Confinement was Unconstitutional' *Thomson Reuters Foundation News* (14 July 2021) <https://news.trust.org/item/20210714132046-i731e/> accessed 16 April 2022.
[80] See Alyssa McMurtry, 'Court Declares Spain's 2nd COVID State of Alarm Unconstitutional' *Anadolu Agency* (27 October 2021) <www.aa.com.tr/en/europe/court-declares-spain-s-2nd-covid-state-of-alarm-unconstitutional/2404881> accessed 13 September 2022.
[81] ibid.
[82] Application No. 49933/20 (13 April 2021). See too Joseph Dute and Tom Goffin, 'Case of *Terheş v Romania*' (2021) 28 *European Journal of Health Law* 407.

a decree enacted by the Romanian Parliament which introduced a 30-day state of emergency, followed by ordinances including a curfew between 10 p.m. and 6 a.m. He asserted that he was personally affected by the decision, maintaining that he had been made subject to arbitrary detention. The Court noted, however, that Mr Terheș had been free to leave his home for various reasons and could go to different places at whatever time of day the situation required and that he had not been subject to individual surveillance by the authorities. He did not claim to have been forced to live in a cramped space and had not been deprived of all social contact. Therefore, it concluded that in view of their degree of intensity, the measures to which he was subject could not be equated to house arrest. In addition, in light of the fact Mr Terheș had not identified specific information about his actual experience in lockdown, he could not be said to have been deprived of his liberty within the meaning of Article 5 section 1 of the *European Convention on Human Rights*.

E. Australian Jurisprudence

Pursuant to emergency powers under the *Public Health and Wellbeing Act 2008* (Vic), directions were made in Victoria, Australia, that were referred to as 'lockdown laws' and that restricted Victorians' movement, for instance by confining them during parts of 2020 to travelling within 25 kilometres of their places of residence.[83] In *Gerner v Victoria*, a hotelier commenced proceedings seeking declarations that the legislative provisions and the lockdown directions were invalid on the basis that they impermissibly burdened an 'implied freedom' for people within Australia 'to move within the State where they reside' that is provided for under the *Australian Constitution*. The High Court of Australia affirmed that freedom of movement or communication in Australia enjoys constitutional protection as an aspect or corollary of the protection of freedom of political communication but held that there is no room for implying more protection by virtue of the mechanism of 'implied prohibition'. The High Court noted[84] that, in *Higgins v The Commonwealth*, Finn J had stated that:

> It is inconceivable ... that the Constitution implicitly puts at risk (subject to considerations of proportionality, etc) a significant range of routine Commonwealth and State laws merely because in particular ways, they limit either freedom of movement or else the making of choices within that freedom.[85]

---

[83] *Gerner v Victoria* [2020] HCA 48 [1]–[2].
[84] ibid [6], [15].
[85] (1998) 79 FCR 528 at 534, 535.

The Human Rights Law Centre has since argued that the *Gerner* decision 'is not a complete rejection of all reasonable challenges on legislative powers. Ultimately, the success of similar constitutional challenges will depend on the merit of arguments made, and whether the subject matter in fact places concerning and unnecessary restrictions on implied freedom drawn within scope of the *Constitution*.'[86]

F. New Zealand Jurisprudence

The *New Zealand Bill of Rights Act 1990* provides that 'everyone lawfully in [New Zealand] has the right to freedom of movement', but this 'may be subject ... to such reasonable limits prescribed by law as can be demonstrably justified in a free and democratic society'.[87] After the government declared a state of emergency the Director-General of Health drew on powers under section 70 of the *Health Act 1956* (NZ) to issue orders restricting that right, 'for the purpose of preventing the outbreak or spread of any infectious disease'.[88]

In *Borrowdale v Director-General of Health, Attorney-General, and New Zealand Law Society*, the High Court of New Zealand rejected a challenge to the lawfulness of state of emergency orders based on points of statutory interpretation (such as that the orders needed to refer to specific individuals, rather than to all New Zealanders).[89] Nevertheless, the Court agreed with the applicant that public announcements by members of the New Zealand government's executive branch in the nine days between issuing the first and second orders, stating or implying that New Zealanders were required to stay at home and that this restriction would be enforced, were not prescribed by law and thus unlawfully limited rights affirmed by the *New Zealand Bill of Rights Act 1990* (NZ), including to freedom of movement.[90] The first order only mandated closure of some premises, and not 'private dwelling houses', and forbade people from congregating, so it was found not to have constituted a requirement to stay at home; by contrast, the second order, which required everyone to remain at their current place of residence except for 'essential personal movement', was considered to require people to stay at home and to have lawfully limited rights protected by that statute.[91]

In addition, two applicants sought a writ of habeas corpus from the High Court of New Zealand to release them from restrictions imposed by the second order

---

[86] Human Rights Law Centre, 'High Court of Australia Rejects Challenge of COVID-19 Lockdown Restrictions' (Human Rights Case Summary, 10 December 2020) <www.hrlc.org.au/human-rights-case-summaries/2020/12/10/high-court-of-australia-rejects-challenge-of-covid-19-lockdown-restrictions> accessed 13 September 2022.
[87] *New Zealand Bill of Rights Act 1990* ss 5, 18(1).
[88] *Borrowdale v Director-General of Health* [2020] NZHC 2090 [25]–[26], [29] (hereafter *Borrowdale*).
[89] ibid [2], [6], [117]–[130].
[90] ibid [5], [191], [197], [225], [240], [280], [292].
[91] ibid [26], [78], [193].

on the basis that the terms of the order subjected them to 'detention' within the meaning of the *Habeas Corpus Act 2001* (NZ).[92] Peters J dismissed these matters, finding that the applicants were not 'detained' according to that statute, as they were 'free to engage in many of their usual activities'.[93] Moreover, even if they were detained, any detention effected by the Director-General of Health's order was lawful under the *Health Act 1956* (NZ).[94]

G. Brazilian Jurisprudence

Brazil's Supremo Tribunal Federal has found that government authorities could use their legislative and administrative powers regarding the right and protection of health, pursuant to the *Constitution of the Federative Republic of Brazil 1988*, to adopt measures restricting the movement of inhabitants of their jurisdictions.[95]

H. United States Jurisprudence

Most courts in the United States of America have supported state governments' use of their legislative police and emergency response powers to issue stay-at-home orders (requiring people to remain at home except to work in essential jobs, or access food or healthcare), finding that they did not unjustifiably infringe rights protected by the *United States Constitution*, including to peaceable assembly.[96] This approach is exemplified by the case of *Givens v Newsom*.[97] Mendez J in the United States District Court for the Eastern District of California dismissed the plaintiffs' application for a temporary restraining order preventing the Governor of California and others from enforcing an order that required that state's residents 'to stay at home or at their place of residence except as needed to maintain continuity of operations of federal critical infrastructure services'.[98] Mendez J did not accept the plaintiffs' argument that, in preventing them from holding 'political demonstrations, rallies, protests, and religious services', the order 'impermissibly [infringed] upon their constitutional rights to speak, assemble, and petition the government' and 'their

---

[92] *A v Ardern* [2020] NZHC 796 [2] (hereafter *A v Ardern*); *B v Ardern* [2020] NZHC 814 [5] (hereafter *B v Ardern*).
[93] *A v Ardern* (n 92) [25], [27], [40]; *B v Ardern* (n 92) [26], [28], [44].
[94] *A v Ardern* (n 92) [44]; *B v Ardern* (n 92) [43].
[95] Pinheiro, Ilarraz, and Mestriner (n 16) 207–208, 210; Supremo Tribunal Federal, 'STF Reaches 2,500 Received Cases Related to Covid-19' (News Release, 28 May 2020) <http://portal.stf.jus.br/noticias/verNoticiaDetalhe.asp?idConteudo=444342&ori=2> accessed 13 September 2022.
[96] Lance Gable, 'Mass Movement, Business and Property Control Measures' in Scott Burris and others (eds), *Assessing Legal Responses to COVID-19* (Public Health Law Watch 2020) 34–37.
[97] 459 F Supp 3d 1302 (ED Cal, 2020).
[98] ibid [2]–[3].

due process rights and their right to liberty under the California Constitution.[99] In reaching this decision, Mendez J found that the stay-at-home order bore 'a real and substantial relation to public health', as it sought 'to slow down the rate of transmission by drastically reducing the number and size of all gatherings'.[100] Mendez J noted that, while the judiciary recognizes that it must protect individuals' rights, 'in the context of this public health crisis', it 'must afford more deference to officials' informed efforts to protect all their citizens, especially their most vulnerable, against such a deadly pandemic'.[101] Mendez J referred to evidence that the 'stay at home order advances the only fool-proof way to prevent the virus from spreading at in-person gatherings', observed that the plaintiffs had not suggested 'a more tailored option that would ensure comparable levels of safety', and concurred with the defendants that ordering only people identified as positive with COVID-19 to stay at home was not 'feasible'.[102] Further, Mendez J considered that the order did 'not prohibit substantially more speech' or 'more expressive association' than was 'necessary to protect public health'.[103]

In the case of *Wisconsin Legislature v Palm*,[104] the Supreme Court of Wisconsin deviated from the trend of upholding stay-at-home orders. However, the relevant order in this case was not issued by the government, but by an executive branch official who the Court found had exceeded her statutory authority and the Court therefore held that the order was unlawful, invalid, and unenforceable.[105] Unusually, the Wisconsin legislature commenced the action, claiming that the emergency order issued by the unelected Secretary-designee of the Department of Health Services requiring all people in Wisconsin to remain in their homes and to abstain from travel, and closing non-essential businesses, 'was promulgated without following required statutory procedures applicable to an emergency, and, in so doing ... impinged upon the Legislature's constitutional core power'.[106] The Court held that statutory rule-making procedures had not been properly followed.[107]

I. Overview

Internationally, for the most part, challenges to lockdowns have not succeeded. While inevitably lockdowns encroach upon a variety of freedoms and rights that otherwise exist and are important, during 2020 and 2021, they were a principal and

---

[99] ibid [2].
[100] ibid [10].
[101] ibid [11]–[12].
[102] ibid [16], [18], [27].
[103] ibid [21].
[104] 391 Wis 2d 497 (Sup Ct 2020).
[105] ibid [6], [37]–[38].
[106] ibid [4], [11]–[12].
[107] ibid [5]–[6], [37]–[38].

often successful strategy for inhibiting the spread of COVID-19. Courts in multiple countries recognized this fact and undertook a balancing exercise, consistently finding that the most important right that needed to be protected was the right to life by the exercise of extraordinary powers pursuant to the terms of public health legislation.

IV. A Challenge to Government Responses under Public Law

One of the most internationally significant challenges to governmental responses to COVID-19 arose from an application for declaratory relief in the High Court of England and Wales in *Gardner & Harris v Secretary of State for Health and Social Care*.[108] The claimants sought declarations that certain policy documents relating to the management of the pandemic that had been issued by the Secretary of State for Health and Social Care in 2020, and the policy decisions recorded in government documentation, constituted breaches of their fathers' rights under the *European Convention on Human Rights* or, in the alternative, were unlawful and susceptible to judicial review on common law principles. The claimants' fathers (Mr Gibson and Mr Harris) had passed away in care homes during the first wave of the pandemic in England during which some 20,000 people had died. The other defendants were the National Health Service Commissioning Board and Public Health England.

The essence of the claim was that the defendants were said to have decided to take steps which would have the effect of introducing or had a risk of introducing COVID-19 into care homes and otherwise failed to take steps to prevent its entering such homes through staff, visitors, and new admissions, opting instead to rely upon strict infection controls as the principal or only means of protecting residents. It was said that this was an inadequate governmental response in circumstances where the defendants knew or should have known that care homes were particularly vulnerable to serious illness and death if COVID-19 entered into them. Multiple criticisms were made by the claimants of the defendants' responses during the early phase of COVID-19, including that:

- There was a lack of expertise in infection control in the homes;
- The defendants knew or should have known that there was a shortage of PPE in many care homes;
- There were no reliable safeguards in place to verify whether care homes could provide adequate levels of infection control;
- The guidance that was provided was reliant on a symptoms-based approach;

[108] [2022] EWHC 967 (Admin) (hereafter *Gardner & Harris*).

- COVID testing was not made available for persons discharged from hospitals to care homes, even where there was sufficient capacity for such testing;
- Inadequate efforts were made to reduce the movement of staff between care homes; and
- Sufficient steps were not taken to restrict visitors to care homes.[109]

In the public law component of the claim, it was alleged too that important relevant considerations were not incorporated into decision-making, such as: assessing the risk to the lives of care residents; considering adoption of a policy of testing persons discharged from hospital, before they were received into care homes; taking into account the potential for transmission of COVID-19 by persons who were not symptomatic; and failing to consider the unsuitability of the care home environment for isolation and infection control.[110] In addition, it was said that there had been an insufficient inquiry by reason of the defendants not considering such matters and consulting expert advisors on their implications. Further it was asserted that irrelevant considerations were taken into account by the defendants, that certain of their decisions were irrational, and that the defendants had breached their duty of transparency by misleading the public when stating that 'from the start we've tried to throw a protective ring around our care homes' and 'we brought in the lockdown in care homes ahead of the general lockdown'.[111]

The claimants submitted that the defendants had a positive obligation to take appropriate steps to safeguard the lives of those within England and to do all that could have been required to prevent life from being avoidably put at risk. This argument was framed by reference to Article 2 of the *European Convention on Human Rights*, which provides that 'Everyone's right to life shall be protected by law.' It was asserted by the claimants that both the defendants' 'systems duty' and 'operational duty' applied and were breached by the defendants during the first wave of the pandemic. The argument advanced in relation to the systems duty was that the defendants were required to put in place a legislative and administrative framework designed to protect against risks to life, whilst the operational duty required the State to take practical steps to safeguard people's right to life from specific dangers in circumstances where was a link to the State's responsibility. It was also argued that the defendants were subject to a negative duty, also known as a '*Munjaz* duty',[112] not to act in a manner or implement policies which would expose those within the jurisdiction to a significant risk of a breach of their Article 2 rights.

The decision was a joint judgment by Bean LJ and Garnham J. They accepted that the systems duty requires the State to have a regulatory framework in place

---

[109] ibid [149].
[110] ibid [150].
[111] ibid [150].
[112] See *R (Munjaz) v Ashworth Hospital* [2006] 2 AC 148.

designed to provide effective structures to protect life,[113] but affirmed that it is a 'high level structural duty' rather than an 'obligation of result'. They held that there was no arguable case that there had been a breach of the systems duty—there was nothing wrong with the framework for the issuing or guidance or policy documents in relation to the pandemic response.[114] They drew from the domestic and European Court of Human Rights' decisions interpreting Article 2 the following principles:

- A real and immediate risk to life is a necessary but not sufficient factor for the existence of an Article 2 operational duty;
- Generally, the other necessary factor is the assumption by the State of responsibility for the welfare and safety of particular individuals, of whom prisoners, detainees under mental health legislation, immigration detainees, and conscripts are paradigm examples since they are under State control;
- However, the duty may exist even in the absence of an assumption by the State of responsibility, where State or municipal authorities have become aware of dangerous situations involving a specific threat to life which arise exceptionally from risks posed by the violent and unlawful acts of others[115] or man-made hazards[116] or natural hazards[117] or from appalling conditions in residential care facilities of which the authorities had become aware;[118]
- in appropriate circumstances (which remain so far undefined), the operational duty may also arise where State or municipal authorities engage in activities which they know or should know pose a real and immediate risk or exceptional risk[119] to the life of a vulnerable individual or group of individuals.[120]

The Court observed that there was no authority from the European Court of Human Rights:

which has gone as far as holding that a State is under an operational duty to take all reasonable steps to avoid the real and immediate risk to life posed by an epidemic or pandemic to as broad and undefined a sector of the population as residents of care homes for the elderly. There is no clear and consistent line of Strasbourg authority which indicates that such a duty exists and we cannot be at

---

[113] *Gardner & Harris* (n 108) [226].
[114] ibid [227].
[115] Citing *Osman v United Kingdom* (2000) 29 EHHR 245.
[116] Citing *Öneryildiz v Turkey* (2005) 41 EHRR 20; *Kolyadenko v Russia* (2013) 56 ECHR 245.
[117] Citing *Budayeva v Russia* (2014) 59 EHRR 2.
[118] Citing *Nencheva v Bulgaria* (Application no 48609-06, European Court of Human Rights, 18 June 2013); *Campeanu v Romania* (Application no 47848-08, European Court of Human Rights, 17 July 2014).
[119] Citing *Watts v United Kingdom* (2010) 51 EHRR SE5.
[120] *Gardner & Harris* (n 108) [230]-[250].

all confident—indeed we gravely doubt—that the ECtHR would we willing to declare that it does. We should keep pace with the Strasbourg jurisprudence, but not run past it and disappear into the distance.[121]

This reasoning led to rejection of the Article 2 claim.

In addition, in light of what it described as 'the highly pressured circumstances of March and April 2020', the Court did not accept that the government could reasonably be criticized for failure to comply with the usual procedural step of carrying out an equalities impact assessment of its policies relating to care homes addressing the need to eliminate discrimination against the elderly and the remainder of the population.[122] It noted too that the public sector equality duty[123] added nothing to the duties of the defendants at common law—'Anyone devising a policy affecting care homes must, if they are to act rationally, bear in mind that a majority of residents of care homes are not only elderly but also have other health issues which make them particularly vulnerable to infections.'[124]

In respect of the public law issues, the Court's approach was to ask whether the decisions that were impugned fell outside the range of reasonable decisions properly open to the government in light of the state of knowledge then available and the circumstances existing at the time.[125] Again the Court explicitly extended latitude to the government:

> We recognise that the Government was having to make judgements in respect of a novel disease against a background of uncertain and rapidly developing scientific knowledge. It was doing so in circumstances of enormous pressure where the matters at stake were of the utmost gravity. Furthermore, in the early months of the pandemic the options available to the Government were constrained by practical limitations as well as scientific uncertainty. The obvious example is the worldwide shortage of PPE in the early months of the pandemic and the worldwide competition for what little PPE there was.[126]

The Court was not prepared to accept criticism of the defendants that they were responsible for an early failure to identify transmission by persons who were asymptomatic. This meant that it did not find irrationality or a failure to take relevant considerations into account by the defendants in drawing up policies which permitted such forms of transmission, given the state of scientific knowledge as at

---

[121] ibid [252]; see too *R (AB) v Secretary of State for Justice* [2021] UKSC 28; [2021] 3 WLR 494 [54]–[59].
[122] *Gardner & Harris* (n 108) [264].
[123] Imposed by s 149(1) of the *Equality Act 2010* (UK).
[124] *Gardner & Harris* (n 108) [264].
[125] ibid [266].
[126] ibid [267].

February and March 2020. It accepted that modelling was available at the time to the government, but highlighted that there was little 'real world evidence' that such transmission was actually occurring:

> Ministers were obliged to weigh up not just the likelihood that non-symptomatic transmission was occurring, but also the very serious consequences if it did so. Non-symptomatic transmission would mean that one elderly patient moved from hospital to a care home could infect other residents before manifesting symptoms or even without ever manifesting symptoms. In this context it is important to recall the emphasis laid by the Defendants on the fact that they were intending to adopt the precautionary principle, in essence preparing on the basis that the worst could happen, throughout their response to COVID-19.[127]

However, importantly, the Court concluded that the growing appreciation that asymptomatic transmission was a 'real possibility' should have prompted a change in the policy of the Secretary of State and Public Policy England concerning care homes earlier than it did.[128] It found no evidence that policy-makers at the relevant time took the view that the risk of serious trauma to a new resident told that they would have a single room for the first week in their new home after being discharged from hospital would have outweighed the risk to other residents of asymptomatic transmission and should have been a part of policy and guidance.[129] It held that the decision to issue admission guidance for care in the form that the guidance was issued, including without such measures, was irrational in that it failed to take account of the risk of asymptomatic transmission and failed to make an assessment on the balance of risks.[130]

The *Gardner & Harris* decision of the High Court is a highly significant precedent in relation to governmental liability for transmission of COVID-19 in aged-care institutions where in many countries large numbers of persons passed away during the early phases of the pandemic. The Court was at pains to emphasize that the decision was not an inquest into the deaths of Mr Gibson or Mr Harris, rather, that it was a judicial review of government action, and that it was not a public inquiry of the kind which the Rt Honourable Baroness Hallett DBE had been appointed in December 2021 to undertake under the *Inquiries Act 2005* (UK).[131]

It is notable that significant latitude was extended by the Court in respect of responsibility for policies and actions that failed to prevent the transmission of COVID-19, having regard to equipment availability issues and the unparalleled challenges faced by public health authorities. The case was argued on the basis of

---
[127] ibid [275].
[128] ibid [278].
[129] ibid [291].
[130] ibid [293].
[131] ibid [3].

evidence as to the evolving state of knowledge in the February–April 2020 period, a time when relatively little was known about the transmissibility of the virus. It is plainly illegitimate to impose responsibility on government or institutions on the basis of information or knowledge that did not exist at the relevant time but which was later acquired.

However, what is apparent from the extensive analysis of precedent and the reasoning employed by Bean LJ and Garnham J is that for England at least the public law lens will focus upon whether relevant matters were ignored by public health officials in discharge of their policy-making, provision of guidance, and making of health directives, whether irrelevant factors were taken into account, and whether reasoning processes underlying the discharge of functions were underpinned by unsatisfactory evaluations to a point where they can be classified as irrational. If, as with the discharge and admission policies that were the subject of adverse determination in *Gardner & Harris*, there were such defects, the decisions may be impugned as having failed to take into account evidence available at the relevant time, and as being irrational. This constitutes imposition of a high level of judicial scrutiny of governmental decision-making in the context of epidemiological and clinical evidence existing during the period in question. In turn, this is likely to open up the potential for many civil actions for negligence.

An unusual attribute of the *Gardner & Harris* decision is that it was not brought to seek damages for pecuniary loss or for mental harm suffered by relatives. Rather, it was an action in which only declaratory relief was sought. However, in a context where significant defects on the part of government (or an institution) are identified, as occurred in *Gardner & Harris*, it is only a modest step away from an adverse finding by a court in negligence—and therefore compensatory orders in the form of damages.

A key component of the decision in *Gardner & Harris* arises from the claimants' argument that the government failed to comply with the deceased persons' right to life under Article 2 of the *European Convention on Human Rights*. The claimants lost this aspect of the claim but it remains open to courts such as the European Court of Human Rights to extend the categories of 'operational duty'. In part this will depend upon the 'margin of appreciation' as a result of which in all instances, including in responding to a pandemic, governments are given a 'wide margin'— 'This is on the well-established grounds both of democratic accountability and institutional competence.'[132] The potential remains that the line of jurisprudence developed by the European Court of Human Rights will be extended to the responsibility of States to broaden the concept of operational duty to take all reasonable

---

[132] See *Dolan v Secretary of State for Health and Social Care* [2020] EWCA Civ 1786; [2021] 1 WLR 2236; [2021] 1 All ER 780 [97]; see too *Richards v Environment Agency* [2022] EWCA Civ 26 [66] [72]; *Budayeva v Russia* (2014) 59 EHHR 2 [134].

steps to avoid real and immediate risks to life by reason of a pandemic to sectors of the community identified to be at particular risk.

V. Challenges to Quarantine

The use of public health powers in relation to the imposition of various forms of quarantine raises delicate questions of human rights and the balance between individual and community interests.[133]

The legality of restricting the human right to freedom of movement through isolation and quarantine may have been questionable where people without appropriate expertise were authorized to determine whether these measures were required to prevent the spread of COVID-19.[134] In the United Kingdom, for instance, the *Coronavirus Act 2020* (UK) empowered 'public health officers', who did not need to be, or act under the guidance of, registered public health consultants, to assess whether isolation and quarantine were proportionate and necessary, and if they deemed them to be so, to detain people.[135] The *European Convention on Human Rights* provides that people may be deprived of their 'right to liberty' through 'lawful detention ... for the prevention of the spreading of infectious diseases'.[136] In *Enhorn v Sweden*, the European Court of Human Rights confirmed that such detention will only be lawful if the deprivation of liberty is proportionate, necessary, and 'the last resort ... because less severe measures have been considered and found to be insufficient to safeguard the public interest'.[137] It has been argued that, given public health officers' possible lack of training, they may have inaccurately evaluated these matters and thus unlawfully required people to isolate or quarantine.[138] However, it is unlikely that this will exculpate government from legal responsibility for the consequences of public health officers' decision-making.

This section reviews challenges to the imposition of quarantine orders in significant decisions made by English, Irish, and United States courts.

---

[133] See eg David M Studdert and Mark A Hall, 'Disease Control, Civil Liberties, and Mass Testing—Calibrating Restrictions During the COVID-19 Pandemic' (2020) 383 *New England Journal of Medicine* 102; Ian Freckelton, 'COVID-19: Criminal Law, Public Assemblies and Human Rights Litigation' (2020) 27(4) *Journal of Law and Medicine* 790.
[134] Jonathan Pugh, 'The United Kingdom's Coronavirus Act, Deprivations of Liberty, and the Right to Liberty and Security of the Person' (2020) 7(1) *Journal of Law and the Biosciences* art lsaa011, 5–7, 12–13.
[135] ibid; *Coronavirus Act 2020* (UK) ss 14(2), (3)(e), 15(1), (5)–(8).
[136] *Convention for the Protection of Human Rights and Fundamental Freedoms* (opened for signature 4 November 1950, entered into force 3 September 1953) 213 UNTS 221 Article 5(1)(e).
[137] Application No 56529/00, 25 January 2005 [36], [44]. See Robyn Martin, 'The Exercise of Public Health Powers in Cases of Infectious Disease: Human Rights Implications' (2006) 14(1) *Medical Law Review* 132; Rebekah McWhirter, 'The Right to Liberty in a Pandemic' (2021) 40(2) *University of Queensland Law Journal* 159.
[138] Pugh (n 134) 12–13.

A. English Jurisprudence

In *R (Khalid) v Secretary of State for the Home Department*,[139] Linden J heard applications by three persons who were British nationals or who had rights of residence in the United Kingdom. Each had travelled to visit his unwell father in Pakistan in March 2021 but on 2 April the United Kingdom placed Pakistan on the 'Red List' under Schedule B1A to the *Health Protection (Coronavirus, International Travel) (England) Regulations 2020* (UK), which had the consequence that upon return from Pakistan each person would be required to 'quarantine' for ten days in a designed hotel and to pay charges for doing so as part of the 'managed quarantine system' (MQS).

The applicants argued that the MQS was irrational, the requirement to quarantine amounted to unlawful deprivation of liberty contrary to Article 5 of the *European Convention on Human Rights*, and the charges levied were excessive. Linden J noted that the aim of the MQS was to reduce the risk posed by people arriving into the United Kingdom and, in particular, the risk associated with 'variants of concern' (VoC) and 'variants under investigation', which were considered at high risk of entering the United Kingdom and then spreading: 'A particular concern was, and remains, the risk of a VoC undermining the vaccination programme and, as a result, having serious economic, health and social consequences and/or putting at risk the Government's plans for the gradual lifting of Covid-related restrictions.'[140] Linden J accepted that decisions about whether to put a given country on the Red List were informed by a range of factors but in particular focused on the views expressed by the experts who gave evidence in the case. He concluded that the risk assessments which were carried out had a particular focus on the public health risk from VoCs posed by incoming travellers to the United Kingdom:

> Regular monitoring and evaluation is undertaken by Public Health England to identify those variants which may be of concern. Where a new VoC is identified, the Joint Biosecurity Centre reviews over 250 countries and territories for evidence of its presence. Direct evidence of the VoC within a country or territory, through VoC surveillance, is taken into account but many countries have limited or no VoC surveillance in place. Indirect indicators are, therefore, also taken into account, including levels of exportation of VoCs to the United Kingdom (which is detected through mandatory testing and sequencing) or to third countries, the strength of travel links with countries known to have the VoC or any rapid deterioration of epidemiological indicators that may suggest the presence of a VoC.[141]

---

[139] [2021] EWHC 2156 (Admin).
[140] ibid [12].
[141] ibid [13].

Thus, the challenge failed.

B. Irish Jurisprudence

The nature of 'hotel quarantine' was scrutinized before O'Moore J of the High Court of Ireland in *Heyns v Tifco Ltd*[142] with a focus being upon the fundamental question of whether it constitutes 'detention'. He concluded that the hotel quarantine system was in accordance with law and not inconsistent with the *Irish Constitution*.

C. United States Jurisprudence

In the initial phase of the pandemic, some United States judges' awareness that use of quarantine could prevent the spread of COVID-19 influenced them to dismiss legal challenges to state governors' orders requiring people entering their jurisdictions to quarantine for 14 days. In so doing, they continued a long tradition of United States courts confirming that, to protect their inhabitants during a health emergency, states can rely on their police powers and restrict citizens' constitutional rights, while acknowledging that this authority is subject to limits.[143]

In *Bayley's Campground v Mills*, Walker USDJ observed that the Governor of Maine's quarantine order 'burdened' citizens' rights recognized in the *United States Constitution* to enter, abide in, and leave states within the United States, and 'be treated as a welcome visitor, rather than an unfriendly alien when temporarily present in the second state'.[144] Yet, significant to Walker USDJ's decision was the fact that the plaintiffs had not produced evidence that there were less restrictive measures that the Governor could have adopted to halt the spread of COVID-19.[145] As will be seen later, this issue of comparators is an increasingly significant theme of United States jurisprudence, in particular from the Supreme Court. When the plaintiffs appealed the decision, the United States Court of Appeals for the First Circuit affirmed Walker USDJ's refusal to grant the requested injunction prohibiting enforcement of the quarantine requirement.[146] The Court agreed that there was sufficient evidence confirming that 'no less restrictive but equally effective

---

[142] [2021] IEHC 329.
[143] Wendy E Parmet and Michael S Sinha, 'COVID-19: The Law and Limits of Quarantine' (2020) 382(15) *New England Journal of Medicine* e28.
[144] 463 F Supp 3d 22 (D Me, 2020) [24]–[25], [28].
[145] ibid [29]–[30].
[146] *Bayley's Campground Inc v Mills* 985 F 3d 153 (1st Cir, 2021) [5], [7], [24]–[25] (2021): by the time of the appeal, the Governor of Maine had rescinded the original order and substituted it with another that included the same quarantine requirement, though also provided for exemptions from it. However, the United States Court of Appeals for the First Circuit considered that the request for an injunction from the original order was 'not moot because it pertains to an executive action that the Governor voluntarily rescinded and could unilaterally reimpose': [25].

alternative was available' to the Governor to lower the spread of COVID-19 in Maine.[147] It took into account the high transmissibility and lethal nature of the virus, its 14-day incubation period, the potential for it to be spread by people who were positive with COVID-19 but asymptomatic, and the unavailability of vaccines or effective treatments for COVID-19 at that time.[148]

In *Carmichael v Ige*, Otake USDJ similarly found that it was 'unclear that there' were 'less restrictive means to achieve' the 'governmental interests' that the Governor of Hawaii's quarantine order was 'narrowly tailored to promote', namely, minimizing the spread of COVID-19 and ensuring the healthcare system was not overwhelmed.[149] For this reason, and an epidemiologist's evidence that Hawaii's low infection and death rates from COVID-19 were attributable to its quarantine and stay-at-home orders, Otake USDJ held that the order was not susceptible to constitutional challenge, as it had a 'real or substantial relation to' a public health crisis.[150] Further, Otake USDJ found that the order was not 'beyond all question, a plain, palpable invasion of rights secured by the fundamental law': it did not prevent people from other states travelling to Hawaii; it was a reasonable restriction, as it was imposed during a pandemic; and it was not discriminatory because it applied equally to residents and non-residents of Hawaii.[151]

VI. Challenges to Curfews

A distinctive category of movement restriction orders made in many countries during the COVID-19 pandemic was the use of orders imposing curfews, which restricted citizens' rights to leave their homes between designated hours of the night. The commencement of curfews varied between 5 p.m. and 10 p.m.

Historically, curfews were a significant public health law measure: in England and various parts of Europe, for instance, fires were required to be covered (*couvrefeu*) at night (usually at about 8 p.m.) in order to reduce the potential for domestic fires and the risks to adjoining residences in villages and towns. The existence of a curfew also had the collateral effect of allowing dispersal of people who would gather around public fires because they did not have private places in which to congregate.[152] Curfew orders in non-pandemic scenarios have been used to constrain the ability of minors to move at will during the night,[153] and curfews have also been

---

[147] ibid [13].
[148] ibid [13]–[17].
[149] 470 F Supp 3d 1133 (D Haw 2020) [24].
[150] ibid [15]–[16].
[151] ibid [15], [21]–[24].
[152] See Ian Freckelton, 'COVID-19 Curfews: Kenyan and Australian Litigation and Pandemic Protection' (2020) 28(1) *Journal of Law and Medicine* 117 (hereafter Freckelton, 'COVID-19 Curfews').
[153] See eg David A Herman, 'Juvenile Curfews and the Breakdown of the Tiered Approach to Equal Protection' (2007) 82(6) *New York University Law Review* 1857; Alexander Korecky, 'Curfew Must Not Ring Tonight: Judicial Confusion and Misperception of Juvenile Curfew Laws' (2016) 44 *Capital*

deployed during wartime[154] and in a variety of terrorism scenarios in which repressive measures have been adjudged necessary for public safety.[155] In the leading United States Supreme Court decision of *Hirabayashi v United States*,[156] a wartime curfew case involving an American citizen of Japanese ancestry, considerable latitude was extended to legislative provisions enabling encroachment on the rights of particular categories of persons of foreign descent during World War II. In 2016, though, the Venice Commission (the European Commission for Democracy through Law), the Council of Europe's advisory body on constitutional matters, recognized the potential for curfews to restrict rights and liberties (albeit in a non-pandemic context dealing with emergency powers in south-eastern Turkey), stating that:

> Curfews are part of the armoury of measures which may be taken by the state to preserve, maintain and restore law and order and to protect the lives and property of its citizens in times of unrest, when there is a high likelihood of violence or when violence escalates (against the state, against the government itself or between different sections of the population).
>
> Secondly, like any exceptional measure, curfews imply restrictions on the everyday rights and freedoms to which everyone is normally entitled for the period of time during which the curfew is in operation. Curfew restrictions a priori designed to prevent and control public disorder, riots and violence are generally considered to be both desirable and necessary or, at worst, a necessary evil.[157]

The Venice Commission emphasized the importance of applying the principle of proportionality in determining whether, and if so how, to use curfews:

> This requirement must apply both to curfew decisions and to their implementation, and to related measures capable of affecting other rights and freedoms, which may consist of additional restrictions that may be imposed on the population during the curfew, such as the closure of schools or businesses, restrictions

---

University Law Review 831; David McDowall, Colin Loftin, and Brian Wiersema, 'The Impact of Youth Curfew Laws on Juvenile Crime Rates' (2000) 46(1) *Crime & Delinquency* 76; Brian Simpson and Cheryl Simpson, 'The Use of Curfews to Control Juvenile Offending in Australia: Managing Crime or Wasting Time?' (1993) 5(2)) *Current Issues in Criminal Justice* 184.

[154] See eg Ninetta Jucker, *Curfew in Paris: A Record of the German Occupation* (Hogarth Press 1960).
[155] See Freckelton, 'COVID-19 Curfews' (n 152), 121–24.
[156] 320 US 81 (1943). See also Gordon K Hirabayashi, *A Principled Stand: The Story of Hirabayashi v United States* (University of Washington Press 2013); William H Rehnquist, *All the Laws But One: Civil Liberties in Wartime* (Knopf Doubleday 2007).
[157] European Commission for Democracy Through Law (Venice Commission), 'Opinion on the Legal Framework Governing Curfews (Turkey)' (107th Plenary Session, Council of Europe, 11 June 2016)[17]–[19]<www.venice.coe.int/webforms/documents/default.aspx?pdffile=CDL-AD(2016)010-e> accessed 13 September 2022.

on the provision of public services or bans on public events, or of security operations carried out in this context by the authorities. Like curfews themselves, all of these measures must be proportionate to the threat and its immediacy, must not last any longer than the threat itself and must only apply to the regions affected by it.[158]

During the COVID-19 pandemic, curfew legislation was subject to challenges in countries as diverse as Kenya, Australia, France, the Netherlands, and Germany, including by reference to the yardstick of proportionality, as discussed in what follows.

A. Kenya

In *Law Society of Kenya v Mutyambai*,[159] the High Court of Kenya was urged to declare unconstitutional the imposition of a night curfew intended to limit the infection of Kenyans with COVID-19. Korir J declined to do so, but held that unreasonable use of force by police in enforcing a curfew order would be unconstitutional. He rejected the proposition that a curfew could only be issued for the purpose of fighting crime, not disease, but observed that 'a curfew is heavy artillery that should be deployed with circumspection'.[160] Korir J further commented that:

> It is important to appreciate that a curfew does not only upset the people's way of life, but it also negatively impacts constitutional rights and fundamental freedoms.... some of the rights limited by a curfew are the freedom of movement, the freedom of association, and the freedom of assembly. Even without the curfew, the insidious nature of coronavirus has *suo moto* robbed us of some aspects of the rights of association and assembly. It is also obvious that curfews limit the hours for earning a living hence limiting socio-economic rights, especially for the vulnerable members of society. It is therefore important to identify the likely negative impacts of a curfew beforehand and put mitigation measures in place. It is also important for those empowered to impose curfews to swiftly lift them if the damage they cause to society far outweighs the benefits.[161]

Korir J concluded that a curfew order should not be issued for an unspecified period and observed that: 'An instrument that restricts rights and freedoms should be

---

[158] ibid [87].
[159] Petition 120 of 2020 (Covid 025) [2020] eKLR, High Court of Kenya, Constitutional and Human Rights Division, 16 April 2020 <http://kenyalaw.org/caselaw/cases/view/193192/> accessed 13 September 2022.
[160] ibid [114].
[161] ibid [115].

clear as to how long the limitation will last.'162 This exemplified reasoning used in a number of public health emergency cases which have sought to ensure checks and balances on executive action, including by reference to circumscribing it within periods of time when it could be justified as necessary by reference to public health exigencies.

Korir J noted that the objective that the curfew order was seeking to achieve, namely, reduction in transmission of the virus, was not measurable: 'No evidence was adduced by either side to show how the curfew will achieve this objective and whether the reduced transmissions, if any, outweighs the hardship visited on the populace by the curfew.'163 However, he accepted that because of the novelty of the pandemic, statistics to assess the issue were not available. Ultimately, he found that: 'The government cannot be faulted for enforcing precautionary and restrictive measures in order to slow the spread of this novel disease in line with the precautionary principle. The use of a curfew order to restrict the contact between persons as advised by the Ministry of Health is a legitimate action.'164

B. Australia

In Victoria, Australia, a challenge was made to curfew orders that commenced first at 8 p.m. and then at 9 p.m until early the following morning.165 A restaurant owner brought the action, alleging that her restaurant had been detrimentally affected by the curfew order, as well as by stay-at-home directions, and contended that her capacity to care for her children was also being adversely affected.166 Ginnane J of the Victorian Supreme Court accepted that the power to impose a curfew could only be exercised where an authorized officer considered it necessary for the protection of public health during a state of emergency.167 He emphasized that, 'Even in an emergency, Victoria is a society of laws and any executive decrees must be made in accordance with law.'168 In this regard, he echoed a similar pronouncement made by the New Zealand High Court in *Borrowdale v Director-General of Health*: 'Even in times of emergency, however, and even when the merits of the Government response are not widely contested, the rule of law matters.... in times of emergency the courts' constitutional role in keeping a weather eye on the rule of law assumes particular importance.'169

---

[162] ibid [119].
[163] ibid [129].
[164] ibid [132].
[165] *Loielo v Giles* [2020] VSC 722 (hereafter *Loielo v Giles*). See too Rosalind Croucher, 'Lockdowns, Curfews and Human Rights: Unscrambling Hyperbole' (2021) 28(3) *Australian Journal of Administrative Law* 137.
[166] *Loielo v Giles* (n 165) [4].
[167] ibid [125].
[168] ibid [16].
[169] *Borrowdale* (n 88) [2], [291].

Ginnane J scrutinized whether the authorized officer had time to take into account the relevant considerations after she was provided with a briefing.[170] He concluded that the authorized officer had abundant evidence on which to reach a decision that the curfew satisfied the proportionality test and that there were no less restrictive means reasonably available to achieve the purpose of reducing the spread of COVID-19.[171] A more geographically targeted approach had not been successful when restrictions were introduced:

> [the authorized officer] had relied on the best possible available evidence, being her daily experience in working with COVID-19 outbreaks, data about infections in Victoria and knowledge of the public health measures that had worked or had not worked. She concluded that the Curfew had assisted in reducing case numbers, particularly by limiting the movement of the residents of Victoria. The plaintiff had called no evidence contrary to that of [the authorized officer]. To the extent that [the authorized officer] was criticised for only having regard to the issue of public health, that was a correct focus because that was the purpose of the emergency powers.[172]

Ginnane J concluded that the human right of freedom of movement was being limited by the curfew directions significantly for the purpose of protecting public health.[173] He found that the reasoning of the authorized officer was that the package of restrictions, including the curfew, had reduced the spread of COVID-19, including by limiting the movement of people in Victoria:

> It is true that she could not point to evidence that the Curfew itself reduced COVID-19 cases, but in the urgency of the circumstances created by the escalating COVID pandemic, [the authorized officer's] decision was not based on conclusions in medical journal articles or from analysing significant scientific evidence, as they were limited. Rather she had made a judgment based on her experience as an infectious diseases physician with added experience of COVID-19 cases.[174]

Ginnane J noted that an alternative to the continuation of the curfew would have been to revoke it and approve the continuation of the other stay-at-home restrictions with modifications. However, he observed that there was equally no evidence that such a course would have continued to achieve the purpose of reducing new cases of COVID-19 at the same rate.[175] Another option would have been to limit

---

[170] *Loielo v Giles* (n 165) [70].
[171] ibid [243].
[172] ibid.
[173] ibid [128].
[174] ibid [249].
[175] ibid [251].

the curfew to high infection areas but the view of the public health officer was that the available evidence did not support the use of localized restrictions. He commented that:

> another option would have been to decide that the Curfew might not reduce the infection rates, as people would have 15 or 16 hours, rather than 24, to shop or exercise, thereby increasing the possibility of infected people spreading the virus to others because they had less time to undertake these activities.[176]

However, Ginnane J emphasized that the existence of other options for addressing the pandemic did not of itself mean that there were 'less restrictive means reasonably available to achieve the purpose' of protecting public health. He found that in determining what means were 'reasonably available', it was appropriate to consider what means had been tried, the consequences of using them, the urgency of the situation, and the risks if infection rates surged again.[177] Ginnane J observed that, at the relevant time, Victoria was in a state of emergency and the stay-at-home directions, including the curfew, had been followed by a significant reduction in infections:

> It might have been reasonably considered that it was not the time to try alternative means of reducing infections as the Curfew did reduce the movement of people. Whether [the authorized officer] should have considered that the restrictions imposed by a Curfew were no longer proportionate to their purpose was a matter of judgment, open to different assessments. A cautious or precautionary approach was to leave the Curfew as modified in place.[178]

C. France

In the period leading up to Christmas 2020, the French government lifted its second lockdown and replaced it with a curfew, which was highly unpopular with some parts of the community.[179] The City Council of Cannes lost a case in which it sought to contest the legality of a 5 p.m. curfew. The Nice Administrative Court rejected arguments that the curfew was contrary to public health interests because it would lead to a high concentration of people as shoppers rushed to stores before

---

[176] ibid [251].
[177] ibid [251].
[178] ibid [252].
[179] 'Confinement allégé: voici la nouvelle attestation de déplacement nécessaire à partir du samedi 28 novembre' *Franceinfo* (28 November 2020) <www.francetvinfo.fr/sante/maladie/coronavirus/confinement/confinement-decouvrez-la-nouvelle-attestation-necessaire-pour-vous-deplacer-a-partir-du-samedi-28-novembre_4199075.html> accessed 23 October 2021.

the early curfew, and that the early evening curfew was an infringement of the right to circulate and do business. The Court stated that the adverse impact of the regulation was 'neither serious nor obviously illegal' and that the measures were necessary and required solidarity and patience.[180] The Conseil d'État upheld the legality of the curfews in both 2020 and 2021.[181]

D. The Netherlands

In February 2021, the Viruswaarheid (Virus Truth) group, formerly Viruswaanzin (Virus Madness), which led a number of anti-lockdown protests in the Netherlands, persuaded the District Court in The Hague that an *avondklok*, a curfew order (the first since the Nazi occupation during World War II[182]), keeping people at home between 9 p.m. and 4.30 a.m. was unlawful because the emergency orders that were said to justify the curfew were not sufficiently clear.[183] The trial judge held that curfews were to be used only in sudden emergencies, such as a dyke breach.[184] However, within days, the Dutch government re-issued the curfew legislation to give the law a sounder footing and an appellate court reversed the first instance decision, holding that the measure was necessary to rein in the pandemic.[185] Presiding Judge Marie-Anne Tan-de Sonnaville held that the interests of the State in fighting the virus 'carry more weight' than those of the anti-lockdown group bringing the lawsuit.[186] Prime Minister Rutte welcomed the ruling, saying: 'I want to ask everyone in the country to keep to the curfew. The good news is that the curfew will remain in place. It's of importance because we're facing the rise of the English virus.'[187]

---

[180] Tribunal Administratif de Nice, Affaire N 2100056, 11 January 2021.
[181] Conseil d'État, 28 October 2020, 445441; Conseil d'État, 9 June 2021, 453247.
[182] See Anna Holligan, 'Covid: Dutch Crisis as Court Orders End to Covid Curfew' *BBC News* (16 February 2021) <www.bbc.com/news/world-europe-56084466> accessed 26 September 2021.
[183] 'Dutch Court Orders Government to Lift Covid Curfew' *France 24* (16 February 2021) <www.france24.com/en/live-news/20210216-dutch-court-orders-government-to-lift-covid-curfew> accessed 13 September 2022.
[184] ibid.
[185] See ECLI: NL: GHDHA: 2021: 252 <https://uitspraken.rechtspraak.nl/inziendocument?id=ECLI:NL:GHDHA:2021:285> accessed 3 November 2021; Molly Quell, 'Dutch Appeals Court Uphold Coronavirus-Minded Curfew' *Courthouse News* (26 September 2021) <www.courthousenews.com/dutch-appeals-court-upholds-coronavirus-minded-curfew/> accessed 13 September 2022; Bart Meijer, 'Dutch Appeals Court Says Coronavirus Curfew was Right Move' US News (26 February 2021) <www.usnews.com/news/world/articles/2021-02-26/dutch-appeals-court-says-coronavirus-curfew-was-right-move> accessed 13 September 2022.
[186] Meijer (n 185).
[187] Toby Sterling and Anthony Deutch, 'Dutch Coronavirus Curfew Upheld Temporarily After Legal Setback' *US News* (16 February 2021) <www.usnews.com/news/world/articles/2021-02-16/dutch-coronavirus-curfew-shot-down-by-court-in-blow-to-government> accessed 13 September 2022.

E. Germany

In Germany, too, the status of curfew laws was subject to legal challenge, having previously been a matter of controversy.[188] In April 2021, the Bundesrat approved laws giving the government stronger powers to fight a third wave of COVID-19. Included amongst them was a power to impose curfews between 10 p.m. and 5 a.m. when cases exceeded 100 per 100,000 residents on three consecutive days.[189] This followed the hesitancy of Germany's 16 states to impose intrusive (and unpopular) public health measures. In May 2021, the Constitutional Court dismissed emergency appeals against the government's decision to impose night curfews in areas with high levels of COVID-19 infections.[190]

F. Overview

A number of themes can be identified from the various challenges to curfews during the COVID-19 pandemic. It has been recognized that curfews significantly impinge on citizens' right of free movement and thus courts have tended to be assiduous to scrutinize them carefully. They have required that the need for curfews and their proportionality to the public risk to which they are responding be established by evidence, usually from public health officials. However, overwhelmingly, the interests of public health have been held to take precedence over individual and commercial interests during the COVID-19 pandemic and thus curfews have generally been found to be a legitimate adjunct to other forms of protection against transmission of the virus.

VII. Challenges to Physical Distancing Orders

Physical distancing was an early bulwark of public health initiatives to reduce the potential for interpersonal contact and thereby transmission of COVID-19.[191] Stay-at-home, shelter-in-place, and lockdown policies constituted some of the most demanding forms of mandated physical distancing policies. The effectiveness of such policies depends on their stringency, as well as on the level of public

---

[188] See Sebastian von Münchow, 'The Legal and Legitimate Combat Against COVID-19: German Curfew-related Case Law' (2020) 19(2) *Connections: The Quarterly Journal* 49.

[189] See Michael Nienaber, 'Germany's Top Court Upholds Night Curfews in COVID-19 Fight' *Reuters* (5 May 2021) <www.reuters.com/world/europe/germany-looks-loosening-lockdown-covid-19-cases-fall-2021-05-05/> accessed 14 September 2022.

[190] ibid.

[191] See Wee C Koh, Lin Naing, and Justin Wong, 'Estimating the Impact of Physical Distancing Measures in Containing COVID-19: An Empirical Analysis' (2020) 100 *International Journal of Infectious Diseases* 42.

compliance with them that is secured by enforcement authorities such as the police.[192] Generally, public health directives have stipulated distances that people should stay apart, ranging from one to two metres. The directives were particularly deployed in workplaces[193] but also in a range of congregate contexts. Physical distancing proved challenging in schools[194] and had impacts on health and well-being for some, including adolescents.[195]

During the pandemic, critiques of the efficacy of such measures commenced to emerge. An example was the argument advanced by Jones and others that rules stipulating required physical distances between individuals were 'based on an outdated, dichotomous notion of respiratory droplet size'.[196] It became apparent that analysis of such issues depended on different modes of respiratory emissions—exhalations, coughs, and sneezes—and that each could be affected by environmental conditions; droplets could travel as far as seven to eight metres.[197] Experimentation suggested that a distance of 2.8 metres was necessary for sneezing, while if there was a breeze 5.8 metres in separation could be needed.[198] Coughing in the context of a gentle breeze needed distancing of 4.5 metres or greater.[199]

In *Sanctuary Ministries v Toronto (City)*,[200] the applicants challenged the Shelter Standards and the 24-Hour Respite Site Standards ('the Standards') of the City of Toronto as unconstitutional in the context of the COVID-19 pandemic.[201] The Standards permitted the use of bunk beds and failed to require a minimum of two-metre spacing between beds. The applicants' motion for an injunction was adjourned when the applicants and the City of Toronto ('the City') signed an interim settlement agreement by which the City undertook various steps to improve the safety and capacity of the shelter system. On the basis of information provided by

---

[192] Ping-Chen Chung and Ta-Chien Chung, 'Impact of Physical Distancing on Reducing Transmission of SARS-CoV-2 Globally: Perspective from Governments' Response and Residents' Compliance' (2021) 16(8) *PLoS One* art e025587.

[193] See Salima Hamouche, 'COVID-19, Physical Distancing in the Workplace and Employees' Mental Health: Implications and Insights for Organizational Interventions—Narrative Review' (2021) 33(2) *Psychiatria Danubina* 202.

[194] See Fatemeh Aminpour, 'Physical Distancing at School is a Challenge. Here Are 5 Ways to Keep Children Safer' *The Conversation* (6 October 2021) <https://theconversation.com/physical-distancing-at-school-is-a-challenge-here-are-5-ways-to-keep-our-children-safer-168072> accessed 14 September 2022.

[195] Sithum Munasinghe and others, 'The Impact of Physical Distancing Policies During the COVID-19 Pandemic on Health and Well-Being Among Australian Adolescents' (2020) 67(5) *Journal of Adolescent Health* 653.

[196] Nicholas R Jones and others, 'Two Metres or One: What is the Evidence for Physical Distancing in COVID-19?' (2020) 370 *British Medical Journal* m3223.

[197] See Lydia Bourouiba, 'Turbulent Gas Clouds and Respiratory Pathogen Emissions: Potential Implications for Reducing Transmission of COVID-19' (2020) 323(18) *Journal of the American Medical Association* 1837.

[198] Branson Chea and others, 'Assessment of Effectiveness of Optimum Physical Distancing Phenomena for COVID-19' (2021) 33(5) *Physics of Fluids* art 051903.

[199] ibid.

[200] (2020) 152 OR (3d) 411.

[201] ibid [6].

Shelter Support & Housing Administration, the City informed the applicants that it had reached compliance with the interim settlement agreement such that the agreement would reach its termination date within two months. However, the applicants submitted that in fact the City of Toronto had breached the agreement by asserting compliance in circumstances where the city had not met its physical distancing obligations, had not met its responsibilities to make available sufficient shelter beds for clients, and had failed to answer relevant and proportionate questions.[202] The applicants brought a notice of motion seeking a remedy for the alleged breaches.

The City acknowledged that by the relevant date (15 June 2020), 32 beds out of 7,152 across seven sites were not in compliance with physical distancing standards.[203] The City argued that this default was negligible and that such instances were the result of isolated human errors not reported due to communication gaps between staff.[204] However, Sossin J of the Ontario Superior Court of Justice found that the City had failed to use its 'best efforts' to achieve the Standards and had not provided relevant and proportionate information sought by the applicants with respect to site visits, site provider verification surveys, and site plans and records. In light of the interpretation of the physical distancing standard, he concluded that the quality assurance system needed to be adjusted so that the requirement to answer questions in those areas would be prospective rather than retrospective. He ordered the City of Toronto to continue its reporting obligations under the settlement agreement until it had met all its obligations.[205] This constituted an important imposition of checks and balances in respect of the City's compliance with its obligation concerning the homeless during the pandemic.

VIII. Challenges to Face Mask Orders

Face masks have constituted a vital part of the armoury for protection against COVID-19[206] with many countries requiring that they be worn in designated circumstances, including at various times in workplaces, in shops, and on public transport.[207] Although there are some who are antagonistic towards wearing

---

[202] ibid [188].
[203] ibid [52].
[204] ibid [59].
[205] ibid [216].
[206] See Derek Chu and others, 'Physical Distancing, Face Masks, and Eye Protection to Prevent Person-to-Person Transmission of SARS-CoV-2 and COVID-19: A Systematic Review and Meta-analysis' (2020) 395(10242) *Lancet* 1973.
[207] See Fiona McDonald and Claire J Horwell, 'Facemasks for Public Use During the COVID-19 Pandemic: An Examination of Responses in Australia and England' in Belinda Bennett and Ian Freckelton (eds), *Pandemics, Public Health Emergencies and Government Powers: Perspectives on Australian Law* (Federation Press 2021).

them,[208] face masks are likely to continue to be worn in congregate circumstances, including on commuter trains and buses, for many years after the waning of the incidence of the pandemic.[209]

In precedent-setting litigation in British Columbia, Canada, fathers of school-aged children sought orders mandating a school's adoption of a mask or face-covering policy for the classroom, as well as enhanced physical distancing.[210] Both the fathers had underlying health conditions that made them subject to an increased risk of harm from COVID-19: one had a wife with cancer who was therefore immunocompromised and the other had a son with viral-induced asthma at risk of being triggered by COVID-19.[211] Basran J observed that, while masks can be used in a variety of settings as 'an additional layer of protection', 'broad mandatory non-medical mask orders in community settings are considered public health measures of last resort. This is because broad-based mandatory mask policies have the most effect when employed where all other more effective forms of control to limit the spread of the virus have broken down or failed.'[212] He found that the evidence adduced before him demonstrated that:

> mandatory mask policies are not without concern, even when used in areas with high community transmission. Mandatory mask policies may result in other more effective means of limiting transmission, such as staying home when sick, proper hand hygiene, and physical distancing, being abandoned because wearing a mask can provide a false sense of security. Mask use is not a replacement for these more effective methods of limiting transmission of COVID-19.[213]

Basran J found no evidence that the fathers had followed the processes of the Ministry of Education for seeking accommodations to in-class instruction based on student or parent and/or caregiver health-related concerns or explored the various transition, virtual, or home-based learning programmes that existed in their schools.[214] He declined the application, finding the public interest was best served by continuing to rely on the public health orders in their then form.[215] He stated that he was satisfied that the advice of British Columbia health officials thoughtfully and comprehensively considered the research and current scientific information regarding the use of masks and concluded that:

---

[208] See Steven Taylor and Gordon JG Amundsen, 'Negative Attitudes About Facemasks During the COVID-19 Pandemic: The Dual Importance of Perceived Ineffectiveness and Psychological Reactance' (2021) 16(2) *PLoS One* art e0246317.
[209] See Ian Freckelton, 'COVID-19 as a Disruptor and a Catalyst for Change' (2021) 28(3) *Journal of Law and Medicine* 597, 607.
[210] *Trest v British Columbia (Minister of Health)* 2020 BCSC 1524.
[211] ibid [2].
[212] ibid [22].
[213] ibid [23].
[214] ibid [36].
[215] ibid [91].

some masking in schools was required, but a widespread mandatory masking policy is not necessary at this time. This is because the evidence shows that in current circumstances, such a policy may be counterproductive because it could detract from the effectiveness of more effective means of limiting transmission, such as staying at home when sick, proper hand hygiene, and physical distancing. This is a reasonable and rational approach to the use of masks in schools.[216]

Once more, this decision extended significant deference to the public health policies in force at the relevant time, on this occasion in the balancing process undertaken in formulating the mandatory masking policies.

IX. Challenges Arising from the Rights to Protest and Assemble

A context in which lockdown directions and physical distancing rules were contested in the courts during the COVID-19 pandemic, as well as within the general community, was in respect of mass gatherings, in particular where protest gatherings were convened and in respect of assemblies that took place for religious purposes. In many countries protests took place in relation to the imposition of lockdown and other government-ordered public health initiatives. A prominent example was in Denmark where after nine days of public demonstrations against legislation which would have allowed government authorities to examine, hospitalize, treat, and isolate people diagnosed with 'dangerous diseases', the amending statute was withdrawn, with Prime Minister Mette Frederiksen conceding that 'a better balance must be found'.[217] Amongst other things, this raised questions about the role of the right of peaceful protest during a public health crisis under provisions such as Articles 19, 21, and 22 of the *International Covenant on Civil and Political Rights (ICCPR)*.[218] In addition, relevantly for the United States, the First Amendment to the *Constitution* provides that:

> Congress shall make no law respecting an establishment of religion, or prohibiting the free exercise thereof; or abridging freedom of speech, or of the press; or the right of the people peaceably to assemble, and to petition the Government for a redress of grievances.

---

[216] ibid [79].
[217] 'Denmark Did Not Scrap its Epidemic Laws Due to "Pots and Pans" Protests' *AAP* (20 August 2021) <www.aap.com.au/factcheck/denmark-did-not-scrap-its-epidemic-laws-due-to-pots-and-pans-protests/> accessed 13 September 2022.
[218] Opened for signature 16 December 1966, entered into force 23 March 1976, 999 UNTS 171. See Victorian Equal Opportunity and Human Rights Commission, 'Explainer: Protests During COVID-19' (September 2021) <www.humanrights.vic.gov.au/resources/explainer-protests-during-covid-19/> accessed 14 September 2022.

A. The Right of Peaceful Protest

Public spaces have a particular symbolic and communicative value in the context of expressions of community aggrievement.[219] This has sometimes been referred to as the 'legal geography of contention'.[220] In *United States v Grace*,[221] for instance, it was held that public places, such as streets, sidewalks, and parks, historically associated with the free exercise of expressive activities, are considered, without more, to be 'public forums': 'In such places, the Government may enforce reasonable time, place, and manner regulations, but additional restrictions, such as an absolute prohibition of a particular type of expression, will be upheld only if narrowly drawn to accomplish a compelling governmental interest.'[222] In the public health law context, then, the question for United States law, is whether a pandemic constitutes such a 'compelling governmental interest'.

Public health and legislative initiatives have been introduced in a number of countries to inhibit rights of protest during COVID-19. One of many instances occurred in 2021 when the British Columbia government introduced legislation to restrict protests around schools, hospitals, and vaccination clinics by establishing 20-metre non-access zones.[223]

However, a contemporary question that arises is whether the option of online protest through the use of social media constitutes an acceptable short-term alternative to persons gathering in person to protest in the context of a pandemic.[224] Archetypally the issues raised involve conflicts between human rights to freedom of expression, peaceful assembly, holding religious views and practising religious beliefs, liberty and security of the person, and liberty of movement, as against protection of the health of the community during a pandemic. The tensions between individual freedoms and public health interests have prompted a variety of court challenges.

Residents of several countries, including Germany and Australia, contravened lockdown orders by attending large demonstrations in public areas to protest against the lockdowns.[225] In so doing, they contested the constraints on their 'right

---

[219] See *Hague v Committee for Industrial Organization*, 307 US 496 (1939); Maria O'Sullivan, 'Protest in a Pandemic: The Special Status of Public Spaces' *Australian Public Law* (27 July 2020) <https://auspublaw.org/2020/07/protest-in-a-pandemic-the-special-status-of-public-spaces/> accessed 14 September 2022.

[220] See eg Javier Auyero, 'The Geography of Popular Contention: An Urban Protest in Argentina' (2003) 28(55/56) *Canadian Journal of Latin American and Caribbean Studies* 37; see also John McCarthy and Clark McPhail, 'Places of Protest: The Public Forum in Principle and Practice' (2006) 11(2) *Mobilization: An International Quarterly* 229; Lucy Finchett-Maddock, *Protest, Property and the Commons: Performances of Law and Resistance* (Routledge 2016).

[221] 461 US 171, 176–78 (1983).

[222] ibid 178.

[223] *Access to Services (COVID-19) Bill 2021* (BC) <www.bclaws.gov.bc.ca/civix/document/id/bills/billscurrent/2nd42nd:gov20-1> accessed 14 September 2022.

[224] See *Commissioner of Police v Gray* [2020] NSWSC 867 [59] (hereafter *Gray*).

[225] Knight (n 58); Lisa Cox, 'Melbourne Anti-lockdown Protesters Arrested and Chased by Police on Horseback' *The Guardian* (19 September 2020) <www.theguardian.com/australia-news/2020/sep/

of peaceful assembly', recognized by Article 21 of the *ICCPR*, and 'stay-at-home' orders that effectively precluded them from attending public gatherings. The *ICCPR* permits restrictions on the exercise of this right if the restrictions conform with the law and 'are necessary in a democratic society in the interests of … the protection of public health'.[226] In the initial phase of the pandemic, several countries, including Guatemala and Latvia, formally sought to derogate from their obligations under Article 21 of the *ICCPR*.[227] The following parts of this section review jurisprudence that evolved during the COVID-19 pandemic in 2020 and 2021 in relation to rights to assemble.

Australian jurisprudence

In New South Wales, Australia, a jurisprudentially significant sequence of decisions was delivered by the Supreme Court in relation to applications to hold public gatherings at different phases of prevalence of the virus within the community.[228] In New South Wales, the Police Commissioner can apply to the Supreme Court for an order prohibiting a public assembly. This occurred on multiple occasions by reason of the Commissioner's concern about the risk of persons becoming infected with COVID-19. Although Australia does not have a bill of rights, and New South Wales has no human rights legislation, the Court expressed itself to be cognizant of the fundamental significance of inhibiting people's right to express themselves in public and frequently used human rights language.

Thus, in *Commissioner of Police (NSW) v Bassi*, Fagan J[229] noted that in such cases the Supreme Court has to strike a balance between two competing public interests—free speech and assembly; and convenience to others, including the risk of violence. He summarized the first consideration as:

> free speech and assembly and in the facilitation of public gatherings at which people with views on matters of public importance may gather together and show their strength, to demonstrate their solidarity with a point of view on a particular issue. The right of assembly and of expression by that means is of great importance in a democracy such as that enjoyed in Australia.
>
> The Court recognises that a strong public interest attaches to any expression of public opinion in this manner. In this case the particular cause that the organiser

---

19/melbourne-anti-lockdown-protesters-arrested-and-chased-by-police-on-horseback> accessed 14 September 2022.

[226] *ICCPR* (n 227) Article 21.

[227] 'Derogations by States Parties from Article 21 ICCPR and Article 11 ECHR on the Basis of the COVID-19 Pandemic' (23 March 2020) <www.rightofassembly.info/assets/downloads/Derogations_by_States_Parties_from_Article_21_ICCPR_on_the_Basis_of_the_COVID_19_Pandemic_(as_of_23_March_2020).pdf> accessed 14 September 2022.

[228] See Freckelton (n 133) 797–85.

[229] [2020] NSWSC 710 [17].

wishes to advance is awareness of what he and others of like mind perceive as unequal treatment of indigenous people in this country by police and concern with respect to deaths of indigenous people that have occurred whilst in custody, and concern with the known high rates of incarceration of indigenous people relative to other members of the community.[230]

He had regard to the fact the *Public Health (COVID-19 Restrictions on Gathering and Movement) Order (No 3) of 2020* (NSW) had been issued by the Health Minister. The *Order* directed by clause 10(1) that: 'a person must not participate in a public gathering of more than 10 persons' and made specific directions with respect to gatherings for weddings, funerals, memorial services, and religious services. In his application for a public gathering, Mr Bassi proposed measures to minimize the risk of the spread of the virus at the proposed assembly, deposing that he had arranged for 50 people who would operate in the capacity of marshals to assist with keeping people separate, and that he had advised through social media that attendees should wear face masks, although he acknowledged that he could not impose that as a prerequisite to participation in the gathering. He said that he had advised attendees 'to be prepared to social distance during the protest' and that arrangements had been made for a stockpile of thousands of face masks to be on hand, given to marshals to hand out to attendees and placed around the perimeter of the assembled people. He also stated that he had arranged for the provision of several hundred bottles of hand sanitizer.

However, Fagan J stated that he could not accept that the proposals advanced by Mr Bassi should take the place of the Public Health Order, which applied to all citizens and which at the relevant time prohibited the formation of gatherings of more than ten people in public places. He did not doubt that the measures proposed by Mr Bassi, if rigorously adopted by attendees, would reduce the risk but would not eliminate it. He commented:

> It is self-evident that the social distancing measures adopted to this point have been the key element in minimising the spread of this disease. A gathering of 5,000 people who are interested in this particular cause, at a time when the entire community is under direction not to gather in groups of more than ten, is an unreasonable proposition.[231]

He held that the exercise of the fundamental right of assembly and of expression of political opinion by gathering in numbers was not taken away by the public health orders but deferred:

---

[230] ibid [17]–[18].
[231] ibid [30].

The public health threat that has been encountered by our community through the spread of this disease has asked a great deal of many people in many respects throughout the community. A great many people have lost their livelihoods for the time being as a result of the need to conform to these restrictions. Others have been unable to attend funeral services for loved ones. Many forms of public gathering have had to be restricted. The conduct of legal proceedings in open court, a most important aspect of the administration of justice in a free society, has had to be curtailed.[232]

Whether 'mere' delay to a public gathering from a scheduled time for a period that cannot be identified with any precision, and which may be lengthy, constitutes a breach of a human right remains to be determined finally in Australia. This aspect of the decision by Fagan J may well be open to challenge in due course.

Mr Bassi urged upon the Court that in fact what would occur if the gathering was not authorized was that those who were interested in the issue would assemble anyway, in disregard of the Public Health Order, and that by not being permitted to spread themselves out over streets and public places, they would be likely to gather in closer proximity on footpaths. Fagan J rejected the submission: 'I do not accept that it would follow upon my refusal to provide authorisation for this assembly that great numbers of people would act so irresponsibly towards the health of their fellow citizens, gather in this manner in circumstances where the application for authorisation has been refused ...'[233] He declined the application.

Shortly afterwards in *Commissioner of Police (NSW) v Supple*,[234] an application was made in comparable circumstances, this time by the Refugee Action Coalition (RAC). Walton J echoed Fagan J in *Bassi* in identifying competing public interests of great importance:

On the one hand there is the right of Australian citizens for free speech and peaceful public assembly for the purposes of promulgating a view about significant public issues, such as the ones sought to be ventilated by the RAC, weighed against public health issues arising from the COVID-19 pandemic and the importance of public health measures that have been put in place to minimise the scope for community transmission of a coronavirus which is, by world experience and as described by the Australia Health Protection Principle Committee ('AHPPC'), highly infectious and dangerous.[235]

---

[232] ibid [31].
[233] ibid [32].
[234] [2020] NSWSC 727 (hereafter *Supple*).
[235] ibid [6].

He observed that there needed to be a balancing exercise that incorporated a balance between the right of assembly and expression, 'rights of great importance in our democracy',[236] and the need to provide protection to the community in relation to health issues arising from a pandemic. He accepted that persons attending the protest would, in good conscience, seek to abide by social distancing measures and other measures designed to restrict the spread of COVID-19, but concluded that the evidence was that the capacity to provide fully effective application of the measures recommended by health authorities dissipates with the circumstances applying in large gatherings of people 'around a subject that naturally and understandably invokes emotional responses'. He concluded that, although fewer people were expected to attend the *Supple* protest than the *Bassi* protest, 'risks nonetheless remain. There are also particular difficulties associated with tracing arising out of public assemblies.'[237] He noted that the best estimates of likely attendance at the march were in the order of 200 people but that that was not a reliable figure. Police evidence was that approximately three to four police officers per ten marchers would need to attend to attempt to enforce the ten-person gathering rule and that the police officers would be required to maintain physical distancing. He accepted the observation that the Public Health Order reflected the professional view of those assisting the government in the interests of community health.

Walton J concluded that while by that time the risk of COVID-19 infections had reduced to 'low levels', the reduction in restrictions needed to be moderate and gradual because of the infectious nature of the virus and the grave consequences of further transmission. He also found an additional factor to be relevant, one which he observed was sometimes overlooked: namely, that the risks associated with public assemblies of this kind invariably involve significant risks for frontline workers such as police officers.[238] He concluded that the balancing of those public health risks, even in their mitigated form, as a result of the success of the government's public health measures, outweighed the rights to public assembly and freedom of speech in the context of the proposed assembly. He commented that Fagan J had been criticized for referring to rights deferred rather than rights extinguished, but:

> it seems to me that the true conclusion is that the balance of these considerations will necessarily shift over time, having regard to the changing public health risks and will be affected as well by the nature and circumstances of any public assembly when viewed against public health restrictions and other factors bearing upon the risks associated with a particular public assembly.[239]

---

[236] See *Commissioner of Police v Gabriel* (2004) 141 A Crim R 566, 567 per Hamilton J; *NSW Commissioner of Police v Keep Sydney Open Ltd* [2017] NSWSC 5 per Lindsay J; *Hirst v Chief Constable of West Yorkshire* (1987) 85 Cr App R 143, 151 per Otton J.
[237] *Supple* (n 234) [22]–[23].
[238] ibid [40].
[239] ibid [42].

He therefore prohibited the proposed public assembly.

In July 2020, at a different stage of the pandemic in New South Wales, a cognate issue returned to the Supreme Court in *Commissioner of Police v Gray*,[240] when the Police Commissioner sought an order to prohibit an assembly arranged by a group known as 'Fighting in Solidarity Towards Treaties' to be held in a park in Newcastle. It was to show solidarity with the Black Lives Matter movement and with Indigenous Australians who had died in police and prison custody. The Commissioner of Police again sought a prohibition order on the grounds of public health considerations, raising concerns as to the safety of march participants, members of the public, and police officers in light of the pandemic. By this stage, the second wave of the pandemic had commenced in Victoria and the decision of the Court took this into account.

Public health expert evidence was given that the risk of community transmission of COVID-19 had become 'low' given what had become the substantially reduced levels of transmission in New South Wales. However, the border between New South Wales and Victoria, which was subject to a fresh wave of the virus, was porous—it had not yet been closed. The Public Health Officer of New South Wales identified the presence of a level of community complacency, as evidenced by the increase in respiratory infections, including influenza, which are transmitted in a similar way to COVID-19.[241] Notwithstanding these matters, she conceded the risk of community transmission as a consequence of the proposed public gathering was low because of the evidence which showed that there was little COVID-19 in the community. She also acknowledged the general health benefits to the population of being able to engage in employment, community activities, and other activities which were beneficial to health. The Public Health Officer sounded a note of caution to the Court, highlighting the increased risk of community transmission posed by a public gathering such as the one proposed whereby people of diverse walks of life and different geographical areas would assemble, thereby increasing the potential spread of the virus if one or more people in the crowd had the virus. Her concern also extended to the difficulties of maintaining social distancing in a crowd of people. She also observed that persons with the virus are most infectious in the 48 hours before the manifestation of initial symptoms.[242]

Adamson J concluded that although public health concerns had not typically been raised by the Commissioner of Police in the past as an objection to a public assembly:

> this circumstance is a reflection of the novelty (at least as far as the case precedents reveal) of a virus such as COVID-19 which is both fatal and readily transmissible

---

[240] *Gray* (n 224).
[241] ibid [33].
[242] ibid [35].

from person to person. I am not persuaded that there is any reason to distinguish the physical danger posed to members of the public by violent groups or the physical inconvenience to members of the public by obstructions to footpaths and roads caused by public assemblies on the one hand, and the increased public health risk occasioned by public gatherings such as proposed in the present case on the other.[243]

She stated that in her view it was also significant that the implied freedom of communication on political and government matters had been recognized as a matter of Australian constitutional law. This combination of factors led her to conclude that if the public assembly was authorized, the participants would not be liable for criminal prosecution. Thus the real question to be determined by the Court was whether the threat posed by the COVID-19 virus was such that public health concerns ought to be viewed (at that time) as outweighing the public interest in free speech and freedom of association.[244] Ultimately, she concluded that the public interest in free speech and freedom of association outweighed the public health concerns and that the order sought by the plaintiff ought to be refused. She was not satisfied that, as long as the assembly was held in substantial accordance with the notice, the participants should be deprived of the protections otherwise existing.[245]

In late July 2020, a further application was made for a public assembly to protest against Aboriginal deaths in custody in the central business district of Sydney. A notice to police was submitted in the prescribed form but then police advised against the holding of the protest, explaining that the public health direction then in force directed that persons not participate in a public gathering of more than 20 persons.[246] The plaintiff argued that the direction was *ultra vires* because it impermissibly burdened the implied freedom of political communication ('the implied freedom') and that the Court was obliged to exercise its powers in conformity with the implied freedom.

Ierace J accepted that considerable progress had been made in confining the COVID-19 virus since March 2020 but noted that the Public Health Order had been amended (on 17 July 2020) to tighten restrictions, limiting group bookings in pubs to a maximum of ten people and the number of customers inside a venue to 300 people. Public health expert evidence before him was that it was accurate to describe the risk from the virus at the time as 'medium'.[247]

Ierace J accepted evidence on behalf of those organizing the gathering that there was a risk of momentum being lost for the campaign if public demonstrations were not allowed and noted that there was no evidence that a 'Black Lives Matter' protest

---

[243] ibid [54]–[55].
[244] ibid [62]–[64].
[245] ibid [70].
[246] *Commissioner of Police (NSW) v Gibson* [2020] NSWSC 953 [5].
[247] ibid [71].

that had recently been held led to any transmissions of the COVID-19 virus, in spite of there being at least 10,000 people in attendance by most estimates. However, he also took into account that the risk of transmission had risen from 'low' to 'medium' as a result of the significant resurgence of the virus in Victoria: 'That current assessment of the level of risk, in spite of relatively low numbers of community transmission, is consistent with New South Wales presently being on the knife-edge of a further escalation in community transmission of the virus.'[248]

He found it also to be relevant that the protest was scheduled to occur on a weekday lunchtime in the heart of the central business district, a location in which it could be expected that large numbers of pedestrians not associated with the protest would move through the public assembly, making physical distancing more difficult. He commented that: 'This is particularly concerning, as the contact particulars of passing pedestrians will be unknown and they may not have taken the same precautionary steps as the protesters, such as wearing masks.'[249] This combination of factors persuaded him that the assembly should not take place:

> In my view, the balancing of the competing concerns of the right to free speech and to demonstrate, as against the safety of the community at large, at this particular phase of the pandemic, necessitates the granting of the order prohibiting the holding of the public assembly. In so finding, I take into account the defendant's proposed safety measures, but also the absence of a mechanism to enforce them and the current rating of the risk of transmission of the COVID-19 virus at public assemblies as being *'medium'*.[250]

An appeal to the Court of Appeal the next day failed.[251]

The series of judgments on assemblies during the 2020 phase of the COVID-19 pandemic by the New South Wales Supreme Court and Court of Appeal addressed technical, constitutional, free speech, freedom of assembly, and public health issues. On each occasion, significant weight was given to public health considerations, although acknowledgment was made of the fact that provision of this form of precedence during the pandemic meant that there would be limitation of people's rights to assemble and express their points of view in public. For as long as the risk of community transmission of COVID-19 was significant, the public health issues were accorded priority over the wishes of those who made applications to assemble for the purpose of engaging in public protest.

---

[248] ibid [82].
[249] ibid [83].
[250] ibid [84].
[251] *Gibson (on Behalf of the Dungay Family) v Commissioner of Police (NSW Police Force)* [2020] NSWCA 160.

B. The Right to Gather for Religious Observance

An issue that has proved particularly contentious in a number of countries has been the asserted entitlement of persons to gather for religious observance during the COVID-19 pandemic in spite of lockdown orders that have precluded congregate gatherings. The issue raises the ambit during a pandemic of provisions such as the right to practise religion.

1. English jurisprudence

In May 2020, the Chairman of the Executive Committee of the Jamiyat Tablighi-Ul Islam Mosque sought an interim injunction to prevent the operation of a restriction imposed under the *Health Protection (Coronavirus Restrictions) (England) Regulations, SI 202/350* that closed places of worship during what was designated 'the emergency period'.[252] The challenge was heard the day before Ramadan. It was argued for the applicant that the Secretary of State's failure to open the mosque for communal prayer was contrary to the applicant's right under Article 9 of the *European Convention on Human Rights* to be permitted to manifest his religious beliefs in worship, teaching, practice, and observance.

Swift J accepted that the restrictions did constitute an infringement of the applicant's right to manifest his religious beliefs as asserted but noted that the restriction concerned 'only one aspect of religious observance—attendance at communal Friday prayers. This is not to diminish the significance of that requirement, yet it is relevant to the scope of the interference that is to be justified.'[253] In addition, the interference was finite, the regulations being time-limited, reviewed every three weeks, and scheduled to expire in September 2020.[254]

Swift J also took into account the position adopted by the British Board of Scholars and Imams (BBSI) in a briefing document published on 16 March 2020, Principles 3 to 6 of which provided that:

> 3. We take seriously our responsibility to minister to the welfare of the Community, both worldly and next-worldly. This involves a recognition of the serious importance that our religion places on life, health, community, and spiritual well-being. To trivialise any aspect of this would be an error. As our scholarly tradition demands, our approach in the Guidance is directed by consideration of what is essential, recommended, and desirable. This includes a keen understanding of when (and which) religious rulings may be suspended due to temporary harms or hardship.

---

[252] *R (Hussain) v Secretary of State for Health and Social Care* [2020] EWHC 1392 (Admin).
[253] ibid [12].
[254] ibid [13].

4. The concern within this guidance does not merely relate to the risk of becoming infected with Coronavirus, but more so to the risk of transmitting it to others, especially the old and infirm. To choose to put oneself in harm's way may be acceptable, unwise, or even prohibited; to put others in harm's way is always more severely censured. The guidance uses a risk matrix approach that considers both likelihood of infection/transmission and consequence of infection, from mild to severe.
5. In the event that government directives are issued over-riding any part of the guidance relating to gathering in public or private spaces, then the government directives would take priority.
6. This document is [not] intended to provide specific guidance to individuals, but a general framework of decision making for institutions and mosques. Given that each mosque and institution is different ... we call for local imams, scholars and mosques to decide on what is in the best interests of their communities. However, our advice is that this should be done when all parties are properly informed and have considered all the principles outlined in this document.[255]

Swift J found Principle 5 to be of significance because the document was published before the 2020 Regulations were made and came into force.[256] He found that on a fair reading of Principle 5, the reference to 'government directives' included instruments such as the 2020 Regulations. Part 5 included 'The Jumu'ah prayer' which read as follows:

It is understood that this is the most contentious question within this guidance, and it has been the subject of significant and vigorous debate among religious scholarship and among the members of the BBSI in particular. Jumu'ah is both an obligation on healthy adult males and a clarion sign of Islam; lifting or suspending that obligation from the community at large is not a step that can or should be taken lightly. Nonetheless, we reiterate that the prime directive for animating this briefing paper is people's health and welfare, particularly protecting the elderly and infirm. Given these factors, the question of Jumu'ah will be explored in some detail. Equally it should be noted that this section primarily refers to the norm of performing Jumu'ah in the mosques.

Two points of consensus emerged from the discussions: (1) If the government issues a directive banning public gatherings this needs to be adhered to, and (2) high risk individuals (as previously identified in the congregational prayers section) SHOULD NOT attend: not only is the obligation of Jumu'ah is lifted from them but their attendance, if any congregation does occur, should be severely and

---
[255] ibid [14].
[256] ibid [15].

proactively precluded. If they are at high risk of transmitting the virus to vulnerable people, it should be unambiguously clarified that their attendance would be immoral and sinful.

With this being understood, two broad opinions are articulated by BBSI members: that of the continuing obligation of Jumu'ah and the position as individuals in the UK are generally exempt from the obligation of Jumu'ah prayers.

Strenuous efforts were made given the extremely short timescales and the difficulty of engaging in detailed legal argumentation remotely, to survey the opinions of over 100 members of the BBSI on their basic stance regarding these two positions. A clear majority of those consulted opined that at this time and until further notice the obligation of Jumu'ah should be lifted from the generality of UK Muslims. These guidelines will be regularly reviewed for continuing relevance and proportionality.[257]

Although the applicant made it clear that his religious beliefs differed from the majority view stated by the BBSI, Swift J noted that the applicant's beliefs about communal Friday prayer in current circumstances were not beliefs shared by all Muslims.[258] He took into account the 'truly exceptional circumstances' presented by the pandemic and found the focus of the regulations to be rationally connected with the objective of protecting public health and scientific advice and that the Secretary of State was entitled to adopt a precautionary stance. He found the infringement of the applicant's Article 9 rights not to be disproportionate. Swift J took into account the fact that in a German decision[259] the Constitutional Court had allowed Friday prayers to take place and concluded that a general prohibition in German law brought in to address the COVID-19 pandemic was in breach of Article 4 of the *German Constitution*.[260] He determined that, given the margin of appreciation properly to be extended to the Secretary of State and the balance of convenience, there was no realistic prospect that the applicant would succeed in his ultimate case so he denied the interim injunction sought.[261]

2. Canadian jurisprudence

In February 2021, Masse JCS of the Supreme Court of Quebec heard a challenge brought by the Quebec Council of Hasidic Jews ('the Council') and several Jewish congregations against government directions which limited religious gatherings to ten persons. Evidence was adduced that under Jewish law a minimum of ten males is needed to form a 'minyan', a representative community of Israel for liturgical purposes. Masse JCS interpreted Quebec's emergency by-law and found that it was

---

[257] ibid [16].
[258] ibid [17].
[259] ibid [25]: *F Bundesverfassungsgericht* [German Constitutional Court], 1BvQ 44/20, 29 April 2020.
[260] *R (Hussain) v Secretary of State for Health and Social Care* [2020] EWHC 1392 (Admin) [25].
[261] ibid [25]–[27].

ambiguous as to whether the ten-person limit referred to an entire building and permitted multiple gatherings in the one building.[262] She urged the Council and its Hassidic community to give rigorous respect to the rule of law, stating everyone has a right to life and everyone is at risk of hospitalization from the virus,[263] concluding, 'Encore un peu de courage, c'est mon souhait pour tous' ('a little more courage, that is my wish for you').[264]

The Quebec government moved the curfew to commence at 9.30 p.m. but again the Council challenged the decision in April 2021. Riordan JCS accepted that, for the petitioners, unfettered access to a synagogue was a question of the highest importance: 'Physical attendance at synagogue three times a day, including once after nightfall, is a mandatory and essential cog in their spiritual life. It is a sincere and serious religious practice and one that is recognized for the purposes of the Canadian Charter of Rights and Freedoms and the Quebec Charter of Human Rights and Freedoms.'[265] The Council members described the decrees as a spiritual, psychological, and social disaster for them, but Riordan JCS emphasized that for the court to strike them down as *ultra vires* it was necessary for the decrees to be shown to be irrelevant, extraneous, or completely unrelated to the purpose of the enabling public health statute. He found as a matter of fact that the government did consider the needs and the special circumstances surrounding religious gatherings in its deliberations over public health policy.[266] He summarized his dismissal of the claim, observing that the Directions squarely and deliberately prioritized public health issues in the knowledge that this would be experienced as a hardship by a number of constituencies:

> The harsh reality of Covid is that the absence of a past outbreak in a particular sector often turns out to be the harbinger of a future outbreak there. This is the battle that the Government is fighting and this is why it feels that it must take what might appear to some to be excessive precautions, even if they might seem to make sense one day, but not the next....
>
> Though we are convinced of the serious distress caused especially to Hassidic males by the Decrees, concern over public health must take priority over our desire to protect their right to practise their religious traditions.[267]

Cognate issues were also raised before Hinkson J of the British Columbia Supreme Court during 2021, when it was asserted by a number of Protestant churches ('the religious petitioners') that their rights under the *Canadian Charter of Rights and*

---

[262] *Conseil des Juifs Hassidiques du Québec, c Procureur Général du Québec*, 2021 QCCS 281.
[263] ibid [186].
[264] ibid [191].
[265] ibid [14].
[266] ibid [31].
[267] ibid [37]–[38].

Freedoms had been infringed by orders made under the *Public Health Act SBC 2008* prohibiting in-person religious services.[268] They claimed that the Public Health Officer had not reasonably balanced the restriction on religious freedom with protection of public health when she imposed the restrictions on religious worship. A related issue arose as a result of a specific petitioner having organized public protests against what he contended was an abuse of government power by the imposition of what he believed were unnecessary and draconian restrictions in the name of safety. He was fined for his conduct. He sought a declaration that his *Charter* rights had been infringed, arguing that the protests in which he participated were peaceful political events that occurred outside and prioritized the safety of attendees, including their physical distancing and their cooperation with police. The British Columbia government conceded that he was justified in this contention[269] and Hinkson J made declarations that the orders prohibiting gatherings and events in November and December 2020 were of no force and effect as they unjustifiably infringed his rights and freedoms.[270]

The position of the religious petitioners was less straightforward. They gave evidence that gathering in-person provided benefits in addition to the fulfilment of their religious beliefs, including accommodating members who did not have the means to use technology; identifying specific needs of vulnerable persons in the church community; providing physical, mental, and emotional care; and providing comfort and encouragement and reducing loneliness, depression, anxiety, and fear. Hinkson J refused their applications for declarations of invalidity, finding the public health orders not to constitute an absolute prohibition on in-person religious gatherings[271] and that the Public Health Officer had acted within the range of reasonable alternatives.[272] He rejected the arguments that the orders were arbitrary, irrational, and disproportionate, finding that they were based on a reasonable assessment of the risk of transmission of the virus during religious and other types of gatherings at the relevant time.[273]

3. United States jurisprudence

Four important cases have been determined by the United States Supreme Court in relation to entitlements of persons to attend religious gatherings in spite of public health orders that such gatherings do not take place.[274]

In the first case, *South Bay United Pentecostal Church v Newsom*,[275] a Californian church, the South Bay Pentecostal Church, applied for an injunction to prevent

---

[268] *Beaudoin v British Columbia*, 2021 BCSC 512.
[269] ibid [147].
[270] ibid [251].
[271] ibid [192].
[272] ibid [223].
[273] ibid [233].
[274] See Josh Blackman, 'The "Essential" Free Exercise Clause' (2021) 4(3) *Harvard Journal of Law & Public Policy* 637.
[275] 140 S Ct 1613 (2020); 207 L Ed 154 (2020).

enforcement of an Executive Order made by the Governor of California limiting attendance at places of worship to 25% of building capacity or a maximum of attendees. The plurality declined the injunctive relief but Thomas, Alito, Gorsuch, and Kavanaugh JJ dissented—they would have granted the relief.

Chief Justice Roberts for the plurality found that the restrictions were consistent with the 'Free Exercise Clause' in the First Amendment to the *Constitution* which disallows any prohibition on the free exercise of religion.[276] He placed emphasis on the fact that:

> Similar or more severe restrictions apply to comparable secular gatherings, including lectures, concerts, movie showings, spectator sports, and theatrical performances, where large groups of people gather in close proximity for extended periods of time. And the Order exempts or treats more leniently only dissimilar activities, such as operating grocery stores, banks, and laundromats, in which people neither congregate in large groups nor remain in close proximity for extended periods.[277]

He observed that when restrictions on particular social activities should be lifted during the pandemic 'is a dynamic and fact-intensive matter subject to reasonable disagreement'.[278] He applied previous authority that when public officials act in areas of medical and scientific uncertainty they must be given latitude that is 'especially broad'.[279] He concluded that: 'Where those broad limits are not exceeded, they should not be subject to second-guessing by an "unelected federal judiciary", which lacks the background, competence, and expertise to assess public health and is not accountable to the people.'[280]

By contrast, Kavanaugh J in dissent expressed the view that California had ample options that would allow it to combat the spread of COVID-19 without discriminating against religion:

> The State could 'insist that the congregants adhere to social-distancing and other health requirements and leave it at that—just as the Governor has done for comparable secular activities.' *Roberts* v *Neace*, 958 F 3d 409, at 415. Or alternatively, the State could impose reasonable occupancy caps across the board. But absent a compelling justification (which the State has not offered), the State may not take a looser approach with, say, supermarkets, restaurants, factories, and offices while imposing stricter requirements on places of worship.[281]

---

[276] 140 S Ct 1613, 1614.
[277] ibid 1614.
[278] ibid 1614.
[279] *Marshall v United States*, 414 US 417, 427 (1974).
[280] *South Bay United Pentecostal Church v Newsom*, 140 S Ct 1613, 1614.
[281] ibid 1615.

In the second case, *Calvary Chapel Dayton Valley v Sisolak*,[282] a church in rural Nevada, the Calvary Chapel Dayton Valley, sought an injunction to permit it to host worship services for about 90 congregants, cutting its services in half, and asking its congregants to adhere to social distancing protocols. However, its proposal was inconsistent with Directive 21, Nevada Governor's Steve Sisolak's phase-two re-opening plan, which limited indoor worship to no more than 50 persons.[283] The Chapel failed but there were powerful dissents from Alito, Gorsuch, and Kavanaugh JJ. Alito J emphasized the inconsistencies in permitting casinos to remain open but restricting attendance at faith services. He stressed that:

> a public health emergency does not give Governors and other public officials *carte blanche* to disregard the Constitution for as long as the medical problem persists. As more medical and scientific evidence becomes available, and as States have time to craft policies in light of that evidence, courts should expect policies that more carefully account for constitutional rights.[284]

Given the passage of time since the Governor's initial declaration of a state of emergency (on 12 May 2020), Alito J classified the 'problem' as 'no longer one of exigency, but one of considered yet discriminatory treatment of places of worship'.[285] He commented that:

> The idea that allowing Calvary Chapel to admit 90 worshippers presents a greater public health risk than allowing casinos to operate at 50% capacity is hard to swallow, and the State's efforts to justify the discrimination are feeble. It notes that patrons at gaming tables are supposed to wear masks and that the service of food at casinos is now limited, but congregants in houses of worship are also required to wear masks, and they do not consume meals during services.
>
> The State notes that facilities other than houses of worship, such as museums, art galleries, zoos, aquariums, trade schools, and technical schools, are also treated less favorably than casinos, but obviously that does not justify preferential treatment for casinos.[286]

Finally, he noted that the State argued that preferential treatment for casinos was justified because the State was in a better position to enforce compliance by casinos, which were under close supervision by state officials and subject to penalties if they

---

[282] 140 S Ct 2603 (2020); 207 L Ed 1129 (2020).
[283] Steve Sisolak, 'Declaration of Emergency Directive 021: Phase Two Reopening Plan' (Emergency Order, 28 May 2020) <https://gov.nv.gov/News/Emergency_Orders/2020/2020-05-28_-_COVID-19_Declaration_of_Emergency_Directive_021_-_Phase_Two_Reopening_Plan_(Attachments)> accessed 14 September 2022.
[284] 140 S Ct 2603, 2605 (2020).
[285] ibid 2605.
[286] ibid 2606.

violate state rules.[287] However, he dismissed this argument summarily, observing that: 'This argument might make some sense if enforcing the 50% capacity rule were materially harder than enforcing a flat 50-person rule. But there is no reason to think that is so, let alone that it would be compelling enough to justify differential treatment of religion.'[288]

In *Roman Catholic Diocese of Brooklyn New York v Cuomo*,[289] an application was made for injunctive relief to the Supreme Court of the United States against an Executive Order issued by the Governor of New York. The order imposed severe restrictions on attendance at religious services in areas classified as 'red', where a cap of attendance by ten persons at each religious service was stipulated, or 'orange' where a cap of attendance by 25 persons was stipulated.[290] The applications were brought by the Roman Catholic Diocese of Brooklyn and by Agudath Israel of America. They contended that the restrictions violated the Free Exercise Clause of the First Amendment and that the regulations treated houses of worship much more harshly than secular facilities.

The applications were allowed on the basis that the applicants showed that their First Amendment claims were likely to prevail, that denying them relief would lead to irreparable injury, and that granting them relief would not harm the public interest.[291] The Court noted that: 'not only is there no evidence that the applicants have contributed to the spread of COVID-19 but there are many other less restrictive rules that could be adopted to minimize the risk to those attending religious services.'[292] It particularly took into account that while constraints were being placed on religious gatherings in red zones, businesses categorized as 'essential' were able to admit as many people as they wished, while in orange zones non-essential businesses could decide how many persons they wished to admit. Justice Gorsuch observed that restrictions applied even to the largest cathedrals and synagogues, which ordinarily hold hundreds of adherents and the restrictions applied no matter the precautions taken, including social distancing, wearing masks, leaving doors and windows open, forgoing singing, and disinfecting spaces between services.[293]

He commented that:

> If only 10 people are admitted to each service, the great majority of those who wish to attend Mass on Sunday or services in a synagogue on Shabbat will be barred. And while those who are shut out may in some instances be able to watch

---

[287] ibid 2606.
[288] ibid 2606.
[289] 141 S Ct 63 (2020); 208 L Ed 206 (2020) (hereafter *Cuomo*).
[290] ibid 65.
[291] ibid 69.
[292] ibid 67.
[293] ibid 67–68.

services on television, such remote viewing is not the same as personal attendance. Catholics who watch a Mass at home cannot receive communion, and there are important religious traditions in the Orthodox Jewish faith that require personal attendance.[294]

In addition, the Court concluded that 'the State has not shown that public health would be imperilled if less restrictive measures were imposed'.[295] It stated that:

> Members of this Court are not public health experts, and we should respect the judgment of those with special expertise and responsibility in this area. But even in a pandemic, the Constitution cannot be put away and forgotten. The restrictions at issue here, by effectively barring many from attending religious services, strike at the very heart of the First Amendment's guarantee of religious liberty. Before allowing this to occur, we have a duty to conduct a serious examination of the need for such a drastic measure.[296]

The next in the sequence of United States authorities was an application for an emergency injunction by Pastor Wong and Karen Busch against California's restriction on in-home worship in *Tandon v Newsom*.[297] The appellants asserted that the Californian law breached the Free Exercise Clause in the First Amendment. The majority upheld the challenge and observed that the government has the burden to establish that a law interfering with the practice of religion satisfied strict scrutiny: 'narrow tailoring requires the government to show that measures less restrictive of the First Amendment activity could not address its interest in reducing the spread of COVID'.[298] The majority applied the *Roman Catholic Diocese* decision and held that where the government 'permits other activities to proceed with precautions, it must show that the religious exercise at issue is more dangerous than those activities even when the same precautions are applied. Otherwise, precautions that suffice for other activities suffice for religious exercise too.'[299] It found that California had treated some comparable secular activities more favourably than at-home religious gatherings, permitting hair salons, retail stores, personal care services, movie theatres, private suites at sporting events and concerts, and indoor restaurants to bring together more than three households at a time without any evidence that such activities would pose any less risk than the applicant's proposed religious exercise at home.[300]

---

[294] ibid 67–68.
[295] ibid 68.
[296] ibid 68.
[297] 141 S Ct 1294 (2021); 209 L Ed 355.
[298] 141 S Ct 1294, 1296–1297 (2021).
[299] ibid 1297.
[300] ibid 1297.

Three Supreme Court judges (Kagan, Breyer, and Sotomayor JJ) dissented. They were prepared to uphold California's laws, observing that:

> California limits religious gatherings in homes to three households. If the State also limits all secular gatherings in homes to three households, it has complied with the First Amendment. And the State does exactly that: It has adopted a blanket restriction on at-home gatherings of all kinds, religious and secular alike. California need not, as the *per curiam* insists, treat at-home religious gatherings the same as hardware stores and hair salons—and thus unlike at-home secular gatherings, the obvious comparator here.[301]

4. Overview

Extensive case law has evolved in relation to the entitlement to assemble for religious purposes during the COVID-19 pandemic. Generally, precedence was given to public health exigencies but it remained necessary for it to be shown that public health orders which inhibited religious practice were necessary and proportionate. In a number of United States cases the necessity of these restrictions was questioned because other forms of interactions by persons in close proximity were taking place, leaving doubts as to the need for and therefore legitimacy of the inhibitions upon religious practice. However, disputes about such matters fundamentally split the United States Supreme Court in a series of cases during 2020 and 2021.

X. Challenges to Mandatory Vaccination Requirements

With the development of vaccines but in the context of ongoing significant levels of persons being infected with COVID-19, 'vaccine mandates' were introduced in a number of countries. Given that such mandates involved the imposition of pressure to submit to a medical intervention which, for a small number of persons, could have adverse consequences, this prompted controversies and community consternation in some countries.[302] Likewise, there was opposition to the requirement that persons be obliged to carry what became known as 'vaccination passports', showing their current vaccination status, in order to be permitted to avail

---

[301] ibid 1298.
[302] See eg Catherine Kyobutungi, 'Kenya Has Imposed a Holiday Season COVID-19 Vaccine Mandate: Why It's Premature' *The Conversation* (4 December 2021) <https://theconversation.com/kenya-has-imposed-a-holiday-season-covid-19-vaccine-mandate-why-its-premature-173155> accessed 14 September 2022; Jan Walter, 'Mandatory COVID Vaccines: A Controversy Across Europe' *DW* (6 November 2021) <www.dw.com/en/mandatory-covid-vaccines-a-controversy-across-europe/a-59742720> accessed 14 September 2022; Lawrence O Gostin, Daniel A Salmon, and Heidi J Larson, 'Mandating COVID-19 Vaccines' (2021) 325(6) *Journal of the American Medical Association* 532.

themselves of the opportunity to work, enter shops, travel, and participate in activities where numbers of persons would be present.[303]

However, especially in the initial phases of the pandemic, courts in a number of countries upheld the validity of mandatory vaccination orders by governments and employers in response to early legal challenges to them.[304] In the United States, several courts cited the 1905 decision of *Jacobson v Massachusetts*,[305] in upholding vaccine mandates, including where they were applied as a precondition to school entry. However, all states granted medical exemptions to these mandates and 45 states and Washington DC granted religious exemptions, with 15 states allowing philosophical exemptions.[306] Nevertheless, as the pandemic progressed, certain cases, most notably in Australia and the United States, indicated disapproval by some judicial officers of vaccine mandates or at least mandates that were imposed in circumstances where particular preconditions, such as consultation with employees or provision of religious exemptions, were not met.

A. Australian Jurisprudence

In Australia, all of the early legal challenges to vaccine mandates were unsuccessful,[307] reflecting courts' apparent propensity to uphold vaccination requirements, whether imposed by governments or employers, where they were reasonable and proportionate in their objective of saving lives and where they rendered workplaces safe during a pandemic. *Kassam v Hazard*, the most high profile of those cases, was a decision of some international significance.[308] Beech-Jones J, the Chief Justice at Common Law in the Supreme Court of New South Wales in Australia, rejected the argument that a requirement for vaccination was unacceptable because

---

[303] See Bridget M Kuehn, 'Vaccine Passports Help Boost Lagging Vaccination Rates' (2020) 327(3) *Journal of the American Medical Association* 209; Kristin Voigt, Evrard Nahimana, and Anat Rosenthal, 'Flashing Red Lights: The Global Implications of COVID-19 Vaccination Passports' (2021) 6(5) *BMJ Global Health* art e006209. See also Chapter 5 for a discussion of mandatory vaccination and vaccine passports.

[304] Michelle M Mello and Wendy E Parmet, 'Public Health Law After COVID-19' (2021) 385(13) *New England Journal of Medicine* 1153, 1155; Dev AS Kevat and others, 'Medico-legal Considerations of Mandatory COVID-19 Vaccination for High Risk Workers' (2021) 215(1) *Medical Journal of Australia* 22.

[305] 197 US 11 (1905); see Wendy K Mariner, George J Annas, and Leonard H Glantz, 'Jacobson v Massachusetts: It's Not Your Great-Great Grandfather's Public Health Law' (2005) 95(4) *American Journal of Public Health* 581; Daniel Farber, 'The Long Shadow of *Jacobson v Massachusetts*: Public Health, Fundamental Rights, and the Courts' (2020) 57(4) *San Diego Law Review* 833; Josh Blackman, 'The Irrepressible Myth of Jacobson v Massachusetts' (2022) 70 *Buffalo Law Review* 131; Wendy E Parmet, 'Rediscovering Jacobson in the Era of COVID-19' (2020) 100 *Boston University Law Review* 117.

[306] Gostin, Salmon, and Larson (n 302) 532.

[307] See Chapter 10. See also Ian Freckelton, 'Mandatory Vaccination Tensions and Litigation' (2021) 28(4) *Journal of Law and Medicine* 913; *Kimber v Sapphire Coast Community Aged Care Ltd* [2021] FWCFB 6015; *Kassam v Hazzard* [2021] NSWSC 1320 (hereafter *Kassam*); *Brassell-Dellow v Queensland (Queensland Police Service)* [2021] QIRC 356.

[308] *Kassam* (n 307).

it contravened the right to earn a living, observing that the privilege against self-incrimination is not a privilege against exoneration.[309] Indeed, Beech-Jones J rejected the proposition that there is a 'right to earn a living' that is protected by the principle of legality.[310] In any event, Beech-Jones J stated that he was not satisfied that the Minister responsible for the mandatory vaccination direction did not appreciate or consider the impact of the impugned orders on freedom of movement, including the capacity to earn a living, or the differential impact on those who are not vaccinated.[311] He concluded that:

> the proper analysis is that the impugned orders curtail freedom of movement which in turn affects a person's ability to work (and socialise). So far as the right to bodily integrity is concerned, it is not violated as the impugned orders do not authorise the involuntary vaccination of anyone. So far as the impairment of freedom of movement is concerned, the degree of impairment differs depending on whether a person is vaccinated or unvaccinated. Curtailing the free movement of persons including their movement to and at work are the very type of restrictions that the [*Public Health Act*] PHA clearly authorises.[312]

Beech-Jones J found that the differential treatment was not arbitrary, but used as a yardstick vaccination status, this being consistent with the objectives of the relevant public health legislation and not an unreasonable exercise of power. Beech-Jones J also repudiated the argument that the direction interfered with a worker's right to bodily integrity.[313] This is likely to be an approach adopted by some other courts during the COVID-19 crisis and its immediate aftermath.[314]

Likewise, entities such as shipping lines and airlines have been observed to have a responsibility to render their places of business safe. Their conditions of carriage that exclude persons who are not vaccinated are also likely to be upheld as lawful.[315]

Notwithstanding this, mandatory vaccination has prompted strong expressions of view during the pandemic and not all judicial officers have approved of it. This is exemplified by the case of *Kimber v Sapphire Coast Community Aged Care Ltd*[316] in

---

[309] ibid [71].
[310] ibid [135]. See generally Dan Meagher and Matthew Groves (eds), *The Principle of Legality in Australia and New Zealand* (Federation Press 2017).
[311] *Kassam* (n 307) [135].
[312] ibid [10]–[11].
[313] ibid [9].
[314] ibid.
[315] See Amy Maguire, Fiona McGaughey and Marco Rizzi, 'Can Governments Mandate a COVID Vaccination? Balancing Public Health with Human Rights – and What the Law Says' *The Conversation* (30 November 2020) < https://theconversation.com/can-governments-mandate-a-covid-vaccination-balancing-public-health-with-human-rights-and-what-the-law-says-150733> accessed 16 May 2022; Tanya Calitz, 'Constitutional Rights in South Africa Protect Against Mandatory COVID-19 Vaccination' *Health and Human Rights Journal* (21 April 2021) <www.hhrjournal.org/2021/04/constitutional-rights-in-south-africa-protect-against-mandatory-covid-19-vaccination/> accessed 13 September 2022.
[316] [2021] FWCFB 6015 [211].

Australia before the Full Bench of the Fair Work Commission. Though in dissent, Deputy President Dean concluded that mandatory vaccination cannot be justified 'in almost every workplace' and asserted that vaccinations constitute clinical trials for which voluntary consent is necessary;[317] there are other options for protecting the community such as testing;[318] and dismissing an employee who elects not to have a COVID-19 vaccine would constitute disability discrimination.[319] She labelled the imposition of a workplace requirement of vaccination as 'medical apartheid',[320] concluding that:

> Blanket rules, such as mandating vaccinations for everyone across a whole profession or industry regardless of the actual risk, fail the tests of proportionality, necessity and reasonableness. It is more than the absolute minimum necessary to combat the crisis and cannot be justified on health grounds. It is a lazy and fundamentally flawed approach to risk management and should be soundly rejected by courts when challenged.[321]

However, these views were in stark contrast to those expressed by judges in another major Australian case on the issue. The decision of Beech-Jones J in *Kassam v Hazzard* was unsuccessfully appealed to the New South Wales Court of Appeal[322] with Bell P (with whom Meagher JA agreed and Leeming JA substantially agreed) commenting that the civil conscription argument advanced by the appellants was 'completely untenable'.[323] The Court of Appeal scrutinized section 7 of the *Public Health Act 2010* (NSW), which permits the Minister for Health in New South Wales, upon considering a situation to have arisen that is (or is likely to be) a threat to public health to take a variety of actions, including declaring a part of the state to be a public health risk area and make such directions as the Minister considers necessary '(a) to reduce or remove any risk to public health in the area, (b) to segregate or isolate inhabitants of the area, and (c) to prevent, or conditionally permit, access to the area.' Bell P found the power given to the Minister to be 'very broad' and held that 'no narrow construction should be afforded to it given its subject matter and the nature of the risk it is designed to address.'[324] He commented that:

> It is inconceivable in my view that the legislature would not have intended to afford the Minister the maximum flexibility possible to counter or address risks

---

[317] ibid [114]–[119].
[318] ibid [139].
[319] ibid [174].
[320] ibid [182].
[321] ibid [181]; compare *Four Aviation Security Service Employees v Minister of Covid-19 Response* [2021] NZHC 3012 [143].
[322] [2021] NSWCA 299.
[323] ibid [38].
[324] ibid [78].

to public health which could be severe, fast-moving and wide-ranging. In that context, it is clear from the second reading speech to which the Court was taken that the *Public Health Act* was enacted with an awareness of the public health risks posed by viruses such as SARS and Ebola.[325]

Bell P rejected the argument that the provision could only be used for 'short, sharp' measures to address a 'short, discrete event', an 'isolated incident', or a 'situation' that had arisen, holding that the provision could be used prophylactically and that the 'situation' may be grave, or potentially so.[326] The Court of Appeal held that the directions, the subject of complaint, were properly made pursuant to section 7. Bell P held that the task of construing the provision should be done in the usual way without being confined by the 'principle of legality',[327] which requires that interference with fundamental rights must be clearly manifested by unmistakable and unambiguous language.[328] He stated that the principle 'must be applied with care'.[329] He emphasized that nothing in the orders '*required*, still less coerced, aged care workers or educational professionals, authorised workers or workers in the construction industry, to be vaccinated'.[330]

Bell P noted that the rights to 'earn a living' and 'to work' were a 'powerful rhetorical refrain',[331] but rejected the proposition that there is a common law right to work 'in any strict sense which would engage the principle of legality'.[332] He dismissed emphatically the proposition that the 'right not to be discriminated against' and the 'right to privacy' could engage the principle of legality (if Parliament intends to interfere with fundamental rights, it must express that intention by clear and unambiguous language) and rejected the argument that the privilege against self-incrimination and the right to silence were breached by the orders.[333]

In a later and extensively reasoned decision,[334] the Full Bench of the Fair Work Commission in Australia upheld a vaccine mandate imposed by a large mining company (BHP), together with a requirement of proof of vaccination status by a form of 'vaccination passport'. It found this to be a reasonable response by the company to COVID-19 as a result of its occupational health and safety obligations[335]

---

[325] ibid [129].
[326] ibid [58].
[327] See *Potter v Minahan* (1908) 7 CLR 277; *Coco v The Queen* (1994) 179 CLR 427, 437.
[328] *Kassam v Hazzard* [2021] NSWCA 299.
[329] ibid [56].
[330] ibid [97].
[331] ibid [100].
[332] ibid [104].
[333] ibid [108]–[109]. See too *Four Midwives v Minister for Covid-19 Response* [2021] NZHC 3064 per Palmer J; *Four Aviation Security Service Employees v Minister of Covid-19 Response* [2021] NZHC 3012 per Cooke J.
[334] *Construction, Forestry, Maritime, Mining and Energy Union v Mt Arthur Coal* [2021] FWCB 6059.
[335] ibid [252], [261].

and the circumstances of a mine site in light of expert evidence from an epidemiologist that:

> the risk of infection for unvaccinated workers will not disappear because they are still at risk of catching COVID-19 from fully vaccinated and unvaccinated workers. Importantly, unvaccinated workers on a work site will increase the risk of spreading COVID-19 to vaccinated workers and other unvaccinated workers. Even one unvaccinated person still poses a significantly higher risk of acquiring the infection and transmitting it to other vaccinated people....
>
> Unvaccinated people at the workplace or places of mass gatherings are still at risk of acquiring infection from an asymptomatic but infected vaccinated person. The risk is lower than acquiring infection from another unvaccinated staff member but household outbreaks report that unvaccinated people are at higher risk of infection (in a mixed household) than vaccinated people. The unvaccinated worker also has a risk of transmitting infection to the vaccinated staff.[336]

The Court concluded that with the opening up of the Australian community in light of high levels of vaccination, in time COVID-19 would spread throughout the community and that when 'COVID-19 does so spread, those who remain unvaccinated are at greatest risk of acquiring COVID-19, becoming seriously ill or dying from acquiring COVID-19, and infecting other people with whom they come into contact.'[337]

However, the Court also concluded that the employer should have provided the employees with a reasonable opportunity to persuade the employer in relation to the proposal to introduce the site access requirement, including by inviting the employees to contribute scientific, medical or safety data or inform them that such information had the potential to influence its assessment and recommendation regarding making vaccination a workplace entry requirement.[338] The Full Bench observed that 'the responsibility to consult carries a responsibility to give those consulted an opportunity to be heard and to express their views so that they can be taken into account; it is not a mere perfunctory exercise'.[339] It accepted that, while persons in the position of the applicants were not being forcibly treated, given they could decline to be vaccinated, 'it is a form of economic and social pressure' 'to surrender their bodily integrity (by undergoing medical treatment) in circumstances where they would prefer not to do so'.[340] It observed that a minority of employees

---

[336] ibid [58].
[337] ibid [62].
[338] This aspect of the decision arose from the fact that s 47 of the *Work Health and Safety Act 2011* (NSW) requires a person conducting a business or undertaking 'so far as is reasonably practicable' to consult with workers who carry out work for the business or undertaking who are or are likely to be directly affected by a matter relating to work health or safety.
[339] *Construction, Forestry, Maritime, Mining and Energy Union v Mt Arthur Coal* [2021] FWCB 6059 [195].
[340] ibid [222]–[223].

felt very strongly about their bodily integrity, and that it is particularly important that these employees be heard.[341] It made no finding as to whether the requirements as to vaccination were in breach of health privacy law, as it did not need to determine the issue.

Thus, the decision gave a significant fillip to requirements for workers to be vaccinated, provided there is compliance with appropriate consultative arrangements with workers pursuant to occupational health and safety requirements. The decision is likely to have ongoing relevance because of the persisting risk at a worksite to persons who are unvaccinated and employers' occupational health and safety obligations toward them.

The overall tenor of decisions in Australia (and New Zealand[342]) is that latitude will be extended by courts to requirements that identifiable categories of workers be required to demonstrate vaccination currency prior to attending the workplace, but the administrative arrangements underpinning such requirements are likely to be scrutinized to ensure that there has been close compliance with procedural, temporal, and fairness obligations. It may be though that, other than for health personnel caring for patients with particular risk features, mandatory vaccination requirements will ease and will not be upheld by courts as the threat posed by COVID-19 variants and sub-variants reduces.

B. The European Court of Human Rights

Consistent with the approaches of many countries' courts to vaccine mandates, the European Court of Human Rights rejected 30 health professionals' requests for interim measures against Greece's requirement for health professionals to have a COVID-19 vaccine in order to continue their occupation (such requests are granted where 'the applicants would otherwise face a real risk of irreversible harm').[343]

---

[341] ibid [224].
[342] See *Four Aviation Security Service Employees v Minister of Covid-19 Response* [2021] NZHC 3012 [124] per Cooke J; *Four Midwives v Minister for Covid-19 Response* [2021] NZHC 3064 per Palmer J.
[343] European Court of Human Rights, 'Refusal of Requests for Interim Measures in Respect of the Greek Law on Compulsory Vaccination of Health-Sector Staff Against COVID-19' (Press Release, 9 September 2021) <https://hudoc.echr.coe.int/app/conversion/pdf/?library=ECHR&id=003-7113391-9633858&filename=Request%20for%20interim%20measures%20against%20Greece%20concerning%20compulsory%20vaccination%20for%20health%20staff.pdf> accessed 13 September 2022.

C. United States Jurisprudence

1. State decisions

Several United States courts at state level upheld COVID-19 vaccine mandates in response to legal challenges. While the approach of the United States Supreme Court in one case heard later in the pandemic was at odds with those decisions, the majority of that Court has demonstrated a preparedness to uphold mandates that apply to healthcare workers. Relevant Supreme Court cases and some decisions that illustrate the approach taken to vaccine mandates at a state level in the United States are now discussed.

The United States District Court for the Southern District of Texas found that the Houston Methodist Hospital's requirement for its employees to have COVID-19 vaccines in order to continue their employment was not coercive.[344]

Subsequently, in *Beckerich v St Elizabeth Medical Centre*, Bunning J in the United States District Court for the Eastern District of Kentucky denied the motion of a group of healthcare workers for a temporary restraining order and/or preliminary injunction prohibiting their employer, the St Elizabeth Medical Center and Summit Medical Group, from enforcing its vaccine mandate.[345] The policy required employees to have a COVID-19 vaccine or apply for a medical or religious exemption—employees who did not comply without an accepted exemption would have their employment terminated.[346] Bunning J noted that 'constitutional rights' were irrelevant to the case because private hospitals are 'not state actors for purposes of constitutional questions'.[347] He considered that the plaintiffs had not established that the defendants had discriminated against employees or breached the *Americans with Disabilities Act of 1990* (US), as it had processed and granted medical and religious exemptions to its policy.[348] Further, Bunning J noted that the plaintiffs did not demonstrate that irreparable harm would follow from failing to grant the injunction (loss of employment is not deemed to constitute irreparable injury) and the plaintiffs were not 'being forcibly vaccinated'.[349]

Bunning J observed that 'actual liberty for all of us cannot exist where individual liberties override potential injury done to others'.[350] He noted that 'the law states that vaccination mandates, both public and private, are permissible with appropriate exceptions', and the defendants' policy was 'well within the confines of the

---

[344] Nathaniel Weixel, 'As COVID-19 Infections Climb, Vaccine Mandates Follow' *The Hill* (8 August 2021) <https://thehill.com/policy/healthcare/566810-as-covid-19-infections-climb-vaccine-mandates-follow?rl=1> accessed 13 September 2022; I Glenn Cohen, 'Can Your Employer Require That You Get Vaccinated? It Depends Where You Live' *Time* (2 August 2021) <https://time.com/6086537/covid-19-vaccine-employer-required/> accessed 13 September 2022.
[345] 64 NDLR P 23 (ED Ky 2021) (hereafter *Beckerich*) [2]–[3].
[346] ibid [2]–[3].
[347] ibid [7]–[8], [17].
[348] ibid [10]–[11], [14].
[349] ibid [16]–[18].
[350] ibid [23].

law, and it appropriately balances the public interests with individual liberties'.[351] The plaintiffs' 'suspicions' concerning 'the efficacy and safety of the COVID-19 vaccines' 'cannot override the law, which recognizes Defendants' right to set conditions of employment'.[352] Bunning J concluded:

> If an employee believes his or her individual liberties are more important than legally permissible conditions on his or her employment, that employee can and should choose to exercise another individual liberty, no less significant—the right to seek other employment.[353]

In *Harsman v Cincinatti Children's Hospital Medical Center*, Black J in the United States District Court for the Southern District of Ohio followed Bunning J's decision in several respects.[354] Black J similarly denied the request of healthcare workers to grant a temporary restraining order or a preliminary injunction restraining the hospital from requiring its employees to have a COVID-19 vaccine and from taking adverse actions against those who did not comply with its mandate.[355] He found that the plaintiffs had not established that their action was likely to succeed, especially given that the hospital had granted medical and religious exemptions to its mandate.[356] Black J referred to the long history of United States judges upholding vaccine mandates as 'constitutionally sound',[357] and noted that 'denying injunctive relief serves the public's interest in combating COVID-19, at an infinitesimally small risk to Plaintiffs' health or liberty'.[358] However, Black J noted that 'against this objective data' 'COVID-19 continues to devastate' and poses a 'very real threat', and that the plaintiffs 'allege unsupported conspiracy theories', which 'are falsehoods'.[359]

In an educational context, the United States District Court for the Northern District of Indiana held that the University of Indiana's COVID-19 vaccine mandate for students was not unconstitutional, as it did not represent 'forced vaccination' because the students could apply for religious and medical exemptions or choose to attend other universities.[360]

---

[351] ibid [22]–[23].
[352] ibid [23]–[24].
[353] ibid [25]–[26].
[354] (SD Ohio, Case No 1:21-cv-597, 20 September 2021) [6].
[355] ibid [3], [6].
[356] ibid [8].
[357] ibid [10].
[358] ibid [14].
[359] ibid [15].
[360] Cohen (n 344).

2. Supreme Court decisions

A major United States authority in relation to mandatory vaccination is the October 2021 refusal of injunctive relief by the Supreme Court.[361] Maine had adopted a regulation requiring certain healthcare workers to receive COVID-19 vaccines if they wished to retain their jobs. Unlike most comparable rules in other parts of the United States, Maine's rule did not contain an exemption for those whose sincerely held religious beliefs precluded them from being vaccinated. The applicants who appeared before the Supreme Court were a physician who operated a medical practice and eight other healthcare workers. One had already lost her job and another faced the imminent loss of his medical practice. They sought injunctive relief to prevent further enforcement of Maine's rule alleging that the Johnson & Johnson vaccine required the use of abortion-related materials in its production and that the Moderna and Pfizer vaccines relied on aborted foetal cell lines.[362] For the purposes of the proceedings Maine did not dispute these propositions.

Maine offered four justifications for its mandate:

(1) Protecting individual patients from contracting COVID-19;
(2) Protecting individual healthcare workers from contracting COVID-19;
(3) Protecting the State's healthcare infrastructure, including the workforce, by preventing COVID-caused absences that could cripple a facility's ability to provide care; and
(4) Reducing the likelihood of outbreaks within healthcare facilities caused by an infected healthcare worker bringing the virus to work.[363]

While the majority declined the application on discretionary grounds, concluding that granting an injunction in such a situation risked an abuse of the emergency procedure,[364] a minority (consisting of Gorsuch, Thomas, and Alito JJ) would have allowed the application. Justice Gorsuch focused on indicia of risk from unvaccinated workers, observing that Maine did not suggest that a worker who was not vaccinated for religious reasons was less likely to spread or contract the virus than someone who was vaccinated.[365] He commented that a government cannot:

> blithely assume those claiming a medical exemption will be more willing to wear protective gear, submit to testing, or take other precautions than someone seeking a religious exemption. A State may not assume 'the best' of individuals engaged in their secular lives while assuming 'the worst' about the habits of religious persons.[366]

---
[361] *John Does 1–3 v Mills*, 142 S Ct 17 (2021); 211 L Ed 2d 243 (2021).
[362] 142 S Ct 17, 19 (2021).
[363] ibid 19.
[364] ibid 18.
[365] ibid 20.
[366] ibid 20.

He reaffirmed the proposition that there continued to be a 'compelling interest' in stemming the spread of COVID-19.[367] He emphasized that 'this interest cannot qualify as such forever', noting that at the time when *Roman Catholic Diocese of Brooklyn New York v Cuomo*[368] was heard in 2020 there were no widely distributed vaccines and few treatments. He noted that: 'If human nature and history teach anything, it is that civil liberties face grave risks when governments proclaim indefinite states of emergency.'[369] This led him to view with reservation the claim by Maine that it was necessary for 90% of its employees at covered health facilities to be vaccinated, as it had not adduced evidence to justify its figure of 90%. He was also troubled by Maine's failure to explain how denying exemptions to religious objectors was essential to achieving its statewide threshold, let alone in the applicants' workplaces. He went as far as to state that 'Maine's decision to deny a religious exemption in these circumstances doesn't just fail the least restrictive means test, it borders on the irrational.'[370]

In a pair of decisions delivered in January 2022, the United States Supreme Court ruled on two further aspects of mandatory vaccination. In the first of those cases, *Biden v Missouri*,[371] the Court upheld (by a five: four majority) a decision by the Secretary of Health and Human Services who administers the Medicare and Medicaid programmes which provide health insurance for United States citizens aged over 65, and those with a disability or with a low income. *Amicus curiae* participation briefs were filed by the American Medical Association and the American Public Health Association. In November 2021, the Secretary announced that, in order to receive Medicare and Medicaid funding, participating facilities were obliged to ensure that their staff—unless exempt for medical or religious reasons—were vaccinated against COVID-19.[372] Two District Courts enjoined enforcement of the rule and the issue argued before the Supreme Court was an application by the federal government to stay the injunctions. The Supreme Court did so by a bare majority.

The plurality noted that the Secretary had the statutory authority to promulgate such regulations 'as may be necessary to the efficient administration of the functions with which [he] is charged'[373] and observed that one such function—'perhaps the most basic, given the Department's core mission—is to ensure that the healthcare providers who care for Medicare and Medicaid patients protect their patients' health and safety.'[374] To that end, Congress authorized the Secretary to promulgate,

---

[367] ibid 20.
[368] 141 S Ct 63 (2020); 208 L Ed 206 (2020) (hereafter *Cuomo*). See the earlier discussion.
[369] ibid 21.
[370] ibid 22.
[371] 142 S Ct 647 (2022); 211 L Ed 433 (2022).
[372] *Medicare and Medicaid Programs; Omnibus COVID-19 Health Care Staff Vaccination*, 86 Fed Reg 61555 (5 November 2021).
[373] 42 USC §1302(a) (2021).
[374] 142 S Ct 650 (2022).

as a condition of a facility's participation in the programmes, such 'requirements as [he] finds necessary in the interest of the health and safety of individuals who are furnished services in the institution'.[375] At the time that the orders, which were the subject of the appeal, were issued, in many facilities 35% or more of staff remained unvaccinated. The plurality found that the rule fitted 'neatly' with the language of the statute:

> After all, ensuring that providers take steps to avoid transmitting a dangerous virus to their patients is consistent with the fundamental principle of the medical profession: first, do no harm. It would be the 'very opposite of efficient and effective administration for a facility that is supposed to make people well to make them sick with COVID-19.' *Florida* v *Department of Health and Human Services*, 19 F 4th 1271, 1288 (CA11 2021).[376]

The plurality noted that the Secretary routinely imposes conditions of participation in the Medicare and Medicaid schemes relating to the qualifications and duties of healthcare workers, illustrating that the obligations extend beyond those of functioning as a 'mere bookkeeper'.[377] Although it accepted that the vaccine mandate went further than the Secretary had done in the past to implement infection control, it observed that: 'he has never had to address an infection of this scale and scope before. In any event, there can be no doubt that addressing infection problems in Medicare and Medicaid facilities is what he does'.[378]

The plurality also factored into its reasoning the fact that vaccination requirements are a common feature of the provision of healthcare in the United States with healthcare workers being ordinarily required to be vaccinated against diseases such as hepatitis B, influenza, measles, mumps, and rubella.[379] It concluded that the Secretary had not exceeded his statutory authority in promulgating the vaccine mandates and rejected the argument that his requirement was either arbitrary or capricious. It also found that there was a good cause exception to his obligation to consult with State agencies given the urgency of the health threat posed by the 'unprecedented circumstances' of the pandemic.[380]

However, in dissent, Alito J, with whom Thomas, Gorsuch, and Barrett JJ agreed, classified as 'obscure' the argument that Congress had authorized the step of compelling ten million healthcare workers to be vaccinated 'on pain of being fired' and

---

[375] 42 USC §1395x(e)(9) (hospitals); see eg §1395x(cc)(2)(J) (outpatient rehabilitation facilities), §1395i-3(d)(4)(B) (skilled nursing facilities), §1395k(a)(2)(F)(i) (ambulatory surgical centers); see also §1396r(d)(4)(B), 1396d(*l*)(1), 1396d(*o*) (corresponding provisions in *Medicaid Act*).
[376] 142 S Ct 647, 650 (2022).
[377] ibid 653.
[378] ibid 653.
[379] Centers for Disease Control and Prevention, State Healthcare Worker and Patient Vaccination Laws (Publication, 28 February 2018).
[380] ibid 654.

denounced the majority's position that the Secretary's failure to engage in a consultative process was justifiable as shifting the presumption against compliance with procedural strictures from the unelected agency to the people they regulate.[381]

In a decision with application to a broader cross-section of the community, however, *National Federation of Independent Business v Department of Labor, Occupational Safety and Health Administration*,[382] the plurality (6:3) led by Breyer J struck down a vaccine mandate enacted for most of the United States workforce by the Secretary of Labor, acting through the Occupational Safety and Health Administration (OSHA). The mandate, which employers were obliged to enforce, applied to approximately 84 million workers, covering nearly all employers with at least 100 employees. It required that covered workers receive a COVID-19 vaccine and pre-empted state laws which provided to the contrary. The only exception was for workers who obtained a medical test each week at their own expense and on their own time, and also wore a mask to work each day. OSHA had never before imposed a comparable mandate. Nor had Congress, which had enacted significant legislation addressing the COVID-19 pandemic, but it had not enacted any measure similar to the mandate that OSHA had promulgated.[383]

OSHA was established by the *Occupational Safety and Health Act* (US) in 1970.[384] It was given responsibility for ensuring occupational safety, namely, 'safe and healthful working conditions'[385] by enforcing occupational safety and health standards promulgated by the Secretary.[386] Such standards must be 'reasonably necessary or appropriate to provide safe or healthful *employment*'.[387] They must also be developed using a rigorous process that includes notice, comment, and an opportunity for a public hearing: §655(b).

The Act contains an exception to ordinary notice-and-comment procedures for 'emergency temporary standards'.[388] Such standards may 'take immediate effect upon publication in the Federal Register'[389] but are permissible only in narrow circumstances: the Secretary must show (1) 'that employees are exposed to grave danger from exposure to substances or agents determined to be toxic or physically new hazards' and (2) 'that the emergency standard is necessary to protect employees from such danger'.[390]

The mandate took place in the context of a wish expressed by President Biden on 9 September 2021 that more Americans be vaccinated, the purpose of the then

---

[381] ibid 659.
[382] 142 S Ct 661 (2022); 211 L Ed 2d 448 (2022).
[383] 142 S Ct 661, 662 (2022).
[384] Pub L No 91-596, 84 Stat 1590 (1970).
[385] §651(b).
[386] §655(b).
[387] §652(8) (emphasis added).
[388] §655(c)(1).
[389] ibid.
[390] ibid.

proposed rule being stated to be to ensure that all employees of employers with 100 employees or more would be fully vaccinated or show their employer a negative COVID-19 test at least once a week. However, the emergency standard was not issued by the Secretary of Labor until 5 November 2021.[391]

The plurality concluded that the applicants were likely to succeed on the merits of their claim that the Secretary lacked authority to impose the mandate. It found that mandate not to be an 'everyday exercise of federal power' permitted by an explicit statutory authorization but, rather, to constitute a significant encroachment into the lives—and health—of a vast number of employees.[392] It observed that, while the authorizing legislation empowered the setting of workplace safety standards, it did not address public health more generally, which was a subject falling outside OSHA's sphere of expertise.[393] It concluded that a vaccine mandate is 'strikingly unlike the workplace regulations that OSHA has typically imposed', observing it 'cannot be undone at the end of the workday'.[394] The plurality conceded that where COVID-19 poses 'a special danger' because of the particular features of an employee's job or workplace, targeted regulations are plainly permissible but classified OSHA's approach as 'indiscriminate' and its mandate as '[taking] on the character of a general public health measure, rather an "*occupational* safety or health standard"'.[395] As Gorsuch J put it, the question was not how to respond to the pandemic but who held the statutory power to do so—'Under the law as it stands today, that power rests with the States and Congress, now OSHA'.[396] He commented that respecting the 'demands' of the division of power:

> may be trying in times of stress. But if this Court were to abide them only in more tranquil conditions, declarations of emergencies would never end and the liberties our Constitution's separation of powers seeks to preserve would amount to little.[397]

The essence of the dissent by Breyer, Sotomayor, and Kagan JJ was that COVID-19 spreads by person-to-person contact in confined indoor spaces, 'so causes harm in nearly all workplace environments'. They described COVID-19 as 'a menace in work settings.... Since the disease's onset, most Americans have seen their workplaces transformed.'[398] They concluded that the vaccine mandate fell within the core of OSHA's mission to protect employees from 'grave danger' and noted OSHA's

---

[391] *COVID-19 Vaccination and Testing; Emergency Temporary Standard*, 86 Fed Reg 61402 (5 November 2021).
[392] 142 S Ct 661, 665 (2022).
[393] ibid 665.
[394] ibid 665.
[395] ibid 666.
[396] ibid 670.
[397] ibid 670.
[398] ibid 670.

estimate that the mandate would be likely to save 6,500 lives and prevent over 250,000 hospitalizations within six months.[399] The dissenting judges lamented that the decision of the majority:

> stymies the Federal Government's ability to counter the unparalleled threat that COVID-19 poses to our Nation's workers. Acting outside of its competence and without legal basis, the Court displaces the judgments of the Government officials given the responsibility to respond to workplace health emergencies.[400]

The minority further observed that COVID-19:

> is most easily transmitted in the shared indoor spaces that are the hallmark of American working life; and that spreads mostly without regard to differences in occupation or industry. Over the past two years, COVID-19 has affected—indeed, transformed—virtually every workforce and workplace in the Nation. Employers and employees alike have recognized and responded to the special risks of transmission in work environments.[401]

This led the minority to classify the majority analysis as 'perverse' as it had the outcome of 'constraining OSHA from addressing one of the gravest workplace hazards in the agency's history'.[402] It expressed regret that the outcome of the case was to undercut the capacity of 'the responsible federal officials, acting well within the scope of their authority, to protect American workers from grave danger'.[403]

The *National Federation of Independent Business* decision by the Supreme Court immediately provoked contrasting reactions. Ohio Attorney-General Dave Yost, one of the Republican officials who challenged the OSHA mandate, stated that: 'Americans have lost too much to this disease already—all of us want this pandemic to end—but it is critical that we do not lose our Constitution, too.' By contrast, Professor Lawrence Gostin focused upon the public health ramifications of the decision, arguing that: 'The court is eviscerating the very ability of the federal government to protect Americans. The justices are overturning decades of precedent upholding federal public health powers.'[404] At a time when only 67% of Americans over the age of five years, and 74% of those over 18 years of age,[405]

---

[399] 86 Fed Reg 61408 (2021).
[400] ibid 670.
[401] ibid 675.
[402] ibid.
[403] ibid 687.
[404] See John Fritze, 'Supreme Court Blocks COVID-19 Vaccine-or-Testing Mandate for Workplaces but Lets Medical Rule Stand' *USA Today* (13 January 2022) <www.usatoday.com/story/news/politics/2022/01/13/supreme-court-halts-bidens-covid-19-mandates-large-employers/9160176002/> accessed 14 September 2022.
[405] 'See How Vaccinations are Going in Your County and State' *New York Times* (14 January 2022) <www.nytimes.com/interactive/2020/us/covid-19-vaccine-doses.html> accessed 14 September 2022.

were fully vaccinated, the decision constitutes a significant setback for reducing the risk of exposure to the pandemic within United States workplaces. It is emblematic of a disinclination on the part of the majority in the Supreme Court to extend latitude for the purposes of statutory interpretation to the power to issue edicts during a public health crisis. While such an approach can be defended from a purist perspective in terms of the need for explicit provision of significant powers to an arm of government, an inability across the board to require vaccination within workplaces will have measurably adverse consequences. Again, this highlights the tension between principles of statutory interpretation and constitutional division of powers and permitted exigencies of responses to a pandemic—a fundamental clash between the application of legal doctrine and what is needed by way of public health initiatives in an emergency. Significantly, it deviates from the longstanding judicial tradition of following the case of *Jacobson v Massachusetts*.[406]

Addressing some of the issues raised by this litigation and other concerns about COVID-19 vaccine mandates, Michelle Mello, Ross Silverman, and Saad Omer suggested that United States governments in particular might legitimately mandate vaccination if the following preconditions are met: as other 'less burdensome' public health measures have failed and there has been insufficient 'voluntary uptake' of vaccines to contain the transmission of COVID-19, it remains a threat to public health, so it is reasonable and necessary to encroach on individuals' autonomy; the Advisory Committee on Immunization Practices has reviewed evidence of the vaccines' safety and efficacy and recommended vaccination; the government has transparently communicated available evidence about vaccines' safety and effectiveness; vaccine supplies are sufficient to immunize the population groups for whom mandatory vaccination is proposed; and governments have arranged for those groups to access vaccination and monitor any side effects of the vaccines.[407]

However, it is clear that there is a significant body of thought on the United States Supreme Court that a heavy burden lies upon those seeking to impose mandatory vaccination in the workplace and probably in other contexts—such as for access to services and participation in civil life. This is only permissible when all other options are proved to be ineffective, when it is established that those seeking a religious exemption would endanger public health by their unpreparedness to comply with mandated vaccination requirements, and when there is an explicit provision of authority for such a mandate.

---

[406] 197 US 11 (1905); see Farber (n 305), ; Gilad Abri and Sebastián Guidi, 'The Pandemic Constitution' (2021) 60(1) *Columbia Journal of Transnational Law* 68.

[407] Michelle M Mello, Ross D Silverman, and Saad B Omer 'Ensuring Uptake of Vaccines against SARS-CoV-2' (2020) 383(14) *New England Journal of Medicine* 1296, 1297–98.

XI. Disputes about Vaccination of Children

Whether or not children should be required, or have an entitlement, to be vaccinated against COVID-19, upon the emergence of suitable vaccines, became a litigated issue in a number of countries during 2021 and the early part of 2022. Generally, it has been held to be reasonable and responsible parental conduct for parents to arrange for a child to be vaccinated against childhood diseases. Yet the issue of whether children should be vaccinated both prior to COVID-19 and during the pandemic has been determined to be the prerogative of their parents when both have responsibility for a child in a number of countries, including England, Australia, New Zealand, and Canada.[408] In some jurisdictions, such as Australia, consequences in terms of access to pre-school facilities and to social security benefits can attach to decisions not to vaccinate children,[409] and there is the potential for such regimes to be extended to parents' refusal to vaccinate their children against COVID-19.

However, particular legal considerations have emerged when one parent is opposed to COVID-19 vaccination. While courts have maintained that the ultimate question is whether vaccination is in the best interests of a child, as identified in what follows, considerations determined to be relevant to decisions about whether children should be vaccinated against COVID-19 have included: the advantages for children to be vaccinated so as to avoid serious and potentially ongoing symptomatology from the virus; the public interest in reducing the risk of children infecting other (often more at risk) parts of the community, such as their grandparents; the availability of only limited information about the long-term risks that might be posed by vaccines that are new; the role of parental preferences, especially when parents disagree; the detriments to unvaccinated children's ability to attend school, participate in extra-curricular activities, engage in gainful employment and travel; and the wishes of children themselves.

In the United Kingdom, MacDonald J observed that 'it is *very* difficult to foresee a situation in which a vaccination against COVID-19 approved for use in children would not be endorsed by the court as being in a child's best interests, absent peer-reviewed research evidence indicating significant concern for the efficacy and/or safety of one or more of the COVID-19 vaccines or a well evidenced

---

[408] See generally Rachael H Jeffrey, 'Vaccination and the Law' (2015) 44(11) *Australian Family Physician* 849; Chloe A Teasdale and others, 'Plans to Vaccinate Children for Coronavirus Disease 2019: A Survey of United States Parents' (2021) 237 *Journal of Pediatrics* 292; Ian Freckelton, 'Vaccinating Children: The COVID-19 Family Law Jurisprudence' (2022) 29(3) *Journal of Law and Medicine* 645; see too *Re T (a child)* [2020] EWHC 220 (Fam); *H (A Child Parental Responsibility: Vaccination* [2020] EWCA 664 (Civ) [21].
[409] See eg Brynley P Hull and others, 'No Jab No Pay: Catch-up Vaccination During Its First Two Years' (2020) 213(8) *Medical Journal of Australia* 364; Raffaela Armiento and others 'Impact of Australian Mandatory "No Jab, No Pay" and "No Jab, No Play" Immunisation Policies on Immunisation Services, Parental Attitudes to Vaccination and Vaccine Uptake, in a Tertiary Paediatric Hospital, the Royal Children's Hospital, Melbourne' (2020) 38(33) *Vaccine* 5231.

contra-indication specific to that subject child.'[410] This has led to a series of English judgments in respect of persons, both adults and children, who are unable to make their own decisions about COVID-19 vaccination that such vaccination is in their best interests.[411]

However, from the time that COVID-19 vaccines became available, arguments were advanced by one parent in dispute with another parent that a failure by the parent with parental responsibility for health matters to vaccinate a child constituted an abrogation of their responsibility to act in the best interests of the child, or alternatively that one parent's preparedness to vaccinate a child was contrary to the child's best interests in light of the risks to the child. A further consideration that has been identified is the entitlement of a child to make their own decisions about COVID-19 vaccination upon achieving sufficient maturity to do so.[412]

Some diversity of approach on these issues is identifiable across decisions in Australia, New Zealand, and Canada. The following paragraphs summarize the divergence in approaches.

A. English Jurisprudence

A leading English judgment in relation to whether it is in a child's best interests to be vaccinated against COVID-19 is the decision of Poole J in *C (Looked After Child (Covid-19 Vaccination)*.[413] The case was about a 13-year-old child, C, who was being looked after by the applicant local authority, which had been given parental responsibility for him. C wanted to be vaccinated against both COVID-19 and the winter flu. C's father had the same view but C's mother was strongly opposed to vaccination of her son. In the context of applying the reasoning of MacDonald J in *M v H and PT*,[414] Poole J noted that the opposition to vaccination by C's mother arose from what she regarded as the absence of compelling evidence that COVID-19 vaccines were safe and effective; she contrasted the COVID-19 vaccine with other vaccines that she regarded as tried and tested;[415] and she relied upon a number of documents which Poole J observed 'can only be described as anti-Covid-19 propaganda.... The material is devoid of evidence or even rational argument and does not point to any peer-reviewed research evidence that raises any significant concern about the efficacy or safety of either vaccine.'[416]

---

[410] *M v H (Private Law Vaccination)* [2020] EWFC 93 [4].
[411] See eg *E (Vaccine)* [2021] EWCOP 7; *SD v Royal Borough of Kensington and Chelsea* [2021] EWCOP 14; *SS v London Borough of Richmond upon Thames* [2021] EWCOP 31; *C (Looked After Child) (Covid-19 Vaccination)* [2021] EWHC 2993 (Fam); *North Yorkshire Clinical Commissioning Group v E (Covid Vaccination)* [2022] EWCOP 15.
[412] *Gillick v West Northwick & Wisbech Health Authority* [1986] AC 112.
[413] [2021] EWHC 2993 (Fam).
[414] [2020] EWFC 93 [4].
[415] *C (Looked After Child (Covid-19 Vaccination)* [2021] EWHC 2993 [14].
[416] ibid [17].

Evidence was placed before the Court by the Children's Guardian that C was very frustrated by his mother's stance and had weighed up evidence about vaccines and formed a settled view that he wanted both vaccinations. He was particularly concerned that there was a disabled child at the placement he shared whom he did not want to infect.

Poole J observed that the COVID-19 vaccination available to C was part of the national programme for vaccination for children, approved by the United Kingdom Health Security Agency, the successor to Public Health England, and held that:

> The court can be satisfied, without the benefit of expert evidence, that the decisions to include the vaccinations in national programmes are based on evidence that they are in the best interests of the children covered by the programmes.... it is worth emphasising that vaccination programmes may be in the best interests of children even though administering the vaccines is not free from risk. Very few activities in medicine or life more generally are free from risk. Administering a vaccine gives rise to a risk of harm to a child. Not giving a vaccine gives risk to a risk of harm to a child. Voluminous evidence establishing the extent and balance of risks and benefits needs to be obtained before a decision is made to roll out a national programme of vaccination or children.[417]

Poole J stated that he had not undertaken an assessment to determine whether C was mature enough to make up his own mind about the COVID-19 vaccination issue, although he commented that C might well be '*Gillick*-competent', namely sufficiently mature to be make an informed decision about whether to be vaccinated. He held that a local authority with a care order is entitled to decide to arrange and consent to a child in its care being vaccinated against COVID-19 and/or the winter flu virus notwithstanding the objections of the child's parents, when: (i) such vaccinations are part of an ongoing national programme approved by the UK Health Security Agency; (ii) the child is either not *Gillick*-competent or is *Gillick*-competent and consents; and (iii) the local authority is satisfied that it is necessary to do so in order to safeguard or promote the individual child's welfare.[418] Poole J commented that he would have had no hesitation in concluding that it was in C's best interests to have the vaccinations given all the circumstances including the balance of risks of having and not having the vaccinations and C's own wishes and feelings.[419]

---

[417] ibid [20].
[418] ibid [23].
[419] ibid [24].

B. Australian Jurisprudence

There have been a number of Australian decisions in relation to vaccination of children against COVID-19 in the context of parental disputation about the issue.

In one of the early judgments, *Makinen & Taube*,[420] Judge Taglieri of the Federal Circuit Court of Australia made final orders giving equal shared responsibility for major long-term issues affecting children aged eight and 12, other than in respect of vaccination. The mother was opposed to the children being vaccinated against COVID-19. She argued that about 5% of the Australian population was unvaccinated and that research showed that it was widely accepted that vaccinations can cause serious illness involving autoimmune disorders/disabilities and neurological disorders.

By contrast, the father and the independent child lawyer (ICL) submitted that it was in the best interests of children to be vaccinated and that if they were not vaccinated, there would be adverse consequences in terms of eligibility for social security entitlements. The position of the ICL was that, without vaccination, there was a likelihood that either or both of the children would be exposed to a risk of contracting COVID-19.

Judge Taglieri accorded little weight to the assertions about risk advanced by the mother. He concluded that the mother had a:

> firm and strong bias against vaccination of any kind. On the evidence, I find that she initially developed a belief about harm of vaccination from hearsay information from a friend/acquaintance prior to the children's birth. This belief has become entrenched consequent to her own interpretation of various publications which she has sought out and read.
>
> Although she is a professional, she is not a medical practitioner or impartial expert witness. Her interpretation of the scientific and medical literature annexed to her affidavits in my view are not wholly supported by the literature itself when read in context and overall.... The literature she relies upon also does not support the view she appears to hold that generally her children should not be vaccinated against any disease because vaccines are harmful to them.[421]

Judge Taglieri observed that the mother had not adduced any evidence about the risk of autoimmune disorders, disabilities, or neurological disorders from vaccinations being greater than the risk of the children contracting any particular disease which vaccination was likely to prevent. She found the mother's attitude against vaccination, while based on her genuine beliefs, not to be reasonable, and ordered

---

[420] [2021] FCCA 1878.
[421] Ibid [59]–[60].

that the father do what was necessary to ensure the children were vaccinated against COVID-19. [422]

In *Palange & Kalhoun*,[423] Judge Smith in the Federal Court and Family Court of Australia took a similar approach. He ordered a 10-year-old child to be vaccinated against COVID-19 with the Pfizer paediatric vaccine in accordance with the Australian Technical Advisory Group on Immunisation (ATAGI) recommendations in place from time to time. The proposed vaccination had been opposed by the child's father who did not want his son vaccinated until the possible long-term effects of the vaccine were known. Judge Smith declined to give 'any weight' to the various opinions on the medical and public health issues associated with COVID-19 infection or vaccinations provided by the father, given that neither parent had any relevant qualifications. He also was not prepared to accord weight to the mother's opinions about medical, psychological, and contagion risks specific to the child. However, he gave substantial weight 'to the evidence of a public health researcher in the area of vaccination who concluded that the risks associated with COVID-19 infection far outweighed the risks associated with vaccination.'[424] Judge Smith concluded that while the risks of COVID-19 infection to young children were comparatively low:

> the risks associated with infection far outweigh the risks associated with vaccination ... there are risks of death, of long term health impacts, of the requirement for hospitalisation including in intensive care, and risk of multisystem inflammatory syndrome, which do not exist to any significant degree in vaccinated children, the risk of myocarditis is significantly increased absent vaccination.[425]

Judge Smith accepted that the father was concerned that the Pfizer vaccine was comparatively new, meaning that there did not exist the history of decades of use that exist for the standard childhood vaccines. However, he observed that there was no material before him to assist in determining what weight to give to 'that possible future unknown':

> I can only take it into account in a general way as a possible risk. Against that unknown risk must be weighed the fact that if the child is not vaccinated now, and on the father's application for an unspecified time until both parties agree, then until he is vaccinated against COVID-19 he is at risk of the known, quantifiable and non-trivial risks from COVID-19 infection which can be significantly reduced by administration of the COVID-19 vaccination.[426]

---

[422] ibid [3].
[423] [2022] FedCFamC2F 149.
[424] *Palange & Kalhoun* [2022] FedCFamC2F 149 [57].
[425] ibid [135]–[136].
[426] ibid [140]–[141].

This led him to conclude that:

> it is in the child's best interests to be vaccinated against COVID-19 with the Pfizer children's vaccine now in order to reduce the known existing risks which, though small, include potentially significant health impacts up to death, rather than to delay and expose the child to the risks of COVID-19 for an unspecified period of time waiting to see whether or not any currently unidentified adverse health side effects arise.[427]

The most significant Australian judgment on the issue thus far, *Clay and Dallas*,[428] is a decision by Sutherland CJ of the Family Court of Western Australia. The issue was whether a 15-year-old child, Child A, should be fully immunized against COVID-19. The evidence before the Court was that Child A wanted such immunization, although in 2015 she had been morbidly obese and experienced raised blood pressure. This raised the issue of whether vaccination posed risks for her, as well as whether she was at especial risk if she contracted COVID-19. By 2022 she had received her first vaccination and wished to proceed with her second and third doses in the usual course. However, her mother did not agree on the basis that she asserted that Child A had pre-existing medical conditions, including a heart murmur, which put her at risk if she had further vaccinations. This meant, the mother contended, that Child A was in the category of being exempt from being required to be vaccinated. The mother stated that she was sceptical about the safety and efficacy of the vaccines.

By invitation, Child A participated in a conference with a Family Consultant who expressed the view that considerable weight should be given to her views—Child A was said to have expressed herself in a clear and articulate manner commensurate with her age and verbalised her opinion in a '"balanced manner"'.[429]

Sutherland CJ noted that in August 2021, ATAGI had recommended COVID-19 vaccination for all individuals from 12 years of age and subsequently for children aged between five and 11 years, taking into account the relevant benefits, risks, uncertainties, and evidence as to matters including safety of the vaccines.

Child A had received her first dose of the Pfizer vaccine in November 2021 without suffering any acute side effects. The mother and the ICL were not aware of the vaccination having been undertaken at the time and had not needed to be informed as a result of the fact that orders for equal shared parental responsibility had been suspended, resulting in the ability for the father to make such decisions unilaterally. Medical evidence adduced before the Court established that Child A had a thyroid condition and a slight heart murmur of which she and her father had

---

[427] ibid [155].
[428] [2022] FCWA 18.
[429] Ibid [15].

been unaware until late in 2021. On the basis of the expert evidence, Sutherland CJ accepted that Child A should have an echocardiogram and if it raised any significant concern she should have a cardiac review before receiving her second dose of the Pfizer vaccine, but that if she had not suffered a new cardiac concern Child A should receive her second and third doses so that she reached the point of being fully vaccinated. He concluded that there was no evidence that Child A had been unduly influenced by anyone—rather, it appeared that her views had been shaped by her own observations and inquiries, together with information supplied to her by her school and her treating family doctor.[430] This combination of factors persuaded Sutherland CJ to accord her views substantial weight.

Sutherland CJ also took into account that Child A's father could be relied upon to take medical advice and that the broader social and other impacts upon Child A of not being vaccinated were relevant considerations. These included that she enjoyed working at a fast-food restaurant and that her employer required her to be vaccinated to continue her employment. The outcome was a decision that it was in Child A's best interests to be vaccinated subject to a satisfactory echocardiogram.

C. New Zealand Jurisprudence

The decision by Judge Coyle of the Family Court in New Zealand in *Long v Steine*[431] is the most authoritative decision to date on the vaccination of children against COVID-19 in New Zealand. It emphasized the significance of children's wishes. Judge Coyle's decision related to a 12-year-old boy, Charlie, who was in his parents' shared care as a result of a parenting order. His mother applied for an order that Charlie be placed into her interim care until he had received his COVID-19 vaccinations, that he receive the vaccinations, that the parties not discuss anti-vaccination views around him, and that any information provided to him about vaccinations be medically approved information presented in a child-friendly form. The lawyer appointed for Charlie presented to the Court a memorandum explaining that Charlie did not wish to be vaccinated and that he wanted to speak directly to the judge. Judge Coyle agreed to this course of action and, after meeting with Charlie, concluded that he was 'an intelligent and articulate young man' and that he was 'thoughtful, intelligent, considered and reasoned'. Coyle J concluded that Charlie's views should be given significant weight. He concluded that it was significant that the New Zealand government had not made COVID-19 vaccination mandatory—'It remains, as enshrined in the Bill of Rights Act, an issue of

---

[430] By contrast, in *F v F* [2013] EWHC 2683 (Fam) [22] Theis J concluded that the expression of views by L and M was likely to have been affected by a lack of maturity and the likelihood of influence by their mother who had strong opinions on the issue.

[431] *Long v Steine* [2022] NZFC 251.

choice.'[432] This meant that Charlie had the right to decline vaccination. Judge Coyle commented:

> I am also aware that if I were to order him to be vaccinated, [Charlie] has made it clear he would tell the health professional giving him the vaccination that he refused to have the vaccination. I cannot accept that any health professional would in those circumstances hold [Charlie] down and force him to have a vaccination. [Counsel's] response was that it is an order of the Court and that the health professional would have to comply. If they do not the only remedy would be to hold the health professional in contempt of Court. In my view that would be a disproportionate response by the Courts to a situation where the health professional vaccinating [Charlie] would simply be applying the Ministry of Health guidelines which state that a child of [Charlie]'s age is able to either consent **or refuse** to have a vaccination (emphasis mine).[433]

Thus, the applications for a change to parenting arrangements and for Charlie to be vaccinated were refused.

D. Canadian Jurisprudence

In *JN v CG*,[434] Pazaratz J of the Ontario Superior Court of Justice heard an application from a father for orders that the mother of children aged 12 and 10 enable them to be vaccinated against COVID-19. The mother informed the Court that she was open to vaccinating her children if safety concerns could be addressed better but that the extensive research she had undertaken had left her with concerns that the potential benefit of the vaccines that were available was outweighed by the risks—'She says that there are too many unknowns, and she worried that "once children are vaxed, they can't be unvaxed".'[435] Both the children had had COVID-19 with minimal symptoms and had recovered completely. The mother referred to medical research that stated that since they had already recovered from COVID-19, the children had greater protection from future infection.

Neither of the children had any medical needs or particular vulnerabilities. Each child expressed a preference not to be vaccinated and was described in a 'Voice of the Child Report' as presenting confidently and thoughtfully.[436] This played a role in Pazaratz J being satisfied that there should be deference to the mother's request

---

[432] ibid [45].
[433] ibid [51].
[434] 2022 ONSC 1198 (Can LII).
[435] ibid [16].
[436] ibid [29].

for a cautious approach to vaccinating the children against COVID-19. He found her position to be:

> compelling, and reinforced by the children's views and preferences which are legitimate and must be respected.... The mother has consistently made excellent, informed, and child-focussed decisions. In every respect she is an exemplary parent, fully attuned to her children's physical and emotional needs. She has demonstrated a clear understanding of the science. She has raised legitimate questions and concerns. I have confidence that she will continue to seek out answers to safeguard the physical and emotional health of her children....
>
> At a certain point, where you have absolute confidence in a parent's insight and decision-making, you have to step back and acknowledge that they love their child; they have always done the right thing for their child ... *and they will continue to do the right thing for their child.*[437]

In another Ontario case, *AM v CD*,[438] there were orders that the parents were to have joint custody of their seven-year-old child and that, if after 'meaningful discussions', the parents were unable to agree on a decision in relation to her health, education, or religion, the mother had final decision-making authority about education and religion, while the father had final decision-making responsibility about her health. Hackland J, also of the Ontario Superior Court of Justice, heard a motion from the mother seeking to be permitted to have her seven-year-old child vaccinated against COVID-19, contrary to the wishes of the father. The father held a degree in health promotion and epidemiology. Like the mother in *JN v CG*, his position was that he was opposed to COVID-19 vaccinations, at least as at March 2022, because he wanted to review further vaccine study data about the safety of the available vaccines. Hackland J based his decision on the evolving state of community vaccination and the nature of COVID-19-variants that had emerged to that point:

> There does indeed seem to be a consensus that the risk of serious harm from the Omicron variant of COVID-19 is not as serious as initially thought. Moreover, vaccine mandates are being withdrawn in many workplaces. Many government mandated health restrictions were withdrawn effective March 1st in this province and mask mandates are expected to be withdrawn shortly. It would appear that vaccinations will continue to be recommended, although not mandated. Hospitalization rates are falling rapidly. Most people recognize that all of these encouraging developments could be reversed in the event that another threatening variant appears. Lastly, and this is not mentioned in the father's affidavit,

---

[437] ibid [83]–[86].
[438] *AM v CD* 2022 ONSC 1516 (CanLII).

there are media reports that the efficacy of the Pfizer vaccination in the 5 to 11 age group may be significantly lower than expected.

In summary, I think the father's views are reasonable that at this point in time (March 2022) we appear to be in a dynamic and rapidly changing and more positive environment so far as managing the public health threat posed by the coronavirus is concerned and a responsible parent is entitled to consider this when assessing their child's need for the Pfizer vaccination.[439]

However, Hackland J found that the fact that the objecting father was the child's decision-maker on matters of health under existing court orders was significant. He assessed the father's interest in the well-being of his daughter as 'sincere, non-dogmatic and supported by reasonable held factual assertions' and noted that 'Importantly, we are currently in a rapidly changing environment as the COVID-19 pandemic subsides and vaccine and masking mandates are being withdrawn. There appears to be particular scrutiny directed at the efficacy of the Pfizer vaccine for children in the 5 to 11 age group.'[440] Thus, he was not prepared to make a change to the previous court orders for the father to have responsibility for decision-making about the child's health.

E. Overview

The vaccination of children against COVID-19 is the decision of parents until such time as children are mature enough to make such a decision themselves. When parents have disagreed about such vaccination, courts have often been deferential to governmental advice and policies. However, in the complex matrix of determining what is in a child's best interests, courts have also taken into account and accorded weight to children's wishes, so long as they have concluded that such expression of wishes has not been influenced by pressure from a parent and is informed and considered.[441] The courts have identified a number of considerations that suggest that it is in the best interests of children to be vaccinated against COVID-19, including their inability to participate in extra-curricular activities if unvaccinated. However, when confronted by strong opposition from a parent otherwise prepared to act in a child's best interests, some courts have been prepared, as in the case of *JN v CG*,[442] to defer to the wishes of a parent, especially if a child is unwilling to be vaccinated.

---

[439] ibid [17]–[18].
[440] ibid [29].
[441] See the factors identified as relevant to the weight to be given to a child's wishes in *Decaen v Decaen* 2013 ONCA 218 [42].
[442] 2022 ONSC 1198 (Can LII).

The approach of the courts will not be static. As the Ontario decision of *AM v CD* discussed earlier demonstrates, the evolving nature of COVID-19 and in particular its less serious variants may affect courts' balancing of the considerations identified as relevant as to whether vaccination of a child, over the wishes of a parent, is in the child's best interests.

XII. Challenges to Denial of Entry of Unvaccinated Persons

In a case that attracted international attention, the world's number one ranked tennis player, Novak Djokovic, contested the decision of Australia's federal government to deny him entry to Australia on the basis of the risk he was alleged to pose to public health due to his refusal to have a COVID-19 vaccination.

The federal government determined to exclude Mr Djokovic, who wished to enter the country to compete in the first Grand Slam of the year, the 2022 Australian Open (which he had won nine times before), by cancelling his entry visa. Under section 133C(3) of the *Migration Act 1958* (Cth) ('the Act'), it was open to the Minister for Immigration, Citizenship, Migrant Services and Multicultural Affairs ('the Minister') to cancel a visa held by a person if the Minister was satisfied that a ground for cancelling the visa existed under section 116 of the Act and that cancellation would be in the public interest. Section 116(1)(e) allowed the Minister to cancel a visa if satisfied that 'the presence of its holder is or may be, or would or might be, a risk to: (i) the health, safety or good order of the Australian community or a segment of the Australian community'.[443]

The Minister took into account that Mr Djokovic had not been vaccinated and that a 'testimonial' was available from a Serbian doctor that he had tested positive to COVID-19 on 16 December 2021 and negative five days later.[444] The Minister concluded that 'the presence of Mr Djokovic in Australia might foster anti-vaccination sentiment leading to (a) other unvaccinated persons refusing to become vaccinated, (b) other unvaccinated persons being reinforced in their existing view not to become vaccinated, and/or (c) a reduction on the uptake of booster vaccines.'[445] This raised the concern that Mr Djokovic's presence in Australia might result in one or more of the following:

---

[443] Initially Mr Djokovic was successful in overturning a decision by a delegate of the Minister to cancel Mr Djokovic's visa on the basis of a denial of procedural fairness: see *Djokovic v Minister for Immigration, Citizenship, Migrant Services and Multicultural Affairs* [2022] FedCFamC2G 7; Ian Freckelton, 'Pandemics, Polycentricity and Perceptions: Lessons from the Djokovic Saga' (2022) 29(1) *Journal of Law and Medicine* 9.

[444] Decision of Minister Hawke (14 January 2022), in affidavit of Natalie Bannister (sworn 15 January 2022) [22] <www.fedcourt.gov.au/__data/assets/pdf_file/0007/95236/Sealed-Affidavit-Bannister-1512 022.pdf> accessed 14 September 2022.

[445] *Djokovic v Minister for Immigration, Citizenship, Migrant Services and Multicultural Affairs* [2022] FCAFC 3 (hereafter *Djokovic*: Full Court) [58].

- An increase in anti-vaccination sentiment, leading to others refusing to become vaccinated or refusing to receive a booster vaccine;
- A reinforcing of views of a minority in the Australian community who remained unvaccinated against COVID-19 and who were at risk of contracting COVID-19;
- An increased number of people deciding not to receive a booster vaccine; and
- Increased pressure placed on the Australian health system, a significant contributing factor being the number of unvaccinated persons contracting COVID-19 and requiring medical attention or assistance.[446]

The decision by the Minister was taken at a time when between 80,000 and 150,000 new cases of COVID-19 were being recorded daily in Australia.

The Minister also took into account Mr Djokovic's high-profile status and potential to be a role model. He determined that:

> Having regard to ... Mr Djokovic's conduct after receiving a positive COVID-19 result [in continuing to associate with people, including without wearing a mask], his publicly stated views, as well as his unvaccinated status, I consider that his ongoing presence in Australia may pose a risk to the good order of the Australian community. In particular, his presence in Australia may encourage other persons to disregard or act inconsistently with public health advice and policies in Australia, including but not limited to, becoming vaccinated against COVID-19 or receiving a booster vaccine.[447]

Mr Djokovic sought judicial review of the Minister's decision. However, on 16 January 2022, the day before the commencement of the Australian Open, the Full Court of the Federal Court of Australia unanimously declined to overturn the decision of the Minister.[448] The tennis player was deported from Australia the same day.[449]

While the Full Court observed that the notions of health and safety did not require elaboration, it applied the analysis of Goldberg J in *Tien v Minister for Immigration and Multicultural Affairs*[450] in respect of the expression 'good order of the Australian community':

---

[446] ibid [64].
[447] ibid [33].
[448] ibid [105].
[449] Paul Karp, 'Novak Djokovic Leaves Australia After Court Upholds Visa Cancellation' *The Guardian* (16 January 2022) <www.theguardian.com/sport/2022/jan/16/novak-djokovic-to-be-deported-from-australia-after-losing-appeal-against-visa-cancellation> accessed 14 September 2022.
[450] (1998) 89 FCR 80, 93–94.

[I]t has, in my opinion, a public order element, that is to say it requires there to be an element of a risk that the person's presence in Australia might be disruptive to the proper administration or observance of the law in Australia or might create difficulties or public disruption in relation to the values, balance and equilibrium of Australian society. It involves something in the nature of unsettling public actions or activities. For example, a person who came to Australia and was found to be committing in Australia serious breaches of the law or criminal acts or was inciting people in the community to violence could properly be said to be a person whose presence in Australia is a risk to the good order of the Australian community. It should be emphasised that it must be the presence of the visa holder 'in Australia' which constitutes or would constitute the risk to the good order of the Australian community.[451]

The Full Court took into account that an important strand of the Minister's reasoning was that Mr Djokovic was a high-profile person with a position as a role model in the sporting and broader community, that Mr Djokovic was widely known to be opposed to being vaccinated, that the Minister concluded that the presence of Mr Djokovic might foster anti-vaccination sentiment, and that anti-vaccination groups in Australia had already participated in civil disturbances and unrest.[452]

The Court found that it was open to the Minister to conclude that Mr Djokovic had a well-known stance that was opposed to vaccination[453] and that the presence of Mr Djokovic might foster anti-vaccination sentiment.[454] It commented that:

It is important to recognise, however, that the Minister's reasons can be seen to encompass the encouragement not only to anti-vaccination groups, some of whom may have extreme views and some of whom may be a risk to the good order or public order in the community, but also to people who may simply be uncertain or wavering as to whether they will be vaccinated.[455]

It found that the evidence before the Minister displayed an affinity between the view of anti-vaccination groups and the view of Mr Djokovic and it observed that:

The possible influence on the second group comes from common sense and human experience: An iconic world tennis star may influence people of all ages, young or old, but perhaps especially the young and the impressionable, to emulate him. This is not fanciful; it does not need evidence. It is the recognition of

---

[451] *Djokovic*: Full Court (above n 445) [40].
[452] ibid [59]–[62].
[453] ibid [71].
[454] ibid [78].
[455] ibid [80].

human behaviour from a modest familiarity with human experience. Even if Mr Djokovic did not win the Australian Open, the capacity of his presence in Australia playing tennis to encourage those who would emulate or wish to be like him is a rational foundation for the view that he might foster anti-vaccination sentiment.[456]

These considerations, together with the fact that rallies and protests had already taken place, were found by the Full Court to entitle the Minister to conclude that the presence of Mr Djokovic may be taken up by such groups in the future in support of their view.[457] It accepted that there was a question, which had not been explored before it, 'as to the extent to which one can or should characterise lawful, even if robust, rallies and protests in the free expression of political or social views (even if unpopular or held only by a few people) as a threat to good order'.[458] However, as this argument had not been pursued before it, the Full Court made no comment in relation to it save to observe that:

> Common recent experience does, however, demonstrate that some rallies and demonstrations concerning COVID-19 and measures to limit movement and activity of the public have involved some violent activity and have been the occasion for the spreading of the disease or at least that is open to be inferred.[459]

The Full Court rejected the proposition that it was irrational for the Minister to be concerned that the asserted support of some anti-vaccination groups for Mr Djokovic's apparent position might encourage rallies and protests that could lead to heightened community transmission and noted that there was evidence that Mr Djokovic 'recently disregarded reasonable public health measures overseas by attending activities unmasked while COVID positive to his knowledge. It was open to infer that this, if emulated, may encourage an attitude of breach of public health regulations'.[460] The essence of the decision by the Full Court was summarized by it to be that: 'Another person in the position of the Minister may have not cancelled Mr Djokovic's visa. The Minister did. The complaints made in the proceeding do not found a conclusion that the satisfaction of the relevant factors and the exercise of discretion were reached and made unlawfully.'[461] This meant that Mr Djokovic failed to discharge the heavy burden on judicial review to establish that the Minister's decision was illogical, irrational, or legally unreasonable.

---

[456] ibid [82].
[457] ibid [83].
[458] ibid [84].
[459] ibid.
[460] ibid [86].
[461] ibid [86], [105].

The decision of the Full Court of the Federal Court of Australia constitutes a significant affirmation of the entitlement of government to take robust action in the public interest during a pandemic. It is important because the key elements of the Minister's decision, which were upheld on judicial review, related to the risk that a high-profile sportsman who was unvaccinated might encourage others to emulate him and constitute a risk to both the health and good order of the community. It is telling that the potential for Mr Djokovic to influence others to decline to have COVID-19 vaccinations, rather than the danger he posed of spreading the virus if he repeated his previous behaviour of failing to isolate after testing positive to it, was treated as the key risk to public health. This appeared to reflect the extent of the government's concern about opposition to its efforts to protect the public. Earlier in the pandemic, Australia's federal government had also cancelled the visa of Katie Hopkins, a British commentator, and deported her. She had proposed to breach hotel quarantine rules and criticized lockdown measures.[462] The possible impact of dissent by a public figure was particularly sensitive at the time Mr Djokovic arrived in Australia, when the public's fatigue from the pandemic and the health measures that limited their freedoms[463] had grown and yet the numbers of those contracting the Omicron variant of the virus were high. The signalling by the Full Court that there was a question, not before it, about whether rallies and protests about vaccination matters could be considered a threat to public order identifies a difficult issue yet to be finally determined in Australia and elsewhere. However, aside from the unsatisfactory nature of the multiple responses from different entities, including various Australian government representatives, which highlights the potential for deficits in decision-making by reference to the lens of polycentricity theory,[464] the action of the Minister and the decision of the Full Court of the Federal Court represent a high water mark of identifying dissent in relation to public health measures such as vaccination as constituting a risk to public health and order. These decisions also reflect the prioritization of public health interests over other significant personal and community interests in relation to the right for views to be expressed about contentious matters such as vaccination during a global health crisis.

---

[462] 'Katie Hopkins Deported From Australia Over Quarantine Rules' *BBC News* (19 July 2021) <www.bbc.com/news/world-australia-57883692> accessed 14 September 2022.

[463] See National Mental Health Commission, Australian Government, 'Pandemic Fatigue' <https://www.mentalhealthcommission.gov.au/Pandemic-Fatigue> accessed 14 September 2021; Chandini R MacIntyre and others, 'Mask Use, Risk-mitigation Behaviours and Pandemic Fatigue During the COVID-19 Pandemic in Five Cities in Australia, the UK and USA: A Cross-sectional Survey' (2021) 106 *International Journal of Infectious Diseases* 199.

[464] See Freckelton (above n 443), in terms of unco-ordinated and inconsistent decision-making; see too Yvonne Hegele and Johanna Schnabel, 'Federalism and the Management of the COVID-19 Crisis: Centralisation, Decentralisation and (Non-)coordination" (2021) 44(5–6) *West European Politics* 1052.

XIII. Conclusion

This chapter has explored the parameters which permit and set limits to the powers of governments to make emergency orders and directions during a pandemic. It has done so by reference to challenges that have been mounted in various countries' courts between 2020 and 2022. The challenges had in common that they have tested the powers and obligations of the State to make orders in the name of public health that have significantly encroached on individuals' rights and liberties, which in some countries are constitutionally entrenched or otherwise protected. Jurisprudential considerations such as necessity, proportionality, and parsimony in terms of imposition of limitations on liberties have figured prominently in courts' decisions, with what complies with such strictures varying at different phases of the COVID-19 pandemic. In the United States there has been particular tension that has played out in courts' decisions between civil liberties to assemble and participate in religious observances, on the one hand, and the risks posed by such gatherings to result in transmission of COVID-19 on the other.

The right to life has emerged as a potent consideration. It has often been given precedence over individuals' personal interests, and has been applied by many courts to justify public health orders, including those which have resulted in closure of borders, imposition of quarantines, and also the requirement that populations or parts of them be locked down for periods of time. The use of curfews has been particularly contentious. However, the point of greatest disputation in the courts has been the making of orders curtailing the right to assemble—whether that be asserted for expression of views by way of civic protest, or for the purposes of religious observance. Generally, orders constraining such rights have been upheld, in spite of the significant civil liberties sensitivities attaching to such decisions.

The chapter has explored a number of sites of disagreement. Generally, where parents have disagreed about their children being vaccinated, courts have determined vaccination to be in children's best interests, although they have accorded weight to the wishes of older children, when these have been able to be expressed in a considered way that is not unduly influenced by the opinions of their parents. The chapter has also reviewed decisions about the imposition of requirements that people be vaccinated in order to enjoy various ways in which they can participate in the community—from working, to attending school and childcare; to being able to go to shops, cafes, and restaurants; and to take public transport. It has described the emergence of a preparedness on the part of a number of countries and also employers within countries during 2021 and 2022 to impose strict measures to inhibit the spread of the virus. The chapter has described a tendency for courts to acquiesce in such measures, most prominently in the *Djokovic* case, provided that it can be shown that the measures are required in the interests of public health and are as focused as possible on the contemporary threat and that, where they involve precluding people from attending their workplace, suitable consultations have taken place between employers and employees and the requirements are clear and time-limited. Where employers have required proof of vaccination status in order to meet their occupational health and safety obligations, the tendency of courts' decision-making has been to uphold such requirements. In Australia, an extra step has been taken, and not disturbed by judicial review—to deny an entry visa where it is adjudged likely that the presence of an unvaccinated person may promote anti-vaccination sentiment, contrary to public health, and disturb good public order.

7
Risk, Impact, and Disadvantage

I. Introduction

As the COVID-19 pandemic has swept the globe, its impact has not only been on the health of those who have contracted the illness. The pandemic has also had a deep effect on the health and well-being of individuals and communities more generally as hospitals have been overwhelmed and burial grounds have filled, lockdowns have limited social interaction and closed businesses, unemployment levels have increased, and homes have become places of work and schooling. Across all of these areas and more, the pandemic has provided dramatic illustrations of the pandemic's social and economic impact, placing a spotlight on, and potentially worsening, existing disadvantage.

This chapter explores the role of law in supporting responses to the broader ramifications of the COVID-19 pandemic. The chapter takes as a starting point a view that developing understandings of these broader dimensions and impacts of the pandemic are key to developing appropriate legal and policy responses. While the risks that COVID-19 poses for the health of older persons are well known, other groups have also experienced significant COVID-19-related consequences, with many of these being social and economic in nature. These effects are discussed in Section II. Recognition of these impacts is important for the ability of individuals and groups to take steps to protect their own health, and for the development of policy responses, as well as for the identification of priority groups for treatments and vaccines. Prevention and treatment of COVID-19 are discussed in Section III. For some individuals, such as those who are homeless or who live in communities without access to clean water, there may be limited opportunities for handwashing and other preventative measures. Furthermore, the lack of universal healthcare in some countries and associated financial costs of accessing healthcare may present a barrier to treatment. In addition, as hospitals became overwhelmed in some countries during waves of the pandemic, rationing of scarce resources such as oxygen and ventilators became necessary, raising important legal and ethical issues about equity and discrimination. More broadly, the pandemic also disrupted health services, with cancellations of elective surgery and disruptions to regular childhood immunizations.

Section IV analyses pandemic-related social isolation. For older persons, the risks of COVID-19 meant prolonged periods of social isolation in the period before the availability of vaccines. However, social isolation was not limited to older

COVID-19, Law & Regulation. Belinda Bennett, Ian Freckelton AO KC, and Gabrielle Wolf, Oxford University Press.
© Belinda Bennett, Ian Freckelton, Gabrielle Wolf 2023. DOI: 10.1093/oso/9780192896742.003.0007

persons, with lockdowns, border closures, and travel restrictions limiting many other people's ability for social interaction. While technology provided some opportunities to enable social interaction, pandemic-related social isolation nonetheless presented risks. As discussed in Section V, there has been widespread recognition of the detrimental effects of the pandemic on people's mental health, and of the potential for women to be at increased risk of domestic violence during the pandemic. Section VI analyses the ramifications of the pandemic for employment. For many employees, the requirements for physical distancing meant a transition to working from home, changing homes into workplaces overnight, and raising complex questions about the obligations of employers to provide safe workplaces. However, for many employees, working from home was not possible which, in some instances, placed these employees at increased risk of exposure to infection. These occupational risks, including those experienced by healthcare workers and other essential services personnel, are discussed further in Chapter 10. The COVID-19 pandemic has also led to widespread loss of employment. In many countries, governments have been required to provide income support for those who lost employment. The legal dimensions of these income supports are also discussed in Section VI.

II. The Uneven Impact of COVID-19

The COVID-19 pandemic was caused by a novel virus, to which there was no natural immunity. In this sense, we were all vulnerable to infection during the pandemic.[1] We were not only all at risk of catching COVID-19, but also of passing the disease on to others, meaning that each one of us can be both 'victim and vector'.[2] As Battin and others have argued, 'Just as physical relationships among human beings may be personal and intimate or accidental and among strangers, victims and vectors may pass disease along either in intimate relationships or without any awareness of each other.'[3] However, the pandemic has also had social and economic dimensions. The pandemic has had widespread consequences for social and economic life across the globe. Although almost everyone has experienced some aspect of these broader consequences of the pandemic, it is also the case that they have fallen particularly heavily on some individuals and communities.[4]

---

[1] For discussion of shared vulnerability to pandemics see Lawrence O Gostin, 'Our Shared Vulnerability to Dangerous Pathogens' (2017) 25(2) *Medical Law Review* 185.
[2] Margaret P Battin and others, *The Patient as Victim and Vector: Ethics and Infectious Disease* (Oxford University Press 2009).
[3] ibid 79.
[4] 'The COVID-19 crisis has exacerbated the vulnerability of the least protected in society': United Nations, *COVID-19 and Human Rights: We Are All in This Together* (April 2020) 2 <https://unsdg.un.org/resources/covid-19-and-human-rights-we-are-all-together> accessed 2 June 2022 (hereafter United Nations, *COVID-19 and Human Rights*)

Commentators have previously argued for the importance of including the needs of vulnerable and disadvantaged groups in preparedness plans.[5] In the context of COVID-19, there has been concern that the pandemic will heighten existing social and economic inequalities.[6] Flood and others have noted that 'COVID-19 has exposed and created vulnerabilities that follow the fault lines of pre-existing structural inequities'.[7]

Differences between the effects of the COVID-19 pandemic on different groups have been evident since the earliest stages of the pandemic. As outlined in Section A, older persons and people with underlying health conditions have been at particular risk of severe illness and mortality associated with COVID-19. However, COVID-19 has also intersected with existing health disparities, revealing existing social and economic factors that contribute to poor health. In Section B we analyse the disproportionate impact of COVID-19 on racial and ethnic minorities. Section C considers the effects of COVID-19 on Indigenous Peoples, which were devastating in some communities. As discussed in Section D, women have also been disproportionately affected by the pandemic, with job losses in female-dominated industries, and increases in their caring responsibilities. Women and children have also been at increased risk of domestic violence during pandemic-related lockdowns. Section E discusses the ways in which the lives of children have been affected by the pandemic. This not only includes the consequences of school closures for children's education, but also through disruption to routine childhood immunizations, and loss of parents and carers due to COVID-related mortality. The challenges for homeless people are considered in Section F. Homeless people have also been at particular risk during the pandemic as they are likely to be adversely affected by lockdowns, likely to experience difficulties in physical distancing, and may lack of access to handwashing facilities. The impact on migrants and refugees is discussed in Section G, including the consequences of border closures for

---

[5] Joshua P Garoon and Patrick S Duggan, 'Discourses of Disease, Discourses of Disadvantage: A Critical Analysis of National Pandemic Influenza Preparedness Plans' (2008) 67(7) *Social Science & Medicine* 1133; Lori Usher-Pines and others, 'Planning for an Influenza Pandemic: Social Justice and Disadvantaged Groups' (2007) 37(4) *Hastings Center Report* 32; Sharona Hoffman, 'Preparing for Disaster: Protecting the Most Vulnerable in Emergencies' (2009) 42(5) *University of California Davis Law Review* 1491; Belinda Bennett and Terry Carney, 'Planning for Pandemics: Lessons from the Past Decade' (2015) 12 *Journal of Bioethical Inquiry* 419, 425; Belinda Bennett and Terry Carney, 'Vulnerability: An Issue for Law and Policy in Pandemic Planning?' in Michael Freeman, Sarah Hawkes and Belinda Bennett (eds), *Law and Global Health: Current Legal Issues* Vol 16 (Oxford University Press 2014). For discussion of the importance of cross-cultural perspectives see Belinda Bennett and Terry Carney, 'Law, Ethics and Pandemic Preparedness: The Importance of Cross-Jurisdictional and Cross-Cultural Perspectives' (2010) 34(2) *Australian and New Zealand Journal of Public Health* 106. For discussion of the importance of compassion see Nigel Stobbs, Belinda Bennett and Ian Freckelton, 'Compassion, Law and COVID-19' (2020) 27 *Journal of Law and Medicine* 865.
[6] Aaron van Dorn, Rebecca E Cooney, and Miriam L Sabin, 'COVID-19 Exacerbating Inequalities in the US' (2020) 395(10232) *Lancet* 1243.
[7] Colleen M Flood and others, 'Overview of COVID-19: Old and New Vulnerabilities' in Colleen M Flood and others (eds), *Vulnerable: The Law, Policy and Ethics of COVID-19* (University of Ottawa Press 2020) 10.

asylum-seekers. In Section H we consider the position of people in detention. Persons with disability have also been at risk during the pandemic. In Section I we identify some of the ways in which the pandemic has affected people with disabilities and recognition of the need for pandemic responses to be disability-inclusive. By analysing these broader social effects of the pandemic, our aim is to recognize the uneven nature of the broader social and economic consequences of the pandemic. Identification of these disparities—in health, social, and economic terms— is essential for the development of informed legal and policy responses.

A. Older Persons and COVID-19

From the outset, the risks of COVID-19 for older persons were clear. Older persons have been at increased risk of COVID-19-related illness and mortality, with those aged 60 or over at increased risk.[8] Older persons have been described as 'the most vulnerable, the hardest hit'.[9] Residents in residential aged care facilities have been particularly at risk during the pandemic. In many countries there were high numbers of deaths among residents of aged care facilities.[10] The risks to older persons from COVID-19 have meant that older persons have been regarded as a priority group for vaccines, with many countries prioritizing those in residential aged care facilities, and older persons living in the community during the early stages of their COVID-19 vaccination programmes.[11]

The implementation of physical distancing measures[12] to limit the spread of disease had a particularly significant impact on older persons. For them, the increased risk of severe disease and mortality associated with COVID-19 meant long periods of social isolation. For those living in residential aged care facilities, there may have been reduced opportunities for social interaction with friends and family during periods when aged care facilities were closed to non-residents in an effort to limit the spread of disease to the vulnerable residents.[13] Older persons with physical

---

[8] World Health Organization, 'Coronavirus Disease (COVID-19)' (13 May 2021) <https://www.who.int/emergencies/diseases/novel-coronavirus-2019/question-and-answers-hub/q-a-detail/coronavirus-disease-covid-19> accessed 28 February 2022.

[9] Tia Powell, Eran Bellin, and Amy R Ehrlich, 'Older Adults and COVID-19: The Most Vulnerable, the Hardest Hit' (2020) 50(3) *Hastings Center Report* 61.

[10] David C Grabowski and Vincent Mor, 'Nursing Home Care in Crisis in the Wake of COVID-19' (2020) 324(1) *Journal of the American Medical Association* 23; William Gardner, David States, and Nicholas Bagley, 'The Coronavirus and the Risks to the Elderly in Long-Term Care' (2020) 32(4–5) *Journal of Aging & Social Policy* 310.

[11] Marcia C Castro and Burton Singer, 'Prioritizing COVID-19 Vaccination by Age' (2021) 118(15) *Proceedings of the National Academy of Sciences of the United States* art e2103700118; Hermann Brenner, 'Focusing COVID-19 Vaccinations on Elderly and High-risk People' (2021) 2 *Lancet Regional Health Europe* art 100044.

[12] As explained in Chapter 5(VII), this term is used in preference to 'social distancing'.

[13] Tamar Rodney, Nia Josiah, and Diana-Lyn Baptiste, 'Editorial: Loneliness in the Time of COVID-19: Impact on Older Adults' (2021) 77(9) *Journal of Advanced Nursing* e24.

disabilities may be at increased risk of depression, anxiety, and loneliness compared to those without a physical disability.[14] Although technology has provided opportunities to maintain some social connection, disparities in IT literacy and access to technology mean that some individuals may remain isolated.[15]

While the COVID-19 pandemic was associated with increased severe disease and mortality amongst older persons with COVID-19, the pandemic was also characterized by increased ageism, negative stereotypes of older persons, and a devaluing of the lives of older persons.[16] As commentators have noted, older persons have heterogeneous abilities and needs.[17] Ehni and Wahl have argued:

> It is tempting to fall into a crude utilitarianism that values lives differently, where we pit one group against another and give lower priority to those who have a lower value attributed to them. Too often, the lives of older people are weighed less than others: they should simply be isolated because they are the most vulnerable; they have lived their lives and have had their chance at living a fulfilling life; they are, in any case, amongst those who are going to die soon. [...] These views contradict the basic values of our society as expressed in the idea of human rights. Importantly, this refers to equal value and respect of each human being and the right to nondiscrimination on the basis of traits such as age, gender, race, or disability.[18]

Consideration of the relevance of age has also been a feature of debates over rationing of scarce resources, such as intensive care beds and ventilators, during the pandemic. These issues are discussed further in Section III and in Chapter 12(III).

B. Race and Ethnicity and COVID-19

The pandemic focused attention on existing disparities in health. In the United States and the United Kingdom, pandemic-related data have revealed the

---

[14] Andrew Steptoe and Giorgio Di Gressa, 'Mental Health and Social Interactions of Older People with Physical Disabilities in England During the COVID-19 Pandemic: A Longitudinal Cohort Study' (2021) 6(6) *Lancet Public Health* e365.

[15] Joanne Brooke and Debra Jackson, 'Editorial: Older People and COVID-19: Isolation, Risk and Ageism' (2020) 29(13–14) *Journal of Clinical Nursing* 2044, 2045. See also Alexander Seifert, Sheila R Cotten, and Bo Xie, 'A Double Burden of Exclusion? Digital and Social Exclusion of Older Adults in Times of COVID-19' (2021) 76(3) *Journals of Gerontology B Psychology Social Sciences* e99. For discussion see also Belinda Bennett and others, 'Australian Law During COVID-19: Meeting the Needs of Older Australians?' (2022) 41(2) *University of Queensland Law Journal* 127, 149-50.

[16] Brooke and Jackson (n 15); Hans-Joerg Ehni and Hans-Werner Wahl, 'Six Propositions Against Ageism in the COVID-19 Pandemic' (2020) 32(4–5) *Journal of Aging & Social Policy* 515; Sarah Fraser and others, 'Ageism and COVID-19: What Does Our Society's Response Say About Us?' (2020) 49(5) *Age & Ageing* 692. For discussion see Bennett and others (n 15) 133.

[17] Ehni and Wahl (n 16) 516; Bennett and others (n 15) 131-32.

[18] Ehni and Wahl (n 16) 521 (citations omitted).

disproportionate impact of COVID-19 on racial and ethnic minorities in terms of infection and mortality. Data from the United Kingdom in May 2020 indicated that patients from racial or ethnic minorities comprised 34% of critically-ill patients despite these groups making up only 14% of the population.[19] Similar disparities were also evident in the United States where data indicate an uneven impact of COVID-19 on African American, Latino, and other minority groups[20] and have exercised a variety of adverse impacts, including high levels of fear, loss, and mistrust.[21]

There has been debate about the causes of these disparities, but it seems that the causes are likely to be complex. While underlying health conditions such as diabetes, obesity, and hypertension are associated with poorer outcomes for COVID-19,[22] accurate data are required in order to draw conclusions about the relationship between co-morbidities and poorer outcomes from COVID-19 for people from racial or ethnic minorities.[23] Other factors are likely to relate to social and economic disadvantage. People from racial or ethnic minorities may hold jobs in essential services, making it more difficult for them to isolate so as to reduce their risk of infection.[24] As Yancy argues, 'consider the aggregate of a higher burden of at-risk comorbidities, the pernicious effects of adverse social determinants of health, and the absence of privilege that does not allow a reprieve from work without dire consequences for a person's sustenance, does not allow safe practices, and does not even allow for 6-foot distancing.'[25] In the United States, those from racial and ethnic minorities may be less likely to have health insurance, thus resulting in reduced access to healthcare.[26] It has been argued that these considerations mean that race and ethnicity need to be analysed in outcomes for COVID-19, alongside factors such as age, sex, gender, and socio-economic status,[27] that health professionals should

---

[19] Neeraj Bhala and others, 'Sharpening the Global Focus on Ethnicity and Race in the Time of COVID-19' (2020) 395(10238) *Lancet* 1673. See too Gregorio A Millett and others, 'Assessing Differential Impacts of COVID-19 on Black Communities' (2020) 47 *Annals of Epidemiology* 37.

[20] Monica Webb Hooper, Anna Maria Nápoles, and Eliseo J Pérez-Stable, 'COVID-19 and Racial/Ethnic Disparities' (2020) 323(24) *Journal of the American Medical Association* 2466; Eboni G Price-Haywood and others, 'Hospitalization and Mortality Among Black Patients and White Patients with Covid-19' (2020) 382(26) *New England Journal of Medicine* 2534; Maritza V Reyes, 'The Disproportional Impact of COVID-19 on African Americans' (2020) 22(2) *Health and Human Rights* 299; Kyla Thomas, 'Pandemic Misery Index Reveals Far-reaching Impact of COVID-19 on American Lives, Especially on Blacks and Latinos' *The Conversation* (2 June 2021) <https://theconversation.com/pandemic-misery-index-reveals-far-reaching-impact-of-covid-19-on-american-lives-especially-on-blacks-and-latinos-159902> accessed 1 October 2022.

[21] Manuel E Jimenez and others, 'Black and Latinx Community Perspectives on COVID-19 Mitigation Behaviors, Testing and Vaccines' (2021) 4(7) *Journal of the American Medical Association Network Open* e2117074; Monica Peek and others, 'COVID-19 Among African Americans: An Action Plan for Mitigating Disparities' (2021) 111(2) *American Journal of Public Health* 286.

[22] Bhala and others (n 19) 1674; Clyde W Yancy, 'COVID-19 and African Americans' (2020) 323(19) *Journal of the American Medical Association* 1891.

[23] Bhala and others (n 19) 1674.

[24] ibid.

[25] Yancy (n 22) 1891–92.

[26] Bhala and others (n 19) 1674.

[27] ibid 1675.

be aware of the potential for existing health inequalities which would affect the health outcomes for patients with COVID-19,[28] and that there is a need to address existing health disparities before the next pandemic.[29]

C. Indigenous Peoples

Previous pandemics have had a disproportionate impact on Indigenous Peoples. For example, during the Spanish flu pandemic, Māori in New Zealand had a death rate that was seven times that of those with a European background,[30] while in Australia some Aboriginal communities were devastated by the pandemic.[31] More recently, Indigenous Peoples were also at increased risk during the 2009 H1N1 influenza pandemic.[32] From an early stage, there were concerns that Indigenous Peoples could be at increased risk from COVID-19, as a result of existing health disparities.[33]

COVID-19 has had a devastating impact on Indigenous Peoples in some countries.[34] The potential impact of COVID-19 on Indigenous Peoples has highlighted the need for accurate data, with one study indicating that only nine countries were able to report COVID-19-related data for Indigenous Peoples, indicating the need for collection of data in relation to Indigenous Peoples.[35] The United Nations Department of Economic and Social Affairs has recommended ensuring 'availability of disaggregated data of indigenous peoples, including on rates of infection, mortality, economic impacts, care burden, and incidence of violence, including gender-based violence'.[36]

---

[28] Diana-Lyn Baptiste and others, 'Editorial: COVID-19: Shedding Light on Racial and Health Inequities in the USA' (2020) 29(15–16) *Journal of Clinical Nursing* 2734.

[29] William F Owen Jr, Richard Carmona, and Claire Pomeroy, 'Failing Another National Stress Test on Health Disparities' (2020) 323(19) *Journal of the American Medical Association* 1905.

[30] Melissa McLeod and others, 'COVID-19: We Must Not Forget About Indigenous Health and Equity' (2020) 44(4) *Australia and New Zealand Journal of Public Health* 253.

[31] See eg Frank Bongiorno, 'How Australia's Response to the Spanish Flu of 1919 Sounds Warnings on Dealing with Coronavirus' *The Conversation* (22 March 2020) <https://theconversation.com/how-australias-response-to-the-spanish-flu-of-1919-sounds-warnings-on-dealing-with-coronavirus-134017> accessed 1 October 2022.

[32] McLeod and others (n 30) 253.

[33] McLeod and others (n 30); Aryati Yashadhana and others, 'Indigenous Australians at Increased Risk of COVID-19 Due to Existing Health and Socioeconomic Inequities' (2020) 1 *Lancet Regional Health: Western Pacific* art 100007; Tamara Power and others, 'Editorial: COVID-19 and Indigenous Peoples: An Imperative for Action' (2020) 29(15–16) *Journal of Clinical Nursing* 2737.

[34] Kaitlin Curtice and Esther Choo, 'Indigenous Populations: Left Behind in the COVID-19 Response' (2020) 395(10239) *Lancet* 1753. See also Aquiles R Henriquez-Trujillo and others, 'COVID-19 Outbreaks Among Isolated Amazonian Indigenous People, Ecuador' (2021) 99(7) *Bulletin of the World Health Organization* 478.

[35] Alistair Mallard and others, 'An Urgent Call to Collect Data Related to COVID-19 and Indigenous Populations Globally' (2021) 6(3) *BMJ Global Health* art e004655.

[36] United Nations Department of Economic and Social Affairs, *The Impact of COVID-19 on Indigenous Peoples* (Policy Brief No 70, May 2020) 2 <https://www.un.org/development/desa/dpad/wp-content/uploads/sites/45/publication/PB_70.pdf> accessed 1 October 2022.

At an early stage of the pandemic, the Australian government used its powers to restrict entry into Australian remote Indigenous communities,[37] and Indigenous communities provided leadership and worked with government to protect their communities.[38] As a result, the infection and mortality rate for Aboriginal and Torres Strait Islander Peoples was lower than their proportion in the population.[39] In Canada, some First Nations communities restricted access to their reserves and discouraged non-residents, including those with seasonal leased cottages on reserves, from visiting, creating tensions over the rights of First Nations peoples and non-residents.[40] In the United States, many tribal communities implemented measures such as quarantine, social distancing orders, curfews, and face mask requirements, designed to limit the spread of COVID-19.[41] However, tensions arose over the relationship between tribal jurisdiction and the jurisdiction of state and federal governments, particularly around checkpoints at entry to tribal lands.[42]

Given the devastating impact of COVID-19 on Indigenous communities around the world, the low infection and mortality rates in Indigenous Peoples in Australia, New Zealand, and Canada stand out as successes. The importance of accurate and high-quality data for these successes has been noted by Mallard and others:

> In all three countries, access to timely, complete and accurate data has both enabled COVID-19 Indigenous-specific preparedness and response plans to be implemented early. In these three countries, Indigenous peoples have also been involved in the development of preparedness and response plans specific to their populations. Australia's comprehensive COVID-19 data collation on notifications, testing rates and outcomes including among Indigenous peoples should be seen as the gold standard. Since the beginning of the pandemic, data are available by region, age and sex for notifications, testing and hospitalisations.[43]

---

[37] *Biosecurity (Human Biosecurity Emergency) (Human Coronavirus with Pandemic Potential) (Emergency Requirements for Remote Communities) Determination 2020* (Cth). For discussion see Chapter 4.

[38] Kristy Crooks, Dawn Casey, and James S Ward, 'First Nations People Leading the Way in COVID-19 Pandemic Planning, Response and Management' (2020) 213(4) *Medical Journal of Australia* 151; Fiona Stanley and others, 'First Nations Health During the COVID Pandemic—Reversing the Gap' in Belinda Bennett and Ian Freckelton (eds), *Pandemics, Public Health Emergencies and Government Powers: Perspectives on Australian Law* (Federation Press 2021). See also George Williams and Sophie Rigney, 'Human Rights in a Pandemic' in Belinda Bennett and Ian Freckelton (eds), *Pandemics, Public Health Emergencies and Government Powers: Perspectives on Australian Law* (Federation Press 2021).

[39] Sandra Eades, Francine Eades, and Daniel McCaullay, 'Australia's First Nations' Response to the COVID-19 Pandemic' (2020) 396(10246) *Lancet* 237; Williams and Rigney (n 38) 145.

[40] Aimée Craft, Deborah McGregor, and Jeffery Hewitt, 'COVID-19 and First Nations' Responses' in Colleen M Flood and others (eds), *Vulnerable: The Law, Policy and Ethics of COVID-19* (University of Ottawa Press 2020) 60–62. For further discussion see Chapter 4.

[41] Aila Hoss and Heather Tanana, 'Upholding Tribal Sovereignty and Promoting Tribal Public Health Capacity During the COVID-19 Pandemic' in Scott Burris and others (eds), *Assessing Legal Responses to COVID-19* (Public Health Law Watch 2020) 79.

[42] ibid.

[43] Mallard and others (n 35) 2.

In the United States, access to public health data, and inclusion of American Indians and Alaskan Natives in demographic data classifications, have been seen as important elements in the development of policy responses.[44]

D. Gender

There has been increasing recognition of the importance of developing understandings of the relevance of gender to the COVID-19 pandemic. Beyond the biological response to COVID-19, 'gender norms and cultural patterns determine the roles women and men play in a society in response to crisis, as well as the differentiated impacts they experience'.[45] The importance of including analysis of gender in emergency preparedness and response has been noted in previous public health emergencies, including in relation to Ebola and Zika virus.[46] With COVID-19 there has been a renewed focus on the gendered effects of the pandemic.[47] Disaggregation of data on the basis of sex has been noted as an important aspect for understanding the gendered impact of the pandemic and developing responses to the pandemic.[48] While much of the focus of the gendered impacts of the pandemic has been on women, the pandemic has also had a distinctive effect on men, highlighting the importance of a gender lens in understanding the pandemic.[49]

The Organisation for Economic Co-operation and Development (OECD) has described women as being 'at the core of the fight against COVID-19 crisis'.[50] This is because women comprise almost 70% of the health workforce, although they remain under-represented in leadership positions.[51] In addition, women also do the majority of unpaid domestic caring work, including child care, but also

---

[44] Hoss and Tanana (n 41) 80.
[45] United Nations Development Program, 'Briefing Note: The Economic Impacts of COVID-19 and Gender Inequality: Recommendations for Policymakers' (April 2020) 4 <https://www.undp.org/publications/economic-impacts-covid-19-and-gender-equality#modal-publication-download> accessed 1 October 2022.
[46] See for example, Sara E Davies and Belinda Bennett, 'A Gendered Human Rights Analysis of Ebola and Zika: Locating Gender in Global Health Emergencies' (2016) 92(5) *International Affairs* 1041.
[47] See, United Nations Development Program (n 45); Clare Wenham and others, 'COVID-19: The Gendered Impacts of the Outbreak' (2020) 395(10227) *Lancet* 846; Workplace Gender Equality Agency (Australia), 'Gendered Impacts of COVID-19' (May 2020); Belinda Bennett and Claire E Bolan, 'Gender and COVID-19: An Australian Perspective' in Belinda Bennett and Ian Freckelton (eds), *Pandemics, Public Health Emergencies and Government Powers: Perspectives on Australian Law* (Federation Press 2021).
[48] The Sex, Gender and COVID-19 Project, 'Gender and Sex-Disaggregated Data: Vital to Inform an Effective Response to COVID-19' (Issue Brief, September 2020) <https://globalhealth5050.org/the-sex-gender-and-covid-19-project/> accessed 1 October 2022.
[49] Myra Betron and others, 'Men and COVID-19: Adding a Gender Lens' (2020) 15(7) *Global Public Health* 1090.
[50] OECD, *Women at the Core of the Fight Against COVID-19 Crisis* (2020) <https://read.oecd-ilibrary.org/view/?ref=127_127000-awfnqj80me&title=Women-at-the-core-of-the-fight-against-COVID-19-crisis> accessed 1 October 2022.
[51] ibid 2.

in caring for adult relatives.[52] Women may be at increased risk of infection due to their caring responsibilities, as healthcare workers and at home.[53] Pandemic-related school closures have also increased the caring responsibilities of parents, with the likelihood being that these additional caring responsibilities particularly affected women,[54] although there are also indications that men increased their child care responsibilities during the pandemic.[55] The combined effect on women of paid and unpaid work as well as community activities has been described as a 'triple burden'.[56] One consequence of physical distancing measures introduced in response to the pandemic has been that households have been regarded as separate and autonomous, with stay-at-home orders advising people not to mix households unless they were part of a 'bubble'.[57] However, it has been argued that such an approach fails to appreciate the interdependencies between households, particularly in relation to caring, and denied people broader support networks outside their households.[58]

The pandemic has also had a particular impact on women's employment in sectors with high female employment such as travel, tourism, retail, hospitality, and accommodation.[59] Women in developing countries are likely to be more vulnerable to pandemic-related job losses. The OECD has noted that 'Compared to women in OECD countries and men everywhere, women in developing countries are more likely to have tenuous ties to labour markets and little access to important social protections like unemployment insurance and contributory health systems.'[60] In addition, women generally have lower average wages than men, higher poverty rates than men, and less wealth than men, placing them at increased risk of poverty,[61] with single parents and elderly women at particular risk of poverty.[62]

COVID-19 may also have affected women's healthcare more generally, including women's reproductive care. At the same time, it has led to regulatory changes in some instances and improved access to care.[63] For example, the increased use of telehealth in some countries has helped to ensure access to

---

[52] ibid 4–5.
[53] ibid 2, 11; United Nations Development Program (n 45) 5, 7.
[54] OECD (n 50) 5. See also Lyn Craig, 'Coronavirus, Domestic Labour and Care: Gendered Roles Locked Down' (2020) 56(4) *Journal of Sociology* 684.
[55] Alice Margaria, 'Fathers, Childcare and COVID-19' (2021) 29 *Feminist Legal Studies* 133.
[56] Helen Jacqueline McLaren and others, 'Covid-19 and Women's Triple Burden: Vignettes from Sri Lanka, Malaysia, Vietnam and Australia' (2020) 9(5) *Social Sciences* 87.
[57] Jackie Gulland, 'Households, Bubbles and Hugging Grandparents: Caring and Lockdown Rules During COVID-19' (2020) 28 *Feminist Legal Studies* 329.
[58] ibid.
[59] OECD (n 50) 7; United Nations Development Program (n 45) 7.
[60] OECD (n 50) 11. See also United Nations Development Program (n 45).
[61] OECD (n 50) 9.
[62] ibid 10.
[63] Deborah J Bateson and others, 'The Impact of COVID-19 on Contraception and Abortion Care Policy and Practice: Experiences from Selected Countries' (2020) 46 *British Medical Journal Sexual and Reproductive Health* 241.

contraception and abortion.[64] The pandemic 'accelerated a shift from surgical to medical abortion',[65] but accessing abortion services during the pandemic was complex.[66] Restrictions on visitors to hospitals during the pandemic also meant that some pregnant women had to give birth without the support of their partner during the labour.[67]

Women and girls are also at increased risk of gender-based violence during periods of crisis or following natural disasters.[68] During the COVID-19 pandemic, women have been at increased risk of domestic violence, particularly during lockdowns, and there have been increased difficulties for women in accessing support services.[69] COVID-related restrictions may also present barriers for access to justice and healthcare by women experiencing domestic violence.[70]

The OECD has noted that 'The COVID-19 pandemic poses a severe threat to the achievement of gender-related SDGs' [Sustainable Development Goals] as it 'will exacerbate existing inequalities and discrimination' and 'might also put a hold to some gender-transformative policies and reforms'.[71] The OECD has noted that the pandemic is particularly likely to affect the achievement of: SDG 5.1 on legislation for gender equality and abolishing discriminatory practices; SDG 5.2 relating to violence against women; SGD 5.3 on eliminating harmful practices such as child marriage and female genital mutilation; SDG 5.4 on achieving equity between men and women in unpaid caring and domestic work; and SDG 5.6 on sexual and reproductive health and rights.[72]

---

[64] ibid; Danielle Mazza, Seema Deb, and Asvini Subasinghe, 'Telehealth: An Opportunity to Increase Access to Early Medical Abortion for Australian Women' (2020) 213(7) *Medical Journal of Australia* 298.

[65] Bateson and others (n 63) 242.

[66] ibid. See also Elizabeth Chloe Romanis, Jordan A Parsons, and Nathan Hodson, 'COVID-19 and Reproductive Justice in Great Britain and the United States: Ensuring Access to Abortion Care During a Global Pandemic' (2020) 7(1) *Journal of Law and the Biosciences* art lsaa027; Marielle S Gross and others, 'Rethinking "Elective" Procedures for Women's Reproduction During COVID-19' (2020) 50(3) *Hastings Center Report* 40.

[67] Jeffrey L Ecker and Howard L Minkoff, 'Laboring Alone? Brief Thoughts on Ethics and Practical Answers During the Coronavirus Disease 2019 Pandemic' (2020) 2(3) *American Journal of Obstetrics and Gynecology Maternal & Fetal Medicine* art 100141.

[68] OECD (n 50) 12.

[69] ibid 12–13. See also Cara Ebert and Janina I Steinert, 'Prevalence and Risk Factors of Violence Against Women and Children During COVID-19, Germany' (2021) 99(6) *Bulletin of the World Health Organization* 429; Diana Nadine Moreira and Mariana Pinto da Costa, 'The Impact of the Covid-19 Pandemic in the Precipitation of Intimate Partner Violence' (2020) 71 *International Journal of Law and Psychiatry* art 101606; Megan L Evans, Margo Lindauer, and Maureen E Farrell, 'A Pandemic Within a Pandemic—Intimate Partner Violence During COVID-19' (2020) 383 *New England Journal of Medicine* 2302; Hayley Boxall, Anthony Morgan, and Rick Brown, 'The Prevalence of Domestic Violence Among Women During the COVID-19 Pandemic' (Statistical Bulletin 28, Australian Institute of Criminology, July 2020).

[70] OECD (n 50) 14. See also UN Women and others, *Justice for Women Amidst COVID-19* (2020) 19.

[71] OECD (n 50) 23.

[72] ibid 24.

E. Children

Although COVID-19 was at first a disease principally affecting adults, with older adults in particular at risk of severe disease and mortality, the emergence of the Delta strain commenced to change that pattern, as did the prioritization of vaccination of adults. For instance, in mid 2021 in England, the highest burden of infection was in children and young adults:[73] those 'aged between 5 and 24 years were overrepresented among infected people [...], contributing 50% of infections (weighted age-standardized) while only representing 25% of the population of England aged 5 years or above'.[74] By September 2021, the highest weighted prevalence was among children aged 5–12 years and 13–17 years of age.[75] While COVID-19 is generally mild in children,[76] McLaws notes the burden of Delta infections in children and young adults and, arguing for expansion of the vaccine roll-out, observed that: 'To assume that COVID-19 will continue to be a mild disease for children is to fail to adjust responses based on knowledge gained earlier in the pandemic'.[77]

The effects of the COVID-19 pandemic on children and adolescents have been identified as extending well beyond physical symptomatology and particularly to include the experience of depression and anxiety symptoms.[78] These were found to be disproportionately in females and older adolescents.[79] Symptomatology was postulated as having been affected by reduced physical activity, delayed sleep time, increased sleep duration, increased screen time, and the adoption of a sedentary lifestyle and a poor quality of life, all contributing to anxiety and depression.[80] Children were also at increased risk of direct and indirect family violence which also had mental health ramifications.[81]

---

[73] Paul Elliott and others, 'Exponential Growth, High Prevalence of SARS-CoV-2, and Vaccine Effectiveness Associated with the Delta Variant' (2021) 374 *Science* art eabl9551.

[74] ibid 3.

[75] Marc Chadeau-Hyam and others, 'SARS-CoV-2 Infection and Vaccine Effectiveness in England (REACT-1): A Series of Cross-Sectional Random Community Surveys' (2022) 10 *Lancet Respiratory Medicine* 355.

[76] Laila F Ibrahim and others, 'The Characteristics of SARS-CoV-2-Positive Children Who Presented to Australian Hospitals During 2020: A PREDICT Network Study' (2021) 215(5) *Medical Journal of Australia* 217.

[77] Mary-Louise McLaws, 'COVID-19 in Children: Time for a New Strategy' (2021) 215(5) *Medical Journal of Australia* 212, 213.

[78] See eg Maria E Loades and others, 'Rapid Systematic Review: The Impact of Social Isolation and Loneliness in the Mental Health of Children and Adolescents in the Context of COVID-19' (2020) 59(11) *Journal of the American Academy of Child and Adolescent Psychiatry* 1218; Nishtha Chawla and others, 'Psychological Impact of COVID-19 on Children and Adolescents; A Systematic Review' (2021) 43(4) *Indian Journal of Psychological Medicine* 294.

[79] Chawla and others (n 78).

[80] Gilbert S Octavius and others, 'Impact of COVID-19 on Adolescents' Mental Health: A Systematic Review' (2020) 27(7) *Middle East Current Psychiatry* n72.

[81] See eg Noemí Pereda and Diego A Díaz-Faes, 'Family Violence Against Children in the Wake of COVID-19 Pandemic: A Review of Current Perspectives and Risk Factors' (2020) 14 *Child and Adolescent Psychiatry and Mental Health* art 40.

Sustainable Development Goal 4 is to 'Ensure inclusive and equitable quality education and promote lifelong learning opportunities for all.' However, the pandemic has had a significant impact on children's education with the United Nations noting that 'The pandemic is deepening the education crisis and widening existing educational inequalities.'[82]

School closures in many countries affected the education of millions of children around the world. The United Nations Educational, Scientific and Cultural Organization (UNESCO) has estimated that pandemic-related school closures have affected approximately 90% of the world's students.[83] The United Nations has warned that 'School closures worldwide may reverse years of progress in access to education.'[84] Although four out of five countries have provided distance-learning opportunities for students during school closures, these options were not available to at least 500 million children and youth.[85] The challenges of remote learning have been particularly acute for children in developing countries. The United Nations estimated that in 2019 approximately 87% of European households had internet access at home, compared to 18% of households in Africa.[86] Furthermore, it notes that 'Successful remote learning also depends on the computer skills of teachers and parents. In about half of the 86 countries for which data are available, less than half of the population possessed basic computer skills.'[87]

The pandemic also poses a risk of an ongoing disruption to the education of children and young people. UNESCO estimated that 24 million students were at risk of not returning to schools, day care centres, and higher education institutions following pandemic-related school closures.[88] Concerns have also been expressed about the potential consequences of school closures for girls, and that they may drop out of school due to pregnancies.[89] In addition, there has been concern that school closures may lead to increased domestic work for girls, which in turn may have an effect on their studying, and a reduced likelihood of their return to school when schools re-open.[90] Concerns have also been expressed that girls are

---

[82] United Nations, *The Sustainable Development Goals Report 2020* (United Nations 2020) (hereafter *Sustainable Development Goals Report 2020*) 32.
[83] UNESCO, 'How Many Students Are At Risk of Not Returning to School?' (Advocacy Paper, UNESCO COVID-19 Education Response, 30 July 2020) 7. See also Wim Van Lancker and Zachary Parolin, 'COVID-19, School Closures, and Child Poverty: A Social Crisis in the Making' (2020) 5(5) *Lancet Public Health* e243.
[84] *Sustainable Development Goals Report 2020* (n 82) 32.
[85] ibid.
[86] ibid 33.
[87] ibid.
[88] UNESCO (n 83) 8.
[89] Katarzyna Burzynska and Gabriela Contreras, 'Gendered Effects of School Closures During the COVID-19 Pandemic' (2020) 395(10242) *Lancet* 1968.
[90] ibid.

at increased risk of child marriages due to school closures and pandemic-related poverty.[91] UNESCO has noted:

> Adolescent girls face a higher risk of not returning to school, especially in sub-Saharan Africa and South Asia, where existing difficulties prevent them from accessing school and completing their education. School closures can aggravate these difficulties as they increase the risks of early and forced marriage, sexual exploitation and abuse, early and unintended pregnancy and female genital mutilation.[92]

In addition, the closure of schools has affected children who have missed out on school meals during periods of school closures.[93] Even with the return of children to school, there can be challenges associated with the lack of handwashing facilities and other basic facilities such as electricity and clean drinking water.[94] Worldwide, basic handwashing facilities are available in only 65% of primary schools, 71% of lower secondary schools, and 76% of upper secondary schools.[95] Globally, access to electricity is available in 89% of upper secondary schools, but in only 57% of upper secondary schools in sub-Saharan Africa.[96] Clean drinking water is available in 85% of upper secondary schools globally, but in only 55% of upper secondary schools in sub-Saharan Africa.[97]

Disruptions to routine childhood immunizations and other healthcare services during the pandemic have also impacted on the lives of children. The United Nations has noted that 'More than half (53 per cent) of the 129 countries where data are available reported moderate-to-severe disruptions or a total suspension of vaccination services during March and April 2020'.[98] One study has estimated an additional 8.5 million children missing third-dose diphtheria-tetanus-pertussis immunization and an estimated additional 8.9 million missing their first-dose measles vaccine in 2020.[99]

The loss of parents and grandparents can also have a devastating impact on the lives of children. Orphanhood and deaths of caregivers have been described as 'a

---

[91] Sophie Cousins, '2.5 million More Child Marriages Due to COVID-19 Pandemic' (2020) 396(10257) *Lancet* 1059; Editorial, 'Prioritising Children's Rights in the COVID-19 Response' (2020) 4(7) *Lancet Child & Adolescent Health* 479.
[92] UNESCO (n 83) 9.
[93] Editorial, 'Generation Coronavirus?' (2020) 395(10242) *Lancet* 1949.
[94] *Sustainable Development Goals Report 2020* (n 82) 33.
[95] ibid.
[96] ibid.
[97] ibid.
[98] ibid 29.
[99] Kate Causey and others, 'Estimating Global and Regional Disruptions to Routine Childhood Vaccine Coverage During the COVID-19 Pandemic in 2020: A Modelling Study' (2021) 398(10299) *Lancet* 522.

hidden pandemic' from COVID-19-related deaths,[100] and represent 'a considerably large group of children in need of support'.[101] Grandparents may live in multi-generational households and may play an important role as caregivers for their grandchildren.[102] Modelling of COVID-19-related deaths in 21 countries between 1 March 2020 and 30 April 2021 estimated that 1,134,000 children experienced the death of a parent or custodial grandparent as their primary caregiver, with an estimated 1,562,000 children experiencing the loss of a primary or secondary caregiver due to COVID-19-related mortality.[103] Countries with high rates of loss due to COVID-19-related mortality of a primary caregiver per 1,000 children included Peru (10.2), South Africa (5.1), Mexico (3.5), and Brazil (2.4).[104]

F. Housing and Homelessness

Lockdowns, stay-at-home orders, and physical distancing all created an increased focus on housing during the pandemic. As Farha and Schwan have argued, 'housing, therefore, has become the front line of defence against the virus. If the centrality of housing to human life were ever in doubt, COVID-19 has powerfully illuminated that having a home is a matter of life or death.'[105] At the same time however, it has been noted that 'in many places, the risks of IPV [intimate partner violence] and other forms of domestic violence means that even in "normal times," the least safe place for women is their own home'.[106]

The COVID-19 pandemic has exacerbated housing insecurity for many families. Pandemic-related job losses or reductions in income have increased the risk of families being unable to afford housing rents or mortgage repayments. The potential scale of the housing crisis led many countries to introduce specific measures to minimize the risk of individuals and families becoming homeless during the pandemic. Measures introduced included: suspending eviction of tenants, subsidizing or deferring rent payments, freezing rent increases, forbearing mortgage payments, suspending foreclosures, supporting mortgage payments, deferring taxes, supporting payments of utility bills, and providing emergency shelter.[107]

---

[100] Susan D Hillis and others, 'Global Minimum Estimates of Children Affected by COVID-19-associated Ophanhood and Deaths of Caregivers: A Modelling Study' (2021) 398(10298) *Lancet* 391.
[101] Rachel A Kentor and Amanda L Thompson, 'Answering the Call to Support Youth Orphaned by COVID-19' (2021) 398(10298) *Lancet* 366, 367.
[102] Hillis and others (n 100).
[103] ibid.
[104] ibid.
[105] Leilani Farha and Kaitlin Schwan, 'The Front Line Defence: Housing and Human Rights in the Time of COVID-19' in Colleen M Flood and others (eds), *Vulnerable: The Law, Policy and Ethics of COVID-19* (University of Ottawa Press 2020) 356.
[106] UN Women and others (n 70) 19.
[107] OECD, *Housing Amid Covid-19: Policy Responses and Challenges* (22 July 2020) 9, 17; Nicholas Pleace and others, *European Homelessness and COVID 19* (European Observatory on Homelessness

In the United States, a number of measures were introduced in relation to housing including: additional funding for public housing operations, mortgage forbearance provisions for loan payments on residential mortgages which prohibited evictions, a moratorium on evictions for non-payment of rent for residents of certain properties, and homelessness assistance grants.[108] In some instances, measures were also introduced at a state level, for example, with a number of states introducing moratoria on evictions of tenants.[109] In a number of states, utilities companies were prohibited from disconnecting utility services during the state of emergency.[110]

In Australia, Canada, and parts of Europe, moratoria on evictions from residential tenancies were also enacted.[111] In Australia, the enactment of these provisions in state and territory legislation followed an announcement on 29 March 2020 by the National Cabinet of a six-month moratorium on evictions from tenancies.[112] Importantly, the moratorium applied to both residential and commercial tenancies.[113] The National Cabinet decision also encouraged negotiation between landlords and tenants over payments of rent,[114] with some jurisdictions establishing formal frameworks for variations of rent.[115] A number of states and territories also introduced provisions preventing landlords from increasing rents for tenancies during the period of the emergency.[116] Other measures introduced in some jurisdictions included land tax rebates for landlords of affected properties.[117]

The pandemic also presented particular challenges for those who were homeless, some of which were associated with both heightened risks of infection and elevated rates of mortality.[118] Roederer and others[119] undertook a serological survey on persons in Paris and its suburbs who had been relocated as a result of experiencing homelessness to emergency shelters, hotels, and other venues. They found that

---

2021)<https://www.feantsaresearch.org/public/user/Observatory/2021/European_Homlessness_and_COVID-19Web_(1).pdf> accessed 1 October 2022.

[108] Courtney Lauren Anderson, 'A Pandemic Meets a Housing Crisis' in Scott Burris and others (eds), *Assessing Legal Responses to COVID-19* (Public Health Law Watch 2020) 188–89. See also Shannon Price, 'Stay at Home: Rethinking Rental Housing Law in an Era of Pandemic' (2020) 28(1) *Georgetown Journal on Poverty Law & Policy* 1, 23–27.

[109] Anderson (n 108) 188–89; Price (n 108).

[110] Anderson (n 108) 189.

[111] Chris Martin, 'Australian Residential Tenancies Law in the COVID-19 Pandemic: Considerations of Housing and Property Rights' (2021) 44(1) *UNSW Law Journal* 197, 203–11; Farha and Schwan (n 105) 363–64; Pleace and others (n 107).

[112] Martin (n 111) 198.

[113] ibid.

[114] ibid.

[115] ibid 211–18.

[116] ibid 211.

[117] ibid 211–17.

[118] Kathryn M Leifheit and others, 'Elevated Mortality Among People Experiencing Homelessness with COVID-19' (2021) 8(7) *Open Forum Infectious Diseases* art ofab301.

[119] Thomas Roederer and others, 'Seroprevalence and Risk Factors of Exposure to COVID-19 in Homeless People in Paris, France: A Cross-sectional Study' (2021) 6(4) *Lancet Public Health* e202.

COVID-19 seropositivity was strongly associated with overcrowding and argued that it is particularly important during a pandemic to provide safe, uncrowded accommodation for persons who have previously been homeless.[120]

Many homeless persons live in congregate communities (such as shelters or informal camps) making physical distancing difficult or impossible.[121] The time they spend in public places may also make compliance with physical distancing difficult.[122] Those who are homeless may lack access to hand-washing and sanitation facilities.[123] While new temporary shelters or temporary housing, such as the provision of hotel rooms, provided a temporary response, it has been argued that there is a need to develop access to permanent post-pandemic housing.[124]

G. Migrants and Refugees

As discussed in Chapter 4, border closures and restrictions on international travel adversely affected migrants and refugees. The United Nations noted the vulnerability of migrants and refugees during the pandemic, identifying that border closures make it difficult for migrants to return home. Furthermore, many countries closed their borders during the pandemic, with at least 57 making no exception for asylum-seekers.[125] It recommended that countries ensure that their response and recovery plans include 'targeted measures to address the disproportionate impact of the virus on certain groups and individuals, including migrants, displaced persons, and refugees',[126] and that countries

> take measures to alleviate the situation of vulnerable groups, including migrants and refugees, outside their country of origin, in particular by granting temporary residence to migrants, imposing a moratorium on deportations and other forced returns, and ensuring that individuals are able to return home voluntarily in safety and dignity.[127]

---

[120] ibid. See too Travis P Baggett and others, 'Prevalence of SARS-CoV-2 Infection in Residents of a Large Homeless Shelter in Boston' (2020) 323(21) *Journal of the American Medical Association* 2191.
[121] Farha and Schwan (n 105) 359; Jack Tsai and Michael Wilson, 'COVID-19: A Potential Public Health Problem for Homeless Populations' (2020) 5(4) *Lancet Public Health* e186.
[122] Terry Skolnik, 'The Punitive Impact of Physical Distancing Laws on Homeless People' in Colleen M Flood and others (eds), *Vulnerable: The Law, Policy and Ethics of COVID-19* (University of Ottawa Press 2020) 295–96. See too *Sanctuary Ministries of Toronto v Toronto (City)* (2020) 152 OR (3d) 411, which is discussed in Chapter 6.
[123] Tsai and Wilson (n 121) e186; Farha and Schwan (n 105) 359.
[124] Farha and Schwan (n 105) 361.
[125] United Nations, *COVID-19 and Human Rights* (n 4) 11.
[126] ibid 21.
[127] ibid 22.

During the pandemic, migrant workers and refugees may not have been eligible for government-provided support measures that were available to citizens and permanent residents.[128] In addition, return migration was expected to increase as migrant workers returned home, creating challenges for origin countries in ensuring the availability of quarantine facilities, and the need to re-settle and find employment for returning migrants.[129] The pandemic also had an impact on the amount of money that migrant workers were able to send home to their families, with the World Bank projecting in 2020 that remittance flows would decline by 14% by 2021 when compared to pre-pandemic levels.[130]

H. People in Detention

Persons in penal and immigration detention live in enclosed, confined spaces—a factor that can exacerbate the health risks posed by COVID-19.[131] From the outset, there was the potential for COVID-19 to spread quickly through a closed environment such as an immigration detention community or a prison, then on to workers, and progressing into the general community. The World Health Organization (WHO) emphasized the need for persons in such forms of detention not to be disadvantaged in terms of medical services made available to them and not to be placed at greater risk of contraction of the virus.[132] To avoid such a scenario, a number of active measures needed to be taken during the COVID-19 pandemic to address risks to detainees.[133]

In the early phases of the COVID-19 pandemic there were many calls for release of prisoners[134] and immigration detainees to reduce the risks of closed

---

[128] Dilip Ratha and others, 'Migration and Development Brief 33: Phase II: COVID-19 Crisis Through a Migration Lens' (KNOMAD-World Bank 2020) 4; Andy Symington. 'Migrant Workers and the COVID-19 Crisis in Australia: An Overview of Governmental Responses' (2020) 26(3) *Australian Journal of Human Rights* 507.

[129] Ratha and others (n 128) 6.

[130] The World Bank, 'COVID-19: Remittance Flows to Shrink 14% by 2021' (Press Release, 29 October, 2020) <https://www.worldbank.org/en/news/press-release/2020/10/29/covid-19-remittance-flows-to-shrink-14-by-2021> accessed 1 October 2022. See also Ratha and others (n 128) 7–16.

[131] See Australian Human Rights Commission, *Management of COVID-19 Risks in Immigration Detention: Review* (June 2021) <https://humanrights.gov.au/our-work/asylum-seekers-and-refugees/publications/management-covid-19-risks-immigration-detention> accessed 1 October 2022.

[132] World Health Organization (Europe), 'Preparedness, Prevention and Control of COVID-19 in Prisons and Other Places of Detention: Interim Guidance' (8 February 2021) <https://apps.who.int/iris/bitstream/handle/10665/339830/WHO-EURO-2021-1405-41155-57257-eng.pdf?sequence=1&isAllowed=y> accessed 1 October 2022.

[133] European Migration Network and OECD, 'The Impact of COVID-19 in the Migration Area in EU and OECD Countries' (April 2001) <https://www.oecd.org/migration/mig/00-eu-emn-covid19-umbrella-inform-en.pdf> accessed 1October 2022.

[134] See eg Stephane Shepherd and Benjamin L Spivak, 'Reconsidering the Immediate Release of Prisoners During COVID-19 Community Restrictions' (2020) 213(2) *Medical Journal of Australia* 58; Elias Visontay, 'Six Victorian Prisons in Covid-19 Lockdown as Lawyers Call for Low-risk Inmates to be Released' *The Guardian* (21 July 2020) <https://www.theguardian.com/australia-news/2020/jul/21/

environment transmission.[135] In some countries such calls were heeded; in others there was a slow response or none at all. In the United States, although some prisoners had been released, by April 2021 the rate of COVID-19 infection in prisons was three times greater than in the general population, with an average of 1,400 new infections and seven deaths every day over the previous year.[136]

Prison overcrowding in many countries exacerbated risks of high levels of transmission. For instance, Human Rights Watch reported in May 2020 that in the Democratic Republic of Congo, where the main prisons were at more than 400% of capacity and over 70% of detainees had not been convicted, fewer than 3,000 of 20,000 detainees had been released.[137] Similarly, Bolivia had released only two detainees out of a prison population of more than 18,000, although the country's prisons held more than twice their capacity and 70% of detainees were awaiting trial.[138] In the United Kingdom where COVID-19 cases had been identified in the majority of prisons, Justice Ministry authorities announced in early April 2020 that up to 4,000 prisoners would be eligible for release, but only 57 had been released by 12 May.[139] New South Wales, in Australia, introduced emergency legislation in late March 2020 enabling the government to release prisoners, but as of September 2021 no prisoners had been released, even though the Delta variant of the virus had entered prisons.[140]

In some countries the situation was a little better in relation to immigration detainees. On 1 January 2020 some 1,200 persons were in immigration detention in the United Kingdom but by 24 March 2020 the number had reduced to 736.[141] Similarly, significant (and unprecedented) numbers of immigration detainees were

six-victorian-prisons-in-covid-19-lockdown-as-lawyers-call-for-low-risk-inmates-to-be-released> accessed 1 October 2022.

[135] See eg Claire Loughnan and others, 'Refugees Need Protection from Coronavirus Too and Must be Released' *The Conversation* (24 April 2020) <https://theconversation.com/refugees-need-protection-from-coronavirus-too-and-must-be-released-136961> accessed 1 October 2022; Anthea Vogl and others, 'COVID-19 and the Relentless Harms of Australia's Punitive Immigration Regime' (2021) 17(1) *Crime, Media, Culture* 43.

[136] Alexander Testa and Chantal Fahmy, 'No Visits and Barely Any Cells—Pandemic Makes Separation Even Scarier for People with a Family Member in Prison' *The Conversation* (2 April 2021) <https://theconversation.com/no-visits-and-barely-any-calls-pandemic-makes-separation-even-scarier-for-people-with-a-family-member-in-prison-158592> accessed 1 October 2022. For further discussion see Chapter 8.

[137] Human Rights Watch, 'Covid-19 Prisoner Releases Too Few, Too Slow' (27 May 2020) <https://www.hrw.org/news/2020/05/27/covid-19-prisoner-releases-too-few-too-slow> accessed 1 October 2022.

[138] ibid.

[139] ibid.

[140] See Rachael Knowles, 'Calls Grow for Low-risk Prisoner Releases as COVID-19 Enters NSW Prisons' *National Indigenous Times* (7 September 2021) <https://nit.com.au/calls-grow-for-low-risk-prisoner-releases-as-covid-19-enters-nsw-prisons/> accessed 1 October 2022; see also Nigel Stobbs and Ian Freckelton, 'The Administration of Justice During Public Health Emergencies' in Belinda Bennett and Ian Freckelton (eds), *Pandemics, Public Health Emergencies and Government Powers: Perspectives on Australian Law* (Federation Press 2021).

[141] *R (Detention Action) v Secretary of State for the Home Department* [2020] EWHC 732 (Admin), [7].

released during the early phases of the pandemic in Canada by decisions of the Immigration and Refugee Board, the administrative tribunal with responsibility for decision-making in relation to asylum-seeker matters.[142] For instance, while on 17 March 2020 353 immigration detainees were being held in provincial jails and immigration holding centres across Canada, by 19 April 2020 that figure had dropped by more than half to 147 detainees, 117 of whom were being held in provincial jails.[143] In Australia, an open letter signed by over 1,100 academics urged a similar course.[144] It was to no avail—the average number of persons detained in Australian immigration facilities in 2019 was 1,340. In 2020, this average increased to 1,487 and was above 1,500 in mid 2021.[145]

However, it became apparent that release from congregate detention did not solve all the issues of risk to health for immigration detainees during COVID-19. Asylum-seekers who were permitted to live in the general community, pending determination of the outcome of their claims for refugee status, typically had limited access to social services and healthcare.[146] During the COVID-19 crisis asylum-seekers had little option but to take jobs that involved heightened risks of contracting the virus.[147] Refugees have been identified as experiencing a range of barriers to healthcare, economic support, education, social support, and border-crossing impediments which have the potential to increase their vulnerability to COVID-19.[148]

Concerns about risks to health in relation to asylum-seekers, particularly those held in detention in England and Australia,[149] were the subject of legal applications.

1. English litigation

In *R (Detention Action) v Secretary of State for the Home Department*,[150] the Court heard an application for interim relief for judicial review challenging the on-going detention of all immigration refugees, in particular those with pre-existing

---

[142] See Rachel Browne, 'Canada in Releasing Immigration Detainees at "Unprecedented" Rates Amid COVID-19 Fears' *Global News* (25 April 2020) <https://globalnews.ca/news/6861756/canada-releasing-immigration-detainees-coronavirus-covid-19/> accessed 1 October 2022; see also Afrat Arbel and Molly Joeck, 'Immigration Detention in the Age of COVID-19' in Catherine Dauvergne (ed), *Research Handbook on the Law and Politics of Migration* (Edward Elgar 2021).
[143] See Browne (n 142).
[144] Vogl and others (n 135) 43.
[145] Australian Human Rights Commission (n 131) 11.
[146] Jennifer Edmonds and Antoine Flahault, 'Refugees in Canada during the First Wave of the COVID-19 Pandemic' (2021) 18(3) *International Journal of Environmental Research and Public Health* art 947.
[147] See Rose D Dalexis and Jude M Cénat, 'Asylum Seekers Working in Quebec (Canada) During the COVID-19 Pandemic: Risk of Deportation, and Threats to Physical and Mental Health' (2020) 292 *Psychiatry Research* art 113299.
[148] Edmonds and Flahault (n 146).
[149] See Sara Dehm, Claire Loughnan, and Linda Steele, 'COVID-19 and Sites of Confinement: Public Health, Disposable Lives and Legal Accountability in Immigration Detention and Aged Care' (2021) 44(1) *University of New South Wales Law Journal* 60.
[150] [2020] EWHC 732 (Admin).

conditions which increased their vulnerability to COVID-19 and what was asserted to be the absence of an effective system for protecting immigration refugees from the virus. The claimant was 'Detention Action', a charity whose purposes were to promote the welfare and protect the rights of persons in immigration detention, together with an Estonian national subject to a deportation order, who was suffering from hypertension for which he had intermittently been prescribed medication. An application was made for his immediate release.

The attention of the Court was directed to 'COVID-19: Prisons and Other Prescribed Places of Detention Guidance'[151] and other government documentation about hygiene practices in detention centres in accordance with Public Health England recommendations; guidance and instructions issued about circumstances in which the Secretary of State would exercise her power to detain; and steps that would be taken to reduce the numbers of persons in immigration detention.[152] Under a policy, 'Guidance on Adults at Risk in Immigration Detention' issued by the Secretary of State,[153] there was a presumption that those identified as vulnerable should be released, provision made for the cessation of social visits for detainees, and for special measures, such as self-isolation and the creation of an individual care plan, to be taken in respect of persons identified as a risk.[154] The Court found that the measures put in place by the Secretary of State were directed to ensuring that, even in the extreme circumstances of the pandemic:

> the immigration detention regime will in systemic terms remain compatible with the obligation to provide safe arrangements for detention.... the Secretary of State is seeking to reduce the numbers of persons detained; steps are being taken to render detention safe for those who are in increased-risk groups but who cannot, for example, for reasons of public protection, be released; those who are not released but are too ill to remain in detention are to be transferred to hospital.[155]

The Court found that, although persons housed in a congregate setting were at particular risk, the measures put in place at the detention centres were not such as to give rise to an arguable claim that the immigration system was failing to meet the

---

[151] It was updated on 18 May 2020: United Kingdom Government, 'COVID-19: Prisons and Other Prescribed Places of Detention Guidance' (18 May 2020) <https://allcatsrgrey.org.uk/wp/download/prisons/COVID-19_-prisons-and-other-prescribed-places-of-detention-guidance-GOV.UK_.pdf> accessed 1 October 2022, and again by the United Kingdom Government, 'Preventing and Controlling Outbreaks of COVID-19 in Prisons and Places of Detention' (9 September 2021) <https://www.gov.uk/government/publications/covid-19-prisons-and-other-prescribed-places-of-detention-guidance/covid-19-prisons-and-other-prescribed-places-of-detention-guidance> accessed 1 October 2022.

[152] *R (Detention Action) v Secretary of State for the Home Department* [2020] EWHC 732 (Admin), [4]–[6].

[153] Pursuant to s 56 of the *Immigration Act 2016* (UK).

[154] *R (Detention Action) v Secretary of State for the Home Department* [2020] EWHC 732 (Admin), [7]–[9].

[155] ibid [24].

required standards. It explicitly warned that too much should not be expected of a government in the circumstances of a pandemic:

> The circumstances presented by the COVID-19 pandemic are unprecedented and are unfolding hour by hour and day by day. Within sensible bounds the Secretary of State must be permitted to anticipate such events as she considers appropriate and respond to events as they unfold. As matters stand, it does seem to us that she has taken and will no doubt continue to take prudent measures, both precautionary and reactive. That being so, the Claimants' evidence does not demonstrate an arguable case that maintaining the immigration detention system including the measures taken to date by the Secretary of State gives rise to a real risk of death or article 3 ill-treatment of persons who remain in detention....
> were it necessary to consider the balance of convenience, given the steps taken so far to reduce the numbers in detention and to protect the health of those remaining in detention, the balance clearly favours permitting the Secretary of State to continue to assess and manage the measures necessary in immigration detention centres as she has done to date.[156]

Prior to the conclusion of the hearing, the Secretary of State agreed to release the claimant from detention, subject to identifying suitable accommodation: 'The guidance already issued by the Secretary of State has as a focus, consideration of individual cases on their own terms. In principle, it seems to us that it is likely that the arrangements already put in place by the Secretary of State, which where necessary include the option of transferring detainees to hospital, will be sufficient to address the risks arising in the vast majority of cases.'[157] The Court pointedly observed that the application for interim relief need not have been brought to court—'sensible co-operation before this case would have led to the same result'.[158]

2. Australian litigation

Arguments in favour of release of a white-collar prisoner during the early phase of the COVID-19 pandemic were canvassed before Murphy J of the Federal Court of Australia in *BNL20 v Minister for Home Affairs*.[159] The applicant was a 68-year-old citizen of Pakistan detained in an interim immigration accommodation centre. He had type-2 diabetes and high cholesterol, amongst other medical conditions. He adduced evidence that it was 'inevitable', 'essentially inevitable' or 'a near certainty' that COVID-19 would enter the custodial facility.[160] He was able to show a range of deficiencies in terms of physical distancing requirements at the accommodation

---

[156] ibid [27]–[28].
[157] ibid [29].
[158] ibid [35].
[159] [2020] FCA 1180.
[160] ibid [6].

centre and that face masks could not be used in the communal dining area. The evidence was that if he contracted COVID-19 he would face a 15% risk of death even if he received the highest quality of medical care, including rapid access to intensive care unit (ICU) facilities.[161]

It was accepted by the Commonwealth of Australia, which ran the accommodation centre, that it owed a duty of care for the health and safety of persons, such as the applicant, who were kept in immigration detention. Justice Murphy concluded that the applicant had made out a prima facie case (sufficient for interlocutory relief) that the Commonwealth government was in breach of its duty to exercise such care for his health and safety in the circumstances and that he should no longer be detained at the accommodation centre. This was because, although to that point (August 2000) there had been no cases of COVID-19 at the accommodation centre, there was a real risk that there would be introduction of the virus and that it would disseminate rapidly among detainees when that occurred—'Because of the applicant's age and medical conditions, if he contracts COVID-19, he is predisposed to suffering a serious form of the disease with devastating health consequences, including a substantially elevated risk of death.'[162]

Justice Murphy was satisfied that there was a real and foreseeable risk that COVID-19 would enter the accommodation centre 'in the near future'[163] and that the applicant was at a materially higher risk than he would have been if he were in the Victorian community under restrictions 'pursuant to which he would only be in contact with persons in his immediate household, would be directed to stay at home unless leaving for one of three specified reasons, and if outside the home required to physically distance and wear a face mask'.[164] Justice Murphy was satisfied that there was a serious question to be tried as to whether in all the circumstances the government had exercised reasonable care to avoid the risk that the applicant would be infected by COVID-19, or at least to take all reasonable steps to minimize that risk.[165] He found that it was open to the government to take a number of actions to reduce the risk but it had not taken them, so he ordered that the applicant cease to be detained at the accommodation centre.[166] After the decision, BNL20 was transferred to a detention centre in another state of Australia.

Issues in relation to the risks of prisoners were also litigated in Victoria, Australia, in the early stages of the pandemic. In *Rowson v Department of Justice and Community Safety*,[167] Ginnane J of the Victorian Supreme Court heard an application brought by a 52-year-old prisoner serving a 64-month sentence for fraud

[161] ibid.
[162] ibid [32].
[163] ibid [58].
[164] ibid [59].
[165] ibid [70].
[166] ibid [103].
[167] [2020] VSC 236.

offences but who was not eligible for parole for nearly two years. The prisoner sought orders that he be released from incarceration to live at his mother's home because of risks to his health on the basis of suffering from chronic atrial fibrillation, angina, asthma, poor blood pressure, and decreased renal function.[168] He had also been prone to lung infections and pneumonia throughout his life. Justice Ginnane heard evidence that prisoners in many parts of the world were being released because of COVID-19 on the basis of their health conditions. Although at that stage there was no COVID-19 in the prison in which the prisoner was serving his sentence, if an infection of prisoners or prison staff should occur, his health would be at high risk.[169]

Evidence was led on behalf of Mr Rowson that, should he contract COVID-19, his chance of developing a severe disease was about 10% and if he were to develop a severe disease, his risk of death was in the order of 30%.[170] Evidence was given that a number of hygiene breaches had been occurring in his prison unit:

> These included that surfaces, such as touch screen kiosks, in the common areas of the Unit that are touched hundreds of times a day by staff and prisoners are not cleaned nor are prisoners given gloves to touch them. Prison officers when conducting a muster have to open the trapdoor to each cell and count the number of prisoners in each cell. They do this without wearing gloves or not changing them. They also have to unlock the cell. Prisoners are provided with one bar of soap a week and have to buy additional bars, but since the beginning of the COVID-19 crisis they have been limited to one bar a week. He has not seen any hand sanitiser in the prison, save for those in the prison clinic that can only be used by health staff.[171]

Expert evidence was given too that there should be strong hygiene regimes, access to diagnostic facilities, and therapeutic assistance, including pharmaceuticals and respiratory support, in prisons.[172] However, evidence was adduced that no risk assessment of the virus as accepted by national guidelines had been undertaken in the prison where Mr Rowson was detained.[173] This meant that a prima facie case had been established that the prison authorities had breached their duty to take reasonable care for his health.

Mr Rowson also pressed arguments based upon the rights of equality before the law, the right to life, and the right to humane treatment when deprived of liberty under the *Charter of Human Rights and Responsibilities Act 2008* (Vic).[174] In

[168] ibid [2].
[169] ibid [10].
[170] ibid [31].
[171] ibid [18].
[172] ibid [34].
[173] ibid [11].
[174] ibid [77]–[81].

addition, he argued that the State's obligation to protect the physical and mental health of prisoners was recognized by the *United Nations Standard Minimum Rules for the Treatment of Prisoners* (the *Nelson Mandela Rules*) which require that prison accommodation meets the requirements of good health, and he asserted that Victoria was in breach of these standards.[175]

Ultimately, Ginnane J declined to release Mr Rowson from prison, although he considered that the Supreme Court had power to make such an order in an extreme case under its inherent jurisdiction to preserve the subject matter of litigation.[175] In light of the fact that at the relevant time no prisoner had been diagnosed with COVID-19, he concluded that no release order should be made on the balance of convenience or the justice of the case. However, he accepted that there was a not insignificant risk that the virus could enter the prison and, if it did, it would spread more rapidly than in the general community. Accordingly, he adjourned the case 'on the basis that a risk assessment should be carried out and, subject to any further submissions about the form of such an order, any recommendations made by it should be implemented. It is an appropriate order to ensure that the subject matter of the litigation is preserved. The justice of the case supports the making of mandatory orders to that effect.'[177]

I. Persons with Disabilities

The United Nations *Convention on the Rights of Persons with Disabilities* (the *Convention*) states that people with disabilities have 'the right to enjoyment of the highest attainable standard of health without discrimination on the basis of disability' (Article 25) and that governments also have a duty to take all necessary measures to ensure the protection and safety of persons with disabilities in situations of risk (Article 11).[178]

People with disabilities were differentially affected by the COVID-19 pandemic in at least three ways: a risk of worse health outcomes from the virus, reduced access to healthcare and rehabilitation services, and adverse social effects from measures introduced in response to the pandemic.[179] It has been suggested that the COVID-19 pandemic provided an opportunity for members of the general community without disabilities to gain better empathy into the lives of those with disabilities.[180] In its 2011 *World Report on*

---

[175] ibid [79].
[176] ibid [93].
[177] ibid [102].
[178] United Nations, *Convention on the Rights of Persons with Disabilities* (adopted 13 December 2006, entered into force 3 May 2008) 2515 UNTS 3.
[179] Tom Shakespeare, Florence Ndagire, and Queen E Seketi, 'Triple Jeopardy: Disabled People and the COVID-19 Pandemic' (2021) 397(10282) *Lancet* 1331.
[180] Ikenna D Ebuenyi and others, 'COVID-19 as Social Disability: The Opportunity of Social Empathy for Empowerment' (2020) 5 *BMJ Global Health* art e003039.

Disability[181] WHO identified a correlation between disability and age (older), poverty, co-morbidities, and gender (female). Another example in this regard is the risk of persons with a disability to have compromised immunity. Early figures from the experience of COVID-19 in England tended to confirm this in the context of COVID-19, with a differential in the most serious effects of the pandemic on persons with disabilities. As Shakespeare and others summarized:

> Risk of death from COVID-19 between Jan 24 and Nov 30, 2020, in England, was 3.1 times greater for men with disabilities and 3.5 times greater for women with disabilities than for men and women without disabilities. People with intellectual disabilities living in congregate residential settings, relevant mainly to high-income settings, had a higher risk of death from COVID-19 than people without disabilities. But even in household settings, people with intellectual disability have an increased risk of COVID-19 death.[182]

Lockdowns also had a more significantly deleterious effect on persons with disabilities including because of reduced access to specialist facilities, therapies and equipment,[183] a sedentary lifestyle,[184] and reduced opportunities for socialization. In addition, compliance with public health guidance and infection control measures was difficult for some persons with a disability to implement.[185] Concerns have also been expressed about the impact of COVID-19 triage policies on people with disabilities. Jackie Leach Scully argued that 'three underlying disablist assumptions' have the potential to 'critically endanger the rights of people with disability in a situation of pandemic triage'.[186] These are assumptions about the health of people with disability, assumptions about the quality of life of people with disability, and assumptions about the social utility of people with disability.[187] Rationing decisions in relation to COVID-19 are discussed further in Chapter 12(III).

A particular concern was expressed in Australia that the federal government failed to incorporate the particular needs of persons with disabilities in its

---

[181] Shakespeare, Ndagire, and Seketi (n 179); World Health Organization and World Bank, *World Report on Disability* (WHO, 14 December 2011).

[182] Shakespeare, Ndagire, and Seketi (n 179) 1331; see too Cieza Alarcos and others, 'Disability and COVID-19: Ensuring No One is Left Behind' (2021) 79 *Archives of Public Health* art 148.

[183] Nicola Theis and others, 'The Effects of COVID-19 Restrictions on Physical Activity and Mental Health of Children and Young Adults with Physical and/or Intellectual Disabilities' (2021) 14(3) *Disability and Health Journal* art 101064. Sohel Ahmed and others, 'Impact of Lockdown on Musculoskeletal Health Due to COVID-19 Outbreak in Bangladesh: A Cross Sectional Survey Study' (2021) 7(6) *Heliyon* art e07335.

[184] Ryan T Conners and others, 'Current and Future Implications of COVID-19 Among Youth Wheelchair Users: 24-Hour Activity Behavior' (2021) 8(8) *Children* 690.

[185] Owen Doody and Paul M Keenan, 'The Reported Effects of the COVID-19 Pandemic on People with Intellectual Disability and their Carers: A Scoping Review' (2021) 53(1) *Annals of Medicine* 786.

[186] Jackie Leach Scully, 'Disability, Disablism, and COVID-19 Pandemic Triage' (2020) 17(4) *Journal of Bioethical Inquiry* 601.

[187] ibid.

messaging during COVID-19—disability-inclusiveness appeared to be inconsistent, leaving persons with disabilities exposed to a greater risk of contracting COVID-19.[188] An aspect of this issue was the absence of comprehensive data about the rates of COVID-19 infection and death among people with disability, precluding ability to understand readily whether better preventative efforts could have reduced the harm caused by the virus to the disability community.[189]

The combination of these issues led the Australian Royal Commission into Violence, Abuse, Neglect and Exploitation of People with Disability to express a 'Statement of Concern' in relation to governmental responses to the COVID-19 pandemic for people with disabilities:

> The Royal Commission calls on all Australian governments to ensure their strategies in responding to the pandemic include the taking of all necessary measures to seek to ensure the protection and safety of persons with disabilities. The emergency planning and responses of the Australian governments should include a specific strategy to provide appropriate guidance, support and funding to meet the particular needs and requirements of people with disability.
>
> The Royal Commission is of the view that Australian governments should seek input from people with disability, leading disability experts and advocates in developing their dedicated strategy, and in particular, in its COVID-19 Coordination Commission initiative.[190]

To a similar effect, the Special Rapporteur on the Rights of Persons with Disabilities stressed that there was not only a need for persons with disabilities to receive information in the course of the pandemic by sign language and accessible means and formats, including digital technology, captioning, relay services, text messages, and in easy-to-read and plain language, but persons with disabilities needed to be consulted and involved in all stages of the pandemic.[191]

---

[188] David Colon-Cabrera and others, 'Examining the Role of Government in Shaping Disability Inclusiveness Around COVID-19: A Framework Analysis of Australian Guidelines' (2021) 20 *International Journal for Equity in Health* art 166; see too Helen Dickinson and Sophie Yates, *More than Isolated: The Experience of Children and Young People with Disability and their Families during the COVID-19 Pandemic* (Report Prepared for Children and Young People with Disability Australia (CYDA), 2020) <https://www.cyda.org.au/images/pdf/covid_report_compressed_1.pdf> accessed 1 October 2022.

[189] Royal Commission into Violence, Abuse, Neglect and Exploitation of People with Disability, *Report on Public Hearing 5: Experiences of People with Disability During the Ongoing COVID-19 Pandemic*, (November 2020) 6 <https://disability.royalcommission.gov.au/system/files/2020-11/Report%20-%20Public%20hearing%205%20-%20Experiences%20of%20people%20with%20disability%20during%20the%20ongoing%20COVID-19%20pandemic.pdf>.

[190] Royal Commission into Violence, Abuse, Neglect and Exploitation of People with Disability, 'Statement of Concern: The Response to the COVID-19 Pandemic for People with Disability' (26 March 2020) < https://disability.royalcommission.gov.au/system/files/2022-02/COVID-19%20Statement%20of%20concern.pdf > accessed 21 October 2022.

[191] United Nations Office of the High Commissioner for Human Rights, 'COVID-19: Who is Protecting the People with Disabilities? – UN Rights Expert' (17 March 2020) <https://www.ohchr.org/EN/NewsEvents/Pages/DisplayNews.aspx?NewsID=25725> accessed 1 October 2022.

Difficult prioritization issues arose in Australia in the early phase of the pandemic between provision of care to aged-care residents and disability care residents. During 2021, too, in the course of the vaccine rollout the Australian Government Department of Health pivoted to deprioritizing people with disability, in favour of those living in aged-care residential facilities.[192] The Disability Royal Commission found that the Department of Health failed to seek advice suitably from people with disabilities, support workers, disability representative organizations, and service providers in relation to the vaccine rollout; its decision-making lacked transparency; and there was a failure to provide vaccine information to persons with a disability in an accessible form.[193] It found that this had led many people with disabilities to lose trust and confidence in the government's handling of the vaccine rollout. Likewise, uncertainty and confusion had been created, potentially leading to vaccine hesitancy among some people with disabilities, and among some disability support workers.[194] This was not only an Australian phenomenon. As Gerard Quinn, the United Nations Special Rapporteur on the Rights of Persons with Disabilities, observed:

> Preventive strategies have tended not to include any consideration of the situation of persons with disabilities. For example, curfew and lockdown measures were not adequately communicated to different groups of persons with disabilities.... One result was that many persons with disabilities unwittingly flouted curfew and lockdown rules with the result that confrontation with the police was inevitable.[195]

It is quite apparent, therefore, that persons with disabilities faced particular challenges during the COVID-19 pandemic and were at risk of being particularly adversely affected by the pandemic in a variety of ways.

III. Prevention and Treatment

Countries need well-resourced and effective public health systems in order to be able to respond effectively to public health emergencies. As outlined in Chapter 3,

---

[192] Royal Commission into Violence, Abuse, Neglect and Exploitation of People with Disability, *Public Hearing 12: The Experiences of People with Disability, in the Context of the Australian Government's Approach to the COVID 19 Vaccine Rollout* (May 2001) 1 < https://disability.royalcommission.gov.au/system/files/2022-02/Report%20-%20Public%20hearing%2012%20-%20The%20experiences%20of%20people%20with%20disability%2C%20in%20the%20context%20of%20the%20Australian%20Government's%20approach%20to%20the%20COVID%2019%20vaccine%20rollout.pdf> accessed 1 October 2022.
[193] ibid 2–3.
[194] ibid 8.
[195] Gerard Quinn, 'COVID-19 and Disability: A War of Two Paradigms' in Morten Kjaerum, Martha F Davis, and Amanda Lyons (eds), *COVID-19 and Human Rights* (Routledge 2021) 120.

the *International Health Regulations (2005)* (*IHR (2005)*) require State Parties to 'develop, strengthen and maintain [...] the capacity to detect, assess, notify and report events in accordance with these Regulations'.[196] Annex 1 of the *IHR (2005)* sets out the core capacity requirements for surveillance and response, and the core capacity requirements for airports, ports, and ground crossings.[197] The *IHR (2005)* came into effect on 15 June 2007.[198] While the *IHR (2005)* required countries to develop these capacities within five years of the *IHR (2005)* coming into effect,[199] the building of national core capacities has been challenging, particularly for some low-resource countries.

During the early stages of the pandemic supplies of personal protective equipment (PPE) were limited,[200] making it difficult to access face masks, gloves, and other PPE. Individuals also needed to practise physical distancing, and to have access to clean water to enable handwashing. For people living in overcrowded conditions, including in slums and refugee camps, there may be little possibility of physical distancing.[201] Furthermore, millions of people live without access to safe drinking water, millions have to fetch and carry water, or have only intermittent water supplies, making access to handwashing very difficult.[202] In 2017, 2 billion people were living without basic sanitation with 673 million of them practising open defecation.[203] In 2017 'only 60% of people had a basic hand-washing facility with soap and water at home' with this figure falling to 28% in the least developed countries.[204] In a pandemic where maintaining distance from others and good hygiene were important, those who were unable to practise these measures because of their living conditions were at increased risk. The United Nations has noted that 'Women-headed households are at particularly risk to increased health risks caused by poor access to clean water and sanitation as they are more likely to have inadequate housing.'[205]

COVID-19 stretched the resources of hospitals and public health systems in some countries, including, for instance, in India, Brazil, and Indonesia. However, even areas with well-resourced health systems were challenged by COVID-19,

---

[196] World Health Organization, *International Health Regulations (2005)* (3rd edn, World Health Organization 2016) (hereafter *IHR (2005)*) Article 5(1).
[197] ibid Annex 1.
[198] ibid 1.
[199] The *IHR (2005)* permitted Member States to request an extension of up to two years, and to request a further extension of not more than two years in exceptional circumstances: *IHR (2005)* Article 5(2).
[200] The Independent Panel for Pandemic Preparedness and Response, 'How An Outbreak Became a Pandemic: The Defining Moments of the COVID-19 Pandemic' 27–29 <https://theindependentpanel.org> accessed 12 December 2021.
[201] United Nations, *COVID-19 and Human Rights* (n 4) 8.
[202] Isha Ray, 'Viewpoint: Handwashing and COVID-19: Simple, Right There ... ?' (2020) 135 *World Development* art 105086.
[203] *Sustainable Development Goals Report* (n 82) 36.
[204] ibid.
[205] United Nations, *A UN Framework for the Immediate Socio-Economic Response to COVID-19* (April 2020) 14.

with Italy and New York City being notable examples during the early stages of the pandemic in 2020. Access to healthcare was also challenging given the lack of universal health coverage in some countries, which can make accessing healthcare expensive and potentially unaffordable. Importantly, universal healthcare is one of the targets for Sustainable Development Goal (SDG) 3.[206]

Such was the demand for healthcare during the pandemic that at times treatments themselves either became scarce or needed to be rationed. Shortages of oxygen supplies were also acute during the pandemic, resulting in dilemmas as to who should be accorded primacy for access to potentially life-saving interventions.[207] In February 2021, WHO and key organizations established the COVID-19 Oxygen Emergency Taskforce under the Access to COVID Tools (ACT)-Accelerator Therapeutics pillar.[208] With limited intensive care beds and limited supplies of ventilators, debates about the ethical[209] and legal[210] aspects of rationing decisions had a new and very practical focus during the pandemic.

---

[206] Sustainable Development Goal 3 is 'Ensure healthy lives and promote well-being for all at all ages.' SDG3.8 is 'Achieve universal health coverage, including financial risk protection, access to quality essential health-care services and access to safe, effective, quality and affordable essential medicines and vaccines for all.' United Nations General Assembly, *Transforming Our World: The 2030 Agenda for Sustainable Development* (A/RES/70/1) (25 September 2015). For discussion of progress on the SDGs see, *Sustainable Development Goals Report* (n 82).

[207] 'Covid-19 in India: Cases, Deaths and Oxygen Supply' *BBC News* (29 April 2021) <https://www.bbc.com/news/world-asia-india-56891016>; Esther Nakkazi, 'Oxygen Supplies and COVID-19 Mortality in Africa' (2021) 9(4) *Lancet Healthy Longevity* e39.

[208] World Health Organization, 'COVID-19 Oxygen Emergency Impacting More Than a Million People in Low- and Middle-Income Countries Every Day, As Demand Surges' (Joint News Release, 25 February 2021) <https://www.who.int/news/item/25-02-2021-covid-19-oxygen-emergency-impacting-more-than-half-a-million-people-in-low--and-middle-income-countries-every-day-as-demand-surges> accessed 1 October 2022. See also Ann D Usher, 'Medical Oxygen Crisis: A Belated COVID-19 Response' (2021) 397(10277) *Lancet* 868.

[209] See for example, Hans Flaatten and others, 'The Good, the Bad, and the Ugly: Pandemic Priority Decisions and Triage' (2021) 47(12) *Journal of Medical Ethics* e75; Douglas B White and Bernard Lo, 'A Framework for Rationing Ventilators and Critical Care Beds During the COVID-19 Pandemic' (2020) 323(18) *Journal of the American Medical Association* 1773; Timothy W Farrell and others, 'Rationing Limited Healthcare Resources in the COVID-19 Era and Beyond: Ethical Considerations Regarding Older Adults' (2020) 68(6) *Journal of the American Geriatrics Society* 1143; Kathleen Liddell and others, 'Who Gets the Ventilator? Important Legal Rights in a Pandemic' (2020) 46(7) *Journal of Medical Ethics* 421; Kristina Orfali, 'What Triage Issues Reveal: Ethics in the COVID-19 Pandemic in Italy and France' (2020) 17 *Journal of Bioethical Inquiry* 675; Dominic Wilkinson, 'ICU Triage in an Impending Crisis: Uncertainty, Pre-emption and Preparation' (2020) 46(5) *Journal of Medical Ethics* 287. See also Julian Savulescu, Ingmar Perrson, and Dominic Wilkinson, 'Utilitarianism and the Pandemic' (2020) 34(6) *Bioethics* 620; Julian Savulescu, James Cameron, and Dominic Wilkinson, 'Equality or Utility? Ethics and Law of Rationing Ventilators' (2020) 125(1) *British Journal of Anaesthesia* 10.

[210] Liddell and others (n 209); I Glenn Cohen, Andrew M Crespo, and Douglas B White, 'Potential Legal Liability for Withdrawing or Withholding Ventilators During COVID-19: Assessing the Risks and Identifying Needed Reforms' (2020) 323(19) *Journal of the American Medical Association* 1901; Eliana Close and others, 'Legal Challenges to ICU Triage Decisions in the COVID-19 Pandemic: How Effectively Does the Law Regulate Bedside Rationing Decisions in Australia?' (2021) 44(1) *UNSW Law Journal* 9; Michelle A Gunn and Fiona McDonald, 'COVID-19, Rationing and the Right to Health: Can Patients Bring Legal Actions if They Are Denied Access to Care?' (2021) 214(5) *Medical Journal of Australia* 207; Lance Gable, 'Allocation of Scarce Medical Resources and Crisis Standards of Care' in Scott Burris and others (eds), *Assessing Legal Responses to COVID-19* (Public Health Law Watch 2020).

Although rationing decisions may be necessary in a situation where the number of patients needing clinical care exceeds the available resources, it is also important to recognize that there are legal and ethical implications that arise from the application of rationing decisions.[211] Many ethical guidelines on rationing are based on saving as many lives as possible, but it has been argued that such an approach 'can occlude the consideration of patients' legal rights—rights that are not suspended merely because a crisis has occurred'.[212] Concerns have been expressed about the potential impact of triage decisions on older persons[213] and on people with disabilities.[214] Where decisions are made to limit care to a certain group or groups of patients, such decisions may be contrary to the human rights or other legal rights of those patients. As Bhatt and others noted:

> One of the many tragic facts about COVID-19 is that epidemiologically relevant determinants of survival rates often coincide at the population level with traits that are 'protected characteristics' under human rights standards, including age and disability. COVID-19 triage procedures must accordingly walk something of a tightrope: incorporating sensitive epidemiological data into clinical decision-making without lapsing into discrimination.[215]

As Bhatt and others observed, however, simply avoiding broad, age-based limits does not in itself provide a safeguard against age discrimination, as indirect discrimination may still arise.[216] These considerations highlight the importance of rationing policies being scrutinized from and shaped by a human rights perspective[217] and ensuring that decision-making processes are transparent and fair.[218]

Finally, it is important to note that the pandemic not only created resource constraints in relation to the care of patients with COVID-19. The increased demands on hospitals and health systems also disrupted healthcare for patients with other health conditions for example, through cancellations of elective surgery, or through patients deferring healthcare visits during the pandemic. Furthermore, cancer screening services were disrupted during the pandemic, with a number of

---

[211] See also Chapter 12(III).
[212] Liddell and others (n 209) 422.
[213] Liddell and others (n 209); For discussion see, Margot NI Kuylen and others, 'Should Age Matter in COVID-19 Triage? A Deliberative Study' (2021) 47(5) *Journal of Medical Ethics* 291.
[214] Liddell and others (n 209); Scully (n 186); Samuel R Bagenstos, 'Who Gets the Ventilator? Disability Discrimination in COVID-19 Medical Rationing Protocols' (2020) 130 *Yale Law Journal Forum* 1. For discussion see, Govind Persad, 'Disability Law and the Case for Evidence-based Triage in a Pandemic' (2020) 130 *Yale Law Journal Forum* 26.
[215] Vivek Bhatt and others, 'Human Rights and COVID-19 Triage: A Comment on the Bath Protocol' (2021) 47(7) *Journal of Medical Ethics* 464, 464.
[216] ibid. See also Sabine Michalowski, 'The Use of Age as a Triage Criterion' in Carla Ferstman and Andrew Fagan (eds), *COVID-19, Law and Human Rights: Essex Dialogues* (School of Law, Human Rights Centre, University of Essex 2020) 99–100.
[217] Bhatt and others (n 215) 465.
[218] Michalowski (n 216) 100.

countries including Australia, Canada, Germany, Italy, the Netherlands, and the United Kingdom pausing breast cancer screening programmes for periods of time during 2020.[219] Concerns have also been expressed that there will be an increase in avoidable cancer deaths in England due to delays in cancer diagnoses as a result of the pandemic.[220] As noted above in Section II(E), there have been pandemic-related disruptions to routine childhood immunizations.

IV. Social Isolation

Governments in many countries implemented lockdowns and distancing measures in response to the pandemic. Some were lengthy—the city of Melbourne in Australia was in lockdown for a total 263 days and Buenos Aires in Argentina for 234 days in total during 2020–2021.[221] Stay-at-home orders, work-from-home orders, curfews, limits on social gatherings, and other measures have all limited social interaction. While these measures played a role in limiting the spread of disease, the social isolation caused by these measures, combined with the stresses caused by job losses and economic insecurity, also presented challenges for the mental health of individuals. The social isolation caused by the pandemic was particularly notable for older people,[222] who faced a higher risk of severe disease or mortality from COVID-19, and for those who lived alone. Furthermore, as discussed above in Section II(D), women and children have been at increased risk of domestic violence during periods of lockdowns. In some countries, including the United Kingdom, the isolation was moderated to some extent by the fact that those who lived alone were able to nominate another household to be part of their 'bubble' to allow social contact within the constraints of physical distancing rules.[223]

Psychological studies have repeatedly emphasized the adverse effects of quarantines and isolation during COVID-19.[224] This was not surprising. A study of

[219] Breast Screening Working Group (WG2) of the Covid-19 and Cancer Global Modelling Consortium and others, 'The Impact of the Covid-19 Pandemic on Breast Cancer Early Detection and Screening' (2021) 151 *Preventive Medicine* art 106585.
[220] Camille Maringe and others, 'The Impact of the COVID-19 Pandemic on Cancer Deaths Due to Delays in Diagnosis in England, UK: A National, Population-Based Modelling Study' (2020) 21(8) *Lancet Oncology* 1023; William Hamilton, 'Cancer Diagnostic Delay in the COVID-19 Era: What Happens Next?' (2020) 21(8) *Lancet Oncology* 1000. See also John M Carethers and others, 'Disparities in Cancer Prevention in the COVID-19 Era' (2020) 13(11) *Cancer Prevention Research* 893.
[221] See Judd Boaz, 'Melbourne Passes Buenos Aires' World Record for Time Spent in COVID-19 Lockdown' *ABC News* (3 October 2021) <https://www.abc.net.au/news/2021-10-03/melbourne-longest-lockdown/100510710> accessed 1 October 2022.
[222] Brooke and Jackson (n 15); Rodney, Josiah, and Baptiste (n 13); Bennett and others (n 15) 147-50; Anthony D Campbell, 'Practical Implications of Physical Distancing, Social Isolation, and Reduced Physicality for Older Adults in Response to COVID-19' (2020) 63(6–7) *Journal of Gerontological Social Work* 688.
[223] Gulland (n 57).
[224] See eg Samantha K Brooks and others, 'The Psychological Impact of Quarantine and How to Reduce It: Rapid Review of the Evidence' (2020) 395(10227) *Lancet* 912; Mahbub Hossain, Abida Sultana, and Neetu Purohit, 'Mental Health Outcomes of Quarantine and Isolation for Infection

Taiwanese hospital staff who might have come into contact with Severe Acute Respiratory Syndrome (SARS) found that having been quarantined was the factor most predictive of symptoms of acute stress disorder.[225] In the same study, quarantined staff were found to be significantly more likely to feel stigmatized and reported exhaustion, detachment from others, anxiety when dealing with febrile patients, irritability, insomnia, poor concentration and indecisiveness, deteriorating work performance, and reluctance to work or consideration of resignation. In another study, the effect of being quarantined was a predictor of post-traumatic stress symptoms in hospital employees even three years later.[226]

Technology also helped to maintain social connections, with both work meetings and social interactions increasingly taking place online. In addition, there was increased use of telehealth services to ensure that individuals could maintain access to healthcare, including mental healthcare, during the pandemic.[227] However, technological solutions to social isolation assume both access to technology and a reasonable level of digital literacy, which may not be available to older persons[228] or to those who are socially or economically disadvantaged.

V. Effects of COVID-19 on Mental Health

Pandemics generate a range of deleterious effects for people's mental health.[229] The COVID-19 pandemic created an environment in which many determinants of poor mental health were exacerbated.[230] There is generally a strong correlation between social isolation and loneliness, and anxiety, depression, self-harm, and

Prevention: A Systematic Umbrella Review of the Global Evidence' (2020) 42 *Epidemiological Health* art e2020038.

[225] YaMei Bai and others, 'Survey of Stress Reactions Among Health Care Workers Involved with the SARS Outbreak' (2004) 55(9) *Psychiatric Services* 1055.

[226] ibid; Ping Wu and others, 'The Psychological Impact of the SARS Epidemic on Health Employees in China: Exposure, Risk Perception, and Altruistic Acceptance of Risk' (2009) 54(5) *Canadian Journal of Psychiatry* 302.

[227] Cason D Schmit and others, 'Telehealth in the COVID-19 Pandemic' in Scott Burris and others (eds), *Assessing Legal Responses to COVID-19* (Public Health Law Watch 2020); Elham Monagesh and Alireza Hajzadeh, 'The Role of Telehealth During COVID-19 Outbreak: A Systematic Review Based on Current Evidence' (2020) 20 *BMC Public Health* 1193; Alan Taylor and others, 'How Australian Health Care Services Adapted to Telehealth During the COVID-19 Pandemic: A Survey of Telehealth Professionals' (2021) 9 *Frontiers in Public Health* art 648009; Sathyanarayanan Doraiswamy and others, 'Use of Telehealth During the COVID-19 Pandemic: Scoping Review' (2020) 22(12) *The Journal of Medical Internet Research* art e24087.

[228] Seifert, Cotten, and Xie (n 15); Bennett and others (n 15) 149-150.

[229] See Damir Huremović (ed), *Psychiatry of Pandemics: A Mental Health Response to Infection Outbreak* (Springer 2019); Steven Taylor, *The Psychology of Pandemics: Preparing for the Next Global Outbreak of Infectious Disease* (Cambridge Scholars Publishing 2019).

[230] See eg Carla Mooney, *Collateral Damage: The Mental Health Effects of the Pandemic* (Reference Point Press 2021).

suicide attempts.[231] Isolation imposed by measures taken to inhibit the spread of COVID-19 resulted in high levels of loneliness, which in turn found expression in anxiety and depression.[232] Mental Health UK issued specific guidance.[233] From October 2020, the Australian government made available additional subsidized psychological therapy sessions for people experiencing severe or enduring mental health impacts from the COVID-19 pandemic.[234] In Canada, a Mental Health Initiative to support decision-making throughout the pandemic was established with participation from the Canadian Institutes of Health Research, Health Canada, and the Public Health Agency of Canada.[235]

The period of lockdowns during the COVID-19 pandemic was also distinguished by an unparalleled level of media coverage which had the potential to be adaptive and positive for mental health. However, many of the messages from the media, including those on social media, had the potential to fuel anxiety by amplifying causes for worry and thereby impairing functionality.[236]

Prior to the COVID-19 pandemic, mental health data had focused on survivors of SARS[237] and Ebola,[238] as well as healthcare workers assisting them. Key issues included fears of exposure to infection, loss of employment, and financial

---

[231] National Academies of Sciences, Engineering, and Medicine, *Social Isolation and Loneliness in Older Adults: Opportunities for the Health Care System* (National Academies Press 2020); Manfred E Beutal and others, 'Loneliness in the General Population: Prevalence, Determinants and Relations to Mental Health' (2017) 17 *BMC Psychiatry* 97; Raheel Mushtaq and others, 'Relationship Between Loneliness, Psychiatric Disorders and Physical Health? A Review of the Psychological Aspects of Loneliness' (2014) 8(9) *Journal of Clinical Diagnostic Research* art WEO1-4.

[232] See Susanna Every-Palmer, 'Psychological Distress, Anxiety, Family Violence, Suicidality, and Wellbeing in New Zealand During the COVID-19 Lockdown: A Cross-sectional Study' (2020) 15(11) *PLoS One* art e0241658; Lokasz Okruszek and others, 'Safe but Lonely? Loneliness, Anxiety and Depression Symptoms and COVID-19' (2020) 11 *Frontiers in Psychology* art 579181; Australian Institute of Health and Welfare, 'Social Isolation and Welfare' (16 September 2021) <https://www.aihw.gov.au/reports/australias-welfare/social-isolation-and-loneliness-covid-pandemic> accessed 1 October 2022.

[233] Mental Health UK, '6 Ways to Boost Your Wellbeing While Staying Indoors' (2021) <https://mentalhealth-uk.org/blog/6-ways-to-boost-your-wellbeing-while-staying-indoors/> accessed 14 November 2021.

[234] Australian Government, Department of Health, 'Looking After Your Mental Health During Coronavirus (COVID-19) Restrictions' <https://www.health.gov.au/news/health-alerts/novel-coronavirus-2019-ncov-health-alert/ongoing-support-during-coronavirus-covid-19/looking-after-your-mental-health-during-coronavirus-covid-19-restrictions> accessed 15 November 2021.

[235] Canadian Institutes of Health Research, 'COVID-19 and Mental Health (CMH) Initiative: Knowledge Mobilization Products' <https://cihr-irsc.gc.ca/e/52033.html> accessed 5 April 2022.

[236] Emily A Holmes and others, 'Multidisciplinary Research Priorities for the COVID-19 Pandemic: A Call for Action for Mental Health Science' (2020) 7(6) *Lancet Psychiatry* 547; Lancet COVID-19 Commission Task Force on Mental Health, 'Early Findings on the Neurological Consequences of COVID-19' (Report, June 2021) <https://static1.squarespace.com/static/5ef3652ab722df11fcb2ba5d/t/60b8d72d1094591797ca475b/1622726446012/Mental+Health+Early+Findings+on+The+Neurological+Consequences+of+COVID-19.pdf> accessed 1 October 2022.

[237] See eg Paula J Gardner and Parvaneh Moallef, 'Psychological Impact on SARS Survivors: Critical Review of the English Language Literature' (2015) 56(1) *Canadian Psychology* 123.

[238] See eg PB James and others, 'Post-Ebola Psychosocial Experiences and Coping Mechanisms among Ebola Survivors: A Systematic Review' (2019) 24(6) *Tropical Medicine and International Health* 671.

pressures. A 2021 study reviewed 236,379 patients diagnosed with COVID-19 and found an incidence of a psychiatric or neurological diagnosis in the following six months as 33.62% with 12.84% receiving their first diagnosis.[239] The COVID-19 cohort had a 17.39% incidence of anxiety disorder, worst with those who had experienced severe symptoms.[240] In addition, post-viral fatigue, an aspect of which is often known as 'long COVID', has the potential to exercise a deleterious impact upon mental health.[241]

A study published in *The Lancet* in October 2021 by Santomauro and others has given a useful empirical perspective on the mental health sequelae of the pandemic.[242] The authors identified an increase in the global prevalence of anxiety disorders during 2020 of 27.9% for females and 21.7% for males, and an increase in major depressive disorder of 29.8% for females and 24.0% for males. They accounted for the gender differential, observing that the prevalence figures were more pronounced during the pandemic than before it:

> females are more likely to be affected by the social and economic consequences of the pandemic. Additional carer and household responsibilities due to school closures or family members becoming unwell are more likely to fall on women. Women are more likely to be financially disadvantaged during the pandemic due to lower salaries, less savings, and less secure employment than their male counterparts. They are also more likely to be victims of domestic violence, the prevalence of which increased during periods of lockdown and stay-at-home orders.[243]

An analysis suggested that, in Australia, at a population level, changes to social and work functioning due to COVID-19 were more strongly associated with deterioration in mental health than the extent of contact with the virus.[244] This was consistent with a finding in the United Kingdom that members of the community were more concerned with how society changes would affect their

---

[239] Maxime Taquet and others, '6-month Neurological and Psychiatric Outcomes in 236,379 Survivors of COVID-19 A Retrospective Cohort Study Using Electronic Health Records' (2021) 8(5) *Lancet Psychiatry* 416.

[240] ibid.

[241] See eg Sindhu B Naidu and others, 'The High Mental Health Burden of "Long COVID" and its Association with On-going Physical and Respiratory Symptoms in All Adults Discharged from Hospital' (2021) 57(6) *European Respiratory Journal* art 2004364; Olalekan L Aiyegbusi and others, 'Symptoms, Complications and Management of Long COVID: A Review' (2021) 114(9) *Journal of the Royal Society of Medicine* 428; Terence Stephenson and others, 'Long COVID and the Mental and Physical Health of Children and Young People: National Matched Cohort Study Protocol (the CLoCk Study)' (2021) 11(8) *BMC Open* art e052838.

[242] Damian F Santomauro and others, 'Global Prevalence and Burden of Depressive and Anxiety Disorders in 204 Countries and Territories in 2020 Due to the COVID-19 Pandemic' (2021) 398(10312) *Lancet* 1700.

[243] ibid 1711.

[244] Amy Dawel and others, 'The Effect of COVID-19 on Mental Health and Wellbeing in a Representative Sample of Australian Adults' (2020) 6(11) *Frontiers of Psychiatry* art 579985.

psychological and financial well-being than with becoming unwell with the virus.[245]

VI. The Impact of COVID-19 on Economies and Employment

Government-imposed lockdowns and other restrictions intended to impose physical distancing became common during 2020 and 2021. With businesses forced to close their doors, and with office buildings and cities emptied of workers, these measures had a dramatic impact on businesses and their employees.[246] In the United States there were large falls on the S&P 500, the Dow Jones Industrial Average, and the Nasdaq. In addition, the United States Federal Reserve reduced interest rates to contain the impact of the virus on the United States economy and purchased large sums in bonds.[247] The European Central Bank determined it necessary to announce a €750 billion asset-purchase programme in order to stabilize and strengthen the Euro.[248] The European Commission relaxed its budget rules in order to encourage public spending and government support of affected businesses.[249] In the United Kingdom, £330 billion of emergency loan guarantees was announced to assist those in financial difficulty and £20 billion of fiscal support for businesses.[250] The United Nations Framework for the Immediate Socio-Economic Response to the COVID-19 Crisis warned that 'while the impact of the pandemic will vary from country, it will most likely increase poverty and inequalities at a global scale, making achievement of SDGs [Sustainable Development Goals] even more urgent'.[251]

Fabricius J of the South African High Court summarized the situation memorably:

---

[245] Emily A Holmes and others, 'Multidisciplinary Research Priorities for the COVID-19 Pandemic: A Call for Action for Mental Health Science' (2020) 7(6) *Lancet Psychiatry* 547.

[246] See Anton Pak and others, 'Economic Consequences of the COVID-19 Outbreak: The Need for Epidemic Preparedness' (2020) 8 *Frontiers in Public Health* art 241.

[247] See Maria Nicola and others, 'The Socio-economic Implications of the Coronavirus Pandemic (COVID-19): A Review' (2020) 78 *International Journal of Surgery* 185, 187–88. See also International Monetary Fund, 'Policy Responses to COVID-19' <https://www.imf.org/en/Topics/imf-and-covid19/Policy-Responses-to-COVID-19> accessed 1 October 2022; Eric Lacey, Joseph Massad, and Robert Utz, *A Review of Fiscal Policy Responses to COVID-19* (World Bank Group 2021) <https://openknowledge.worldbank.org/bitstream/handle/10986/35904/A-Review-of-Fiscal-Policy-Responses-to-COVID-19.pdf?sequence=1&isAllowed=y> accessed 1 October 2022.

[248] Nicola (n 247) 187.

[249] ibid.

[250] ibid.

[251] United Nations, *A UN Framework for the Immediate Socio-economic Response to COVID-19* (April 2020) 3 <https://unsdg.un.org/sites/default/files/2020-04/UN-framework-for-the-immediate-socio-economic-response-to-COVID-19.pdf> accessed 1 October 2022.

the present lock-down measures will result in massive unemployment with all its consequences relating to the inability to provide each particular family with sustenance and an income. It is clear that thousands of small businesses have been adversely affected and many of them will probably never be re-established. Unemployment will become worse and many families, in fact most likely millions, will think about the future with a great deal of insecurity and despair. Added to that is that both the Commissioner of South African Revenue Services and the Minister of Finance have told the public about the billions of Rand that are lost every month, unrecoverable in my view, as a result of the lock-down Regulations, and the fact that thousands of businesses have ground to a halt. This has of course a snowball effect in as much as the State is deprived of revenue that it would receive by way of various forms of taxes.[252]

As discussed below, the economic impact of the pandemic has been considerable, with many losing employment either permanently or during lockdown periods.

A. Work and Workplaces

For those still employed during 2020 and 2021, working from home became a new norm for many people around the world, either as a result of mandated government lockdowns, or as a matter of choice for those able to work remotely. Working from home added new complexities for both employers and employees. Given the legal obligations on employers for workplace health and safety, challenges arose in ensuring that homes were safe workplaces.[253] For employees, the transition to working from home potentially meant greater flexibility in working hours and raised questions about whether working from home will become a 'new normal'.[254] For parents of school-aged children, working from home became a complex juggling act.[255]

There are several additional points to note in this respect. First, even after the lifting of lockdowns and stay-at-home orders, the increasing numbers of workers who were working from home had a dramatic impact on businesses (cafes, restaurants, retail stores, and others) that depended on workers being in their usual workplaces. Around the world, cities introduced measures to respond to and recover

---

[252] *Khosa v Minister of Defence* [2020] 3 ALL SA 190; [2020] ZAGPPHC 147, [19].
[253] For further discussion of these issues see Chapter 10.
[254] Sue Williamson, Linda Colley, and Sally Hanna-Osborne, 'Will Working from Home Become the "New Normal" in the Public Sector?' (2020) 79(4) *Australian Journal of Public Administration* 601; Nicola Green, David Tappin, and Tim Bentley, 'Working From Home Before, During and After the COVID-19 Pandemic: Implications for Workers and Organisations' (2020) 45(2) *New Zealand Journal of Employment Relations* 5.
[255] OECD (n 50) 4–5.

from the impact of the pandemic.[256] Changing patterns of work for office-based workers also affected those employed in sectors such as hospitality and retail in cities and other areas that depend on those office-based businesses for their customers. The number of visitors to city centres declined during the pandemic with an impact on city-based businesses.[257]

Second, the pandemic highlighted the importance of paid leave entitlements for workers to support them staying at home and not presenting for work when unwell. However, paid sick leave entitlements vary between countries and between different groups of workers.[258] It has been argued that the COVID-19 period has shown that it is particularly important for essential workers to be provided with paid sick leave.[259]

The third point is that although working from home became a new norm for many, it was not an option available for all. Yancy has argued, 'Being able to maintain social distancing while working from home, telecommuting, and accepting a furlough from work but indulging in the plethora of virtual social events are issues of *privilege*.'[260] For people working in essential services, such as supermarkets, transport, emergency services, and healthcare, even during lockdown periods, working from home was not possible. Furthermore, the nature of their work meant that they were in regular contact with large numbers of people. For these individuals, their employment was potentially a source of risk during the pandemic.[261] The pandemic raised important questions about the duties of employers to provide safe workplaces for their employees.[262]

From early in the pandemic, there were reports of healthcare workers contracting, and dying, in substantial numers from COVID-19.[263] These risks of work-related infections and deaths raised important legal and ethical issues about the obligations of hospitals and employers to provide healthcare workers with safe

---

[256] OECD, 'Cities Policy Responses' (23 July 2020) <https://www.oecd.org/coronavirus/policy-responses/cities-policy-responses-fd1053ff/> accessed 1 October 2022.

[257] Paul J Maggin and Gary Mortimer, 'How COVID All But Killed the Australian CBD' (*The Conversation*, 30 October 2020) <https://theconversation.com/how-covid-all-but-killed-the-australian-cbd-147848> accessed 1 October 2022.

[258] Jody Heymann and others, 'Protecting Health During COVID-19 and Beyond: A Global Examination of Paid Sick Leave Design in 193 Countries' (2020) 15(7) *Global Public Health* 925.

[259] Ruqaiijah Yearby, 'Protecting Workers That Provide Essential Services' in Scott Burris and others (eds), *Assessing Legal Responses to COVID-19* (Public Health Law Watch 2020); Sharon Terman, 'Protecting Workers' Jobs and Income During COVID-19' in Scott Burris and others (eds), *Assessing Legal Responses to COVID-19* (Public Health Law Watch 2020).

[260] Yancy (n 22) 1891.

[261] Editorial, 'The Plight of Essential Workers During the COVID-19 Pandemic' (2020) 395(10237) *Lancet* 1587.

[262] Joellen Riley Munton, 'Work Health and Safety: Regulating for Safe and Sustainable Work Practices in a Post-Pandemic World' in Belinda Bennett and Ian Freckelton (eds), *Pandemics, Public Health Emergencies and Government Powers: Perspectives on Australian Law* (Federation Press 2021); Katherine Lippel, 'Occupational Health and Safety and COVID-19: Whose Rights Come First in a Pandemic?' in Colleen M Flood and others (eds), *Vulnerable: The Law, Policy and Ethics of COVID-19* (University of Ottawa Press 2020).

[263] See Chapter 10.

workplaces. This included through the provision of adequate PPE[264] and raised issues concerning the professional and ethical duties of workers to continue to work when at risk to their own health. While these debates are not new,[265] they came to the fore once again with the COVID-19 pandemic.[266] Furthermore, although health professionals have often been referred to as 'heroes' during the pandemic, it has been argued that 'the dominant heroism narrative [...] stifles meaningful, and much needed, discussion about under what obligations healthcare workers have to work'.[267] While most of these debates have arisen in the context of the obligations of health professionals, the pandemic has revealed the complexities of risk and work for many essential workers and for their employers.[268]

B. Loss of Work

As the World Bank noted in June 2020, 'The COVID-19 crisis is exacting a massive toll on the poor and vulnerable. Millions of people will fall into extreme poverty, while millions of existing poor will experience even deeper deprivation—the first increase in global poverty since 1998.'[269] From April 2020 to March 2021, the World Bank Group committed over US$200 billion in an effort to address the effects of the pandemic.[270]

---

[264] See Ian Freckelton, 'COVID-19 and Occupational Health and Safety: Ethical and Legal Issues for Hospitals and Health Centres' (2020) 27(3) *Journal of Law and Medicine* 590; Danuta Mendelson and others, 'Legal Implications of Personal Protective Equipment Use When Treating Patients for COVID-19 (SARS-CoV-2)' (2020) 27(4) *Journal of Law and Medicine* 856; Rosalind J McDougall and others, 'Balancing Health Worker Well-being and Duty to Care: An Ethical Approach to Staff Safety in COVID-19 and Beyond' (2021) 47(5) *Journal of Medical Ethics* 318; Udo Schüklenk, 'What Healthcare Professionals Owe Us: Why Their Duty to Treat During a Pandemic is Contingent on Personal Protective Equipment' (2020) 46(7) *Journal of Medical Ethics* 432; Jessica M Dean and others, 'Obligations of Australian Health Services as Employers During COVID-19' (2021) 45(5) *Australian Health Review* 622.

[265] Heidi Malm and others, 'Ethics, Pandemics and the Duty to Treat' (2008) 8(8) *American Journal of Bioethics* 4; Lynette Reid, 'Diminishing Returns? Risk and the Duty to Care in the SARS Epidemic' (2005) 19(4) *Bioethics* 348; Belinda Bennett, Terry Carney, and Caroline Saint, 'Swine Flu, Doctors and Pandemics: Is There a Duty to Treat During a Pandemic?' (2010) 17(5) *Journal of Law and Medicine* 736.

[266] See Stephanie B Johnson and Frances Butcher, 'Doctors During the COVID-19 Pandemic: What Are Their Duties and What is Owed to Them?' (2021) 47(1) *Journal of Medical Ethics* 12; Michael Dunn and others, '"Your Country Needs You": The Ethics of Allocating Staff to High-Risk Clinical Roles in the Management of Patients with COVID-19' (2020) 46(7) *Journal of Medical Ethics* 436.

[267] Caitríona L Cox, '"Healthcare Heroes": Problems with Media Focus on Heroism from Healthcare Workers During the COVID-19 Pandemic' (2020) 46(8) *Journal of Medical Ethics* 510, 511. See also Wendy Lipworth, 'Beyond Duty: Medical "Heroes" and the COVID-19 Pandemic' (2020) 17(4) *Journal of Bioethical Inquiry* 723.

[268] For discussion see Chapter 10.

[269] World Bank Group, 'Saving Lives, Scaling-up Impact and Getting Back on Track' (World Bank Group COVID-19 Crisis Response Approach Paper, June 2020) vi; see too Maria Nicol and others (n 247).

[270] World Bank Group, 'How the World Bank Group is Helping Countries Address COVID-19 (Coronavirus)' (6 April 2022) <https://www.worldbank.org/en/news/factsheet/2020/02/11/how-the-world-bank-group-is-helping-countries-with-covid-19-coronavirus> accessed 20 May 2022.

Loss of income due to the pandemic also diminished the food security of individuals and families, particularly those who are already economically disadvantaged.[271] Individuals with a high level of dependence on labour-based income were at risk of food insecurity as a result of lost income due to pandemic-related physical distancing measures and lockdowns, although it has been noted that the impact of such income shocks can be reduced through government social security payments.[272]

In response to the economic impact of the pandemic, many governments introduced a range of income support and social security measures. In the United Kingdom, the government introduced a Job Retention Scheme which supported employers to pay 80% of pre-pandemic wages (up to a maximum limit) for employees who had been furloughed due to the pandemic.[273] In addition, a Self-Employment Income Support Scheme was introduced to support those who were self-employed, and there were increases to various social security benefits.[274] In the United States, the *Families First Coronavirus Response Act* introduced a federal paid leave policy from April to December 2020 for workers of organizations with fewer than 500 workers.[275] In addition, a number of states also introduced paid pandemic-related sick leave for workers.[276] In March 2020 the *Coronavirus Aid, Relief and Economic Security Act* (US) created new temporary assistance through the Pandemic Unemployment Assistance program, which provided assistance for those not eligible for state unemployment insurance, and the Pandemic Unemployment Compensation program which provided an additional US$600 per week for those on unemployment benefits, and an additional 13 weeks of benefits at the expiration of state unemployment benefits.[277] Some states also introduced disaster relief grants or payments.[278] It has been noted however, that undocumented workers are excluded from the unemployment insurance system, leaving them particularly vulnerable if they experienced pandemic-related unemployment and loss of income.[279]

---

[271] Christophe Béné, 'Resilience of Local Food Systems and Links to Food Security—A Review of Some Important Concepts in the Context of COVID-19 and Other Shocks' (2020) 12 *Food Security* 805; Stephen Devereux, Christophe Béné, and John Hoddinott, 'Conceptualising COVID-19's Impacts on Household Food Security' (2020) 12 *Food Security* 769; Mathew Swinburne, 'Using SNAP to Address Food Insecurity During the COVID-19 Pandemic' in Scott Burris and others (eds), *Assessing Legal Responses to COVID-19* (Public Health Law Watch 2020).
[272] Channing Arndt and others, 'Covid-19 Lockdowns, Income Distribution, and Food Security: An Analysis for South Africa' (2020) 26 *Global Food Security* art 100410.
[273] Mike Brewer and Laura Gardiner, 'The Initial Impact of COVID-19 and Policy Responses on Household Incomes' (2020) 36(S1) *Oxford Review of Economic Policy* S187, S188.
[274] ibid S188–S189.
[275] Terman (n 259) 206.
[276] ibid.
[277] ibid 206–207.
[278] ibid 207.
[279] ibid 208.

In Australia, the federal government also introduced a range of temporary additional social security measures to support those affected by the economic impact of the pandemic. In March 2020 the government introduced a fortnightly Jobkeeper payment to eligible employers of A$1,500 for each eligible employee so that employers could continue to pay their employees.[280] Employers were eligible if their turnover had been reduced by at least a specified minimum percentage compared to their turnover in a comparable period in the previous year.[281] While Jobkeeper applied to both full-time and part-time employees, casual employees were only included if they had been employed by the employer for at least 12 months, and were not a permanent employee of another employer.[282] From March 2020 the government also expanded eligibility for the Jobseeker payment for those looking for employment, and from April 2020 also provided a Coronavirus Supplement of A$550 per fortnight for those receiving the Jobseeker payment and other eligible social security payments.[283] In addition, two payments of A$750 were paid to recipients of some social security payments and veterans' payments.[284] The mutual obligation requirements, which include requirements for recipients of some social security payments to search for jobs, were suspended until June 2020.[285] The number of people receiving income support payments for unemployed persons increased from approximately 820,000 in December 2019 to 1,640,000 at the end of May 2020.[286] Approximately 2.2 million recipients of social security payments were receiving the Coronavirus Supplement by the end of June 2020.[287]

In July 2020, the Australian government announced a number of changes to the COVID-19 income support measures. These included a reduction in the Coronavirus Supplement from A$550 per fortnight to A$250 per fortnight, reinstatement of assets tests for eligibility, reintroduction of modified mutual obligation requirements, and changes to the income test which would allow recipients to earn more income before their payment is reduced.[288] The Jobkeeper payments were originally scheduled to end in September 2020 but this was

---

[280] Geoff Gilfillan, 'COVID-19: Impacts on Casual Workers in Australia—A Statistical Snapshot' (Research Paper, Parliament of Australia, Updated 8 May 2020) 3; see too Terry Carney, 'Economic Hardship Payments in Health Emergencies' in Belinda Bennett and Ian Freckelton (eds), *Pandemics, Public Health Emergencies and Government Powers: Perspectives on Australian Law* (Federation Press 2021).
[281] Gilfillan (n 280) 3.
[282] ibid.
[283] ibid 3–4.
[284] Michael Klapdor, 'Changes to the COVID-19 Social Security Measures: A Brief Assessment' (Research Paper, Parliament of Australia, 30 July 2020) 3.
[285] ibid.
[286] ibid.
[287] ibid.
[288] ibid 1–5. For further discussion of COVID-related social security payments in Australia see Carney (n 280).

extended until March 2021, although payments were made at a reduced rate.[289] In June 2021 the government announced a COVID-19 Disaster Payment, which was a lump sum payment for those who had lost income or employment due to a lockdown in response to COVID-19. The rate for the payment was based on the number of hours of work per week lost as a result of the lockdown. In September 2021, the government announced that automatic renewal of the payment would cease once 70% of the population aged 16 years and older in the jurisdiction were fully vaccinated with two doses of a COVID-19 vaccine, and would be phased out once 80% of the population in the jurisdiction was fully vaccinated.[290] The government also introduced a Pandemic Leave Disaster Payment of A$1,500 for every 14-day period that an individual was unable to work because they were required to self-isolate, quarantine, or care for someone with COVID-19. To be eligible for the Pandemic Disaster Leave Payment a person needed also not to be receiving an Australian government income support payment, must not have received an equivalent state payment, and must have had insufficient paid leave entitlements. A financial hardship test applied from January 2022. In September 2021 the government announced that the payment would continue until 30 June 2022.[291]

VII. Conclusion

The COVID-19 pandemic affected all parts of society. Older people; women; children; people of Black, Hispanic, and Indigenous backgrounds; refugees and migrants; homeless people; asylum-seekers and people in detention; those with a mental illness; and people with disabilities all experienced particular challenges during the pandemic. In addition, vulnerabilities became apparent due to poorly resourced health systems, as well as through poverty-related aspects such as inadequate housing or lack of access to clean water and sanitation. In some instances, the reality that hospitals were overwhelmed resulted in decisions being made about rationing of healthcare, an issue we discuss in more detail in Chapter 12. Pandemic-related lockdowns and stay-at-home orders have changed patterns of work with many people working from home during the crisis but also continuing to do so after the lockdowns.[292] However, as already

---

[289] Carney (n 280) 190.
[290] Michael Klapdor and Anthony Lotric, 'Australian Government COVID-19 Disaster Payments: A Quick Guide' (Parliament of Australia, 21 January 2022) 2–5.
[291] ibid 9–10.
[292] See Josh Butler and Rafqa Touma, 'Working from Home: Major Australian Employers Respond to Latest Covid Health Advice' (20 July 2022) *The Guardian* <https://www.theguardian.com/australia-news/2022/jul/20/working-from-home-major-australian-employers-respond-to-latest-covid-health-advice> accessed 1 October 2022.

discussed, this was a privilege not available to all. These changing work patterns have raised new, complex issues for workplace health and safety. We discuss these issues in Chapter 10. Finally, COVID-19 has had a severe impact on economic activity around the world, resulting in increases in unemployment and in some instances the payment of government support as people lost their jobs during the pandemic.

8
Criminal Justice Issues and the COVID-19 Pandemic

I. Introduction

COVID-19 and attempts to minimize the harm it causes have precipitated significant changes to the criminal justice systems of many countries. Conduct that has threatened to exacerbate this health crisis has been criminalized, altering (at least temporarily) the scope of behaviour that can attract penal sanctions. Internationally, COVID-19 has also led to shifts in the rate and nature of crimes committed, including a rise in certain offences that have targeted some disadvantaged groups in particular. In addition, the pandemic has disrupted the usual mechanisms for obtaining legal assistance, investigating allegations of criminal offending, and hearing and determining criminal law matters. Some of these changes, and the heightened risk of COVID-19 spreading within prisons, have influenced decision-making about incarcerating people who have been charged with or convicted of criminal offending.

This chapter examines prominent examples of these developments across a number of countries and their implications for the rule of law and human rights. Humanitarian organizations and scholars have emphasized the potential for the overreach of the criminal law and obstructions to access to justice in a public health emergency, and the consequent risk of unjustifiably encroaching on civil liberties, notwithstanding this context.[1] The experience of the COVID-19 pandemic has nonetheless also led to some constructive innovations and highlighted systemic problems, which could encourage future criminal law reforms that enhance protection of human rights.[2] Sections II and III of this chapter consider changes to substantive and procedural aspects, respectively, of the criminal justice systems of

---

[1] See eg Terry Skolnik, 'Criminal Law During (and After) COVID-19' (2020) 43(4) *Manitoba Law Journal* 145, 146; United Nations, *COVID-19 and Human Rights: We Are All in This Together* (April 2020) 15 <https://unsdg.un.org/resources/covid-19-and-human-rights-we-are-all-together> accessed 11 July 2021 (hereafter United Nations, *COVID-19 and Human Rights*); UN Women and others, *Justice for Women Amidst COVID-19* (22 May 2020) 13, 15 <www.undp.org/publications/justice-women-amidst-covid-19> accessed 4 August 2021 (hereafter UN Women and others, *Justice for Women Amidst COVID-19*).
[2] Skolnik (n 1) 146.

several countries that have taken place during the COVID-19 pandemic and their possible ramifications. Section IV examines the impact of the pandemic on the use of incarceration in relation to accused persons and offenders who have been convicted. The chapter concludes by reflecting on potentially enduring effects of COVID-19 on criminal justice systems, including opportunities it has highlighted for improvements to be made to them.

II. Changes to Substantive Aspects of Criminal Justice Systems

In striving to slow the transmission of COVID-19, governments of many countries have turned to the criminal law as a means of influencing behaviour, including deterring conduct that has facilitated the spread of the virus.[3] As discussed in Chapters 4 and 5, laws have been passed to implement a range of public health measures intended to impede the spread of COVID-19, ranging from requirements to stay at home to mask-wearing. Violations of these public health rules have sometimes been treated as involving the commission of established criminal offences.[4] Yet in some countries, as discussed later, legislative changes have also created new criminal offences and/or prescribed sanctions specifically for non-compliance with health measures related to COVID-19.[5] Other conduct that could increase the spread of COVID-19 or threaten to do so, or obstruct efforts to halt its dissemination and reduce the harm it causes, has been penalized by both pre-existing and recently created criminal offences. Although governments have attempted to protect public health, these developments have drawn attention to the risk in a public health emergency for them to lose sight of their obligations to uphold the rule of law and give adequate respect to human rights.[6] A recent increase in some types of crimes, which has been attributed to COVID-19 and responses to it, has reinforced the imperative for states to focus on these values, especially during a public health crisis. Discussion of examples of these substantive changes to the criminal law follows.

---

[3] Nina Sun and Livio Zilli, 'COVID-19 Symposium: The Use of Criminal Sanctions in COVID-19 Responses—Exposure and Transmission, Part I' *Opinio Juris* (3 April 2020) <http://opiniojuris.org/2020/04/03/covid-19-symposium-the-use-of-criminal-sanctions-in-covid-19-responses-exposure-and-transmission-part-i/> accessed 10 September 2022 (hereafter Sun and Zilli, 'Part I').

[4] Skolnik (n 1) 146; Sun and Zilli, 'Part I' (n 3).

[5] Sun and Zilli, 'Part I' (n 3); see eg in South Africa *Regulations Issued in Terms of Section 27(2) of the Disaster Management Act 57 of 2002* (18 March 2020) regs 3, 11; Nicola Canestrini, 'COVID-19 Italian Emergency Legislation and Infection of the Rule of Law' (2020) 11(2) *New Journal of European Criminal Law* 116, 120–21; Joseph Lelliott, Andreas Schloenhardt, and Ruby Ioannou, 'Pandemics, Punishment, and Public Health: COVID-19 and Criminal Law in Australia' (2021) 44(1) *University of New South Wales Law Journal* 167, 178–79.

[6] United Nations, *COVID-19 and Human Rights* (n 1) 2–3.

A. Criminalization of Conduct Related to COVID-19

As already noted, a number of governments, including China, France, the United States, Italy, and Turkey, have relied on the criminal law to enforce public health measures that they have implemented during the COVID-19 pandemic.[7] In some countries, people have been charged for breaching public health orders under categories of criminal offences that were created before the pandemic and were not originally intended to apply to such conduct. For example, French authorities have reportedly prosecuted those who contravened lockdown rules for the criminal offence of 'endangering the lives of others', an offence which is punishable by a fine or prison term.[8]

Yet other governments, such as that of the Australian state of New South Wales, have passed legislation imposing criminal sanctions for contravention of public health orders made to hinder the spread of COVID-19.[9] Also in Victoria, Australia, clause 165BN of the *Public Health and Wellbeing Amendment (Pandemic Management) Act 2021* (Vic)[10] imposed penalties of up to A$10,904 for individuals and over A$54,522 for bodies corporate that failed to comply with a 'pandemic order'. By April 2021, more than 400 New Zealanders had been convicted for breaching coronavirus restrictions,[11] with one in five sentenced to prison terms,

---

[7] Sergii Starodubov, Viktoriia Vladyshevska, and Maryna Pyzhova, 'Liability for Violation of Quarantine: Novelties of Administrative and Criminal Legislation' (2020) 9(2) *Ius Humani Law Journal* 137, 144; Canestrini (n 5) 120; Estelle Chambas and Thomas Perroud, 'France: Legal Response to Covid-19' in Jeff King and Octávio LM Ferraz (eds), *The Oxford Compendium of National Legal Responses to Covid-19* (Oxford University Press 2021); Hera Asad and others, 'Health Care Workers and Patients as Trojan Horses: A COVID19 Ward Outbreak' (2020) 2(3) *Infection Prevention in Practice* art 100073; Serban Köybaşı, Volkan Aslan, and Naciye Betül Haliloğlu, 'Turkey: Legal Response to Covid-19' in Jeff King and Octávio LM Ferraz (eds), *The Oxford Compendium of National Legal Responses to Covid-19* (Oxford University Press 2021); Zhiqiong June Wang and Jianfu Chen, 'The People's Republic of China: Legal Response to Covid-19' in Jeff King and Octávio LM Ferraz (eds), *The Oxford Compendium of National Legal Responses to Covid-19* (Oxford University Press 2021).

[8] Oliver Rowland, 'French Covid-19 Lockdown Extension "Probable"' *The Connexion* (21 March 2020) <https://www.connexionfrance.com/article/French-news/france-expected-to-extend-covid-19-lockdown-period-beyond-initial-two-week-period-as-virus-spreads> accessed 28 May 2022; 'France Arrests People for Flouting Confinement Rules' *The Connexion* (20 March 2020) <https://www.connexionfrance.com/article/French-news/France-arrests-people-for-flouting-confinement-rules-as-Macron-calls-for-confinement-rules-to-be-taken-more-seriously> accessed 28 May 2022; Jean-Michel Décugis and Jérémie Pham-Lê, 'Confinement: Premières Gardes à Vue Pour Mise en Danger de la vie d'Autrui' *Le Parisien* (19 March 2020) <https://www.leparisien.fr/faits-divers/confinement-premieres-gardes-a-vue-en-france-pour-non-respect-des-regles-19-03-2020-8284038.php> accessed 28 May 2022. Likewise, in South Africa, two people were charged with attempted murder where they flouted quarantine requirements after testing positive to COVID-19 and thus exposed others to the virus: S Abdool Karim, 'Criminalisation of Transmission of SARS-CoV-2: A Potential Challenge to Controlling The Outbreak in South Africa' (2020) 110(6) *South African Medical Journal* 458, 458.

[9] Antonia Miller, 'Lawcodes Report: New Criminal Penalties for COVID-19 Related Offences' (2020) 32(4) *Judicial Officers Bulletin* 33, 34.

[10] This Act was passed following considerable public and parliamentary debate: see eg 'Marathon Debate Over Victorian Government's Pandemic Bill Ends, Amendments Sent to Lower House' *ABC News* (1 December 2021) <www.abc.net.au/news/2021-12-01/debate-ends-over-victorian-pandemic-bill-in-upper-house/100663740> accessed 8 December 2021.

[11] See eg *Police v Harris* [2020] NZDC 27024; *Police v Woods* [2020] NZDC 6614.

a disproportionate number of whom were Māori.[12] Large numbers of fines have been imposed for non-compliance with physical distancing measures in Quebec, Canada,[13] and requirements to wear masks in public in Turkey.[14] Quarantine is one of the most common public health measures, violation of which governments (including in Italy, Ukraine, Lithuania, Bulgaria, Argentina, and Norway) penalized during the COVID-19 pandemic,[15] and, from Hawaii in the United States to the Philippines, people have been arrested for this offence.[16]

Some governments have sought to use the criminal law to curb other behaviour that could impede efforts to slow the transmission of COVID-19 and mitigate its harm. For instance, a Ukrainian bill, introduced in 2020, created a criminal offence of illegally exporting from Ukraine (including by concealing from customs control) 'anti-epidemic goods' 'necessary to prevent the introduction and spread of acute respiratory disease caused by' COVID-19.[17] In some countries, dissemination of false information about COVID-19 and/or treatments for it have been classified as a crime.[18] For example, in Hungary, by as early as 15 May 2020, police had commenced 90 proceedings for the offence of 'scaremongering' pursuant to the Criminal Code in response to the alleged spread of fabricated information relating to COVID-19.[19] The Hungarian government had amended this legislation, so it proscribed 'at a site of public danger and in front of a large audience, [stating or disseminating] any untrue fact or any misrepresented true fact with regard to the public danger that is capable of causing disturbance or unrest in a larger group of persons at the site of public danger'.[20] In one case, the Pécs District Court

---

[12] See Tess McClure, 'Dozens Jailed in New Zealand for Coronavirus Breaches' *The Guardian* (6 April 2021) <www.theguardian.com/world/2021/apr/06/new-zealand-coronavirus-breaches-jailed-convicti ons> accessed 30 October 2021. Under the *Public Health Response Amendment Act (No 2) 2021* (NZ), enacted on 20 November 2021, penalties were increased and a person intentionally failing to comply with a COVID-19 order, such as travelling without permission within New Zealand, became subject to a court-imposed infringement fine of up to NZ$12,000 or six months' imprisonment.

[13] Skolnik (n 1) 176.

[14] Starodubov, Vladyshevska, and Pyzhova (n 7) 145.

[15] Nina Sun and Livio Zilli, 'COVID-19 Symposium: The Use of Criminal Sanctions in COVID-19 Responses—Enforcement of Public Health Measures, Part II' *Opinio Juris* (3 April 2020) <http://opin iojuris.org/2020/04/03/covid-19-symposium-the-use-of-criminal-sanctions-in-covid-19-responses-enforcement-of-public-health-measures-part-ii/> accessed 3 August 2021 (hereafter Sun and Zilli, 'Part II'); Starodubov, Vladyshevska, and Pyzhova (n 7) 145–46.

[16] Mark E Wojcik and David W Austin, 'Criminal Justice and COVID-19' (2020) 35(3) *Criminal Justice* 44; Starodubov, Vladyshevska, and Pyzhova (n 7) 146.

[17] Law of Ukraine, 'On Amendments to the Law of Ukraine "on Foreign Economic Activities"' <https://www.wto.org/english/thewto_e/acc_e/ukr_e/wtaccukr139_leg_11.pdf> accessed 10 April 2022; see too Svitlana Mazepa, 'COVID-19 and Its Impact on Ukrainian Criminal Law' *Intersentia Online* (20 September 2020) <www.intersentiaonline.com/permalink/5e82010d2fb0e95a07b4d00a1 ef0ed5b> accessed 4 August 2021.

[18] United Nations, *COVID-19 and Human Rights* (n 1) 17. For a debate on whether such conduct should be criminalized, see Melinda C Mills and Jonas Sivelä, 'Should Spreading Anti-vaccine Misinformation be Criminalised?' (2021) 372 *British Medical Journal* n272.

[19] András Koltay, 'The Punishment of Scaremongering in the Hungarian Legal System. Freedom of Speech in the Times of the COVID-19 Pandemic' (2020) Working Paper, No ID 3735867 14 <https:// papers.ssrn.com/sol3/papers.cfm?abstract_id=3735867> accessed 4 August 2021.

[20] ibid 10.

reprimanded for this offence an individual who had stated on a social media platform that COVID-19 did not exist and thus that there was no reason to fear its risk to health.[21]

In some jurisdictions, high numbers of penalties have been imposed, although the effectiveness of such enforcement measures is unclear.[22] For instance, in England and Wales, 117,213 fixed penalty notices were issued for breaches of laws related to COVID-19 between 27 March 2020 and 20 June 2021.[23] In New South Wales, Australia, the Police Minister reported that, up to 1 October 2021, 51,642 people had been issued with infringement notices for 'public health order breaches' and 15,924 people had been given fines for failing to wear masks when required.[24] Enforcement of the penalties, however, proved not to be straightforward in some jurisdictions. In Victoria, Australia, for instance, by 17 June 2021, of the 37,939 fines that had been imposed, only 25% had been paid; in addition it was mostly the poor and the young who had been fined.[25] The Canadian Civil Liberties Association argued that harsher measures introduced by some provinces, such as an evening curfew in Quebec, a stay-at-home order in Ontario, both enforced by fines, and the hiring of a 'private security force' to levy fines in Manitoba did not

---

[21] ibid 14.

[22] Alex Luscombe and Alexander McClelland, 'An Extreme Last Resort': Monetary Penalties and the Policing of COVID-19 in Canada (Report, Centre for Media, Technology and Democracy, November 2020) <www.mediatechdemocracy.com/work/extreme-last-resort-monetary-penalties-and-the-policing-of-covid19-in-canada> accessed 3 March 2022; Canadian Civil Liberties Association, COVID-19 and Law Enforcement in Canada: The Second Wave (May 2021) 4 <https://ccla.org/wp-content/uploads/2021/06/2021-05-13-COVID-19-and-Law-Enforcement-The-second-wave.pdf> accessed 30 October 2021.

[23] Jennifer Brown, 'Coronavirus: Enforcing Restrictions' (House of Commons Library, Research Briefing Paper No 9024, 27 July 2021) <https://researchbriefings.files.parliament.uk/documents/CBP-9024/CBP-9024.pdf> accessed 30 October 2021; Jamie Grierson and Tobi Thomas, 'Covid Fines Surge in England and Wales as Police Adopt Hardline Approach' The Guardian (26 February 2021) <www.theguardian.com/world/2021/feb/25/covid-fines-surge-in-england-and-wales-as-police-adopt-hardline-approach> accessed 30 October 2021; House of Commons Justice Committee, Covid-19 and the Criminal Law (Report, 21 September 2021) <https://committees.parliament.uk/publications/7439/documents/77794/default/> accessed 10 April 2022.

[24] See Catie McLeod, 'NSW Police Minister David Elliott Faces Questions over Covid Compliance' The West Australian (29 October 2021) <https://thewest.com.au/news/nsw-police-minister-david-elliott-faces-questions-over-covid-compliance-c-4367242> accessed 30 October 2021.

[25] Simone F Koob and Craig Butt, 'Nearly 38,000 Fines Issued for Breaching Coronavirus Restrictions But Only a Quarter Paid' The Age (17 June 2021) <www.theage.com.au/national/victoria/nearly-38-000-fines-issued-for-breaching-coronavirus-restrictions-but-only-a-quarter-paid-20210617-p581rj.html> accessed 30 October 2021. See too Simone F Koob, '"No Surprise": The Young and Poor Most Likely to Get a COVID Fine' The Age (23 November 2021) <https://www.theage.com.au/national/victoria/no-surprise-the-young-and-poor-most-likely-to-get-a-covid-fine-20211111-p5985s.html> accessed 5 December 2021. By contrast, in New South Wales, 3,338 fines, totalling A$4,409,800, were issued for breaches of public health orders between March 2000 and June 2021, 88% of which were for individuals: Elyse Methven and Samantha Lee, 'Why $5000 COVID Fines Might Backfire' Sydney Morning Herald (16 August 2021) <www.smh.com.au/national/why-5000-covid-fines-might-backfire-20210815-p58iw8.html> accessed 30 October 2021. Further, 34,649 public health order infringements were issued in New South Wales between 1 January and 31 August 2021, of which 34,627 were being prosecuted: Hannah Ryan, 'NSW Police Drop 22 of 34,000 COVID Fines' Canberra Times (16 October 2021) <www.canberratimes.com.au/story/7472034/nsw-police-drop-22-of-34000-covid-fines/> accessed 30 October 2021.

correlate with an overall reduction in the number of people testing positive to the virus.[26]

By creating new criminal offences or applying pre-existing ones, several countries have penalized conduct that has the potential to or does transmit COVID-19.[27] Some laws have specified particular types of behaviour that are proscribed due to their risk of spreading the virus. This is exemplified by sanctions that have been imposed for spitting and/or coughing on others during the pandemic, including in New South Wales,[28] China's Hubei province,[29] and Canada (where this behaviour has been deemed to constitute assault).[30] Other governments have criminalized exposure of other people to COVID-19 generally, which could encompass diverse forms of conduct. Regulations made pursuant to South Africa's *Disaster Management Act 2002*, for instance, provided that 'any person who intentionally exposes another person to COVID-19 may be prosecuted for an offence, including assault, attempted murder or murder'.[31] One individual who attended work following his receipt of a positive COVID-19 test is reported to have been arrested for 'attempted murder' under these rules.[32]

Some people have been prosecuted for criminal offending where they have been alleged to have exposed others to COVID-19 recklessly. For example, an individual on Canada's Prince Edward Island was charged with contravening an order to isolate.[33] Similarly, in New Zealand, a person was charged with assault for propelling spittle towards the face of a person who was immunocompromised by reason of receiving chemotherapy.[34] In other instances, people have been charged with criminal offences that require proof of intent to expose others to or transmit COVID-19. This is illustrated by the potential for charges to be brought under New South Wales's *Public Health (COVID-19 Spitting and Coughing) Order (No 2) 2021* (NSW), which provides that 'a person must not intentionally spit at or cough on' a 'public official' or 'another [specified] worker' 'in a way that would reasonably

---

[26] Canadian Civil Liberties Association (n 22).
[27] Sun and Zilli, 'Part I' (n 3).
[28] Miller (n 9) 34; *Public Health Amendment (COVID-19 Spitting and Coughing) Regulation 2020* (NSW).
[29] Alex Lin, 'Carriers of the Wuhan Coronavirus Face Criminal Charges if They Knowingly Infect Others in Hubei' *CNN* (30 January 2020) <https://edition.cnn.com/asia/live-news/coronavirus-outbreak-01-30-20-intl-hnk/h_f66290a211493ac108b20f9bd7921d1e?utm_source=The+Appeal&utm_campaign=8d62ad4821-EMAIL_CAMPAIGN_2018_08_09_04_14_COPY_01&utm_medium=email&utm_term=0_72df992d84-8d62ad4821-58431075>; see also in India 'Spitting in Public Now an Offence under Disaster Management Act: MHA' *The Economic Times* (15 April 2020) <https://economictimes.indiatimes.com/news/politics-and-nation/spitting-in-public-now-an-offence-under-disaster-management-act-mha/articleshow/75161291.cms> accessed 10 April 2022.
[30] Skolnik (n 1) 153; Eric Mykhalovskiy and others, 'Human Rights, Public Health and COVID-19 in Canada' (2020) 111(6) *Canadian Journal of Public Health* 975, 976–77.
[31] *Regulations Issued in Terms of Section 27(2) of the Disaster Management Act 2002* (18 March 2020) reg 11(6).
[32] Sun and Zilli, 'Part I' (n 3).
[33] Mykhalovskiy and others (n 30) 977.
[34] *Allen v Police* [2021] NZHC 981.

be likely to cause fear about the spread of COVID-19'.[35] In principle, advances in genomic sequencing that have enabled tracing of the sources of COVID-19 infection[36] have the potential to lessen difficulties that existed earlier in the pandemic in establishing the requisite *actus reus* of offences involving transmission of COVID-19 (namely, that the victim contracted COVID-19 from the accused person).[37]

In several states of the United States, behaviour that intentionally exposes others to or spreads COVID-19, or threatens to do so, has been classified as a terrorist offence with COVID-19 being conceptualized as a 'biological agent'.[38] For instance, New Jersey's Attorney-General is reported to have charged a man with making a 'terroristic threat' for coughing at a woman whom he informed he had COVID-19.[39] Likewise, a person who filmed himself licking deodorant sticks in a shop in Virginia was charged with the offence of 'making a terrorist threat in the second degree', which is defined as including 'recklessly [disregarding] the risk of causing the evacuation, quarantine or closure of any portion of a building ... and knowingly ... [causing] a false belief or fear that an incident has occurred or that a condition exists involving danger to life'.[40] Individuals were charged with perpetrating a biological weapons hoax in Florida and Texas, respectively—one was alleged to have stated falsely that they had COVID-19 and coughed on a police officer, and the other was a person who was alleged to have posted a message on social media claiming that he had engaged someone to spread COVID-19 in grocery shops.[41]

B. Implications for Human Rights and the Rule of Law of Criminalizing Conduct Related to COVID-19

Concerns have been raised that, in criminalizing behaviour that could increase the spread of COVID-19 and its harmful effects, some governments have neglected to prioritize human rights and the rule of law, and thus compromised effective responses to the crisis.[42] During the pandemic, many governments have necessarily focused on fulfilling their obligations under the *International Covenant on*

---

[35] *Public Health (COVID-19 Spitting and Coughing) Order (No 2) 2021* (NSW) ord 5(1).
[36] Elias Visontay, 'Genomic Sequencing: What it is and How it's Being Used Against COVID-19 in Victoria' *The Guardian* (5 July 2020) <www.theguardian.com/world/2020/jul/05/genomic-sequencing-testing-coronavirus-what-is-it-how-used-australia-victoria-melbourne-covid-19-clusters-hotspots-outbreak> accessed 4 August 2021.
[37] Skolnik (n 1) 161.
[38] Chad Flanders and others, '"Terroristic Threats" and COVID-19: A Guide for the Perplexed' (2020) 169(4) *University of Pennsylvania Law Review Online* 63, 64; see generally Lucia Binding, 'Coronavirus: Two Charged with Terror Offences Over Threats to Spread COVID-19' *Sky News* (10 April 2020) <https://news.sky.com/story/coronavirus-two-charged-with-terror-offences-over-threats-to-spread-covid-19-11970802> accessed 10 April 2022.
[39] Sun and Zilli, 'Part I' (n 3).
[40] Flanders and others (n 38) 74.
[41] Wojcik and Austin (n 16).
[42] United Nations, *COVID-19 and Human Rights* (n 1) 15–16.

Civil and Political Rights (ICCPR) to protect 'the inherent right to life',[43] and under the *International Covenant on Economic, Social and Cultural Rights* (*ICESCR*) to take steps 'necessary for ... the prevention, treatment and control of epidemic ... diseases' to help realize people's right 'to the enjoyment of the highest attainable standard of ... health'.[44] While criminalizing certain conduct may have assisted governments in this regard, it had the potential to inhibit people from exercising other human rights also enshrined in national and international legal instruments.

In particular, to avoid incurring criminal sanctions, people may have complied with laws that required them to remain in isolation, quarantine, or under curfew or lockdown, which in turn precluded them from exercising their 'right to liberty of movement' and 'right of peaceful assembly', which the *ICCPR* recognizes.[45] Likewise, the imposition of criminal sanctions for disseminating certain forms of information about COVID-19 could have infringed people's exercise of their right also recognized in the *ICCPR* to 'freedom of expression', which includes 'freedom to seek, receive and impart information and ideas of all kinds'.[46]

Moreover, some governments' use and application of the criminal law during this pandemic may not have met preconditions for legitimately restricting these human rights. COVID-19 has posed a major risk to public health and many governments have criminalized conduct that had the potential to aggravate that threat. As discussed in Chapter 5, the *ICCPR* may allow limitations on human rights that address 'a serious threat to the health of the population' by 'preventing disease'.[47] Further, signatories to the *ICCPR* can 'take measures derogating from' their 'obligations' under it if 'faced with a situation of exceptional and actual or imminent danger which threatens ... the physical integrity of the population'.[48] Yet some governments may have had difficulty demonstrating, as required by the *ICCPR*, that their imposition of limitations on the above-mentioned human rights through their use of the criminal law were always strictly necessary to address, and proportionate to, the public health emergency, and were non-discriminatory.[49] It was important for governments to consider and review regularly whether their reliance

---

[43] *International Covenant on Civil and Political Rights* (opened for signature 16 December 1966, entered into force 23 March 1976) 999 UNTS 171, Article 6(1) (hereafter *ICCPR*); United Nations, *COVID-19 and Human Rights* (n 1) 2, 4.

[44] *International Covenant on Economic, Social and Cultural Rights* (opened for signature 16 December 1966, entered into force 3 January 1976) 993 UNTS 3, Article 12.

[45] *ICCPR* (n 43) Articles 12, 21.

[46] United Nations, *COVID-19 and Human Rights* (n 1) 17; *ICCPR* (n 43) Article 19. See also Chapter 9 in relation to regulation of the entitlements of health practitioners and legal practitioners.

[47] UN Commission on Human Rights, *The Siracusa Principles on the Limitation and Derogation Provisions in the International Covenant on Civil and Political Rights* (Resolution E/CN.4/1985/4, 28 September 1984), cl 25 (hereafter *Siracusa Principles*).

[48] ibid cl 39.

[49] Mykhalovskiy and others (n 30) 976–77; *ICCPR* (n 43) Articles 4, 12(3), 19(3), 21, 26; *Siracusa Principles* (n 47); United Nations, *COVID-19 and Human Rights* (n 1) 4.

on the criminal law met these preconditions to encroaching upon human rights;[50] otherwise, governments risked 'normalizing' excessive use of coercive measures for responding to behaviour that could be managed more appropriately and effectively through less punitive means.[51]

Although the aim by governments around the world to inhibit the spread of COVID-19 and its harmful effects was 'legitimate', it was important to ensure that encroachments on human rights through criminalizing certain conduct were not more restrictive and severe than was necessary to achieve it, as required by the *Siracusa Principles*.[52] This was an aspect of the requirement for responses to be proportionate to the risks posed. Medical science and epidemiological data informed many governments' decisions to implement public health measures, as these sources of information indicated that the measures would heighten the chances of reducing the transmission and the detrimental impact of COVID-19.[53]

However, it has been argued that some governments appear not to have relied on such evidence in determining whether it was necessary to penalize violation of public health rules in order to deter this conduct.[54] As highlighted above, it appears that attempts to enforce compliance with public health measures were often ineffective.[55] In Italy, for example, more than 40,000 people were charged with contravening quarantine rules, notwithstanding the threat of a €4,000 fine or a one to five-year prison term for this offence.[56] Likewise, in Canada, between 1 April and 15 June 2020, more than 10,000 fines were issued for violation of various public health rules.[57] It has been argued that use of non-coercive measures—including coherent public health messaging and education—may have been more effective in persuading people to adhere to health measures than imposing criminal penalties.[58] Other suggestions include that governments could have improved rates of compliance with public health rules by addressing factors that influenced them, such as by ensuring that: people who were required to remain in isolation, quarantine, or lockdown had adequate accommodation, food, and other provisions, and financial and social support; masks were available and affordable; and COVID-19 testing was accessible.[59] In addition, some have contended that public

---

[50] Mykhalovskiy and others (n 30) 978; United Nations, *COVID-19 and Human Rights* (n 1) 17.
[51] Sun and Zilli, 'Part II' (n 15); Skolnik (n 1) 155; Starodubov, Vladyshevska, and Pyzhova (n 7) 146.
[52] *Siracusa Principles* (n 47) cls 10–11, 51, 54; *ICCPR* (n 43) Article 4.
[53] See eg *Loielo v Giles* (2020) 63 VR 1, 18 [40]–[41], 25 [70].
[54] Starodubov, Vladyshevska, and Pyzhova (n 7) 154.
[55] ibid 144.
[56] ibid 144–45.
[57] Mykhalovskiy and others (n 30) 977. Notably, substantial fines and costs were also imposed in the case of *AG of Ontario v Trinity Bible Chapel* 2021 ONSC 1169 [78]. In this case, various churches and pastors were found to have engaged in 'flagrant', 'intentional', and 'public' contempt of orders previously made to restrain them from holding gatherings of more than 10 persons.
[58] Starodubov, Vladyshevska, and Pyzhova (n 7) 147; Sun and Zilli, 'Part II' (n 15); Kristina Murphy and others, 'Why People Comply with COVID-19 Social Distancing Restrictions: Self-interest or Duty?' (2020) 53(4) *Australian and New Zealand Journal of Criminology* 477.
[59] Starodubov, Vladyshevska, and Pyzhova (n 7) 147; Sun and Zilli, 'Part II' (n 15). Some or all of these supports were available in some countries, as discussed throughout this book.

condemnation, especially through commentary in social media and other forms of media, of violation of health rules might have had the effect of discouraging this conduct sufficiently to make the threat of criminal sanctions redundant.[60]

Concerns have been expressed about some governments using the health crisis to quash dissent.[61] Some governments may have used what they asserted to be the risk of information worsening the health crisis as a pretext for suppressing public debate about their actions.[62] A tool by which they may have done this, while recognizing that its purpose may have been legitimate in principle, is criminalizing dissemination of false information. Pomeranz and Schwid usefully assembled possible examples of this phenomenon:

> In March 2020, the interim president of Bolivia signed an emergency decree criminalizing acts that 'misinform or generate uncertainty to the population.' Botswana's April 2020 Emergency Powers (COVID-19) Regulations criminalized relaying 'any information to the public about COVID-19 from a source other than the Director of Health Services' or the World Health Organization. Hungary's parliament passed an emergency law that gave the prime minister powers to rule by decree and penalize people who spread 'fake news' about the virus or measures against it. The Philippines 'Bayanihan to Heal as One Act' penalized 'creating, perpetrating, or spreading false information regarding the COVID-19 crisis.' And Zimbabwe enacted a regulation clarifying that the government could prosecute 'any person who publishes or communicates false news' about officials enforcing the national lockdown. People prosecuted under these countries' new laws could be fined and imprisoned for up to 20 years.[63]

To meet the test of strict necessity, a derogation measure should be 'directed to an actual, clear, present, or imminent danger and may not be imposed merely because of an apprehension of potential danger'.[64] However, 'mere' apprehension that spreading fabricated information could lead to the further transmission of COVID-19 and undermine efforts to contain it and minimize its impact, rather

---

[60] Flanders and others (n 38) 66, 87.
[61] United Nations Office of the High Commissioner for Human Rights, 'COVID-19: States Should Not Abuse Emergency Measures to Suppress Human Rights—UN Experts' (16 March 2020) <www.ohchr.org/en/NewsEvents/Pages/DisplayNews.aspx?NewsID=25722&LangID=E> accessed 16 November 2021.
[62] United Nations, *COVID-19 and Human Rights* (n 1) 3, 17; Koltay (n 19) 11–12, 15; Fadhilah Fitri Primandari, 'Democracy and Human Rights During the COVID-19: The Case of Indonesia' (2020) 26(3) *Australian Journal of Human Rights* 529, 532.
[63] Jennifer L Pomeranz and Aaroin R Schwid, 'Governmental Actions to Address COVID-19 Misinformation' (2021) 42(2) *Journal of Public Health Policy* 201, 205. See too Human Rights Watch, 'COVID-19 Triggers Wave of Free Speech Abuse: Scores of Countries Target Media, Activists, Medics, Political Opponents' (Human Rights Watch, 11 February 2021) <www.hrw.org/news/2021/02/11/covid-19-triggers-wave-free-speech-abuse#> accessed 16 November 2021.
[64] *Siracusa Principles* (n 47) cl 54.

than evidence that it would have these effects, might prompt governments to penalize such conduct.

The imposition of criminal sanctions for certain conduct during the pandemic may not only have been unnecessary for, but in fact thwarted achievement of, public health objectives.[65] Arresting and imprisoning those who violated public health rules, for example, would have increased the number of people in custody at a time when it was especially important to lower incarceration rates.[66] As discussed further in Section IV below, the risk of contracting COVID-19 was elevated in prisons.[67] A person held in custody for a short period could contract COVID-19 and infect others after being released into the community.[68] In addition, concerns have been expressed that it was possible that criminalization of exposing others to and transmitting COVID-19 would have the same impact as similar laws that applied to HIV, which increased fear about and stigmatization of people with AIDS, and deterred people with HIV symptoms from undergoing testing and seeking treatment.[69]

The United Nations cautioned that, while 'law enforcement has a role to support the fight against the disease and protect people' and 'coercive measures may be justified in certain situations, they can backfire if applied in a heavy-handed, disproportionate way, undermining the whole pandemic response'.[70] In some circumstances, the restriction of people's capacity to exercise their human rights through criminalizing certain conduct may not have been proportionate to the aim of protecting public health and the 'nature and extent' of the threat that COVID-19 posed to it, as required by the *Siracusa Principles*.[71] Further, it has not always been apparent that any benefits attained from infringing on human rights through use of the criminal law during the pandemic were greater than harm caused by doing so.[72]

It seems that some governments that relied on the criminal law nonetheless attempted to respond proportionately to behaviour that potentially jeopardized public health. This was evident in their stipulation that conduct that risked spreading COVID-19 attracted harsher sanctions if in fact it had this impact.

---

[65] Sun and Zilli, 'Part I' (n 3).
[66] Flanders and others (n 38) 89.
[67] Jessica Bresler and Leo Beletsky, 'COVID-19, Incarceration, and the Criminal Legal System' in Scott Burris and others (eds), *Assessing Legal Responses to COVID-19* (Public Health Law Watch 2020) 230; Jacqueline Beard, 'Coronavirus: Prisons (England and Wales)' (House of Commons Library, Briefing Paper No 8892, 18 May 2020) 1 <https://commonslibrary.parliament.uk/research-briefings/cbp-8892/> accessed 4 August 2021.
[68] Skolnik (n 1) 167–68.
[69] Sun and Zilli, 'Part I' (n 3); Skolnik (n 1) 158–59; see too Matthew M Kavanagh and others, 'Law, Criminalization and HIV in the World: Have Countries that Criminalise Achieved More or Less Successful Pandemic Response?' (2021) 6(8) *BMJ Global Health* art e006315.
[70] United Nations, *COVID-19 and Human Rights* (n 1) 15.
[71] *Siracusa Principles* (n 47) cls 10, 51.
[72] Damian A Gonzalez-Salzberg, 'Protecting Human Rights in the Americas Amid a Pandemic: A Reflection on Resolution 1/2020 of the Inter-American Commission' (2020) 26(3) *Australian Journal of Human Rights* 556, 559.

For instance, in Germany, a person could be imprisoned for up to five years where their violation of quarantine rules resulted in infection of someone else with COVID-19.[73] In other cases, though, there was the risk of imposition of disproportionate penalties.[74] In any event, the imposition of criminal sanctions generally to enforce compliance with public health measures was excessive if, as noted earlier, it was unnecessary for, and other less severe means were as effective, if not more, in stemming the spread of COVID-19 and protecting the public.[75]

The imposition of criminal sanctions for contravention of public health laws during this pandemic in some instances also discriminated against those experiencing various hardships and, consequently, entrenched and exacerbated social inequities.[76] Disadvantaged and marginalized people, who have a high risk of contracting and suffering from COVID-19, have also often had difficulty adhering to public health measures.[77] They may have lacked access to accommodation in which they could quarantine or isolate, or were employed in roles that required them to leave home during lockdowns and that they could not afford to discontinue.[78] The impecunious could not pay for legal counsel to defend them against criminal charges relating to breaches of public health laws,[79] let alone fines imposed for these offences.[80] This left them dependent upon government-funded legal aid, where that existed. A person's failure to pay fines could lead to their incarceration and the debt could undermine their capacity to obtain accommodation in which they could comply with stay-at-home orders.[81] Notwithstanding these issues, homeless people have reportedly been fined for breaching public health laws during the COVID-19 pandemic, for instance, in certain cities in France, Canada, and Australia.[82] As discussed later in this chapter, the threat of criminal penalties for violating stay-at-home orders may also have inhibited some victims of domestic violence from escaping their abusers.

---

[73] Starodubov, Vladyshevska, and Pyzhova (n 7) 145.
[74] ibid 144.
[75] Gonzalez-Salzberg (n 72) 559; Mazepa (n 17).
[76] Mykhalovskiy and others (n 30) 977.
[77] ibid 977; United Nations, *COVID-19 and Human Rights* (n 1) 7; Gonzalez-Salzberg (n 72) 558.
[78] Gonzalez-Salzberg (n 72) 558–60.
[79] Skolnik (n 1) 162.
[80] Mykhalovskiy and others (n 30) 977.
[81] Skolnik (n 1) 177–78.
[82] Mykhalovskiy and others (n 30) 977; Skolnik (n 1) 177; Pauline Bock, 'Coronavirus: France's Homeless "Fined For Not Staying Indoors" During COVID-19 Lockdown' *euronews* (20 March 2020) <https://www.euronews.com/2020/03/20/coronavirus-france-s-homeless-fined-for-not-staying-indoors-during-covid-19-lockdown> accessed 28 May 2022; Christopher Knaus, 'Unfair Covid Fines Causing Hardship and Should Not be Enforced, Advocates Say' *The Guardian* (7 December 2021) <https://www.theguardian.com/australia-news/2021/dec/07/unfair-covid-fines-causing-hardship-and-should-not-be-enforced-advocates-say> accessed 28 May 2022.

C. Changes to the Nature and Rate of Crimes Committed

The COVID-19 pandemic and measures implemented to halt its spread have led to shifts in the type and volume of crimes committed in many countries. Enforcement of stay-at-home orders in particular altered people's opportunities to commit certain kinds of crimes. The introduction of other public health laws also led to criminal offending, not only by virtue of their violation, but also due to disputes regarding compliance with them. Victims of criminal offences whose rate of commission rose during the pandemic have often been those least able to defend themselves, including people trapped in homes that are sites of domestic violence and older people who are isolated and susceptible to becoming victims of offenders. In addition, people of Asian descent have become targets of crimes in non-Asian countries owing to speculation that COVID-19 originated in China. These changes to the nature and rate of criminal offending have highlighted the imperative for governments to focus on upholding the rule of law and protecting those who are especially vulnerable during a public health emergency.

Markedly similar fluctuations in the type and volume of crimes committed following the issuing of public health orders to stay at home have been observed in several countries. During lockdowns, the rates of commission of theft, shoplifting, home burglaries, minor aggravated battery and assault, and minor drug-related offences declined in a range of countries, including the United States, United Kingdom, India, China, Australia, Mexico, Canada, and European countries.[83] These changes have been attributed to restrictions on people's movement and thus opportunities for offenders to commit crimes and, in the case of crimes typically perpetrated by groups of young people, for offenders to congregate and engage in criminal activity together.[84] After lockdowns ended, the volume of commission of these crimes appeared to revert to their preceding levels.[85] By contrast, seemingly there have been no significant changes during the pandemic to rates of homicide and other serious violent crimes, which are often committed by individuals acting alone, but also to the volume of organized crime, including major drug offences.[86]

---

[83] Jose Roberto Balmori de la Miyar, Lauren Hoehn-Velasco, and Adan Silverio-Murillo, 'The U-Shaped Crime Recovery During COVID-19: Evidence from National Crime Rates in Mexico' (2021) 10(1) *Crime Science* art 14, 1-4; Samuel Langton, Anthony Dixon, and Graham Farrell, 'Six Months in: Pandemic Crime Trends in England and Wales' (2021) 10(1) *Crime Science* art 6, 2, 11.

[84] John H Boman IV and Owen Gallupe, 'Has COVID-19 Changed Crime? Crime Rates in the United States During the Pandemic' (2020) 45 *American Journal of Criminal Justice* 537, 540, 542; Langton, Dixon, and Farrell (n 83) 12; Balmori de la Miyar, Hoehn-Velasco, and Silverio-Murillo (n 83) 2-4, 12.

[85] Balmori de la Miyar, Hoehn-Velasco, and Silverio-Murillo (n 83) 2-4; Langton, Dixon, and Farrell (n 83) 13.

[86] Ezekiel Edwards and others, 'The Other Epidemic: Fatal Police Shootings in the Time of COVID-19' (Research Report, American Civil Liberties Union, 2020) <www.aclu.org/sites/default/files/field_document/aclu_the_other_epidemic_fatal_police_shootings_2020.pdf> accessed 30 October 2021; Boman and Gallupe (n 84) 541-42; Balmori de la Miyar, Hoehn-Velasco, and Silverio-Murillo (n 83) 12.

Also, in periods of lockdown, the volume of commission of some types of crimes in fact increased. Some of this offending was opportunistic and the United Nations and certain countries appreciated the importance of trying to pre-empt it. The United Nations cautioned that 'at this time, we need to push back against those who seek opportunistically to use the crisis to further their position or steal through corruption resources intended for the pandemic response'.[87] For instance, a Ukrainian bill sought to create a criminal offence of breaching legislation regarding price setting during the declared state of emergency.[88] Taking advantage of changes to commerce, robberies of businesses that had been forced to close, such as restaurants, rose in the United States.[89] In addition, some offenders turned to forms of crime that they could commit while they and their victims remained at home, including fraud and cyber-crime.[90] Various fraud offences, many of which were committed online or by telephone, increased during the COVID-19 period, including the sending of fraudulent text messages, false online shopping complaints, technical support scams, romance scams, and, as discussed further in Chapter 9, false claims that certain products could protect against contracting or could cure infection from COVID-19.[91] The United States Federal Trade Commission warned early in the pandemic that 'scammers are taking advantage of fears surrounding the coronavirus. They're ... using fake emails, texts, and social media posts as a ruse to take your money and get your personal information'.[92] Some offenders pretended to be undertaking contact-tracing in order to obtain details from victims that they could use to steal their identities or money.[93] Persons were reported to have been charged in the United States with conspiracy to commit 'wire fraud' where they attempted to sell a large volume of surgical marks that did not in fact exist.[94] In one case, an offender advertised on his website and sold stolen COVID-19 test kits, falsely claiming he was connected to laboratories that would test the results, but he did not provide test results to purchasers.[95]

---

[87] United Nations, *COVID-19 and Human Rights* (n 1) 15.
[88] Mazepa (n 17).
[89] Wojcik and Austin (n 16).
[90] Brian K Payne, 'Criminals Work from Home During Pandemics Too: A Public Health Approach to Respond to Fraud and Crimes Against Those 50 and Above' (2020) 45(4) *American Journal of Criminal Justice* 563, 564. See also Steven Kemp and others, 'Empty Streets, Busy Internet: A Time-Series Analysis of Cybercrime and Fraud Trends During COVID-19' (2021) 37(4) *Journal of Contemporary Criminal Justice* 480.
[91] ibid 565.
[92] ibid 566.
[93] Wojcik and Austin (n 16).
[94] Neil Vigdor, 'Two Sought $4 Million for Face Masks That Didn't Exist, US Says' *The New York Times* (27 April 2020) <https://www.nytimes.com/2020/04/27/us/california-coronavirus-ppe-face-mask-scam.html> accessed 28 May 2022. See also United States Attorney's Office Southern District of Texas, 'Local Man Sentenced For $317 Million N95 Mask Scam' (16 February 2022) <https://www.just ice.gov/usao-sdtx/pr/local-man-sentenced-317-million-n95-mask-scam> accessed 28 May 2022.
[95] United States Attorney's Office Western District of Pennsylvania, 'New York City Man Arrested on Fraud Charges for Selling Stolen COVID-19 Testing Services Through His Website, YouHealth, Inc., Without Sending Promised Test Results' (7 May 2020) <https://www.justice.gov/usao-wdpa/pr/

It seems that older people in particular have been victims of fraud, but also other criminal offences during the pandemic.[96] In some instances, including in the United States, they have been targeted by offenders who have attempted to steal money from them by falsely claiming that their relatives needed it for COVID-19-related emergencies, offering them fraudulent medical treatments, proposing to perform errands that they were unable to undertake, or engaging in fraud related to social security administration.[97] Owing to their increased social isolation during the pandemic, older people were especially vulnerable to such fraud, as well as to elder abuse more generally.[98] Their usual carers may have neglected them for fear of contracting COVID-19, and their carers or relatives may have stolen money or goods from them to mitigate economic effects of the pandemic.[99] Oversight of nursing, psychiatric, and other facilities might have been diminished during lockdowns, potentially exposing older people and also people with disabilities to an increased risk of experiencing abuse.[100]

Increases in the commission of another form of crime—domestic violence—during the pandemic, and lockdowns in particular,[101] have similarly reinforced the need to take extra measures to maintain the rule of law and protect those who may be vulnerable during a public health emergency. Anecdotal evidence and data from reports to police and domestic abuse hotlines in many countries, including China, the United Kingdom, United States, and Argentina, have documented this rise.[102] In Victoria, Australia, up to 31 March 2021, there had been an 11.3% increase in

---

new-york-city-man-arrested-fraud-charges-selling-stolen-covid-19-testing-services> accessed 28 May 2022.
[96] Payne (n 90) 565–66, 568.
[97] ibid 568.
[98] ibid 570–71.
[99] ibid 570.
[100] UN Women and others, *Justice for Women Amidst COVID-19* (n 1) 19; World Health Organization, 'Elder Abuse' (Fact Sheet, 4 October 2021) <https://www.who.int/news-room/fact-sheets/detail/elder-abuse> accessed 10 April 2022; Lena K Makaroun, Rachel L Bachrach, and Ann-Marie Rosland, 'Elder Abuse in the Time of COVID-19—Increased Risks for Older Adults and Their Caregivers' (2020) 28(8) *American Journal of Geriatric Psychiatry* 876; S Duke Han and Laura Mosqueda, 'Elder Abuse in the COVID-19 Era' (2020) 68(7) *Journal of the American Geriatric Society* 1386; E-Shien Chang and Becca R Levy, 'High Prevalence of Elder Abuse During the COVID-19 Pandemic: Risk and Resilience Factors' (2021) 29(11) *American Journal of Geriatric Psychiatry* 1152.
[101] United Nations, *COVID-19 and Human Rights* (n 1) 11; Jennifer Koshan, Janet Mosher, and Wanda Wiegers, 'COVID-19, the Shadow Pandemic, and Access to Justice for Survivors of Domestic Violence' (2020) 57(3) *Osgoode Hall Law Journal* 739, 740–41; Boman and Gallupe (n 84) 541; Wojcik and Austin (n 16); Pastilí T Vasquez, *The Impact of COVID-19 on Criminal Justice: System Responses of Gender-based Violence Against Women: A Global Review of Emerging Evidence* (Report, United Nations Office on Drugs and Crime, April 2021) 36–52 <www.unodc.org/documents/justice-and-prison-reform/Assessment_COVID-19_and_CJS_responses_to_GBVAW_23Mar2021.pdf>; Zarizana A Aziz and Janine Moussa, 'COVID-19 and Violence Against Women: Unprecedented Impacts and Suggestions for Mitigation' in Morten Kjaerum, Martha F Davis, and Amanda Davis (eds), *COVID-19 and Human Rights* (Routledge 2021).
[102] Koshan, Mosher, and Wiegers (n 101) 746–47; Boman and Gallupe (n 84) 541; UN Women and others, *Justice for Women Amidst COVID-19* (n 1) 19.

family violence offences, driven by breaches of family violence orders (up 18.4%) and family violence-related assaults (up 5.9%) for the preceding 12 months.[103] Yet this information probably does not reflect the extent of the escalation in domestic violence; under-reporting of this crime, which already occurred before the pandemic, was likely to have been greater during lockdowns, as many victims would have been unable to communicate with people outside their homes (for instance, by telephone or email) without their abusers' knowledge.[104]

Various changes, attributable to the pandemic and public health laws, would probably have contributed to an increase in the commission of crimes of domestic violence. Financial hardship due to job losses and preclusion from working during lockdowns, emotional stress associated with interruptions to usual routines, and restrictions on leaving home, may have intensified tensions within many families.[105] Lockdowns have resulted in victims being trapped with their abusers and prevented from seeking assistance from social services.[106] As noted earlier, victims might have remained in abusive homes to avoid incurring penalties for violating stay-at-home orders. Some may also have been reluctant to escape from violent households to refuges if they were concerned that they could contract COVID-19 there.[107] If they lost employment during the pandemic, victims of domestic violence may have lacked the resources to move away from their homes because they were financially dependent on their abusers.[108] Lockdowns have also enhanced some abusers' capacity to exercise coercive control over their victims, as they were already isolated socially and physically, and would often have had difficulty accessing support.[109]

Disputes over people's contravention of public health orders, and mask-wearing in particular, have also precipitated the commission of criminal offences during the pandemic. For instance, a customer in the United States was reported to have fatally shot a security guard at a store after he stated that her child needed to wear a mask to enter it and, in Germany, a man is reported as having confessed, in a suicide note, to killing his wife and three children after authorities discovered he had faked a vaccination certificate.[110] Also in the United States, a man was convicted of

---

[103] Koob and Butt (n 25).
[104] Koshan, Mosher, and Wiegers (n 101) 750; Boman and Gallupe (n 84) 540; UN Women and others, *Justice for Women Amidst COVID-19* (n 1) 19.
[105] Wojcik and Austin (n 16); Koshan, Mosher, and Wiegers (n 101) 753.
[106] Wojcik and Austin (n 16); Koshan, Mosher, and Wiegers (n 101) 741; Boman and Gallupe (n 84) 541; Santiago M Perez-Vincent and others, *COVID-19 Lockdowns and Domestic Violence* (Report, Inter-American Development Bank, July 2020) <https://publications.iadb.org/publications/english/document/COVID-19-Lockdowns-and-Domestic-Violence-Evidence-from-Two-Studies-in-Argentina.pdf> accessed 10 April 2022.
[107] Wojcik and Austin (n 16).
[108] Koshan, Mosher, and Wiegers (n 101) 754.
[109] ibid 741, 752–53.
[110] Timothy Bella, 'Man Gets 10-Year Sentence for Attacking and Coughing on Person Who Asked Him to Pull up Mask' *The Washington Post* (12 June 2021) <www.washingtonpost.com/nation/2021/06/12/shane-michael-mask-assault-iowa/> accessed 13 July 2021; Emily Crane, 'Dad Murders Family After Being Caught with Fake COVID Vaccine Card' *News.com.au* (8 December 2021) <https://www.

wilful injury causing serious injury and sentenced to ten years' imprisonment for attacking, coughing, and spitting in the face of another man in an optometrist shop who requested him to comply with a public health order requiring mask wearing in 'establishments providing personal services'.[111] The Mayor of Stillwater, Oklahoma, is reported to have felt compelled to modify an order requiring customers to wear masks in stores and restaurants after employees were 'threatened with physical violence and showered with verbal abuse' when they attempted to enforce it.[112]

Also coinciding with the COVID-19 pandemic, and in the United States in particular, has been a rise in the commission of 'hate crimes'. Asian Americans especially reported becoming targets of racially driven attacks, which encompassed verbal harassment, physical violence, and vandalization of and other damage to their businesses.[113] As discussed in Chapter 2, pandemics have often incited xenophobia, scapegoating, and mistreatment of those perceived as foreign, for causing and spreading illness, as Chinese residents of San Francisco experienced during the bubonic plague in 1900.[114] A rise in crimes against Asian Americans appears to be attributable to people linking them with the emergence and transmission of COVID-19.[115] The United States Federal Bureau of Investigation warned of the risk of this occurring, noting, 'a portion of the US public will associate COVID-19 with China and Asian American populations'.[116] Encouraging Americans to connect Chinese people with COVID-19 have been references to the disease as the 'Wuhan', 'Chinese', and 'China' virus in media reports and other public communications by the then United States President Donald Trump and other officials.[117] This nomenclature was at odds with the World Health Organization's guidance to refrain from naming a pandemic after the region in which the disease was first reported to avoid stigmatizing its residents.[118] It also tapped into historical fears and perceptions by some white persons of an association between non-white persons and disease.[119]

The United Nations reminded Member States of their obligations to 'counter discrimination' in the wake of the increase in 'incidents of discrimination, xenophobia, racism and attacks against people scapegoated for spreading the virus'.[120]

---

news.com.au/lifestyle/real-life/news-life/dad-murders-family-after-being-caught-with-fake-covid-vaccine-card/news-story/79edb6737f3e23237a11f9fb99e056c5> accessed 10 December 2021.

[111] Bella (n 110).
[112] Wojcik and Austin (n 16).
[113] Angela R Gover, Shannon B Harper, and Lynn Langton, 'Anti-Asian Hate Crime During the COVID-19 Pandemic: Exploring the Reproduction of Inequality' (2020) 45(4) *American Journal of Criminal Justice* 647, 648, 659; Hannah Tessler, Meera Choi, and Grace Kao, 'The Anxiety of Being Asian American: Hate Crimes and Negative Biases During the COVID-19 Pandemic' (2020) 45(4) *American Journal of Criminal Justice* 636, 640.
[114] Gover, Harper, and Langton (n 113) 652–53.
[115] ibid 648.
[116] Tessler, Choi, and Kao (n 113) 638.
[117] Gover, Harper, and Langton (n 113) 653–54; Tessler, Choi, and Kao (n 113) 637.
[118] Gover, Harper, and Langton (n 113) 653–54.
[119] Tessler, Choi, and Kao (n 113) 640.
[120] United Nations, *COVID-19 and Human Rights* (n 1) 11.

Until recently, however, it was largely activists and community organizations that sought to curb this offending in the United States.[121] Indeed, 12 senators wrote to the United States Commission on Civil Rights expressing their concern about the lack of 'a concerted effort from federal agencies to prevent and address anti-Asian sentiment related to the COVID-19 pandemic'.[122] Finally, however, in May 2021, the United States Congress passed the *COVID-19 Hate Crimes Act*, which defines a COVID-19 hate crime as a violent crime motivated by '(1) the actual or perceived characteristic (e.g., race) of any person, and (2) the actual or perceived relationship to the spread of COVID-19 of any person because of that characteristic'.[123] This statute requires a Department of Justice officer or employee 'to facilitate the expedited review of hate crimes and reports of hate crimes'. It also stipulates that the Department should 'issue guidance for state, local, and tribal law enforcement agencies on establishing online hate crime reporting processes' and 'guidance aimed at raising awareness of hate crimes' during the pandemic.[124] In other countries, existing anti-discrimination laws may also have been relevant.[125]

III. Issues for Criminal Justice Systems

The COVID-19 pandemic and measures implemented to contain its spread have also had a significant impact on many procedural aspects of criminal justice systems across the world. They interrupted usual processes for obtaining legal assistance, accumulating evidence for use in proceedings, and managing and hearing criminal law matters. These changes risked hindering access to justice,[126] with potentially dire consequences for victims of crime, accused persons, and convicted offenders. Even in a public health emergency, access to justice remains fundamental to protecting human rights and maintaining the rule of law.[127] Attempts

---

[121] Tessler, Choi, and Kao (n 113) 642.
[122] As quoted in Gover, Harper, and Langton (n 113) 660.
[123] Congressional Research Service, 'H.R. 6721 (116th): COVID-19 Hate Crimes Act' 34 USC 10101 (2021) (GovTrack, 5 May 2020) <www.govtrack.us/congress/bills/116/hr6721/summary> accessed 10 September 2022.
[124] Congressional Research Service, 'Summary: S.937—117th Congress (2021–2022)' <www.congress.gov/bill/117th-congress/senate-bill/937> accessed 4 August 2021; see also 'Remarks by President Biden at Signing of the COVID-19 Hate Crimes Act' (20 May 2021) <https://www.whitehouse.gov/briefing-room/speeches-remarks/2021/05/20/remarks-by-president-biden-at-signing-of-the-covid-19-hate-crimes-act/> accessed 10 April 2022.
[125] For instance, in Australia, s 18C of the *Racial Discrimination Act 1975* (Cth) states: 'It is unlawful for a person to do an act, otherwise than in private, if: (a) the act is reasonably likely, in all the circumstances, to offend, insult, humiliate or intimidate another person or a group of people; and (b) the act is done because of the race, colour or national or ethnic origin of the other person or of some or all of the people in the group'.
[126] UN Women and others, *Justice for Women Amidst COVID-19* (n 1) 13, 15.
[127] ibid 2.

were made to overcome possible obstacles to access to justice during the COVID-19 pandemic, but they had mixed success.

The COVID-19 pandemic generated a range of obstacles to people obtaining timely access to legal services and to courts determining their charges. The baseline for a meeting of the Organisation for Economic Co-operation and Development (OECD) Global Roundtables on Access to Justice in April 2020 was that increased vulnerabilities were likely to lead to a surge of legal needs and that any pathway for recovery would have to integrate accessible and people-centred justice systems to assist in restoring social cohesion, economies, and confidence in institutions.[128]

The pandemic presented serious challenges for the administration of justice. In many countries, including Australia,[129] Canada,[130] various member states of the European Union,[131] and the United States,[132] courts moved rapidly to online proceedings. However, this was not feasible in all countries. In some other countries a hybrid position was adopted. In South Korea, for instance, a reform bill for Civil Procedural Rules for video-conferencing supported using this technology for pre-trial conferences and pre-trial hearings, subject to both parties' consent, but it was not allowed for the trials themselves.[133]

The continued operation of the courts during the pandemic was important, but access to them was reduced for many due to technical and logistical difficulties. This resulted in problems for many people to have access to decision-making and support services associated with courts. In turn, this caused backlogs, including for jury trials in countries that have juries in criminal matters. Some jurisdictions,

---

[128] OECD, *Impact of COVID-19 on Access to Justice: Online Meeting of the OECD Global Roundtable on Equal Access to Justice* (28 April 2020) <www.oecd.org/governance/global-roundtables-access-to-justice/Final_agenda_28%20April_meeting.pdf> accessed 26 October 2021.

[129] Michael Legg and Anthony Song, 'The Courts, the Remote Hearing and the Pandemic: From Action to Reflection' (2021) 44(1) *University of New South Wales Law Journal* 126; Michael Legg, 'The COVID-19 Pandemic, the Courts and Online Hearings: Maintaining Open Justice, Procedural Fairness and Impartiality' (2021) 49(2) *Federal Law Review* 161; Nigel Stobbs and Ian Freckelton, 'The Administration of Justice During Public Health Emergencies' in Belinda Bennett and Ian Freckelton (eds), *Pandemics, Public Health Emergencies and Government Powers: Perspectives on Australian Law* (Federation Press 2021).

[130] Richard Haigh and Bruce Preston, 'The Court System in a Time of Crisis: COVID-19 and Issues in Court Administration' (2020) 57(3) *Osgoode Hall Law Journal* 869; Kate Puddister and Tamara A Small, 'Trial by Zoom? The Response to COVID-19 by Canada's Courts' (2020) 53 *Canadian Journal of Political Science* 373.

[131] OECD and the Law and Justice Foundation of New South Wales, *Access to Justice and the COVID-19 Pandemic: Compendium of Country Practices* (25 September 2020) 13 <www.lawfoundation.net.au/ljf/site/articleIDs/5BEBDA8F5FA5EF7E852586B100025DB7/$file/oecd-access-to-justice-covid19.pdf> accessed 9 April 2022; Anne Sanders, 'Video-Hearings in Europe Before, During and After the COVID-19 Pandemic' (2020) 12(2) *International Journal for Court Administration* art 3; Costas Popotas, 'COVID-19 and the Courts. The Case of the Court of Justice of the European Union (CJEU)' (2021) 12(2) *International Journal for Court Administration* art 4.

[132] Julie Marie Baldwin, John M Eassey, and Erika J Brooke, 'Court Operations During the COVID-19 Pandemic' (2020) 45(4) *American Journal of Criminal Justice* 743; Alicia L Bannon and Douglas Keith, 'Remote Court: Principles for Virtual Proceedings During the COVID-19 Pandemic and Beyond' (2021) 115(6) *Northwestern University Law Review* 1875.

[133] OECD and the Law and Justice Foundation of New South Wales (n 131) 3.

such as the United Kingdom and Australia, moved some of their trials to online platforms, while countries such as Portugal[134] and Chile extended regimes for authenticating documents and signature acknowledgments online.[135] In civil matters, online mediations in Canada and Australia became standard and it has been suggested that this may become 'the new normal in a post-COVID-19 world'.[136]

The United Kingdom commissioned a 'rapid review' of its move to remote hearings, concluding by June 2020[137] that the transition had gone well, with 71.5% respondents to a survey confirming that they were satisfied with their experience,[138] although 44.7% reported having had technical difficulties.[139] Concern was expressed, though, that the feasibility of people's participation in hearings relied upon lay parties having access to multiple devices and good standards of written comprehension; the absence of these created barriers to effective participation.[140] Concern was expressed that remote hearings had an adverse impact upon both the quality of criminal trials (including where hearings were particularly complex),[141] and the openness of justice, although some journalists reported that their capacity to attend hearings had been improved by their being accessible online.[142]

A joint OECD/Australian analysis of access to justice during COVID-19 emphasized the need to engage proactively with communities, especially with 'vulnerable and marginalised groups such as racial minorities, the elderly, youth, and children, people with disabilities, indigenous people, refugees and migrants', to ensure they were aware of existing supports and how they could gain access to them.[143] This analysis drew attention to initiatives such as the use of traditional media and newspapers to inform people of the availability of support services in Israel, and public awareness campaigns in Chile for women to learn about their options.[144]

In addition, deferrals of pre-trial hearings and trials exposed victims of crimes, including women, children, people with disabilities, and older people, to a risk of experiencing further harm from offenders who were not subject to police or judicial scrutiny. In many countries, including the United States, Canada, the United

---

[134] eportugal, 'COVID-19 Justice' (27 September 2021) <https://eportugal.gov.pt/en/covid-19/justica> accessed 27 October 2021.
[135] OECD and the Law and Justice Foundation of New South Wales (n 131) 39.
[136] Mitchell Rose, 'Mediation by Zoom Addresses Social Distancing, Shuttered Courtrooms' *The Lawyer's Daily* (31 March 2020) <www.thelawyersdaily.ca/articles/18393> accessed 27 October 2021. See also Justin Monahan, 'Enemy at the Gates: Online Dispute Resolution in the Time of COVID-19' *Schulich Law Scholars* (2021) <https://digitalcommons.schulichlaw.dal.ca/cgi/viewcontent.cgi?article=1002&context=lawpostpandemic> accessed 27 October 2021.
[137] Natalie Byrom, Sarah Beardon, and Abby Kendrick, *Rapid Review: The Impact of COVID-19 on the Civil Justice System* (Report, June 2020) <www.judiciary.uk/wp-content/uploads/2020/06/FINAL-REPORT-CJC-4-June-2020.v2-accessible.pdf> accessed 26 October 2021.
[138] ibid 1.15.
[139] ibid 1.17.
[140] ibid 1.22.4.
[141] See *R v Macdonald* [2020] NSWSC 382, [29].
[142] Byrom, Beardon, and Kendrick (n 137) 1.24.
[143] OECD and the Law and Justice Foundation of New South Wales (n 131) 13.
[144] ibid.

Kingdom, Afghanistan, and Uganda, the threat of COVID-19 transmission and stay-at-home orders resulted in the suspension of investigations of allegations of criminal offending, pre-trial hearings, and trials.[145] Among those detrimentally affected by these interruptions were witnesses to and victims of crimes.[146] In addition, due to lockdowns and border closures, on occasions it was not possible for investigations to be undertaken at sites of mass atrocity crimes.[147] Victims of domestic violence in Lebanon confronted barriers to obtaining evidence of abuse they had experienced, as forensic doctors had been reluctant to examine patients for fear of contracting COVID-19.[148]

Delays in running criminal proceedings disadvantaged accused persons, too, especially where their pre-trial detention was protracted as a consequence.[149] Indeed, German courts mostly did not rely on a legislative increase to the maximum term of suspension of a criminal trial before it needed to continue or begin again (from three weeks to three months and ten days) during the pandemic because they did not wish to extend defendants' pre-hearing custody unduly.[150] The postponement of hearings and prolonging of pre-trial incarceration may have encroached on legally recognized human rights, including the right to timely proceedings, of people who are charged with criminal offences. For instance, the *ICCPR* provides that: 'anyone arrested or detained on a criminal charge shall be brought promptly before a judge or other officer authorized by law to exercise judicial power and shall be entitled to trial within a reasonable time or to release'; and 'anyone who is deprived of his liberty by arrest or detention shall be entitled to take proceedings before a court, in order that that court may decide without delay on the lawfulness of his detention and order his release if the detention is not lawful'.[151] According to the *Siracusa Principles*, 'protections against arbitrary arrest and detention ... may be subject to legitimate limitations if strictly required by the exigencies of an emergency situation'.[152] However, they also provide that, even during an 'emergency situation', 'no person shall be detained for an indefinite period of time ... pending

---

[145] UN Women and others, *Justice for Women Amidst COVID-19* (n 1) 15–16; Skolnik (n 1) 155; Sun and Zilli, 'Part I' (n 3); Larysa Bielik and others, 'Features of Criminal Proceedings (Pre-Trial and Trial Investigation) in the Time of Pandemic Covid-19' (2020) 9(2) *Ius Humani Law Journal* 203, 213, 220; Hirad Abtahi, 'The International Criminal Court during the COVID-19 Pandemic' (2020) 18 *Journal of International Criminal Justice* 1069, 1072–73.
[146] Donald Nicolson and Jago Russell, 'Covid-19 and Criminal Justice: Temporary Fixes or Long Term Reform?' in Carla Ferstman and Andrew Fagan (eds), *Covid-19, Law and Human Rights: Essex Dialogues* (School of Law and Human Rights Centre, University of Essex 2020) 207.
[147] Abtahi (n 145) 1072–73.
[148] UN Women and others, *Justice for Women Amidst COVID-19* (n 1) 19–20.
[149] Nicolson and Russell (n 146) 207; Skolnik (n 1) 155.
[150] Christian Ritscher, 'COVID-19 and International Criminal Trials in Germany' (2020) 18(5) *Journal of International Criminal Justice* 1077, 1077–78.
[151] ICCPR (n 43) Articles 9(3)–(4). See also *Convention for the Protection of Human Rights and Fundamental Freedoms* (opened for signature 4 November 1950, entered into force 3 September 1953) 213 UNTS 221, Articles 5(3)–(4) (hereafter *European Convention on Human Rights*).
[152] *Siracusa Principles* (n 47) cl 70.

judicial investigation or trial', and 'any person charged with a criminal offense shall be entitled to ... be informed of the charges promptly'.[153]

Several countries sought to address impediments to timely court proceedings during the pandemic, though they have not always succeeded in preserving access to justice and protecting persons with particular vulnerabilities. Some courts prioritized hearing urgent matters, while postponing other proceedings.[154] Nevertheless, determinations of which matters were pressing may have been contentious and varied between jurisdictions.[155] In certain instances, violation of public health laws might have been deemed most urgent and diverted police and judicial officers' attention from other matters.[156] Convicted offenders' appellate cases in particular may not have been prioritized. Probably less controversial were some courts' decisions to continue hearing proceedings in which the safety of alleged victims of crimes was threatened, and courts' willingness to make urgent interim orders, such as initiating or extending existing protection and restraining orders.[157]

Courts in some jurisdictions continued to hold hearings subject to the implementation of various measures that were intended to minimize the risk of transmission of COVID-19. These included limits on the number of attendees (and especially people who were not participating in the trials),[158] and requirements for attendees to wear masks, physically distance from one another, sanitize their hands, and submit health declarations prior to their attendance.[159] Some German courts built individual transparent booths for participants in trials to occupy.[160] The pandemic resulted in the adoption of a number of other procedural innovations, including the use of physically distanced juries sitting in cinemas and increased use of digital technology.[161] In Victoria, Australia, jury boxes were widened to allow more space between seats and a virtual jury pool was initiated, with empanelment restricted to up to 30 persons in a room, with each potential juror required to walk up to a camera and unmask, allowing for lawyers

---

[153] ibid cls 70(b), (g).
[154] UN Women and others, *Justice for Women Amidst COVID-19* (n 1) 15; Bielik and others (n 145) 211–12, 217; Koshan, Mosher, and Wiegers (n 101) 743; John Sorabji and Steven Vaughan, '"This Is Not A Rule": COVID-19 in England and Wales and Criminal Justice Governance via Guidance' (2021) 12(1) *European Journal of Risk Regulation* 143, 144.
[155] UN Women and others, *Justice for Women Amidst COVID-19* (n 1) 16; Koshan, Mosher, and Wiegers (n 101) 795–96.
[156] Bielik and others (n 145) 220.
[157] UN Women and others, *Justice for Women Amidst COVID-19* (n 1) 5, 15–16, 29; Koshan, Mosher, and Wiegers (n 101) 743, 795.
[158] Ritscher (n 150) 1079; Bielik and others (n 145) 212.
[159] UN Women and others, *Justice for Women Amidst COVID-19* (n 1) 29; Sorabji and Vaughan (n 154) 144, 154.
[160] Ritscher (n 150) 1078.
[161] 'Coming Soon—Juries to Sit in Cinemas' *Scottish Law News* (14 August 2020) <www.scottishlegal.com/article/coming-soon-juries-to-sit-in-cinemas> accessed 30 October 2021.

and the accused person to see their face and exercise their rights of peremptory challenge.[162]

Introduction of these measures did not always succeed in preventing the spread of COVID-19, however. Sufficient physical distancing between attendees at hearings was often not feasible, due to the relatively small size of many courtrooms, the need for parties to have confidential communications with their legal representatives during proceedings,[163] and the high number of participants frequently involved in criminal trials (including the defendant, defence and prosecution legal representatives, witnesses, judges, and jurors).[164] Indeed, 599 people who attended criminal courts in the United Kingdom between 24 November 2020 and 11 January 2021 (including court staff and judges) reportedly contracted COVID-19, which was attributed to crowded courtrooms, failure to wear masks, and accused persons contracting the virus during pre-trial custody.[165]

Although these measures enabled some criminal law hearings to proceed, in certain respects they may still have compromised access to justice. For instance, wearing of masks prevented judges and jurors from viewing and drawing important inferences from witnesses' and defendants' facial expressions and there are a number of limitations to 'distributed hearings'.[166] Restrictions on the number of people who could attend hearings might have prevented those charged with criminal offences from exercising their human right, enshrined in various legal instruments including the *ICCPR*, to a genuinely public hearing.[167] In some criminal trials in the United Kingdom, a number of court rooms were used simultaneously to accommodate and maintain physical distance between all the participants, but this increased the backlog of cases, further delaying hearings.[168]

Due to the risk of transmission of COVID-19 in a courtroom, it was often considered preferable not to assemble juries or a full bench at a hearing, even with health measures in place. In some countries, jury trials were suspended, particularly during lockdowns.[169] Legislation was also passed allowing for trials to proceed adjudicated by judges sitting alone.[170] Nevertheless, this change generated concerns, including in Scotland and parts of Australia, on the basis that it could

---

[162] Tammy Mills, 'Masks, Makeover and Privacy Screens: What Jury Trials Look Like After COVID-19' *The Age* (15 January 2021) <www.theage.com.au/national/victoria/masks-seat-shifting-and-privacy-screens-what-jury-trials-look-like-after-covid-19-20210113-p56tur.html> accessed 30 October 2021.
[163] Ritscher (n 150) 1079; Sorabji and Vaughan (n 154) 144.
[164] Nicolson and Russell (n 146) 211.
[165] Howard Riddle, Anthony Edwards, and Matthew Hardcastle, 'COVID-19 and the Criminal Courts' (2021) 3 *Criminal Law Review* 159, 160.
[166] Ritscher (n 150) 1079.
[167] Sorabji and Vaughan (n 154) 144; *ICCPR* (n 43) Article 14(1); *Siracusa Principles* (n 47) cl 70(g); *European Convention on Human Rights* (n 151) Article 6.
[168] Nicolson and Russell (n 146) 212.
[169] Sorabji and Vaughan (n 154) 153; Nicolson and Russell (n 146) 212.
[170] Riddle, Edwards, and Hardcastle (n 165) 159; Ian Freckelton, 'COVID-19: Criminal Law, Public Assemblies and Human Rights Litigation' (2020) 27(4) *Journal of Law and Medicine* 790, 795.

prevent the accused person from receiving a fair hearing, which is a recognized human right.[171] However, in Australia, in the Supreme Court of the Australian Capital Territory, in *R v Ali (No 3)*,[172] Murrell CJ was at pains to emphasize that a fair criminal trial was not synonymous with a trial before a jury and observed that:

> During an emergency, be it a public health emergency or another sort of emergency, short-term legislation may restrict personal freedom and confer unusually broad powers on administrators. In such times, it is even more important than usual that the courts continue to operate effectively, independently and impartially, and be seen to do so.
>
> It is accepted that, generally, it is preferable that accused persons be tried by a jury. Although a trial by a judge alone will be a fair trial, in a democracy it is preferable that a serious allegation be judged by a body that represents the community. At present that is not possible. Yet the criminal courts must continue to operate. The willingness and capacity of courts to fairly conduct criminal trials is the lodestar by which the effectiveness of the criminal justice system will be seen and judged. It is critical to the maintenance of public confidence in the administration of justice.[173]

Diverse approaches were taken to the temporary expedient of judge-alone trials. In Victoria, Australia, judge-alone trials were only held if each of the accused persons agreed to this occurring, the court was satisfied that each accused person had obtained legal advice on whether to give such consent, and the court considered it in the interests of justice to make the order.[174] Given these hurdles, judge-alone trials hardly ever occurred in that state. In the Australian Capital Territory in Australia, judge-alone trials during the COVID-19 pandemic were introduced if a trial judge concluded that such a procedure: '(a) will ensure the orderly and expeditious discharge of the business of the court; and (b) is otherwise in the interests of justice'.[175] This required analysis of what constituted the 'interests of justice' and was not straightforward. In *R v UD (No 2)*,[176] Elkaim J noted the accused person's lack of consent to a judge-alone trial, and accepted it was a relevant factor, but in *R v Ali (No 3)*,[177] Murrell CJ concluded that 'while regard may be had to the fact that the accused does not consent to trial by a judge alone, much more weight should be attached to whether there are good reasons for the accused's attitude'.[178]

---

[171] Nicolson and Russell (n 146) 211–12; Freckelton (n 170) 795. See eg *ICCPR* (n 43) Article 14(1).
[172] [2020] ACTSC 103 (hereafter *R v Ali (No 3)*).
[173] ibid [91]–[92].
[174] *Criminal Procedure Act 2009* (Vic) s 420D(1).
[175] *COVID-19 Emergency Response Act 2020* (ACT) sch 1, cl 68BA(3).
[176] [2020] ACTSC 90 [42].
[177] *R v Ali (No 3)* (n 172) [108].
[178] ibid [109].

Various courts sought to surmount the above-mentioned problems and continue proceedings during the pandemic by relying on information and communication technology to conduct hearings remotely.[179] In many countries, including the United Kingdom and Australia, legislative and other changes permitted participants in trials to make submissions electronically over email, and attend hearings using audio or audio-visual technology.[180] Yet remote hearings did not necessarily secure access to justice, particularly for accused persons. Defendants who lacked access to and/or were unfamiliar with this technology, or who did not have a private space in which to attend a virtual hearing, would have had difficulty taking advantage of these changes.[181] Further, they might in fact have diminished their capacity to participate effectively in hearings if, for example: their legal representatives were not physically present with them and they were unable to communicate expansively, confidentially, and continuously with them during the trial; requisite technical equipment broke down; their internet connection was poor; they had only a partial view of the hearing and its other participants; and/or they experienced disabilities or mental health conditions that affected their ability to comprehend proceedings occurring remotely and/or express themselves meaningfully using this technology.[182] In addition, there was the risk that witnesses may have been influenced in giving evidence by other people who were hidden from the camera's view or not audible when a telephone was used.[183] However, it might have been easier to make remote than in-person hearings publicly accessible.[184]

In determining whether to hold criminal hearings remotely during the pandemic, certain courts considered some of these issues. For instance, on 23 June 2020, the Presidency of the International Criminal Court published 'Guidelines for the Judiciary Concerning the Holding of Court Hearings During the COVID-19 Pandemic'.[185] It advised that the judges could choose whether to hold hearings remotely, but needed to assess first whether they would comply sufficiently with 'rights and protections under the Rome Statute of the International Criminal Court' and the 'Rules of Procedure and Evidence'.[186] The impact on access to justice of holding a criminal hearing remotely was also evaluated in the New South Wales

---

[179] UN Women and others, *Justice for Women Amidst COVID-19* (n 1) 5, 15, 29; Bielik and others (n 145) 211–12.
[180] UN Women and others, *Justice for Women Amidst COVID-19* (n 1) 5, 15, 29; Bielik and others (n 145) 211–12; Nicolson and Russell (n 146) 207, 211; National Conference of State Legislatures, *COVID-19 and the Criminal Justice System: A Guide for State Lawmakers* (Report, 19 August 2020) <www.ncsl.org/research/civil-and-criminal-justice/covid-19-and-the-criminal-justice-system-a-guide-for-state-lawmakers.aspx> accessed 5 August 2021; *R v Macdonald* [2020] NSWSC 382 [7] (hereafter *R v Macdonald*).
[181] UN Women and others, *Justice for Women Amidst COVID-19* (n 1) 15–16; Bielik and others (n 145) 218; Riddle, Edwards, and Hardcastle (n 165) 160–61.
[182] Nicolson and Russell (n 146) 213; Riddle, Edwards, and Hardcastle (n 165) 161.
[183] Nicolson and Russell (n 146) 213.
[184] Sorabji and Vaughan (n 154) 153.
[185] Abtahi (n 145) 1073.
[186] ibid 1074.

Supreme Court case of *R v Macdonald*.[187] Fullerton J adjourned a criminal trial where the Chief Justice of that Court had directed that 'there be no physical appearances in trial proceedings' due to the threat of transmission of COVID-19. She found that 'the accused's right to a fair trial would be at risk' if the trial continued 'in a virtual courtroom'.[188] The parties had technical difficulties remaining connected to the online hearing, probably due to the high usage of the Court's internet service at that time.[189] Further, Fullerton J accepted that one of the accused persons lacked sufficient skills in computer use and typing 'to provide satisfactory instructions by email' to his legal representative during the hearing, and took into account that his internet connection frequently failed.[190]

As the incidence of various crimes rose during the pandemic, their victims, but also accused persons, often faced new impediments to obtaining legal assistance, though some steps were taken to address them.[191] The operation of services that can help victims of crime obtain legal advice, such as community legal services and domestic violence hotlines, was frequently limited, especially during lockdowns.[192] Even if such services continued to operate remotely, there was the risk that victims may have had difficulty accessing them if they lacked the requisite technology, skills or privacy to do so.[193] Examples of attempts undertaken to meet these challenges are a mechanism, created with the support of the International Development Law Organization, for women experiencing violence in Tunisia to obtain legal assistance online, and the use by Italian police of a telephone application for victims of domestic violence to send messages to police without their abusers' knowledge.[194]

Also during lockdowns, those charged with criminal offending (whether in custody or free) faced additional difficulties in securing legal representation. This had the potential to compromise their right to a fair trial, central to which is the opportunity to communicate confidentially with and defend themselves with the assistance of legal representatives of their choice or free legal assistance if they could not afford to pay for it.[195] In some circumstances, however, information and communication technology was deployed to facilitate contact between accused persons and their legal representatives. For instance, in England and Wales, lawyers were enabled to consult with accused persons who were held in custody and attend police interviews remotely (through phone or videoconferencing).[196]

---

[187] [2020] NSWSC 382.
[188] ibid [29]–[30].
[189] ibid [13], [21].
[190] ibid [24]–[25].
[191] Koshan, Mosher, and Wiegers (n 101) 743.
[192] UN Women and others, *Justice for Women Amidst COVID-19* (n 1) 15; Koshan, Mosher, and Wiegers (n 101) 755.
[193] Koshan, Mosher, and Wiegers (n 101) 755.
[194] UN Women and others, *Justice for Women Amidst COVID-19* (n 1) 27–28.
[195] See eg *Siracusa Principles* (n 47) cl 70(g); ICCPR (n 43) Article 14; *European Convention on Human Rights* (n 151) Article 6.
[196] Nicolson and Russell (n 146) 209.

IV. The Impact of COVID-19 on the Use of Detention and Incarceration

The COVID-19 pandemic also had an impact on decision-making in many countries about whether to remand in custody people accused of committing crimes pending trial, and whether at sentencing to incarcerate offenders and, if so, the duration of detention that should be imposed on people who had been charged with or convicted of criminal offences. The risks of COVID-19 spreading rapidly through prisons and causing suffering and potentially deaths of inmates were clear from the outset of the pandemic[197] and have been well documented.[198]

These risks of infection, in addition to delays in court proceedings attributable to the pandemic and public health measures, incited calls to reduce the incarcerated population.[199] These issues were discussed in Chapter 7. In response to these circumstances, as discussed below, some jurisdictions succeeded in lowering rates of pre-trial detention and did not require certain categories of convicted offenders to serve their full prison sentences. These developments have been welcomed due to longstanding concerns about the implications for human rights of excessive use of incarceration as a criminal law sanction.[200] Yet it appears that, during the pandemic, the human rights to life and enjoyment of the highest attainable standard of health of those still incarcerated were not always adequately protected.[201]

Due to many prisons' lack of adequate ventilation, tightly confined spaces, and overcrowding, physical distancing inside their walls has generally not been feasible.[202] Moreover, during the pandemic, many prisons did not have adequate or sufficient hand sanitizers and personal protective equipment, or tested inmates for infection with COVID-19 before or while they have been imprisoned.[203]

---

[197] Benjamin A Barsky and others, 'Vaccination Plus Decarceration—Stopping Covid-19 in Jails and Prisons' (2021) 384(17) *New England Journal of Medicine* 1583, 1584; Nadine Kronfli and Matthew J Akiyama, 'Prioritizing Incarcerated Populations for COVID-19 Vaccination and Vaccine Trials' (2021) 31 *eClinical Medicine* art 100659; American Civil Liberties Union, 'Flattening the Curve: Why Reducing Jail Populations is Key to Beating COVID-19' *ACLU* (2020) <www.aclu.org/sites/default/files/field_document/aclu_covid19-jail-report_2020-8_1.pdf> accessed 30 October 2021; Hope Metcalf, 'Life and Death in Prisons' in Morten Kjaerum, Martha F Davis, and Amanda Davis (eds), *COVID-19 and Human Rights* (Routledge 2021); Carlos Franco-Paredes and others, 'Decarceration and Community Re-entry in the COVID-19 Era' (2021) 21(1) *Lancet Infectious Diseases* art e11.

[198] See eg Amnesty International, *Forgotten Behind Bars: COVID-19 and Prisons* (Report, 18 March 2021) <www.amnesty.org/en/wp-content/uploads/2021/05/POL4038182021ENGLISH.pdf> accessed 16 October 2021.

[199] United Nations, *COVID-19 and Human Rights* (n 1) 12; Wojcik and Austin (n 16); Sun and Zilli, 'Part I' (n 3); Barsky and others (n 197) 1584.

[200] See eg Skolnik (n 1) 145.

[201] Adelina Iftene, 'COVID-19 in Canadian Prisons: Policies, Practices and Concerns' in Colleen M Flood and others (eds), *Vulnerable: The Law, Policy and Ethics of COVID-19* (University of Ottawa Press 2020) 367, 378–79. See also *Rowson v Department of Justice and Community Safety* [2020] VSC 236.

[202] Sun and Zilli, 'Part I' (n 3); Iftene (n 201) 367, 374; Wojcik and Austin (n 16); Bresler and Beletsky (n 67) 230; UN Women and others, *Justice for Women Amidst COVID-19* (n 1) 24.

[203] Amnesty International (n 198) 4.5; Barsky and others (n 197) 1584; Wojcik and Austin (n 16); Catherine D Marcum, 'American Corrections System Response to COVID-19: An Examination of

COVID-19 was disseminated swiftly through prisons in many parts of the world,[204] without adequate prioritization being given to vaccinating prisoners.[205] Strodel and others have pointed out that the failure to prioritize people who are incarcerated for vaccination will 'deny them access to fundamental health care and place them at risk of morbidity, long-term sequelae, and mortality'.[206]

In the United States, for instance, the COVID-19 infection rate within prisons was almost six times higher than amongst the free population.[207] A major study of United States prisons up to 3 April 2021 found that the standardized mortality rate from COVID-19 per 100,000 persons was 199.6 deaths for the prison population compared to 80.9 deaths for the United States population.[208] Prisoners were particularly susceptible to poor outcomes from contracting COVID-19, too, owing to the high rate among them of comorbid conditions that are risk factors for COVID-19 and their often minimal access to vaccination, adequate health services, and medical treatment.[209] Indeed, it is estimated that prisoners who contracted COVID-19 have been three times more likely than persons in the general community who contract the virus to die from it.[210]

The heightened risks of contracting COVID-19 in prison, and the indefinite suspension of and delays in court proceedings owing to public health measures, influenced decisions to lower the number of accused persons who are detained before trial and the length of pre-trial custody.[211] As noted above, even if accused persons were held in custody for a brief period of time, they had the potential to introduce COVID-19 to the prison if they already had the virus, or contracted it there and spread it to the community on release.[212] Further, the longer defendants were held in custody without a hearing, the greater their chances of conviction, loss of employment and access to housing, and emotional stress.[213] Inmates'

---

the Procedures and Policies Used in Spring 2020' (2020) 45(4) *American Journal of Criminal Justice* 759, 761.

[204] UN Women and others, *Justice for Women Amidst COVID-19* (n 1) 24; Wojcik and Austin (n 16).

[205] See eg Rachel Strodel and others, 'COVID-19 Vaccine Prioritization of Incarcerated People Relative to Other Vulnerable Groups: An Analysis of State Plans' (2021) 16(6) *PLoS One* art e0253208. See Justin Berk, 'Why We Vaccinate Incarcerated People First' (2021) 35 *eClinical Medicine* 100864; Anne C Spaulding and Chad Zawitz, 'Vaccination in Prisons and Jails: Corrections Needed in Future Plans' (2022) 20 *Clinical Infectious Diseases* art ciab1031; Hannah Kim and others, 'The Health Impacts of the COVID-19 Pandemic on Adults Who Expereince Imprisonment Globally: A Mixed Methods Systematic Review' (2022) 17(5) *PLoS One* art e0268866.

[206] See eg Strodel and others (n 205).

[207] Bresler and Beletsky (n 67) 228; Barsky and others (n 197) 1584.

[208] Neal Marquez and others, 'COVID-19 Incidence and Mortality in Federal and State Prisons Compared with the US Population April 5, 2020, to April 3, 2021' (2021) 326(18) *Journal of the American Medical Association* 1865.

[209] Skolnik (n 1) 166; Sun and Zilli, 'Part I' (n 3); Iftene (n 201) 370–71; UN Women and others, *Justice for Women Amidst COVID-19* (n 1) 24.

[210] Barsky and others (n 197) 1584.

[211] Skolnik (n 1) 168.

[212] ibid 167–78.

[213] ibid 156, 164.

fear of contracting COVID-19 in prison also ran the risk of harming their mental health.[214] Consequently, in several countries, including the United States, which has the world's highest incarceration rate,[215] courts and governments released from custody prior to their trials people who had been charged with committing crimes for which, before the pandemic, they would have been held in detention (on remand) until their hearings took place.[216] In some instances, the imposition of non-custodial measures, such as electronic monitoring and/or house arrest of accused, was contemplated in order to ensure the protection of the community prior to court proceedings.[217]

Significant percentages of prisoner populations are made up of pre-trial detainees: for instance, 81.3% of the prison population in Bangladesh;[218] 73.5% in Nigeria;[219] and 69.1% in India.[220] The advent of COVID-19 led some to advocate for significant liberalization of the granting of bail to unsentenced prisoners during the pandemic.[221] In Nigeria, a further step was taken with the Chief Justice identifying to state judges that 52,226 persons in custodial centres were 'Awaiting Trial Persons' for whom new measures needed to be adopted as a result of the pandemic:

> Most of these custodial centres are presently housing inmates beyond their capacities and the overcrowded facilities pose a potent threat to the health of the inmates and the public in general in view of the present circumstances, hence the need for urgent steps to bring the situation under control.
>
> Considering the above, it has become imperative for Your Lordships to embark on an immediate visit to all custodial/correctional centres within your respective States to identify and release deserving inmates, where that has not been done already.
>
> During the requested visit, the Chief Judges are enjoined to consider the conditional or unconditional release of Awaiting Trial Persons who have spent 6 years or more in custody.

---

[214] ibid 165.
[215] Paola Scommegna, 'US Has World's Highest Incarceration Rate' *Population Reference Bureau* (10 August 2021) <www.prb.org/resources/u-s-has-worlds-highest-incarceration-rate/> accessed 5 August 2021.
[216] Bresler and Beletsky (n 67) 229; Wojcik and Austin (n 16).
[217] Skolnik (n 1) 173.
[218] World Prison Brief, 'Bangladesh' (March 2021) <www.prisonstudies.org/country/bangladesh> accessed 30 October 2021.
[219] World Prison Brief, 'Nigeria' (30 August 2021) <www.prisonstudies.org/country/nigeria> accessed 30 October 2021.
[220] World Prison Brief, 'India' (31 December 2019) <https://www.prisonstudies.org/country/india> accessed 30 October 2021.
[221] See eg Rick Sarre, Lorana Bartels, and Toni Makkai, 'We Need to Consider Granting Bail to Unsentenced Prisoners to Stop the Spread of Coronavirus' *The Conversation* (26 March 2020) <https://theconversation.com/we-need-to-consider-granting-bail-to-unsentenced-prisoners-to-stop-the-spread-of-coronavirus-134526> accessed 30 October 2021.

ATPs who have no confirmed criminal cases against them, aged inmates and terminally ill may be discharged.[222]

In determining whether to grant bail to people charged with criminal offences, courts in a number of countries took into account factors associated with the COVID-19 pandemic. In several Australian cases, for instance, courts held that COVID-19 did not itself give rise to a compelling reason for bail, but was a consideration to which the courts needed to have regard when considering the particular grounds of an application.[223] This was particularly so where there were likely to be lengthy delays in bringing a hearing to trial, especially if the delays would be longer than the sentence that might ultimately be imposed, and if the imposition of conditions could ameliorate the risks to the public associated with releasing an accused person from custody.[224] An initiative to address this problem was the introduction of 'Nightingale courts' in England to provide additional courts, as well as to lengthen courts' sitting hours.[225] Another consideration identified was whether the extent to which the COVID-19 crisis may make time in remand more difficult than it otherwise would be, for example, due to isolation of detainees, limits on their contact with family members and friends, or restriction of their opportunities for education and/or rehabilitation.[226]

In the Australian case of *Rakielbakhour v DPP*,[227] Hamill J identified the following 11 factors as being relevant to the application for bail during 2020: (1) 'Gaols and similar institutions are particularly susceptible to the rapid spread of the COVID-19 virus. It is difficult, if not impossible, to enforce or facilitate the kinds of restrictions currently being encouraged upon people in the community'; (2) minimal (at the time) existence of the virus in New South Wales prisons; (3) inmates were 'subject to more onerous conditions of incarceration' without 'personal visits' and with extended periods in their cells; (4) many cases were being adjourned; (5) an eight-week adjournment would occur whether or not the release application was granted; (6) longer delays were likely; (7) it was to be expected

---

[222] 'CJN Orders Speedy Trial of Cases, Decongestion of Custodial Centres' *Channels TV* (15 May 2020) <www.channelstv.com/2020/05/15/cjn-orders-speedy-trial-of-cases-decongestion-of-custodial-centres/> accessed 30 October 2021 (hereafter 'CJN Orders').

[223] Brendon Murphy and Tahli Ferrari, 'Bail in the Time of COVID-19' (2020) 44(4) *Criminal Law Journal* 247; Freckelton (n 170) 794; Natalia Antolak-Saper, 'COVID-19: An Exceptional or Surrounding Circumstance for the Purposes of Bail and Sentencing?' (2020) 30(1) *Journal of Judicial Administration* 81.

[224] See eg *Re Broes* [2020] VSC 128, [46]-[47]; *Re McCann* [2020] VSC 138, [39]; *Re Tong* [2020] VSC 141, [35].

[225] See Mike McConville and Luke Marsh, 'Resuscitating Criminal Courts after COVID-19: Trialling a Cure Worse than the Disease' (2021) 26(2) *International Journal of Evidence & Proof* 103; Rabah Kherbane, 'Covid-19: Entitlement of Defendants Awaiting Trial to Apply for Bail' *Law Society Gazette* (16 April 2020) <www.lawgazette.co.uk/practice-points/covid-19-entitlement-of-defendants-awaiting-trial-to-apply-for-bail/5103885.article>.

[226] *Re Diab* [2020] VSC 196, [14]-[15].

[227] [2020] NSWSC 323, [14].

that inmates waiting in gaol would have 'significant anxiety levels arising from the possibility that the virus is capable of spreading quickly within the prison', if introduced; (8) official information demonstrated an 'exponential' increase in the prevalence of the virus; (9) the number of cases in the community had risen significantly; (10) legislative responses had included the option for release of prisoners by Corrective Services; and (11) jury trials had been suspended and a backlog in trials was developing.

A similar approach was taken in Canada. For instance, in *R v Baidwan*,[228] Skarica J in the Superior Court of Justice in Ontario outlined matters that a court should take into account in 'assessing risk to a detained accused, in the context of whether there has been a material change in circumstances due to the COVID-19 pandemic' that justifies bail review.[229] These include: 'recent reliable data regarding the general risk ... of being infected by COVID-19'; 'the specific risk of an accused due to his/her age and underlying medical conditions'; 'the specific risk of an accused in a particular institution'; 'development of vaccines, cures or technological advances in the testing/treatment of COVID-19'; and 'whether detention is necessary for the protection or safety of the public' because an accused is likely to breach 'social distancing and stay at home rules' if released.[230] In this case, Skarica J refused the application for bail, finding that the accused man had a very low risk of dying from COVID-19 if infected, no inmates at the time had been infected at the detention facility where he was held, and due to his previous infractions when subject to bail terms and probation, he was unlikely to adhere to public health recommendations.[231]

Influencing some courts' determinations about whether to grant bail, as well as their sentencing decisions, was also their recognition of changes made to prison routines, such as confinement of prisoners to their cells for large numbers of hours per day, reduction or suspension of educational and work opportunities, and cessation of contact with friends and loved ones, in response to the pandemic.[232] These modifications, in addition to the heightened risk of contracting and suffering from COVID-19 while incarcerated, especially in prisons experiencing overcrowding, increased the hardship of inmates' experience of incarceration.[233] In 2001, Maycock and Dickson undertook a participatory correspondence study in relation to inmates at the Scottish Prison Estate[234] in order to understand better

---

[228] 2020 ONSC 2349.
[229] ibid [61], [79].
[230] ibid [61].
[231] ibid [75]–[79], [85]–[86].
[232] Freckelton (n 170) 792–94; Stobbs and Freckelton (n 129); Amine Ghram and others, 'COVID-19 Pandemic and Physical Exercise: Lessons Learnt for Confined Communities' (2021) 12 *Frontiers in Psychology* art 618585.
[233] Freckelton (n 170) 792–94; Onyeka Otugo and Brooke Wages, 'COVID-19: The Additional Sentence for the Incarcerated' (2020) 4(1) *Health Equity* 403.
[234] Matthew Maycock and Graeme Dickson, 'Analysing the Views of People in Custody about the Management of the COVID-19 Pandemic in the Scottish Prison Estate' (2021) 17(3) *International Journal of Prisoner Health* 320; Matthew Maycock, '"Covid-19 Has Caused a Dramatic Change to

the experience of being a prisoner during the pandemic. Significantly, they found that COVID-19 was 'transformative for everyday prison life' and that it caused a major reduction to prisoners' perceptions of their autonomy and an increase in their sense of being subject to an oppressive and constrained regime of incarceration. It intensified their feelings of the restrictiveness of imprisonment.[235]

To curb the potential for COVID-19 to be introduced into and disperse within prisons, many prisons confined inmates to their cells more often, and restricted their opportunities to meet visitors, exercise, and engage in work, educational, and rehabilitative activities.[236] Where courts sentenced offenders to prison terms during the pandemic, they sometimes adapted their sentences in light of these matters. For instance, some Canadian courts reduced the duration of prison terms that they imposed at the time of sentencing by giving offenders credit for pre-trial custody they had served or permitted them to serve some of their prison terms on probation.[237] Thus, for instance, in *R v Persad*,[238] Schreck J took into account that the accused had been under prison lockdown for approximately 47% of his time on remand. He accepted Persad's evidence regarding the experience of being confined to a small cell with lack of access to a shower, a telephone, and fresh air, the prison's unsanitary conditions, and the tense atmosphere amongst inmates. This led Schreck J to classify the conditions as 'inhumane' and failing to 'comport with basic standards of human decency',[239] and to accord 'enhanced credit' of 1.5 days for each day the accused spent in lockdown.[240]

Some countries took active measures to reduce the incidence of the imposition of imprisonment during COVID-19. For instance, in Nigeria, the Chief Justice issued a directive to all state judges to impose fines instead of imprisonment for people convicted of less serious offences,[241] while in Spain and Norway, governments increased the availability of electronic monitoring as an alternative to imposition of custodial dispositions.[242] Also in response to these issues, governments in some countries released offenders from prison before they had completed serving their entire sentences, and relied on non-custodial sanctions to protect the public. For example, given the overcrowding in Italy's prisons, its government ordered that inmates who had under 18 months of their prison terms to complete could

---

Prison Life"': Analysing the Impacts of the Covid-19 Pandemic on the Pains of Imprisonment in the Scottish Prison Estate' (2021) 62(1) *British Journal of Criminology* 218.

[235] The authors used the taxonomy in Gresham M Sykes, *The Society of Captives: A Study of a Maximum Security Prison* (Princeton University Press 1958).
[236] Marcum (n 203) 762; Freckelton (n 170) 794, 796; Beard (n 67) 2–3; Iftene (n 201) 373.
[237] Skolnik (n 1) 174.
[238] 2020 ONSC 188.
[239] ibid.
[240] See too *R v OK* 2020 ONCJ 189.
[241] 'CJN Orders' (n 222).
[242] DLA Piper, *A Global Analysis of Prisoner Releases in Response to COVID-19* (Report, 2020) 14.

serve the remainder of their sentences at home under house arrest.[243] Likewise, American federal and state governments released offenders from detention, particularly where they had served the majority of their prison terms and/or had committed low-level or non-violent offences and, in some instances, ordered that they complete their sentences in home confinement or under parole supervision.[244] The British government also released temporarily from prison, subject to electronic tagging, pregnant women, prisoners with children, and other offenders within two months of completing their prison terms, who had been assessed as posing a low risk to public safety.[245] Australian state legislation permitted the release of inmates earlier than the end of their non-parole period,[246] and some Canadian provinces released from prison offenders who had served most of their sentences.[247]

An administrative mechanism adopted to recognize the harshness of sentences during the COVID-19 period and to encourage cooperative behaviour in confinement was a reduction in sentences through the use of 'emergency management days'.[248] This resulted in prisoners in jails in Victoria, Australia, having almost a month deducted from their sentences by January 2021; statistics provided to a committee of the Victorian Parliament showed that 4,927 prisoners had accumulated a total of 129,568 days off their sentences during the COVID-19 lockdown.[249] However, the measure was politically sensitive and was criticized by the opposition Shadow Minister for Corrections as an effective 'get out of jail free card'.[250]

Changes were also made in some countries to conditions of parole and probation to minimize the risk of spreading COVID-19. For instance, in some American states, parole and probation officers used video technology or telephone calls, rather than in-person meetings, to communicate with offenders.[251] In Mysuru, India, jail authorities began releasing prisoners and remandees on 90-day 'COVID-19 parole' to decongest the prison.[252] However, ironically, eight prisoners declined the

---

[243] Andrea Cioffi, 'COVID-19 and the Release of Mafia Bosses: The Importance of Medico-Legal Evaluations' (2020) 60(3) *Medicine, Science and the Law* 239.
[244] Marcum (n 203) 764–65; Wojcik and Austin (n 16); Bresler and Beletsky (n 67) 229.
[245] Beard (n 67) 3–4.
[246] Freckelton (n 170) 792.
[247] Iftene (n 201) 372.
[248] An emergency management day is a day deducted from a prisoner's sentence due to the impact of particular circumstances on a prisoner: see *Corrections Act 1986* (Vic) s 58E(1).
[249] Public Accounts and Estimates Committee, Parliament of Victoria, *Inquiry into the Victorian Government's Response to the COVID-19 Pandemic* (Victorian Government Printer 2021) 286–87 <www.parliament.vic.gov.au/file_uploads/PAEC_59-08_Vic_Gov_response_to_COVID-19_pandemic_YKNbjt2Y.pdf> accessed 30 October 2021.
[250] 'Victorian Prisoners Get Unfair Sentence Reductions as a Result of COVID-19 Restrictions, Opposition Says' *ABC News* (31 January 2021) <www.abc.net.au/news/2021-01-31/get-out-of-jail-free-cards-for-victorian-prisoners-locked-down-/13106620> accessed 30 October 2021.
[251] Marcum (n 203) 764.
[252] Laiqh A Khan, 'Eight Convicts Refuse to Go Home on COVID-19 Parole' *The Hindu* (18 July 2021) <www.thehindu.com/news/national/karnataka/eight-convicts-refuse-to-go-home-on-covid-19-parole/article34706288.ece> accessed 30 October 2021.

offer as they feared the chances of contracting the virus were higher outside prison and that they might not be able to earn a living during the lockdown.[253]

Only a small number of jurisdictions implemented programmes to provide specific support to prisoners who were released in response to COVID-19. DLA Piper reported that 'The new supports were typically minor and involved small grants of financial or in-kind support such as in Nigeria, where the government provided prisoners with small sums of money on release and funded transport back to their home towns'.[254] Further, 'In England and Wales mobile phones were also given to prisoners to ensure they could remain in contact with corrections staff remotely'.[255]

V. Conclusion

This chapter has canvassed some of the significant changes that have occurred to the operation of criminal justice systems in response to the COVID-19 pandemic and attempts to slow its spread and minimize its detrimental impact. These shifts have illuminated some longstanding problems within criminal justice and have the potential to precipitate constructive reforms.[256] The experience of the pandemic has underscored the importance of respecting human rights and maintaining the rule of law to ensure that the health and safety of the 'most vulnerable'—who include victims of crime, accused persons, and convicted offenders—are protected at all times, including during public health emergencies.[257] Particular complexities have been identified in extending bail to and sentencing persons in the course of a pandemic when confinement on remand and in prison may carry especial burdens and risks. Learning from experiences during the COVID-19 pandemic, recognition of human rights and the importance of upholding the rule of law might be reflected in the future in criminal justice systems through: the imposition of criminal sanctions for violation of health measures only in circumstances where it is established that they are effective in deterring breaches of the law; overcoming obstructions to access to justice for victims of crime, accused persons, and convicted offenders, including through the use of technology; the increased use of non-custodial measures that can still protect the public from people who have been charged with and convicted of criminal offending, especially non-violent crimes;[258] and improved conditions for those who are held in custody.

---

[253] ibid.
[254] DLA Piper (n 242) 40.
[255] ibid.
[256] Skolnik (n 1) 146.
[257] United Nations, *COVID-19 and Human Rights* (n 1) 2.
[258] Skolnik (n 1) 146, 148, 174, 179; Marcum (n 203) 765.

9
Civil Liability, Regulation, and Accountability

I. Introduction

The COVID-19 pandemic has posed major and challenging accountability and liability issues for litigation brought against governments, institutions, corporations, employers and, to a lesser degree, individuals. The high incidence of death, ongoing impairment, including through 'long COVID',[1] and economic loss caused by COVID-19 throughout the world has provided an impetus for the institution of significant numbers of civil claims in the courts. Amongst other things, civil claims have been brought by persons who have contracted the virus when they have asserted they should not have done, by dependents of persons who have died of COVID-19, or been adversely affected by its symptoms, and by businesses that have lost revenue as a result of lockdowns or other measures taken by government to inhibit the spread of the virus. The claims have targeted action, inaction, and inadequate action by defendants and sought the award of damages and the securing of injunctive relief to prohibit impugned or dangerous responses to actions engaged in during the pandemic.

The claims have arisen through actions in tort, as well as actions for breach of contract, and have prompted consideration of the capacity of the civil law to deal fairly and responsively with hardships and loss caused by a pandemic. This has raised questions about when indemnity from such actions should be provided to health practitioners and what should be the criteria for the award of compensation when adverse consequences ensue for persons who have been vaccinated at the urging of the State.

---

[1] This is now recognized by WHO: 'Post COVID-19 condition occurs in individuals with a history of probable or confirmed SARS CoV-2 infection, usually 3 months from the onset of COVID-19 with symptoms and that last for at least 2 months and cannot be explained by an alternative diagnosis. Common symptoms include fatigue, shortness of breath, cognitive dysfunction but also others and generally have an impact on everyday functioning. Symptoms may be new onset following initial recovery from an acute COVID-19 episode or persist from the initial illness. Symptoms may also fluctuate or relapse over time.' See World Health Organization, 'A Clinical Case Definition of Post COVID-19 Condition by a Delphi Consensus' (Report, 6 October 2021) <www.who.int/publications/i/item/WHO-2019-nCoV-Post_COVID-19_condition-Clinical_case_definition-2021.1> accessed 14 September 2022.

In addition, discharge of obligations under insurance contracts has become controversial internationally, particularly in respect of business interruption insurance. This has been in the context of businesses sustaining losses against which they have assumed they were protected by insurance. There has been a need too to understand causes of death from the pandemic that have required analysis by forensic pathologists, often in the context of deaths that relatives of deceased persons felt could or should have been avoided. In countries with the institution of the coroner, this has generated inquests in a number of high profile instances that have probed whether different and better action should have been taken to protect persons with particular vulnerabilities. Part of coroners' investigations has been an attempt to learn public health lessons from identified insufficiencies in responses to the pandemic.

In terms of consumer protection, government instrumentalities in a number of countries have sought to inhibit and deter predatory conduct by the unscrupulous who have attempted to profit from the COVID-19 crisis. This has included actions by corporate regulators, regulators of medicines and devices, and consumer protection and fair trading regulators. In addition, entities with responsibility for maintaining professional standards amongst health practitioners, both registered and unregistered, have sought to prevent and deter practitioners who have undermined public health strategies and attempted to use their position of influence to urge members of the public not to believe in the reality of the pandemic or the efficacy of vaccines.

Section II of this chapter deals with actions in tort that have been commenced against governments for failure to respond adequately, for instance, to the risks of penetration of the virus into residential care facilities for older people, and to supervise the disembarkation of passengers from cruise ships where a significant incidence of COVID-19 should have been anticipated. It also examines the potential for future litigation against those who have engaged in careless, intentional, or reckless transmission of the virus. Section III deals with actions in contract for breach of agreements during the crisis. It wrestles with the relevance of the doctrine of frustration of contract and the effect of 'force majeure' clauses on the ongoing operation of contracts whose implementation was obstructed by the virus. Section IV engages with the difficult issues that arise from insurers' disinclination to make payments for unanticipated scenarios relating to COVID-19, such as business interruption, highlighting contrasting approaches taken in England and Australia. Sections V and VI summarize the provision of immunity from legal action, both in tort and contract, for persons harmed by vaccinations and the availability of compensation for harm suffered by persons who have received COVID-19 vaccinations. Section VII scrutinizes medico-legal ramifications of investigations of death by forensic pathologists and medical examiners, as well as important coroners' inquests that have taken place in relation to deaths arising from COVID-19. Section VIII analyses the international response by regulatory agencies to false and misleading representations about treatments or forms of prevention for COVID-19. Section IX reviews prominent actions taken by regulators of health practitioners to dissuade and deter practitioners from engaging in communications that reduce community confidence in public health initiatives to reduce transmission of the virus or that discourage patients from receiving vaccinations against it.

II. Tort Law

The COVID-19 pandemic has generated a range of issues and litigation that are tortious in nature, namely, that constitute actionable civil wrongs. It has been observed that: 'This crisis has the potential to test the boundaries of the law of tort on several fronts.'[2] The testing of such limits is likely to continue to raise issues in respect of the formulation of the duty of care in negligence actions against government, those responsible for aged-care and other residences, as well as employers. There is the potential too (already realized in some countries) for class actions to be brought by cohorts of the community that assert that they have been wrongfully dealt with by those with a responsibility to safeguard their interests during the COVID-19 health crisis. This Section of the chapter examines some examples of tortious actions that might arise from incidents related to COVID-19.

A. Trespass to the Person and Intentional Torts

Trespasses to the person in tort law are constituted by either assault or battery, the first where there is the threat of unwelcome physical contact, the second where the threat is acted upon.[3] With the increase in awareness about the risks of person-to-person contact, the potential for actions for the tort of trespass to the person arises. Similarly, given the risks of transmission of COVID-19 by droplets, deliberate coughing or sneezing by a person who is aware that they have or may have COVID-19, or adoption of an unduly close physical position to another person, may well constitute a trespass to the person.

Conventionally, in such a context, the question posed in respect of the tort of assault is whether the conduct constitutes an act that causes another person to apprehend the infliction of immediate, unlawful harm to their person.[4] It has been held, for instance, that the flashing of a bright light into another's eyes may amount

---

[2] Michael Douglas and John Eldridge, 'Coronavirus and the Law of Obligations' (2020) 3 *UNSW Law Journal Forum* 1, 6.
[3] See Mark Lunney, Donal Nolan, and Ken Oliphant, *Tort Law: Text and Materials* (6th edn, Oxford University Press 2017) 49–57; Rachael Mulheron, *Principles of Tort Law* (2nd edn, Cambridge University Press 2020) 685–748.
[4] See eg *Collins v Wilcock* [1984] 1 WLR 1172, 1177 per Robert Goff LJ.

to battery,[5] so a cough or sneeze by a person who is aware that they have or may have COVID-19 may well constitute an assault. However, in some circumstances, the awareness or belief on the part of the 'victim' that the perpetrator had not contracted COVID may preclude the perpetrator's liability.

Actual physical contact (as against apprehension of it: assault), without consent, can constitute the tort of battery. Throwing water on a person has been held to be battery,[6] as has spitting in a person's face.[7] Consequently, deliberate spitting, but also coughing or sneezing in the direction of another person by a person who is aware that they are or may be infected with COVID-19, may similarly be found to constitute battery.[8]

Whether spitting, coughing, or sneezing deliberately into a person's face during a pandemic would constitute an intentional tort depends on whether it can be proved to have been intended to cause physical harm in the sense of communicating the virus.[9]

B. Negligence

The tort of negligence is committed when it is proved that there is a duty of care, that the duty has been breached, and that the breach of the duty has caused harm.[10] The harm for which there can be recovery in tort may be physical, emotional, economic, or mental harm that is suffered by the individual concerned or their dependents. Mental harm (formerly termed 'the tort of nervous shock') in the form of a recognized psychiatric disorder, as a result of what has happened to someone close to them, usually a relative, can be compensable. Engaging in conduct where a foreseeable outcome is facilitation of the transmission of an infectious disease may amount to tortious conduct because it could constitute the breach of a duty of care to a person who would foreseeably suffer adverse consequences from such a breach.

A variety of scenarios have the potential to give rise to an action for negligence in the context of a pandemic. Tort law has been described as a 'social mediator' that balances the conflicting interests of individuals in order to achieve a 'desirable

---

[5] *Kaye v Robertson* [1991] FSR 62, 68 [3].
[6] *Pursell v Horn* (1838) 8 Ad & E 602, 112 ER 966.
[7] See *R v Cotesworth* (1704) 6 Mod 180, 87 ER 928; *Majindi v Northern Territory* [2012] NTSC 25.
[8] See Chapter 8. An instance of such a scenario was asserted when the Cardiff coroner was informed in the course of an inquest into the death of a worker at the University Hospital of Wales, that the deceased man had been approached by a patient from a mental health unit, who claimed to have COVID-19 and coughed on him. Ultimately, the coroner found that there was not sufficient evidence to establish that this was the cause of death: see John Jones, 'Dad-of-two Hospital Worker Aged Just 55 Died with Covid' *WalesOnline* (6 December 2021) <www.walesonline.co.uk/news/wales-news/hospital-worker-died-covid0cardiff-22379270> accessed 15 May 2022.
[9] See Douglas and Eldridge (n 2) 8–9.
[10] See Mulheron (n 3) 35–121.

social result'.[11] This highlights the need for tort law to adjust to deal with new social connections and to impose liability where there is culpability for which there ought to be compensation to a person who has been adversely affected. It has been observed that, 'To be stricken with disease through another's negligence is in legal contemplation as it often is in the seriousness of consequences no different from being struck with an automobile through another's negligence.'[12] Liability for reckless or negligent transmission of sexually communicable diseases has been recognized for many years,[13] in spite of the fact that such liability raises a range of challenges for relationships and for the role of the law,[14] including issues arising from the voluntary assumption of risk. It is therefore inevitable and appropriate that the tort of negligence will play a significant role in determining as a matter of legal principle whether there have been breaches of duties to take suitable steps to protect against foreseeable risks during a pandemic such as COVID-19 when such breaches have caused harm and loss.

Further, the potential exists for negligence law to be a catalyst for significant improvements in areas such as working conditions and in the care of persons such as those living in congregate circumstances, for instance residential care,[15] and for those who undertake travel (such as on cruise ships) that brings them into close proximity to other people when infection is reasonably foreseeable. A failure to provide suitably safe working conditions, including personal protective equipment (PPE), hygiene facilities, and arrangements for physical distancing may constitute actionable negligence. So too may a failure to institute safe living circumstances for persons living in congregate care who are especially vulnerable to contracting and suffering from COVID-19. If, during the pandemic, for instance, an aged-care residential home or a prison failed to follow procedures formulated by government for the safe care of residents, this may well constitute a breach of their duty of care. Should persons contract the virus as a result of such a compromise to the obligation to take reasonable measures to provide a safe living environment, this could constitute actionable negligence.

---

[11] See William L Prosser, *Handbook of the Law of Torts* (4th edn, West Publishing Co 1971) 14–15; see too Daniel Hemelk and Daniel B Rodriguez, 'A Public Health Framework for COVID-19 Business Liability' (2020) 7(1) *Journal of Law and the Biosciences* lsaa074.

[12] *Billo v Allegheny Steel Co* 195 A 110, 111 (PA 1937).

[13] See eg William S Donnell, 'You Wouldn't Give Me Anything, Would You? Tort Liability for Genital Herpes' (1983) 20(1) *California Western Law Review* 60; Louis A Alexander, 'Liability in Tort for the Sexual Transmission of Disease: Genital Herpes and the Law' (1984) 70(1) *Cornell Law Review* 101; Timothy J Hasken, 'A Duty to Kiss and Tell? Examining the Uncomfortable Relationship between Negligence and the Transmission of HPV' (2010) 95 *Iowa Law Review* 985; Douglas W Baruch, 'AIDS in the Courts: Tort Liability for the Sexual Transmission of Acquired Immune Deficiency Syndrome' (1987) 22(2) *Tort & Insurance Law Journal* 165.

[14] See Deana A Pollard, 'Sex Torts' (2007) 91(3) *Minnesota Law Review* 769 ; Deana Pollard Sacks, 'Intentional Sex Torts' (2008) 77(3) *Fordham Law Review* 1051.

[15] See Nicolas P Terry, 'How COVID-19 Could Drive Improvements in Care Facilities: Part II' *Harvard Law School Petrie-Flom Center* (10 June 2020) <https://blog.petrieflom.law.harvard.edu/2020/06/10/covid19-nursing-homes-care-facilities-part-2/> accessed 14 September 2022.

This reality has led to the institution of class action lawsuits based on allegations of negligence as a result of how authorities have managed the pandemic. An early example was an action involving approximately 2,500 (mostly German) tourists in Austria against the response to the pandemic in the sports resort of Ischgl in Tyrol province.[16] The Austrian Consumer Protection Association, Verbraucherschutzverein (VSV), which brought the action, maintained that the tortious conduct consisted of an unacceptably delayed response to the beginning of the COVID-19 pandemic and that, while the outbreak constituted a frustrating event, keeping a ski resort open when the authorities should have known of the risk of mass infection constituted actionable negligence.[17] Such actions are often brought in tort for negligence and also in contract for breach of an implied term of the contract to provide facilities that maintain the health and safety of persons involved.

A large number of class actions in relation to persons contracting COVID-19 that have their foundation in negligence have been initiated. Over 1,400 class actions were filed in Canada in 2020 alone.[18] Some class actions initiated in Australia have related to deaths in nursing home facilities where it has been claimed on behalf of relatives of deceased persons that a duty of care towards residents was breached by the facilities.[19] Another has arisen as a shareholder class action out of the handling of business interruption claims,[20] allegedly triggering an emergency raising of capital and propelling an insurer into deficit.[21]

A prominent category of these actions arises from alleged dilatoriness in cruiseliners' suspension of operations between 9 and 26 March 2020 and consequent endangerment of their passengers.[22] The dilemma was global. John Ioannidis, a Stanford University epidemiologist, observed: 'Cruise ships are like an ideal experiment of a closed population. You know who is there and at risk and you can measure everyone.'[23]

---

[16] See Nadine Schmidt, 'Austrian Officials Face Lawsuit from 2,500 Tourists over Ski Resort Outbreak' *CNN Travel* (1 April 2020) <https://edition.cnn.com/travel/article/austria-ski-resort-ischgl-coronavirus-intl/index.html> accessed 14 September 2022.
[17] See ibid.
[18] Pierce Atwood, 'Class Action Litigation Related to COVID-19: Filed and Anticipated Cases in 2020' (Alert, 3 September 2021) <www.pierceatwood.com/alerts/class-action-litigation-related-covid-19-filed-and-anticipated-cases-2020> accessed 14 September 2022.
[19] See Lyle Steffensen, 'COVID-19 Class Actions Against Aged Care Providers' *Marsh* (2021) <www.marsh.com/au/risks/pandemic/insights/aged-care-covid-19-class-actions.html> accessed 14 September 2022.
[20] See Section IV.
[21] See Charlotte Grieve, 'Extraordinary Oversight: IAG Faces Class Action over COVID-19 Bungle' *Sydney Morning Herald* (29 November 2021) <www.smh.com.au/business/companies/extraordinary-oversight-iag-faces-class-action-over-covid-19-bungle-20211129-p59cyt.html> accessed 3 March 2022.
[22] See Angela T de Paula and Vanie BM Herédia, 'COVID-19 and Cruise Ships: A Drama Announced' (2020) 47 *Études Caribéennes* <https://doi.org/10.4000/etudescaribeennes.20047> accessed 3 March 2022.
[23] See Smriti Mallapaty, 'What the Cruise-ship Outbreaks Reveal about COVID-19' (2020) 580(7801) *Nature* 18; Eilif Dahl, 'Coronavirus (Covid-19) Outbreak on the Cruise Ship Diamond Princess' (2020)

Cruise ships were stranded in the early stages of the pandemic in many parts of the world. A prominent example of civil action taken by passengers on such cruise ships is an Australian action against the owner and operator of the Ruby Princess cruise ship. The statement of claim alleged that there was a failure to take appropriate measures to ensure that the passengers were safe and protected from contracting COVID-19 on the ship. It asserted that this failure arose from breaches of the cruise owner and operator's duty of care to its passengers, as well as breaches of consumer guarantees and other provisions under the *Australian Consumer Law*.[24] Over 700 passengers were diagnosed with symptoms of COVID-19. The passengers on the Ruby Princess included citizens from multiple countries. Similarly, actions have been instituted against the owners of the cruise ships, the Diamond Princess,[25] on which 712 people contracted COVID-19 and 13 died, and the Grand Princess.[26]

Of course, during a pandemic, there are limits to the preventative actions that can be taken where the incidence of transmission of a virus is high. Tort law is flexible and generally avoids the unreasonable imposition of liability; it is capable of addressing rigorously whether a defendant's duty of care in particular, even unusual, circumstances is established on the balance of probabilities. In addition, some tort legislation provides scope for a defendant to argue that they bear no duty of care in some situations. For instance, section 5B of the *Civil Liability Act 2002* (NSW) in the Australian state of New South Wales provides that:

(1) A person is not negligent in failing to take precautions against a risk of harm unless:
    (a) the risk was foreseeable (that is, it is a risk of which the person knew or ought to have known), and
    (b) the risk was not insignificant, and
    (c) in the circumstances, a reasonable person in the person's position would have taken those precautions.

71(1) *International Maritime Health* 5; Wai Leung and others, 'Presumed COVID-19 Index Case on Diamond Princess Cruise Ship and Evacuees to Hong Kong' (2020) 27(5) *Journal of Travel Medicine* taaa073.

[24] See *Karpik v Carnival PLC (The Ruby Princess) (Stay Application)* [2021] FCA 1082.

[25] See Eisuke Nakazawa, Hiroyasa Ino, and Akira Akabayashi, 'Chronology of COVID-19 Cases on the Diamond Princess Cruise Ship and Ethical Considerations: A Report from Japan' (2020) 14(4) *Disaster Medicine Public Health Preparedness* 506.

[26] See Hugo Martin, 'Death on the High Seas: Cruise Passengers Face Head Winds with COVID Lawsuits' *Los Angeles Times* (3 November 2021) <www.latimes.com/business/story/2021-11-03/covid-cruises-lawsuits-maritime-law-princess-battles> accessed 3 December 2021.

(2) In determining whether a reasonable person would have taken precautions against a risk of harm, the court is to consider the following (amongst other relevant things)--
   (a) the probability that the harm would occur if care were not taken,
   (b) the likely seriousness of the harm,
   (c) the burden of taking precautions to avoid the risk of harm,
   (d) the social utility of the activity that creates the risk of harm.

In principle, this may enable some defendants to mount a plausible argument that in their particular circumstances it was reasonable for them to have acted as they did, namely, not to take precautions (or at least certain precautions) against a foreseeable risk of harm, because of the burden that would have been posed by taking such precautions. Generally, the exceptional circumstances in which persons (including healthcare practitioners) have been required to provide services are likely to be taken into account by courts in determining whether there has been a breach of a duty of care. As Poole has observed:

> Some negligent conduct will have nothing to do with the crisis; it will just be plainly negligent. In other cases, the courts might find that, notwithstanding the pressures placed upon them by the crisis, a defendant has even so given unacceptably poor care to a patient. The expected standards of care will reflect the stresses imposed on the particular healthcare providers and professionals, but those standards may yet be breached by unacceptably poor care.[27]

It can confidently be said that COVID-19 tort litigation mounted by persons who contend that they have contracted the virus, themselves or indirectly (such as by a person upon whom they are financially dependent having contracted it), will require curial analysis globally about where to fix the limits of foreseeability and obligation to respond to risks of a pandemic and its effects on identifiable cohorts of the community.

III. Contract Law

To take into account the potential for frustration of a contract, it is common for contracting parties to incorporate clauses within their agreements that address supervening events that have the potential to frustrate the contract in the sense of making fulfilment of the terms of the contract physically, legally, or commercially

---

[27] Nigel Poole, 'Coronavirus and Clinical Negligence' (2020) 25(3) *Journal of Patient Safety and Risk Management* 97, 98.

impossible. These clauses, generally referred to as force majeure clauses, take different forms—in construction contracts, for instance, a contractor adversely affected by a force majeure event is often entitled to extra time to complete the contract but not necessarily to be remunerated for it.[28]

The concept of force majeure is not generally recognized as a stand-alone legal concept; it is the product of commercial agreement between contracting parties. The concept of force majeure has its origins in Roman law,[29] but it has become globally ubiquitous.[30] It is described in French law as an event that prevents a party from performance, as it is irresistible and unforeseeable. Article 1218 of the French Civil Code provides that an event of force majeure justifies the suspension or termination of a contract, even if the contract does not contain a provision to that effect. To a similar effect, section 1511(2) of the Californian Civil Code in the United States provides that

> The want of performance of an obligation, or of an offer of performance, in whole or in part, or any delay therein, is excused by the following causes, to the extent to which they operate ... 2. When it is prevented or delayed by an irresistible, superhuman cause, or by the act of public enemies of this state or of the United States, unless the parties have expressly agreed to the contrary.

A pandemic raises confronting issues for society about the enforceability of contractual arrangements at a time when financial relationships are profoundly disrupted and the availability of labour is reduced, whether that be attributable to illness, death, quarantine arrangements, or stay-at-home orders. As noted in Chapter 2, the Black Death prompted many changes to the law,[31] including to industrial law through the *Ordinance of Labourers 1349* (Eng) and then the *Statute of Labourers 1351* (Eng),[32] the role of the Court of Chancery, and the law of contract. Conditional bonds with punitive terms also became more common as a mechanism to ensure adherence to contractual commitments.[33] More latterly, Article 79

---

[28] J Hunter Robinson and others, 'Use the Force? Understanding Force Majeure Clauses' (2020) 44(1) *American Journal of Trial Advocacy* 1, 6–7; Andrew A Schwartz, 'Frustration, the MAC Clause, and COVID-19' (2022) 55 *University of California Davis Law Review* 1771.

[29] Robinson and others (n 28) 2–6.

[30] See eg John W Carter, *Contract Law in Australia* (7th edn, LexisNexis Butterworths 2018) 776; Fareya Azfar, 'The Force Majeure "Excuse"' (2012) 26(2) *Arab Law Quarterly* 249; Peter J Mazzacano, 'Force Majeure, Impossibility, Frustration and the Like: Excuses for Non-performance; the Historical Origins and Development of an Autonomous Commercial Norm in the CISG' (2011) 2 *Nordic Journal of Commercial Law* 1.

[31] See Robert C Palmer, *English Law in the Age of the Black Death, 1348–1381: A Transformation of Governance and Law* (University of North Carolina Press 1993).

[32] See Michael Bennett, 'The Impact of the Black Death on English Legal History' (1995) 11 *Australian Journal of Law and Society* 191.

[33] See Katy Barnett and Matthew Harding, 'Contract in the Time of COVID-19' in Belinda Bennett and Ian Freckelton (eds), *Pandemics, Public Health Emergencies and Government Powers: Perspectives on Australian Law* (The Federation Press 2021).

of the *United Nations Convention on Contracts for the Sale of Goods* specifies that there are three main requirements for the invocation of inability to perform contractual obligations: they must be beyond parties' control; they must not be foreseeable at the time of the execution of the contract; and they must not be able to be avoided or overcome.[34]

It is likely that the evolution of contract law will be given a fillip by COVID-19 with a rethinking of the doctrine of frustration of contract and of the effect of force majeure provisions in light of the incidence of parties defaulting on agreements into which they entered prior to the commencement of the pandemic. Yet there has been some resistance to revisiting fundamental legal principles in one-off cases and the question has been raised as to whether this should be the responsibility of legislatures. For instance, Richard Salter QC, sitting as a Deputy Judge of the High Court of England and Wales in *TKC London Ltd v Allianz Insurance PLC*,[35] commented:

> Some readers of this judgment may ... have the instinctive reaction that an 'all risks' business interruption policy ... ought in justice to provide cover to [small and medium enterprises] ... against the significant damage to their businesses caused by government measures such as the Coronavirus Regulations, which have been implemented for the benefit of everyone but which have had their most damaging effect on particular sectors. Some may also argue that the common law should therefore change its approach to such policies, and should adapt its principles of contractual interpretation and implication to the present unprecedented circumstances, so that they assist in transferring the burden of the present emergency to those, such as insurance companies and other major financial institutions, who may perhaps better be able to bear it. However, as the authors of the BIICL Concept Note '*Breathing Space*' wisely observed: 'In times of uncertainty, the law must provide a solid, practical and predictable foundation for the resolution of disputes and the confidence necessary for an eventual recovery ... Contractual rights are to be evaluated by applying settled principles to the contract in question. Legal certainty remains paramount and gives the surest basis for resolution ...'[36]

During the pandemic, some contracts ceased to be able to be performed (or at least were made much more difficult to perform) because the circumstances had

---

[34] *United Nations Convention on Contracts for the International Sale of Goods* (opened for signature, 11 April 1980, entered into force 1 January 1988) 1489 UNTS 3<www.jus.uio.no/lm/un.contracts.international.sale.of.goods.convention.1980/79.html> accessed 1 November 2021. See S Esra Kiraz and Esra Y Üstün, 'COVID-19 and Force Majeure Clauses: An Examination of Arbitral Tribunal's Awards' (2020) 25(4) *Uniform Law Review* 437.
[35] [2020] EWHC 2710 (Comm), [133].
[36] See too *Bank of New York Mellon (International) Ltd v Cone-UK Ltd* [2021] EWHC 1013 (QB), [251]–[252].

radically changed from what the parties had agreed upon when they entered into their agreements. In these circumstances, some claimed that it was possible to assert as a matter of principle 'non haec in foedera veni. It was not this that I promised to do'.[37] Such a characterization constitutes frustration of the contract and automatically brings the contract to an end.

Most contracts, though, including those which are international trade contracts, contain one form or another of a clause enabling parties to be excused from their obligations when they are prevented from performance, either completely or partially, by defined events or circumstances.[38] These are forms of force majeure clauses. Questions have arisen as to whether such clauses extend to cover the ramifications of the COVID-19 pandemic. Force majeure clauses can also provide a right for contractual termination, most often if the force majeure event subsists for a defined period. In these circumstances, the clauses may specify which party is to retain the benefit of monies paid or work done under the contract upon termination. Normally, the defined events that are required to occur are matters that are beyond the reasonable control of either party.

Because of the disproportionality between the likelihood and impact of such events, force majeure clauses are negotiated between parties as a part of allocating risks between them. Force majeure clauses take different forms—in construction contracts, for instance, a contractor adversely affected by a force majeure event is often entitled to extra time for completion of the contract but not necessarily to extra remuneration for the costs involved.[39]

Another aspect of force majeure clauses is that they require a party to be put on notice as to what has occurred and its impact upon contractual performance. Some of the time, in fact, the requirement is more demanding. A force majeure provision commonly mandates the party affected to give a specific form of notice within a designated time of the occurrence of a relevant event indicating its relevance for their performance of their contractual obligations. Compliance with a notice requirement, including within the designated time frame, may be a condition precedent; it depends on the contractual terms.[40]

---

[37] *Davis Contractors Ltd v Fareham Urban District Council* [1956] AC 696, 729. See too *Codelfa Construction Pty Ltd v State Rail Authority of New South Wales* (1982) 149 CLR 337, 357 (Mason J), 408 (Brennan J).
[38] See Anthony Groom, 'Force Majeure Clauses' (2004) *AMPLA Yearbook* 286.
[39] William J Shaughnessy, William E Underwood, and Chris Gazenave, 'COVID-19's Impact on Construction: Is There a Remedy? Time Extension, Force Majeure, or More?' (2020) XII(134) *National Law Review* <www.natlawreview.com/article/covid-19-s-impact-construction-there-remedy-time-extension-force-majeure-or-more> accessed 14 September 2022; Douglas V Bartman, 'Force Majeure in Construction and Real Estate Claims' *American Bar Association* (17 July 2020) < https://www.americanbar.org/groups/litigation/committees/commercial-business/articles/2020/spring2020-force-majeure-construction-real-state-claims/> accessed 14 September 2022.
[40] Robinson and others (n 28) 7.

The party that relies upon the force majeure event generally has the burden of proving the frustrating event.[41] They must therefore prove not only that the event occurred, but that it had a frustrating outcome, including one that is more than temporary or 'just' challenging.[42] Similarly, these clauses will be subject to the *contra proferentem* rule, which stipulates that any ambiguity in the term of a contract must be construed against the party that is seeking to rely on the term. The result is that a force majeure clause is construed strictly[43] and, to the extent of any ambiguity in its terms, is interpreted against the interests of the party that seeks to rely on it. A force majeure term will usually state expressly that the force majeure event must be an event that is beyond the reasonable control of either party. However, if it does not, such a term may be implied into the contract. For instance, a seller of generic goods is not usually relieved, even by a force majeure clause, from a duty to appropriate such goods simply because a particular source of supply becomes unavailable or there is a shortage of materials, especially if it can be overcome at a cost. In some jurisdictions, such as the United States, a force majeure event cannot retrospectively alter an unfulfilled contractual obligation for which complete performance was due prior to the force majeure event.[44]

It is unlikely that a pandemic would satisfy the term 'an act of God', to which many force majeure clauses refer and that more conventionally consists of 'elementary forces of nature unconnected with the agency of man or other cause',[45] such as storms, flooding, lightning, or heavy snowfalls. Notably, in a decision by the Royal Court of Jersey, COVID-19 was described by the Commissioner not as a force majeure but 'akin to force majeure'.[46] Importantly, during the COVID-19 pandemic, it is not only the impact of the virus, but also laws, orders, and directions from government and the executive, that might prevent performance of contracts. This raises complex questions requiring close construction of contractual terms and the parties' intention.

An example of this phenomenon in the context of force majeure clauses (with the potential for relevance to COVID-19 litigation) occurred in *Kyocera Corp v*

---

[41] See eg *Channel Island Ferries Ltd v Sealink UK Ltd* [1988] 1 Lloyd's Rep 323; *North Queensland Pipeline No 1 Pty Ltd v QNI Resources Pty Ltd* [2021] QSC 190, [1110].

[42] See generally *Gulf Oil Corp v FERC*, 706 F 2d 444 (3rd Cir 1983); *Associated Acquisitions, LLC v Carbone Properties of Audobon, LLC* 962 So 2d 1102, 1103–1104 (La Ct App, 2007); *South32 Aluminium (RAA) Pty Ltd v Alinta Sales Pty Ltd* [2015] WASC 450, [34]. In respect of COVID-19, see *Bank of New York Mellon (International) Ltd v Cine-UK Ltd* [EWHC 1013 (QB)]; *Salam Air SAOC v Latam Airlines Groups SA* [2020] EWHC 2414 (Comm). In *Dwyer (UK Franchising) Ltd v Fredbar Ltd* [2021] EWHC 1218 (Ch), a force majeure clause granted a franchisor the power to designate an event as 'a supervening event'. The franchisor refused to designate COVID-19 as such an event because the emergency plumbing business was an essential service and could still operate during lockdowns. The Court disagreed, holding that the franchisor had fallen below the standard of acting honestly, genuinely, and in good faith by failing to make such a designation.

[43] See eg *LNCP002 Pty Ltd v Feridun Akcan* [2021] NSWSC 848.

[44] See eg *Wartsila Diesel, Inc v Sierra Rutile, Ltd* WL (ED Pa, Civ A 95-2958, 16 December 1996).

[45] *Nugent v Smith* (1876) 1 CPD 423, 444.

[46] *Representation of Pearmain re St Clement Parish Elections* [2021] JRC 213, [10].

Hemlock Semiconductor, LLC,[47] where the force majeure controversy occurred in the aftermath of a Japanese solar manufacturer entering into a 'take-or-pay' contract with a United States supplier of silicon used to make solar panels. After the execution of the contract, the Chinese government provided subsidies to its domestic manufacturers to make the Chinese products more price-competitive. The response of the United States government was to impose retaliatory tariffs on Chinese solar panels. When this 'trade war' resulted in a dramatic reduction in the price of silicon, the Japanese manufacturer informed its supplier that it would cease payments under the take-or-pay contract because the actions of the Chinese government, and the response of the United States government, constituted a force majeure event. The manufacturer sought a declaration that the force majeure provision excused its failure to perform its contractual obligations. However, the trial court, and the appellate court,[48] declined the relief, finding that the position of the manufacturer was that the depression in prices in the solar panel market caused it to lose profitability rather than conduct by the Chinese and United States governments. The reasoning in this case has the potential to be applied in the complex commercial oscillations during and in the aftermath of the COVID-19 pandemic.

By contrast, in *International Minerals & Chemical Corp v Llano, Inc*,[49] a force majeure clause was found to have been properly invoked. A mining facility that purchased natural gas under a take-or-pay contract became subject to new government-imposed emission controls, which compelled it to decommission processing equipment that consumed about six percent of its natural gas requirements under the contract that provided that if the facility was 'unable to receive gas as provided ... an appropriate adjustment in the minimum purchase requirements ... shall be made'.[50] The Tenth Circuit Court in the United States concluded that it was necessary to construe 'unable', not in a literal sense but in a way which comported with the contractual intention of the parties so that it meant 'impracticable'. It concluded that the change in emission standards and the resulting operational changes to the facility rendered it 'unable, for reasons beyond its reasonable control, to receive its minimum purchase obligation of natural gas', with the result that the force majeure provision excused it from paying 'for any natural gas it did not take'.[51]

If comparable reasoning were applied in the context of the COVID-19 pandemic, given the stay-at-home obligations imposed repeatedly by governments in many parts of the world, a plausible argument may well be made that force majeure clauses in many contracts had the potential to be invoked, upon the giving of proper and timely notice. Thereafter, the obligation of the party invoking the

---

[47] 886 NW 2d 445 (Mich Ct App, 2015).
[48] ibid 450.
[49] 770 F 2d 879 (10th Cir, 1989).
[50] ibid 883–84.
[51] ibid 887.

clause was to engage in suitable efforts at mitigation. However, it can confidently be predicted that the efforts made by persons seeking to rely on force majeure clauses to mitigate their losses during the pandemic will fall under close scrutiny by the courts.

IV. Construction of Insurance Contracts

COVID-19 and the public health measures taken by governments have caused heavy financial burdens for many businesses, which have looked to their insurance policies to cover their losses arising from interruption to their work. Large numbers of insurance claims have been made around the world by business owners with insurers frequently declining to pay on the ground that their policies do not cover effects, or at least certain effects, of the pandemic. Important, but not wholly consistent, guidance has been provided by decisions of the United Kingdom Supreme Court and the Australian Federal Court on the issue. More decisions in many countries are likely to be delivered. The issues raised go to how insurance contracts should be interpreted in the context of a global health crisis which of its nature has been responsible (both directly and indirectly) for heavy losses for all sectors of the world's economies.

A. United Kingdom Jurisprudence

The United Kingdom Supreme Court's judgment in a test case in relation to coverage of insurance policies for COVID-19-related losses was delivered in 2021. The case was brought by the Financial Conduct Authority for the benefit of shareholders, many of whom were small and medium enterprises, under the Financial Markets Test Case Scheme.[52] The defendants were eight insurers that were the leading providers of business interruption insurance. Business interruption policies operate on the basis that the insured can recover financial losses caused by the relevant insured peril for an indemnity period as stipulated in the policy. Typically, the insured peril is physical loss of or damage to property (damage clauses). If, for instance, an insured hotel is damaged as a result of a fire, the existence of the material damage confers the right to recover both repair costs and consequential business insurance losses. Insurance for lost revenue may also be offered through an extension to the policy (non-damage clauses), so that, irrespective of any physical damage, cover for pure business insurance losses might still be available.[53]

---

[52] *The Financial Conduct Authority v Arch Insurance (UK) Ltd* [2021] UKSC 1 (hereafter 'the *Arch Insurance* decision').

[53] See generally Paul McHugh, 'Business Interruption Insurance in the Time of COVID-19: Who Should Foot the Bill?' (2021) 29(2) *Journal of Law and Policy* 491.

The aim of the proceedings which resulted in the *Arch Insurance* decision was to achieve as much clarity as possible for the maximum number of policy-holders and their insurers, consistent with the need for expedition and proportionality.[54] The approach taken by the Court was to consider a representative sample of standard form business interruption policies in the light of agreed and assumed facts. 'In addition to the particular policies chosen for the test case, some 700 types of policies across over 60 different insurers and 370,000 policy-holders were anticipated to be affected by the outcome of the litigation.'[55]

The issue traversed in the judgment was the proper interpretation of four types of clauses, which are found in the wording of many policies:

(i) 'Disease clauses': clauses providing cover for business interruption losses resulting from the occurrence of a notifiable disease, such as COVID-19, at or within a specified distance of the business premises);
(ii) 'Prevention of access clauses': clauses providing cover for business interruption losses resulting from public authority intervention preventing or hindering access to, or use of, the business premises);
(iii) 'Hybrid clauses': clauses combining the main elements of the disease and prevention of access clauses); and
(iv) 'Trends clauses': clauses providing for business interruption loss to be quantified by reference to what the performance of the business would have been had the insured peril not occurred).

The plurality (Lord Hamblen and Lord Leggatt, Lord Reed agreeing) noted that disease clauses provide indemnity for notifiable diseases, which include cholera, typhus, plague, yellow fever, and Severe Acute Respiratory Syndrome (SARS), all of which, like COVID-19, are capable of spreading rapidly and widely.[56] The list was also open-ended so that if at any time a new disease emerged as a threat to public health, it could be added, as happened with COVID-19. An outbreak of such a disease could potentially affect a substantial number of businesses and cause interruption to businesses over a wide area:

> a risk clearly contemplated by the policy, which recognises that the occurrence of a notifiable disease up to 25 miles away might lead to interruption of business at the insured premises. The parties must also have contemplated that the authorities would be likely to take action in response to an outbreak of a notifiable disease as a whole, and not to particular parts of an outbreak, and that it would be

---

[54] The *Arch Insurance* decision (n 52) 3.
[55] Ibid. See generally McHugh (n 53).
[56] The *Arch Insurance* decision (n 52) [57]; *Djokovic v Minister for Immigration, Citizenship, Migrant Services and Multicultural Affairs* [2022] FCAFC 3 (hereafter *Djokovic*: Full Court)..

irrelevant to any action taken whether cases fell within or outside a line 25 miles away from the insured premises.[57]

The plurality provided important definitional guidance in relation to key terms and therefore to the scope of insurance coverage. It held that 'prevention means stopping something from happening or making an intended act impossible and is different from mere hindrance', 'but that in the context of closing the dining part of a restaurant which remained open to takeaway custom access to a discrete part of the premises or access to the premises for a discrete purpose will have been completely stopped from happening'.[58] The plurality also found that 'inability to use' premises in terms of entitlement to coverage could include a policy-holder's inability to use either the whole or a discrete part of its premises for all or a part of its business activities.[59] It held that the ordinary meaning of 'interruption' is:

> quite capable of encompassing interference or disruption which does not bring about a complete cessation of business or activities, and which may even be slight (although it will only be relevant if it has a material effect on the financial performance of the business). Furthermore, the possibility that interruption may be partial is inherent in the policy provisions which deal with the calculation of loss and which envisage that the business may continue operating during a period of interruption but with reduced income or increased costs of working.[60]

The Supreme Court held that all individual cases of COVID-19 that had occurred by the date when government-ordered measures were put into place were equally effective proximate causes of loss. Accordingly, policy-holders needed only to establish that there was at least one case of COVID-19 within the relevant geographical area set out in the policy. It rejected the insurers' argument that one event cannot in law be a cause of another unless it can be said that the second event would not have occurred in the absence of ('but for') the first.[61] Thus, in respect of certain of the insurance policies, a key clause ('the public authority clause') was found to have the effect of indemnifying the policy-holder against the risk of all the elements of the insured peril acting in causal combination to bring about business interruption loss; but it did so regardless of whether the loss was concurrently caused by other (uninsured but non-excluded) consequences of the COVID-19 pandemic which was the underlying or originating cause of the insured peril. This constituted a significant win for insured policy-holders.[62]

---

[57] The *Arch Insurance* decision (n 52) [57].
[58] ibid [151].
[59] ibid [134].
[60] ibid [138].
[61] ibid [182], [195], [220], [228].
[62] ibid [243].

The Supreme Court held that trends clauses should not be construed so as to take away cover for losses prima facie covered by the insuring clauses on the basis of concurrent causes of those losses which do not prevent them from being covered by the insuring clauses.[63] The trends for which clauses require adjustment were held not to include circumstances arising out of the same underlying or originating cause as the insured peril. Thus, there was no need to adjust losses actually suffered on the basis that if the insured peril (COVID-19) had not occurred, the results of the business would still have been affected by other consequences of the COVID-19 pandemic.[64]

In important respects, the Supreme Court rejected contentions on behalf of insurers to read down standard clauses which would have had the effect of precluding an insured's recovery of losses for business interruptions occasioned as a result of the pandemic.

B. Australian Jurisprudence

In Australia, the law in respect of the operation of business interruption clauses has not been determined finally, but there have been two important decisions on this issue.

In the first decision, *HDI Global Security SE v Wonkana No 3 Pty Ltd*,[65] the first, second, and third defendants were insured against interruption to their tourist park business between February 2020 and February 2021 under a business interruption policy issued by HDI. The retail business of the fourth defendant was insured under a similar policy between May 2019 and May 2020 by Hollard. Each of the policies provided cover for interruption of business caused by outbreaks of certain infectious diseases within a 20 kilometre radius of the insured's premises (the Disease Benefit clauses). In both policies, the extension was subject to an exclusion clause in relevantly indistinguishable terms. In the HDI policy, the exclusion clause read:

> The cover ... does not apply to any circumstances involving 'Highly Pathogenic Avian Influenza in Humans' *or other diseases declared to be quarantinable diseases under the Australian Quarantine Act 1908 and subsequent amendments*.[66]

On 16 June 2016, well before the period of cover for either policy commenced, the *Quarantine Act 1908* (Cth) was repealed and the *Biosecurity Act 2015* (Cth) came

---

[63] ibid [264].
[64] ibid [288].
[65] [2020] NSWCA 296.
[66] ibid [11] [emphasis added].

into force. The *Biosecurity Act* did not provide for declarations of quarantinable diseases by the Governor-General. Instead, in certain circumstances, the Director of Human Biosecurity was able to classify a disease as a 'listed human disease'. Before the repeal of the *Quarantine Act 1908* (Cth), COVID-19 was not declared to be a quarantinable disease. However, on 21 January 2020, COVID-19 was determined to be a listed human disease under the *Biosecurity Act 2015* (Cth).[67]

The defendant insured parties claimed indemnity from HDI and Hollard under the Disease Benefit clauses in their respective policies for business interruption caused by COVID-19. Those claims were declined. By a summons filed in the Supreme Court of New South Wales, the insurers commenced proceedings seeking declarations that on the proper construction of each clause, the words 'declared to be a quarantinable disease under the *Quarantine Act 1908* (Cth) should be read so as to cover diseases under the *Biosecurity Act 2015* (Cth)'. However, they did not succeed. The Court of Appeal held that COVID-19 was not a disease 'declared to be a quarantinable disease under the *Quarantine Act 1908* (Cth) and subsequent amendments', and accordingly was not excluded from the Disease Benefit clauses.[68] Special leave to appeal to the High Court of Australia was declined.

The second significant Australian authority on the issue arose from litigation in the Federal Court of Australia in *Swiss Re International Se v LCA Marrickville Pty Ltd*.[69] It involved nine separate policy-holders, each of which had been issued a commercial insurance policy containing a business interruption coverage section. In her judgment at first instance, Jagot J held that closure or restriction orders from the Commonwealth or state governments were not made as a result of disease, damage or threat at or near the insured parties' premises. To this extent, she did not apply the reasoning in the United Kingdom's *Arch Insurance* case:

> it cannot be concluded in the context of these matters that each and every known case of COVID-19 in any location in a State was an equally effective cause of the State government actions (in contrast to the threat or risk to each and every person in a State presented by known and unknown cases of COVID-19 given its highly contagious nature).[70]

Jagot J was unable to conclude on the facts that any State Government action was caused by, or resulted from, or was in consequence of, the existence of any case of COVID-19 at the location or within the area required by the insuring provisions.[71] To the extent that any insuring provision required the action of an authority to be caused by, to result from, or be in consequence of an occurrence or outbreak

---

[67] ibid [13].
[68] ibid [121].
[69] [2021] FCA 1206.
[70] ibid [79]–[80].
[71] ibid [81].

of COVID-19 at a specific location or within a specified area, she could not reach such a conclusion. In particular, she was unable to find that each and every case of COVID-19, including any case within the area required by the insuring clause, was an equally effective cause of the taking of the state government action.[72] That meant that Jagot J concluded that the relevant state government actions were caused by the existence of COVID-19 cases in the state (known) and the associated threat or risk of COVID-19 to persons (from cases both known and unknown) across the state as a whole. Thus, she inferred that the state government acted because it knew cases of COVID-19 existed in certain (but not all) locations in the state and because it considered that there was a threat or risk of COVID-19 to persons (from cases both known and unknown) across the state as a whole.[73]

On this basis, it was Jagot J's view that the state government actions were caused by, or resulted from, or were in consequence of, the threat or risk of COVID-19 to persons in each and every part of the state including at or within the location or area required by the insuring provisions. Accordingly, an insuring provision requiring the action of the authority to be caused by or result from or be in consequence of the threat or risk of infectious or contagious disease at a location or within a specified area was satisfied, as the threat or risk to each and every person was an equally effective cause of the action of the state government.[74]

In dealing with the application of the principles of causation and trends in business clauses to the assessment of loss, the distinction between Commonwealth and state meant that, in the case of action of the Commonwealth government, the cause or fortuity (chance event) underlying the insured perils was different from the cause or fortuity underlying the uninsured perils. The insured perils concerned action of an authority caused by, resulting from or in consequence of infectious or contagious diseases at a location or within a specified area—that was not the same as the cause of the uninsured peril if that uninsured peril involved the actions of the Commonwealth government, involving actions caused by the existence of COVID-19 cases overseas and the threat this presented to Australia by reason of persons (including travelling Australian residents) from overseas entering Australia.[75]

As such, cover was not available to the insured parties under the business interruption clauses. Most of the policy-holders operated across the sectors most affected financially by the presence of the COVID-19 pandemic in Australia. Those included gymnasiums, cafes, restaurants, health, travel, and hospitality industries. While all policy-holders asserted they had been adversely affected by the pandemic, each industry type faced its own unique difficulties. Cafes, for instance,

---

[72] ibid.
[73] ibid.
[74] ibid [82].
[75] ibid.

recorded losses where foot traffic was reduced. Travel agencies recorded losses where international travel bans had been imposed.

Jagot J took note of the idiosyncrasies of each policy-holder's business and issued a reminder that no two policy-holders would experience the identical factual circumstances. She also noted that the insurance policies in question—although similar—differed in some ways from one another. The insuring provisions of each policy could be categorized as one of four types:

- Prevention of Access Clauses—these clauses provided cover where the order or action of a competent authority prevented or restricted access to insured premises because of damage or a threat of damage to property or persons (often within a specified radius of the insured premises);
- Disease Clauses—these clauses covered loss arising from the presence or outbreak of infectious disease at the insured premises or within a specified radius of the insured premises;
- Hybrid Clauses—these were a hybrid of the first two, providing cover for loss where the orders/actions of a competent authority had closed or restricted access to premises, and the orders/actions were made or taken as a result of the presence or outbreak of infectious disease within a specified radius of the insured premises;
- Catastrophe Clauses—these clauses provided cover to a policy-holder when he or she suffered loss resulting from the action of a civil authority during a 'catastrophe' for the purpose of retarding the catastrophe.[76]

She held that only the Disease Clause was capable of providing cover in the circumstances. None of the Hybrid, Prevention of Access, or Catastrophe Clauses would be activated in respect of the COVID-19 pandemic for a number of reasons. The primary reason was that none of the orders of the Commonwealth or state governments were made as a result of the particular presence or outbreak of COVID-19 at the relevant policyholder's premises. Jagot J identified—in the case of one particular policy-holder—that there could be cover for policies where there was an identified case of COVID-19 at the premises and that was the cause of loss. However, in those circumstances it would also be up to the particular policy-holder to show that the cause of their loss was the presence of COVID-19 and not some other cause such as an international travel ban. Inevitably, there was a risk that this would not be an easy burden to discharge and therefore would limit effective recourse to the policy.

In short, the *Swiss Re International Se judgment* determined that in many cases policy-holders would not be entitled to coverage under the Hybrid, Prevention of Access, or Catastrophe Clauses save in very specific circumstances. Where

---

[76] Ibid [99].

policy-holders could identify specific considerations (such as the actual presence of COVID-19 or an order directed to that particular policy-holder to close their business premises), they would then have several further matters to establish, including: the loss resulting from that particular matter, that there is no exclusion that would preclude cover, and that their loss had not been otherwise compensated—for instance, by way of government benefits made to compensate for losses during the pandemic. The decision of Jagot J was appealed to the Full Court of the Federal Court with a judgment delivered in February 2022.[77] The Full Court upheld the decision of Jagot J in all save two matters. The first was as to whether, if an insured was entitled to recover, it would need to account for certain payments or government benefits received from third parties. The Full Court also came to a different view as to the payment of interest by an insurer, in the event that an insurer was liable to provide indemnity. Special leave to appeal this decision has been sought from the High Court of Australia but at the time of writing the decision is reserved. However, the essence of the position in Australia, unless it is reversed by the High Court, is that, by contrast with the position in the United Kingdom under the *Arch Insurance* decision, most business interruption policies will not be regarded as providing cover for losses caused by a pandemic. In turn, this will have major ramifications for the role of business interruption insurance policies internationally.[78]

C. The Interpretive Issue

However, there is a broader international issue—how insurance policies should be interpreted in the context of a pandemic. Knutsen and Stempel have argued convincingly against engaging in a literalist or dictionary-focused interpretation of insurance policies in such a context, instead contending that equitable and predictable insurance coverage determinations require a contextual assessment grounded in the role of insurance as a risk-based financial instrument, and giving effect in an integrative way to the intent, purpose, and operation of key clauses.[79] Broadly characterized, the *Arch Insurance* decision has taken this approach, but thus far decisions in Australia have not.

---

[77] LCA Marrickville Pty Ltd v Swiss Re International SE [2022] FCAFC 17.
[78] See Elena Nebolsina, 'The Impact of the Covid-19 Pandemic on the Business Interruption Insurance Demand in the United States' (2021) 7(11) *Heliyon* art e08357.
[79] Erik S Knutsen, 'The COVID-19 Pandemic and Insurance Coverage for Business Interruption in Canada' (2021) 46(2) *Queen's Law Journal* 431; see too Erik S Knutsen and Jeffrey W Stempel, 'Infected Judgment: Problematic Rush to Conventional Wisdom and Insurance Coverage Denial in a Pandemic' (2021) 27 *Connecticut Insurance Law Journal* 185; Christopher C French, 'COVID-19 Business Interruption Insurance Losses: The Cases for and Against Coverage' (2020) 27 *Connecticut Insurance Law Journal* 1; Jeffrey W Stempel and Eric S Knutsen, 'Rejecting Word Worship: An Integrative Approach to Judicial Construction of Insurance Policies' (2021) 90(2) *University of Cincinnati Law Review* 562.

V. Immunity for Healthcare Workers

During the COVID-19 pandemic, an issue that proved controversial (and the subject of litigation in New York,[80] Florida,[81] New Jersey, and Michigan) was whether immunity from negligence actions should be bestowed on health practitioners for acts or omissions undertaken in good faith when working in the exceptionally challenging environment of provision of healthcare[82] during a pandemic.[83] Issues of potential unfairness, in the absence of such protection, arose when hospitals were experiencing shortages of staff and essential equipment, pressures on clinicians were extreme, and doctors and nurses who were not fully qualified, or retired practitioners, were being asked to perform clinical functions.[84] It has been argued that it is reasonable in such exceptional circumstances to recognize the reality of altered operations in a healthcare emergency and not appropriate to impose a test for a duty of care applicable during ordinary times.[85]

Generally, though, it is rare for special protection to be given to a class of defendants for the reason that their fulfilment of their professional obligations is particularly challenging[86] and this has played a role in rendering such protection highly unusual internationally. Notably, section 3215 of the *Coronavirus Aid, Relief, and Economic Security Act* of 2000 (US)[87] provided an extension of protection to

---

[80] See Wendy Teo, Lawrence H Brenner, and B Sonny Bal, 'Medicolegal Sidebar: Legal Immunity for Healthcare Workers During COVID-19' (2020) 478(10) *Clinical Orthopaedics and Related Research* 2218.

[81] See Butler Weihmuller Katz Craig LLP, Paola Solano, and Eric Zivitz, 'Florida's New COVID-19 Liability Protection Legislation: What it Means and the Legal Effect Moving Forward' *JDSupra* (6 April 2021) <www.jdsupra.com/legalnews/florida-s-new-covid-19-liability-5501778/> accessed 5 December 2021.

[82] See Kieran Duignan and Chloe Bradbury, 'Covid-19 and Medical Negligence Litigation: Immunity for Healthcare Professionals?' (2020) 88(1 Supp) *Medico-Legal Journal* 31; Owen Bowcott, 'Union Seeks Legal Immunity for NHS Medics in Pandemic' *The Guardian* (19 April 2020) <www.theguardian.com/society/2020/apr/19/coronavirus-nhs-risks-facing-billions-of-pounds-in-negligence-claims#main content> accessed 4 October 2022.

[83] See too Medical Defence Union, 'MDU Calls for National Debate over Protecting NHS from COVID-19 Clinical Negligence Claims' (Press Release, 20 April 2020) <www.themdu.com/press-centre/press-releases/mdu-calls-for-national-debate-over-protecting-nhs-from-covid-19-clinical-negligence-claims> accessed 14 September 2022; Christine Tomkins and others, 'Should Doctors Tackling Covid-19 be Immune from Negligence Liability Claims?' (2020) 370 *British Medical Journal* m2487; Hilary Young, 'Governments Shouldn't Shield Essential Workers from COVID-19 Lawsuits' *The Conversation* (4 October 2020) <https://theconversation.com/governments-shouldnt-shield-essential-workers-from-covid-19-lawsuits-146514> accessed 14 September 2022.

[84] James Todd and Emma Corkill, 'Standards of Care during COVID-19' *Local Government Lawyer* (24 April 2020) <www.localgovernmentlawyer.co.uk/healthcare-law/174-healthcare-features/43475-what-standard-of-care-should-hospitals-be-held-to-in-the-covid-19-outbreak> accessed 14 September 2024. See too I Glenn Cohen, Andrew M Crespo, and Douglas B White, 'Potential Legal Liability for Withdrawing or Withholding Ventilators During COVID-19' (2020) 323(19) *Journal of the American Medical Association* 1901.

[85] See eg Viorel Rotila, 'Physicians Professional Immunity in the COVID-19 Pandemic: Problems and Solutions' (2021) 12(1Sup1) *Postmodern Openings* 356.

[86] See Rob Heywood, 'Systemic Negligence and NHS Hospitals: An Underutilised Argument' (2021) 32(3) *King's Law Journal* 437.

[87] 15 USC 9001.

'volunteers'[88] under Federal or State law in the United States in relation to their provision of 'health care services' in their capacity as a volunteer as long as they have 'a good faith belief that the individual being treated is in need of health care services'.

In some countries, healthcare workers involved in the administration of vaccinations, including for COVID-19, were accorded statutory protection against liability for injuries sustained by those who received vaccinations.[89] An example is the United States *Public Readiness and Emergency Preparation Act* of 2005 (US) (*PREP Act*),[90] which authorizes the Secretary of the Department of Health and Human Services to issue declarations that provide immunity from liability (except for wilful misconduct) for certain claims. For COVID-19, the Secretary initially issued a declaration on 17 March 2020 providing for immunity from liability for 'covered persons', including employers, for liability for claims:

> of loss caused, arising out of, relating to, or resulting from administration or use of countermeasures to diseases, threats and conditions determined by the Secretary to constitute a present, or credible risk of a future public health emergency to entities and individuals involved in the development, manufacture, testing, distribution, administration, and use of such countermeasures.

With respect to the COVID-19 vaccines, the declaration provides a liability shield for 'covered persons' involved in the administration of a vaccine approved by government authorities (except in cases of wilful misconduct) when acting in accordance with applicable directions, guidelines, or recommendations issued by the Secretary regarding administration and use of a countermeasure. 'Covered persons' under the *PREP Act* include categories of individuals such as 'program planners' and 'qualified persons'. A 'qualified person' is defined to mean:

> A licensed health professional or other individual who is authorized to prescribe, administer, or dispense covered countermeasures under the law of the state in which the countermeasure was prescribed, administered, or dispensed; or a person within a category identified as "qualified" in a declaration, such as volunteers.[91]

The initial declaration has been amended on multiple occasions with the Secretary expanding coverage by broadening the definition of who is a 'qualified person' and

---

[88] Defined by s 3215(4) as persons not receiving compensation or anything in lieu of compensation.
[89] See Randy G Mungwira and others, 'Global Landscape Analysis of No-fault Compensation Programmes for Vaccine Injuries: A Review and Survey of Implementing Countries' (2020) 15(5) *PLoS One* art e0233334. See also the discussion in Chapter 12.
[90] 42 USC § 247d-6d.
[91] 42 USC 247d-6d(i)(8).

thereby permitted to prescribe, dispense, and administer authorized COVID-19 vaccines. As of 16 February 2021, for instance, the Acting Secretary issued a 'Sixth Amendment to the Declaration', adding a further category of qualified persons under section 247d-6d(i)(8)(B): federal employees, contractors, and volunteers authorized by their Department or agency to prescribe, administer, deliver, distribute, or dispense the 'Covered Countermeasure' as any part of their duties or responsibilities. This was done on the basis of an identification of:

> an urgent need to expand the pool of available COVID-19 vaccinators in order to respond effectively to the pandemic. As vaccine supply is made more widely available over the coming months, health care system capacity and the vaccination workforce are likely to become increasingly strained throughout the Nation. The United States is deploying federal personnel, contractors and volunteers to assist in the national COVID-19 vaccination program. While the United States is a covered person under the PREP Act and the Declaration, this amendment clarifies that federal employees, contractors and volunteers are also qualified persons authorized by the Secretary to prescribe, dispense, or administer covered countermeasures, consistent with the terms and conditions of the Declaration.[92]

This set of protections in relation to vaccination administration has the potential to provide a further fillip to the impetus for provision of vaccines, as well as protection for those involved in the process, in respect of whom it is in the community's interest that they continue to provide their services.

VI. Vaccination Compensation

A. Adverse Vaccination Effects

There is a small but important incidence of adverse effects from the vaccines that are currently available against COVID-19. As of 10 November 2021, the United Kingdom Medicines and Healthcare products Regulatory Agency documented that 24.2 million first doses of the COVID-19 Pfizer/BioNTech vaccine and 24.8 million first doses of the COVID-19 vaccine AstraZeneca had been administered, and around 20.6 million and 24.1 million second doses of the COVID-19 Pfizer/BioNTech vaccine and the COVID-19 vaccine AstraZeneca respectively. Approximately 1.5 million first doses and approximately 1.3 million second doses

---

[92] United States Government, 'Sixth Amendment to Declaration Under the Public Readiness and Emergency Preparedness Act for Medical Countermeasures Against COVID-19' 86 Fed Reg 9516 (16 February 2021) <www.federalregister.gov/documents/2021/02/16/2021-03106/sixth-amendment-to-declaration-under-the-public-readiness-and-emergency-preparedness-act-for-medical> accessed 14 September 2022.

of the COVID-19 vaccine Moderna had also been administered. Over 9.5 million booster doses of vaccines had been administered.[93]

In the case of the mRNA vaccines from Pfizer and Moderna, there is a small increased risk of pericarditis (inflammation of the protective sac around the heart) and/or myocarditis (inflammation of the heart muscle),[94] and other cardiac complications.[95] Up to 10 November 2021, the Medicines and Healthcare products Regulatory Agency in the United Kingdom had received 413 reports of myocarditis and 320 reports of pericarditis following the Pfizer vaccine and 148 reports of myocarditis and 185 of pericarditis after the Moderna vaccine, with three fatalities after the Pfizer vaccine and nine after the Moderna vaccine.[96]

People with a history of any of the following conditions were advised in Australia to:

consult a general practitioner, immunization specialist service, or cardiologist about the best timing of vaccination and whether any additional precautions were recommended:

- Recent (i.e., within the last 3 months) myocarditis or pericarditis
- Acute rheumatic fever or acute rheumatic heart disease (i.e., with evidence of active inflammation)
- Acute decompensated heart failure[97]

The other risk from mRNA vaccines is severe allergic reactions. This was recognized early.[98] A United States study found that of 64,900 employees who received a first dose of the Pfizer or Moderna vaccines, allergic reactions were reported by 1,365 employees with a mean age of 41 and 94% of whom were female. One patient was admitted to intensive care, and nine received intramuscular epinephrine, but all recovered.[99] As of 10 November 2021, the United Kingdom Medicines and

---

[93] United Kingdom Government, 'Coronavirus Vaccine—Weekly Summary of Yellow Card Reporting (Research and Analysis, 19 November 2021) <www.gov.uk/government/publications/coronavirus-covid-19-vaccine-adverse-reactions/coronavirus-vaccine-summary-of-yellow-card-reporting> accessed 14 September 2022 (hereafter UK Government, 'Coronavirus Vaccine').

[94] See too George A Diaz and others, 'Myocarditis and Pericarditis after Vaccination for COVID-19' (2021) 326(12) *Journal of the American Medical Association* 1210.

[95] ibid.

[96] UK Government, 'Coronavirus Vaccine' (n 93).

[97] Australian Government, Department of Health, Guidance on Myocarditis and Pericarditis after RNA COVID-19 Vaccines' (2 December 2021) <www.health.gov.au/resources/publications/covid-19-vaccination-guidance-on-myocarditis-and-pericarditis-after-mrna-covid-19-vaccines> accessed 4 March 2022; see also Australian Government, Department of Health, 'Guidance on Myocarditis and Pericarditis after mRNA COVID-19 Vaccines' (29 April 2022) accessed 15 May 2022.

[98] Centers for Disease Control and Prevention, 'Allergic Reactions Including Anaphylaxis after Receipt of the First Dose of Pfizer-BioNTech COVID-19 Vaccine—United States, December 14–23, 2020' (2021) 70(2) *Morbidity and Mortality Weekly Report* 46 <www.cdc.gov/mmwr/volumes/70/wr/mm7002e1.htm> accessed 14 September 2022.

[99] Kimberly G Blumenthal and others, 'Acute Allergic Reactions to mRNA COVID-19 Vaccines; (2021) 325(15) *Journal of the American Medical Association* 1562, 1563–1564. See too Tom T Shimabukuro, Matthew Cole, and John R Su, 'Reports of Anaphylaxis after Receipt of mRNA COVID-19 Vaccine

Healthcare products Regulatory Agency had received 540 reports of severe allergic reaction after administration of the Pfizer vaccine, 41 after the Moderna vaccine, and 843 after the AstraZeneca vaccine.[100]

The major risk from the AstraZeneca vaccine is thrombotic events (blood clots),[101] disproportionately in young people. It was this that resulted in a pausing of the vaccine's administration in a number of European countries as a result of 30 cases of thrombotic events (predominantly venous) that came to the attention of the European Medicines Agency. However, up to 10 November 2021, the Medicines and Healthcare products Regulatory Agency had received Yellow Card reports of 425 cases of major thromboembolic events (blood clots) with concurrent thrombocytopenia (low platelet counts) in the United Kingdom following vaccination with AstraZeneca. Forty-six of the 425 reports were reported after a second dose.[102] Of the 425 reports, 215 occurred in females, and 206 occurred in males aged from 18 to 93 years. There had been 73 deaths, six of which occurred after the second dose.[103]

Although the side effects from the vaccines were rare, some of them, and particularly those associated with the AstraZeneca vaccine, received a high level of publicity. The history of vaccination, including the 'Cutter incident' in which children were immunized with a contaminated polio vaccine (discussed in Chapter 2),[104] includes an unfortunate incidence of adverse outcomes for a small number of those receiving them. The notoriety of such effects, and the fear of there being no recourse, played a role in discouraging some people from being vaccinated against COVID-19 while leaving others who did suffer adverse effects from those vaccines without compensation in some countries. For this reason, as well as reasons of equity, there has been an international impetus to provide compensation for ill effects of the COVID-19 vaccines to those who have been adversely affected by them.

---

in the US—December 12 2020—January 18, 2021' (2021) 325(11) *Journal of the American Medical Association* 1101.

[100] UK Government, 'Coronavirus Vaccine' (n 93).

[101] Paul R Hunter, 'Thrombosis after COVID-19 Vaccination' (2021) 373 *British Medical Journal* n958; Nina H Schultz and others, 'Thrombosis and Thrombocytopenia after ChAdOx1 nCOV-19 Vaccination' (2021) 384(22) *New England Journal of Medicine* 2124; Massimo Franchini, Giancarlo M Liumbruno, and Mario Pezzo, 'Covid-19 Vaccine-associated Immune Thrombosis and Thrombocytopenia (VITT): Diagnostic and Therapeutic Recommendations for a New Syndrome' (2021) 107(2) *European Journal of Haematology* 173; Australian Government, Department of Health, 'Primary Care Approach to Thrombosis with Thrombocytopenia Syndrome after Vaxzevria (AstraZeneca) Vaccine' (15 September 2021) <https://www.health.gov.au/resources/publications/covid-19-vaccination-primary-care-approach-to-thrombosis-with-thrombocytopenia-syndrome-after-covid-19-astrazeneca-vaccine> accessed 4 October 2022.

[102] UK Government, 'Coronavirus Vaccine' (n 93).

[103] ibid.

[104] See Paul A Offit, 'The Cutter Incident, 50 Years Later' (2005) 352(14) *New England Journal of Medicine* 1411; Alison Day, '"An American Tragedy": The Cutter Incident and its Implications for the Salk Polio Vaccine in New Zealand 1955–1960' (2009) 11(2) *Health History* 42.

B. The Advance Market Commitment (AMC) Eligible Economies Compensation Scheme

The Gavi Vaccine Alliance[105] is an entity, allied with WHO, UNICEF, the World Bank, and the Bill and Melinda Gates Foundation, which, amongst other things, works towards equitable distribution of vaccines through the COVAX scheme.[106] An important aspect of the scheme is a no-fault compensation regime for AMC Eligible Economies.[107] At the time of writing, AMC Eligible Economies consist of 92 low- and middle-income economies designated as eligible to have their participation in the COVAX Facility supported by the COVAX Scheme (discussed further in Chapters 11 and 12).[108]

The no-fault compensation scheme is the first and only international vaccine injury compensation scheme. It provides what it describes as 'fair, no-fault, lump sum compensation to eligible individuals who suffer certain serious adverse events after receiving a COVID-19 vaccine distributed through the COVAX Facility'.[109] It was initially scheduled to run until 30 June 2022. The scheme is funded by a small levy on each vaccine dose distributed through COVAX to various countries and economies.

The scheme does not provide compensation for any 'non-serious adverse events' or for any serious or non-serious adverse events arising from any COVID-19 vaccine that has not been received through the COVAX Facility or has been administered in any country, territory, or economy which is not an 'AMC Eligible Economy'. In the event that a government of any AMC Eligible Economy authorizes, recommends, or permits the use of a vaccine in a manner other than in accordance with that vaccine's label, serious adverse events arising from such use are only eligible for compensation under the scheme if use of the vaccine complies with the recommendations of the WHO Strategic Advisory Group of Experts on Immunization (SAGE) and WHO guidance relating to the implementation of such recommendations.[110]

---

[105] Gavi, 'About Our Alliance' (13 October 2021) <www.gavi.org/our-alliance/about> accessed 14 September 2022.
[106] World Health Organization, 'COVAX: Working for Global Equitable Access to COVID-19 Vaccines' <www.who.int/initiatives/act-accelerator/covax> accessed 14 September 2022.
[107] World Health Organization, 'COVAX No-Fault Compensation Program' <www.who.int/initiatives/act-accelerator/covax/no-fault-compensation#:~:text=COVAX%20No%2DFault%20Compensation%20Program%20is%20the%20first%20and%20only,19%20vaccines%20in%20record%20time.> accessed 14 September 2022 (hereafter WHO, 'COVAX No-Fault').
[108] Gavi, 'AMC-Eligible Economies' (12 May 2021) <www.gavi.org/sites/default/files/covid/pr/COVAX_CA_COIP_List_COVAX_PR_12-05-21.pdf> accessed 14 September 2022. See also Chapter 12.
[109] WHO, 'COVAX No-Fault' (n 107).
[110] COVAX, 'COVAX No-Fault Compensation Program for AMC Eligible Economies' *World Health Organization* (5 July 2021) <www.who.int/publications/m/item/covax-no-fault-compensation-program-for-amc-eligible-economies> accessed 13 September 2022.

There is a waiting period of 30 days following the administration of a vaccine to the patient (or, in the case of birth defects, to the patient's mother) before any steps towards initiating an application for compensation under the scheme can be taken. However, the waiting period does not apply if a patient has died following the administration of a vaccine and the death is considered by a registered healthcare professional to have been caused by the vaccine or its administration.[111]

Payments of compensation under the scheme are made from financial reserves established out of a fund specifically created for this purpose, based on a per dose levy charged on each vaccine procured or made available through the COVAX Facility for use in AMC Eligible Economies. The Administrator of the scheme has the capacity to review up to 25,000 applications and receivable claims within any consecutive thirty-day period.

C. National No-fault Vaccination Compensation Schemes

Beyond the Advance Market Commitment countries in which the Gavi Vaccine Alliance no-fault compensation scheme operates, as of 2020 in at least 25 countries, people adversely affected by vaccinations, including by COVID-19 vaccinations, were eligible for compensation.[112] However, criteria for eligibility and quantum of compensation vary significantly from country to country. In most countries, the process is initiated by a claim made by the injured person and a lump sum is paid pursuant to a calculation matrix that is predetermined by reference to the extent of the injury, proven medical needs, loss of capacity to work, and pain and suffering caused. Most such no-fault compensation schemes are administered at the central government level, with only Germany, Italy, the Republic of China, and the Canadian Province of Quebec administering them at a province or state level. In Finland and Sweden the programmes are administered by the insurance sector.[113]

The United States *National Childhood Vaccine Injury Act* of 1986 (US)[114] enables compensation for vaccine-related injuries or death to be paid out of a fund created by an excise tax on every vaccine administered under the National Vaccine Injury Compensation Program (VICP).[115] Modest amounts of compensation have been paid through this non-adversarial scheme, but it has functioned as a significant

---

[111] ibid.
[112] See Mungwira and others (n 89); Stefano D'Errico and others, '"First Do No Harm". No-Fault Compensation Program for COVID-19 Vaccines as Feasibility and Wisdom of a Policy Instrument to Mitigate Vaccine Hesitancy' (2021) 9(10) *Vaccines* 116.
[113] See Mungwira and others (n 89); D'Errico and others (n 112).
[114] 42 USC § 300aa-10, et seq.
[115] See Alexandra M Stewart, 'When Vaccine Injury Claims Go to Court' (2009) 360(24) *New England Journal of Medicine* 2498; Ian Freckelton, 'Vaccination Litigation: The Need for Rethinking Compensation for Victims of Vaccination Injury' (2018) 25(2) *Journal of Law and Medicine* 293.

source of community reassurance in the United States in relation to concerns about the safety of vaccines and the research underpinning them. Under the *PREP Act*,[116] the Countermeasures Injury Compensation Program exists. It is less generous than the VICP.[117] To qualify for eligibility a person who asserts that they have suffered an injury from a 'covered countermeasure', which includes a COVID-19 vaccine, can submit a claim for a 'covered injury' or a death to the Secretary of the Department of Health and Human Services. Under the *PREP Act* compensation is only made based on compelling, reliable, valid, medical, and scientific evidence. Benefits include medical expenses, lost employment income up to US$50,000 for each year of work, and survivor death benefits. It does not include compensation for pain, suffering, or emotional distress. Reimbursement for attorneys' fees is not available.

In the United Kingdom a person is eligible for a 'vaccine damage payment' under the *Vaccine Damage Payments Act 1979* (UK) if the government's Department of Work and Pensions is satisfied that the person is, or was immediately before their death, 'severely disabled', defined as at least 60% disability, which can be mental or physical, based on evidence from doctors or hospitals involved in the person's treatment as a result of a COVID-19 vaccination carried out in the United Kingdom or the Isle of Man.[118] The claimant must be over the age of two at the time of making the claim. There is provision for a tax-free one-off payment of the 'statutory sum' (currently set at £120,000), which is payable to any person who meets the eligibility requirements.

As part of its measures to encourage members of the community to vaccinate against COVID-19, in October 2021 Australia joined other countries in creating a no-fault scheme to reimburse people 'who suffer a moderate to significant impact' following an adverse reaction to an approved COVID-19 vaccine.[119] The scheme covers the costs of injuries above A$1,000. Claims are assessed by independent experts and the compensation paid is based on recommendations and fully funded by the Commonwealth government.[120] For claims between A$1,000 and A$20,000,

---

[116] 42 USC §§ 247d-6d, 247d-6e.
[117] See Katharine Van Tassel, Carmel Shachar, and Sharona Hoffman, 'Covid-19 Vaccine Injuries—Preventing Inequities in Compensation' (2021) 384(10) *New England Journal of Medicine* art e34.
[118] COVID-19 Vaccines were included in the scheme by the *Vaccine Damage Payments (Specified Diseases) Order 2020*, SI 2020/1411 (UK).
[119] Greg Hunt, 'No Fault COVID-19 Indemnity Scheme' (Media Release, 28 August 2021) <www.health.gov.au/ministers/the-hon-greg-hunt-mp/media/no-fault-covid-19-indemnity-scheme> accessed 14 September 202 www.health.gov.au/ministers/the-hon-greg-hunt-mp/media/no-fault-covid-19-indemnity-scheme 2.
[120] The threshold was lowered from A$5,000 in November 2021: see Australian Government, Department of Health, 'Reduction in Threshold of No Fault COVID-19 Vaccine Claims Scheme' (News, 24 November 2021) <www.health.gov.au/news/reduction-in-threshold-of-no-fault-covid-19-vaccine-claims-scheme> accessed 14 September 2024 (hereafter Australian Government, 'Reduction in Threshold').

claimants need to have been hospitalized for at least one night, nominate they are seeking less than A$20,000, and provide applicable evidence of:

- the nature of the injury and medical documentation of its likely relationship to a COVID-19 vaccination
- hospitalisation, due to a vaccine-related injury
- medical costs
- lost wages.[121]

By 17 November 2021, 10,000 potential claims had been registered.[122]

Similarly, after criticisms of the absence of such a scheme,[123] in June 2021, Canada launched a national vaccine injury compensation scheme for people who experienced severe adverse reactions to an approved COVID-19 vaccine, other than persons in Quebec who receive compensation under the longstanding Quebec programme. The pan-Canadian Vaccine Support Program (VISP) sets a high bar for eligibility, though.[124] It provides no-fault compensation for those ascertained to have experienced a serious and permanent injury[125] after receiving a Health Canada-authorized vaccine with financial support also being available for persons who have died after receiving a vaccination. The amount of financial support an individual will receive is determined on a case-by-case basis with amounts paid based on a pre-determined financial support payment framework. The framework aligns with compensation provided under the Quebec Vaccine Injury Compensation Program and informed by other public and private sector injury compensation practices. A committee comprised of three physicians reviews claimants' medical records to determine whether a probable link exists between the injury and the vaccine that has been administered. There is a physician committee empowered to hear appeals.[126]

---

[121] Australian Government, 'Reduction in Threshold' (n 120).

[122] Jolyon Attwooll, 'Processing for COVID-19 Vaccine Compensation Scheme to Begin Next Month' *News GP* (17 November 2021) <www1.racgp.org.au/newsgp/professional/processing-for-covid-19-vaccine-compensation-schem> accessed 14 September 2022.

[123] See eg Roger Collier, 'No-fault Compensation Program Overdue, Experts Say' (2011) 183(5) *Canadian Medical Association Journal* E263; Jennifer Keelan and Kumanan Wilson, *Designing a No-Fault Vaccine-Injury Compensation Programme for Canada: Lessons Learned from an International Analysis of Programmes* (Munk School Briefing, University of Toronto, February 2011) <https://munkschool.utoronto.ca/wp-content/uploads/2012/07/Keelan-Wilson_NoFaultVaccine_CPHS_2011.pdf> accessed 14 September 2022; Kumanan Wilson and Jennifer Keelan, 'The Case for a Vaccine Injury Compensation Program for Canada' (2012) 103(2) *Canadian Journal of Public Health* 122.

[124] Vaccine Injury Support Program, 'Frequently Asked Questions' <https://vaccineinjurysupport.ca/en/faq#eligibility> accessed 14 September 2022.

[125] ibid: defined as 'a severe, life-threatening or life-altering injury that may require in-person hospitalization, or a prolongation of existing hospitalization, and results in persistent or significant disability or incapacity, or where the outcome is a congenital malformation or death'.

[126] See Vaccine Injury Support Program (n 124).

VII. Pathology and Medico-legal Investigations into COVID-19 Deaths

It is in the community's interest to understand as much as possible from the phenomenology of COVID-19 deaths so that lessons can be learned and applied. This has several aspects. It incorporates the practice of pathologists, particularly forensic pathologists, who are the principal medical investigators of the causes of death. In countries following the English tradition, coroners are the legal investigators of death.[127] In countries that do not follow the English tradition, there are other governmental processes for reviewing what might be avoidable causes of death. The succeeding paragraphs make reference to methods of death investigation in the pandemic context which are relevant to potential legal issues. The methods are themselves a form of legal process which can give rise to litigation—an outcome of any form of death investigation in relation to a pandemic has the potential to be a civil action for wrongful contribution to death, as well as litigation brought by those who are dependent upon or closely connected with the deceased person.

In countries that respond formally by way of investigation into unexpected deaths or clusters of deaths, the first challenge is to determine whether the deaths have been caused or contributed to by COVID-19. Moretti and others have observed that the COVID-19 virus requires four areas of attention from medico-legal examiners: (i) risk assessment; (ii) pathological determinations; (iii) universal standard preventative measures; and (iv) standard operating procedures for handling specific organisms.[128] If 'universal preventative measures are effectively used, they mitigate against inaccurate or incomplete data used in risk assessment.'[129]

A. Medico-legal Investigations

The role of the forensic pathologist or medico-legal examiner is vital in disease surveillance and, in particular, as a conduit for epidemiological data collection.[130] In the United States the approach of Nolte and others in deploying a model surveillance system has been internationally influential in classifying and extrapolating information from pandemic data obtained from autopsies.[131]

---

[127] See Ian Freckelton and David Ranson, *Death Investigation and the Coroner's Inquest* (Oxford University Press 2006).
[128] Matteo Moretti and others, 'The Roles of Medical Examiners in the COVID-19 Era: A Comparison Between the United States and Italy' (2021) 17 *Forensic Science, Medicine and Pathology* 262.
[129] ibid 265.
[130] ibid 266.
[131] Kurt B Nolte and others, '"Med-X": A Medical Examiner Surveillance Model for Bioterrorism and Infectious Disease Mortality' (2007) 38(5) *Human Pathology* 718.

Much was learned from a pathology perspective from the SARS and Middle East Respiratory Syndrome (MERS) experiences and also from the Ebola epidemic in West Africa between 2014 and 2015. During SARS it was pathologists' autopsies that began to shed light on the atypical pneumonia and diffuse alveolar damage that was lethal in many cases, as well as on the phenomenon of sudden unexpected death. Such information in turn assisted with prioritizing the treatment measures best deployed for those who were infected.[132] This has proved to be relevant to responses to COVID-19, which is another form of coronavirus.

Sessa, Salerno and Pomara have pointed out that, based on experiences with SARS and MERS, 'the post-mortem examination may be considered the gold standard method to understand the pathophysiological mechanisms, contributing to clarify morphological and virology features, suggesting unexplored therapeutic approaches and new frontiers of research'.[133] A failure to learn from and apply such lessons in a cognate context—COVID-19, for instance—has the potential to have adverse public health outcomes, and also to have medico-legal consequences. An issue with accumulating understanding of MERS was the dearth of autopsy studies of the infection[134] which continues to leave limits to the understanding of the infection. By contrast, the landmark study by He and others in 2006 documented from post-mortem samples the effects of SARS on angiotensin-converting enzyme 2 (ACE-2) expressing cells, the primary target of the infection, which produced high levels of pro-inflammatory cytokines, generating immune-mediated damage.[135] It has emerged that in respect of COVID-19, the virus uses the ACE-2 as a cell receptor to invade human cells. As Li and others have put it, 'ACE2 is the key to understanding the mechanism of SARS-CoV-2 infection'.[136]

Aside from the understanding of the mechanisms of disease learned from previous experiences with coronaviruses, a lesson learned from the Ebola crisis of 2014–2015 was that handling of bodies of the dead was one of the main vectors for transmission of the disease which ultimately claimed over 11,300 lives.[137]

---

[132] Pek Y Chong and others, 'Analysis of Deaths During the Severe Acute Respiratory Syndrome (SARS) Epidemic in Singapore: Challenges in Determining a SARS Diagnosis' (2004) 128(2) *Archives of Pathology and Laboratory Medicine* 195.

[133] Francesco Sessa, Monica Salerno, and Cristoforo Pomara, 'Autopsy Tool in Unknown Diseases: The Experience with Coronaviruses (SARS-CoV, MERS-CoV, SARS-CoV-2)' (2021) 57(4) *Medicina* 309, 310.

[134] The two principal papers are: Dianna L Ng and others, 'Clinicopathologic, Immunohistochemical, and Ultrastructural Findings of a Fatal Case of Middle East Respiratory Syndrome Coronavirus Infection in the United Arab Emirates, April 2014' (2016) 186(3) *American Journal of Pathology* 652; Khaled O Alsaad and others, 'Histopathology of Middle East Respiratory Syndrome Coronavirus (MERS-CoV) Infection—Clinicopathological and Ultrastructural Study' (2018) 72(3) *Histopathology* 516.

[135] L He and others, 'Expression of Elevated Levels of Pre-inflammatory Cytokines in SARS-CoV-infected ACE2+ Cells in SARS Patients: Relation to the Acute Lung Injury and Pathogenesis of SARS' (2006) 210(3) *Journal of Pathology* 288.

[136] Meng-Yuan Li and others, 'Expression of the SARS-CoV-2 Cell Receptor Gene ACE2 in a Wide Variety of Human Tissues' (2020) 9(1) *Infectious Diseases of Poverty* 45.

[137] See Ahmad Samarji, 'Overloaded Morgues, Mass Graves and Infectious Remains: How Forensic Pathologists Handle the Coronavirus Dead' *The Conversation* (9 April 2020) <https://theconversation.

This understanding played a major role in generating the revised manual on 'Management of Dead Bodies Following Disasters', published in 2016 by WHO and the International Federation of the Red Cross and Red Crescent Societies.[138] The manual has been drawn upon internationally for discharge of occupational health and safety obligations in relation to those who are suspected of having died of COVID-19.[139]

A suite of procedures to achieve the objective of accurate medico-legal investigations of large numbers of deaths and to protect those undertaking the investigative processes from themselves becoming infected has been integral to the COVID-19 response and to the discharge of occupational health and safety responsibilities by offices of medico-scientific investigation.[140] This is a familiar issue for forensic technicians and forensic pathologists who are required to deal with many circumstances in which a deceased person's body poses risks of infectiousness. It has been found that the COVID-19 virus has strong 'survivability' and resistance to cold environments.[141] This means that there is a particular need for rigorous care to be taken with both the death scene and the site of autopsy or other form of death investigation, including the use of one-piece protective clothing, 'N95' masks, protective goggles, protective shoe covers, at least two layers of latex gloves, use of a special autopsy location with a process of buffer zones, and a suitable ventilation and air conditioning system.[142] Particular care also needs to be taken in the aftermath of a medico-legal or other autopsy, or even with a superficial investigation. Scrupulous decontamination procedures need to be deployed[143] and in some countries there was a need for upgrading of mortuaries and infrastructure, as well as training of

---

com/overloaded-morgues-mass-graves-and-infectious-remains-how-forensic-pathologists-handle-the-coronavirus-dead-135275> accessed 14 September 2022.

[138] Stephen Cordner and others (eds), *Management of Dead Bodies after Disasters: A Field Manual for First Responders* (2nd edn, WHO, ICRC and International Federation of Red Cross and Red Crescent Societies 2016) <www.paho.org/disasters/dmdocuments/DeadBodiesFieldManual-2ndEd.pdf> accessed 14 September 2022.

[139] See Chapter 10.

[140] See eg David Ranson, 'COVID-19 and Forensic Medical Practice' (2020) 27(4) *Journal of Law and Medicine* 807, 809; Antonio SF dos Santos, Richard S Dias, and Wendell da Luz Silva, 'Imaging Protocols for the Autopsy Service in a Time of Pandemic Emergency Minimising the Contagion of SARS-CoV-2 Expert Government Agents' (2021) 10(6) *Research, Society and Development* art e28810615860.

[141] See Ye Xue and others, 'Perspectives on the Death Investigation During the COVID-19 Pandemic' (2020) 2 *Forensic Science International: Synergy* 126.

[142] See eg World Health Organization, 'Infection Prevention and Control for the Safe Management of a Dead Body in the Context of COVID-19' (Interim Guidance, 4 September 2020) <www.who.int/publications/i/item/infection-prevention-and-control-for-the-safe-management-of-a-dead-body-in-the-context-of-covid-19-interim-guidance> accessed 14 September 2021; Brian Hanley and others, 'Autopsy in Suspected COVID-19 Cases' (2020) 73 *Journal of Clinical Pathology* 239; J Matthew Lacy and others, 'COVID-19: Postmortem Diagnostic and Biosafety Considerations' (2020) 41(3) *American Journal of Forensic Medicine and Pathology* 143; Danmi Mao and others, 'Guide to Forensic Pathology Practice for Death Cases Related to Coronavirus Disease 2019 (COVID-19) Trial Draft' (2020) 5(1) *Forensic Sciences Research* 1.

[143] Lacy and others (n 141).

stakeholders and assessment of facilities where bodies of persons who had died of COVID-19 were being housed.[144]

Forensic radiology has also been found to be particularly helpful as a form of non-intrusive forensic investigation of COVID-19 deaths. Post-mortem CT scanning and MRI scanning have the potential to demonstrate forms of lung change which are distinctive to COVID-19.[145] One of the advantages of such forms of investigative technology is that they involve significantly reduced workplace risks to medico-legal workers because of the reduced interaction with the body of the deceased person.[146]

A variety of issues have arisen in the course of medico-legal investigations due to difficulties in distinguishing between 'death caused by COVID-19' and 'death with COVID-19', both of which designations are important for the integrity of mortality data.[147] In Australia, the Bureau of Statistics published formal guidance on how COVID-19 should be recorded on the medical certificate of cause of death.[148] It required use of terminology recommended by WHO of 'COVID-19' or 'Coronavirus Disease 2019'[149] and discouraged use of the imprecise term, 'coronavirus', on the basis that it could introduce 'uncertainty for coding cause of death which may lead to under reporting in national statistics'. It also mandated the recording of existing conditions, especially those which are chronic in nature, that may have contributed to death and specification of the causal pathway leading to death by certifying doctors, including pathologists:

> For example, in cases when COVID-19 causes pneumonia and fatal respiratory distress, both pneumonia and respiratory distress should be included along with COVID-19 ... alongside the duration of each disease and symptom. Certifiers should include as much detail as possible based on their knowledge of the case, medical records, laboratory testing, etc.[150]

---

[144] Vikas P Meshram, Tanuj Kanchan, and Raghvendra S Shekhawat, 'Management of the Dead During Coronavirus Disease 2019 Outbreak: Practices and Procedures of Forensic Practitioners from India' (2021) 62(1) *Medicine, Science and the Law* 38.

[145] See Wolf Schweitzer and others, 'Implications for Forensic Death Investigations from First Swiss Post-mortem CT in a Case of Non-Hospital Treatment with COVID-19' (2020) 21 *Forensic Imaging* art 200378; Tanuj Kanchan and others, 'The Advantages of Virtopsy During the Covid-19 Pandemic' (2020) 88(1 Suppl) *Medico-Legal Journal* 55.

[146] Kanchan and others (n 145) 56.

[147] See Milenko Bogdanovic and others, 'Is the Role of Forensic Medicine in the COVID-19 Pandemic Underestimated?' (2020) 17(1) *Forensic Science, Medicine and Pathology* 136.

[148] Australian Bureau of Statistics, 'Guidance for Certifying Deaths Due to COVID-19' (25 March 2020) <www.abs.gov.au/ausstats/abs@.nsf/mf/1205.0.55.001> accessed 14 September 2022.

[149] ibid—utilizing the WHO emergency code of 'UO7.1 COVID-19': see World Health Organization, 'Emergency Use ICD Codes for COVID-19 Disease Outbreak' (2021) <https://www.who.int/standards/classifications/classification-of-diseases/emergency-use-icd-codes-for-covid-19-disease-outbreak> accessed 14 September 2022.

[150] ibid.

In England the threshold for a coroner's determination that an act, omission, or pathology caused a death is that it must have 'more than minimally, negligibly or trivially contributed to the death'.[151] This means that the threshold for a decision at inquest that COVID-19 played a role in bringing about a death is low. Under an initiative introduced by the *Coronavirus Act 2020* (Eng and Wales), a doctor who was not the attending doctor was permitted to sign the medical certificate cause of death within 28 days of death, further reducing the requirement for an inquest to be convened to determine the causes of death.[152]

B. English Coronial Investigations

In March 2020, the Chief Coroner issued important guidance that limited the role of coroners' inquests in England and Wales in respect of COVID-19 deaths. He stated that as COVID-19 is a 'naturally occurring disease', inquests into COVID-19 deaths would normally not be necessary unless a person died due to additional factors, such as neglect.[153] In April 2020, he issued further, clarifying guidance that 'If the medical cause of death is COVID-19 and there is no reason to suspect that any culpable human failure contributed to the particular death, there will usually be no requirement for an investigation to be opened.'[154] He explained that:

> a death which is believed to be due to COVID-19 may require a coroner's investigation and inquest in some circumstances. For instance, if there were reason to suspect that some human failure contributed to the person being infected with the virus, an investigation and inquest may be required. If the coroner decides to open an investigation, then he or she may need to consider whether any failures of precautions in a particular workplace caused the deceased to contract the virus and so contributed to death. Also, if there were reason to suspect that some failure of clinical care of the person in their final illness contributed to death, it may be necessary to have an inquest and consider the clinical care. If the person died in state detention (eg in prison or secure mental health ward), an inquest would have to take place.[155]

---

[151] *R (Dawson) v HM Coroner for East Riding and Kingston upon Hull Coroners District* [2001] EWHC 352, [65]–[67].
[152] David Oliver, 'The Medical Examiner Role Could Transform Our Approach to Handling Death' (2020) 379 *British Medical Journal* m3035.
[153] Mark Lucraft, 'Chief Coroner Guidance 34—COVID-19' (26 March 2020) paras 17, 19 <www.judiciary.uk/wp-content/uploads/2020/03/Chief-Coroner-Guidance-No.-34-COVID-19_26_March_2020-.pdf> accessed 14 September 2022.
[154] Mark Lucraft, 'Chief Coroner Guidance 37—COVID-19 Deaths and Possible Exposure in the Workplace' (28 April 2020) para 9 <www.judiciary.uk/wp-content/uploads/2020/04/Chief-Coroners-Guidance-No-37-28.04.20.pdf> accessed 14 September 2022 (hereafter Chief Coroner, 'Guidance 37').
[155] ibid para 12.

He cautioned that an inquest would not be a satisfactory means of determining the adequacy of general policies[156] or whether arrangements were in place for provision of PPE to healthcare workers in the country or a part of it.[157] The guidance was controversial with concern being expressed that, amongst other things, it was steering coroners 'away from investigating policy failures in the provision of protective equipment in the workplace'[158] and would limit and frustrate the convening of inquests into the deaths of frontline workers from COVID-19.[159]

Section 7 of the *Coroners and Justice Act 2009* (Eng and Wales) requires a coroner to sit with a jury (among other things) if the coroner has reason to suspect that a death was caused by a notifiable disease. However, a government innovation first under the *Coronavirus Act 2020* (Eng and Wales) and then under the *Judicial Review and Courts Bill 2021* (Eng and Wales) was to provide that COVID-19 is not a notifiable disease for the purposes of the need for coroners to sit with juries, although a coroner retains the discretion to sit with a jury.[160]

A high profile inquest into the cause of death of a 51-year-old woman shortly after she was vaccinated with the AstraZeneca vaccine on 23 March 2021 concluded in England in November 2021. Bolton Senior Coroner Tim Brennand found that the woman was wrongly diagnosed with gastroenteritis at the Royal Albert Infirmary in Wigan and may have received suboptimal care contributed to by 'confirmation bias' on the part of doctors who originally arrived at a wrong diagnosis for her.[161] Ultimately, she was found to have died of multiple organ failure caused by vaccine-induced immune thrombotic thrombocytopenia, a condition not recognized at the time of her death. The pathologist gave evidence that of the 425 cases of major blood clots that had been identified to the time of his report, 215 were in women and 101 were in the age group of 50 to 59. He said that 24.8 million people in the United Kingdom had been given the first dose of the AstraZeneca vaccine and 24.1 million had had two doses of the same vaccine.[162] Senior Coroner Brennand concluded he could not say whether the woman would have lived had doctors recognized sooner that she was having an adverse reaction to the vaccine

---

[156] Applying *Scholes v SSHD* [2006] HRLR 44, [69]; *R (Smith) v Oxfordshire Assistant Deputy Coroner* [2011] 1 AC 1, [81].

[157] Chief Coroner, 'Guidance 37' (n 154) para 13.

[158] See Clare Dyer, 'Covid-19: Coroners Needn't Investigate PPE Policy Failure in Deaths of NHS Staff, New Guidance Says' (2020) 369 *British Medical Journal* art m1806.

[159] INQUEST, 'Coroners Guidance Will Stymie and Limit Investigations into COVID-19 Deaths of Frontline Workers' (News 29 May 2020) <www.inquest.org.uk/cc-guidance> accessed 14 September 2022.

[160] See Catherine Fairbairn and Georgina Sturge, 'Reforms to the Coroner Service in England and Wales' (Research Briefing, House of Commons Library, 23 September 2021) 22–23 <https://researchbriefings.files.parliament.uk/documents/CBP-9328/CBP-9328.pdf> accessed 14 September 2021.

[161] See Thomas George, '"Healthy" Mum-of-Two, 51, Died from Blood Clot "Likely" to have been Caused by "Very Rare" Vaccine Side-effect' *Manchester Evening News* (25 November 2021) <www.manchestereveningnews.co.uk/news/greater-manchester-news/healthy-mum-two-51-died-22279053?> accessed 14 September 2022.

[162] See ibid.

but he observed that 'The deceased died as a consequence of the unrecognized, rare complications of a recently administered elective and necessary Covid-19 vaccination.'[163]

Another significant inquest in England during the COVID-19 era was conducted into the death of a patient who was found by the Senior Coroner for Manchester South, Alison Mutch, to have died as a result of COVID-19 pneumonia and right-sided neck of femur fracture, hypertension, and atrial fibrillation.[164] She found the deceased man to have been admitted to hospital for surgery for a fractured hip and placed in a bay where patients were exposed to a COVID-19 positive patient. He contracted the virus, deteriorated rapidly, and passed away.

Regulation 28 of the *Coroners (Investigations) Regulations 2013* (Eng and Wales), made under paragraph 7(1) of Schedule 5 to the *Coroners and Justice Act 2009* (England and Wales), requires a coroner to make a report about anything revealed by their investigation that gives rise to a concern that circumstances creating a risk of other deaths will occur, or will continue to exist, in the future, and 'in the coroner's opinion, action should be taken to prevent the occurrence or continuation of such circumstances, or to eliminate or reduce the risk of death created by such circumstances'. Regulation 29 mandates a response to such a report.[165]

Pursuant to Regulation 28, Senior Coroner Mutch reported her concern about the implementation of guidance from Public Health England (PHE) about placement of patients who were COVID-19 positive, observing that as a result of reflection and concern about interpreting the guidance, the Trust responsible for the care of the patient had changed its policy so that such movement of patients no longer took place. 'However, the guidance from PHE has not been amended and it was unknown how other trusts were choosing to interpret the guidance and as such putting potentially vulnerable patients at risk of developing Covid-19 whilst an in-patient.'[166] She noted that her report of PHE England and NHS England required a response within 56 days with details of action taken or proposed to be taken, setting out the timetable for action, or explaining why no such action would be taken.[167] Both of these inquests are illustrative of the constructive contribution able to be made by coroners in relation to lessons that need to be learned from suboptimal responses to a pandemic.

---

[163] See ibid.
[164] Alison Mutch, 'Regulation 28 Report to Prevent Future Deaths: Inquest into the Death of Leslie Harris' (9 December 2020) <www.judiciary.uk/wp-content/uploads/2021/01/Leslie-Harris-2020-0280_Redacted.pdf> accessed 14 September 2022 (hereafter 'Regulation 28 Report').
[165] See generally Alison Leary and others, 'A Thematic Analysis of the Prevention of Future Deaths Reports in Healthcare from HM Coroners in England and Wales 2016–2019' (2021) 26(1) *Journal of Patient Safety and Risk Management* 14.
[166] 'Regulation 28 Report' (n 164).
[167] ibid.

C. Scottish Procurator Fiscal Investigations

By contrast with the death investigation system in England and Wales, in Scotland there is no system of coroners or inquests. Instead, there is the option for formal investigation of a death that appears to be accidental, unexplained, sudden, suspicious, or giving rise to 'public anxiety'. An independent investigation can be undertaken by a local Crown agent, namely, a Procurator Fiscal. Such investigations are the constitutional responsibility of the Lord Advocate of Scotland. The Lord Advocate, James Wolffe QC, announced in May 2020 that the following categories of death were to be reported to the Procurator Fiscal:

- 'all Covid-19 or presumed Covid-19 deaths where the deceased might have contracted the virus in the course of their employment or occupation, including the deaths of care home workers, front-line National Health Service staff, public transport employees and emergency services personnel'; and
- 'all Covid-19 or presumed Covid-19 deaths where the deceased was resident in a care home when the virus was contracted'.[168]

He stated that this approach was to 'ensure that all deaths within the two categories ... will be registered within the Crown system of death investigation, and that each of those deaths can be investigated' by a dedicated team under the Lord Advocate's remit so as to ensure that 'society will learn lessons for the future'.[169] This appeared to mean that the categories of death that would be formally investigated in Scotland would be significantly broader than those in England and Wales.

A consequence of the announcement was the establishment in May 2020 of a dedicated COVID-19 Death Investigation Team (CDIT) to prove the circumstances of coronavirus-related deaths in care homes across Scotland. By 21 January 2021, the CDIT had received 2,242 such reports[170] and, by 30 September, it had received 3,491 reports.[171] Later in 2021 the ambit of the CDIT was extended to 827 deaths in Scotland's hospitals, with a judge-led public inquiry into Scotland's handling of the pandemic expected to commence late in 2021,[172] ahead of a United

---

[168] Crown Office and Procurator Fiscal Service, 'Revised Guidance on Reporting of Deaths During Coronavirus Outbreak' (News, 15 May 2020) <www.copfs.gov.uk/media-site-news-from-copfs/1883-revised-guidance-on-reporting-of-deaths-during-coronavirus-outbreak> accessed 14 September 2022.
[169] ibid.
[170] See Caitlyn Dewar, 'Crown Office Investigating More than 450 Care Homes in Scotland over Covid Deaths' *The Scotsman* (22 January 2021) <www.scotsman.com/health/coronavirus/crown-office-investigating-more-450-care-homes-scotland-over-covid-deaths-3109120> accessed 14 September 2022.
[171] See Andrew Picken, 'Covid: Hospital-linked Deaths in Scotland Under Investigation' *BBC News* (4 November 2021) <www.bbc.com/news/uk-scotland-59140798> accessed 14 September 2022.
[172] Scottish Government, 'Setting up the Scottish COVID-19 Public Inquiry' (Consultation, 30 September 2021) <https://consult.gov.scot/digital-communications/setting-up-the-scottish-covid-19-public-inquiry/> accessed 14 September 2022; Andrew Watterson, 'Scotland's COVID Inquiry Must be Credible, Timely and Thorough—Here's What Needs to Happen' *The Conversation* (2 September

Kingdom-wide inquiry by the Right Honourable Baroness Hallett, scheduled for Spring 2022.[173]

D. Canadian Coronial Investigations

In Canada, the Deputy Chief Coroner for Ontario undertook an investigation into the COVID-19-related deaths of temporary foreign agricultural workers (TFAWs) during 2020.[174] The investigation arose from the deaths by reason of COVID-19 of three Mexican citizens in May/June 2020. The investigation found an absence of specific pandemic-related preparations or guidelines for TFAWs, some of whom were undocumented by reason of not having been granted refugee status or having been the subject of human trafficking, and who, by reason of living in congregate circumstances and the nature of their working conditions, were at higher risk of contracting a disease such as COVID-19.[175] Amongst other things, the investigation recommended better documentation of TFAWs so as to facilitate contact-tracing and the creation and management of COVID-19 isolation centres,[176] as well as the development of culturally appropriate education campaigns in relation to the risks and benefits of COVID-19 vaccines.[177] This was an example of an inquest that advanced public health recommendations in relation to circumstances presented by the pandemic.

High profile coroners' inquests were convened during 2021 into deaths in aged-care facilities in Quebec in Canada and Victoria in Australia. They are also illustrative of the preventative role of coronership in both jurisdictions[178] as well as the public health role of coroners to conduct open investigations into deaths about whose occurrence there is community concern and from which it is necessary to learn lessons to avoid recurrence.

2021) <https://theconversation.com/scotlands-covid-inquiry-must-be-credible-timely-and-thorough-heres-what-needs-to-happen-167009> accessed 14 September 2022.

[173] William James and Alistair Smout, 'UK's Johnson Announces COVID-19 Inquiry Next Year' *Reuters* (12 May 2021) <www.reuters.com/world/uk/uks-pm-johnson-announces-covid-19-public-inquiry-2021-05-12/> accessed 14 September 2022; United Kingdom COVID-19 Inquiry, 'The Independent Public Inquiry to Examine the COVID-19 Pandemic in the UK' (2022) <https://covid19.public-inquiry.uk> accessed 15 May 2022.

[174] Deputy Chief Coroner of Ontario, 'COVID-19 Related Deaths of Temporary Foreign Agricultural Workers in 2020' (Review, October 2021) <www.mcscs.jus.gov.on.ca/sites/default/files/content/mcscs/docs/Report%20-%20DCC%27s%20Review%20of%20COVID-19%20Related%20Deaths%20of%20TFAWs%20in%202020.pdf> accessed 20 November 2021.

[175] ibid 9.
[176] ibid 13–14.
[177] ibid 22.
[178] *Coroners Act 2008* (Vic) s 1(c); *An Act Respecting the Determination of the Causes and Circumstances of Death* RSQ 1983, c R-0.2, ss 3, 92(5).

In the Quebec inquest before Coroner Kamel, evidence was given by a former Health Minister that 'systemic ageism, outdated health care facilities and government reforms all contributed to the deaths of nearly 10 per cent of the province's long-term care patients, a rate that was five times higher than that in Canada overall'.[179] In her extensive inquest report Coroner Kamel found that aged-care residents in Quebec had been seriously overlooked during the first wave of the pandemic and that structural weaknesses had become apparent.[180] These included a lack of suitably trained and remunerated staff, particularly beneficiary attendants and nursing assistants.[181] Coroner Camel made a series of recommendations directed to the Ministry of Health and Social Services with a view to creating greater accountability for long-term care home managers for the care of frail elderly people and to ensure that there is an adequate supply of PPE at all times.[182] She proposed that the precautionary principle be introduced at the centre of all risk evaluation.[183] Coroner Kamel also recommended that the training of nursing assistants be reviewed to enable them to perform tasks such as the provision of respiratory care and the use of ventilators.[184] The decision is one of the most significant critiques of governmental and institutional decision-making in relation to aged-care residences where so many deaths took place in the early stages of the COVID-19 pandemic.

E. Australian Coronial Investigations

In Victoria, Australia, an inquest was commenced in November 2021 before State Coroner John Cain into deaths of residents at St Basil's Home for the Aged. It followed an independent report commissioned by the Australian Department of Health into deaths at that facility and a second facility which found that:

- Emergency planning and preparedness was inadequate;
- Infection prevention and control were suboptimal;
- Leadership and effective management faltered;
- Surge workforce planning was inadequate to manage the scale of the outbreak; and

---

[179] See Clara Descurninges, '"Systemic Ageism" to Blame for COVID-19 Deaths in Quebec Care Homes, Inquest Hears' *The Globe and Mail* (1 November 2021) <www.theglobeandmail.com/canada/article-systemic-ageism-to-blame-for-covid-19-deaths-in-quebec-care-homes/> accessed 14 September 2024.
[180] Rapport d'enquête concernant 53 décès survenus dans des milieux d'hébergement au cours de la première vague de la pandemie de la COVID-19 au Québec (Quebec Coroner's Court, 10 May 2022) 119.
[181] ibid 120–21.
[182] ibid 122.
[183] ibid 122.
[184] ibid 123.

- Pathology testing was delayed.[185]

Throughout July and August 2020, 94 residents and the same number of staff members contracted COVID-19, with 45 residents dying from the virus and a further five dying of neglect as the workforce succumbed to the virus. The focuses of the November/December 2021 inquest were upon how St Basil's management and staff and the state and federal governments prepared for COVID-19 in aged care; their responses when it took hold; the timeliness of information provided to staff, residents, and families; whether the state and federal governments co-ordinated their response to the outbreak appropriately; and the adequacy of the replacement workforce deployed to St Basil's. A key aspect of the coronial inquest was compliance with occupational health and safety obligations[186] at St Basil's,[187] as well as scrutiny of an assessment by the Chief Nursing and Midwifery Officer that St Basil's was 'fit for purpose' as an aged-care facility.[188]

F. Overview of Medico-legal Investigations

Attempts have been made globally to achieve consistency of approach in relation to designation and description of COVID-19 deaths.[189] Much in this regard is dependent upon uniform and correct description and registration of deaths, especially in a medico-legal context where forensic pathology, armed with techniques of forensic radiology, has emerged for some countries as a useful diagnostic tool. Death investigative procedures have played a crucial role in evaluating where gaps in service delivery have occurred and lessons that need to be learned from them. For countries that have inherited the English medico-legal investigation of the coroner, this has provided an opportunity for the convening of important public inquests in which contentious aspects of the rollout of COVID-19 procedures

---

[185] Lyn Gilbert and Alan Lilly, *Independent Review of COVID-19 Outbreaks at St Basil's Home for the Aged in Fawkner, Victoria, and Heritage Care Epping Gardens in Epping, Victoria* (Report, 30 November 2020) <www.health.gov.au/sites/default/files/documents/2020/12/coronavirus-covid-19-independent-review-of-covid-19-outbreaks-at-st-basil-s-and-epping-gardens-aged-care-facilities.pdf> accessed 20 November 2021. See also Ian Freckelton, 'Government Inquiries, Investigations and Reports During the COVID-19 Pandemic' in Belinda Bennett and Ian Freckelton (eds), *Pandemics, Public Health Emergencies and Government Powers: Perspectives on Australian Law* (Federation Press 2021).

[186] See Chapter 10.

[187] See Mary Sinanidis, 'St Basil's Coronial Inquest: Timeline of Events Which Have Unfolded So Far' *Neos Kosmos* (19 November 2021) <https://neoskosmos.com/en/2021/11/19/news/st-basils-coronial-inquest-timeline-of-events-which-have-unfolded-so-far/> accessed 14 September 2022.

[188] See Clay Lucas, 'Aged Care Sector under Fire as Top Nurse Details St Basil's "Fit for Purpose" Decision' *The Age* (1 December 2021) <www.theage.com.au/politics/victoria/aged-care-sector-under-fire-as-top-nurse-details-st-basil-s-fit-for-purpose-decision-20211130-p59dft.html> accessed 14 September 2022; see *Kontis v Coroners Court of Victoria* [2022] VSC 422.

[189] See Thomas Beaney and others, 'Excess Mortality: The Gold Standard in Measuring the Impact of COVID-19 Worldwide' (2020) 113(9) *Journal of the Royal Society of Medicine* 329.

and protections against contracting the virus have been able to be scrutinized. In Scotland too, which operates under a medico-legal death investigation system closer to the European model, the decision has been taken to undertake rigorous investigations so as to obtain independent perspectives on key aspects of government and other responses to the pandemic.

VIII. Consumer Protection Litigation

During a pandemic, fear, anxiety, and even paranoia can lead members of the public to resort to unorthodox measures to protect themselves against or treat symptoms of the disease. There can be a tendency for members of the public, especially when they are isolated, to trust and suspend discernment when otherwise they would be more critical and circumspect in their responses to promises and representations.[190] In addition, such times provide opportunities for the unscrupulous and the predatory to exploit people's anxieties by promoting products and interventions that have no prospect of efficacy, for significant commercial gain. This is a global phenomenon[191] and, in relation to the COVID-19 pandemic, has provoked expressions of concern from many health practitioners.[192] The issue is not without precedent. Similar issues have arisen in previous pandemics, particularly during the Spanish flu.[193] As a consequence, while concerted efforts have been made to engage in accurate public information campaigns by governments during the COVID-19 pandemic,[194] the role of state consumer authorities to take action against those making false representations proved to be very important

---

[190] See Steven W Taylor, *The Psychology of Pandemics: Preparing for the Next Global Outbreak of Infectious Disease* (Cambridge Scholars Publishing 2019); Ian Freckelton, 'COVID-19: Fear, Quackery, False Representations and the Law' (2020) 72 *International Journal of Law and Psychiatry* art 101611 (hereafter Freckelton, 'COVID-19'); Jon Roozenbeek and others, 'Susceptibility to Misinformation about COVID-19 Around the World' (2020) 7(1) *Royal Society Open Science* e202199; Jay P Kennedy, Melisssa Rorie, and Michael L Benson, 'COVID-19 Frauds: An Exploratory Study of Victimization During a Global Crisis' (2021) 20(3) *Criminology & Public Policy* 493.

[191] See Freckelton, 'COVID-19' (n 190). See too Hannah Jose, 'As India's Health System Falters, COVID Quackery Gets a Boost with Officials Promoting Coronavirus Misinformation' *ABC News* (16 May 2021) <www.abc.net.au/news/2021-05-16/india-covid-19-cow-dung-fake-remedies-alternative-medicine/100132838> accessed 14 September 2021.

[192] See eg Stewart Carr, 'Yoga and HULA HOOPS Join List of Quack Cures for Covid on Social Media as Doctors Warn of Misinformation on Treatments' *Daily Mail* (24 October 2021) <www.dailymail.co.uk/news/article-10125147/Yoga-HULA-HOOPS-join-quack-cures-Covid-social-media-doctors-warn-misinformation.html> accessed 14 September 2022.

[193] See Michael Levi and Russell G Smith, 'Fraud and its Relationship to Pandemics and Economic Crises: From Spanish Flu to COVID-19' (Report 19, Australian Institute of Criminology Research, 2021) <www.aic.gov.au/sites/default/files/2021-04/rr19_fraud_and_its_relationship_to_pandemics_and_economic_crises.pdf> accessed 14 September 2022. See also Chapter 2.

[194] See Heidi Oi-Yee Li and others, 'YouTube as a Source of Information on COVID-19: A Pandemic of Misinformation' (2020) 5(5) *British Medical Journal Global Health* art e002604; Calvin Chan and others, 'The Reliability and Quality of YouTube Videos as a Source of Public Health Information Regarding COVID-19 Vaccination: Cross-sectional Study' (2021) 7(7) *JMIR Public Health Surveillance* art e29942.

both from the perspective of preventing the proliferation of inaccurate information and deterring those minded to distribute such information for their pecuniary advantage.[195]

An early phase of consumer protection provided by the law during a pandemic was initiated through litigation arising from the 'Russian Flu'. As discussed in Chapter 2, the Carbolic Smoke Ball was promoted as an effective protection against the virus. It consisted of a rubber ball filled with powdered carbolic acid.[196] The patient squeezed the ball, sending a puff of acidic smoke up a tube inserted into the nostrils. It was widely advertised, including in the *Pall Mall Gazette*, with testimonials provided by well-known personalities, as was common at the time. A £100 reward was offered to anyone using the Smoke Ball correctly who then contracted influenza.[197] The Carbolic Smoke Ball Company ('the Company') deposited £1,000 in the Alliance Bank in Regent Street to demonstrate the bona fides of its financial offer.[198]

Louisa Elizabeth Carlill purchased a smoke ball from a chemist in Oxford Street, London, and used it, as directed, three times a day for nearly two months. However, she contracted the flu. Ms Carlill duly claimed her 'reward', but was rebuffed by the Company, which replied to correspondence from her husband, who had trained as a solicitor, saying that, if used properly, it had total confidence in its product. It declined to return her money. This resulted in her suing the Company in the High Court for breach of contract. She succeeded[199] but the Company appealed to the Court of Appeal, arguing that its advertisement was 'mere puff'. However, this argument was rejected on the basis that the Company had deposited £1,000 to show its seriousness. As McGinnis observed:

> a legal decision supporting that type of argument would only serve to encourage the telling of even more outrageous untruths. Advertisers could attempt with impunity to trap consumers with progressively bigger lies and then avoid liability by laughing at the gullibility of the gulled. Instead, the court said that it was going to look at the contract as printed and to interpret it according to its plain meaning, on the sensible assumption that what is exactly what Mrs Carlill and other buyers like her would have done.[200]

---

[195] See also Chapter 11.
[196] See NJC Snell, 'The Carbolic Smoke Ball' (2001) 15 *International Journal of Pharmaceutical Medicine* 195. It has been suggested that the Carbolic Smoke Ball Company was a homoeopathic company: Raphael N Obu, 'Medical Law and Misrepresentation in the Practice of Homeopathy and Alternative Medicine in Ghana: Lessons Learnt in Studying Law and Practicing Holistic Medicine' (2020) 3(4) *Law, Crime Justice* 99.
[197] Janice D McGinnis, '*Carlill v Carbolic Smoke Ball Company*: Influenza, Quackery, and the Unilateral Contract' (1988) 5 *Canadian Journal of Medical History* 121, 124.
[198] See Clive Coleman, 'Carbolic Smoke Ball: Fake or Cure' *BBC News* (5 November 2009) <http://news.bbc.co.uk/2/hi/business/8340276.stm> accessed 14 September 2022.
[199] *Carlill v Carbolic Smoke Ball Co* [1892] 2 QB 484 (hereafter '*Carlill*').
[200] McGinnis (n 197) 127–28.

Secondly, the Company maintained that it had no way of ascertaining whether Mrs Carlill had followed its instructions correctly. This contention was rejected by the Court of Appeal out-of-hand.[201] Thirdly, the Company argued that an offer such as it had made could not be understood to have been made to the whole world. This argument too failed. The Court of Appeal found that the offer was clear and made to a group of consumers—anyone fulfilling its terms could be deemed to have accepted the offer. Finally, the company argued that the requisite consideration for a contract did not exist. However, the Court of Appeal rejected this contention too, concluding that any use of the smoke ball would be likely to promote sales and thus be of value to the company. Thus, Mrs Carlill's use of the smoke ball constituted valuable consideration.

The outcome of the decision was an emphatic endorsement of contract law as a means by which the vulnerable could be protected against false representations, which were not honoured, during a pandemic. The editors of the *Lancet* exulted:

> We are glad to learn that in spite of the ingenuity of their legal advisers the defendants have been held liable to make good their promise. People who are silly enough to adopt a medicine simply because a tradesman is reckless enough to make extravagant promises and wild representations as to its efficacy may thank themselves chiefly for any disappointment that ensues. Still for this folly, which is only foolish and nothing worse, it is possible to feel sympathy when the disappointment comes. It is a pleasant alternative to learn that the dupe has been able, as in the present instance to enforce a sharp penalty and that the process of reaping a harvest from the simplicity of one's neighbours is attended with dangers of miscarriage which must materially diminish its attractiveness in the eyes of those people who supply the popular demand for quack medicines.[202]

The *Carlill* decision was one of the bases for the development of consumer protection law to safeguard persons vulnerable to the representations made by unethical purveyors of medical products and devices, including during a pandemic.

The Organisation for Economic Co-operation and Development (OECD) responded early during the COVID-19 pandemic by observing that the crisis had 'upended the global consumer landscape' and identifying that there were:

> increasing reports of unfair, misleading and fraudulent commercial practices online. These include financial scams, false claims of coronavirus treatment or prevention, price gouging of essential goods and the promotion of unsafe or

---

[201] *Carlill* (n 199).
[202] Editorial, '*Carlill v The Carbolic Smoke-Ball Company*' (1892) 140(3593) *Lancet* 102; AW Brian Simpson, 'Quackery and Contract Law: The Case of the Carbolic Smoke Ball' (1985) 14(2) *Journal of Legal Studies* 345.

counterfeit products. Many governments must strike a balance between protecting consumers' health and safety, strengthening consumer trust, and addressing challenges to business and workers.[203]

During the COVID-19 era, there was a marked rise in disinformation across social media, and some of the claims garnered considerable traction.[204] This led the United States Congress to enact the *COVID-19 Consumer Protection Act* (US), which was directed towards inhibiting deceptive acts and practices in connection with COVID-19. Section 2(a) of that Act provides that for the duration of a public health emergency declared under the *Public Health Services Act* (42 USC 247d), 'it is unlawful for any person, partnership, or corporation to engage in a deceptive act or practice in or affecting commerce ... that is associated with (1) the treatment, cure, prevention, mitigation, or diagnosis of COVID-19; or (2) a government benefit related to COVID-19.'

This was one of the early examples of consumer protection intervention through legislation during the COVID-19 pandemic. It was replicated by non-legislative measures taken in many other countries. For instance, as early as 27 February 2020, the Autorità Garante della Concorrenza e del Mercato (the Italian Antitrust Authority) sent a request for information to leading online sales platforms and other sales sites about the marketing of hand sanitizers and disposable respiratory protection masks. Its action was a response to numerous complaints lodged by consumers and associations concerning, on the one hand, claims relating to the alleged effectiveness of these products in terms of protection and/or counteraction against COVID-19 and, on the other, the unjustified and significant increase in the prices of such products.[205] The result of its communication was that companies were required to communicate within three days the measures they had adopted to eliminate advertising slogans that could mislead consumers about the effectiveness of products in preventing or treating COVID-19 as well as the steps they had taken to avoid unjustified and disproportionate price increases.[206]

Another early action was initiated by the Polish Office of Competition and Consumer Protection ('UOKiK') in March 2020 after it received information that two wholesalers had terminated contracts with hospitals to supply PPE to them because they had opportunities to secure more lucrative supply arrangements, in

---

[203] OECD, 'Protecting Online Consumers during the COVID-19 Crisis' (Policy Response, 28 April 2020) <www.oecd.org/coronavirus/policy-responses/protecting-online-consumers-during-the-covid-19-crisis-2ce7353c/> accessed 14 September 2022.

[204] See David R Grimes, 'Medical Disinformation and the Unenviable Nature of COVID-19 Conspiracy Theories' (2021) 16(3) *PLoS One* art e0245900.

[205] Autorità Garante della Concorrenza e del Mercato, 'Coronavirus, the Authority Intervenes in the Sale of Sanitizing Products and Masks' (Press Release, 27 February 2020) <https://en.agcm.it/en/media/press-releases/2020/3/ICA-Coronavirus-the-Authority-intervenes-in-the-sale-of-sanitizing-products-and-masks> accessed 14 September 2022.

[206] ibid.

particular for surgical masks.[207] The UOKiK communicated that the maximum fine that it was able to impose for such conduct was 10% of the company's turnover and there was also the potential for such conduct to constitute both an infraction of the Polish Public Procurement Law, which allows exclusion of a company from eligibility for future government contracts, as well as to be an infraction of the Penal Code of Poland by constituting conduct that caused a state of widespread danger to life or health.[208]

The United States Associate Commissioner for Regulatory Affairs, observed in March 2021 that:

> It has been said that there is *good fishing in troubled waters* and that has been the case with fraudsters seeking to profit from anxiety and fears associated with COVID-19. Accordingly, the US Food and Drug Administration is on the lookout for charlatans seeking to profit from the pandemic.[209]

The tendency of regulators in a number of countries during the COVID-19 pandemic was to communicate initially with those responsible for problematic representations by sending warning letters. Typical of this was the strategy adopted by the United States Food and Drug Administration, which started with sending warning letters to firms that had offered to sell products with spurious claims to prevent, treat, mitigate, diagnose, or cure COVID-19. Its broader strategy was to send warning letters but also to engage in seizures, apply for injunctions in the courts and, where necessary, initiate criminal prosecutions against firms that persisted in violating the law.[210]

Other entities in the United States provided ancillary consumer protection support. For instance, the Federal Trade Commission warned consumers against those seeking to charge for vaccinations or to provide a national vaccination app, certificate, or passport.[211] It also noted that:

> More and more places are requiring proof that you've had a COVID-19 vaccine or have recently tested negative before giving you access. Scammers see this as an

---

[207] Office of Competition and Consumer Protection of Poland, 'UOKiK's Proceedings on Wholesalers' Unfair Conduct Towards Hospitals' (Press Release, Polish Government, 4 March 2020) <www.uokik.gov.pl/news.php?news_id=16277> accessed 14 September 2022.
[208] ibid.
[209] Judy McMeekin, 'National Consumer Protection Week: FDA is Vigilant in Protecting Consumers Against COVID-19 Vaccine Scams' (FDA Voices, Food and Drug Administration, 3 February 2021) <www.fda.gov/news-events/fda-voices/national-consumer-protection-week-fda-vigilant-protecting-consumers-against-covid-19-vaccine-scams> accessed 14 September 2022.
[210] Food and Drug Administration, United States, 'Fraudulent Coronavirus Disease 2019 (COVID-19) Products' (30 September 2021) <www.fda.gov/consumers/health-fraud-scams/fraudulent-coronavirus-disease-2019-covid-19-products> accessed 25 October 2021.
[211] Federal Trade Commission, 'Coronavirus Advice for Consumers' <www.ftc.gov/coronavirus/scams-consumer-advice> accessed 14 September 2022.

opportunity to profit by selling fake verification tools or products, like fake vaccination cards, certificates, and test results.'[212]

This led it to urge consumers to file reports with it so that consumer protection action could be taken. As of 18 October 2021, it publicized that it had received 625,989 such reports and estimated that US$588.2 million had been incurred in fraud losses as a result of COVID-19 scams.[213]

The Office of Criminal Investigations (OCI), which is part of the Food and Drug Administration, took many actions to deal with misrepresentations in relation to misbranded drugs advertised to treat COVID-19. An example was action taken against a man and his company in Georgia, which claimed that his US$19 'Immune Shot' could 'LOWER your risk of COVID-19 by nearly 50%'. The suspect targeted individuals aged 50 and older with sales pitches, including company website statements such as 'The NEXT FIVE MINUTES could save your life', 'Immune Shot could be the most important formula in the WORLD right now due to the new pandemic', 'Immune Shot is Not a Luxury, It is a Necessity Right Now', 'Point Blank, if YOU Leave, YOU are at Risk' and 'Is Your Life Worth $19? Seriously, Is It?'[214] In another case,[215] an agent from the OCI went undercover to arrest a fraudster who was posing as a biotech expert. The suspect claimed to have created an injectable COVID-19 vaccine that he offered to inject into customers for US$400–$1,000 each. In early March 2020, undercover OCI agents contacted a suspect through social media, where he had uploaded posts in which he claimed he had developed and administered vaccines for cancer and COVID-19. Around the same time, the state of Washington Attorney-General issued a cease-and-desist letter, telling the suspect to stop making claims and offering his 'vaccine' for COVID-19. Undeterred, however, the suspect indicated to undercover agents that the warning

---

[212] Colleen Tressler, 'Don't Buy Fake COVID-19 Vaccine Cards or Negative Test Results. Here's Why' (Blog Post, Federal Trade Commission, 20 August 2021) <www.consumer.ftc.gov/blog/2021/08/dont-buy-fake-covid-19-vaccine-cards-or-negative-test-results-heres-why> accessed 14 September 2022.

[213] Federal Trade Commission, 'FTC COVID-19 and Stimulus Reports' (18 October 2021) <https://public.tableau.com/app/profile/federal.trade.commission/viz/COVID-19andStimulusReports/Map> accessed 14 September 2022.

[214] Food and Drug Administration, United States, 'Georgia Man and his Company Charged with Selling Misbranded Drug Advertised to Treat COVID-19' (Press Release, 10 August 2020) <www.fda.gov/inspections-compliance-enforcement-and-criminal-investigations/press-releases/georgia-man-and-his-company-charged-selling-misbranded-drug-advertised-treat-covid-19> accessed 4 October 2022.

[215] Food and Drug Administration, United States, 'Purported Biotech Executive Charged with Introducing Misbranded Drug into Interstate Commerce for Distribution of "COVID-19 Vaccine"' (Press Release, 21 January 2021) <www.fda.gov/inspections-compliance-enforcement-and-criminal-investigations/press-releases/purported-biotech-executive-charged-introducing-misbranded-drug-interstate-commerce-distribution> accessed 4 October 2022 (hereafter FDA, 'Purported Biotech Executive'). See too Food and Drug Administration, United States, 'Three Baltimore-Area Men Facing Federal Charges for Fraud Scheme Purporting to Sell Covid-19 Vaccines' (Press Release, 11 February 2021) <www.fda.gov/inspections-compliance-enforcement-and-criminal-investigations/press-releases/three-baltimore-area-men-facing-federal-charges-fraud-scheme-purporting-sell-covid-19-vaccines> accessed 14 September 2022 (hereafter FDA, 'Three Baltimore-Area Men').

had just increased demand for his injections, which he now called an 'immunogen' instead of a vaccine. Despite entering a consent decree with the state of Washington to stop selling his purported vaccines, the suspect continued to communicate with the undercover OCI agent and travelled to Idaho to 'vaccinate' the agent. This resulted in his arrest.[216]

A high-profile action was also brought by the Australian Competition and Consumer Commissioner (ACCC) against a clothing manufacturer which resulted in an order by the Federal Court that it pay A$5 million in penalties for making false and misleading representations to consumers and engaging in conduct liable to mislead the public in connection with the promotion and supply of its activewear for women.[217] The defendant admitted that, in July 2020, it falsely represented to consumers that its activewear 'eliminated', 'stopped the spread' of, and 'protected wearers' against 'viruses including COVID-19'.[218] The misleading representations were made on in-store signage, on its website, on Instagram, in emails to consumers, and in media releases. When appearing before the Federal Court of Australia, the clothing company admitted that it had falsely represented that it had a scientific or technological basis for making the 'anti-virus' claims about its clothing when no such basis existed, and that it did not have any scientific testing results showing the effectiveness of its shield activewear on viruses, including COVID-19. In imposing the civil penalties,[219] Rangiah J concluded that:

> Lorna Jane sought to exploit the fear and concern of the public through the use of misleading, deceptive, and untrue representations about the properties of LJ Shield Activewear. The behaviour of Lorna Jane can only be described as exploitative, predatory, and potentially dangerous.[220]

In a later Australian case,[221] Rofe J of the Federal Court of Australia imposed penalties of A$2 million against a company and A$1 million against a former chiropractor for representations made on the company's website and on Facebook that were precluded under the *Therapeutic Goods Act 1989* (Cth). Justice Rofe also made injunctions to preclude repetition of the conduct. The representations promoted hyperbaric oxygen therapy ('HBOT') as a treatment for a number of conditions including COVID-19. Justice Rofe classified the COVID-19 posts as 'pseudoscientific'[222] and targeted at a 'vulnerable audience'[223] at a time when 'community anxiety was building as to this new pandemic'.[224] In the context of the former

---

[216] FDA, 'Purported Biotech Executive' (n 215). See too FDA, 'Three Baltimore-Area Men' (n 215).
[217] See also Chapter 11.
[218] *Australian Competition and Consumer Commission v Lorna Jane Pty Ltd* [2021] FCA 852, [1].
[219] ibid [4].
[220] ibid [19].
[221] *Secretary, Department of Health v Oxymed Australia Pty Ltd* [2021] FCA 1518.
[222] ibid [93].
[223] ibid.
[224] ibid [243].

chiropractor's 'zealous enthusiasm'[225] for hyperbaric oxygen treatment and his lack of insight into the contravening conduct,[226] Rofe J noted that:

> The expert medical evidence was that there was a risk of harm to consumers who might not pursue the orthodox treatment for their condition, and the risk that vulnerable consumers also might suffer financial harm as a result of the cost of a course of HBOT.[227]

In Japan advertisements that make false or exaggerated medical claims are illegal under consumer protection legislation that prohibits the making of misleading representations in respect of goods and services.[228] In addition, advertisements for uncertified products claiming to prevent or treat medical conditions are a violation of Japan's pharmaceutical and medical device law.[229] Early in the COVID-19 pandemic, the Consumer Affairs Agency of Japan took the approach of monitoring online advertisements that falsely represented preventative characteristics of products and demanding improvement. It informed companies that were non-compliant with its requirements that they needed to curtail their conduct.[230]

By June 2020, concerns about the phenomenon had grown and it was being theorized that entrepreneurial e-commerce site operators were taking advantage of inadequate regulatory oversight at a time when people were staying at home and were relying more heavily on e-commerce. Surveys of infringing products showed substantial increases in the availability of products that were making false claims on marketing sites.[231] Japan's Ministry for Health made it clear that selling products as anti-viral agents for use on the body, rather than as a deodorizer or cleanser, were breaching pharmaceutical and medical device laws and the Tokyo Metropolitan Government, which monitors legal compliance for commercial products sold in the capital and provides guidance where necessary, provided clear messages to a similar effect. However, research by *Nikkei Asia* found that a significant number of e-commerce operators were circumventing the law by using suggestive language connoting antiviral efficacy for their products.[232]

---

[225] ibid [259].
[226] ibid [260].
[227] ibid [243].
[228] See Oki Mori and Mai Umezawa, 'Japan: Consumer Protection Laws and Regulations 2021' (ICLG, 4 May 2021) <https://iclg.com/practice-areas/consumer-protection-laws-and-regulations/japan> accessed 14 September 2022.
[229] Consumer Affairs Agency of Japan, 'White Paper on Consumer Affairs 2021' (2021) <www.caa.go.jp/en/publication/annual_report/2021/assets/en_summary_2021_210824.pdf> accessed 14 September 2022.
[230] ibid.
[231] See Yuichiro Kanematsu, 'Ads Touting Quack Coronavirus Cures Rampant in Japan' *Nikkei Asia* (9 June 2020) <https://asia.nikkei.com/Spotlight/Coronavirus/Ads-touting-quack-coronavirus-cures-rampant-in-Japan> accessed 14 September 2022.
[232] ibid.

In the United Kingdom, too, efforts were made to inhibit false advertising about products asserted to be able to prevent, treat, and cure COVID-19. The United Kingdom's Medicines and Healthcare products Regulatory Agency (MHRA) warned the public not to be fooled by products ranging from self-testing kits to anti-viral misting sprays. It announced that in the early stages of COVID-19 it had disabled nine domain names and social media accounts that were selling fake coronavirus-related products, and that it was investigating five further cases.[233] Lynda Scammell, a Senior Enforcement Advisor to the MHRA, made the point that at the time:

> There is no medicine licensed specifically to treat or prevent COVID-19, therefore any claiming to do so are not authorised and have not undergone regulatory approvals required for sale on the UK market. We cannot guarantee the safety or quality of the product and this poses a risk to your health. The risk of buying medicines and medical devices from unregulated websites are that you just don't know what you will receive and could be putting your health at risk.[234]

The MHRA stated on 19 March 2020 that its annual operation in relation to the illegal online sale of medicine 'identified a disturbing trend of criminals who are taking advantage of the COVID-19 outbreak by exploiting the high market demand for personal protection and hygiene products'.[235] It also noted that:

> Globally, 2,000 online advertisements related to COVID-19 were found and more than 34,000 unlicensed and fake products, advertised as "corona spray", "coronavirus medicines" or, "coronaviruses packages" were seized. Whilst there were no coronavirus related products found to have reached UK borders on this occasion, Operation Pangea aims to tackle serious organized crime globally and the MHRA plays a big role in ensuring unlicensed medicines and medical devices are not making their way onto UK markets.[236]

By May 2020, Ms Scammell explained the MHRA strategy:

---

[233] Medicines and Healthcare products Regulatory Agency, 'UK Medicines and Medical Devices Regulator Investigating 14 Cases of Fake or Unlicensed COVID-19 Medical Products' (Press Release, 4 April 2020) <www.gov.uk/government/news/uk-medicines-and-medical-devices-regulator-investigating-14-cases-of-fake-or-unlicensed-covid-19-medical-products> accessed 14 September 2021.

[234] Medicines and Healthcare products Regulatory Agency, 'Coronavirus: Global Crackdown Sees a Rise in Unlicenced Medical Products Related to COVID-19' (Press Release, 19 March 2020) <www.gov.uk/government/news/coronavirus-global-crackdown-sees-a-rise-in-unlicenced-medical-products-related-to-covid-19> accessed 14 September 2022 (hereafter 'Coronavirus: Global Crackdown'); Samuel Lovett, 'Coronavirus: Surge in Fake Treatments Sold Online Spark Warning from UK Authorities' *The Independent* (4 April 2020) <www.independent.co.uk/news/health/coronavirus-fake-cure-treatment-sold-online-latest-a9447496.html> accessed 14 September 2022.

[235] 'Coronavirus: Global Crackdown' (n 234).

[236] ibid.

We want to caution people that products claiming to do so are not authorised and have not undergone regulatory approvals required for sale on the UK market. We cannot guarantee the safety or quality of these products and this poses a risk to your health. We have been receiving reports of 'miracle cures', 'antiviral misting sprays', antiviral medicines being sold through websites. Offering to sell unauthorised medicines is against the law.[237]

Criminal charges have also been brought, including by the City of London Intellectual Property Crime Unit, for fraud and unlawful manufacture of medicinal products for the treatment of COVID-19.[238] In addition, an investigation was launched by the Charity Commission (which regulates charities in England and Wales), as well as Trading Standards, into the Camberwell Kingdom Church that had been reported to be selling coronavirus 'protection kits'. However, the Church then relaunched the kits, priced at £91, claiming them to be 'divine cleansing oil'.[239]

During the COVID-19 pandemic the tendency of regulators was to communicate to those making problematic representations, initially, by sending warning letters. However, as discussed earlier, in a number of symbolic actions regulators sought pecuniary penalties and requested court injunctions against purveyors of precluded representations. This aspect of consumer protection policy constituted an important reinforcement of governments' attempts to prohibit predatory behaviour during a time when consumers could be vulnerable to those who wanted to take advantage of anxiety, mistrust, and desperation within the community.

IX. Regulation of Healthcare Practitioners

Another source of problematic representations about a pandemic is from health practitioners, in particular medical practitioners. Such practitioners who are registered or licensed (depending on the jurisdiction) occupy positions of significant influence at such a time and are looked to for guidance and provision of reliable information by their patients and by the community generally. When they

---

[237] Medicines and Healthcare products Regulatory Agency, 'Senior Enforcement Advisor at UK Medicines Regulator Warns Against Purchasing Fake or Unlicensed Coronavirus (COVID 19) Medicines' (Press Release, 7 May 2020) <www.gov.uk/government/news/senior-enforcement-advisor-at-uk-medicines-regulator-warns-against-purchasing-fake-or-unlicensed-coronavirus-covid-19-medicines> accessed 14 September 2022.
[238] 'Coronavirus: Man in Court Over Fake COVID-19 Treatment Kits' *BBC News* (21 March 2020) <www.bbc.com/news/uk-england-london-51991245> accessed 14 September 2022.
[239] 'Coronavirus: Camberwell Church Continuing to Sell Fake Covid-19 Cure' *BBC News* (30 April 2020) <www.bbc.com/news/uk-england-london-52480133> accessed 14 September 2022.

fail significantly in this regard, or when they communicate misinformation, professional regulators can be called upon to intervene to protect the public as well as the standing of the relevant profession.[240] In Australia, the Australian Health Practitioner Regulation Agency (AHPRA) and the National Health Boards warned in March 2020:

> the public is likely to seek reassurance and answers about COVID-19 from their trusted health professional. While the vast majority of health practitioners are responding professionally to the COVID-19 emergency and focusing on providing safe care, Ahpra and National Boards are seeing some examples of false and misleading advertising on COVID-19.
>
> During these challenging times, it is vital that health practitioners only provide information about COVID-19 that is scientifically accurate and from authoritative sources, such as a state, territory or Commonwealth health department or the World Health Organization (WHO). According to these authoritative sources, there is currently no cure or evidence-based treatment or therapy which prevents infection by COVID-19 and work is currently underway on a vaccine.
>
> Other than sharing health information from authoritative sources, registered health practitioners should not make advertising claims on preventing or protecting patients and health consumers from contracting COVID-19 or accelerating recovery from COVID-19. To do so involves risk to public safety and may be unlawful advertising.[241]

Notwithstanding such advice, regulatory intervention was required on multiple occasions in relation to individual practitioners during the pandemic. Cases during the COVID-19 pandemic, one from Australia, three from England, one from Canada, and the other from Ireland, are examples of regulatory approaches during the crisis.[242]

---

[240] Compare the refusal of a visa to the tennis player, Novak Djokovic, on the ground that his presence may act as a fillip to those opposed to vaccination and influence others, discussed in Chapter 6. Issues can arise also in relation to the regulation of lawyers who attempt to use their trusted position to urge anti-vaccination stances or opposition to public health measures, including on social media: see Marta Rychert, Kate Diesfeld, and Ian Freckelton, 'Professional Discipline for Vaccine Misinformation Posts on Social Media: Issues and Controversies for the Legal Profession' (2022) 29(3) *Journal of Law and Medicine* 895 (hereafter Rychert and others, 'Vaccine Misinformation Posts').

[241] AHPRA and the National Boards, 'False and Misleading Advertising on COVID-19' (News, 31 March 2020) <www.ahpra.gov.au/News/2020-03-31-false-and-misleading-advertising-on-covid-19.aspx> accessed 14 September 2022.

[242] See generally Ian Freckelton, 'COVID-19 Denialism, Vaccine Scepticism and the Regulation of Health Practitioners' (2021) 28(3) *Journal of Law and Medicine* 613 (hereafter Freckelton, 'COVID-19 Denialism').

A. English Jurisprudence

In England, a consultant surgeon, Mr Mohammad Adil, who had worked in the National Health System for nearly 30 years, was suspended for an interim period of 12 months after posting videos on social media claiming that COVID-19 was a hoax and orchestrated by the elite to control the world.[243] Dr Anne McCloskey, a family doctor in Derry and a former Aontú (political party) councillor, was also suspended, in her case for 18 months, while the General Medical Council investigated disinformation for which it was said she was responsible for promulgating in relation to COVID-19 vaccines. Among claims allegedly made by Dr McCloskey were assertions that many people had been 'coerced, bribed or bullied' into being vaccinated and that COVID-19 vaccines were 'malevolent'.[244]

However, in *White v General Medical Council*,[245] the issue was as to how health practitioners' rights to free speech during the COVID-19 pandemic can be reconciled with their ongoing right to practise. Dr White was a general practitioner with an unblemished career. A video expressing views that he held about COVID-19 was posted by him on YouTube. He was then suspended by NHS England South East but subsequently reinstated.[246] The General Medical Council then referred him to the Immediate Orders Tribunal for it to consider imposition of restrictions on his practice[247] on three bases:

- Spreading 'misinformation and inaccurate details about COVID-19 and how it is diagnosed and treated, including saying the vaccine is a form of genetic manipulation which can cause serious illness and death and that he advised against wearing masks.'
- Potentially putting 'patients at risk and diminishing the public's trust in the medical profession by disseminating misinformation and inaccurate details about the measures taken to tackle the Coronavirus pandemic.'
- Signposting viewers of his online video to 'comments and articles of others on the internet who shared the same views, raising concerns on the basis that those individuals were also promoting information which was inaccurate or untrue.'[248]

---

[243] See Clare Dyer, 'Surgeon Who Said COVID-19 Was a Hoax Has Been Suspended Pending GMC Investigation' (2020) 370 *British Medical Journal* m2714.

[244] See Garrett Hargan, 'Derry GP Handed 18-month Suspension Over COVID Misinformation' *Belfast Telegraph* (24 September 2021) <www.belfasttelegraph.co.uk/news/northern-ireland/derry-gp-handed-18-month-suspension-over-covid-misinformation-40883032.html> accessed 14 September 2022.

[245] [2021] EWHC 3286 (Admin).

[246] ibid [4].

[247] Pursuant to rule 27 of the *General Medical Council (Fitness to Practise) Rules Order of Council 2004*, SI 2004/2608 (England and Wales).

[248] *White v General Medical Council* [2021] EWHC 3286 (Admin), [5].

Dr White accepted that in the video he stated that he was leaving his employment in conventional medicine to pursue a career in 'functional medicine' because of lies about the National Health Service and the government about the pandemic which he could no longer tolerate and that he identified hydroxychloroquine, budesonide inhalers, and ivermectin as drugs that he regarded as 'safe and proven treatments' that he had been prevented from prescribing.[249] He also agreed that he had aired doubts about the safety of vaccination, argued that 99% of those who died from COVID-19 suffered from multiple medical problems, raised concerns about polymerase chain reaction (PCR) testing, saying it was a 'fraud that vitiates everything', expressed concerns about the side effects of vaccines, and contended that 'masks do absolutely nothing'.[250]

Before the Interim Orders Tribunal, counsel for Dr White and for the General Medical Council addressed the issue of whether the statements made by Dr White fell within the bounds of legitimate freedom of speech, the right to which is protected by Article 10 of the *European Convention on Human Rights*,[251] or whether they went beyond 'legitimate medical comment to conspiracy theories, accusing the government of a campaign of lies and a hoax' and thereby breaching 'Good Medical Practice', undermining confidence in the profession, and raising concerns as to patient safety.[252] However, the Immediate Orders Tribunal did not make reference to these issues in its reasons for imposing conditions on Dr White, save to state that it had taken into account his right to freedom of expression. The Tribunal instead focused on the risk posed by his expression of views about patient safety and his responsibility to provide sufficient and balanced information about the virus.[253] It precluded him from using social media to put forward or share any views he had about COVID-19 or associated matters and required him to remove any such posts for which he had been responsible.[254]

Justice Dove allowed the appeal, noting that section 12 of the *Human Rights Act 1998* (UK) required the Immediate Orders Tribunal to take into account the right of freedom of expression in its decision-making by asking itself whether Dr White would probably succeed at any later tribunal hearing. This required explicit

---

[249] ibid [6].
[250] ibid [7].
[251] '1. Everyone has the right to freedom of expression. This right shall include freedom to hold opinions and to receive and impart information and ideas without interference by public authority and regardless of frontiers. This Article shall not prevent States from requiring the licensing of broadcasting, television or cinema enterprises.
2. The exercise of these freedoms, since it carries with it duties and responsibilities, may be subject to such formalities, conditions, restrictions or penalties as are prescribed by law and are necessary in a democratic society, in the interests of national security, territorial integrity or public safety, for the prevention of disorder or crime, for the protection of health or morals, for the protection of the reputation or rights of others, for preventing the disclosure of information received in confidence, or for maintaining the authority and impartiality of the judiciary.'
[252] *White v General Medical Council* [2021] EWHC 3286 (Admin), [10].
[253] ibid [10].
[254] ibid [1].

reference to and consideration of his right to freedom of expression.[255] Justice Dove also noted that a further deficit in the orders made by the Immediate Orders Tribunal was that the prohibition imposed on Dr White would preclude him from changing his mind and expressing himself on social media in support of the position expressed by the General Medical Council. He drew attention to the need for proportionality in any order which inhibited a practitioner's freedom of expression, even on an interim basis, by being specific about the views or opinions they are not allowed to express.[256] The decision by Dove J constitutes an important precedent for the incorporation of entitlements to freedom of expression as a consideration to be balanced against concerns held by a regulator that a health practitioner is expressing views which may be inconsistent with, and even play a role in undermining, public health policies in force from time to time during a pandemic.

B. Irish Jurisprudence

In an important judgment in 2021, the President of the Irish High Court, Irvine J, heard an application for an interim suspension order in relation to the registration of a 71-year-old general medical practitioner, Dr Waters.[257] Amongst other issues that raised the concern of the regulator, the Irish Medical Council, was the presence in the waiting room of the doctor's surgery of a photocopied pamphlet entitled, 'No Pandemic Killing Us', as well as the fact that during a consultation that he undertook, a patient maintained that he (the patient) 'was treated to a barrage of nonsense about the "hoax that is Covid-19" and that "the state and the government are scamming the people"'.[258] Furthermore, Dr Waters was said to have advised the complainant that wearing masks was causing his illness and that COVID-19 was a hoax. The complainant also stated that Dr Waters made the claim that people who were confirmed to have died of COVID-19 had not actually died from that disease and those that did were 'terribly old'.[259]

The patient expressed the concern that Dr Waters'

> behaviour is very dangerous as he is openly undermining the messages being delivered by public health professionals who are trying their best to manage the current public health emergency. Dr Waters I fear is influencing patients of his to become sceptical about the severity of this situation and I would worry about those who are vulnerable ... I fear Dr Waters has patients who are in vulnerable

---

[255] ibid [23].
[256] ibid [28].
[257] *Medical Council v Waters* [2021] IEHC 252 (hereafter '*Medical Council v Waters*'). See generally Freckelton, 'COVID-19 Denialism' (n 242).
[258] *Medical Council v Waters* (n 257) [5].
[259] ibid [4].

categories and I would worry for those patients who take his opinions at face value due to his status as medical professional.[260]

Justice Irvine found that, although Dr Waters had known for many months of the government's vaccination programme, he had not taken steps to inform his patients as soon as possible of his objection to administering vaccines or of their right to have vaccines administered by another practitioner.

Justice Irvine observed that:

> In circumstances where he does not deny that Covid-19 can kill, particularly the elderly, and he does not deny that Covid-19 is contagious or that its onwards transmission is prevented by testing and tracing close contacts of those infected and by ensuring that an infected person remains distanced or in isolation from others, the Respondent will have difficulty in relying upon his rights in that regard.
>
> Furthermore, it is hard to see how the Respondent's rights of conscientious objection could entitle him to make decisions for his patients regarding the risks he believes they should be willing to accept when visiting his practice. His failure to refer patients for testing when they present with Covid-19 symptoms and in failing to advise such patients to self-isolate and knowingly to operate his surgery in a manner which increases his patients' risks of contracting or spreading Covid-19 are difficult to excuse on any grounds.[261]

She also concluded that:

> His failure to refer patients for Covid-19 testing may have very real and severe consequences for his patients and those with whom they have close contact. At the risk of stating the obvious, to fail to test patients suspected of having Covid-19 may lead to undetected cases in the community and result in the uncontrolled spread of the virus. Similarly, the Respondent's failure and that of his staff to wear masks and the fact that mask wearing, physical distancing and other preventative measures are not encouraged or followed at his practice as well as the continuance of walk-in appointments make his premises unnecessarily dangerous for his patients. Non-adherence to these measures in a general practitioner's practice is particularly dangerous having regard to the fact that the general practitioner's surgery is often the first port of call for many who display symptoms of Covid-19. In this kind of environment, adherence to basic public health advice is vital.[262]

---

[260] ibid [5].
[261] ibid [34]–[35].
[262] ibid [36].

C. Canadian Jurisprudence

In Ontario, Canada, the College of Physicians and Surgeons suspended an emergency room doctor, Dr Rochagné Kilian, on an interim basis for a variety of public pronouncements about the safety and efficacy of COVID-19 vaccines.[263] She had been a speaker at several rallies organized by the 'Grey-Bruce Freedom Fighters', a group that campaigned against mandatory vaccination and against lockdowns, allegedly with some 3,000 members,[264] and was reported to have resigned her position as an emergency room doctor owing to the way that the Grey Bruce Health Services had handled the pandemic. She campaigned about what she asserted was a rise in 'D-dimer levels' in patients after receiving a COVID-19 vaccine and argued that the consequential phenomenon of 'micro-clotting' was likely to be associated with the development of an autoimmune disorder.[265] She and three other Ontario doctors had previously been precluded from providing medical exemptions to mandates on masks and COVID-19 vaccinations and testing for the virus.[266]

D. Australian Jurisprudence

In the Australian state of Victoria,[267] a medical practitioner, Dr Ellis, campaigned against government policies in relation to treatment of COVID-19, advocated the use of vitamin C to treat it, disputed the utility of vaccinations against the virus, and expressed doubts to patients and in the media (including social media) about the seriousness of the pandemic. A complaint was made about his conduct and he was given the opportunity to recant and commit to adhering to the conventional medical position about the treatment and prevention of the virus. He was equivocal in relation to such matters. The Victorian Civil and Administrative Tribunal upheld a decision of the Medical Board of Australia to suspend the practitioner, finding that Dr Ellis posed a serious risk to the community and commenting that: 'The

---

[263] Chris Herhalt, 'Ontario Regulator Says Anti-COVID-19 Vaccine Doctor Can No Longer Practice Medicine' *CP24* (28 October 2021) <www.cp24.com/news/ontario-regulator-says-anti-covid-19-vaccine-doctor-can-no-longer-practice-medicine-1.5642086> accessed 4 October 20zo.

[264] See Keith Dempsey, 'Rally Against Vaccine Protests Held in Hanover' *The Post* (12 October 2021) <www.thepost.on.ca/news/local-news/rally-against-vaccine-passports-held-in-hanover> accessed 4 October 2022.

[265] See Canadian Covid Care Alliance, 'Dr Rochagné Kilian—Blowing the Whistle on Covid-19 Vaccines and D-Dimer Levels' (Video, 29 October 2021) <www.canadiancovidcarealliance.org/media-resources/dr-rochagne-kilian-blowing-the-whistle-on-covid-19-vaccines-and-d-dimer-levels/> accessed 14 September 2022.

[266] Chris Fox, 'Two Doctors Banned from Issuing Medical Exemptions for COVID-19 Vaccines, Mandatory Mask Requirements' *CP24* (18 October 2021) <www.cp24.com/news/two-doctors-barred-from-issuing-medical-exemptions-for-covid-19-vaccines-mandatory-mask-requirements-1.5627317> accessed 14 September 2022.

[267] *Ellis v Medical Board of Australia* [2020] VCAT 862.

coronavirus pandemic has increased the risk that vulnerable or unqualified persons would, out of fear or desperation, turn to "advice" from unreliable sources.'[268]

E. Summary

The decision by Irvine J to suspend Dr Waters and by the Victorian Civil and Administrative Tribunal to affirm the suspension of Dr Ellis were conventional in terms of their approach to discouragement of non-evidence-based medical practice and conduct likely to bring disrepute upon the medical profession. They were consistent with the decision of the Immediate Orders Tribunal in relation to Dr White. However, the appellate decision of Dove J in relation to Dr White provided a salutary reminder that the entitlement of health practitioners to express their views must be incorporated explicitly as part of the decision-making process about whether sanctions should be imposed for the expression of heterodox views.

The extent to which and the manner in which health practitioners should be permitted to express their dissent against current clinical orthodoxy during a pandemic is far from straightforward.[269] It exemplifies tensions in respect of the exercise of rights to free speech by health practitioners during a medical emergency; some asserted that there was an excessive degree of coercion exercised to comply with the positions taken by public health officials during the COVID-19 pandemic.[270] A communication to the CBC News by the College of Physicians and Surgeons of Ontario, Canada, illustrates the issue:

> It's important that physicians recognize the influence that they may have on social media, particularly when it comes to public health. The [College of Physicians and Surgeons of Ontario] believes questioning the value of vaccinations or countering public health best practices during COVID-19 represents a risk to the public and is not acceptable behaviour. Physicians who are found to be spreading misleading medical information that may bring harm towards patients can face practice restrictions or suspension for their actions.[271]

Highlighting the importance of the issue from the perspective of public health, it has been identified that propagation of erroneous, 'scientific-sounding

---

[268] ibid [82].
[269] See Kamran Abbasi, 'Covid-19 Dissenters—Or the Virtue in Being Less Cheerful' (2021) 372 *British Medical Journal* n731.
[270] See Human Rights Watch, *COVID-19 Triggers Wave of Free Speech Abuse* (Report, 11 February 2021) <www.hrw.org/news/2021/02/11/covid-19-triggers-wave-free-speech-abuse#> accessed 14 September 2022.
[271] See Katie Nicholson and Andrea Bellemare, 'Ontario Doctor Subject of Complaints After COVID-19 Tweets' *CBC News* (10 August 2021) <www.cbc.ca/news/canada/toronto/kulvinder-kaur-gill-tweets-cpso-1.5680122> accessed 14 September 2022.

misinformation' about vaccination, for instance, is associated with a decline in preparedness to submit to vaccination.[272]

The problematic aspect of what needs to be a balancing exercise is the extent to which, within the bounds of adherence to evidence-based practice, health practitioners should be precluded from expressing genuinely held views that are inconsistent with the status quo and with the position being promoted at any given time by the government.[273] Put another way, how pluralistic is professional discourse permitted to be during a pandemic? Is it reasonable to impose more constraints on health practitioners than are required of others?[274] There is much to be said for constructive professional discussion and questioning of prevailing assumptions in a temperate and analytical tone. Disagreement can be healthy—what is public health policy at one time can be jettisoned later when other data become available. Ultimately, the question is where the line should be drawn, particularly in the midst of a 'battle' against a pandemic. The controversies tend to arise where health professionals are considered by a regulator to be contradicting scientifically established matters relating to the pandemic or the safety and advisability of vaccination.

It is apparent from the decisions and regulatory responses to which reference has been made in this part of the chapter that, during the COVID-19 pandemic, primacy was given by regulators and disciplinary tribunals in a number of countries to enforce consistency with government messaging in relation to the pandemic. Health practitioners who departed from the prevailing orthodoxy were at risk of being deprived of their entitlement to practise their profession, at least for a time. It became apparent that it was generally regarded as a responsibility of registered health practitioners to abstain from anything that might be construed as the provision of misinformation and which could thereby imperil public health. Practitioners who flouted or were seen to be non-compliant with such obligations risked being deprived of the privileges of registration. However, the decision of Dove J in *White v General Medical Council*[275] constitutes a salutary reminder of the need for meaningful attention to be paid on every occasion to the reality that imposition of constraints upon health practitioners' public expression of views is an

---

[272] See Sahi Loomba and others, 'Measuring the Impact of COVID-19 Vaccine Misinformation on Vaccination Intent in the UK and USA' (2021) 5 *Nature Human Behaviour* 337. See too World Health Organization, 'Fighting Misinformation in the Time of COVID-19, One Click at a Time' (Feature Story, 27 April 2021) <www.who.int/news-room/feature-stories/detail/fighting-misinformation-in-the-time-of-covid-19-one-click-at-a-time> accessed 14 September 2022.

[273] See Vinay Prasad and Jeffrey S Flier, 'Scientists Who Express Different Views on COVID-19 Should Be Heard, Not Demonized' *STAT* (27 April 2020) <www.statnews.com/2020/04/27/hear-scientists-different-views-covid-19-dont-attack-them/> accessed 14 September 2022.

[274] See Erik Baekkeskov, Olivier Rubin, and Perola Öberg, 'Monotonous or Pluralistic Public Discourse? Reason-giving and Dissent in Denmark's and Sweden's Early 2020 COVID-19 Responses' (2021) 28(8) *Journal of European Public Policy* 1321. See too in the context of lawyers Rychert and others, 'Vaccine Misinformation Posts' (n 239).

[275] [2021] EWHC 3286 (Admin).

encroachment on the right to freedom of expression—a valuable entitlement in a democratic society.

X. Conclusion

The COVID-19 pandemic has generated a variety of bases upon which persons who have been adversely affected by lockdowns and stay-at-home orders have sought recourse in civil actions. More will follow. Most of these actions are likely to be claims under the tort of negligence, and the preponderance will probably be brought against governments, but some are also being brought against institutions, such as providers of congregate care, and employers. Some actions might also be brought under contract law when the pandemic has made compliance with the terms of agreements impossible or very difficult. In this regard, the pandemic is shining a new light on the doctrine of frustration of contract and the ambit of force majeure clauses. Protections have been created in a number of countries for those administering vaccinations so as to engage participation in the process by health practitioners. However, concerns about the potential for adverse effects from vaccinations, although significant side effects are rare, has created an impetus for no-fault vaccination schemes. Such schemes exist for some participants in the COVAX scheme but pressure has been building for other countries also to create such schemes.

An issue that is continuing to be resolved by appellate courts in a number of countries is the efficacy of business interruption insurance. This area is highly technical and depends upon national jurisprudence and the precise terms of such clauses. A policy tension can be identified between giving effect to the apparent intention of such clauses, namely to protect insured persons and business entities against commercial interruptions which could not have been foreseen, and the effects of a broad reading of such clauses to permit insurance companies to deny liability to claimants. Consumer protection in the face of false, inflated, and misconceived claims by proponents of products and services has proved difficult to apply globally. Medico-legal investigations into COVID-19 deaths have generated many challenges in relation to their findings and what can be learned from them. In countries with coronial systems, such as England, Canada, and Australia, inquests have commenced into certain categories of deaths, seeking to learn lessons that can be applied in the future. In other jurisdictions too, such as Scotland, formal measures have been deployed to inquire into deaths that may have been avoidable to allay public concerns about such deaths and to protect against them in the future.

Diverse regulatory measures, ranging from the conciliatory, to civil enforcement, to the deployment of the criminal law have been utilized in order to provide consumer protection to persons at risk of being exploited by the unscrupulous. In addition, the pandemic has posed challenges for regulators of health practitioners.

Action has been taken in a number of countries that has had the effect of significantly inhibiting the expression of unconventional opinions that have been inconsistent with governments' health directives. This has raised difficult issues in relation to the suppression of unorthodox views during a pandemic. It highlights the need for recognition that suppression of dissenting views, even by health practitioners, involves a serious encroachment upon rights of free speech and expression.

10
COVID-19 and Workplace and Occupational Health and Safety

I. Introduction

During the COVID-19 pandemic, the workplace became a focus of regulation and legal intervention by reason of its constituting a forum for congregate gatherings and thereby for potential transmission of a virus in a way that had not occurred for a century. This has placed pressure upon occupational health and safety laws to adapt to the reality of workplaces foreseeably constituting a vector for the spread of a potentially fatal illness. It has required rethinking of responsibilities in respect of the conditions for entry into, departure from, and interaction within workplaces, as well as for practices permitted to take place within workplaces.

The nature of many workplaces has changed, too, in response to the pandemic. Section II of this chapter reviews key aspects of these changes. The pandemic has disrupted workforce trends and been the catalyst for new ones. For instance, there are likely for some time to be offices of reduced size within central business districts[1] and potentially fewer people working within such districts at any given time. In addition, the pandemic has provided additional impetus to the digitalization of work with remote contact with employees, contractors, clients, and patients assuming a much higher profile.[2] The use of remote conferencing facilities is likely to result longer term in far less travelling for work.[3] Another consequence of the pandemic has been the need for adaptation of working arrangements so that, when

---

[1] See eg Douglas Broom, 'Home or Office? Survey Shows Opinions About Work after COVID-19' *World Economic Forum* (21 July 2021) <www.weforum.org/agenda/2021/07/back-to-office-or-work-from-home-survey/> accessed 14 September 2022; Daniel Davis, '5 Models for the Post-Pandemic Workplace' *Harvard Business Review* (3 June 2021) <https://hbr.org/2021/06/5-models-for-the-post-pandemic-workplace> accessed 14 September 2022;Piyush Tiwari and Jyoti Shukla, 'The Future of Offices in Post-COVID Melbourne' *Pursuit* (2021) <https://pursuit.unimelb.edu.au/articles/the-future-of-offices-in-post-covid-melbourne> accessed 14 September 2022.

[2] See Fareed Zakaria, *Ten Lessons for a Post-Pandemic World* (Allen Lane 2021) 103.

[3] See Peter Caputo and others, 'Return to a World Transformed: How the Pandemic is Reshaping Corporate Travel' (Deloitte Insight, 2 August 2021) <www2.deloitte.com/us/en/insights/focus/transportation/future-of-business-travel-post-covid.html> accessed 14 September 2022; Alana Semuels, 'Business Travel's Demise Could Have Far-Reaching Consequences' *Time* (20 October 2021) <https://time.com/6108331/business-travel-decline-covid-19/> accessed 14 September 2022; David Koenig, '"Things Have Changed": Business Travel May Never Go Back to the Way It was Before COVID-19' *USA Today* (26 July 2021) <www.usatoday.com/story/travel/2021/07/26/business-travel-changes-covid-pandemic-zoom-meetings-in-person-gatherings/5374153001/> accessed 1 December 2021.

required by public health directives, as many people as possible could work from home and be managed and monitored remotely.[4] This, too, is a change to working patterns that to some degree is likely to endure after the pandemic in the form of what are often now termed 'hybrid work arrangements'.[5]

Health and safety responsibilities in the context of a pandemic generate particular legal obligations for employers, employees, and contractors. The nature of these obligations is scrutinized in Section III of this chapter. The changes in working arrangements between 2020 and 2022 also raised the question of how occupational health and safety should be maintained as far as practicable and how new forms of workplace, including the home, should be regulated for that purpose. COVID-19 generated debates about who is differentially affected by such changes in working arrangements, because of the limitations that some have in working remotely—for instance, by reason of the suitability of their home for online work, responsibilities for childcare, and availability of adequate internet facilities.

The profiles of those in work changed too. For instance, during surges in need, workers in the health sector who were not traditionally the providers of certain services were asked to return from retirement, diversify their work skills, or accelerate their acquisition of skills so as to fill gaps. As discussed in Section IV of this chapter, this required legislative authorization for some categories of workers, such as healthcare workers, and flexibility for management and employees alike. Debates took place about whether essential workers could ethically or legally opt out of the workplace during the public health crisis, prioritizing their own health (and that of their families) over the needs of others, including their clients/patients. Later in the pandemic, some workers were resistant to returning to the workplace, or at least to the traditional workplace, while risks of viral transmission periodically re-emerged during new waves of the pandemic and as long as risks from the virus could not be eliminated. These matters are explored in Section V of this chapter.

With the increasing availability of vaccines, another set of issues emerged surrounding the entitlement or obligations of employers to exclude workers, patrons, and customers who had not been tested for or vaccinated against COVID-19—or, put another way, the measures that a workplace could reasonably impose to limit its premises playing an unacceptable role in facilitating spread of the virus. This is an aspect of the mandatory vaccination or 'no jab, no work' debate, which had the

---

[4] See Productivity Commission, *Working From Home* (Research Paper, 2021) <www.pc.gov.au/research/completed/working-from-home/working-from-home.pdf> accessed 14 September 2022.

[5] See Susan Lund and others, *The Future of Work After COVID-19* (Report, McKinsey Global Institute 18 February 2021) <www.mckinsey.com/featured-insights/future-of-work/the-future-of-work-after-covid-19> accessed 14 September 2022; Antoni Wontorczyk and Bohan Roznowski, 'Remote, Hybrid and On-Site Work during the SARSCo-V-2 Pandemic and the Consequences for Stress and Work Engagement' (2022) 19(4) *International Journal of Environmental Public Health* art 2400; Saba Aziz, 'Canadians Favour Hybrid Work Amid COVID-19. Can Employers Force Them Back?' *Toronto Star* (23 March 2022) <https://globalnews.ca/news/8702634/covid-return-to-office-employee-rights/> accessed 21 May 2022.

potential to place a newly stigmatized section of the community, 'the unvaccinated', at a disadvantage in a variety of respects, including in their capacity to maintain employment. These issues are scrutinized in Section VI of the chapter.

II. Changing Workplace Culture

It has been part of the culture in many workplaces, and encouraged by employers, that employees should not take sick leave without proper cause,[6] and that they should show commitment to undertaking their work responsibilities by working through minor symptoms of illness.[7] The latter is often termed 'presenteeism'.[8] The decision by workers to attend the workplace when unwell has been recognized as being influenced by a number of factors, including sick leave policies, an increasingly casualized workforce, and cultures of obligation experienced in some sectors of the workforce, such as that which employs healthcare practitioners and emergency services personnel.[9] A systematic review of presenteeism found three principal themes:

1. Organisational factors (organisational policy, presenteeism culture, disciplinary action);
2. Job characteristics (lack of cover, professionalism, job demand); and
3. Personal reasons (burden on colleagues, colleague perceptions, threshold of sickness absence and financial concerns).[10]

Concerns about the dangers of the culture of 'soldiering on' have been raised for some years, independently of pandemics, in part because the culture has the potential to result in workers placing their health at risk and becoming more unwell than if they assisted their recovery by taking a short break away from the workplace.[11]

---

[6] Known in some countries, including Australia, as 'sickies': see John R Schermerhorn Jr and others, *Management* (7th edn, Wiley 2020) ch 12. See too Sophie Toomey, 'Sickies Unmask Offices' *The Australian* (6 October 2017) <www.theaustralian.com.au/news/sickies-unmask-offices/news-story/4fb5c991479797770847f8d04e7308b7> accessed 25 November 2021.
[7] See Maria Karanika-Murray and Caroline Biron, 'The Health-performance Framework of Presenteeism Towards Understanding an Adaptive Behavior' (2020) 73(2) *Human Relations* 242.
[8] See Hesan Quazi, *Presenteeism: The Invisible Cost to Organizations* (Palgrave Macmillan 2013).
[9] See Kian Preston-Suni, Manuel A Celedon, and Kristina M Cordasco, 'Patient Safety and Ethical Implications on Healthcare Sick Leave Policies on the Pandemic Era' (2021) 47(10) *The Joint Commission Journal on Quality and Patient Safety* 673.
[10] Rebecca K Webster and others, 'A Systematic Review of Infectious Illness Presenteeism: Prevalence, Reasons and Risk Factors' (2019) 19 *BMC Public Health* art 799, 1.
[11] See Evans R Fernández Pérez, 'Soldiering on the Job When Ill: Productivity Costs in Connective Tissue Disease-Associated Interstitial Lung Disease' (2020) 17(9) *Annals of the American Thoracic Society* 1058; Eric Widera, Anna Chang, and Helen L Chang, 'Presenteeism: A Public Health Hazard' (2010) 25(11) *Journal of General Internal Medicine* 1244; Christine Long, 'Should You Soldier On at Work?' *The Sydney Morning Herald* (23 July 2015) <www.smh.com.au/business/small-business/should-you-soldier-on-at-work-20150710-gi9n7u.html> accessed 5 December 2021.

In addition, such conduct has facilitated the spread of conditions such as seasonal influenza, norovirus, and rotavirus, including amongst co-workers.[12] It has even been suggested that the economic consequences of presenteeism may be greater than those of absenteeism.[13] This has given a fillip to lobbying for paid sick leave to reduce the phenomenon of presenteeism,[14] as well as for improvements in staff numbers.[15]

Ironically, the phenomenon of 'presenteeism' has been identified as particularly prevalent amongst healthcare workers who too often experience a sense of obligation to work even when symptomatic with illness.[16] For instance, a 2020 study of 533 respondents from 49 countries (Europe 69.2%, Asia-Pacific 19.1%, the Americas 10.9%, and Africa 0.8%) representing 249 healthcare workers (46.7%) and 284 non-healthcare workers (53.2%) found that 58.5% of respondents stated they continued to work when unwell with an influenza-like illness with no variation between the two categories. Sixty-seven (26.9%) healthcare workers and forty-six (16.2%) non-healthcare workers would work with fever alone. Most healthcare workers (89.2–99.2%) and non-healthcare workers (80%–96.5%) would work with 'minor' influenza-like symptoms, such as sore throat, sinus cold, fatigue, sneezing, runny nose, mild cough, and reduced appetite.[17]

However, COVID-19 has stigmatized presenteeism in a potent way, highlighting the fact that attendance at work by workers who may be symptomatic with the virus has the potential to be seriously irresponsible by endangering the health of colleagues and, if the workers are healthcare workers, of those patients whose health they should be safeguarding. In this context, healthcare workers have been described as 'Trojan Horses'.[18] The risk of such workers themselves being

---

[12] See Erin Garrity, 'Guacamole is Extra but the Norovirus Comes Free: Implementing Paid Sick Days for American Workers' (2017) 58(2) *Boston College Law Review* 703.

[13] See Tammy Prater and Kim Smith, 'Underlying Factors Contributing to Presenteeism and Absenteeism' (2011) 9(6) *Journal of Business and Economics Research* 1. See too Paul Hemp, 'Presenteeism: At Work—But Out of It' *Harvard Business Review* (October 2004) <https://hbr.org/2004/10/presenteeism-at-work-but-out-of-it> accessed 14 September 2022.

[14] See Abay Asfaw, Roger Rosa, and Regina Pana-Cryan, 'Potential Economic Benefits of Paid Sick Leave in Reducing Absenteeism Related to the Spread of Influenza-like Illness' (2017) 59(9) *Journal of Occupational and Environmental Medicine* 822. See too Jody Heymann and others, 'Protecting Health During COVID-19 and Beyond: A Global Examination of Paid Sick Leave in 193 Countries' (2020) 15(7) *Global Public Health* 925.

[15] See RM Wrate, 'Increase in Staff Numbers May Reduce Doctors' "Presenteeism"' (1999) 319(7223) *British Medical Journal* 1502.

[16] See Webster and others (n 10); Filipa Pereira and others, 'Presenteeism Among Nurses in Switzerland and Portugal and its Impact on Patient Safety and Quality of Care: Protocol for a Qualitative Study' (2021) 10(5) *JMIR Research Protocols* art e27963; Anupam B Jena and others, 'Presenteeism Among Resident Physicians' (2010) 304(11) *Journal of the American Medical Association* 1166; Ian Freckelton and Patricia Molloy, 'The Health of Health Practitioners: Remedial Programs, Regulation and the Spectre of the Law' (2007) 15(3) *Journal of Law and Medicine* 366.

[17] Ermira Tartari and others, 'Not Sick Enough to Worry? "Influenza-like" Symptoms and Work-related Behavior among Healthcare Workers and other Professionals: Results of a Global Survey' (2020) 15(5) *PLoS One* art e0232168.

[18] See H Asad and others, 'Health Care Workers and Patients as Trojan Horses: A COVID-19 Ward Outbreak' (2020) 2(3) *Infection Prevention in Practice* art 100073.

a precipitant to nosocomial infection spread during a pandemic was identified during the Severe Acute Respiratory Syndrome (SARS) pandemic, prompting discussion about the responsibilities of healthcare workers if they are suffering from symptoms with the potential to result in disease transmission.[19] However, with the high incidence of COVID-19 in workplaces (as discussed later in this chapter), the risks of healthcare workers being vehicles for spreading the virus were very great if they attended work when there was any potential of them being symptomatic. This is playing a role in changing workplace culture generally and especially in the environments where healthcare practitioners provide patient care.

III. Legislative Occupational Health and Safety Obligations

Countries and, in some instances, states or provinces, have diverse obligations under occupational health and safety law. These are generally set out in detailed legislative provisions. Awareness of occupational health and safety dangers conventionally tracks back to the father of industrial injury awareness, Bernardino Ramazzini, who published his first book on occupational diseases in 1713: *De Morbis Artificum Diatriba*.[20] A legislative response to regulating safety in the workplace evolved in the early nineteenth century in a number of countries, including the United Kingdom. Such a response was characterized by the laying down of minimum standards of safe work practice in legislation and regulations, rendering non-compliance with standards in some circumstances a criminal offence, and providing for enforcement of the standards by an independent inspectorate.[21] By the 1960s, there was a perception that occupational health and safety processes in Britain were not achieving their objectives and, in 1970, a Committee of Inquiry chaired by Lord Robens was established to inquire into whether law reform was required. Its 1972 report found the law to be convoluted and 'intrinsically unsatisfactory', and its administration fragmented. The Robens report, which has been internationally influential and resulted, amongst other things, in the *Health and Safety at Work Act 1974* (UK), recommended a more unified and integrated system with better enunciation of obligations, increased cooperation between workers and their representatives, and the use of safety committees and safety representatives.[22]

---

[19] See AK Simonds and DK Sokol, 'Lives on the Line? Ethics and Practicalities of Duty of Care in Pandemics and Disasters' (2009) 34(2) *European Respiratory Journal* 303, 306.

[20] See Bernardinho Ramazzini, *De Morbis Artificum Diatriba: Diseases of Workers* (1713, revised with translation and notes by Wilmer C Wright, rev edn, University of Chicago Press 1940). See too Bernardinho Ramazzini, 'De Morbis Artificum Diatriba [Diseases of Workers]' (2021) 91(9) *American Journal of Public Health* 1380.

[21] See Jacky Steemson, *Labourer's Law: A History of Occupational Health and Safety Legislation* (Royal Society for the Prevention of Accidents 1983); Paul Weindling (ed), *The Social History of Occupational Health* (Croom Helm 1985); Jacqueline K Corn, *Response to Occupational Health Hazard: A Historical Perspective* (Van Nostrand Reinhold 1992).

[22] Alfred Robens (Lord), *Safety and Health at Work: Report of the Committee* (HMSO 1972).

The *Occupational Safety and Health Convention 1981* of the International Labour Organization (ILO)[23] also played an internationally significant role in improving health and safety standards in many countries' workplaces. It required signatory states to 'formulate, implement and periodically review a coherent national policy on occupational safety, occupational health and the working environment' in order to 'prevent accidents and injury to health arising out of, linked with or occurring in the course of work, by minimising, so far as is reasonably practicable, the causes of hazards inherent in the working environment'.[24] This was followed in 2006 by the ILO's Promotional Framework for the *Occupational Safety and Health Convention*,[25] which requires:

(a) 'a national tripartite advisory body, or bodies, addressing occupational safety and health issues;
(b) information and advisory services on occupational safety and health;
(c) the provision of occupational safety and health training;
(d) occupational health services in accordance with national law and practice;
(e) research on occupational safety and health;
(f) a mechanism for the collection and analysis of data on occupational injuries and diseases, taking into account relevant ILO instruments;
(g) provisions for collaboration with relevant insurance or social security schemes covering occupational injuries and diseases; and
(h) support mechanisms for a progressive improvement of occupational safety and health conditions in micro-enterprises, in small and medium-sized enterprises and in the informal economy.'

Pursuant to these Conventions, occupational health and safety legislation tends to impose a higher standard of care than does negligence law—for instance, requiring employers to take steps 'so far as is reasonably practicable' to render workplaces safe.

As noted above, such obligations apply to employers, and often extend to subcontractors,[26] as well as to persons in orthodox roles as employees. For instance, section 2 of the *Health and Safety at Work Act 1974* (UK) provides that:

(1) It shall be the duty of every employer to ensure, so far as is reasonably practicable, the health, safety and welfare at work of all his employees.

---

[23] International Labour Organization, *Occupational Safety and Health Convention (No 155) Concerning Occupational Safety and Health and the Working Environment* (opened for signature 22 June 1981, entered into force 11 August 1983) 1331 UNTS 279.
[24] ibid Article 4.
[25] International Labour Organization, *Promotional Framework for Occupational Safety and Health Convention (No 187) Concerning the Promotional Framework for Occupational Safety and Health* (opened for signature 15 June 2006, entered into force 20 February 2009) 2564 UNTS 291, art 4(3).
[26] See *Health and Safety at Work Act 1974* (UK), s 3.

(2) Without prejudice to the generality of an employer's duty under the preceding subsection, the matters to which that duty extends include in particular—
  (a) the provision and maintenance of plant and systems of work that are, so far as is reasonably practicable, safe and without risks to health;
  (b) arrangements for ensuring, so far as is reasonably practicable, safety and absence of risks to health in connection with the use, handling, storage and transport of articles and substances;
  (c) the provision of such information, instruction, training and supervision as is necessary to ensure, so far as is reasonably practicable, the health and safety at work of his employees;
  (d) so far as is reasonably practicable as regards any place of work under the employer's control, the maintenance of it in a condition that is safe and without risks to health and the provision and maintenance of means of access to and egress from it that are safe and without such risks;
  (e) the provision and maintenance of a working environment for his employees that is, so far as is reasonably practicable, safe, without risks to health, and adequate as regards facilities and arrangements for their welfare at work.

Section 2(6) of the same legislation also requires an employer to engage in consultation 'with a view to the making and maintenance of arrangements which will enable him and his employees to co-operate effectively in promoting and developing measures to ensure the health and safety at work of the employees, and in checking the effectiveness of such measures'. Put another way, employers cannot unilaterally, without consultation, impose measures that they assert to be for the purposes of workplace health safety—rather, discharge of such a function is required to be collaborative. As discussed in Chapter 6, if it is not, the measures imposed by employers may not be lawful.[27]

In *Edwards v National Coal Board*,[28] Asquith LJ of the Court of Appeal of England and Wales explained in the context of a mine owner's obligations that the words 'reasonably practicable' constitute a narrower term than 'physically possible' and imply that a computation must be made in which the degree of risk is placed in one scale and the sacrifice involved in the measures necessary for averting the risk is placed in the other.

---

[27] See *Construction, Forestry, Maritime, Mining and Energy Union, Mr Howard v Mt Arthur Coal Pty Ltd* [2021] FWCB 6059.
[28] [1949] 1 KB 704, 712. See too *Commission v United Kingdom* [2007] All ER 126; [2007] IRLR 720.

Section 7 of the *Health and Safety at Work Act 1974* (UK) specifies the reciprocal obligations of employees in respect of workplace safety:

It shall be the duty of every employee while at work—
(a) to take reasonable care for the health and safety of himself and of other persons who may be affected by his acts or omissions at work; and
(b) as regards any duty or requirement imposed on his employer or any other person by or under any of the relevant statutory provisions, to co-operate with him so far as is necessary to enable that duty or requirement to be performed or complied with.

A key question that arose during the emergence and persistence of COVID-19 concerned the extent of such duties in relation to the pandemic. One of the many issues that has arisen has been about an employer's obligations when the employee's home becomes their workplace, which may be deficient in a variety of safety respects, such as ergonomic standards. For instance, Australia's national work health and safety workers' compensation authority acknowledged that 'Employers' duties extend to workers who work from home or remotely, and they must take steps to ensure, so far as is reasonably practicable, the health and safety of their workers'. It recommended that employers

- 'Ensure a safe workspace in the home with a designated work area, comfortable and hazard-free access, and adequate lighting and ventilation.
- Stay connected and supported—create an effective communication structure with regular check-ins, and team and individual catch-ups.
- Maintain work-life balance—define the workplace, avoid distractions and follow routines.
- Monitor absenteeism and incident reports and patterns.[29]'

In Ireland, the Health and Safety Authority published a detailed checklist for employers and employees in relation to health and safety issues for remote working.[30]

---

[29] Australian Government, Comcare, 'Working from Home' (2021) <www.comcare.gov.au/office-safety-tool/spaces/work-areas/working-from-home> accessed 14 September 2022. See too Australian Government, Fair Work Ombudsman, *Alternative Work Arrangements* (Report, 25 November 2021) <https://coronavirus.fairwork.gov.au/coronavirus-and-australianworkplace-laws/alternative-work-arrangements> accessed 3 December 2021; Michael Tooma and Mary-Louise McLaws, *Managing COVID-19 Risks in the Workplace: A Practical Guide* (LexisNexis 2021).

[30] Health and Safety Authority of Ireland, 'Guidance on Working from Home for Employers and Employees' (2020) <www.hsa.ie/eng/publications_and_forms/publications/safety_and_health_management/guidance_on_working_from_home_for_employers_and_employees.html> accessed 1 December 2021.

It has been the obligation of employers and employees alike to comply with governmental directives during lockdowns, curfews, and other public health restrictions. However, merely following public health directives is not sufficient to discharge health and safety obligations in the workplace.[31] In Great Britain, the Health and Safety Executive required employers to update their risk assessment processes to protect workers against transmission of the virus in the workplace and committed to:

- help businesses in Great Britain work safely by providing advice and guidance
- check that appropriate workplace measures are in place to protect workers from transmission of COVID-19
- proactively inspect high risk industries
- inspect critical areas and activities in major hazard offshore oil and gas and the onshore chemical, explosives and microbiological industries
- investigate work-related deaths, serious major injuries, dangerous occurrences and reported concerns across all industry sectors. This includes those related to COVID-19
- regulate how employers meet their responsibilities[32]

Upon the identification of a cluster of COVID-19 cases in a workplace, or the declaration of a workplace pandemic, the role of the Health and Safety Executive was acknowledged to be to inspect COVID-19 transmission risk controls in the workplace and how a business has implemented their COVID-19 risk controls.[33]

As perhaps was to be expected, the effectiveness of both government and employers in regulating workplace risks has been controversial. For instance, Watterson lambasted British politicians and government bodies alike, noting that: 'several trade unions, health professional bodies, and nongovernmental organizations identified COVID-19 threats from poor personal protection equipment, working practices, and knowledge gaps and offered solutions for health care workers, social care workers, production workers, and service workers in "essential" occupations'.[34] The concern identified was that there was significantly inadequate response to such threats.

---

[31] See Stephen Duckett, 'Keeping Workers COVID-safe Requires More than Just Following Public Health Orders' *The Conversation* (12 October 2021) <https://theconversation.com/keeping-workers-covid-safe-requires-more-than-just-following-public-health-orders-169617> accessed 14 September 2022.

[32] Health and Safety Executive, 'Regulating Occupational Health and Safety During the Coronavirus (COVID-19) Pandemic' <www.hse.gov.uk/coronavirus/regulating-health-and-safety/index.htm> accessed 5 March 2022.

[33] ibid.

[34] Andrew Watterson, 'COVID-19 in the UK and Occupational Health and Safety: Predictable not Inevitable Failures by Government, and Trade Union and Nongovernmental Organization Responses' (2020) 30(2) *New Solutions: A Journal of Environmental and Occupational Health Policy* 86.

IV. Changes to Workplace Legislation

From the outset of the pandemic, it was identified that particular occupational groups, especially those in the healthcare workforce, and, for instance, in food packaging and processing facilities, were at heightened risk from exposure to the COVID-19 virus.[35] This necessitated taking a number of preventative measures, including the adequate provision of effective protective equipment, an obligation that at first was met insufficiently in most countries[36] and then progressively improved. Meat-processing plants played a particular role in the early phase of the COVID-19 pandemic in spreading the virus. In Brazil, for instance, it was alleged by union officials by August 2020 that one in five of Brazil's meat-plant workers had contracted the coronavirus.[37] Similarly, over 1,500 workers at Tönnies, one of Germany's largest meat-processing companies, were reported to have contracted COVID-19 early in the pandemic.[38]

Prior to COVID-19, research had established a relationship between climate and the occurrence of SARS and Middle East Respiratory Syndrome (MERS) cases, highlighting the risks in such working conditions and the role of humidity,[39] as well as the risk of strenuous labour conducted by workers in close proximity to one another on a production line in cool and moist conditions.[40] This was consistent with a 2017 study that had compared 81 workers in slaughterhouses with 81 office workers and found that the prevalence of respiratory disorders, such as cough, productive cough, breathlessness, phlegm, and wheezing, was 3.17, 4.02, 3.07, 4.66, and 3.94 times, respectively, higher among workers in slaughterhouses compared with office workers.[41] It demonstrated the need from an occupational health and safety perspective for changes to work conditions within abattoirs.

---

[35] See eg European Centre for Disease Prevention and Control, 'COVID-19 Clusters and Outbreaks in Occupational Settings in the EU/EEA and the UK' (Technical Report, 11 August 2020) <www.ecdc.europa.eu/sites/default/files/documents/COVID-19-in-occupational-settings.pdf> accessed 14 September 2022; Ian Freckelton, 'COVID-19, Negligence and Occupational Health and Safety: Ethical and Legal Issues for Hospitals and Health Centres' (2020) 27(3) *Journal of Law and Medicine* 590 (hereafter Freckelton, 'COVID-19, Negligence').

[36] See eg Dejene Hailu and others, 'Occupational Health Safety of Health Professionals and Associated Factors During COVID-19 Pandemics at North Showa Zone, Oromia Regional State, Ethiopia' (2021) 14 *Risk Management Healthcare Policy* 1299.

[37] See Tatiana Freitas, 'Covid Hit 20% of Meat Workers in No 1 Chicken Exporter Brazil' *Bloomberg* (19 August 2020) <www.bloombergquint.com/onweb/a-fifth-of-meat-workers-caught-covid-in-biggest-chicken-supplier> accessed 12 December 2022.

[38] Clara Nack, 'Europe's Meat Industry is a Coronavirus Hot Spot' *DW* (23 June 2020) <www.dw.com/en/europes-meat-industry-is-a-coronavirus-hot-spot/a-53961438> accessed 14 September 2022.

[39] Michael P Ward, Shuang Xiao, and Zhijie Zhang, 'The Role of Climate during the COVID-19 Epidemic in New South Wales, Australia' (2020) 67(6) *Transboundary and Emerging Diseases* 2313.

[40] See Shelley Marshall and Carla Chan Unger, 'Treating Workers like Meat: What We've Learnt from COVID-19 Outbreaks in Abattoirs' *The Conversation* (14 October 2020) <https://theconversation.com/treating-workers-like-meat-what-weve-learnt-from-covid-19-outbreaks-in-abattoirs-145444> accessed 14 September 2022.

[41] Abbasali Kasaeinasab and others, 'Respiratory Disorders Among Workers in Slaughterhouses' (2017) 8(1) *Safety and Health at Work* 84.

In the European Union, this translated to an increased focus on testing for COVID-19 in some workplace settings, combined with the development of robust policies on matters such as physical distancing, hygiene and cleaning, appropriate use of personal protective equipment (PPE), where necessary, and hand hygiene, particularly in closed settings and situations where workers had extended contact or shared transport or accommodation.[42]

Rather than surveying legislative initiatives in relation to occupational health and safety across many countries during the pandemic, it is useful to focus on some of the legislative initiatives in one western European nation—Germany—as an illustration of this trend. On 19 November 2020, the *Third Act to Protect the Public in the Event of an Epidemic Situation of National Significance* ('the *Third Act*') entered into force in Germany. It amended several laws, in particular the *Infectious Diseases Protection Act* (*Infektionsschutzgesetz, IfSG*), to ensure that measures taken to contain the spread of COVID-19 were proportionate and did not infringe constitutional rights. In addition, the *Third Act* provided for enhanced laboratory capacities by also using veterinary facilities; rapid antigen testing; uniform requirements for travellers returning from risk areas; compensation for hospitals postponing surgery to keep intensive care beds available for COVID-19 patients; and digitization of health services.

In September 2021, a new federal occupational health and safety regulation was promulgated in Germany.[43] It maintained an obligation for employers to offer COVID-19 tests to employees twice a week and it required employers to release employees from work for appointments to receive their vaccines.[44] It also mandated employees to be informed about the health risks of a COVID-19 infection and about the possibility of protective vaccinations. The legislative amendments clarified that, when determining and implementing occupational infection protection measures, employers were entitled to take into account any vaccination or recovery status of their employees that was known to them, but they did not provide for a statutory right to inquire into the vaccination status of employees.[45] This was followed in November 2021 by further amendments requiring employers to offer the option of working from home 'wherever possible'.[46] Employers had to offer their employees who performed office work or comparable activities the opportunity to work from home, unless there were 'compelling operational reasons'

---

[42] European Centre for Disease Prevention and Control (n 35).
[43] Federal Government of Germany, 'Occupational Health and Safety Regulation to be Adapted' (1 September 2021) <www.bundesregierung.de/breg-en/news/covid-health-and-safety-regulation-1956814> accessed 14 September 2022.
[44] ibid.
[45] ibid.
[46] See Nils Neumann and Lara Wengenmayr, 'New German Workplace Restrictions: Mandatory Work from Home and Entry Restrictions for Office Access' *National Law Review* (23 November 2021) <www.natlawreview.com/article/covid-19-new-german-covid-19-workplace-restrictions-mandatory-work-home-and-entry> accessed 14 September 2022.

for not doing so. The amended provisions did not specify what constituted such 'compelling operational reasons'.[47]

With the re-opening of many countries, it is clear that workplaces need to give consideration to a wide range of factors, including how work practices should adapt to minimize the risk of transmission of the virus depending on the vaccination status of employees,[48] as well as those who might visit the work site; how the safety of indoor air can be monitored; whether rapid antigen testing should be required as a condition for entry into the workplace; when the wearing of face masks should be mandated; and what the procedures should be for contact tracing and also temporary preclusion from the workplace when persons in the workplace are found to have been positive for COVID-19 or in close proximity to persons who have tested positive. All of these matters are not static—they will evolve as the incidence of the virus changes and will also depend upon the specific workplace environment, some being much more hazardous in terms of the potential transmission of COVID-19 than others.[49] However, it can be identified that tolerance levels for poor ventilation and for the presence of unwell employees will change long-term in the aftermath of COVID-19.

V. Healthcare Workers During COVID-19

Healthcare workers have a range of vulnerabilities to contracting diseases in the workplace. These are exacerbated during a pandemic and require the adoption of particular measures to make the workplace environment as safe as is reasonably practicable.

A. The Health of Healthcare Workers

The healthcare industry is routinely described as one of the most hazardous environments in which to work.[50] Healthcare workers run particular risks on the frontline of a pandemic.[51]

---

[47] ibid.
[48] See too Chapter 5.
[49] See Geraldo C de Oliveira Neto and others, 'Performance Evaluation of Occupational Health and Safety in Relation to the COVID-19 Fighting Practices Established by WHO: Survey in Multinational Industries' (2021) 141 *Safety Science* art 105331.
[50] See National Institute for Occupational Safety and Health, 'Healthcare Workers' (Centers for Disease Control and Prevention, 13 January 2017) <www.cdc.gov/niosh/topics/healthcare/default.html> accessed 1 December 2021; Bobby Joseph and Merlyn Joseph, 'The Health of the Healthcare Workers' (2016) 20(2) *Indian Journal of Occupational and Environmental Medicine* 71.
[51] See Ulf Karlsson and Carl-Johan Fraenkel, 'COVID-19: Risks to Healthcare Workers and their Families' (2020) 371 *British Medical Journal* m3944.

Frontline health practitioners have been recognized as at particular risk of contracting a variety of infectious diseases; this was identified, for instance, during the Ebola outbreaks.[52] They are also at risk of coming into contact with blood-borne pathogens and diseases such as tuberculosis.[53] Infectious diseases have posed particular risks for healthcare workers in a number of contexts. SARS was identified as a new disease by World Health Organization (WHO) physician, Dr Carlo Urbani, in a Chinese-American businessman, two days after he had been admitted to Hanoi's Vietnam-France Hospital. The patient passed away from the illness and a month and a day later Dr Urbani died from SARS too.[54] SARS had a death toll of 8,096 individuals globally (as discussed in Chapter 2), 21% of whom were healthcare workers.[55] In outbreaks in Hong Kong and Toronto, 62%[56] and 51%[57] respectively of the patients with COVID-19 were healthcare workers.

Both the original whistleblower in relation to reporting the identification of COVID-19 in China, Dr Li Wenliang,[58] and one of Wuhan's hospital directors, were among many other medical practitioners who died from the virus in its early phases.[59]

From its inception, the COVID-19 pandemic has placed a heavy burden on healthcare workers.[60] This has proved tragically to be the case with COVID-19 internationally as time has gone on too, and as a greater perspective on healthcare worker risk and its specific causes has become possible.[61] It seems likely that in a number of countries there was a serious occupational safety deficit—an early issue was that the PPE made available during the first phases of the pandemic was

---

[52] See eg Ibrahim Yusuf and others, 'Ebola and Compliance with Infection Prevention Measures in Nigeria' (2014) 14(11) *Lancet Infectious Diseases* 1045.

[53] See eg Iacopo Baussano and others, 'Tuberculosis among Health Care Workers' (2011) 17(3) *Emergency Infectious Diseases* 488.

[54] David P Fidler, *SARS, Governance and the Globalization of Disease* (Palgrave MacMillan 2004) 76–77, 86; see too Ivan Oransky, 'Carlo Urbani' (2003) 361(9367) *Lancet* 1481; Fiona Fleck, 'Carlo Urbani' (2003) 326(7393) *British Medical Journal* 825.

[55] See LLM Poon and others, 'The Aetiology, Origins and Diagnosis of Severe Acute Respiratory Syndrome' (2004) 4(11) *Lancet Infectious Diseases* 663; PL Ho, M Becker, and MM Chan-Yeung, 'Emerging Occupational Lung Infections' (2005) 11(7) *International Journal of Tuberculosis and Lung Disease* 710.

[56] See Nelson Lee and others, 'Major Outbreak of Severe Acute Respiratory Syndrome in Hong Kong' (2003) 348(2) *New England Journal of Medicine* 1986.

[57] See Christopher M Booth and others, 'Clinical Features and Short Term Outcomes of 44 Patients with SARS in the Greater Toronto Area' (2003) 289(21) *Journal of the American Medical Association* 2801.

[58] See 'Li Wenliang: Coronavirus Kills Chinese Whistleblower' *BBC News* (7 February 2020) <www.bbc.com/news/world-asia-china-51403795> accessed 2 November 2021.

[59] 'Hospital Director Dies in China's Wuhan, Epicentre of Coronavirus COVID-19 Outbreak' *ABC News* (18 February 2020) <www.abc.net.au/news/2020-02-18/hospital-director-dies-in-chinas-wuhan-epicentre-of-coronavir/11977268> accessed 14 Septeember 2022.

[60] See Freckelton, 'COVID-19, Negligence' (n 35).

[61] See eg Albert Nienhaus and Rozita Hod, 'COVID-19 Among Health Workers in Germany and Malaysia' (2020) 17(13) *International Journal of Research in Public Health* art 4881; Nicola Davis, 'Who Is Most at Risk of Contracting Coronavirus?' *The Guardian* (22 February 2020) <www.theguardian.com/world/2020/feb/21/who-is-most-at-risk-of-contracting-coronavirus> accessed 14 September 2022.

insufficient and ineffectual.[62] The risks have been particularly pronounced for older and immunocompromised healthcare workers.[63] A report as early as mid-February 2020 suggested that 1,717 healthcare workers in China had contracted the virus.[64] A later analysis argued that more than 3,300 nurses, doctors, and other hospital staff workers across China became COVID-positive, many because they lacked sufficient PPE. At the stage when Italy had about 41,000 COVID-19 cases, alarmingly, at least 2,609 were among healthcare workers.[65] By 20 March 2020, it was estimated that 9% of COVID-19 deaths in Italy were of healthcare workers.[66] Similarly, at a time when Spain had 11,178 confirmed COVID-19 cases, it was reported that 455 healthcare workers had contracted the virus.[67]

In a large register-based cohort study, comprising the entire Scottish healthcare workforce, the risks of COVID-19-related hospital admission between patient-facing and non-patient-facing workers, their household members, and the general population were compared.[68] Absolute risks were low, but during the first three months of the pandemic, patient-facing healthcare workers were three times more likely to be admitted to hospital with COVID-19 than non-patient-facing healthcare workers. Risk was doubled among household members of patient-facing workers, in analyses adjusted for sex, age, ethnicity, socioeconomic status, and co-morbidity.[69]

WHO Director-General, Tedros Adhanom Ghebreyesus, observed early in the pandemic that: 'Health workers are the glue that holds the health system and outbreak response together. We need to know more about how they are getting sick'.[70] As the pandemic evolved, there was a recognition of the need for the adoption of

---

[62] See Médecins Sans Frontières, 'Help and Solidarity Needed in Europe to Protect Medical Staff from COVID-19' (Press Release, 16 March 2020) <www.msf.org/covid-19-urgent-help-needed-across-european-borders-protect-medical-staff> accessed 14 September 2022.

[63] See Peter I Buerhaus, David I Auerbach, and Douglas O Staiger, 'Older Clinicians and the Surge in Novel Coronavirus Disease 2019 (COVID-19)' (2020) 323(18) *Journal of the American Medical Association* 1777; Carmelle Peisah and others, 'Just When I Thought I was Out, They Pull Me Back In: The Older Physician in the COVID-19 Pandemic' (2020) 32(10) *International Psychogeriatrics* 1211.

[64] See Rhea Mahbubani, 'The Coronavirus Has Infected More Than 1,700 Healthcare Workers in China, Killing 6 of Them' *Business Insider Australia* (15 February 2020) <www.businessinsider.com.au/coronavirus-infects-healthcare-workers-china-deaths-2020-2?r=US&IR=T> accessed 14 September 2022.

[65] See International Council of Nurses, 'High Proportion of Healthcare Workers with COVID-19 in Italy is a Stark Warning to the World' (20 March 2020) <www.icn.ch/news/high-proportion-healthcare-workers-covid-19-italy-stark-warning-world-protecting-nurses-and> accessed 14 September 2022.

[66] See Gemma Mitchell, 'Nurses Among Confirmed Deaths from COVID-19 Around the World' *Nursing Times* (20 March 2020) <www.nursingtimes.net/news/coronavirus/nurses-among-confirmed-deaths-from-covid-19-around-the-world-20-03-2020/> accessed 14 September 2022.

[67] See Alyssa McMurtry, 'Coronavirus: Spain Reports 182 Deaths in a Day' *Anadolu Agency* (17 March 2020) <www.aa.com.tr/en/europe/coronavirus-spain-reports-182-deaths-in-a-day/1769214> accessed 14 September 2022.

[68] Anoop SV Shah and others, 'Risk of Hospital Admission with Coronavirus Disease 2019 in Healthcare Workers and Their Households: Nationwide Linkage Cohort Study' (2020) 371 *British Medical Journal* m3582.

[69] ibid.

[70] Mahbubani (n 64).

especial and pandemic-informed measures to protect healthcare workers—both ethically and legally. During 2020, healthcare workers were hailed as superheroes and received a variety of high-profile forms of public applause and accolades. WHO declared 2021 'The Year of Health and Care Workers'.[71]

Healthcare workers have been called upon to continue to provide care through successive waves of the pandemic despite their exhaustion, ongoing risks of infection, and fears of transmission of the virus to family members, the illness and death of colleagues, and the loss in tragic circumstances of large numbers of patients.[72] Long shifts have been common and have taken a toll.[73] For many, fear, excessive workloads, and sleep deprivation have had adverse physical and mental health consequences.[74] Burnout and mental health sequelae have emerged as a significant workplace challenge for healthcare workers. In an Italian study in which 330 health professionals participated, for instance, 235 (71.2%) had scores for anxiety above the clinical cut-off, 88 (26.8%) had clinical levels for depression, 103 (31.3%) for anxiety, 113 (34.3%) for stress, and 121 (36.7%) for post-traumatic stress. In terms of burnout, 107 (35.7%) had moderate and 105 (31.9%) severe levels of emotional exhaustion; 46 (14.0%) had moderate and 40 (12.1%) severe levels of depersonalization; and 132 (40.1%) had moderate and 113 (34.3%) severe levels of a sense of reduced personal accomplishment, prompting the authors to observe that monitoring and treatment of the conditions were 'needed'.[75] A similar study involving healthcare workers in Victoria, Australia, also found high levels of psychological distress and called for 'targeted supportive interventions during the current and future outbreaks of infectious diseases'.[76] The need for such interventions was classified as urgent by a study in Pakistan.[77] A comparable review of healthcare

---

[71] World Health Organization, 'Year of Health and Care Workers 2021' (Campaign 2021) <www.who.int/campaigns/annual-theme/year-of-health-and-care-workers-2021> accessed 14 September 2022.

[72] See Sangeeta Mehta and others, 'COVID-19: A Heavy Toll on Health-care Workers' (2021) 9(3) *Lancet Respiratory Medicine* 226.

[73] Natasha Shaukat, Daniyal M Ali, and Junaid Razzak, 'Physical and Mental Health Impacts of COVID-19 on Healthcare Workers: A Scoping Review' (2020) 13(1) *International Journal of Emergency Medicine* art 40.

[74] Sonja Cabarkapa, Joel A King, and Chee H Ng, 'The Psychiatric Impact of COVID-19 on Healthcare Workers' (2020) 49(12) *Australian Journal of General Practice* 791. See too 'The Mental Health of Health Workers in the Pandemic' (2021) 99(6) *Bulletin of the World Health Organization* 410; Svenja Hummel and others, 'Mental Health Among Medical Professionals During the COVID-19 Pandemic in Eight European Countries: Cross-sectional Survey Study' (2021) 23(1) *Journal of Medical Internet Research* art e24983.

[75] Emanuele M Giusti and others, 'The Psychological Impact of the COVID-19 Outbreak on Health Professionals: A Cross-sectional Study' (2020) 11(11) *Frontiers in Psychology* 1684, 1. See too Feras I Hawari and others, 'The Inevitability of COVID-19 Related Distress Among Healthcare Workers: Findings from a Low Caseload Country Under Lockdown' (2021) 16(4) *PLoS One* art e0248741. See too Heather Hall, 'The Effect of the COVID-19 Pandemic on Healthcare Workers' Mental Health' (2020) 33(7) *Journal of the American Academy of Physician Assistants* 45.

[76] Sara Holton and others, 'Psychological Well-being of Australian Hospital Clinical Staff During the COVID-19 Pandemic' (2021) 45(3) *Australian Health Review* 297, 304.

[77] Khezar Hayat and others, 'Impact of COVID-19 on the Mental Health of Healthcare Workers: A Cross-sectional Study from Pakistan' (2021) 9 *Frontiers in Public Health* art 603602; Mohammed G

workers in Singapore and India also recommended the provision of psychological support and interventions for healthcare workers presenting with physical symptoms (once physical infection had been excluded).[78]

Healthcare workers, other than those working in hospitals, such as general practitioners, have also been significantly adversely affected by the pandemic.[79] This impact has extended beyond the need for additional education about the pandemic,[80] and included increased administrative tasks, reduced billable time, pivoting to telehealth service provision,[81] some of which may have lasting impacts on the delivery of general practice care,[82] and created diverse areas of stress, including, in the early phases, difficulties ensuring access to suitable PPE.[83] A review of social media usage by general practitioners has also suggested stresses arising from low morale, feeling undervalued, and a perception of lack of support from government, media, and the general public.[84]

B. Diversifying the Healthcare Workforce

A variety of strategies were deployed during 2020 and 2021 to augment the healthcare workforce, especially during surge periods. An option availed of in many countries was to add to the workforce by recruiting retired health practitioners.[85]

Elbqry and others, 'Effect of COVID-19 Stressors on Healthcare Workers' Performance and Attitude at Suez Canal University Hospitals' (2021) 28(1) *Middle East Current Psychiatry* art 4.

[78] Nicholas WS Chew and others, 'A Multinational, Multicentre Study on the Psychological Outcomes and Associated Physical Symptoms Amongst Healthcare Workers During COVID-19 Outbreak' (2020) 88 *Brain, Behaviour and Immunity* 559, 565.

[79] See David Kamerow, 'COVID-19: Don't Forget the Impact on US Family Physicians' (2020) 368 *British Medical Journal* m1260; Rita Rubin, 'COVID-19's Crushing Effects on Medical Practices, Some of Which Might Not Survive' (2020) 324(4) *Journal of the American Medical Association* 321; Marion Dutour and others, 'Family Medicine Practitioners' Stress During the COVID-19 Pandemic: A Cross-sectional Survey' (2021) 22 *BMC Family Practice* 36.

[80] See Tessa Copp and others, 'COVID-19 Challenges Faced By General Practitioners in Australia: A Survey Study Conducted in March 2021' (2021) 27(5) *Australian Journal of Primary Health* 357.

[81] See Rubin (n 79); Rebecca Kippen and others, 'A National Survey of COVID-19 Challenges, Responses and Effects in Australian General Practice' (2020) 49(11) *Australian Journal of General Practice* 745; Robyn Homeniuk and Claire Collins, 'How COVID-19 Has Affected General Practice Consultations and Income: General Practitioner Cross-sectional Population Survey Evidence from Ireland' (2021) 11(4) *BMJ Open* art e044685.

[82] See Jacqui Thornton, 'COVID-19: How Coronavirus Will Change the Face of General Practice Forever' (2020) 368 *British Medical Journal* m1279.

[83] Anthony Scott, *The Impact of COVID-19 on GPs and Non-GP Specialists in Private Practice* (Health Sector Report, Melbourne Institute 2020) 16 <https://melbourneinstitute.unimelb.edu.au/__data/ass ets/pdf_file/0003/3436014/UoM-MI-ANZ_Brochure-FV.pdf> accessed 14 September 2022.

[84] Su Golder and others, 'General Practitioner Perspectives and Wellbeing During the COVID-19 Pandemic: A Mixed Method Social Media Analysis' (medRxiv, 2021) <www.medrxiv.org/content/10.1101/2021.10.19.21265194v1.full> accessed 1 October 2022.

[85] See eg in Italy: Eileen AJ Connelly, 'Italy Calls in Retired Doctors to Help Combat Coronavirus Epidemic' *New York Post* (7 March 2020) <https://nypost.com/2020/03/07/italy-calls-in-retired-doct ors-to-help-combat-coronavirus-epidemic/> accessed 27 14 December 2022. See in New Zealand: Jo McKenzie-McLean, 'Coronavirus: "Call to Arms" for Retired Doctors and Nurses to Help Hospitals

However, as noted above, this involved those individuals assuming particular risks as they frequently had especial vulnerabilities by reason of the co-morbidities that often accompany age, leading Sabath and Colt to call for attempts to explore how we might 'take advantage of' health practitioners' medical skills and altruism 'while optimizing caution and safety'.[86] However, many such practitioners were recruited for the provision of primary care. In New York, as early as late March 2020, 52,000 health professionals had responded to a call by Governor Cuomo for retired health professionals and students to help provide care for the rapidly rising confirmed COVID-19 cases.[87] By the same time, large numbers of retired healthcare workers had also agreed to assist with the outbreak in England.[88] In Australia, the Australian Health Practitioner Regulatory Agency added categories of practitioners to a temporary pandemic response sub-register, creating an opt-out pool of general practitioners, nurses, midwives, pharmacists, psychologists, physiotherapists, diagnostic radiographers, and Aboriginal and Torres Strait Islander health practitioners from which an augmented workforce could be drawn.[89] During India's battle against the increase in cases as a result of the Delta variant of the virus, retired doctors and nurses were also recruited,[90] while the issue became politicized in Sri Lanka with the main opposition party making a call for such an initiative in May 2021.[91] In Turkey, in October 2020, the Health Ministry placed a ban on healthcare workers leaving or retiring in the context of a surge in COVID-19 cases.[92] When a similar order was made in April 2021, the Health and Social

---

Fight Infection' *Stuff* (20 March 2020) <www.stuff.co.nz/national/health/coronavirus/120441250/coronavirus-call-to-arms-for-retired-doctors-and-nurses-to-help-hospitals-fight-infection> accessed 14 December 2022. See in Canada: Farrah Merali, 'Hundreds of Ontario Doctors Have Come Out of Retirement or Offered to Redeploy During Pandemic' *CBC News* (30 April 2020) <www.cbc.ca/news/canada/toronto/ontario-doctors-offer-to-be-redeployed-or-come-out-of-retirement-1.5549656> accessed 14 September 2022.

[86] Bruce F Sabath and Henri G Colt, 'Sending Retirees to the Frontlines?' (2020) 10(5) *Journal of Community Hospital Internal Medicine Perspectives* 386.

[87] Sanya Mansoor, '"I've Been Missing Caring for People." Thousands of Retired Health Care Workers Are Volunteering to Help Areas Overwhelmed by Coronavirus' (*Time*, 6 March 2020) <https://time.com/5810120/retired-health-care-workers-coronavirus/> accessed 14 September 2022.

[88] Lucia Binding, 'Coronavirus: 4,500 Retired Doctors and Nurses Sign Up to Battle COVID-19 Pandemic' *Sky News* (22 March 2020) <https://news.sky.com/story/coronavirus-4-500-retired-doctors-and-nurses-sign-up-to-battle-covid-19-pandemic-11961685> accessed 14 September 2022.

[89] Ahpra and National Boards, 'Pandemic Response Sub-register' (26 September 2022) < https://www.ahpra.gov.au/News/COVID-19/Pandemic-response-sub-register.aspx > accessed 5 October 2022.

[90] 'COVID-19: Retired Doctors, Nurses to be Roped in to Augment Trained Manpower' *The Hindu* (18 July 2021) <www.thehindu.com/news/national/karnataka/covid-19-retired-doctors-nurses-to-be-roped-in-to-augment-trained-manpower/article34490985.ece> accessed 14 September 2022.

[91] See Imesh Ranasinghe, 'Recall Retired Doctors, Nurses to Combat COVID-19, Sri Lanka Opposition SJB Tells Govt' *Economynext* (14 May 2021) <https://economynext.com/recall-retired-doctors-nurses-to-combat-covid-19-sri-lanka-opposition-sjb-tells-govt-81963/> accessed 14 September 2022.

[92] 'Turkey Bans Resignation for Healthcare Workers as COVID-19 Figures Continue to Rise' *Ahval* (27 October 2020) <https://ahvalnews.com/healthcare/turkey-bans-resignation-healthcare-workers-covid-19-figures-continue-rise> accessed 14 September 2022.

Service Laborers Union asserted that the government measure was inconsistent with the *Turkish Constitution*.[93]

Another option availed of in some countries was to draw upon those who had partially completed their credentialling, namely healthcare students. For instance, Spain brought into the healthcare workforce students who had not yet completed their medical or nursing qualifications.[94] Recruitment from overseas was a further strategy that was utilized. An example was in Victoria, Australia, where by late 2021, the decision was made by the government to recruit 1,000 healthcare workers who were living overseas, primarily Australians, to help ease the pressures on local hospital staff.[95]

Lieutenant General John Frewen, who headed the Australian COVID Shield Taskforce, urged a further option—the use of health practitioners who had relevantly cognate qualifications to those who usually provided certain forms of clinical services. He argued for the recruiting of dietitians, speech pathologists, dentists, and podiatrists to help the vaccination effort and relieve a 'fatigued and burnt out' workforce.[96] In the United Kingdom, an amendment to the law meant that doctors in England did not need to be on the 'national performers list' to support the vaccination effort,[97] although they were not able to work beyond the remit of the registered vaccination roles. Suitably trained non-registered members of staff, such as paramedics, physiotherapists, chiropodists, podiatrists, dietitians, occupational therapists, orthoptists, prosthetists, radiographers, and speech and language therapists, under the supervision of registered healthcare professionals who carried out clinical assessments and secured patient consent, were permitted to administer vaccines.[98] In addition, the Chartered Institute of Environmental Health established a register of people in the United Kingdom who were willing to volunteer to provide support services during the pandemic. This included persons with public health and administrative skills currently working in the private and

---

[93] SES Union, 'Denying Health Workers their Right to Leave is Against the Constitution' *Bianet* (16 April 2021) <https://m.bianet.org/english/labor/242597-denying-health-workers-their-right-to-leave-is-against-the-constitution> accessed 14 September 2024.

[94] See Helena Legido-Quigley and others 'The Resilience of the Spanish Health System against the COVID-19 Pandemic' (2020) 5(5) *Lancet Public Health* art E251.

[95] Naveen Razik, 'Victoria to Recruit Overseas Healthcare Workers to Help with COVID-19 Outbreak' *SBS News* (12 October 2021) <www.sbs.com.au/news/victoria-to-recruit-overseas-healthcare-workers-to-help-with-covid-19-outbreak/381df855-33b8-490e-ab5b-04d94170c417> accessed 14 September 2022.

[96] See Sarah Martin, 'Dentists, Midwives and Physiotherapists Could Deliver Covid Jabs to Bolster Australia's Rollout' *The Guardian* (5 August 2021) <www.theguardian.com/australia-news/2021/aug/05/dentists-midwives-and-physiotherapists-could-deliver-covid-jabs-to-bolster-australias-rollout> accessed 14 September 2022.

[97] See the *National Health Service (Performers Lists, Coronavirus) (England) Amendment Regulations 2021* (Eng).

[98] See British Medical Association, 'COVID-19 Vaccination Programme: Extra Workforce' (4 June 2021) <www.bma.org.uk/advice-and-support/covid-19/vaccines/covid-19-vaccination-programme-extra-workforce> accessed 14 September 2022.

business sectors.[99] Such forms of recruitment raise difficult medico-legal issues in terms of the discharge of duties of care by persons with deficits in their skills and experience.

However, there was another side to the impact of the COVID-19 pandemic upon health practitioners. It had the potential to result in a reconfiguration of the ongoing healthcare workforce. Many practitioners chose to retire, some citing stress from the pandemic and others specifically identifying unacceptable risks to their health from continuing to work. For instance, as early as August 2020, the Physicians Foundation in the United States identified that 8% of physicians had closed their practices as a result of COVID-19 and 59% expressed the view that COVID-19 would lead to a reduction in the number of independent physician practices in their communities.[100] Another survey that reported in September 2020 found that 19% of primary carers stated that clinicians in their practice had retired early because of COVID-19 or were planning to do so.[101] In the United Kingdom, too, it was reported in May 2021 that more than one in three general practitioners were planning early retirement as the pandemic and their workload took a toll on them.[102] These changes to the numbers and profile of the healthcare workforce as a result of the COVID-19 pandemic are likely to have major ramifications for patient care in many parts of the world.

C. WHO and ILO Guidance

WHO identified hazards for healthcare workers at the frontline of the COVID-19 outbreak response, including exposure to the virus, long working hours, psychological distress, fatigue, occupational burnout, stigma, and physical and psychological violence.[103] Typically, occupational health and safety legislation

---

[99] See Chartered Institute of Environmental Health, 'Environmental Health Together Register' (2021) <www.cieh.org/policy/coronavirus-covid-19/environmental-health-together/> accessed 13 September 2022.

[100] The Physicians Foundation, '2020 Survey of America's Physicians: COVID-19 Impact Edition' Physicians Foundation (2020) <https://physiciansfoundation.org/wp-content/uploads/2020/08/20-1278-Merritt-Hawkins-2020-Physicians-Foundation-Survey.6.pdf> accessed 14 September 2022.

[101] Larry A Green Center, 'Quick COVID-19 Primary Care Survey, Series 21 Fielded September 18–21, 2020' <https://static1.squarespace.com/static/5d7ff8184cf0e01e4566cb02/t/5f75da37bde1f0691fc28b0d/1601559097041/C19+Series+21+National+Executive+Summary.pdf> accessed 14 September 2022.

[102] Nick Bostock, 'More than One in Three GPs Plan Early Retirement as Pandemic and Workload Take Toll' *GP Online* (4 May 2021) <www.gponline.com/one-three-gps-plan-early-retirement-pandemic-workload-toll/article/1714669> accessed 14 September 2022.

[103] World Health Organization, 'Coronavirus Disease (COVID-19) Outbreak: Rights, Roles and Responsibilities of Health Workers, Including Key Considerations for Occupational Health and Safety' (Interim Guidance, 19 March 2020) <https://apps.who.int/iris/bitstream/handle/10665/331510/WHO-2019-nCov-HCWadvice-2020.2-eng.pdf> accessed 14 September 2022.

imposes duties on both employers and employees in relation to ensuring and maintaining safety in the workplace. WHO identified the following healthcare worker rights, including the expectations that employers and managers in health facilities:

- assume overall responsibility to ensure that all necessary preventive and protective measures are taken to minimize occupational safety and health risks', including implementation of occupational safety and health management systems to identify hazards and assess risks to health and safety; IPC measures; and zero-tolerance policies towards workplace violence and harassment
- provide information, instruction, and training on occupational safety and health, including;
  refresher training on infection prevention and control (IPC);
  use, putting on, taking off and disposal of personal protective equipment (PPE);
- provide adequate IPC and PPE supplies (masks, gloves, goggles, gowns, hand sanitizer, soap and water, cleaning supplies) in sufficient quantity to those caring for suspected or confirmed COVID-19 patients, such that workers do not incur expenses for occupational safety and health requirements;
- familiarize personnel with technical updates on COVID-19 and provide appropriate tools to assess, triage, test, and treat patients, and to share IPC information with patients and the public;
- provide appropriate security measures as needed for personal safety;
- provide a blame-free environment in which health workers can report on incidents, such as exposures to blood or bodily fluids from the respiratory system, or cases of violence, and adopt measures for immediate follow up, including support to victims;
- advise health workers on self-assessment, symptom reporting, and staying home when ill;
- maintain appropriate working hours with breaks;
- consult with health workers on occupational safety and health aspects of their work, and notify the labour inspectorate of cases of occupational diseases;
- allow health workers to exercise the right to remove themselves from a work situation that they have reasonable justification to believe presents an imminent and serious danger to their life or health, and protect health workers exercising this right from any undue consequences;
- not require health workers to return to a work situation where there has been a serious danger to life or health until any necessary remedial action has been taken;
- honour the right to compensation, rehabilitation, and curative services for health workers infected with COVID-19 following exposure in the workplace—considered as an occupational disease arising from occupational exposure;
- provide access to mental health and counselling resources; and

- enable cooperation between management and health workers and their representatives.[104]

In terms of the obligations of healthcare workers, it stated that they should:

- follow established occupational safety and health procedures, avoid exposing others to health and safety risks, and participate in employer-provided occupational safety and health training;
- use provided protocols to assess, triage, and treat patients;
- treat patients with respect, compassion, and dignity;
- maintain patient confidentiality;
- swiftly follow established public health reporting procedures of suspected and confirmed cases;
- provide or reinforce accurate IPC and public health information, including to concerned people who have neither symptoms nor risk;
- put on, use, take off, and dispose of PPE properly;
- self-monitor for signs of illness and self-isolate and report illness to managers, if it occurs;
- advise management if they are experiencing signs of undue stress or mental health challenges that require supportive interventions; and
- report to their immediate supervisor any situation which they have reasonable justification to believe presents an imminent and serious danger to life or health.

In February 2021, the ILO and WHO issued updated guidance.[105] It emphasized that:

- 'Health workers should continue to enjoy their right to decent, healthy and safe working conditions in the context of COVID-19.
- Primary prevention of COVID-19 among health workers should be based on risk assessment and introduction of appropriate measures.
- Other occupational risks amplified by the COVID-19 pandemic, including violence, harassment, stigma, discrimination, heavy workload and prolonged use of personal protective equipment (PPE) should be addressed.

---

[104] ibid.
[105] World Health Organization and International Labour Organization, 'COVID-19: Occupational Health and Safety for Health Workers' (Interim Guidance, 2 February 2021) <www.ilo.org/wcmsp5/groups/public/---ed_dialogue/---sector/documents/publication/wcms_769309.pdf> accessed 4 October 2022.

- Occupational health services, mental health and psychosocial support, adequate sanitation, hygiene and rest facilities should be provided to all health workers.
- Health-care facilities should have occupational health programmes in conjunction with programmes for infection prevention and control.
- Employers have the overall responsibility to ensure that all necessary preventive and protective measures are taken to minimize occupational risks to health workers.
- Health workers are responsible for following established rules for the protection of their health and safety at work.'[106]

The ILO/WHO Guidance noted occupational hazards that put healthcare workers at risk of disease, injury, and death in the context of the COVID-19 response, including: infections with COVID-19; skin disorders and heat stress from prolonged use of PPE; exposures to toxins because of increased use of disinfectants; psychological distress; chronic fatigue; stigma; discrimination; physical and psychological violence; and harassment.[107] It stated that:

> Mitigating these hazards and protecting the health, safety and well-being of health workers requires well-coordinated and comprehensive measures for infection prevention and control, occupational health and safety, health workforce management and mental health and psychosocial support. Insufficient occupational health and safety measures can result in increased rates of work-related illness among health workers, high rates of absenteeism, reduced productivity and diminished quality of care.[108]

Acknowledging that workplace risk, even within the same workplace, may vary, based on healthcare workers' tasks and roles, the ILO/WHO Guidance suggested classification of risk levels according to a straightforward taxonomy:

1. *Lower risk* – jobs or tasks without frequent, close contact with the public or others and that do not require contact with people known or suspected of being infected with SARS-CoV-2.
2. *Medium risk* – jobs or tasks with close frequent contact with patients, visitors, suppliers and co-workers but that do not require contact with people known or suspected of being infected with SARS-CoV-2.

---

[106] ibid.
[107] ibid.
[108] ibid.

3. *High risk* – jobs or tasks with high potential for close contact with people who are known to be or suspected of being infected with SARS-CoV-2 or contact with objects and surfaces possibly contaminated with the virus.
4. *Very high risk* – jobs and tasks with risk of exposure to aerosols containing SARS-CoV-2, in settings where aerosol-generating procedures are regularly performed on patients with COVID-19 or working with infected people in indoor, crowded places without adequate ventilation.'[109]

The ILO/WHO Guidance also recommended that in relation to lower risk assessments where caution is required, healthcare facilities should 'organize remote work and teleservices wherever possible and appropriate; provide natural or mechanical ventilation without recirculation; and organize regular environmental clean-ups and disinfection'. It urged the introduction of 'measures for avoiding crowding and social mixing, and encouraging workers to observe safe physical distancing; the implementation of measures to prevent the sharing of work stations and equipment; and the establishment of flexible sick leave policies'. It recommended that workers 'stay home if unwell; observe hand and respiratory hygiene; use fabric masks in common areas and face-to-face meetings'.

In respect of assessments of medium risk, this Guidance suggested that healthcare facilities should:

- consider alternatives to face-to-face outpatient visits using telehealth services wherever feasible and appropriate;
- provide sneeze screens, barriers, workplace modifications and natural or mechanical ventilation without recirculation;
- organize screening and triage for early recognition of patients with suspected COVID-19 and rapid implementation of source control measures;
- organize regular environmental clean-up and disinfection;
- introduce measures to avoid crowding and social mixing, such as restricting visitors and designating areas where patients are not allowed;
- encourage workers to observe safe physical distancing when not wearing PPE (e.g. in break rooms and cafeterias);
- provide IPC [infection prevention control] training and adequate PPE in sufficient quantity and quality;
- establish flexible sick leave policies. [110]

---

[109] ibid.
[110] ibid.

It recommended that workers should 'stay home if unwell; observe hand and respiratory hygiene; wear medical masks and other PPE according to their tasks and apply standard precautions in providing patient care'.

Where risk was categorized as high, it recommended that healthcare facilities:

- implement engineering, environmental and administrative controls for IPC, and provide adequate PPE in sufficient quantity and quality;
- provide enhanced ventilation without recirculation, with 'clean to less clean' directional design for airflows;
- organize regular environmental clean-up and disinfection;
- introduce measures for avoiding crowding and social mixing and restricting non-essential workers and visitors;
- provide regular IPC training, including on the use of PPE;
- establish flexible sick leave policies.[111]

It proposed that workers and caregivers 'use personal protective equipment based on transmission-based precautions (medical mask, gown, gloves, eye protection) and apply standard precautions in providing patient care; stay home if unwell; and observe hand and respiratory hygiene'.[112]

Finally, where risk was assessed as very high, it proposed that healthcare facilities implement engineering, environmental, and administrative controls for infection prevention and control and provide adequate PPE in sufficient quantity and quality:

- provide mechanical ventilation with high efficiency particulate air filters without recirculation;
- introduce measures for avoiding crowding and social mixing and for restricting access of non-essential workers and visitors;
- provide regular infection prevention and control training, and training in donning and doffing personal protective equipment; and
- establish flexible sick leave policies.[113]

It proposed that where risk was categorized as high, workers should 'stay home if unwell; observe hand and respiratory hygiene; use personal protective equipment; and apply standard precautions in providing patient care'.[114] It may well be that a failure to institute such measures would be regarded as constituting actionable negligence on the part of employers. It may also leave them open to allegations of breaches of occupational health and safety obligations.

---

[111] ibid.
[112] ibid.
[113] ibid.
[114] ibid.

D. Declining to Provide Healthcare Services During a Pandemic

The COVID-19 pandemic has renewed a debate that took place during previous periods of global infection about when workers, in particular healthcare workers, can ethically and legally decline to perform their duties out of concern for their own well-being. For employees, the issue arises when the prevalence of a pandemic is high and essential workers who have significant levels of personal contact with members of the public are put at risk of contracting the disease in the course of their employment—for example, police, workers in food shops and pharmacies, workers with the homeless, providers of care to persons who are institutionalized, taxi drivers and transport workers, to name but some. However, it is healthcare workers who are most frequently and extensively exposed to those who have tested positive to a disease the subject of a pandemic. For them, the question of their provision of services arises in many contexts, including those engaging in overseas aid work to supplement available healthcare workers in a foreign country in crisis; hospital workers in emergency wards; general practitioners seeing their usual patients in person; and workers who staff vaccination centres. Most of the debate regarding declining to perform work during a pandemic has focused upon healthcare workers, sometimes describing their work as supererogatory[115]—beyond the call of duty—so it is upon them that this part of the chapter focuses.

It was pointed out in the context of the Ebola outbreak of 2014 that resort to the concept of 'duty of care' in this regard is an inadequate moral guide.[116] It also has limitations in terms of utility as a matter of tort law.[117] In the aftermath of SARS, where a disproportionate percentage of deaths were amongst healthcare workers,[118] and in Toronto, Canada, where the figure was approximately half of all deaths,[119] at a time when avian flu was anticipated, Daniel Sokol made the important point that the terminology of 'duty of care' in the context of healthcare workers' ethical obligations to care for patients during a health crisis is 'at best, too vague and, at worst, dangerous'.[120] He argued that the duty of care is 'neither fixed nor absolute but heavily dependent on context', with the normal risk level in the

---

[115] See Caitríona L Cox, '"Healthcare Heroes": Problems with Media Focus on Heroism from Healthcare Workers During the COVID-19 Pandemic' (2020) 46 *Journal of Medical Ethics* 510–511 discussing heroism in the context of James O Urmson, 'Saints and Heroes' in Abraham I Melden (ed), *Essays in Moral Philosophy* (University of Washington Press 1958).

[116] Aminu Yakubu and others, 'The Ebola Outbreak in Western Africa: Ethical Obligations for Care' (2016) 42(4) *Journal of Medical Ethics* 209.

[117] See Chapter 9.

[118] See Carly Ruderman and others, 'On Pandemics and the Duty to Care: Whose Duty? Who Cares?' (2006) 7 *BMC Medical Ethics* art 5.

[119] See Heidi Malm and others, 'Ethics, Pandemics, and the Duty to Treat' (2008) 8 *American Journal of Bioethics* 4.

[120] Daniel K Sokol, 'Virulent Epidemics and Scope of Healthcare Workers' Duty of Care' (2006) 12(8) *Emerging Infectious Diseases* 1238.

working environment, the healthcare worker's area of work, and the likely harm and the benefits of treatment, as well as competing obligations from diverse roles played by the healthcare worker, all influencing the content and limits of what from time to time in a pandemic might be regarded as a duty of care. Sokol called for such issues to be tackled 'in times of relative calm, rather than in times of pandemic turbulence'.[121]

Like many other workers, the jobs of healthcare workers during a pandemic are imperilled if they decline to attend the frontline workplace themselves.[122] During 2020 and 2021, there were many reports of healthcare workers feeling ethically conflicted between their duties to consider the well-being of their patients, but also to promote and maintain their own health.[123] An example of the latter is the statement in the American Nurses Association Code of Ethics that 'The nurse owes the same duties to self as to others, including the responsibility to preserve integrity and safety'.[124] The situation can be complicated by vocational and workplace cultures in which sacrifice to others, in particular to patients, is expected.[125] Ethical dilemmas concerning provision of care during the COVID-19 pandemic were found by a Swiss study to be a major source of stress for nurses.[126]

It has been argued that healthcare workers have a duty to treat patients during a pandemic, in spite of risks to themselves, by reason of their role and their duties of beneficence.[127] Other factors that have been cited have included their possession of special skills, acquired by their training and experience, meaning that they are uniquely positioned to meet their patients' therapeutic needs, and their decision to pursue a healthcare profession, an intrinsic component of their role being to provide care, including to those who are infectious (namely, to an extent they have provided implied informed consent to running risks). In addition, there is what has been asserted to be the social contract between healthcare workers and society.[128] In the context of the Ebola outbreak in West Africa too there was the consideration of healthcare workers' limited capacity to provide protection for themselves

---

[121] ibid 1241.
[122] University of Toronto Joint Centre for Bioethics Pandemic Influenza Working Group, *Stand on Guard for Thee: Ethical Considerations in Preparedness Planning for Pandemic Influenza* (Report, November 2005) 10 <https://jcb.utoronto.ca/wp-content/uploads/2021/03/stand_on_guard.pdf> accessed 14 September 2022.
[123] See Hugh McKenna, 'COVID-19—Ethical Issues for Nurses' (2020) 110 *International Journal of Nursing Studies* art 103673.
[124] American Nurses Association, 'Code of Ethics for Nurses wth Interpretive Statements' (2015) Provision 5 <www.nursingworld.org/coe-view-only> accessed 27 November 2021.
[125] Junhong Zhu, Teresa Stone, and Marcia Petrini, 'The Ethics of Refusing to Care for Patients During the Coronavirus Pandemic: A Chinese Perspective' (2020) 28(1) *Nursing Inquiry* art e12380.
[126] Michele Villa and others, 'Ethical Conflict and its Psychological Correlates Among Hospital Nurses in the Pandemic: A Cross-Sectional Study within Swiss COVID-19 and Non-COVID-19 Wards' (2021) 18(22) *International Journal of Environmental Research Public Health* art 12012.
[127] See Sokol (n 120).
[128] See eg Chalmers C Clark, 'In Harm's Way: AMA Physicians and the Duty to Treat' (2005) 30(1) *Journal of Medicine and Philosophy* 65; Malm and others (n 119) 9.

as a result of deficiencies in the healthcare system,[129] an issue that was replicated to some degree in a number of countries early in the COVID-19 pandemic due to the scarcity of adequate PPE.

Relevant ethical considerations evolve during the course of a pandemic. There are particular issues, which are very difficult to manage, during the early phase of a pandemic when the nature of the threat is not well understood.[130] By contrast, when there is more knowledge about effective preventative measures and treatments, the option for healthcare workers to adopt self-protective measures falling short of complete withdrawal of labour is increased.

Another relevant consideration is that opting out by any individual healthcare worker is likely to impose extra burdens on their colleagues, such as young healthcare practitioners who do not have children, and those who may be placed under pressure by state authorities to work excessive numbers of hours in fraught conditions.[131] In 2003, Alexander and Wynia reported that in a random survey of 1,000 physicians selected from the American Medical Association master file of United States physicians, only a little over half of those who responded reported believing they had a duty to treat patients in the event of an unknown but deadly illness.[132] A later survey found that prior experience in a comparable scenario positively affected intention to respond in a crisis.[133] When employers institute stress-reducing measures, this may reduce disinclination by healthcare workers to take on risks during a pandemic crisis,[134] as may enhanced provision of ethical guidance on the basis of stakeholder consultation.[135] A number of scenarios have been identified that have the potential to legitimize healthcare workers declining to provide frontline assistance, such as if the work is beyond their skill set or if they have especial health vulnerabilities by reason of age or morbidities.

Perhaps the most important scenario in which workers are ethically and legally entitled to decline to perform duties is when their workplace is not safe. In 2020, in the United Kingdom, the Royal College of Nursing issued guidance on this issue, focusing upon whether nurses were being supplied with appropriate PPE.[136] It

---

[129] Yakubu and others (n 116).

[130] See Stephanie B Johnson and Frances Butcher, 'Doctors During the COVID-19 Pandemic: What are their Duties and What is Owed to Them?' (2021) 47(1) *Journal of Medical Ethics* 12.

[131] See Lynette Reid, 'Diminishing Returns? Risk and the Duty to Care in the SARS Epidemic' (2005) 19(4) *Bioethics* 348.

[132] G Caleb Alexander and Matthew K Wynia, 'Ready and Willing? Physicians' Sense of Preparedness for Bioterrorism' (2003) 22(5) *Health Affairs* 189.

[133] Jiaying Li and others, 'Intention to Response, Emergency Preparedness and Intention to Leave Among Nurses During COVID-19' (2020) 7(6) *Nursing Open* 1867.

[134] Beesan Maraqa, Zaher Nazzal, and Therese Zink, 'Mixed Method Study to Explore Ethical Dilemmas and Health Care Workers' Willingness to Work Amid COVID-19 Pandemic in Palestine' (2021) 7 *Frontiers in Medicine (Lausanne)* art 576820.

[135] Belinda Bennett, Terry Carney, and Caroline Saint, 'Swine Flu, Doctors and Pandemics: Is there a Duty to Treat During a Pandemic?' (2010) 17(5) *Journal of Law and Medicine* 736.

[136] Royal College of Nursing, 'Guidance for Members: Refusal to Treat Due to Lack of Adequate PPE During the Pandemic' (9 April 2020) <www.rcn.org.uk/professional-development/publications/rcn-refusal-to-treat-covid-19-uk-pub-009231> accessed 27 December 2021. See too Paul Joseph,

emphasized that the Nursing and Midwifery Council requires registered nurses to be accountable for the safety of themselves, their patients, and the public, 'and this must empower them to speak up'.[137] It identified considerations beyond the safety of nurses themselves in relation to the decision to work if their safety is not properly safeguarded:

> When considering the weight to be placed on your own safety, you are not simply taking your personal wellbeing into account. If you become unwell, you might spread infection through your community, including to high-risk patients. You will not be available to provide care to others. You might put your own family at risk including more vulnerable relatives and you may have a vulnerability yourself that makes infection a greater risk.[138]

It required that nurses who were concerned about safety in their workplace during the pandemic attempt to identify changes to the way they work, that might reduce the risk to them, rather than refuse to provide treatment at all:

> Can treatment be delayed or provided differently? Can alternative practices reduce the risk of transmission? Can staff with greater vulnerability be placed into roles that carry lower risk? Working with your manager and colleagues, your clinical expertise and knowledge of your patients will be invaluable.[139]

Ultimately, though, if nurses could not identify feasible options, the guidance affirmed that nurses 'are entitled to refuse to work' although 'this will be a last resort'. It stated that nurses should:

> [r]est assured that if you refuse to treat for lack of PPE, and are criticised subsequently, the RCN will provide you with legal representation and other support in any proceedings that ensue, without judgement. These are enormously difficult circumstances for our members and RCN support will be there.[140]

In the United States of America, the Occupational Safety and Health Administration (OSHA) of the Department of Labor provides similar guidance, albeit not directed specifically to the pandemic context:

'Coronavirus: Can Nurses Refuse to Work if they Don't Have Adequate PPE?' *The Conversation* (21 May 2020) <https://theconversation.com/coronavirus-can-nurses-refuse-to-work-if-they-dont-have-adequate-ppe-138545> accessed 13 September 2022.
[137] Royal College of Nursing (n 136).
[138] ibid.
[139] ibid.
[140] ibid.

Your right to refuse to do a task is protected if **all** of the following conditions are met:

- Where possible, you have asked the employer to eliminate the danger, and the employer failed to do so; and
- You refused to work in 'good faith.' This means that you must genuinely believe that an imminent danger exists; and
- A reasonable person would agree that there is a real danger of death or serious injury; and
- There isn't enough time, due to the urgency of the hazard, to get it corrected through regular enforcement channels, such as requesting an OSHA inspection.[141]

It advises that the following steps should be taken:

- Ask your employer to correct the hazard, or to assign other work;
- Tell your employer that you won't perform the work unless and until the hazard is corrected; and
- Remain at the worksite until ordered to leave by your employer.[142]

Similarly, in British Columbia in Canada, regulation 3.12 of the *Occupational Health and Safety Regulation*, which applies to all workplaces under the inspectional jurisdiction of WorkSafe British Columbia, sets out a process for refusal to work, commencing with the proposition that: 'A person must not carry out or cause to be carried out any work process or operate or cause to be operated any tool, appliance or equipment if that person has reasonable cause to believe that to do so would create an undue hazard to the health and safety of any person.' When a person refuses to carry out a work process, they must report the circumstances to their supervisor or employer. When they do so, no adverse actions can be taken against them for that reason.[143] As Davies and Shaul have usefully summarized,[144] labour boards across Canada have affirmed that workers must satisfy four criteria to justify refusing to work because of dangerous or unsafe conditions:

- 'Workers must *honestly* believe that their health or well-being is endangered. They cannot refuse to work for a reason unrelated to safety.

---

[141] Occupational, Safety and Health Administration, 'Workers' Right to Refuse Dangerous Work' United States Department of Labor <www.osha.gov/workers/right-to-refuse> accessed 27 November 2021.
[142] ibid.
[143] *Occupational Health and Safety Regulation* (British Columbia), s 3.13.
[144] Cara E Davies and Randi Z Shaul, 'Physicians' Legal Duty of Care and Legal Right to Refuse to Work During a Pandemic' (2010) 182(2) *Canadian Medical Association Journal* 167, 169.

- Workers must *reasonably* believe that their health or well-being is endangered. That is, another worker with the same training and experience would also believe that the circumstances represent an unacceptable hazard.
- Workers must communicate their concerns to their supervisor in a reasonable and adequate manner. This usually requires workers to notify their supervisor of their refusal to work, and the reasons for their refusal, as soon as possible.
- The danger must be sufficiently serious to justify the action; it must be immediate and more than a matter of repugnancy, unpleasantness or fear of minor injury.'

This short review of the literature and guidance on rights to decline to work during a pandemic highlights the obligation of employers and government to take all available measures to protect essential workers, and especially healthcare workers, by instituting processes to reduce risks of transmission of disease, providing facilities for minimizing stress and other consequences of working in a dangerous environment, and providing suitable remuneration for their work and compensation for those who suffer adverse effects from the pandemic while at work.

VI. Mandatory Vaccination in Workplaces

During the COVID-19 pandemic, employers have mandated vaccination of their workers. This is not a new phenomenon. For instance, on 5 February 1777, after heavy losses in Boston and Quebec, in a letter to John Hancock, who was president of the Second Continental Congress, General George Washington issued the order to have all troops in the Continental Army inoculated. In another letter to Dr William Shippen Jr signed the next day, Washington ordered all recruits arriving in Philadelphia to be inoculated:

> Finding the small pox to be spreading much and fearing that no precaution can prevent it from running thro' the whole of our Army, I have determined that the Troops shall be inoculated. This Expedient may be attended with some inconveniences and some disadvantages, but yet I trust, in its consequences will have the most happy effects. Necessity not only authorizes but seems to require the measure, for should the disorder infect the Army, in the natural way, and rage with its usual virulence, we should have more to dread from it, than from the Sword of the Enemy. Under these circumstances, I have directed Doctr. Bond to prepare immediately for inoculating in this Quarter, keeping the matter as secret as possible, and request that you will without delay inoculate all the Continental Troops that are in Philadelphia and those that shall come in as fast as they arrive.[145]

---

[145] See Hugh Thursfield, 'Smallpox in the American War of Independence' (1940) 2(4) *Annals of Medical History* 312; Dan Liebowitz, 'Smallpox Vaccination: An Early Start of Modern Medicine in America' (2017) 7(1) *Journal of Community Hospital Internal Medicine Perspectives* 61.

In late 2021, a wide range of governments as well as individual companies in different parts of the world required their staff and/or contractors to receive a COVID-19 vaccination in order to continue working for them at their premises or at all. In Chapter 5 we discuss the introduction of mandatory vaccination requirements and in Chapter 6 analyse some of the key challenges mounted to such requirements. Some educational institutions, including universities and colleges in many jurisdictions, including several European countries, Canada, the United States of America, and Australia, required staff and students to have COVID-19 vaccines to attend their campuses.[146] Although young people were less likely than adults to suffer serious symptoms from COVID-19, they could still contract and spread the virus to fellow students and teachers in the close confines of classrooms and lecture theatres.[147] The issue of coercing vaccination by precluding the right to work for those who could not produce evidence of their vaccination status became both controversial and politicized late in 2021.[148] An example of this is a dissenting decision on the issue in the Fair Work Commission of Australia where Dean DP argued that:

> Blanket rules, such as mandating vaccinations for everyone across a whole profession or industry regardless of the actual risk, fail the tests of proportionality, necessity and reasonableness. It is more than the absolute minimum necessary to combat the crisis and cannot be justified on health grounds. It is a lazy and fundamentally flawed approach to risk management and should be soundly rejected by courts when challenged.[149]

Employers' COVID-19 vaccine mandates had the potential to assist in protecting public health if they had the effect of leveraging increases in the number

---

[146] Peter A Newman and Adrian Guta, 'Mandatory COVID-19 Vaccines on University Campuses: An Obvious Solution or a Problem?' *The Conversation* (3 August 2021) <https://theconversation.com/mandatory-covid-19-vaccines-on-university-campuses-an-obvious-solution-or-a-problem-164738> accessed 5 October 2021; 'Which European Universities Require a COVID-19 Vaccine?' *Schengenvisainfo news* (28 September 2021) <www.schengenvisainfo.com/news/which-european-universities-require-a-covid-19-vaccine/> accessed 5 October 2021; Giulia Hayward, 'Who Can Make You Get a Covid Vaccine?' *New York Times* (24 September 2021) <www.nytimes.com/article/covid-vaccine-mandates.html> accessed 5 October 2021; Tess Bennett, 'Vaccine Mandates Lead the Way for Campus Reopenings' *Australian Financial Review* (27 September 2021) <www.afr.com/work-and-careers/education/vaccine-mandates-lead-the-way-for-campus-reopenings-20210924-p58uk6> accessed 5 October 2021.

[147] Dorit Rubinstein Reiss and Arthur Caplan, 'Considerations in Mandating a New COVID-19 Vaccine in the USA for Children and Adults' (2020) 7(1) *Journal of Law and the Biosciences* art lsaa025; Lawrence O Gostin, Daniel A Salmon, and Heidi J Larson, 'Mandating COVID-19 Vaccines' (2021) 325(6) *Journal of American Medical Association* 532.

[148] See eg Ian Freckelton, 'Mandatory Vaccination Tensions and Litigation' (2021) 28(4) *Journal of Law and Medicine* 913.

[149] *Kimber v Sapphire Coast Community Aged Care Ltd* [2021] FWCFB 6015, [181].

of vaccinated people.[150] Moreover, arguably, some employers had legal obligations to require their staff to be vaccinated so that they could maintain healthy and safe workplaces.[151] This was especially the case in employment settings that had a high risk of transmission of the virus, such as healthcare facilities.[152] Healthcare workers could contract COVID-19 from unwell people and spread it to patients, other staff, such as cleaners, and the public outside their workplaces.[153] Further, by preventing these employees from suffering illness and dying from COVID-19, mandatory vaccination had the potential to help ensure that there was a sufficient volume of healthcare workers to meet patient demand.[154]

Although at the time of writing no evidence has emerged of any governments or employers physically forcing people to have a COVID-19 vaccine, and vaccine mandates were intended to protect people's health, they constituted a significantly coercive measure in that they did apply pressure to workers to submit to vaccination if they wished to retain their employment.[155] There has been something of a move towards the use of overt compulsion internationally, with the unvaccinated becoming increasingly stigmatized and classified as failing to conform to a standard that is responsible as it is in the interests of fellow workers and the general community.[156] The first country to make a clear move in this regard was Saudi Arabia where, on 7 May 2021, the Ministry of Human Resources and Social Development announced that, as of 1 August 2021, it would be mandatory for all public and private sector workers to be vaccinated to attend the workplace.[157]

In Greece, Prime Minister Kyriakos Mitsotakis announced plans in November 2021 to penalize people aged 60 and over who refused to have COVID-19 vaccines, whether or not they were working, with a monthly fine of €100 to be imposed from

---

[150] Stephen Duckett and others, *Race to 80: Our Best Shot at Living With COVID* (Report, Grattan Institute 29 July 2021) 40 <https://grattan.edu.au/report/race-to-80/> accessed 14 September 2022.
[151] Gostin, Salmon, and Larson (n 147) 532; Gabrielle Wolf, Jason Taliadoros, and Penny Gleeson, 'A Panacea for Australia's COVID-19 Crisis? Weighing Some Legal Implications of Mandatory Vaccination' (2021) 28(4) *Journal of Law and Medicine* 993.
[152] Gostin, Salmon, and Larson (n 147) 532.
[153] ibid; Owen N Bradfield and Alberto Giubilini, 'Spoonful of Honey or a Gallon of Vinegar? A Conditional COVID-19 Vaccination Policy for Front-line Healthcare Workers' (2021) 47(7) *Journal of Medical Ethics* 467; Rachel Gur-Arie, Euzebiusz Jamrozik, and Patricia Kingori, 'No Jab, No Job? Ethical Issues in Mandatory COVID-19 Vaccination of Healthcare Personnel' (2021) 6(2) *BMJ Global Health* art e004877.
[154] Gostin, Salmon, and Larson (n 147) 532; Gur-Arie, Jamrozik, and Kingori (n 153).
[155] World Health Organization, 'COVID-19 and Mandatory Vaccination: Ethical Considerations and Caveats' Policy Brief (13 April 2021) <www.who.int/publications/i/item/WHO-2019-nCoV-Policy-brief-Mandatory-vaccination-2021.1> accessed 14 September 2022 (hereafter WHO, 'COVID-19 and Mandatory Vaccination').
[156] See Rebecca Weisser, 'Covid's Lepers: The Vaccinated Not the Unvaccinated are Driving the Pandemic' *Spectator Australia* (23 October 2021) <https://spectator.com.au/2021/10/covids-lepers/> accessed 14 September 2022.
[157] See Abdulrahman Alajlan and others, 'Saudi Arabia: Mandatory Vaccination to Attend the Workplace' *Global Compliance News* (2 September 2021) <www.globalcompliancenews.com/2021/09/02/saudi-arabia-mandatory-vaccination-to-attend-the-workplace-16082021/> accessed 14 September 2022. For Turkmenistan see Owen Dyer, 'COVID-19: Turkmenistan Becomes First Country to Make Vaccination Mandatory for All Adults' (2021) 374 *British Medical Journal* n1766.

16 January 2022.[158] European Union President, Ursula von der Leyen, commented, in the context of the proliferation of the Omicron variant in December 2021, that poor vaccine take-up meant that mandatory vaccination 'needed to be on the table as a policy response'.[159]

In the United Kingdom, the government required all National Health Service personnel to be vaccinated by April 2022 or risk being dismissed.[160] In the United States of America, the Biden administration announced plans to require all United States companies with 100 or more workers to vaccinate their staff or introduce regular testing procedures.[161] This move proved to be controversial with, amongst others, the Republican Party opposing it[162] and the legislation implementing it ultimately being struck down by the Supreme Court.[163]

In the Philippines, President Duterte made vaccination or frequent testing compulsory for those working in offices,[164] before signalling preparedness to mandate universal vaccination after meeting with the country's National Task Force Against COVID-19 to discuss the emergence of the Omicron variant.[165] Reflecting global debate on the issue, Philippines Interior Secretary Eduardo Año stated that he preferred to avoid making vaccination mandatory, but noted that several local governments had compelled vaccination already by using section 16 of the *Local Government Code* (Phil), which allowed the executive to issue orders or ordinances that will protect constituents and this 'is considered legal unless stopped by the court'.[166]

---

[158] Samantha Vanderslott, 'Greece to Make COVID Vaccines Mandatory for Over-60s, but do Vaccine Mandates Work?' *The Conversation* (2 December 2021) <https://theconversation.com/greece-to-make-covid-vaccines-mandatory-for-over-60s-but-do-vaccine-mandates-work-172672> accessed 14 September 2022.

[159] See Daniel Boffey and Helena Smith, 'EU Must Consider Mandatory Covid Jabs, Says Von der Leyen' (2 December 2021) *The Guardian* <www.theguardian.com/world/2021/dec/01/eu-must-consider-mandatory-covid-jabs-says-von-der-leyen> accessed 14 September 2022.

[160] See Dennis Campbell, '"Tens of Thousands" of NHS and Care Home Staff Could Quit Over COVID Jabs' *The Guardian* (10 November 2021) <www.theguardian.com/society/2021/nov/09/covid-vaccine-to-be-compulsory-for-all-nhs-england-staff-by-april> accessed 14 September 2022.

[161] See Eric Berger, 'Republicans Slam Biden Vaccine Rule for Businesses as Health Groups Defend it' *The Guardian* (8 November 2021) <www.theguardian.com/us-news/2021/nov/08/biden-covid-vaccine-mandate-large-companies-republicans> accessed 14 September 2022.

[162] See Sheryl L Stolberg, 'GOP Seethes at Biden Mandate, Even in States Requiring Other Vaccines' *New York Times* (16 October 2021) <www.nytimes.com/2021/09/12/us/politics/vaccine-mandates-republicans.html> accessed 14 September 2022; Lev Facher, 'GOP Opposition to Vaccine Mandates Extends Far Beyond Covid-19' STAT (17 November 2021) <www.statnews.com/2021/11/17/gop-opposition-to-vaccine-mandates-extends-far-beyond-covid-19/> accessed 14 September 2022.

[163] See *National Federation of Independent Business v Department of Labor, Occupational Safety and Health Administration*, 142 S Ct 661 (2022); 211 L Ed 2d 448 (2022). See Chapter 6.

[164] See 'Philippines to Require Vaccination for Employees Working On-site' *Reuters* (12 November 2021) <www.reuters.com/world/asia-pacific/philippines-require-vaccination-employees-working-on-site-2021-11-12/> accessed 30 November 2021.

[165] See Zacarian Sarao, 'Duterte Open to Making Jabs Mandatory; Cabinet Mulls "Pressuring" the Unvaccinated' *Inquirer* (29 November 2021) <https://newsinfo.inquirer.net/1521567/duterte-says-he-agrees-with-making-vaccines-mandatory-cabinet-mulls-pressuring-the-unvaccinated> accessed 14 September 2022.

[166] ibid. The Federated States of Micronesia has also made vaccination compulsory in all contexts as a 'necessary step to achieve herd immunity': Mala Darmadi, 'Federated States of Micronesia Makes

In many instances, the consequences of non-compliance with such mandates might have deprived people of a substantive choice not to have a vaccine.[167] The measures exercised a high level of leverage. Healthcare professionals who resisted Italy's requirement for them to have a COVID-19 vaccine faced the option of either being transferred to duties that did not risk spreading the virus or being suspended without pay for up to a year.[168] Failure to adhere to employers' vaccine mandates would also have led in some cases to loss of employment and of a livelihood if all workplaces in that industry required vaccination.[169] Initial surveys generated varied results concerning whether people would accept employer-mandated COVID-19 vaccination.[170] Yet, as more businesses required their staff to have COVID-19 vaccines and authorities approved their actions (for instance, the United States Equal Employment Opportunity Commission determined that employers could require their employees to receive a COVID-19 vaccine and prohibit them from entering the workplace if they did not do so),[171] people often had little option but to submit to vaccination directions in order to remain in employment. In addition, students who did not comply with a COVID-19 vaccine mandate could lose their educational opportunities if they were unable to continue their studies remotely.

Vaccination is a requirement for professional practice and work in healthcare services in many countries, including the United States[172] and Italy,[173] with minimal exemptions being permitted (one example of an exemption is the case where vaccination would pose a threat to the individual's personal health due to their particular clinical conditions). In Italy, there is an enforcement procedure: lists of healthcare workers are transmitted to healthcare services, which subsequently invite workers who are not already recorded as immunized to prove that their vaccination has been administered, and the services can request the record or document the individual's special clinical conditions that are impediments to them having a

---

COVID-19 Vaccine Mandatory' *ABC* (30 July 2021) <www.abc.net.au/radio-australia/programs/pacificbeat/fsm-president-iv/13477078> accessed 14 September 2022.

[167] Bradfield and Giubilini (n 153) 467.

[168] Michele Massa, 'The Italian "No Jab, No Job" Law' *Verfassunblog on Matters Constitutional* (7 April 2021) <https://verfassungsblog.de/the-italian-no-jab-no-job-law/> accessed 14 September 2022.

[169] Bradfield and Giubilini (n 153) 469; Anna Odone and others, 'Current Understandings of the Impact of Mandatory Vaccination Laws in Europe' (2021) 20(5) *Expert Review of Vaccines* 559, 560–61.

[170] See eg Jeffrey V Lazarus and others, 'A Global Survey of Potential Acceptance of a COVID-19 Vaccine' (2020) 27(2) *Nature Medicine* 225; Emily Largent and others, 'US Public Attitudes Toward COVID-19 Vaccine Mandates' (2020) 3(12) *Journal of American Medical Association Network Open* art e2033324 <https://jamanetwork.com/journals/jamanetworkopen/fullarticle/2774317> accessed 14 September 2022.

[171] Gostin, Salmon, and Larson (n 147) 532.

[172] See *Biden v Missouri*, 142 S Ct 647 (2022); 211 L Ed 433 (2022). See Chapter 6.

[173] Marta Paterlini, 'Covid-19: Italy Makes Vaccination Mandatory for Healthcare Workers' (2021) 373 *British Medical Journal* n905. See too Jacqui Wise, 'Covid-19: France and Greece Make Vaccination Mandatory for Healthcare Workers' (2021) 374 *British Medical Journal* n1797.

vaccine. Healthcare workers must comply within five days, or the local healthcare unit will communicate the non-compliance to the relevant employers and professional associations. After such communication, non-compliant healthcare workers must be removed from every activity involving interpersonal contact, or any other risk of infection. They can be employed in other positions, including at a lower level with a correspondingly lower salary if this is possible; otherwise, their employment is suspended without income. This arrangement lasts as long as the vaccination is not administered (in other words, they retain the key to reinstatement), or until the national vaccination programme is fully executed, but no longer than 31 December 2021.[174] This new COVID-19 law is likely to be found to comply with Article 32 of the *Italian Constitution*, which provides that no one can be compelled to undertake any medical treatment without a specific statutory requirement and provided that requirement is not incompatible with human dignity. However, the period of time during which such stern stipulations remain justified, with the number of those who are vaccinated rising, and the severity of the COVID-19 infection appearing for the present to be reducing in successive variants, remains to be seen.

A further issue that has proved contentious has been whether it is unethical and potentially a disciplinary infraction for a frontline healthcare practitioner to refrain from having a COVID-19 vaccination. Laura Palazzani, Deputy Vice-President of the National Bioethics Committee of Italy, has taken a robust stand on the issue, maintaining that, 'vaccines are an ethical obligation for health professionals: their professional duty to treat the sick obliges them to avoid transmitting the infection, to operate in safe conditions, and to provide reliable information on the significance of vaccines for the protection of public health'.[175]

'No jab, no job' policies have been highly controversial and generated divisive public protests in many countries. As Gur-Arie, Jamrozik, and Kingori have argued,[176] winning the trust of workers by incremental education in order to improve vaccination rates is preferable to the use of coercion. This too has been the approach of WHO, which at first went no further than urging that ethical considerations be carefully weighed in considering whether mandatory vaccination is a justifiable policy option,[177] but then contended that mandates should be an 'absolute last resort and only applicable when all other feasible options to improve vaccination uptake have been exhausted'.[178] Similarly, the option of providing inducements in cash or kind to persuade or encourage people to submit to vaccination, as urged by Savulescu, is constructive.[179]

---

[174] Massa (n 168).
[175] See Paterlini (n 173).
[176] Gur-Arie, Jamrozik, and Kingori (n 153).
[177] WHO, 'COVID-19 and Mandatory Vaccination' (n 155).
[178] Hans Kluge, Regional Director of WHO for Europe, as quoted in Ashleigh Furlong, 'WHO Cautions Against Mandatory Vaccination' *Politico* (7 December 2021) <https://www.politico.eu/article/who-cautions-against-mandatory-vaccination/> accessed 14 September 2022.
[179] Julian Savulescu, 'Good Reasons to Vaccinate: Mandatory or Payment for Risk?' (2021) 47(2) *Journal of Medical Risks* 78.

Another issue that has been highlighted is that imposition of mandatory vaccination as a precondition for entry to the workplace or, put another way, as a basis for excluding workers from the work site, should be the subject of consultation between employers and employees. In a key Australian Fair Work Commission decision in relation to mandatory vaccination, a failure to engage in such consultation was held to have rendered such a step unlawful.[180]

Two significant decisions of the United States Supreme Court, discussed in detail in Chapter 6, concerned COVID-19 vaccine mandates for workers. By a five: four majority in the case of *Biden v Missouri*,[181] the Supreme Court upheld a decision by the Secretary of Health and Human Services to require of facilities receiving Medicaid and Medicare funding that they ensure that their staff were vaccinated against COVID-19. However, the same court in *National Federation of Independent Business v Department of Labor, Occupational Safety and Health Administration*[182] struck down a vaccine mandate promulgated by OSHA that had been applicable to 84 million United States workers, employed in corporations with more than 100 employees. It did so by a six: three majority on the basis that the legislation establishing OSHA did not sufficiently authorize such a step, with Gorsuch J expressing concern that provision of such latitude could result in a declaration of a public health emergency never coming to an end and citizens' liberties and the separation of powers 'amount[ing] to little'.

VII. Conclusion

The nature of work, the supervision of workers, the location of workplaces and whether continuity of employment would be disrupted by 'the Great Resignation'[183] all became matters of controversy as a result of the COVID-19 pandemic. With the imposition of public health measures such as lockdowns and edicts that persons should work from home if they could has come a reconsideration of the need for traditional workplaces in which workers cluster together physically in the same area. Many expressed the desire during the COVID-19 pandemic to continue to work at least part of the time online away from their central workplace. For some, this has been regarded as a positive development.[184] However, the new forms of

---

[180] *Construction, Forestry, Maritime, Mining and Energy Union v Mt Arthur Coal Pty Ltd* [2021] FWCFB 6059, discussed in Chapter 6.
[181] 142 S Ct 647 (2022); 211 L Ed 433 (2022).
[182] *National Federation of Independent Business v Occupational Safety and Health Administration*, 142 S Ct 661 (2020).
[183] Carlos Carrillo-Tudela, Alex Clymo and David Zentler-Munro, 'The Truth About the "Great Resignation" – Who Changed Jobs, Where They Went and Why' *The Conversation* (29 March 2022) <https://theconversation.com/the-truth-about-the-great-resignation-who-changed-jobs-where-they-went-and-why-180159> accessed 14 September 2022.
[184] See Martin Tusl, 'Impact of the COVID-19 Crisis on Work and Private Life, Mental Well-being and Self-rated Health in German and Swiss Employees: A Cross-sectional Online Survey' (2021) 21 *BMC Public Health* art 641.

working have posed challenges in terms of management and mentoring of workers. In addition, for some workers, such an option has not been feasible because of the nature of their work or their own circumstances and obligations.

The pandemic has caused a rethinking of workers' responsibilities, especially in the healthcare industry, but also more broadly, to take personal charge for maintaining the health of those within the workplace by staying away from work when unwell. This has become part of a new debate about reciprocal obligations by employers and employees for health and safety within the workplace, prioritizing the health of the workplace against previous cultures of 'soldiering on' and presenteeism. It is increasingly accepted that it is an obligation of employers to have not just hand sanitizers and appropriate forms of PPE in the workplace, where necessary, but also policies that actively discourage workers from attending if they may be symptomatic with the virus.

Ethical and legal issues have needed to be explored too about when workers are entitled to refrain from working or to withdraw their labour completely during a pandemic, making more pressing the concomitant needs experienced by the community and exacerbating the burdens placed upon fellow workers. This has been an issue especially for healthcare workers who have been at disproportionate risk during the pandemic. The debate in this regard remains unresolved, but it is clear that COVID-19 has asked a great deal of healthcare workers and for some has exacted a very serious toll, aspects of which have been ongoing, and led a percentage of them to discontinue their vocation permanently. These persons need to be looked after and, where necessary, the workforce needs to be supplemented in a variety of ways.

While mandatory vaccination in the workplace continues to be a difficult ethical and legal issue, the legally recognized human right to life is likely to be accorded precedence as a consideration during a public health emergency; so long as government or employer edicts requiring vaccination of people in the workplace are necessary and proportionate, and suitable consultation takes place between employers and employees, they will generally be determined by courts to be lawful. However, an ongoing issue worthy of community debate is the steps that may need to be taken to avoid stigmatization and discrimination against an increasingly marginalized group in the community—those who choose not to be vaccinated.

11
Development of COVID-19 Treatments and Vaccines

I. Introduction

Soon after its emergence, it was apparent that COVID-19 could have a catastrophic effect on the world: it spread extremely easily and swiftly between people and, in serious cases, caused severe symptoms, including difficulty breathing, and death. In due course it also became apparent that it could have ongoing effects. Only some jurisdictions, such as China, Australia, New Zealand, South Pacific nations, and, to a degree, Thailand, Vietnam, and Taiwan, successfully suppressed outbreaks of COVID-19 during early waves of the pandemic, largely through restricting people's movement, as discussed in Chapters 4 and 5. However, in most countries, given their detrimental economic and social impact, these measures were not sustainable indefinitely.[1] Further, many people, and particularly populations in low- and middle-income countries, faced barriers to adhering to hygiene and physical distancing practices that could impede the dissemination of the virus.[2]

Consequently, it was imperative to meet two challenges as quickly as possible. The first was to develop COVID-19 treatments (to cure the disease or at least reduce the severity of its symptoms) and vaccines (to prevent people from contracting and suffering or dying from it).[3] The second was to produce treatments and vaccines that were proven to be safe and effective and distribute them as widely as possible within countries and internationally.[4] This chapter and Chapter 12 examine the first and second challenges respectively, with a focus on legal, regulatory, and ethical issues that have been relevant to addressing them.

---

[1] World Health Organization, 'WHO Concept for Fair Access and Equitable Allocation of COVID-19 Health Products' (9 September 2020) 5 <www.who.int/docs/default-source/coronaviruse/who-covid19-vaccine-allocation-final-working-version-9sept.pdf> accessed 1 February 2021; Muhammad Zaheer Abbas, 'Treatment of the Novel COVID-19: Why Costa Rica's Proposal for the Creation of a Global Pooling Mechanism Deserves Serious Consideration?' (2020) 7(1) *Journal of Law and the Biosciences* art lsaa049, 2.

[2] Leila Abdullahi and others, 'Community Interventions in Low- and Middle-Income Countries to Inform Covid-19 Control Implementation Decisions in Kenya: A Rapid Systematic Review' (2020) 15(12) *PLoS One* art e0242403, 1, 18–20, 22; Tony Kirby, 'Evidence Mounts on the Disproportionate Effect of COVID-19 on Ethnic Minorities' (2020) 8(6) *Lancet Respiratory Medicine* 547, 548.

[3] Abbas (n 1) 3, 9.

[4] ibid.

Section II of this chapter considers these issues in the context of research undertaken to develop COVID-19 treatments and vaccines. It discusses the role played by the World Health Organization (WHO) in encouraging scientific collaboration, and strategies that were adopted to accelerate this research, including the use of human challenge trials. Section III of the chapter focuses on participation in this research and explores the challenge that researchers faced to develop COVID-19 treatments and vaccines as quickly as possible while ensuring that the subjects of clinical trials were protected. It examines aspects of human rights law and ethical guidelines that govern provision of consent to participate in clinical trials, and matters that have been relevant to involving in this research people who could not provide their voluntary or informed consent to participate in them. This Section also considers the importance of enrolling a diverse range of subjects in COVID-19 clinical trials. Section IV of this chapter discusses issues arising from the publication of results of research into COVID-19 treatments and vaccines. It delves into the dilemma that it was optimal to disseminate evidence that might assist in combatting the pandemic as soon as possible, but publication of research results before they had been reviewed pursuant to traditional, rigorous scholarly processes potentially had highly adverse consequences. Section V of the chapter provides some brief concluding observations.

II. Research into COVID-19 Treatments and Vaccines

From the beginning of the pandemic, it was clear that rapid development of COVID-19 treatments and vaccines could only be accomplished through researchers' extensive collaboration. Substantial efforts were therefore invested in facilitating co-ordination and co-operation among scientists and health professionals working on COVID-19 research across the globe.[5] The international collaboration of research teams during this pandemic, the 'breakneck speed' at which they worked to investigate and develop treatments and vaccines, and the immense financial investment by governments, private companies, and philanthropic organizations in such research, were unprecedented.[6] Notwithstanding

---

[5] Sarah Boseley, 'The Race to Make a COVID-19 Vaccine' (2021) 398(1303) *Lancet* 832; Sarah Gilbert and Catherine Green, *Vaxxers: The Inside Story of the Oxford AstraZeneca Vaccine and the Race Against the Virus* (Hodder & Stoughton 2021); World Health Organization, 'A Coordinated Global Research Roadmap: 2019 Novel Coronavirus' (March 2020) 19 <https://www.who.int/publications/m/item/a-coordinated-global-research-roadmap> accessed 6 September 2022 (hereafter World Health Organization, 'A Roadmap').

[6] World Health Organization, 'A Roadmap' (n 5) 19; Gilbert and Green (n 5); Gregory Zuckerman, *A Shot to Save the World: The Remarkable Race and Groundbreaking Science Behind the Covid-19 Vaccines* (Penguin 2021); Jason W Nickerson and Matthew Herder, 'COVID-19 Vaccines as Global Public Goods' in Colleen M Flood and others (eds), *Vulnerable: The Law, Policy and Ethics of COVID-19* (University of Ottawa Press 2020) 594–95; Jemima Stratford, Emily McKenzie, and Emma Mockford, 'Balancing Speed and Safety: The Authorisation of COVID-19 Vaccines and Medicines' (2020) 25(2) *Judicial Review* 105–106.

the achievements in research and development and their altruistic motives, national and international authorities and researchers recognized the importance of ensuring that they were subject to appropriate and effective legal and regulatory governance and oversight, and conformed to accepted ethical standards.[7] This was especially apparent from the work undertaken by WHO during the pandemic.

A. Involvement of the World Health Organization

WHO began encouraging and co-ordinating collaborative COVID-19 research within the international scientific community shortly after its Director-General declared on 30 January 2020 that the COVID-19 outbreak was a public health emergency of international concern.[8] At that stage, there were no proven treatments or vaccines for COVID-19.[9] Together with the Global Research Collaboration for Infectious Disease Preparedness and Response, in February 2020, WHO organized a 'Global Forum on Research and Innovation for COVID-19' to 'accelerate innovative research to help contain the spread of the epidemic and facilitate care for those affected'.[10] Four hundred people, including scientists and public health professionals, attended the forum, which WHO convened on 11 and 12 February 2020 at its Geneva headquarters.[11]

Participants in the forum assessed the then state of knowledge about SARS-CoV-2 (the virus that causes the COVID-19 disease) and 'shared scientific data'; discussed several research topics and 'ethical considerations for research'; determined 'research priorities'; and explored opportunities for collaborative research work.[12] The participants agreed to eight 'immediate research actions', which included 'broadly and rapidly [sharing] virus materials, clinical samples and [associated] data'.[13] Another action involved 'rapidly developing master protocols for clinical trials' to 'accelerate the evaluation of investigational therapeutics and vaccines', 'improve collaboration and comparison across different studies', and 'streamline ethics review'.[14]

After the forum, WHO proceeded to follow the 'R&D Blueprint Strategy', which medical, scientific, and regulatory experts had created in the wake of the 2016

---

[7] Lawrence O Gostin, Safura Abdool Karim, and Benjamin Mason Meier, 'Facilitating Access to a COVID-19 Vaccine Through Global Health Law' (2020) 48(3) *Journal of Law, Medicine & Ethics* 622, 623–25.
[8] World Health Organization, 'R&D Blueprint and COVID-19' <www.who.int/teams/blueprint/covid-19> accessed 4 October 2022 (hereafter World Health Organization, 'R&D Blueprint and COVID-19').
[9] World Health Organization, 'A Roadmap' (n 5) 3.
[10] World Health Organization, 'R&D Blueprint and COVID-19' (n 8).
[11] World Health Organization, 'A Roadmap' (n 5) 2.
[12] ibid.
[13] ibid 8.
[14] ibid 8.

Ebola epidemic.[15] This is 'a global strategy and preparedness plan' that aims to facilitate 'rapid activation of research and development activities during epidemics' in order to 'fast-track the availability of effective tests, vaccines and medicines'.[16] The plan contemplated a broad global coalition of experts to develop and implement an 'R&D Blueprint' to '[facilitate] a coordinated and accelerated response to COVID-19', which included 'an unprecedented program to develop a vaccine, research into potential pharmaceutical treatments and strengthened channels for information sharing between countries'.[17] The R&D Blueprint also outlined a 'governance structure'.[18] This involved a Scientific Advisory Group to provide 'strategic and scientific advice on research priorities', which in turn contributed to information given by the Strategic and Technical Advisory Group for Infectious Hazards to WHO's Health Emergencies Programme.[19] Scientists and institutions across the world working on COVID-19 research were divided into working parties, which were described as 'thematic areas', to focus on specific research priorities.[20] Experts in the different thematic areas would collaborate with each other and report on the advances they made to the Scientific Advisory Group.[21]

On 2 March 2020, the Scientific Advisory Group met to review the progress of COVID-19 research since the Global Research Forum and 'advise WHO on additional prioritization of research actions'.[22] WHO then developed an 'R&D Roadmap' that articulated 'immediate, mid-term and longer-term priorities' for the 'global research response' to COVID-19.[23] The Roadmap noted that 'the intense communications and information sharing among researchers is unprecedented and has resulted in a level of collaboration among scientists that, together with innovation advances, has led to research actions being implemented faster than ever before during an outbreak'.[24] Also, according to the Roadmap, 'a comprehensive collaborative research agenda' had been drafted and its implementation commenced.[25] The Roadmap recorded WHO's intention 'to maintain a high-level discussion platform which enables consensus on strategic directions, nurtures scientific collaborations, and supports optimal and rapid research to address crucial gaps, without duplication of efforts'.[26]

---

[15] ibid 2; World Health Organization, 'R&D Blueprint and COVID-19' (n 8).
[16] World Health Organization, 'R&D Blueprint About Us' <www.who.int/teams/blueprint/about> accessed 10 September 2022.
[17] World Health Organization, 'A Roadmap' (n 5) 19; World Health Organization, 'R&D Blueprint and COVID-19' (n 8).
[18] World Health Organization, 'A Roadmap' (n 5) 19.
[19] ibid.
[20] ibid.
[21] ibid.
[22] ibid 3.
[23] ibid.
[24] ibid 4.
[25] Ibid 3.
[26] ibid.

In April 2020, WHO, together with the European Commission, the Bill and Melinda Gates Foundation, and France, launched the 'framework for collaboration' known as the 'Access to COVID-19 Tools (ACT) Accelerator' (ACT Accelerator).[27] It comprised diverse other partners, too, including health organizations, researchers, and philanthropists.[28] One of the key means by which the ACT Accelerator sought to achieve its aim of '[ending] the COVID-19 pandemic as quickly as possible' was to 'accelerate development' of COVID-19 'therapeutics and vaccines', and two of its 'four pillars' were devoted to this endeavour.[29] Unitaid and the Wellcome Trust led the 'therapeutics pillar', in which WHO was also involved, that sought to develop COVID-19 treatments.[30] A global alliance named 'COVAX' constituted the pillar that was dedicated to accelerating development and manufacture of COVID-19 vaccines.[31] COVAX was led by: WHO; the Coalition for Epidemic Preparedness Innovations (CEPI) ('a global partnership', which was formed in 2017 'to facilitate access to new vaccines' in order to halt 'future pandemics');[32] and Gavi (a vaccine alliance comprising public and private partners, which was created in 2000 to improve children's access to vaccines in low- and middle-income countries).[33] Nevertheless, the ACT Accelerator appeared to struggle to secure sufficient funding to provide substantial support for the development of COVID-19 treatments and vaccines.[34]

B. Strategies to Accelerate COVID-19 Research

Teams of scientists used varied strategies to hasten their COVID-19 research. Thorough scientific research into treatments and vaccines for diseases

---

[27] World Health Organization, 'The ACT-Accelerator Frequently Asked Questions' <www.who.int/initiatives/act-accelerator/faq> accessed 4 October 2022 (hereafter World Health Organization, 'The ACT-Accelerator').
[28] ibid.
[29] ibid.
[30] ibid.
[31] ibid.
[32] Gostin, Karim, and Meier (n 7) 624; CEPI, 'Preparing for Future Pandemics' <https://cepi.net/> accessed 4 October 2022.
[33] Gostin, Karim, and Meier (n 7) 624; GAVI, 'About Our Alliance' (13 October 2021) <www.gavi.org/our-alliance/about> accessed 1 February 2021.
[34] World Health Organization, 'ACT-Accelerator Update' (26 June 2020) <www.who.int/news/item/26-06-2020-act-accelerator-update> accessed 4 October 2022; United Nations, 'UN Welcomes Nearly $1 Billion in Recent Pledges—to Bolster Access to Lifesaving Tests, Treatments and Vaccines to End COVID-19' (News Release, 30 September 2020) <www.un.org/sites/un2.un.org/files/v16_press_release_unga_act-ac_300920final.pdf> accessed 1 February 2021; ACT-Accelerator Therapeutics Partnership, 'COVID-19 Therapeutics Investment Case' (2020) <https://unitaid.org/assets/Therapeutics-Partnership-Investment-Case.pdf> accessed 4 October 2022; World Health Organization, 'G20 Leaders Boost Support of the Access to COVID-19 Tools (ACT) Accelerator but Urgent and Immediate Action is Needed to Maintain Momentum' (News Release, 21 May 2021) <www.who.int/news/item/21-05-2021-g20-leaders-boost-support-of-the-access-to-covid-19-tools-(act)-accelerator-but-urgent-and-immediate-action-is-needed-to-maintain-momentum>.

typically takes years, and in the case of vaccines at least a decade, to complete.[35] Conventionally, a medical product's safety and effectiveness is assessed in the following stages:[36]

- 'preclinical testing' (the product is tested on human cells or animals);
- 'phase 0 trials' (a low dosage of the product is administered to a small number of people);
- 'phase 1 safety trials' (a larger number of people receive a higher dosage of the product);
- 'phase 2 expanded trials' (hundreds of people receive the product in the highest dosage deemed safe during phase 1 trials and, in certain trials, some participants receive a comparable product or placebo); and
- 'phase 3 efficacy trials' (randomized controlled trials involving thousands of people, who receive either the product or a placebo).[37]

Obstacles to these trials proceeding swiftly can include the need to:

- recruit a sufficiently large and diverse pool of participants (for example, researchers working on the COVID-19 vaccine, Moderna, struggled to reach its target of 30,000 participants for its clinical trials);
- monitor participants for a significant period of time after they have received the product to check its impact (for example, the United States of America's Food and Drug Administration requires a minimum of six months' follow-up);
- in the case of vaccines, wait for participants to become exposed to the virus and to determine if any immunity they provide endures;
- analyse the data; and
- revisit phases of the trials that fail (more than 80% of products fail a trial phase).[38]

---

[35] Patricia J Zettler, Micah L Berman, and Efthimios Parasidis, 'Drug and Vaccine Development and Access' in Scott Burris and others (eds), *Assessing Legal Responses to COVID-19* (Public Health Law Watch 2020) 166.
[36] Stratford, McKenzie, and Mockford (n 6) 108.
[37] ibid 109; Carl Zimmer, Jonathan Corum, and Sui-Lee Wee, 'Coronavirus Vaccine Tracker' *New York Times* (31 January 2021) <www.nytimes.com/interactive/2020/science/coronavirus-vaccine-tracker.html> accessed 1 February 2021; Jill Seladi-Schulman, 'What Happens in a Clinical Trial?' *Healthline* (21 June 2019) <www.healthline.com/health/clinical-trial-phases#phase-iv> accessed 10 September 2022.
[38] Zettler, Berman, and Parasidis (n 35) 163, 166; Dorit R Reiss, 'The COVID-19 Vaccine Dilemma' (2020) 6(1) *Administrative Law Review Accord* 29, 37–38; Philip R Krause and Marion F Gruber, 'Emergency Use Authorization of Covid Vaccines—Safety and Efficacy Follow-up Considerations' (2020) 383(19) *New England Journal of Medicine* e107(1), e107(2); Zimmer, Corum, and Wee (n 37).

To counterbalance such impediments, scientists undertook multiple different trials simultaneously, aiming to find safe and effective treatments and vaccines in the record time of a year.[39] As discussed further below, they also attempted to 're-purpose' some existing drugs—such as remdesivir, dexamethasone, and actemra—by testing their effectiveness for COVID-19.[40] Scientists sometimes ran two phases of tests concurrently or combined phases.[41] For instance, in the second human trial for a COVID-19 vaccine, Oxford University researchers blended phase 1 and phase 2 trials, with ten participants initially receiving two doses of the vaccine separated by four weeks and then 1,102 other participants receiving the vaccine or a comparator.[42] In some cases, preclinical testing was abbreviated or abandoned.[43] Researchers developing the Moderna vaccine candidate, for example, bypassed the preclinical stage of testing their product on animals before administering it to humans, even though it was a new substance.[44] Certain trials involved fewer participants than would typically be enrolled and, in some cases, 'observational studies' were used instead of randomized, controlled trials.[45] The vaccines were not always tested on young people, at least until late in the testing process. For instance, it was not until December 2020 that Moderna announced that it would test its vaccine on children aged between 12 and 17.[46]

The most expedited process for COVID-19 vaccine production involved Russia's Sputnik V vaccine (also known as Gam-COVID-Vac), a heterologous recombinant vaccine, which was developed by the Gamaleya Research Institute of Epidemiology and Microbiology in Moscow. Concerns were raised internationally both as to the efficacy and safety of this vaccine. Like the Oxford-AstraZeneca and Johnson & Johnson vaccines, it used an engineered adenovirus, but by contrast, two vectors—rAd26 and rAd5 – for its first and second doses respectively.[47]

---

[39] Stratford, McKenzie, and Mockford (n 6) 109; European Commission, 'EU Strategy for COVID-19 Vaccines' (Communication from the Commission, 17 June 2020) COM/2020/245 <https://eur-lex.europa.eu/legal-content/EN/TXT/?qid = 1597339415327&uri = CELEX:52020DC0245> accessed 26 October 2021.

[40] Wendy Lipworth and others, 'Science at Warp Speed: Medical Research, Publication, and Translation During the COVID-19 Pandemic' (2020) 17(4) *Journal of Bioethical Inquiry* 555; Tina Hesman Saey, 'Why It's Still So Hard to Find Treatments for Early COVID-19' *Science News* (27 July 2021) <www.sciencenews.org/article/coronavirus-covid-19-why-early-treatment-drugs> accessed 4 October 2022.

[41] Zimmer, Corum, and Wee (n 37); Reiss (n 38) 50–51.

[42] Stratford, McKenzie, and Mockford (n 6) 109.

[43] Lipworth and others (n 40) 555.

[44] Paul Komesaroff, Ian Kerridge, and Lyn Gilbert, 'The US is Fast-tracking a Coronavirus Vaccine, but Bypassing Safety Standards May Not be Worth the Cost', *The Conversation* (24 March 2020) <https://theconversation.com/the-us-is-fast-tracking-a-coronavirus-vaccine-but-bypassing-safety-standards-may-not-be-worth-the-cost-134041> accessed 10 September 2022.

[45] Lipworth and others (n 40) 555.

[46] See Denise Grady, 'Moderna Plans to Begin Testing its Coronavirus Vaccine in Children' *New York Times* (18 December 2020) <www.nytimes.com/2020/12/02/health/Covid-Moderna-vaccine-children.html> accessed 10 September 2022.

[47] See eg Elizabeth Mahase, 'Covid-19: Russian Vaccine Efficacy is 91.6%, Show Phase III Trial Results' (2021) 372 *British Medical Journal* n309.

Logunov and others maintained that this vaccine, which had been tested on 76 volunteers, '[induced] strong humoral and cellular immune responses on 100% of healthy participants' and generated only mild adverse reactions.[48] On 11 August 2020, Russia's Ministry of Health issued a registration certificate for the vaccine, so that it could be administered to 'a small number of citizens from vulnerable groups'.[49] The certificate stated that it could not be used widely until 1 January 2021,[50] although the website for Sputnik V stated that a phase III efficacy trial involving more than 2,000 people was scheduled to begin in August 2020 in Russia, the United Arab Emirates, Saudi Arabia, Brazil, and Mexico, with mass production of the vaccine scheduled to begin in September.[51] Svetlana Zavidova, a lawyer heading the Association of Clinical Research Organizations in Russia, is reported as having denounced the acceleration in the trial process as 'ridiculous'.[52]

Others, too, voiced concerns. For instance, Andreev and others (including Bucci) accepted that the results were 'potentially significant' and published an open letter setting out their worries.[53] In a separate article, Bucci and others (including Andreev) emphasized the absence of the numerical values for each studied individual and an indication of how many of those who had recovered from the virus were included in the analysis, and a failure to make available key data to verify the overlap of percentages in the graphs that had been published.[54] However, further data were published in February 2021 as a result of a randomized, controlled phase 3 trial involving approximately 20,000 persons in each of the actual and placebo groups. It showed high efficacy (91.6% immunogenicity), and a good tolerability profile in participants aged 18 years or older.[55] Again concerns were expressed about discrepancies in the data and what was said to be

---

[48] Denis Logunov and others, 'Safety and Immunogenicity of an rAD26 and rAD5 Vector-based Heterologous Prim-boost COVID-19 Vaccine in Two Formulations: Two Open, Non-Randomised Phase 1/2 Studies from Russia' (2020) 396(10255) *Lancet* 887.

[49] See Jon Cohen, 'Russia's Approval of a COVID-19 Vaccine is Less Than Meets the Press Release' *Science Insider* (11 August 2020) <www.science.org/content/article/russia-s-approval-covid-19-vaccine-less-meets-press-release> accessed 4 October 2022.

[50] ibid.

[51] Logunov and others (n 48); Kirill Dmitriev, 'Questions on Russia's Sputnik V Vaccine Answered, Time for Critics to Look for Plank in Own Eyes' *Sputnik V* (7 September 2020) <https://sputnikvaccine.com/newsroom/kirill-dmitriev-questions-on-russia-s-sputnik-v-vaccine-answered-time-for-critics-to-look-for-plank-/> accessed 22 November 2021.

[52] Cohen (n 49).

[53] Konstantin Andreev and others, 'Note of Concern' *Cattivi Scienziati* (7 September 2020) <https://cattiviscienziati.com/2020/09/07/note-of-concern/> accessed 4 October 2022.

[54] Enrico Bucci and others, 'Safety and Efficacy of the Russian COVID-19 Vaccine: More Information Needed' (2020) 396(10256) *Lancet* E53. See also Kylie Quinn and Holly Seale, 'Russia's Coronavirus Vaccine Hasn't Been Fully Tested. Doling it Out Risks Side Effects and False Protection' *The Conversation* (12 August 2020) <https://theconversation.com/russias-coronavirus-vaccine-hasnt-been-fully-tested-doling-it-out-risks-side-effects-and-false-protection-144347> accessed 26 October 2021.

[55] Denis Logunov and others, 'Safety and Efficacy of an rAD26 and rAd5 Vector-based Heterologous Prime-boost COVID-19 in Vaccine: An Interim Analysis of a Randomised Controlled Phase 3 Trial in Russia' (2021) 397(10275) *Lancet* 671.

substandard reporting of interim data.[56] In general, the new data resulted in a reduction in concern about it,[57] although concerns persisted until late 2021 about its efficacy against COVID-19 variants,[58] as well as in respect of its one-dose sibling, 'Sputnik light'.[59]

In March 2021, the European Medicines Agency instituted a 'rolling review' of Sputnik V.[60] As discussed further in Chapter 12, this is a measure deployed to assess a promising drug in a situation such as a public health emergency. While usually all data on the effectiveness, safety, and quality of a medicine or vaccine, as well as all required documentation, must be ready prior to the European Medicines Agency's evaluation, in the case of a rolling review, the European Medicines Agency's Committee for Medicinal Products for Human Use reviews data as they become available from ongoing studies. Once that Committee decides that sufficient data are available, it can authorize use of the medical product sooner than would otherwise be the case. During the rolling review, and throughout the COVID-19 pandemic, the European Medicines Agency and its scientific committees were supported by the COVID-19 European Medicines Agency pandemic task force. As of October 2021,[61] the European Medicines Agency and WHO through its Strategic Advisory Group of Experts on Immunization were still reviewing data about Sputnik V, although by March 2022 the WHO review of Sputnik V was suspended because of the Russian invasion of Ukraine.[62] Nonetheless its use was permitted in many countries, including Brazil, Hungary, India, and the Philippines.[63] However, ironically, uptake of the local vaccine proved to be slow in Russia, not just because of the unusual haste with which the vaccine was made available to the

---

[56] Enrico Bucci and others, 'Data Discrepancies and Substandard Reporting of Interim Data of Sputnik V Phase 3 Trial' (2021) 397(10288) *Lancet* 1881.

[57] See eg Ian Jones and Polly Roy, 'Sputnik V COVID-19 Vaccine Candidate Appears Safe and Effective' (2021) 397(10275) *Lancet* 642; Bianca Nogrady, 'Mounting Evidence Suggests Sputnik COVID Vaccine is Safe and Effective' (2021) 595(7867) *Nature* 339.

[58] Mario Cazzola and others, 'Controversy Surrounding the Sputnik V Vaccine' (2021) 187 *Respiratory Medicine* art 106569.

[59] ibid. See Haya Karima, 'Egypt Approves Russian Single-component Sputnik Light Vaccine Against COVID-19: RDIF' (25 September 2021) <www.egypttoday.com/Article/1/108162/Egypt-approves-Russian-single-component-Sputnik-Light-vaccine-against-COVID accessed 4 October 2022.

[60] European Medicines Agency, 'EMA Starts Rolling Review of the Sputnik V COVID-19 Vaccine' (4 March 2021) <https://www.ema.europa.eu/en/news/ema-starts-rolling-review-sputnik-v-covid-19-vaccine> accessed 4 October 2022.

[61] Jamey Keaten, 'WHO Still Reviewing Sputnik V Vaccine, as Russia Presses Bid' *AP News* (6 October 2021) <https://apnews.com/article/coronavirus-pandemic-united-nations-world-health-organization-europe-russia-3e8159d00b525c187864f8b68252691e> accessed 4 October 2022.

[62] World Health Organization, 'Vaccines Guidance Document' (29 September 2021) <https://extranet.who.int/pqweb/sites/default/files/documents/Status_COVID_VAX_29Sept2021.pdf> accessed 13 October 2021; Mrinalika Roy, 'WHO Delays Review of Russia's Sputnik V Vaccine on Ukraine Conflict' *Reuters* (17 March 2022) <https://www.reuters.com/business/healthcare-pharmaceuticals/who-delays-review-russias-sputnik-v-vaccine-ukraine-conflict-2022-03-16/> accessed 19 May 2022.

[63] Nogrady (n 57).

local population, but because mistrust of both vaccines and medical professionals in that country is significant.[64]

The pace of COVID-19 research and development was remarkable. Within six months of scientists sequencing SARS-CoV-2, six vaccine candidates were in phase 3 clinical trials.[65] By January 2021, 67 vaccines were undergoing human clinical trials and 20 had reached the final testing stages.[66] By October 2021, 194 vaccines were in preclinical development, 126 were in human clinical trials, including phases I, II, and III, 26 were in phase III clinical trials, and 8 were in phase IV post-licensure surveillance.[67] By mid-October 2021, the United States Food and Drug Administration issued an 'Emergency Use Authorization' in relation to the Moderna vaccine for certain populations.[68]

'The Solidarity Trial' was a momentous undertaking to identify potential COVID-19 treatments.[69] WHO, together with some partners, launched this international, randomized clinical trial, which enrolled almost 12,000 patients in 500 hospital sites in over 30 countries.[70] WHO played a critical role in organizing the trial, including by arranging for manufacturers to donate treatment courses for participants.[71] This trial evaluated the effects of four treatments—remdesivir, hydroxychloroquine, lopinavir/ritonavir, and interferon—on three outcomes in COVID-19 patients: mortality; need for assisted ventilation; and duration of hospital stay.[72] It published interim results on 15 October 2020, which indicated that all four treatments had little or no effect on those outcomes.[73] The trial was adaptive, meaning that drugs adjudged not to be promising were abandoned, while others were added.[74] For instance, hydroxychloroquine and lopinavir/ritonavir trials were discontinued on 20 June and 4 July 2020 respectively.[75] However, by

---

[64] Arik Burakovsky, 'Russia's COVID-19 Response Slowed by Population Reluctant to Take Domestic Vaccine' *The Conversation* (26 August 2021) <https://theconversation.com/russias-covid-19-response-slowed-by-population-reluctant-to-take-domestic-vaccine-165925> accessed 4 October 2022.

[65] Lawrence O Gostin, 'The Great Coronavirus Pandemic of 2020—7 Critical Lessons' (2020) 324(18) *Journal of the American Medical Association* 1816.

[66] Zimmer, Corum, and Wee (n 37).

[67] National Centre for Immunisation Research and Surveillance, 'COVID-19 Vaccine Development Landscape' (13 October 2021) <www.ncirs.org.au/covid-19/covid-19-vaccine-development-landscape> accessed 4 October 2022.

[68] See Amy McKeever, 'Here's the Latest on COVID-19 Vaccines' *National Geographic* (15 October 2021) <www.nationalgeographic.com/science/article/coronavirus-vaccine-tracker-how-they-work-latest-developments-cvd> accessed 4 October 2022.

[69] World Health Organization, 'WHO COVID-19 Solidarity Therapeutics Trial' <www.who.int/emergencies/diseases/novel-coronavirus-2019/global-research-on-novel-coronavirus-2019-ncov/solidarity-clinical-trial-for-covid-19-treatments> accessed 4 October 2022 (hereafter World Health Organization, 'Solidarity Trial').

[70] ibid.
[71] ibid.
[72] ibid.

[73] WHO Solidarity Trial Consortium, 'Repurposed Antiviral Drugs for COVID-19—Interim WHO Solidarity Trial Results' (2021) 384(6) *New England Journal of Medicine* 497.

[74] World Health Organization, 'Solidarity Trial' (n 69).
[75] ibid.

August 2021, WHO announced a new phase in its Solidarity trial, which involved enrolling patients to test three new drugs in hospitalized COVID-19 patients:

- Artesunate (a drug prescribed for severe malaria);
- Imatinib (a drug prescribed for the treatment of chronic myelogenous leukaemia, acute lymphoblastic leukaemia, and various gastrointestinal stromal tumours by blocking the abnormal protein that signals cancers cells to multiply); and
- Infliximab (a drug prescribed for diseases of the immune system such as Crohn's disease and rheumatoid arthritis).[76]

WHO adopted an approach of maintaining a 'living guideline' for COVID-19 therapeutics.[77] By September 2021, the guidelines contained:

- 'a strong recommendation for systemic corticosteroids' in 'patients with severe or critical COVID-19';
- 'a conditional recommendation against systemic corticosteroids' in 'patients with non-severe COVID-19';
- 'a conditional recommendation against remdesivir in patients with critical COVID-19';
- 'a strong recommendation against hydroxychloroquine' in patients with COVID-19 of any severity;
- 'a strong recommendation against lopinavir-ritonavir' in patients with COVID-19 of any severity;
- 'a recommendation against ivermectin' in patients with COVID-19 of any severity, 'except in the context of a clinical trial'; and
- a recommendation for treatment with 'IL-6 receptor blockers (tocilizumab or sarilumab)' for 'patients with severe or critical COVID-19' infection.[78]

However, individual countries continued to make their own decisions. For instance, in August 2021, the Australian Therapeutic Goods Administration provisionally approved GlaxoSmith Kline's monoclonal antibody treatment, sotrovimab (XEVUDY), 'for the treatment of adults and adolescents (aged 12 years and over and weighing at least 40 kg) with coronavirus disease 2019 (COVID-19) who do not require initiation of oxygen due to COVID-19 and who are at increased risk

---

[76] World Health Organization, 'WHO's Solidarity Clinical Trial Enters a New Phase with Three New Candidate Drugs' (News Release, 11 August 2021) <www.who.int/news/item/11-08-2021-who-s-solidarity-clinical-trial-enters-a-new-phase-with-three-new-candidate-drugs> accessed 27 September 2022.
[77] See eg World Health Organization, 'Therapeutics and COVID-19: Living Guideline' (6 July 2021) < https://www.who.int/publications/i/item/WHO-2019-nCoV-therapeutics-2022.4> accessed 2 October 2022.
[78] ibid.

of progression to hospitalization or death'.[79] This treatment was approved even though Australia's National COVID-19 Clinical Evidence Taskforce gave the drug at best a qualified endorsement:

> The available research does not currently provide enough evidence to determine the benefits of sotrovimab in specific subgroups of patients. In the absence of definitive evidence, the Taskforce has arrived at a consensus recommendation based on their combined clinical expertise to guide clinical decisions about which patients are most likely to benefit from sotrovimab.
>
> There is no evidence evaluating the effectiveness of sotrovimab in fully vaccinated patients, a low likelihood of development of severe disease, and a small risk of adverse events. Given this and the lower risk of deterioration in these patients, it is unlikely that sotrovimab will be particularly valuable in fully vaccinated patients, unless the patient is immunosuppressed.
>
> There is no evidence on the effectiveness of sotrovimab in immunosuppressed patients. However, given the likely higher risk of deterioration in these patients, and the absence of reasons to believe otherwise, it is likely that sotrovimab will be beneficial for immunosuppressed patients.[80]

However, this pronouncement was made after the European Medicines Agency confirmed on 21 May 2021 that sotrovimab could be used to treat some patients,[81] and the United States Food and Drug Administration issued an 'Emergency Use Authorization' on 26 May 2021 similarly permitting use of sotrovimab.[82] By

---

[79] Therapeutic Goods Administration, 'TGA Provisionally Approves GlaxoSmithKline's COVID-19 Treatment: Sotrovimab (XEVUDY)' Australian Government Department of Health (20 August 2021) <www.tga.gov.au/media-release/tga-provisionally-approves-glaxosmithklines-covid-19-treatment-sotrovimab-xevudy> accessed 10 September 2022. See also Elise Schubert, Lifeng Kang, and Nial Wheate, 'What Is Sotrovovimab, the COVID Drug the Government Has Bought Before Being Approved for Use in Australia?' *The Conversation* (9 August 2021) <https://theconversation.com/what-is-sotrovimab-the-covid-drug-the-government-has-bought-before-being-approved-for-use-in-australia-155802?> accessed 10 September 2022.

[80] National COVID-19 Clinical Evidence Taskforce, 'Australian Guidelines for the Clinical Care of People with COVID-19' (26 August 2021) <https://app.magicapp.org/#/guideline/5571> accessed 4 October 2022.

[81] European Medicines Agency, 'EMA Issues Advice on Use of Sotrovimab (VIR-7831) for Treating COVID-19' (21 May 2021) <www.ema.europa.eu/en/news/ema-issues-advice-use-sotrovimab-vir-7831-treating-covid-19> accessed 4 October 2022.

[82] United States Food and Drug Administration, 'Coronavirus (COVID-19) Update: FDA Authorizes Additional Monoclonal Antibody for Treatment of COVID-19' (News Release, 26 May 2021) <www.fda.gov/news-events/press-announcements/coronavirus-covid-19-update-fda-authorizes-additional-monoclonal-antibody-treatment-covid-19> accessed 4 October 2021. On 22 December 2021, the United States Food and Drug Administration issued an Emergency Use Authorization in relation to another medication, the first oral pill treatment for COVID-19—Pfizer's Paxlovid (nirmatrelvir and ritonavir tablets)—that was similarly prescribed 'for the treatment of mild-to-moderate coronavirus disease (COVID-19) in adults and pediatric patients (12 years of age and older weighing at least 40 kilograms or about 88 pounds) with positive results of direct SARS-CoV-2 testing, and who are at high risk for progression to severe COVID-19, including hospitalization or death': United States Food and Drug Administration, 'Coronavirus (COVID-19) Update: FDA Authorizes First Oral Antiviral for Treatment of COVID-19' (News Release, 22 December 2021) <https://www.fda.gov/news-events/press-announceme

October 2021, however, studies were showing clear evidence that sotrovimab was significantly reducing the risk of progression of COVID-19 symptoms among high-risk patients with mild-to-moderate symptoms.[83]

C. Human Challenge Trials

Human challenge trials (also known as controlled human infection trials) involve the intentional infection of patients with diseases to learn how to improve treatment or prevent diseases. A number of ethically indefensible human challenge trials have taken place since World War II. Each stands as a warning against the risks attendant upon the advancement of medical knowledge by the intentional infliction of diseases upon subjects without their informed consent and to their detriment. Notwithstanding this history, human challenge trials have been proposed and in fact commenced during the COVID-19 pandemic. One notorious previous human challenge trial—the 'Tuskegee Study of Untreated Syphilis in the Negro Male' between 1932 and 1972—highlighted the need to ensure that those who are not in a position to provide informed consent to their participation in such research are explicitly and adequately protected.[84] The 623 participants in this study were informed that they would be treated for 'bad blood', were not told they were involved in a study, did not provide informed consent to participating in it, were not offered proper treatment when it became available, and were not told they could withdraw from the study and obtain treatment from other sources.[85]

Concerns were similarly raised following public exposure of the 'Willowbrook' studies that were undertaken in the United States between the 1950s and the 1970s.[86] Fifty-one residents of a state school for children with intellectual disabilities were infected with various strains of hepatitis by being intentionally fed

---

nts/coronavirus-covid-19-update-fda-authorizes-first-oral-antiviral-treatment-covid-19> accessed 10 May 2022.

[83] See eg Anil Gupta and others, 'Early Treatment for Covid-19 with SARS-CoV-2 Neutralizing Antibody Sotrovimab' (2021) 385(21) *New England Journal of Medicine* 1941.

[84] See James H Jones, *Bad Blood: The Tuskegee Syphilis Experiment* (The Free Press 1993); Susan M Reverby (ed), *Tuskegee's Truths: Rethinking the Tuskegee Syphilis Study* (University of North Carolina Press 2000) (hereafter Reverby, *Tuskegee's Truths*); Susan M Reverby, *Examining Tuskegee: The Infamous Syphilis Study and its Legacy* (University of North Carolina Press 2009) (hereafter Reverby, *Examining Tuskegee*); Fred D Gray, *The Tuskegee Syphilis Study: The Real Story and Beyond* (NewSouth Books 2013).

[85] See Jones (n 84); Reverby, *Tuskegee's Truths* (n 84); Reverby, *Examining Tuskegee* (n 84); Gray (n 84).

[86] See Eugene F Diamond, 'The Willowbrook Experiments' (1973) 40(2) *The Linacre Quarterly* 133; Franz J Ingelfinger, 'Ethics of Experiments on Children' (1973) 288(15) *New England Journal of Medicine* 791; David Goode and others, *A History and Sociology of the Willowbrook State School* (American Association on Intellectual and Developmental Disabilities 2013). For a defence by the researchers, see Saul Krugman, 'The Willowbrook Hepatitis Studies Revisited: Ethical Aspects' (1986) 8(1) *Reviews of Infectious Diseases* 157.

infectious faecal extracts.[87] Willowbrook was closed after the publicity,[88] litigation ensued in relation to the constitutional right to protection from harm,[89] and a fillip was given to deinstitutionalization of persons with intellectual disabilities.[90] Another key legacy of the exposure of the unethical exploitation of the residents of Willowbrook was recognition of the need to enable persons with disabilities to provide informed consent to medical research in which they participate, so far as this is possible.[91]

In 2010, the public learned that medical research in Guatemala between 1946 and 1948, which was supported by the Venereal Disease Research Laboratory of the United States Public Health Service, had involved deliberate exposure of 1,308 prisoners, soldiers, patients in a state-run psychiatric hospital, and commercial sex workers, to syphilis, gonorrhea, and chancroid.[92] As the Presidential Commission for the Study of Bioethical Issues observed, 'the events in Guatemala serve as a cautionary tale of how the quest for scientific knowledge without regard to relevant ethical standards can blind researchers to the humanity of the people they enlist into research'.[93]

Despite these scandals, in a variety of other circumstances, human challenge trials have enabled significant advances in the development of vaccines and treatments, for instance, for yellow fever,[94] and cholera.[95] From the early phases of the COVID-19 pandemic, to speed up the pursuit of an effective vaccine, proposals were advanced in several countries to undertake 'human challenge trials'. Such an option in respect of vaccine research could involve subjects being given

---

[87] See Diamond (n 86); Ingelfinger (n 86); Goode and others (n 86). For a defence by the researchers, see Krugman (n 86).
[88] See David J Rothman and Sheila M Rothman, *The Willowbrook Wars: Bringing the Mentally Disabled into the Community* (Routledge 2004).
[89] *New York State Association for Retarded Children Inc v Rockefeller* 357 F Supp 752 (1973); *New York State Association for Retarded Children v Carey* 706 F 2d 956 (1983).
[90] See Goode and others (n 86).
[91] See eg Licia Carlson, 'Research Ethics and Intellectual Disability: Broadening the Debates' (2013) 86(3) *Yale Journal of Biology and Medicine* 303.
[92] See Susan M Reverby, '"Normal Exposure" and Inoculation Syphilis: A PHS "Tuskegee" Doctor in Guatemala, 1946–1948' (2011) 23(1) *Journal of Policy History* 6; Presidential Commission for the Study of Bioethical Issues, '*Ethically Impossible': STD Research in Guatemala from 1946 to 1948* (Report, September 2011) <https://bioethicsarchive.georgetown.edu/pcsbi/sites/default/files/Ethically%20Impossible%20(with%20linked%20historical%20documents)%202.7.13.pdf> accessed 6 March 2022; Kayte Spector-Bagdady and Paul A Lombardo, '"Something of an Adventure": Postwar NIH Research Ethos and the Guatemala STD Experiments' (2013) 41(3) *Journal of Law, Medicine & Ethics* 697; Kayte Spector-Bagdady and Paul A Lombardo, 'US Public Health Service STD Experiments in Guatemala (1946–1948) and Their Aftermath' (2019) 41(2) *Ethics & Human Research* 29.
[93] Presidential Commission for the Study of Bioethical Issues (n 92) 7.
[94] See Enrique Chaves-Carballo, 'Clara Maass, Yellow Fever and Human Experimentation' (2013) 178(5) *Military Medicine* 557; Akhil Mehra, 'Politics of Participation: Walter Reed's Yellow-Fever Experiments' (2009) 11(4) *Virtual Mentor* 326.
[95] See Myron M Levine, 'Experimental Challenge Studies in the Development of Vaccines for Infectious Diseases' (1998) 95 *Developments in Biological Standardization* 169; Debbie-Ann T Shirley and Monica A McArthur, 'The Utility of Human Challenge Studies in Vaccine Development: Lessons Learned from Cholera' (2011) 1 *Vaccine: Development and Therapy* 3.

SARS-CoV-2 as a substitute for phase 3 trials.[96] The proposal for these trials was controversial,[97] due to the risks of participants experiencing severe illness or dying,[98] the potential for trial participants to spread the virus to others, difficulty establishing the authenticity of participants' consent, and abuse of the subjects in some past human challenge studies.[99] Nevertheless, they attracted support from early in the pandemic.[100] Advocates for 'controlled human challenge trials of SARS-CoV-2 vaccine candidates' argued that they 'could accelerate the testing and potential rollout of efficacious vaccines' and thereby 'reduce the global burden of coronavirus-related mortality and morbidity'.[101] WHO similarly acknowledged the potential value of such trials, observing that:

> They can be substantially faster to conduct than vaccine field trials, in part because far fewer participants need to be exposed to experimental vaccines in order to provide (preliminary) estimates of efficacy and safety. Such studies can be used to compare the efficacy of multiple vaccine candidates and thus select the most promising vaccines for larger studies. Well designed challenge studies might thus not only accelerate COVID-19 vaccine development, but also make it more likely that the vaccines ultimately deployed are more effective.[102]

---

[96] Sean O'Neill McPartlin and others, 'Covid-19 Vaccines: Should We Allow Human Challenge Studies to Infect Healthy Volunteers with SARS-CoV-2? (2020) 371 *British Medical Journal* m4258, 1; Reiss (n 38) 57; Euzebiusz Jamrozik, George S Heriot, and Michael J Selgelid, 'Coronavirus Human Infection Challenge Studies: Assessing Potential Benefits and Risks' (2020) 17 *Journal of Bioethical Inquiry* 709–10.

[97] See Ian Freckelton, 'Human Challenge Trials: Ethical and Legal Issues for COVID-19 Research' (2021) 28(2) *Journal of Law and Medicine* 311 (hereafter Freckelton, 'Human Challenge Trials'); UK COVID Challenge, 'About Our COVID-19 Volunteer Trials' <https://ukcovidchallenge.com/covid-19-volunteer-trials/>; Ewen Callaway, 'Dozens to be Deliberately Infected with Coronavirus in UK "Human Challenge" Trials' (2020) 586(7831) *Nature* 651; Theresa Machemer, 'A Brief History of Human Challenge Trials' *Smithsonian Magazine* (16 December 2020) <www.smithsonianmag.com/science-nature/brief-history-human-challenge-trials-180976556/>; Daniel P Sulmasy, 'Are SARS-CoV-2 Human Challenge Trials Ethical?' (2021) 181(8) *Journal of the American Medical Association Internal Medicine* 1031.

[98] Reiss (n 38) 57; Nir Eyal, Marc Lipsitch, and Peter G Smith, 'Human Challenge Studies to Accelerate COVID Vaccine Licensure' (2020) 221(11) *Journal of Infectious Diseases* 1752.

[99] See Holly Fernandez Lynch, 'The Rights and Wrongs of Intentional Exposure Research: Contextualising the Guatemala STD Inoculation Study' (2012) 38(8) *Journal of Medical Ethics* 513; Takashi Tsuchiya, 'The Imperial Japanese Experiments in China' in Ezekiel J Emanuel and others (eds), *The Oxford Textbook of Clinical Research Ethics* (Oxford University Press 2008); Paul J Weindling, 'The Nazi Medical Experiments' in Ezekiel J Emanuel and others (eds), *The Oxford Textbook of Clinical Research Ethics* (Oxford University Press 2008); Euzebiusz Jamrozik and Michael J Selgelid, *Human Challenge Studies in Endemic Settings: Ethical and Regulatory Issues* (Springer 2021); Euzebiusz Jamrozik and Michael J Selgelid, 'Ethical Issues Surrounding Controlled Human Infection Challenge Studies in Endemic Low- and Middle-Income Countries' (2020) 34(8) *Bioethics* 797.

[100] See Ewen Callaway, 'Should We Infect Healthy People with Coronavirus?' (2020) 580(7801) *Nature* 17.

[101] Eyal, Lipsitch, and Smith (n 98). See also Garth Rapeport and others, 'SARS-CoV-2 Human Challenge Studies—Establishing the Model During an Evolving Pandemic' (2021) 385 *New England Journal of Medicine* 961.

[102] World Health Organization, 'Key Criteria for the Ethical Acceptability of COVID-19 Human Challenge Studies' (6 May 2020) <https://apps.who.int/iris/bitstream/handle/10665/331976/WHO-2019-nCoV-Ethics_criteria-2020.1-eng.pdf?ua=1> accessed 1 February 2021.

In April 2020, 35 members of the United States House of Representatives encouraged Congress to consider allowing volunteers to be infected with COVID-19 to accelerate vaccine testing.[103] '1DaySooner', a non-profit organization advocating for human challenge studies, asserted that 38,659 people had indicated their willingness to participate in such trials.[104] On 14 October 2020, a group of prominent scientists and ethicists wrote an open letter on behalf of 1DaySooner to the United Kingdom's Secretary of State for Health and Social Care, urging:

> you and other international institutions and governments around the world to endorse and advance immediate preparations for human challenge trials, including supporting safe and reliable production of the virus, design of an infectious dosing study, and any biocontainment facilities necessary to house participants.[105]

The United Kingdom government subsequently invested £30 million to fund COVID-19 challenge trials.[106]

Risks associated with human challenge trials have previously prompted identification of ethical and regulatory considerations that might need to be taken into account in deciding whether to conduct them. For instance, in 2016, an expert committee commissioned by the National Institute of Allergy and Infectious Diseases and the Walter Reed Army Institute of Research articulated such matters (which it found had not been met by proposals to undertake a Zika virus human challenge trial), including whether the risks are 'reasonable, minimized, and justified by the potential social value of the trial', 'vulnerable populations' are 'protected', and there is 'a robust informed consent process'.[107] In response to the COVID-19 pandemic, on 6 May 2020, WHO similarly published the following recommendations of eight 'key criteria for the ethical acceptability of COVID-19 Human Challenge Studies' (Table 11.1).[108]

---

[103] Letter from Bill Foster and others to Alex M Azar II and Stephen Hahn (Congress of the United States, 20 April 2020) <https://foster.house.gov/sites/foster.house.gov/files/2020.04.20_Ltr%20to%20HHS%20%20FDA%20on%20Rapid%20Vaccine%20Deployment%20for%20COVID-19%20-%20Signed.pdf> accessed 4 October 2022.
[104] 1Day Sooner <www.1daysooner.org/> accessed 10 May 2022; McPartlin and others (n 96).
[105] Scott Aaronson and others, 'UK: Challenge Trials for COVID-19' *1Day Sooner* (14 October 2020) <www.1daysooner.org/uk-open-letter> accessed 4 October 2022.
[106] See Natalie Grover, 'UK to Spend £30m on Trials Infecting Young People to Hasten Covid Vaccine' *The Guardian* (20 October 2020) <www.theguardian.com/world/2020/oct/20/covid-firm-secures-10m-to-infect-young-volunteers-to-hasten-vaccine> accessed 4 October 2022.
[107] Seema K Shah and others, 'Ethical Considerations for Zika Virus Human Challenge Trials: Report and Recommendations' (February 2017) <www.niaid.nih.gov/sites/default/files/EthicsZikaHumanChallengeStudiesReport2017.pdf> accessed 26 October 2021.
[108] World Health Organization, 'Key Criteria for the Ethical Acceptability of COVID-19 Human Challenge Studies' (6 May 2020) 4–5 <https://apps.who.int/iris/bitstream/handle/10665/331976/WHO-2019-nCoV-Ethics_criteria-2020.1-eng.pdf?ua = 1> accessed 4 October 2022.

Table 11.1 Key criteria for the ethical acceptability of COVID-19 Human Challenge Studies

	Scientific and ethical assessments	
Criterion 1	Scientific justification	SARS-CoV-2 challenge studies must have strong scientific justification
Criterion 2	Assessment of risks and potential benefits	It must be reasonable to expect that the potential benefits of SARS-CoV-2 challenge studies outweigh risks
	Consultation and coordination	
Criterion 3	Consultation and engagement	SARS-CoV-2 challenge research programmes should be informed by consultation and engagement with the public as well as relevant experts and policy-makers
Criterion 4	Coordination	SARS-CoV-2 challenge study research programmes should involve close coordination between researchers, funders, policy-makers and regulators
	Selection criteria	
Criterion 5	Site selection	SARS-CoV-2 challenge studies should be situated where the research can be conducted to the highest scientific, clinical and ethical standards
Criterion 6	Participant selection	SARS-CoV-2 challenge study researchers should ensure that participant selection criteria limit and minimize risk
	Review and consent	
Criterion 7	Expert review	SARS-CoV-2 challenge studies should be reviewed by a specialized independent committee
Criterion 8	Informed consent	SARS-CoV-2 challenge studies must involve rigorous informed consent

Scholars Nir Eyal, Marc Lipsitch, and Peter Smith, also suggested introducing a safeguard to COVID-19 human challenge trials pertaining to the selection and treatment of participants:

> Volunteers in such studies could autonomously authorize the risks to themselves, and their *net* risk could be acceptable if participants comprise healthy young adults, who are at relatively low risk of serious disease following natural infection, if they have a high baseline risk of natural infection, and if during the trial they receive frequent monitoring and, following any infection, the best available care.[109]

Another sensitive point is what pecuniary and other benefits are given to human challenge trial participants. The risk is that monetary payment will induce people to enrol in these trials where they otherwise might have refrained from doing so due to concerns about their safety; as Macklin has put it, 'The likely result is that a disproportionate number of volunteers would come from lower-income brackets, including many people who lost their jobs because of the pandemic. It is also likely that many volunteers would be members of racial and ethnic minorities.'[110] Lynch and others[111] have argued that the framework generally applied to clinical research should be adapted, dividing benefits into reimbursement, compensation, and incentives, focusing upon fairness and promoting adequate recruitment and retention of participants as counterweights to the potential for inducements to be excessive and intrude upon participants' voluntariness.[112] They have contended that within the basic framework, several factors are especially salient for human challenge trials involving COVID-19 vaccines, including the nature of participants' confinement, their anticipated discomfort, risks and uncertainty relating to the trials, participants' motivations, and their trust in those running the trials.[113] Their argument is that these factors need to be reflected in a payment worksheet created to help sponsors, researchers, and ethics reviewers systematically develop and assess ethically justifiable payment amounts.[114]

---

[109] Eyal, Lipsitch, and Smith (n 98) 1752.
[110] Ruth Macklin, 'Human Challenge Studies for Covid-19 Vaccine: Questions about Benefits and Risks' *The Hastings Center* (15 June 2020) <www.thehastingscenter.org/human-challenge-studies-for-covid-19-vaccine-questions-about-benefits-and-risks/> accessed 4 October 2022.
[111] Holly Fernandez Lynch and others, 'Promoting Ethical Payment in Human Infection Challenge Studies' (2021) 21(3) *American Journal of Bioethics* 11.
[112] ibid.
[113] ibid.
[114] ibid.

After COVID-19 vaccines had commenced to be rolled out early in 2021, scholars Nir Eyal, Arthur Caplan, and Stanley Plotkin continued to promote the utility of human challenge trials.[115] They pointed out the dearth of knowledge about rates of infection and infectiousness in vaccinated and unvaccinated people. They accepted that participants in human challenge trials would need to be young and healthy, and that such persons should receive priority access to any necessary care during and after the trials:

> While standard phase III field trials have already proven multiple vaccines to be safe and efficacious, and many countries are already rolling these vaccines out, it remains important to test whether these vaccines block infections (a crucial role not yet elucidated) and how long that protection lasts. The world also needs to test whether next generation vaccines competitively prevent infection, especially for vaccines that aren't restricted by cold chains, the need for repeat doses, limited global vaccine production, or unaffordable pricing. Human challenge trials can offer insights in these areas.[116]

These scholars argued that challenge trials could, amongst other things, 'discern the efficacy of vaccines in ... preventing infection to the vaccinated person', 'measure rapidly the comparative efficacy of different vaccines', including 'against new viral variants', and 'discern the duration and breadth of vaccine immunity'.[117] However, a contrasting perspective was aired in a letter to the *British Medical Journal* from Professor Hasford, the President of the Association of Medical Ethics Committees in Germany.[118] He raised concerns about the risk of underprivileged and vulnerable members of the community disproportionately participating in human challenge trials, as well as about the generalizability of outcomes.[119] He expressed the hope that 'human challenge trials with SARS-CoV-2 will not be performed as human beings should not become just a means to an end'.[120] Daniel Sulmasy argued that, while the COVID-19 pandemic presented urgent needs:

> the ethical justification for ... challenge studies using SARS-CoV-2 fall short of the mark: there are alternatives; the study population may not give generalizable

---

[115] Nir Eyal, Arthur Caplan, and Stanley Plotkin, 'Human Challenge Trials of COVID-19 Vaccines Still Have Much to Teach Us' *The BMJ Opinion* (8 January 2021) <https://blogs.bmj.com/bmj/2021/01/08/human-challenge-trials-of-covid-19-vaccines-still-have-much-to-teach-us/> accessed 22 September 2022.
[116] ibid.
[117] ibid.
[118] Joerg Hasford, 'Re: Covid-19: Human Challenge Studies will see People Purposefully Infected with Virus' (Rapid Response, *British Medical Journal*, 22 October 2020) <www.bmj.com/content/371/bmj.m4101/rr-0> accessed 4 October 2022.
[119] ibid.
[120] ibid.

results; there is no rescue therapy; the long-term risks of infection are unknown; and the level of remuneration is suspiciously high.[121]

Notwithstanding these issues, in February 2021, a specially constituted research committee, recognized by the United Kingdom Ethics Committee Authority and forming part of the Health Research Authority of the National Health Service,[122] approved a fast-tracked COVID-19 human infection challenge trial.[123] This made the United Kingdom the first country to run a formally constituted COVID-19 human challenge trial. Initially, the trial was programmed to involve 90 healthy adult volunteers who would be overseen rigorously by the Royal Free London Hospital where participants would be required to remain during the trial.[124] The arrangement was that participants would be paid £4,500 for their involvement. However, by June 2021, it had evolved with two trials underway, utilizing the original strain of the COVID-19 virus. The University of Oxford and Imperial College were conducting parallel tests; the University used a dose-escalation approach by infecting sero-negative people, while Imperial College infected sero-positive people with a documented history of COVID-19 infection in an effort to gain a better understanding of protective immunity. Helen McShane, an Oxford University vaccines expert leading the trial, explained that the aspiration was to identify a challenge dose that was safe, but then, ideally, a dose that would re-infect persons who had previously been infected with SARS-CoV-2:

> We can then interrogate the baseline immune response in all of our subjects and determine, what is it about the immune response in those subjects who cannot be reinfected, compared with those who can? ... We may see, for example, that people who have a level of neutralizing antibodies above a certain point cannot be reinfected. That then tells us [about] the immune response we want to induce with a new vaccine. And that then feeds very directly into vaccine design, but more importantly, vaccine testing. So that's what our model is for.[125]

---

[121] Sulmasy (n 97) 1032.

[122] See National Health Service Health Research Authority, 'COVID-19 Human Infection Challenge Vaccine Studies' (5 November 2020) <www.hra.nhs.uk/about-us/news-updates/covid-19-human-infection-challenge-vaccine-studies/> accessed 4 October 2022.

[123] Department for Business, Energy, and Industrial Strategy and Kwasi Kwarteng, 'World's First Coronavirus Human Challenge Study Receives Ethics Approval in the UK' Press Release (17 February 2021) <www.gov.uk/government/news/worlds-first-coronavirus-human-challenge-study-receives-ethics-approval-in-the-uk> accessed 22 September 2022.

[124] See Freckelton, 'Human Challenge Trials' (n 97); Nicola Davis, 'Covid: Trial to Study Effect of Immune System on Reinfection' The Guardian (19 April 2021) <www.theguardian.com/science/2021/apr/19/trial-to-study-effect-of-immune-system-on-covid-reinfection> accessed 4 October 2022.

[125] See Jef Akst, 'Q & A: Human Challenge Studies of COVID-19 Underway in UK' The Scientist (18 June 2021) <www.the-scientist.com/news-opinion/q-a-human-challenge-studies-of-covid-19-underway-in-uk-68908> accessed 4 October 2022.

The model developed by Imperial College had similar aims to the Oxford University test, but was slightly different from it, as it sought to develop a human challenge model that could be used to 'test vaccine efficacy'.[126] It may well be that the United Kingdom COVID-19 human challenge tests give an impetus internationally to this form of research. However, it is notable that the protocols utilized in the COVID-19 trials provide significant levels of protection to participants.

III. Participation in COVID-19 Treatments and Vaccines Research

To develop treatments and vaccines for COVID-19 and confirm their safety and efficacy, scientists undertook a large number of human clinical trials.[127] Given the risks of such trials harming and even killing participants, the trials clearly engaged the human rights to 'life' and 'to the enjoyment of the highest attainable standard of physical and mental health', which are recognized in international and domestic legal instruments.[128] Many countries have regulatory authorities that guide, monitor, and/or control the conduct of clinical trials to ensure that human rights are protected.[129] Concerns were raised, however, that, in the face of desperate pleas for a rapid solution to the escalating infection and mortality rates from COVID-19, the usual safeguards to protect human subjects in clinical trials might be sacrificed.[130] Yet, given the urgent need for treatments and vaccines for the virus, it was important to consider whether any protocols for clinical trials could be modified, while still ensuring participants' safety.[131] A major concern was to ensure that participants gave informed consent to enrol in COVID-19 clinical trials and, if it was important to involve participants who were unable to consent to their enrolment, that they were protected from exploitation. Another challenge posed by this pandemic and the pace at which clinical trials needed to proceed was to enrol a sufficiently diverse range of participants in them.

---

[126] See Akst (n 125). See further Ryan O'Hare, 'COVID-19 Human Challenge Study Reveals Detailed Insights into Infection' (Imperial College London, 31 March 2022) <https://www.imperial.ac.uk/news/233514/covid-19-human-challenge-study-reveals-detailed/> accessed 4 October 2022; Ewen Callaway, 'Scientists Deliberately Gave People COVID – Here's What They Learnt' (2022) 602(7896) *Nature* 191.

[127] Zimmer, Corum, and Wee (n 37).

[128] Sarah Joseph, 'International Human Rights Law and the Response to the COVID-19 Pandemic' (2020) 11(2) *Journal of International Humanitarian Legal Studies* 249; *International Covenant on Economic, Social and Cultural Rights* (opened for signature 16 December 1966, entered into force 3 January 1976) 993 UNTS 3, Article 12(1); *International Covenant on Civil and Political Rights* (opened for signature 16 December 1966, entered into force 23 March 1976) 999 UNTS 171, Article 6(1) (hereafter *ICCPR*).

[129] Holly Fernandez Lynch and others, 'Regulatory Flexibility for COVID-19 Research' (2020) 7(1) *Journal of Law and the Biosciences* art lsaa057, 9 (hereafter Lynch and others, 'Regulatory Flexibility').

[130] Alex John London and Jonathan Kimmelman, 'Against Pandemic Research Exceptionalism' (2020) 368(6490) *Science* 476; Joseph (n 128).

[131] Lynch and others, 'Regulatory Flexibility' (n 129).

A. Consent to Participate in COVID-19 Clinical Trials

1 Human rights law

One of the principal protections for human subjects involved in clinical trials—to which those undertaking COVID-19 research needed to have regard—is the requirement under human rights law that they provide informed consent to participate in them. The notion of informed consent as a foundation for contemporary ethical principles for research dates to the Nuremberg Code that was developed in the period following World War II.[132] Article 5 of the *Universal Declaration of Human Rights* provides that 'no one shall be subject to torture or to cruel, inhuman or degrading treatment'.[133] With greater specificity on this issue, Article 7 of the *International Covenant on Civil and Political Rights* states that 'no one shall be subjected without his free consent to medical or scientific experimentation'.[134] More recently, the 2005 *Universal Declaration on Bioethics and Human Rights*[135] has set out precise principles regarding this subject. For instance, Article 6 provides that:

1. Any preventive, diagnostic and therapeutic medical intervention is only to be carried out with the prior, free and informed consent of the person consent of the person concerned, based on adequate information. The consent should, where appropriate, be express and may be withdrawn by the person concerned at any time and for any reason without disadvantage or prejudice.
2. Scientific research should only be carried out with the prior, free, express and informed consent of the person concerned. The information should be adequate, provided in a comprehensible form and should include modalities for withdrawal of consent. Consent may be withdrawn by the person concerned at any time and for any reason without any disadvantage or prejudice. Exceptions to this principle should be made only in accordance with ethical and legal standards...
3. In appropriate cases of research carried out on a group of persons or a community, additional agreement of the legal representatives of the group or community concerned may be sought. In no case should a collective community agreement or the consent of a community leader or other authority substitute for an individual's informed consent.

---

[132] See George J Annas and Michael A Grodin, *The Nazi Doctors and the Nuremberg Code: Human Rights in Human Experimentation* (Oxford University Press 1992).
[133] United Nations General Assembly, *Universal Declaration of Human Rights* (Resolution A/RES/3/217A, 10 December 1948).
[134] *ICCPR* (n 128).
[135] UNESCO General Conference, *Universal Declaration on Bioethics and Human Rights* (33rd Sess, 19 October 2005).

Article 7 of the *Universal Declaration on Bioethics and Human Rights* deals specifically with persons who are unable, for any reason, to provide consent. It states:

> In accordance with domestic law, special protection is to be given to persons who do not have the capacity to consent:
> (a) authorization for research and medical practice should be obtained in accordance with the best interest of the person concerned and in accordance with domestic law. However, the person concerned should be involved to the greatest extent possible in the decision-making process of consent, as well as that of withdrawing consent;
> (b) research should only be carried out for his or her direct health benefit, subject to the authorization and the protective conditions prescribed by law, and if there is no research alternative of comparable effectiveness with research participants able to consent. Research which does not have potential direct health benefit should only be undertaken by way of exception, with the utmost restraint, exposing the person only to a minimal risk and minimal burden and, if the research is expected to contribute to the health benefit of other persons in the same category, subject to the conditions prescribed by law and compatible with the protection of the individual's human rights. Refusal of such persons to take part in research should be respected.

Article 8 of the *Universal Declaration on Bioethics and Human Rights* states that 'human vulnerability should be taken into account', 'individuals and groups of special vulnerability should be protected and the personal integrity of such individuals respected'. Article 15 of the *Convention on the Rights of Persons with Disabilities*[136] too not only reiterates that 'no one shall be subjected to torture or to cruel, inhuman or degrading treatment or punishment', but it provides explicitly that 'no one shall be subjected without his or her free consent to medical or scientific experimentation'.

The temptations for researchers to disregard these protections of human rights and undertake clinical research that is contrary to the best interests of participants who are not in a position to provide informed consent to the risks they are running can be potent. Past scandals, including those perpetrated by Nazi doctors[137] and the Japanese military in World War II,[138] demonstrated in the most extreme ways

---

[136] *Convention on the Rights of Persons with Disabilities* (opened for signature 13 December 2006, entered into force 3 May 2008) 2515 UNTS 3.

[137] See Robert Jay Lifton, *The Nazi Doctors: Medical Killing and the Psychology of Genocide* (rev edn, Basic Books 2017); Annas and Grodin (n 132).

[138] See eg Jing-Bao Nie and others (eds), *Japan's Wartime Medical Atrocities: Comparative Inquiries in Science, History and Ethics* (Routledge 2010); Hal Gold, *Japan's Infamous Unit 731: Firsthand Accounts of Japan's Wartime Human Experimentation Program* (Tuttle 2019).

the potential for exploitation of vulnerable research subjects.[139] These and other atrocities in fact prompted the development of protections for research subjects though case law[140] and bioethical principles.[141]

Since the Tuskegee, Willowbrook, and Guatemala scandals discussed in Section II above, attempts have been made to identify capacities that prospective subjects of clinical trials must demonstrate in order to provide genuinely informed consent to their participation in them. These include their: understanding of the facts of the study (for example, its purpose, design, and the subjects' responsibilities); appreciation of the study's personal relevance and potential consequences of participating in it (for instance, its risks and benefits, and limitations on personalized treatment decisions); ability to reason logically about their options (such as to assess the risk-to-benefit ratio of participating in it); and ability to express a personal choice about whether or not to participate in it.[142]

2 Ethical guidelines on human research

The need to ensure protection of human research participants is also reflected in international and national ethical guidelines that govern human research. For example, the World Medical Association's *Declaration of Helsinki*, first adopted in 1964,[143] requires that consent to participate in research must be informed and voluntary.[144] In the United States, the *National Research Act of 1974* provided for the implementation of a surrogate mechanism for protecting prospective subjects of clinical trials who lack the capacity to provide informed consent to participating in them by establishing Institutional Review Boards (IRBs) to protect their rights.[145] Subsequently, the 1979 Belmont Report of the National Commission for the Protection of Human Subjects of Biomedical and Behavioral Research also sought to protect these participants in clinical trials.[146] This report influenced the 1991

---

[139] See eg Paul Weindling and others, 'The Victims of Unethical Human Experiments and Coerced Research under National Socialism' (2016) 40(1) *Endeavour* 1; Sheldon Rubenfeld and Susan Benedict, *Human Subjects Research After the Holocaust* (Springer 2014).
[140] See eg *Salgo v Leland Stanford Jr University Board of Trustees* 154 Cal App 2d 560, 317 P 2d 170 (1957).
[141] See George J Annas, 'Beyond Nazi War Crimes Experiments: The Voluntary Consent Requirement of the Nuremberg Code at 70' (2018) 108(1) *American Journal of Public Health* 42.
[142] See eg Paul S Appelbaum and Loren H Roth, 'Competency to Consent to Research: A Psychiatric Overview' (1982) 39(8) *Archives of General Psychiatry* 951; Laura B Dunn and others, 'Assessing Decisional Capacity for Clinical Research or Treatment: A Review of Instruments' (2006) 163(8) *American Journal of Psychiatry* 1323; Edward D Sturman, 'The Capacity to Consent to Treatment and Research: A Review of Standardized Assessment Tools' (2005) 25(7) *Clinical Psychology Review* 954; Juana I Acosta, 'Vaccines, Informed Consent, Effective Remedy and Integral Reparation: An International Human Rights Perspective' (2015) 131 *Vniversitas* 19.
[143] World Medical Association General Assembly, *Declaration of Helsinki—Ethical Principles for Medical Research Involving Human Subjects* (adopted June 1964) (hereafter *Declaration of Helsinki*).
[144] 'Participation by individuals capable of giving informed consent as subjects in medical research must be voluntary': *Declaration of Helsinki* (n 143) para 25.
[145] National Commission for the Protection of Human Subjects of Biomedical and Behavioral Research, *Belmont Report* (United States Department of Health and Human Services, 18 April 1979).
[146] ibid.

Federal Policy for the Protection of Human Subjects, which was codified by 15 federal departments and agencies in the so-called 'Common Rule'.[147] Key elements of this policy are: requirements for assuring research institutions' compliance with it; requirements for researchers; obtaining and documenting informed consent; and requirements pertaining to the IRB's membership, function, operations, review of research, and record-keeping.[148] It incorporated additional protections for particularly vulnerable research subjects before it was again revised in 2018.[149]

Similarly, the United Kingdom's 'Code of Practice for Research' requires researchers on projects involving human subjects to satisfy themselves that participants are enabled, by the provision to them of adequate, accurate information in an appropriate form through suitable procedures, to give informed consent, having particular regard to the needs and capacities of vulnerable groups.[150] Similar requirements are set out in the 2019 'Concordat to Support Research Integrity'.[151] In Australia, paragraph 1.4 of the 'National Statement on Ethical Conduct in Human Research' precludes 'exploitation of participants in the conduct of research',[152] and Chapter 4.4 provides detailed guidance for research involving persons who may be unable to give consent. Perhaps most importantly from an international perspective, the Council for International Organizations for Medical Sciences, founded under the auspices of WHO and the United Nations Educational, Scientific and Cultural Organization, in its fourth edition of its *International Ethical Guidelines for Health-related Research Involving Humans*, released in 2016,[153] stated without equivocation that 'researchers have a duty to provide potential research participants with the information and the opportunity to give their free and informed consent to participate in research, or to decline to do so, unless a research ethics

---

[147] See Jerry Menikoff, 'The Common Rule, Updated' (2017) 376 *New England Journal of Medicine* 613; Kathy L Hudson and Francis S Collins, 'Bringing the Common Rule into the 21st Century' (2015) 373 *New England Journal of Medicine* 2293.

[148] See *Protection of Human Subjects*, 45 CFR § 46 (2017) <www.govinfo.gov/content/pkg/CFR-2016-title45-vol1/pdf/CFR-2016-title45-vol1-part46.pdf> accessed 4 October 2022.

[149] *Federal Policy for the Protection of Human Subjects*, 82 Fed Reg 7149, 7259, 7273, 19 January 2017 (with effect from 21 January 2019) <www.govinfo.gov/content/pkg/FR-2017-01-19/pdf/2017-01058.pdf> accessed 4 October 2022. See Grace Gartel, Heather Scuderi, and Christine Servay, 'Implementation of Common Rule Changes to the Informed Consent Form: A Research Staff and Institutional Review Board Collaboration' (2020) 20(1) *The Ochsner Journal* 76.

[150] United Kingdom Research Integrity Office, 'Code of Practice for Research: Promoting Good Practice and Preventing Misconduct' (2021) s 3.7.10 <https://ukrio.org/wp-content/uploads/UKRIO-Code-of-Practice-for-Research.pdf> accessed 4 October 2022.

[151] Universities UK, 'The Concordat to Support Research Integrity' (25 October 2019).

[152] National Health and Medical Research Council, Australian Research Council, and Universities Australia, *National Statement on Ethical Conduct in Human Research (2007)* (Updated 2018) (National Health and Medical Research Council 2018) <www.nhmrc.gov.au/about-us/publications/national-statement-ethical-conduct-human-research-2007-updated-2018#block-views-block-file-attachments-content-block-1> accessed 10 September 2022.

[153] Council for International Organizations for Medical Sciences and World Health Organization, *International Ethical Guidelines for Health-related Research Involving Humans* (4th edn, CIOMS 2016) guideline 9 <https://cioms.ch/wp-content/uploads/2017/01/WEB-CIOMS-EthicalGuidelines.pdf> accessed 10 September 2022.

committee has approved a waiver or modification of informed consent'. Guideline 10 provides that:

> Before a waiver of informed consent is granted, researchers and research ethics committees should first seek to establish whether informed consent could be modified in a way that would preserve the participant's ability to understand the general nature of the investigation and to decide whether to participate.

A research ethics committee may approve a modification or waiver of informed consent to research if:

- the research would not be feasible or practicable to carry out without the waiver or modification;
- the research has important social value; and
- the research poses no more than minimal risks to participants.

3 Involvement in COVID-19 research of subjects without their voluntary and informed consent

Important issues arise about the propriety of involving in clinical research people who are so unwell that they are unable to communicate their wishes, such as where they have been admitted to an intensive care unit (ICU) or have experienced significant cognitive deterioration.[154] Yet, in clinical trials of COVID-19 treatments and vaccines, it was critical to involve elderly people who did or could potentially require ICU care because they were especially at risk of suffering severe complications or dying from this disease.[155] Indeed, the British Geriatrics Society contended that 'it is unacceptable to use age as an exclusion criterion for clinical studies; such an approach is unethical, particularly in conditions such as COVID-19 infection that older people suffer from disproportionately'.[156]

> COVID-19 illness has three main phases:
> In phase 1, SARS-CoV-2 binds with the angiotensin converting enzyme (ACE)2 receptor on alveolar macrophages and epithelial cells, triggering toll like receptor (TLR) mediated nuclear factor kappa-light-chain-enhancer of activated B cells

---

[154] See Ian Freckelton, 'Clinical Research Without Consent: Challenges for COVID-19 Research' (2020) 28(1) *Journal of Law and Medicine* 90 (hereafter Freckelton, 'Clinical Research Without Consent').

[155] See Jennifer L Watson and others, 'Obstacles and Opportunities in Alzheimer's Clinical Trial Recruitment' (2014) 33(4) *Health Affairs (Millwood)* 574; Ginger E Nicol and others, 'Action at a Distance: Geriatric Research during a Pandemic' (2020) 68(5) *Journal of the American Geriatric Society* 922; British Geriatrics Society, 'COVID-19: BGS Statement on Research for Older People during the COVID-19 Pandemic' (1 April 2020) <www.bgs.org.uk/resources/covid-19-bgs-statement-on-research-for-older-people-during-the-covid-19-pandemic> accessed 4 October 2022.

[156] British Geriatrics Society (n 155).

(NF-ƙB) signaling. It effectively blunts early (IFN) response allowing unchecked viral replication. Phase 2 is characterized by hypoxia and innate immunity mediated pneumocyte damage as well as capillary leak. Some patients further progress to phase 3 characterized by a cytokine storm with worsening respiratory symptoms, persistent fever, and haemodynamic instability.[157]

As knowledge developed about means of treating seriously ill COVID-19 patients effectively, it became apparent that the use of drugs to inhibit the production of cytokines that result in progressive organ damage, and strategies to deal with Acute Respiratory Distress Syndrome (ARDS), had the potential to lower their fatality rates.[158] However, such patients tended to be received into ICU in a condition in which they were incapable of giving consent and/or by reason of age-related conditions had an impaired capacity to provide informed consent.

In a significant decision, the Guardianship Division of the Civil and Administrative Tribunal ('the Tribunal') in the Australian State of New South Wales was called on to consider whether to permit participation in a clinical trial of a new medication—STC3141—developed to treat people with COVID-19 and ARDS, subjects who were unable to consent to doing so.[159] In New South Wales, the *Guardianship Act 1987* (NSW) governs the provision of medical treatment, including in a clinical trial, to those who are incapable of giving consent to receiving it. In *Shehabi v Attorney General (NSW)*,[160] the Appeal Panel of the Tribunal described this legislation as establishing a three-step process for obtaining consent for such individuals to receive medical treatment as part of a clinical trial as follows:

(1) First, the Tribunal must determine whether to approve the trial ... but that approval does not operate, by itself, as consent to the participation in the trial by any particular patient.
(2) Second, if the Tribunal is satisfied in accordance with ... the Act that the clinical trial should be approved, the Tribunal then has to determine whether consent to treatment as part of that trial should be given by the 'person responsible' or by the Tribunal.

---

[157] Sumanth Khadke and others, 'Harnessing the Immune System to Overcome Cytokine Storm and Reduce Viral Load in COVID-19: A Review of the Phases of Illness and Therapeutic Agents' (2020) 17 *Virology Journal* art 154.
[158] See Yufang Shi and others, 'COVID-19 Infection: The Perspectives on Immune Responses' (2020) 27 *Cell Death and Differentiation* 1451.
[159] See *Guardianship Act 1987* (NSW) s 45AA(2); *STC3141—An Open Label, Multi-Centre Study to Determine the Safety and Efficacy of STC3141 Administered as an Infusion for up to 5 Days in Subjects with COVID-19 Respiratory Distress Syndrome Requiring Intensive Care* [2020] NSWCATGD 16 (hereafter *STC3141*).
[160] [2016] NSWCATAP 137.

(3) Third, depending on whether the consent is to be obtained from the person responsible or the Tribunal, consent must then be obtained for the medical treatment in the course of the trial to be carried out on the patient.[161]

The Tribunal followed this process in the *STC3141* case in responding to an application by researchers for approval of a phase 2 clinical trial of the drug, which was intended to involve 160 adult ICU patients with confirmed COVID-19 infection and ARDS.[162] The researchers proposed to test the hypothesis that treatment with STC3141 would improve clinical outcomes for COVID-19 patients in the ICU by enhancing respiratory function in those experiencing respiratory distress as a result of the virus. The applicants maintained that the study needed to involve critically ill patients who would be unable to provide consent to participate in it because they were subject to mechanical ventilation and continuous sedation.

The Tribunal approved the trial, finding that it met the statutory requirements.[163] Specifically, the Tribunal was satisfied that the potential benefits of STC3141 were an alleviation of COVID-19 symptoms by reducing the damage caused by circulating histones (proteins that are critical in the packing of DNA into the cell and into chromatin and chromosomes), which in turn would result in faster recovery times, a reduced number and severity of medical complications from ARDS, and increased survival rates.[164] Importantly, the Tribunal found that the trial would not involve any substantial risk to participants.[165] In addition, it accepted that STC3141 had 'reached a stage at which safety and ethical considerations make it appropriate that STC3141 be made available to patients who suffer from COVID-19 even though those patients will be not able to consent to taking part in the Trial'.[166] The Tribunal found, too, that it was 'in the best interests of patients suffering from COVID-19 and meeting the clinical trial protocol criteria for inclusion [to] be able to take part in the Trial'.[167] Those participants would 'be critically unwell without recourse to disease-specific treatment and subject to a significant risk of death' (there were, at that time, no proven treatments for COVID-19) and could 'receive the best form of available ICU setting care, or, that same care as well as the trial drug, for which there are no know [sic] significant risk of adverse events'.[168] Finally, the Tribunal noted that the relevant ethics committee

---

[161] ibid [67].
[162] *STC3141* (n 159) [15]. See Freckelton, 'Clinical Research Without Consent' (n 154).
[163] *STC3141* (n 159) [48].
[164] ibid [48].
[165] ibid [36]. The Tribunal was informed of important data that confirmed that STC3141 had been well-tolerated by healthy volunteers in short infusions and continuous long-term infusions without deaths or serious adverse events or any need to discontinue them due to adverse events: [16], [33].
[166] ibid [41].
[167] ibid [45].
[168] ibid [45], [34].

had approved the trial.[169] The decision-making in the *SCT3141* case constitutes a useful model pursuant to which testing of proposed innovative treatments can be made subject to checks and balances in a scenario in which trial subjects may be unable to provide informed consent.

4 Research involving incarcerated persons

Issues surrounding participants' consent to involvement in COVID-19 clinical trials also arose in considering whether incarcerated people could or should be enrolled in them. The ethical dilemma of enrolling prisoners in COVID-19 clinical trials was heightened due to the collective memory of medical practitioners having carried out potentially harmful research experiments on human subjects in prisons in the past. These issues were highlighted during the trial of Nazi doctors before the Nuremberg Tribunal for atrocities committed in the name of medical science.[170] The Nuremberg Code articulated requirements of voluntary consent for participation in research, and 'constituted the first international normative framework regulating the standards of research clinical trials'.[171] While the Nuremberg Code has been superseded by other ethical guidance for research, such as the *Declaration of Helsinki*, the requirement for voluntary consent remained.[172]

A number of serious issues had previously arisen in relation to United States practitioners' experimentation on prisoners.[173] For instance, a United States doctor, Richard Strong, had performed a series of experiments after the turn of the twentieth century on inmates of the Bilibid Prison.[174] Dr Joseph Goldberger too had performed experiments on inmates at Rankin Prison in Mississippi in 1915, inducing pellagra in them after a promise of a pardon.[175] Dr Leo Stanley had supervised the use of testicular injections from animals in hundreds of inmates at San Quentin Prison between 1919 and 1922,[176] and Dr Cooper had used

---

[169] ibid [46].
[170] Germany (Territory under Allied Occupation, 1945–1955), *Trials of War Criminals before the Nuremberg Military Tribunals under Control Council Law No 10* (United States Government Printing Office, 1949).
[171] Udo Schüklenk and Richard E Ashcroft, 'International Research Ethics' (2000) 14(2) *Bioethics* 158, 159. See also Annas and Grodin (n 132).
[172] Schüklenk and Ashcroft (n 171) 159; Annas (n 141).
[173] See Keramet Reiter, 'Experimentation on Prisoners: Persistent Dilemmas in Rights and Regulations' (2009) 97(2) *California Law Review* 501.
[174] See Eli Chernin, 'Richard Pearson Strong and the Iatrogenic Plague Disaster in Bilibid Prison, Manila, 1906' (1989) 11(6) *Reviews of Infectious Diseases* 996; See also David Salinas-Flores, 'One Hundred Years after the Expedition by Harvard University to Peru to Investigate Carrion's Disease' (2016) 64(3) *Revista de la Facultad de Medicina* 517.
[175] See Alan Kraut, 'Dr Joseph Goldberger and the War on Pellagra' (National Institutes of Health: Office of National Institutes of Health History and Stetten Museum) <https://history.nih.gov/pages/viewpage.action?pageId=8883184> accessed 6 March 2022.
[176] See Ethan Blue, 'The Strange Career of Leo Stanley: Remaking Manhood and Medicine at San Quentin State Penitentiary, 1913–1951' (2009) 78(2) *Pacific Historical Review* 210; Katie Dowd, 'The San Quentin Prison Doctor Who Performed over 10,000 Human Experiments' *SFGATE* (13 August 2019) <https://www.sfgate.com/sfhistory/article/leo-stanley-gland-rejuvenation-surgery-14298920.php> accessed 4 October 2022.

'volunteers' from the Colorado Penitentiary for attempts to develop a tuberculosis vaccine.[177] More than 400 prisoners were persuaded to participate in malaria studies at Stateville Penitentiary in Illinois.[178] Such practices continued until the 1960s with 75 prisoners at Holmesburg Prison in Pennsylvania being exposed to high doses of dioxin, the main toxic ingredient in Agent Orange,[179] in spite of the Nuremberg Code.

In 1976, the National Commission for the Protection of Human Subjects of Biomedical and Behavioral Research in the United States intervened robustly in relation to experimentation on prisoners. It released a report condemning the use of prisoners in human subjects research,[180] which in turn led to regulations in 1998 that substantially prohibited the practice.[181] However, by 2006, the Institutes of Medicine (now the National Academy of Medicine) revisited the issue and recommended changes so that prisoners could participate in limited clinical trials, particularly those with minimal risks and interventions and whose safety and efficacy had been established, including phase 3 clinical trials.[182]

United States prisons in particular were potentially a fruitful source of research subjects with COVID-19.[183] The risk of inmates contracting COVID-19 was particularly high due to the close confines of their environment and, in some instances, their poor health and the quality of the healthcare available to them.[184] Yet their capacity to provide authentically voluntary consent to participate in clinical trials had the potential to be compromised if they felt compelled to enrol in trials by the prison authorities or due to the high risk of contracting COVID-19 in prison.[185]

Prisoners' possible participation in or exclusion from COVID-19 clinical trials raised other dilemmas. If they participated in trials and, consequently, experienced

---

[177] See Michael J Selgelid and Lee B Reichman, 'Ethical Issues in Tuberculosis Diagnosis and Treatment' (2011) 15(Supp 2) *International Journal of Tuberculosis and Lung Disease* 9; Allen M Hornblum, 'They Were Cheap and Available: Prisoners as Research Subjects in Twentieth Century America' (1997) 315(7120) *British Medical Journal* 1437.

[178] See Franklin G Miller, 'The Stateville Penitentiary Malaria Experiments: A Case Study in Retrospective Ethical Assessment' (2013) 56(4) *Perspectives in Biological Medicine* 548; Katelyn Kalata, 'The Exploitation of Inmates: Stateville Penitentiary Malaria Experiment' (2020) XI (Spring) *Western Illinois Historical Review* 2153.

[179] See Allen M Hornblum, *Acres of Skin: Human Experiments at Holmesburg Prison* (Routledge 1999).

[180] National Commission for the Protection of Human Subjects of Biomedical and Behavioral Research (n 145).

[181] 45 Code of Federal Regulations (CFR) § 46.306(a)(2)(i)–(iv) (2007), describing the four categories of research in which prisoners might permissibly be included: (i) research about the effects of incarceration, (ii) research about prisons as institutions, (iii) research about conditions particularly affecting prisoners, and (iv) research about practices expected to improve the health of individual subjects.

[182] See Lawrence O Gostin, Cori Vanchieri, and Andrew Pope (eds), *Ethical Considerations for Research Involving Prisoners* (National Academies Press 2007).

[183] Camila Strassle and others, 'Covid-19 Vaccine Trials and Incarcerated People—The Ethics of Inclusion' (2020) 383(20) *New England Journal of Medicine* 1897. See also Brendan Saloner and others, 'COVID-19 Cases and Deaths in Federal and State Prisons' (2020) 324(6) *Journal of the American Medical Association* 602.

[184] Strassle and others (n 183) 1897; Lynch and others, 'Regulatory Flexibility' (n 129).

[185] Strassle and others (n 183) 1898.

COVID-19 symptoms, they may have neglected to report them for fear of being placed in isolation or other unpleasant conditions in prison.[186] Further, they might have been more likely to suffer adverse effects from the medications being tested than non-incarcerated people if they did not receive suitable clinical assistance for those symptoms.[187] Enrolment of prisoners in clinical trials might also have been exploitative of this population, unless prisoners were guaranteed first access to treatments or vaccines that were proven to be safe and effective.[188] Yet it was feasible that scientists might not have included any prisoners in clinical trials and thereby potentially prevented them from benefiting from new treatments and vaccines.[189] Emily Wang, Jonathan Zenilman, and Lauren Brinkley-Rubinstein argued in 2020 that a panel of experts should be convened to discuss the possible inclusion of incarcerated people in phase 3 COVID-19 vaccine trials and consider the following recommendations:

1. Obtain input from currently and formerly incarcerated individuals and those who work in corrections: The IOM report suggested the need for 'collaborative responsibility', whereby incarcerated people and correctional staff are involved in the design of research proposals and setting a research agenda. Vaccine trials should be person-centered and acknowledge the unique logistics of conducting research in correctional facilities without impeding good science or violating research ethics. In the longer-term, incarcerated people should also be part of revising regulations of clinical research in correctional facilities.
2. Make racial equity a guiding lens: COVID-19 and incarceration disproportionately affect Black communities. One in 3 Black men will interface with the US prison system in their lifetime (this does not account for time in jail), making vaccine trial data from prisons and jails likely generalizable to the general population of Black men. Recruitment for vaccine trials in prisons and jails may improve participation of racial and ethnic minorities, thereby improving external validity of COVID-19 vaccine trials, which, as of yet, have disproportionately recruited White participants. Clinical trials conducted in the community should obtain permission to follow trial participants into correctional settings, as necessary, to help minimize loss to follow-up among minority participants.
3. Learn from history: The urgency of the current pandemic and of past and future respiratory pandemics may lead to the desire for quick, easier

---

[186] ibid.
[187] ibid.
[188] ibid; Emily A Wang, Jonathan Zenilman, and Lauren Brinkley-Rubinstein, 'Ethical Considerations for COVID-19 Vaccine Trials in Correctional Facilities' (2020) 324(11) *Journal of the American Medical Association* 1031.
[189] Lynch and others, 'Regulatory Flexibility' (n 129).

solutions. The present sense of urgency to find a vaccine makes it difficult to take time to support inclusive decision-making and consider long-term consequences. The need for quick results may minimize the interests of vulnerable populations.

4. Ensure receipt of efficacious vaccines and care after the trial concludes: Many correctional settings are not well equipped to deal with screening for and treating COVID-19, much less aftercare following vaccine trials. Inclusion of incarcerated individuals in clinical trials must also include resources for correctional health systems to attend to vaccine complications and, once the trials conclude, universal access to these vaccines. Funding for aftercare, like any community setting, should be guaranteed by the study sponsor and universal access to vaccines proven to be effective and safe should be guaranteed by federal legislation, as there currently is no mandate to provide vaccines to those who are incarcerated.

5. Convene a federal oversight board: Aside from the specific IRB processes outlined in the current regulations, a federal oversight board should be convened that monitors all COVID-19 vaccine trials conducted in correctional settings, regardless of whether the trials are funded by the federal government.

6. Study implementation of vaccines in correctional systems: Implementing clinical trials in correctional facilities, especially in prisons where sentence lengths are typically longer than a year, could help to enable high levels of adherence and follow-up, including antibody testing. However, once efficacious and safe COVID-19 vaccines are developed, additional research will be needed to determine how best to administer and improve uptake of vaccines in correctional systems. In jails where the risk for COVID-19 is still high but the population throughput is much higher, effective strategies for follow-up within the facility and after release must be identified.[190]

B. Diversity of Participants in COVID-19 Clinical Trials

In recent years, there has been increased recognition of the importance of quantitative and qualitative clinical research reflecting the diversity of the population, which can be achieved through enrolling a varied range of participants.[191] Ethical guidelines for research have encouraged scientists to enrol in their clinical trials

---

[190] Wang, Zenilman, and Brinkley-Rubinstein (n 188) 1032.
[191] See eg Peter Allmark, 'Should Research Samples Reflect the Diversity of the Population?' (2004) 30(2) *Journal of Medical Ethics* 185; Vivian Pinn, 'Achieving Diversity and its Benefits in Clinical Research' (2004) 6(12) *American Medical Association Journal of Ethics* 561; David H Strauss, Sarah A White, and Barbara B Bierer, 'Justice, Diversity and Research Ethics Review' (2021) 371(6535) *Science* 1209; Editorial, 'Striving for Diversity in Research Studies' (2021) 385(15) *New England Journal of Medicine* 1429; Janet Woodcock and others, 'Integrating Research into Community Practice—Toward Increased Diversity in Clinical Trials' (2021) 385 *New England Journal of Medicine* 1351.

people from diverse backgrounds to ensure that the research and its outcomes are equitable: the benefits that it produces, but also the 'burdens of participation in research' would be shared equally among a cross-section of society.[192] Moreover, scientists could confirm the effectiveness of treatments and vaccines for different social groups and, in particular, people who were most at risk of contracting the disease.[193] Although older persons have a higher risk of severe disease and mortality from COVID-19, there is a risk that they will be under-represented in clinical trials.[194]

There have also been calls to ensure that pregnant and breastfeeding women are included in research for COVID-19 vaccines and treatments,[195] in part because of the escalated rate of hospitalization and death among women with COVID-19 who are pregnant, as against those who are not.[196] For instance, it was important to include pregnant women in COVID-19 clinical trials because some data indicated that women who contracted the virus while pregnant may have been more likely to experience spontaneous abortions[197] or to give birth prematurely.[198] Historically, women and especially those who are pregnant, have been underrepresented in clinical research,[199] though regulatory authorities in some countries, such as the United States, have introduced rules seeking to redress this imbalance.[200]

---

[192] Council for International Organizations of Medical Sciences and World Health Organization (n 153) 8.

[193] Jared S Hopkins, 'COVID-19 Vaccine Trials Have a Problem: Minority Groups Don't Trust Them' *The Wall Street Journal* (5 August 2020) <www.wsj.com/articles/covid-19-vaccine-trials-have-a-problem-minority-groups-dont-trust-them-11596619802> accessed 4 October 2022; Allison M Whelan, 'Unequal Representation: Race, Sex, and Trust in Medicine—COVID-19 and Beyond' *Harvard Law School Petrie-Flom Center* (30 November 2020) <https://blog.petrieflom.law.harvard.edu/2020/11/30/covid-race-gender-clinical-trials-disparities/> accessed 4 October 2022.

[194] Virginie Prendki and others, 'A Systematic Review Assessing the Under-Representation of Elderly Adults in COVID-19 Trials' (2020) 20 *BMC Geriatrics* art 538.

[195] Melanie M Taylor and others, 'Inclusion of Pregnant Women in COVID-19 Treatment Trials: A Review and Global Call to Action' (2021) 9(3) *Lancet Global Health* E366; Devin D Smith and others, 'Exclusion of Pregnant Women from Clinical Trials During the Coronavirus Disease 2019 Pandemic: A Review of International Registries' (2020) 37(8) *American Journal of Perinatology* 792.

[196] See eg Rita Rubin, 'Pregnant People's Paradox—Excluded from Vaccine Trials Despite Having a Higher Risk of COVID-19 Complications' (2021) 325(11) *Journal of the American Medical Association* 1027. See also Erica M Lokken and others, 'Disease Severity, Pregnancy Outcomes, and Maternal Deaths among Pregnant Patients with Severe Acute Respiratory Syndrome Coronavirus 2 Infection in Washington State' (2021) 225(1) *American Journal of Obstetrics & Gynecology* 77.

[197] See Rahul K Gajbhiye and others, 'Increased Rate of Miscarriage during Second Wave of COVID-19 Pandemic in India' (2021) 58(6) *Ultrasound in Obstetrics and Gynaecology* 946.

[198] Emily H Adhikari and Catherine Y Spong, 'COVID-19 Vaccination in Pregnant and Lactating Women' (2021) 325(11) *Journal of the American Medical Association* 1039; Diana W Bianchi, Lisa Kaeser, and Alison N Cernich, 'Involving Pregnant Individuals in Clinical Research on COVID-19 Vaccines' (2021) 325(11) *Journal of the American Medical Association* 1041; Whelan (n 193).

[199] For discussion see Belinda Bennett and others, 'Gender Inequities in Health Research: An Australian Perspective' in Michael Freeman (ed), *Law and Bioethics: Current Legal Issues Volume 11* (Oxford University Press 2008); Belinda Bennett and Isabel Karpin, 'Regulatory Options for Gender Equity in Health Research' (2008) 1(2) *International Journal of Feminist Approaches to Bioethics* 80; Françoise Baylis and Angela Ballantyne (eds), *Clinical Research Involving Pregnant Women* (Springer 2016).

[200] Bennett and Karpin (n 199); Whelan (n 193).

Across the world, a disproportionate percentage of people from racial and ethnic minorities contracted and died from COVID-19,[201] so it was crucial that they were represented among participants in clinical trials.[202] This disparity was attributable to their comorbid health conditions, inadequate healthcare, and socio-economic factors (such as that they were less likely to be employed in roles that could be continued from home and more likely to need to take public transport to workplaces and live in high density accommodation, which made physical distancing difficult).[203] Yet concerns were raised that racial and ethnic diversity in COVID-19 research was deemed a priority due to racist attributions of biological and genetic differences between people based on the colour of their skin.[204]

It nonetheless proved difficult to encourage people from minorities to participate in COVID-19 clinical trials.[205] This has been attributed to previous exploitation of people of colour generally in unethical medical experiments from which they did not gain any benefit (the treatments and vaccines produced from such research were prioritized for wealthy, white people), and their consequent distrust of governments and healthcare institutions.[206] Furthermore, there is a need to ensure that information for research participants is available in their first languages, and that culturally sensitive recruitment methods are used.[207] Efforts have been made, in the United States, for instance, by researchers, doctors, advocacy groups, and community leaders, to counter misinformation that was circulating about COVID-19 clinical trials and convey the importance of people of colour enrolling in the trials to guarantee the effectiveness and safety of treatments and vaccines for them.[208]

The risk of 'medical neocolonialism' also needed to be addressed in seeking to recruit people from developing countries to participate in COVID-19 clinical trials.[209] It has been recognized as important to involve Africans in particular in

---

[201] See eg Krishnan Bhaskaran and others, 'Factors Associated with Deaths due to COVID-19 Versus Other Causes: Population-based Cohort Analysis of UK Primary Care Data and Linked National Death Registrations within the OpenSAFELY Platform' (2021) 6 *Lancet Regional Health—Europe* art 100109.

[202] Editorial (n 191); Woodcock and others (n 191); Shaun Treweek and others, 'COVID-19 and Ethnicity: Who Will Research Results Apply to?' (2020) 395(10242) *Lancet* 1955; Mary Chris Jaklevic, 'Researchers Strive to Recruit Hard-Hit Minorities Into COVID-19 Vaccine Trials' (2020) 324(9) *Journal of the American Medical Association* 826, 826; Bisola O Ojikutu and others, 'Building Trust in COVID-19 Vaccines and Beyond Through Authentic Community Investment' (2021) 111(3) *American Journal of Public Health* 366, 366; Whelan (n 193); Hopkins (n 193).

[203] Jaklevic (n 202) 826–27; Hopkins (n 193).

[204] Colleen Campbell 'Racial Inclusivity in COVID-19 Vaccine Trials' *Harvard Law School Petrie-Flom Center* (22 September 2020) <https://blog.petrieflom.law.harvard.edu/2020/09/22/racial-inclusivity-covid19-vaccine-trials/> accessed 4 February 2021.

[205] Hopkins (n 193); Whelan (n 193); Matiangai Sirleaf, 'Expendable Lives and COVID-19' *Harvard Law School Petrie-Flom Center* (8 October 2020) <https://blog.petrieflom.law.harvard.edu/2020/10/08/expendable-lives-and-covid-19/> accessed 4 October 2022.

[206] Ojikutu and others (n 202) 366; Natasha Crooks, Geri Donenberg, and Alicia Matthews, 'Ethics of Research at the Intersection of COVID-19 and Black Lives Matter: A Call to Action' (2021) 47(4) *Journal of Medical Ethics* 205; Treweek and others (n 202); Hopkins (n 193); Sirleaf (n 205).

[207] Treweek and others (n 202) 1956.

[208] Hopkins (n 193).

[209] Sirleaf (n 205).

clinical trials given the high rate of HIV and AIDS, and COVID-19 on their continent: this research could confirm the effectiveness of COVID-19 treatments and vaccines for people suffering from both diseases.[210] A collaboration between Oxford and Witwatersrand universities, the South African Medical Research Council, and the Bill and Melinda Gates Foundation therefore sought to test a COVID-19 vaccine (ChAdOx1) on 2,000 South Africans.[211] Protesters feared that the trials were designed to exploit African people as 'guinea pigs'.[212] Adherence to legal and regulatory measures (such as obtaining approval from the South African Health Products Regulatory Authority) and ethical guidelines (such as those produced by human research ethics committees) was essential for securing community trust in the research.[213]

It was also important to test COVID-19 vaccines on children to ensure that they were safe and effective for this age group.[214] As the United States Food and Drug Administration observed:

> It's important that the public recognize that, because young children are still growing and developing, it's critical that thorough and robust clinical trials of adequate size are completed to evaluate the safety and the immune response to a COVID-19 vaccine in this population. Children are not small adults—and issues that may be addressed in pediatric vaccine trials can include whether there is a need for different doses or different strength formulations of vaccines already used for adults.[215]

In the initial phase of the pandemic, older people faced the most significant risks of contracting and suffering serious illness and/or dying from COVID-19, but the emergence of the Delta variant raised the spectre of substantial numbers of children becoming very unwell, too, including with multi-inflammatory syndrome in children.[216] In addition, the emergence of information about the incidence and symptoms of 'long COVID' escalated the need to protect children from contracting

---

[210] Jeffrey Mphahlele, 'COVID-19 Vaccine: The Challenges of Running a Trial in the Middle of a Pandemic' *The Conversation* (7 July 2020) <https://theconversation.com/covid-19-vaccine-the-challenges-of-running-a-trial-in-the-middle-of-a-pandemic-141728> accessed 4 October 2022.
[211] ibid.
[212] Sirleaf (n 205).
[213] ibid.
[214] Kevin Mintz and others, 'Enrolling Minors in COVID-19 Trials' (2021) 147(3) *Pediatrics* art e2020040717, 1; Xiaohui Zou and Bin Cao, 'COVID-19 Vaccines for Children Younger than 12 Years: Are We Ready?' (2021) 21(12) *Lancet Infectious Diseases* 1614.
[215] Janet Woodcock and Peter Marks, 'FDA Will Follow the Science on COVID-19 Vaccines for Young Children' United States Food and Drug Administration (10 September 2021) <https://www.fda.gov/news-events/press-announcements/fda-will-follow-science-covid-19-vaccines-young-children> accessed 11 September 2022.
[216] See Leora R Feldstein and others, 'Multisystem Inflammatory Syndrome in US Children and Adolescents' (2020) 383 *New England Journal of Medicine* 334.

the virus.[217] This provided a new impetus for assessing whether vaccines could safely be administered to children, in spite of the desire not to involve children prematurely in experimental research trials. As pressures built for immunization of children under 12 years of age against COVID-19, some scholars argued that the a priori exclusion of children from COVID-19 vaccination was unjust and that there should be a graduated inclusion of children in vaccinations against COVID-19 with rigorous monitoring.[218] This issue was particularly sensitive due to past controversies about vaccinating children that followed the dissemination of false information indicating that the MMR vaccine could cause autism.[219]

As Kevin Mintz and others noted, COVID-19 researchers faced the dilemma that 'enrolling minors too soon [for instance, before there was evidence of the safety and efficacy of the vaccines in adults] runs the risk of exposing them to excessive research risks', but 'waiting too long could unjustly deny minors and their families the benefits of a vaccine and has the potential to delay an effective response to the pandemic by a year or longer'.[220] In addition, a potentially significant obstacle to minors' participation in clinical trials is that many of them are unable to provide informed consent to this participation.[221] To reduce the risk that minors are not 'exposed to excessive research risk', the parents or guardians of minors are often required to provide consent on their behalf to their enrolment in clinical trials.[222] Nevertheless, in the case of COVID-19 vaccine trials, it appears that many parents were reluctant to consent to their children's participation in them. In one study that involved 2,768 participants, only 18.4% of parents stated they would enrol their child in a clinical trial for a COVID-19 vaccine and 14.4% indicated that they would agree to their children's participation in a randomized placebo-controlled study.[223] Factors associated with willingness to participate were parents agreeing to enrol in a COVID-19 vaccine trial themselves, having an older child,

---

[217] See Heidi Ledford, 'Should Children Get COVID Vaccines? What the Science Says' (2021) 595(7869) *Nature* 638; Phoebe Roth, 'Should We Vaccinate Children Against COVID-19? We Asked 5 Experts' *The Conversation* (2 August 2021) <https://theconversation.com/should-we-vaccinate-children-against-covid-19-we-asked-5-experts-165316> accessed 4 October 2022; Helen Thomson, 'Children are Getting Long Covid and Being Left with Lasting Problems' *New Scientist* (24 February 2021) <www.newscientist.com/article/mg24933233-600-children-are-getting-long-covid-and-being-left-with-lasting-problems/> accessed 11 September 2022.

[218] See eg Margherita Brusa and Yechiel M Barilkan, 'Voluntary COVID-19 Vaccination of Children: A Social Responsibility' (2021) 47(8) *Journal of Medical Ethics* 543. See too the analysis in Dan M Cooper and others, 'SARS CoV-2 Vaccine Testing and Trials in the Pediatric Population: Biologic, Ethical, Research and Implementation Challenges' (2021) 90 *Pediatric Research* 966.

[219] See Fiona Godlee, Jane Smith, and Harvey Marcovitch, 'Wakefield's Article Linking MMR Vaccine and Autism was Fraudulent' (2011) 342 *British Medical Journal* c7452; Ian Freckelton, *Scholarly Misconduct: Law, Regulation and Practice* (OUP 2016) (hereafter Freckelton, *Scholarly Misconduct*).

[220] Mintz and others (n 214) 1–2.

[221] ibid 1.

[222] ibid 2.

[223] Ran D Goldman and others, 'Factors Associated with Parents' Willingness to Enroll their Children in Trials for COVID-19 Vaccination' (2021) 17(6) *Human Vaccines and Immunotherapeutics* 1607.

having children who received all vaccinations based on their country's vaccination schedule, and parents with high school education or lower.[224]

Finally, as discussed earlier, it is important to include a diverse range of participants in COVID-19 research. However, it is also important to ensure that research results provide disaggregated data so that the efficacy of treatments and vaccines for particular groups can be scrutinized and evaluated.[225]

IV. Publication of Results of COVID-19 Research

In the race to develop COVID-19 treatments and vaccines, a large number of research projects were registered on 'ClinicalTrials.gov', a database of clinical studies from across the world that are privately and publicly funded.[226] Concerns were raised that some of those studies commenced prematurely, before usual steps that assess such projects' viability had been taken, and that they proposed to deploy research methods that 'are easy to implement but unlikely to yield unbiased effect estimates'.[227] Similarly worrying was that researchers could be tempted to compromise orthodox research standards, and curtail peer review and other rigorous processes that are traditionally used to verify research results.[228] The bulwarks against such conduct became the quality of reviewing by journals, individual scientists' repetition of studies and/or analyses of them, and alerts that they published on blogs.

Scholars and scientists debated whether 'research exceptionalism'—the notion that, in light of extraordinary threats to public health, it is legitimate for researchers to take shortcuts—was warranted by reason of the pandemic.[229] Yet, in mid-2020, the precipitate publication of research results about the efficacy of hydroxychloroquine as a treatment, which were subsequently proven to be fraudulent, dramatically brought the appropriateness of this approach into doubt.[230] The issue came into further focus during 2020 and 2021 in relation to publications about the effectiveness of ivermectin as a treatment for COVID-19.

Some argued that fastidious adherence to orthodox research standards during this pandemic (including using substantial sample sizes, randomization, and placebo comparators) constituted an unaffordable indulgence given the clinical

---

[224] ibid.
[225] Lavanya Vijayasingham, Evelyne Bischof, and Jeannette Wolfe, 'Sex-disaggregated Data in COVID-19 Vaccine Trials' (2021) 397(10278) *Lancet* 966. See Chapter 3 for further discussion of the importance of disaggregated data.
[226] US National Library of Medicine, 'ClinicalTrials.gov' <https://clinicaltrials.gov/> accessed 4 October 2022.
[227] London and Kimmelman (n 130) 476.
[228] ibid.
[229] See Jan Solbakk and others, 'Back to WHAT? The Role of Research Ethics in Pandemic Times' (2021) 24 *Medicine, Health Care and Philosophy* 3; London and Kimmelman (n 130) 476.
[230] See Section IV(A) below.

exigencies to deal with the overwhelming tide of medical emergencies.[231] Even WHO argued that it needed 'to balance scientific rigor against speed' in justifying the decision not to design the Solidarity Trial as a double-blind study (where some participants are given the trial product while others receive a placebo, and the participants and researchers do not initially know who is receiving each).[232]

By contrast, Alex London and Jonathan Kimmelman maintained that, especially during a pandemic, it is critical that research generates information on which 'caregivers, health systems, and policy-makers' can confidently depend in order to make crucial 'decisions that implicate health, welfare, and the use of scarce resources'.[233] They articulated 'five conditions of informativeness and social value' that 'research should embody' so that these stakeholders can 'efficiently discharge' their 'moral' and 'social responsibilities'.[234] First, research should be important in the sense that it addresses key evidence gaps, with interventions selected for testing that capture the most promising therapeutic and prophylactic options as judged from reviews of evidence and trials that have already been conducted.[235] Second, research should be designed rigorously to detect clinically meaningful effects so that both positive and negative results serve the informational needs of clinicians and health systems, neither eschewing randomization nor using surrogate end points.[236] Third, research should be characterized by analytical integrity, with 'designs' 'prespecified in protocols' that are 'prospectively registered and analyzed in accordance with prespecification'.[237] Fourth, 'research should be reported comprehensively, promptly, and consistently with prespecified analyses'.[238] Finally, research must also be feasible in the sense that studies should have 'a credible prospect of reaching their recruitment target and being completed within a time frame where the evidence is still actionable'.[239]

London and Kimmelman also made the useful points that:

> One reporting challenge present in the best of times, and likely to re-emerge during pandemics, is the deposition of positive findings in preprint servers earlier than nonpositive studies. Another challenge is quality control. Qualified peer reviewers are a scarce resource, and the proliferation of low-quality papers saps the ability of scientists to place findings into context before they are publicized.[240]

---

[231] London and Kimmelman (n 130) 476.
[232] Kai Kupferschmidt and Jon Cohen, 'WHO Launches Global Megatrial of the Four Most Promising Coronavirus Treatments' *ScienceInsider* (22 March 2020) <www.sciencemag.org/news/2020/03/who-launches-global-megatrial-four-most-promising-coronavirus-treatments> accessed 4 February 2021.
[233] London and Kimmelman (n 130) 476.
[234] ibid.
[235] ibid.
[236] ibid.
[237] ibid 477.
[238] ibid.
[239] ibid.
[240] ibid.

It has previously been recognized as crucial that the best available research evidence and data that can help combat a public health emergency are made widely available.[241] Recognizing this imperative, in January 2020, Wellcome, an independent charitable foundation that addresses health challenges, issued a statement '[calling] on researchers, journals and funders to ensure that research findings and data relevant to this outbreak are shared rapidly and openly to inform the public health response and help save lives'.[242] Signatories to this statement, including research institutions and journals, expressed their commitment:

to work together to help ensure:
- all peer-reviewed research publications relevant to the outbreak are made immediately open access, or freely available at least for the duration of the outbreak
- research findings relevant to the outbreak are shared immediately with the WHO upon journal submission, by the journal and with author knowledge
- research findings are made available via preprint servers before journal publication, or via platforms that make papers openly accessible before peer review, with clear statements regarding the availability of underlying data
- researchers share interim and final research data relating to the outbreak, together with protocols and standards used to collect the data, as rapidly and widely as possible—including with public health and research communities and the WHO
- authors are clear that data or preprints shared ahead of submission will not preempt its publication in these journals.[243]

The risks of disseminating results of research into COVID-19 treatments before the quality and accuracy of those studies had been rigorously evaluated was brought into sharp relief by the publication of purported research into repurposing existing drugs to treat this virus. Perhaps because the safety of these drugs for other purposes, namely, as anti-malarial and anti-parasitic treatments, had been established, assessments of data regarding the efficacy and safety of their redeployment to treat COVID-19 were limited, with potentially dangerous consequences.

---

[241] Wellcome, 'Statement on Data Sharing in Public Health Emergencies' (Press Release, 1 February 2016) <https://wellcome.org/press-release/statement-data-sharing-public-health-emergencies> accessed 4 October 2022.
[242] Wellcome, 'Sharing Research Data and Findings Relevant to the Novel Coronavirus (COVID-19) Outbreak' (Press Release, 31 January 2020) <https://wellcome.org/coronavirus-covid-19/open-data> accessed 4 October 2022.
[243] ibid.

A. The Hydroxychloroquine Saga

A cautionary example of the importance of adhering to rigorous scholarly protocols in publishing the results of clinical research, even during a public health emergency, was the publication of two controversial articles in *The Lancet*[244] and *The New England Journal of Medicine*[245] respectively regarding the repurposing of an existing drug—hydroxychloroquine—to treat COVID-19.[246]

In *The Lancet* article, its authors, Professor Mandeep Mehra and others, claimed that research had found that use of hydroxychloroquine or chloroquine (previously approved for treating conditions including malaria and arthritis),[247] 'or their combination with a macrolide', to treat COVID-19 patients 'was associated with an increased hazard for de-novo ventricular arrhythmia and death in hospital'.[248] They concluded that their 'findings suggest that these drug regimens should not be used outside of clinical trials and urgent confirmation from randomised clinical trials is needed'.[249] The authors maintained that their results derived from a multinational registry of the use of hydroxychloroquine or chloroquine with or without a macrolide for treatment of COVID-19.[250] They claimed to have analysed de-identified data obtained from a cloud-based healthcare analytics platform hosted by the Surgical Outcomes Collaborative (Surgisphere).[251] The number of patients was asserted to be substantial: 96,032 hospitalized patients who had tested positive to COVID-19 and been admitted to no fewer than 671 hospitals on six continents between 20 December 2019 and 14 April 2020.[252] It was asserted, though, that the funder of the study, which was associated with Surgisphere, had played no role in the study design, data collection, data analysis, data interpretation, or writing of the report.[253]

---

[244] Mandeep R Mehra and others, 'RETRACTED: Hydroxychloroquine or Chloroquine with or without a Macrolide for Treatment of COVID-19: A Multinational Registry Analysis' *Lancet* (22 May 2020) <https://doi.org/10.1016/S0140-6736(20)31180-6> accessed 4 October 2022 (hereafter Mehra and others, 'Hydroxychloroquine').

[245] Mandeep R Mehra and others, 'Cardiovascular Disease, Drug Therapy, and Mortality in Covid-19' (2020) 382 *New England Journal of Medicine* e102(1) (retracted) <https://www.nejm.org/doi/full/10.1056/NEJMoa2007621> accessed 4 October 2022 (hereafter Mehra and others, 'Cardiovascular Disease').

[246] See Ian Freckelton, 'Perils of Precipitate Publication: Fraudulent and Substandard COVID-19 Research' (2020) 27(4) *Journal of Law and Medicine* 779 (hereafter Freckelton, 'Perils of Precipitate Publication').

[247] For a summary of the use of chloroquine and hydroxychloroquine in treating COVID-19, see Elengovan Manivannen, 'The Rise and Fall of Chloroquine/Hydroxychloroquine as Compassionate Therapy of COVID-19' (2021) 12 *Frontiers in Pharmacology* art 584940.

[248] Mehra and others, 'Hydroxychloroquine' (n 244).
[249] ibid.
[250] ibid.
[251] ibid.
[252] ibid.
[253] ibid.

Prior to the publication of these articles, United States President Donald Trump had endorsed hydroxychloroquine in press conferences and social media as a possible cure for COVID-19,[254] and a statement from the Chinese government had recommended it be included in the next version of the Guidelines for the Prevention, Diagnosis, and Treatment of Pneumonia Caused by COVID-19 issued by the National Health Commission of the People's Republic of China.[255] Further, the United States Food and Drug Administration had granted an 'Emergency Use Authorization' permitting use of hydroxychloroquine and chloroquine to treat hospitalized patients who could not participate in clinical trials.[256] For a time, this led to stockpiling of the drugs with consequential shortages of them for treating auto-immune diseases such as lupus and rheumatoid arthritis.[257]

The articles had a substantial and immediate impact. WHO announced the cessation of the hydroxychloroquine arm of the Solidarity Trial.[258] The governments of a number of countries moved to halt the use of hydroxychloroquine to treat COVID-19 patients.[259] In addition, the United Kingdom's Medicines and Healthcare products Regulatory Agency (MHRA) required clinical trials that were using hydroxychloroquine in the United Kingdom to treat or prevent COVID-19 'to suspend recruitment of further participants'.[260]

Nevertheless, doubts quickly emerged about the integrity, validity, and veracity of the dataset that had been relied upon, as well as the statistical analysis undertaken and conclusions reached.[261] On 28 May 2020, *The Lancet* published an open letter about the article that had been written by 182 scientists from 24 countries, in which they identified flaws that suggested the data had been fabricated or riddled with errors.[262] Both articles were retracted soon

---

[254] Zettler, Berman, and Parasidis (n 35) 166; Jennifer Martin and others, 'COVID-19: The Rise and Fall of Hydroxychloroquine' *Insight* (7 September 2020) <https://insightplus.mja.com.au/2020/35/covid-19-the-rise-and-fall-of-hydroxychloroquine/> accessed 11 September 2022.

[255] See Jianjun Gao, Zhenxue Tian, and Xu Yang, 'Breakthrough: Chloroquine Phosphate Has Shown Apparent Efficacy in Treatment of COVID-19 Associated Pneumonia in Clinical Studies' (2020) 14(1) *Bioscience Trends* 72.

[256] Martin and others (n 254).

[257] See Christine A Peschken, 'Possible Consequences of a Shortage of Hydroxychloroquine for Patients with Systemic Lupus Erythematosus Amid the COVID-19 Pandemic' (2020) 47(6) *Journal of Rheumatology* 787.

[258] Lipworth and others (n 40) 556.

[259] Catherine Offord, 'The Surgisphere Scandal: What Went Wrong?' *The Scientist* (1 October 2020) <www.the-scientist.com/features/the-surgisphere-scandal-what-went-wrong--67955> accessed 4 October 2022.

[260] Medicines and Healthcare products Regulatory Agency, 'MHRA Suspends Recruitment to COVID-19 Hydroxychloroquine Trials' (Press Release, 16 June 2020) <www.gov.uk/government/news/mhra-suspends-recruitment-to-covid-19-hydroxychloroquine-trials> accessed 4 October 2022.

[261] Lipworth and others (n 40) 556; Offord (n 259).

[262] James Watson on behalf of 182 signatories, 'An Open Letter to Mehra et al and The Lancet' *Zenodo* (28 May 2020) <https://zenodo.org/record/3865253#.Xu2gmS97HGB> accessed 4 October 2022; *Lancet* Editors, 'Expression of Concern: Hydroxychloroquine or Chloroquine with or without a Macrolide for Treatment of COVID-19: A Multinational Registry Analysis' (2020) 395(10240) *Lancet* art E102.

afterwards.[263]

The scandal was deemed an 'unwanted diversion' during the pandemic,[264] but this description did not capture the seriousness of the scholarly misconduct and its potential consequences.[265] Major deficiencies were exposed in the reviewing processes undertaken by both journals and thereby in the scholarly fabric.[266] During 2020, pre-print servers were deluged with postings of articles that concerned COVID-19 studies that had not yet been peer-reviewed, and scholarly journals were placed under intense strain.[267] James Heathers observed in *The Guardian*:

> Peer-review during a pandemic faces a brutal dilemma—the moral importance of releasing important information with planetary consequences quickly, versus the scientific importance of evaluating the presented work fully—while trying to recruit scientists, already busier than usual due to their disrupted lives, to review work for free. And, after this process is complete, publications face immediate scrutiny by a much larger group of engaged scientific readers than usual, who treat publications which affect the health of every living human being with the scrutiny they deserve.[268]

Dr Marcia Angell, a former Editor-in-Chief of *The New England Journal of Medicine*, similarly opined, 'there is always a tension between getting it fast and getting it right … in the current pandemic, that balance may have shifted too far toward getting it fast'.[269] Late in 2020, the Editors of the *Lancet* Group announced in 'Learning from a Retraction' that a review of the peer-review processes had resulted in changes to the declarations sought from authors, the data-sharing statements required for research papers, and the peer-review process for similar papers based on large datasets or real-world data.[270]

---

[263] Mehra and others, 'Hydroxychloroquine' (n 244); Mehra and others, 'Cardiovascular Disease' (n 245).

[264] See Issam Ahmed, 'COVID-19 Research Scandal: Unwanted Diversion During Pandemic' *MedicalXpress* (6 June 2020) <https://medicalxpress.com/news/2020-06-covid-scandal-unwanted-diversion-pandemic.html> accessed 4 October 2022.

[265] See Freckelton, 'Perils of Precipitate Publication' (n 246).

[266] See Lindsay McKenzie, 'Debunking Bad COVID-19 Research' *Inside Higher Ed* (29 June 2020) <https://www.insidehighered.com/news/2020/06/29/new-mit-press-journal-debunk-bad-covid-19-research> accessed 4 October 2022; see more generally Freckelton, *Scholarly Misconduct* (n 219).

[267] See eg Diana Kwon, 'How Swamped Preprint Servers Are Blocking Bad Coronavirus Research' (2020) 581(7807) *Nature* 130; Holly Else, 'How to Bring Preprints to the Charged Field of Medicine' *Nature* (6 June 2019) <https://www.nature.com/articles/d41586-019-01806-2> accessed 11 September 2022.

[268] James Heathers, 'The Lancet Has Made One of the Biggest Retractions in Modern History. How Could This Happen?' *The Guardian* (5 June 2020) <www.theguardian.com/commentisfree/2020/jun/05/lancet-had-to-do-one-of-the-biggest-retractions-in-modern-history-how-could-this-happen> accessed 4 October 2022.

[269] See Roni Caryn Rabin, 'The Pandemic Claims New Victims: Prestigious Medical Journals' *New York Times* (14 June 2020) <www.nytimes.com/2020/06/14/health/virus-journals.html> accessed 4 October 2022.

[270] Lancet Group Editors, 'Learning from a Retraction' (2020) 396(10257) *Lancet* P1056.

B. The Ivermectin Saga

Significant controversies were also generated by publications about ivermectin and, in particular, a pre-print article published in *Research Square* by Ahmed Elgazzar and others.[271] That article went through four versions, commencing on 12 November 2020 and concluding on 14 July 2021, after which it was withdrawn. Ivermectin is a well known anti-parasitic (deworming) medication that has broad anti-viral activity through inhibition of viral proteins.[272] WHO and the United States Food and Drugs Administration, among others, have approved its use for this purpose. The Elgazzar study purported to evaluate the efficacy of the medication provided along with standard care in the treatment of mild, moderate, and severely ill persons who had COVID-19. It found a substantial improvement and reduction in mortality rate in ivermectin-treated groups and a significant reduction in the incidence of infection in healthcare and household contacts when used as a prophylaxis.

A systematic review and meta-analysis of 15 trials, including the Elgazzar study, by Andrew Bryant and others concluded that the use of ivermectin to treat COVID-19 provides a 'significant benefit of survival' and that:

> Overall, the evidence also suggests that early use of ivermectin may reduce morbidity and mortality from COVID-19. This is based on (1) reductions in COVID-19 infections when ivermectin was used as prophylaxis, (2) the more favorable effect estimates for mild to moderate disease compared with severe disease for death due to any cause, and (3) evidence demonstrating reductions in deterioration.[273]

This prompted Bryant and his co-authors to contend that 'Ivermectin is likely to be an equitable, acceptable, and feasible global intervention against COVID-19. Health professionals should strongly consider its use, in both treatment and prophylaxis'.[274]

Questions were soon raised about the Elgazzar study's design, possible plagiarism in its wording, and the potential for its data to have been fabricated, amid

---

[271] Ahmed Elgazzar and others, 'Efficacy and Safety of Ivermectin for Treatment and Prophylaxis of COVID-19 Pandemic' *Research Square* (14 July 2021) <https://doi.org/10.21203/rs.3.rs-100956/v2> accessed 11 September 2022.

[272] See Ricardo Peña-Silva and others, 'Pharmacokinetic Considerations on the Repurposing of Ivermectin for Treatment of COVID-19' (2020) 87(3) *British Journal of Clinical Pharmacology* 1589.

[273] Andrew Bryant and others, 'Ivermectin for Prevention and Treatment of COVID-19 Infection: A Systematic Review, Meta-analysis, and Trial Sequential Analysis to Inform Clinical Guidelines' (2021) 28(4) *American Journal of Therapeutics* e434; see also Pierre Kory and others, 'Review of the Emerging Evidence Demonstrating the Efficacy of Ivermectin in the Prophylaxis and Treatment of COVID-19' (2021) 28(3) *American Journal of Therapeutics* e299.

[274] Bryant and others (n 273).

claims that at least 79 of the patient records were clones of other records.[275] Review of the analysis undertaken by Bryant and others showed that the studies they used were small—one only included 24 patients—many of them were not double-blinded, a significant number were open-label (the health providers and the patients were aware of the medication being given), and its methodology involved questionable pooling of the data.[276] By March 2021, WHO, the United States Food and Drug Administration, and the European Medicines Agency recommended that ivermectin only be used within clinical trials[277] and, by April 2021, ivermectin was lambasted as 'the new hydroxychloroquine'.[278] In June 2021, another systematic review and meta-analysis concluded that ivermectin did not reduce mortality, length of hospital stay, or viral clearance in randomized controlled trials and was 'not a viable option to treat patients with COVID-19'.[279] In July 2021, a Cochrane Review Group confirmed that it had found 'no evidence to support the use of ivermectin for treating or preventing COVID-19 infection'.[280] Conspiracy theorists resisted the criticisms and responses of regulators by arguing, amongst other things,

---

[275] See Melissa Davey, 'Huge Study Supporting Ivermectin as Covid Treatment Withdrawn over Ethical Concerns' *The Guardian* (16 July 2021) <www.theguardian.com/science/2021/jul/16/huge-study-supporting-ivermectin-as-covid-treatment-withdrawn-over-ethical-concerns> accessed 11 September 2022; Jack Lawrence, 'Why Was a Major Study on Ivermectin for COVID-19 Just Retracted?' *Grifter Analysis and Review* (15 July 2021) <https://grftr.news/why-was-a-major-study-on-ivermectin-for-covid-19-just-retracted/> accessed 4 October 2022; Nick Brown, 'Some Problems in the Dataset of a Large Study of Ivermectin for the Treatment of COVID-19' *Nick Brown's Blog* (15 July 2021) <http://steamtraen.blogspot.com/2021/07/Some-problems-with-the-data-from-a-Covid-study.html> accessed 11 September 2022.

[276] David Gorski, 'Ivermectin is the New Hydroxychloroquine, Take 2' *Science-Based Medicine* (21 June 2021) <https://sciencebasedmedicine.org/ivermectin-is-the-new-hydroxychloroquine-take-2/> accessed 11 September 2022.

[277] See World Health Organization, 'WHO Advises that Ivermectin Only be Used to Treat COVID-19 Within Clinical Trials' (31 March 2021) <www.who.int/news-room/feature-stories/detail/who-advises-that-ivermectin-only-be-used-to-treat-covid-19-within-clinical-trials> accessed 11 September 2022. Similarly, the United States Food and Drug Administration warned on 9 March 2021 that: 'The FDA has not authorized or approved ivermectin for the treatment or prevention of COVID-19 in people or animals. Ivermectin has not been shown to be safe or effective for these indications': United States Food and Drug Administration, 'Why You Should Not Use Ivermectin to Treat or Prevent COVID-19' (9 March 2021) <www.fda.gov/consumers/consumer-updates/why-you-should-not-use-ivermectin-treat-or-prevent-covid-19> accessed 11 September 2022. See also European Medicines Agency, 'EMA Advises Against Use of Ivermectin for the Prevention or Treatment of COVID-19 Outside Randomised Clinical Trials' (22 March 2021) <https://www.ema.europa.eu/en/news/ema-advises-against-use-ivermectin-prevention-treatment-covid-19-outside-randomised-clinical-trials> accessed 11 September 2022.

[278] See Scott Gavura, 'Ivermectin the New Hydroxychloroquine' *Science-Based Medicine* (15 April 2021) <https://sciencebasedmedicine.org/ivermectin-is-the-new-hydroxychloroquine/> accessed 8 September 2021.

[279] Yuani M Roman and others, 'Ivermectin for the Treatment of Coronavirus Disease 2019: A Systematic Review and Meta-analysis of Randomized Controlled Trials' (2022) 74(6) *Clinical Infectious Diseases* 1022.

[280] Maria Popp and others, 'Ivermectin for Preventing and Treating COVID-19' *Cochrane* (28 July 2021) <www.cochrane.org/CD015017/HAEMATOL_ivermectin-preventing-and-treating-covid-19> accessed 11 September 2022.

that 'discussion' about ivermectin was being 'suppressed' by 'Big-Pharma' because of the 'threat' it posed to the 'billion-dollar vaccine business'.[281]

However, in February 2021, the manufacturer of ivermectin, Merck, had issued a caution that:

> Company scientists continue to carefully examine the findings of all available and emerging studies of ivermectin for the treatment of COVID-19 for evidence of efficacy and safety. It is important to note that, to-date, our analysis has identified:
> - No scientific basis for a potential therapeutic effect against COVID-19 from pre-clinical studies;
> - No meaningful evidence for clinical activity or clinical efficacy in patients with COVID-19 disease, and;
> - A concerning lack of safety data in the majority of studies.[282]

By 14 July 2021, the Elgazzar study had been withdrawn due to a concern communicated to the publisher, which had commenced to undertake a 'formal investigation'.[283] Although research into the potential efficacy of ivermectin as an anti-viral agent continues,[284] the more significant question is how the drug was able to assume legitimacy as a suitable COVID-19 treatment based on methodologically flawed studies that were published in the uncritical environment of COVID-19 anxiety. It has been argued that:

> research related to ivermectin in COVID-19 has serious methodological limitations resulting in very low certainty of the evidence, and continues to grow. The use of ivermectin, among others [sic] repurposed drugs for prophylaxis or treatment for COVID-19, should be done based on trustable [sic] evidence, without conflicts of interest, with proven safety and efficacy in patient-consented, ethically approved, randomised clinical trials.[285]

---

[281] See Matt Taibbi, 'Why Has "Ivermectin" Become a Dirty Word?' *TK News* (19 June 2021) <https://taibbi.substack.com/p/why-has-ivermectin-become-a-dirty-7bd> accessed 11 September 2022.

[282] Merck, 'Merck Statement on Ivermectin Use During the COVID-19 Pandemic' (Company Statement, 4 February 2021) <https://www.merck.com/news/merck-statement-on-ivermectin-use-during-the-covid-19-pandemic/> accessed 11 September 2022.

[283] 'Editorial Note' *Research Square* (19 July 2021) <www.researchsquare.com/article/rs-100956/v4> accessed 11 September 2022.

[284] See Andrew McLachlan, 'A Major Ivermectin Study Has Been Withdrawn, So What Now for the Controversial Drug?' *The Conversation* (22 July 2021) <https://theconversation.com/a-major-ivermectin-study-has-been-withdrawn-so-what-now-for-the-controversial-drug-164627> accessed 11 September 2022.

[285] Luis Ignacio Garegnani, Eva Madrid, and Nicolás Meza, 'Misleading Clinical Evidence and Systematic Reviews on Ivermectin for COVID-19' (2022) 27(3) *BMJ Evidence-Based Medicine* 156.

The claims made regarding the effectiveness of ivermectin in treating COVID-19 (though not by the manufacturer) generated increased demand for the drug in many parts of the world. Use of ivermectin for off-label purposes in the context of COVID-19 surged in many countries, especially Peru, Bolivia, Guatemala, and a number of other Latin American countries.[286] In Australia, imports of ivermectin were reported to have increased tenfold,[287] prompting a warning from the Therapeutic Goods Administration that it was not approved for treatment of COVID-19.[288] This highlights not just 'the challenges of investigating drug efficacy during a pandemic',[289] and the fact that 'scientific rigor is needed, even in pandemic times',[290] but also the risk that people will rely on published research that is unsubstantiated and use therapies to treat COVID-19 whose efficacy and safety for this application are unproven.

V. Conclusion

The COVID-19 pandemic has generated major achievements in scientific research and development. The speed at which treatments and vaccines have been developed and tested has been highly unusual, and the collaboration and co-operation between scientists and health professionals from across the world was remarkable. Time was saved, knowledge pooled, and discoveries shared. WHO played a vital role in facilitating this progress. Yet WHO, like other authorities, scientists, and commentators, was wary about the risks of failure to comply fully or at all with legal, regulatory, and ethical requirements surrounding research and development in the haste to discover life-saving medical products. Some shortcuts that were taken in research and development during the pandemic highlighted the reasonableness of these concerns and the perils of precipitate publication of research and loosened checks on the quality of studies prior to disseminating their results. Reliance on studies of COVID-19 treatments that lacked a sound research base could potentially have adverse consequences for patients. The experience

---

[286] See Emiliano Rodríguez Mega, 'Latin America's Embrace of an Unproven COVID Treatment is Hindering Drug Trials' (2020) 586(7830) *Nature* 481.
[287] See Josh Taylor, 'Australian Imports of Ivermectin Increase Tenfold, Prompting Warning from TGA' *The Guardian* (31 August 2021) <www.theguardian.com/world/2021/aug/30/australian-imports-of-ivermectin-increase-10-fold-prompting-warning-from-tga> accessed 11 September 2022.
[288] See Therapeutic Goods Administration, 'Risks of Importing Ivermectin for Treatment of COVID-19' (Media Release and Statement, 23 August 2021) <https://www.tga.gov.au/media-release/risks-importing-ivermectin-treatment-covid-19> accessed 11 September 2022.
[289] Sara Reardon, 'Flawed Ivermectin Preprint Highlights Challenges of COVID Drug Studies' (2021) 596(7871) *Nature* 173.
[290] Carlos Chaccour, 'Ivermectin and COVID-19: How a Flawed Database Shaped the Pandemic Response of Several Latin-American Countries' *IS Global* (29 May 2020) <www.isglobal.org/en/healthisglobal/-/custom-blog-portlet/ivermectin-and-covid-19-how-a-flawed-database-shaped-the-covid-19-response-of-several-latin-american-countries/2877257/0> accessed 11 September 2022.

of developing COVID-19 treatments and vaccines can inspire confidence in the potential to meet major public health challenges in the future, but it should also remind researchers, scholarly publishers, and governments of the importance of maintaining and adhering to ethical, regulatory, and legal standards. The next chapter discusses the production, regulation, and distribution of COVID-19 treatments and vaccines.

12
Production, Regulation, and Distribution of COVID-19 Treatments and Vaccines

I. Introduction

Given the rapid dissemination of COVID-19, it became clear early in the pandemic that arresting its detrimental effects would depend on the global availability of safe and effective treatments and vaccines for the virus. This was a matter of equity, too. Participants in the Global Research Collaboration for Infectious Disease Preparedness and Response at the World Health Organization's (WHO) headquarters in Geneva in February 2020 nominated as an 'immediate research action' facilitating 'fair and equitable access to any medical products or innovations that are developed using' shared 'virus materials, clinical samples and associated data'.[1] However, as discussed in this chapter, it was a major challenge to produce enough of these medical products to meet demand, and distribute them as quickly and broadly as needed to all countries and all populations within them. There were several obstacles to achieving these objectives. While attempts were made to use legal and regulatory mechanisms to overcome them, in some instances, the mechanisms employed in fact contributed to these impediments.

Section II of this chapter examines the imperative recognized during the COVID-19 pandemic to ensure equitable access to treatments and vaccines both within national populations and globally. It explores the human rights that such access could protect and some attempts that were made to help achieve it. Section III of the chapter discusses considerations that were relevant to decision-making about how to ration and allocate COVID-19 treatments and vaccines within some countries when they were in limited supply. Section IV considers the challenges faced by regulatory authorities during this health emergency to protect the public by both tackling the proliferation of fraudulent COVID-19 therapies and accelerating the processes of evaluating whether medical products were safe and effective to treat the virus and thus whether to permit their distribution. Section V of this chapter examines the potential for intellectual property laws to impede equitable

---

[1] World Health Organization, *A Coordinated Global Research Roadmap: 2019 Novel Coronavirus* (Report, March 2020) 8 <https://www.who.int/publications/m/item/a-coordinated-global-research-roadmap> accessed 2 June 2022.

global access to COVID-19 treatments and vaccines, and attempts to surmount these hurdles.

II. Access to COVID-19 Treatments and Vaccines

In the initial phase of the COVID-19 pandemic, both effective treatments and a cure for the disease were not yet available and, in most countries, public health measures proved unsustainable or inadequate to stem its spread.[2] As the pandemic progressed, and once safe and effective COVID-19 vaccines had been developed, and effective treatments were becoming available, it became apparent that extensive distribution of them was an important means of significantly halting escalations in infection and mortality rates.[3] The quest for treatments to address symptoms of the virus gathered momentum during 2021 with the prospect that the focus would shift towards their being made available, as had been the challenge with vaccines once they were developed.[4]

Many scholars and commentators argued that international human rights law required countries to ensure equitable, non-discriminatory access to safe and effective COVID-19 vaccines and treatments, once they were developed, within and beyond their own jurisdictions.[5] It was also increasingly recognized that it was essential to develop global governance frameworks that facilitated global distributive justice[6] and international cooperation to share the fruits of COVID-19 research equally throughout the world.[7] Various initiatives, many of them sponsored by WHO, sought to encourage collaboration for this purpose, but 'treatment parochialism' and 'vaccine nationalism', where countries prioritized the needs of their

---

[2] Lawrence O Gostin, Safura Abdool Karim, and Benjamin Mason Meier, 'Facilitating Access to a COVID-19 Vaccine Through Global Health Law' (2020) 48(3) *Journal of Law, Medicine & Ethics* 622, 622; Ashlee Beazley, 'Contagion, Containment, Consent: Infectious Disease Pandemics and the Ethics, Rights and Legality of State-enforced Vaccination' (2020) 7(1) *Journal of Law and the Biosciences* art lsaa021.

[3] Gostin, Karim, and Meier (n 2) 622; Jason W Nickerson and Matthew Herder, 'COVID-19 Vaccines as Global Public Goods' in Colleen M Flood and others (eds), *Vulnerable: The Law, Policy and Ethics of COVID-19* (University of Ottawa Press 2020) 592; Beazley (n 2); Brook K Baker, 'Campaigning for Both Innovation and Equitable Access to COVID-19 Medicines' in Morten Kjaerum, Martha F Davis, and Amanda Lyons (eds), *COVID-19 and Human Rights* (Routledge 2021).

[4] Gostin, Karim, and Meier (n 2) 622–23; Seth Berkley, 'COVAX Explained' *Gavi* (3 September 2020) <www.gavi.org/vaccineswork/covax-explained> accessed 4 October 2022.

[5] See eg Katharina Ó Cathaoir, 'Human Rights in Times of Pandemics: Necessity and Proportionality' in Morten Kjaerum, Martha F Davis, and Amanda Lyons (eds), *COVID-19 and Human Rights* (Routledge 2021); Gostin, Karim, and Meier (n 2) 623; Kevin Bell, 'COVID-19 and Human Rights in Australia: Part 1' *Castan Centre for Human Rights Law* (21 April 2020) <www.monash.edu/law/research/centres/castancentre/our-areas-of-work/covid19/policy/covid19-and-human-rights-in-australia/covid19-and-human-rights-in-australia-part-1> accessed 11 September 2022.

[6] Jane H Williams and Angus Dawson, 'Prioritising Access to Pandemic Influenza Vaccine: A Review of the Ethics Literature' (2020) 21(1) *BMC Medical Ethics* 40.

[7] Gostin, Karim, and Meier (n 2) 623, 625; Nickerson and Herder (n 3) 591; Editorial, 'Global Governance for COVID-19 Vaccines' (2020) 395(10241) *Lancet* 1883.

own populations, threatened to undermine such collaboration. An example was the United States programme known as 'Operation Warp Speed', a partnership between the Departments of Health and Human Services and Defense,[8] which involved government funding of US$18 billion for vaccines intended solely for the United States population.[9]

A. Ensuring Equitable Access

Prior to the COVID-19 pandemic, the United Nations had acknowledged that access to treatments and vaccines could be integral to protecting three recognized human rights in particular.[10] First, enabling access to treatments and vaccines could help to protect the right 'to the enjoyment of the highest attainable standard of physical and mental health' ('right to health'), which is recognized in many international instruments, including the *International Covenant on Economic, Social and Cultural Rights* (*ICESCR*).[11] Indeed, that Covenant provides that 'steps taken ... to achieve the full realization of this right shall include those necessary for ... the prevention, treatment and control of ... diseases'.[12] Second, if a treatment or vaccine could prevent premature death from disease, access to it would also promote the 'right to life', which is recognized in the *International Covenant on Civil and Political Rights*.[13] Third, where treatments and vaccines are produced through

---

[8] United States Government Accountability Office, 'Operation Warp Speed: Accelerated COVID-19 Vaccine Development Status and Efforts to Address Manufacturing Challenges' (11 February 2021) <www.gao.gov/products/gao-21-319> accessed 15 September 2022.

[9] Lancet Commission on COVID-19 Vaccines and Therapeutics Task Force Members, 'Operation Warp Speed: Implications for Global Vaccine Security' (2021) 9(7) *Lancet Global Health* art e1017; Congressional Research Service, 'Operation Warp Speed Contracts for COVID-19 Vaccines and Ancillary Vaccination Materials' (1 March 2021) <https://crsreports.congress.gov/product/pdf/IN/IN11560> accessed 11 September 2022; Arthur Herman, 'Why Operation Warp Speed Worked' *Wall Street Journal* (1 February 2021) <www.wsj.com/articles/why-operation-warp-speed-worked-11612222129> accessed 11 September 2022.

[10] United Nations General Assembly, *Report of the Special Rapporteur on the Right of Everyone to the Enjoyment of the Highest Attainable Standard of Physical and Mental Health* (13 September 2006) UN Doc A/61/338, 10–11 < https://documents-dds-ny.un.org/doc/UNDOC/GEN/N06/519/97/PDF/N0651997.pdf?OpenElement > accessed 11 September 2022 (hereafter UNGA, *Report of the Special Rapporteur*); see too Paul Hunt, 'Interpreting the International Right to Health in a Human Rights-Based Approach to Health' (2016) 18(2) *Health and Human Rights Journal* 109.

[11] *International Covenant on Economic, Social and Cultural Rights* (opened for signature 16 December 1966, entered into force 3 January 1976) 993 UNTS 3, Article 12(1) (hereafter *ICESCR*). See Alexandra L Phelan and others, 'Legal Agreements: Barriers and Enablers to Global Equitable COVID-19 Vaccine Access' (2020) 396(10254) *Lancet* 800, 801.

[12] *ICESCR* (n 11) Article 12 (2)(c). Such steps could include enhancing trust in vaccination by publicizing accurate information about it: OECD, 'Enhancing Public Trust in COVID-19 Vaccination: The Role of Governments' (10 May 2021) <www.oecd.org/coronavirus/policy-responses/enhancing-public-trust-in-covid-19-vaccination-the-role-of-governments-eae0ec5a/> accessed 11 September 2022.

[13] *International Covenant on Civil and Political Rights* (opened for signature 16 December 1966, entered into force 23 March 1976) 999 UNTS 171, Article 6(1).

research, facilitating access to them would uphold the right 'to enjoy the benefits of scientific progress and its application', which is also recognized in the *ICESR*.[14]

The *Universal Declaration on Bioethics and Human Rights*[15] also refers to the imperative of ensuring equitable access to the fruits of research at local and global levels. For instance, Article 15 of that instrument provides that 'benefits resulting from any scientific research and its applications should be shared within society as a whole and within the international community', and Article 24 states that 'states should foster international dissemination of scientific information and encourage the free flow and sharing of scientific and technological knowledge'.

Countries' international legal obligations to ensure universal access to a COVID-19 treatment or vaccine in order to protect these rights would be triggered especially if they and/or WHO classified it as an 'essential medicine'.[16] WHO's list of 'essential medicines' comprises drugs that are required to 'satisfy the priority health care needs of the population' in light of 'disease prevalence' and 'evidence' of their 'efficacy' and 'safety'.[17] Countries' duties to provide access to COVID-19 treatments and vaccines that meet this definition would entail ensuring that they are made 'available in sufficient quantities' in 'all parts' of 'their jurisdictions' 'without discrimination', and that they are 'affordable' for everyone, including vulnerable populations.[18] To protect the rights to health, life, and enjoyment of the benefits of scientific progress, countries would also need to ensure access to good quality COVID-19 treatments and vaccines for other jurisdictions, and especially low- and middle-income countries that otherwise could not afford to purchase them.[19] If a COVID-19 treatment or vaccine was only available in some regions, every individual's health and life would remain in jeopardy due to the persistent risks of recurrent outbreaks and further spread or mutation of the virus.[20] Indeed, WHO identified COVID-19 'variants of interest' and 'variants of concern' (classified according to the threat they represent), which spread outside their places of origin,[21] including: during 2021, the Lambda and Mu 'variants of interest', which

---

[14] *ICESCR* (n 11) Article 15(1)(b); Phelan and others (n 11) 801.
[15] UNESCO General Conference, *Universal Declaration on Bioethics and Human Rights* (33rd Sess, 19 October 2005).
[16] Hans V Hogerzeil, 'Essential Medicines and Human Rights: What Can They Learn from Each Other?' (2006) 84(5) *Bulletin of the World Health Organization* 371, 371, 373; Gostin, Karim, and Meier (n 2) 623; World Health Organization, 'WHO Model Lists of Essential Medicines' <www.who.int/groups/expert-committee-on-selection-and-use-of-essential-medicines/essential-medicines-lists> accessed 11 September 2022.
[17] Hogerzeil (n 16) 371.
[18] UNGA, *Report of the Special Rapporteur* (n 10) 13–14; Gostin, Karim, and Meier (n 2).
[19] Gostin, Karim, and Meier (n 2) 623; Dainius Pūras and others, 'The Right to Health Must Guide Responses to COVID-19' (2020) 395(10241) *Lancet* 1888. See more generally UNGA, *Report of the Special Rapporteur* (n 10) 15–16.
[20] Gostin, Karim, and Meier (n 2) 622–23; Thomas J Bollyky, Lawrence O Gostin, and Margaret A Hamburg, 'The Equitable Distribution of COVID-19 Therapeutics and Vaccines' 323(24) (2020) *Journal of the American Medical Association* 2462, 2463.
[21] World Health Organization, 'Tracking SARS-CoV-2 Variants' (Activities, 3 May 2022) <www.who.int/en/activities/tracking-SARS-CoV-2-variants/> accessed 16 May 2022 (hereafter World Health Organization, 'Tracking').

dispersed beyond Peru and Colombia respectively;[22] and the Delta and Omicron variants of concern, which were first identified in India and South Africa in March and November 2021, respectively, and spread globally.[23]

International collaboration and planning have been vital to the attempt to ensure equitable global access to COVID-19 treatment and vaccines.[24] As noted in Chapter 2, smallpox was only eradicated through worldwide co-operation.[25] The COVID-19 pandemic highlighted the need for global governance structures to co-ordinate governments, non-government organizations, funding bodies, and pharmaceutical companies, and facilitate production and distribution of vaccines on a mass scale.[26] During this pandemic, a number of schemes were developed to encourage such cooperation, the most substantial of which was the 'Access to COVID-19 Tools (ACT) Accelerator' ('ACT Accelerator'), discussed briefly in Chapter 11.[27] In addition to accelerating development of COVID-19 treatments and vaccines, with its aphorism, 'no one is safe unless everyone is safe',[28] the ACT Accelerator also sought to 'accelerate … production, and equitable access to COVID-19' treatments and vaccines.[29] The 'therapeutics pillar' of the ACT Accelerator aimed to 'manufacture, procure and distribute 245 million treatments for populations in low- and middle-income countries within 12 months'.[30] The ACT-Accelerator articulated four priorities for 2021:

1. Rapidly scale up the delivery of at least 2 billion doses of vaccines through COVAX to the most high risk and highly exposed populations globally;

---

[22] Adam Taylor, 'The Lambda Variant: Is it More Infectious, and Can It Escape Vaccines? A Virologist Explains' *The Conversation* (21 July 2021) <https://theconversation.com/the-lambda-variant-is-it-more-infectious-and-can-it-escape-vaccines-a-virologist-explains-164156> accessed 11 September 2022; Luke O'Neill, 'Mu: Everything You Need to Know about the New Coronavirus Variant of Interest' *The Conversation* (3 September 2021) <https://theconversation.com/mu-everything-you-need-to-know-about-the-new-coronavirus-variant-of-interest-167154> accessed 11 September 2022.

[23] World Health Organization, 'Tracking' (n 21); Ed Yong, 'The 3 Simple Rules that Underscore the Danger of Delta' *The Atlantic* (1 July 2021) <www.theatlantic.com/health/archive/2021/07/3-principles-now-define-pandemic/619336/> accessed 11 September 2022.

[24] Gostin, Karim, and Meier (n 2) 623; Nickerson and Herder (n 3) 591, 599.

[25] Gostin, Karim, and Meier (n 2) 623.

[26] Editorial (n 7); Bollyky, Gostin, and Hamburg (n 20) 2463.

[27] World Health Organization, 'The ACT-Accelerator Frequently Asked Questions' <www.who.int/initiatives/act-accelerator/faq> accessed 4 October 2022 (hereafter World Health Organization, 'The ACT-Accelerator').

[28] World Health Organization, 'COVAX: Working for Global Equitable Access to COVID-19 Vaccines' <www.who.int/initiatives/act-accelerator/covax> accessed 4 October 2022.

[29] World Health Organization, 'The ACT-Accelerator' (n 27). See too Mark Eccleston-Turner and Harry Upton, 'International Collaboration to Ensure Equitable Access to Vaccines for COVID-19: The ACT-Accelerator and the COVAX Facility' (2021) 99(2) *Milbank Quarterly* 426. See also Chapter 7(III) regarding the supply of oxygen through the ACT-Accelerator.

[30] World Health Organization, 'The ACT-Accelerator' (n 27).

2. Bolster the R&D agenda, product evaluation, and regulatory pathways for new and modified tests, treatments, and vaccines to respond to emerging variants and programmatic needs;
3. Stimulate rapid and effective uptake and use of COVID-19 tests, treatments, and PPE in low and middle income countries; and
4. Ensure a robust supply pipeline of essential tests, treatments, and PPE to support broader access in [low- and middle-income countries] and protect vital health infrastructure.[31]

B. COVAX

Several high-income countries were initially able to secure access to vaccines faster than others and to a higher number of doses of them than other less wealthy countries.[32] Anticipating this inequity, WHO developed the 'Concept for Fair Access and Equitable Allocation of Covid-19 Health Products'.[33] WHO's Strategic Advisory Group of Experts on Immunization also created a 'Values Framework for the Allocation and Prioritization of COVID-19 Vaccination' ('Values Framework'), a core principle of which is 'global equity', with the associated objective of ensuring that 'vaccine allocation takes into account the special epidemic risks and needs of all countries' and especially low- and middle-income countries.[34] The Values Framework recommends that 'financially able countries' 'support approaches', such as the COVAX Facility, 'to ensure access to COVID-19 vaccine for resource constrained populations'.[35]

COVAX, the 'vaccine pillar' of the ACT Accelerator, attempted to ensure that vaccines would be 'manufactured at the right volumes ... and delivered to those that need them most', and 'all participating countries, regardless of income levels, will have equal access to these vaccines once they are developed'.[36] The 'COVAX Facility' was established as 'an actively managed portfolio of vaccine candidates'

---

[31] ACT Accelerator, 'ACT-Accelerator Prioritized Strategy & Budget for 2021' *World Health Organization* (12 April 2021) <www.who.int/publications/m/item/act-a-prioritized-strategy-and-budget-for-2021> accessed 4 October 2022.

[32] Sarah Joseph, 'International Human Rights Law and the Response to the COVID-19 Pandemic' (2020) 11(2) *Journal of International Humanitarian Legal Studies* 249.

[33] World Health Organization, 'WHO Concept for Fair Access and Equitable Allocation of COVID-19 Health Products' (9 September 2020) <www.who.int/docs/default-source/coronaviruse/who-covid19-vaccine-allocation-final-working-version-9sept.pdf> accessed 11 September 2022.

[34] World Health Organization, 'WHO SAGE Values Framework for the Allocation and Prioritization of COVID-19 Vaccination' (14 September 2021) 11 <https://apps.who.int/iris/bitstream/handle/10665/334299/WHO-2019-nCoV-SAGE_Framework-Allocation_and_prioritization-2020.1-eng.pdf?ua=1> accessed 11 September 2022 (hereafter WHO, 'SAGE').

[35] ibid.

[36] World Health Organization, 'The ACT-Accelerator' (n 27).

whose manufacture high-income countries would fund in order to subsidize vaccine doses for low- and middle-income countries.[37]

On behalf of the Facility, the Gavi Vaccine Alliance aimed to reach agreements with vaccine manufacturers to provide two billion doses by the end of 2021.[38] Self-financing governments would make up-front payments for a designated number of vaccine doses from manufacturers.[39] In exchange, they would receive access at low, negotiated prices to enough doses of any vaccines in COVAX's portfolio that received regulatory approval to immunize 20% of their population.[40] Low- and middle-income countries participating in the Facility would also receive sufficient vaccine doses to immunize the most vulnerable 20% of their populations, after which the self-financing participants could potentially obtain doses for up to 50% of their populations.[41] Approximately 5% of the doses would be allocated to 'humanitarian organizations' so they could vaccinate refugees and others who might otherwise not obtain access to vaccines.[42] In this way, the Facility would ensure equitable access to COVID-19 vaccines for people in low- and middle-income countries which could not afford vaccines, but also in high-income countries that lacked bilateral agreements with vaccine manufacturers or whose agreements had failed.[43]

The 'Gavi COVAX Advance Market Commitment' was created to raise monetary donations to enable low- and middle-income countries to participate in the Facility.[44] Gavi used these funds to enter advance purchase agreements with vaccine manufacturers, whereby it committed to buying high volumes of vaccine candidates prior to their regulatory approval to ensure manufacturers produced sufficient doses to be distributed to countries 'according to need, rather than ability to pay'.[45] These agreements provided incentives to manufacturers to boost their capacity to produce vaccines (in which they usually would not risk investing while they awaited regulators' decisions) to reduce delays and initial shortages in production of vaccines that ultimately proved to be safe and effective.[46] For instance, on 18 December 2020, COVAX announced that it had signed an advance purchase agreement with AstraZeneca for 170 million doses of the AstraZeneca/Oxford

---

[37] Berkley (n 4); Eric A Friedman and others, 'Joining COVAX Could Save American Lives' *Foreign Policy* (15 September 2020) < https://foreignpolicy.com/2020/09/15/covax-vaccine-covid-19-trump-save-lives-equitable-distribution/ > accessed 11 September 2022.
[38] World Health Organization, 'The Covax Facility: Global Procurement for COVID-19 Vaccines' (6 August 2020) 3 <www.who.int/publications/m/item/the-covax-facility> accessed 4 October 2022 (hereafter World Health Organization, 'The Covax Facility').
[39] ibid; Berkley (n 4).
[40] World Health Organization, 'The Covax Facility' (n 38) 5–6; Friedman and others (n 37).
[41] Berkley (n 4); World Health Organization, 'The Covax Facility' (n 38) 5.
[42] Berkley (n 4).
[43] ibid.
[44] ibid.
[45] Editorial (n 7); Ann D Usher, 'COVID-19 Vaccines for All?' (2020) 395(10240) *Lancet* 1822, 1822; Phelan and others (n 11) 801.
[46] Berkley (n 4).

vaccine candidate, and executed a memorandum of understanding with Johnson & Johnson for 500 million doses of the Janssen vaccine candidate.[47] These contracts were:

> in addition to [COVAX's] existing agreements ... with the Serum Institute of India for 200 million doses—with options for up to 900 million doses more—of either the AstraZeneca/Oxford or Novavax vaccine candidates, as well as a statement of intent for 200 million doses of the Sanofi/GSK vaccine candidate.[48]

In September 2020, the WHO Secretariat released an 'allocation framework for fair and equitable access to COVID-19 health products', which articulated principles and ethical values, such as 'transparency' and 'equity and fairness', to inform the distribution of vaccines and treatments for this disease.[49] However, the framework was not formally adopted in an international legal instrument or agreement,[50] and the basis upon which governments might agree to share vaccines pursuant to this model was unclear.[51] Moreover, COVAX was criticized for failing to conform with some of the standards enshrined in this framework; for instance, it was accused of lacking transparency in its communications about the operation of the Advance Market Commitment and Gavi's contracts with vaccine manufacturers.[52] Further, as many high-income countries in the Facility also entered their own bilateral arrangements with vaccine manufacturers, they were potentially able to 'double-dip', giving them greater access to vaccines than low- and middle-income countries.[53] In any event, although over 190 countries joined COVAX, the refusal of the United States during Donald Trump's presidency to participate in COVAX impaired the capacity of COVAX to access sufficient finances and encourage the increased production of COVID-19 vaccine candidates so that there was ultimately a sufficient global supply of them.[54] Some ethicists questioned the prioritization of COVAX of, first, equal distribution among participating countries

---

[47] World Health Organization, 'COVAX Announces Additional Deals to Access Promising COVID-19 Vaccine Candidates; Plans Global Rollout Starting Q1 2021' (News Release, 18 December 2020) <www.who.int/news/item/18-12-2020-covax-announces-additional-deals-to-access-promising-covid-19-vaccine-candidates-plans-global-rollout-starting-q1-2021> accessed 4 October 2022.
[48] ibid.
[49] World Health Organization, 'WHO Concept for Fair Access and Equitable Allocation of COVID-19 Health Products' (9 September 2020) 5–7 <www.who.int/docs/default-source/coronaviruse/who-covid19-vaccine-allocation-final-working-version-9sept.pdf> accessed 4 October 2022.
[50] Phelan and others (n 11) 801.
[51] Editorial (n 7).
[52] Phelan and others (n 11) 801; Usher (n 45) 1822; Editorial (n 7).
[53] Julia Belluz, '171 Countries are Teaming up for a COVID-19 Vaccine. But not the US' *Vox* (9 October 2020) <www.vox.com/21448719/covid-19-vaccine-covax-who-gavi-cepi> accessed 11 September 2022.
[54] ibid; Friedman and others (n 37).

and then, second, access according to need, arguing that the initial determinant of vaccine allocation should simply be countries' relative needs.[55]

Several countries, including the United States, entered advance purchase agreements with COVID-19 vaccine manufacturers to supply doses to their own populations exclusively.[56] In entering into these bilateral legal agreements, governments committed to buy a certain number of doses of potential vaccines from vaccine manufacturers if they were ultimately developed, licensed, and produced in exchange for securing the doses and priority access to them at a negotiated price.[57] For instance, the governments of the United States and United Kingdom paid to secure 300 and 30 million doses respectively of AstraZeneca in advance for their citizens.[58] These governments could have obtained the vaccine doses more quickly and cheaply under the advance purchase agreements than they could through COVAX, but it was only useful if the vaccine candidates that were the subject of the advance purchase agreements proved efficacious.[59] If those candidates ultimately proved not to be safe and effective, the governments may have been left without immediate or sufficient access to successful vaccines.[60]

Moreover, in facilitating some countries' stockpiling and hoarding of prospective vaccines, the advance purchase agreements were a manifestation of 'vaccine nationalism', which became a major obstacle to global collaboration and equitable access to COVID-19 vaccines.[61] Another example of vaccine nationalism was certain governments' investment in the manufacture of vaccines solely for their populations. For instance, the National Research Council of Canada paid for CanSino Biologics Inc to develop and undertake clinical trials of a COVID-19 vaccine candidate in exchange for CanSino agreeing to supply Canada with the vaccine.[62] These initiatives marked a shift away from conceptualizing vaccines as a 'global public good' during the phases of their development, production, and distribution.[63] In protecting themselves first and depriving other countries of such advantages and, particularly low- and middle-income countries, of access to vaccines when they initially became available, these governments may have thereby extended the duration of the pandemic.[64] This was not the first occasion on which

---

[55] See Siddhanth Sharma, Nisrine Kawa, and Apoorva Gomber, 'WHO's Allocation Framework for COVAX: Is it Fair?' (2022) 48(7) *Journal of Medical Ethics* 434; Nancy S Jecker, Aaron G Wightman, and Douglas S Diekema, 'Vaccine Ethics: An Ethical Framework for Global Distribution of COVID-19 Vaccines' (2021) 47(5) *Journal of Medical Ethics* 308.

[56] Phelan and others (n 11) 801; Friedman and others (n 37); David P Fidler, 'Vaccine Nationalism's Politics' (2020) 369(6505) *Science* 749 (hereafter Fidler, 'Vaccine Nationalism').

[57] Phelan and others (n 11) 800–801.

[58] Editorial (n 7).

[59] Phelan and others (n 11) 800–801; Friedman and others (n 37); Fidler, 'Vaccine Nationalism' (n 56).

[60] Phelan and others (n 11) 801.

[61] ibid 800; Friedman and others (n 37).

[62] Nickerson and Herder (n 3) 597–99.

[63] Phelan and others (n 11) 801; Nickerson and Herder (n 3) 591–92, 599–600; Gostin, Karim, and Meier (n 2) 623.

[64] Phelan and others (n 11) 800.

such a phenomenon occurred. During the 2009 H1N1 pandemic, governments of high-income countries similarly purchased most of the supply of vaccine doses in advance before they became widely available.[65]

Another initiative that was developed during the COVID-19 pandemic to improve equitable access to vaccines may nonetheless have similarly prioritized the needs of one region at the expense of people living in other areas. In June 2020, Italy, France, Germany, and the Netherlands created the 'Inclusive Vaccines Alliance' to encourage pharmaceutical companies to manufacture COVID-19 vaccines in Europe and supply them at affordable prices to European Union Member States.[66] On their behalf, the European Commission entered into advance purchase agreements (financed by the 'Emergency Support Instrument', a fund that enables the European Union to support its Member States when a crisis reaches the point of having an exceptional scale and impact)[67] with at least three pharmaceutical companies that would enable them to purchase vaccine doses at particular prices when they became available 'to be distributed on a population-based pro-rata basis'.[68] Although it was intended that the Alliance would donate some of the vaccine doses it purchased to low- and middle-income countries, it was less than straightforward which countries would obtain them, how many they could obtain, and who would determine the allocation.[69]

COVAX sought to encourage countries that had 'secured sufficient doses' of COVID-19 vaccines and vaccine manufacturers to contribute a 'portion' of their doses to the Facility to 'complement the early doses' that COVAX had procured and 'facilitate their equitable global distribution'.[70] In December 2020, COVAX

---

[65] David P Fidler, 'Negotiating Equitable Access to Influenza Vaccines: Global Health Diplomacy and the Controversies Surrounding Avian Influenza H5N1 and Pandemic Influenza H1N1' (2010) 7(5) *PLoS Medicine* art e1000247; Phelan and others (n 11) 800; Nickerson and Herder (n 3) 599.

[66] Usher (n 45) 1822; Editorial (n 7); Gerardo Fortuna, 'Coalition of Countries Aims to Keep COVID-19 Vaccine Manufacturing in Europe' *Euractiv* (29 June 2020) <www.euractiv.com/section/coronavirus/news/coalition-of-countries-aims-to-keep-covid-19-vaccine-manufacturing-in-europe/> accessed 4 October 2022.

[67] European Commission, 'Emergency Support Instrument' (Fact Sheet, 7 September 2021) <https://ec.europa.eu/echo/what/civil-protection/emergency-support-instrument_en> accessed 11 September 2022 (hereafter EC, 'Emergency Support Instrument').

[68] European Commission, 'EU Strategy for COVID-19 Vaccines' Communication from the Commission COM (2020) 245 final <https://eur-lex.europa.eu/legal-content/EN/TXT/?qid=1597339415327&uri=CELEX:52020DC0245> accessed 11 September 2022 (hereafter EC, 'EU Strategy'); EC, 'Emergency Support Instrument' (n 67); European Commission, 'Coronavirus: The Commission Signs First Contract with AstraZeneca' (Press Release, 27 August 2020) <https://ec.europa.eu/commission/presscorner/detail/en/ip_20_1524> accessed 4 October 2022 (hereafter EC, 'Coronavirus').

[69] Editorial (n 7); EC, 'Coronavirus' (n 68).

[70] COVAX, 'Principles for Sharing COVID-19 Vaccine Doses with COVAX' *Gavi* (3 February 2020) 2 <www.gavi.org/sites/default/files/covid/covax/COVAX_Principles-COVID-19-Vaccine-Doses-COVAX.pdf> accessed 11 September 2022.

published the following 'Principles for Sharing COVID-19 Vaccine Doses with COVAX':

1. Safe and effective: shared doses must be of assured quality with, at a minimum, WHO prequalification/emergency use listing or licensure/authorization from an SRA [stringent regulatory authority]. Vaccine doses could be transferred to countries most rapidly if they are already in the COVAX Portfolio; other vaccines can be considered if they meet WHO's Target Product Profile and the standards set by the Independent Product Group for vaccines in the COVAX portfolio.
2. Early availability: shared doses should be made available as soon as possible and ideally concurrently by the sharing country as it receives vaccines to increase equitable access and have maximum impact. Dose sharing should begin very early in 2021. Doses provided later in 2021 and beyond could still help increase coverage in countries and impact the pandemic.
3. Rapidly deployable: sharing of doses should be signaled as early as possible in the manufacturing process, with the dose-sharing country facilitating authorizations, so that doses are shipped directly from the manufacturer with universal labelling and packaging, allowing rapid deployment and maximizing shelf-life.
4. Unearmarked: to facilitate equitable access and in keeping with COVAX's allocation mechanism, doses should not be earmarked for specific geographies or populations.
5. Substantive quantity: shared doses should be of sufficient and predictable volumes to have a substantive impact in achieving the goals of the Facility.[71]

During 2021, the issue of making vaccines that were surplus to high-income countries' needs available to other countries became politically sensitive,[72] and the concept of 'vaccine justice' emerged as a concern. By late April 2021, more than 80% of the world's available COVID-19 vaccines had been distributed to high-income countries, with just 0.3% of them delivered to low-income countries despite the COVAX initiative.[73] By July 2021, COVAX had obtained commitments directly from manufacturers and dose-sharing countries for 5.1 billion vaccine doses (3.8 billion doses were secured through legally binding contracts with manufacturers).[74] COVAX forecast that it would have 1.2 billion vaccine

---

[71] ibid.
[72] See Sophie Harman, Eugene Richardson, and Parsa Erfani, 'To End COVID-19 We Need Vaccine Justice for Developing Countries Not Outdated Charity' *The Conversation* (21 June 2021) <https://theconversation.com/to-end-covid-19-we-need-vaccine-justice-for-developing-countries-not-outdated-charity-viewpoint-162818> accessed 11 September 2022.
[73] See Sophie Harman and others, 'Global Vaccine Equity Demands Reparative Justice—Not Charity' (2021) *BMJ Global Health* art e006504.
[74] COVAX, 'COVAX Global Supply Forecast' (12 July 2021) <www.gavi.org/sites/default/files/covid/covax/COVAX-Supply-Forecast.pdf> accessed 4 October 2022.

doses available for supply to the 92 countries of the Gavi COVAX Advance Market Commitment by the end of 2021, corresponding to 40% coverage of Advance Market Commitment adult populations (excluding India).[75] By the end of 2021 only 9% of people in Africa had been fully vaccinated against the virus, WHO targets had been comprehensively missed, and there was a troubling incidence of vaccine hesitancy.[76] An assessment by WHO showed in October 2021 that only 14.2% (about one in seven) COVID-19 infections were being detected in Africa and WHO observed that:

> vaccination rates remain low, with only 30% of the continent's 54 nations having fully vaccinated 10% of their population against the disease—compared with almost 90% of high-income countries. Meanwhile, just under half of the African countries that have received COVID-19 vaccines have fully vaccinated just 2% or less of their populations.[77]

By 28 October 2021, just five African countries, less than 10% of Africa's 54 nations, were projected to hit the end-of-year target of fully vaccinating 40% of their people.[78] Moreover, Africa had a higher mortality rate from COVID-19 than Asia, Europe, Australia, and North and South America, which was associated, unsurprisingly, with a range of factors, including the high prevalence of co-morbidities of HIV/AIDS, diabetes, chronic liver disease, and organ dysfunction on that continent.[79] The low vaccination rate in Africa increased the potential for the emergence of new mutations of COVID-19, which in due course could affect the whole world.[80]

---

[75] ibid.
[76] See Peter Mwai, 'Covid-19 Vaccinations: African Nations Miss WHO Target' *BBC News* (31 December 2021) <https://www.bbc.com/news/56100076> accessed 19 May 2022; AbdulAzeez A Anjorin and others, 'Will Africans Take COVID-19 Vaccination?' (2021) 16(12) *PLoS One* art e0260575.
[77] World Health Organization Africa, 'Six in Seven COVID-19 Infections Go Undetected in Africa' (14 October 2021) <www.afro.who.int/news/six-seven-covid-19-infections-go-undetected-africa> accessed 11 September 2022. See too Sara Jerving, 'The Long Road Ahead for COVID-19 Vaccination in Africa' (2021) 398(10303) *Lancet* 827; Catherine Kyobutungi, 'Want to Know About Vaccine Rollouts in Africa? Click on a Country Here and Find Out' *The Conversation* (29 September 2021) <theconversation.com/want-to-know-about-vaccine-rollouts-in-africa-click-on-a-country-here-and-find-out-168621> accessed 11 September 2022. See too Jean B Nachega, 'Scaling Up Covid-19 Vaccination in Africa—Lessons from the HIV Pandemic' (2021) 385(3) *New England Journal of Medicine* 196.
[78] World Health Organization Africa, 'Less than 10% of African Countries to Hit Key COVID-19 Vaccination Goal' (28 October 2021) <https://www.afro.who.int/news/less-10-african-countries-hit-key-covid-19-vaccination-goal> accessed 11 September 2022.
[79] African COVID-19 Critical Care Outcomes Study Investigators, 'Patient Care and Clinical Outcomes for Patients with COVID-19 Infection Admitted to African High-care or Intensive Care Units (ACCCOS): A Multicentre, Prospective, Observational Cohort Study' (2021) 397(10288) *Lancet* 1885.
[80] See Ed Rybicki and others, 'How the Coronavirus Mutates and What This Means for the Future of COVID-19' *The Conversation* (17 February 2021) <https://theconversation.com/how-the-coronavirus-mutates-and-what-this-means-for-the-future-of-covid-19-154499?> accessed 11 September 2022.

Sophie Harman and her co-authors identified three limited approaches that were being taken to address vaccine distribution inequity during the pandemic: 'bilateral charity, multilateral charity, and temporary waivers or suspensions of intellectual property'.[81] The first—'bilateral charity'—involved states with excess vaccines sharing them with low- and middle-income countries. However, these authors argued that such arrangements left the recipients beholden to the largesse of donors in terms of both timing of distribution of vaccines and conditions that might be attached to the donations. In using the term 'multilateral charity', Harman and her co-authors were referring to the COVAX initiative about which they expressed reservations because of its limited funding and problems in relation to supply chains. They directed their main criticisms of the COVAX scheme towards rich countries and pharmaceutical companies that they claimed used it as a 'shield' against requests for intellectual property waivers (discussed in Section V), and they argued that such waivers were fundamental to the achievement of vaccine justice:

> Vaccine justice starts with moving beyond aid models of vaccine donation, in which poorer countries are gifted vaccine leftovers. It demands rapidly achieving global consensus for the IP waiver, democratising vaccine IP and know-how and supporting low-income and middle-income countries to build manufacturing capacity for this pandemic *and the next*. These steps can mark the start of a reparative justice movement in global health that demands we confront and overturn colonial legacies that continue to devastate the health of low- and middle-income countries.[82]

The 'People's Vaccine Alliance'—'a coalition of organisations and activities united under a common aim of campaigning for a "people's vaccine"' for COVID-19—also criticized COVAX for its alleged failure to use its 'purchasing power' to pressure corporations into sharing the 'science, knowledge and technology behind their vaccines, which could lead to scaled up production'.[83] It also expressed concern about the potential for COVAX to consider a tiered pricing model, which would have the result that many middle-income countries might not be able to afford COVID-19 vaccines or would be forced deeper into debt. It contended that for COVAX to succeed, it needed to:

- Be transparent about decision-making
- Publish the deals it makes with pharmaceutical companies
- Meaningfully involve developing country governments and civil society in decision-making

---

[81] Harman and others (n 73).
[82] ibid.
[83] The People's Vaccine, 'FAQ' <https://peoplesvaccine.org/faq/> accessed 11 September 2022.

- Ensure maximum production of vaccine doses by pushing pharmaceutical companies and research institutions to share the science, technology and know-how behind their vaccines with the WHO COVID-19 Technology Access Pool (C-TAP)
- Secure low and transparent vaccine prices
- Ensure equitable distribution of doses according to the WHO's equitable allocation framework.[84]

The COVID-19 Technology Access Pool (C-TAP) was another WHO initiative during the pandemic that was intended to facilitate timely, equitable, and affordable access to COVID-19 health products by boosting their supply. It aimed to provide:

a global one-stop shop for developers of COVID-19 therapeutics, diagnostics, vaccines, and other health products to share their intellectual property, knowledge, and data, with quality assured manufacturers through public health-driven voluntary, non-exclusive and transparent licenses.[85]

C-TAP was launched by WHO, in partnership with the government of Costa Rica under a global Solidarity Call to Action.[86] Uptake was slow.[87]

Ironically, by mid- to late-2021, despite the lack of equitable access to COVID-19 vaccines globally, some countries' stores of vaccines remained unused close to their expiry dates. For instance, in late July 2021, states within the United States were reported to have around 26 million unused doses of COVID-19 vaccines, including a significant number of Pfizer doses that were due to expire in August 2021. Although in some cases unused doses were distributed to low- and middle-income countries, they were often unable to administer them prior to the expiry of their use-by-dates. For instance, on 26 March 2021, Malawi, a country of 18 million people with a high COVID-19 infection rate, acquired 102,000 doses of the AstraZeneca vaccine through the African Union. However, the expiry date on the labels was 13 April so all doses that could not be administered in time were destroyed with the government explaining that it needed to reassure the community that it was not administering out-of-date vaccines.[88] As Jane Feinmann put it, this

---

[84] ibid.

[85] World Health Organization, 'WHO COVID-19 Technology Access Pool' <https://www.who.int/initiatives/covid-19-technology-access-pool> accessed 7 March 2022 (hereafter WHO, 'COVID-19 Technology Access Pool').

[86] World Health Organization, 'Solidarity Call to Action' <www.who.int/initiatives/covid-19-technology-access-pool/solidarity-call-to-action> accessed 11 September 2022 (hereafter WHO, 'Solidarity Call to Action').

[87] See Ed Silverman, 'The WHO Launched a Voluntary Covid-19 Product Pool. What Happens Next?' *Stat* (29 May 2020) <www.statnews.com/pharmalot/2020/05/29/who-covid19-coronavirus-patents/> accessed 11 September 2022.

[88] See Rhoda Odhiambo, 'Malawi Burns Thousands of Expired AstraZeneca Covid-19 Vaccine Doses' *BBC News* (19 May 2021) <www.bbc.com/news/world-africa-57168841> accessed 11 September 2022.

problem threatened to discourage wealthy countries from making donations to COVAX, and exacerbated the offensive impression that it was 'giving leftovers to the needy'.[89]

In response, WHO issued guidance on using COVID-19 vaccines before their expiry dates, which urged national programmes to 'maintain focus on the primary objectives of COVID-19 vaccination in a supply-constrained situation' and 'ensure equitable distribution' of the vaccines.[90] It recommended using 'monitoring data to estimate capacity to utilize vaccines' before they expired and paying close attention to the reasons for slow utilization of vaccines, namely: the limitation of the vaccine rollout to certain geographic or administrative areas within a country and on an inadequate scale; an inadequate number of vaccination sites; and insufficient planning and commitment of resources, 'sub-optimal implementation of delivery strategies, or vaccine hesitancy among priority target groups'.[91] WHO also urged reviews of whether choices made to accelerate utilization were likely to result in consumption of the available vaccine doses before they expired and, if not, the taking of corrective action.[92]

III. Rationing and Allocation of COVID-19 Treatments and Vaccines

Scarcity of key therapeutic resources in some countries inhibited their capacity to respond adequately and safely to the pandemic. There were shortages initially of personal protective equipment (PPE)[93] and then of COVID-19 treatments, including ventilators,[94] and later of vaccines.[95] As a consequence, governments, policy-makers, health professionals, and hospitals were compelled to make difficult decisions about how to allocate their limited resources.[96] This chapter

---

[89] Jane Feinmann, 'How the World is (Not) Handling Surplus Doses and Expiring Vaccines' (2021) 374 *British Medical Journal* art n2062.

[90] World Health Organization, 'Guidance on Utilization of COVID-19 Vaccines Before the Date of Expiry' (Scientific Brief, 19 July 2021) <www.who.int/publications/i/item/guidance-on-utilization-of-covid-19-vaccines-before-the-date-of-expiry> accessed 11 September 2022.

[91] ibid.

[92] ibid.

[93] See Jennifer Cohen and Yana van der Meulen Rodgers, 'Contributing Factors to Personal Protective Equipment Shortages during the COVID-19 Pandemic' (2020) 141 *Preventive Medicine* art 106263; Talha Burki, 'Global Shortage of Personal Protective Equipment' (2020) 20(7) *Lancet Infectious Diseases* 785.

[94] See Megan L Ranney, Valerie Griffeth, and Ashish K Jha, 'Critical Supply Shortages—The Need for Ventilators and Personal Protective Equipment during the COVID-19 Pandemic' (2020) 382(18) *New England Journal of Medicine* e41(1).

[95] See Anne Moore, 'COVID Vaccines: Why Waiving Patents Won't Fix Global Shortage—Scientist Explains' *The Conversation* (4 May 2021) <https://theconversation.com/covid-vaccines-why-waiving-patents-wont-fix-global-shortage-scientist-explains-158643> accessed 11 September 2022.

[96] Angus Dawson and others, 'An Ethics Framework for Making Resource Allocation Decisions within Clinical Care: Responding to COVID-19' (2020) 17(4) *Journal of Bioethical Inquiry* 749; Kristina Orfali, 'What Triage Issues Reveal: Ethics in the COVID-19 Pandemic in Italy and France' (2020) 17(4)

concentrates on these issues insofar as they arose in respect of COVID-19 treatments and vaccines.

Existing guidelines, policies, and protocols were relied upon or adapted, and new ones created to assist decision-makers in rationing COVID-19 treatments and vaccines, and determining the priority in which different populations within countries and internationally would receive them.[97] The ethical implications of those decisions have been the subject of considerable debate, which is beyond the scope of this book. Yet they also raised important legal issues, as they engaged the human rights to life, health, and enjoyment of the benefits of scientific progress, and the exercise of those rights without discrimination, which are protected in domestic and international law.[98]

A. Rationing of Treatments

In many countries in the early phases of the COVID-19 pandemic, shortages of critical care equipment[99] and facilities to provide respiratory support to the approximately 2.5% of patients who required them highlighted the need for triage protocols for allocation of ventilators.[100] The issue was both ethical and legal.[101] The most problematic form of medical care during the COVID-19 pandemic was the use of ventilators, and the most confronting aspect of their use was their withdrawal from patients who needed them.[102] These challenges were summarized in an early article published in *The Lancet Respiratory Medicine*:

> Existing ventilator triage guidelines facilitate ventilator allocation on the basis of illness severity, giving priority to the sickest patients with a reasonable chance of a desired outcome. More controversially, priority might be given to certain patient

---

Journal of Bioethical Inquiry 675; Jackie L Scully, 'Disability, Disablism, and COVID-19 Pandemic Triage' (2020) 17(4) *Journal of Bioethical Inquiry* 601, 601.

[97] Scully (n 96); Deborah Hellman and Kate M Nicholson, 'Rationing and Disability: The Civil Rights and Wrongs of Clinical Triage Protocols' (2020) 78(4) *Washington and Lee Law Review* 3; Dawson and others (n 96) 749; Orfali (n 675); C de V Castelyn and others, 'Resource Allocation During COVID-19: A Focus on Vulnerable Populations' (2020) 13(2) *South African Journal of Bioethics* 83, 83.

[98] Kathleen Liddell and others, 'Who Gets the Ventilator? Important Legal Rights in a Pandemic' (2020) 46(7) *Journal of Medical Ethics* 421, 423; Bo Chen and Donna Marie McNamara, 'Disability Discrimination, Medical Rationing and COVID-19' (2020) 12(4) *Asian Bioethics Review* 511, 511–12; Hellman and Nicholson (n 97) 3.

[99] See Ranney, Griffeth, and Jha (n 94).

[100] Liddell and others (n 98) 421.

[101] See eg Michelle A Gunn and Fiona J McDonald, 'COVID-19, Rationing and the Right to Health: Can Patients Bring Legal Actions if They are Denied Access to Care?' (2021) 214(5) *Medical Journal of Australia* 207.

[102] Robert Truog, Christine Mitchell, and George Q Daley, 'The Toughest Triage—Allocating Ventilators in a Pandemic' (2020) 382 *New England Journal of Medicine* 1973, 1973.

populations, such as younger patients, with a higher likelihood of recovery and maximisation of life-years saved. Health-care providers with COVID-19 might also be prioritised on the basis of their role in treating patients affected by the pandemic.[103]

Developing criteria to determine which patients' needs should be met was challenging as patients could require ventilation for up to three weeks and around half of those who obtained ventilation might die.[104] Ezekiel Emanuel and his co-authors noted that previous proposals for allocating resources in public health crises had identified four fundamental values that should guide decision-making about allocation of resources during a pandemic: 'maximizing the benefits produced by scarce resources, treating people equally, promoting and rewarding instrumental value, and giving priority to the worst off'.[105] They argued that the most important consideration should be maximizing benefits in discharging scarce resources, having regard to the objectives of saving as many lives and the most years of life as possible. Controversially, they contended that:

> Because young, severely ill patients will often comprise many of those who are sick but could recover with treatment, this operationalization also has the effect of giving priority to those who are worst off in the sense of being at risk of dying young and not having a full life.
> Because maximizing benefits is paramount in a pandemic, we believe that removing a patient from a ventilator or an ICU bed to provide it to others in need is also justifiable and that patients should be made aware of this possibility at admission.[106]

Emanuel and his co-authors also urged that, because of their instrumental value to the community, critical interventions—testing, PPE, intensive care unit (ICU) beds, ventilators, therapeutics, and vaccines—should be allocated first to frontline healthcare workers and others who care for ill patients and who keep critical infrastructure operating, and particularly workers who face a high risk of infection and whose training makes them difficult to replace. However, for patients with similar prognoses to one another, they contended that the principle that should operate to determine who received scarce resources should be equality, and that it should

---

[103] Max M Feinstein and others, 'Considerations for Ventilator Triage During the COVID-19 Pandemic' (2020) 8(6) *Lancet Respiratory Medicine* art e53.

[104] Liddell and others (n 98) 421; Chen and McNamara (n 98) 514.

[105] Ezekiel J Emanuel and others, 'Fair Allocation of Scarce Medical Resources in the Time of Covid-19' (2021) 382 *New England Journal of Medicine* 2049, 2051.

[106] ibid 2052. For a contrasting view, including in relation to withdrawing life support from one patient and transferring it to another, see Douglas B White and Bernard Lo, 'A Framework for Rationing Ventilators and Critical Care Beds During the COVID-19 Pandemic' (2020) 323(18) *Journal of the American Medical Association* 1773.

be applied by random allocation of resources, such as through a lottery, rather than pursuant to a first-come, first-served allocation process.[107] Donna Chen and her co-authors engaged with the argument in relation to healthcare workers and considered that instrumental justifications are insufficient to override the moral commitment to value lives equally. They also argued that institutional policies prioritizing healthcare workers over other patients violate other ethical norms, including the commitment to put patients first, and that such decisions could engender or deepen existing distrust of the clinicians, hospitals, and health systems where such policies are instituted, even if they are never invoked.[108]

While in the early phase of the COVID-19 pandemic, most countries did allocate scarce treatments first to healthcare workers and also older people, especially those in residential care,[109] the emergence of the Delta variant necessitated recalibration of this prioritization of which patients initially required protection. For instance, at that time, a new profile emerged in Australia of the patients who most required COVID-19 treatments. In the state of New South Wales, people aged 30–49 represented the highest number of COVID-19 hospitalizations in June to July 2021,[110] and in the state of Victoria, close to 50% of people admitted with COVID-19 to ICUs from 3 August to 17 September 2021 were aged 40 or younger.[111] This may have been a product of the greater protection of older people from the virus, including through their high vaccination rate, but also the growing willingness of younger people to be tested for COVID-19.[112] Although older persons and those who were immunocompromised remained most at risk, the profile of those who contracted COVID-19 changed and the number of persons under 40 who were hospitalized increased significantly.

Few triage policies recommended a lottery system for deciding who should receive ventilation during the COVID-19 pandemic, which would have reflected an egalitarian approach of treating all patients equally.[113] However, influenced by the utilitarian objective of achieving the greatest good for the greatest number, many such policies endorsed prioritizing for treatment those patients who were most

---

[107] Emanuel and others (n 105) 2052–53.

[108] Donna Chen and others, 'Who Will Receive the Last Ventilator: Why COVID-19 Policies Should Not Prioritise Healthcare Workers' (2021) 47(9) *Journal of Medical Ethics* 599.

[109] Víctor M Becerra-Muñoz and others, 'Clinical Profile and Predictors of In-hospital Mortality among Older Patients Hospitalised for COVID-19' (2021) 50(2) *Age and Ageing* 326.

[110] See Peter Wark, 'Younger Adults Can Get Very Sick from COVID Too. Here's What the Data Tell Us' *The Conversation* (6 August 2021) <https://theconversation.com/younger-adults-can-get-very-sick-and-die-from-covid-too-heres-what-the-data-tell-us-165250> accessed 20 September 2021; Aisha Dow, 'The Face of the COVID Pandemic Has Fundamentally Changed in Victoria' *The Age* (19 September 2021) <www.theage.com.au/national/victoria/the-face-of-the-covid-pandemic-has-fundamentally-changed-in-victoria-20210918-p58ssw.html> accessed 4 October 2022.

[111] Dow (n 110).

[112] See Jennifer Abbasi, 'Younger Adults Caught in COVID-19 Crosshairs as Demographics Shift' (2020) 324(21) *Journal of the American Medical Association* 2141.

[113] Julian Savulescu, James Cameron, and Dominic Wilkinson, 'Equality or Utility? Ethics and Law of Rationing Ventilators' (2020) 125(1) *British Journal of Anaesthesia* 10, 10.

likely to survive, in order to save the most lives.[114] Some commentators urged the use of triage teams, with advice from hospital ethics committees, to make such decisions.[115]

This ground for allocating scarce therapeutic resources is not generally regarded as contravening human rights law.[116] Yet, in the context of the COVID-19 pandemic, concerns were raised that triage protocols did not encourage assessing each individual's likelihood of survival following ventilation, but rather suggested that certain characteristics of patients, such as their age or capacity, should be relied upon as the sole determinants of their chances of living and thus of decisions for rationing ventilators.[117] Implementing such policies risked breaching anti-discrimination laws; while the aim of maximizing benefits from limited resources was legitimate, reference to those traits was potentially disproportionate to and unnecessary to achieve it.[118]

In addition, rationing decisions that were based on patients' health status had the potential to lead to denial of treatment to people whose poorer prospects of positive health outcomes were attributable to socio-economic factors, thereby further entrenching inequities.[119] For instance, it was feared that the Canadian Medical Association's guidance framework, which recommended that triage decisions be based on clinical predictions of mortality and prioritize those with 'reasonable life expectancy', would disproportionately affect marginalized populations such as the homeless, Indigenous people, and refugees.[120] United Nations human rights experts, including human rights rapporteurs, issued a pointed statement confirming that 'everyone ... has the right to life-saving interventions', 'scarcity of resources ... should never be a justification to discriminate against certain groups of patients', and that 'states must take additional social protection measures so that their support reaches those who are at most risk of being disproportionately affected by the crisis' (such as 'people with disabilities, older persons, minority communities, indigenous peoples ... homeless people, migrants and refugees').[121]

---

[114] Savulescu, Cameron, and Wilkinson (n 113) 11–13; Chen and McNamara (n 98) 512; Hellman and Nicholson (n 97) 9–10.

[115] Feinstein and others (n 103); Douglas B White and others, 'Who Should Receive Life Support During a Public Health Emergency? Using Ethical Principles to Improve Allocation Decisions' (2009) 150(2) *Annals of Internal Medicine* 132.

[116] Joseph (n 32) 266. See *Soobramoney v Minister of Health, KwaZulu-Natal* [1997] ZACC 17; 1998 (1) SA 765 where the South African Constitutional Court found that hospitals did not infringe the right to health where they made decisions regarding rationing of limited therapeutic resources based upon whether an individual's health condition could be treated. See also *R v Cambridge Health Authority, ex parte B* [1995] 2 All ER 129; Savulescu, Cameron, and Wilkinson (n 113) 12.

[117] Savulescu, Cameron, and Wilkinson (n 113) 12.

[118] ibid; Liddell and others (n 98); see also Chapter 7.

[119] Liddell and others (n 98) 422; Dawson and others (n 96) 751.

[120] Trudo Lemmens and Roxanne Mykitiuk, 'Disability Rights Concerns and Clinical Triage Protocol Development During the COVID-19 Pandemic' (2020) 40(4) *Health Law in Canada* 103, 106–7.

[121] United Nations Office of the High Commissioner for Human Rights, 'No Exceptions with COVID-19: "Everyone has the Right to Life-Saving Interventions"—UN Experts Say' (26 March 2020) <www.ohchr.org/EN/NewsEvents/Pages/DisplayNews.aspx?NewsID=25746&LangID=E> accessed 11 September 2022.

That advice was promulgated in March 2020 following the release of controversial guidelines by the Italian College of Anesthesia, Analgesia, Resuscitation and Intensive Care (SIAARTI) in response to the lack of triage policies in northern Italy (the first area in the West to confront ventilator shortages during the pandemic).[122] These guidelines recommended that 'patients with the highest chance of therapeutic success ... retain access to intensive care' and, if required, health professionals should 'establish an age limit for access to intensive care', potentially excluding people over a certain age.[123] Around this time, Italian hospitals began lowering the age at which patients could access ventilators (from 80 to 75), as demand for them surged.[124] The guidelines also suggested that health professionals might need to refuse to treat patients with co-morbid health conditions who could be more likely to die or require longer treatment.[125]

The 'COVID-19 Rapid Guidance' that the United Kingdom's National Institute for Health and Care Excellence (NICE) published (after the government did not develop its proposed national COVID-19 triage policy) was the subject of similar criticism.[126] In its first iteration, this guidance suggested using a 'Clinical Frailty Scale' (CFS) to ascertain which patients were 'at increased risk of poor outcomes' and might 'not benefit from critical care interventions', and thus to triage COVID-19 patients' admission to intensive care.[127] The CFS was created to apply to elderly patients and its criteria pertaining to ability to perform daily activities could be irrelevant to the likelihood of COVID-19 patients' survival following ventilation.[128] Moreover, assessments based on patients' frailty had the potential to discriminate against older people and those with disabilities, who might be evaluated as being especially frail.[129] The United Nations Office of the High Commissioner for Human Rights (OHCHR) observed that 'triage guidelines for allocation of scarce resources with exclusion criteria based on ... "frailty"' 'reveal medical bias against persons with disabilities concerning their quality of life and social value' and contribute to the 'greater inequalities' they face 'in accessing healthcare'.[130]

NICE amended its guidance so that assessments of COVID-19 patients' likelihood of survival would determine triage decisions,[131] but recommended that the

---

[122] Orfali (n 96) 676–77; Yascha Mounk, 'The Extraordinary Decisions Facing Italian Doctors' *The Atlantic* (12 March 2020) <www.theatlantic.com/ideas/archive/2020/03/who-gets-hospital-bed/607807/> accessed 11 September 2022.
[123] Mounk (n 122); Orfali (n 96) 677.
[124] Orfali (n 96) 677.
[125] Mounk (n 122).
[126] Liddell and others (n 98) 421; Savulescu, Cameron, and Wilkinson (n 113) 10.
[127] Scully (n 96) 604; Liddell and others (n 98) 421.
[128] Scully (n 96) 604.
[129] ibid; Savulescu, Cameron, and Wilkinson (n 113) 12–13.
[130] United Nations Office of the High Commissioner for Human Rights, 'COVID-19 and the Rights of Persons with Disabilities: Guidance' (29 April 2020) <www.ohchr.org/Documents/Issues/Disability/COVID-19_and_The_Rights_of_Persons_with_Disabilities.pdf> accessed 11 September 2022 (hereafter OHCHR, 'COVID-19 and the Rights of Persons with Disabilities').
[131] Scully (n 96) 604; Savulescu, Cameron, and Wilkinson (n 113) 10.

CFS should not inform them where patients were under 65 years of age and/or had a stable disability, and that 'assessments should be individualized and holistic'.[132] The guidance did not advise specifically on rationing ventilators among patients admitted to intensive care.[133] Leaving this evaluation to the discretion of doctors, hospitals, and National Health Service Clinical Commissioning Groups (which manage health services) created a risk of decision-making about withholding and withdrawing ventilation that was inconsistent, disproportionate, discriminatory, and arbitrary, and thus contravened relevant laws.[134]

In the United States, too, the Department of Health and Human Services' Office for Civil Rights received complaints that 'crisis standards of care' adopted by some states' hospitals and agencies during the pandemic breached disability discrimination laws.[135] For instance, Alabama's Crisis Standards of Care (which were subsequently withdrawn) permitted denial of ventilation to people with intellectual disabilities, seemingly due to the inaccurate and discriminatory presumption that they were less likely to benefit from this treatment.[136] Disability Rights Washington contended that application of the Washington State Department of Health's advice to triage COVID-19 patients based on 'loss of reserves in energy, physical ability, cognition and general health' could discriminate against older persons, those with disabilities, and/or those with co-morbid health conditions.[137] The Office for Civil Rights issued a bulletin confirming that:

> persons with disabilities should not be denied medical care on the basis of stereotypes, assessments of quality of life, or judgments about a person's relative "worth" based on the presence or absence of disabilities or age. Decisions ... concerning whether an individual is a candidate for treatment should be based on an individualized assessment of the patient based on the best available objective medical evidence.[138]

In the face of various countries' potentially discriminatory guidelines, the OHCHR endorsed the Bioethics Committee of the San Marino Republic's COVID-19 guidance that 'correct application of triage' involves 'respecting every human life, based on the criteria of clinical appropriateness and proportionality of the treatments'.[139] That guidance also stated that 'other selection criteria, such

---

[132] Scully (n 96) 604; Savulescu, Cameron, and Wilkinson (n 113) 10–11, 13.
[133] Liddell and others (n 98) 421.
[134] ibid 421–24.
[135] Samuel R Bagenstos, 'Who Gets the Ventilator? Disability Discrimination in COVID-19 Medical-Rationing Protocols' (2020) 130 *Yale Law Journal Forum* 1, 2–3.
[136] ibid 2; Scully (n 96) 602.
[137] Chen and McNamara (n 98) 513.
[138] HHS Office for Civil Rights in Action, 'Civil Rights, HIPAA, and the Coronavirus Disease 2019 (COVID-19)' (Bulletin, 28 March 2020) 1 <www.hhs.gov/sites/default/files/ocr-bulletin-3-28-20.pdf> accessed 11 September 2022; Hellman and Nicholson (n 97) 3.
[139] OHCHR, 'COVID-19 and the Rights of Persons with Disabilities' (n 130); Chen and McNamara (n 98) 515–16.

as age, gender, social or ethnic affiliation, disability, is ethically unacceptable, as it would implement a ranking of lives only apparently more or less worthy of being lived, constituting an unacceptable violation of human rights'.[140] However, a consequence of such guidance is that few ethical and clinical reference points remain for clinicians' decision-making about how to allocate scarce therapeutic resources.

B. Allocation of Vaccines

Protocols, policies, and frameworks that guided decisions about the priority in which COVID-19 vaccines were administered to various populations within countries proved to be comparatively uncontentious. Seeking to pre-empt decision-making that was discriminatory or lacked a sound ethical basis, WHO's Strategic Advisory Group of Experts on Immunization articulated values and ethical considerations that it maintained should inform decisions about allocating COVID-19 vaccines after regulatory authorities approved them, but when their supply was still limited.[141] The 'overarching goal' of its 'Values Framework' was to treat these vaccines as a 'global public good' and it set out six core principles 'to guide distribution', which it translated into objectives and then into priority groups for vaccination.[142]

The recommendation of the Values Framework to prioritize vaccination of 'older adults' and 'groups with comorbidities' was inverse to the approach often taken in allocating ventilators during the initial phase of the pandemic.[143] This suggestion aligned with the principle of 'human well-being' and fulfilled its associated objective of lowering 'deaths and disease burden' from COVID-19.[144] The Values Framework also suggested prioritizing vaccination of 'health and other essential workers' to achieve this aim, as well as the goal of '[protecting] those who bear significant additional risks and burdens of COVID-19 to safeguard the welfare of others' (which is aligned to the principle of 'reciprocity').[145] It was recognized that these people had a heightened risk of contracting COVID-19 (for instance, from patients) and transmitting the disease to vulnerable people. Further, their good health was critical to ensuring they could continue to help others.[146] To address the principle of 'national equity', the Values Framework articulated the objective of

---

[140] OHCHR, 'COVID-19 and the Rights of Persons with Disabilities' (n 130); Chen and McNamara (98) 515–16.
[141] World Health Organization, 'Coronavirus Disease (COVID-19): Vaccine Access and Allocation' (Q&A, 12 December 2020) <www.who.int/news-room/q-a-detail/coronavirus-disease-(covid-19)-vaccine-access-and-allocation> accessed 11 September 2022; WHO, 'SAGE' (n 34).
[142] WHO, 'SAGE' (n 34).
[143] ibid 10.
[144] ibid.
[145] ibid 4, 7, 10–11.
[146] Alberto Giubilini, Julian Savulescu, and Dominic Wilkinson, 'COVID-19 Vaccine: Vaccinate the Young to Protect the Old?' (2020) 7(1) *Journal of Law and the Biosciences* art lsaa050, 3.

ensuring 'vaccine prioritization within countries takes into account the vulnerabilities, risks and needs of groups who, because of underlying societal, geographic or biomedical factors, are at risk of experiencing greater burdens' from COVID-19, and suggested that 'socially disadvantaged populations', including 'people living in poverty', should have priority access to vaccines.[147]

Initial allocations of COVID-19 vaccines in many countries were largely consistent with the Values Framework. In the United Kingdom, one of the first countries to immunize against COVID-19, the Joint Committee on Vaccination and Immunization (which advises health departments) recommended an initial phase of preventing 'mortality' and maintaining 'health and social care systems' by prioritizing for vaccination 'groups' that, according to epidemiological and other data and mathematical modelling of the impact of vaccination, 'taken together ... represent around 99% of preventable mortality from COVID-19'.[148] The Committee suggested vaccinating people in residential facilities and their carers first, frontline health and social care workers (who were at high risk of contracting COVID-19 and/or transmitting it to vulnerable people and other healthcare staff), and those in older age groups.[149] In addition, the Committee noted that prioritizing vaccination of people who are clinically vulnerable due to underlying health conditions would help to mitigate inequalities stemming from socio-economic factors that Black, Asian, and minority ethnic groups experience and contribute to their increased risk of contracting, and having poor health outcomes from and dying of COVID-19.[150]

Likewise, the United States Centers for Disease Control and Prevention (CDC) recommended that governments distribute the limited vaccine supply in phases that prioritized healthcare staff and long-term care facility residents, followed by frontline essential workers, then older aged people, people with underlying health conditions, and other essential workers.[151] The CDC relied on advice from the Advisory Committee on Immunization Practices, an independent panel of medical and public health experts, which in turn received recommendations, commissioned by the CDC and National Institutes of Health, from the National

---

[147] WHO, 'SAGE' (n 34) 4, 11. Another approach is to prioritize those who are likely to be vectors of the disease: see Rosamond Rhodes, 'Justice in COVID-19 Vaccine Prioritisation: Rethinking the Approach' (2021) 47(9) *Journal of Medical Ethics* 623.

[148] Joint Committee on Vaccination and Immunisation, 'Advice on Priority Groups for COVID-19 Vaccination, 30 December 2020' (Independent Report, 6 January 2021) <www.gov.uk/government/publications/priority-groups-for-coronavirus-covid-19-vaccination-advice-from-the-jcvi-30-december-2020/joint-committee-on-vaccination-and-immunisation-advice-on-priority-groups-for-covid-19-vaccination-30-december-2020#vaccine-priority-groups-advice-on-30-december-2020> accessed 11 September 2022.

[149] ibid.

[150] ibid.

[151] Centers for Disease Control and Prevention, 'CDC's COVID-19 Vaccine Rollout Recommendations' (3 February 2021) <www.cdc.gov/coronavirus/2019-ncov/vaccines/recommendations.html> accessed 11 February 2021.

Academies of Sciences Engineering Medicine (NASEM).[152] NASEM developed the 'Framework for Equitable Allocation of COVID-19 Vaccine',[153] which bears similarities to the Values Framework.[154] It also seeks to maximize societal benefit by lowering morbidity and mortality from COVID-19, protect people from discrimination, and mitigate 'health inequities', including by prioritizing for vaccination certain social groups, such as racial minorities, who face higher risks of contracting, and having severe health outcomes from and dying of COVID-19.[155] To 'complement' such guidelines for allocating vaccines in the United States, public health researchers created an 'online calculator' that could be used to assess people's risk of mortality from COVID-19 (based on factors including their age, health conditions, and ethnicity) and thus identify 'high-risk populations' to prioritize for immunization.[156] However, it became apparent that one group at high risk of contracting and suffering from COVID-19 that did not receive vaccination prioritization in many countries was prisoners.[157] Another was persons with disabilities.[158]

IV. Regulation of COVID-19 Treatments and Vaccines

The chief gatekeepers to public access to medical treatments and vaccines in many countries are authorities that regulate such products and the practice of health professionals who can prescribe and dispense them.[159] During the COVID-19 pandemic, regulatory authorities faced pressure to permit the release of some of those

---

[152] ibid; Harald Schmidt, Lawrence O Gostin, and Michelle A Williams, 'Is it Lawful and Ethical to Prioritize Racial Minorities for COVID-19 Vaccines?' (2020) 324(20) *Journal of the American Medical Association* 2023, 2023.

[153] National Academies of Sciences Engineering Medicine, 'A Framework for Equitable Allocation of Vaccine for the Novel Coronavirus' <www.nationalacademies.org/our-work/a-framework-for-equitable-allocation-of-vaccine-for-the-novel-coronavirus> accessed 4 October 2022.

[154] Schmidt, Gostin, and Williams (n 152) 2023.

[155] National Academies of Sciences Engineering Medicine (n 153) 92–93; Schmidt, Gostin, and Williams (n 152) 2023; Centers for Disease Control and Prevention (n 151).

[156] Annika Weder and Carly Kempler, 'Online COVID-19 Mortality Risk Calculator Could Help Determine Who Should Get Vaccine First' *Johns Hopkins University Hub* (12 December 2020) <https://hub.jhu.edu/2020/12/11/covid-mortality-risk-calculator-nilanjan-chatterjee/?mc_cid=4432da8080&mc_eid=cf81ce4b09>; Jin Jin and others, 'Individual and Community-Level Risk for COVID-19 Mortality in the United States' (2021) 27(2) *Nature Medicine* 264.

[157] See eg Rachel Strodel and others, 'COVID-19 Vaccine Prioritization of Incarcerated People Relative to Other Vulnerable Groups: An Analysis of State Plans' (2021) 16(6) *PLoS ONE* art e0253208.

[158] See Royal Commission into Violence, Abuse, Neglect and Exploitation of People with Disability, *Report on Public Hearing 5: Experiences of People with Disability During the Ongoing COVID-19 Pandemic* (Public Hearing Report, November 2020) <https://disability.royalcommission.gov.au/system/files/2020-11/Report%20-%20Public%20hearing%205%20-%20Experiences%20of%20people%20with%20disability%20during%20the%20ongoing%20COVID-19%20pandemic.pdf> accessed 4 October 2022; Sara Rotenberg, Matthew B Downer, and Jane Cooper, 'Making COVID-19 Vaccinations Accessible for People with Disabilities' (2021) 49(4) *Vaccine* 5727.

[159] Patricia J Zettler, Micah L Berman, and Efthimios Parasidis, 'Drug and Vaccine Development and Access' in Scott Burris and others (eds), *Assessing Legal Responses to COVID-19* (Public Health Law Watch 2020) 164.

medical products to the public as quickly as possible.[160] This pandemic therefore tested their capacity to accelerate and adapt their processes to meet the demands of a public health emergency, while still protecting the public by ensuring that no treatment or vaccine was made widely available unless its safety and effectiveness for use in humans had been established through rigorous scientific testing.[161] Also during the COVID-19 pandemic, authorities needed to combat a proliferation of quackery, false claims, and fraudulent medications.[162]

A. Fraudulent COVID-19 Therapies

During the COVID-19 pandemic, there was a significant incidence of predatory proffering of spurious medications and preventative agents. This was unsurprising in light of the occurrence of a similar phenomenon during previous pandemics, including the 1889–92 'Russian flu' and the 1918–20 'Spanish flu'.[163] As noted in Chapter 2, during the former, Louisa Carlill sued the Carbolic Smoke Ball Company for breach of contract over its spurious claim that its 'smoke ball' was a medical preparation that could prevent those who inhaled its smoke from contracting influenza.[164] The decisions of the High Court of England and the Court of Appeal in that case are often regarded as initiating modern consumer protection law.[165]

During the Spanish flu, those fearful of contracting the influenza and those suffering from its symptoms sought the assistance of orthodox medicine, but conventional medical practitioners had little in their medicine cabinet to assist them. Clinical drug development was in its early stages, few human trials had been conducted, and double-blind, placebo-controlled trials were almost unknown. Anxiety generated commercial opportunities for the entrepreneurial as well as the unscrupulous. Familiar proprietary brands 'bought advertising space alongside quacks and snake oil salesmen, all keen to persuade a desperate public to purchase their wares. Alongside over-the-counter products, frightened families also turned to folk remedies, traditional cures familiar to their heritage'.[166] As the mortality rates from Spanish flu soared, so, too, did the willingness of the community 'to try something, anything, to save themselves and their loved ones from a horrible

---

[160] Dorit R Reiss, 'The COVID-19 Vaccine Dilemma' (2020) 6 *Administrative Law Review Accord* 29, 32.

[161] Jemima Stratford, Emily MacKenzie, and Emma Mockford, 'Balancing Speed and Safety: The Authorisation of COVID-19 Vaccines and Medicines' (2020) 25(2) *Judicial Review* 105, 115, 117.

[162] See Ian Freckelton, 'COVID-19: Fear, Quackery, False Representations and the Law' (2020) 72 *International Journal of Law and Psychiatry* art 101611.

[163] See Catharine Arnold, *Pandemic 1918: The Story of the Deadliest Influenza in History* (Michael O'Mara Books 2018).

[164] *Carlill v Carbolic Smoke Ball Company* [1892] 2 QB 484.

[165] *Carlill v Carbolic Smoke Ball Company* [1893] 1 QB 256.

[166] See Arnold (n 163) 153.

death'.[167] This desperation was met with a proliferation of advertisements in the West for influenza-related remedies: 'from the *Times of London* to the *Washington Post*, page after page was filled with dozens of advertisements for preventive measures and over-the-counter remedies'.[168] A host of alternative healers emerged around the world. Aspirin and drugs such as quinine, known for its utility with malaria, were promoted by entrepreneurial healers, as were arsenic, digitalis, and strychnine concoctions, as well as a variety of alcohol-based remedies. In some countries, people turned to traditional healers or traditional medicines.[169]

The repetition of these phenomena during the COVID-19 pandemic, and propagation of conspiracy theories and misinformation about, and bogus cures for, the virus prompted WHO to respond to these developments early in the pandemic. On 15 February 2020, WHO's Director-General, Dr Tedros Adhanom Ghebreyesus, identified that the world was not 'just fighting an epidemic; we're fighting an infodemic'.[170] WHO published an extensive list of 'myth-busters', endeavouring to counter false information that had been disseminated, which confirmed matters such as that: adding pepper to food and vaccines against pneumonia did not prevent or cure this disease; hot or cold weather, hot baths, and hand-dryers could not kill the virus; 5G networks did not spread COVID-19; ingesting bleach and methanol can be lethal; and ultra-violet lamps do not disinfect skin.[171]

In several countries, regulatory authorities tackled false claims regarding protecting and curing COVID-19. In Australia, the Therapeutic Goods Administration fined: a celebrity chef for claims he made on Facebook that his 'BioCharger' device could be used in relation to the 'Wuhan Coronavirus';[172] a company for alleged misleading advertising about its 'anti-virus activewear';[173] and a deregistered chiropractor for his allegedly false and misleading advertisements that his hyperbaric oxygen chambers could treat COVID-19 (and a variety of other

---

[167] ibid; Fred Andayi, 'How the Spanish Flu Affected Kenya—And its Similarities to Coronavirus' *The Conversation* (22 April 2020) <https://theconversation.com/how-the-spanish-flu-affected-kenya-and-its-similarities-to-coronavirus-136515> accessed 4 October 2022.
[168] Arnold (n 163) 154.
[169] Laura Spinney, *Pale Rider: The Spanish Flu of 1918 and How It Changed the World* (Public Affairs 2017) 125.
[170] World Health Organization, 'Munich Security Conference' (Speech, 15 February 2020) <www.who.int/director-general/speeches/detail/munich-security-conference> accessed 11 September 2022.
[171] World Health Organization, 'Coronavirus Disease (COVID-19) Advice for the Public: Myth Busters' (23 November 2020) <www.who.int/emergencies/diseases/novel-coronavirus-2019/advice-for-public/myth-busters> accessed 11 September 2022.
[172] Therapeutic Goods Administration, 'Pete Evans' Company Fined for Alleged COVID-19 Advertising Breaches' (Media Release and Statement, 24 April 2020) <www.tga.gov.au/media-release/pete-evans-company-fined-alleged-covid-19-advertising-breaches#:~:text=Pete%20Evans'%20company%20fined%20for%20alleged%20COVID%2D19%20advertising%20breaches,-24%20April%202020&text=The%20Therapeutic%20Goods%20Administration%20(TGA,Act%201989%20(the%20Act)> accessed 11 September 2022.
[173] Therapeutic Goods Administration, 'Lorna Jane Fined Almost $40,000 for Alleged Advertising Breaches in Relation to COVID-19 and "Anti-Virus Activewear"' (Media Release and Statement, 17 July 2020) <www.tga.gov.au/media-release/lorna-jane-fined-almost-40000-alleged-advertising-breaches-relation-covid-19-and-anti-virus-activewear> accessed 11 September 2022.

maladies).[174] Similarly, the United States Food and Drug Administration issued many warning letters in relation to misbranded and unapproved products related to COVID-19.[175] It also issued a 'Consumer Update' early in 2021, entitled 'Beware of Fraudulent Coronavirus Tests, Vaccines and Treatments',[176] which stated:

> The FDA is particularly concerned that these deceptive and misleading products might cause Americans to delay or stop appropriate medical treatment, leading to serious and life-threatening harm. It's likely that the products do not do what they claim, and the ingredients in them could cause adverse effects and could interact with, and potentially interfere with, essential medications.

In the United Kingdom, the Medicines and Healthcare products Regulatory Agency (MHRA) issued warnings and advice about such conduct,[177] and a similar approach was adopted in Singapore and Japan.[178]

Concerns were expressed during the pandemic that some groups of scientists were developing, promoting, and administering products they claimed were vaccines for COVID-19, but whose safety and efficacy was not tested using rigorous

---

[174] Therapeutic Goods Administration, 'TGA Initiates Court Proceedings Against Oxymed Australia and Director Malcolm Hooper for Alleged Unlawful Advertising' (Media Release and Statement, 3 September 2020) <www.tga.gov.au/media-release/tga-initiates-court-proceedings-against-oxymed-australia-and-director-malcolm-hooper-alleged-unlawful-advertising> accessed 11 September 2022.

[175] See Katrina A Bramstedt, 'Unicorn Poo and Blessed Waters: COVID-19 Quackery and FDA Warning Letters' (2021) 55(1) *Therapeutic Innovation and Regulatory Science* 239; United States Food and Drug Administration, 'Warning Letter Genesis 2 Church' (8 April 2020) <www.fda.gov/inspections-compliance-enforcement-and-criminal-investigations/warning-letters/genesis-2-church-606459-04082020> accessed 11 September 2022; United States Food and Drug Administration, 'Fraudulent Coronavirus Disease 2019 (COVID-19) Products' (30 September 2021) <www.fda.gov/consumers/health-fraud-scams/fraudulent-coronavirus-disease-2019-covid-19-products> accessed 11 September 2022.

[176] United States Food and Drug Administration, 'Beware of Fraudulent Coronavirus Tests, Vaccines and Treatments' (3 January 2021) <www.fda.gov/consumers/consumer-updates/beware-fraudulent-coronavirus-tests-vaccines-and-treatments> accessed 11 September 2022.

[177] Samuel Lovett, 'Coronavirus: Surge in Fake Treatments Sold Online Spark Warning from UK Authorities' *The Independent* (4 April 2020) <www.independent.co.uk/news/health/coronavirus-fake-cure-treatment-sold-online-latest-a9447496.html> accessed 11 September 2022; Medicines and Healthcare products Regulatory Agency, 'UK Medicines and Medical Devices Regulator Investigating 14 Cases of Fake or Unlicensed COVID-19 Medical Products' (Press Release, 4 April 2020) <www.gov.uk/government/news/uk-medicines-and-medical-devices-regulator-investigating-14-cases-of-fake-or-unlicensed-covid-19-medical-products> accessed 11 September 2022; Medicines and Healthcare products Regulatory Agency, 'Senior Enforcement Advisor at UK Medicines Regulator Warns Against Purchasing Fake or Unlicensed Coronavirus (COVID-19) Medicines' (Press Release, 7 May 2020) <www.gov.uk/government/news/senior-enforcement-advisor-at-uk-medicines-regulator-warns-against-purchasing-fake-or-unlicensed-coronavirus-covid-19-medicines> accessed 11 September 2022.

[178] Yuichiro Kanematsu, 'Ads Touting Quack Coronavirus Cures Rampant in Japan' *Nikkei Asia* (9 June 2020) <https://asia.nikkei.com/Spotlight/Coronavirus/Ads-touting-quack-coronavirus-cures-rampant-in-Japan> accessed 11 September 2022; 'Japan Govt Warns About Online Ads for "Anti-Coronavirus" Goods' *Nippon.com* (11 March 2020) <www.nippon.com/en/news/yjj2020031100921/japan-govt-warns-about-online-ads-for-anti-coronavirus-goods.html> accessed 4 October 2022.

scientific methods or proven.[179] These 'citizen scientists' risked harming themselves and the public.[180] Yet regulatory authorities' jurisdiction to control their activities was unclear. A failure by bodies such as the United States Food and Drug Administration to intervene could result in a lack of protection for the public and also, by conveying the message that standards were lowered, diminish public trust in vaccines whose efficacy had in fact been proven.[181]

B. Fast-tracked Regulatory Approval

Processes undertaken by many regulatory authorities to evaluate carefully proposals to release to the public new medical products or repurpose existing ones are usually lengthy.[182] In order to assess the safety and efficacy of a product for its specified uses, regulators generally review all available evidence in relation to it, including its 'therapeutic indications, contra-indications and adverse reactions', and results of trials (many regulators require new treatments and vaccines to complete successfully all the testing phases outlined in Chapter 11).[183] They must then determine whether standards, often prescribed in legislation, have been met.[184] For instance, before approving use of a medical product, the United States Food and Drug Administration requires 'substantial evidence' of the product's effectiveness,[185] while the United Kingdom's MHRA must be satisfied that the 'therapeutic efficacy of the product ... outweigh[s] the risks' to the public.[186] If a regulator does approve use of a medical product, it often still requires 'phase 4 trials' to be conducted in order to review its long-term safety and efficacy, and will continue to monitor its production to ensure there is no contamination.[187]

Given the escalating hospitalization and death toll from COVID-19, and detrimental social and economic effects of this disease and restrictions implemented to contain its spread, the urgent release to the public of safe and effective treatments and vaccines was a priority.[188] Many regulatory authorities therefore contemplated and/or followed pathways to 'fast-track' their assessment of new COVID-19

---

[179] Christie J Guerrini and others, 'Self-experimentation, Ethics, and Regulation of Vaccines' (2020) 369(6511) *Science* 1570, 1570; Linda J Birkin, Eleftheria Vasileiou, and Helen R Stagg, 'Citizen Science in the Time of COVID-19' (2021) 76(7) *Thorax* 636; Livio Provenzi and Serena Barello, 'The Science of the Future: Establishing a Citizen-Scientists Collaborative Agenda after Covid-19' (2020) 8 *Frontiers in Public Health* art 282.
[180] Guerrini and others (n 179) 1572.
[181] ibid 1570.
[182] See eg Stratford, McKenzie, and Mockford (n 161) 108; Zettler, Berman, and Parasidis (n 159) 163.
[183] Zettler, Berman, and Parasidis (n 159) 163; Reiss (n 160) 34; Stratford, McKenzie, and Mockford (n 161) 108.
[184] Zettler, Berman, and Parasidis (n 159) 163; Reiss (n 160) 34.
[185] Zettler, Berman, and Parasidis (n 159) 163.
[186] Stratford, McKenzie, and Mockford (n 161) 107.
[187] Reiss (n 160) 38–39; Stratford, McKenzie, and Mockford (n 161) 109.
[188] Reiss (n 160) 44–45.

medical products and proposals to repurpose existing ones to treat the virus.[189] In so doing, regulators needed to balance risks associated with taking a long time to approve the use of these products against those inherent in rushing to do so.[190] The latter included the possible release to the community of unsafe or ineffective products, which could harm and kill people and, consequently, undermine public confidence in medical products and regulatory authorities, and discourage people from receiving future treatments and vaccines that could otherwise have prevented further disease outbreaks.[191] Shortcuts that certain governments or regulatory authorities took during this pandemic appeared not to have placed significant weight on these risks. For instance, China and Russia authorized release of vaccines to the public without first publicizing data from phase 3 trials in relation to them.[192]

Other countries embraced existing or created new procedures for responding flexibly and quickly to applications for permission to use medical products, while seeking to maintain appropriate safeguards.[193] Before making their medical products publicly available, developers in the European Union were required to obtain 'marketing authorization' of them from regulators in one or more Member States or from the European Medicines Agency.[194] In April 2020, the European Medicines Agency established a 'Covid-19 Pandemic Task Force' to assist regulators to take 'quick and coordinated regulatory action on the development, authorisation and safety monitoring of treatments and vaccines intended for the treatment and prevention of Covid-19'.[195] The European Medicines Agency promised to provide free, 'rapid scientific advice' to developers about the design of and methods used in their studies.[196]

In addition, the European Medicines Agency proposed to use 'an emergency "rolling review" procedure', whereby the European Medicines Agency's Committee for Medicinal Products for Human Use would evaluate data as they became available during the course of developing treatments or vaccines.[197] The Committee for Medicinal Products for Human Use applied this process in considering the use of remdesivir to treat COVID-19, which enabled it to complete its evaluation earlier than it otherwise would have.[198] The European Medicines Agency also published

---

[189] Wendy Lipworth and others, 'Science at Warp Speed: Medical Research, Publication, and Translation During the COVID-19 Pandemic' (2020) 17(4) *Journal of Bioethical Inquiry* 555, 555.
[190] Stratford, McKenzie, and Mockford (n 161) 115, 117; Reiss (n 160) 30, 32.
[191] Stratford, McKenzie, and Mockford (n 161) 115, 117; Reiss (n 160) 30, 32, 49; Zettler, Berman, and Parasidis (n 159) 166.
[192] Carl Zimmer, Jonathan Corum, and Sui-Lee Wee, 'Coronavirus Vaccine Tracker' *New York Times* (31 January 2021) <www.nytimes.com/interactive/2020/science/coronavirus-vaccine-tracker.html> accessed 1 February 2021.
[193] Stratford, McKenzie, and Mockford (n 161) 111–12; EC, 'EU Strategy' (n 68).
[194] Stratford, McKenzie, and Mockford (n 161) 106–108.
[195] ibid 113.
[196] ibid 114.
[197] ibid.
[198] ibid.

guidance advising that 'applications for a marketing authorisation for products intended for prevention or treatment of Covid-19 will be treated in an expedited manner'.[199] In so doing, it proposed to draw on the 'accelerated assessment procedure' that it is permitted to undertake where a product that is the subject of an application for marketing authorization is 'of major interest from the point of view of public health'.[200] The MHRA similarly advised that it would provide 'expedited scientific advice and rapid reviews of clinical trial applications to support manufacturers and researchers on potential treatments for Covid-19'.[201]

Certain proposed COVID-19 medical products comprised 'genetically modified organisms' (GMOs) and therefore needed to comply with the European Parliament's Directive regarding evaluation of environmental risks associated with clinical trials of such products before testing them.[202] As fulfilling those requirements would delay the trial process, the European Commission recommended 'a Regulation to derogate ... for the period during which COVID-19 is regarded as a public health emergency from certain provisions of the GMO Directive for clinical trials with COVID-19 vaccines' and treatments that 'contain or consist of GMOs'.[203]

During the COVID-19 pandemic, some regulators also drew on their powers to grant temporary permission for use of medical products in a public health emergency where complete information concerning their safety and effectiveness is not yet available, so they are unable to approve their use definitively.[204] For instance, the European Medicines Agency can provide 'conditional' marketing authorization for a product that is subject to ongoing clinical trials where: it is proposed to be used in 'emergency situations in response to public health threats' recognized by WHO and the European Union; the Committee for Medicinal Products for Human Use considers that 'the benefit to public health of the immediate availability on the market of the medicinal product concerned outweighs the risk inherent in the fact that additional data is still required'; and the applicant will probably be able to 'provide comprehensive clinical data in due course'.[205]

The MHRA in the United Kingdom was the first Western regulatory authority to grant temporary authorization of use of a COVID-19 vaccine.[206] On 2 December 2020, it permitted supply (except to pregnant and breastfeeding women) of batches

---

[199] ibid 112.
[200] ibid.
[201] ibid 115.
[202] EC, 'EU Strategy' (n 68).
[203] ibid.
[204] Reiss (n 160) 52–53.
[205] Stratford, McKenzie, and Mockford (n 161) 113; EC, 'EU Strategy' (n 68).
[206] 'Pfizer and BioNTech Achieve First Authorization in the World for a Vaccine to Combat COVID-19' *GlobeNewswire* (2 December 2020) <www.globenewswire.com/news-release/2020/12/02/2138011/0/en/Pfizer-and-BioNTech-Achieve-First-Authorization-in-the-World-for-a-Vaccine-to-Combat-COVID-19.html> accessed 11 September 2022; Zimmer, Corum, and Wee (n 192).

of the vaccine produced by Pfizer and BioNTech.[207] The United Kingdom usually awaits European Medicines Agency approval of a vaccine before distributing it, but its government amended the *Human Medicines Regulations 2012* (UK) so that the MHRA could temporarily authorize COVID-19 vaccines without first obtaining the European Medicines Agency's permission.[208] The MHRA claimed it used the 'rolling review' process described above and relied on preliminary evidence of the vaccine's safety and efficacy,[209] but it lacked information about its interaction with other drugs.[210]

The United States Food and Drug Administration similarly used this mechanism, termed an 'Emergency Use Authorization' in the United States, to address issues arising during the COVID-19 pandemic.[211] The Food and Drug Administration (which is given authority by the *Food, Drug and Cosmetic Act* to oversee the safety of drugs and medical devices) can authorize use of unapproved medical products or unapproved uses of already approved products if the Secretary of the Department of Health and Human Services declares there is a 'public health emergency' and the Food and Drug Administration determines that several statutory preconditions have been met.[212] Those criteria include: the emergence of a 'serious or life-threatening illness' caused by a biological agent; 'reasonable belief that the product may be effective in diagnosing, treating, or preventing the illness or condition ... based on totality of scientific data'; 'the product's known and potential benefits outweigh known and potential risks when used for disease'; and 'there is no adequate approved, available alternative'.[213]

On 4 February 2020, the Secretary of the Department of Health and Human Services issued an emergency declaration for COVID-19.[214] As described in Chapter 11, the United States Food and Drug Administration granted Emergency Use Authorizations in relation to hydroxychloroquine and chloroquine to treat hospitalized patients who could not participate in clinical trials.[215] Nevertheless, the Food and Drug Administration revoked those Emergency Use Authorizations

---

[207] Elisabeth Mahase, 'Vaccinating the UK: How the Covid Vaccine was Approved, and Other Questions Answered' (2020) 371 *British Medical Journal* m4759.

[208] ibid 1.

[209] ibid 1; Zimmer, Corum, and Wee (n 192).

[210] Mahase (n 207) 2.

[211] Reiss (n 160) 52–53.

[212] John D Blum and Jordan Paradise, 'Public Health Preparedness & Response: An Exercise in Administrative Law' (2018) 20 *DePaul Journal of Health Care Law* 2; Reiss (160) 52–53; Zettler, Berman, and Parasidis (n 159) 164; Philip R Krause and Marion F Gruber, 'Emergency Use Authorization of Covid Vaccines—Safety and Efficacy Follow-up Considerations' (2020) 383(19) *New England Journal of Medicine* e107(1).

[213] Reiss (n 160) 52–53; Zettler, Berman, and Parasidis (n 159) 164; Krause and Gruber (n 212) e107(1).

[214] Zettler, Berman, and Parasidis (n 159) 164.

[215] Jennifer Martin and others, 'COVID-19: The Rise and Fall of Hydroxychloroquine' *InSight* (7 September 2020) <https://insightplus.mja.com.au/2020/35/covid-19-the-rise-and-fall-of-hydroxychloroquine/> accessed 4 October 2022; Zettler, Berman, and Parasidis (n 159) 165.

in June and issued guidance against using hydroxychloroquine outside clinical trials, noting its adverse side-effects.[216] This decision was prompted by the publication of the results of research whose validity was ultimately brought into question, as discussed in Chapter 11.[217] However, subsequent high quality research demonstrated that treating COVID-19 patients with hydroxychloroquine provides no clinical benefit and it does not prevent development of the disease.[218]

Emergency Use Authorizations are granted on the basis of available evidence in an emergency and on the understanding that they will be revoked if further evidence emerges confirming that the preconditions for their issue are no longer satisfied or the product is unsafe or ineffective.[219] Yet the revocation of the Emergency Use Authorizations for hydroxychloroquine and chloroquine raised concerns that the United States Food and Drug Administration may have granted them too hastily and in response to political pressure, unnecessarily jeopardizing people's health and lives.[220] On 15 May 2020, President Trump announced the formation of 'Operation Warp Speed', a public-private partnership between various government agencies (including the Department of Health and Human Services and the Food and Drug Administration, which falls within it) and industry representatives to accelerate research, medical product development, and wide distribution of COVID-19 vaccines by January 2021.[221] When the Food and Drug Administration issued these Emergency Use Authorizations, there were very limited data indicating their efficacy in treating COVID-19, and risks associated with their use, including of inducing serious heart arrhythmias, were well known.[222] Moreover, it was asserted that the Food and Drug Administration's Commissioner confirmed that President Trump had 'directed' the Food and Drug Administration to investigate the potential for hydroxychloroquine to treat COVID-19,[223] and the Food and Drug Administration granted the Emergency Use Authorizations just days after

---

[216] Zettler, Berman, and Parasidis (n 159) 165; Elizabeth Y McCuskey, 'FDA in the Time of COVID-19' (2020) 45(3) *Administrative and Regulatory Law News* 7, 9.

[217] Lipworth and others (n 189) 556; Catherine Offord, 'The Surgisphere Scandal: What Went Wrong?' *The Scientist* (1 October 2020) <www.the-scientist.com/features/the-surgisphere-scandal-what-went-wrong--67955> accessed 4 October 2022.

[218] April Jorge, 'Hydroxychloroquine in the Prevention of COVID-19 Mortality' (2021) 3(1) *Lancet Rheumatology* e2, e2–e3; Martin and others (n 215).

[219] Zettler, Berman, and Parasidis (n 159) 165; Itay Moshkovits, 'Emergency Use Authorizations of COVID-19-Related Medical Products' (2022) 182(2) *Journal of the American Medical Association Internal Medicine* 228; Alan Tran and Theodore J Witek Jr, 'The Emergency Use Authorization of Pharmaceuticals: History and Utility During the COVID-19 Pandemic' (2021) 35(4) *Pharmaceutical Medicine* 203; Adarsh Bhimraj and others, 'Therapeutic Emergency Use Authorisations (EUAs) During Pandemics: Double-edged Swords' (2022) 74(9) *Clinical Infectious Diseases* 1686.

[220] Zettler, Berman, and Parasidis (n 159) 165; Reiss (n 160) 8–49.

[221] Lawrence O Gostin and Daniel A Salmon, 'The Dual Epidemics of COVID-19 and Influenza: Vaccine Acceptance, Coverage, and Mandates' (2020) 324(4) *Journal of the American Medical Association* 335, 336; Zettler, Berman, and Parasidis (n 159) 165; Reiss (n 160) 49–50.

[222] Zettler, Berman, and Parasidis (n 159) 165; Martin and others (n 215) 160; Reiss (n 160) 48.

[223] McCuskey (n 216) 8.

President Trump publicly endorsed hydroxychloroquine in press conferences and social media as a possible cure for this disease.[224]

In addition to compromising public safety, fast-tracking release of these treatments, which did not ultimately prove to be safe and effective, had the potential to diminish public confidence and trust in the Food and Drug Administration and other future treatments and vaccines.[225] Initially, it may also have hindered further research if it became more difficult to recruit participants for clinical trials because COVID-19 treatments were already available.[226] Granting an Emergency Use Authorization in relation to a product can give the public the false impression that the Food and Drug Administration has in fact approved it.[227] The issuing of these Emergency Use Authorizations also had the potential to constitute a waste of manufacturing resources and money: it is reported that, following their revocation, the United States' Strategic National Stockpile retained 63 million doses of hydroxychloroquine.[228] Yet the Food and Drug Administration fulfilled its promise to continue assessing emerging data about the treatments after it granted the Emergency Use Authorizations.[229]

In August 2020, the Food and Drug Administration granted an Emergency Use Authorization to permit use of convalescent plasma to treat COVID-19 in hospitalized patients.[230] This therapy involves extracting antibodies to the virus that causes COVID-19 from blood donated by people who have contracted and recovered from COVID-19, and transfusing them into patients with COVID-19, with the aim of assisting their bodies to combat the virus and thereby lower the duration and/or severity of infection.[231] The Food and Drug Administration noted that convalescent plasma 'should not be considered a new standard of care' and

---

[224] Zettler, Berman, and Parasidis (n 159) 165; Martin and others (n 215).

[225] Nicole Lurie, Joshua M Sharfstein, and Jesse L Goodman, 'The Development of COVID-19 Vaccines: Safeguards Needed' (2020) 324(5) *Journal of the American Medical Association* 439, 440; Krause and Gruber (n 212) e107(1).

[226] Zettler, Berman, and Parasidis (n 159) 165; Sravya Chary, 'Benefits and Drawbacks of Emergency Use Authorizations for COVID Vaccines' *Harvard Law School Petrie-Flom Center* (10 December 2020) <https://blog.petrieflom.law.harvard.edu/2020/12/10/emergency-use-authorization-covid-vaccines/> accessed 4 October 2022 (hereafter Chary, 'Benefits and Drawbacks').

[227] Zettler, Berman, and Parasidis (n 159) 165; Lurie, Sharfstein, and Goodman (n 225) 440.

[228] Martin and others (n 215).

[229] United States Food and Drug Administration, 'Emergency Use Authorizations' (10 February 2021) <www.fda.gov/emergency-preparedness-and-response/mcm-legal-regulatory-and-policy-framework/emergency-use-authorization#coviddrugs> accessed 4 October 2022; Krause and Gruber (n 212) e107(1).

[230] United States Food and Drug Administration, 'FDA Issues Emergency Use Authorization for Convalescent Plasma as Potential Promising COVID-19 Treatment, Another Achievement in Administration's Fight Against Pandemic' (23 August 2020) <www.fda.gov/news-events/press-announcements/fda-issues-emergency-use-authorization-convalescent-plasma-potential-promising-covid-19-treatment> accessed 4 October 2022.

[231] Mayo Clinic, 'Convalescent Plasma Therapy' (29 August 2020) <www.mayoclinic.org/tests-procedures/convalescent-plasma-therapy/about/pac-20486440> accessed 121 September 2022; Stratford, McKenzie, and Mockford (n 161) 106, fn 4.

clinical trials pertaining to it must continue.[232] The National Institutes of Health COVID-19 Treatment Guidelines Panel and the Infectious Diseases Society of America agreed that '[t]here are insufficient data to recommend either for or against the use of convalescent plasma for the treatment of COVID-19' and convalescent plasma should only be used within a clinical trial.[233] Rigorous, randomized, controlled trials subsequently found that convalescent plasma did not reduce progression to severe COVID-19 or mortality in adults.[234] As of September 2022 the Food and Drug Administration has revised, but not yet revoked its Emergency Use Authorization for convalescent plasma.[235]

In December 2020, the Food and Drug Administration issued Emergency Use Authorizations for the Pfizer-BioNTech and Moderna COVID-19 vaccines.[236] The Food and Drug Administration sought to reassure the public that: the vaccines had been 'rigorously tested'; it had determined that their 'known and potential benefits outweigh the known and potential risks'; vaccine manufacturers must submit extensive information and data to the Food and Drug Administration, which its scientists and physicians, 'who have globally recognized expertise in the complexity of vaccine development and in evaluating the safety and effectiveness of all vaccines', assess; and the Food and Drug Administration and CDC would continue to undertake 'post-authorization vaccine safety monitoring'.[237] Further, the Food and Drug Administration asserted that 'efforts to speed vaccine development ... have not sacrificed scientific standards, the integrity of the vaccine review process, or safety'.[238] It advised that COVID-19 vaccines had been developed 'so

---

[232] Holly Fernandez Lynch, Alison Bateman-House, and Steven Joffe, 'Emergency Approvals for COVID-19: Evolving Impact on Obligations to Patients in Clinical Care and Research' (2021) 174(2) *Annals of Internal Medicine* 256.

[233] ibid.

[234] Federal Drug Administration, 'Recommendations for Investigational COVID-19 Convalescent Plasma' (10 January 2022) < https://www.fda.gov/vaccines-blood-biologics/investigational-new-drug-applications-inds-cber-regulated-products/recommendations-investigational-covid-19-convalescent-plasma> accessed 11 September 2022; Ventura A Simonovich and others, 'A Randomized Trial of Convalescent Plasma in Covid-19 Severe Pneumonia' (2020) 384(7) *New England Journal of Medicine* 619; Elizabeth B Pathak, 'Convalescent Plasma is Ineffective for COVID-19: Lessons from the Placid Trial' (2020) 371 *British Medical Journal* m4072.

[235] American Hospital Association, 'FDA Updates EUA for COVID-19 Convalescent Plasma' (8 February 2021) <https://www.aha.org/news/headline/2021-02-08-fda-updates-eua-covid-19-convalescent-plasma> accessed 11 September 2022.

[236] United States Food and Drug Administration, 'FDA Takes Key Action in Fight Against COVID-19 by Issuing Emergency Use Authorization for First COVID-19 Vaccine' (11 December 2020) <www.fda.gov/news-events/press-announcements/fda-takes-key-action-fight-against-covid-19-issuing-emergency-use-authorization-first-covid-19> accessed 11 September 2022; United States Food and Drug Administration, 'FDA Takes Additional Action in Fight Against COVID-19 by Issuing Emergency Use Authorization for Second COVID-19 Vaccine' (18 December 2020) <www.fda.gov/news-events/press-announcements/fda-takes-additional-action-fight-against-covid-19-issuing-emergency-use-authorization-second-covid> accessed 11 September 2022 (hereafter FDA, 'Additional Action').

[237] United States Food and Drug Administration, 'Emergency Use Authorization for Vaccines Explained' (20 November 2020) <www.fda.gov/vaccines-blood-biologics/vaccines/emergency-use-authorization-vaccines-explained> accessed 11 September 2022 (hereafter FDA, 'Emergency Use Authorization'); FDA, 'Additional Action' (n 236).

[238] FDA, 'Emergency Use Authorization' (n 237).

quickly' because the United States government 'coalesced' many organizations and companies 'to develop a coordinated strategy for prioritizing and speeding development of the most promising vaccines' and 'made investments in the necessary manufacturing capacity'.[239]

In August 2021, the Food and Drug Administration authorized additional vaccine doses for certain categories of immunocompromised persons.[240] In addition, on 29 October 2021, the Food and Drug Administration granted an Emergency Use Authorization permitting the Pfizer-BioNTech vaccine to be administered to children aged between 5 and 11 years.[241]

Concerns were nonetheless expressed that the Food and Drug Administration's issuing of Emergency Use Authorizations for vaccines had the potential to lead to participants in vaccine trials withdrawing from them and discourage people from participating in new vaccine trials, thus hindering the progress of vital research.[242] After Emergency Use Authorizations were issued, those running vaccine trials would be ethically obliged to inform participants in the placebo arms of the trials that they had the option to obtain a vaccine.[243] If the subjects of trials received a placebo, and were informed of this at any stage (which may not be feasible), they would be likely to withdraw from them in order to obtain the vaccine.[244] Further, if vaccines were available by virtue of Emergency Use Authorizations, potential new participants in vaccine trials would probably prefer to receive a vaccine outside of the trials than participate in them, including because they risked obtaining a placebo rather than the vaccine.[245]

A so-called 'expanded access' or 'compassionate use' programme is another regulatory mechanism for authorizing use of medical products that regulators have not yet approved, which was relied upon during the COVID-19 pandemic.[246] Through this pathway, patients who are at the greatest risk of severe illness or death can access an investigational product outside a clinical trial.[247] The Food and Drug Administration permitted expanded access use of remdesivir for individual

---

[239] ibid.

[240] United States Food and Drug Administration, 'Coronavirus (COVID-19) Update: FDA Authorizes Additional Vaccine Dose for Certain Immunocompromised Individuals' (News Release, 12 August 2021) <www.fda.gov/news-events/press-announcements/coronavirus-covid-19-update-fda-authorizes-additional-vaccine-dose-certain-immunocompromised> accessed 11 September 2022.

[241] US Food and Drug Administration, 'FDA Authorizes Pfizer-BioNTech COVID-19 Vaccine for Emergency Use in Children 5 Through 11 Years of Age' (News Release, 29 October 2021) <https://www.fda.gov/news-events/press-announcements/fda-authorizes-pfizer-biontech-covid-19-vaccine-emergency-use-children-5-through-11-years-age> accessed 11 September 2022.

[242] Holly Fernandez Lynch, Alison Bateman-House, and Arthur Caplan, 'Authorize Emergency Vaccines for COVID-19, But Do It Well' *Harvard Law School Petrie-Flom Center* (10 December 2020) <https://blog.petrieflom.law.harvard.edu/2020/12/10/covid-vaccine-eua-emergency-use-authorization/> accessed 11 September 2022.

[243] Chary, 'Benefits and Drawbacks' (n 226).

[244] Fernandez Lynch, Bateman-House, and Caplan (n 242).

[245] ibid.

[246] Zettler, Berman, and Parasidis (n 159) 164; Stratford, McKenzie, and Mockford (n 161) 114.

[247] Chary, 'Benefits and Drawbacks' (n 226).

patients with COVID-19 and a 'multi-patient expanded access program' that the manufacturer of remdesivir, Gilead Sciences, led.[248] As noted in Chapter 11, remdesivir was already available, but had been approved to treat viral infections other than COVID-19, and it was hoped that it might lessen the duration and/or severity of this disease.[249] In response to several countries' requests for the opinion on the compassionate use of remdesivir by the Committee for Medicinal Products for Human Use, the European Medicines Agency also recommended remdesivir for compassionate use programmes in European Union Member States, which involved patients who required invasive mechanical ventilation due to confirmed or suspected COVID-19 and who were not participating in clinical trials.[250]

Regulatory authorities' full approvals of some COVID-19 medical products were also controversial, such as the Food and Drug Administration's first approval for a COVID-19 treatment—remdesivir (known commercially as Veklury)—on 22 October 2020.[251] After granting expanded access in relation to this drug, the Food and Drug Administration had issued an Emergency Use Authorization for its use in patients aged over 12 who required hospitalization for COVID-19, following the release of preliminary results from a randomized, double-blind, controlled phase 3 clinical trial involving 1,062 hospitalized patients with COVID-19, which indicated that they recovered more quickly than they otherwise would have.[252] The Food and Drug Administration expedited its review of the repurposing of remdesivir and granted Gilead Sciences a fast-track designation, which included a rolling review of new evidence about it.[253]

Before approving remdesivir for the treatment of COVID-19, the Food and Drug Administration undertook a risk-benefit assessment.[254] A multi-disciplinary team reviewed remdesivir's safety and efficacy, and independent analyses were conducted of the results from three randomized, controlled clinical trials in

---

[248] United States Food and Drug Administration, 'Coronavirus (COVID-19) Update: FDA Issues Emergency Use Authorization for Potential COVID-19 Treatment' (1 May 2020) <www.fda.gov/news-events/press-announcements/coronavirus-covid-19-update-fda-issues-emergency-use-authorization-potential-covid-19-treatment> accessed 11 September 2022 (hereafter FDA, 'Emergency Use Authorization for Potential COVID-19 Treatment'); Zettler, Berman, and Parasidis (n 159) 164.

[249] Zettler, Berman, and Parasidis (n 159) 164; FDA, 'Emergency Use Authorization for Potential COVID-19 Treatment' (n 248); Stratford, McKenzie, and Mockford (n 161) 106.

[250] Stratford, McKenzie, and Mockford (n 161) 114; Nigyar Dzhafer and Jannis V Papathanasiou, 'Compassionate Drug Use—Time Arising for a New Law in Bulgaria in the Era of COVID-19' (2020) 62(3) *Folia Medica* 592, 594.

[251] Zachary Brennan, 'FDA Approves Remdesivir as First Coronavirus Drug' *Politico* (22 October 2020) <www.politico.com/news/2020/10/22/fda-approves-remdesivir-coronavirus-431336> accessed 11 September 2022; Sravya Chary, 'Experts Question FDA Approval of Remdesivir for COVID-19' *Harvard Law School Petrie-Flom Center* (10 November 2020) <https://blog.petrieflom.law.harvard.edu/2020/11/10/remdesivir-veklury-covid-fda-approval/> accessed 11 September 2022 (hereafter Chary, 'Remdesivir').

[252] Zettler, Berman, and Parasidis (n 159) 165; Daniel Rubin and others, 'FDA Approval of Remdesivir—A Step in the Right Direction' (2020) 383 *New England Journal of Medicine* 2598; Brennan (n 251).

[253] Rubin and others (n 252).

[254] ibid.

hospitalized patients, indicating that remdesivir could reduce the duration of hospitalization (though not the risk of death) and the likelihood that patients would require oxygen.[255] Yet many considered that there was not 'substantial evidence' of the effectiveness of remdesivir in treating COVID-19 because the studies supporting its use were 'underpowered', its efficacy was uncertain,[256] and the available evidence was insufficient to support the Food and Drug Administration's finding that the benefits of remdesivir outweighed its risks in treating COVID-19 patients, which were preconditions to approving it. In its risk-benefit assessment, the Food and Drug Administration did not refer to the preliminary results relating to remdesivir from the largest COVID-19 treatment study at the time—the Solidarity Trial, discussed in Chapter 11—which were released a week before the Food and Drug Administration issued its approval.[257] As noted in Chapter 11, that study found that remdesivir had 'little to no effect' in hospitalized patients 'as indicated by overall mortality, initiation of ventilation and duration of hospital stay'.[258] In addition, the Food and Drug Administration did not convene an independent advisory committee to review remdesivir before approving it, claiming that the application 'did not raise significant safety or efficacy issues'.[259] Following its approval, the optimal dosing of remdesivir for paediatric and pregnant patients and those with renal or hepatic impairment was still unclear.[260]

Bodies that regulate doctors and pharmacists can also prevent the public from accessing treatments and vaccines by prohibiting 'off-label' prescribing and dispensing of medical products that regulatory authorities have approved.[261] For example, they might prohibit use of the product by a patient group, for particular symptoms or diseases, or through certain methods, which the regulator has not specifically approved.[262] During the COVID-19 pandemic, regulatory authorities in some states in the United States restricted off-label prescribing and dispensing of hydroxychloroquine and chloroquine for COVID-19 in response to reports

---

[255] Brennan (n 251); Rubin and others (n 252); Chary, 'Remdesivir' (n 251).

[256] See eg John D Norrie, 'Remdesivir for COVID-19: Challenges of Underpowered Studies' (2020) 395(10236) *Lancet* 1525; World Health Organization, 'WHO Recommends Against the Use of Remdesivir in COVID-19 Patients' (20 November 2020) <https://www.who.int/news-room/feature-stories/detail/who-recommends-against-the-use-of-remdesivir-in-covid-19-patients> accessed 11 September 2022; Iwein Gyselinck and Wim Janssens, 'Remdesivir, on the Road to DisCoVeRY' (2021) 22(2) *Lancet Infectious Diseases* 153; see even in July 2021 Joyce M Hoek and others, 'Rethinking Remdesivir for COVID-19: A Bayesian Reanalysis of Trial Findings' (2021) 16(7) *PLoS One* art e0255093.

[257] Brennan (n 251); Chary, 'Remdesivir' (n 251).

[258] Chary, 'Remdesivir' (n 251); Brennan (n 251).

[259] Brennan (n 251).

[260] Rubin and others (n 252); World Health Organization, 'WHO Recommends Against the Use of Remdesivir in COVID-19 Patients' (20 November 2020) <https://www.who.int/news-room/feature-stories/detail/who-recommends-against-the-use-of-remdesivir-in-covid-19-patients> accessed 11 September 2022.

[261] Zettler, Berman, and Parasidis (n 159) 163–64.

[262] Richard Day, 'Off-label Prescribing' (2013) 36(6) *Australian Prescriber* 182 <www.nps.org.au/australian-prescriber/articles/off-label-prescribing> accessed 11 September 2022.

that health professionals were hoarding it and thereby depriving patients suffering from malaria, lupus, and rheumatoid arthritis from using them.[263] These authorities also conveyed the absence of comprehensive evidence of their efficacy in treating COVID-19.[264] Nevertheless, it seems that these authorities did not prevent health professionals from prescribing and dispensing 'off-label' dexamethasone, 'a long-approved corticosteroid', for patients with COVID-19, following reports that it could reduce fatalities in some patients who were very unwell.[265]

A key challenge for distributing COVID-19 treatments and vaccines globally and ensuring equitable access to them was that each government had varied regulatory requirements that the treatments needed to meet before their roll-out was permitted[266] Further, some of the treatments were onerous and even redundant, particularly in instances where another country's regulatory authority had approved them.[267] For those countries that lacked efficient regulatory processes, the distribution of treatments and vaccines could be tardy and potentially result in people resorting to using inferior products and/or products whose efficacy was unproven.[268] Some scholars therefore recommended using global health law to achieve consistency in treatment and vaccine regulations.[269] WHO attempted to harmonize approval processes internationally, but without success.[270]

V. Intellectual Property Law and COVID-19 Treatments and Vaccines

Intellectual property law has the potential to enhance or obstruct the capacity for countries, especially low- and middle-income countries, to obtain or manufacture and distribute treatments and vaccines in required quantities and at affordable prices.[271] These possibilities for the application of intellectual property law were evident in 1997 when 39 pharmaceutical companies took action against the South African government in an attempt to stop the promulgation of legislation aimed

---

[263] Zettler, Berman, and Parasidis (n 159) 164.
[264] ibid.
[265] ibid.
[266] Gostin, Karim, and Meier (n 2) 624–25.
[267] ibid 624.
[268] ibid 625.
[269] ibid 624.
[270] ibid 625.
[271] ibid 624; Enrico Bonadio and Andrea Baldini, 'COVID-19, Patents and the Never-Ending Tension Between Proprietary Rights and the Protection of Public Health' (2020) 11(2) *European Journal of Risk Regulation* 390, 393; Nirmalya Syam, 'Intellectual Property, Innovation and Access to Health Products for COVID-19: A Review of Measures Taken by Different Countries' *The South Centre* (June 2020) <www.southcentre.int/policy-brief-80-june-2020/#> accessed 14 February 2021.

at lowering the cost of medication, particularly medication for treatment of HIV/ AIDS, in South Africa.[272]

The risk of intellectual property regimes constraining effective responses to past pandemics, including avian influenza[273] and swine influenza,[274] prompted calls by WHO to relax these legal constraints. As discussed in Chapter 2, a precipitant to the stance adopted by WHO was Indonesia breaking with a long tradition of free international sharing of flu virus specimens in December 2006 when it stopped sending H5N1 influenza virus samples to WHO in protest against the high cost of commercial vaccines derived from such samples.[275] In response, in 2007, WHO approved a resolution that was intended to make gene sequencing of newly isolated virus strains and vaccines developed using them available globally, regardless of the patent protection claimed by vaccine developers. This resolution called for the establishment of 'an international stockpile of vaccines for H5N1 or other influenza viruses of pandemic potential, and to formulate mechanisms and guidelines aimed at ensuring fair and equitable distribution of pandemic-influenza vaccines at affordable prices in the event of a pandemic'.[276]

The response to the 2009 H1N1 swine flu pandemic also illustrated the potential for intellectual property laws to impede equitable global access to treatments and vaccines during major public health emergencies.[277] The swine flu pandemic prompted public health authorities to encourage the public to be vaccinated. However, for some time, vaccine supplies were limited and debates took place about rationing vaccines and two anti-viral treatments, Tamiflu and Relenza.[278] The United States government's solution was to purchase 250 million vaccine doses from the relevant pharmaceutical companies and distribute them to healthcare

---

[272] The action by the companies was ultimately abandoned after an intense lobbying campaign: see Pat Sidley, 'Drug Companies Withdraw Law Suit Against South Africa' (2000) 322(7293) *British Medical Journal* 1011; Chris McGreal, 'Shamed and Humiliated—The Drugs Firms Back Down' *The Guardian* (20 April 2001) <www.theguardian.com/uk/2001/apr/19/highereducation.world> accessed 4 October 2022.

[273] Dawn Dziuba, 'TRIPS Article 31Bis and H1N1 Swine Flu: Any Emergency or Urgency Exception to Patent Protection' (2010) 20(2) *Indiana International and Comparative Law Review* 195.

[274] World Health Organization, 'Patent Landscape for the H5 Virus' (Interim Report, 17 November 2007) <www.who.int/influenza/resources/documents/avian_flu_landscape.pdf?ua=1> accessed 1 November 2021; World Intellectual Property Organization, 'WIPO Patent Search Report on Pandemic Influenza Preparedness (PIP)-Related Patents and Patent Applications' (1 April 2011) <www.who.int/influenza/resources/Influenza_FullReport_01Apr2011.pdf> accessed 1 November 2021.

[275] See Donald G McNeil Jr, 'Indonesia May Sell, Not Give, Bird Flu Virus to Scientists' *New York Times* (7 February 2007) <www.nytimes.com/2007/02/07/world/asia/07birdflu.html> accessed 1 November 2021.

[276] Centre for Infectious Disease Research and Policy, 'WHO Adopts Resolution of Flu Virus Sharing' (23 May 2007) <www.cidrap.umn.edu/news-perspective/2007/05/who-adopts-resolution-flu-virus-sharing> accessed 4 October 2022.

[277] See Michelle Kaplan, 'The 2009 H1N1 Swine Flu Pandemic: Reconciling Goals of Patents and Public Health Initiatives' (2010) 20(3) *Fordham Intellectual Property, Media & Entertainment Law Journal* 991.

[278] See eg Lawrence O Gostin and Benjamin E Berkman, 'Pandemic Influences, Ethics, Law and the Public's Health' (2007) 59(1) *Administrative Law Review* 121.

providers and ultimately the American public free of charge in accordance with prioritization recommended by the Centers for Disease Control and Prevention's Advisory Committee on Immunization. While this side-stepped patent problems and benefited Americans, it did not facilitate other countries' access to vaccines and treatments. On 17 September 2009, the United States government pledged to donate 10% of its vaccines to WHO, but by 28 October the Secretary of Health reneged, stating that the donation would not occur until all Americans who needed them had access to them, as production problems had caused shortages of the vaccines. Vaccine nationalism prevailed.[279] This highlighted the fact that countries in which vaccines and treatments are manufactured have sovereignty over access to them, provided they negotiate successfully with the holders of patents for these medical products (usually pharmaceutical companies).[280] It was also apparent that advance procurement agreements entered into by low- and middle-income countries were unlikely to enable them to obtain sufficient quantities of vaccine doses during a subsequent pandemic.[281]

Unsurprisingly, the COVID-19 pandemic resulted in renewed calls for waiving intellectual property protections for medical treatments and vaccines.[282] Yet several countries again relied on intellectual property laws to engage in treatment nationalism during the COVID-19 pandemic.[283] For instance, on 16 June 2020, the United Kingdom stockpiled and banned the export of dexamethasone.[284] As noted

---

[279] See Ana S Rutschman, 'Is There a Cure for Vaccine Nationalism?' (2021) 120(822) *Current History* 9.

[280] See David P Fidler, 'Negotiating Equitable Access to Influenza Vaccines: Global Health Diplomacy and the Controversies Surrounding Avian Influenza H5N1 and Pandemic Influenza H1N1' (2010) 7(5) *PLoS Medicine* art e1000247.

[281] Mark Turner, 'Vaccine Procurement During an Influenza Pandemic and the Role of Advance Purchase Agreements: Lessons from 2009-H1N1' (2016) 11(3) *Global Public Health* 322.

[282] See eg Nancy S Jecker and Caesar A Atuire, 'What's Yours is Ours: Waiving Intellectual Property Protections for COVID-19 Vaccines' (2021) 47(9) *Journal of Medical Ethics* 595; Sophie McNeill, 'Australia Should Back COVID-19 Waiver of Intellectual Property Rules' *Human Rights Watch* (25 July 2021) <www.hrw.org/news/2021/07/25/australia-should-back-covid-19-waiver-intellectual-property-rules> accessed 4 October 2022; Etienne Billette de Villemeur, Bruno Versaevel, and Vianney Dequiedt, 'Intellectual Property and Covid-19: How Can We Accelerate Vaccination Globally?' *The Conversation* (26 April 2021) <https://theconversation.com/intellectual-property-and-covid-19-how-can-we-acc elerate-vaccination-globally-159467> accessed 4 October 2022; Melody Okereke, 'Toward Vaccine Equity: Should Big Pharma Waive Intellectual Property Rights for COVID-19 Vaccines?' (2021) 2 *Public Health in Practice* art 100165.

[283] See eg Godwell Nhamo and others, 'COVID-19 Vaccines and Treatments Nationalism: Challenges for Low-income Countries and the Attainment of the SDGs' (2021) 16(3) *Global Public Health* 319; Graham Dutfield, 'Coronavirus: It is Morally Indefensible for a Nation to Keep Life-saving Drugs for Itself' *The Conversation* (2 July 2020) <https://theconversation.com/coronavirus-it-is-morally-indef ensible-for-a-nation-to-keep-life-saving-drugs-for-itself-141734> accessed 10 September 2021.

[284] See Medicine and Healthcare products Regulatory Agency, 'List of Medicines that Cannot be Exported from the UK or Hoarded' (Guidance, 3 August 2021) <https://assets.publishing.service. gov.uk/government/uploads/system/uploads/attachment_data/file/1010617/Restricted_Medicines_ List_August_2021.csv/preview> accessed 10 September 2021; David C Gaze, 'Dexamethasone: What is the Breakthrough Treatment for COVID-19?' *The Conversation* (18 June 2020) <https://theconve rsation.com/dexamethasone-what-is-the-breakthrough-treatment-for-covid-19-140966> accessed 4 October 2022.

earlier, this is a steroid medication with anti-inflammatory properties, used since the 1960s for the treatment of allergies, asthma, lupus, and rheumatoid arthritis, which was repurposed to treat COVID-19.[285] Similar problems occurred in the United States in relation to the hepatitis C drug, remdesivir, as outlined below.

While patents issued for COVID-19 treatments and vaccines had the potential to stimulate research and development, they also risked restricting their availability to low- and middle-income countries.[286] Patents would grant their owners—the products' developers—exclusive rights to prevent others from producing and distributing them without their consent.[287] Therefore, unless these patent owners granted licences to use their treatments or vaccines, others could not manufacture or supply them.[288] Several countries turned to compulsory licensing and government use authorization as mechanisms for circumventing the obstacle that patents posed to accessing COVID-19 treatments and vaccines.[289] Governments passed legislation and instituted administrative measures to enable them to permit production of patented products without obtaining the patent owners' consent to do so.[290]

On 19 May 2020, the 73rd World Health Assembly called for 'urgent removal of unjustified obstacles' to 'universal, timely and equitable access to, and fair distribution of ... products ... required in the response to the COVID-19 pandemic', 'consistent with ... international treaties'.[291] Those treaties included the World Trade Organization's (WTO) 'Agreement on Trade-Related Aspects of Intellectual Property Rights' (TRIPS) and WTO's 'Doha Declaration on the TRIPS Agreement and Public Health' ('Doha Declaration').[292] TRIPS permits international enforcement of intellectual property rights, including in relation to medical products.[293] In response to difficulties for low- and middle-income countries in accessing

---

[285] See RECOVERY Collaborative Group, 'Dexamethasone in Hospitalized Patients with Covid-19' (2021) 384(8) *New England Journal of Medicine* 693.
[286] Ronald Labonte and Mira Johri, 'COVID-19 Drug and Vaccine Patents Are Putting Profit Before People' *The Conversation* (6 November 2020) <https://theconversation.com/covid-19-drug-and-vaccine-patents-are-putting-profit-before-people-149270> accessed 7 March 2022.
[287] World Intellectual Property Organization, 'Patents' <www.wipo.int/patents/en/> accessed 15 February 2021.
[288] Syam (n 271) 2.
[289] ibid; Jorges L Contreras, 'Deconstructing Moderna's COVID-19 Patent Pledge' *Harvard Law School Petrie-Flom Center* (21 October 2020) <https://blog.petrieflom.law.harvard.edu/2020/10/21/moderna-covid19-patent-pledge/> accessed 12 December 2021.
[290] ibid; World Trade Organization, 'Compulsory Licensing of Pharmaceuticals and TRIPS' <www.wto.org/english/tratop_e/trips_e/public_health_faq_e.htm#:~:text=Compulsory%20licensing%20is%20when%20a,the%20patent%2Dprotected%20invention%20itself> accessed 11 September 2022 (hereafter WTO, 'Compulsory Licensing').
[291] World Health Assembly, 'COVID-19 Response' (Resolution WHA 73.1, 19 May 2020) <https://apps.who.int/gb/ebwha/pdf_files/WHA73/A73_R1-en.pdf> accessed 11 September 2022.
[292] ibid; *Marrakesh Agreement Establishing the World Trade Organization* (opened for signature 15 April 1994, entered into force 1 January 1995) 1867 UNTS 3, Annex 1C ('Agreement on Trade-Related Aspects of Intellectual Property Rights'); World Trade Organization, 'Declaration on The TRIPS Agreement and Public Health' (Resolution WT/Min(01)/Dec/2, 14 November 2001)<www.wto.org/english/thewto_e/minist_e/min01_e/mindecl_trips_e.htm> accessed 11 September 2022 (hereafter 'Doha Declaration').
[293] Gostin, Karim, and Meier (n 2) 624.

affordable patented HIV treatments, TRIPS was amended to permit compulsory licensing in the context of public health crises.[294] The Doha Declaration, adopted on 14 November 2001, states that TRIPS 'does not and should not prevent [WTO's 164] members from taking measures to protect public health', and affirmed a commitment to interpreting and implementing TRIPS to support their 'right to protect public health' and 'promote access to medicines for all'.[295] Those 'flexibilities' were stated as including that: 'each member has the right to grant compulsory licences and the freedom to determine the grounds upon which such licences are granted', and 'each member has the right to determine what constitutes a national emergency or other circumstances of extreme urgency', on the understanding that 'public health crises' could 'represent' them.[296]

Consistent with this Declaration, from early in the pandemic, governments of several countries had been adopting measures to combat obstacles posed by intellectual property laws to reducing the price of and facilitating access to COVID-19 treatments and vaccines.[297] For instance, on 17 March 2020, Chile adopted a resolution declaring that the COVID-19 'outbreak justifies the use of compulsory licensing to facilitate access to vaccines, drugs ... and other technologies useful for the ... prevention ... and treatment of the coronavirus'.[298] The Canadian government passed the *COVID-19 Emergency Response Act 2020* (Can), which amended its compulsory licensing law to enable the government and anyone it authorized to obtain a one-year licence to 'make ... use and sell a patented invention to the extent necessary to respond to the public health emergency' through an application to the patent office.[299] Although the patent owner needed to be paid, the government could issue compulsory licences without needing to negotiate the terms of the access.[300]

The Israeli government adopted a similar measure after AbbVie, an American pharmaceutical company that was the patent owner and manufacturer of lopanivir/ritonavir (known as 'Kaletra'), stated that it was unable to provide sufficient supplies of this product, which had been used to treat HIV and was being

---

[294] Sarah Joseph, 'COVID-19 and Human Rights: Past, Present and Future' (2020) Griffith Law School Research Paper No. 20-23, 10 <https://papers.ssrn.com/sol3/papers.cfm?abstract_id=3574491> accessed 12 September 2022; WTO, 'Compulsory Licensing' (n 290). See too Justin Malbon, 'Obtaining COVID-19 Vaccines: How the Government Sold the Parachutes' in Belinda Bennett and Ian Freckelton (eds), *Pandemics, Public Health Emergencies and Government Powers: Perspectives on Australian Law* (Federation Press 2021).
[295] World Trade Organization, 'Doha Declaration' (n 292).
[296] ibid.
[297] Contreras (n 289).
[298] See Syam (n 271) 2–3.
[299] Jeremy De Beer and E Richard Gold, 'International Trade, Intellectual Property, and Innovation Policy: Lessons from a Pandemic' in Colleen M Flood and others (eds), *Vulnerable: The Law, Policy and Ethics of COVID-19* (University of Ottawa Press 2020) 582; *COVID-19 Emergency Response Act 2020* (Can) s 51, inserting *Patent Act 1985* (Can) s 19.4.
[300] De Beer and Gold (n 299) 582; Syam (n 271) 2.

tested for its efficacy in treating COVID-19.[301] The government issued a compulsory licence or government use authorization to permit an Israeli company, on behalf of the Ministry of Health, to import a generic version of Kaletra from an Indian manufacturing company (Hetero) to treat COVID-19 patients.[302] AbbVie subsequently announced that it would not enforce its Kaletra patent during the COVID-19 pandemic.[303]

C-TAP, discussed in Section II(B) above, was also intended to overcome restrictions on access to COVID-19 treatments and vaccines induced by intellectual property laws. WHO announced its establishment on 1 June 2020 to gather patents and other forms of intellectual property to increase development and production of new technologies needed for responding to COVID-19.[304] It sought to 'compile, in one place, pledges of commitment ... to voluntarily share COVID-19 health technology related knowledge, intellectual property and data'.[305] A model for C-TAP was the Medicines Patent Pool, which resulted in all intellectual property for HIV treatments that WHO had endorsed being licensed to this patent pool.[306] Especially because C-TAP was a voluntary mechanism, its likely success was unclear.[307]

In October 2020, India and South Africa put a proposal to the World Trade Association TRIPS Council that, for the duration of the pandemic, it should permit countries to suspend intellectual property protections in relation to COVID-19 treatments and prophylactic medications in order to accelerate their production and distribution.[308] However, the International Federation of Pharmaceutical Manufacturers and Associations clearly signalled its continuing commitment to traditional intellectual property protections in stating on 16 October 2020:

> One-size-fits all proposals advocating for diluting or suspending IP rights during this pandemic disregard the specific circumstances of each situation, each product and each country—all facing very different challenges regarding the

---

[301] Bonadio and Baldini (n 271) 392; Thiru, 'Israel Issues Compulsory License to Allow the Government to Import Generic Versions of Kaletra' *Knowledge Ecology International* (23 March 2020) <www.keionline.org/32503> accessed 4 October 2022.
[302] Bonadio and Baldini (n 271) 392; Thiru (n 301).
[303] Bonadio and Baldini (n 271) 393.
[304] WHO, 'COVID-19 Technology Access Pool' (n 85).
[305] Integrated People-Centred Health Services, 'COVID-19 Technology Access Pool' (10 June 2020) <www.integratedcare4people.org/contents/tags/intellectual%20property/> accessed 12 September 2022.
[306] Medicines Patent Pool, 'Expanding Access to Public Health' (Brochure, 2020) <https://medicinespatentpool.org/news-publications/mpp-publications/> accessed 9 June 2021.
[307] Gostin, Karim, and Meier (n 2) 624.
[308] See Ellen 't Hoen, 'The Indian/South African Proposal for a WTO Waiver on IP for COVID-19 Related Health Products—What It Means?' *Health Policy Watch* (14 October 2020) <https://healthpolicy-watch.news/77719-2/> accessed 7 March 2022; see also Dilan Thampapillai, 'The Controversy to Come? Patent Law and a COVID-19 Vaccine' *ANU College of Law* (10 June 2020) <https://law.anu.edu.au/research/essay/covid-19-and-international-law/controversy-come-patent-law-and-covid-19-vaccine> accessed 12 September 2022.

manufacture and distribution of COVID-19 treatments and vaccines. The international IP system already has rules and practices to permit customized solutions to real-world problems that may arise.

Long before the SARS CoV-2 pandemic, pharmaceutical companies have engaged in many voluntary licensing initiatives as part of their business model, with IP providing them the necessary confidence to engage in such transactions ... The biopharmaceutical industry's record of engaging with multiple stakeholders through various innovative access initiatives and research collaborations showcases that a strong IP incentive system is not incompatible with a rapid and robust response to a health crisis.[309]

Although supported by more than 100 countries within the WTO and a global campaign for the 'People's Vaccine',[310] the proposal was blocked at committee meetings by a number of wealthy countries with large pharmaceutical industries, including the United Kingdom, Japan, and European Union member states.[311] However, the United States of America (under the Biden administration) on 5 May 2021,[312] and then Russia and China, announced their support for a waiver of intellectual property protection on COVID-19 vaccines, prompting an editorial in *Nature* to call for other countries to join the initiative.[313]

Bangladesh was able to circumvent some of its intellectual property obligations under TRIPS during the COVID-19 pandemic. In 2020, after the Food and Drug Administration issued an Emergency Use Authorization and the European Medicines Agency granted conditional marketing authorization for the use of remdesivir to treat COVID-19, there were major international shortages of this product, as its manufacturer, Gilead Sciences, had sold all of its stock to the United States government.[314] Gilead entered licensing agreements with Indian and Pakistani generic manufacturing companies to supply remdesivir to 127 low- and

---

[309] International Federation of Pharmaceutical Manufacturers and Associations, 'IFPMA Statement on "Intellectual Property and COVID-19"' (16 October 2020) <www.ifpma.org/resource-centre/ifpma-statement-on-intellectual-property-and-covid-19/> accessed 15 February 2021.
[310] See 'The People's Vaccine' <https://peoplesvaccine.org> accessed 12 September 2022.
[311] See Leah Ferris, 'Intellectual Property Agreements and COVID-19 Proposals to Ensure Access to Treatments' (Parliament of Australia, 14 September 2021) <www.aph.gov.au/About_Parliament/Parliamentary_Departments/Parliamentary_Library/FlagPost/2021/September/Intellectual_property_agreements_and_COVID-19> accessed 12 September 2022.
[312] Office of the United States Trade Representative, 'Statement from Ambassador Katherine Tai on the Covid-19 Trips Waiver' (Press Release, 5 May 2021) <https://ustr.gov/about-us/policy-offices/press-office/press-releases/2021/may/statement-ambassador-katherine-tai-covid-19-trips-waiver> accessed 12 September 2022.
[313] Editorial, 'A Patent Waiver on COVID Vaccines is Right and Fair' (2021) 593(7860) *Nature* 478. See too Priri Krishtel and Rohit Malpani, 'Suspend Intellectual Property Rights for COVID-19 Vaccines' (2021) 373 *British Medical Journal* n1344; see too John Zaracostas, 'Mixed Response to COVID-19 Intellectual Property Waiver' (2022) 399(10345) *Lancet* 1292.
[314] See 'Covid-19 Surge: Bangladesh to Send Remdesivir to India Next Week' *Healthworld.com* (30 April 2020) <www.business-standard.com/article/current-affairs/bangladesh-to-send-remdesivir-drug-medical-supplies-to-india-next-week-121043000092_1.html> accessed 9 June 2021.

middle-income countries.[315] The Bangladesh government issued an emergency decree, pursuant to which Beximco, which was not one of the companies that entered those agreements, could provide a generic version of remdesivir to state hospitals for free and sell it to private clinics.[316] The government was acting under a WTO agreement that permits 'least developed country members' to have an exemption from obligations under TRIPS and, in particular, allows them to grant a company a licence to copy a patented medicine without the patent holder's consent.[317]

Individual companies and coalitions of organizations also adopted measures which took different forms and were variously described, to make their intellectual property rights freely available to address the suffering caused by COVID-19.[318] They pertained to different types of intellectual property rights, including patents, copyrights, and designs, and imposed varied restrictions and limitations.[319] In some instances, companies holding patents for medical products that could treat COVID-19 unilaterally pledged to refrain from asserting their intellectual property rights in relation to them if doing so would undermine 'efforts to contain the outbreak or treat its symptoms'.[320] For example, Moderna held seven patents in the United States covering aspects of its COVID-19 vaccine candidate.[321] On 8 October 2020, Moderna 'publicly pledged not to enforce its COVID-19 related patents against "those making vaccines intended to combat the pandemic"'.[322] As noted earlier, AbbVie similarly pledged not to enforce its patent in relation to Kaletra.[323]

Pledges were also made through co-ordinated efforts of organizations that committed to comparable terms. A prominent example of this was the 'Open COVID Pledge', which was developed by a coalition of scientists, engineers, and legal experts, and permitted any interested organization the right to use the licensed rights without preparing further paperwork.[324] It expressed its intentions clearly as follows:

---

[315] Ed Silverman, 'First Generic Version of Gilead's Remdesivir Will Be Sold by a Bangladesh Drug Maker' *Stat* (22 May 2020) <www.statnews.com/pharmalot/2020/05/22/gilead-remdesivir-covid19-coronavirus-beximco-patent/> accessed 4 October 2022.

[316] ibid.

[317] ibid; Nirmalya Syam, 'The TRIPS Council on 15–16 October Should Agree to Extend the Transition Period that Exempts Least Developed Countries from Implementation of the WTO TRIPS Agreement' *InfoJustice* (7 October 2020) <http://infojustice.org/archives/42666> accessed 12 September 2022.

[318] Jorge L Contreras and others, 'Pledging Intellectual Property for COVID-19' (2020) 38(10) *Nature Biotechnology* 1146.

[319] ibid.

[320] Contreras (n 289).

[321] ibid.

[322] ibid.

[323] ibid.

[324] Open COVID Pledge, 'The Pledge' <https://opencovidpledge.org/the-pledge/> accessed 4 October 2022.

Immediate action is required to halt the COVID-19 Pandemic and treat those it has affected. It is a practical and moral imperative that every tool we have at our disposal be applied to develop and deploy technologies on a massive scale without impediment.

We therefore pledge to make our intellectual property available free of charge for use in ending the COVID-19 pandemic and minimizing the impact of the disease.

We will implement this pledge through a license that details the terms and conditions under which our intellectual property is made available.[325]

Other similar commitments, such as the Harvard–MIT–Stanford pledge, provided a framework (in that instance, the COVID-19 Technology Access Framework),[326] but still required organizations that wished to use pledged intellectual property rights to negotiate a separate licence agreement with the rights holder.[327]

The COVID-19 pandemic thus gave rise to a multi-pronged critique of traditional intellectual property protections that provide advantages to holders of patents for pharmaceutical products, including during public health emergencies. Measures were identified and, in some instances, implemented to attempt to overcome those protections and make COVID-19 treatments and vaccines available equitably across the world. The extent to which these initiatives benefited low- and middle-income countries during the pandemic and in its aftermath remains to be evaluated.

VI. Conclusion

Production in sufficient volumes of COVID-19 treatments and vaccines that had been proven to be safe and effective, and distribution of them equitably within countries and across the world could protect human rights and lower the incidence of or even eradicate this disease. Yet, during the pandemic, several major obstacles to achieving these objectives became apparent. These included some countries' treatment and vaccine nationalism, and intellectual property laws that bolstered this attitude, as well as the extensive time required to evaluate rigorously the safety and efficacy of new medical products. In spite of these challenges, various initiatives, epitomized by COVAX and C-TAP,

---

[325] Open COVID Pledge, 'The Pledge' <https://opencovidpledge.org/the-pledge/> accessed 4 October 2022.
[326] MIT Technology Licensing Office, 'COVID-19 Technology Access Framework' (7 April 2020) <https://tlo.mit.edu/engage-tlo/covid-19/covid-19-technology-access-framework> accessed 12 September 2022.
[327] Contreras and others (n 318).

demonstrated the potential for nations to work together to surmount such hurdles. The COVID-19 pandemic has also necessitated engagement with, and in some circumstances creation of novel solutions to, dilemmas concerning how to ration and allocate critical treatments and vaccines when they are in limited supply.

13
Law, Regulation, and Rights: Reflections on the COVID-19 Pandemic

I. Introduction

Early in the COVID-19 pandemic, Arundhati Roy observed that:

> Historically pandemics have forced humans to break with the past and imagine their world anew. This one is no different. It is a portal, a gateway between one world and the next. We can choose to walk through it, dragging the carcasses of our prejudice and hatred, our avarice, our data banks and dead ideas, our dead rivers and smoky skies behind us. Or we can walk through it lightly, with little luggage, ready to imagine another world. And ready to fight for it.[1]

In this final chapter, we take up Roy's challenge. We reflect on the legal and regulatory responses to the COVID-19 pandemic that we have analysed throughout the book and explore possibilities they have illuminated for effectively tackling global health crises in the future. In particular, the COVID-19 pandemic has demonstrated that management of global health crises can be collaborative, informed by a number of disciplines, and cognizant of the diversity of the challenges such crises may pose.

COVID-19 has proved to be the most severe pandemic that the world has experienced in a century. As was the case during the Spanish flu of 1918–19, there are few, if any, places that have been untouched by COVID-19. As observed in Chapters 1 and 2, increased contact between humans and animals, including as a consequence of environmental degradation and the nature and volume of production of meat and poultry, has greatly increased the potential for the development of new zoonotic diseases.[2] Further, unprecedented globalization and the rapidity with which goods and humans move across the planet has exponentially heightened the opportunities for infectious diseases to spread.[3] Indeed, given these developments,

---

[1] Arundhati Roy, 'The Pandemic Is a Portal' *Financial Times* (4 April 2020) <https://ft.com/content/10d8f5e8-74eb-11ea-95fe-fcd274e920ca> accessed 14 September 2022.
[2] Mark Honigsbaum, *The Pandemic Century: One Hundred Years of Panic, Hysteria and Hubris* (C Hurst and Company (Publishers) Limited 2019) xi; David Morens and others, 'Pandemic COVID-19 Joins History's Pandemic Legion' (2020) 11(3) *American Society for Microbiology* art e00812-20, 2–3.
[3] Honigsbaum (n 2) 262; S Harris Ali, 'Globalized Complexity and the Microbial Traffic of New and Emerging Infectious Disease Threats' in Tamara Giles-Vernick, Susan Craddock, with Jennifer

it is crucial that the world heeds lessons from its management of COVID-19 to prepare for future pandemics. Principally, this involves medico-scientific readiness, but it also incorporates administrative and legal operationalization of the guidance provided by epidemiologists, clinicians, and scientists.

The Spanish flu is estimated to have killed at least 50 million people in two years.[4] Recent estimates indicate that the COVID-19 pandemic has led to 14.9 million excess deaths.[5] Both pandemics have thus taken a tragic toll on human life around the world.

However, in contrast to Spanish flu, one notable characteristic of the COVID-19 pandemic has been the unprecedented speed with which treatments and vaccines for a new virus have been developed. In addition, the capacity today to detect and monitor the progress of disease transmission and the impact of public health measures, and the ability to analyse such data, have vastly improved.[6] As we have demonstrated in this book, the law has played a pivotal role in facilitating and putting into operation these scientific and epidemiological achievements and in combating the detrimental effects of COVID-19. As discussed in Chapters 4, 5, and 8, informed by relevant data, governments have relied on domestic emergency laws to impose a raft of public health measures that have inhibited (or at least delayed) the spread of COVID-19, and they have often drawn on the criminal law to enforce them. Such laws have been controversial, and even divisive within the community. At the same time, various uses and adaptations of regulatory structures and mechanisms have facilitated the rapid international collaboration between scientists working on COVID-19 treatments and vaccines, and acceleration of their research, as examined in Chapter 11. Despite these advances in science and medicine, it is also the case that before and even after the development of COVID-19 vaccines, we have relied on public health tools that, as discussed in Chapter 2,

---

Gunn (eds), *Influenza and Public Health: Learning from Past Pandemics* (Earthscan 2010) 22–23; Nita Madhav and others, 'Pandemics, Risks, Impacts and Mitigation' in Dean R Jamison and others (eds), *Disease Control Priorities: Improving Health and Reducing Poverty* (3rd edn International Bank for Reconstruction and Development/World Bank 2017); Nathan Wolfe, *The Viral Storm: The Dawn of a New Pandemic Age* (Allen Lane 2011) 3.

[4] Anthea Hyslop, 'Forewarned, Forearmed: Australia and the Spanish Influenza Pandemic, 1918–1919' in John Lack (ed), *1919: The Year Things Fell Apart?* (Australian Scholarly Publishing 2019) 2; Centers for Disease Control and Prevention, '1918 Pandemic (H1N1 Virus)' <https://cdc.gov/flu/pandemic-resources/1918-pandemic-h1n1.html> accessed 24 December 2021. For further discussion see Chapter 2.

[5] World Health Organization, '14.9 Million Excess Deaths Associated with the COVID-19 Pandemic in 2020 and 2021' News Release (5 May 2022) <https://www.who.int/news/item/05-05-2022-14.9-million-excess-deaths-were-associated-with-the-covid-19-pandemic-in-2020-and-2021> accessed 19 May 2022.

[6] Alexandra Minna Stern and Howard Markel, 'International Efforts to Control Infectious Diseases, 1851 to the Present' (2004) 292(12) *Journal of the American Medical Association* 1474. See Chapter 3 for discussion of the role of data during the COVID-19 pandemic.

have been used for centuries to curb disease transmission, including quarantine, wearing of face masks, and physical distancing.

Notwithstanding the beneficial impact of many laws promulgated during the COVID-19 pandemic, some have had deleterious social and economic effects, discussed in Chapter 7, and indeed, as explored in Chapter 6, various laws have been challenged in many court actions. This litigation has brought into sharp relief the tensions between the desire to pursue individual liberties and the imperative to protect public health during an ongoing emergency. At times governments were unable to protect all rights and freedoms and needed to strike a delicate balance between competing priorities during the pandemic.

As noted above, in this conclusion to the book, we reflect on insights that can be gained from the legal and regulatory responses to COVID-19 for the management of future pandemics. At the beginning of the pandemic, some of the issues that would become relevant to managing it were not immediately apparent. After two and a half years, however, those matters are now largely identifiable. It is therefore possible to reflect on the ways in which the responses to COVID-19 have illuminated how law and regulation can operate best in future public health emergencies. Also in this conclusion, we discuss some issues that appear, at the time of writing, to pose ongoing dilemmas and challenges for the law to address in tackling this pandemic and future pandemics.

II. Layers of Law and Polycentricity

This book has highlighted the layers of law involved in, and the polycentricity of, responses to the COVID-19 pandemic. As outlined in Chapter 1, the notion of polycentricity provides a useful lens through which government responses to a pandemic can be evaluated. The theory, which derives from the initial work of Vincent and Elinor Ostrom,[7] emphasizes the complexities of government decision-making and governance at multiple levels, and the potential for overlap, conflict, and lack of co-ordination if there is a lack of harmonious common purpose.[8] Risks identified by scholars include a failure to deal adequately with crises and a lack of accountability on the part of government.[9] In the context of governance during a pandemic, it has been argued that it is unhelpful for government to impose

---

[7] See Vincent Ostrom, Charles M Tiebout, and Robert Warren, 'The Organization of Government in Metropolitan Areas: A Theoretical Inquiry' (1961) 55(4) *American Political Science* 831; Elinor Ostrom, 'Polycentric Systems for Coping with Collective Action and Global Environmental Change' (2010) 20(4) *Global Environmental Change* 550.

[8] Ostrom, Tiebout, and Warren (n 7); see also Keith Carlisle and Rebecca L Gruby, 'Polycentric Systems of Governance: A Theoretical Model for the Commons' (2017) 47(4) *Policy Studies Journal* 927, 930–31.

[9] See eg Julia Black, 'Constructing and Contesting Legitimacy and Accountability in Polycentric Regulatory regimes' (2008) 2(2) *Regulation & Governance* 137.

measures directed towards prevention of disease dissemination; the community is more likely to be persuaded to embrace and implement government initiatives if such measures are 'nested' within collective action.[10] In addition, scholars have observed that, while there may be a certain amount of co-operation and respect between governments during a pandemic, it may be a challenge to maintain such co-operation in the longer term.[11]

Existing and new domestic and international laws have been integral to attempts by individual countries and globally to arrest the spread of COVID-19 and minimize its detrimental impact. In Chapters 4 and 5, we analysed relevant public health laws that have been introduced and applied in countries around the world at national, state, and provincial levels, and even at the local government level,[12] during the pandemic. These layers of law and regulation have been placed under pressure throughout the pandemic and have exposed the need for effective co-ordination during, and a co-operative 'whole-of-government' response to, the public health crisis.[13] At each of these layers, public health legislation, rules, and directions have shaped the response to the pandemic, with public health measures, such as lockdowns and restrictions on movement, having significant effects on individuals, families, and communities. Where there has been a high level of co-ordination and agreement between different layers of government, including

---

[10] Pablo Paniagua and Veeshan Rayamajhee, 'A Polycentric Approach for Pandemic Governance: Nested Externalities and Co-production Challenges' (2021) 17(1) *Journal of Institutional Economics* 71.

[11] See Johanne Poirier and Jessica Michelin, 'Facing the Coronavirus Pandemic in the Canadian Federation: Reinforced Dualism and Muted Cooperation?' in Nico Steytler (ed), *Comparative Federalism and Covid-19: Combating the Pandemic* (Routledge 2021) 216.

[12] See eg Organisation for Economic Co-operation and Development, 'The Territorial Impact of COVID-19: Managing the Crisis and Recovery Across Levels of Government' (Policy Response, 10 May 2021) <www.oecd.org/coronavirus/policy-responses/the-territorial-impact-of-covid-19-managing-the-crisis-and-recovery-across-levels-of-government-a2c6abaf/> accessed 31 December 2021; Commonwealth Local Government Forum, 'Local Government Response to COVID-19' (2021) <www.clgf.org.uk/whats-new/local-government-action-on-covid-19/> accessed 14 September 2022; United Kingdom Local Government Association, 'COVID-19: Good Council Practice' <www.local.gov.uk/our-support/coronavirus-council-information-and-support/covid-19-good-council-practice> accessed 14 September 2022; Australian Housing and Urban Research Institute, 'The Role of Local Government in Pandemic Recovery for Australia' (2 June 2021) <www.ahuri.edu.au/research/brief/role-local-government-pandemic-recovery-australia> accessed 14 September 2022; Dylan Talabis and others, 'Local Government Responses for COVID-19 Management in the Philippines' (2021) 21(1) *BMC Public Health* 1711.

[13] See Anne Twomey, 'Federal and State Powers to Deal with Pandemics—Cooperation, Conflict and Confusion' in Belinda Bennett and Ian Freckelton (eds), *Pandemics, Public Health Emergencies and Government Powers: Perspectives on Australian Law* (Federation Press 2021); Cheryl Saunders, 'Grappling with the Pandemic: Rich Insights into Intergovernmental Relations' in Nico Steytler (ed), *Comparative Federalism and Covid-19: Combating the Pandemic* (Routledge 2021) 378–79; Lawrence O Gostin and James G Hodge Jr, 'US Emergency Legal Responses to Novel Coronavirus: Balancing Public Health and Civil Liberties' (2020) 323(12) *Journal of the American Medical Association* 1131; Jonathan Pugh, 'The United Kingdom's Coronavirus Act, Deprivations of Liberty, and the Right to Liberty and Security of the Person' (2020) 7(1) *Journal of Law and the Biosciences* lsaa011; Nico Steytler, Jaap de Visser, and Tinashe Chigwata, 'South Africa: Surfing Toward Centralisation on the Covid-19 Wave' in Nico Steytler (ed), *Comparative Federalism and Covid-19: Combating the Pandemic* (Routledge 2021).

in the laws governments have imposed to support the response to the pandemic, and community acceptance of such measures, these different layers have presented comparatively few difficulties in most countries. However, in some instances, different layers of law and government have presented challenges for co-ordination. This has particularly been the case in federal countries where there are different responsibilities at national and state levels,[14] at times leading to differing approaches between federal and state governments and between state governments over issues such as border closures and quarantine requirements for domestic travellers.[15] Further, as Studdert, Rothstein, and Mello note, the variety and consequent 'patchwork nature' of regulatory responses in different jurisdictions in the United States of America, for example, has been reflected in 'different trajectories' for the spread of COVID-19 in those areas.[16] It will be important to reflect upon the differing policy and regulatory responses that have been adopted by countries at the national, state or provincial, and local levels, and their integration and co-ordination with one another (while also allowing for regional differentiations in approach), as well as their relative success in inhibiting dispersal of the virus and obtaining and maintaining community support for them.[17] For the present, what can be observed is that significant advantages can be identified in consistency of approaches, particularly when such approaches by government are informed by expert medico-scientific analysis of data.

As discussed in Chapter 3, at an international level, the *International Health Regulations 2005 (IHR (2005))* have provided the global regulatory frameworks that enabled the Director-General of the World Health Organization (WHO) to declare a public health emergency of international concern in relation to the spread of COVID-19. Also at a global level, the COVID-19 pandemic and measures that were successful in responding to it have demonstrated the importance of international co-operation and collaboration in addressing global public health emergencies. As identified in Chapters 11 and 12, WHO has played a leading role in mobilizing such international efforts to inhibit the spread of COVID-19, including through developing, producing, and distributing globally both treatments

---

[14] See eg John Kincaid and J Wesley Leckrone, 'American Federalism and Covid-19: Party Trumps Policy' in Nico Steytler (ed), *Comparative Federalism and Covid-19: Combating the Pandemic* (Routledge 2021); Nicholas Aroney and Michael Boyce, 'The Australian Federal Response to the COVID-19 Crisis: Momentary Success or Enduring Reform' in Nico Steytler (ed), *Comparative Federalism and Covid-19: Combating the Pandemic* (Routledge 2021). For an earlier discussion see Belinda Bennett, 'Legal Rights During Pandemics: Federalism, Rights and Public Health Laws – A View from Australia' (2009) 123 *Public Health* 232.
[15] For discussion see Paula O'Brien and Eliza Waters, 'COVID-19: Public Health Emergency Powers and Accountability Mechanisms in Australia' (2021) 28(2) *Journal of Law and Medicine* 346; Holly Mclean and Ben Huf, 'Emergency Powers, Public Health and COVID-19' Research Paper No 2, Parliament of Victoria (August 2020) 35–38; David M Studdert, Mark A Hall, and Michelle M Mello, 'Partitioning the Curve—Interstate Travel Restrictions During the COVID-19 Pandemic' (2020) 383(13) *New England Journal of Medicine* e83.
[16] Studdert, Hall, and Mello (n 15) e83(1).
[17] See Aroney and Boyce (n 14) 314.

and vaccines. The pandemic has highlighted the need for adaptation of intellectual property laws to facilitate equitable international access to such medical products, and internationally consistent laws for monitoring their safety and efficacy. Innovations such as COVAX, a collaboration led by Gavi, the Coalition for Epidemic Preparedness Innovations (CEPI), and WHO to accelerate the development, manufacture, and equitable distribution of COVID-19 vaccines,[18] demonstrate the capacity for international collaboration, but also potential impediments to their effectiveness, including continuing assertions of intellectual property entitlements, treatment parochialism, and vaccine nationalism.

Significant initiatives during this pandemic have demonstrated that it can be vital to use global governance arrangements to facilitate international cooperation. Following the COVID-19 pandemic, it will be important to review the impact of the ACT Accelerator and COVAX, WHO's 'Concept for Fair Access and Equitable Allocation of COVID-19 Health Products',[19] and other policies that were applied to determine how therapeutic resources should be allocated while in scarce supply. Even as 2021 was concluding, simple measures to diagnose COVID-19— by rapid-flow (rapid antigen) or polymerase chain reaction (PCR) testing—were in problematically short supply in a number of countries,[20] in the same way that personal protective equipment had been scarce nearly two years before, at the beginning of the pandemic.

The COVID-19 pandemic has focused international attention on the need to improve global governance structures to prepare for future pandemics. As discussed in Chapter 3, this has prompted interest in developing a 'pandemic treaty', which will constitute an international agreement on strategies for preventing and addressing future pandemics.[21] In light of the decision by the World Health Assembly in November 2021 to begin work on a new convention, agreement, or instrument on pandemic prevention, preparedness, and response,[22] there will be

---

[18] World Health Organization, 'COVAX: Working for Global Equitable Access to COVID-19 Vaccines' <www.who.int/initiatives/act-accelerator/covax> accessed 14 September 2022.

[19] World Health Organization, 'WHO Concept for Fair Access and Equitable Allocation of COVID-19 Health Products' (9 September 2020) <www.who.int/docs/default-source/coronaviruse/who-covid19-vaccine-allocation-final-working-version-9sept.pdf> accessed 14 September 2022.

[20] See Oliver Barnes, John Burn-Murdoch and Laura Hughes, 'Why Are There Covid Test Shortages in the UK?' (31 December 2021) *Financial Times* <https://www.ft.com/content/25c9aa67-2b7e-4b8d-a25b-0b7b7ac48452> accessed 4 October 2022; Yuki Noguchi, 'Why the US's Supply of COVID Tests Has been Unpredictable—and How That Can Change' *NPR* (23 December 2021) <www.npr.org/2021/12/23/1067598843/why-the-u-s-s-supply-of-covid-tests-has-been-unpredictable-and-how-that-can-chan> accessed 4 October 2022.

[21] See eg Ronald Labonté and others, 'A Pandemic Treaty, Revised International Health Regulations, or Both?' (2021) 17 *Globalization and Health* art 128; Lawrence O Gostin, Sam F Halabi, and Kevin A Klock, 'An International Agreement on Pandemic Prevention and Preparedness' (2021) 326(13) *Journal of the American Medical Association* 1257.

[22] World Health Organization, 'World Health Assembly Agrees to Launch Process to Develop Historic Global Accord on Pandemic Prevention, Preparedness and Response' (News Release, 1 December 2021) <www.who.int/news/item/01-12-2021-world-health-assembly-agrees-to-launch-process-to-develop-historic-global-accord-on-pandemic-prevention-preparedness-and-response> accessed 14 September 2022.

international discussion and debate for the foreseeable future about how the global community can best work together to prevent and respond to future pandemics.

As analysed in this book, the legal and regulatory responses to the pandemic have been characterized by polycentricity. A multiplicity of agencies, institutions, non-government organizations, and government departments have contributed to them. This has created a risk of overlap and inconsistency of approach within and between countries in terms of the measures that they have adopted to slow or restrict spread of this disease. For individual countries, the pandemic has also required action and guidance from a range of bodies across society. As discussed in Chapter 7, the pandemic and efforts to halt its dissemination have had widespread social and economic impacts to which some governments have been responsive, such as by developing policies and programmes to provide income support for those who have lost employment due to the imposition of public health measures. In addition, as explored in Chapter 8, criminal justice systems played an important role, for example, by enforcing compliance with public health orders, managing the continued operation of the courts as an essential service during the pandemic, and permitting early release from prison of low-risk offenders in efforts to minimize their risks of contracting and suffering from COVID-19.[23] Employers also faced dilemmas in continuing to function during the pandemic. The potential for COVID-19 to spread within work environments, as examined in Chapter 10, presented new challenges for workplace health and safety, and necessarily engaged employers and employees alike in tackling risks posed by the pandemic.

A distinctive element of governments' responses to the COVID-19 pandemic was their support for the collaboration between clinicians, epidemiologists, and scientific researchers in their pandemic-related work, as well as governments' reliance upon this research. More than has been possible previously, responses to the risks of pandemic transmission were informed and, at times, driven by data assembled in relation to the virus and its variants, its spread, and the relative success of measures intended to limit its transmission. Indeed, public health officials and governments often emphasized that their responses were influenced by medical science. This has been more than political rhetoric. The synergy between medicine, science, and law was a phenomenon of the COVID-19 pandemic and is likely to constitute a template for future responses to pandemics.

However, as discussed in Chapter 3, the emphasis given to data-based action by public health authorities globally has highlighted the need for consistent definitions in respect of deaths and hospital admissions caused by a pandemic and for

---

[23] Benjamin Barsky and others, 'Vaccination Plus Decarceration—Stopping Covid-19 in Jails and Prisons' (2021) 384(17) *New England Journal of Medicine* 1583; Hope Metcalf, 'Life and Death in Prisons' in Morten Kjaerum, Martha F Davis, and Amanda Lyons (eds), *COVID-19 and Human Rights* (Routledge 2021); Adelina Iftene, 'COVID-19 in Canadian Prisons: Policies, Practices and Concerns' in Colleen M Flood and others (eds), *Vulnerable: The Law, Policy and Ethics of COVID-19* (University of Ottawa Press 2020).

countries to compile data accurately and make reports of data accessible. It is only by reference to sound data, including, wherever available, genomic sequencing showing genetic variations in a disease, that it is possible to identify local and international trends and patterns in disease spread and evolution.[24] Genomic sequencing of a disease that spread internationally first occurred during the 2013–16 Ebola outbreak and then during the Zika epidemic of 2015–16, thereby laying the foundations for responses to COVID-19 and making it the most highly tested outbreak in history.[25] In turn, this focus upon analysis of the constituents of a disease and its variants is likely to constitute a template for how future epidemics and pandemics are managed.[26]

This book's examination of the wide range of laws and regulations that were utilized to address the COVID-19 pandemic, and the broad range of organizations and institutions that were engaged in this endeavour, reveals the complexity of meeting challenges posed by a global health emergency. In particular, it has highlighted the importance of resolving inconsistencies between laws and regulations made at local, state or provincial, national, and international levels. Further, while the pandemic has demonstrated that various bodies can contribute valuably to responding to a health crisis, clarifying their distinct roles and decision-making authority at the outset is crucial to avoid misunderstandings or conflict. Legal and regulatory responses to the COVID-19 pandemic have illuminated the need to develop sophisticated, collaborative, and multifaceted plans and frameworks for future public health emergencies to ensure consistency between and effectiveness of laws and regulations, and co-operation and co-ordination between bodies that impose and implement them.

III. The Role and Scope of Law

In this book we have explored the essential roles played by a wide range of laws and regulations in responding to the challenges posed by the COVID-19 pandemic. This analysis highlights that an important aspect of pandemic preparedness is consideration of how the law can be used to improve people's prospects of positive

---

[24] See eg Courtney Lane, 'Genomic-informed Responses in the Elimination of COVID-19 in Victoria, Australia: An Observational, Genomic Epidemiological Study' (2021) 6(8) *Lancet Public Health* E547; Public Health Ontario, 'SARS-CoV-2 Whole Genome Sequencing in Ontario' (Weekly Epidemiologcal Summary, 29 December 2021) <www.publichealthontario.ca/-/media/documents/ncov/epi/covid-19-sars-cov2-whole-genome-sequencing-epi-summary.pdf?sc_lang=en> accessed 15 September 2022.

[25] See Angela Beckett and Samuel Ronson, 'How COVID-19 Transformed Genomics and Changed the Handling of Disease Outbreaks Forever' *The Conversation* (2 January 2022) <https://theconversation.com/how-covid-19-transformed-genomics-and-changed-the-handling-of-disease-outbreaks-forever-173299> accessed 15 September 2022.

[26] Yuki Furuse, 'Genomic Sequencing Effort for SARS-CoV-2 by Country During the Pandemic' (2021) 103 *International Journal of Infectious Diseases* 305.

health, social, and economic outcomes. In addition, such planning needs to contemplate safeguards that can be introduced to mitigate the potential for unnecessary overreach of the law despite the emergency context.

As discussed in Chapter 5, under international human rights law, governments can impose measures in emergencies that encroach upon some human rights—some rights are non-derogable—provided the restrictions meet certain requirements, including by being the least restrictive, feasible, necessary, proportionate, and time-limited.[27] As we move to the period after the COVID-19 pandemic, it will be important for the exceptional laws that were introduced in response to the emergency (often justified through use of war or battle language)[28] to be limited (if they are still necessary to respond to the impact of the pandemic) or repealed when they are no longer required.[29] Exceptional laws that encroach on human rights and were enacted in response to an emergency should not be retained when the emergency has passed. We consider these issues in more detail below in Section V.

The notion of pandemic exceptionalism—relaxing usual laws and increasing the flexibility and agility of regulation to tackle exigencies posed by a public health emergency—has also arisen in the context of research undertaken into COVID-19 treatments and vaccines.[30] There is the potential for inappropriate research shortcuts to be taken under cover of the need for breakthroughs. The outcomes can be detrimental to research trajectories and create erroneous expectations of the efficacy of treatments and prevention agents that are in fact ineffective or even dangerous. As identified in Chapter 11, requiring adherence to orthodox ethical obligations in research contributes to protecting the public.

Chapter 11 also discussed significant dilemmas faced by regulators and the international scholarly and research community in seeking to develop and make urgently available to the public safe and effective medical products. It will be important to reflect on the impact of some of the decisions that were taken during the pandemic in this regard, such as to: expedite the usual steps involved in conducting clinical trials; undertake human challenge trials; enrol in trials people who were unable to provide informed consent to their participation in them; distribute research results before they had been subjected to substantial peer review; and enable access

---

[27] United Nations Economic and Social Council Commission on Human Rights, *The Siracusa Principles on the Limitation and Derogation Provisions in the International Covenant on Civil and Political Rights* (Resolution E/CN.4/1985/4, 28 September1984) (hereafter *Siracusa Principles*). For discussion see Audrey Lebret, 'COVID-19 Pandemic and Derogation to Human Rights' (2020) 7(1) *Journal of Law and the Biosciences* art lsaa015 .

[28] See Jessica Kirk and Matt McDonald, 'The Politics of Exceptionalism: Securitization and COVID-19' (2021) 1(3) *Global Studies Quarterly* art ksab024.

[29] For a discussion of the politics of exceptionalism in law-making, see Julian Arato, Kathleen Claussen, and J Benton Heath, 'The Perils of Pandemic Exceptionalism' (2020) 114(4) *American Journal of International Law* 627.

[30] Holly Fernandez Lynch and others, 'Regulatory Flexibility for COVID-19 Research' (2020) 7(1) *Journal of Law and the Biosciences* art lsaa057; Alex John London and Jonathan Kimmelman, 'Against Pandemic Research Exceptionalism' (2020) 368(6490) *Science* 476.

to treatments and vaccines before they had completed orthodox testing phases. While there may be scope for research exceptionalism, and while there may be justifications for methodologies such as human challenge trials during a pandemic, there needs to be rigorous oversight and adherence to accepted processes to ensure that research is consistent with appropriate ethical and legal standards.

The breadth of legal issues that have arisen during the COVID-19 pandemic has demonstrated for the future that responding effectively to the impact of a public health crisis may necessitate the application of laws and regulatory measures beyond public health orders. For example, as identified in Chapter 9, regulatory authorities have needed to take steps to protect consumers from false or misleading advertising about products that purport to treat or prevent COVID-19. Medical regulatory agencies have also taken action at times in relation to health practitioners whose communications with patients have been regarded as contrary to accepted public health advice. Further, Chapter 12 examined use of intellectual property law to meet the challenge of distributing COVID-19 vaccines across the globe.

In other contexts, a wide variety of inquiries and reports have reviewed decision-making during the pandemic and made important recommendations for the future. For instance, a panel constituted by WHO has asserted that available evidence 'has revealed failures and gaps in international and national responses that must be corrected. Current institutions, public and private, failed to protect people from a devastating pandemic':[31]

> Without change, they will not prevent a future one. That is why the Panel is recommending a fundamental transformation designed to ensure commitment at the highest level to a new system that is coordinated, connected, fast-moving, accountable, just, and equitable — in other words, a complete pandemic preparedness and response system on which citizens can rely to keep them safe and healthy.[32]

A further example of such independent reports from which lessons can be learned about the requirement for fairness in responses to the onset of a pandemic is the 2021 report of the European Court of Auditors. It concluded that air passengers were not informed adequately about their rights during the COVID-19 crisis and recommended that the European Commission should: better protect the rights of air passengers and inform them about their rights; enhance the co-ordination of national measures and better link State aid to airlines to ensure their reimbursement

---

[31] The Independent Panel for Pandemic Preparedness and Response, 'COVID-19: Make it the Last Pandemic' (Report, May 2021) 4 <https://theindependentpanel.org/wp-content/uploads/2021/05/COVID-19-Make-it-the-Last-Pandemic_final.pdf> accessed 5 October 2022.
[32] ibid.

of passengers' payment for flights that were cancelled; and improve the tools and legislation for safeguarding air passengers' rights.[33]

In 2021, Imperial College London generated an overview of the pandemic's threat with a specific focus on outbreak size, severity, intervention policy, and genetics.[34] It described work assessing the interventions, health impacts, transmission patterns, and indirect effects of COVID-19, as well as an overview of the support provided by real-time modelling, the Real-time Assessment of Community Transmission (REACT) studies, the European and global response, and various forms of software and tools that had been developed. Both the United Kingdom[35] and Australian[36] governments have commissioned an unparalleled series of investigations and reports into responses to the COVID-19 pandemic. In the United Kingdom a COVID-19 Committee[37] and in New Zealand an Epidemic Response Committee[38] were established to table reports to Parliament on the COVID-19 response. The various inquiries and reports that have been published, some of which have been tabled in parliaments, provide valuable insights into the role and scope of law during a pandemic, and into changes that should be made prior to a further pandemic.

Another important issue that emerged during the COVID-19 pandemic is how to determine the most effective means for understanding and evaluating the effects on population health of laws and legal practices. For instance, writing by reference to 'legal epidemiology', Burris and others have pointed out that:

Laws are not pills and cannot be developed, pretested, dosed, and delivered like pills. That said, the relative neglect of research on law as a factor in the level and distribution of health is a matter of habit and culture, not the limits of scientific possibility.[39]

---

[33] European Court of Auditors, 'Air Passenger Rights During the COVID-19 Pandemic: Key Rights Not Protected Despite Commission Efforts' Special Report 15 (2021) <https://op.europa.eu/webpub/eca/special-reports/passenger-rights-15-2021/en/> accessed 5 October 2021.

[34] Centre for Infectious Disease Analysis, *Imperial College COVID-19 Response Team Report 2020– 2021* (Report, 2021) <www.imperial.ac.uk/media/imperial-college/medicine/mrc-gida/Imperial-College-COVID-19-Response-Team-2020-2021-Report-(22-03-2021).pdf> accessed 3 June 2022.

[35] For an extensive list of the parliamentary committees' reports, see United Kingdom Parliament, 'Inquiries and Reports' <www.parliament.uk/business/publications/coronavirus/inquiries-and-reports/> accessed 15 September 2022.

[36] See Ian Freckelton, 'Government Inquiries, Investigations and Reports During the COVID-19 Pandemic' in Belinda Bennett and Ian Freckelton (eds), *Pandemics, Public Health Emergencies and Government Powers: Perspectives on Australian Law* (Federation Press 2021).

[37] United Kingdom Parliament, 'COVID-19 Committee Lords Select Committee' <https://committees.parliament.uk/committee/460/covid19-committee/> accessed 15 September 2022.

[38] See New Zealand Parliament, 'Epidemic Response Committee: COVID-19 2020' <www.parliament.nz/en/visit-and-learn/history-and-buildings/special-topics/epidemic-response-committee-covid-19-2020/> accessed 15 September 2022.

[39] Scott Burris, Evan D Anderson, and Alexander C Wagenaar, 'The "Legal Epidemiology" of Pandemic Control' (2021) 384(21) *New England Journal of Medicine* 1973, 1974. 'Legal epidemiology' has been defined as 'the scientific study and deployment of law as a factor in the cause, distribution, and prevention of disease and injury in a population': see Scott Burris, Lindsay K Cloud, and Matthew

This observation has led these scholars to call for an escalation of research into: the mechanisms, effects, side-effects, and implementation of laws designed to influence matters such as the dispersal of a communicable virus; how the legal infrastructure of the health system influences its effectiveness; and diverse issues of health equity, including how laws that may appear to have no purpose of improving health outcomes in fact shape the social determinants of health.[40]

A related area of further research, which is also relevant to risk issues discussed in Section IV, that could usefully be undertaken concerns how the COVID-19 pandemic has affected the social determinants of health. The pandemic has exposed that the longstanding structural drivers of health inequities are particularly susceptible to exacerbation during a public health crisis. These factors include precarious and adverse working conditions, economic disparities, and insufficiently democratic political processes and institutions.[41] Abrams and Szefler have properly called for the social determinants of health to be prioritized as part of pandemic research, public health policy development, and policy implementation.[42] An associated challenge is to ascertain the means by which law, including international law, can be harnessed to enhance the social determinants of health and reduce inequity.

IV. Understandings of and Legal Responses to Risk

Evaluations of the nature and level of risk that the virus has posed to human health have prompted legal and regulatory responses to the COVID-19 pandemic during each of its phases. However, as the pandemic evolved, it became increasingly apparent that individuals faced different forms and degrees of risk, and that risks they faced varied depending on the country in which they lived. This public health emergency thus highlighted for the future the need for the law to address the disproportionate impact of a pandemic both within countries and globally, as well as how the laws that are used to inhibit its spread affect all aspects of the community—both directly and indirectly. Simultaneously, the emergence of COVID-19 has amplified appreciation internationally of the threats that zoonotic diseases pose to all of humanity, and accelerated scientific investigation into and consideration of

---

Penn, 'The Growing Field of Legal Epidemiology' (2020) 26(2) *Journal of Public Health Management and Practice* S4, S4.

[40] Burris, Anderson, and Wagenaar (n 39) 1975.

[41] See Lauren Paremoer and others, 'Covid-19 Pandemic and the Social Determinants of Health' (2021) 372 *British Medical Journal* 129.

[42] Elissa M Abrams and Stanley J Szefler, 'COVID-19 and the Impact of Social Determinants of Health' (2020) 8(7) *Lancet Respiratory Medicine* 659, 660; see too William C Cockerham and Geoffrey B Cockerham, *The Covid-19 Reader: The Science and What it Says About the Social* (Routledge 2021).

approaches that can mitigate those risks. It will be important to review how legal structures and requirements can best support these developments in the future.

As discussed in Chapter 7, it emerged that some people and communities had a higher probability of experiencing poor outcomes during the COVID-19 pandemic. For instance, those who lived in crowded accommodation or were homeless and/or lack access to means of maintaining sound hygiene practices, were at increased risk of contracting the virus. People with comorbidities and those of older age were especially vulnerable to experiencing severe symptoms of illness and dying from COVID-19 if they contracted it. Indigenous communities in many countries have been identified as having been at particular risk during the pandemic, both directly and indirectly, because of their health disadvantages and inequitable access to healthcare.[43] Using disease tracking methodologies and other measures to evaluate the impact of a public health crisis will be important to develop strategies to optimize protection of Indigenous communities in future pandemics.[44]

In addition, emergency domestic laws on which governments relied during the COVID-19 pandemic to impose public health measures had especially adverse effects on particular social groups, such as people who have been unable to continue their work remotely and thus lost employment, business owners who have needed to discontinue their operations during lockdowns, and people for whom stay-at-home orders heightened their risk of experiencing domestic violence or mental illness. Certain industries, such as those involved in tourism and hospitality, were especially affected and will need to evolve to regain their viability.[45] As discussed in Chapter 7, children also experienced significant impacts from the COVID-19 pandemic, including interruption to schooling, disruption of childhood vaccination programs, and loss of caregivers due to pandemic-related mortality. Many members of the community in receipt of medical treatment or in need of medical investigations were not able to access medical services that in normal times are more available.[46] In addition, the pandemic and legal and regulatory responses to

---

[43] See eg David Follent and others, 'The Indirect Impacts of COVID-19 on Aboriginal Communities Across New South Wales' (2021) 214(5) *Medical Journal of Australia* 199.

[44] See Stephanie R Carroll and others, 'Indigenous Peoples' Data During COVID-19: From External to Internal' (2021) 6 *Frontiers in Sociology* 62; Alistair Mallard and others, 'An Urgent Call to Collect Data Related to COVID-19 and Indigenous Populations Globally' (2021) 6(3) *BMC Global Health* art e004655.

[45] See Dogan Gursoy and Christina G Chi, 'Effects of COVID-19 Pandemic on Hospitality Industry: Review of the Current Situations and Research Agenda' (2020) 29(5) *Journal of Hospitality, Marketing & Management* 527; David Y Aharon and others, 'COVID-19, Government Measures and Hospitality Industry Performance' (2021) 16(8) *PLoS One* art e0255819; Muhammad Rahman and others, 'Effect of Covid-19 Pandemic on Tourist Travel and Management Perceptions' (2021) 16(9) *PloS One* art e0256486; Gagan D Sharma, Asha Thomas, and Justin Paul, 'Reviving Tourism Industry Post-COVID-19: A Resilience-based Framework' (2021) *Tourism Management Perspectives* art 100786.

[46] See eg World Health Organization, 'COVID-19 Significantly Impacts Health Services for Communicable Diseases' (News Release, 1 June 2020) <www.who.int/news/item/01-06-2020-covid-19-significantly-impacts-health-services-for-noncommunicable-diseases> accessed 15 September 2022; Ray Moynihan and others, 'Impact of COVID-19 Pandemic on Utilisation of Healthcare

it generated a range of problematic mental health consequences, including heightened fears and new anxieties, which will take time to resolve after the pandemic has completely passed. In these respects, the pandemic has highlighted that in future it will be crucial for governments to consider how they can support members of the population who are at heightened risk during a pandemic and minimize the deleterious effects of public health measures introduced as part of efforts to curb the spread of infectious disease.

Some issues of risk have been considered in the context of litigation. For example, in Canadian litigation, as discussed in Chapter 6, an issue arose relating to whether the state or its instrumentalities were obliged to maintain certain physical distances between bunk beds in shelter support,[47] or to require the wearing of face masks or face-coverings by children in schools in order to protect their family members.[48] Interestingly, in these challenges to state power there was the assertion of a requirement that there be the adoption by government of more stringent measures to protect sectors of the community identified as being at particular risk by reason of their health status.

Issues relating to risk have also arisen in the context of debates over vaccine mandates, as discussed in Chapters 5 and 10. The mandates potentially protected many people's health and lives; if they increased the vaccination rate, they may have reduced the risk of contracting and transmitting COVID-19, and developing severe illness or dying from it.[49] As the United States District Court for South Carolina held in October 2021 in response to a legal challenge to a vaccine mandate, 'While plaintiffs may remain unvaccinated at their own risk, the balance of equities and public interest do not require defendants to allow plaintiffs to spread that risk in their workplace and, by extension, into the communities they serve.'[50]

The COVID-19 pandemic has also drawn attention to the disparities in global health. People in many low- and middle-income countries and poor communities in high-income countries suffered disproportionately high rates of infection and mortality from COVID-19 due to factors such as overcrowding, and the nature of their employment in dense and unhygienic working conditions. In addition, as examined in Chapter 12, low- and middle-income countries did not have access to COVID-19 treatment and vaccines comparable to that which was available in high-income countries. This is relevant to attainment and implementation of the

---

Services: A Systematic Review' (2021) 11(3) *BMJ Open* art e045343; Mikko Uimonen, 'The Impact of the COVID-19 Pandemic on Waiting Times for Elective Surgery Patients: A Multicenter Study' (2021) 16(7) *PLoS One* art e0253875.

[47] *Sanctuary Ministries of Toronto v Toronto (City)* (2020) 152 OR (3d) 411.
[48] *Trest v British Columbia (Minister of Health)* 2020 BCSC 1524.
[49] See Gabrielle Wolf, Jason Taliadoros, and Penny Gleeson, 'A Panacea for Australia's COVID-19 Crisis? Weighing Some Legal Implications of Mandatory Vaccination' (2021) 28(4) *Journal of Law and Medicine* 993, 996–97.
[50] *Bauer v Summey* 568 F Supp 3d 573 (DSC 2021) [606].

Sustainable Development Goals.[51] While compromises have been made to intellectual property rights during the development of these medical products, they did not result in the equitable availability of vaccines and treatments throughout the world. In fact, the inequities were confronting, and vaccine nationalism and treatment parochialism resulted in a gross disparity between access to the highest attainable standard of health in high-income countries by contrast with countries with lower incomes.

Gleeson and multiple organizations have highlighted that this inequity is more than an ethical issue; it has the potential to have global consequences if it enables further waves of preventable illness to emanate from countries that are unable to access vaccines and where, as a result, COVID-19 spreads at high rates and mutations proliferate.[52] At a time when levels of vaccination in Africa were well below 10%, and a number of countries were reliant upon 'leftover vaccines', high-income countries were in a position to focus on providing booster vaccinations to their populations. The People's Vaccine Alliance ('the Alliance') documented on 21 November 2021 that 49% of the vaccines sold by AstraZeneca, Pfizer/BioNTech, Moderna, and Johnson and Johnson had been delivered to high-income countries, even though such countries only comprise 16% of the world's entire population.[53] Moreover, as of that date, while the countries of the African Union have a collective population three times larger than the countries of the European Union, the African Union Vaccine Acquisition Trust, a vaccine procurement platform, had been able to purchase only 100 million doses from Pfizer/BioNTech and Johnson and Johnson, compared to the European Union, which had purchased nearly 1.5 billion doses from AstraZeneca, Pfizer/BioNTech, Moderna, and Johnson and Johnson, or approximately 15 times the number of doses compared to the African Union.[54] The Alliance asserted that, via bilateral contractual arrangements, Moderna had sold in the order of nine of every ten doses to high-income countries,

---

[51] Babatunde Abidoye and others, 'Leaving No One Behind: Impact of COVID-19 on the Sustainable Development Goals (SDGs)' (Report, United Nations Development Program and Frederick S Pardee Center for International Futures, 2021) < https://data.undp.org/wp-content/uploads/2021/04/Leaving-No-One-Behind-COVID-impact-on-the-SDGs-second-flagship-2.pdf > accessed 15 September 2022.

[52] Deborah Gleeson, 'Wealthy Nations Starved the Developing World of Vaccines. Omicron Shows the Cost of this Greed' *The Conversation* (30 November 2021) <https://theconversation.com/wealthy-nations-starved-the-developing-world-of-vaccines-omicron-shows-the-cost-of-this-greed-172763> accessed 15 September 2022. See also Seth Berkley, 'No One is Safe Until Everyone is Safe' (29 October 2021) <www.gavi.org/vaccineswork/no-one-safe-until-everyone-safe> accessed 15 September 2022; World Health Organization, 'A Global Pandemic Requires a World Effort to End it: None of us Will be Safe Until Everyone is Safe' (30 September 2020) <www.who.int/news-room/commentaries/detail/a-global-pandemic-requires-a-world-effort-to-end-it-none-of-us-will-be-safe-until-everyone-is-safe> accessed 15 September 2022.

[53] Rohit Malpani and Alex Maitland, 'Dose of Reality: How Rich Countries and Pharmaceutical Corporations are Breaking their Vaccine Promises' (*The People's Vaccine*, 21 October 2021) <https://app.box.com/s/hk2ezb71vf0sla719jx34v0ehs0l22os> accessed 15 Septembember 2022; see too World Health Organization, 'Vaccine Equity' (2021) <www.who.int/campaigns/vaccine-equity> accessed 15 September 2022.

[54] Malpani and Maitland (n 53).

while Pfizer/BioNTech had sold eight times as many doses to high-income countries compared to doses sold to low- and middle-income countries.[55]

Prior to the COVID-19 pandemic, the extent of the zoonotic threat to the world was understood in principle, with up to three quarters of emerging infectious diseases recognized as having a zoonotic origin.[56] However, COVID-19 has generated a much higher level of awareness about the many sources of risk of the emergence and transmission of new zoonotic diseases.[57] As we discussed in Chapter 1, during the COVID-19 pandemic an increased global interest in One Health emerged. One Health constitutes a collaborative, multisectoral, and transdisciplinary approach—working at local, regional, national, and global levels—with the goal of achieving improved health outcomes by recognizing the interconnectedness of people, animals, plants, and their shared environment.[58] One Health can be relevant for the design and implementation of programmes, policies, legislation, and research.[59]

The United States' Centers for Disease Control and Prevention has observed that COVID-19 has highlighted the multiple relationships and intersections between humans and the natural world.[60] The virus infected companion, wildlife, zoo, and production animals and, although animals did not play a significant ongoing role in the spread of the virus, the virus has demonstrated the importance of rigorous surveillance of signs of emerging diseases to identify the potential for new hosts and reservoirs where diseases, including COVID-19, may be able to mutate and potentially become a threat to humans.[61] The United States' Centers for Disease Control and Prevention stated in November 2021: 'One of the lessons learned from COVID-19 is that emerging zoonotic infectious diseases are here to stay and fighting new disease threats such as COVID-19, Ebola, and Zika requires One Health collaboration across human, animal, and environmental health organizations'.[62]

---

[55] ibid.
[56] Kate E Jones, 'Global Trends in Emerging Infectious Diseases' (2008) 451(7181) *Nature* 990.
[57] See eg Michael Greger, *How to Survive a Pandemic* (Bluebird Books 2021) 335–36; Odette K Lawler and others, 'The COVID-19 Pandemic is Intricately Linked to Biodiversity Loss and Ecosystem Health' (2021) 5(11) *Lancet Planetary Health* E840.
[58] See eg Mohamed E El Zowalaty and Josef D Järhult, 'From SARS to COVID-19: A Previously Unknown SARS-related Coronavirus (SARS CoV-2) of Pandemic Potential Infecting Humans—Call for a One Health Approach' (2020) 9 *One Health* art 100124; Arne Ruckert and others, 'What Role for One Health in the COVID-19 Pandemic?' (2020) 111 *Canadian Journal of Public Health* 641.
[59] World Health Organization Regional Office for Europe, 'One Health' <https:euro.who.int/en/health-topics/health-policy/one-health> accessed 21 December 2021.
[60] Centers for Disease Control and Prevention, 'Importance of One Health for COVID-19 and Future Pandemics' (Media Statement, 3 November 2021) <www.cdc.gov/media/releases/2021/s1103-one-health.html> accessed 15 September 2022.
[61] ibid.
[62] ibid. The emergence of Monkeypox as a public health emergency of international concern has further emphasised this: see Mark Eccleston-Turner, 'Monkeypox as a PHEIC: Implications for Global Health Governance' (1 August 2022) *Lancet*; Ian Freckelton and Gabrielle Wolf, 'Responses to Monkeypox: Learning from Previous Public Health Emergencies' (2022) 29(4) *Journal of Law and Medicine* (in press).

A key outcome of COVID-19 has been the launch of a new 'One Health High-Level Expert Panel', which is intended to improve understanding of how diseases with the potential to trigger pandemics emerge and spread.[63] Operating under the One Health approach, the panel will advise four international organizations— the Food and Agriculture Organization of the United Nations (FAO); the World Organisation for Animal Health (OIE); the United Nations Environment Programme (UNEP); and WHO—on the development of a long-term global plan of action to avert outbreaks of diseases like H5N1 avian influenza, Middle East Respiratory Syndrome (MERS), Ebola, Zika, and, possibly, COVID-19.[64] Key first steps will include: systematic analyses of scientific knowledge about the factors that lead to transmission of a disease from animal to human and vice versa; development of risk assessment and surveillance frameworks; identification of capacity gaps; as well as agreement on good practices to prevent and prepare for zoonotic outbreaks.[65] It is planned that the panel will consider the impact of human activity on the environment and wildlife habitats and, specifically, the critical areas of: food production and distribution; urbanization and infrastructure development; international travel and trade; activities that lead to biodiversity loss and climate change; and those that put increased pressure on the natural resource base—all of which can lead to the emergence of zoonotic diseases. It is hoped that the panel will guide development of a dynamic new research agenda and draw up evidence-based recommendations for global, regional, national, and local action.[66]

Legal structures and legislative support for One Health are fundamental to entrenching consciousness of and implementation of One Health approaches.[67] Ruckert and others[68] have correctly pointed out that until now there has been little integration of One Health principles in international treaties and regulations. However, COVID-19 has provided an impetus for addressing this deficit. The proposed pandemic treaty has the potential to 'help establish a permanent global One

---

[63] World Health Organization, 'New International Expert Panel to Address the Emergence and Spread of Zoonotic Diseases' (Joint News Releaase, 20 May 2021) <www.who.int/news/item/20-05-2021-new-international-expert-panel-to-address-the-emergence-and-spread-of-zoonotic-diseases> accessed 15 September 2022.
[64] ibid.
[65] ibid.
[66] ibid.
[67] Alexandra L Phelan and Lawrence O Gostin, 'Law as a Fixture Between the One Health Interfaces of Emerging Diseases' (2017) 111(6) *Transactions of the Royal Society of Tropical Medicine and Hygiene* 241; Guirong Fang and Qunli Song, 'Legislative Advancement of One Health in China in the Context of the COVID-19 Pandemic: From the Perspective of the Wild Animal Conservation Law' (2021) 12 *One Health* art 100195; Food and Agriculture Organization of the United Nations, 'One Health Legislation: Contributing to Pandemic Prevention Through Law' (Policy Brief, 2020) <www.fao.org/3/ca9729en/ca9729en.pdf> accessed 21 December 2021, ranging through sanitary and phytosanitary regulation, environmental protection legislation, legislation for the conservation and sustainable use of biodiversity, forestry, wildlife, and fisheries legislation and antimicrobial resistance legislation.
[68] Arne Ruckert and others, 'One Health as a Pillar for a Transformative Pandemic Treaty' Global Health Centre Policy Brief, 2021 <www.graduateinstitute.ch/sites/internet/files/2021-11/policybrief-onehealth-v3.pdf> accessed 15 September 2022.

Health structure that, among other tasks, could oversee and provide technical and scientific support during treaty implementation, review and resolve evolving policy issues, and contribute to current and forthcoming pandemic protocol and guideline negotiations'.[69]

As discussed in many of the chapters in this book, the law has supported the extraordinary medico-scientific achievements and collaborations that have ameliorated risks to human health posed by the COVID-19 pandemic. These successes have laid the foundations for future medico-scientific developments to which the law will need to respond, including by facilitating further research and implementing various innovations. In this way, the pandemic has provided an important spur to inter-disciplinary research collaboration.[70]

Major early research achievements during the COVID-19 pandemic were the expedited genomic sequencing of the virus by the Institut Pasteur by 29 January 2020,[71] and the prompt international availability of the sequencing.[72] Genomic understanding of the virus allowed the mapping of the 'human genetic architecture' of COVID-19,[73] which in turn enabled understanding of particular susceptibilities to the virus, and improvements to be made to the sensitivity and specificity of means of detecting variants of the virus. This process provided a roadmap for how we shall need to respond to other pandemic threats. As Sylvie Briand, Director of Global Infectious Hazard Preparedness for WHO, has identified:

> As more countries move to implement sequencing programmes, there will be further opportunities to better understand the world of emerging pathogens and their interactions with humans and animals in a variety of climates, ecosystems, cultures, lifestyles and biomes. This knowledge will shape a new vision of

---

[69] ibid 3; see too Hélène Carabin, 'One Health: A Crucial Approach to Preventing and Preparing for Future Pandemics' *The Conversation* (24 December 2021) <https://theconversation.com/one-health-a-crucial-approach-to-preventing-and-preparing-for-future-pandemics-173637> accessed 15 September 2022.

[70] See Ryosuke L Ohniwa and others, 'COVID-19 as a Research Dynamic Transformer: Emerging Cross-Disciplinary and National Characteristics' (2021) 4 *Frontiers in Big Data* art 631073; Merrill Singer and others, 'Syndemics: A Cross-Disciplinary Approach to Complex Epidemic Events like COVID-19' (2021) 50 *Annual Review of Anthropology* 41; Yojana Sharma, 'COVID-19 Starts Push for More Interdisciplinary Research' *University World News* (25 July 2021) <www.universityworldnews.com/post.php?story=20200724125405567> accessed 17 September 2022.

[71] Institut Pasteur, 'Whole Genome of Novel Coronavirus, 2019-nCoV, Sequenced' *Science Daily* (31 January 2020) <www.sciencedaily.com/releases/2020/01/200131114748.htm> accessed 17 September 2022.

[72] See Azadeh Rahimi, Azin Mirzazadeh, and Soheil Tavakolpour, 'Genetics and Genomic of SARS-CoV-2: A Review of the Literature with the Special Focus on Genetic Diversity and SARS-CoV-2 Genome Detection' (2021) 113(1) *Genomics* 1221.

[73] Mari EK Niemi and others, 'Mapping the Human Genetic Architecture of COVID-19' (2021) 600(7889) *Nature* 472.

the world and open new paradigms in epidemic and pandemic prevention and control.[74]

These developments have also facilitated the global tracking of the spread of mutations of the virus and the creation of a growing number of appropriately researched and tested COVID-19 vaccines. Sir Jeremy Farrar, Director of the Wellcome Trust, has aptly described the medico-scientific accomplishments during the COVID-19 pandemic as follows:

This is one of the most epic and pioneering moments in human history, comparable to the race to put a man on the moon, the discovery of DNA, or the first ascent of Everest. ... Science is the exit strategy, as long as we make that science equitably available to the world.[75]

V. Human Rights

The legal and regulatory responses to the COVID-19 pandemic engaged human rights that are recognized under domestic and international law. Human rights organizations and scholars have rightly cautioned against neglecting human rights in the haste to address the exigencies of an emergency situation.[76] Moreover, they have emphasized that respect for human rights should meaningfully inform decision-making during a pandemic.[77] Yet the COVID-19 pandemic has highlighted that, during a public health crisis, protecting some human rights will necessarily involve encroaching upon other human rights. In the balances that governments, regulatory authorities, and courts have struck between different interests and rights lie important lessons for responding to future health crises.

In Chapters 3, 4, 5, 6, and 8, we examined a range of existing laws and regulations that were applied and new ones that were enacted in an attempt to inhibit the spread of the highly contagious COVID-19 virus. They largely reflected governments' prioritization of protecting the human rights to life and 'the highest

---

[74] Sylvie Briand, 'Preface' to World Health Organization, 'Genomic Sequencing of SARS-CoV-2: A Guide to Implementation for Maximum Impact on Public Health' (8 January 2021) <www.who.int/publications/i/item/9789240018440> accessed 15 September 2022.

[75] Jeremy Farrar, 'Endorsement' in Sarah Gilbert and Catherine Green, *Vaxxers: The Inside Story of the Oxford AstraZeneca Vaccine and the Race Against the Virus* (Hodder & Stoughton, 2021) ii. See too Brendan Borrell, *The First Shots: The Epic Rivalries and Heroic Science Behind the Race to the Coronavirus Vaccine* (Text Publishing 2021)in relation to Operation Warp Speed.

[76] See eg United Nations, *COVID-19 and Human Rights: We Are All in This Together* (April 2020) 2–3 <https://unsdg.un.org/sites/default/files/2020-04/COVID-19-and-Human-Rights.pdf> accessed 21 December 2021 (hereafter United Nations, *COVID-19 and Human Rights*; Morten Kjaerum, Martha F Davis, and Amanda Lyons (eds), *COVID-19 and Human Rights* (Routledge 2021); Stefan Kirchner (ed), *Governing the Crisis: Law, Human Rights and COVID-19* (Lit Verlag 2021).

[77] See eg United Nations, *COVID-19 and Human Rights* (n 76) 2–3.

attainable standard' of 'health' ('right to health'), which are recognized in, amongst other things, the *International Covenant on Civil and Political Rights (ICCPR)*,[78] above promoting other human rights. Key examples of such laws discussed in this book were intended to prevent people from contracting, becoming ill, and dying from COVID-19. They required people to adhere to public health measures (including isolation of individuals who tested positive for the virus; quarantine of individuals who may have been exposed to the virus; stay-at-home orders; lockdowns; curfews; and closure of borders to local areas, larger regions, states and countries), and criminalized conduct that could increase the spread of COVID-19. While these laws may have protected the rights to life and health, they also restricted other rights, which are recognized in various legal instruments, such as the *ICCPR*, including people's exercise of rights of freedom of movement, expression, peaceful assembly, and religious practice.[79] Some laws explicitly affected these rights by prohibiting public protests and gatherings for religious observance, ostensibly due to the risks they posed for transmission of COVID-19.

As discussed in Chapter 6, across the world, these laws and their intrusion on the enjoyment of human rights were often subject to legal challenges, many of which were unsuccessful. Courts' support for laws that placed public health and community interests above individuals' liberties may give governments confidence to enforce laws that restrict human rights in future public health emergencies and set a precedent for judicial endorsement of these responses. This potential reinforces the imperative for introducing and maintaining safeguards against unjustifiable limits on human rights especially in public health crises.

Central to many of the challenges to laws imposing public health measures during the COVID-19 pandemic were claims that they did not satisfy preconditions for legitimately encroaching upon human rights. As discussed in Chapters 3, 4, 5, and 6, domestic and international human rights laws permit limitations on and derogations from obligations to protect some (though not all) human rights where, amongst other things, they are: responding to an urgent public need; pursuing a legitimate objective; proportionate to that objective; necessary to achieve it; and non-discriminatory.[80] Litigants frequently argued that non-coercive measures (such as physical distancing, testing for COVID-19 infection, and tracing contacts of positive cases) that were less restrictive of human rights than the laws that were enforced could have prevented or delayed the spread of COVID-19. These legal actions underscore the importance during a health emergency of placing limits on the duration of public health laws, being specific about the parameters of such

---

[78] See eg *International Covenant on Civil and Political Rights* (opened for signature 15 December 1966, entered into force 23 March 1976) 999 UNTS 171, Article 6(1) (hereafter *ICCPR*); *International Covenant on Economic, Social and Cultural Rights* (opened for signature 16 December 1966, entered into force 3 January 1976) 993 UNTS 3, Article 12(1) (hereafter *ICESCR*).

[79] See eg *ICCPR* (n 78) Articles 12(1)–(2), 18, 19(2), 21.

[80] See eg *Siracusa Principles* (n 27) cls 25, 39, 51–54, 58; *ICCPR* (n 78) Article 4.

limitations, and repeatedly undertaking evidence-based evaluations of their effectiveness to determine if their encroachment on human rights remains warranted.[81]

Other aspects of the legal and regulatory responses to the COVID-19 pandemic similarly highlight the importance of ensuring there are checks on the imposition of measures that limit human rights in future public health crises. As explored in Chapter 5, authorities often relied on their powers to make public health orders urgently in an emergency context that were not subject to usual processes of parliamentary scrutiny. It will be crucial to reflect on this experience, including to consider which situations might justify such exceptional actions. As discussed above, equally critical will be to ensure that intrusions on the enjoyment of human rights are temporary and do not endure once a health crisis has passed; otherwise, civil liberties may be permanently eroded.[82] In addition, consideration needs to be given to any concerns raised, as they have been during the COVID-19 pandemic, that authorities are using emergency circumstances to justify encroachments on human rights that are intended to achieve objectives unrelated to protecting public health (such as expansion of power, suppression of dissent, and discrimination against certain sectors of the community).[83]

Chapters 4 and 7 emphasized that certain populations may be at heightened risk during a public health emergency of experiencing limitations on their human rights, which laws can alleviate or exacerbate. For instance, given their susceptibility to experiencing poor health outcomes from COVID-19, it was deemed essential to take special steps to protect the rights to life and health of Indigenous Peoples by preventing others from entering their communities. Conversely, travel restrictions had a more substantial effect on the exercise of human rights by some people who were facing the threat of persecution than on many other people. For some people on the move, such laws intruded not only on their right to freedom of movement, but also on their rights to life and health, to 'seek and to enjoy... asylum from persecution', and to be free from 'torture' and 'cruel, inhuman or degrading treatment or punishment'.[84] Once the COVID-19 pandemic has fully passed, it

---

[81] See eg United Nations, *COVID-19 and Human Rights* (n 76) 17; Eric Mykhalovskiy and others, 'Human Rights, Public Health and COVID-19 in Canada' (2020) 111(6) *Canadian Journal of Public Health* 975, 978.

[82] European Group on Ethics in Science and Technologies, 'Statement on European Solidarity and the Protection of Fundamental Rights in the COVID-19 Pandemic' (2 April 2020) 3 <https://ec.europa.eu/info/sites/info/files/research_and_innovation/ege/ec_rtd_ege-statement-covid-19.pdf> accessed 15 September 2022.

[83] Klaus Dodds and others, 'The COVID-19 Pandemic: Territorial, Political and Governance Dimensions of the Crisis' (2020) 8(3) *Territory, Politics, Governance* 289, 292–93; United Nations Human Rights, Office of the High Commissioner, 'COVID-19: States Should Not Abuse Emergency Measures to Suppress Human Rights—UN Experts' (16 March 2020) <www.ohchr.org/en/NewsEvents/Pages/DisplayNews.aspx?NewsID=25722&LangID=E> accessed 15 September 2022.

[84] See eg *ICCPR* (n 78) Article 7; *Universal Declaration of Human Rights* (Resolution A/RES/3/217A, 10 December 1948) Article 14; United Nations, *Policy Brief: COVID-19 and People on the Move* (June 2020) 1–2 <https://unsdg.un.org/resources/policy-brief-covid-19-and-people-move> accessed 15 September 2022.

will be prudent to assess the benefits of public health laws that were imposed by reference to their differential effects on the exercise of human rights by various populations, and consider whether supports for those social groups could improve protection of their rights in an emergency context.

Other individuals who confronted an increased risk of encroachment on their human rights during the COVID-19 pandemic were victims of crime, accused persons, and people convicted of committing crimes. As discussed in Chapter 8, the pandemic and measures implemented to curb its spread posed obstacles to access to justice, which is fundamental to several human rights. For example, disruptions to usual processes for obtaining legal assistance and representation jeopardized some individuals' exercise of their human right to a fair trial.[85] Likewise, suspension and postponement of criminal hearings potentially resulted in encroachment on the human rights to prompt trials for people arrested or detained on criminal charges,[86] and to protection from indefinite detention pending a trial.[87]

Yet some innovations to criminal justice systems during the COVID-19 pandemic may lead to enduring law reforms that enhance protection of human rights.[88] For instance, after the pandemic, many courts may still rely on technology to hear matters online, which facilitates expeditious progression and resolution of proceedings where not all participants can be physically present together. This has advantages in terms of access to justice, although it can create problems, such as reductions in the immediacy of interaction between accused persons, their representatives, and judicial officers, and in the therapeutic potential of the accused's experience of the criminal justice system.[89] Further, the increased risks of contracting COVID-19 in prison, and the indefinite suspension of trials and extensive delays in some proceedings, influenced courts to reduce pre-trial detention and prison sentences, impose alternative sanctions to custodial sentences, and, as noted above, release some offenders before they completed their prison terms. These developments have the potential to reduce excessive resort to incarceration as a response to criminal offending and associated encroachments on people's human rights.[90]

Criminal penalties for breach of public health laws, directives and orders should be proportionate to the risks created and should not exceed what is necessary for specific and general deterrence at the time. The particular phase of the pandemic may be relevant to the invocation of the criminal law in order to impose obligations, but where offences are created, it is important that they are enforced;

---

[85] See eg *ICCPR* (n 78) Article 14; *Siracusa Principles* (n 27) cl 70(g).
[86] See eg *ICCPR* (n 78) Article 9.
[87] See eg *Siracusa Principles* (n 27) cl 70(b).
[88] Terry Skolnik, 'Criminal Law During (and After) COVID-19' (2020) 43(4) *Manitoba Law Journal* 145, 146.
[89] See Tania Sourdin, *Judges, Technology and Artificial Intelligence: The Artificial Judge* (Elgar 2021) 98–108; Michael Legg and Anthony Song, 'The Courts, the Remote Hearing and the Pandemic: From Action to Reflection' (2021) 44(1) *University of New South Wales Law Journal* 126.
[90] Skolnik (n 88) 145.

otherwise, a gap may develop between government rhetoric and follow-through, resulting in community disillusionment and loss of respect for the public measures that have been announced.[91]

The law in relation to emergency measures has been clarified in the crucible of challenges in many countries to emergency public health legislation, directions, and orders. We have reviewed significant examples of those challenges in Chapter 6. The many cases that have been determined by the courts, including appellate courts, have involved a weighing of public health considerations against assertion of rights by individuals or sectors of the community. The factor of necessity, taking into account the severity of the threat posed to public health at the relevant time, has generally been held to take primacy over interference with liberties, such as the human rights to freedom of expression, belief, assembly, movement, and the right to be free from arbitrary detention. The right to life has also been identified as a critical right, legitimizing interference with other rights, and permitting lockdowns; closures of schools; restrictions on access to groups of persons at particular medical risk, such as persons in a variety of closed communities; curfews; and prohibitions on congregate religious practices and gatherings to make protests. However, proportionality of the state response and the specificity of provisions restricting rights, as well as their being clear and time-limited, have also been important considerations in ensuring both transparency and accountability of public health legislation and delegated legislation.

Community tolerance for encroachments on individuals' rights and freedoms waned as weariness induced by the pandemic and responses to it grew. In this context, as discussed in Chapter 6, governments were increasingly called upon to justify ongoing measures to curb transmission of the virus amid claims that their efforts constituted excessive intrusions into civil life and liberties. This has raised issues about whether it is more efficacious for the state to take an assertive role in imposing public health measures or simply to leave it to individuals to recognize and fulfil their personal responsibilities to protect their own and others' health.[92] It has also generated debate about whether pandemic-specific legislative provisions,[93] with carefully crafted checks and balances, are preferable to generic public health legislation that is responsive to a variety of temporary public health emergencies. A subset of this issue is whether it is preferable to have Ministers formally

---

[91] See Simone F Koob, '"No Surprise": The Young and Poor Most Likely to Get a COVID Fine' *The Age* (23 November 2021) <www.theage.com.au/national/victoria/no-surprise-the-young-and-poor-most-likely-to-get-a-covid-fine-20211111-p5985s.html> accessed 15 September 2022.

[92] For instance, Sweden took the latter approach, see eg: Mariam Claeson and Stefan Hanson, 'COVID-19 and the Swedish Enigma' (2021) 397(10271) *Lancet* 259; Swapnil Mishra and others, 'Comparing the Responses of the UK, Sweden and Denmark to COVID-19 Using Counterfactual Modelling' (2021) 11 *Scientific Reports* art 16342.

[93] See eg *Public Health and Wellbeing Amendment (Pandemic Management) Act 2021* (Vic).

making decisions about pandemic declarations and directions on expert public health advice, or to have public health officials making such decisions.[94]

We can also heed lessons for responding to future health emergencies from human rights issues that have arisen in the context of developing, producing, and distributing COVID-19 treatments and vaccines. In Chapter 11, we emphasized that, notwithstanding the urgent search for treatments, cures, and preventative agents such as vaccinations for COVID-19, it remains crucial to protect the human rights of potential participants in clinical trials to life, health, and freedom from undergoing medical or scientific experimentation without providing informed consent.[95] Once safe and effective treatments and vaccines have been developed, as discussed in Chapter 12, it is fundamental as a matter of equity that they are distributed evenly across the world in order to protect everyone's rights to life, health, non-discrimination, and enjoyment of 'the benefits of scientific progress and its applications'.[96] As Cohn, Mahon, and Walensky have pointed out, 'Vaccines do not save lives. Vaccinations do.'[97]

Another issue for future consideration will be the engagement of human rights through governments' and employers' introduction of COVID-19 vaccine mandates in many countries, as examined in Chapters 5, 6, and 10. An evaluation of the mandates' benefits will need to take into account that they encroached upon the human rights to life and health when people experienced adverse effects from vaccination, and also other human rights, such as to 'freedom of thought, conscience and religion' for those who opposed vaccination, and who felt alienated by the use of coercion imposed by governments and employers.[98] Mandates have provided another example of the requirement for a balance between rights and liberties in the context of a pandemic. The litigation experience from the COVID-19 pandemic has the potential to provide insights into the duration for which any vaccine mandates should last once a certain percentage of the population is vaccinated.

In a similar vein, it will be important to assess the impact on enjoyment of human rights of the legal requirements imposed on people who were unvaccinated once vaccines became available. An uncomfortable question in this regard is whether there should be restrictions on the entitlements of persons who choose not to be vaccinated, and the extent to which there should be any form of state-sanctioned discrimination against or stigmatization of persons falling into this category, so as

---

[94] See Gabrielle Appleby and others, 'Victoria's Controversial Pandemic Bill: 6 Ways for the Government to Show It is Serious About Scrutiny' *The Conversation* (15 November 2021) <https://theconversation.com/victorias-controversial-pandemic-bill-6-ways-for-the-government-to-show-it-is-serious-about-scrutiny-171600> accessed 15 September 2022.

[95] See eg *ICCPR* (n 78) Article 7.

[96] See eg *ICESCR* (n 78) Article 15(1)(b); Lawrence O Gostin, Safura Abdool Karim, and Benjamin Mason Meier, 'Facilitating Access to a COVID-19 Vaccine Through Global Health Law' (2020) 48(3) *Journal of Law, Medicine & Ethics* 622.

[97] Amanda C Cohn, Barbara E Mahon, and Rochelle P Walensky, 'One Year of COVID-19 Vaccines: A Shot of Hope, A Dose of Reality' (2021) 327(2) *Journal of the American Medical Association* 119.

[98] See Wolf, Taliadoros, and Gleeson (n 49) 997–99.

to optimize protection for those who are vaccinated.[99] These can raise ethical issues, including in the contexts of clinical practice[100] and epidemiology.[101]

As discussed in Chapters 5 and 6, during the pandemic, people needed at times in many countries to provide evidence of their COVID-19 vaccination (a vaccine passport) to enter public venues, to leave their homes for reasons other than accessing essential services and work in some places, such as Germany and Austria,[102] and to qualify for exemptions from long periods of quarantine. Vaccine passports thus engaged the human rights to freedom of movement and freedom from discrimination for a group in the community, namely, 'the unvaccinated',[103] and led to their stigmatization and removal from them of important civic opportunities to participate in the community. Further, like vaccine mandates, vaccine passports may have intruded on the human right to privacy, as people were required to disclose their vaccination status.[104]

Once the COVID-19 pandemic has fully passed, it will be crucial to repeal (or invoke sunset clauses in relation to) laws and regulations that were promulgated to inhibit the spread of the virus but reduced people's opportunities to exercise their human rights. As the United Nations has observed, protection of human rights will also be integral to the world's 'recovery' from COVID-19.[105] So, too, concerns for human rights must be at the forefront of preparations for the next pandemic.

VI. Civil Litigation and Regulatory Obligations

The COVID-19 pandemic has prompted a fundamental reassessment of the obligations owed by individuals and entities in many contexts and especially in areas, such as the workplace, where persons congregate, interact, and thus can potentially act as vectors for the spread of disease. The pandemic has raised for evaluation the intersections between four organizations with varied forms of regulatory

---

[99] In Illinois a bill was introduced in December 2021 into the state legislature to preclude discrimination against a person's refusal to obtain, receive or accept a vaccination contrary to his or her belief: see COVID-19 Religious Exemption Act, HB4239, 102nd Illinois General Assembly (2021) <www.ilga.gov/legislation/BillStatus.asp?DocNum=4239&GAID=16&DocTypeID=HB&LegId=137251&SessionID=110&GA=102> accessed 15 September 2022.
[100] See American Medical Association, 'Can Physicians Decline Unvaccinated Patients?' (15 September 2021) <www.ama-assn.org/delivering-care/ethics/can-physicians-decline-unvaccinated-patients> accessed 15 September 2022.
[101] See Editorial, 'Discriminating against the Unvaccinated' *Jakarta Post* (12 August 2021) <www.thejakartapost.com/academia/2021/08/12/discriminating-against-the-unvaccinated.html> accessed 15 Septmber 2022.
[102] Scott Neuman, 'Austria and Germany Impose Restrictions on Unvaccinated as People as COVID Cases Surge' *NPR* (15 November 2021) <https:npr.org/sections/coronavirus-live-updates/2021/11/15/1055839727/austria-and-germany-impose-restrictions-on-unvaccinated-people-as-covid-cases-su> accessed 15 September 2022.
[103] See Wolf, Taliadoros, and Gleeson (n 49) 1000.
[104] See *ICCPR* (n 78) Article 17; Wolf, Taliadoros, and Gleeson (n 49) 998–99.
[105] See eg United Nations, *COVID-19 and Human Rights* (n 76) 2.

responsibility: (i) international bodies such as WHO, which is responsible for administering the *IHR (2005)*, but also has distributed guidance and developed policies; (ii) governments that are empowered to generate policies and impose public health requirements (such as vaccine mandates and vaccine passports); (iii) employers, which are required to provide safe workplaces; and (iv) employees, who are obliged to refrain from engaging in conduct has the potential to imperil the health and safety of others in many contexts, including in workplaces.

As discussed in Chapter 3, WHO has played a central role in responding to the COVID-19 pandemic. The *IHR (2005)* have provided a framework for the obligations of countries regarding reporting cases of COVID-19 to WHO, as well as broader obligations in relation to development of their national public health capacities. In addition, as discussed in Chapters 11 and 12, WHO has played an important role in leading global initiatives, such as COVAX, to ensure the equitable distribution of vaccines globally.

The principal focus of legal challenges during the COVID-19 pandemic has been on the obligations of national and state or provincial governments to protect the community by imposing rules and requirements to limit the spread of the virus. However, it has been significant that there have been disputes between individuals too, including in family law litigation in respect of the well-being of children. We discuss these issues in Chapter 6. Some governments have fulfilled their obligations more effectively than others. All have faced extraordinary challenges posed by the pandemic, and some have learned from their own and others' mistakes, and honed their procedures and policies. Official reports and inquiries,[106] as well as medico-legal investigations such as inquests, discussed in Chapter 9, have provided opportunities for analysis of public health processes and responses, and for lessons to be learned from the extent to which governments and institutions such as hospitals have met their responsibilities. Amongst other things, such reports and inquiries have constituted a vital perspective on government action, including the administration of various forms of quarantine, as well as policies, procedures, and conduct in places such as hospitals and residential care facilities. The legacy of such analyses will be a suite of important insights that have the potential to assist in future pandemic responsiveness, reinforcing for governments their obligations in such emergency circumstances.

A particular challenge that has emerged for governments is to continue to fulfil their obligations during a prolonged, multi-phase public health emergency. While members of the community have tended to be relatively compliant during the early throes of a public health crisis, there can be the emergence of two impediments to decision-making when there are months and even years of strictures and

---

[106] See Ian Freckelton, 'Government Inquiries, Investigations and Reports During the COVID-19 Pandemic' in Belinda Bennett and Ian Freckelton (eds), *Pandemics, Public Health Emergencies and Government Powers: Perspectives on Australian Law* (Federation Press 2021).

challenges. The first is pandemic fatigue, a 'chafing at the bit' to return to personal and commercial normality, and bring constraints to an end, to remove government from personal life, and to return to the way things were before the pandemic.[107] This dynamic can make government decision-making in particular about reversion to lockdowns, in the face of new waves of a pandemic, politically difficult and can even stand in the way of the reimposition of relatively unintrusive public health measures such as the wearing of face masks.[108] The other potential impediment to decision-making is community complacency.[109] After a certain time, there can be an inurement to figures of new infections and rates of pandemic mortality, resulting in people failing to ensure their vaccinations are current and neglecting to adopt prudent measures to reduce the potential for contracting the virus.[110] While in part this an issue for public health messaging, it is also a challenge for long-term management of vaccination awareness and maintenance of preventative strategies through legal measures when the immediacy of a crisis has passed.

As discussed in Chapter 10, in many countries, COVID-19 has resulted in long-term changes to work, requirements to attend the workplace, and central business district office occupancy. It has also raised issues concerning requirements of employers to maintain a safe workplace and employees' responsibilities to refrain from attendance at a work site when unwell. While 'no jab, no work' policies of employers have generated consternation and resentment, some of which have been traversed in the courts, as discussed in Chapter 6, the dialogue about what is needed for a safe and healthy workplace has had constructive aspects. It has drawn attention to the reciprocity in responsibilities between employers and employees in the interests of maintaining a healthy and safe workplace. There is the potential

---

[107] See eg Danny Dorling, 'When Will Life Return to Normal after the Pandemic' *The Conversation* (3 December 2021) <https://theconversation.com/when-will-life-return-to-normal-after-the-pandemic-172726> accessed 15 September 2022. However, by contrast, see Ullrich Ecker and Stephan Lewandowsky, 'Life after COVID: Most People Don't Want a Return to Normal—They Want a Fairer, More Sustainable Future' (University of Western Australia, 6 January 2022) <www.uwa.edu.au/news/Article/2022/January/Life-after-COVID-most-people-dont-want-a-return-to-normal-they-want-a-fairer-more-sustainable-future> accessed 15 September 2022.

[108] Mark Santora and Isabella Kwai, 'As Virus Surges in Europe, Resistance to New Restrictions Also Grows' *New York Times* (9 October 2020) <www.nytimes.com/2020/10/09/world/europe/coronavirus-europe-fatigue.html> accessed 15 September 2021. See too Sabina Kleitman and others, 'To Comply or Not Comply. A Latent Profile Analysis of Behaviour and Attitudes Toward the COVID-19 Pandemic' (2021) 16(7) *PLoS One* art e0255268.

[109] Editorial, 'COVID-19 Vaccines: No Time for Complacency' (2020) 396(10263) *Lancet* 1607; Geetika Dang and Sansiddha Pani, 'Vaccine Complacency: A Reality' *The Hindu* (21 December 2021) <www.thehindu.com/news/national/vaccine-complacency-a-reality/article38002654.ece> accessed 15 September 2022; Tom Dusevic, 'Why There's No Time for Covid Complacency' *The Australian* (10 December 2021) <www.theaustralian.com.au/inquirer/why-theres-no-time-for-covid-complacency/news-story/56f72b7024735527a93d41c8c4618bf0> accessed 22 December 2021.

[110] See eg Viswa C Chandu and others, 'Vaccination Induced Complacency in Adherence to COVID-19 Precautionary Measures Among Oral Health Care Professionals in India and the United States: A Retrospective Pretest-Posttest Design' (2021) 17(12) *Human Vaccines and Immunotherapeutics* 5105; Jim Reed, 'Will Complacency Damage Covid Booster Rollout?' *BBC News* (3 November 2021) <www.bbc.com/news/health-59122646> accessed 15 September 2022.

for the COVID-19 pandemic to be the catalyst for eroding the culture of presenteeism whereby employees have felt an obligation to attend the workplace, when they are unwell and/or providing care to others in order to meet employers' and colleagues' expectations. If this occurs, it will be a positive development as it may lead to requirements for employers to develop relevant policies, in consultation with employees, for ensuring suitable measures to protect their employees' health, and to requirements for employees to take actions that ensure they do not imperil the health of others in their workplace.

Public health laws are ultimately only as effective as people's preparedness to comply with them. The COVID-19 pandemic has highlighted the need to understand better those who have a tendency to decline to comply with such measures, and how they can be assisted to identify advantages for such compliance in everyone's interest.[111] In addition, it raises an issue that is well recognized in public health and implemented in public health laws, namely, that coercive measures should be minimized so far as is possible. Non-coercive strategies, such as public education, including contemporary and non-alarmist explanations of medico-scientific data, are likely to prompt less of a backlash from the community and to result in greater levels of trust and co-operation than coercive laws. Similarly, it has been argued that provision of incentives for taking various precautions such as physical distancing from others, hand hygiene, compliance with coughing and sneezing etiquette, wearing of masks in public transport, and submission to testing for a contagious virus if symptomatic, has the potential for being effective in persuading people to abide by public health measures.[112]

The other side to this, though, is the need for robust responses where irresponsible or egregiously anti-social conduct is engaged in that places in jeopardy the wellbeing of the community during a pandemic. In this regard, too, there is a need for balance and moderation.

Chapter 9 has explored the rights of persons, including healthcare workers, to withdraw their labour during a pandemic. This is a sensitive ethical and legal issue. Healthcare workers assume particular obligations to provide care and assistance during a public health crisis. However, it must also be acknowledged that they are on the frontline during such an emergency and so are at heightened risk of contracting disease, and that some have particular physical and mental health vulnerabilities that need to be protected. In addition, there is the risk that they will suffer exhaustion and burnout from the demands made of them, especially if the pandemic continues for a lengthy period.[113] Risks and vulnerabilities in this regard

---

[111] Santora and Kwai (n 108).

[112] See Julian Savulescu, Jonathan Pugh, and Dominic Wilkinson, 'Balancing Incentives and Disincentives for Vaccination in a Pandemic' (2021) 27(9) *Nature Medicine* 1500.

[113] See Sangheeta Mehta and others, 'COVID-19: A Heavy Toll on Health-care Workers' (2021) 9(3) *Lancet Respiratory Medicine* 226; Yeonhoon Jang and others, 'Burnout and Peritraumatic Distress of Healthcare Workers in the COVID-19 Pandemic' (2021) 21 *BMC Public Health* art 2075; Robert Maunder and Gillian Strudwick, 'High Rates of COVID-19 Burnout Could Lead to Shortage of

that have been identified deserve further analysis so that lessons can be learned for retaining and nurturing staff during an extended public health emergency.[114] During the COVID-19 pandemic, initiatives were pursued to address labour shortages in various workforces through recruitment of supplementary workers and role diversification. What is clear is that a range of persons who are designated emergency workers, especially healthcare workers, paid a high price for their dedication to their jobs. Maintaining a functional essential workforce during surges in need, and supporting healthcare workers during a pandemic, are issues that need to be the subject of further workforce planning before another pandemic.

A pandemic generates many situations in which persons and entities are adversely affected. Some losses and damage are necessary incidents of a global public health crisis. However, some are generated by negligence, or recklessly dangerous conduct, or by virtue of obligations created by contractual agreements. Another distinctive feature of the COVID-19 pandemic is that in many countries the public health crisis and legal and regulatory responses to it have prompted a significant level of litigation that is in the process of making its way through the courts. In the course of such cases there have been challenges to public health orders, but also claims by persons that they have been adversely affected by phenomena such as negligent provision of care in a context where harm as a result of a breach of duty was reasonably foreseeable.[115] Litigation during the COVID-19 pandemic also shone a light upon force majeure provisions in contracts and caused them to be interpreted in a pandemic context, and recalibrated to account for future vicissitudes, including potential business losses.

Regulators have a particular set of responsibilities during a pandemic. Members of the community can invest inappropriate reliance on representations made by unscrupulous purveyors of remedies and preventative measures in such a crisis. Governments have a responsibility to protect consumers by taking firm action to inhibit the making and dissemination of false and misleading representations during a pandemic so that individuals are not exploited. Chapter 9 has explored examples of such measures that government agencies took in diverse countries

---

Health-care Workers' *The Conversation* (29 August 2021) <https://theconversation.com/high-rates-of-covid-19-burnout-could-lead-to-shortage-of-health-care-workers-166476> accessed 15 September 2022; Irene Teo and others, 'Healthcare Worker Stress, Anxiety and Burnout During the COVID-19 Pandemic in Singapore: A 6-month Multi-centre Prospective Study' (2021) 16(10) *PLoS One* art e0258866.

[114] See eg Amy V Ferry and others, 'Predictors of UK Healthcare Worker Burnout During the COVID-19 Pandemic' (2021) 114(6) *QJM: An International Journal of Medicine* 374; Antonio Lasalvia and others, 'The Sustained Psychological Impact of the COVID-19 Pandemic on Healthcare Workers One Year After the Outbreak: A Repeated Cross-Sectional Study in a Tertiary Hospital of North-East Italy' (2021) 18(24) *International Journal of Environmental Research and Public Health* art 13374.

[115] See Robert Booth, 'Rights Watchdog Backs Court Action over Covid Deaths in English Care Homes' *The Guardian* (4 September 2021) <www.theguardian.com/society/2020/sep/03/rights-watchdog-backs-court-action-over-covid-deaths-in-english-care-homes> accessed 15 September 2022.

and court decisions that permitted enforcement action to deter unacceptable conduct by those promising curative and preventative options that are unsupported by orthodox medico-scientific evidence.

A challenge during the COVID-19 pandemic was to calibrate the ethical responsibilities of health (and other) practitioners, especially medical practitioners, to refrain from making statements that were not justified by reference to peer-reviewed medical literature, or had the potential to undermine governments' public health initiatives. There is a balance to be struck between the interests of public health and the rights of health professionals, in particular, who have views that are to some degree at odds with those of the government of the day or of public health authorities, to express their genuinely held opinions. The regulatory lines in this regard remain to be resolved with finality, but it is important that health practitioners do not engage in dishonest conduct, such as providing exemptions to vaccination requirements without proper cause, and that they refrain from deceptive and misleading statements upon which their patients may rely to their detriment. The provision of guidance from health practitioner regulators that is respectful of rights to free speech, belief, and opinion is important but, as shown in Chapter 9, far from straightforward.

VII. Conclusion

As 2021 drew to a close and we moved into 2022, the Omicron variant of COVID-19 prompted a resurgence of government actions to inhibit the spread of the virus. As was the case during 2020 and early 2021, such measures varied greatly, ranging from lockdowns to encouraging members of the community to exercise personal responsibility. In the Netherlands, there was a Christmas lockdown.[116] In the Australian State of Western Australia, the borders were almost completely sealed in an effort to prevent people who tested positive to the Omicron variant from entering that State.[117] In the Northern Territory in Australia there were 'lockouts', similar to stay-at-home orders, for those who were not vaccinated.[118] Canada lifted additional restrictions that it had imposed 'out of prudence' for travellers returning from ten specified countries, but significantly increased on-arrival

---

[116] 'COVID: Dutch Go Into Christmas Lockdown Over Omicron Wave' *BBC News* (19 December 2021) <www.bbc.com/news/world-europe-59713503> accessed 15 September 2022.

[117] Government of Western Australia, 'COVID-19 Coronavirus: Travel and Border: Statewide' (23 December 2021) <www.wa.gov.au/government/document-collections/covid-19-coronavirus-travel-and-border-state-wide> accessed 15 September 2022.

[118] See Savannah Meacham and Joe Attanasio, 'Northern Territory Introduces Lockout for Unvaccinated After Recording 256 COVID-19 Cases' *Channel 9 News* (6 January 2022) <www.9news.com.au/national/coronavirus-update-nt-northern-territory-introduces-lockout-for-unvaccinated-after-recording-256-covid-19-cases/a5d10238-ca71-4fd4-9cf4-00f9cbd8df72> accessed 15 September 2022.

testing resources and advised its citizens to avoid travelling outside Canada.[119] In England, face coverings were required by law in most indoor public places and on public transport and in taxis, although not in hospitality venues where food and drink were consumed or during exercise or dancing, although the requirements were withdrawn on 1 April 2022[120] The German Ethics Council recommended extension of the vaccination mandate for certain healthcare workers to all adults,[121] and the United States Supreme Court convened an emergency hearing to rule on the legitimacy of vaccine mandates.[122]

Other important developments at this time were also afoot. On 22 December 2021, the United States Food and Drug Administration issued an emergency use authorization for Pfizer's Paxlovid, tablets to be taken orally, 'for the treatment of mild-to-moderate COVID-19 in adult and paediatric patients ... with positive results of direct SARS-CoV-2 testing, and who are at high risk for progression to severe COVID-19, including hospitalization or death'.[123] This had the potential to constitute a significant breakthrough as it was the first oral anti-viral treatment for COVID-19 that was able to be administered outside a hospital setting.

In the latter stages of 2021, the United Kingdom House of Lords COVID-19 Committee commenced an inquiry into 'Life Beyond COVID', inviting members of the community 'to share their hopes and fears about what the pandemic might mean in the long-term for our home and working lives, and for how we function as a society—what it might mean for social cohesion, for (in)equality, for our environment or for arts and culture'.[124] In addition, Lady Hallett had been announced as chair of a comprehensive public inquiry into the COVID-19 pandemic.[125]

---

[119] Government of Canada, 'Government of Canada Announces Additional Measures to Contain the Spread of the Omicron Variant' (News Release, 17 December 2021) <www.canada.ca/en/public-hea lth/news/2021/12/government-of-canada-announces-additional-measures-to-contain-the-spread-of-the-omicron-variant.html> accessed 15 September 2022.

[120] United Kingdom Government, 'Face Coverings: When to Wear One, Exemptions, and How to Make Your Own' (Guidance, 10 December 2021) <www.gov.uk/government/publications/face-coveri ngs-when-to-wear-one-and-how-to-make-your-own/face-coverings-when-to-wear-one-and-how-to-make-your-own> accessed 15 September 2022.

[121] 'COVID: German Ethics Council Approves Mandatory Vaccines' *DW* (22 December 2021) <www. dw.com/en/covid-german-ethics-council-approves-mandatory-vaccines/a-60220179> accessed 15 September 2022.

[122] See *National Federation of International Business v Occupational Safety and Health Administration*, 142 S Ct 661 (2022); 211 L Ed 448 (2022); *Biden v Missouri*, 142 S Ct 647 (2022); 211 L Ed 433 (2022), discussed in Chapter 6.

[123] United States Food and Drug Administration, 'Coronavirus (COVID-19) Update: FDA Authorizes First Oral Antiviral for Treatment of COVID-19' (22 December 2021) <www.fda.gov/news-events/press-announcements/coronavirus-covid-19-update-fda-authorizes-first-oral-antiviral-treatm ent-covid-19> accessed 15 September 2022. See too World Health Organization, 'Therapeutics and COVID-19' (Living Guideline, 21 September 2021) <https://www.who.int/publications/i/item/WHO-2019-nCoV-therapeutics-2021.3> accessed 15 September 2022.

[124] COVID-19 Committee, United Kingdom Parliament, 'Life Beyond COVID' <https://committees. parliament.uk/work/421/life-beyond-covid/> accessed 15 September 2022.

[125] Cabinet Office Prime Minister's Office, and the Rt Hon Boris Johnson, 'Prime Minister Announces COVID-19 Inquiry Chair' (15 December 2021) <https://www.gov.uk/government/news/prime-minis ter-announces-covid-19-inquiry-chair> accessed 15 September 2022.

At a global level, on 22 December 2021, the Director-General of WHO called for a moratorium on COVID-19 booster vaccinations, noting that, while 126 countries worldwide had issued recommendations on booster or additional vaccinations against COVID-19, the majority were high-income or upper-middle-income countries and such a programme did not exist in any low-income country:

> In the context of ongoing global vaccine supply constraints and inequities, broad-based administration of booster doses risks exacerbating vaccine access by driving up demand in countries with substantial vaccine coverage and diverting supply while priority populations in some countries, or in subnational settings, have not yet received a primary vaccination series.[126]

Thus, by the beginning of 2022, approximately two years since the emergence of COVID-19, there had been remarkable achievements in international collaboration to develop effective treatments and vaccines for this virus. While there remained substantial disparity in equitable global distribution of both, compromising the protection of many people's human rights to health and life, some progress was being made in that regard and in spite of impediments such as intellectual property laws. WHO continued to co-ordinate a wide variety of responses to the effects of the virus by promulgating diverse guidance on measures to inhibit its spread. Debates were intensifying about the funding of WHO so that it could undertake its functions more effectively and sustainably.[127] Courts continued to hear challenges to public health measures, as well as to the commercial and other consequences of the pandemic, and policy-makers were commencing, through initiatives such as the proposed pandemic treaty, to direct their minds to the lessons that could be learned from the experience of the COVID-19 pandemic and to actions that might need to be taken to reduce the potential for a further pandemic with a similar or worse level of suffering and disruption to that caused by COVID-19.

It is vital that, when the passage of time permits the experience of the COVID-19 pandemic to be analysed with greater perspective, the synergies of science, medicine, and public health law are reviewed through all relevant lenses. It is only through such reflection that we can ready ourselves for the challenges that will be posed by the pandemics to come.

---

[126] World Health Organization, 'Interim Statement on Booster Doses for COVID-19 Vaccination' (Statement, 22 December 2021) <www.who.int/news/item/22-12-2021-interim-statement-on-booster-doses-for-covid-19-vaccination---update-22-december-2021> accessed 15 September 2022.

[127] See eg Lawrence O Gostin and others, 'Financing the Future of WHO' (2022) 399(10334) *Lancet* 1445. In relation to a decision in 2022 by the World Health Assembly on sustainable financing to enhance the independence of WHO, see John Zarocostas, 'WHA Sees Changes to Health Regulations and WHO Funding' (2022) 399(10341) *Lancet* 2090.

Bibliography

For those references associated with websites, the full URLs can be found in the main text.

1Day Sooner, 'UK: Challenge Trials for COVID-19' (*1Day Sooner,* 14 October 2020)

Aavitsland, Preben and others, 'Functioning of the International Health Regulations During the COVID-19 Pandemic' (2021) 398(10308) *Lancet* 1283

Abbas, Muhammad Z, 'Treatment of the Novel COVID-19: Why Costa Rica's Proposal for the Creation of a Global Pooling Mechanism Deserves Serious Consideration?' (2020) 7(1) *Journal of Law and the Biosciences* art lsaa049

Abbasi, Jennifer, 'Younger Adults Caught in COVID-19 Crosshairs as Demographics Shift' (2020) 324(21) *Journal of the American Medical Association* 2141

Abbasi, Kamran, 'Covid-19 Dissenters—Or the Virtue in Being Less Cheerful' (2021) 372 *British Medical Journal* art n731

Abdul Aziz, Zarizana and Janine Moussa, 'COVID-19 and Violence Against Women: Unprecedented Impacts and Suggestions for Migration' in Morten Kjaerum, Martha F Davis and Amanda Lyons (eds), *COVID-19 and Human Rights* (Routledge 2021)

Abdullahi, Leila and others, 'Community Interventions in Low—and Middle-Income Countries to Inform COVID-19 Control Implementation Decisions in Kenya: A Rapid Systematic Review' (2020) 15(12) *PLoS One* art e0242403

Abidoye, Babatunde and others, *Leaving No One Behind: Impact of COVID-19 on the Sustainable Development Goals (SDGs)* (Report, United Nations Development Program and Frederick S Pardee Center for International Futures 2021)

Abiri, Gilad and Sebastián Guidi, 'The Pandemic Constitution' (2021) 60(1) *Columbia Journal of Transnational Law* 68

AbouZahr, Carla and others, 'The COVID-19 Pandemic: Effects on Civil Registration of Births and Deaths and on Availability and Utility of Vital Events Data' (2021) 111(6) *American Journal of Public Health* 1123

AbouZahr, Carla and others, 'Towards Universal Civil Registration and Vital Statistics Systems: The Time is Now' (2015) 386(10001) *Lancet* 1407

Abrams, Elissa M and Stanley J Szefler, 'COVID-19 and the Impact of Social Determinants of Health' (2020) 8(7) *Lancet Respiratory Medicine* 659

Abtahi, Hirad, 'The International Criminal Court during the COVID-19 Pandemic' (2020) 18(5) *Journal of International Criminal Justice* 1069

Acosta, Juana I, 'Vaccines, Informed Consent, Effective Remedy and Integral Reparation: An International Human Rights Perspective' (2015) 131 *Vniversitas* 19

ACT Accelerator, 'ACT-Accelerator Prioritized Strategy & Budget for 2021' (World Health Organization 12 April 2021)

Adhikari, Emily H and Catherine Y Spong, 'COVID-19 Vaccination in Pregnant and Lactating Women' (2021) 325(11) *Journal of the American Medical Association* 1039

African COVID-19 Critical Care Outcomes Study Investigators, 'Patient Care and Clinical Outcomes for Patients with COVID-19 Infection Admitted to African High-care or Intensive Care Units (ACCCOS): A Multicentre, Prospective, Observational Cohort Study' (2021) 397(10288) *Lancet* 1885

Ahamad, Mazbahul G and others, 'Officially Confirmed COVID-19 and Unreported COVID-19–Like Illness Death Counts: An Assessment of Reporting Discrepancy in Bangladesh' (2021) 104(2) *American Journal of Tropical Medicine and Hygiene* 546

Ahmed, Issam, 'COVID-19 Research Scandal: Unwanted Diversion During Pandemic' *MedicalXpress* (6 June 2020)

Ahmed, Sohel and others, 'Impact of Lockdown on Musculoskeletal Health Due to COVID-19 Outbreak in Bangladesh: A Cross-sectional Survey Study' (2021) 7(6) *Heliyon* art e07335

Ahmed, Warish and others, 'First Confirmed Detection of SARS-CoV-2 in Untreated Wastewater in Australia: A Proof of Concept for the Wastewater Surveillance of COVID-19 in the Community' (2020) 728 *Science of the Total Environment* art 138764

AHPRA and National Boards (Aus), 'False and Misleading Advertising on COVID-19' (News, 31 March 2020)

AHPRA and National Boards (Aus), 'Pandemic Response Sub-registers' (1 November 2021)

Aiyegbusi, Olalekan L and others, 'Symptoms, Complications and Management of Long COVID: A Review' (2021) 114(9) *Journal of the Royal Society of Medicine* 428

Akinbi, Alex, Mark Forshaw, and Victoria Blinkhorn, 'Contact Tracing Apps for the COVID-19 Pandemic: A Systematic Literature Review of Challenges and Future Directions for Neo-liberal Societies' (2021) 9(1) *Health Information Science and Systems* 18

Akst, Jef, 'Q&A: Human Challenge Studies of COVID-19 Underway in UK' *The Scientist* (18 June 2021)

Alarcos, Cieza and others, 'Disability and COVID-19: Ensuring No One is Left Behind' (2021) 79 *Archives of Public Health* art 148

Alexander, G Caleb and Matthew K Wynia, 'Ready and Willing? Physicians' Sense of Preparedness for Bioterrorism' (2003) 22(5) *Health Affairs* 189

Alexander, Louis A, 'Liability in Tort for the Sexual Transmission of Disease: Genital Herpes and the Law' (1984) 70(1) *Cornell Law Review* 101

Ali, S Harris, 'Globalized Complexity and the Microbial Traffic of New and Emerging Infectious Disease Threats' in Tamara Giles-Vernick and Susan Craddock with Jennifer Gunn (eds), *Influenza and Public Health: Learning from Past Pandemics* (Routledge 2010)

Ali, S Harris and Roger Keil (eds), *Networked Disease: Emerging Infections in the Global City* (Wiley-Blackwell 2008)

Allmark, Peter, 'Should Research Samples Reflect the Diversity of the Population?' (2004) 30(2) *Journal of Medical Ethics* 185

Alsaad, Khaled O and others 'Histopathology of Middle East Respiratory Syndrome Coronavirus (MERS-CoV) Infection—Clinicopathological and Ultrastructural Study' (2018) 72(3) *Histopathology* 516

Alteri, Luca and others, 'Covid-19 and the Structural Crisis of Liberal Democracies. Determinants and Consequences of the Governance of Pandemic' (2021) 14(1) *Partecipazione e Conflitto* 1

Alvarez, José E, 'The WHO in the Age of the Coronavirus' (2020) 114(4) *American Journal of International Law* 578

Amann, Julia, Joanna Sleigh, and Effy Vayena, 'Digital Contact-tracing During the COVID-19 Pandemic: An Analysis of Newspaper Coverage in Germany, Austria, and Switzerland' (2021) 16(2) *PLoS One* art e0246524

American Civil Liberties Union, 'Flattening the Curve: Why Reducing Jail Populations is Key to Beating COVID-19' (ACLU 2020)

American Hospital Association, 'FDA Updates EUA for COVID-19 Convalescent Plasma' (8 February 2021)

American Medical Association, 'Can Physicians Decline Unvaccinated Patients?' (15 September 2021)
American Nurses Association, 'Code of Ethics for Nurses with Interpretive Statements' (2015)
Aminnejad, Reza and Rosa Alikhani, 'Physical Distancing or Social Distancing: That is the Question' (2020) 67(8) *Canadian Journal of Anaesthesia* 1457
Aminpour, Fatemeh, 'Physical Distancing at School is a Challenge. Here are 5 Ways to Keep Children Safer' *The Conversation* (6 October 2021)
Amnesty International, *Forgotten Behind Bars: COVID-19 and Prisons* (Report, 18 March 2021)
Amoretti, Maria C and Elisabetta Lalumera, 'COVID-19 as the Underlying Cause of Death: Disentangling Facts and Values' (2021) 43(1) *History and Philosophy of the Life Sciences* art 4
Andayi, Fred, 'How the Spanish Flu Affected Kenya—And its Similarities to Coronavirus' *The Conversation* (22 April 2020)
Anderson, Courtney L, 'A Pandemic Meets a Housing Crisis' in Scott Burris and others (eds), *Assessing Legal Responses to COVID-19* (Public Health Law Watch 2020)
Anderson, Evan and Scott Burris, 'Is Law Working? A Brief Look at the Legal Epidemiology of COVID-19' in Scott Burris and others (eds), *Assessing Legal Responses to COVID-19* (Public Health Law Watch 2020)
Anjorin, AbdulAzeez A and others, 'Will Africans Take COVID-19 Vaccination?' (2021) 16(12) *PLoS One* art e0260575
Annas, George J, 'Beyond Nazi War Crimes Experiments: The Voluntary Consent Requirement of the Nuremberg Code at 70' (2018) 108(1) *American Journal of Public Health* 42
Annas, George J and Michael A Grodin, *The Nazi Doctors and the Nuremberg Code: Human Rights in Human Experimentation* (Oxford University Press, 1992)
Antolak-Saper, Natalia, 'COVID-19: An Exceptional or Surrounding Circumstance for the Purposes of Bail and Sentencing?' (2020) 30(1) *Journal of Judicial Administration* 81
Appelbaum, Paul S and Loren H Roth, 'Competency to Consent to Research: A Psychiatric Overview' (1982) 39(8) *Archives of General Psychiatry* 951
Appleby, Gabrielle and others, 'Victoria's Controversial Pandemic Bill: 6 Ways for the Government to Show It Is Serious About Scrutiny' *The Conversation* (15 November 2021)
Arato, Julian, Kathleen Claussen, and J Benton Heath, 'The Perils of Pandemic Exceptionalism' (2020) 114(4) *American Journal of International Law* 627
Arbel, Efrat and Molly Joeck, 'Immigration Detention in the Age of COVID-19' in Catherine Dauvergne (ed), *Research Handbook on the Law and Politics of Migration* (Edward Elgar 2021)
Arctic Council, 'The Impact of COVID-19 on Inuit Communities' (16 July 2020)
Arndt, Channing and others, 'Covid-19 Lockdowns, Income Distribution, and Food Security: An Analysis for South Africa' (2020) 26 *Global Food Security* art 100410
Arnold, Catharine, *Pandemic 1918: The Story of the Deadliest Influenza in History* (Michael O'Mara Books 2018)
Arnold, Catharine, *Pandemic 1918: Eyewitness Accounts from the Greatest Medical Holocaust in Modern History* (St Martin's Press, 2020)
Aroney, Nicholas and Michael Boyce, 'The Australian Federal Response to the Covid-19 Crisis: Momentary Success or Enduring Reform?' in Nico Steytler (ed), *Comparative Federalism and Covid-19: Combating the Pandemic* (Routledge 2021)

Arora, Alisha and others, 'Understanding Coronaphobia' (2020) 54 *Asian Journal of Psychiatry* art 102384

Asad, H and others, 'Health Care Workers and Patients as Trojan Horses: A COVID19 Ward Outbreak' (2020) 2(3) *Infection Prevention in Practice* art 100073

Asfaw, Abay, Roger Rosa, and Regina Pana-Cryan, 'Potential Economic Benefits of Paid Sick Leave in Reducing Absenteeism Related to the Spread of Influenza-Like Illness' (2017) 59(9) *Journal of Occupational and Environmental Medicine* 822

Asmundson, Gordon J and Steven Taylor, 'Coronaphobia: Fear and the 2019-nCoV Outbreak' (2020) 70 *Journal of Anxiety Disorders* art 102196

Atrey, Shreya, 'India' in Bonavero Institute of Human Rights, *A Preliminary Human Rights Assessment of Legislative and Regulatory Responses to the COVID-19 Pandemic Across 11 Jurisdictions* (Bonavero Report No 3/2020, 6 May 2020)

Attwooll, Joylon, 'Processing for COVID-19 Vaccine Compensation Scheme to Begin Next Month' *News GP* (17 November 2021)

Atwood, Pierce, 'Class Action Litigation Related to COVID-19: Filed and Anticipated Cases in 2020' (Alert, 3 September 2021)

Australia Institute, 'Privacy Concerns Cast Shadow Over Vaccination Passports' (Media Release, 10 September 2021)

Australian Bureau of Statistics, 'Guidance for Certifying Deaths Due to COVID-19' (Catalogue No 1205.0.55.001, 25 March 2020)

Australian Government, 'Guidance on Myocarditis and Pericarditis after mRNA COVID-19 Vaccines' (30 July 2021, updated 29 April 2022)

Australian Government, 'Is it True? Does the Vaxzevria (AstraZeneca) COVID-19 Vaccine Cause Blood Clots?' (Department of Health 4 September 2021)

Australian Government, Comcare, 'Working from Home' (2021)

Australian Government, Department of Health, 'Looking After Your Mental Health During Coronavirus (COVID-19) Restrictions' (March 2020)

Australian Government, Fair Work Ombudsman, 'Alternative Work Arrangements' (25 November 2021)

Australian Housing and Urban Research Institute, 'The Role of Local Government in Pandemic Recovery for Australia' (Brief, 2 June 2021)

Australian Human Rights Commission, *Management of COVID-19 Risks in Immigration Detention* (June 2021)

Australian Institute of Health and Welfare, 'Social Isolation and Welfare' (16 September 2021)

Autorità Garante della Concorrenza e del Mercato, 'Coronavirus, the Authority Intervenes in the Sale of Sanitizing Products and Masks' (Press Release, 27 February 2020)

Auyero, Javier, 'The Geography of Popular Contention: An Urban Protest in Argentina' (2003) 28 (55/56) *Canadian Journal of Latin American and Caribbean Studies* 37

Azfar, Fareya, 'The Force Majeure "Excuse"' (2012) 26(2) *Arab Law Quarterly* 249

Baekkeskov, Erik, Olivier Rubin, and PerOla Öberg, 'Monotonous or Pluralistic Public Discourse? Reason-giving and Dissent in Denmark's and Sweden's Early 2020 COVID-19 Responses' (2021) 28(8) *Journal of European Public Policy* 1321

Bagenstos, Samuel R, 'Who Gets the Ventilator? Disability Discrimination in COVID-19 Medical Rationing Protocols' (2020) 130 *Yale Law Journal Forum* 1

Baggett, Travis P and others, 'Prevalence of SARS-CoV-2 Infection in Residents of a Large Homeless Shelter in Boston' (2020) 323(21) *Journal of the American Medical Association* 2191

Bai, YaMei and others, 'Survey of Stress Reactions Among Health Care Workers Involved with the SARS Outbreak' (2004) 55(9) *Psychiatric Services* 1055

Baker, Brook K, 'Campaigning for Both Innovation and Equitable Access to COVID-19 Medicines' in Morten Kjaerum, Martha F Davis and Amanda Lyons (eds), *COVID-19 and Human Rights* (Routledge 2021)

Baldwin, Julie Marie, John M Eassey, and Erika J Brooke, 'Court Operations During the COVID-19 Pandemic' (2020) 45(4) *American Journal of Criminal Justice* 743

Ball, Philip, 'Anti-Vaccine Movement Might Undermine Pandemic Efforts' (2020) 581(7808) *Nature* 251

Balmori de la Miyar, Jose Roberto and others, 'The U-Shaped Crime Recovery During COVID-19: Evidence from National Crime Rates in Mexico' (2021) 10(1) *Crime Science* art 14

Banholzer, Nicolas and others, 'Estimating the Effects of Non-pharmaceutical Interventions on the Number of New Infections with COVID-19 During the First Epidemic Wave' (2021) 16(6) *PLoS One* e0252827

Bannon, Alicia L and Douglas Keith, 'Remote Court: Principles for Virtual Proceedings During the COVID-19 Pandemic and Beyond' (2021) 115(6) *Northwestern University Law Review* 1875

Baptiste, Diana-Lyn and others, 'COVID-19: Shedding Light on Racial and Health Inequities in the USA' (2020) 29(15-16) *Journal of Clinical Nursing* 2734

Baqui, Pedro and others, 'Ethnic and Regional Variations in Hospital Mortality from COVID-19 in Brazil: A Cross-Sectional Observational Study' (2020) 8 *Lancet Global Health* e1018

Barnett, Daniel J, 'Pandemic Influenza and its Definitional Implications' (2011) 89(7) *Bulletin of the World Health Organization* 539

Barnett, Katy and Matthew Harding, 'Contract in the Time of COVID-19' in Belinda Bennett and Ian Freckelton (eds), *Pandemics, Public Health Emergencies and Government Powers: Perspectives on Australian Law* (Federation Press 2021)

Barry, John M, *The Great Influenza: The Story of the Deadliest Pandemic in History* (Penguin Books 2005)

Barsky, Benjamin A and others, 'Vaccination Plus Decarceration—Stopping Covid-19 in Jails and Prisons' (2021) 384(17) *New England Journal of Medicine* 1583

Bartel, Robyn and others, 'Legal Geography: An Australian Perspective' (2013) 51(4) *Geographical Research* 339

Bartman, Douglas V, 'Force Majeure in Construction and Real Estate Claims' (American Bar Association 17 July 2020)

Baruch, Douglas W, 'AIDS in the Courts: Tort Liability for the Sexual Transmission of Acquired Immune Deficiency Syndrome' (1987) 22(2) *Tort & Insurance Law Journal* 165

Bashford, Alison, 'At the Border: Contagion, Immigration, Nation' (2002) 33(120) *Australian Historical Studies* 344

Bashford, Alison, *Imperial Hygiene: A Critical History of Colonialism, Nationalism and Public Health* (Palgrave Macmillan 2004)

Bassiouni, M Cherif, *International Extradition: United States Law and Practice* (6th edn, Oxford University Press 2016)

Bateson, Deborah J and others, 'The Impact of COVID-19 on Contraception and Abortion Care Policy and Practice: Experiences from Selected Countries' (2020) 46 *British Medical Journal Sexual and Reproductive Health* 241

Batniji, Rajaie, 'Historical Evidence to Inform COVID-19 Vaccine Mandates' (2021) 397(10276) *Lancet* 791

Battin, Margaret P and others, *The Patient as Victim and Vector: Ethics and Infectious Disease* (Oxford University Press 2009)

Baussano, Iacopo and others, 'Tuberculosis among Health Care Workers' (2011) 17(3) *Emerging Infectious Diseases* 488

Bayer, Ronald and Laurence Dupuis, 'Tuberculosis, Public Health, and Civil Liberties' (1995) 16 *Annual Review of Public Health* 307

Baylis, Françoise and Angela Ballantyne (eds), *Clinical Research Involving Pregnant Women* (Springer 2016)

Baylis, Françoise and Natalie Kofler, 'A Public Health Ethic Should Inform Policies on COVID-19 Immunity Passports' (2021) 21(4) *Lancet Infectious Diseases* 456

Beaney, Thomas and others, 'Excess Mortality: The Gold Standard in Measuring the Impact of COVID-19 Worldwide' (2020) 113(9) *Journal of the Royal Society of Medicine* 329

Beard, Jacqueline, 'Coronavirus: Prisons (England and Wales)' (House of Commons Library Briefing Paper No 8892, 18 May 2020)

Beaumont, Paul R and Peter E McEleavy, *The Hague Convention on International Child Abduction* (Oxford University Press 1999)

Beazley, Ashlee, 'Contagion, Containment, Consent: Infectious Disease Pandemics and the Ethics, Rights and Legality of State-enforced Vaccination' (2020) 7(1) *Journal of Law and the Biosciences* art lsaa021

Becerra-Muñoz and others, 'Clinical Profile and Predictors of In-hospital Mortality among Older Patients Hospitalised for COVID-19' (2021) 50(2) *Age and Ageing* 326

Beckett, Angela and Samuel Robson, 'How COVID-19 Transformed Genomics and Changed the Handling of Disease Outbreaks Forever' *The Conversation* (2 January 2022)

Bell, Kevin, 'COVID-19 and Human Rights in Australia: Part 1' *Castan Centre for Human Rights Law* (21 April 2020)

Belluz, Julia, '171 Countries are Teaming up for a COVID-19 Vaccine. But not the US' *Vox* (9 October 2020)

Béné, Christophe, 'Resilience of Local Food Systems and Links to Food Security—A Review of Some Important Concepts in the Context of COVID-19 and Other Shocks' (2020) 12 *Food Security* 805

Bennett, Belinda, 'Editorial: Law, Global Health and Sustainable Development: The Lancet Commission on the Legal Determinants of Health' (2020) 27(3) *Journal of Law and Medicine* 505

Bennett, Belinda, 'Legal Rights During Pandemics: Federalism, Rights and Public Health Laws—A View from Australia' (2009) 123(3) *Public Health* 232

Bennett, Belinda, 'Travel in a Small World: SARS, Globalization and Public Health Laws' in Belinda Bennett and George F Tomossy (eds), *Globalization and Health: Challenges for Health Law and Bioethics* (Springer 2006)

Bennett, Belinda and Claire E Brolan, 'Gender and COVID-19: An Australian Perspective' in Belinda Bennett and Ian Freckelton (eds), *Pandemics, Public Health Emergencies and Government Powers: Perspectives on Australian Law* (Federation Press 2021)

Bennett, Belinda and Terry Carney, 'Law, Ethics and Pandemic Preparedness: The Importance of Cross-Jurisdictional and Cross-Cultural Perspectives' (2010) 34(2) *Australian and New Zealand Journal of Public Health* 106

Bennett, Belinda and Terry Carney, 'Planning for Pandemics: Lessons from the Past Decade' (2015) 12(3) *Journal of Bioethical Inquiry* 419

Bennett, Belinda and Terry Carney, 'Public Health Emergencies of International Concern: Global, Regional and Local Responses to Risk' (2017) 25(2) *Medical Law Review* 223

Bennett, Belinda and Terry Carney, 'Vulnerability: An Issue for Law and Policy in Pandemic Planning?' in Michael Freeman, Sarah Hawkes, and Belinda Bennett (eds) *Law and Global Health: Current Legal Issues Volume 16* (Oxford University Press 2014)

Bennett, Belinda and Isabel Karpin, 'Regulatory Options for Gender Equity in Health Research' (2008) 1(2) *International Journal of Feminist Approaches to Bioethics* 80

Bennett, Belinda, Terry Carney, and Richard Bailey, 'Emergency Powers and Pandemics: Federalism and the Management of Public Health Emergencies in Australia' (2012) 31(1) *University of Tasmania Law Review* 37

Bennett, Belinda, Terry Carney, and Caroline Saint, 'Swine Flu, Doctors and Pandemics: Is There a Duty to Treat During a Pandemic?' (2010) 17(5) *Journal of Law and Medicine* 736

Bennett, Belinda, Ian Freckelton, and Gabrielle Wolf, 'COVID-19 and the Future of Australian Public Health Law' (2022) 43(1) *Adelaide Law Review* (forthcoming)

Bennett, Belinda and others, 'Australian Law During COVID-19: Meeting the Needs of Older Australians?' (2022) 41(2) *University of Queensland Law Journal* 127

Bennett, Belinda and others, 'Gender Inequities in Health Research: An Australian Perspective' in Michael Freeman (ed), *Law and Bioethics: Current Legal Issues Volume 11* (Oxford University Press 2008)

Bennett, Luke and Antonia Layard, 'Legal Geography: Becoming Spatial Detectives' (2015) 9(7) *Geography Compass* 406

Bennett, Michael, 'The Impact of the Black Death on English Legal History' (1995) 11 *Australian Journal of Law and Society* 191

Bennett, Tess, 'Vaccine Mandates Lead the Way for Campus Reopenings' *Australian Financial Review* (27 September 2021)

Bennoune, Karima, '"Lest We Should Sleep": COVID-19 and Human Rights' (2020) 114(4) *American Journal of International Law* 666

Benvenisti, Eyal, 'The WHO—Destined to Fail? Political Cooperation and the COVID-19 Pandemic' (2020) 114(4) *American Journal of International Law* 588

Berk, Justin, 'Why We Vaccinate Incarcerated People First' (2021) 35 *eClinical Medicine* art 100864

Berkley, Seth, 'COVAX Explained' *Gavi* (3 September 2020)

Berkley, Seth, 'No One is Safe Until Everyone is Safe' *Gavi* (29 October 2021)

Bernal, Jamie L and others, 'Effectiveness of Covid-19 Vaccines Against the B.1.617.2 (Delta) Variant' (2021) 385(7) *New England Journal of Medicine* 585

Betron, Myra and others, 'Men and COVID-19: Adding a Gender Lens' (2020) 15(7) *Global Public Health* 1090

Beutel, Manfred E and others, 'Loneliness in the General Population: Prevalence, Determinants and Relations to Mental Health' (2017) 17 *BMC Psychiatry* 97

Beyrer, Chris, 'A Pandemic Anniversary: 40 Years of HIV/AIDS' (2021) 397(10290) *Lancet* 2142

Bhala, Neeraj and others, 'Sharpening the Global Focus on Ethnicity and Race in the Time of COVID-19' (2020) 395(10238) *Lancet* 1673

Bhaskaran, Krishnan and others, 'Factors Associated with Deaths due to COVID-19 Versus Other Causes: Population-based Cohort Analysis of UK Primary Care Data and Linked National Death Registrations within the OpenSAFELY Platform' (2021) 6 *Lancet Regional Health—Europe* art 100109

Bhatt, Vivek and others, 'Human Rights and COVID-19 Triage: A Comment on the Bath Protocol' (2021) 47(7) *Journal of Medical Ethics* 464

Bhimraj, Adarsh and others, 'Therapeutic Emergency Use Authorisations (EUAs) During Pandemics: Double-edged Swords' (2022) 74(9) *Clinical Infectious Diseases* 1686

Bianchi, Diana W, Lisa Kaeser, and Alison N Cernich, 'Involving Pregnant Individuals in Clinical Research on COVID-19 Vaccines' (2021) 325(11) *Journal of the American Medical Association* 1041

Biehl, João, Lucas EA Prates, and Joseph J Amon, 'Supreme Court v Necropolitics: The Chaotic Judicialization of COVID-19 in Brazil' (2021) 23(1) *Health and Human Rights Journal* 151

Bielik, Larysa and others, 'Features of Criminal Proceedings (Pre-Trial and Trial Investigation) in the Time of Pandemic Covid-19' (2020) 9(2) *Ius Humani Law Journal* 203

Birkin, Linda J, Eleftheria Vasileiou, and Helen Ruth Stagg, 'Citizen Science in the Time of COVID-19' 76(7) *Thorax* 636.

Black, Julia, 'Constructing and Contesting Legitimacy and Accountability in Polycentric Regulatory Regimes' (2008) 2(2) *Regulation & Governance* 137

Blackman, Josh, 'The "Essential" Free Exercise Clause' (2021) 4(3) *Harvard Journal of Law & Public Policy* 637

Blackman, Josh, 'The Irrepressible Myth of *Jacobson v Massachusetts*' (2021) 70(1) *Buffalo Law Review* 131

Blake, Paul A, 'Historical Perspectives on Pandemic Cholera' in Kaye Wachsmuth, Paul A Blake, and Ørjan Olsvik (eds), *Vibrio Cholerae and Cholera: Molecular to Global Perspectives* (Wiley 1994)

Blue, Ethan, 'The Strange Career of Leo Stanley: Remaking Manhood and Medicine at San Quentin State Penitentiary, 1913–1951' (2009) 78(2) *Pacific Historical Review* 210

Blum, John D and Paradise, Jordan, 'Public Health Preparedness & Response: An Exercise in Administrative Law' (2018) 20 *DePaul Journal of Health Care Law* 2

Blumenthal, Kimberly G and others, 'Acute Allergic Reactions to mRNA COVID-19 Vaccines' (2021) 325(15) *Journal of the American Medical Association* 1562

Boccaccio, Giovanni, *The Decameron of Giovanni Boccaccio* (Frances Winwar tr, Modern Library 1955)

Bogdanović, Milenko and others, 'Is the Role of Forensic Medicine in the COVID-19 Pandemic Underestimated?' (2020) 17(1) *Forensic Science, Medicine and Pathology* 136

Bogler, Anne and others, 'Rethinking Wastewater Risks and Monitoring in Light of the COVID-19 Pandemic' (2020) 3(12) *Nature Sustainability* 981

Bollyky, Thomas J, Lawrence O Gostin, and Margaret A Hamburg, 'The Equitable Distribution of COVID-19 Therapeutics and Vaccines' 323(24) (2020) *Journal of the American Medical Association* 2462

Boman IV, John H and Owen Gallupe, 'Has COVID-19 Changed Crime? Crime Rates in the United States During the Pandemic' (2020) 45(4) *American Journal of Criminal Justice* 537

Bonadio, Enrico and Andrea Baldini, 'COVID-19, Patents and the Never-Ending Tension Between Proprietary Rights and the Protection of Public Health' (2020) 11(2) *European Journal of Risk Regulation* 390

Bonavero Institute of Human Rights, *A Preliminary Human Rights Assessment of Legislative and Regulatory Responses to the COVID-19 Pandemic Across 11 Jurisdictions* (Bonavero Report No 3/2020, 6 May 2020)

Bongiorno, Frank, 'How Australia's Response to the Spanish Flu of 1919 Sounds Warnings on Dealing with Coronavirus' *The Conversation* (22 March 2020)

Booth, Christopher M and others, 'Clinical Features and Short-Term Outcomes of 144 Patients with SARS in the Greater Toronto Area' (2003) 289(21) *Journal of the American Medical Association* 2801

Borrell, Brendan, *The First Shots: The Epic Rivalries and Heroic Science Behind the Race to the Coronavirus Vaccine* (Text Publishing 2021)

Boseley, Sarah, 'The Race to Make a COVID-19 Vaccine' (2021) 398(1303) *Lancet* 832

Boserup, Brad, Mark McKenney, and Adel Elkbuli, 'Alarming Trends in US Domestic Violence during the COVID-19 Pandemic' (2020) 38(12) *American Journal of Emergency Medicine* 2753

Bostock, Nick, 'More than One in Three GPs Plan Early Retirement as Pandemic and Workload Take Toll' *GP Online* (4 May 2021)

Boughey, Janina, 'Executive Power in Emergencies: Where is the Accountability?' (2020) 45(3) *Alternative Law Journal* 168

Bourouiba, Lydia, 'Turbulent Gas Clouds and Respiratory Pathogen Emissions: Potential Implications for Reducing Transmission of COVID-19' (2020) 323(18) *Journal of the American Medical Association* 1837

Boxall, Hayley, Anthony Morgan, and Rick Brown, 'The Prevalence of Domestic Violence Among Women During the COVID-19 Pandemic' (Statistical Bulletin 28, Australian Institute of Criminology, July 2020)

Bradbury-Jones, Caroline and Louise Isham, 'The Pandemic Paradox: The Consequences of COVID-19 on Domestic Violence' (2020) 29(13–14) *Journal of Clinical Nursing* 2047

Braden, Roger N, 'AIDS: Dealing with the Plague' (1992) 19(2) *Northern Kentucky Law Review* 277

Bradfield, Owen M and Alberto Giubilini, 'Spoonful of Honey or a Gallon of Vinegar? A Conditional COVID-19 Vaccination Policy for Front-line Healthcare Workers' (2021) 47(7) *Journal of Medical Ethics* 467

Bradford, Laura, Mateo Aboy, and Kathleen Liddell, 'COVID-19 Contact Tracing Apps: A Stress Test for Privacy, the GDPR and Data Protection Regimes' (2020) 7(1) *Journal of Law and the Biosciences* art lsaa034

Braithwaite, Isobel and others, 'Automated and Partly Automated Contact Tracing: A Systematic Review to Inform the Control of COVID-19' (2020) 2(11) *Lancet Digital Health* e607

Bramstedt, Katrina A, 'Unicorn Poo and Blessed Waters: COVID-19 Quackery and FDA Warning Letters' (2021) 55(1) *Therapeutic Innovation and Regulatory Science* 239

Breast Screening Working Group (WG2) of the Covid-19 and Cancer Global Modelling Consortium and others, 'The Impact of the Covid-19 Pandemic on Breast Cancer Early Detection and Screening' (2021) 151 *Preventive Medicine* art 106585

Brennan, Zachary, 'FDA Approves Remdesivir as First Coronavirus Drug' *Politico* (22 October 2020)

Brenner, Hermann, 'Focusing COVID-19 Vaccinations on Elderly and High-risk People' (2021) 2 *Lancet Regional Health Europe* art 100044

Bresler, Jessica and Leo Beletsky, 'COVID-19, Incarceration, and the Criminal Legal System' in Scott Burris and others (eds), *Assessing Legal Responses to COVID-19* (Public Health Law Watch 2020)

Brewer, Mike and Laura Gardiner, 'The Initial Impact of COVID-19 and Policy Responses on Household Incomes' (2020) 36(S1) *Oxford Review of Economic Policy* S187

Bristow, Nancy, *American Pandemic: The Lost Worlds of the 1918 Influenza Epidemic* (Oxford University Press 2012)

British Geriatrics Society, 'COVID-19: BGS Statement on Research for Older People during the COVID-19 Pandemic' (1 April 2020)

British Medical Association, 'COVID-19 Vaccination Programme: Extra Workforce' (4 June 2021)

British Medical Journal, 'WHO Guideline Development Group Advises Against Use of Remdesivir for Covid-19' (19 November 2020)

Brolan, Clair E and Hebe Gouda, 'Civil Registration and Vital Statistics, Emergencies, and International Law: Understanding the Intersection' (2017) 25(2) *Medical Law Review* 314

Brooke, Joanne and Debra Jackson, 'Older People and COVID-19: Isolation, Risk and Ageism' (2020) 29(13–14) *Journal of Clinical Nursing* 2044

Brooks, John T and Jay C Butler, 'Effectiveness of Mask Wearing to Control Community Spread of SARS-CoV-2' (2021) 325(10) *Journal of the American Medical Association* 998

Brooks, Samantha K and others, 'The Psychological Impact of Quarantine and How to Reduce It: Rapid Review of the Evidence' (2020) 395(10227) *Lancet* 912

Broom, Douglas, 'Home or Office? Survey Shows Opinions About Work after COVID-19' *World Economic Forum* (21 July 2021)

Brown, Jennifer, 'Coronavirus: Enforcing Restrictions' (House of Commons Library Research Briefing Paper No 9024, 27 July 2021)

Brown, Nick, 'Some Problems in the Dataset of a Large Study of Ivermectin for the Treatment of COVID-19' *Nick Brown's Blog* (15 July 2021)

Brown, Rebecca CH and others, 'Passport to Freedom? Immunity Passports for COVID-19' (2020) 46(10) *Journal of Medical Ethics* 652

Brown, Rebecca CH and others, 'The Scientific and Ethical Feasibility of Immunity Passports' (2021) 21(3) *Lancet Infectious Diseases* e58

Bruno, Bethany, David I Shalowitz, and Kavita S Arora, 'Ethical Challenges for Women's Healthcare Highlighted by the COVID-19 Pandemic' (2021) 47(2) *Journal of Medical Ethics* 69

Brusa, Margherita and Yechiel M Barilan, 'Voluntary COVID-19 Vaccination of Children: A Social Responsibility' (2021) 47(8) *Journal of Medical Ethics* 543

Bruun, Christer, 'The Antonine Plague and the "Third Century Crisis"' in Olivier Hekster, Gerda de Kleijn, and Daniëlle Slootjes (eds), *Crises and the Roman Empire: Proceedings of the Seventh Workshop of the International Network Impact of Empire* (Brill 2007)

Bryant, Andrew and others, 'Ivermectin for Prevention and Treatment of COVID-19 Infection: A Systematic Review, Meta-analysis, and Trial Sequential Analysis to Inform Clinical Guidelines' (2021) 28(4) *American Journal of Therapeutics* e434

Bucci, Enrico M and others. 'Data Discrepancies and Substandard Reporting of Interim Data of Sputnik V Phase 3 Trial' (2021) 397(10288) *Lancet* 1881

Bucci, Enrico M and others, 'Safety and Efficacy of the Russian COVID-19 Vaccine: More Information Needed' (2020) 396(10256) *Lancet* E53

Budd, Jobie and others, 'Digital Technologies in the Public Health Response to COVID-19' (2020) 26(8) *Nature Medicine* 1183

Buerhaus, Peter I, David I Auerbach, and Douglas O Staiger, 'Older Clinicians and the Surge in Novel Coronavirus Disease 2019 (COVID-19)' (2020) 323(18) *Journal of the American Medical Association* 1777

Burakovsky, Arik, 'Russia's COVID-19 Response Slowed by Population Reluctant to Take Domestic Vaccine' *The Conversation* (26 August 2021)

Burdon, Mark and Brydon Wang, 'Implementing COVIDSafe: The Role of Trustworthiness and Information Privacy Law' (2021) 3(1) *Law, Technology and Humans* 35

Burki, Talha, 'Global Shortage of Personal Protective Equipment' (2020) 20(7) *Lancet Infectious Diseases* 785

Burkle, Frederick M, 'The World Health Organization Global Health Emergency Workforce: What Role Will the United States Play?' (2016) 10(4) *Disaster Medicine and Public Health Preparedness* 531

Burnett, Garrett W and others, 'Managing COVID-19 From the Epicenter: Adaptations and Suggestions Based on Experience' (2021) 35(3) *Journal of Anesthesia* 366

Burris, Scott, Evan D Anderson, and Alexander C Wagenaar, 'The "Legal Epidemiology" of Pandemic Control' (2021) 384(21) *New England Journal of Medicine* 1973

Burris, Scott, Lindsay K Cloud, and Matthew Penn, 'The Growing Field of Legal Epidemiology' (2020) 26(Supp2) *Journal of Public Health Management and Practice* S4

Burzynska, Katarzyna and Gabriela Contreras, 'Gendered Effects of School Closures During the COVID-19 Pandemic' (2020) 395(10242) *Lancet* 1968

Butler Weihmuller Katz Craig LLP, Paola Solano, and Eric Zivitz, 'Florida's New COVID-19 Liability Protection Legislation: What it Means and the Legal Effect Moving Forward' *JDSupra* (6 April 2021)

Bynum, Helen, *Spitting Blood: The History of Tuberculosis* (Oxford University Press 2012)

Byrne, Joseph P, and Jo N Hays, *Epidemics and Pandemics: From Ancient Plagues to Modern-Day Threats* (Greenwood 2021)

Byrom, Natalie, Sarah Beardon, and Abby Kendrick, *Rapid Review: The Impact of COVID-19 on the Civil Justice System* (Report, June 2020)

Cabarkapa, Sonja, Joel A King, and Chee H Ng, 'The Psychiatric Impact of COVID-19 on Healthcare Workers' (2020) 49(12) *Australian Journal of General Practice* 791

Calain, Philippe and Marc Poncin, 'Reaching out to Ebola Victims: Coercion, Persuasion or an Appeal for Self-Sacrifice?' (2015) 147 *Social Science & Medicine* 126

Calitz, Tanya, 'Constitutional Rights in South Africa Protect Against Mandatory COVID-19 Vaccination' *Health and Human Rights Journal* (21 April 2021)

Callaway, Ewen, 'Dozens to be Deliberately Infected with Coronavirus in UK "Human Challenge" Trials' (2020) 586(7831) *Nature* 651

Callaway, Ewen, 'Scientists Deliberately Gave People COVID—Here's What They Learnt' (2022) 602(7896) *Nature* 191

Callaway, Ewen, 'Should We Infect Healthy People with Coronavirus?' (2020) 580(7801) *Nature* 17

Campbell, Anthony D, 'Practical Implications of Physical Distancing, Social Isolation, and Reduced Physicality for Older Adults in Response to COVID-19' (2020) 63(6–7) *Journal of Gerontological Social Work* 688

Campbell, Colleen, 'Racial Inclusivity in COVID-19 Vaccine Trials' *Harvard Law School Petrie-Flom Center* (22 September 2020)

Campbell, Judy, 'Smallpox in Aboriginal Australia, 1829–31' (1983) 20(81) *Historical Studies* 536

Canadian Civil Liberties Association, *COVID-19 and Law Enforcement in Canada: The Second Wave* (Report, May 2021)

Canadian Covid Care Alliance, 'Dr Rochagné Kilian—Blowing the Whistle on Covid-19 Vaccines and D-Dimer Levels' (Video, October 29, 2021)

Canadian Federal, Provincial and Territorial Privacy Commissioners, 'Privacy and COVID-19 Vaccine Passports' (Joint Statement, 19 May 2021)

Canadian Institutes of Health Research, 'COVID-19 and Mental Health (CMH) Initiative: Knowledge Mobilization Products'

Canestrini, Nicola, 'COVID-19 Italian Emergency Legislation and Infection of the Rule of Law' (2020) 11(2) *New Journal of European Criminal Law* 116

Caputo, Peter and others, 'Return to a World Transformed: How the Pandemic is Reshaping Corporate Travel' *Deloitte Insights* (2 August 2021)

Carabin, Hélène, 'One Health: A Crucial Approach to Preventing and Preparing for Future Pandemics' *The Conversation* (24 December 2021)

Carethers, John M and others, 'Disparities in Cancer Prevention in the COVID-19 Era' (2020) 13(11) *Cancer Prevention Research* 893

Carlisle, Keith and Rebecca L Gruby, 'Polycentric Systems of Governance: A Theoretical Model for the Commons' (2017) 47(4) *Policy Studies Journal* 927

Carlson, Licia, 'Research Ethics and Intellectual Disability: Broadening the Debates' (2013) 86(3) *Yale Journal of Biology and Medicine* 303

Carney, Terry, 'Economic Hardship Payments in Health Emergencies' in Belinda Bennett and Ian Freckelton (eds) *Pandemics, Public Health Emergencies and Government Powers: Perspectives on Australian Law* (Federation Press 2021)

Carney, Terry and Belinda Bennett, 'Framing Pandemic Management: New Governance, Science or Culture?' (2014) 23(2) *Health Sociology Review* 136

Carrasco, Sandra, Majdi Faleh, and Neeraj Dangol, 'Our Lives Matter: Melbourne's Public Housing Residents Talk About Why COVID-19 Hits Them Hard' *The Conversation* (24 July 2020)

Carrilo-Tudela, Carlos, Clymo, Alex, and Zentler-Muynro, David, 'The Truth About the "Great Resignation" —Who Changed Jobs, Where They Went and Why' *The Conversation* (29 March 2022)

Carrington, Kerry and others, 'The Impact of COVID-19 Pandemic on Australian Domestic and Family Violence Services and their Clients' (2021) 56(4) *Australian Journal of Social Issues* 539

Carroll, Stephanie Russo and others, 'Indigenous Peoples' Data During COVID-19: From External to Internal' (2021) 6 *Frontiers in Sociology* 617895

Carter, David J, 'Transmission of HIV and the Criminal Law: Examining the Impact of Pre-Exposure Prophylaxis and Treatment-as-Prevention' (2020) 43(3) *Melbourne University Law Review* 937

Carter, John W, *Contract Law in Australia* (7th edn, LexisNexis Butterworths 2018)

Cassier, Maurice, 'Flu Epidemics, Knowledge Sharing and Intellectual Property' in Tamara Giles-Vernick and Susan Craddock with Jennifer Gunn (eds), *Influenza and Public Health: Learning from Past Pandemics* (Routledge 2010)

Castelyn, C de V and others, 'Resource Allocation During COVID-19: A Focus on Vulnerable Populations' (2020) 13(2) *South African Journal of Bioethics and Law* 83

Castro, Marcia C and Burton Singer, 'Prioritizing COVID-19 Vaccination by Age' (2021) 118(15) *Proceedings of the National Academy of Sciences of the United States of America* art e2103700118

Cathaoir, Katharina Ó, 'Human Rights in Times of Pandemics: Necessity and Proportionality' in Morten Kjaerum, Martha F Davis, and Amanda Lyons (eds), *COVID-19 and Human Rights* (Routledge 2021)

Causey, Kate and others, 'Estimating Global and Regional Disruptions to Routine Childhood Vaccine Coverage During the COVID-19 Pandemic in 2020: A Modelling Study' (2021) 398(10299) *Lancet* 522

Cazzola, Mario and others, 'Controversy Surrounding the Sputnik V Vaccine' (2021) 187(106569) *Respiratory Medicine*

Centers for Disease Control and Prevention (US), '1918 Pandemic (H1N1 Virus)' (20 March 2019)

Centers for Disease Control and Prevention (US), '1918 Pandemic Influenza Historic Timeline' (20 March 2018)

Centers for Disease Control and Prevention (US), 'Allergic Reactions Including Anaphylaxis After Receipt of the First Dose of Pfizer-BioNTech COVID-19 Vaccine—United States, December 14-23, 2020' (2021) 70(2) *Morbidity and Mortality Weekly Report* 46

Centers for Disease Control and Prevention (US), 'CDC's COVID-19 Vaccine Rollout Recommendations' (3 February 2021)
Centers for Disease Control and Prevention (US), 'Importance of One Health for COVID-19 and Future Pandemics' (Media Statement, 3 November 2021)
Centers for Disease Control and Prevention (US), 'Pneumocystis Pneumonia—Los Angeles' (1981) 30(21) *Morbidity and Mortality Weekly Report* 250
Centers for Disease Control and Prevention (US), 'Pneumocystis Pneumonia—Los Angeles' (1996) 45(34) *Morbidity and Mortality Weekly Report* 729
Centers for Disease Control and Prevention (US), 'Severe Acute Respiratory Syndrome (SARS)' (Basics Fact Sheet, 13 January 2004)
Centers for Disease Control and Prevention (US), 'State Healthcare Worker and Patient Vaccination Laws' (Publication, 28 February 2018)
Centre for Human Rights (SA), 'Derogations by States Parties from Article 21 ICCPR and Article 11 ECHR on the Basis of the COVID-19 Pandemic' (University of Pretoria, 23 March 2020)
Chaccour, Carlos, 'Ivermectin and COVID-19: How a Flawed Database Shaped the Pandemic Response of Several Latin-American Countries' *IS Global* (29 May 2020)
Chadeau-Hyam, Marc and others, 'SARS-CoV-2 Infection and Vaccine Effectiveness in England (REACT-1): A Series of Cross-Sectional Random Community Surveys' (2022) 10 *Lancet Respiratory Medicine* 355
Chambas, Estelle and Perroud, Thomas, 'France: Legal Response to Covid-19' in Jeff King and Octávio LM Ferraz (eds), *The Oxford Compendium of National Legal Responses to Covid-19* (Oxford University Press 2021)
Chan, Calvin and others, 'The Reliability and Quality of YouTube Videos as a Source of Public Health Information Regarding COVID-19 Vaccination: Cross-sectional Study' (2021) 7(7) *JMIR Public Health Surveillance* art e29942
Chan, Eunice YS, Davy Cheng, and Janet Martin, 'Impact of COVID-19 on Excess Mortality, Life Expectancy, and Years of Life Lost in the United States' (2021) *PLoS One* art e0256835
Chan, Margaret, 'World Now at the Start of 2009 Influenza Pandemic' (11 June 2009)
Chandu, Viswa Chaitanya and others, 'Vaccination Induced Complacency in Adherence to COVID-19 Precautionary Measures Among Oral Health Care Professionals in India and the United States: A Retrospective Pretest-Posttest Design' (2021) 17(12) *Human Vaccines and Immunotherapeutics* 5105
Chang, E-Shien and Becca R Levy, 'High Prevalence of Elder Abuse During the COVID-19 Pandemic: Risk and Resilience Factors' (2021) 29(11) *American Journal of Geriatric Psychiatry* 1152
Chaplin, Steven, 'Protecting Parliamentary Democracy in "Plague" Times: Accountability and Democratic Institutions During the Pandemic' (2020) 46(1) *Commonwealth Law Bulletin* 110
Chartered Institute of Environmental Health, 'Environmental Health Together Register' (2021)
Chary, Sravya, 'Benefits and Drawbacks of Emergency Use Authorizations for COVID Vaccines' *Harvard Law School Petrie-Flom Center* (10 December 2020)
Chary, Sravya, 'Experts Question FDA Approval of Remdesivir for COVID-19' *Harvard Law School Petrie-Flom Center* (10 November 2020)
Chaslot, Arthur, 'The Plague in Modern Times and the Role of Law' (2012) 2(1) *Journal of Biosecurity, Biosafety and Biodefense Law* art 10

Chatmon, Benita N and Ecoee Rooney, 'Taking Care of the Caretaker: Navigating Compassion Fatigue Through a Pandemic' (2021) 38(3) *Australian Journal of Advanced Nursing* 1

Chaves-Carballo, Enrique, 'Clara Maass, Yellow Fever and Human Experimentation (2013) 178(5) *Military Medicine* 557

Chawla, Nishtha and others, 'Psychological Impact of COVID-19 on Children and Adolescents: A Systematic Review' (2021) 43(4) *Indian Journal of Psychological Medicine* 294

Chea, Branson and others, 'Assessment of Effectiveness of Optimum Physical Distancing Phenomena for COVID-19' (2021) 33(5) *Physics of Fluids* art 051903

Chen, Bo and Donna Marie McNamara, 'Disability Discrimination, Medical Rationing and COVID-19' (2020) 12(4) *Asian Bioethics Review* 511

Chen, Chun-Mei, 'Public Health Messages About COVID-19 Prevention in Multilingual Taiwan' (2020) 39(5) *Multilingua* 597

Chen, Donna T and others, 'Who Will Receive the Last Ventilator: Why COVID-19 Policies Should Not Prioritise Healthcare Workers' (2021) 47(9) *Journal of Medical Ethics* 599

Cheng, Kar K, Tai H Lam, and Chi C Leung, 'Wearing Face Masks in the Community During COVID-19: Altruism and Solidarity' (2022) 399(10336) *Lancet* e39

Cheng, Vincent CC and others, 'Severe Acute Respiratory Syndrome Coronavirus as an Agent of Emerging and Reemerging Infection' (2007) 20(4) *Clinical Microbiology Reviews* 660

Chernin, Eli, 'Richard Pearson Strong and the Iatrogenic Plague Disaster in Bilibid Prison, Manila, 1906' (1989) 11(6) *Reviews of Infectious Diseases* 996

Chew, Nicholas WS and others, 'A Multinational, Multicentre Study on the Psychological Outcomes and Associated Physical Symptoms Amongst Healthcare Workers During COVID-19 Outbreak' (2020) 88 *Brain, Behavior, and Immunity* 559

Chhun, Maura, '"A Good Winter Rain Will Put Everything Right": The British Government in India's Response to the 1918 Influenza Pandemic and Famine' (2019–20) 19 *The Middle Ground Journal* 1

Chin, James, *The AIDS Pandemic: The Collision of Epidemiology with Political Correctness* (Radcliffe Publishing 2007)

Chong, Pek Y and others, 'Analysis of Deaths During the Severe Acute Respiratory Syndrome (SARS) Epidemic in Singapore: Challenges in Determining a SARS Diagnosis' (2004) 128(2) *Archives of Pathology and Laboratory Medicine* 195

Chu, Derek K and others, 'Physical Distancing, Face Masks, and Eye Protection to Prevent Person-to-Person Transmission of SARS-CoV-2 and COVID-19: A Systematic Review and Meta-analysis' (2020) 395(10242) *Lancet* 1973

Chung, Ping-Chen and Ta-Chien Chung, 'Impact of Physical Distancing on Reducing Transmission of SARS-CoV-2 Globally: Perspective from Government's Response and Residents' Compliance' (2021) 16(8) *PLoS One* art e0255873

Cioffi, Andrea, 'COVID-19 and the Release of Mafia Bosses: The Importance of Medico-Legal Evaluations' (2020) 60(3) *Medicine, Science and the Law* 239

Claeson, Mariam and Stefan Hanson, 'COVID-19 and the Swedish Enigma' (2020) 397(10271) *Lancet* 259

Claeson, Mariam and Stefan Hanson, 'The Swedish COVID-19 Strategy Revisited' (2021) 397(10285) *Lancet* 1619

Clark, Chalmers C, 'In Harm's Way: AMA Physicians and the Duty to Treat' (2005) 30(1) *Journal of Medicine and Philosophy* 65

Clark, Cendra and others, 'US-Affiliated Pacific Island Responses to COVID-19: Keys to Success and Important Lessons' (2022) 28(1) *Journal of Public Health Management & Practice* 10

Clinton, Chelsea and Devi Sridhar, *Governing Global Health: Who Runs the World and Why?* (Oxford University Press 2017)

Close, Eliana and others, 'Legal Challenges to ICU Triage Decisions in the COVID-19 Pandemic: How Effectively Does the Law Regulate Bedside Rationing Decisions in Australia?' (2021) 44(1) *University of New South Wales Law Journal* 9

Cloud, Lindsay K and others, 'A Chronological Overview of the Federal, State and Local Response to COVID-19' in Scott Burris and others (eds), *Assessing Legal Responses to COVID-19* (Public Health Law Watch 2020)

Coalition for Epidemic Preparedness Innovations, 'New Vaccines for a Safer World'

Cockerham, William C and Geoffrey B Cockerham, *The Covid-19 Reader: The Science and What it Says About the Social* (Routledge 2020)

Coggon, John and Lawrence O Gostin, 'Global Health with Justice: Controlling the Floodgates of the Upstream Determinants of Health Through Evidence-Based Law' (2020) 13(1) *Public Health Ethics* 4

Cohen, I Glenn, Andrew M Crespo, and Douglas B White, 'Potential Legal Liability for Withdrawing or Withholding Ventilators During COVID-19: Assessing the Risks and Identifying Needed Reforms' (2020) 323(19) *Journal of the American Medical Association* 1901

Cohen, Jennifer and Yana van der Meulen Rodgers, 'Contributing Factors to Personal Protective Equipment Shortages during the COVID-19 Pandemic' (2020) 141 *Preventive Medicine* art 106263

Cohen, Jon, 'Russia's Approval of a COVID-19 Vaccine is Less than Meets the Press Release' *ScienceInsider* (11 August 2020)

Cohen, Odeya and others, 'Promoting Public Health Legal Preparedness for Emergencies: Review of Current Trends and Their Relevance in Light of the Ebola Crisis' (2015) 8 *Global Health Action* art 28871

Cohn, Amanda C, Barbara E Mahon, and Rochelle P Walensky, 'One Year of COVID-19 Vaccines: A Shot of Hope, A Dose of Reality' (2021) 327(2) *Journal of the American Medical Association* 119

Cohn, Samuel K, 'The Black Death and the Burning of Jews' (2007) 196(1) *Past and Present* 3

Cohn, Samuel K, 'After the Black Death: Labour Legislation and Attitudes Towards Labour in Late-Medieval Western Europe' (2007) 60(3) *Economic History Review* 457

Coker, Richard and others, 'Towards a Conceptual Framework to Support One-Health Research for Policy on Emerging Zoonoses' (2011) 11(4) *Lancet Infectious Diseases* 326

Colet, Anna and others, 'The Black Death and its Consequences for the Jewish Community in Tàrrega: Lessons From History and Archeology' in Monica H Green (ed), *Pandemic Disease in the Medieval World* (Arc Medieval Press 2015)

Collier, Roger, 'No-fault Compensation Program Overdue, Experts Say' (2011) 183(5) *Canadian Medical Association Journal* E263

Colon-Cabrera, David and others, 'Examining the Role of Government in Shaping Disability Inclusiveness Around COVID-19: A Framework Analysis of Australian Guidelines' (2021) 20 *International Journal for Equity in Health* 166

Committee on Economic, Social and Cultural Rights (UN), 'General Comment No 14: The Right to the Highest Attainable Standard of Health (Article 12) of the International Covenant on Economic, Social and Cultural Rights' (United Nations, E/C.12/2000/4, 11 August 2000)

Committee on Economic, Social and Cultural Rights (UN), 'Statement on the Coronavirus Disease (COVID-19) Pandemic and Economic, Social and Cultural Rights' (United Nations E/C.12/2020/1, 17 April 2020)

Commonwealth Local Government Forum, 'Local Government Response to COVID-19' (2021)

Condon, Bradly J and Tapen Sinha, *Global Lessons from the AIDS Pandemic: Economic, Financial, Legal and Political Implications* (Springer 2008)

Congressional Research Service, 'H.R. 6721 (116th): COVID-19 Hate Crimes Act Summary' *GovTrack* (5 May 2020)

Congressional Research Service (US), 'Operation Warp Speed Contracts for COVID-19 Vaccines and Ancillary Vaccination Materials' (1 March 2021)

Congressional Research Service (US), 'Summary: S.937—117th Congress (2021–2022)'

Conners, Ryan T and others, 'Current and Future Implications of COVID-19 Among Youth Wheelchair Users: 24-Hour Activity Behavior' (2021) 8(8) *Children* 690

Consumer Affairs Agency, 'White Paper on Consumer Affairs 2021' (Japanese Government, 2021)

Contreras, Jorge L, 'Deconstructing Moderna's COVID-19 Patent Pledge' *Harvard Law School Petrie-Flom Center* (21 October 2020)

Contreras, Jorge L and others, 'Pledging Intellectual Property for COVID-19' (2020) 38(10) *Nature Biotechnology* 1146

Cooper, Dan M and others, 'SARS-CoV-2 Vaccine Testing and Trials in the Pediatric Population: Biologic, Ethical, Research and Implementation Challenges' (2021) 90 *Pediatric Research* 966

Cooper, Donna, 'Post-Separation Parenting During COVID-19' in Belinda Bennett and Ian Freckelton (eds), *Pandemics, Public Health Emergencies and Government Powers: Perspectives on Australian Law* (Federation Press 2021)

Copeland, Glenn, 'Timely and Accurate Data From Vital Records Registration, Merged with Disease-Reporting System Data, Can Truly Empower Public Health Officials' (2021) 111(6) *American Journal of Public Health* 990

Copp, Tessa and others, 'COVID-19 Challenges Faced By General Practitioners in Australia: A Survey Study Conducted in March 2021' (2021) 27(5) *Australian Journal of Primary Health* 357

Cordner, Stephen and others (eds), *Management of Dead Bodies After Disasters: A Field Manual for First Responders* (2nd edn, Pan American Health Organization 2016)

Cormacain, Ronan, 'Keeping Covid-19 Emergency Legislation Socially Distant from Ordinary Legislation: Principles for the Structure of Emergency Legislation' (2020) 8(3) *The Theory and Practice of Legislation* 245

Corn, Jacqueline Karnell, *Response to Occupational Health Hazard: A Historical Perspective* (Van Nostrand Reinhold 1992)

Costa, Miguel João, *Extradition Law: Reviewing Grounds for Refusal from the Classic Paradigm to Mutual Recognition and Beyond* (Brill Nijhoff 2019)

Council for International Organizations for Medical Sciences and World Health Organization, *International Ethical Guidelines for Health-related Research Involving Humans* (4th edn, CIOMS 2016)

Cousins, Sophie, '2.5 Million More Child Marriages Due to COVID-19 Pandemic' (2020) 396(10257) *Lancet* 1059

COVAX, 'COVAX Global Supply Forecast' (12 July 2021)

COVAX, 'COVAX No-Fault Compensation Program for AMC Eligible Economies' (Publication, World Health Organization 5 July 2021)

COVAX, 'Principles for Sharing COVID-19 Vaccine Doses With COVAX' *Gavi* (3 February 2020)
COVID-19 Committee, United Kingdom Parliament, 'Life Beyond COVID'
COVID-19 Excess Mortality Collaborators, 'Estimating Excess Mortality Due to the COVID-19 Pandemic: A Systematic Analysis of COVID-19-Related Mortality, 2020–21' (2022) 399(10334) *Lancet* 1513
Cox, Caitríona L, '"Healthcare Heroes": Problems with Media Focus on Heroism from Healthcare Workers During the COVID-19 Pandemic' (2020) 46(8) *Journal of Medical Ethics* 510
Craddock, Susan and Tamara Giles-Vernick, 'Introduction' in Tamara Giles-Vernick and Susan Craddock with Jennifer Gunn (eds), *Influenza and Public Health: Learning from Past Pandemics* (Routledge 2010)
Craft, Aimée, Deborah McGregor, and Jeffery Hewitt, 'COVID-19 and First Nations' Responses' in Colleen M Flood and others (eds), *Vulnerable: The Law, Policy and Ethics of COVID-19* (University of Ottawa Press 2020)
Craig, Lyn, 'Coronavirus, Domestic Labour and Care: Gendered Roles Locked Down' (2020) 56(4) *Journal of Sociology* 684
Cronin, Christopher J, and William N Evans, 'Excess Mortality from COVID and Non-COVID Causes in Minority Populations' (2021) 118(39) *Proceedings of the National Academy of Sciences of the United States of America* art e2101386118
Crooks, Kristy, Dawn Casey, and James S Ward, 'First Nations People Leading the Way in COVID-19 Pandemic Planning, Response and Management' (2020) 213(4) *Medical Journal of Australia* 151
Crooks, Natasha, Geri Donenberg, and Alicia Matthews, 'Ethics of Research at the Intersection of COVID-19 and Black Lives Matter: A Call to Action' (2021) 47(4) *Journal of Medical Ethics* 205
Crosby, Alfred W, *America's Forgotten Pandemic: The Influenza of 1918* (2nd edn, Cambridge University Press 2003)
Croucher, Rosalind, 'Lockdowns, Curfews and Human Rights: Unscrambling Hyperbole' (2021) 28(3) *Australian Journal of Administrative Law* 137
Crown Office and Procurator Fiscal Service (Scot), 'Revised Guidance on Reporting of Deaths During Coronavirus Outbreak' (News, 15 May 2020)
Curtice, Kaitlin and Esther Choo, 'Indigenous Populations: Left Behind in the COVID-19 Response' (2020) 395(10239) *Lancet* 1753
Cutler, Sally J, Anthony R Fooks, and Wim HM van der Poel, 'Public Health Threat of New, Reemerging, and Neglected Zoonoses in the Industrialized World' (2010) 16(1) *Emerging Infectious Diseases* 1
D'Errico, Stefano and others, '"First Do No Harm": No-Fault Compensation Program for COVID-19 Vaccines as Feasibility and Wisdom of a Policy Instrument to Mitigate Vaccine Hesitancy' (2021) 9(10) *Vaccines* 116
Da Silva, Michael, 'COVID-19 and Health-Related Authority Allocation Puzzles' (2021) 30(1) *Cambridge Quarterly of Healthcare Ethics* 25
Dahl, Eilif, 'Coronavirus (Covid-19) Outbreak on the Cruise Ship Diamond Princess' (2020) 71(1) *International Maritime Health* 5
Dalexis, Rose Darly and Jude Mary Cénat, 'Asylum Seekers Working in Quebec (Canada) During the COVID-19 Pandemic: Risk of Deportation, and Threats to Physical and Mental Health' (2020) 292 *Psychiatry Research* art 113299
David Nelken, 'Between Comparison and Commensuration: A Case Study of COVID-19 Rankings' (2021) 17(2) *International Journal of Law in Context* 215

Davies, Cara E and Randi Zlotnik Shaul, 'Physicians' Legal Duty of Care and Legal Right to Refuse to Work During a Pandemic' (2010) 182(2) *Canadian Medical Association Journal* 167

Davies, Sara E and Belinda Bennett, 'A Gendered Human Rights Analysis of Ebola and Zika: Locating Gender in Global Health Emergencies' (2016) 92(5) *International Affairs* 1041

Davies, Sara E and Jeremy Youde, 'The IHR (2005), Disease Surveillance, and the Individual in Global Health Politics' (2013) 17(1) *International Journal of Human Rights* 133

Davies, Sara E, Adam Kamradt-Scott, and Simon Rushton, *Disease Diplomacy: International Norms and Global Health Security* (Johns Hopkins University Press 2015)

Davis, Daniel, '5 Models for the Post-Pandemic Workplace' *Harvard Business Review* (3 June 2021)

Dawel, Amy and others, 'The Effect of COVID-19 on Mental Health and Wellbeing in a Representative Sample of Australian Adults' (2020) 11 *Frontiers of Psychiatry* art 579985

Dawson, Angus and others, 'An Ethics Framework for Making Resource Allocation Decisions Within Clinical Care: Responding to COVID-19' (2020) 17(4) *Journal of Bioethical Inquiry* 749

Day, Alison, '"An American Tragedy": The Cutter Incident and its Implications for the Salk Polio Vaccine in New Zealand 1955–1960' (2009) 11(2) *Health History* 42

Day, Richard, 'Off-label Prescribing' (2013) 36(6) *Australian Prescriber* 182

De Beer, Jeremy and E Richard Gold, 'International Trade, Intellectual Property, and Innovation Policy: Lessons From a Pandemic' in Colleen M Flood and others (eds), *Vulnerable: The Law, Policy and Ethics of COVID-19* (University of Ottawa Press 2020)

De Cock, Kevin M, Harold W Jaffe, and James W Curran, 'Reflections on 40 Years of AIDS' (2021) 27(6) *Emerging Infectious Diseases* 1553

de Haas, Samuel, Georg Goetz, and Sven Heim, 'Measuring the Effects of COVID-19-related Night Curfews: Empirical Evidence from Germany' (2021) (MGKS Discussion Paper Series in Economics, Universität Marburg No 18-2021)

De Oliveira Neto, GC and others, 'Performance Evaluation of Occupational Health and Safety in Relation to the COVID-19 Fighting Practices Established by WHO: Survey in Multinational Industries' (2021) 141 *Safety Science* art 105331

de Paula, Angela T and Vania BM Herédia, 'COVID-19 and Cruise Ships: A Drama Announced' (2020) 47 *Études Caribéennes*

de Villemeur, Etienne Billette, Bruno Versaevel, and Vianney Dequiedt, 'Intellectual Property and Covid-19: How Can We Accelerate Vaccination Globally?' *The Conversation* (26 April 2021)

Dean, Jessica M and others, 'Obligations of Australian Health Services as Employers During COVID-19' (2021) 45(5) *Australian Health Review* 622

Decision of Minister Hawke (14 January 2022) in 'Affidavit of Natalie Bannister' (sworn 15 January 2022)

Degeling, Chris and others, 'Implementing a One Health Approach to Emerging Infectious Disease: Reflections on the Socio-Political, Ethical and Legal Dimensions' (2015) 15 *BMC Public Health* 1307

Dehingia, Nabamallika and Anita Raj, 'Sex Differences in COVID-19 Case Fatality: Do We Know Enough?' (2021) 9(1) *Lancet Global Health* e14

Dehm, Sara, Claire Loughnan, and Linda Steele, 'COVID-19 and Sites of Confinement: Public Health, Disposable Lives and Legal Accountability in Immigration Detention and Aged Care' (2021) 44(1) *University of New South Wales Law Journal* 60

Department for Business, Energy, and Industrial Strategy and Kwasi Kwarteng (UK), 'World's First Coronavirus Human Challenge Study Receives Ethics Approval in the UK' (Press Release, 17 February 2021)

Department of Health (Aus), 'Guidance on Myocarditis and Pericarditis After, RNA COVID-19 Vaccines' (Publication, Australian Government, 2 December 2021)

Department of Health (Aus), 'Primary Care Approach to Thrombosis with Thrombocytopenia Syndrome after Vaxzevria (AstraZeneca) Vaccine' (Australian Government, 15 September 2021)

Deputy Chief Coroner of Ontario, 'COVID-19 Related Deaths of Temporary Foreign Agricultural Workers in 2020' (Review, October 21 2021)

Detsky, Allan S and Isaac I Bogoch, 'COVID-19 in Canada: Experience and Response' (2020) 324(8) *Journal of the American Medical Association* 743

Devereux, Stephen, Christophe Béné, and John Hoddinott, 'Conceptualising COVID-19's Impacts on Household Food Security' (2020) 12 *Food Security* 769

Dhillon, Ranu S and J Daniel Kelly, 'Community Trust and the Ebola Endgame' (2015) 373(9) *New England Journal of Medicine* 787

Diamond, Eugene F, 'The Willowbrook Experiments' (1973) 40(2) *The Linacre Quarterly* 133

Diaz, Adrian and others, 'Elective Surgery in the Time of COVID-19' (2020) 219(6) *American Journal of Surgery* 900

Diaz, George A and others, 'Myocarditis and Pericarditis After Vaccination for COVID-19' (2021) 326(12) *Journal of the American Medical Association* 1210

Diaz, Theresa and others, 'A Call for Standardised Age-Disaggregated Health Data' (2021) 2(7) *Lancet Healthy Longevity* 436

Dickinson, Helen and Sophie Yates, *More than Isolated: The Experience of Children and Young People with Disability and their Families during the COVID-19 Pandemic* (Report prepared for Children and Young People with Disability Australia (CYDA), May 2020)

DLA Piper, *A Global Analysis of Prisoner Releases in Response to COVID-19* (Report, December 2020)

Dmitriev, Kirill, 'Questions on Russia's Sputnik V Vaccine Answered, Time for Critics to Look for Plank in Own Eyes' *Sputnik V* (7 September 2020)

Dodds, Klaus and others, 'The COVID-19 Pandemic: Territorial, Political and Governance Dimensions of the Crisis' (2020) 8(3) *Territory, Politics, Governance* 289

Doherty, Peter, *An Insider's Plague Year* (Melbourne University Press 2021)

Dolgin, Janet L, 'AIDS: Social Meanings and Legal Ramifications' (1985) 14(1) *Hofstra Law Review* 193

Donley, Greer, Beatrice A Chen, and Sonya Borrero, 'The Legal and Medical Necessity of Abortion Care Amid the COVID-19 Pandemic' (2020) 7(1) *Journal of Law and the Biosciences* art lsaa013

Donnell, William S, 'You Wouldn't Give Me Anything, Would You? Tort Liability for Genital Herpes' (1983) 20(1) *California Western Law Review* 60

Doody, Owen and Paul M Keenan, 'The Reported Effects of the COVID-19 Pandemic on People with Intellectual Disability and their Carers: A Scoping Review' (2021) 53(1) *Annals of Medicine* 786

Doraiswamy, Sathyanarayanan and others, 'Use of Telehealth During the COVID-19 Pandemic: Scoping Review' (2020) 22(12) *The Journal of Medical Internet Research* art e24087

Dorling, Danny, *Public Health: Cholera to the Coalition* (Policy Press 2013)

Dorling, Danny, 'When Will Life Return to Normal after the Pandemic?' *The Conversation* (3 December 2021) dos Santos, Antonio SF, Richard S Dias, and Wendell da Luz Silva, 'Imaging Protocols for the Autopsy Service in a Time of Pandemic Emergency Minimising the Contagion of SARS-CoV-2 Expert Government Agents' (2021) 10(6) *Research, Society and Development* art e28810615860

Doshi, Peter, 'The Elusive Definition of Pandemic Influenza' (2011) 89(7) *Bulletin of the World Health Organization* 532

Douglas, Michael and John Eldridge, 'Coronavirus and the Law of Obligations' [2020] 3 *UNSW Law Journal Forum*

Dowd, Katie, 'The San Quentin Prison Doctor Who Performed over 10,000 Human Experiments' *SFGATE* (13 August 2019)

Dowdle, Walter R, 'The Principles of Disease Elimination and Eradication' (Centers for Disease Control and Prevention, 31 December 1999)

Dowling, John M and Chin F Yap, *Communicable Diseases in Developing Countries: Stopping the Global Epidemics of HIV/AIDS, Tuberculosis, Malaria and Diarrhea* (Palgrave MacMillan 2014)

Dowling, Peter, *Fatal Contact: How Epidemics Nearly Wiped Out Australia's First Peoples* (Monash University Publishing 2021)

Dreisbach, Jeconiah L and Sharon Mendoza-Dreisbach, 'The Integration of Emergency Language Services in COVID-19 Response: A Call for the Linguistic Turn in Public Health' (2021) 43(2) *Journal of Public Health* e248

Dreisbach, Jeconiah L and Sharon Mendoza-Dreisbach, 'Unity in Adversity: Multilingual Crisis Translation and Emergency Linguistics in the COVID-19 Pandemic' (2021) 14 *Open Public Health Journal* 94

Droznin, Maxwell, Allen Johnson, and Asal M Johnson, 'Multidrug Resistant Tuberculosis in Prisons Located in Former Soviet Countries: A Systematic Review' (2017) 12(3) *PLoS One* art e0174373.

Dubov, Alex and Steven Shoptawb, 'The Value and Ethics of Using Technology to Contain the COVID-19 Epidemic' (2020) 20(7) *American Journal of Bioethics* W7

Duckett, Stephen, 'Keeping Workers COVID-safe Requires More than Just Following Public Health Orders' *The Conversation* (12 October 2021)

Duckett, Stephen and others, *Race to 80: Our Best Shot at Living With COVID* (Report No 2021-09, Grattan Institute 29 July 2021)

Duff, Johnathan H and others, 'A Global Public Health Convention for the 21st Century' (2021) 6(6) *Lancet Public Health* e428

Duignan, Kieran and Chloe Bradbury, 'Covid-19 and Medical Negligence Litigation: Immunity for Healthcare Professionals?' (2020) 88(1 Supp) *Medico-Legal Journal* 31

Dunn, Laura B and others, 'Assessing Decisional Capacity for Clinical Research or Treatment: A Review of Instruments' (2006) 163(8) *American Journal of Psychiatry* 1323

Dunn, Michael and others, '"Your Country Needs You": The Ethics of Allocating Staff to High-Risk Clinical Roles in the Management of Patients with COVID-19' (2020) 46(7) *Journal of Medical Ethics* 436

Dute, Joseph and Tom Goffin, '*Case of Terheş v Romania*, 20 May 2021, no. 49933/20 ' (2021) 28(2) *European Journal of Health Law* 407

Dutfield, Graham, 'Coronavirus: It is Morally Indefensible for a Nation to Keep Life-saving Drugs for Itself' *The Conversation* (2 July 2020)

Dutour, Marion and others, 'Family Medicine Practitioners' Stress During the COVID-19 Pandemic: A Cross-Sectional Survey' (2021) 22 *BMC Family Practice* art 36

Dwyer, Dominic E, 'Surveillance of Illness Associated With Pandemic (H1N1) 2009 Virus Infection Among Adults Using a Global Clinical Site Network Approach: The INSIGHT FLU 002 and FLU 003 Studies' (2011) 29S *Vaccine* B56

Dyer, Clare, 'Covid-19: Coroners Needn't Investigate PPE Policy Failure in Deaths of NHS Staff, New Guidance Says' (2020) 369 *British Medical Journal* m1806

Dyer, Clare, 'Surgeon Who Said COVID-19 Was a Hoax Has Been Suspended Pending GMC Investigation' (2020) 370 *British Medical Journal* m2714

Dyer, Owen, 'Covid-19: Turkmenistan Becomes First Country to Make Vaccination Mandatory for All Adults' (2021) 374 *British Medical Journal* n1766

Dzau, Victor J and Peter Sands, 'Beyond the Ebola Battle—Winning the War Against Future Epidemics' (2016) 375(3) *New England Journal of Medicine* 203

Dzhafer, Nigyar and Jannis V Papathanasiou, 'Compassionate Drug Use—Time Arising for a New Law in Bulgaria in the Era of COVID-19' (2020) 62(3) *Folia Medica* 592

Dziuba, Dawn, 'TRIPS Article 31Bis and H1N1 Swine Flu: Any Emergency or Urgency Exception to Patent Protection?' (2010) 20(2) *Indiana International and Comparative Law Review* 195

Eades, Sandra and others, 'Australia's First Nations' Response to the COVID-19 Pandemic' (2020) 396(10246) *Lancet* 237

Ebert, Cara and Janina I Steinert, 'Prevalence and Risk Factors of Violence Against Women and Children During COVID-19, Germany' (2021) 99(6) *Bulletin of the World Health Organization* 429

Ebuenyi, Ikenna D and others, 'COVID-19 as Social Disability: The Opportunity of Social Empathy for Empowerment' (2020) 5 *BMJ Global Health* art e003039

Eccleston-Turner, Mark and Harry Upton, 'International Collaboration to Ensure Equitable Access to Vaccines for COVID-19: The ACT-Accelerator and the COVAX Facility' (2021) 99(2) *Milbank Quarterly* 426

Ecker, Jeffrey L and Howard L Minkoff, 'Laboring Alone? Brief Thoughts on Ethics and Practical Answers During the Coronavirus Disease 2019 Pandemic' (2020) 2(3) *American Journal of Obstetrics and Gynecology Maternal and Fetal Medicine* art 100141

Ecker, Ullrich and Stephan Lewandowsky, 'Life after COVID: Most People Don't Want a Return to Normal—They Want a Fairer, More Sustainable Future' (University of Western Australia, 6 January 2022)

Editorial, 'A Patent Waiver on COVID Vaccines is Right and Fair' (2021) 593(7860) *Nature* 478

Editorial, 'Ageing Unequally' (2021) 2(5) *Lancet Healthy Longevity* e231

Editorial, 'Compounding Inequalities: Racism, Ageism, and Health' (2021) 2(3) *Lancet Healthy Longevity* e112

Editorial, 'Generation Coronavirus?' (2020) 395(10242) *Lancet* 1949

Editorial 'Genomic Sequencing in Pandemics' (2021) 397(10273) *Lancet* 445

Editorial, 'India Under COVID-19 Lockdown' (2020) 395(10233) *Lancet* 1315

Editorial, 'India's COVID-19 Emergency' (2021) 397(10286) *Lancet* 1683

Editorial, 'Learn from COVID before Diving Into a Pandemic Treaty' (2021) 592(7853) *Nature* 165

Editorial, 'Prioritising Children's Rights in the COVID-19 Response' (2020) 4(7) *Lancet Child & Adolescent Health* 479

Editorial, 'Striving for Diversity in Research Studies' (2021) 385(15) *New England Journal of Medicine* 1429

Editorial, 'The Plight of Essential Workers During the COVID-19 Pandemic' (2020) 395(10237) *Lancet* 1587

Editorial, 'We Need a Global Conversation on the 2020 Olympic Games' (2021) 397(10291) *Lancet* 2225

Edmonds, Jennifer and Antoine Flahault, 'Refugees in Canada during the First Wave of the COVID-19 Pandemic' (2021) 18(3) *International Journal of Environmental Research and Public Health* art 947

Edwards, Ezekiel and others, 'The Other Epidemic: Fatal Police Shootings in the Time of COVID-19' (Research Report, American Civil Liberties Union 2020)

Ehni, Hans-Joerg and Hans-Werner Wahl, 'Six Propositions Against Ageism in the COVID-19 Pandemic' (2020) 32(4–5) *Journal of Aging & Social Policy* 515

Eisinger, Robert W and Anthony S Fauci, 'Ending the HIV/AIDS Pandemic' (2018) 24(3) *Emerging Infectious Diseases* 413

Elbqry, Mohammed G and others, 'Effect of COVID-19 Stressors on Healthcare Workers' Performance and Attitude at Suez Canal University Hospitals' (2021) 28(1) *Middle East Current Psychiatry* art 4

Elgazzar, Ahmed and others, 'Efficacy and Safety of Ivermectin for Treatment and Prophylaxis of COVID-19 Pandemic' *Research Square* (14 July 2021)

Elliott, Paul and others, 'Exponential Growth, High Prevalence of SARS-CoV-2, and Vaccine Effectiveness Associated with the Delta Variant' (2021) 374 *Science* art eabl9551

Else, Holly, 'How to Bring Preprints to the Charged Field of Medicine' *Nature* (6 June 2019)

Emanuel, Ezekiel J and others, 'Fair Allocation of Scarce Medical Resources in the Time of Covid-19' (2021) 382(21) *New England Journal of Medicine* 2049

Engel, Jonathan, *The Epidemic: A Global History of AIDS* (HarperCollins 2006)

ePortugal, 'COVID-19: Justice' (27 September 2021)

ETIAS, 'Difference Between the European Union vs the Schengen Area'

European Centre for Disease Prevention and Control, 'COVID-19 Clusters and Outbreaks in Occupational Settings in the EU/EEA and the UK' (Technical Report, 11 August 2020)

European Centre for Disease Prevention and Control, 'Surveillance Definitions for COVID-19' (15 March 2021)

European Commission, 'Coronavirus: The Commission Signs First Contract with AstraZeneca' (Press Release, 27 August 2020)

European Commission, 'Emergency Support Instrument' (Factsheet, 7 September 2021)

European Commission, 'EU Strategy for COVID-19 Vaccines' (Communication from the Commission, 17 June 2020) COM/2020/245

European Commission, 'Temporary Reintroduction of Border Control'

European Commission for Democracy Through Law, 'Opinion on the Legal Framework Governing Curfews (Turkey)' (107th Plenary Session, Council of Europe 11 June 2016)

European Court of Auditors, 'Air Passenger Rights During the COVID-19 Pandemic: Key Rights Not Protected Despite Commission Efforts' (Special Report 15, 2021)

European Court of Human Rights, 'Refusal of Requests for Interim Measures in Respect of the Greek Law on Compulsory Vaccination of Health-Sector Staff Against COVID-19' (Press Release, 9 September 2021)

European Group on Ethics in Science and Technologies, 'Statement on European Solidarity and the Protection of Fundamental Rights in the COVID-19 Pandemic' (2 April 2020)

European Medicines Agency, 'EMA Advises Against Use of Ivermectin for the Prevention or Treatment of COVID-19 Outside Randomised Clinical Trials' (22 March 2021)

European Medicines Agency, 'EMA Issues Advice on Use of Sotrovimab (VIR-7831) for Treating COVID-19' (21 May 2021)

European Medicines Agency, 'EMA Starts Rolling Review of the Sputnik V COVID-19 Vaccine' (4 March 2021)

European Migration Network and OECD, 'The Impact of COVID-19 in the Migration Area in EU and OECD Countries' (April 2021)
European Union Agency for Fundamental Rights, 'Fundamental Rights of Refugees, Asylum Applicants and Migrants at the European Borders' (27 March 2020)
Evagora-Campbell, Mireille and others, 'From Routine Data Collection to Policy Design: Sex and Gender Both Matter in COVID-19' (2021) 397(10293) *Lancet* 2447
Evans, Kylie and Nicholas Petrie, 'COVID-19 and the Australian Human Rights Acts' (2020) 45(3) *Alternative Law Journal* 175
Evans, Megan L, Margo Lindauer, and Maureen E Farrell, 'A Pandemic Within a Pandemic—Intimate Partner Violence during Covid-19' (2020) 383(24) *New England Journal of Medicine* 2302
Every-Palmer, Susanna and others, 'Psychological Distress, Anxiety, Family Violence, Suicidality, and Wellbeing in New Zealand During the COVID-19 Lockdown: A Cross-sectional Study' (2020) 15(11) *PloS One* e0241658
Eyal, Nir, Arthur Caplan, and Stanley Plotkin, 'Human Challenge Trials of COVID-19 Vaccines Still Have Much to Teach Us' *The BMJ Opinion* (8 January 2021)
Eyal, Nir, Marc Lipsitch, and Peter G Smith, 'Human Challenge Studies to Accelerate Coronavirus Vaccine Licensure' (2020) 221(11) *Journal of Infectious Diseases* 1752
Fairbairn, Catherine and Georgina Sturge, 'Reforms to the Coroner Service in England and Wales' (Research Briefing, House of Commons Library 23 September 2021)
Fairchild, Amy, Lawrence Gostin, and Ronald Bayer, 'Vexing, Veiled and Inequitable: Social Distancing and the "Rights" Divide in the Age of COVID-19' (2020) 20(7) *American Journal of Bioethics* 55
Family Court of Australia, 'Statement from the Hon Will Alstergren—Parenting Orders and COVID-19' (Media Release, 26 March 2020)
Fang, Guirong and Qunli Song, 'Legislative Advancement of One Health in China in the Context of the COVID-19 Pandemic: From the Perspective of the Wild Animal Conservation Law' (2021) 12 *One Health* art 100195
Farber, Daniel, 'The Long Shadow of *Jacobson v Massachusetts*: Public Health, Fundamental Rights, and the Courts' (2020) 57(4) *San Diego Law Review* 833
Farha, Leilani and Kaitlin Schwan, 'The Front Line Defence: Housing and Human Rights in the Time of COVID-19' in Colleen M Flood and others (eds), *Vulnerable: The Law, Policy and Ethics of COVID-19* (University of Ottawa Press 2020)
Farmer, Paul, *Fevers, Feuds and Diamonds: Ebola and the Ravages of History* (Farrar, Straus, and Giroux 2020)
Farrell, Timothy W and others, 'Rationing Limited Healthcare Resources in the COVID-19 Era and Beyond: Ethical Considerations Regarding Older Adults' (2020) 68(6) *Journal of the American Geriatrics Society* 1143
Fauci, Anthony S and Hilary D Marston, 'Ending the HIV-AIDS Pandemic—Follow the Science' (2015) 373(23) *New England Journal of Medicine* 2197
Faust, Jeremy S and Carlos del Rio, 'Assessment of Deaths from COVID-19 and from Seasonal Influenza' (2020) 180(8) *Journal of the American Medical Association Internal Medicine* 1045
Federal Government of Germany, 'Occupational Health and Safety Regulation to be Adapted' (1 September 2021)
Federal Trade Commission (US), 'Coronavirus Advice for Consumers'
Federal Trade Commission (US), 'FTC COVID-19 and Stimulus Reports' (18 October 2021)
Feinmann, Jane, 'How the World is (Not) Handling Surplus Doses and Expiring Vaccines' (2021) 374 *British Medical Journal* art n2062

Feinstein, Max M and others 'Considerations for Ventilator Triage During the COVID-19 Pandemic' (2020) 8(6) *Lancet Respiratory Medicine* art e53

Feldstein, Leora R and others, 'Multisystem Inflammatory Syndrome in US Children and Adolescents' (2020) 383(4) *New England Journal of Medicine* 334

Ferris, Leah, 'Intellectual Property Agreements and COVID-19 Proposals to Ensure Access to Treatments' (Parliament of Australia, 14 September 2021)

Ferry, Amy V and others, 'Predictors of UK Healthcare Worker Burnout During the COVID-19 Pandemic' (2021) 114(6) *QJM: An International Journal of Medicine* 374

Fidler, David P, 'From International Sanitary Conventions to Global Health Security: The New International Health Regulations' (2005) 4(2) *Chinese Journal of International Law* 325

Fidler, David P, 'International Law and Equitable Access to Vaccines and Antivirals in the Context of 2009-H1N1 Influenza' in David A Relman, Eileen R Choffnes, and Alison Mack (eds), *The Domestic and International Impacts of the 2009-H1N1 Influenza A Pandemic* (The National Academies Press 2010)

Fidler, David P, 'Negotiating Equitable Access to Influenza Vaccines: Global Health Diplomacy and the Controversies Surrounding Avian Influenza H5N1 and Pandemic Influenza H1N1' (2010) 7(5) *PloS Medicine* art e1000247

Fidler, David P, *SARS, Governance and the Globalization of Disease* (Palgrave Macmillan 2004)

Fidler, David P, 'The COVID-19 Pandemic, Geopolitics, and International Law' (2020) 11(2) *Journal of International Humanitarian Legal Studies* 237

Fidler, David P, 'Vaccine Nationalism's Politics' (2020) 369(6505) *Science* 749

Fidler, David P, Lawrence O Gostin, and Howard Markel, 'Through the Quarantine Looking Glass: Drug-Resistant Tuberculosis and Public Health Governance, Law and Ethics' (2007) 35(4) *Journal of Law, Medicine & Ethics* 616

Filho, Walter L and others, 'Coronavirus: COVID-19 Transmission in Pacific Small Island Developing States' (2020) 17(15) *International Journal of Environmental Research and Public Health* art 5409

Finchett-Maddock, Lucy, *Protest, Property and the Commons: Performances of Law and Resistance* (Routledge 2016)

Flaatten, Hans and others, 'The Good, the Bad, and the Ugly: Pandemic Priority Decisions and Triage' (2021) 47(12) *Journal of Medical Ethics* e75

Flanders, Chad and others, '"Terroristic Threats" and COVID-19: A Guide for the Perplexed' (2020) 169(4) *University of Pennsylvania Law Review Online* 63

Flaxman, Seth and others, 'Estimating the Effects of Non-pharmaceutical Interventions on COVID-19 in Europe' (2020) 584(7820) *Nature* 257

Fleck, Fiona, 'Carlo Urbani' (2003) 326(7393) *British Medical Journal* 825

Flood, Colleen M, Bryan Thomas, and Kumanan Wilson, 'Civil Liberties vs. Public Health' in Colleen M Flood and others (eds) *Vulnerable: The Law, Policy and Ethics of COVID-19* (University of Ottawa Press 2020)

Flood, Colleen M and others, 'Overview of COVID-19: Old and New Vulnerabilities' in Colleen M Flood and others (eds), *Vulnerable: The Law, Policy and Ethics of COVID-19* (University of Ottawa Press 2020)

Flood, Colleen M and others, 'Reconciling Civil Liberties and Public Health in the Response to COVID-19' (2020) 5(1) *FACETS* 887

Flores, Stefan and others, 'COVID-19: New York City Pandemic Notes from the First 30 Days' (2020) 38(7) *American Journal of Emergency Medicine* 1534

Florey, Katherine, 'Toward Tribal Regulatory Sovereignty in the Wake of the COVID-19 Pandemic' (2021) 63(2) *Arizona Law Review* 399

Follent, David and others, 'The Indirect Impacts of COVID-19 on Aboriginal Communities Across New South Wales' (2021) 214(5) *Medical Journal of Australia* 199

Food and Agriculture Organization of the United Nations, 'Indigenous Peoples' Health and Safety at Risk Due to Coronavirus (COVID-19)'

Food and Agriculture Organization of the United Nations, 'One Health Legislation: Contributing to Pandemic Prevention Through Law' (Policy Brief, July 2020)

Forman, Lisa and Jillian C Kohler, 'Global Health and Human Rights in the Time of COVID-19: Response, Restrictions and Legitimacy' (2020) 19(5) *Journal of Human Rights* 547

Fortuna, Gerardo, 'Coalition of Countries Aims to Keep COVID-19 Vaccine Manufacturing in Europe' *Euractiv* (29 June 2020)

Foster, Michelle, Hélène Lambert, and Jane McAdam, 'Refugee Protection in the COVID-19 Crisis and Beyond: The Capacity and Limits of International Law' (2021) 44(1) *University of New South Wales Law Journal* 104

Franchini, Massimo, Giancarlo M Liumbruno, and Mario Pezzo, 'Covid-19 Vaccine-associated Immune Thrombosis and Thrombocytopenia (VITT): Diagnostic and Therapeutic Recommendations for a New Syndrome' (2021) 107(2) *European Journal of Haematology* 173

Franco-Paredes, Carlos and others, 'Decarceration and Community Re-entry in the COVID-19 Era' (2021) 21(1) *Lancet Infectious Diseases* art e11

Fraser, Sarah and others, 'Ageism and COVID-19: What Does Our Society's Response Say About Us?' (2020) 49(5) *Age and Ageing* 692

Freckelton, Ian, 'Clinical Research Without Consent: Challenges for COVID-19 Research' (2020) 28(1) *Journal of Law and Medicine* 90

Freckelton, Ian, 'COVID-19 as a Disruptor and a Catalyst for Change' (2021) 28(3) *Journal of Law and Medicine* 597

Freckelton, Ian, 'COVID-19 and Family Law Decision-Making' (2020) 27(4) *Journal of Law and Medicine* 846

Freckelton, Ian, 'COVID-19: Criminal Law, Public Assemblies and Human Rights Litigation' (2020) 27(4) *Journal of Law and Medicine* 790

Freckelton, Ian, 'COVID-19 Curfews: Kenyan and Australian Litigation and Pandemic Protection' (2020) 28(1) *Journal of Law and Medicine* 117

Freckelton, Ian, 'COVID-19 Denialism, Vaccine Scepticism and the Regulation of Health Practitioners' (2021) 28(3) *Journal of Law and Medicine* 613

Freckelton, Ian, 'COVID-19: Fear, Quackery, False Representations and the Law' (2020) 72 *International Journal of Law and Psychiatry* art 101611

Freckelton, Ian, 'COVID-19, Negligence and Occupational Health and Safety: Ethical and Legal Issues for Hospitals and Health Centres' (2020) 27(3) *Journal of Law and Medicine* 590

Freckelton, Ian, 'Government Inquiries, Investigations and Reports During the COVID-19 Pandemic' in Belinda Bennett and Ian Freckelton (eds), *Pandemics, Public Health Emergencies and Government Powers: Perspectives on Australian Law* (Federation Press 2021)

Freckelton, Ian, 'Human Challenge Trials: Ethical and Legal Issues for COVID-19 Research' (2021) 28(2) *Journal of Law and Medicine* 311

Freckelton, Ian, 'Mandatory Vaccination Tensions and Litigation' (2021) 28(4) *Journal of Law and Medicine* 913

Freckelton, Ian, 'Pandemics, Polycentricity and Public Perceptions: Lessons from the Djokovic Saga' (2022) 29(1) *Journal of Law and Medicine* 9

Freckelton, Ian, 'Perils of Precipitate Publication: Fraudulent and Substandard COVID-19 Research' (2020) 27(4) *Journal of Law and Medicine* 779

Freckelton, Ian, *Scholarly Misconduct: Law, Regulation and Practice* (Oxford University Press 2016)

Freckelton, Ian, 'Vaccinating Children: The COVID-19 Family Law Jurisprudence' (2022) 29(3) *Journal of Law and Medicine* 645

Freckelton, Ian, 'Vaccination Litigation: The Need for Rethinking Compensation for Victims of Vaccination Injury' (2018) 25(2) *Journal of Law and Medicine* 293

Freckelton, Ian and Patricia Molloy, 'The Health of Health Practitioners: Remedial Programs, Regulation and the Spectre of the Law' (2007) 15(3) *Journal of Law and Medicine* 366

Freckelton, Ian and David Ranson, *Death Investigation and the Coroner's Inquest* (Oxford University Press 2006)

Freckelton, Ian and Vera L Raposo, 'International Access to Public Health Data: An Important Brazilian Legal Precedent' (2020) 27(4) *Journal of Law and Medicine* 895

Freckelton, Ian and Wolf, Gabrielle, 'Responses to Monkeypox: Learning from Previous Public Health Emergencies' (2022) 29(4) *Journal of Law and Medicine* (in press)

French, Christopher C, 'COVID-19 Business Interruption Insurance Losses: The Cases for and Against Coverage' (2020) 27(1) *Connecticut Insurance Law Journal* 1

Frieden, Thomas R and Marine Buissonnière, 'Will a Global Preparedness Treaty Help or Hinder Pandemic Preparedness?' (2021) 6 *BMJ Global Health* art 006297

Friedman, Eric A and others, 'Joining COVAX Could Save American Lives' *Foreign Policy* (15 September 2020)

Fukuda-Parr, Sakiko, Paulo Buss, and Alicia E Yamin, 'Pandemic Treaty Needs to Start With Rethinking the Paradigm of Global Health Security' (2021) 6 *BMJ Global Health* art e006392

Furlong, Ashleigh, 'WHO Cautions Against Mandatory Vaccination' *Politico* (7 December 2021)

Furuse, Yuki, 'Genomic Sequencing Effort for SARS-CoV-2 by Country During the Pandemic' (2021) 103 *International Journal of Infectious Diseases* 305

Gabarron, Elia, Sunday O Oyeyemi, and Rolf Wynn, 'COVID-19-related Misinformation on Social Media: A Systematic Review' (2021) 99(6) *Bulletin of the World Health Organization* 455

Gable, Lance, 'Allocation of Scarce Medical Resources and Crisis Standards of Care' in Scott Burris and others (eds), *Assessing Legal Responses to COVID-19* (Public Health Law Watch 2020)

Gable, Lance, 'Mass Movement, Business and Property Control Measures' in Scott Burris and others (eds), *Assessing Legal Responses to COVID-19* (Public Health Law Watch 2020)

Gable, Lance, Natalie Ram, and Jeffrey L Ram, 'Legal and Ethical Implications of Wastewater Monitoring of SARS-CoV-2 for COVID-19 Surveillance' (2020) 7(1) *Journal of Law and the Biosciences* art lsaa039

Gajbhiye, Rahul and others, 'Increased Rate of Miscarriage during Second Wave of COVID-19 Pandemic in India' (2021) 58(6) *Ultrasound in Obstetrics and Gynecology* 946

Gao, Jianjun, Zhenxue Tian, and Xu Yang, 'Breakthrough: Chloroquine Phosphate Has Shown Apparent Efficacy in Treatment of COVID-19 Associated Pneumonia in Clinical Studies' (2020) 14(1) *Bioscience Trends* 72

Gardner, Paula J and Parvaneh Moallef, 'Psychological Impact on SARS Survivors: Critical Review of the English Language Literature' (2015) 56(1) *Canadian Psychology* 123

Gardner, William, David States, and Nicholas Bagley, 'The Coronavirus and the Risks to the Elderly in Long-Term Care' (2020) 32(4–5) *Journal of Aging & Social Policy* 310

Garegnani, Luis Ignacio, Eva Madrid, and Nicolás Meza, 'Misleading Clinical Evidence and Systematic Reviews on Ivermectin for COVID-19' (2022) 27(3) *BMJ Evidence-Based Medicine* 156

Garoon, Joshua P and Patrick S Duggan, 'Discourses of Disease, Discourses of Disadvantage: A Critical Analysis of National Pandemic Influenza Preparedness Plans' (2008) 67(7) *Social Science & Medicine* 1133

Garrity, Erin, 'Guacamole is Extra but the Norovirus Comes Free: Implementing Paid Sick Days for American Workers' (2017) 58(2) *Boston College Law Review* 703

Gartel, Grace, Herather Scuderi, and Christine Servay, 'Implementation of Common Rule Changes to the Informed Consent Form: A Research Staff and Institutional Review Board Collaboration' (2020) 20(1) *The Ochsner Journal* 76

GAVI, 'About Our Alliance' (13 October 2021)

GAVI, 'AMC-Eligible Economies' (12 May 2021)

Gavura, Scott, 'Ivermectin the New Hydroxychloroquine' (*Science-Based Medicine*, 15 April 2021)

Gaze, David C, 'Dexamethasone: What is the Breakthrough Treatment for COVID-19?' *The Conversation* (18 June 2020)

Genicot, Nathan, 'Epidemiological Surveillance and Performance Assessment: The Two Roles of Health Indicators During the COVID-19 Pandemic' (2021) 17(2) *International Journal of Law in Context* 186

Gensini, Gian Franco, Magdi H Yacoub, and Andrea A Conti, 'The Concept of Quarantine in History: From Plague to SARS' (2004) 49(4) *Journal of Infection* 257

Germany (Territory Under Allied Occupation, 1945–1955), *Trials of War Criminals Before the Nuernberg Military Tribunals under Control Council Law No 10* (United States Government Printing Office 1949)

Gerussi, Valentina and others, 'Vaccine Hesitancy among Italian Patients Recovered from COVID-19 Infection Towards Influenza and SARS-CoV-2 Vaccination' (2021) 9(2) *Vaccines* 172

Ghezelbash, Daniel and Nikolas F Tan, 'The End of the Right to Seek Asylum? COVID-19 and the Future of Refugee Protection' (2020) 32(4) *International Journal of Refugee Law* 668

Ghráinne, Bríd Ní, 'COVID-19, Border Closures and International Law' (Institute of International Relations Prague, 4 May 2020)

Ghram, Amine and others, 'COVID-19 Pandemic and Physical Exercise: Lessons Learnt for Confined Communities' (2021) 12 *Frontiers in Psychology* art 618585

Gilbert, Geoff, 'Forced Displacement in a Time of a Global Pandemic' in Carla Ferstman and Andrew Fagan (eds), *Covid-19, Law and Human Rights: Essex Dialogues* (School of Law and Human Rights Centre, University of Essex 2020)

Gilbert, Lyn and Alan Lilly, *Independent Review of COVID-19 Outbreaks at St Basil's Home for the Aged in Fawkner, Victoria; Heritage Care Epping Gardens in Epping, Victoria* (Report, 30 November 2020)

Gilbert, Sarah and Catherine Green, *Vaxxers: The Inside Story of the Oxford AstraZeneca Vaccine and the Race Against the Virus* (Hodder & Stoughton 2021)

Gilfillan, Geoff, 'COVID-19: Impacts on Casual Workers in Australia—A Statistical Snapshot' (Research Paper, Parliament of Australia, updated 8 May 2020)

Giubilini, Alberto, Julian Savulescu, and Dominic Wilkinson, 'COVID-19 Vaccine: Vaccinate the Young to Protect the Old?' (2020) 7(1) *Journal of Law and the Biosciences* art lsaa050

Giubilini, Alberto, Julian Savulescu, and Dominic Wilkinson, 'Queue Questions: Ethics of COVID-19 Vaccine Prioritization' (2021) 35(4) *Bioethics* 348

Giusti, Emanuele M and others, 'The Psychological Impact of the COVID-19 Outbreak on Health Professionals: A Cross-Sectional Study' (2020) 11 *Frontiers in Psychology* art 1684

Gleeson, Deborah, 'Wealthy Nations Starved the Developing World of Vaccines. Omicron Shows the Cost of This Greed' *The Conversation* (30 November 2021)

Global Fund, *Results Report 2021* (Report, 8 September 2021)

Global Outbreak Alert and Response Network, 'About Us'

Godlee, Fiona, Jane Smith, and Harvey Marcovitch, 'Wakefield's Article Linking MMR Vaccine and Autism was Fraudulent' (2011) 342 *British Medical Journal* c7452

Goetz, Klaus H and Dorte S Martinsen, 'COVID-19: A Dual Challenge to European Liberal Democracy' (2021) 44(5–6) *West European Politics* 1003

Goggin, Gerard, 'COVID-19 Apps in Singapore and Australia: Reimagining Healthy Nations with Digital Technology' (2020) 177(1) *Media International Australia* 61

Gold, Hal, *Japan's Infamous Unit 731: Firsthand Accounts of Japan's Wartime Human Experimentation Program* (Tuttle 2019)

Golder, Su and others, 'General Practitioner Perspectives and Wellbeing During the COVID-19 Pandemic: A Mixed Method Social Media Analysis' *medRxiv* (2021)

Goldman, Ran D and others, 'Factors Associated with Parents' Willingness to Enroll their Children in Trials for COVID-19 Vaccination' (2021) 17(6) *Human Vaccines and Immunotherapeutics* 1607

Gonzalez-Salzberg, Damian A, 'Protecting Human Rights in the Americas Amid a Pandemic: A Reflection on Resolution 1/2020 of the Inter-American Commission' (2020) 26(3) *Australian Journal of Human Rights* 556

Goode, David and others, *A History and Sociology of the Willowbrook State School* (American Association on Intellectual and Developmental Disabilities 2013)

Gorman, Anna and Kaiser Health News, 'Medieval Diseases Are Infecting California's Homeless' *The Atlantic* (8 March 2019)

Gorski, David, 'Ivermectin is the New Hydroxychloroquine, Take 2' *Science-Based Medicine* (21 June 2021)

Gostin, Lawrence O, Ronald Bayer and Amy L Fairchild, 'Ethical and Legal Challenges Posed by Severe Acute Respiratory Syndrome: Implications for the Control of Severe Infectious Disease Threats' (2003) 290(24) *Journal of the American Medical Association* 3229

Gostin, Lawrence O, *Global Health Law* (Harvard University Press 2014)

Gostin, Lawrence O, *Global Health Security: A Blueprint for the Future* (Harvard University Press 2021)

Gostin, Lawrence O, 'Our Shared Vulnerability to Dangerous Pathogens' (2017) 25(2) *Medical Law Review* 185

Gostin, Lawrence O, 'Reforming the World Health Organization After Ebola' (2015) 313(14) *Journal of the American Medical Association* 1407

Gostin, Lawrence O, 'The Great Coronavirus Pandemic of 2020—7 Critical Lessons' (2020) 324(18) *Journal of American Medical Association* 1816

Gostin, Lawrence O and Benjamin E Berkman, 'Pandemic Influenza: Ethics, Law and the Public's Health' (2007) 59(1) *Administrative Law Review* 121

Gostin, Lawrence O and Eric A Friedman, 'A Retrospective and Prospective Analysis of the West African Ebola Virus Disease Epidemic: Robust National Health Systems at the Foundation and an Empowered WHO at the Apex' (2015) 385(9980) *Lancet* 1902

Gostin, Lawrence O and James G Hodge Jr, 'US Emergency Legal Responses to Novel Coronavirus: Balancing Public Health and Civil Liberties' (2020) 323(12) *Journal of the American Medical Association* 1131

Gostin, Lawrence O and Rebecca Katz, 'The International Health Regulations: The Governing Framework for Global Health Security' (2016) 94(2) *Milbank Quarterly* 264

Gostin, Lawrence O and Zita Lazzarini, *Human Rights and Public Health in the AIDS Pandemic* (Oxford University Press 1997)

Gostin, Lawrence O and Daniel A Salmon, 'The Dual Epidemics of COVID-19 and Influenza: Vaccine Acceptance, Coverage, and Mandates' (2020) 324(4) *Journal of the American Medical Association* 335

Gostin, Lawrence O and Sarah Wetter, 'Using COVID-19 to Strengthen the WHO: Promoting Health and Science Above Politics' (2020) *Milbank Quarterly Opinion*

Gostin, Lawrence O, and Lindsay F Wiley, 'Governmental Public Health Powers During the COVID-19 Pandemic: Stay-at Home Orders, Business Closures, and Travel Restrictions' (2020) 323(21) *Journal of the American Medical Association* 2137

Gostin, Lawrence O and Lindsay F Wiley, *Public Health Law: Power, Duty, Restraint* (3rd edn, University of California Press 2016)

Gostin, Lawrence O, Sam F Halabi, and Kevin A Klock, 'An International Agreement on Pandemic Prevention and Preparedness' (2021) 326(13) *Journal of the American Medical Association* 1257

Gostin, Lawrence O, Safura A Karim, and Benjamin M Meier, 'Facilitating Access to a COVID-19 Vaccine Through Global Health Law' (2020) 48(3) *Journal of Law, Medicine & Ethics* 622

Gostin, Lawrence O, Benjamin M Meier, and Barbara Stocking, 'Developing an Innovative Pandemic Treaty to Advance Global Health Security' (2021) 49(3) *Journal of Law, Medicine & Ethics* 503

Gostin, Lawrence O, Daniel A Salmon, and Heidi J Larson, 'Mandating COVID-19 Vaccines' (2021) 325(6) *Journal of American Medical Association* 532

Gostin, Lawrence O, Cori Vanchieri, and Andrew Pope (eds), *Ethical Considerations for Research Involving Prisoners* (National Academies Press 2007)

Gostin, Lawrence O and others, 'Financing the Future of WHO' (2022) 399(10334) *Lancet* 1445

Gostin, Lawrence O and others, 'The Legal Determinants of Health: Harnessing the Power of Law for Global Health and Sustainable Development' (2019) 393(10183) *Lancet* 1857

Gostin, Lawrence O and others, 'Toward a Common Secure Future: Four Global Commissions in the Wake of Ebola' (2016) 13(5) *PLoS Medicine* art e1002042

Gottfried, Robert S, *The Black Death: Natural and Human Disaster in Medieval Europe* (The Free Press 1983)

Gover, Angela R, Shannon B Harper, and Lynn Langton, 'Anti-Asian Hate Crime During the COVID-19 Pandemic: Exploring the Reproduction of Inequality' (2020) 45(4) *American Journal of Criminal Justice* 647

Government of Canada, 'Government of Canada Announces Additional Measures to Contain the Spread of the Omicron Variant' (News Release, 17 December 2021)

Government of Western Australia, 'COVID-19 Coronavirus: Travel and Border: Statewide' (23 December 2021)

Grab, Alexander, 'Smallpox Vaccination in Napoleonic Italy (1800–1814)' (2017) 30(3) *Napoleonica La Revue* 38

Grabowski, David C and Vincent Mor, 'Nursing Home Care in Crisis in the Wake of COVID-19' (2020) 324(1) *Journal of the American Medical Association* 23

Gray, Fred D, *The Tuskegee Syphilis Study: The Real Story and Beyond* (NewSouth Books 2013)

Greely, Henry T, 'COVID-19 Immunity Certificates: Science, Ethics, Policy and Law' (2020) 7(1) *Journal of Law and the Biosciences* art lsaa035

Green, Manfred S, 'Did the Hesitancy in Declaring COVID-19 a Pandemic Reflect a Need to Refine the Term?' (2020) 395(10229) *Lancet* 1034

Green, Monica H, 'Editor's Introduction to Pandemic Disease in the Medieval World: Rethinking the Black Death' in Monica H Green (ed), *Pandemic Disease in the Medieval World* (Arc Medieval Press 2015)

Green, Nicola, David Tappin, and Tim Bentley, 'Working From Home Before, During and After the COVID-19 Pandemic: Implications for Workers and Organisations' (2020) 45(2) *New Zealand Journal of Employment Relations* 5

Greene, Alan, *Emergency Powers in a Time of Pandemic* (Bristol University Press 2020)

Greger, Michael, *How to Survive a Pandemic* (Bluebird Books 2021)

Greitens, Sheena C, 'Surveillance, Security, and Liberal Democracy in the Post-COVID World' (2020) 74(S1) *International Organization* art 169

Greyling, Talita, Stephanie Rossouw, and Tamanna Adhikari, 'The Good, the Bad and the Ugly of Lockdowns During COVID-19' (2021) 16(1) *PLoS One* art e0245546

Griglio, Elena, 'Parliamentary Oversight Under the Covid-19 Emergency: Striving Against Executive Dominance' (2020) 8(1–2) *The Theory and Practice of Legislation* 49

Grimes, David R, 'Medical Disinformation and the Unenviable Nature of COVID-19 Conspiracy Theories' (2021) 16(3) *PLoS One* art e0245900

Groom, Anthony, 'Force Majeure Clauses' (2004) *AMPLA Yearbook* 286

Gross, Marielle S and others, 'Rethinking "Elective" Procedures for Women's Reproduction During COVID-19' (2020) 50(3) *Hastings Center Report* 40

Grothe-Hammer, Michael and Steffen Roth, 'Dying is Normal, Dying with the Coronavirus is Not: A Sociological Analysis of the Implicit Norms Behind the Criticism of Swedish "Exceptionalism"' (2021) 23(Sup1) *European Societies* S332

Guénel, Annick, and Sylvia Klingberg, 'Biosecurity in the Time of Avian Influenza, Vietnam' in Tamara Giles-Vernick and Susan Craddock with Jennifer Gunn (eds), *Influenza and Public Health: Learning from Past Pandemics* (Routledge 2010)

Guerrini, Christi J and others, 'Self-experimentation, Ethics, and Regulation of Vaccines' (2020) 369(6511) *Science* 1570

Gulland, Jackie, 'Households, Bubbles and Hugging Grandparents: Caring and Lockdown Rules During COVID-19' (2020) 28 *Feminist Legal Studies* 329

Gunn, Michelle A and Fiona J McDonald, 'COVID-19, Rationing and the Right to Health: Can Patients Bring Legal Actions if They Are Denied Access to Care?' (2021) 214(5) *Medical Journal of Australia* 207

Gupta, Anil and others, 'Early Treatment for Covid-19 with SARS-CoV-2 Neutralizing Antibody Sotrovimab' (2021) 385(21) *New England Journal of Medicine* 1941

Gur-Arie, Rachel, Euzebiusz Jamrozik, and Patricia Kingori, 'No Jab, No Job? Ethical Issues in Mandatory COVID-19 Vaccination of Healthcare Personnel' (2021) 6(2) *BMJ Global Health* art e004877

Gursoy, Dogan and Christina G Chi, 'Effects of COVID-19 Pandemic on Hospitality Industry: Review of the Current Situations and a Research Agenda' (2020) 29(5) *Journal of Hospitality, Marketing & Management* 527

Gyselinck, Iwein and Wim Janssens, 'Remdesivir, on the Road to DisCoVeRY' (2021) 22(2) *Lancet Infectious Diseases* 153

Habib, Heba, 'Has Sweden's Controversial Covid-19 Strategy Been Successful?' (2020) 369 *British Medical Journal* m2376

Habibi, Roojin and others, 'Do Not Violate the International Health Regulations During the COVID-19 Outbreak' (2020) 395(10225) *Lancet* 664

Haddock, David D and Lynne Kiesling, 'The Black Death and Property Rights' (2002) 31(2) *Journal of Legal Studies* S545

Hague Conference on Private International Law, 'COVID-19 Toolkit' (2020)

Haigh, Richard and Bruce Preston, 'The Court System in a Time of Crisis: COVID-19 and Issues in Court Administration' (2020) 57(3) *Osgoode Hall Law Journal* 869

Hailu, Dejene and others, 'Occupational Health Safety of Health Professionals and Associated Factors During COVID-19 Pandemics at North Showa Zone, Oromia Regional State, Ethiopia' (2021) 14 *Risk Management Healthcare Policy* 1299

Hall, Heather, 'The Effect of the COVID-19 Pandemic on Healthcare Workers' Mental Health' (2020) 33(7) *Journal of the American Academy of Physician Assistants* 45

Hall, Mark A, and David M Studdert, '"Vaccine Passport" Certification—Policy and Ethical Considerations' (2021) 385(11) *New England Journal of Medicine* e32

Hamilton, William, 'Cancer Diagnostic Delay in the COVID-19 Era: What Happens Next?' (2020) 21(8) *Lancet Oncology* 1000

Hamlin, Christopher, *Cholera: The Biography* (Oxford University Press 2009)

Hamouche, Salima, 'COVID-19, Physical Distancing in the Workplace and Employees' Mental Health: Implications and Insights for Organizational Interventions—Narrative Review' (2021) 33(2) *Psychiatria Danubina* 202

Han, Duke and Laura Mosqueda, 'Elder Abuse in the COVID-19 Era' (2020) 68(7) *Journal of the American Geriatric Society* 1386

Han, Emeline and others, 'Lessons Learnt from Easing COVID-19 Restrictions: An Analysis of Countries and Regions in Asia Pacific and Europe' (2020) 396(10261) *Lancet* 1525

Hanley, Brian and others, 'Autopsy in Suspected COVID-19 Cases' (2020) 73 *Journal of Clinical Pathology* 239

Harman, Sophie, Eugene Richardson and Parsa Erfani, 'To End COVID-19 We Need Vaccine Justice for Developing Countries Not Outdated Charity' *The Conversation* (21 June 2021)

Harman, Sophie and others, 'Global Vaccine Equity Demands Reparative Justice—Not Charity' (2021) 6 *BMJ Global Health* art e006504

Hasell, Joe and others, 'A Cross-Country Database of COVID-19 Testing' (2020) 7 *Scientific Data* art 345

Hasford, Joerg, 'Re: Covid-19: Human Challenge Studies will see People Purposefully Infected with Virus' Rapid Response, *British Medical Journal* (25 October 2020)

Hasken, Timothy J, 'A Duty to Kiss and Tell? Examining the Uncomfortable Relationship between Negligence and the Transmission of HPV' (2010) 95(3) *Iowa Law Review* 985

Haug, Nina and others, 'Ranking the Effectiveness of Worldwide COVID-19 Government Initiatives' (2020) 4(12) *Nature Human Behaviour* 1303

Hawari, Feras I and others, 'The Inevitability of Covid-19 Related Distress Among Healthcare Workers: Findings from a Low Caseload Country Under Lockdown' (2021) 16(4) *PLoS One* art e0248741

Hayat, Khezar and others, 'Impact of COVID-19 on the Mental Health of Healthcare Workers: A Cross-Sectional Study from Pakistan' (2021) 9 *Frontiers in Public Health* art 603602

Hays, JN, *The Burdens of Disease: Epidemics and Human Response in Western History* (rev edn, Rutgers University Press 2009)

He, L and others, 'Expression of Elevated Levels of Pre-inflammatory Cytokines in SARS-CoV-infected ACE2+ Cells in SARS Patients: Relation to the Acute Lung Injury and Pathogenesis of SARS' (2006) 210(3) *Journal of Pathology* 288

Health and Safety Authority of Ireland, 'Guidance on Working from Home for Employers and Employees' (2020)

Health and Safety Executive (UK), 'Regulating Occupational Health and Safety During the Coronavirus (COVID-19) Pandemic'

Heffer, Simon, 'What the Spanish Flu Pandemic Teaches us Today' *The New Statesman* (London, 8–14 May 2020)

Hegele, Yvonne and Schnabel, Johanna, 'Federalism and the Management of the COVID-19 Crisis: Centralisation, Decentralisation and (Non-)coordination' (2021) 44(5–6) *West European Politics* 1052

Heggen, Kristin, Tony J Sandset, and Eivind Engebretsen, 'COVID-19 and Sustainable Development Goals' (2020) 98(10) *Bulletin of the World Health Organization* 646

Hellman, Deborah and Kate M Nicholson, 'Rationing and Disability: The Civil Rights and Wrongs of Clinical Triage Protocols' (2020) 78(4) *Washington and Lee Law Review* 3

Hemelk, Daniel and Rodriguez, Daniel B, 'A Public Health Framework for COVID-19 Business Liability' (2020) 7(1) *Journal of Law and the Biosciences* art lsaa074

Hemp, Paul, 'Presenteeism: At Work—But Out of It' *Harvard Business Review* (October 2004)

Hennock, EP, 'The Urban Sanitary Movement in England and Germany, 1838–1840: A Comparison' (2000) 15 *Continuity and Change* 269

Henriquez-Trujillo, Aquiles R and others, 'COVID-19 Outbreaks Among Isolated Amazonian Indigenous People, Ecuador' (2021) 99(7) *Bulletin of the World Health Organization* 478

Herman, David A, 'Juvenile Curfews and the Breakdown of the Tiered Approach to Equal Protection' (2007) 82(6) *New York University Law Review* 1857

Herreros, Benjamin, Pablo Gella, and Diego R de Asua, 'Triage During the COVID-19 Epidemic in Spain: Better and Worse Ethical Arguments' (2020) 46(7) *Journal of Medical Ethics* 455

Heymann, David L and Nahoko Shindo, 'COVID-19: What is Next for Public Health?' (2020) 395(10224) *Lancet* 542

Heymann, David L and others, 'Zika Virus and Microcephaly: Why is This Situation a PHEIC?' (2016) 387(10020) *Lancet* 719

Heymann, Jody and others, 'Protecting Health During COVID-19 and Beyond: A Global Examination of Paid Sick Leave Design in 193 Countries' (2020) 15(7) *Global Public Health* 925

Heywood, Rob, 'Systemic Negligence and NHS Hospitals: An Underutilised Argument' (2021) 32(3) *King's Law Journal* 437

HHS Office for Civil Rights in Action, 'Civil Rights, HIPAA, and the Coronavirus Disease 2019 (COVID-19)' (Bulletin, 28 March 2020)

Hillis, Susan D and others, 'Global Minimum Estimates of Children Affected by COVID-19-associated Orphanhood and Deaths of Caregivers: A Modelling Study' (2021) 398(10298) *Lancet* 391

Hippisley-Cox, Julia and others, 'Risk of Thrombocytopenia and Thromboembolism After COVID-19 Vaccination and SARS-CoV2 Positive Testing: Self-Controlled Case Series Study' (2021) 374 *British Medical Journal* n1931

Hirabayashi, Gordon K, *A Principled Stand: The Story of Hirabayashi v United States* (University of Washington Press 2013)

Ho, PL, M Becker, and MM Chan-Yeung, 'Emerging Occupational Lung Infections' (2005) 11(7) *International Journal of Tuberculosis and Lung Disease* 710

Hodgson, Patrick G, 'Flu, Society and the State: The Political, Social and Economic Implications of the 1918–1920 Influenza Pandemic in Queensland' (PhD Thesis, James Cook University 2017)

Hoek, Joyce M and others, 'Rethinking Remdesivir for COVID-19: A Bayesian Reanalysis of Trial Findings' (2021) 16(7) *PloS One* art e0255093

Hoffman, Sharona, 'Preparing for Disaster: Protecting the Most Vulnerable in Emergencies' (2009) 42(5) *UC Davis Law Review* 1491

Hogerzeil, Hans V, 'Essential Medicines and Human Rights: What Can They Learn From Each Other?' (2006) 84(5) *Bulletin of the World Health Organization* 371

Holmes, Emily A and others, 'Multidisciplinary Research Priorities for the COVID-19 Pandemic: A Call for Action for Mental Health Science' (2020) 7(6) *Lancet Psychiatry* 547

Holton, Sara and others, 'Psychological Well-being of Australian Hospital Clinical Staff During the COVID-19 Pandemic' (2021) 45(3) *Australian Health Review* 297

Homeniuk, Robyn and Claire Collins, 'How COVID-19 Has Affected General Practice Consultations and Income: General Practitioner Cross-Sectional Population Survey Evidence from Ireland' (2021) 11(4) *BMJ Open* art e044685

Honigsbaum, Mark, *A History of the Great Influenza Pandemics: Death, Panic and Hysteria, 1830–1920* (IB Tauris 2014)

Honigsbaum, Mark, 'Regulating the 1918-19 Pandemic: Flu, Stoicism and the Northcliffe Press' (2013) 57(2) *Medical History* 165

Honigsbaum, Mark, 'Spanish Influenza Redux: Revisiting the Mother of all Pandemics' (2018) 391(10139) *Lancet* 2492

Honigsbaum, Mark, *The Pandemic Century: One Hundred Years of Panic, Hysteria and Hubris* (C Hurst and Company (Publishers) Limited 2019)

Honigsbaum, Mark, 'The "Russian" Influenza in the UK: Lessons Learned, Opportunities Missed' (2011) 29S *Vaccine* B11

Honigsbaum, Mark and Lakshmi Krishnan, 'Taking Pandemic Sequelae Seriously: From the Russian Influenza to COVID-19 Long-haulers' (2020) 396(10260) *Lancet* 1389

Hooper, Monica W, Anna M Nápoles, and Eliseo J Pérez-Stable, 'COVID-19 and Racial/Ethnic Disparities' (2020) 323(24) *Journal of the American Medical Association* 2466

Hopkins, Donald R, *The Greatest Killer: Smallpox in History* (University of Chicago Press 2002)

Hornblum, Allen M, *Acres of Skin: Human Experiments at Holmesburg Prison* (Routledge 1999)

Hornblum, Allen M, 'They Were Cheap and Available: Prisoners as Research Subjects in Twentieth Century America' (1997) 315(7120) *British Medical Journal* 1437

Horne, Nicholas, 'COVID-19 and Parliamentary Sittings (Current as at 2 April 2020)' (Parliamentary Library, Parliament of Australia)

Horton, Richard, 'Offline: COVID-19 is Not a Pandemic' (2020) 396(10255) *Lancet* 874

Hoss, Aila and Heather Tanana, 'Upholding Tribal Sovereignty and Promoting Tribal Public Health Capacity During the COVID-19 Pandemic' in Scott Burris and others (eds), *Assessing Legal Responses to COVID-19* (Public Health Law Watch 2020)

Hossain, Mahbub, Abida Sultana, and Neetu Purohit, 'Mental Health Outcomes of Quarantine and Isolation for Infection Prevention: A Systematic Umbrella Review of the Global Evidence' (2020) 42 *Epidemiological Health* art e2020038

Howard, Jeremy and others, 'An Evidence Review of Face Masks Against COVID-19' (2021) 118(4) *Proceedings of the National Academy of Sciences of the United States of America* art e2014564118

Hsin, Lisa, 'New Zealand' in Bonavero Institute of Human Rights, *A Preliminary Human Rights Assessment of Legislative and Regulatory Responses to the COVID-19 Pandemic Across 11 Jurisdictions* (Bonavero Report No 3/2020, 6 May 2020)

Huang, Irving Yi-Feng, 'Fighting COVID-19 Through Government Initiatives and Collaborative Governance: The Taiwan Experience' (2020) 80(4) *Public Administration Review* 665

Huber, Martin, and Henrika Langen, 'Timing Matters: The Impact of Response Measures on COVID-19-Related Hospitalization and Death Rates in Germany and Switzerland' (2020) 156(1) *Swiss Journal of Economic Statistics* 10

Huber, Valeska, 'Pandemics and the Politics of Difference: Rewriting the History of Internationalism Through Nineteenth-Century Cholera' (2020) 15(3) *Journal of Global History* 394

Hudson, Kathy L and Francis S Collins, 'Bringing the Common Rule into the 21st Century' (2015) 373(24) *New England Journal of Medicine* 2293

Human Rights Law Centre, 'High Court of Australia Rejects Challenge of COVID-19 Lockdown Restrictions' (Human Rights Case Summary, 10 December 2020)

Human Rights Watch, 'Covid-19 Prisoner Releases Too Few, Too Slow' (27 May 2020)

Human Rights Watch, 'COVID-19 Triggers Wave of Free Speech Abuse: Scores of Countries Target Media, Activists, Medics, Political Opponents' (11 February 2021)

Hummel, Svenja and others, 'Mental Health Among Medical Professionals During the COVID-19 Pandemic in Eight European Countries': Cross-Sectional Survey Study' (2021) 23(1) *Journal of Medical Internet Research* art e24983

Hunt, Greg, 'No Fault COVID-19 Indemnity Scheme' (Media Release, 28 August 2021) Department of Health, 'Reduction in Threshold of No Fault COVID-19 Vaccine Claims Scheme' (News, Australian Government, 24 November 2021)

Hunt, Paul, 'Interpreting the International Right to Health in a Human Rights-Based Approach to Health' (2016) 18(2) *Health and Human Rights Journal* 109

Hunter, Paul R, 'Thrombosis After COVID-19 Vaccination' (2021) 373 *British Medical Journal* n958

Huremović, Damir (ed), *Psychiatry of Pandemics: A Mental Health Response to Infection Outbreak* (Springer 2019)

Hyslop, Anthea, 'Forewarned, Forearmed: Australia and the Spanish Influenza Pandemic, 1918–1919' in John Lack (ed), *1919: The Year Things Fell Apart?* (Australian Scholarly Publishing 2019)

Iacobucci, Gareth, 'Covid and Flu: What Do the Numbers Tell Us About Morbidity and Deaths?' (2021) 375 *British Medical Journal* n2514

Ibrahim, Laila F and others, 'The Characteristics of SARS-CoV-2-Positive Children Who Presented to Australian Hospitals During 2020: A PREDICT Network Study' (2021) 215(5) *Medical Journal of Australia* 217

Iftene, Adelina, 'COVID-19 in Canadian Prisons: Policies, Practices and Concerns' in Colleen M Flood and others (eds), *Vulnerable: The Law, Policy and Ethics of COVID-19* (University of Ottawa Press 2020)

Iliffe, John, *The African AIDS Epidemic: A History* (Ohio University Press 2005)

Imperial College COVID-19 Response Team, *Imperial College COVID-19 Response Team 2020–2021* (Report, 2021)

Independent Panel for Pandemic Preparedness and Response, 'COVID-19: The Authoritative Chronology, December 2019-March 2020' Background Paper 2a (May 2021)
Independent Panel for Pandemic Preparedness and Response, *COVID-19: Make it the Last Pandemic* (Report, May 2021)
Independent Panel for Pandemic Preparedness and Response, 'How an Outbreak Became a Pandemic: The Defining Moments of the COVID-19 Pandemic' (May 2021)
Ingelfinger, Franz J, 'Ethics of Experiments on Children' (1973) 288(15) *New England Journal of Medicine* 791
INQUEST, 'Chief Coroners Guidance Will Stymie and Limit Investigations Into COVID-19 Deaths of Frontline Workers' (News, 29 May 2020)
Institut Pasteur, 'Whole Genome of Novel Coronavirus, 2019-nCoV, Sequenced' *Science Daily* (31 January 2020)
Integrated People-Centred Health Services, 'COVID-19 Technology Access Pool' (Toolkit, 10 June 2020)
International Federation of Pharmaceutical Manufacturers and Associations, 'IFPMA Statement on "Intellectual Property and COVID-19"' (Statement, 16 October 2020)
International Monetary Fund, 'Policy Responses to COVID-19'
Islam, Nazrul and others, 'Excess Deaths Associated with Covid-19 Pandemic in 2020: Age and Sex Disaggregated Time Series Analysis in 29 High Income Countries' (2021) 373 *British Medical Journal* n1137
Jackman, Martha, 'Fault Lines: COVID-19, the *Charter*, and Long-Term Care' in Colleen M Flood and others (eds), *Vulnerable: The Law, Policy and Ethics of COVID-19* (University of Ottawa Press 2020)
Jacobs, Lesley A, 'Rights and Quarantine During the SARS Global Health Crisis: Differentiated Legal Consciousness in Hong Kong, Shanghai and Toronto' (2007) 41(3) *Law & Society Review* 511
Jaklevic, Mary Chris, 'Researchers Strive to Recruit Hard-Hit Minorities Into COVID-19 Vaccine Trials' (2020) 324(9) *Journal of American Medical Association* 826
James, Peter B and others, 'Post-Ebola Psychosocial Experiences and Coping Mechanisms among Ebola Survivors: A Systematic Review' (2019) 24(6) *Tropical Medicine and International Health* 671
Jamrozik, Euzebiusz and Michael J Selgelid, 'Ethical Issues Surrounding Controlled Human Infection Challenge Studies in Endemic Low-and Middle-Income Countries' (2020) 34(8) *Bioethics* 797
Jamrozik, Euzebiusz and Michael J Selgelid, *Human Challenge Studies in Endemic Settings: Ethical and Regulatory Issues* (Springer 2021)
Jamrozik, Euzebiusz, George S Heriot, and Michael J Selgelid, 'Coronavirus Human Infection Challenge Studies: Assessing Potential Benefits and Risks' (2020) 17 *Journal of Bioethical Inquiry* 709
Jamshidi, Maryam, 'The Federal Government Probably Can't Order Statewide Quarantines' *The University of Chicago Law Review Online* (20 April 2020)
Jang, Yeonhoon and others, 'Burnout and Peritraumatic Distress of Healthcare Workers in the COVID-19 Pandemic' (2021) 21(1) *BMC Public Health* 2075
Jecker, Nancy S and Caesar A Atuire, 'What's Yours is Ours: Waiving Intellectual Property Protections for COVID-19 Vaccines' (2021) 47(9) *Journal of Medical Ethics* 595
Jecker, Nancy S, Aaron G Wightman, and Douglas S Diekema, 'Vaccine Ethics: An Ethical Framework for Global Distribution of COVID-19 Vaccines' (2021) 47(5) *Journal of Medical Ethics* 308

Jedwab, Remi, Noel D Johnson, and Mark Koyama, 'Negative Shocks and Mass Persecutions: Evidence from the Black Death' (2019) 24(4) *Journal of Economic Growth* 345

Jena, Anupam B and others, 'Presenteeism Among Resident Physicians' (2010) 304(11) *Journal of the American Medical Association* 1166

Jensen, Steven LB, '"Human Rights against Human Arbitrariness": Pandemics in a Human Rights Historical Perspective' in Morten Kjaerum, Martha F Davis, and Amanda Lyons (eds), *COVID-19 and Human Rights* (Routledge 2021)

Jerving, Sara, 'The Long Road Ahead for COVID-19 Vaccination in Africa' (2021) 398(10303) *Lancet* 827

Jimenez, Manuel E and others, 'Black and Latinx Community Perspectives on COVID-19 Mitigation Behaviors, Testing and Vaccines' (2021) 4(7) *Journal of the American Medical Association Network Open* art e2117074

Jin, Jin and others, 'Individual and Community-Level Risk for COVID-19 Mortality in the United States' (2021) 27(2) *Nature Medicine* 264

Johnson, Stephanie B and Frances Butcher, 'Doctors During the COVID-19 Pandemic: What Are Their Duties and What is Owed to Them?' (2021) 47(1) *Journal of Medical Ethics* 12

Joint Committee on Vaccination and Immunisation, *Advice on Priority Groups for COVID-19 Vaccination, 30 December 2020* (Independent Report, 6 January 2021)

Jones, Ian and Polly Roy, 'Sputnik V COVID-19 Vaccine Candidate Appears Safe and Effective' (2021) 397(10275) *Lancet* 642

Jones, James H, *Bad Blood: The Tuskegee Syphilis Experiment* (Free Press 1993)

Jones, Kate E and others, 'Global Trends in Emerging Infectious Diseases' (2008) 451(7181) *Nature* 990

Jones, Nicholas R and others, 'Two Metres or One: What is the Evidence for Physical Distancing in COVID-19?' (2020) 370 *British Medical Journal* art n3223

Jorge, April, 'Hydroxychloroquine in the Prevention of COVID-19 Mortality' (2021) 3(1) *Lancet Rheumatology* e2

Joseph, Bobby and Merlyn Joseph, 'The Health of the Healthcare Workers' (2016) 20(2) *Indian Journal of Occupational and Environmental Medicine* 71

Joseph, Paul, 'Coronavirus: Can Nurses Refuse to Work if They Don't Have Adequate PPE?' *The Conversation* (21 May 2020)

Joseph, Sarah, 'Civil and Political Rights' in Mashood A Baderin and Manisuli Ssenyonjo (eds), *International Human Rights Law: Six Decades after the UDHR and Beyond* (Ashgate 2010)

Joseph, Sarah, 'COVID-19 and Human Rights: Past, Present and Future' (2020) Griffith Law School Research Paper No. 20-23

Joseph, Sarah, 'International Human Rights Law and the Response to the COVID-19 Pandemic' (2020) 11(2) *Journal of International Humanitarian Legal Studies* 249

Jucker, Ninetta, *Curfew in Paris: A Record of the German Occupation* (Hogarth Press 1960)

Kalata, Katelyn, 'The Exploitation of Inmates: Stateville Penitentiary Malaria Experiment' (2020) XI (Spring) *Western Illinois Historical Review* 2153

Kaldor, Jenny C and others, 'The *Lancet*-O'Neill Institute/Georgetown University Commission on Global Health and Law: The Power of Law to Advance the Right to Health' (2020) 13(1) *Public Health Ethics* 9

Kallings, LO, 'The First Postmodern Pandemic: 25 Years of HIV/AIDS' (2008) 263(3) *Journal of Internal Medicine* 218

Kamerlin, Shina CL and Peter M Kasson, 'Managing Coronavirus Disease 2019 Spread with Voluntary Public Health Measures: Sweden as a Case Study for Pandemic Control' (2020) 71(12) *Clinical Infectious Diseases* 3174

Kamerow, Douglas, 'COVID-19: Don't Forget the Impact on US Family Physicians' (2020) 368 *British Medical Journal* art m1260

Kampf, Günter, 'COVID-19: Stigmatising the Unvaccinated is Not Justified' (2021) 398(10314) *Lancet* 1871

Kanchan, Tanuj and others, 'The Advantages of Virtopsy During the Covid-19 Pandemic' (2020) 88(1 suppl) *Medico-Legal Journal* 55

Kanematsu, Yuichiro, 'Ads Touting Quack Coronavirus Cures Rampant in Japan' *Nikkei Asia* (9 June 2020)

Kaplan, Michelle, 'The 2009 H1N1 Swine Flu Pandemic: Reconciling Goals of Patents and Public Health Initiatives' (2010) 20(3) *Fordham Intellectual Property, Media & Entertainment Law Journal* 991

Karanika-Murray, Maria and Caroline Biron, 'The Health-Performance Framework of Presenteeism: Towards Understanding an Adaptive Behaviour' (2020) 73(2) *Human Relations* 242

Karim, S Abdool, 'Criminalisation of Transmission of SARS-CoV-2: A Potential Challenge to Controlling the Outbreak in South Africa' (2020) 110(6) *South African Medical Journal* 458

Karlinsky, Ariel and Dmitry Kobak, 'Tracking Excess Mortality Across Countries During the COVID-19 Pandemic with the World Mortality Dataset' (2021) 10 *eLife* art e60336

Karlsson, Ulf and Carl-Johan Fraenkel, 'COVID-19: Risks to Healthcare Workers and Their Families' (2020) 371 *British Medical Journal* m3944

Kasaeinasab, Abbasali and others, 'Respiratory Disorders Among Workers in Slaughterhouses' (2017) 8(1) *Safety and Health at Work* 84

Katz, Rebecca, and Julie Fischer, 'The Revised International Health Regulations: A Framework for Global Pandemic Response' (2010) 3(2) *Global Health Governance* 1

Kavaliunas, Andrius and others, 'Swedish Policy Analysis for COVID-19' (2020) 9(4) *Health Policy and Technology* 598

Kavanagh, Matthew M and others, 'Law, Criminalization and HIV in the World: Have Countries that Criminalise Achieved More or Less Successful Pandemic Response' (2021) 6(8) *BMJ Gobal Health* art e0066315

Keelan, Jennifer and Kumanan Wilson, *Designing a No-Fault Vaccine-Injury Compensation Programme for Canada: Lessons Learned from an International Analysis of Programmes* (Munk School Briefing, University of Toronto February 2011)

Keller, Marcel and others, 'Ancient Yersinia Pestis Genomes from Across Western Europe Reveal Early Diversification during the First Pandemic (541–750)' (2019) 116(25) *Proceedings of the National Academy of the Sciences of the United States of America* 12363

Kelly, David, Kate Shaw, and Libby Porter, 'Melbourne Tower Lockdowns Unfairly Target Already Vulnerable Public Housing Residents' *The Conversation* (6 July 2020)

Kelly, Heath, 'The Classical Definition of a Pandemic is not Elusive' (2011) 89(7) *Bulletin of the World Health Organization* 540

Kelso, Jane, 'When Masks Were Compulsory' (Sydney Living Museums, 25 August 2020)

Kemp, Steven and others, 'Empty Streets, Busy Internet: A Time-Series Analysis of Cybercrime and Fraud Trends During COVID-19' (2021) 37(4) *Journal of Contemporary Criminal Justice* 480

Kennedy, Jay P, Melissa Rorie, and Michael L Benson, 'COVID-19 Frauds: An Exploratory Study of Victimization During a Global Crisis' (2021) 20(3) *Criminology & Public Policy* 493

Kent, Susan K, *The Influenza Pandemic of 1918-1919: A Brief History With Documents* (Bedford/St Martin's 2013)

Kentor, Rachel A and Amanda L Thompson, 'Answering the Call to Support Youth Orphaned by COVID-19' (2021) 398(10298) *Lancet* 366

Kettl, Donald F, 'States Divided: The Implications of American Federalism for COVID-19' (2020) 80(4) *Public Administration Review* 595

Kevat, Dev AS and others, 'Medico-legal Considerations of Mandatory COVID-19 Vaccination for High Risk Workers' (2021) 215(1) *Medical Journal of Australia* 22

Khadke, Sumanth and others, 'Harnessing the Immune System to Overcome Cytokine Storm and Reduce Viral Load in COVID-19: A Review of the Phases of Illness and Therapeutic Agents' (2020) 17 *Virology Journal* art 154

Khatatbeh, Moawiah, 'Efficacy of Nationwide Curfew to Encounter Spread of COVID-19: A Case from Jordan' (2020) 8 *Frontiers in Public Health* 394

Kherbane, Rabah, 'Covid-19: Entitlement of Defendants Awaiting Trial to Apply for Bail' *The Law Society Gazette* (16 April 2020)

Kim, Young S, 'World Health Organization and Early Global Response to HIV/AIDS: Emergence and Development of International Norms' (2015) 22(1) *Journal of International and Area Studies* 19

Kincaid, John and J Wesley Leckrone, 'American Federalism and Covid-19: Party Trumps Policy' in Nico Steytler (ed), *Comparative Federalism and Covid-19: Combating the Pandemic* (Routledge 2021)

Kippen, Rebecca and others, 'A National Survey of COVID-19 Challenges, Responses and Effects in Australian General Practice' (2020) 49(11) *Australian Journal of General Practice* 745

Kiraz. S Esra and Esra Y Üstün, 'COVID-19 and Force Majeure Clauses: An Examination of Arbitral Tribunal's Awards' (2020) 25(4) *Uniform Law Review* 437

Kirby, Amy E and others, 'Using Wastewater Surveillance Data to Support the COVID-19 Response—United States, 2020–2021' (2021) 70(36) *Morbidity and Mortality Weekly Reports* 1242

Kirby, Tony, 'Evidence Mounts on the Disproportionate Effect of COVID-19 on Ethnic Minorities' (2020) 8 *Lancet Respiratory Medicine* 547

Kirby, Tony, 'When Should the UK Lift its Lockdown?' (2021) 9 *Lancet Respiratory Medicine* e44

Kirchner, Stefan (ed), *Governing the Crisis: Law, Human Rights and COVID-19* (LIT Verlag 2021)

Kirk, Jessica and Matt McDonald, 'The Politics of Exceptionalism: Securitization and COVID-19' (2021) 1(3) *Global Studies Quarterly* art ksab024

Kjaerum, Morten, Martha F Davis, and Amanda Lyons (eds), *COVID-19 and Human Rights* (Routledge 2021)

Klapdor, Michael, 'Changes to the COVID-19 Social Security Measures: A Brief Assessment' (Research Paper, Parliament of Australia, 30 July 2020)

Klapdor, Michael and Anthony Lotric, 'Australian Government COVID-19 Disaster Payments: A Quick Guide' (Quick Guide, Parliament of Australia, 4 August 2021)

Klein, Natalie, 'International Law Perspectives on Cruise Ships and COVID-19' (2020) 11(2) *Journal of International Humanitarian Legal Studies* 282

Kleinman, Arthur and James L Watson (eds), *SARS in China: Prelude to Pandemic?* (Stanford University Press 2005)

Kleitman, Sabina and others, 'To Comply or Not Comply? A Latent Profile Analysis of Behaviours and Attitudes During the COVID-19 Pandemic' (2021) 16(7) *PLoS One* art 0255268

Kluge, Hans Henri P and others, 'Refugee and Migrant Health in the COVID-19 Response' (2020) 395(10232) *Lancet* 1237

Knutsen, Erik S, 'The COVID-19 Pandemic and Insurance Coverage for Business Interruption in Canada' (2021) 46(2) *Queen's Law Journal* 431

Knutsen, Erik S and Jeffrey W Stempel, 'Infected Judgment: Problematic Rush to Conventional Wisdom and Insurance Coverage Denial in a Pandemic' (2021) 27 *Connecticut Insurance Law Journal* 185

Kofler, Natalie and Françoise Baylis, 'Ten Reasons Why Immunity Passports Are a Bad Idea' (2020) 581(7809) *Nature* 379

Koh, Wee C, Lin Naing, and Justin Wong, 'Estimating the Impact of Physical Distancing Measures in Containing COVID-19: An Empirical Analysis' (2020) 100 *International Journal of Infectious Diseases* 42

Koltay, András 'The Punishment of Scaremongering in the Hungarian Legal System: Freedom of Speech in the Times of the COVID-19 Pandemic' (2020) Working Paper

Komesaroff, Paul, Ian Kerridge, and Lyn Gilbert, 'The US is Fast-Tracking a Coronavirus Vaccine, But Bypassing Safety Standards May Not be Worth the Cost' *The Conversation* (24 March 2020)

Korecky, Alexander, 'Curfew Must Not Ring Tonight: Judicial Confusion and Misperception of Juvenile Curfew Laws' (2016) 44(4) *Capital University Law Review* 831

Korobkin, Russell, 'Three Choice Architecture Paradigms for Healthcare Policy' in IG Cohen, Holly Fernandez Lynch, and Christopher T Robertson (eds), *Nudging Health: Health Law and Behavioral Economics* (Johns Hopkins University Press 2016)

Kory, Pierre Kory and others, 'Review of the Emerging Evidence Demonstrating the Efficacy of Ivermectin in the Prophylaxis and Treatment of COVID-19' (2021) 28(3) *American Journal of Therapeutics* e299

Koshan, Jennifer, Janet Mosher, and Wanda Wiegers, 'COVID-19, the Shadow Pandemic, and Access to Justice for Survivors of Domestic Violence' (2020) 57(3) *Osgoode Hall Law Journal* 739

Kotar, SL and JE Gessler, *Smallpox: A History* (McFarland & Co 2013)

Köybaşı, Serkan, Volkan Aslan, and Naciye Betül Haliloğlu, 'Turkey: Legal Response to Covid-19', in Jeff King and Octávio LM Ferraz (eds), *The Oxford Compendium of National Legal Responses to Covid-19* (Oxford University Press 2021)

Kozyreva, Anastasia and others, 'Psychological Factors Shaping Public Responses to COVID-19 Digital Contact Tracing Technologies in Germany' (2021) 11 *Scientific Reports* art 18716

Krasser, Anja, 'Compulsory Vaccination in a Fundamental Rights Perspective: Lessons from the ECtHR' (2021) 15(2) *Vienna Journal on International Constitutional Law* 207

Krause, Philip R and Marion F Gruber, 'Emergency Use Authorization of Covid Vaccines—Safety and Efficacy Follow-up Considerations' (2020) 383(19) *New England Journal of Medicine* e107(1)

Krause, Philip R and others, 'Considerations in Boosting COVID-19 Vaccine Immune Responses' (2021) 398(10308) *Lancet* 1377

Kraut, Alan, 'Dr Joseph Goldberger and the War on Pellagra' (National Institutes of Health: Office of National Institutes of Health History and Stetten Museum)

Krieger, Nancy and others, 'Missing Again: US Racial and Ethnic Data for COVID-19 Vaccination' (2021) 397(10281) *Lancet* 1259

Krishtel, Priti and Rohit Malpani, 'Suspend Intellectual Property Rights for COVID-19 Vaccines' (2021) 373 *British Medical Journal* n1344

Kronfli, Nadine and Matthew J Akiyama, 'Prioritizing Incarcerated Populations for COVID-19 Vaccination and Vaccine Trials' (2021) 31 *eClinical Medicine* Article art 100659

Krugman, Saul, 'The Willowbrook Hepatitis Studies Revisited: Ethical Aspects' (1986) 8(1) *Reviews of Infectious Diseases* 157

Kuehn, Bridget M, 'Vaccine Passports Help Boost Lagging Vaccination Rates' (2020) 327(3) *Journal of the American Medical Association* 209

Kupferschmidt, Kai and Jon Cohen, 'WHO Launches Global Megatrial of the Four Most Promising Coronavirus Treatments' *ScienceInsider* (22 March 2020)

Kuppalli, Krutika and others, 'India's COVID-19 Crisis: A Call for International Action' (2021) 397(10290) *Lancet* 2132

Kuylen, Margot NI and others, 'Should Age Matter in COVID-19 Triage? A Deliberative Study' (2021) 47(5) *Journal of Medical Ethics* 291

Kwon, Diana, 'How Swamped Preprint Servers Are Blocking Bad Coronavirus Research' (2020) 581(7807) *Nature* 130

Kyobutungi, Catherine, 'Kenya Has Imposed a Holiday Season COVID-19 Vaccine Mandate: Why it's Premature' *The Conversation* (4 December 2021)

Kyobutungi, Catherine, 'Want to Know About Vaccine Rollouts in Africa? Click on a Country Here and Find Out' *The Conversation* (29 September 2021)

Kypraios, Christos, 'Italy' in Bonavero Institute of Human Rights, *A Preliminary Human Rights Assessment of Legislative and Regulatory Responses to the COVID-19 Pandemic Across 11 Jurisdictions* (Bonavero Report No 3/2020, 6 May 2020)

Labonté, Ronald and Mira Johri, 'COVID-19 Drug and Vaccine Patents Are Putting Profit Before People' *The Conversation* (6 November 2020)

Labonté, Ronald and others, 'A Pandemic Treaty, Revised International Health Regulations, or Both?' (2021) 17 *Globalization and Health* art 128

Laborde, David and others, 'COVID-19 Risks to Global Food Security' (2020) 369 *Science* 500

Labrague, Leonardo J and Janet Alexis A De Los Santos, 'Prevalence and Predictors of Coronaphobia Among Frontline Hospital and Public Health Nurses' (2021) 38(3) *Public Health Nursing* 382

Labuschaigne, Melodie, 'Ethicolegal Issues Relating to the South African Government's Response to COVID-19' (2020) 13(1) *South African Journal of Bioethics and Law* 23

Lacey, Eric, Joseph Massad, and Robert Utz, *A Review of Fiscal Policy Responses to COVID-19* (World Bank Group 2021)

Lacy, J Matthew and others, 'COVID-19: Postmortem Diagnostic and Biosafety Considerations' (2020) 41(3) *American Journal of Forensic Medicine and Pathology* 143

Lancet, '*Carlill v The Carbolic Smoke-Ball Company*' (1892) 140 *Lancet* 102

Lancet, 'COVID-19 Vaccines: No Time for Complacency' (2020) 396(10263) *Lancet* 1607

Lancet, 'Global Governance for COVID-19 Vaccines' (2020) 395(10241) *Lancet* 1883

Lancet Commission on COVID-19 Vaccines and Therapeutics Task Force Members, 'Operation Warp Speed: Implications for Global Vaccine Security' (2021) 9(7) *Lancet Global Health* e1017

Lancet COVID-19 Commission Task Force on Mental Health, *Early Findings on the Neurological Consequences of COVID-19* (Report, June 2021)

Lancet Editors, 'Expression of Concern: Hydroxychloroquine or Chloroquine With or Without a Macrolide for Treatment of COVID-19: A Multinational Registry Analysis' (2020) 395 *Lancet* E102

Lancet Group Editors, 'Learning from a Retraction' (2020) 396(10257) *Lancet* P1056

Lane, Courtney R and others, 'Genomic-informed Responses in the Elimination of COVID-19 in Victoria, Australia: An Observational, Genomic Epidemiological Study' (2021) 6(8) *Lancet Public Health* E547

Langton, Samuel, Anthony Dixon, and Graham Farrell, 'Six Months in: Pandemic Crime Trends in England and Wales' (2021) 10 *Crime Science* art 6

Largent, Emily A, Govind Persad, and Samantha Sangenito, 'US Public Attitudes Toward COVID-19 Vaccine Mandates' (020) 3(12) *Journal of American Medical Association Network Open* art e2033324

Larry A Green Center, 'Quick COVID-19 Primary Care Survey: Series 21 Fielded September 18–21, 2020'

Larsen, David A and Krista R Wigginton, 'Tracking COVID-19 with Wastewater' (2020) 38(10) *Nature Biotechnology* 1151

Lasalvia, Antonio and others, 'The Sustained Psychological Impact of the COVID-19 Pandemic on Health Care Workers One Year After the Outbreak: A Repeated Cross-Sectional Study in a Tertiary Hospital of North-East Italy' (2021) 18(24) *International Journal of Environmental Research and Public Health* art 13374

Lau, H and others, 'Evaluating the Massive Underreporting and Undertesting of COVID-19 Cases in Multiple Global Epicenters' (2021) 27(2) *Pulmonology* 110

Lawler, Odette K and others, 'The COVID-19 Pandemic is Intricately Linked to Biodiversity Loss and Ecosystem Health' (2021) 5(11) *Lancet Planetary Health* E840

Lawrence, Jack, 'Why Was a Major Study on Ivermectin for COVID-19 Just Retracted?' *Grftr* (15 July 2021)

Lazarus, Jeffrey V and others, 'A Global Survey of Potential Acceptance of a COVID-19 Vaccine' (2021) 27(2) *Nature Medicine* 225

Le Bert, Nina and others, 'SARS-CoV-2-specific T Cell Immunity in Cases of COVID-19 and SARS, and Uninfected Controls' (2020) 584(7821) *Nature* 457

Le Bouthillier, Yves and Delphine Nakache, 'The Right of Citizens Abroad to Return During a Pandemic' in Colleen M Flood and others (eds), *Vulnerable: The Law, Policy and Ethics of COVID-19* (University of Ottawa Press 2020)

Leary, Alison and others, 'A Thematic Analysis of the Prevention of Future Deaths Reports in Healthcare from HM Coroners in England and Wales 2016–2019' (2021) 26(1) *Journal of Patient Safety and Risk Management* 14

Leask, Julie and others, 'Policy Considerations for Mandatory Covid-19 Vaccination from the Collaboration on Social Science in Immunisation' (2021) 215(11) *Medical Journal of Australia* 499

Lebret, Aubrey, 'COVID-19 Pandemic and Derogation to Human Rights' (2020) 7(1) *Journal of Law and the Biosciences* art lsaa015

Ledford, Heidi, 'Should Children Get COVID Vaccines? What the Science Says' (2021) 595(7869) *Nature* 638

Lee, Kelley and others, 'Global Coordination on Cross-Border Travel and Trade Measures Crucial to COVID-19 Response' (2020) 395(10237) *Lancet* 1593

Lee, Nelson and others, 'Major Outbreak of Severe Acute Respiratory Syndrome in Hong Kong' (2003) 348(20) *New England Journal of Medicine* 1986

Legg, Michael, 'The COVID-19 Pandemic, the Courts and Online Hearings: Maintaining Open Justice, Procedural Fairness and Impartiality' (2021) 49(2) *Federal Law Review* 161

Legg, Michael and Anthony Song, 'The Courts, the Remote Hearing and the Pandemic: From Action to Reflection' (2021) 44(1) *University of New South Wales Law Journal* 126

Legido-Quigley, Helena and others, 'The Resilience of the Spanish Health System against the COVID-19 Pandemic' (2020) 5(5) *Lancet Public Health* art E251

Leifheit, Kathryn M and others, 'Elevated Mortality Among People Experiencing Homelessness with COVID-19' (2021) 8(7) *Open Forum Infectious Diseases* art ofab301

Lekfuangfu, Warn N and others, 'On Covid-19: New Implications of Job Task Requirements and Spouse's Occupational Sorting' (2020) 12 *Covid Economics* 87

Lelliott, Joseph, Andreas Schloenhardt, and Ruby Ioannou, 'Pandemics, Punishment, and Public Health: COVID-19 and Criminal Law in Australia' (2021) 44(1) *University of New South Wales Law Journal* 167

Lemmens, Trudo and Roxanne Mykitiuk, 'Disability Rights Concerns and Clinical Triage Protocol Development During the COVID-19 Pandemic' (2020) 40(4) *Health Law in Canada* 103

Leonard, Arthur S, 'AIDS and Employment Law Revisited' (1985) 14(1) *Hofstra Law Review* 11

Leslie, Emily and Riley Wilson, 'Sheltering in Place and Domestic Violence: Evidence from Calls for Service during COVID-19' (2020) 189 *Journal of Public Economics* art 104241

Letter from Bill Foster and others to Alex M Azar II and Stephen Hahn (Congress of the United States, 20 April 2020)

Leung, Wai S and others, 'Presumed COVID-19 Index Case on Diamond Princess Cruise Ship and Evacuees to Hong Kong' (2020) 27(5) *Journal of Travel Medicine* taaa073

Levi, Michael and Russell G Smith, *Fraud and its Relationship to Pandemics and Economic Crises: From Spanish Flu to COVID-19* (Research Report 19, Australian Institute of Criminology 2021)

Levin, Yuval, 'A Mirror of the Plague: Pandemics Ancient and Modern and the Lessons They Teach' *Commentary* (New York City, May 2020) 18

Levine, Myron M, 'Experimental Challenge Studies in the Development of Vaccines for Infectious Diseases' (1998) 95 *Developments in Biological Standardization* 169

Lewis, Dyani, 'Where COVID Contact Tracing Went Wrong' (2021) 588(7838) *Nature* 384

Li, Heidi OY and others, 'YouTube as a Source of Information on COVID-19: A Pandemic of Misinformation?' (2020) 5(5) *BMJ Global Health* art e002604

Li, Jiaying and others, 'Intention to Response, Emergency Preparedness and Intention to Leave Among Nurses During COVID-19' (2020) 7(6) *Nursing Open* 1867

Li, Meng-Yuan and others, 'Expression of the SARS-CoV-2 Cell Receptor Gene ACE2 in a Wide Variety of Human Tissues' (2020) 9(1) *Infectious Diseases of Poverty* 45

Liddell, Kathleen and others, 'Who Gets the Ventilator? Important Legal Rights in a Pandemic' (2020) 46(7) *Journal of Medical Ethics* 421

Liebowitz, Dan, 'Smallpox Vaccination: An Early Start of Modern Medicine in America' (2017) 7(1) *Journal of Community Hospital Internal Medicine Perspectives* 61

Lifton, Robert J, *The Nazi Doctors: Medical Killing and the Psychology of Genocide* (rev edn, Basic Books 2017)

Lippel, Katherine, 'Occupational Health and Safety and COVID-19: Whose Rights Come First in a Pandemic?' in Colleen M Flood and others (eds) *Vulnerable: The Law, Policy and Ethics of COVID-19* (University of Ottawa Press 2020)

Lipworth, Wendy, 'Beyond Duty: Medical "Heroes" and the COVID-19 Pandemic' (2020) 17(4) *Journal of Bioethical Inquiry* 723

Lipworth, Wendy and others, 'Science at Warp Speed: Medical Research, Publication, and Translation During the COVID-19 Pandemic' (2020) 17(4) *Journal of Bioethical Inquiry* 555

Littman, RJ and ML Littman, 'Galen and the Antonine Plague' (1973) 94(3) *American Journal of Philology* 243

Littman, Robert J, 'The Plague of Athens: Epidemiology and Paleopathology' (2009) 76(5) *Mount Sinai Journal of Medicine* 456

Loades, Maria Elizabeth and others, 'Rapid Systematic Review: The Impact of Social Isolation and Loneliness in the Mental Health of Children and Adolescents in the Context of COVID-19' (2020) 59(11) *Journal of the American Academy of Child and Adolescent Psychiatry* 1218

Logunov, Denis Y and others, 'Safety and Efficacy of an rAd26 and rAd5 Vector-Based Heterologous Prime-Boost COVID-19 in Vaccine: An Interim Analysis of a Randomised Controlled Phase 3 Trial In Russia' (2021) 397(10275) *Lancet* 671

Logunov, Denis Y and others, 'Safety and Immunogenicity of an rAd26 and rAd5 Vector-Based Heterologous Prim-Boost COVID-19 Vaccine in Two Formulations: Two Open, Non-Randomised Phase 1/2 Studies from Russia' (2020) 396(10255) *Lancet* 887

Lokken, Erica M and others, 'Disease Severity, Pregnancy Outcomes, and Maternal Deaths among Pregnant Patients with Severe Acute Respiratory Syndrome Coronavirus 2 Infection in Washington State' (2021) 225(1) *American Journal of Obstetrics & Gynecology* 77

London, Alex John and Jonathan Kimmelman, 'Against Pandemic Research Exceptionalism' (2020) 368(6490) *Science* 476

Loomba, Sahi and others, 'Measuring the Impact of COVID-19 Vaccine Misinformation on Vaccination Intent in the UK and USA' (2021) 5(3) *Nature Human Behaviour* 337

Lopez III, Leo, Louis H Hart III, and Mitchell H Katz, 'Racial and Ethnic Health Disparities Related to COVID-19' (2021) 325 *Journal of the American Medical Association* 719

Loughnan, Claire and others, 'Refugees Need Protection from Coronavirus Too, and Must be Released' *The Conversation* (24 April 2020)

Lowth, Mary, 'Plagues, Pestilence and Pandemics: Deadly Diseases and Humanity' (2012) 42(16) *Practice Nurse* 42

Löwy, Ilana, 'Comment: Influenza and Historians: A Difficult Past' in Tamara Giles-Vernick and Susan Craddock with Jennifer Gunn (eds), *Influenza and Public Health: Learning from Past Pandemics* (Routledge 2010)

Lucivero, Federica and others, 'COVID-19 and Contact Tracing Apps: Ethical Challenges for a Social Experiment on a Global Scale' (2020) 17(4) *Journal of Bioethical Inquiry* 835

Lucraft, Mark, 'Chief Coroner's Guidance—Covid-19' (26 March 2020)

Lucraft, Mark, 'Chief Coroner's Guidance No 37: Covid-19 Deaths and Possible Exposure in the Workplace' (28 April 2020)

Lund, Susan and others, *The Future of Work After COVID-19* (Report, McKinsey Global Institute, 18 February 2021)

Lunney, Mark, Donal Nolan, and Ken Oliphant, *Tort Law: Text and Materials* (6th edn, Oxford University Press 2017)

Lurie, Nicole, Joshua M Sharfstein, and Jesse L Goodman, 'The Development of COVID-19 Vaccines: Safeguards Needed' (2020) 324(5) *Journal of the American Medical Association* 439

Luscombe, Alex and Alexander McClelland, *'An Extreme Last Resort': Monetary Penalties and the Policing of COVID-19 in Canada* (Centre for Media, Technology and Democracy, Report, November 2020)

Lynch, Holly F, 'The Rights and Wrongs of Intentional Exposure Research: Contexualising the Guatemala STD Inoculation Study' (2012) 38(8) *Journal of Medical Ethics* 513

Lynch, Holly F, Alison Bateman-House, and Arthur Caplan, 'Authorize Emergency Vaccines for COVID-19, But Do it Well' *Harvard Law School Petrie-Flom Center* (10 December 2020)

Lynch, Holly F, Alison Bateman-House, and Steven Joffe, 'Emergency Approvals for COVID-19: Evolving Impact on Obligations to Patients in Clinical Care and Research' (2021) 174(2) *Annals of Internal Medicine* 256

Lynch, Holly F and others, 'Promoting Ethical Payment in Human Infection Challenge Studies' (2021) 21(3) *American Journal of Bioethics* 11

Lynch, Holly F and others, 'Regulatory Flexibility for COVID-19 Research' (2020) 7(1) *Journal of Law and the Biosciences* art lsaa057

Lyu, Wei and George L Wehby, 'Community Use of Face Masks and COVID-19: Evidence from a Natural Experiment of State Mandates in the US' (2020) 39(8) *Health Affairs* 1419

MacDonald, Noni E and the SAGE Working Group on Vaccine Hesitancy, 'Vaccine Hesitancy: Definition, Scope and Determinants' (2015) 33(34) *Vaccine* 4161

MacDonnell, Vanessa, 'Ensuring Executive and Legislative Accountability in a Pandemic' in Colleen M Flood and others (eds), *Vulnerable: The Law, Policy and Ethics of COVID-19* (University of Ottawa Press 2020)

Machemer, Theresa, 'A Brief History of Human Challenge Trials' *Smithsonian Magazine* (16 December 2020)

MacIntyre, Chandini R and others, 'Mask Use, Risk-mitigation Behaviours and Pandemic Fatigue During the COVID-19 Pandemic in Five Cities in Australia, the UK and USA: A Cross-sectional Survey' (2021) 106 *International Journal of Infectious Diseases* 199

Mackenzie, John S and others, 'The Global Outbreak Alert and Response Network' (2014) 9(9) *Global Public Health* 1023

Mackey, Tim K, 'The Ebola Outbreak: Catalyzing a "Shift" in Global Health Governance?' (2016) 16 *BMC Infectious Diseases* art 699

Macklin, Ruth, 'Human Challenge Studies for Covid-19 Vaccine: Questions about Benefits and Risks' *The Hastings Center* (15 June 2020)

Madhav, Nita and others, 'Pandemics: Risks, Impacts, and Mitigation' in Dean T Jamison, and others (eds), *Disease Control Priorities: Improving Health and Reducing Poverty* (3rd edn, International Bank for Reconstruction and Development/World Bank 2017)

Maginn, Paul J and Gary Mortimer, 'How COVID All But Killed the Australian CBD' *The Conversation* (30 October, 2020)

Maglen, Krista, 'A World Apart: Geography, Australian Quarantine, and the Mother Country' (2005) 60(2) *Journal of the History of Medicine and Allied Sciences* 196

Maguire, Amy, Fiona McGaughey, and Marco Rizzi, 'Can Governments Mandate a COVID Vaccination? Balancing Public Health with Human Rights—And What the Law Says' *The Conversation* (30 November 2020)

Mahase, Elisabeth, 'Covid-19: Russian Vaccine Efficacy is 91.6%, Show Phase III Trial Results' (2021) 372 *British Medical Journal* n309

Mahase, Elisabeth, 'Vaccinating the UK: How the Covid Vaccine was Approved, and Other Questions Answered' (2020) 371 *British Medical Journal* 4759

Makaroun, Lena K, Rachel L Bachrach, and Ann-Marie Rosland, 'Elder Abuse in the Time of COVID-19—Increased Risks for Older Adults and Their Caregivers' (2020) 28(8) *American Journal of Geriatric Psychiatry* 876

Malbeuf, Jilene and others, 'The Plague of Athens Shedding Light on Modern Struggles with COVID-19' (2021) 22(43) *Journal of Classics Teaching* 47

Malbon, Justin, 'Obtaining COVID-19 Vaccines: How the Government Sold the Parachutes' in Belinda Bennett and Ian Freckelton (eds), *Pandemics, Public Health Emergencies and Government Powers: Perspectives on Australian Law* (Federation Press 2021)

Mallapaty, Smriti, 'What the Cruise Ship Outbreaks Reveal About COVID-19' (2020) 580(7801) *Nature* 18

Mallapaty, Smriti, 'Where Did COVID Come From? Five Mysteries that Remain' (2021) 591(7849) *Nature* 188

Mallard, Alistair and others, 'An Urgent Call to Collect Data Related to COVID-19 and Indigenous Populations Globally' (2021) 6(3) *BMC Global Health* art 004655

Malloy, Jonathan, 'The Adaptation of Parliament's Multiple Roles to COVID-19' (2020) 53(2) *Canadian Journal of Political Science* 305

Malm, Heidi and others, 'Ethics, Pandemics and the Duty to Treat' (2008) 8(8) *American Journal of Bioethics* 4

Malpani, Rohit and Alex Maitland, 'Dose of Reality: How Rich Countries and Pharmaceutical Corporations are Breaking their Vaccine Promises' *The People's Vaccine* (21 October 2021)

Manivannan, Elangovan and others, 'The Rise and Fall of Chloroquine/Hydroxychloroquine as Compassionate Therapy of COVID-19' (2021) 12 *Frontiers in Pharmacology* art 584940

Mansoor, Sanya, '"I've Been Missing Caring for People." Thousands of Retired Health Care Workers Are Volunteering to Help Areas Overwhelmed by Coronavirus' *Time* (26 March 2020)

Mao, Danmi and others, 'Guide to Forensic Pathology Practice for Death Cases Related to Coronavirus Disease 2019 (COVID-19) (Trial draft)' (2020) 5(1) *Forensic Sciences Research* 1

Maragakis, Lisa L, 'Coronavirus, Social and Physical Distancing and Self-Quarantine' *Johns Hopkins Medicine* (15 July 2020)

Maraqa, Beesan, Zaher Nazzal, and Therese Zink, 'Mixed Method Study to Explore Ethical Dilemmas and Health Care Workers' Willingness to Work Amid COVID-19 Pandemic in Palestine' (2021) 7 *Frontiers in Medicine* art 576820

Marcum, Catherine D, 'American Corrections System Response to COVID-19: An Examination of the Procedures and Policies Used in Spring 2020' (2020) 45(4) *American Journal of Criminal Justice* 759

Margaria, Alice, 'Fathers, Childcare and COVID-19' (2021) 29 *Feminist Legal Studies* 133

Mariner, Wendy K, George J Annas, and Leonard H Glantz, 'Jacobson v Massachusetts: It's Not Your Great-Great-Grandfather's Public Health Law' (2005) 95(4) *American Journal of Public Health* 581

Maringe, Camille and others, 'The Impact of the COVID-19 Pandemic on Cancer Deaths Due to Delays in Diagnosis in England, UK: A National, Population-Based Modelling Study' (2020) 21(8) *Lancet Oncology* 1023

Marisam, Jason, 'Local Governance and Pandemics: Lessons From the 1918 Flu' (2008) 85(3) *University of Detroit Mercy Law Review* 347

Marquez, Neal and others, 'COVID-19 Incidence and Mortality in Federal and State Prisons Compared with the US Population April 5, 2020, to April 3, 2021' (2021) 326(18) *Journal of the American Medical Association* 1865

Marshall, Shelley and Carla Chan Unger, 'Treating Workers like Meat: What We've Learnt from COVID-19 Outbreaks in Abattoirs' *The Conversation* (14 October 2020)

Marston, Cicely, Alicia Renedo, and Sam Miles, 'Community Participation is Crucial in a Pandemic' (2020) 395(10238) *Lancet* 1676

Martin, Chris, 'Australian Residential Tenancies Law in the COVID-19 Pandemic: Considerations of Housing and Property Rights' (2021) 44(1) *University of New South Wales Law Journal* 197

Martin, Jennifer and others, 'COVID-19: The Rise and Fall of Hydroxychloroquine' *InSight* (7 September 2020)

Martin, Robyn, 'The Exercise of Public Health Powers in Cases of Infectious Disease: Human Rights Implications' (2006) 14(1) *Medical Law Review* 132

Massa, Michele, 'The Italian "No Jab, No Job" Law' *Verfassunblog on Matters Constitutional* (7 April 2021)

Mathen, Carissima, 'Resisting the Siren's Call: Emergency Powers, Federalism, and Public Policy' in Colleen M Flood and others (eds) *Vulnerable: The Law, Policy and Ethics of COVID-19* (University of Ottawa Press 2020)

Matteucci, Stefano C, 'Italy: Between Mandatory and Conditional Covid-19 Vaccination Policies' *Lex-Atlas: Covid-19* (4 May 2021)

Maunder, Robert and Gillian Strudwick, 'High Rates of COVID-19 Burnout Could Lead to Shortage of Health-care Workers' *The Conversation* (29 August 2021)

Maycock, Matthew, '"Covid-19 Has Caused a Dramatic Change to Prison Life": Analysing the Impacts of the Covid-19 Pandemic on the Pains of Imprisonment in the Scottish Prison Estate' (2021) 62(1) *British Journal of Criminology* 218

Maycock, Matthew and Graeme Dickson, 'Analysing the Views of People in Custody about the Management of the COVID-19 Pandemic in the Scottish Prison Estate' (2021) 17(3) *International Journal of Prisoner Health* 320

Mayo Clinic, 'Convalescent Plasma Therapy' (29 August 2020)

Mazepa, Svitlana, 'COVID-19 and Its Impact on Ukrainian Criminal Law' *Intersentia Online* (20 September 2020)

Mazza, Danielle, Seema Deb, and Asvini Subasinghe, 'Telehealth: An Opportunity to Increase Access to Early Medical Abortion for Australian Women' (2020) 213(7) *Medical Journal of Australia* 298

Mazzacano, Peter J, 'Force Majeure, Impossibility, Frustration & the Like: Excuses for Non-performance; the Historical Origins and Development of an Autonomous Commercial Norm in the CISG' (2011) 2 *Nordic Journal of Commercial Law* 1

McCarthy, John and Clark McPhail, 'Places of Protest: The Public Forum in Principle and Practice' (2006) 11(2) *Mobilization: An International Quarterly* 229

McConville, Mike and Luke Marsh, 'Resuscitating Criminal Courts after COVID-19: Trialling a Cure Worse than the Disease' (2021) 26(2) *International Journal of Evidence & Proof* 103

McCuskey, Elizabeth Y, 'FDA in the Time of COVID-19' (2020) 45(3) *Administrative and Regulatory Law News* 7

McDonald, Fiona and Claire J Howell, 'Facemasks for Public Use During the COVID-19 Pandemic: An Examination of Responses in Australia and England' in Belinda Bennett and Ian Freckelton (eds), *Pandemics, Public Health Emergencies and Government Powers: Perspectives on Australia Law* (Federation Press 2021)

McDonald, Fiona and others, 'Facemask Use for Community Protection from Air Pollution Disasters: An Ethical Overview and Framework to Guide Agency Decision Making' (2020) 43 *International Journal of Disaster Risk Reduction* art 101376

McDougal, Lotus and others, 'Strengthening Gender Measures and Data in the COVID-19 Era: An Urgent Need for Change' (Brief, 6 March 2021)

McDougall, Rosalind J and others, 'Balancing Health Worker Well-Being and Duty to Care: An Ethical Approach to Staff Safety in COVID-19 and Beyond' (2021) 47(5) *Journal of Medical Ethics* 318

McDowall, David, Colin Loftin, and Brian Wiersema, 'The Impact of Youth Curfew Laws on Juvenile Crime Rates' (2000) 46(1) *Crime & Delinquency* 76

McGinnis, Janice D '*Carlill v Carbolic Smoke Ball Company*: Influenza, Quackery, and the Unilateral Contract' (1988) 5 *Canadian Journal of Medical History* 121

McGuirl, Marlene C and Robert N Gee, 'AIDS: An Overview of the British, Australian, and American Responses' (1985) 14(1) *Hofstra Law Review* 107

McHugh, Paul, 'Business Interruption Insurance in the Time of COVID-19: Who Should Foot the Bill?' (2021) 29(2) *Journal of Law and Policy* 491

McKeever, Amy, 'Here's the Latest on COVID-19 Vaccines' *National Geographic* (30 October 2021)

McKenna, Hugh, 'COVID-19: Ethical Issues for Nurses' (2020) 110 *International Journal of Nursing Studies* art 103673

McKenzie, Lindsay, 'Debunking Bad COVID-19 Research' *Inside Higher Ed* (29 June 2020)

McLachlan, Andrew, 'A Major Ivermectin Study Has Been Withdrawn, So What Now for the Controversial Drug?' *The Conversation* (22 July 2021)

McLaren, Helen J and others, 'COVID-19 and Women's Triple Burden: Vignettes from Sri Lanka, Malaysia, Vietnam and Australia' (2020) 9(5) *Social Sciences* 87

McLaws, Mary-Louise, 'COVID-19 in Children: Time for a New Strategy' (2021) 215(5) *Medical Journal of Australia* 212

Mclean, Holly and Ben Huf, 'Emergency Powers, Public Health and COVID-19' (Research Paper No 2, Parliament of Victoria August 2020)

McLeod, Melissa A and others, 'Protective Effect of Maritime Quarantine in South Pacific Jurisdictions, 1918–19 Influenza Pandemic' (2008) 14(3) *Emerging Infectious Diseases* 468

McLeod, Melissa A and others, 'COVID-19: We Must Not Forget About Indigenous Health and Equity' (2020) 44(4) *Australia and New Zealand Journal of Public Health* 253

McMeekin, Judy, 'National Consumer Protection Week: FDA is Vigilant in Protecting Consumers Against COVID-19 Vaccine Scams' (FDA Voices, Food and Drug Administration, 3 February 2021)

McNeill, Sophie, 'Australia Should Back Covid-19 Waiver of Intellectual Property Rules' *Human Rights Watch* (25 July 2021)

McPartlin, Seán O'Neill and others, 'Covid-19 Vaccines: Should We Allow Human Challenge Studies to Infect Healthy Volunteers with SARS-CoV-2?' (2020) 371 *British Medical Journal* art m4258

McQueen, Humphery, 'The Spanish Influenza Pandemic in Australia, 1918–19' in Jill Roe (ed), *Social Policy in Australia: Some Perspectives 1901–1975* (Cassell Australia 1976)

McWhirter, Rebekah, 'The Right to Liberty in a Pandemic' (2021) 40(2) *University of Queensland Law Journal* 159

Meagher, Dan and Matthew Groves, *The Principle of Law and Legality in Australia and New Zealand* (Federation Press 2017)

Médecins Sans Frontières, 'Help and Solidarity Needed in Europe to Protect Medical Staff from COVID-19' (Press Release, 16 March 2020)

Medical Defence Union (UK), 'MDU Calls for National Debate over Protecting NHS from COVID-19 Clinical Negligence Claims' (Press Release, 20 April 2020)

Medicines and Healthcare products Regulatory Agency (UK), 'Coronavirus: Global Crackdown Sees a Rise in Unlicenced Medical Products Related to COVID-19' (Press Release, 19 March 2020)

Medicines and Healthcare products Regulatory Agency (UK), 'List of Medicines that Cannot be Exported from the UK or Hoarded' (Guidance, 3 August 2021)

Medicines and Healthcare products Regulatory Agency (UK), 'MHRA Suspends Recruitment to COVID-19 Hydroxychloroquine Trials' (Press Release, 16 June 2020)

Medicines and Healthcare products Regulatory Agency (UK), 'Senior Enforcement Advisor at UK Medicines Regulator Warns Against Purchasing Fake or Unlicensed Coronavirus (COVID 19) Medicines' (Press Release, 7 May 2020)

Medicines and Healthcare products Regulatory Agency (UK), 'UK Medicines and Medical Devices Regulator Investigating 14 Cases of Fake or Unlicensed COVID-19 Medical Products' (Press Release, 4 April 2020)

Medicines Patent Pool, 'Expanding Access to Public Health' (Brochure, 2020)

Mega, Emiliano Rodríguez, 'Latin America's Embrace of an Unproven COVID Treatment is Hindering Drug Trials' (2020) 586(7830) *Nature* 481

Mehra, Akhil, 'Politics of Participation: Walter Reed's Yellow-Fever Experiments' (2009) 11(4) *Virtual Mentor* 326

Mehra, Mandeep R and others, 'Cardiovascular Disease, Drug Therapy, and Mortality in Covid-19' (2020) 382(26) *New England Journal of Medicine* e102(1) (retracted)

Mehra, Mandeep R and others, 'RETRACTED: Hydroxychloroquine or Chloroquine With or Without a Macrolide for Treatment of COVID-19: A Multinational Registry Analysis' *Lancet* (22 May 2020)

Mehta, Sangeeta and others, 'COVID-19: A Heavy Toll on Health-Care Workers' (2021) 9(3) *Lancet Respiratory Medicine* 226

Meier, Benjamin M, Roojin Habibi, and Y Tony Yang, 'Travel Restrictions Violate International Law' (2020) 367(6485) *Science* 1436

Melden, Abraham I (ed), *Essays in Moral Philosophy* (University of Washington Press 1958)

Mello, Michelle M and Wendy E Parmet, 'Public Health Law After COVID-19' (2021) 385(13) *New England Journal of Medicine* 1153

Mello, Michelle M, Ross D Silverman, and Saad B Omer, 'Ensuring Uptake of Vaccines against SARS-CoV-2' (2020) 383(14) *New England Journal of Medicine* 1296

Mendelson, Danuta and others, 'Legal Implications of Personal Protective Equipment Use When Treating Patients for COVID-19 (SARS-CoV-2)' (2020) 27(4) *Journal of Law and Medicine* 856

Menikoff, Jerry, 'The Common Rule, Updated' (2017) 376(7) *New England Journal of Medicine* 613

Mental Health UK, '6 Ways to Boost Your Wellbeing While Staying Indoors' (2021)

Merck, 'Merck Statement on Ivermectin Use During the COVID-19 Pandemic' (Company Statement, 4 February 2021)

Merson, Michael and Stephen Inrig, *The AIDS Pandemic: Searching for a Global Response* (Springer 2018)

Meshram, Vikas P, Tanuj Kanchan, and Raghvendra S Shekhawat, 'Management of the Dead During Coronavirus Disease 2019 Outbreak: Practices and Procedures of Forensic Practitioners from India' (2021) 62(1) *Medicine, Science and the Law* 38

Metcalf, Hope, 'Life and Death in Prisons' in Morten Kjaerum, Martha F Davis, and Amanda Lyons (eds), *COVID-19 and Human Rights* (Routledge 2021)

Meyerowitz-Katz, Gideon and others, 'Is the Cure Really Worse than the Disease? The Health Impacts of Lockdowns During COVID-19' (2021) 6(8) *BMJ Global Health* art e006653

Michalowski, Sabine, 'The Use of Age as a Triage Criterion' in Carla Ferstman and Andrew Fagan (eds), *Covid-19, Law and Human Rights: Essex Dialogues* (School of Law and Human Rights Centre, University of Essex 2020)

Miller, Antonia, 'Lawcodes Report: New Criminal Penalties for COVID-19 Related Offences' (2020) 32(4) *Judicial Officers Bulletin* 33

Miller, Franklin G, 'The Stateville Penitentiary Malaria Experiments: A Case Study in Retrospective Ethical Assessment' (2013) 56(4) *Perspectives in Biological Medicine* 548

Millett, Gregorio A and others, 'Assessing Differential Impacts of COVID-19 on Black Communities' (2020) 47 *Annals of Epidemiology* 37

Mills, Melinda C and Jonas Sivelä, 'Should Spreading Anti-vaccine Misinformation Be Criminalised?' (2021) 372 *British Medical Journal* art n272

Mintz, Kevin and others, 'Enrolling Minors in COVID-19 Trials' (2021) 147(3) *Pediatrics* art e2020040717

Mirzayev, Fuad and others, 'World Health Organization Recommendations on the Treatment of Drug-resistant Tuberculosis, 2020 Update' (2021) 57(6) *European Respiratory Journal* art e2003300

Mishra, Swapnil and others, 'Comparing the Responses of the UK, Sweden and Denmark to COVID-19 Using Counterfactual Modelling' (2021) 11 *Scientific Reports* art 16342

MIT Technology Licensing Office, 'COVID-19 Technology Access Framework' (7 April 2020)

Monaghesh, Elham and Alireza Hajizadeh, 'The Role of Telehealth During COVID-19 Outbreak: A Systematic Review Based on Current Evidence' (2020) 20 *BMC Public Health* 1193

Monahan, Justin, *Enemy at the Gates: Online Dispute Resolution in the Time of COVID-19* (Schulich Law Scholars 2021)

Mooney, Carla, *Collateral Damage: The Mental Health Effects of the Pandemic* (ReferencePoint Press 2021)

Mooney, Graham, '"A Menace to the Public Health" —Contact Tracing and the Limits of Persuasion' (2020) 383(19) *New England Journal of Medicine* 1806

Moore, Anne, 'COVID Vaccines: Why Waiving Patents Won't Fix Global Shortage—Scientist Explains' *The Conversation* (4 May 2021)

Moorthy, Vasee and others, 'Data-sharing for Novel Coronavirus (COVID-19)' (2020) 98(3) *Bulletin of the World Health Organization* 150

Moreira, Diana Nadine and Mariana P da Costa, 'The Impact of the Covid-19 Pandemic in the Precipitation of Intimate Partner Violence' (2020) 71 *International Journal of Law and Psychiatry* art 101606

Morens, David M and others, 'Pandemic COVID-19 Joins History's Pandemic Legion' (2020) 11(3) *American Society for Microbiology* art e00812-20

Moretti, Matteo and others, 'The Roles of Medical Examiners in the COVID-19 Era: A Comparison Between the United States and Italy' (2021) 17 *Forensic Science, Medicine and Pathology* 262

Mori, Oki and Mai Umezawa, 'Japan: Consumer Protection Laws and Regulations 2021' *ICLG* (4 May 2021)

Moriarty, Leah F and others, 'Public Health Responses to COVID-19 Outbreaks on Cruise Ships—Worldwide, February–March 2020' (2020) 69(12) *Morbidity and Mortality Weekly Report* 347

Morley, Ian, 'City Chaos, Contagion, Chadwick and Social Justice' (2007) 80(2) *Yale Journal of Biological Medicine* 61

Morley, Jeremy D, *The Hague Abduction Convention: Practical Issues and Procedures for Family Lawyers* (2nd edn, American Bar Association 2017)

Morley, Jessica and others, 'Ethical Guidelines for COVID-19 Tracing Apps' (2020) 582(7810) *Nature* 29

Moshkovits, Itay, 'Emergency Use Authorizations of COVID-19-Related Products' (2022) 182(2) *Journal of the American Medical Association Internal Medicine* 228

Moukaddam, Nidal, 'Fears, Outbreaks, and Pandemics: Lessons Learned' (2019) 36(11) *Psychiatric Times* 28

Mounk, Yascha, 'The Extraordinary Decisions Facing Italian Doctors' *The Atlantic* (12 March 2020)

Moynihan, Ray and others, 'Impact of COVID-19 Pandemic on Utilisation of Healthcare Services: A Systematic Review' (2021) 11(3) *BMJ Open* e045343

Mphahlele, Jeffrey, 'COVID-19 Vaccine: The Challenges of Running a Trial in the Middle of a Pandemic' *The Conversation* (7 July 2020)

Mulheron, Rachael, *Principles of Tort Law* (2nd edn, Cambridge University Press 2020)

Mullen, Lucia and others, 'An Analysis of International Health Regulations Emergency Committees and Public Health Emergency of International Concern Designations' (2020) 5(6) *BMJ Global Health* art e002502

Munasinghe, Sithum and others, 'The Impact of Physical Distancing Policies During the COVID-19 Pandemic on Health and Well-Being Among Australian Adolescents' (2020) 67(5) *Journal of Adolescent Health* 653

Mungwira, Randy G and others, 'Global Landscape Analysis of No-fault Compensation Programmes for Vaccine Injuries: A Review and Survey of Implementing Countries' (2020) 15(5) *PLoS One* art e0233334

Munton, Joellen R, 'Work Health and Safety: Regulating for Safe and Sustainable Work Practices in a Post-Pandemic World' in Belinda Bennett and Ian Freckelton (eds) *Pandemics, Public Health Emergencies and Government Powers: Perspectives on Australian Law* (Federation Press 2021)

Murphy, Brendon and Tahlia Ferrari, 'Bail in the Time of COVID-19' (2020) 44(4) *Criminal Law Journal* 247

Murphy, Jim and Alison Blank, *Invincible Microbe: Tuberculosis and the Never-ending Search for a Cure* (Houghton Mifflin Harcourt 2012)

Murphy, Kristina and others, 'Why People Comply with COVID-19 Social Distancing Restrictions: Self-interest or Duty?' (2020) 53(4) *Australian and New Zealand Journal of Criminology* 477

Mushtaq, Raheel and others, 'Relationship Between Loneliness, Psychiatric Disorders and Physical Health? A Review of the Psychological Aspects of Loneliness' (2014) 8(9) *Journal of Clinical Diagnostic Research* art WEO1-4

Mutch, Alison, 'Regulation 28: Report to Prevent Future Deaths' (9 December 2020)

Mykhalovskiy, Eric and others, 'Human Rights, Public Health and COVID-19 in Canada' (2020) 111(6) *Canadian Journal of Public Health* 975

Nabarro, David, 'COVID19: Do What is Needed to Hold the Virus at Bay' *Skills, Systems & Synergies for Sustainable Development* (14 October 2020)

Nachega, Jean B and others, 'Scaling Up Covid-19 Vaccination in Africa—Lessons from the HIV Pandemic' (2021) 385(3) *New England Journal of Medicine* 196

Naidu, Sindhu B and others, 'The High Mental Health Burden of "Long COVID" and its Association with On-going Physical and Respiratory Symptoms in All Adults Discharged from Hospital' (2021) 57(6) *European Respiratory Journal* art 2004364

Nakazawa, Eisuke, Hiroyasa Ino, and Akira Akabayashi, 'Chronology of COVID-19 Cases on the Diamond Princess Cruise Ship and Ethical Considerations: A Report from Japan' (2020) 14(4) *Disaster Medicine Public Health Preparedness* 506

Nakkazi, Esther, 'Oxygen Supplies and COVID-19 Mortality in Africa' (2021) 9(4) *Lancet Healthy Longevity* e39

National Academies of Sciences, Engineering and Medicine (US), *A Framework for Equitable Allocation of Vaccine for the Novel Coronavirus* (National Academies Press 2020)
National Academies of Sciences, Engineering, and Medicine (US), *Social Isolation and Loneliness in Older Adults: Opportunities for the Health Care System* (National Academies Press 2020)
National Centre for Immunisation Research and Surveillance (US), 'COVID-19 Vaccine Development Landscape' (13 October 2021)
National Commission for the Protection of Human Subjects of Biomedical and Behavioral Research (US), 'The Belmont Report' (United States Department of Health and Human Services, 18 April 1979)
National Conference of State Legislatures (US), *COVID-19 and the Criminal Justice System: A Guide for State Lawmakers* (Report, 19 August 2020)
National COVID-19 Clinical Evidence Taskforce (Aus), 'Australian Guidelines for the Clinical Care of People with COVID-19' (26 August 2021)
National Health and Medical Research Council, Australian Research Council and Universities Australia, *National Statement on Ethical Conduct in Human Research (2007) (Updated 2018)* (National Health and Medical Research Council 2018)
National Health Service Health Research Authority (UK), 'COVID-19 Human Infection Challenge Vaccine Studies' (5 November 2020)
National Institute for Occupational Safety and Health (US), 'Healthcare Workers' *Centres for Disease Control and Prevention* (13 January 2017)
National Mental Health Commission (Aus), 'Pandemic Fatigue' (Australian Government)
Nebolsina, Elena, 'The Impact of the Covid-19 Pandemic in the Business Interruption Insurance Demand in the United States' (2021) 7(100) *Heliyon* e08357
Neumann, Nils and Lara Wengenmayr, 'New German COVID-19 Workplace Restrictions: Mandatory Work from Home and Entry Restrictions for Office Access' *National Law Review* (23 November 2021)
New Zealand Parliament, 'Epidemic Response Committee: COVID-19 2020'
Newfoundland and Labrador, House of Assembly, *Hansard*, 48th Leg, 3rd Sess, Vol XLVIII, No 44 (20 November 2018)
Newman, Peter A and Adrian Guta, 'Mandatory COVID-19 Vaccines on University Campuses: An Obvious Solution or a Problem?' *The Conversation* (3 August 2021)
Ng, Dianna L and others, 'Clinicopathologic, Immunohistochemical, and Ultrastructural Findings of a Fatal Case of Middle East Respiratory Syndrome Coronavirus Infection in the United Arab Emirates, April 2014' (2016) 186(3) *American Journal of Pathology* 652
Nhamo, Godwell and others, 'COVID-19 Vaccines and Treatments Nationalism: Challenges for Low-income Countries and the Attainment of the SDGs' (2021) 16(3) *Global Public Health* 319
Nichols, Lionel, 'Australia' in Bonavero Institute of Human Rights, *A Preliminary Human Rights Assessment of Legislative and Regulatory Responses to the COVID-19 Pandemic Across 11 Jurisdictions* (Bonavero Report No 3/2020, 6 May 2020)
Nickerson, Jason W and Matthew Herder, 'COVID-19 Vaccines as Global Public Goods' in Colleen M Flood and others (eds), *Vulnerable: The Law, Policy and Ethics of COVID-19* (University of Ottawa Press 2020)
Nicol, Dianne and others, 'Australian Perspectives on the Ethical and Regulatory Considerations for Responsible Data Sharing in Response to the COVID-19 Pandemic' (2020) 27(4) *Journal of Law and Medicine* 829
Nicol, Ginger E and others, 'Action at a Distance: Geriatric Research during a Pandemic' (2020) 68(5) *Journal of the American Geriatrics Society* 922

Nicola, Maria and others, 'The Socio-Economic Implications of the Coronavirus Pandemic (COVID-19): A Review' (2020) 78 *International Journal of Surgery* 185

Nicolson, Donald and Jago Russell, 'Covid-19 and Criminal Justice: Temporary Fixes or Long Term Reform?' in Carla Ferstman and Andrew Fagan (eds), *Covid-19, Law and Human Rights: Essex Dialogues* (School of Law and Human Rights Centre, University of Essex 2020)

Nie, Jing-Bao and others, *Japan's Wartime Medical Atrocities: Comparative Inquiries in Science, History and Ethics* (Routledge 2010)

Niemi, Mari EK and others, 'Mapping the Human Genetic Architecture of COVID-19' (2021) 600(7889) *Nature* 472

Nienhaus, Albert and Rozita Hod, 'COVID-19 Among Health Workers in Germany and Malaysia' (2020) 17(13) *International Journal of Research in Public Health* art 4881

Nikogosian, Haik and Ilona Kickbusch, 'The Case for an International Pandemic Treaty' (2021) 372 *British Medical Journal* n527

Nilsson, Anna, 'Is Compulsory Childhood Vaccination Compatible with the Right to Respect for Private Life? A Comment on *Vavřička and Others v the Czech Republic*' (2021) 28(3) *European Journal of Health Law* 323

Nogrady, Bianca, 'Mounting Evidence Suggests Sputnik COVID Vaccine is Safe and Effective' (2021) 595(7867) *Nature* 339

Nolte, Kurt B and others, '"Med-X": A Medical Examiner Surveillance Model for Bioterrorism and Infectious Disease Mortality' (2007) 38(5) *Human Pathology* 718

Noppert, Grace A and Lauren C Zalla, 'Who Counts and Who Gets Counted? Health Equity in Infectious Disease Surveillance' (2021) 111(6) *American Journal of Public Health* 1004

Nordberg, Ana and Titti Mattsson, 'COVID-19 Pandemic in Sweden: Measures, Policy Approach and Legal and Ethical Debates' (2020) 1S *BioLaw Journal: Rivista di BioDiritto* 731

Norrie, John David, 'Remdesivir for COVID-19: Challenges of Underpowered Studies' (2020) 395(10236) *Lancet* 1525

NSW Government, 'COVID-19 Check-in Mandate Expanded' (30 June 2021)

O'Brien, Paula and Eliza Waters, 'COVID-19: Public Health Emergency Powers and Accountability Mechanisms in Australia' (2021) 28(2) *Journal of Law and Medicine* 345

O'Neill, Luke, 'Mu: Everything You Need to Know about the New Coronavirus Variant of Interest' *The Conversation* (3 September 2021)

O'Sullivan, Maria, 'Protest in a Pandemic: The Special Status of Public Spaces' *Australian Public Law* (27 July 2020)

Obu, Raphael N, 'Medical Law and Misrepresentation in the Practice of Homeopathy and Alternative Medicines in Ghana: Lessons Learnt in Studying Law and Practicing Holistic Medicine' (2020) 3(4) *Scholars International Journal of Law, Crime Justice* 99

Occupational Safety and Health Administration (US), 'Workers' Right to Refuse Dangerous Work' (United States Department of Labor)

Octavius, Gilbert Sterling and others, 'Impact of COVID-19 on Adolescents' Mental Health: A Systematic Review' (2020) 27 *Middle East Current Psychiatry* n72

Odone, Anna and others, 'Current Understandings of the Impact of Mandatory Vaccination Laws in Europe' (2021) 20(5) *Expert Review of Vaccines* 559

OECD, 'Cities Policy Responses' (Policy Response, 23 July 2020)

OECD, 'Enhancing Public Trust in COVID-19 Vaccination: The Role of Governments (Policy Response, 10 May 2021)

OECD, 'Housing Amid Covid-19: Policy Responses and Challenges' (22 July 2020)

OECD, 'Impact of COVID-19 on Access to Justice: Online Meeting of the OECD Global Roundtable on Equal Access to Justice' (Agenda, 28 April 2020)

OECD, 'Protecting Online Consumers during the COVID-19 Crisis' (Policy Response, 28 April 2020)

OECD, 'The Territorial Impact of COVID-19: Managing the Crisis and Recovery Across Levels of Government' (Policy Response, 10 May 2021)

OECD, 'Tracking and Tracing COVID: Protecting Privacy and Data While Using Apps and Biometrics' (23 April 2020)

OECD, *Women at the Core of the Fight Against COVID-19 Crisis* (2020)

OECD and Law and Justice Foundation of New South Wales, *Access to Justice and the COVID-19 Pandemic: Compendium of Country Practices* (25 September 2020)

Office of Competition and Consumer Protection of Poland, 'UOKiK's Proceedings on Wholesalers' Unfair Conduct Towards Hospitals' (Press Release, Polish Government 4 March 2020)

Office of the High Commissioner for Human Rights, 'CCPR General Comment No. 27: Article 12 (Freedom of Movement)' (adopted 2 November 1999, 67th Session, CCPR/C/21/Rev.1/Add.9)

Office of the United States Trade Representative, 'Statement from Ambassador Katherine Tai on the Covid-19 Trips Waiver' (Press Release, 5 May 2021)

Offit, Paul A, 'The Cutter Incident, 50 Years Later' (2005) 352(14) *New England Journal of Medicine* 1411

Offord, Catherine, 'The Surgisphere Scandal: What Went Wrong?' *The Scientist* (1 October 2020)

Ogden, Lesley E, 'A Brief Biological History of Quarantine' (2021) 71(9) *BioScience* 899

Ogg, Kate, 'COVID-19 Travel Bans: The Right to Seek Asylum When You Cannot Leave Your Homeland' (Kaldor Centre for International Refugee Law, 16 April 2020)

Ohlin, Jens D, 'Pandemics, Quarantines, Utility, and Dignity' [2021] *Michigan State Law Review* 539

Ohniwa, Ryosuke L and others 'COVID-19 as a Research Dynamic Transformer: Emerging Cross-Disciplinary and National Characteristics' (2021) 4 *Frontiers in Big Data* art 631073

Ojikutu, Bisola O and others, 'Building Trust in COVID-19 Vaccines and Beyond Through Authentic Community Investment' (2021) 111(3) *American Journal of Public Health* 366

Okereke, Melody, 'Toward Vaccine Equity: Should Big Pharma Waive Intellectual Property Rights for COVID-19 Vaccines?' (2021) 2 *Public Health in Practice* art 100165

Okruszek, Łukasz and others, 'Safe but Lonely? Loneliness, Anxiety and Depression Symptoms and COVID-19' (2020) 11 *Frontiers in Psychology* art 579181

Oliver, David, 'The Medical Examiner Role Could Transform Our Approach to Handling Death' (2020) 370 *British Medical Journal* m3035

Oransky, Ivan, 'Carlo Urbani' (2003) 361(9367) *Lancet* 1481

Orfali, Kristina, 'What Triage Issues Reveal: Ethics in the COVID-19 Pandemic in Italy and France' (2020) 17(4) *Journal of Bioethical Inquiry* 675

Ostrom, Elinor, 'Polycentric Systems for Coping with Collective Action and Global Environmental Change' (2010) 20(4) *Global Environmental Change* 550

Ostrom, Vincent, Charles M Tiebout, and Robert Warren, 'The Organization of Government in Metropolitan Areas: A Theoretical Inquiry' (1961) 55(4) *American Political Science Review* 831

Ottersen, Trygve, Steven J Hoffman, and Gaëlle Groux, 'Ebola Again Shows the International Health Regulations are Broken: What Can Be Done Differently to Prepare for the Next Epidemic?' (2016) 42(2–3) *American Journal of Law & Medicine* 356

Otugo, Onyeka and Brooke Wages, 'COVID-19: The Additional Sentence for the Incarcerated' (2020) 4(1) *Health Equity* 403

Owen Jr, William F, Richard Carmona, and Claire Pomeroy, 'Failing Another National Stress Test on Health Disparities' (2020) 323(19) *Journal of the American Medical Association* 1905

Oyeniran, OI, T Chia, and MI Oraebosi, 'Combating Covid-19 Pandemic in Africa: An Urgent Call to Scale Up Laboratory Testing Capacities' (2020) 15 *Ethics, Medicine and Public Health* art 100552

Paakkari, Leena and Orkan Okan, 'COVID-19: Health Literacy is an Underestimated Problem' (2020) 5(5) *Lancet Public Health* e249

Pai, Madhukar 'Covidization of Research: What Are the Risks?' (2020) 26(8) *Nature Medicine* 1159

Pak, Anton and others, 'Economic Consequences of the COVID-19 Outbreak: The Need for Epidemic Preparedness' (2020) 8 *Frontiers in Public Health* art 241

Palmer, Robert C, *English Law in the Age of the Black Death, 1348–1381: A Transformation of Governance and Law* (University of North Carolina Press 2001)

Paniagua, Pablo and Veeshan Rayamajhee, 'A Polycentric Approach for Pandemic Governance: Nested Externalities and Co-production Challenges' (2021) 17 *Journal of Institutional Economics* 211

Parasidis, Efthimios, 'Recalibrating Vaccination Laws' (2017) 97 *Boston University Law Review* 2153

Paremoer, Lauren and others, 'Covid-19 Pandemic and the Social Determinants of Health' (2021) 372 *British Medical Journal*

Parker, Melissa, Hayley MacGregor, and Grace Akello, 'COVID-19, Public Authority and Enforcement' (2020) 39(8) *Medical Anthropology* 666

Parmet, Wendy E, 'AIDS and Quarantine: The Revival of an Archaic Doctrine' (1985) 14(1) *Hofstra Law Review* 53

Parmet, Wendy, 'Immigration Law's Adverse Impact on COVID-19' in Scott Burris and others (eds), *Assessing Legal Responses to COVID-19* (Public Health Law Watch 2020)

Parmet, Wendy E, 'Pandemics, Populism and the Role of Law in the H1N1 Vaccine Campaign' (2010) 4(1) *Saint Louis University Journal of Health Law and Policy* 113

Parmet, Wendy E, *Populations, Public Health, and the Law* (Georgetown University Press 2009)

Parmet, Wendy E, 'Rediscovering Jacobson in the Era of COVID-19' (2020) 100 *Boston University Law Review Online* 117

Parmet, Wendy E and Michael S Sinha, 'Covid-19: The Law and Limits of Quarantine' (2020) 382(15) *New England Journal of Medicine* e28

Paterlini, Marta, 'Covid-19: Italy Makes Vaccination Mandatory for Healthcare Workers' (2021) 373 *British Medical Journal* n905

Pathak, Elizabeth B, 'Convalescent Plasma is Ineffective for COVID-19: Lessons from the Placid Trial' (2020) 371 *British Medical Journal* m4072

Payne, Brian K, 'Criminals Work from Home During Pandemics Too: A Public Health Approach to Respond to Fraud and Crimes Against Those 50 and Above' (2020) 45(4) *American Journal of Criminal Justice* 563

Peccia, Jordan and others, 'Measurement of SARS-CoV-2 RNA in Wastewater Tracks Community Infection Dynamics' (2020) 38(10) *Nature Biotechnology* 1164

Peek, Monica E and others, 'COVID-19 Among African Americans: An Action Plan for Mitigating Disparities' (2021) 111(2) *American Journal of Public Health* 286

Peisah, Carmelle and others, 'Just When I Thought I Was Out, They Pull Me Back In: The Older Physician in the COVID-19 Pandemic' (2020) 32(10) *International Psychogeriatrics* 1211

Pellecchia, Umberto and others, 'Social Consequences of Ebola Containment Measures in Liberia' (2015) 10(12) *PLoS One* art e0143036

Peña-Silva, Ricardo and others, 'Pharmacokinetic Considerations on the Repurposing of Ivermectin for Treatment of COVID-19' (2020) 87(3) *British Journal of Clinical Pharmacology* 1589

Pereda, Noemí and Diego A Díaz-Faes, 'Family Violence Against Children in the Wake of COVID-19 Pandemic: A Review of Current Perspectives and Risk Factors' (2020) 14 *Child and Adolescent Psychiatry and Mental Health* art 40

Pereira, Filipa and others, 'Presenteeism Among Nurses in Switzerland and Portugal and its Impact on Patient Safety and Quality of Care: Protocol for a Qualitative Study' (2021) 10(5) *JMIR Research Protocols* art e27963

Pérez, Evans RF, 'Soldiering on the Job When Ill: Productivity Costs in Connective Tissue Disease-Associated Interstitial Lung Disease' (2020) 17(9) *Annals of the American Thoracic Society* 1058

Perez-Vincent, Santiago M and others, *COVID-19 Lockdowns and Domestic Violence* (Report, Inter-American Development Bank, July 2020)

Perry, Robert D and Jacqueline D Fetherston, 'Yersinia Pestis—Etiologic Agent of Plague' (1997) 10(1) *Clinical Microbiological Reviews* 35

Persad, Govind, 'Disability Law and the Case for Evidence-Based Triage in a Pandemic' (2020) 130 *Yale Law Journal Forum* 26

Persad, Govind, Monica E Peek, and Ezekiel J Emanuel, 'Fairly Prioritizing Groups for Access to COVID-19 Vaccines' (2020) 324(16) *Journal of the American Medical Association* 1601

Peschken, Christine A, 'Possible Consequences of a Shortage of Hydroxychloroquine for Patients with Systemic Lupus Eryhthematosus Amid the COVID-19 Pandemic' (2020) 47(6) *Journal of Rheumatology* 787

Petrov, Andrey N and others, 'Lessons on COVID-19 from Indigenous and Remote Communities of the Arctic' (2021) 27(9) *Nature Medicine* 1491

Phelan, Alexandra L, 'COVID-19 Immunity Passports and Vaccination Certificates: Scientific, Equitable, and Legal Challenges' (2020) 395(10237) *Lancet* 1595

Phelan, Alexandra L and Lawrence O Gostin, 'Law as a Fixture Between the One Health Interfaces of Emerging Diseases' (2017) 111(6) *Transactions of the Royal Society of Tropical Medicine and Hygiene* 241

Phelan, Alexandra L and others, 'Legal Agreements: Barriers and Enablers to Global Equitable COVID-19 Vaccine Access' (2020) 396(10254) *Lancet* 800

Physicians Foundation (US), '2020 Survey of America's Physicians: COVID-19 Impact Edition' (Physicians Foundation 2020)

Pierre, Jon, 'Nudges Against Pandemics: Sweden's COVID-19 Containment Strategy in Perspective' (2020) 39(3) *Policy and Society* 478

Piller, Ingrid, Jie Zhang, and Jia Li, 'Linguistic Diversity in a Time of Crisis: Language Challenges of the COVID-19 Pandemic' (2020) 39(5) *Multilingua* 503

Pinheiro, Victor M, Marcelo Ilarraz, and Melissa T Mestriner, 'The Impacts of the COVID-19 Crisis on the Brazilian Legal System: A Report on the Functioning of the Branches of the Government and on the Legal Scrutiny of Their Activities' (2020) 8(1–2) *The Theory and Practice of Legislation* 193

Pinn, Vivian W, 'Achieving Diversity and its Benefits in Clinical Research' (2004) 6(12) *American Medical Association Journal of Ethics* 561

Piroth, Lionel and others, 'Comparison of the Characteristics, Morbidity, and Mortality of COVID-19 and Seasonal Influenza: A Nation-wide, Population-based Retrospective Cohort Study' (2021) 9(3) *Lancet Respiratory Medicine* 251

Pleace, Nicholas and others, 'European Homelessness and COVID 19' (European Observatory on Homelessness, March 2021)

Poirier, Johanne and Jessica Michelin, 'Facing the Coronavirus Pandemic in the Canadian Federation: Reinforced Dualism and Muted Cooperation?' in Nico Steytler (ed), *Comparative Federalism and Covid-19: Combating the Pandemic* (Routledge 2021)

Pollard, Deana A, 'Sex Torts' (2007) 91(3) *Minnesota Law Review* 769

Pollard Sacks, Deana, 'Intentional Sex Torts' (2008) 77(3) *Fordham Law Review* 1051

Pomeranz, Jennifer L and Aaron R Schwid, 'Governmental Actions to Address COVID-19 Misinformation' (2021) 42(2) *Journal of Public Health Policy* 201

Poole, Nigel, 'Coronavirus and Clinical Negligence' (2020) 25(3) *Journal of Patient Safety and Risk Management* 97

Poon, LLM and others, 'The Aetiology, Origins and Diagnosis of Severe Acute Respiratory Syndrome' (2004) 4(11) *Lancet Infectious Diseases* 663

Popotas, Costas, 'COVID-19 and the Courts. The Case of the Court of Justice of the European Union (CJEU)' (2021) 12(2) *International Journal for Court Administration* art 4

Popp, Maria and others, 'Ivermectin for Preventing and Treating COVID-19' *Cochrane* (28 July 2021)

Powell, Cathleen, 'Rule of Law Has Moved Centre Stage in Lockdown: What it Is and Why it Matters' *The Conversation* (22 May 2020)

Powell, Tia, Eran Bellin, and Amy R Ehrlich, 'Older Adults and COVID-19: The Most Vulnerable, the Hardest Hit' (2020) 50(3) *Hastings Center Report* 61

Power, Tamara and others, 'COVID-19 and Indigenous Peoples: An Imperative for Action' (2020) 29(15–16) *Journal of Clinical Nursing* 2737

Prater, Tammy and Kim Smith, 'Underlying Factors Contributing to Presenteeism and Absenteeism' (2011) 9(6) *Journal of Business and Economics Research* 1

Premier of Victoria, 'Vaccination Required to Protect Workers and Victoria' (Media Release, 1 October 2021)

Prendki, Virginie and others, 'A Systematic Review Assessing the Under-Representation of Elderly Adults in COVID-19 Trials' (2020) 20 *BMC Geriatrics* art 538

President of the Family Division and Head of Family Justice [England and Wales], 'Coronavirus Crisis: Guidance on Compliance with Family Court Child Arrangement Orders' (24 March 2020)

Presidential Commission for the Study of Bioethical Issues, '*"Ethically Impossible"*: STD Research in Guatemala from 1946 to 1948* (Report, 13 September 2011)

Preston-Suni, Kian, Manuel A Celedon, and Kristina M Cordasco, 'Patient Safety and Ethical Implications of Health Care Sick Leave Policies on the Pandemic Era' (2021) 47(10) *The Joint Commission Journal on Quality and Patient Safety* 673

Price, Shannon, 'Stay at Home: Rethinking Rental Housing Law in an Era of Pandemic' (2020) 28(1) *Georgetown Journal on Poverty Law and Policy* 1

Price-Haywood, Eboni G and others, 'Hospitalization and Mortality Among Black Patients and White Patients with Covid-19' (2020) 382(26) *New England Journal of Medicine* 2534

Primandari, Fadhilah F, 'Democracy and Human Rights During the COVID-19: The Case of Indonesia' (2020) 26(3) *Australian Journal of Human Rights* 529

Procedure and Privileges Committee, *The Legislative Assembly's Response to the COVID-19 Pandemic* (Parliament of Western Australia, 17 November 2020)

Productivity Commission (Australia), 'Working From Home' (Research Paper, September 2021)

Prosser, William L, *Handbook of the Law of Torts* (4th edn, West Publishing Co 1971)

Provenzi, Livio and Serena Barello, 'The Science of the Future: Establishing a Citizen-Scientists Collaborative Agenda after Covid-19' (2020) 8 *Frontiers in Public Health* art 282

Public Accounts and Estimates Committee, Parliament of Victoria, *Inquiry into the Victorian Government's Response to the COVID-19 Pandemic* (Victorian Government Printer 2021)

Public Health Ontario, 'SARS-CoV-2 Whole Genome Sequencing in Ontario' *Weekly Epidemiological Summary* (29 December 2021)

Public Safety Canada, 'Guidance on Essential Services and Functions in Canada During the COVID-19 Pandemic' (14 October 2021)

Puddister, Kate and Tamara A Small, 'Trial by Zoom? The Response to COVID-19 by Canada's Courts' (2020) 53(2) *Canadian Journal of Political Science* 373

Pugh, Jonathan, 'The United Kingdom's Coronavirus Act, Deprivations of Liberty, and the Right to Liberty and Security of the Person' (2020) 7(1) *Journal of Law and the Biosciences* art lsaa011

Pūras, Dainius and others, 'The Right to Health Must Guide Responses to COVID-19' (2020) 395(10241) *Lancet* 1888

Quammen, David, *Ebola: The Natural and Human History of a Deadly Virus* (WW Norton & Co 2014)

Quammen, David, *The Chimp and the River: How AIDS Emerged from an African Forest* (The Bodley Head 2015)

Quazi, Hesan, *Presenteeism: The Invisible Cost to Organizations* (Palgrave Macmillan 2013)

Quick, Jonathan D, *The End of Epidemics: How to Stop Viruses and Save Humanity Now* (Scribe 2020)

Quinn, Gerard, 'COVID-19 and Disability: A War of Two Paradigms' in Morten Kjaerum, Martha F Davis, and Amanda Lyons (eds), *COVID-19 and Human Rights* (Routledge 2021)

Quinn, Kylie and Holly Seale, 'Russia's Coronavirus Vaccine Hasn't Been Fully Tested. Doling it Out Risks Side Effects and False Protection' *The Conversation* (12 August 2020)

Qureshi, Adnan, *Ebola Virus Disease: From Origin to Outbreak* (Academic Press 2016)

Rader, Benjamin and others, 'Mask-wearing and Control of SARS-CoV-2 Transmission in the USA: A Cross-sectional Study' (2021) 3(3) *Lancet Digital Health* e148

Rahimi, Azadeh, Azin Mirzazadeh, and Soheil Tavakolpour, 'Genetics and Genomics of SARS-CoV-2: A Review of the Literature with the Special Focus on Genetic Diversity and SARS-CoV-2 Genome Detection' (2021) 113(1) *Genomics* 1221

Rahman, Muhammad KR and others, 'Effect of Covid-19 Pandemic on Tourist Travel Risk and Management Perceptions' (2021) 16(9) *PLoS One* art e0256486

Rajan, SI, P Sivakumar and Aditya Srinivasan, 'The COVID-19 Pandemic and Internal Labour Migration in India: A "Crisis of Mobility"' (2020) 63 *Indian Journal of Labour Economics* 1021

Ram, Natalie and David Gray, 'Mass Surveillance in the Age of COVID-19' (2020) 7(1) *Journal of Law and the Biosciences* art lsaa023

Ramazzini, Bernardino, *De Morbis Artificum Diatriba: Diseases of Workers* (tr Wilmer Cave Wright, rev edn, University of Chicago Press 1940)

Ramazzini, Bernardino, 'De Morbis Artificum Diatriba [Diseases of Workers]' (2001) 91(9) *American Journal of Public Health* 1380

Ranasinghe, Imesh, 'Recall Retired Doctors, Nurses to Combat COVID-19, Sri Lanka Opposition SJB Tells Govt' *Economynext* (14 May 2021)

Ranney, Megan L, Valerie Griffeth, and Ashish K Jha, 'Critical Supply Shortages—The Need for Ventilators and Personal Protective Equipment during the COVID-19 Pandemic' (2020) 382(18) *New England Journal of Medicine* e41(1)

Ranson, David, 'COVID-19 and Forensic Medical Practice' (2020) 27(4) *Journal of Law and Medicine* 807

Rapeport, Garth and others, 'SARS-CoV-2 Human Challenge Studies—Establishing the Model During an Evolving Pandemic' (2021) 385(11) *New England Journal of Medicine* 961

Raposo, Vera L, 'Portugal: Fighting COVID-19 in the Edge of Europe' (2020)(1S) *BioLaw Journal: Rivista di BioDiritto* 723

Rasmussen, Anne, 'Prevent or Heal, Laissez-Faire or Coerce? The Public Health Politics of Influenza in France, 1918–1919' in Tamara Giles-Vernick and Susan Craddock with Jennifer Gunn (eds), *Influenza and Public Health: Learning from Past Pandemics* (Routledge 2010)

Ratha, Dilip and others, 'Migration and Development Brief 33: Phase II: COVID-19 Crisis Through a Migration Lens' (KNOMAD-World Bank, October 2020)

Ray, Isha, 'Viewpoint—Handwashing and COVID-19: Simple, Right There … ?' (2020) 135 *World Development* art 105086

Rayment, Erica and Jason VandenBeukel, 'Pandemic Parliaments: Canadian Legislatures in a Time of Crisis' (2020) 53(2) *Canadian Journal of Political Science* 379

Reardon, Sara, 'Flawed Ivermectin Preprint Highlights Challenges of COVID Drug Studies' (2021) 596(7871) *Nature* 173

RECOVERY Collaborative Group, 'Dexamethasone in Hospitalized Patients with Covid-19' (2021) 384(8) *New England Journal of Medicine* 693

Rehnquist, William H, *All the Laws But One: Civil Liberties in Wartime* (Knopf Doubleday 2007)

Reid, Lynette, 'Diminishing Returns? Risk and the Duty to Care in the SARS Epidemic' (2005) 19(4) *Bioethics* 348

Reiss, Dorit R, 'Religious Exemptions to Vaccines and the Anti-vax Movement' *Harvard Law School Petrie-Flom Center* (16 July 2021)

Reiss, Dorit R, 'The COVID-19 Vaccine Dilemma' (2020) 6(1) *Administrative Law Review Accord* 49

Reiss, Dorit R and Arthur L Caplan, 'Considerations in Mandating a New COVID-19 Vaccine in the USA for Children and Adults' (8 May 2020) 7(1) *Journal of Law and the Biosciences* art lsaa025

Reiss, Dorit R and Y Tony Yang, 'Why a COVID-19 Vaccine Shouldn't be Mandatory' *Harvard Law School Petrie-Flom Center* (15 September 2020)

Reiter, Keramet, 'Experimentation on Prisoners: Persistent Dilemmas in Rights and Regulations' (2009) 97(2) *California Law Review* 501

Relman, David A, Eileen R Choffnes, and Alison Mack (eds), *The Domestic and International Impacts of the 2009-H1N1 Influenza A Pandemic* (The National Academies Press 2010)

Research Square, 'Editorial Note' *Research Square* (19 July 2021)

Reverby, Susan M, *Examining Tuskegee: The Infamous Syphilis Study and its Legacy* (University of North Carolina Press 2009)

Reverby, Susan M, '"Normal Exposure" and Inoculation Syphilis: A PHS "Tuskegee" Doctor in Guatemala, 1946-1948' (2011) 23(1) *Journal of Policy History* 6

Reverby, Susan M (ed), *Tuskegee's Truths: Rethinking the Tuskegee Syphilis Study* (University of North Carolina Press 2000)

Reyes, Maritza V, 'The Disproportional Impact of COVID-19 on African Americans' (2020) 22(2) *Health and Human Rights Journal* 299

Rhodes, John, *The End of Plagues: The Battle Against Infectious Diseases* (St Martin's Press 2013)

Rhodes, Rosamond, 'Justice in COVID-19 Vaccine Prioritisation: Rethinking the Approach' (2021) 47(9) *Journal of Medical Ethics* 623

Ribeiro, Helena, Viviana M Lima, and Eliseu A Waldman, 'In the COVID-19 Pandemic in Brazil, Do Brown Lives Matter?' (2020) 8(8) *Lancet Global Health* e976

Rice, Geoffrey W, 'How Reminders of the 1918–19 Pandemic Helped Australia and New Zealand Respond to COVID-19' (2020) 15(3) *Journal of Global History* 421

Rice, Geoffrey W, 'Remembering 1918: Why did Māori Suffer More Than Seven Times the Death Rate of Non-Māori New Zealanders in the 1918 Influenza Pandemic?' (2019) 53(1) *New Zealand Journal of History* 90

Riddle, Howard, Anthony Edwards, and Matthew Hardcastle, 'COVID-19 and the Criminal Courts' (2021) 3 *Criminal Law Review* 159

Ripperger, Tyler J and others, 'Orthogonal SARS-CoV-2 Serological Assays Enable Surveillance of Low-prevalence Communities and Reveal Durable Humoral Immunity' (2020) 53(5) *Immunity* 925

Ritscher, Christian, 'COVID-19 and International Criminal Trials in Germany' (2020) 18(5) *Journal of International Criminal Justice* 1077

Robens, Lord Alfred, *Safety and Health at Work: Report of the Committee* (Her Majesty's Stationery Office 1972)

Robinson, JH and others, 'Use the Force? Understanding Force Majeure Clauses' (2020) 44(1) *American Journal of Trial Advocacy* 1

Rodney, Tamar, Nia Josiah, and Diana-Lyn Baptiste, 'Loneliness in the Time of COVID-19: Impact on Older Adults' (2021) 77(9) *Journal of Advanced Nursing* e24

Rodríguez-Ocaña, Esteban, 'Barcelona's Influenza: A Comparison of the 1889–1890 and 1918 Autumn Outbreaks' in Tamara Giles-Vernick and Susan Craddock with Jennifer Gunn (eds), *Influenza and Public Health: Learning from Past Pandemics* (Routledge 2010)

Roederer, Thomas and others, 'Seroprevalence and Risk Factors of Exposure to COVID-19 in Homeless People in Paris, France: A Cross-sectional Study' (2021) 6(4) *Lancet Public Health* e202

Roesch, Elizabeth and others, 'Violence Against Women During COVID-19 Pandemic Restrictions' (2020) 369 *British Medical Journal* m1712

Roman, Yuani M and others, 'Ivermectin for the Treatment of Coronavirus Disease 2019: A Systematic Review and Meta-analysis of Randomized Controlled Trials' (2022) 74(6) *Clinical Infectious Diseases* 1022

Romanis, Elizabeth C, Jordan A Parsons, and Nathan Hodson, 'COVID-19 and Reproductive Justice in Great Britain and the United States: Ensuring Access to Abortion Care During a Global Pandemic' (2020) 7(1) *Journal of Law and the Biosciences* art lsaa027

Romero, Marta M and others, 'COVID-19 Outbreak in Long-Term Care Facilities from Spain. Many Lessons to Learn' (2020) 15(10) *PLoS One* art e0241030

Roozenbeek, Jon and others, 'Susceptibility to Misinformation about COVID-19 Around the World' (2020) 7(1) *Royal Society Open Science* art e202199

Rose, Mitchell, 'Mediation by Zoom Addresses Social Distancing, Shuttered Courtrooms' *The Lawyer's Daily* (31 March 2020)

Rosen, William, *Justinian's Flea: Plague, Empire and the Birth of Europe* (Jonathan Cape 2007)

Rotenberg, Sara, Matthew B Downer, and Jane Cooper, 'Making COVID-19 Vaccinations Accessible for People with Disabilities' (2021) 49(4) *Vaccine* 5727

Roth, Phoebe, 'Should We Vaccinate Children Against COVID-19? We Asked 5 Experts' *The Conversation* (2 August 2021)

Rothman, David J and Sheila M Rothman, *The Willowbrook Wars: Bringing the Mentally Disabled into the Community* (Routledge 2004)

Rothman, Sheila M, *Living in the Shadow of Death: Tuberculosis and the Social Experience of Illness in American History* (Johns Hopkins University Press 1995)

Rothstein, Mark A, 'From SARS to Ebola: Legal and Ethical Considerations for Modern Quarantine' (2015) 12(1) *Indiana Health Law Review* 227

Rotila, Viorel, 'Physicians Professional Immunity in the COVID-19 Pandemic: Problems and Solutions' (2021) 12 (1Sup1) *Postmodern Openings* 356

Roy, Arundhati, 'The Pandemic Is a Portal' *Financial Times* (4 April 2020)

Royal College of Nursing (UK), 'Guidance for Members: Refusal to Treat Due to Lack of Adequate PPE During the Pandemic' (9 April 2020)

Royal Commission into Violence, Abuse, Neglect and Exploitation of People with Disability (Aus), *Public Hearing 5: Experiences of People with Disability During the Ongoing COVID-19 Pandemic* (Public Hearing Report, November 2020)

Royal Commission into Violence, Abuse, Neglect and Exploitation of People with Disability (Aus) *Public Hearing 12: The Experiences of People with Disability, in the Context of the Australian Government's Approach to the COVID-19 Vaccine Rollout* (Public Hearing Report, October 2021)

Royal Commission into Violence, Abuse, Neglect and Exploitation of People with Disability (Aus), 'Statement of Concern: The Response to the COVID-19 Pandemic for People with Disability' (26 March 2020)

Rubenfeld, Sheldon and Susan Benedict, *Human Subjects Research after the Holocaust* (Springer 2014)

Rubin, Daniel and others, 'FDA Approval of Remdesivir—A Step in the Right Direction' (2020) 383(27) *New England Journal of Medicine* 2598

Rubin, Rita, 'COVID-19's Crushing Effects on Medical Practices, Some of Which Might Not Survive' (2020) 324(4) *Journal of the American Medical Association* 321

Rubin, Rita, 'Pregnant People's Paradox—Excluded from Vaccine Trials Despite Having a Higher Risk of COVID-19 Complications' (2021) 325(11) *Journal of the American Medical Association* 1027

Ruckert, Arne and others, 'One Health as a Pillar for a Transformative Pandemic Treaty' (Global Health Centre Policy Brief, 2021)

Ruckert, Arne and others, 'What Role for One Health in the COVID-19 Pandemic?' (2020) 111 *Canadian Journal of Public Health* 641

Ruderman, Carly and others, 'On Pandemics and the Duty to Care: Whose Duty? Who Cares?' (2006) 7 *BMC Medical Ethics* art 5

Rutschman, Ana S, 'Is There a Cure for Vaccine Nationalism?' (2021) 120(822) *Current History* 9

Ryan, Nessa E and Alison M El Ayadi, 'A Call for a Gender-Responsive, Intersectional Approach to Address COVID-19' (2020) 15(9) *Global Public Health* 1404

Rybicki, Ed and others, 'How the Coronavirus Mutates and What This Means for the Future of COVID-19' *The Conversation* (17 February 2021)

Rychert, Marta, Kate Diesfeld, and Ian Freckelton, 'Professional Discipline for Vaccine Misinformation Posts on Social Media: Issues and Controversies for the Legal Profession' (2022) 29(3) *Journal of Law and Medicine* 895

Sabath, Bruce F and Henri G Colt, 'Sending Retirees to the Frontlines?' (2020) 10(5) *Journal of Community Hospital Internal Medicine Perspectives* 386

Saey, Tina H, 'Why It's Still So Hard to Find Treatments for Early COVID-19' *Science News* (27 July 2021)

Sage Working Group on Vaccine Hesitancy, 'Report of the SAGE Working Group on Vaccine Hesitancy' (1 October 2014)

Salinas-Flores, David, 'One Hundred Years after the Expedition by Harvard University to Peru to Investigate Carrion's Disease' (2016) 64(3) *Revista de la Facultad de Medicina* 517

Salman, Ahmad and others, 'The Psychological and Social Impacts of Curfew During the COVID-19 Outbreak in Kuwait: A Cross-Sectional Study' (2021) 13(5) *Sustainability* art 8464

Saloner, Brendan and others, 'COVID-19 Cases and Deaths in Federal and State Prisons' (2020) 324(6) *Journal of the American Medical Association* 602

Samarji, Ahmad, 'Overloaded Morgues, Mass Graves and Infectious Remains: How Forensic Pathologists Handle the Coronavirus Dead' *The Conversation* (9 April 2020)

Sanders, Anne, 'Video-Hearings in Europe Before, During and After the COVID-19 Pandemic' (2020) 12(2) *International Journal for Court Administration* art 3

Sanmarchi, Francesco and others, 'Exploring the Gap Between Excess Mortality and COVID-19 Deaths in 67 Countries' (2021) 4(7) *Journal of the American Medical Association Network Open* art e2117359

Santomauro, Damian F and others, 'Global Prevalence and Burden of Depressive and Anxiety Disorders in 204 Countries and Territories in 2020 Due to the COVID-19 Pandemic' (2021) 398(10312) *Lancet* 1700

Sarang, Anya and others, 'Prisons as a Source of Tuberculosis in Russia' (2016) 12(1) *International Journal of Prisoner Health* 45

Sarre, Rick, Lorana Bartels, and Toni Makkai, 'We Need to Consider Granting Bail to Unsentenced Prisoners to Stop the Spread of Coronavirus' *The Conversation* (26 March 2020)

Sátiro, Renato M, Jessica V Martins, and Marcos de Moraes Sousa, 'The Courts in the Face of the COVID-19 Crisis: An Analysis of the Measures Adopted by the Brazilian Judicial System' (2021) 12(2) *International Journal for Court Administration* 10

Satoh, Suzuka and Elisa Boyer, 'HIV in South Africa' (2019) 394(10197) *Lancet* 467

Saunders, Cheryl, 'Grappling with the Pandemic: Rich Insights into Intergovernmental Relations' in Nico Steytler (ed), *Comparative Federalism and Covid-19: Combating the Pandemic* (Routledge 2021)

Savulescu, Julian, 'Good Reasons to Vaccinate: Mandatory or Payment for Risk?' (2021) 47(2) *Journal of Medical Risks* 78

Savulescu, Julian, James Cameron, and Dominic Wilkinson, 'Equality or Utility? Ethics and Law of Rationing Ventilators' (2020) 125(1) *British Journal of Anaesthesia* 10

Savulescu, Julian, Ingmar Persson, and Dominic Wilkinson, 'Utilitarianism and the Pandemic' (2020) 34(6) *Bioethics* 620

Savulescu, Julian, Jonathan Pugh, and Dominic Wilkinson, 'Balancing Incentives and Disincentives for Vaccination in a Pandemic' (2021) 27(9) *Nature Medicine* 1500

Schermerhorn Jr, John R and others, *Management* (7th edn, Wiley 2020)

Schloenhardt, Andreas, 'From Black Death to Bird Flu: Infectious Diseases and Immigration Restrictions in Asia' (2006) 12(2) *New England Journal of International and Comparative Law* 263

Schmidt, Harald, Lawrence O Gostin, and Michelle A Williams, 'Is it Lawful and Ethical to Prioritize Racial Minorities for COVID-19 Vaccines?' (2020) 324(20) *Journal of the American Medical Association* 2023

Schmit, Cason D and others, 'Telehealth in the COVID-19 Pandemic' in Scott Burris and others (eds), *Assessing Legal Responses to COVID-19* (Public Health Law Watch 2020)

Schneider, Lindsey, Joshua Sbicca, and Stephanie Malin, 'Native American Tribes' Pandemic Response Is Hamstrung by Many Inequities' *The Conversation* (1 June 2020)

Schubert, Elise, Lifeng Kang, and Nial Wheate, 'What Is Sotrovimab, the COVID Drug the Government Has Bought Before Being Approved for Use in Australia?' *The Conversation* (9 August 2021)

Schüklenk, Udo, 'What Healthcare Professionals Owe Us: Why Their Duty to Treat During a Pandemic is Contingent on Personal Protective Equipment (PPE)' (2020) 46(7) *Journal of Medical Ethics* 432

Schüklenk, Udo and Richard E Ashcroft, 'International Research Ethics' (2000) 14(2) *Bioethics* 158

Schultz, Nina H and others, 'Thrombosis and Thrombocytopenia after ChAdOx1 nCOV-19 Vaccination' (2021) 384(22) *New England Journal of Medicine* 2124

Schwartz, Andrew A, 'Frustration, the MAC Clause, and COVID-19' (2022) 55 *University of California Davis Law Review* 1771

Schweitzer, Wolf and others, 'Implications for Forensic Death Investigations from First Swiss Post-mortem CT in a Case of Non-Hospital Treatment with COVID-19' (2020) 21 *Forensic Imaging* art 200378

Scommegna, Paola, 'US Has World's Highest Incarceration Rate' *Population Reference Bureau* (10 August 2021)

Scott, Anthony, 'The Impact of COVID-19 on GPs and Non-GP Specialists in Private Practice' (Health Sector Report, Melbourne Institute 2020)

Scott, Nick and others, 'The Introduction of a Mandatory Mask Policy was Associated with Significantly Reduced COVID-19 Cases in a Major Metropolitan City' (2021) 16(7) *PLoS One* art e0253510

Scottish Government, 'Setting up the Scottish COVID-19 Public Inquiry' (Consultation, 30 September 2021)

Scully, Jackie L, 'Disability, Disablism, and COVID-19 Pandemic Triage' (2020) 17(4) *Journal of Bioethical Inquiry* 601

Seifert, Alexander, Sheila R Cotten, and Bo Xie, 'A Double Burden of Exclusion? Digital and Social Exclusion of Older Adults in Times of COVID-19' (2021) 76(3) *Journals of Gerontology B Psychology Social Sciences* e99

Seladi-Schulman, Jill, 'What Happens in a Clinical Trial?' *Healthline* (21 June 2019)

Selgelid, Michael J and LB Reichman, 'Ethical Issues in Tuberculosis Diagnosis and Treatment' (2011) 15(Supp 2) *International Journal of Tuberculosis and Lung Disease* 9

Semuels, Alana, 'Business Travel's Demise Could Have Far-Reaching Consequences' *Time* (20 October 2021)

Senanayake, Sanjaya N, and Mark J Ferson, 'Detention for Tuberculosis: Public Health and the Law' (2004) 180(11) *Medical Journal of Australia* 573

Sendziuk, Paul, *Learning to Trust: Australian Responses to AIDS* (UNSW Press 2003)

Senn, Mark A, 'English Life and Law in the Time of the Black Death' (2003) 38(3) *Real Property, Probate and Trust Journal* 507

SES Union, 'Denying Health Workers their Right to Leave is Against the Constitution' *Bianet* (16 April 2021)

Sessa, Francesco, Monica Salerno, and Cristoforo Pomara, 'Autopsy Tool in Unknown Diseases: The Experience with Coronaviruses (SARS-CoV, MERS-CoV, SARS-CoV-2)' (2021) 57(4) *Medicina* 309

Sex, Gender and COVID-19 Project, 'Gender and Sex-Disaggregated Data: Vital to Inform an Effective Response to COVID-19' (Issue Brief, September 2020)

Sex, Gender and COVID-19 Project, 'The COVID-19 Sex-Disaggregated Data Tracker' (24 December 2021)

Seytre, Bernard and Mary Shaffer, *The Death of a Disease: A History of the Eradication of Poliomyelitis* (Rutgers University Press 2005)

Shah, Anoop SV and others, 'Effect of Vaccination on Transmission of SARS-Cov-2' (2021) 385(18) *New England Journal of Medicine* 1718

Shah, Anoop SV and others, 'Risk of Hospital Admission with Coronavirus Disease 2019 in Healthcare Workers and Their Households: Nationwide Linkage Cohort Study' (2020) 371 *British Medical Journal* art m3582

Shah, Seema K and others, 'Ethical Considerations for Zika Virus Human Challenge Trials: Report and Recommendations' (February 2017)

Shah, Sonia, *Pandemic: Tracking Contagions, from Cholera to Ebola and Beyond* (Picador 2016)

Shakespeare, Tom, Florence Ndagire, and Queen E Seketi, 'Triple Jeopardy: Disabled People and the COVID-19 Pandemic' (2021) 397(10282) *Lancet* 1331

Sharif, Ahmed and others, 'A Pragmatic Approach to COVID-19 Vaccine Passport' (2021) 6 *BMJ Global Health* art e006956

Sharma, Gagan Deep, Asha Thomas, and Justin Paul, 'Reviving Tourism Industry Post-COVID-19: A Resilience-based Framework' (2021) 37 *Tourism Management Perspectives* art 100786

Sharma, Siddhanth, Nisrine Kawa, and Apoorva Gomber, 'WHO's Allocation Framework for COVAX: Is it Fair?' (2022) 48 *Journal of Medical Ethics* 434

Sharma, Yojana, 'COVID-19 Starts Push for More Interdisciplinary Research' *University World News* (25 July 2020)

Shaughnessy, William J, William E Underwood, and Chris Cazenave, 'COVID-19's Impact on Construction: Is There a Remedy? Time Extension, Force Majeure, or More?' (2020) XII(134) *National Law Review*

Shaukat, Natasha, Daniyal Mansoor Ali, and Junaid Razzak, 'Physical and Mental Health Impacts of COVID-19 on Healthcare Workers: A Scoping Review' (2020) 13 *International Journal of Emergency Medicine* art 40

Shelby, Tyler and others, 'Lessons Learned from COVID-19 Contact Tracing During a Public Health Emergency: A Prospective Implementation Study' (2021) 9 *Frontiers in Public Health* art 721952

Shepherd, Stephane and Benjamin L Spivak, 'Reconsidering the Immediate Release of Prisoners During COVID-19 Community Restrictions' (2020) 213(2) *Medical Journal of Australia* 58

Shi, Yufang and others, 'COVID-19 Infection: The Perspectives on Immune Responses' (2020) 27 *Cell Death and Differentiation* 1451

Shimabukuro, Tom T, Matthew Cole, and John R Su, 'Reports of Anaphylaxis after Receipt of mRNA COVID-19 Vaccines in the US—December 12 2020—January 18, 2021' (2021) 325(11) *Journal of the American Medical Association* 1101

Shirley, Debbie-Ann T and Monica A McArthur, 'The Utility of Human Challenge Studies in Vaccine Development: Lessons Learned from Cholera' (2011) 1 *Vaccine: Development and Therapy* 3

Sidley, Pat, 'Drug Companies Withdraw Law Suit Against South Africa' (2000) 322 *British Medical Journal* 1011

Silverman, Ed, 'First Generic Version of Gilead's Remdesivir Will Be Sold by a Bangladesh Drug Maker' *Stat* (22 May 2020)

Silverman, Ed, 'The WHO Launched a Voluntary Covid-19 Product Pool. What Happens Next?' *Stat* (29 May 2020)

Silverman, Ross D, 'Contact Tracing, Intrastate and Interstate Quarantine, and Isolation' in Scott Burris and others (eds), *Assessing Legal Responses to COVID-19* (Public Health Law Watch 2020)

Simonds, AK and DK Sokol, 'Lives on the Line? Ethics and Practicalities of Duty of Care in Pandemics and Disasters' (2009) 34(2) *European Respiratory Journal* 303

Simonovich, Ventura A and others, 'A Randomized Trial of Convalescent Plasma in Covid-19 Severe Pneumonia' (2020) 384(7) *New England Journal of Medicine* 619

Simpson, AWB, 'Quackery and Contract Law: The Case of the Carbolic Smoke Ball' (1985) 14(2) *Journal of Legal Studies* 345

Simpson, Brian and Cheryl Simpson, 'The Use of Curfews to Control Juvenile Offending in Australia: Managing Crime or Wasting Time?' (1993) 5(2) *Current Issues in Criminal Justice* 184

Singer, Audrey, 'COVID-19: Restrictions on Travelers at US Land Borders' *Congressional Research Service* (6 July 2020)

Singer, Merrill and others, 'Syndemics: A Cross-Disciplinary Approach to Complex Epidemic Events like COVID-19' (2021) 50 *Annual Review of Anthropology* 41

Singh, Pranveer (ed), *Tuberculosis and Co-infection with HIV-AIDS: Its History, Cause and Spread* (Cambridge Scholars Publishing 2019)

Singh, Sudhvir and others, 'How an Outbreak Became a Pandemic: A Chronological Analysis of Crucial Junctures and International Obligations in the Early Months of the COVID-19 Pandemic' (2021) 398(10316) *Lancet* 2109

Sirleaf, Ellen J and Helen Clark, 'Report of the Independent Panel for Pandemic Preparedness and Response: Making COVID-19 the Last Pandemic' (2021) 398(10295) *Lancet* 101

Sirleaf, Matiangai, 'Expendable Lives and COVID-19' *Harvard Law School Petrie-Flom Center* (8 October 2020)

Skolnik, Terry, 'Criminal Law During (and After) COVID-19' (2020) 43(4) *Manitoba Law Journal* 145

Skolnik, Terry, 'The Punitive Impact of Physical Distancing Laws on Homeless People' in Colleen M Flood and others (eds), *Vulnerable: The Law, Policy and Ethics of COVID-19* (University of Ottawa Press 2020)

Slack, Paul, 'Responses to Plague in Early Modern Europe: The Implications of Public Health' (1988) 55(3) *Social Research* 433

Sleat, Daniel, Kirsty Innes, and Imogen Parker, 'Are Vaccine Passports and Covid Passes a Valid Alternative to Lockdowns?' (2021) 375 *British Medical Journal* n2571

Smallman-Raynor, MR and AD Cliff, *Poliomyelitis: Emergence to Eradication* (Oxford University Press 2006)

Smith, Devin D and others, 'Exclusion of Pregnant Women from Clinical Trials During the Coronavirus Disease 2019 Pandemic: A Review of International Registries' (2020) 37(8) *American Journal of Perinatology* 792

Snell, NJC, 'The Carbolic Smoke Ball' (2001) 15 *International Journal of Pharmaceutical Medicine* 195

Snowden, Frank M, *Epidemics and Society: From the Black Death to the Present* (Yale University Press 2019)

Soares, Andreia A, 'The Mental Health of Health Workers in the Pandemic' (2021) 99(6) *Bulletin of the World Health Organization* 410

Sokol, Daniel K, 'Virulent Epidemics and Scope of Healthcare Workers' Duty of Care' (2006) 12(8) *Emerging Infectious Diseases* 1238

Solbakk, Jan H and others, 'Back to WHAT? The Role of Research Ethics in Pandemic Times' (2021) 24 *Medicine, Health Care and Philosophy* 3

Soltesz, Kristian and others, 'The Effect of Interventions on COVID-19' (2020) 588(7839) *Nature* E26

Sorabji, John and Steven Vaughan, '"This Is Not A Rule": COVID-19 in England and Wales and Criminal Justice Governance via Guidance' (2021) 12(1) *European Journal of Risk Regulation* 143

Søreide, K and others, 'Immediate and Long-Term Impact of the COVID-19 Pandemic on Delivery of Surgical Services' (2020) 107(10) *British Journal of Surgery* 1250

Sørensen, Kristine and others, 'Rebranding Social Distancing to Physical Distancing: Calling for a Change in the Health Promotion Vocabulary to Enhance Clear Communication During a Pandemic' (2021) 28(1) *Global Health Promotion* 5

Sourdin, Tania, *Judges, Technology and Artificial Intelligence: The Artificial Judge* (Edward Elgar 2021)

Spadaro, Alessandra, 'COVID-19: Testing the Limits of Human Rights' (2020) 11(2) *European Journal of Risk Regulation* 317

Spaulding, Anne C and Chad Zawitz, 'Vaccination in Prisons and Jails: Corrections Needed in Future Plans' (2022) *Clinical Infectious Diseases* art ciab1031

Spector-Bagdady, Kayte and Paul A Lombardo, ' "Something of an Adventure": Postwar NIH Research Ethos and the Guatemala STD Experiments' (2013) 41(3) *Journal of Law, Medicine & Ethics* 697

Spector-Bagdady, Kayte and Paul A Lombardo, 'US Public Health Service STD Experiments in Guatemala (1946–1948) and Their Aftermath' (2019) 41(2) *Ethics & Human Research* 29

Spinks, Harriet, 'Boat "Turnbacks" in Australia: A Quick Guide to the Statistics since 2001' (Parliament of Australia, 20 July 2018)

Spinks, Harriet, 'Seeking Asylum in the Time of Coronavirus: COVID-19 Pandemic Effects on Refugees and People Seeking Asylum' (Parliament of Australia, 19 May 2020)

Spinney, Laura, *Pale Rider: The Spanish Flu of 1918 and How It Changed the World* (Public Affairs 2017)

Stanley, Fiona and others, 'First Nations Health During the COVID Pandemic—Reversing the Gap' in Belinda Bennett and Ian Freckelton (eds), *Pandemics, Public Health Emergencies and Government Powers: Perspectives on Australian Law* (Federation Press 2021)

Stanton, Catherine and Hannah Quirk, *Criminalising Contagion: Legal and Ethical Challenges of Disease Transmission and the Criminal Law* (Cambridge University Press, 2016)

Starodubov, Sergii, Viktoriia Vladyshevska, and Maryna Pyzhova, 'Liability for Violation of Quarantine: Novelties of Administrative and Criminal Legislation' (2020) 9(2) *Ius Humani Law Journal* 137

Steemson, Jacky, *Labourer's Law: A History of Occupational Health and Safety Legislation* (Royal Society for the Prevention of Accidents 1983)

Steffensen, Lyle, 'COVID-19 Class Actions Against Aged Care Providers' *Marsh* (2021)

Stempel, Jeffrey W and Eric S Knutsen, 'Rejecting Word Worship: An Integrative Approach to Judicial Construction of Insurance Policies' (2021) 90(2) *University of Cincinnati Law Review* 561

Stephenson, Peta, Ian Freckelton, and Belinda Bennett, 'Public Health Emergencies in Australia' in Belinda Bennett and Ian Freckelton (eds), *Pandemics, Public Health Emergencies and Government Powers: Perspectives on Australian Law* (Federation Press 2021)

Stephenson, Terence and others, 'Long COVID and the Mental and Physical Health of Children and Young People: National Matched Cohort Study Protocol (the CLoCk Study)' (2021) 11(8) *BMJ Open* art 3052838

Steptoe, Andrew and Giorgio Di Gessa, 'Mental Health and Social Interactions of Older People with Physical Disabilities in England During the COVID-19 Pandemic: A Longitudinal Cohort Study' (2021) 6(6) *Lancet Public Health* e365

Stern, Alexandra M and Howard Markel, 'International Efforts to Control Infectious Diseases, 1851 to the Present' (2004) 292(12) *Journal of the American Medical Association* 1474

Stewart, Alexandra M, 'When Vaccine Injury Claims Go to Court' (2009) 360(24) *New England Journal of Medicine* 2498

Steytler, Nico (ed), *Comparative Federalism and Covid-19: Combating the Pandemic* (Routledge 2021)

Steytler, Nico, Jaap de Visser, and Tinashe Chigwata, 'South Africa: Surfing Toward Centralisation on the Covid-19 Wave' in Nico Steytler (ed), *Comparative Federalism and Covid-19: Combating the Pandemic* (Routledge 2021)

Stobbs, Nigel, Belinda Bennett, and Ian Freckelton, 'Compassion, Law and COVID-19' (2020) 27(4) *Journal of Law and Medicine* 865

Stobbs, Nigel and Ian Freckelton, 'The Administration of Justice During Public Health Emergencies' in Belinda Bennett and Ian Freckelton (eds), *Pandemics, Public Health Emergencies and Government Powers: Perspectives on Australian Law* (Federation Press 2021)

Stojanovic, Jovana and others, 'COVID-19 is Not the Flu: Four Graphs from Four Countries' (2021) 9 *Frontiers in Public Health* art 628479

Strassle, Camila and others, 'Covid-19 Vaccine Trials and Incarcerated People—The Ethics of Inclusion' (2020) 383(20) *New England Journal of Medicine* 1897

Stratford, Jemima, Emily MacKenzie, and Emma Mockford, 'Balancing Speed and Safety: The Authorisation of COVID-19 Vaccines and Medicines' (2020) 25(2) *Judicial Review* 105

Strauss, David H, Sarah A White, and Barbara E Bierer, 'Justice, Diversity and Research Ethics Review' (2021) 371(6535) *Science* 1209

Strodel, Rachel and others, 'COVID-19 Vaccine Prioritization of Incarcerated People Relative to Other Vulnerable Groups: An Analysis of State Plans' (2021) 16(6) *PLoS One* art e0253208

Studdert, David M and Mark A Hall, 'Disease Control, Civil Liberties, and Mass Testing—Calibrating Restrictions During the COVID-19 Pandemic' (2020) 383(2) *New England Journal of Medicine* 102

Studdert, David M, Mark A Hall, and Michelle M Mello, 'Partitioning the Curve—Interstate Travel Restrictions During the COVID-19 Pandemic' (2020) 383(13) *New England Journal of Medicine* e83

Stulpin, Caitlyn, 'Q&A: Is Convalescent Plasma Effective for COVID-19?' *Healio* (2 November 2020)

Sturman, Edward D, 'The Capacity to Consent to Treatment and Research: A Review of Standardized Assessment Tools' (2005) 25(7) *Clinical Psychology Review* 954

Sulmasy, Daniel P, 'Are SARS-CoV-2 Human Challenge Trials Ethical?' (2021) 181(8) *Journal of the American Medical Association Internal Medicine* 1031

Sun, Nina and Livio Zilli, 'COVID-19 Symposium: The Use of Criminal Sanctions in COVID-19 Responses—Enforcement of Public Health Measures, Part II' *Opinio Juris* (3 April 2020)

Suñer, Clara and others, 'A Retrospective Cohort Study of Risk Factors for Mortality Among Nursing Homes Exposed to COVID-19 in Spain' (2021) 1 *Nature Aging* 579

Supremo Tribunal Federal, 'STF Reaches 2,500 Received Cases Related to Covid-19' (News Release, 28 May 2020)

Swinburne, Mathew, 'Using SNAP to Address Food Insecurity During the COVID-19 Pandemic' in Scott Burris and others, *Assessing Legal Responses to COVID-19* (Public Health Law Watch 2020)

Syam, Nirmalya, 'Intellectual Property, Innovation and Access to Health Products for COVID-19: A Review of Measures Taken by Different Countries' *The South Centre* (June 2020)

Syam, Nirmalya, 'The TRIPS Council on 15–16 October Should Agree to Extend the Transition Period that Exempts Least Developed Countries from Implementation of the WTO TRIPS Agreement' *InfoJustice* (7 October 2020)

Sykes, Gresham M, *The Society of Captives: A Study of a Maximum Security Prison* (Princeton University Press 1958)

Sylvie Briand, 'Preface' to World Health Organization, 'Genomic Sequencing of SARS-CoV-2: A Guide to Implementation for Maximum Impact on Public Health' (Implementation Guide, 8 January 2021)

Symington, Andy, 'Migrant Workers and the COVID-19 Crisis in Australia: An Overview of Governmental Responses' (2020) 26(3) *Australian Journal of Human Rights* 507

't Hoen, Ellen, 'The Indian/South African Proposal for a WTO Waiver on IP for COVID-19 Related Health Products—What It Means?' *Health Policy Watch* (14 October 2020)

Talabis, Dylan Antonio S and others, 'Local Government Responses for COVID-19 Management in the Philippines' (2021) 21(1) *BMC Public Health* art 1711

Tanner, Ryan and Colleen M Flood, 'Vaccine Passports Done Equitably' (2021) 2(4) *Journal of the American Medical Association Health Forum* art e210972

Taquet, Maxime and others, '6-Month Neurological and Psychiatric Outcomes in 236,379 Survivors of COVID-19: A Retrospective Cohort Study Using Electronic Health Records' (2021) 8(5) *Lancet Psychiatry* 416

Tartari, Ermira and others, 'Not Sick Enough to Worry? "Influenza-Like" Symptoms and Work-Related Behavior among Healthcare Workers and Other Professionals: Results of a Global Survey' (2020) 15(5) *PLoS One* art e0232168

Tartof, Sara Y and others, 'Effectiveness of mRNA BNT162b2 COVID-19 Vaccine Up to 6 Months in a Large Integrated Health System in the USA: A Retrospective Cohort Study' (2021) 398(10309) *Lancet* 1407

Taylor, Adam, 'The Lambda Variant: Is It More Infectious, and Can It Escape Vaccines? A Virologist Explains' *The Conversation* (21 July 2021)

Taylor, Alan and others, 'How Australian Health Care Services Adapted to Telehealth During the COVID-19 Pandemic: A Survey of Telehealth Professionals' (2021) 9 *Frontiers in Public Health* art 648009

Taylor, Melanie M and others, 'Inclusion of Pregnant Women in COVID-19 Treatment Trials: A Review and Global Call to Action' (2021) 9(3) *Lancet Global Health* e366

Taylor, Steven, *The Psychology of Pandemics: Preparing for the Next Global Outbreak of Infectious Disease* (Cambridge Scholars Publishing 2019)

Taylor, Steven and Gordon JG Asmundson, 'Negative Attitudes About Facemasks During the COVID-19 Pandemic: The Dual Importance of Perceived Ineffectiveness and Psychological Reactance' (2021) 16(2) *PLoS One* art e0246317

Tedeschi, Miriam, 'The Body and the Law Across Boundaries During the COVID-19 Pandemic' (2020) 10(2) *Dialogues in Human Geography* 178

Teo, Irene and others, 'Healthcare Worker Stress, Anxiety and Burnout During the COVID-19 Pandemic in Singapore: A 6-month Multi-centre Prospective Study' (2021) 16(10) *PLoS One* art e0258866

Teo, Wendy, Lawrence H Brenner, and B Sonny Bal, 'Medicolegal Sidebar: Legal Immunity for Healthcare Workers During COVID-19' (2020) 478(10) *Clinical Orthopaedics and Related Research* 2218

Terman, Sharon, 'Protecting Workers' Jobs and Income During COVID-19' in Scott Burris and others (eds), *Assessing Legal Responses to COVID-19* (Public Health Law Watch 2020)

Terry, Nicolas P, 'How COVID-19 Could Drive Improvements in Care Facilities (Part II)' *Harvard Law School Petrie-Flom Center* (10 June 2020)

Tessler, Hannah, Meera Choi, and Grace Kao, 'The Anxiety of Being Asian American: Hate Crimes and Negative Biases During the COVID-19 Pandemic' (2020) 45(4) *American Journal of Criminal Justice* 636

Testa, Alexander and Chantal Fahmy, 'No Visits and Barely Any Cells—Pandemic Makes Separation Even Scarier for People with a Family Member in Prison' *The Conversation* (2 April 2021)

Thacker, Brenda, 'The Antonine Plague: Unknown Death within the Roman Empire, 165–180 CE' in Rebecca M Seaman (ed), *Epidemics and War: The Impact of Disease on Major Conflicts in History* (ABC-CLIO 2018)

Thaler, Jeff, 'Can Governors Close Their Borders to Pandemic Risks? *Just Security* (20 April 2020)

Thaler, Richard H and Cass R Sunstein, *Nudge: Improving Decisions About Health, Wealth and Happiness* (Penguin Books 2009)

Thampapillai, Dilan, 'The Controversy to Come? Patent Law and a COVID-19 Vaccine' *ANU College of Law*

Theis, Nicola and others, 'The Effects of COVID-19 Restrictions on Physical Activity and Mental Health of Children and Young Adults with Physical and/or Intellectual Disabilities' (2021) 14(3) *Disability and Health Journal* art 101064

Therapeutic Goods Administration, 'Lorna Jane Fined Almost $40,000 for Alleged Advertising Breaches in Relation to COVID-19 and "Anti-Virus Activewear"' (Media Release and Statement, 17 July 2020)

Therapeutic Goods Administration, 'Pete Evans' Company Fined for Alleged COVID-19 Advertising Breaches' (Media Release and Statement, 24 April 2020)

Therapeutic Goods Administration, 'Risks of Importing Ivermectin for Treatment of COVID-19' (Media Release and Statement, 23 August 2021)

Therapeutic Goods Administration, 'TGA Initiates Court Proceedings Against Oxymed Australia and Director Malcolm Hooper for Alleged Unlawful Advertising' (Media Release and Statement, 3 September 2020)

Therapeutic Goods Administration, 'TGA Provisionally Approves GlaxoSmithKline's COVID-19 Treatment: Sotrovimab (XEVUDY)' *Australian Government Department of Health* (20 August 2021)

Thiru, 'Israel Issues Compulsory License to Allow the Government to Import Generic Versions of Kaletra' *Knowledge Ecology International* (23 March 2020)

Thomas, Amanda J, *Cholera: The Victorian Plague* (Pen & Sword History 2015)

Thomas, Kyla, 'Pandemic Misery Index Reveals Far-reaching Impact of COVID-19 on American Lives, Especially on Blacks and Latinos' *The Conversation* (2 June 2021)

Thompson, Janelle R and others, 'Making Waves: Wastewater Surveillance of SARS-CoV-2 for Population-Based Health Management' (2020) 184 *Water Research* art 116181

Thomson, Helen, 'Children are Getting Long Covid and Being Left with Lasting Problems' *New Scientist* (24 February 2021)

Thornton, Jacqui, 'Covid-19: How Coronavirus Will Change the Face of General Practice Forever' (2020) 368 *British Medical Journal* m1279

Thucydides, *History of the Peloponnesian War* (first published 4th century BC, Penguin 1972)

Thursfield, Hugh, 'Smallpox in the American War of Independence' (1940) 2(4) *Annals of Medical History* 312

Tiwari, Piyush and Jyoti Shukla, 'The Future of Offices in Post-COVID Melbourne' *Pursuit* (21 October 2020)

Todd, James and Emma Corkill, 'Standards of Care during COVID-19' *Local Government Lawyer* (24 April 2020)

Todrys, KW, E Howe, and JJ Amon, 'Failing Siracusa: Governments' Obligations to Find the Least Restrictive Options for Tuberculosis Control' (2013) 3(1) *Public Health Action* 7

Tomkins, Christine and others, 'Should Doctors Tackling Covid-19 be Immune from Negligence Liability Claims?' (2020) 370 *British Medical Journal* art m2487

Tooma, Michael and Mary-Louise McLaws, *Managing COVID-19 Risks in the Workplace: A Practical Guide* (LexisNexis 2021)

Townsend, Jeffrey P and others, 'The Durability of Immunity Against Reinfection by SARS-CoV-2: A Comparative Evolutionary Study' (2021) 2(12) *Lancet Microbe* art e666

Tran, A and Theodore J Witek, 'The Emergency Use Authorization of Pharmaceuticals: History and Utility During the COVID-19 Pandemic' (2021) 35(4) *Pharmaceutical Medicine* 203

Trauer, James M and Allen C Cheng, 'Multidrug-resistant Tuberculosis in Australia and Our Region' (2016) 204(7) *Medical Journal of Australia* 251

Tressler, Colleen, 'Don't Buy Fake COVID-19 Vaccine Cards or Negative Test Results. Here's Why' (Blog Post, Federal Trade Commission 20 August 2021)

Treweek, Shaun and others, 'COVID-19 and Ethnicity: Who Will Research Results Apply To?' (2020) 395(10242) *Lancet* 1955

Truog, Robert, Christine Mitchell, and George Q Daley, 'The Toughest Triage—Allocating Ventilators in a Pandemic' (2020) 382(21) *New England Journal of Medicine* 1973

Tsai, Jack and Michal Wilson, 'COVID-19: A Potential Public Health Problem for Homeless Populations' (2020) 5(4) *Lancet Public Health* e186

Tsuchiya, Takashi, 'The Imperial Japanese Experiments in China' in Ezekiel J Emanuel and others (eds), *The Oxford Textbook of Clinical Research Ethics* (Oxford University Press 2008)

Turner, Mark, 'Vaccine Procurement During an Influenza Pandemic and the Role of Advance Purchase Agreements: Lessons from 2009-H1N1' (2016) 11(3) *Global Public Health* 322

Tusl, Martin, 'Impact of the COVID-19 Crisis on Work and Private Life, Mental Well-being and Self-rated Health in German and Swiss Employees: A Cross-sectional Online Survey' (2021) 21 *BMC Public Health* art 641

Twomey, Anne, 'Federal and State Powers to Deal with Pandemics: Cooperation, Conflict and Confusion' in Belinda Bennett and Ian Freckelton (eds), *Pandemics, Public Health Emergencies and Government Powers: Perspectives on Australian Law* (Federation Press 2021)

Ueki, Hiroshi and others, 'Effectiveness of Face Masks in Preventing Airborne Transmission of SARS-CoV-2' (2020) 5(5) *mSphere* art 00637-20

Uimonen, Mikko and others, 'The Impact of the COVID-19 Pandemic on Waiting Times for Elective Surgery Practices: A Multicenter Study' (2021) 16(7) *PLoS One* art e0253875

UK COVID Challenge, 'About Our COVID-19 Volunteer Trials'
UN Women and others, *Justice for Women Amidst COVID-19* (22 May 2020)
UNAIDS, 'About: Saving Lives, Leaving No One Behind' (Who We Are)
UNAIDS, *Countdown to Zero* (Report, 9 June 2011)
UNESCO General Conference, 'Universal Declaration on Bioethics and Human Rights' (33rd Sess, 19 October 2005)
UNESCO, 'How Many Students Are at Risk of Not Returning to School?' (Advocacy Paper, UNESCO COVID-19 Education Response, 30 July 2020)
United Kingdom Government, 'Coronavirus Vaccine—Weekly Summary of Yellow Card Reporting' (Research and Analysis, 19 November 2021)
United Kingdom Government, 'COVID-19: Prisons and Other Prescribed Places of Detention Guidance' (Guidance, 18 May 2020)
United Kingdom Government, 'Face Coverings: When to Wear One, Exemptions, and How to Make Your Own' (Guidance, 10 December 2021)
United Kingdom Government, 'Preventing and Controlling Outbreaks of COVID-19 in Prisons and Places of Detention' (Guidance, 9 September 2021)
United Kingdom Local Government Association, 'COVID-19: Good Council Practice'
United Kingdom Parliament, 'COVID-19 Committee: Lords Select Committee'
United Kingdom Parliament, 'Inquiries and Reports'
United Kingdom Research Integrity Office, 'Code of Practice for Research: Promoting Good Practice and Preventing Misconduct' (2021)
United Nations, *COVID-19 and Human Rights: We Are All in This Together* (April 2020)
United Nations, *Policy Brief: The Impact of COVID-19 on Older Persons* (May 2020)
United Nations, *Policy Brief: COVID-19 and People on the Move* (June 2020)
United Nations, *A UN Framework for the Immediate Socio-Economic Response to COVID-19* (April 2020)
United Nations, 'Sustainable Development Goals' (United Nations Department of Economic and Social Affairs: Sustainable Development)
United Nations, *The Sustainable Development Goals Report 2020* (United Nations, 2020)
United Nations Department of Economic and Social Affairs, 'COVID-19 and Indigenous Peoples'
United Nations Department of Economic and Social Affairs, *The Impact of COVID-19 on Indigenous Peoples* (Policy Brief No 70, May 2020)
United Nations Development Program, 'Briefing Note: The Economic Impacts of COVID-19 and Gender Inequality: Recommendations for Policymakers' (April 2020)
United Nations Economic and Social Commission on Human Rights, *The Siracusa Principles on the Limitation and Derogation Provisions in the International Covenant on Civil and Political Rights* (Resolution E/CN.4/1985/4, 28 September 1984)
United Nations General Assembly, *Report of the Special Rapporteur on the Right of Everyone to the Enjoyment of the Highest Attainable Standard of Physical and Mental Health* (UN Doc A/61/338, 13 September 2006)
United Nations General Assembly, 'Transforming Our World: The 2030 Agenda for Sustainable Development' (Resolution A/RES/70/1, United Nations 25 September 2015)
United Nations General Assembly, 'United Nations Declaration on the Rights of Indigenous Peoples' (Resolution A/RES/61/295, 13 September 2007)
United Nations General Assembly, 'Universal Declaration of Human Rights' (Resolution A/RES/3/217A, 10 December 1948)

United Nations High Commissioner for Refugees, 'Key Legal Considerations on Access to Territory for Persons in Need of International Protection in the Context of the Covid-19 Response' (16 March 2020)
United Nations Human Rights Committee, 'Article 6: Right to Life' (General Comment No 36 CCPR/C/GC/36, 3 September 2019)
United Nations Human Rights Committee, 'Statement on Derogations From the Covenant in Connection With the COVID-19 Pandemic' (30 April 2020, CCPR/C/128/2)
United Nations Office of the High Commissioner for Human Rights, 'COVID-19 and the Human Rights of Migrants: Guidance' (7 April 2020)
United Nations Office of the High Commissioner for Human Rights, 'Monitoring Civil and Political Rights'
United Nations Office of the High Commissioner for Human Rights, 'No Exceptions With COVID-19: "Everyone has the Right to Life-Saving Interventions"—UN Experts Say' (26 March 2020)
United Nations Office of the High Commissioner for Human Rights, 'COVID-19: States Should Not Abuse Emergency Measures to Suppress Human Rights' (16 March 2020)
United Nations Office of the High Commissioner for Human Rights, 'COVID-19 and the Rights of Persons With Disabilities: Guidance' (29 April 2020)
United Nations Office of the High Commissioner for Human Rights, 'COVID-19: Who is Protecting the People with Disabilities?—UN Rights Expert' (17 March 2020)
United Nations Network on Migration, 'Forced Returns of Migrants Must be Suspended in Times of COVID-19' (Press Release, 14 May 2020)
Universities UK, 'The Concordat to Support Research Integrity' (25 October 2019)
University of Toronto Joint Centre for Bioethics Pandemic Influenza Working Group, 'Stand on Guard for Thee: Ethical Considerations in Preparedness Planning for Pandemic Influenza' (Report, November 2005)
Urmson, JO, 'Saints and Heroes' in AI Melden (ed), *Essays in Moral Philosophy* (University of Washington Press 1958)
US Food and Drug Administration, 'Beware of Fraudulent Coronavirus Tests, Vaccines and Treatments' (3 January 2021)
US Food and Drug Administration, 'Coronavirus (COVID-19) Update: FDA Authorizes Additional Monoclonal Antibody for Treatment of COVID-19' (News Release, 26 May 2021)
US Food and Drug Administration, 'Coronavirus (COVID-19) Update: FDA Authorizes Additional Vaccine Dose for Certain Immunocompromised Individuals' (News Release, 12 August 2021)
US Food and Drug Administration, 'Coronavirus (COVID-19) Update: FDA Authorizes First Oral Antiviral for Treatment of COVID-19' (News Release, 22 December 2021)
US Food and Drug Administration, 'Coronavirus (COVID-19) Update: FDA Issues Emergency Use Authorization for Potential COVID-19 Treatment' (News Release, 1 May 2020)
US Food and Drug Administration, 'Emergency Use Authorizations' (10 February 2021)
US Food and Drug Administration, 'Emergency Use Authorization for Vaccines Explained' (20 November 2020)
US Food and Drug Administration, 'FDA Authorizes Pfizer-BioNTech COVID-19 Vaccine for Emergency Use in children 5 Through 11 Years of Age' (News Release, 29 October 2021)
US Food and Drug Administration, 'FDA Issues Emergency Use Authorization for Convalescent Plasma as Potential Promising COVID-19 Treatment, Another

Achievement in Administration's Fight Against Pandemic' (News Release, 23 August 2020)

US Food and Drug Administration, 'FDA Takes Additional Action in Fight Against COVID-19 by Issuing Emergency Use Authorization for Second COVID-19 Vaccine' (News Release, 18 December 2020)

US Food and Drug Administration, 'FDA Takes Key Action in Fight Against COVID-19 by Issuing Emergency Use Authorization for First COVID-19 Vaccine' (News Release, 11 December 2020)

US Food and Drug Administration, 'Fraudulent Coronavirus Disease 2019 (COVID-19) Products' (30 September 2021)

US Food and Drug Administration, 'Georgia Man and his Company Charged with Selling Misbranded Drug Advertised to Treat COVID-19' (Press Release, 10 August 2020)

US Food and Drug Administration, 'Purported Biotech Executive Charged with Introducing Misbranded Drug into Interstate Commerce for Distribution of "COVID-19 Vaccine"' (Press Release, 21 January 2021)

US Food and Drug Administration, 'Three Baltimore-Area Men Facing Federal Charges for Fraud Scheme Purporting to Sell Covid-19 Vaccines' (Press Release, 11 February 2021)

US Food and Drug Administration, 'Warning Letter Genesis 2 Church' (8 April 2020)

US Food and Drug Administration, 'Why You Should Not Use Ivermectin to Treat or Prevent COVID-19' (9 March 2021)

US Government Accountability Office, 'Operation Warp Speed: Accelerated COVID-19 Vaccine Development Status and Efforts to Address Manufacturing Challenges' (11 February 2021)

US National Library of Medicine, 'ClinicalTrials.gov'

Uscher-Pines, Lori and others, 'Planning for an Influenza Pandemic: Social Justice and Disadvantaged Groups' (2007) 37(4) *Hastings Center Report* 32

Usher, Ann D, 'COVID-19 Vaccines for All?' (2020) 395(10240) *Lancet* 1822

Usher, Ann D, 'Medical Oxygen Crisis: A Belated COVID-19 Response' (2021) 397(10277) *Lancet* 868

Vaccine Injury Support Program, 'Frequently Asked Questions'

Valleron, AJ, S Meurisse, and PY Boelle, 'Historical Analysis of the 1889–1890 Pandemic in Europe' (2008) 12(1) *International Journal of Infectious Diseases* e95

van der Werf, Sylvie, 'Past Influenza Epidemics and Implications for Contemporary Influenza Research' in Tamara Giles-Vernick and Susan Craddock with Jennifer Gunn (eds), *Influenza and Public Health: Learning from Past Pandemics* (Routledge 2010)

van Dorn, Aaron, Rebecca E Cooney, and Miriam L Sabin, 'COVID-19 Exacerbating Inequalities in the US' (2020) 395(10232) *Lancet* 1243

Van Lancker, Wim and Zachary Parolin, 'COVID-19, School Closures, and Child Poverty: A Social Crisis in the Making' (2020) 5(5) *Lancet Public Health* e243

Van Tassel, Katharine, Carmel Shachar, and Sharona Hoffman, 'Covid-19 Vaccine Injuries—Preventing Inequities in Compensation' (2021) 384(10) *New England Journal of Medicine* e34

Vanderslott, Samantha, 'Greece to Make COVID Vaccines Mandatory for Over-60s, but do Vaccine Mandates Work?' *The Conversation* (2 December 2021)

Vasquez, Pastilí T, *The Impact of COVID-19 on Criminal Justice: System Responses of Gender-based Violence Against Women: A Global Review of Emerging Evidence* (Report, United Nations Office on Drugs and Crime, April 2021)

Velias, Alina, Sotiris Georganas, and Sotiris Vandoros, 'COVID-19: Early Evening Curfews and Mobility' (2022) 292 *Social Science & Medicine* art 114538

Vicentini, C and others, 'Early Assessment of the Impact of Mitigation Measures on the COVID-19 Outbreak in Italy' (2020) 185 *Public Health* 99

Victorian Equal Opportunity and Human Rights Commission, 'Explainer: Protests During COVID-19' (September 2021)

Victorian Government, 'Authorised Provider and Authorised Worker List' (5 October 2021)

Victorian Government, 'Guidelines for Meeting Your Contact Tracing Obligation' (1 July 2021)

Victorian Ombudsman, 'Investigation into Decision-making under the Victorian Border Crossing Permit Directions' (Parliamentary Paper No 309 Session 2018-21, December 2021)

Victorian Ombudsman, 'Investigation into the Detention and Treatment of the Public Housing Residents Arising from a COVID-19 "Hard Lockdown" in July 2020' (Parliamentary Paper No 192 Session 2018-20, December 2020)

Vijayasingham, Lavanya, Evelyne Bischof and Jeannette Wolfe, 'Sex-disaggregated Data in COVID-19 Vaccine Trials' (2021) 397(10278) *Lancet* 966

Villa, Michele and others, 'Ethical Conflict and its Psychological Correlates Among Hospital Nurses in the Pandemic: A Cross-Sectional Study within Swiss COVID-19 and Non-COVID-19 Wards' (2021) 18(22) *International Journal of Environmental Research and Public Health* art 12012

Vinceti, Marco and others, 'Lockdown Timing and Efficacy in Controlling Covid-19 Using Mobile Phone Tracking' (2020) 25 *EClinical Medicine* art 100457

Vogl, Anthea and others, 'COVID-19 and the Relentless Harms of Australia's Punitive Immigration Detention Regime' (2021) 17(1) *Crime, Media, Culture* 43

Voigt, Kristin, Evrard Nahimana, and Anat Rosenthal, 'Flashing Red Lights: The Global Implications of COVID-19 Vaccination Passports' (2021) 6(5) *BMJ Global Health* art e006209

Vollmar, Lewis C, 'The Effect of Epidemics on the Development of English Law from the Black Death Through the Industrial Revolution' (1994) 15(3) *Journal of Legal Medicine* 385

von Münchow, Sebastian, 'The Legal and Legitimate Combat Against COVID-19: German Curfew-related Case Law' (2020) 19(2) *Connections: The Quarterly Journal* 49

von Tigerstrom, Barbara and Kumanan Wilson, 'COVID-19 Travel Restrictions and the International Health Regulations (2005)' (2020) 5 *BMJ Global Health* art e002629

Walby, Sylvia, 'The COVID Pandemic and Social Theory: Social Democracy and Public Health in the Crisis' (2021) 24(1) *European Journal of Social Theory* 22

Wamoyi, Joyce, Meghna Ranganathan, and Heidi Stöckl, 'COVID-19 Social Distancing Measures and Informal Urban Settlements' (2021) 99(6) *Bulletin of the World Health Organization* 475

Wandwalo, Eliud, 'Why Drug-resistant Tuberculosis Poses a Major Risk to Global Health Security' *The Global Fund* (19 November 2020)

Wang, Emily A, Jonathan Zenilman, and Lauren Brinkley-Rubinstein, 'Ethical Considerations for COVID-19 Vaccine Trials in Correctional Facilities' (2020) 324(11) *Journal of the American Medical Association* 1031

Wang, Zhiqiong June, and Jianfu Chen, 'The People's Republic of China: Legal Response to Covid-19', in Jeff King and Octávio LM Ferraz (eds), *The Oxford Compendium of National Legal Responses to Covid-19* (Oxford University Press 2021)

Wang, Zijun and others, 'Naturally Enhanced Neutralizing Breadth Against SARS-CoV-2 One Year After Infection' (2021) 595(7867) *Nature* 426

Ward, Michael P, Shuang Xiao, and Zhijie Zhang, 'The Role of Climate during the COVID-19 Epidemic in New South Wales, Australia' (2020) 67(6) *Transboundary and Emerging Diseases* 2313

Wark, Peter, 'Younger Adults Can Get Very Sick from COVID Too. Here's What the Data Tell Us' *The Conversation* (6 August 2021)

Watson, James, 'An Open Letter to Mehra et al and The Lancet' *Zenodo* (28 May 2020)

Watson, Jennifer L and others, 'Obstacles and Opportunities in Alzheimer's Clinical Trial Recruitment' (2014) 33(4) *Health Affairs (Millwood)* 574

Watterson, Andrew, 'COVID-19 in the UK and Occupational Health and Safety: Predictable Not Inevitable Failures by Government, and Trade Union and Nongovernmental Organization Responses' (2020) 30(2) *New Solutions: A Journal of Environmental and Occupational Health Policy* 86

Watterson, Andrew, 'Scotland's COVID Inquiry Must be Credible, Timely and Thorough—Here's What Needs to Happen' *The Conversation* (2 September 2021)

Webber, Grégorie, 'The Duty to Govern and the Rule of Law in an Emergency' in Colleen M Flood and others, (eds) *Vulnerable: The Law, Policy and Ethics of COVID-19* (University of Ottawa Press 2020)

Webster, Rebecca and others, 'A Systematic Review of Infectious Illness Presenteeism: Prevalence, Reasons and Risk Factors' (2019) 19(1) *BMC Public Health* art 799

Weder, Annika and Carly Kempler, 'Online COVID-19 Mortality Risk Calculator Could Help Determine Who Should Get Vaccine First' *Johns Hopkins University Hub* (12 December 2020)

Weijers, Robert J and Björn B de Koning, 'Nudging to Increase Hand Hygiene During the COVID-19 Pandemic: A Field Experiment' (2021) 53(3) *Canadian Journal of Behavioural Science* 353

Weindling, Paul (ed), *The Social History of Occupational Health* (Croom Helm 1985)

Weindling, Paul J, 'The Nazi Medical Experiments' in Ezekiel J Emanuel and others (eds), *The Oxford Textbook of Clinical Research Ethics* (Oxford University Press 2008)

Weindling, Paul and others, 'The Victims of Unethical Human Experiments and Coerced Research under National Socialism' (2016) 40(1) *Endeavour* 1

Weisser, Rebecca, 'Covid's Lepers: The Vaccinated, Not the Unvaccinated, Are Driving the Pandemic' *Spectator Australia* (23 October 2021)

Wellcome, 'Sharing Research Data and Findings Relevant to the Novel Coronavirus (COVID-19) Outbreak' (Press Release, 31 January 2020)

Wellcome, 'Statement on Data Sharing in Public Health Emergencies' (Press Release, 1 February 2016)

Wenham, Clare, Mark Eccleston-Turner, and Maike Voss, 'The Futility of the Pandemic Treaty: Caught Between Globalism and Statism' (2022) 98(3) *International Affairs* 837

Wenham, Clare and Mark Eccleston-Turner, 'Monkeypox as a PHEIC: Implications for Global Health Governance' (1 August 2022) *Lancet*

Wenham, Clare and others, 'COVID-19: The Gendered Impacts of the Outbreak' (2020) 395(10227) *Lancet* 846

Wenham, Clare and others, 'Preparing for the Next Pandemic' (2021) 373 *British Medical Journal* n1295

Wenham, Clare and others, 'Problems with Traffic Light Approaches to Public Health Emergencies of International Concern' (2021) 397(10287) *Lancet* 1856

Western Australia Government, 'COVID-19 Coronavirus: Controlled Border' (20 January 2022)

Westhaus, Sandra and others, 'Detection of SARS-CoV-2 in Raw and Treated Wastewater in Germany—Suitability for COVID-19 Surveillance and Potential Transmission Risks' (2021) 751 *Science of the Total Environment* art 141750

Whaley, Floyd and Osman D Mansoor, 'SARS Chronology' in World Health Organization, *SARS: How a Global Epidemic Was Stopped* (Report, 2006)

Whelan, Allison M, 'Unequal Representation: Race, Sex, and Trust in Medicine—COVID-19 and Beyond' *Harvard Law School Petrie-Flom Center* (30 November 2020)

White, Douglas B and Bernard Lo, 'A Framework for Rationing Ventilators and Critical Care Beds During the COVID-19 Pandemic' (2020) 323(18) *Journal of the American Medical Association* 1773

White, Douglas B and others, 'Who Should Receive Life Support During a Public Health Emergency? Using Ethical Principles to Improve Allocation Decisions' (2009) 150(2) *Annals of Internal Medicine* 132

WHO Ebola Response Team, 'After Ebola in West Africa—Unpredictable Risks, Preventable Epidemics' (2016) 375(6) *New England Journal of Medicine* 587

WHO Scientific Advisory Group for the Origins of Novel Pathogens (SAGO), *Preliminary Report*, 9 June 2022 (World Health Organization, 2022)

WHO Solidarity Trial Consortium, 'Repurposed Antiviral Drugs for COVID-19—Interim WHO Solidarity Trial Results' (2021) 384(6) *New England Journal of Medicine* 497

Widera, Eric, Anna Chang, and Helen L Chen, 'Presenteeism: A Public Health Hazard' (2010) 25(11) *Journal of General Internal Medicine* 1244

Wiley, Lindsay F, 'Federalism in Pandemic Prevention and Response' in Scott Burris and others (eds), *Assessing Legal Responses to COVID-19* (Public Health Law Watch 2020)

Wiley, Lindsay F, 'Public Health Law and Science in the Community Mitigation for Covid-19' (2020) 7(1) *Journal of Law and the Biosciences* art lsaa019

Wiley, Lindsay F, Micah L Berman, and Doug Blanke, 'Who's Your Nanny? Choice, Paternalism and Public Health in the Age of Personal Responsibility' (2013) 41(S1) *Journal of Law, Medicine & Ethics* 88

Wilkinson, Dominic, 'ICU Triage in an Impending Crisis: Uncertainty, Pre-emption and Preparation' (2020) 46(5) *Journal of Medical Ethics* 287

Williams, Gareth, *Angel of Death: The Story of Smallpox* (Palgrave Macmillan 2010)

Williams, George and Sophie Rigney, 'Human Rights in a Pandemic' in Belinda Bennett and Ian Freckelton (eds), *Pandemics, Public Health Emergencies and Government Powers: Perspectives on Australian Law* (Federation Press 2021)

Williams, Jane H and Angus Dawson, 'Prioritising Access to Pandemic Influenza Vaccine: A Review of the Ethics Literature' (2020) 21(1) *BMC Medical Ethics* 40

Williamson, Sue, Linda Colley, and Sally Hanna-Osborne, 'Will Working from Home Become the "New Normal" in the Public Sector?' (2020) 79(4) *Australian Journal of Public Administration* 601

Wilson, Kumanan and Colleen M Flood, 'Implementing Digital Passports for SARS-CoV-2 Immunization in Canada' (2021) 193(14) *Canadian Medical Association Journal* E486

Wilson, Kumanan and Jennifer Keelan, 'The Case for a Vaccine Injury Compensation Program for Canada' (2012) 103(2) *Canadian Journal of Public Health* 122

Wilson, Kumanan and others, 'Strategies for Implementing the New International Health Regulations in Federal Countries' (2008) 86(3) *Bulletin of the World Health Organization* 215

Wise, Jacqui, 'Covid-19: France and Greece Make Vaccination Mandatory for Healthcare Workers' (2021) 374 *British Medical Journal* n1797

Wise, Jacqui, 'Covid-19: Is the UK Heading Towards Mandatory Vaccination of Healthcare Workers?' (2021) 373 *British Medical Journal* n1056

Witzleb, Normann and Moira Paterson, 'The Australian COVIDSafe App and Privacy: Lessons for the Future of Privacy Regulation' in Belinda Bennett and Ian Freckelton (eds), *Pandemics, Public Health Emergencies and Government Powers: Perspectives on Australian Law* (Federation Press 2021)

Wojcik, Mark E and David W Austin, 'Criminal Justice and COVID-19' (2020) 35(3) *Criminal Justice* 44

Wolf, Gabrielle, Jason Taliadoros, and Penny Gleeson, 'A Panacea for Australia's COVID-19 Crisis? Weighing Some Legal Implications of Mandatory Vaccination' (2021) 28(4) *Journal of Law and Medicine* 993

Wolfe, Nathan, *The Viral Storm: The Dawn of a New Pandemic Age* (Allen Lane 2011)

Wontorczyk, Antoni and Bohan Roznowski, 'Remote, Hybrid and On-Site Work during the SARSCo-V-2 Pandemic and the Consequences for Stress and Work Engagement' (2022) 19(4) *International Journal of Environmental Public Health* art 2400

Woodcock, Janet and Peter Marks, 'FDA Will Follow The Science on COVID-19 Vaccines for Young Children' (Statement, *US Food and Drug Administration*, 10 September 2021)

Woodcock, Janet and others, 'Integrating Research into Community Practice—Toward Increased Diversity in Clinical Trials' (2021) 385(15) *New England Journal of Medicine* 1351

Woolf, Steven H, Ryan K Masters, and Laudan Y Aron, 'Effect of the Covid-19 Pandemic in 2020 on Life Expectancy Across Populations in the USA and Other High Income Countries: Simulations of Provisional Mortality Data' (2021) 373 *British Medical Journal* n1343

Workplace Gender Equality Agency (Australia), 'Gendered Impacts of COVID-19' (May 2020)

World Bank Group, 'COVID-19: Remittance Flows to Shrink 14% by 2021' (Press Release, 29 October, 2020)

World Bank Group, 'How the World Bank Group is Helping Countries Address COVID-19 (Coronavirus)' (6 April 2022)

World Bank Group, 'Poverty and Shared Prosperity 2020: Reversals of Fortune' (Report, 2020)

World Bank Group, 'Saving Lives, Scaling Up Impact and Getting Back on Track' (COVID-19 Crisis Response Approach Paper, June 2020)

World Bank Group, 'World Bank Group's Operational Response to COVID-19 (coronavirus)—Projects List' (Brief, 25 October 2021)

World Health Assembly, 'COVID-19 Response' (Resolution WHA 73.1, 19 May 2020)

World Health Assembly, 'Global Eradication of Poliomyelitis by the Year 2000' (Resolution WHA41.28, 13 May 1988)

World Health Assembly, 'International Health Regulations' (Resolution WHA22.46, 25 July 1969)

World Health Assembly, 'Revision of the International Health Regulations' (Resolution WHA58.3, 23 May 2005)

World Health Assembly, 'Revision and Updating of the International Health Regulations' (Resolution WHA48.7, 12 May 1995)

World Health Assembly, 'Severe Acute Respiratory Syndrome (SARS)' (Resolution WHA56.29, 28 May 2003)

World Health Assembly, 'Special Session of the World Health Assembly to Consider Developing a WHO Convention, Agreement or Other International Instrument on Pandemic Preparedness and Response' (Decision WHA74(16), 31 May 2021)

World Health Organization, 'ACT-Accelerator Update' (News Release, 26 June 2020)
World Health Organization, 'Advice on the Use of Masks in the Context of COVID-19: Interim Guidance' (6 April 2020)
World Health Organization, 'Cholera' (Fact Sheet, 30 March 2022)
World Health Organization, 'Classification of Omicron (B.1.1.529): SARS-CoV-2 Variant of Concern' (26 November 2021)
World Health Organization, 'A Clinical Case Definition of Post COVID-19 Condition by a Delphi Consensus' (Report, 6 October 2021)
World Health Organization, 'Contact Tracing in the Context of COVID-19: Interim Guidance' (1 February 2021)
World Health Organization, 'Contingency Fund for Emergencies'
World Health Organization, *A Coordinated Global Research Roadmap: 2019 Novel Coronavirus* (Report, March 2020)
World Health Organization, 'Coronavirus Disease (COVID-19)' (13 May 2021)
World Health Organization, 'Coronavirus Disease (COVID-19) Advice for the Public: Myth Busters' (23 November 2020)
World Health Organization, 'Coronavirus Disease (COVID-19) Outbreak: Rights, Roles and Responsibilities of Health Workers, Including Key Considerations for Occupational Health and Safety' (Interim Guidance, 19 March 2020)
World Health Organization, 'Coronavirus Disease 2019 (COVID-19)—Situation Report—50' (10 March 2020)
World Health Organization, 'Coronavirus Disease 2019 (COVID-19)—Situation Report—51' (11 March 2020)
World Health Organization, 'Coronavirus Disease 2019 (COVID-19)—Situation Report—60' (19 March 2020)
World Health Organization, 'Coronavirus Disease 2019 (COVID-19)—Situation Report—61' (20 March 2020)
World Health Organization, 'Coronavirus Disease 2019 (COVID-19)—Situation Report—68' (28 March 2020)
World Health Organization, 'Coronavirus Disease 2019 (COVID-19)—Situation Report—70' (30 March 2020)
World Health Organization, 'Coronavirus Disease (COVID-19): Vaccine Access and Allocation' (Q&A, 12 December 2020)
World Health Organization, 'COVAX Announces Additional Deals to Access Promising COVID-19 Vaccine Candidates; Plans Global Rollout Starting Q1 2021' (News Release, 18 December 2020)
World Health Organization, 'COVAX No-Fault Compensation Program'
World Health Organization, 'COVAX: Working for Global Equitable Access to COVID-19 Vaccines'
World Health Organization, 'COVID-19 and Mandatory Vaccination: Ethical Considerations and Caveats' Policy Brief (13 April 2021)
World Health Organization, 'COVID-19 Oxygen Emergency Impacting More Than Half a Million People in Low- and Middle-Income Countries Every Day, As Demand Surges' (Joint News Release, 25 February 2021)
World Health Organization, 'COVID-19 Significantly Impacts Health Services for Noncommunicable Diseases' (News Release, 1 June 2020)
World Health Organization, 'COVID-19 Strategy Update—14 April 2020'
World Health Organization, 'COVID-19 Weekly Epidemiological Update' (4 May 2021)
World Health Organization, 'COVID-19 Weekly Epidemiological Update' (11 May 2021)
World Health Organization, 'Digital Tools for COVID-19 Contact Tracing: Annex: Contact Tracing in the Context of COVID-19' (2 June 2020)

World Health Organization, 'Ebola Outbreak in the Democratic Republic of the Congo Declared a Public Health Emergency of International Concern' (News Release, 17 July 2019)

World Health Organization, 'Elder Abuse' (Fact Sheet, 4 October 2021)

World Health Organization, 'Emergency Use ICD Codes for COVID-19 Disease Outbreak' (2021)

World Health Organization, 'Estimating Mortality from COVID-19: Scientific Brief' (4 August 2020)

World Health Organization, 'Ethical Considerations to Guide the Use of Digital Proximity Tracking Technologies for COVID-19 Contact Tracing' (Interim Guidance, 28 May 2020)

World Health Organization, 'Fighting Misinformation in the Time of COVID-19, One Click at a Time' (Feature Story, 27 April 2021)

World Health Organization, 'G20 Leaders Boost Support of the Access to COVID-19 Tools (ACT) Accelerator but Urgent and Immediate Action is Needed to Maintain Momentum' (News Release, 21 May 2021)

World Health Organization, 'A Global Pandemic Requires a World Effort to End it: None of us will be Safe Until Everyone is Safe' (Commentaries, 30 September 2020)

World Health Organization, 'Global Tuberculosis Report 2021' (14 October 2021)

World Health Organization, 'Guidance on Utilization of COVID-19 Vaccines Before the Date of Expiry' (Scientific Brief, 19 July 2021)

World Health Organization, *Health in 2015: From MDGs, Millennium Development Goals to SDGs, Sustainable Development Goals* (World Health Organization 2015)

World Health Organization, 'HIV/AIDS' (Fact Sheet, 30 November 2021)

World Health Organization, 'How WHO is Working to Track Down the Animal Reservoir of the SARS-CoV-2 Virus' (6 November 2020)

World Health Organization, 'Implementation of the International Health Regulations (2005): Report of the Review Committee on the Role of the International Health Regulations (2005) in the Ebola Outbreak and Response' (WHA A69/21, 13 May 2016)

World Health Organization, 'Infection Prevention and Control for the Safe Management of a Dead Body in the Context of COVID-19' (Interim Guidance, 4 September 2020)

World Health Organization, 'Interim Statement on Booster Doses for COVID-19 Vaccination' (22 December 2021)

World Health Organization, *International Health Regulations (2005)* (3rd edn, World Health Organization 2016)

World Health Organization, *Joint External Evaluation Tool: International Health Regulations (2005)* (2nd edn, World Health Organization 2018)

World Health Organization, 'Key Criteria for the Ethical Acceptability of COVID-19 Human Challenge Studies' (6 May 2020)

World Health Organization, 'Looking Back at a Year That Changed the World: WHO's Response to COVID-19' (24 February 2021)

World Health Organization, 'Mask Use in the Context of COVID-19: Interim Guidance' (1 December 2020)

World Health Organization, 'Munich Security Conference' (Speech, 15 February 2020)

World Health Organization, 'New International Expert Panel to Address the Emergence and Spread of Zoonotic Diseases' (Joint News Release, 20 May 2021)

World Health Organization, 'Novel Coronavirus (2019-nCoV)—Situation Report 10' (30 January 2020)

World Health Organization, 'Novel Coronavirus (2019-nCoV)—Situation Report 11' (31 January 2020)

World Health Organization, 'Novel Coronavirus (2019-nCoV)—Situation Report 18' (Emergency Situational Update, 7 February 2020)
World Health Organization, 'Novel Coronavirus (2019-nCoV)—Situation Report 19' (8 February 2020)
World Health Organization, 'Novel Coronavirus (2019-nCoV)—Situation Report 22' (11 February 2020)
World Health Organization, 'Past Pandemics' (Health Topic)
World Health Organization, 'Patent Landscape for the H5 Virus' (Interim Report, 17 November 2007)
World Health Organization, 'Plague' (Fact Sheet, 31 October 2017)
World Health Organization, 'Poliomyelitis' (Fact Sheet, 22 July 2019)
World Health Organization, 'R&D Blueprint: About Us'
World Health Organization, 'R&D Blueprint and COVID-19'
World Health Organization, 'Report of the Review Committee on the Functioning of the International Health Regulations (2005) During the COVID-19 Response' (Report, Final Draft WHA A74/9 Add.1, 30 April 2021)
World Health Organization, 'Severe Acute Respiratory Syndrome (SARS)' (Health Topic)
World Health Organization, 'Situation Report—Ebola Virus Disease' (30 March 2016)
World Health Organization, 'Smallpox' (Health Topic)
World Health Organization, 'Solidarity Call to Action'
World Health Organization, 'Special Programme on AIDS: Strategies and Structure, Projected Needs' (WHO/SPA/GEN/87.1, March 1987)
World Health Organization, 'Statement on the 1st Meeting of the IHR Emergency Committee on the 2014 Ebola Outbreak in West Africa' (8 August 2014)
World Health Organization, 'Statement on the 9th Meeting of the IHR Emergency Committee Regarding the Ebola Outbreak in West Africa' (29 March 2016)
World Health Organization, 'Statement on the Second Meeting of the International Health Regulations (2005) Emergency Committee Regarding the Outbreak of Novel coronavirus (2019-nCoV)' (30 January 2020)
World Health Organization, 'Statement of the Twenty-ninth Polio IHR Emergency Committee' (Statement, 20 August 2021)
World Health Organization, 'Status of Environmental Surveillance for SARS-CoV-2 Virus: Scientific Brief' (5 August 2020)
World Health Organization, 'Strengthening Response to Pandemics and Other Public-Health Emergencies: Report of the Review Committee on the Functioning of the International Health Regulations (2005) and on Pandemic Influenza (H1N1) 2009 (April 2011)
World Health Organization, 'The ACT-Accelerator Frequently Asked Questions'
World Health Organization, 'The COVAX Facility: Global Procurement for COVID-19 Vaccines' (6 August 2020)
World Health Organization, 'The Impact of COVID-19 on Health and Care Workers: A Closer Look at Deaths' (September 2021)
World Health Organization, 'The True Death Toll of COVID-19: Estimating Excess Global Mortality'
World Health Organization, 'Therapeutics and COVID-19: Living Guideline' (6 July 2021)
World Health Organization, 'Tracking SARS-CoV-2 Variants' (3 May 2022)
World Health Organization, 'Tuberculosis' (Fact Sheet, 14 October 2021)
World Health Organization, 'UN Welcomes Nearly $1 Billion in Recent Pledges—to Bolster Access to Lifesaving Tests, Treatments and Vaccines to end COVID-19' (News Release, 30 September 2020)

World Health Organization, 'Update on Omicron' (Statement, 28 November 2021)
World Health Organization, 'Vaccine Equity'
World Health Organization, 'Vaccines' (Guidance Document, 29 September 2021)
World Health Organization, 'Weekly Epidemiological Update on COVID-19: Edition 72' (Emergency Situational Update, 28 December 2021)
World Health Organization, 'Weekly Operational Update on COVID-19: Issue No 83' (7 December 2021)
World Health Organization, 'WHO Advises that Ivermectin Only be Used to Treat COVID-19 Within Clinical Trials' (31 March 2021)
World Health Organization, 'WHO and Partners Call for Action to Better Protect Health and Care Workers From COVID-19' (News Release, 21 October 2021)
World Health Organization, 'WHO Concept for Fair Access and Equitable Allocation of COVD-19 Health Products' (9 September 2020)
World Health Organization, *WHO-Convened Global Study of Origins of SARS-CoV-2: China Part*, Joint WHO-China Report (30 March 2021)
World Health Organization, 'WHO COVID-19 Solidarity Therapeutics Trial'
World Health Organization, 'WHO COVID-19 Technology Access Pool'
World Health Organization, 'WHO Director-General, 'Opening Remarks at the Media Briefing on COVID-19' (24 June 2020)
World Health Organization, 'WHO Director-General's Opening Remarks at the Media Briefing on COVID-19' (11 March 2020)
World Health Organization, 'WHO Director-General's Statement on Tanzania and COVID-19' (20 February 2021)
World Health Organization, 'WHO Model Lists of Essential Medicines'
World Health Organization, 'WHO Public Health Research Agenda for Managing Infodemics' (World Health Organization, 2021)
World Health Organization, 'WHO Recommends Against the Use of Remdesivir in COVID-19 Patients' (20 November 2020)
World Health Organization, 'WHO SAGE Values Framework for the Allocation and Prioritization of COVID-19 Vaccination' (14 September 2021)
World Health Organization, 'WHO Statement on the First Meeting of the International Health Regulations (2005) (IHR (2005)) Emergency Committee on Zika Virus and Observed Increase in Neurological Disorders and Neonatal Malformations' (1 February 2016)
World Health Organization, 'WHO Statement on the Second Meeting of the International Health Regulations Emergency Committee Concerning the International Spread of Wild Poliovirus' (3 August 2014)
World Health Organization, 'WHO's Solidarity Clinical Trial Enters a New Phase with Three New Candidate Drugs' (News Release, 11 August 2021)
World Health Organization, 'World Health Assembly Agrees to Launch Process to Develop Historic Global Accord on Pandemic Prevention, Preparedness and Response' (News Release, 1 December 2021)
World Health Organization, 'World Health Organization Best Practices for the Naming of New Human Infectious Diseases' (Technical Document, 15 May 2015)
World Health Organization, 'Year of Health and Care Workers 2021' (Campaign, 2021)
World Health Organization Africa, 'Less than 10% of African Countries to Hit Key COVID-19 Vaccination Goal' (28 October 2021)
World Health Organization Africa, 'Six in Seven COVID-19 Infections Go Undetected in Africa' (14 October 2021)

World Health Organization (Europe), 'Preparedness, Prevention and Control of COVID-19 in Prisons and Other Places of Detention: Interim Guidance' (8 February 2021)
World Health Organization Regional Office for Europe, 'One Health'
World Health Organization and International Labour Organization, 'COVID-19: Occupational Health and Safety for Health Workers' (Interim Guidance, 2 February 2021)
World Health Organization and UNAIDS, 'The Treatment 2.0 Framework for Action: Catalysing the Next Phase of Treatment, Care and Support' (Report, 2011)
World Health Organization and UNICEF, 'Advice on the Use of Masks for Children in the Community in the Context of COVID-19' (Annex to the Advice on the Use of Masks in the Context of COVID-19, 21 August 2020)
World Health Organization and World Bank Group, *World Report on Disability* (14 December 2011)
World Intellectual Property Organization, 'Patents'
World Intellectual Property Organization, 'WIPO Patent Search Report on Pandemic Influenza Preparedness (PIP)-Related Patents and Patent Applications' (1 April 2011)
World Medical Association General Assembly, *Declaration of Helsinki—Ethical Principles for Medical Research Involving Human Subjects* (adopted June 1964)
World Prison Brief, 'Bangladesh' (March 2021)
World Prison Brief, 'India' (31 December 2019)
World Prison Brief, 'Nigeria' (30 August 2021)
World Trade Organization, 'Compulsory Licensing of Pharmaceuticals and TRIPS'
World Trade Organization, 'Declaration on The TRIPS Agreement and Public Health' (Resolution WT/Min(01)/Dec/2, 14 November 2001)
Wrate, RM, 'Increase in Staff Numbers May Reduce Doctors' "Presenteeism"' (1999) 319 *British Medical Journal* art 1502,
Wu, Ping and others, 'The Psychological Impact of the SARS Epidemic on Hospital Employees in China: Exposure, Risk Perception, and Altruistic Acceptance of Risk' (2009) 54(5) *Canadian Journal of Psychiatry* 302
Xue, Ye and others, 'Perspectives on the Death Investigation During the COVID-19 Pandemic' (2020) 2 *Forensic Science International: Synergy* 126
Yakubu, Aminu and others, 'The Ebola Outbreak in Western Africa: Ethical Obligations for Care' (2016) 42(4) *Journal of Medical Ethics* 209
Yancey, Diane, *Cholera* (Lucent Books 2013)
Yancy, Clyde W, 'COVID-19 and African Americans' (2020) 323(19) *Journal of the American Medical Association* 1891
Yashadhana, Aryati and others, 'Indigenous Australians at Increased Risk of COVID-19 Due to Existing Health and Socioeconomic Inequities' (2020) 1 *Lancet Regional Health Western Pacific* art 100007
Yaylymova, Aynabat, 'COVID-19 in Turkmenistan: No Data, No Health Rights' (2020) 22(2) *Health and Human Rights* 325
Yeamans, Robin, 'Constitutional Attacks on Vagrancy Laws' (1968) 20(4) *Stanford Law Review* 782
Yearby, Ruqaiijah, 'Protecting Workers That Provide Essential Services' in Scott Burris and others (eds), *Assessing Legal Responses to COVID-19* (Public Health Law Watch 2020)
Yekini, Abubakri, *The Hague Judgments Convention and Commonwealth Model Law: A Pragmatic Perspective* (Hart 2021)
Yellow Horse, Aggie J, and Kimberly R Huyser, 'Indigenous Data Sovereignty and COVID-19 Data Issues for American Indian and Alaska Native Tribes and Populations' (2021) *Journal of Population Research*

Yong, Ed 'The 3 Simple Rules that Underscore the Danger of Delta' *The Atlantic* (1 July 2021)

Youde, Jeremy, *Global Health Governance* (Polity 2012)

Young, Hilary, 'Governments Shouldn't Shield Essential Workers from COVID-19 Lawsuits' *The Conversation* (4 October 2020)

Yusuf, Ibrahim and others, 'Ebola and Compliance with Infection Prevention Measures in Nigeria' (2014) 14(11) *Lancet Infectious Diseases* 1045

Zakaria, Fareed, *Ten Lessons for a Post-Pandemic World* (Allen Lane 2021)

Zaracostas, John, 'Mixed Response to COVID-19 Intellectual Property Waiver' (2022) 399(10332) *Lancet* 1292

Zarocostas, John, 'WHA Sees Changes to Health Regulations and WHO Funding' (2022) 399(10341) *Lancet* 2090

Zettler, Patricia J, Micah L Berman, and Efthimios Parasidis, 'Drug and Vaccine Development and Access' in Scott Burris and others (eds), *Assessing Legal Responses to COVID-19* (Public Health Law Watch 2020)

Zhan, Mingkun and others, 'Lesson Learned from China Regarding Use of Personal Protective Equipment' (2020) 48(12) *American Journal of Infection Control* 1462

Zhu, Junhong, Teresa Stone, and Marcia Petrini, 'The Ethics of Refusing to Care for Patients During the Coronavirus Pandemic: A Chinese Perspective' (2020) 28(1) *Nursing Inquiry* art e12380

Zidar, Andraž, 'WHO International Health Regulations and Human Rights: From Allusions to Inclusion' (2015) 19(4) *International Journal of Human Rights* 505

Zou, Xiaohui and Bin Cao, 'COVID-19 Vaccines for Children Younger than 12 Years: Are We Ready?' (2021) 21(12) *Lancet Infectious Diseases* 1614

Zowalaty, Mohamed E El and Josef D Järhult, 'From SARS to COVID-19: A Previously Unknown SARS-related Coronavirus (SARS-CoV-2) of Pandemic Potential Infecting Humans—Call for a One Health Approach' (2020) 9 *One Health* art 100124

Zuckerman, Gregory, *A Shot to Save the World: The Remarkable Race and Groundbreaking Science Behind the Covid-19 Vaccines* (Penguin 2021)

Index

For the benefit of digital users, indexed terms that span two pages (e.g., 52–53) may, on occasion, appear on only one of those pages.

Access to COVID-19 Tools (ACT) Accelerator, 459, 506–7. *See also* COVAX
access to justice, 340–41
   deferral of hearings, 342–43
   remote hearings, 342
acquired immune deficiency syndrome, 61–62. *See also* human immunodeficiency virus
   discrimination against, 62–63
Acute Respiratory Distress Syndrome (ARDS), 481
Agreement on Trade-Related Aspects of Intellectual Property Rights (TRIPS), 69–70, 542–43
AIDS. *See* acquired immune deficiency syndrome
anthrax, vii
anti-vaccination, 48, 276
anxiety, 398–99
assaults, 328, 359–60. *See also* coughing; sneezing; spitting; torts
assumpsit writs, 46–47
asylum-seekers, 140–43, 297–304
   refoulement, 142–43
   Rohingya, 140
Australia
   asylum-seeker litigation, 301–4
   Australian Health Practitioner Regulation Agency, 433–35
   bail, 352–53
   coroners' investigations, 396–97
   curfew litigation, 221–23
   fraudulent treatments, 527–28
   immigration detention litigation, 301–2
   insurance contract jurisprudence, 373–77
   lockdown jurisprudence, 205–6
   mandatory vaccination litigation, 248–53
   National Cabinet, 152, 295
   National COVID-19 Clinical Evidence Taskforce, 465–66
   no-fault vaccine compensation scheme, 384–85
   prisoner detention litigation, 302–4
   public protest litigation, 231–37
   regulation of health practitioners, 407–16
   Royal Commission into Violence, Abuse, Neglect and Exploitation of People with Disability, 306
   Spanish flu, 57–58
   Therapeutic Goods Administration, 456–57, 527–28
   vaccination of children litigation, 266–69
   widening of jury boxes, 344–45
Austria
   cordon, 45
avian influenza, 24, 56–57

bail, 350–54
   Australia, 352–53
   Canada, 353
Bangladesh
   pre-trial detention, 351
   intellectual property, 545–46
battery, 359–60
Belgium, 131–32
Biden, President, viii–ix, 259–60
biological agent, 329
Black Death, 42–43, 45, 46–47
borders, 113
   closures, 115–20
   litigation, 191–99
Brazil, 6–7
   disclosure of COVID-19, 107–8
   Gamma variant, 11
   Indigenous communities, 131
   lockdown jurisprudence, 207
   meat plants, 427
British Board of Scholars and Imams, 238–40
business interruption insurance, 358. *See also* insurance contracts

Canada
   bail, 353, 354
   coroners' investigations, 395–96
   face mask litigation, 228–29
   fines, 331–32
   Indigenous communities, 124–25

Canada (*cont.*)
  intellectual property, 543
  Privacy Commissioners, 179–80
  regulation of health practitioners, 413
  religious observance litigation, 240–42
  severe acute respiratory syndrome, 67
  vaccination of children litigation, 270–72
Carbolic Smoke Ball Company, 55, 399–401, 526
Carlill, Louise, 55, 399–401, 526
case fatality ratio, 105
Centers for Disease Control and Prevention, vii, 524–25, 540–41, 564
central business districts, 316–17
childcare, 289
children, 126–32, 291–94
  Family Court of Australia, 126–27
  Greece, 129
  Hague Convention, 129–30
  Poland, 131
  school closures, 292–93
  Spain, 130–31
  Superior Court of Justice of Ontario, 127–28
  Tonga, 129
  vaccination, 263–72
Chile
  authenticating documents, 341–42
  intellectual property, 543
China
  Dynamic Zero COVID policy, viii
  numbers of cases, 6
  reporting of COVID-19, ix
cholera, 49–53, 77
  notification, 77
  trials, 468–69
  vaccine, 51–52
citizen scientists, 528–29
civil liability, 357–417
civil registration, 109–10
class actions, 362. *See also* negligence
Coalition for Epidemic Preparedness Innovations (CEPI), 459
compassionate use, 536–37
compensation
  Advance Market Commitment (AMC) Eligible Economies Compensation Scheme, 383–84
  national no-fault schemes, 384–86
conspiracy theories, 527
consumer protection, 371, 398–407
  Australian, 404–5
  Carbolic Smokeball Company case, 399–401
  Italian, 401
  Japanese, 405
  Polish, 401–2
  United Kingdom, 406–7
  United States, 401–4
consumption. *See* tuberculosis
contact tracing, 3, 181–84
  digital technology, 182–83
contract litigation, 357, 364–70
  force majeure clauses, 365–70
  insurance contracts, 370–77
contra proferentem rule, 368
cordon sanitaire, vii–viii. *See also* quarantine
coronaphobia, 42
coroners. *See also* medico-legal investigations
  Australian investigations, 396–97
  Canadian investigations, 395–96
  English investigations, 391–90
  threshold for investigation, 391
coughing, 328, 360
courts. *See also* access to justice
  audio-visual technology, 347
  authenticating documents, 341–42
  backlogs, 341–42
  delays, 343–44
  distributed hearings, 345
  face masks, 345
  judge-alone trials, 345–46
  jury boxes, 344–45
  online proceedings, 341
  physical distancing, 345
  remote hearings, 342
  signature acknowledgments, 341–42
  transparent booths, 344–45
  virtual hearings, 347–48
COVAX, x, 459, 512–13, 514. *See also* Access to COVID-19 Tools (ACT) Accelerator
  access to treatments, 507–16
  criticism of, 509–10
  Principles for Sharing COVID-19 Vaccine Doses with COVAX, 511–12
COVID-19. *See also* COVID-19 treatment
  asymptomatic presentation, 114–15
  biological agent, 329
  boosters, 580
  characteristics, 1
  conspiracy theories, 527
  deaths, 106, 387–98. (*see also* medico-legal investigations)
  death toll, 2–3
  Delta variant, 104
  emergence, 4–5
  ethnicity, 284–86
  gender, 288–90
  genome, 5
  humidity, 427
  independent inquiry, viii–ix
  Indigenous peoples, 286–88

infectiousness, 113
infodemic, 103, 527
'Life Beyond COVID', 579
Long Covid, 284, 357, 489–90
misdiagnosis, 105–6
older persons, 111, 190–284
Oxygen Emergency Taskforce, 309
Pacific islands, 115–16
pandemic, 80
phases, 480–81
prevention, 307–11
public health emergency of international concern, 75–76, 80
race, 284–86
remdesivir, 537–39, 545–46
survivability of virus, 389–90
treatments, 307–11 (*see also* COVID-19 treatment)
underestimate, 105–6
uneven impact, 281–307
unprecedented speed, 505
vaccines (*see* vaccines)
variants, 10–11
Wuhan outbreak, viii
COVID-19 Technology Access Pool (C-TAP), 515
COVID-19 treatment, 455–501. *See also* COVID-19
access, 503–7
Clinical Frailty Scale, 521
compassionate use, 536–37
convalescent plasma, 534–35
'COVID-19 Rapid Guidance', 521
dexamethasone, 541–42
fast-tracked, 529–39
fraudulent, 526
genetically modified organisms, 531
hydroxychloroquine, 494–96, 532–33
ivermectin, 497–500
Paxlovid, 579
rationing, 517–23
regulation, 525–39
remdesivir, 537–39, 541–42, 545–46
respiratory support, 517–4
sotrovimab, 465–67
stockpiling, 541–42
covidization
research, 23
criminalization of conduct, 325
human rights, 329–30
Hungary COVID-19 misrepresentations, 326–27
prisons, 333
Ukraine export law, 326–27

criminal justice, 323–56
appeals, 344–45
delays, 343–44
face masks, 345
judge-alone trials, 345–46
criminal offending, 335. *See also* assault; spitting
domestic violence, 337–38
fraud, 336
hate crimes, 339
theft, 336
victims, 337
cruise ships, 143–44, 363
curfews, 161–63
Australian litigation, 221–23
avondklok, 224
effects of, 162–63
English litigation, 216–17
European Court of Human Rights litigation, 215
French litigation, 223–24
German litigation, 225
Greece, 162–63
Kenya litigation, 220–21
Kuwait, 162–63
legality, 215
Netherlands litigation, 224
Cutter Laboratories, 60

Data
accurate, 29
age-related, 111
based action, 555–56
case fatality ratio, 105
civil registration, 109–10
disaggregated, 29–30, 110–12
epidemiological, 29
excess mortality statistics, 29
gender, 288
importance, 103–8
infection fatality ratio, 105
reporting, 104
timely, 29, 30
underreporting, 107
vital statistics, 109–10
wastewater surveillance, 185–87
deaths
death caused by COVID-19, 390
death with COVID-19, 390
excess mortality, 2–3
healthcare workers, 2–3
decarceration, 350–51, 355–56
Democratic Republic of the Congo
Ebola, 71

666 INDEX

Demonstrators, 188, 230–31
　Australian, 230–31
　German, 230–31
digital technology
　apps, viii
　digital technology, 183
　QR codes, 182–84
disabilities. *See* persons with disabilities
discrimination
　Asian persons, 335
　countering, 339–40
　human immunodeficiency syndrome, 62–63
disease surveillance, 3
disease-tracking methodologies, 560–61
dissent
　quashing, 332
Djokovic, Novak, 273–77
　deportation, 273–76
Doha Declaration on the TRIPS Agreement and Public Health, 542–43
domestic violence, 290, 334, 337–38, 348

Ebola, 15–16, 24, 71–72, 82–84
　duty of care of health practitioners, 442–43
　mental health consequences, 313–14
　pathology, 388
　public health emergency of international concern, 80–81
　International Health Regulations (2005), 95–97
economies, 315–21
electronic monitoring, 354–55
emergency laws, 147–81
　curfews, 161–63
　decision-making, 156–57
　emergency declarations, 148–51
　law-making, 151–53, 156
　rationality, 156
emergency use authorization, 532–35
　vaccines, 535–36
employment, 315–21
England
　asylum-seeker litigation, 299–301
　coroners' investigations, 391–90 (*see also* coroners)
　immigration detainee litigation, 299–301
　lockdown litigation, 202
　penalty notices, 326–27
　public law litigation, 209–15
　quarantine litigation, 216–17
　regulation of health practitioners, 409–11
　religious observance litigation, 238–40
　vaccination of children litigation, 264–65
environmental surveillance, 186. *See also* wastewater surveillance

epidemiology, 39–40, 555
ethical issues
　health practitioners' withdrawal of labour, 442–47
　rationing of treatment, 517–23
European Medicines Agency, 530–31
evictions, 295
exceptionalism. *See* pandemic exceptionalism
excess mortality statistics, 2–3, 29, 106–7
extradition, 132–36

face masks, 164–67
　bushfires, 164–65
　courts, 345
　litigation, 227–29
　N95 masks, 389–90
　pollution, 164–65
　volcanic eruptions, 164–65
　World Health Organization views, 165
families. *See* children
fear, 398–99
fines, 201. *See also* criminalization of conduct; penalty notices
　Canada, 331–32
　Canadian Civil Liberties Association, 327–28
　Italy, 331–32
　Nigeria, 354–55
First Nations. *See* Indigenous communities
Flagellants, 45–46
flattening the curve, 29
Florence
　board of public health, 44–45
Food and Agriculture Organization (FAO), 18, 122–23
force majeure clauses, 365–70
　Californian statute law, 365
　French law, 365
　Japanese law, 368–69
forensic radiology, 390
France
　asylum-seekers, 140
　curfew litigation, 223–24
　force majeure clauses, 365
frauds, 336
　therapies, 525–39

Gavi – The Vaccine Alliance, 15–16, 459, 508
　Advance Market Commitment, 508–9
gender, 27, 110–11, 159, 288–90
general practitioners. *See* health practitioners
genomic sequencing, 5, 555–56
Germany
　curfew litigation, 225
　occupational health and safety, 428–29

INDEX 667

transparent booths, 344–45
violation of quarantine, 333–34
germ theory, 51–52
Ghebreyesus, Tedros Adhanom, 75, 104, 431, 527
Global Fund to Fight AIDS, Tuberculosis and Malaria, 15–16
global health, 15–16
  disparities, 562–63
global surveillance systems, 108
Global Outbreak Alert and Response Network (GOARN) 67
governance
  inequities, ix
Great Influenza Pandemic. *See* Spanish flu
Greece
  curfews, 162–63
  Hague Convention, 129–30
  vaccination mandate, 449–50
Grey-Bruce Freedom Fighters, 413
Guinea
  Ebola, 71

H1N1 (swine flu) influenza, 70
  intellectual property, 506–41
  pork import bans, 93
  public health emergency of international concern, 80–81
  purchase of vaccines, 510–11
  International Health Regulations (2005), 92–95
H5N1 (bird flu), 62–63, 68, 93–94
  intellectual property, 540
haemorrhagic fevers, 82–84
Hague Convention, 129–30
hand sanitizing, 186–87, 228, 229, 232, 296, 303, 344–45, 516–17, 518–19. *See also* personal protective equipment
  marketing, 401
  prisons, 349–50
hate crimes, 339–40
health
  determinants, 28, 31
  magistrates, 44
health practitioners
  Australian, 408
  declining to provide services, 442–47
  dentists, 435–36
  dietitians, 435–36
  distress, 432–33
  diversifying, 433–36
  ethical issues, 442–47
  general practitioners, 433
  health of, 429–33
  immunity from negligence actions, 378–80
  podiatrists, 435–36

regulation, 407–16
retired, 433–35
retirements, 436
risks to, 429–33
speech pathologists, 435–36
Trojan Horses, 421–22
HIV, 61–62. *See also* human immunodeficiency virus
hoax, 329
homelessness, 294–96
Hong Kong, H5N1, 68
  physical distancing, 163
  Severe Acute Respiratory Syndrome, 67
Hopkins, Katie, 277
housing, 294–96
human challenge trials, 467–75. *See also* human subject research; research
  '1 Day Sooner', 470
  cholera trials, 468–69
  controversies, 468–75
  financial benefits, 472
  syphilis, gonorrhea, and chancroid trials, 468
  Tuskegee Study of Untreated Syphilis in the Negro Male, 467
  United Kingdom trials, 474–75
  volunteers, 472
  World Health Organization recommendations, 470
  Willowbrook studies, 467–68
  yellow fever trials, 468–69
human immunodeficiency virus. *See also* Acquired Immunodeficiency Virus
  criminalization, 63–64
  discrimination, 62–63
  negligence, 64
  South Africa, 64
  stigmatization, 333
human rights, 14, 30–32, 567–73
  assembly, 30, 330
  education, 202
  freedom of expression, 328
  freedom of speech, 410
  freedom of movement, 199–200, 330
  International Health Regulations (2005), 88–89
  right to health, 30–31, 329–30, 504–5
  right to life, 31, 210, 329–30, 504–5
  right to protest, 230
  right to religious observance, 238–47
human subject research
  cholera, 51–52
Hungary
  COVID-19 misrepresentations, 326–27
  immigration detainees, 297–99

hydroxychloroquine
  controversies, 494–96
  Emergency use authorization, 532–33

immorality, 45–46
Inclusive Vaccines Alliance, 511
Independent Panel for Pandemic Preparedness and Response, 100–1, 108
India, 9, 121
  Delta variant, 11–12
  intellectual property waiver, 544
  parole, 355–56
  pre-trial detention, 351
Indigenous communities
  Australia, 123–24
  Brazil, 124
  Canada. 124–25
  data, 122–23, 287
  effects of COVID-19, 284–86
  Elders, 122
  leaders, 123–24
  susceptibility to COVID-19, 121
  United States, 124–25
  women, 122
individual obligations, 14
Indonesia
  bird flu specimens, 69–70
infection fatality ratio, 105
insurance contracts, 358, 370–77. *See also* business interruption insurance
  Australian jurisprudence, 373–77
  construction, 370–77
  United Kingdom jurisprudence, 370
intellectual property, 539–47
  Agreement on Trade-Related Aspects of Intellectual Property Rights (TRIPS), 69–70, 542–43
  Doha Declaration on the TRIPS Agreement and Public Health, 542–43
  global issues, 79
  Harvard–MIT–Stanford pledge, 547
  International Federation of Pharmaceutical Manufacturers and Associations, 544–45
  Open COVID Pledge, 546–47
  patents, 542
  waiver of protections, 541–42, 544
International Covenant on Civil and Political Rights
  right to life, 116–17, 118, 148, 476, 504–5
International Covenant on Economic, Social and Cultural Rights, 30–31, 504–5
International Health Regulations, ix, 69, 76–92
  1969, 78
  adoption, 78

  consultation obligation, 86
  contraventions, 119–20
  Ebola, 97–99
  H1N1 influenza, 92–95
  human rights approach, 88–90
  national capacity building, 87
  National Focal Point, 87
  public health emergency of international concern, 80–84
  public health risk, 82
  purpose, 79
  reforms in 2005, 79
  reporting, 85
  sharing information, 86–87
  temporary recommendations, 90
International Labour Organization, 423
  health workers, 423–24, 425
International Negotiation Body (INB), x
International Sanitary Convention, 52
International Sanitary Regulations, 69, 77
  notification of diseases, 77
Ireland, 131–32
  Health and Safety Authority, 426
  lockdown litigation, 203
  quarantine litigation, 217
  regulation of health practitioners, 411–12
isolation, 3, 154–58
  Prince Edward Island, 328–29
Israel
  intellectual property, 543
Italy, 7
  asylum-seekers, 140, 142
  consumer protection, 401
  fines, 331–32
  overcrowding of prisons, 354–55
ivermectin controversies, 497–500

Japan, 5–6, 163
  consumer protection, 405
Jenner, Edward, 41, 47–48
Jews
  discrimination against, 45–46
judge-alone trials, 345–46

Kenya
  curfew litigation, 220–21
Korea, 5–6
Kuwait
  curfews, 162–63

Lassa fever, 82–84
law. *See also* emergency laws
  global, 14–16
  layers of, 13, 551–53 (*see also* polycentricity)

national, 16–17
public, 209–15
role, 13–14, 19–23, 40
scope, 13–14
Siracusa Principles, 149–50
lawyers
regulation, 408
Lebanon, 342–43
legal representation, 340–41
life expectancy
reduction, 9
United States, 9–10
Lithuania
restrictions on movement, 118
litigation
asylum-seeker, 297–304
border closures, 191–99
consumer protection, 398–407
contract, 357, 364–70
coroners' decisions, 391–97
curfews, 220–25
face mask, 227–29
insurance contracts, 370–77
mandatory vaccination, 247–62
physical distancing, 225–27
public law, 209–15
quarantine, 215–18
rights to protest and assemble, 229–47
tort, 357, 360–64
lockdown orders, 30, 158–61
Australian jurisprudence, 205–6
compliance, 201
criminal offending, 336
enforcement, 335
European Court of Human Rights jurisprudence, 204–5
fines, 201
hard, 200
Ireland jurisprudence, 202–3
New Zealand jurisprudence, 206–7
Singapore, 6
South African jurisprudence, 201–2
Spain jurisprudence, 203–4
United States jurisprudence, 207–8
Wuhan, 6
Long-Covid. *See* COVID-19

Malawi, 515–16
Malaysia
asylum-seekers, 140
Malta
asylum-seekers, 140
mandatory vaccination. *See* vaccination mandates
Marburg virus, 82–84

mask mandates, vii–viii, 166–67
masks. *See* face masks; mask mandates
medical historians, 39–40
Medicines and Healthcare products Regulatory Agency. *See* United Kingdom Medicines: Healthcare products Regulatory Agency
medico-legal investigations, 387–98
Australian coroners' investigations, 396–97
Canadian coroners' investigations, 395–96
death caused by COVID-19, 390
death with COVID-19, 390
English coroners' investigations, 391–90
forensic radiology, 390
Scottish Procurator Fiscal investigations, 394–95
Mehra, Mandeep. *See* hydroxychloroquine controversies
meningococcal disease, 82–84
mental health, 312–15, 561–62
MERS. *See* Middle East Respiratory Syndrome
Middle East Respiratory Syndrome, 24, 80–81
pathology, 388
migrants, 296
Milan, 44–45
Millennium Development Goals, 186–87
Monkeypox, 564
Morocco, 121
movement restrictions, 113–45
asylum-seekers, 140–43
border restrictions, 115–20
Brazilian jurisprudence, 207
children, 126–32
extradition, 132–36
impact, 126–32
international legal obligations, 116–17
litigation, 191–99
non-citizens, 136–39
Portugal, 114–15
quarantine, 154–58
Sweden, 114–15
Taiwan, 114–15
travel restrictions, 153–54
myocarditis. *See* vaccination

National Commission for the Protection of Human Subjects of Biomedical and Behavioral Research, 478–79
Nazi doctors, 477–78
negligence, 360–64
Netherlands
curfew litigation, 224
New Zealand
lockdown litigation, 206–7
vaccination of children litigation, 269–70

Nigeria
  decarceration, 351
  fines, 354–55
no-fault vaccination compensation schemes, 384–86
  Australian scheme, 385–86
  Canadian scheme, 386
  United Kingdom scheme, 385
  United States scheme, 384–85
no jab, no work, 170, 419–20, 451, 452
North Korea, 104
Norway, 163
nosocomial infections, 421–22
Nuremberg Code, 476

occupational health and safety, 317–18, 418–54
  dead bodies, 389–90
  legislative obligations, 422–26
  litigation, 424
  origins, 422
  Robens report, 422
  United Kingdom legislation, 423–24, 425
older persons, 3, 111, 283–84
Olympic Games
  postponement, 10, 12–13
Ombudsman (Victoria)
  lockdown report, 200–1
One Health, 25, 565–66
Organisation for Economic Co-operation and Development (OECD), 288–89, 290
  consumers, 400–1

Pakistan, 121
  quarantine litigation, 216–17
pandemic
  declaration, 7
  exceptionalism, 22–23
  Framework Convention, 101
  jurisprudence, 189
  litigation, 188–279
  measuring, 103
  treaty (*see* pandemic treaty)
pandemic treaty, 100–3, 554–55
Paralympic Games
  postponement, 10, 12–13
Paris School of Medicine, 49–50
parole, 355–56
patents, 542. *See also* intellectual property
pathologists, 389–90
penalty notices. *See also* fines
  England and Wales, 327–28
People's Vaccine Alliance, 563–64
pericarditis. *See* vaccination
persecution, 40–41

personal protective equipment (PPE), 308, 317–18, 428, 430–31
persons with disabilities, 304–7
  Australian Royal Commission into Violence, Abuse, Neglect and Exploitation of People with Disability, 306
pesthouses, 44, 49
PHEIC. *See* public health emergency of international concern
Philippines
  vaccination mandate, 450
physical distancing, 30, 152–53, 163–64
  courts, 345
  East Africa, 164
  Hong Kong, 163
  Japan, 163
  litigation, 225–27
  Norway, 163
  Singapore, 163
  South Korea, 163
plague, 39–40, 77
  Antonine, 42
  Athens, 39–40
  Black Death, 42–43
  bubonic, 42–43
  Galen, 42, 43
  Justinian, 42–43
  Marseille, 39–40
  notification, 78
  pneumonic, 82–84
  white, 52–53
Poland, 131
  consumer protection, 401–2
police interviews, 348
polio. *See* poliomyelitis
poliomyelitis, 60–61
  public health emergency of international concern, 80–81
  vaccination, 60–61
polycentricity, 13, 17–19, 551–52
  Djokovic saga, 270
  governance of pandemic, 551–52
  International Health Regulations (2005), 85–86
  Ostrom theory, 551–52
  whole-of-government response, 506
ports
  closure, 143–44
Portugal
  authenticating documents, 341–42
  movement restrictions, 114–15
pre-trial detention. *See* bail
presenteeism, 420–22
prisons, 300, 301–2
  COVID-19 risks, 333

INDEX 671

decarceration, 354–55
  harshness, 355
  infection rate, 350
  overcrowding, 298
  pre-trial custody, 350–51 (*see also* bail)
  release on parole, 355–56
  sentencing, 349–56
  ventilation, 349–50
protesters. *See* demonstrators
public health emergency, 58
public health emergency of international concern (PHEIC), 1, 6, 22, 75–76
  COVID-19, 75–76
  declaration, 84–85
  H1N1 influenza, 80–81
  Ebola, 80–81
  elements, 84
  International Health Regulations (2005), 80
  polio, 60–61, 80–81
  Zika virus, 80–81
public health law, 1–2, 20–22, 576
  criminal penalties, 331–32
public law
  litigation, 209–15
public spaces, 230

quarantine, 44
  Ebola, 154
  Germany, 333–34
  lazaretti, 44
  litigation, 215–18
  Severe Acute Respiratory Syndrome, 67, 154
  Spanish flu, 57–58, 154
  tuberculosis, 53–54, 155
  United States, 57–58
  unlawful, 48

Ramazzini, Bernardino, 422
rapid antigen testing, 117
rationing, 309–11
Rector of Ragusa, 44
Red Cross
  American, 59
refoulement, 142–43
refugees, 296–97. *See also* asylum-seekers
regulation of health practitioners, 407–16. *See also* health practitioners
  Australian, 407–8, 413–14
  Canadian, 413
  English, 409–11
  Irish, 411–12
regulatory tools, 22
Relenza, 540–41
remdesivir, 537–39, 541–42, 545–46

repatriation of citizens, 120–21
  Canada, 120
Republic of the Congo
  Ebola, 71
research
  Access to COVID-19 Tools (ACT) Accelerator, 459
  British Geriatrics Society, 480
  children, 489, 490–91
  consent, 476–86
  conventional stages, 459–60
  Council for International Organizations for Medical Sciences, 479–80
  diversity of participation, 486–91
  ethical guidelines, 478–80
  ethnic minorities, 488
  exceptionalism, 491, 496
  Global Forum on Research and Innovation for COVID-19, 457
  human challenge trials (*see* human challenge trials)
  human rights, 476–78
  hydroxychloroquine controversies, 494–96
  incarcerated persons, 483–86
  ivermectin controversies, 497–500
  medical neocolonialism, 488–89
  Nuremberg Code, 476
  older persons, 489–90
  Oxford University, 461
  participation, 475
  pregnant and breastfeeding women, 487
  publication of results, 491–500
  R & D Blueprint Strategy, 457–58
  R & D Roadmap, 458
  Solidarity Trial, 464–65
  strategies, 459–67
  United Kingdom Code of Practice for Research, 479–80
  World Health Organization living guidelines, 465
Rift Valley fever, 82–84
rights. *See* human rights
risk, 14, 23–24
  legal responses, 560–61
  mapping, 29–30
Roy, Arundhati, 502–49
Russian Flu, 54–49
  Carbolic Smoke Ball Company, 55, 399–400
  fraudulent treatments, 526

Sabin, Albert, 60–61
Salk, Jonas, 60
sanitary cordons
  Spanish flu, 57
San Marino, 522–23

SARS. *See* Severe Acute Respiratory Syndrome
SARS-CoV-2, 1
Saudi Arabia
  vaccination mandate, 449
scapegoating (*see also* discrimination), 40–41, 339
scaremongering, 326–27
school closures, 292–93
Scotland
  Procurator Fiscal Investigations, 394–95
Severe Acute Respiratory Syndrome (SARS), 24, 66–68, 293
  Canada, 67
  China, 67
  health workers, 421–22, 430, 442–43
  Hong Kong, 67
  impetus for reform, 78
  mental health consequences, 313–14
  notification, 82–84
  origin, 66–67
  pathology, 388
  quarantine, 67
  Singapore, 67
  Taiwan, 311–12
Sierra Leone
  Ebola, 71, 72
Singapore, 6, 163
Siracusa Principles, 148–49, 331, 343–44
smallpox, 47–48, 77
  inoculation, 47–48
  notification, 82–84
  vaccination, 49
sneezing, 359
social distancing. *See* physical distancing
social isolation, 311–12
solidarity trial, 7
sotrovimab, 465–67
South Africa
  Beta variant, 11
  human immunodeficiency virus, 64, 539–40
  intellectual property waiver, 544
  lockdown litigation, 201–2
  Omicron variant, 11
  spitting, 328
  unemployment, 315–16
South Korea, 163
Spain, 8, 130–31
  lockdown litigation, 203–4
Spanish flu, 1, 55–60, 549–51
  closure of entertainment venues, 58
  fraudulent treatments, 526–27
  mandatory reporting, 57
  mortality rate, 59–60
  sanitary cordons, 57
spitting, 328–29, 338–39, 359–60. *See also* assaults
Statute of Labourers, 46–47
stay-at-home orders. *See* lockdown orders
stigmatizing conduct, 339, 421–22
Sustainable Development Goals, 26–28, 181–82, 186–87, 290, 292, 308–9, 562–63
Sweden
  approach, 160–61
  recommendations, 114–15

Taiwan, 130, 157
Tamiflu, 69–70, 540–41
Tanzania, 105
technology, 312
  audio-visual, 347
  virtual hearings, 347
telecommuting, 317
tenants, 295
testing, 117. *See also* rapid antigen testing
Thailand, 5–6
Thucydides, 40–41
Tonga, 129
tort litigation, 357, 359–64
  assault, 359
  battery, 359
  catalyst, 361
  class actions, 362
  intentional torts, 359–60
  trespass to the person, 359–60
travel
  reduced, 418–19
travel bans, 119–20, 153–54. *See also* movement restrictions
travellers, 89
TRIPS. *See* Agreement on Trade-Related Aspects of Intellectual Property Rights
Trump, President, ix, 15–16, 339, 509–10, 533–34
tuberculosis (TB), 3, 52–54, 77
  quarantine, 53–54
Tunisia, 348
Turkey
  ban on health practitioner retirements, 433–35
Turkmenistan, 104–5
Tuskegee Study of Untreated Syphilis in the Negro Male, 467
typhoid, 49–50

Ukraine
  exporting anti-epidemic goods, 326–27
  price-setting, 336
  unemployment, 315–16
United Kingdom. *See also* England
  alpha variant, 11

Code of Practice for Research, 479–80
consumer protection, 406–5
human challenge trials, 474–75
insurance contracts jurisprudence, 370–73, 406
Joint Committee on Vaccination and Immunization, 524
Medicines and Healthcare products Regulatory Agency, 380–81, 528, 529, 531
National Institute for Health and Care Excellence (NICE), 521–22
no-fault vaccine compensation scheme, 385
occupational health and safety legislation, 423–24, 425
purchase of vaccines, 510
vaccination mandate, 450
United Nations
AIDS, 65
Committee on Economic, Social and Cultural Rights, 30–31, 150
Convention on Contracts for the Sale of Goods, 365–66
Convention on the Rights of Persons with Disabilities, 304
Declaration on the Rights of Indigenous Peoples, 122–23, 125–293
Educational, Scientific and Cultural Organization (UNESCO), 292
Food and Agriculture Organization (FAO), 18, 122–23
Human Rights Committee (HRC), 116–17
International Children's Emergency Fund (UNICEF), 18
Joint United Nations Programme on HIV and AIDS (UNAIDS), 18
United States
Advisory Committee on Immunization Practices, 524–25
Centers for Disease Control and Prevention, 524–25, 540–41, 564
consumer protection, 402–4
Food and Drug Administration, 466–67, 527–28, 529, 532–33
Framework for Equitable Allocation of COVID-19 Vaccine, 524–25
Indigenous people's health, 125–26
lockdown jurisprudence, 207–8
mandatory vaccination litigation, 254–62
no-fault vaccine compensation scheme, 384–85
numbers of cases, 8–9
purchase of vaccines, 510
quarantine litigation, 217–18

reduction in life expectancy, 9–10
religious observance litigation, 242–47
Universal Declaration on Bioethics and Human Rights, 476–77, 505–6
Universal Declaration of Human Rights, 117–18, 142
universities
closure, 57

Vaccine Alliance. *See* Gavi
vaccine passports, 176–81
vaccination
Advance Market Commitment (AMC) Eligible Economies Compensation Scheme, 383–84
adverse effects, 380–82
children, 263–73
compensation, 380–81
destruction, 515–16
expiration dates, 516
Malawi, 515–16
myocarditis, 381
national compensation schemes, 384–86
pericarditis, 381
rates, 512–13
vaccination mandates, vii–viii, 167–76, 447–53
Fair Work Commission (Australia), 448
Italy, 451–52
litigation, 247–62
Philippines, 450
Saudi Arabia, 449
United Kingdom, 450
United States, 451–52
Washington, George, 447
vaccines
access, ix
advance purchase agreements, 510
allocation, 523–25
AstraZeneca, 380–82, 508–9, 510
Cutter Laboratories, 60, 374
distribution inequity, 514
expedited, 461, 464
Johnson & Johnson, 461
justice, 514
Moderna, 381, 461, 535–36
mRNA, 381–82
nationalism, 510–11, 540–41
Novavax, 509
'People's Vaccine Alliance', 514, 545, 563–64
Pfizer, 380–81, 535–36
poliomyelitis, 60
rationing, 516–25
Sputnik V, 461–63
vagrancy, 46–47

variants, 10–12. *See also* COVID-19
　Alpha, 11
　Beta, 11
　Delta, 11, 104, 291, 505–6
　Delta Plus, 104
　Gamma, 11
　Lambda, 505–6
　Mu, 505–6
　Omicron, 11–12, 139, 161, 166–67, 169–70, 178–79, 270, 449–50, 505–6
　variants of concern, 10–11, 29, 505–6
　variants of interest, 10–11, 505–6
ventilation, 349–50
ventilators, 309
　rationing, 517–23
victims of crime, 342–43
virtual hearings, 347–48. *See also* courts; technology
vital statistics, 109–10

Washington, George, 47–48
World Bank, 15–16
wastewater surveillance, 185–87
Western Samoa, 57–58
West Nile fever, 82–84
Willowbrook studies, 467–68
Women, 288–90
work
　changes, 575–76
　conditions, 427
　essential, 419
　home, 316
　healthcare, 429–33
　loss of, 318–21 (*see also* unemployment)
　no jab, no work, 419–20
　paid leave entitlements, 317
　remote conferencing, 418–19
　surge needs, 419
workforce
　diversifying, 433–36
workplaces
　culture, 420–22
　European Union testing, 423
　German, 428–29

meat-processing plants, 427
presenteeism, 420–22
safety, 418–54 (*see also* occupational health and safety)
World Bank Group, 158
World Health Assembly, x, 15, 25, 60–61, 66, 69–70, 77–79, 96–97, 100, 101–3, 542–43, 554–55
　pandemic prevention, 102–3
　polio, 60–61
World Health Organization
　Concept for Fair Access and Equitable Allocation of COVID-19 Health Products, 554
　COVID-19 Technology Access Pool (C-TAP), 515, 544
　face masks, 165–66
　Global Research Collaboration for Infectious Disease Preparedness and Response, 502
　healthcare workers, 436–41
　living guidelines for COVID-19 therapeutics, 465
　myth-busters, 527
　recommendations for human challenge trials, 470
　Strategic Advisory Group of Experts on Immunization, 523
　success, 77
　United States, viii–ix
　Values Framework, 523–24
World Medical Association
　Declaration of Helsinki, 478–79
Wuhan outbreak, viii

xenophobia, 339

yellow fever, 51, 77, 82–84
　trials, 468–69

Zika virus, 555–56
　public health emergency of international concern, 80–81
zoonotic diseases, 4–5, 24–25, 72–73, 564
　epidemics, 39–40